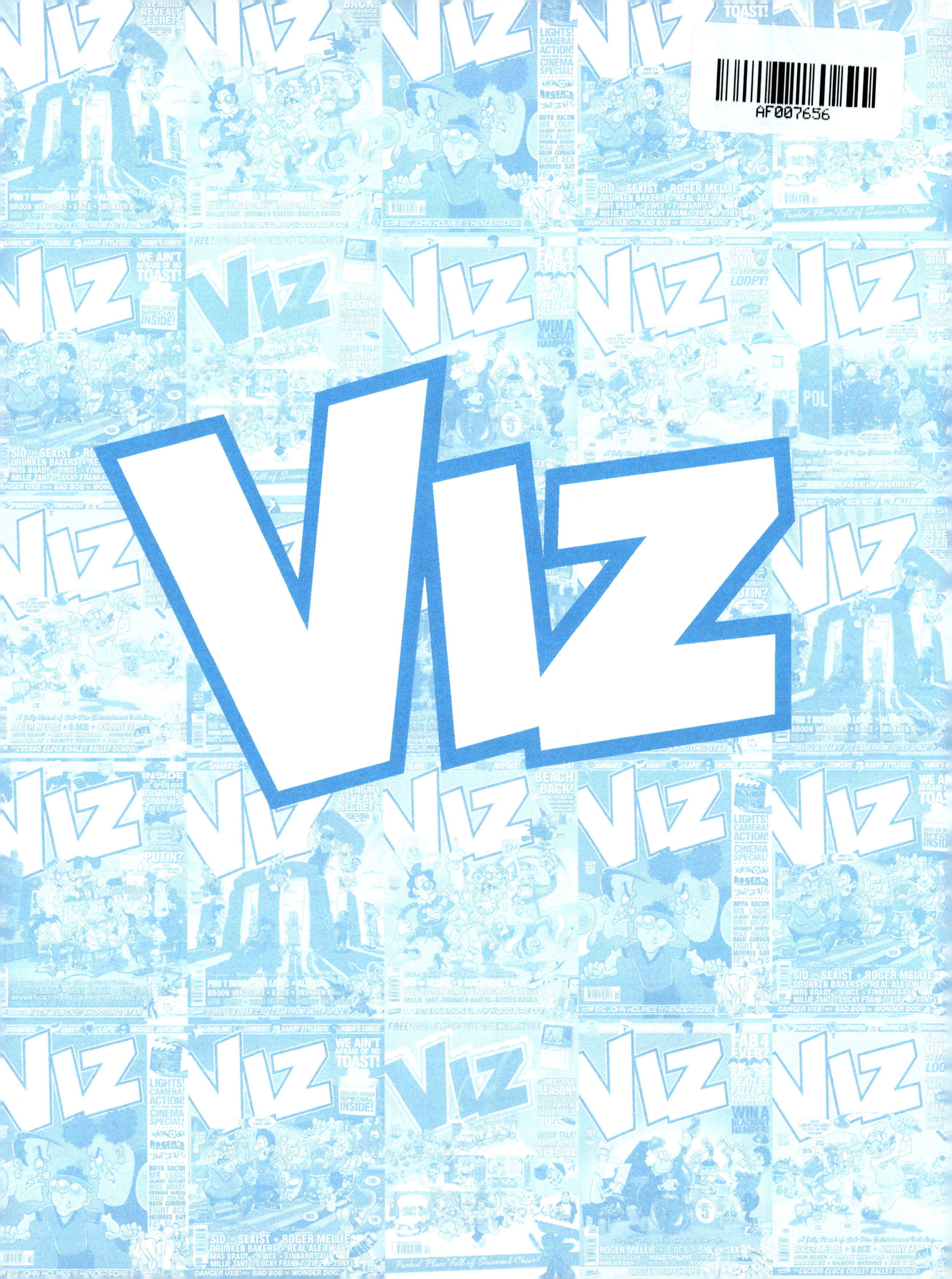
VIZ

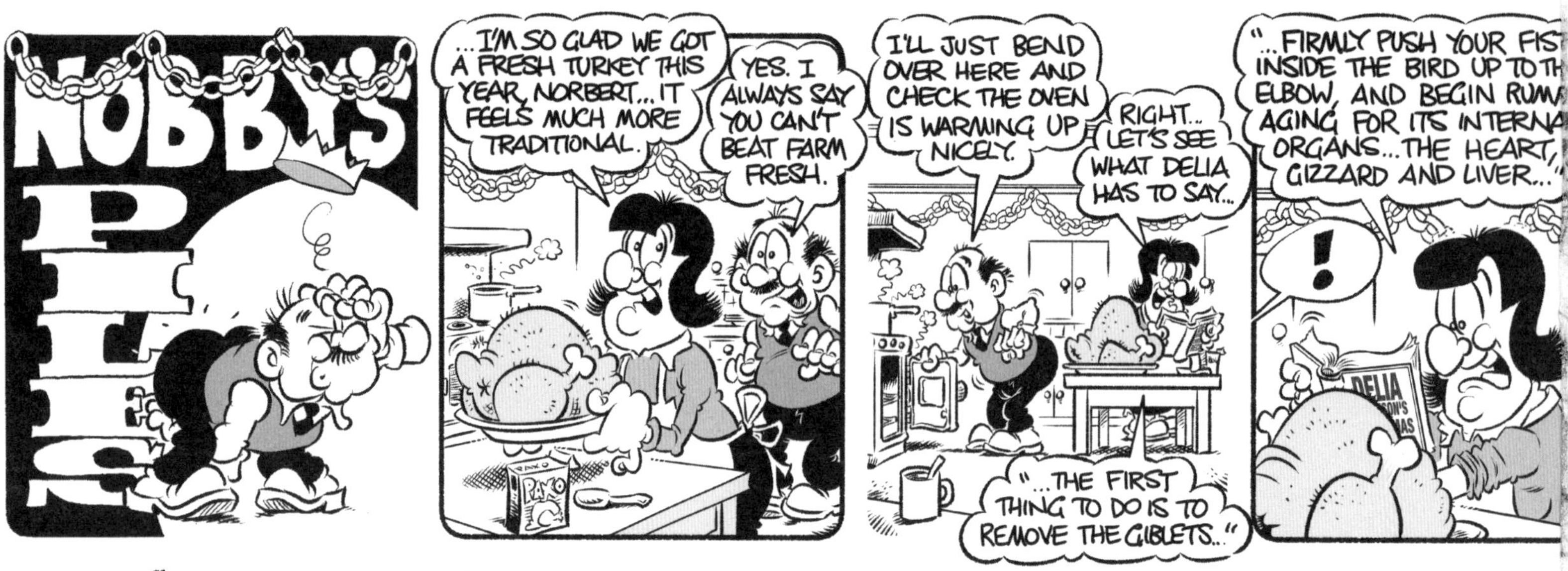
NOBBY'S PILES
...I'M SO GLAD WE GOT A FRESH TURKEY THIS YEAR, NORBERT... IT FEELS MUCH MORE TRADITIONAL.
YES. I ALWAYS SAY YOU CAN'T BEAT FARM FRESH.
I'LL JUST BEND OVER HERE AND CHECK THE OVEN IS WARMING UP NICELY.
RIGHT.. LET'S SEE WHAT DELIA HAS TO SAY...
"...THE FIRST THING TO DO IS TO REMOVE THE GIBLETS.."
"...FIRMLY PUSH YOUR FIS
INSIDE THE BIRD UP TO TH
ELBOW, AND BEGIN RUMA
AGING FOR ITS INTERNA
ORGANS...THE HEART,
GIZZARD AND LIVER..."
!
DELIA

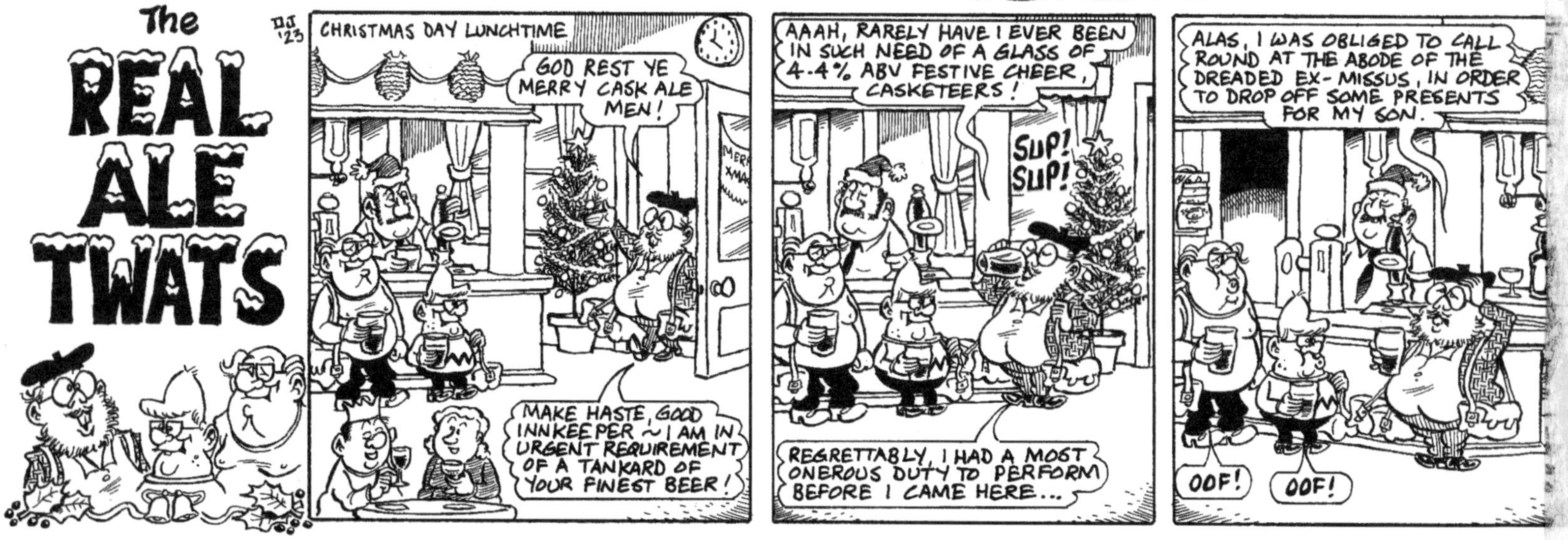
The REAL ALE TWATS
CHRISTMAS DAY LUNCHTIME
GOD REST YE MERRY CASK ALE MEN!
MAKE HASTE, GOOD INNKEEPER ~ I AM IN URGENT REQUIREMENT OF A TANKARD OF YOUR FINEST BEER!
AAAH, RARELY HAVE I EVER BEEN IN SUCH NEED OF A GLASS OF 4.4% ABV FESTIVE CHEER, CASKETEERS!
SUP! SUP!
REGRETTABLY, I HAD A MOST ONEROUS DUTY TO PERFORM BEFORE I CAME HERE...
ALAS, I WAS OBLIGED TO CALL ROUND AT THE ABODE OF THE DREADED EX-MISSUS, IN ORDER TO DROP OFF SOME PRESENTS FOR MY SON.
OOF!
OOF!

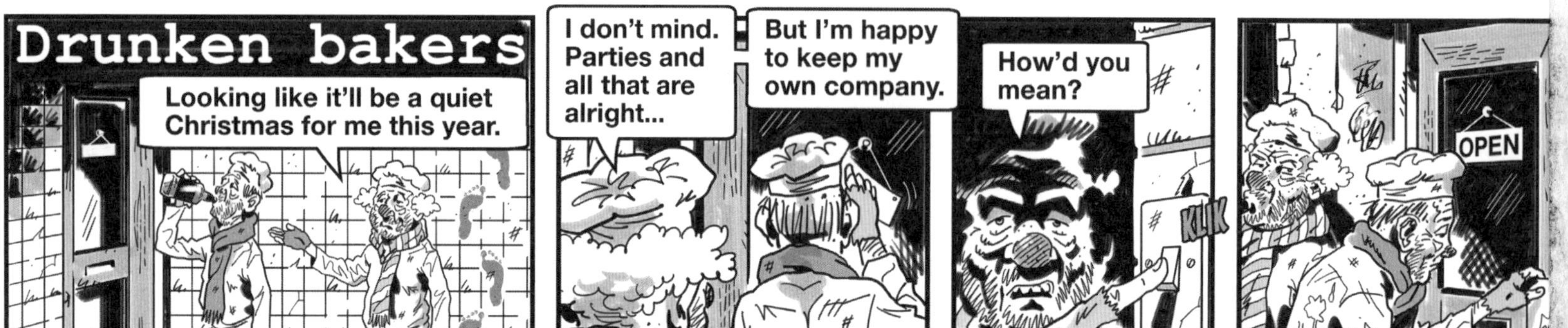
Drunken bakers
Looking like it'll be a quiet Christmas for me this year.
Yeah...
I don't mind. Parties and all that are alright...
But I'm happy to keep my own company.
Just as well.
How'd you mean?
KLIK
No fucker else is.
OPEN

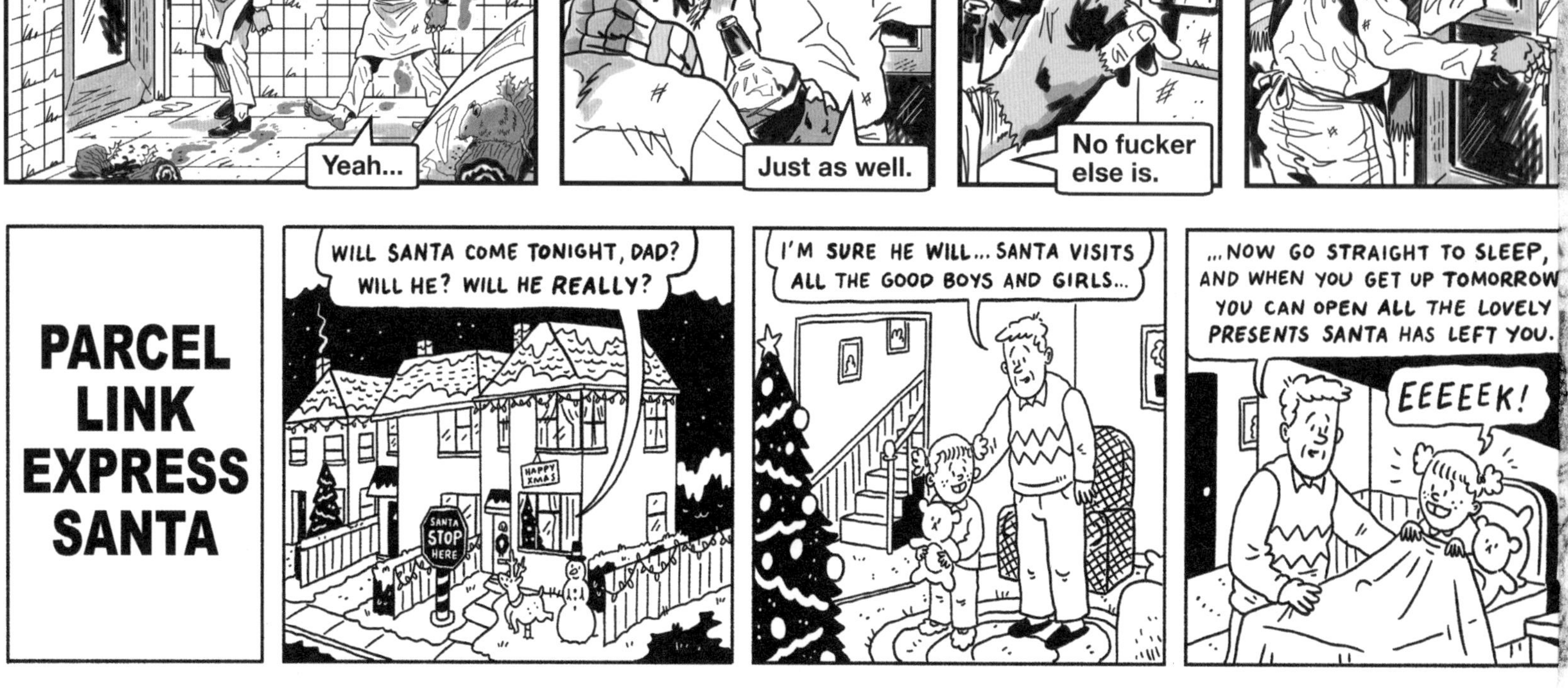
PARCEL LINK EXPRESS SANTA
WILL SANTA COME TONIGHT, DAD? WILL HE? WILL HE REALLY?
HAPPY XMAS
SANTA STOP HERE
I'M SURE HE WILL... SANTA VISITS ALL THE GOOD BOYS AND GIRLS...
...NOW GO STRAIGHT TO SLEEP, AND WHEN YOU GET UP TOMORROW YOU CAN OPEN ALL THE LOVELY PRESENTS SANTA HAS LEFT YOU.
EEEEEK!

..ONCE YOU'VE GOT A GOOD
RIP ON THEM, GIVE THEM A
RM PULL UNTIL THEY SNAP
FF..." OH DEAR, MINE DON'T
EEM TO BE COMING AWAY...
!
DELIA
RECIPES
...PERHAPS I SHOULD TENDERIZE THE CARTILAGE BY STRIKING IT REPEATEDLY WITH MY MEAT HAMMER...
YAAAARGH! ME FUCKING MICHAELS!!
WALLOP! WALLOP!
WALLOP!
WALLOP! WALLOP!
"OOF" IS THE VERY WORD, MES FRÈRES!
N ENCOUNTER WITH MY FORMER ROUBLE-AND-STRIFE ON HER OORSTEP WAS NOT EXACTLY ONDUCIVE TO MY MOOD OF SEASONAL MERRIMENT!
HOWEVER, THESE THINGS ARE SENT TO TRY US, AND ONE CANNOT SHIRK ONE'S PARENTAL DUTIES.
AFTER ALL, CHRISTMAS IS A TIME FOR SELFLESSNESS ~ WE MUST PUT ASIDE OUR OWN PERSONAL DESIRES, AND DO WHAT WE CAN FOR OTHER PEOPLE.
AND YOU KNOW, CASKETEERS... ≥SNIFF≤... CALL ME AN OLD SENTIMENTALIST IF YOU WISH...
WIPE WIPE
...BUT THE THOUGHT OF YOUNG PERTWEE'S LITTLE FACE BEING SUFFUSED WITH JOY AS HE UNWRAPS THOSE PRESENTS IS BRINGING A WARM GLOW TO MY HEART!
MEANWHILE
CAMRA GOOD BEER GUIDE 1996
OWLD THROBBER'S BEST BITTER 5.5% MINI KEG
From your biological Daddy
Christmas still a *funny* time for you, I expect.
OPEN
What with it being when your missus upped and fucked off with the kid...
Never think about it.
Aye, best idea. Forget the pair of 'em. *Bitches.*
OPEN
Any road... A very *merry* Christmas to you, *mate*.
And you.
JACK DANIEL-SAN
"Bourbon with a KICK!"
Oh Joanne.
24/7
Twat.
ATER...
THUMP!
WOOSH!
NEXT MORNING...
DADDY... WHAT DOES IT MEAN?
PARCEL LINK EXPRESS SANTA
Our Santa called but was unable to deliver your presents.
We will attempt to deliver them again next year.
Alternatively, you could call in to the depot at the North Pole to collect them, 9:00-18:00 any day except Christmas Eve.
LM

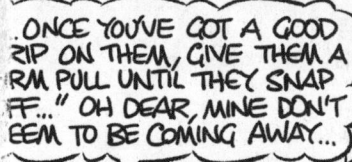

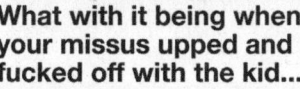

Bad Bob The Randy Wonder Dog

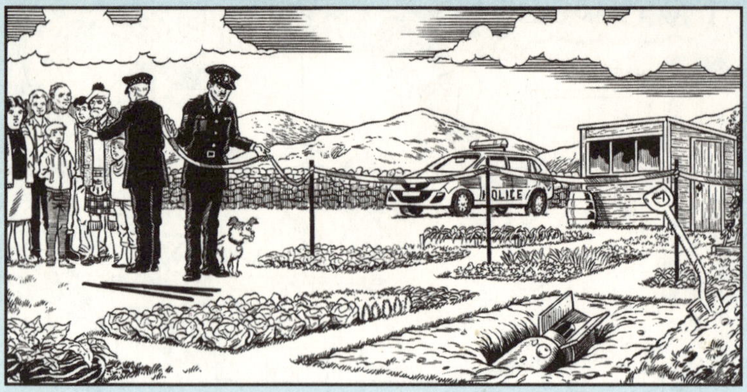

THERE was great excitement in the village of Peebles. Digging tatties on his allotment, old Mr Arbroath had unearthed an unexploded WWII bomb! Sergeant Greenock was called and soon had the area cordoned off, and the bomb squad from the Glencatterick barracks were on their way.

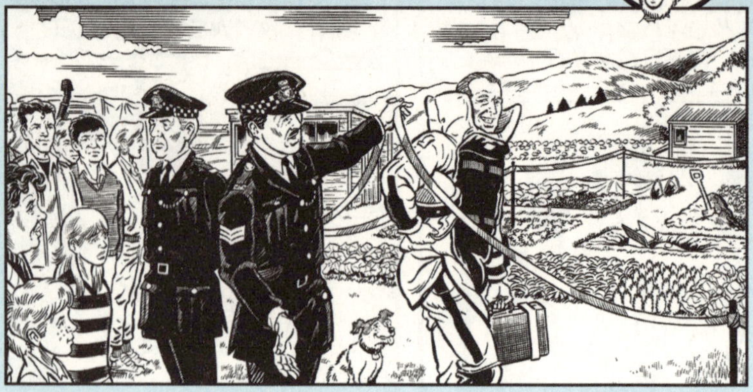

CAPTAIN Firth of the Dundee Highland Fusiliers - an expert at defusing antiquated munitions - was soon on the scene in his protective suit. "Keep everyone back, Sergeant Greenock, this is delicate work," he said. "One wee vibration could detonate this bomb and blow us a' tae kingdom come!"

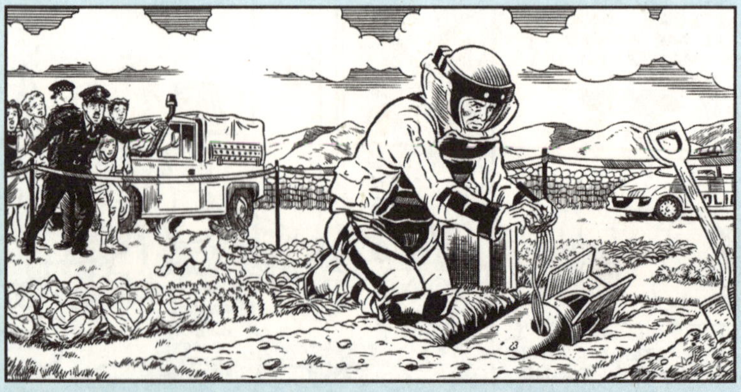

AT A SAFE distance behind the cordon, everyone held their breath as the brave captain began his work. But suddenly, Bob, Sergeant Greenock's feisty wee dog, dashed towards the soldier performing his delicate task. "Bob! Bob! Get back here!" cried the anguished policeman.

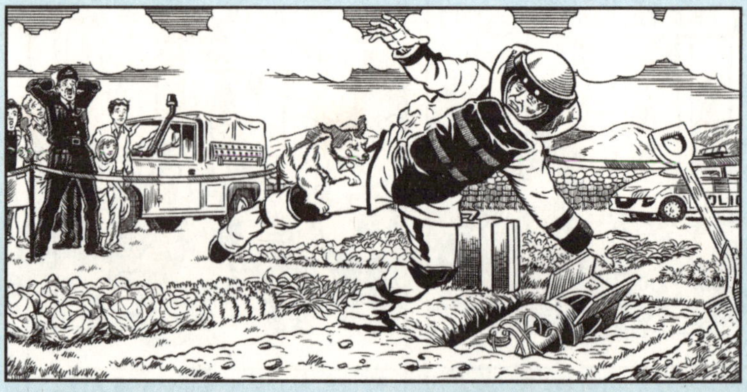

IN A STATE of arousal, the randy terrier leapt up and grabbed the poor captain's thigh in an amorous embrace. "Jesus!" cried the soldier in alarm. "Get yir dog under control, man. I'm trying tae diffuse a bomb, here!" But unable to cross the cordon, Sergeant Greenock could only shout threats towards Bob.

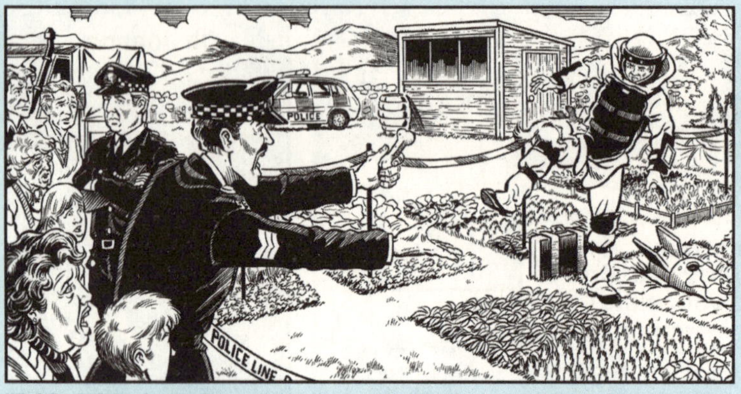

"BOB! BOB! Come here, Bob! I've a wee Bonio fur ye!" he called. But Bob was in his stride, thrusting rhythmically against the thick protective suit of the captain's leg. "Get this wee bas aff me, man!" cried the captain. "I cannae concentrate oan whit I'm doing!" But Bob showed no sign of stopping.

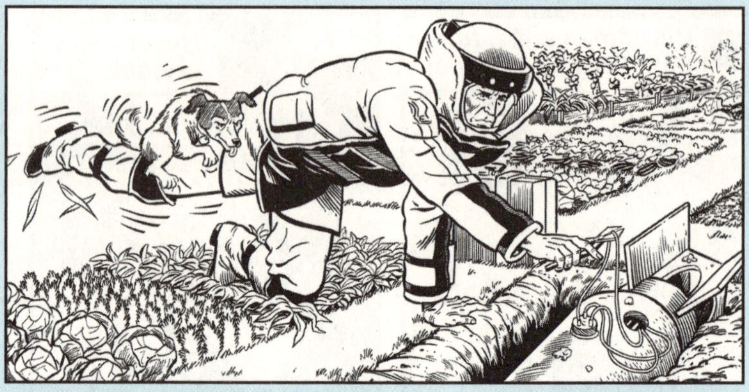

CAPTAIN Firth struggled with the bomb as the vibrations from Bob's thrustings travelled up his leg and through his body, disturbing his usually rock-steady hand. "Stop it, Bob! Bad dog! I'll hae yir guts f' garters!" cried Greenock from afar. But Bob's wee paws were already wearing the jester's shoes.

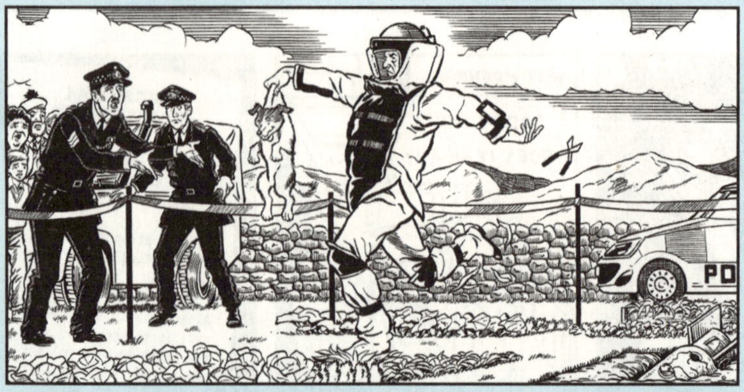

SUDDENLY, the onlookers heard Captain Firth cry out, and saw him stumble backwards to the ground. "Guid heavens!" cried Sergeant Greenock. *"He must have cut the wrang wire and started the detonation countdown!"* Captain Firth picked himself up and began to run from the bomb as fast as he could.

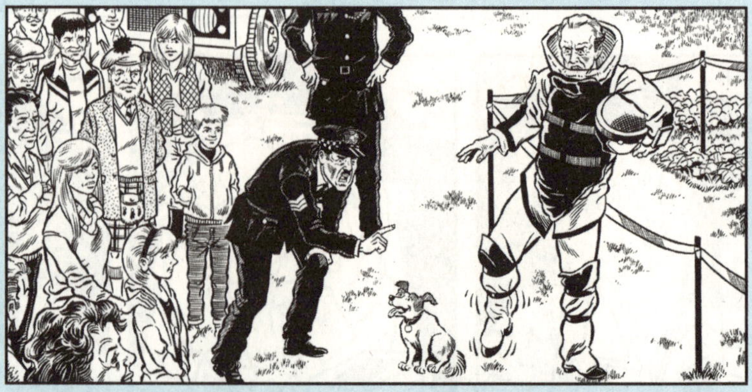

"WHIT'S happened, Captain? Is the bomb going tae go aff?" asked Greenock. "Ach, no. Yon bomb's a dud!" replied the captain. "But yir wee bluidy dog went aff... a' awa ma leg!" Sergeant Greenock looked at the mess all over the leg of the the soldier's bomb-proof suit. "Bad Bob! Bad Bob! Nae biscuit!"

Seconds out... Round 40! It's

THE WRESTLER'S NECK

A SWEATY RINGFUL OF PILEDRIVERS SMACKED DOWN FROM ISSUES 322~331

Boston Crabs
Graham Dury, Simon Thorp, Alex Morris

Half Nelsons
Thomas Armstrong, Adrian Bamforth, Mark Bates, Mark Baxter, Christian Boston, Alex Collier, Simon Ecob, Tom Ellen, Barney Farmer, Peter Green, Lee Healey, Davey Jones, Marc Jones, Luke McGarry, Paul Palmer, Tom Paterson, Paul Roberts, Simon Robinson, Joe Shooman, Anthony Smith, Paul Solomons, Cat Sullivan, Kent Taylor, Neil Tollfree, Nick Tolson, Dominic Twose and Stevie White.

Camel Clutches
David Saunders and Lee Boyman

Published by Diamond Publishing Ltd,
part of the Metropolis Group
4th Floor, Harmsworth House,
13-15 Bouverie Street,
London EC4Y 8DP

ISBN 978-1-9164219-8-1
First Printing Summer 2025

© Fulchester Industries/Diamond Publishing Ltd. All rights reserved. No part of this book may be trash-talked before being hit with a flimsy, lightweight chair without the written permission of Fulchester Industries and/or Diamond Publishing.

Subscribe online at www.viz.co.uk

Find us at:
facebook.com/vizcomic   bluesky.com/vizcomic
Instagram.com/vizcomicofficial   TikTok.com/vizcomic

BIFFA BACON
LOVE
HATE
31ST OCT...
HOO, SON... IT'S THE THORTY FORST O' FUCKIN' OCTURBAH!.. Y'KNAA WOT THAT MEANS, DIVVEN'T YUZ?
AYE!.. IT'S HALLUR-WEEN
HALLUR-WEEN MY FUCKIN' ARSE! IT'S TIME T'GET W' CHRISMUS TREE
EH!?.. FUCKIN' CHRISMUS TREE?
THERE WIVVEN'T BE NEE CHRISMUS TREES IN THE SHOPS, YET
SHOPS!?! YUZ DIVVEN'T GET CHRISMUS TREES IN THE FUCKIN' SHOPS, YUZ DAFT TWAT.. THE COUNTRYSIDE'S FUCKIN' FULL O' THE FUCKIN' FUCKAZ
SLOO!
LET'S GAN GET ONE
AYE!.. C'MON, SON.. GERRIN' T' THE FESTIVE SPIRIT, Y' MISERABLE BASTAAD
SHORTLY...
HOO.. YUZ'RE REET, FATHA.. THEZ MILLIONS O' THE FUCKAZ... ANY O' THESE BASTAADS'LL DEE
NAH, SON..
...THEZ A CANNY BIG FUCKAH ON HADRIAN'S WAALL... IT'S A FUCKIN' FANTAKKA SPECIMEN O' A TREE.
THARRIDIS, FATHA.. THARRIT FUCKIN' IS
IT'S THE MURST PHURTURGRAPHED TREE IN THE FUCKIN WORLD... BIN ON THOOSANDS O' CALENDAZ AN MILLIONS O' FUCKIN' PICK-CHAZ!
AYE.. AN ICONIC SYMBOL O' THE COONTY, SON... IT'S STOOD SENTINAL ON THE RURMAN WAALL F' FUCKIN' CENTURIES!...
EEH!.. THE THINGS IT MUST HEV SEEN IF IT COULD SEE.. THE STORIES IT COULD TELL IF IT COULD FUCKIN TAALK!
ANYHOO.. DID YUZ BRING THE FUCKIN' SAW, SON?
AYE!
CHAMPION.. WUZ'LL HEV THE FUCKER DOON IN NEE TIME
SO...
REET... THAT'S AS FAR AS WUZ CAN GAN IN THE MURTAH... WUZ'LL HEV T' WAALK THE REST O' THE FUCKIN' WAY
WAALK!?!... IS IT FAR, LIKE?
NAH, SON!
KEEP GANNIN', SON
PUFF!! PANT!! GASP!!
...JUST ROOND THIS RIDGE, Y' SOFT SHITE!
FUCKIN' GASP!!
SOME FUCKAZ CURRIT DOON AALREADY!
WELL, THAT'S SAVED US THE FUCKIN' JOB, MUTHA
AYE! YUZ CAN HOY THAT FUCKIN' SAW AWAY, BIFFA, SON!
IT'S A CANNY BIG TREE, THOUGH BUT, FATHA
AYE! BUT THEZ NEE POINT HEVVIN A FUCKIN' PIDDLIN' CHRISMUS TREE, SON
THAT'S REET, BIFFA.. SMAALL TREES IS F' SOFT FUCKIN' SHITES
NOO SHUT YUZ FUCKIN' WHINGIN' AN' GERRA HURLD O' THE OTHER END.. THEN WUZZLE GET THE FUCKAH BACK T' THE FUCKIN' CAR!
REET, MUTHA
HOO! THE FUCK'S GANNIN' ON 'ERE, LIKE?
EH?.. THE FUCK'S IT GORRA DEE WI' YEE?

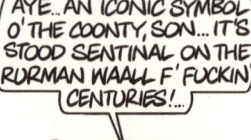

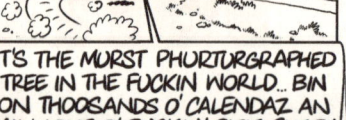

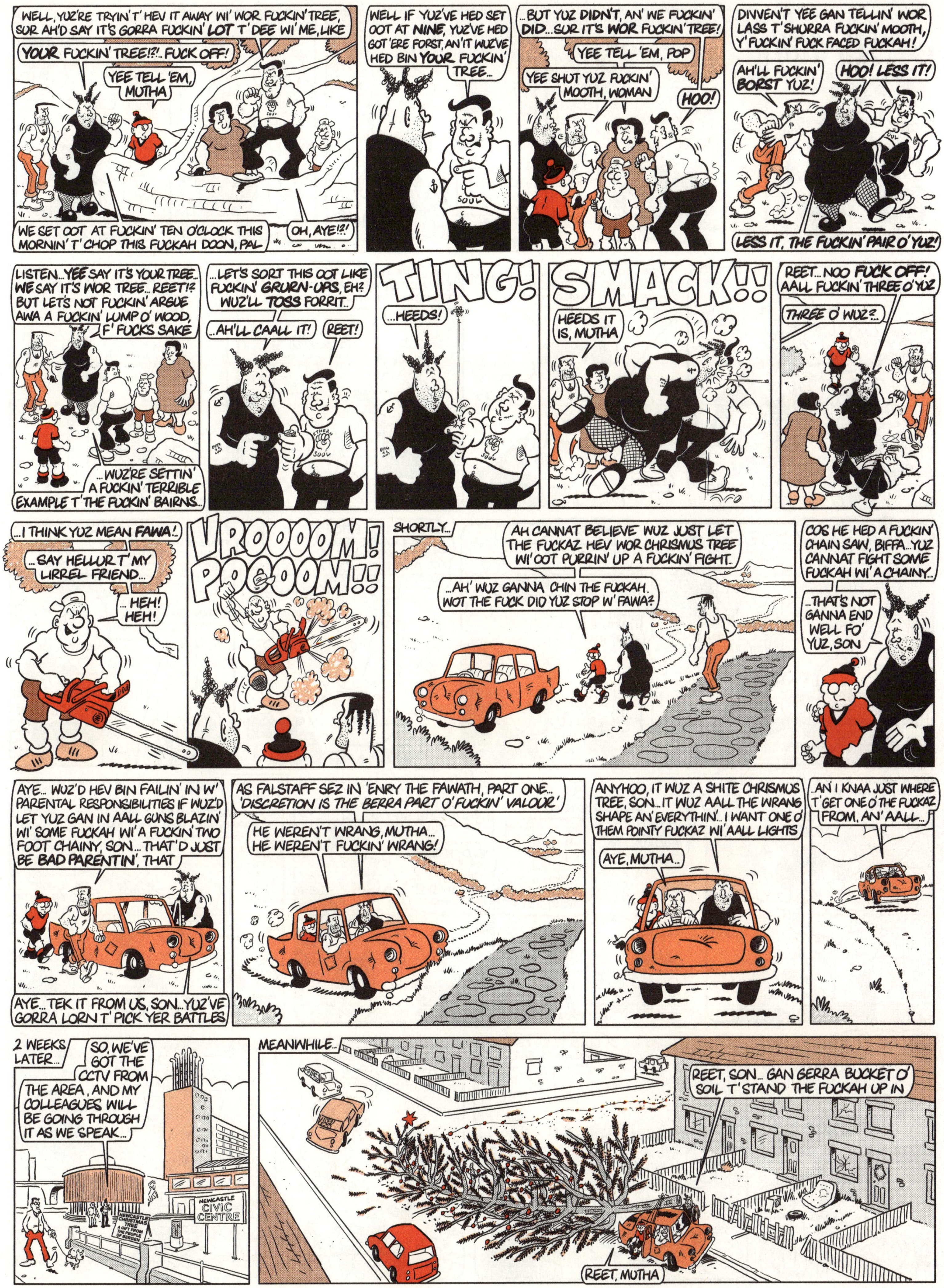
WELL, YUZ'RE TRYIN' T' HEV IT AWAY WI' WOR FUCKIN' TREE, SUR AH'D SAY IT'S GORRA FUCKIN' LOT T' DEE WI' ME, LIKE
YOUR FUCKIN' TREE!?'.. FUCK OFF!
YEE TELL 'EM, MUTHA
WE SET OOT AT FUCKIN' TEN O'CLOCK THIS MORNIN' T' CHOP THIS FUCKAH DOON, PAL
OH, AYE!?!
WELL IF YUZ'VE HED SET OOT AT NINE, YUZ'VE HED GOT 'ERE FORST, AN' IT WUZ'VE HED BIN YOUR FUCKIN' TREE...
...BUT YUZ DIDN'T, AN' WE FUCKIN' DID... SUR IT'S WOR FUCKIN' TREE!
YEE TELL 'EM, POP
YEE SHUT YUZ FUCKIN' MOOTH, WOMAN
HOO!
DINVEN'T YEE GAN TELLIN' WOR LASS T' SHURRA FUCKIN' MOOTH, Y' FUCKIN' FUCK FACED FUCKAH!
AH'LL FUCKIN' BORST YUZ!
HOO! LESS IT!
LESS IT, THE FUCKIN' PAIR O' YUZ!
LISTEN... YEE SAY IT'S YOUR TREE... WE SAY IT'S WOR TREE... REET!? BUT LET'S NOT FUCKIN' ARGUE AWA A FUCKIN' LUMP O' WOOD, F' FUCKS SAKE
...WUZ'RE SETTIN' A FUCKIN' TERRIBLE EXAMPLE T' THE FUCKIN' BAIRNS...
...LET'S SORT THIS OOT LIKE FUCKIN' GRURN-UPS, EH? WUZ'LL TOSS FORRIT...
...AH'LL CAALL IT!
REET!
TING!
...HEEDS!
SMACK!!
HEEDS IT IS, MUTHA
REET... NOO FUCK OFF! AALL FUCKIN' THREE O' YUZ
THREE O' WUZ?..
...I THINK YUZ MEAN FAWA!
...SAY HELLUR T' MY LIRREL FRIEND...
...HEH! HEH!
VROOOOM! POOOOM!!
SHORTLY...
AH CANNAT BELIEVE WUZ JUST LET THE FUCKAZ HEV WOR CHRISMUS TREE WI'OOT PURRIN' UP A FUCKIN' FIGHT.
...AH' WUZ GANNA CHIN THE FUCKAH. WOT THE FUCK DID YUZ STOP W' FAWA?
COS HE HED A FUCKIN' CHAIN SAW, BIFFA... YUZ CANNAT FIGHT SOME FUCKAH WI' A CHAINY...
...THAT'S NOT GANNA END WELL FO' YUZ, SON
AYE... WUZ'D HEV BIN FAILIN' IN W' PARENTAL RESPONSIBILITIES IF WUZ'D LET YUZ GAN IN AALL GUNS BLAZIN' WI' SOME FUCKAH WI' A FUCKIN' TWO FOOT CHAINY, SON... THAT'D JUST BE BAD PARENTIN', THAT
AYE... TEK IT FROM US, SON... YUZ'VE GORRA LORN T' PICK YER BATTLES
AS FALSTAFF SEZ IN 'ENRY THE FAWATH, PART ONE... 'DISCRETION IS THE BERRA PART O' FUCKIN' VALOUR'
HE WEREN'T WRANG, MUTHA... HE WEREN'T FUCKIN' WRANG!
ANYHOO, IT WUZ A SHITE CHRISMUS TREE, SON... IT WUZ AALL THE WRANG SHAPE AN' EVERYTHIN'... I WANT ONE O' THEM POINTY FUCKAZ WI' AALL LIGHTS
AYE, MUTHA...
...AN' I KNAA JUST WHERE T' GET ONE O' THE FUCKAZ FROM, AN' AALL...
2 WEEKS LATER...
SO, WE'VE GOT THE CCTV FROM THE AREA, AND MY COLLEAGUES WILL BE GOING THROUGH IT AS WE SPEAK...
NEWCASTLE CIVIC CENTRE
MEANWHILE...
REET, SON... GAN GERRA BUCKET O' SOIL T' STAND THE FUCKAH UP IN
REET, MUTHA

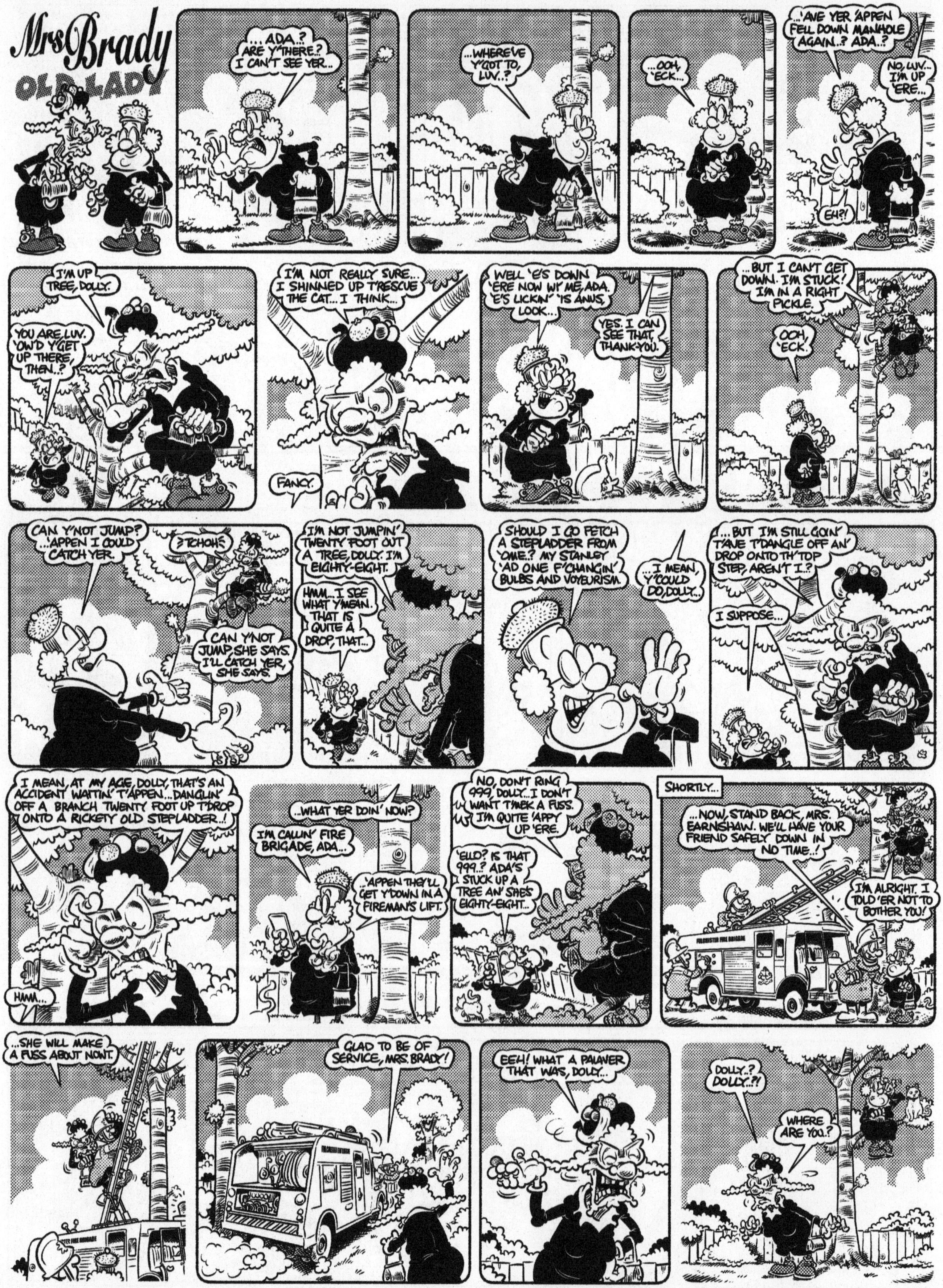
Mrs Brady
OLD LADY
...ADA..? ARE Y'THERE..? I CAN'T SEE YER...
...WHEREVE Y'GOT TO, LUV..?
...OOH, 'ECK...
...'AVE YER 'APPEN FELL DOWN MANHOLE AGAIN..? ADA..?
NO, LUV... I'M UP 'ERE...
EH?!
I'M UP TREE, DOLLY.
YOU ARE, LUV. 'OW'D Y'GET UP THERE, THEN..?
I'M NOT REALLY SURE... I SHINNED UP T'RESCUE THE CAT... I THINK...
FANCY.
WELL 'E'S DOWN 'ERE NOW WI' ME, ADA. 'E'S LICKIN' 'IS ANUS, LOOK...
YES. I CAN SEE THAT, THANK-YOU.
...BUT I CAN'T GET DOWN. I'M STUCK! I'M IN A RIGHT PICKLE.
OOH, 'ECK.
CAN Y'NOT JUMP? ...'APPEN I COULD CATCH YER.
TCHOH!
CAN Y'NOT JUMP, SHE SAYS. I'LL CATCH YER, SHE SAYS.
I'M NOT JUMPIN' TWENTY FOOT OUT A TREE, DOLLY. I'M EIGHTY-EIGHT.
HMM... I SEE WHAT Y'MEAN. THAT IS QUITE A DROP, THAT...
SHOULD I GO FETCH A STEPLADDER FROM 'OME..? MY STANLEY 'AD ONE F'CHANGIN' BULBS AND VOYEURISM.
...I MEAN, Y'COULD DO, DOLLY...
...BUT I'M STILL GOIN' T'AVE T'DANGLE OFF AN' DROP ONTO TH'TOP STEP, AREN'T I..?
I SUPPOSE...
I MEAN, AT MY AGE, DOLLY, THAT'S AN ACCIDENT WAITIN' T'APPEN... DANGLIN' OFF A BRANCH TWENTY FOOT UP T'DROP ONTO A RICKETY OLD STEPLADDER...!
HMM...
...WHAT YER DOIN' NOW?
I'M CALLIN' FIRE BRIGADE, ADA...
...'APPEN THEY'LL GET Y'DOWN IN A FIREMAN'S LIFT.
NO, DON'T RING 999, DOLLY... I DON'T WANT T'MEK A FUSS. I'M QUITE 'APPY UP 'ERE.
'ELLO? IS THAT 999..? ADA'S STUCK UP A TREE AN' SHE'S EIGHTY-EIGHT...
SHORTLY...
...NOW, STAND BACK, MRS. EARNSHAW. WE'LL HAVE YOUR FRIEND SAFELY DOWN IN NO TIME...!
I'M ALRIGHT. I TOLD 'ER NOT TO BOTHER YOU!
...SHE WILL MAKE A FUSS ABOUT NOWT.
GLAD TO BE OF SERVICE, MRS. BRADY!
EEH! WHAT A PALAVER THAT WAS, DOLLY...
DOLLY..? DOLLY..?!
WHERE ARE YOU..?

FOODIE BOLLOCKS
Look, mate, the bacon is just bacon, alright?
Bob's Butty Bar
FULL ENGLISH IN A BOX £4
BACON SAUSAGE OR EGG BARM £2
Plain or smoky, take or leave it.
Sigh, you leave me little choice.
But, F-Y-I, your attitude to provenance is literally terrifying.
Oh. My. God.
FULL ENGLISH IN A BO £4
What do you call that?
Er, a bacon barm?
Barm as in barmcake?
Yes.
Then you deserve to be closed down.
What? Why?
Passing off generic white bread rolls as barmcakes?
I think Trading Standards might take a dim view.
Nah, bap, roll, barm, all different words for the same thing ain't they?
Un. Be. Lievable.
Baps and barms are types of roll, but not all rolls are baps or barms.
Well my old mum called 'em barms.
I suppose she explains your ignorance.
Forget her. Trust me, traditional barmcakes are nothing like this factory offering.
Broader, flatter, the bread is leavened with fresh barm, a yeasty scum which forms on fermenting ales, making for a fuller, quite distinctive flavour.
If it's the real deal you're after source from Borough Market.
Little PAINS
Fran Hingelby's bi-weekly pop-up heritage roll concept.
In May he told FEAST artisanal focus on loaves had unwittingly undermined historic small breads.
Feast
Rock and Roll Tsar
Threatening baked diversity.
His book on extinct varieties of once common British rolls topped the Times Bestsellers for a month.
WATERSTON
Roll Play
Roll Play
Not to hyperbolise... But there was a genocide.
The brave thing is that not two years ago Fran'd never so much as touched a bag of flour.
Poor guy was stuck in the City!
Managing the Hingelby family's £5billion property portfolio.
Then he had a dreadful experience at the annual BlackRock summer garden party.
It's the old story, great burger – in this case single cow organic wagyu – on an average bun!
We've all been there! But Fran had the passion to fight back.
Quit the City, walked, taking nothing but his 25 percent stake in the firm, and threw himself straight into rolls.
No fear. No quarter.
Now his are probably the only historically legitimate barmcakes out there.
Best yet, he brings them in at a fair price, just four pounds a piece.
What's burrow market?
Ha ha, incredible.
You, are a disgrace.

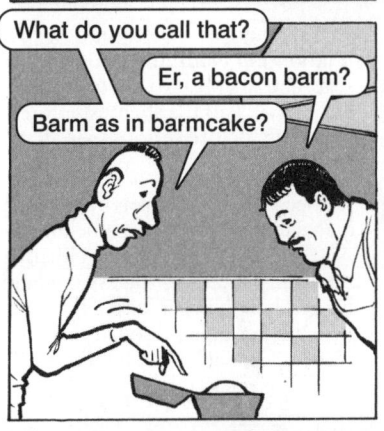

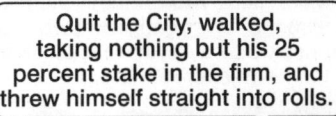

HURT OF HEART-TRANSPLANT HERO IN HEARTBREAK HOTEL

HEART OF DARKNESS: Office manager Vin Trickle points to where he thinks doctors transplanted his heart ... and ruined his life.

A TYESLEY heart-transplant recipient is poised to drag the NHS through the courts, accusing failing quacks of derailing an 18-year marriage and costing him his wife and home.

Office manager Vin Trickle parted from his wife Monica in April, a little over two years after surgical boffins at the University Hospital in Birmingham removed his failing heart and replaced it with the healthy cardiovascular pump of a young donor whose head had been crushed by a steam-hammer the previous day.

hospital

Initially, 17-stoner plus Vin was delighted to have survived his dance with death, and the 59-year-old 50-a-day smoker even went so far as to post a glowing review on the NHS's Check-a-Trade page.

"The docs and nurses got eight out of ten from me," he told the *Sparkhill World News*. "They literally saved my life. I only knocked the two off because the nurses were wearing trousers instead of skirts, and the food was fucking horrible."

"But for a time I was a man reborn," he sighed, tears sparkling in his small brown eyes. "In my naive joy, all I could think of was that I wouldn't be unceremoniously dumped into infinite nothingness in the near future. Gratitude, I suppose you'd call it."

"If only I'd known that what they actually put into my chest was a heart-shaped ball of heartbreak."

deliberate

Vin responded well to treatment and two months after his op left hospital and returned to work at Tyesley International Paperclips where life resumed as normal. Or so he thought.

"In all honesty I felt no different in myself, but within a few weeks of being back in the office, I'd embarked upon a full-blown love affair with a female employee," he said. "It was so out of character for me to have done anything even remotely like that, and I can't believe I didn't notice at the time," marvelled Vin.

cassock

"I'd enjoyed a casual sexual relationship with this woman for several years prior to the transplant, but I never had the slightest interest in anything more serious than that," he said.

"Becca's a cleaner and I'm management, so she's a bit below me. And she's not very bright, either. If she hadn't been so attractive, I would happily have had her sacked that time I caught her going through the petty cash tin," he said. "I wish I had now."

choreography

But Vin's casual workplace affair took a dramatic turn once he received his new heart. Before he knew what was happening, he had set Becca up in a swanky flat above a chip shop in Acock's Green.

"All of a sudden I found myself telling the bloody woman that I loved her, and that I was ready to give up my gorgeous house of all those years. And my wife," he said. "I mean, that's just not me. I know which side my bread is buttered. Although now I have to use that low-fat alternative now, which is bloody awful stuff. It just makes your toast wet."

HOW TO DO IT!

SURGEONS are often put on a pedestal simply for performing life saving operations. But few people actually realise how easy these procedures are to perform. And the heart transplant is possibly the easiest of all. *Viz* science correspondent PROFESSOR STANLEY JORDAN takes us step by step through this piece of piss procedure.

"A heart transplant is not a difficult thing to do. In fact, it's a little like changing a plug – as long as you connect the wires correctly, then the electricity will flow. It's slightly trickier, in that it is pipes with blood in rather than wires with leccy, and there are four pipes as opposed to three wires. But's here's how it's done."

1. Open up the chest

THE HEART is towards the centre of the body slightly towards the left. However, a few people have a mutation where all their organs are on the wrong side of the body, a mirror image of how it should be, so surgeons doing heart transplants always open patients up in the middle, just in case. There are a few ribs in the way, but just push them to the side with a medical clamp and you will see the heart beating away between the lungs.

2. Take out the old heart

WHEN changing a gearbox on a car, you can't put the new one in until the old one is out, and it's the same with hearts. Snip the four pipes coming out the top and bottom, left and right, leaving about an inch or so of pipe attached to the heart. They are not colour coded like wires, so make sure you know which is which. Once they are cut, take out the old heart. A good tip is to throw it away at this point – it's no good to anybody, and it's not unheard of for doctors to get a bit confused and accidentally put the old one back in.

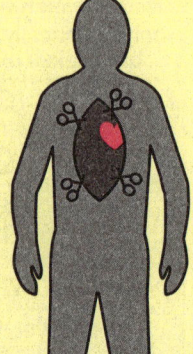

3. Put the new heart in

TAKE the new heart and put in into place between the lungs, making sure you've got it the right way round, pointy side down. Then take each of the four pipes and connect them with medical stitches to the corresponding inch or so of pipe on the new heart. Make sure you connect them to the correct bit, or else the new heart won't work properly. After a final check that everything is all water-tight, it's time get the new ticker running.

4. Finishing off

GET a defibrillator and put the two paddles on the patient's chest. Then, after everyone is standing clear, give them a blast of leccy – a few thousand volts should do the trick – and check that the new heart is beating. If it is, that's great. If it's not, give them another jolt or two until it gets going. When it's all up and running, a quick check to see if you haven't left any instruments in the chest cavity and it's time to close up. Pull the flaps of skin together on the chest and sew them up and job done. Easy as pissing in the shower.

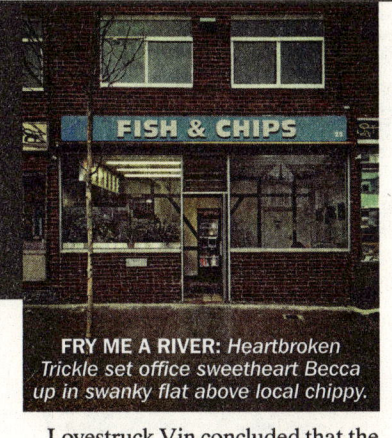

FRY ME A RIVER: Heartbroken Trickle set office sweetheart Becca up in swanky flat above local chippy.

Lovestruck Vin concluded that the NHS had given him the wrong kind of heart, one that was full of emotion, completely incompatible with his self-styled goals-driven mind.

"The bloke who donated must of been someone really soppy, probably a socialist, or a bloody poet or something," he said. "And I think the docs knew what they were doing when they gave me this soft ticker."

"I'm your meat and two vegetables sort of bloke, and the hospital staff knew that fine well. I'd kicked-off on a couple of occasions in the run-up to my op, once when they wouldn't let me watch telly after midnight and again when some foreign staff tried to help me, so they knew the heart of some soft-arse would be no good for me," he said. "I think they stuck it in to get back at me."

Vin's wife Monica confronted her husband over the affair after seeing a credit card statement revealing a £218 transaction at a local exotic underwear shop in town. Vin explained what had happened and was surprised and disappointed when Monica didn't believe him. "The rotten cow threw me out that night," he said.

"I've been living in the Premier Inn ever since and, worse still, thanks to the restraining order I'm effectively *cancelled* from pressuring Monica to change her thinking," he said. "My hands are tied."

balustrade

And it was losing everything that led to Vin taking legal action against the Birmingham University Hospital.

"The NHS obviously *saved* my life, obviously," he said. "But in the long-run, they *destroyed* it, and working on the principle that you are only as good as your last match, they owe me big-time."

"Half of a four-bed detached, enclosed garden front and rear in a nice part of town, to spell it out," he said. "And I'd just had a Whirlpool bath put in, sixteen grand on its own."

Staff at the University Hospital were asked to confirm or deny whether or not the donor was soft, perhaps a socialist or poet, but they declined to comment.

BILLIARDS FITNESS MACHINE MANUFACTURERS

RUN AWAY WITH THIS YEAR'S 'MUST-HAVE' HOME GYM MACHINE
BAIZE RUNNER™
The Original Snooker Treadmill

prices from **£1,500**

The fitness craze that swept the East off its feet has finally landed in the West.

Gufftronics Leisure Machines has secured exclusive European distribution rights to the *Baize Runner* series of tournament-grade Billiards Treadmills, so there's now no excuse not to enjoy a frame of snooker while you get in shape!

Features:
- Finest Italian slate bed ensures sure-footing and no ball bounce on impact.
- Tough, scuff resistant baize running surface available in choice of three colours.
- Adjustable incline targets calves and upperbody while increasing ball speed.
- Ingenious ball return system quickly sends pocketed balls back up the body of the machine ready for play.
- Supplied with set of snooker balls and US-style 'spots and stripes' pool balls for play variation.

Model shown BR-500XL

Buy NOW to receive your FREE trainer chalk!

"My doctor recommended I buy a Baize Runner BR-1000 to help keep my joints supple, and I've not looked back. Last week I made a 147 break while attempting to climb onto the machine!"
Mrs D. Gravitas, Esher

BAIZE RUNNER™

Distributed in the Europe by Gufftronics Lesiure Machines Ltd, Unit 253b Gravy Ind. Estate, Milton Keynes

GOD HELPS MAN WHO HELPS HIMSELF

HOLY SPIRIT: *Terry Corndolly believes a higher hand turned his bleach into vodka.*

Doncaster man's supermarket miracle confounds filth

WE are all familiar with the Bible story recounting how Jesus transformed water into wine. But last week, shoppers in a Doncaster branch of Sainsbury's witnessed an arguably even greater act of divine intervention. For after shopper Terry Corndolly purchased a 1litre bottle of thin bleach, he discovered to his amazement that it had miraculously turned into 70cl of *vodka!*

EXCLUSIVE!

Even more remarkably Corndolly, 63, was unaware that the miraculous divine transubstantiation had occurred until he was stopped by a security guard as he was leaving the shop.

"Being community-minded, I normally shop at my local multi-mart as I feel it's my civic duty to support local businesses," the former warehouse worker told reporters at a sparsely attended press conference in his local pub. "However, after a recent incident which ended up with the owner displaying my photograph in his shop window, I felt it was best to spread my custom a little further afield."

turtle

Terry said he believes that it was Heavenly interference that led him to the supermarket on that morning after he discovered he needed some bleach to put down his toilet.

"I got the bleach from the household aisle and headed for the tills," he said. "It was a snip at 75p a bottle."

"I normally go to any empty till, but that day something led me away from the manned tills and towards the self service bit. I don't know what it was, call it divine intervention, but I felt an unseen hand guiding me towards the tills where you bleep the things through yourself."

macrandrous

Corndolly admits to being in a bit of a hurry as his ankle tag only afforded him another 30 minutes away from the half-way house where he lives following a misunderstanding. So he quickly scanned the bleach, put it in his rucksack and headed for the exit.

Little did he realise that while he walked towards the door, a miracle was unfolding.

As he was leaving the store, a security guard attempted to stop the clinically obese dad of six, who he claimed to have observed behaving suspiciously in the self service area.

"I naturally assumed that I was their millionth customer and they wanted to give me a cash prize or something," said Terry. "I've got no interest in such earthly bounty, so I quickly sold him a dummy and tried to leg it. But I didn't realise they work in pairs and he had a colleague waiting outside."

Corndolly was frogmarched to the manager's office where the details of the holy phenomenon revealed themselves.

"I couldn't believe my eyes," said Terry. "The bottle of bleach that I'd purchased had somehow transubstantiated into vodka. Not only that but the security tag had been snipped off and the bar code for the cleaning product was stuck to the voddy with chewing gum."

"Talk about moving in mysterious ways. I mean, if that's not a rock-solid miracle, I don't know what is."

But rather than call the Archbishop of Canterbury or the Pope to report this deific occurrence, the store manager called the police, and a surprised Terry was taken to the local station and charged with theft.

"I've always been religious," said Corndolly. "So I immediately recognised this as part of the Almighty's grand plan."

He continued: "I honestly think that this bleach turning into voddy was a transcendent act from up on high. Sadly, the security guards and the titheads weren't as quick to see the light. It would seem that we are truly living in a secular society."

ritzy

Despite what he considers a gross miscarriage of justice, online porn aficionado Terry has managed to retain an air of graceful calm throughout his legal tribulations, that culminated in him being bailed pending trial at a local magistrates court. "Our Lord told us to turn the other cheek and forgive our neighbours' trespasses, so I'll face this utter stitch-up by the filth with pious equanimity," he said. "It's in this spirit of tolerance and compassion that I've also asked for several other legally questionable miraculous events to be taken into consideration."

And Terry was equally philosophical about his upcoming court appearance. "Given all my priors, I'll probably get sent down as usual," he said. "But my spirituality allows me to face such adversity with grace and humility, such that my next stretch in the nick can be used for reflection, contemplation and reconnecting with my spice habit."

"Amen to that," he added.

Bill WeetaBixby
MILD-MANNERED BILL BIXBY HID A TERRIFYING SECRET...
GIVE US YER WALLET, GRANDAD!
WHEN ANGRY HE WOULD TRANSFORM INTO A RAGING MONSTER!
DON'T MAKE ME ANGRY...
IF YOU KNOW WHAT'S GOOD FOR YOU!
GAAAAHHHHHH!!
WHAT THE FU-
-CK IS THAT?!
C'MON THEN YOU TITCHY BREAKFASTS!
I'VE GOT HIS WALLET.
STAMP

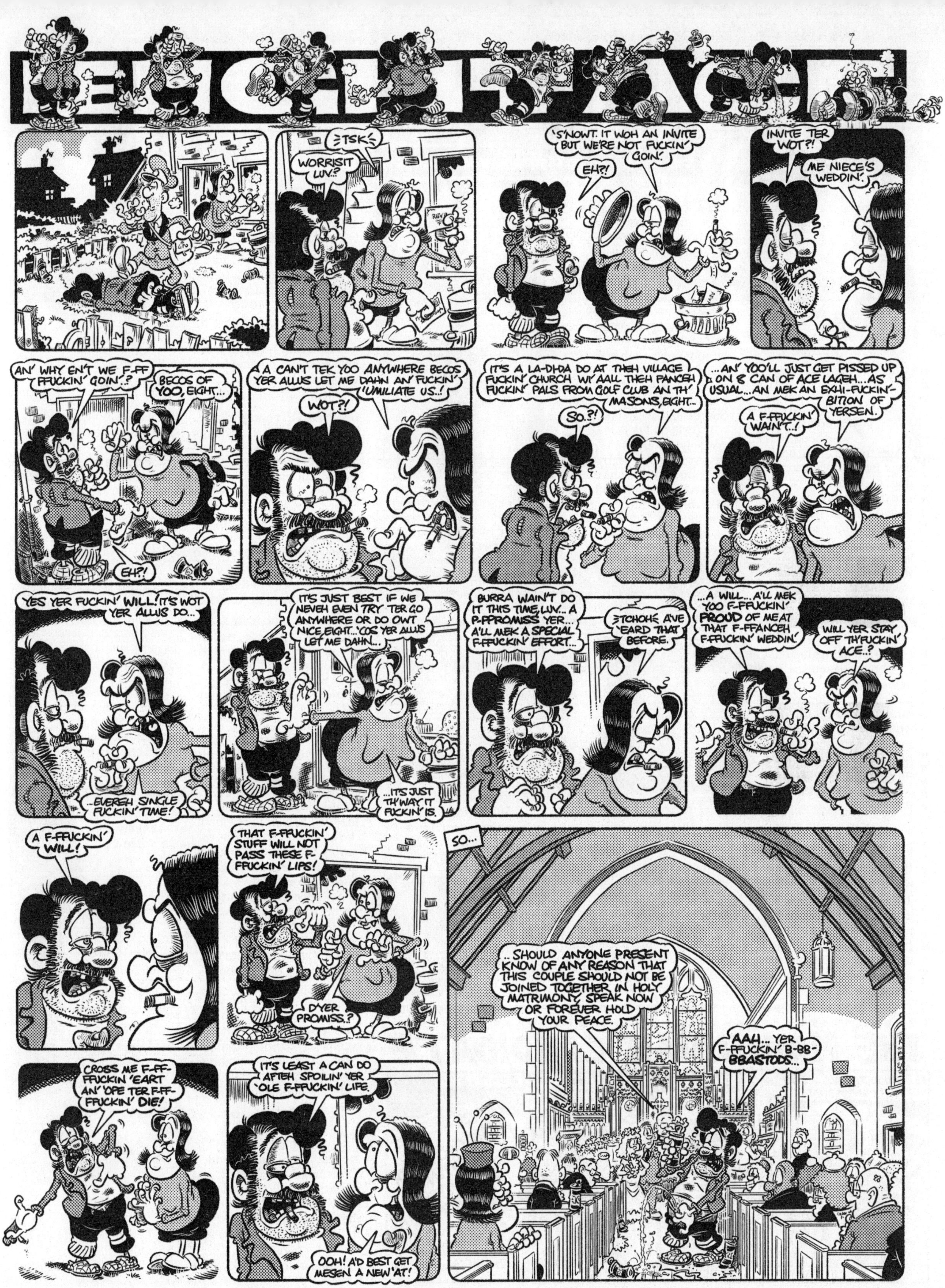
TSK
WORRISIT LUV..?
'S'NOWT. IT WOH AN INVITE BUT WE'RE NOT FUCKIN' GOIN'.
EH?!
INVITE TER WOT?!
ME NIECE'S WEDDIN'.
AN' WHY EN'T WE F-FF FFUCKIN' GOIN'..?
BECOS OF YOO, EIGHT...
EH?!
A CAN'T TEK YOO ANYWHERE BECOS YER ALLUS LET ME DAHN AN' FUCKIN' 'UMILIATE US..!
WOT?!
IT'S A LA-DHDA DO AT THEH VILLAGE FUCKIN' CHURCH WI' AALL THEH FANCEH FUCKIN' PALS FROM GOLF CLUB AN TH' MASONS, EIGHT...
SO..?!
...AN' YOO'LL JUST GET PISSED UP ON 8 CAN OF ACE LAGEH...AS USUAL...AN MEK AN EXHI-FUCKIN'-BITION OF YERSEN.
A F-FFUCKIN' WAIN'T..!
YES YER FUCKIN' WILL! IT'S WOT YER ALLUS DO...
...EVEREH SINGLE FUCKIN' TIME!
IT'S JUST BEST IF WE NEVEH EVEN TRY TER GO ANYWHERE OR DO OWT NICE EIGHT...'COS YER ALLUS LET ME DAHN...
...IT'S JUST TH' WAY IT FUCKIN' IS.
BURRA WAIN'T DO IT THIS TIME, LUV... A P-PPROMISS YER... A'LL MEK A SPECIAL F-FFUCKIN' EFFORT...
TCHOH! A'VE 'EARD THAT BEFORE.
...A WILL...A'LL MEK YOO F-FFUCKIN' PROUD OF ME AT THAT F-FFANCEH F-FFUCKIN' WEDDIN'.
WILL YER STAY OFF TH'FUCKIN' ACE..?
A F-FFUCKIN' WILL!
THAT F-FFUCKIN' STUFF WILL NOT PASS THESE F-FFUCKIN' LIPS!
DYER PROMISS..?
CROSS ME F-FF-FFUCKIN' 'EART AN' 'OPE TER F-FF-FFUCKIN' DIE!
IT'S LEAST A CAN DO AFTEH SPOILIN' YER 'OLE F-FFUCKIN' LIFE.
OOH! A'D BEST GET MESEN A NEW 'AT!
SO...
...SHOULD ANYONE PRESENT KNOW OF ANY REASON THAT THIS COUPLE SHOULD NOT BE JOINED TOGETHER IN HOLY MATRIMONY, SPEAK NOW OR FOREVER HOLD YOUR PEACE.
AAH... YER F-FFUCKIN' B-BB-BBASTODS...

LETTERBOCKS

...co.uk letters@viz.co.uk

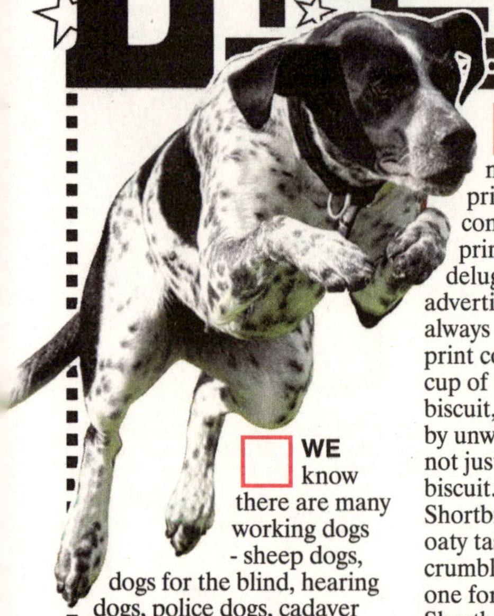

WE know there are many working dogs - sheep dogs, dogs for the blind, hearing dogs, police dogs, cadaver dogs and those big bear-like dogs who dole out rum up mountains. This might all sound impressive, but unemployment amongst dogs is actually well over 99%. So the scrounging, parasitic shit machines aren't as great as they like to think they are.

Damien Woodhouse, Hessle

I FIND the high-pitched squeals and screams of babies and children utterly intolerable. I am sure they would find grown-ups much more welcoming if they made their noises in lower, more soothing tones.

Julian Wiseman, email

IN the event of a catastrophic oil-spill at sea, haven't the likes of Shell and BP considered throwing a load of sliced mushrooms on the slick? Them bastards hoover up all the oil in the pan when I'm trying to do a fry-up. Plus, a bedraggled cormorant might appreciate a snack whilst waiting to be rescued.

Eldon Furse, email

IT seems to me that the major advantage of print media over web content is that with print, the reader is not deluged with aggressive advertising. This is why I always enjoy reading my print copy of *Viz* with a nice cup of tea and a shortbread biscuit, unencumbered by unwanted adverts. But not just any shortbread biscuit. A Barbara's Orkney Shortbread, with its sweet, oaty taste and delicious crumbly texture is the only one for me. Yes, Barbara's Shortbread. Much nicer than Morag's Shetland Shortbread, which is fucking horrible.

Barbara Q. Sauce, Hoy

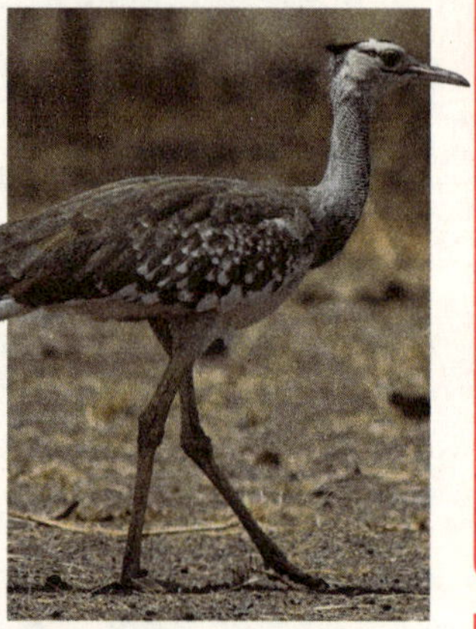

WHAT is Joe Williams from Leeds talking about *(previous annual, p209)*, when he says that all things that rhyme with custard are yellow? I'm eating some chocolate custard which is brown not yellow, quite like the colour of a bustard. Mr Williams needs to have his eyes tested and have a long, hard think before writing this nonsense.

Tom Dixon, York

STAR LETTER

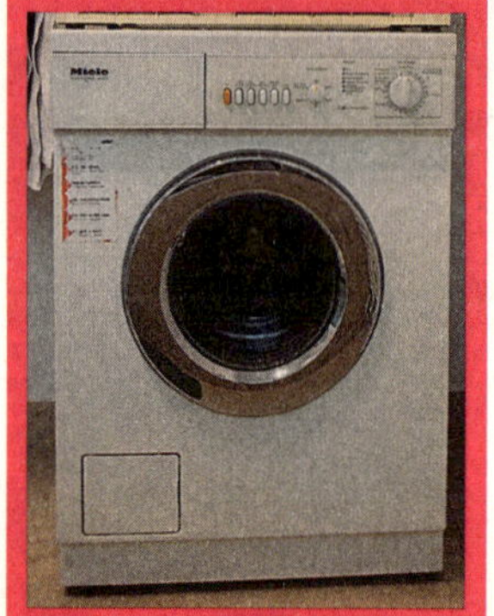

DOES anyone know what's going on inside a washing machine between the point when it's finished the wash cycle and emptied the water out, and the point 2 or 3 minutes later when the door unlocks? I have watched intently through the washer door many times during these periods of forced laundry detainment, and I simply can't see anything happening. Am I missing something, or are the washing machine designers just trying to waste our time?

Brian Flinn, St Helens

I'M confused by Vladimir Putin's hatred of the west. I live in Alaska, so he's actually 'the west' as far as I'm concerned. Honestly, it's one perspective for us civvies, and one for diminutive, bloated despots.

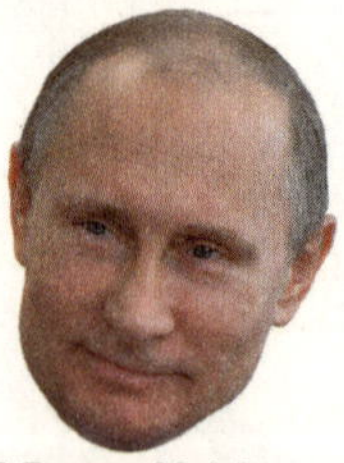

Val Dees, Valdez

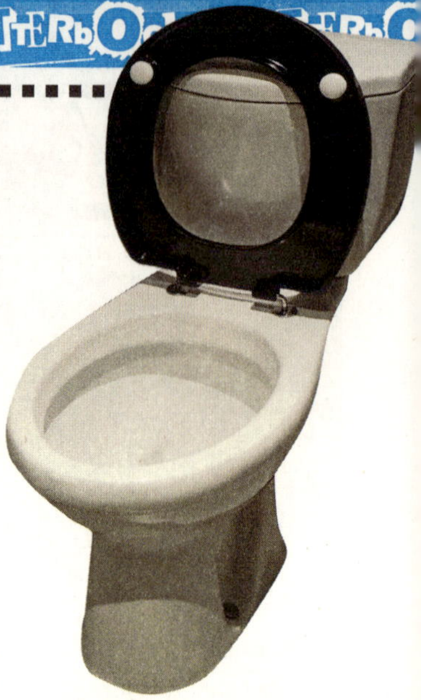

THE toilets in some fancy hotels play the sound of tinkling water, presumably to assist with urination. Why then, in the cubicles, do they not have a flat screen TV on the back of the door showing videos of mudslides? As usual, it is one rule for urinators and another for defecators.

Paul Skinback, London

MY wife bought a cheap rim-block from ASDA the other day. It's certainly helping to keep our toilet clean, as the smell from it is so acrid that I'm now doing my business at the bottom of the garden like the neighbours' cats do.

Joe Hartshorn, Alness

WATER companies always complain about people using moist wipes, saying that they clog the filters. I'm sure they do, but I bet when faced with either an arduous 20-minute bog roll session, or 30 seconds with a couple of moist wipes, all the CEOs of these companies would plump for the latter on the quiet.

Eldon Furse, email

IF all blue-badge parking spaces were not gritted and left covered with extremely slippery ice each winter, then selfish non-disabled drivers would more likely be deterred from using them.

Ian Webb, Bury St Edmunds

I WOULD like to thank the hoodie-wearing youth who took the time to chat to my mum the other day as she was paying for her shopping in the supermarket. It might only have been small talk about sausage rolls, but having a friendly chat with a young stranger made her day. Unfortunately, the lad's friend was nothing like him, and took the opportunity to sneak up behind my mum and steal her purse from her bag whilst she was distracted. If this scoundrel took a leaf out of his pal's book, the world would be a much better place.

Frank Badclown, Leeds

PEOPLE always employ the phrase "you couldn't make it up" in response to actual events. This remarkable lack of imagination in these people beggars belief to the extent that, honestly, one struggles to mentally concoct such a state of affairs.

Prince Asbo, Folkestone

MAYBE the people who stick Barbie Dolls and Action Men up their arses don't derive any sexual pleasure from it at all. Perhaps what really gets them off is the conversation where they explain how it got up there to a world weary consultant.

Duncan White, Southampton

I DON'T know why people say "it's not rocket science" as a means of explaining how simple something is. Rocket science is fairly simple itself. All you have to do is make sure that the thrust the engines produce is greater than the weight of the rocket and off they go. "It's not getting an appointment with your GP" would be a better phrase, as this is virtually fucking impossible.

Tommy Tanksworth, Crewe

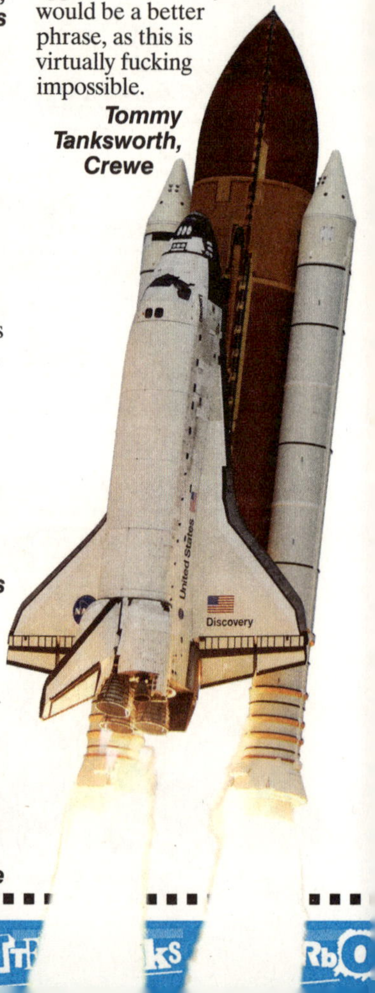

THE MANCUNIAN CANDIDATE

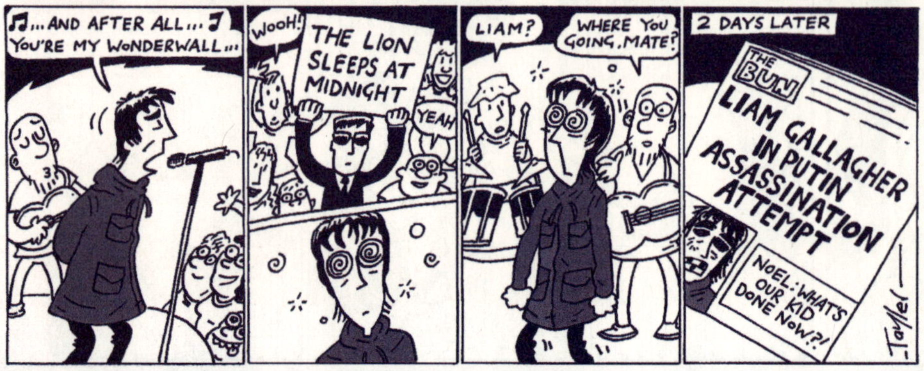

...AND AFTER ALL... YOU'RE MY WONDERWALL...
WOOH!
THE LION SLEEPS AT MIDNIGHT
YEAH
LIAM?
WHERE YOU GOING, MATE?
2 DAYS LATER
THE BUN
LIAM GALLAGHER IN PUTIN ASSASSINATION ATTEMPT
NOEL: WHAT'S OUR KID DONE NOW?!
Tayler

TOP TIPS

COLOURBLIND learner drivers. At traffic lights, the top grey light means "stop" and the bottom grey light means "go". Don't bother with the middle grey light as no-one really knows what that is for anyway.

T O'Neill, Glasgow

SAVE on washing dirty breakfast bowls by pouring your cereal and milk straight into a plugged sink. When you're finished, simply unplug it and rinse the remaining milk away.

Adam, Manchester

TOY manufacturers. Instead of making pretend vacuum cleaners for toddlers, make them actually work, then my 2-year-old old grandson can vacuum the entire house and save me getting off my arse.

Eldon Furse, email

PUT a Euro in a supermarket trolley coin slot, then loiter near the entrance. By taking £1 from unassuming customers in return for the trolley and presumed pound coin, you make 12p on each transaction. Repeat until 1 Euro is worth more than £1 or until you are arrested.

Harry Dobby, The Potteries

MAKE sure dropped toast lands butter-side down by leaving it unbuttered and covering your kitchen floor with a thin layer of butter.

Mark, Stockport

CEOS. Having a number plate on your Range Rover starting with "B055" is only relevant to your immediate employees, and even then only within working hours. Perhaps a plate including "TW4T" would be a more accurate substitute?

Eldon Furse, email

toptips@viz.co.uk

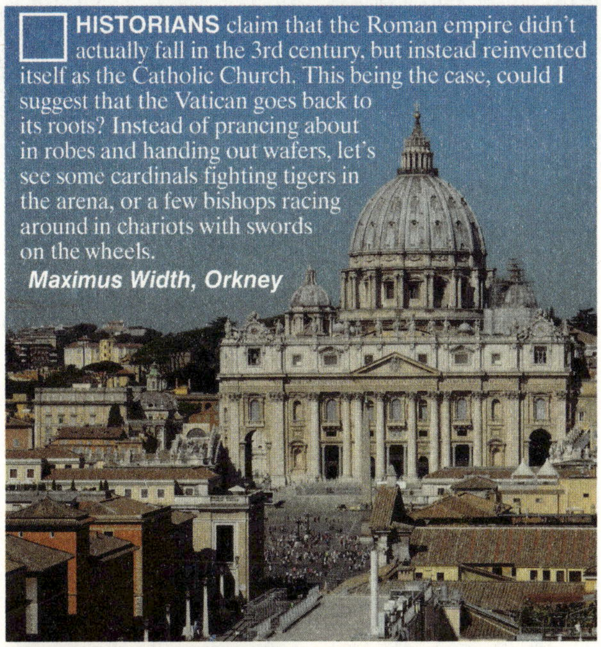

HISTORIANS claim that the Roman empire didn't actually fall in the 3rd century, but instead reinvented itself as the Catholic Church. This being the case, could I suggest that the Vatican goes back to its roots? Instead of prancing about in robes and handing out wafers, let's see some cardinals fighting tigers in the arena, or a few bishops racing around in chariots with swords on the wheels.

Maximus Width, Orkney

WHEN it was built in 1957, the Lovell Telescope at Jodrell Bank was the largest steerable dish radio telescope in the world but has since been overtaken by two larger telescopes built in America and Germany. If astronomers aimed it upwards and filled it to the brim with cornflakes and milk, we would be able to get our record back, in the 'World's largest cereal bowl' category. It might interfere slightly with the sensitivity of the instrument readings but it'd be worth it to see the look on America and Germany's faces.

Wendy Garibaldi, Cardiff

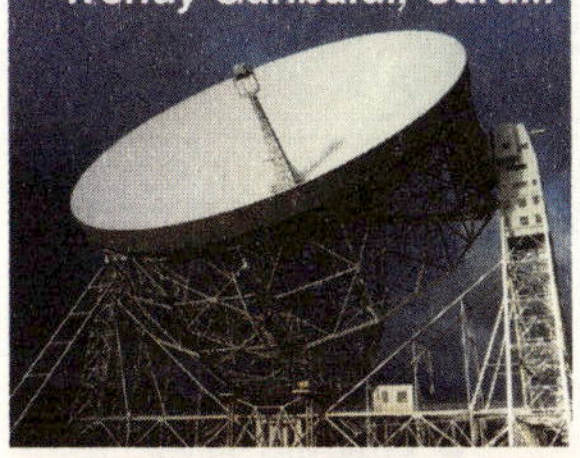

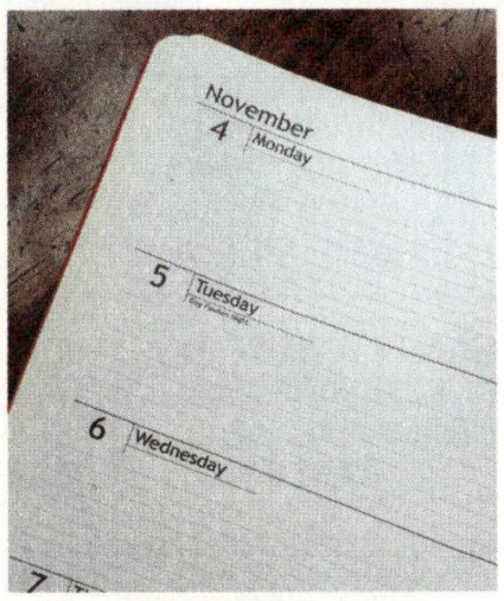
November
4 Monday
5 Tuesday
6 Wednesday

I RECENTLY read that when quarries have served their purpose, they are turned into either lakes or landfill sites. It struck me that these two choices of 'afterlife' – one beautiful and serene, the other rancid, horrifying and putrid – is a bit like the quarry version of Heaven and Hell. Except, in this case it's actually real – unlike all that stupid God and the Devil bollocks.

Prof. R Dawkins, Oxford

THREE months of the year end in -ember and "the 5th" is not actually rhymed with anything in the poem. But apart from that, *"Remember, remember, the 5th of November"* is a great mnemonic device.

Christina Martin, Bexhill-on-Sea

WHAT are you doing, using clever analogies of the current state of social media disinformation? I've also noticed hidden references to well-known works of art in prior issues. Stop it now. I expect fart and knob gags and nothing more cerebral, thank you very much.

Nick Haskell, Adelaide

I WAS disgusted to read that Prince Charles has followed in the footsteps of notoriously ego-centric celebrities such as P Diddy and The Artist Formerly Known as Prince by changing his name to "King Charles". And it hasn't gone unnoticed that he waited until his mother died before embarking on this vanity project. He must have known that her late majesty would never have stood for such nonsense.

Rachel Zani, Reading

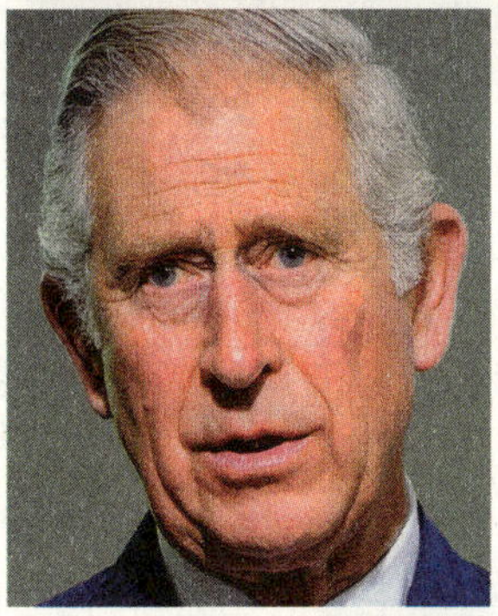

I FELL down a ditch recently whilst walking home paralytic through our local woods. Since then, I have been obsessed by wondering what would have happened if I had been bitten by a radioactive badger during my ordeal. Fighting nocturnal crimes in a stripy black and white outfit sounds the business. Do you think DC Comics or Marvel would be interested?

Les Lloyd, email

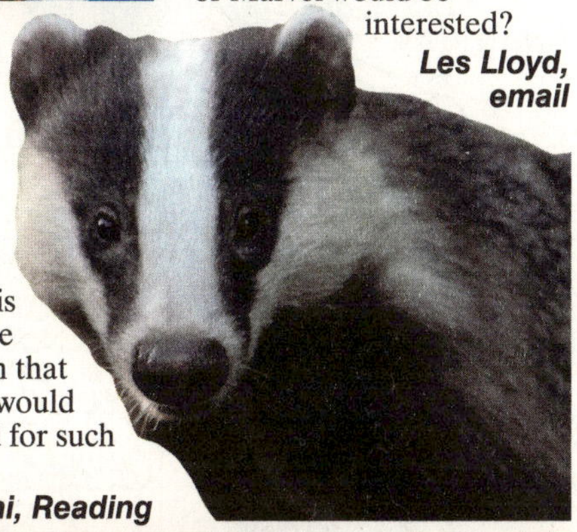

Windbreak Corner

YOU'VE all been farting like thunder and writing in to tell us about it, as if we're the slightest bit interested. Here's a selection of the best wind-related letters we've received.

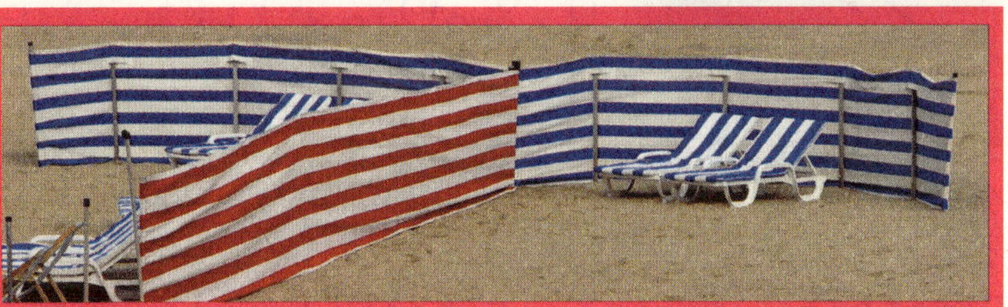

I RECENTLY farted the Da! Da! Da! bit after singing the title line of the song *Shall We Dance*, from the musical *The King and I*. It was absolutely pitch perfect. I might be a lousy singer, but I can fart like Dame Kiri Te Kanawa.

Hector Prowse, Cheam

EVERYONE in the Zoom meeting knows you have just farted when you click mute for 5 seconds. Especially if, when you unmute, your wife yells at you from the next room to stop farting.

Prince Asbo, Fokestone

IT HAS just struck me that my earlier letter may have been misconstrued. When I said I could fart like Dame Kiri Te Kanawa, I meant that I can fart like she sings, not fart like she farts. Could I take this opportunity to apologise to Dame Kiri for any offence caused?

Hector Prowse, Cheam

I WAS waiting for my missus outside Dunelm today when I let fly with a massive fart – and the automatic doors opened! Can any of your readers beat that?

Bob Jones, email

I HAVE just done the loudest fart since records began. And I can say this with confidence because there seem to be no official flatulence volume records currently established. I must therefore be the record holder. Now that the "since records began" on flatulence is officially underway, let battle commence.

J Smotherbox, Newark

REGARDING my earlier letter, I was not implying that Dame Kiri Te Kanawa sounds like me farting when she sings. I was merely trying to communicate to your readers how tuneful my farting was. I realise now that it was a rather poor analogy on many levels, and once again offer my sincere apologies to Dame Kiri.

Hector Prowse, Cheam

I HAD a Goblin meat pudding last night – one of those that you boil in the tin. And this morning whilst singing *O Mio Babbino Caro* from Puccini's opera *Gianni Schicchi*, I dropped a gut that sounded like someone with a smoker's cough blowing a vuvuzela.

Dame Kiri Te Kanawa, New Zealand

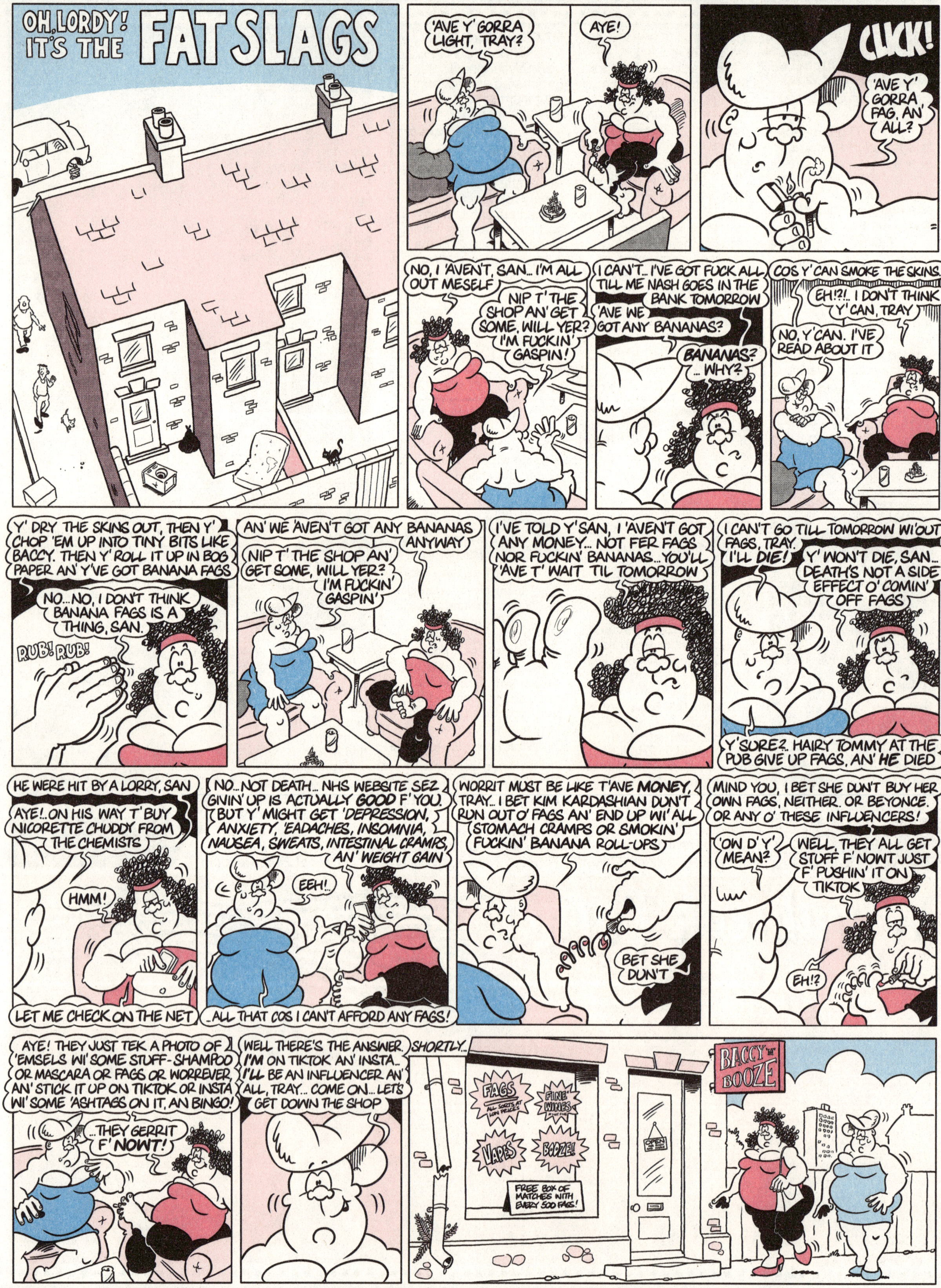
OH, LORDY! IT'S THE FAT SLAGS
'AVE Y' GORRA LIGHT, TRAY?
AYE!
CLICK!
'AVE Y' GORRA FAG, AN' ALL?
NO, I 'AVEN'T, SAN... I'M ALL OUT MESELF
NIP T' THE SHOP AN' GET SOME, WILL YER? I'M FUCKIN' GASPIN!
I CAN'T... I'VE GOT FUCK ALL TILL ME NASH GOES IN THE BANK TOMORROW
'AVE WE GOT ANY BANANAS?
BANANAS? ...WHY?
COS Y' CAN SMOKE THE SKINS
EH!?!... I DON'T THINK Y' CAN, TRAY
NO, Y' CAN. I'VE READ ABOUT IT
Y' DRY THE SKINS OUT, THEN Y' CHOP 'EM UP INTO TINY BITS LIKE BACCY. THEN Y' ROLL IT UP IN BOG PAPER AN' Y'VE GOT BANANA FAGS
NO... NO, I DON'T THINK BANANA FAGS IS A THING, SAN.
RUB! RUB!
AN' WE 'AVEN'T GOT ANY BANANAS ANYWAY
NIP T' THE SHOP AN' GET SOME, WILL YER? I'M FUCKIN' GASPIN'
I'VE TOLD Y' SAN, I 'AVEN'T GOT ANY MONEY... NOT FER FAGS NOR FUCKIN' BANANAS... YOU'LL 'AVE T' WAIT TIL TOMORROW
I CAN'T GO TILL TOMORROW WI'OUT FAGS, TRAY. I'LL DIE!
Y' WON'T DIE, SAN... DEATH'S NOT A SIDE EFFECT O' COMIN' OFF FAGS
Y' SURE?.. HAIRY TOMMY AT THE PUB GIVE UP FAGS, AN' HE DIED
HE WERE HIT BY A LORRY, SAN
AYE!.. ON HIS WAY T' BUY NICORETTE CHUDDY FROM THE CHEMISTS
HMM!
LET ME CHECK ON THE NET
NO... NOT DEATH... NHS WEBSITE SEZ GIVIN' UP IS ACTUALLY GOOD F' YOU. BUT Y' MIGHT GET 'DEPRESSION, ANXIETY, 'EADACHES, INSOMNIA, NAUSEA, SWEATS, INTESTINAL CRAMPS, AN' WEIGHT GAIN'
EEH!
...ALL THAT COS I CAN'T AFFORD ANY FAGS!
WORRIT MUST BE LIKE T'AVE MONEY, TRAY... I BET KIM KARDASHIAN DUN'T RUN OUT O' FAGS AN' END UP WI' ALL STOMACH CRAMPS OR SMOKIN' FUCKIN' BANANA ROLL-UPS
BET SHE DUN'T
MIND YOU, I BET SHE DUN'T BUY HER OWN FAGS, NEITHER. OR BEYONCE. OR ANY O' THESE INFLUENCERS!
'OW D'Y' MEAN?
WELL, THEY ALL GET STUFF F' NOWT JUST F' PUSHIN' IT ON TIKTOK
EH!?
AYE! THEY JUST TEK A PHOTO OF 'EMSELS WI' SOME STUFF- SHAMPOO OR MASCARA OR FAGS OR WORREVER AN' STICK IT UP ON TIKTOK OR INSTA WI' SOME 'ASHTAGS ON IT, AN BINGO!
...THEY GERRIT F' NOWT!
WELL THERE'S THE ANSWER. I'M ON TIKTOK AN' INSTA... I'LL BE AN INFLUENCER AN' ALL, TRAY... COME ON... LET'S GET DOWN THE SHOP
SHORTLY...
BACCY 'N' BOOZE
FAGS
FINE WINES
VAPES
BOOZE!
FREE BOX OF MATCHES WITH EVERY 500 FAGS!
OPEN

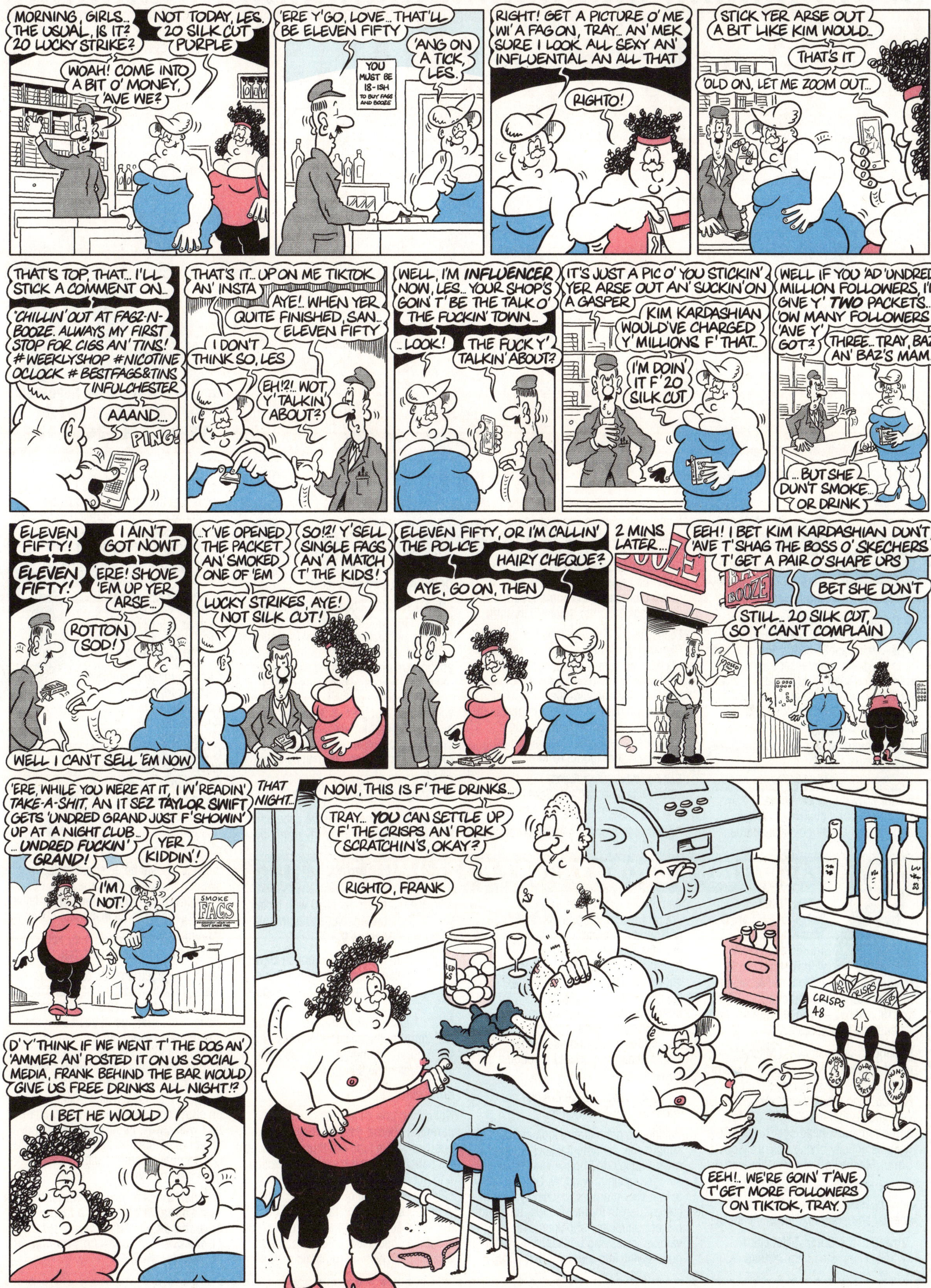
MORNING, GIRLS... THE USUAL, IS IT? 20 LUCKY STRIKE?
NOT TODAY, LES. 20 SILK CUT PURPLE
WOAH! COME INTO A BIT O' MONEY, 'AVE WE?
'ERE Y'GO, LOVE... THAT'LL BE ELEVEN FIFTY
YOU MUST BE 18-18H TO BUY FAGS AND BOOZE
'ANG ON A TICK, LES.
RIGHT! GET A PICTURE O' ME WI' A FAG ON, TRAY... AN' MEK SURE I LOOK ALL SEXY AN' INFLUENTIAL AN ALL THAT
RIGHTO!
STICK YER ARSE OUT A BIT LIKE KIM WOULD...
THAT'S IT
'OLD ON, LET ME ZOOM OUT...
THAT'S TOP, THAT... I'LL STICK A COMMENT ON...
'CHILLIN' OUT AT FAGZ-N-BOOZE. ALWAYS MY FIRST STOP FOR CIGS AN' TINS! #WEEKLYSHOP #NICOTINE OCLOCK #BESTFAGS&TINS INFULCHESTER
AAAND...
PING!
THAT'S IT... UP ON ME TIKTOK AN' INSTA
AYE!.. WHEN YER QUITE FINISHED, SAN... ELEVEN FIFTY
I DON'T THINK SO, LES
EH!?!.. WOT Y' TALKIN' ABOUT?
WELL, I'M INFLUENCER NOW, LES... YOUR SHOP'S GOIN' T' BE THE TALK O' THE FUCKIN' TOWN...
...LOOK!
THE FUCK Y' TALKIN' ABOUT?
IT'S JUST A PIC O' YOU STICKIN' YER ARSE OUT AN' SUCKIN' ON A GASPER
KIM KARDASHIAN WOULD'VE CHARGED Y' MILLIONS F' THAT...
I'M DOIN' IT F' 20 SILK CUT
WELL IF YOU 'AD 'UNDRED MILLION FOLLOWERS, I'D GIVE Y' TWO PACKETS... 'OW MANY FOLLOWERS 'AVE Y' GOT?
THREE... TRAY, BAZ, AN' BAZ'S MAM...
...BUT SHE DUN'T SMOKE... OR DRINK
ELEVEN FIFTY!
I AIN'T GOT NOWT
ELEVEN FIFTY!
'ERE! SHOVE 'EM UP YER ARSE...
ROTTON SOD!
WELL I CAN'T SELL 'EM NOW
...Y'VE OPENED THE PACKET AN' SMOKED ONE OF 'EM
SO!?! Y'SELL SINGLE FAGS AN' A MATCH T' THE KIDS!
LUCKY STRIKES, AYE! NOT SILK CUT!
ELEVEN FIFTY, OR I'M CALLIN' THE POLICE
HAIRY CHEQUE?
AYE, GO ON, THEN
2 MINS LATER...
EEH! I BET KIM KARDASHIAN DUN'T 'AVE T' SHAG THE BOSS O' SKECHERS T' GET A PAIR O' SHAPE UPS
BET SHE DUN'T
STILL... 20 SILK CUT, SO Y' CAN'T COMPLAIN
'ERE, WHILE YOU WERE AT IT, I W' READIN' TAKE-A-SHIT, AN IT SEZ TAYLOR SWIFT GETS 'UNDRED GRAND JUST F' SHOWIN' UP AT A NIGHT CLUB...
...'UNDRED FUCKIN' GRAND!
YER KIDDIN'!
I'M NOT!
SMOKE FAGS
D'Y'THINK IF WE WENT T' THE DOG AN' 'AMMER AN' POSTED IT ON US SOCIAL MEDIA, FRANK BEHIND THE BAR WOULD GIVE US FREE DRINKS ALL NIGHT!?
I BET HE WOULD
THAT NIGHT...
NOW, THIS IS F' THE DRINKS...
TRAY... YOU CAN SETTLE UP F' THE CRISPS AN' PORK SCRATCHIN'S, OKAY?
RIGHTO, FRANK
CRISPS 48
EEH!.. WE'RE GOIN' T'AVE T'GET MORE FOLLOWERS ON TIKTOK, TRAY.

ROMANCING THE DRONE!

FROM LAND'S END to Kerberos – the fourth moon of Pluto, located on the outer rim of the Keiper Belt – we all love Valentine's Day.

Come February 14th, every one of us likes to do something romantic for that extra-special person in our lives. Whether it's knocking up a candlelit Champagne dinner for a certain someone, whisking our sweetheart off for a glamorous weekend in Paris, or paying over the odds at the Shell garage for a bouquet of wilting roses for the missus, Valentine's Day brings out the true romantic in us all.

And our favourite A-List stars are no different. Like all of us, these icons of stage and screen love nothing more than to lavish affection onto their other halves during the most amorous 24 hours of the year, showering them with flowers, chocolates and all manner of luxurious, expensive gifts.

Or so you would think. But is that really the case?

We sent top investigative journalist MAHATMA MACAROON out and about on Valentine's Day, to find out just how 'romantic' Tinseltown's best and brightest REALLY are.

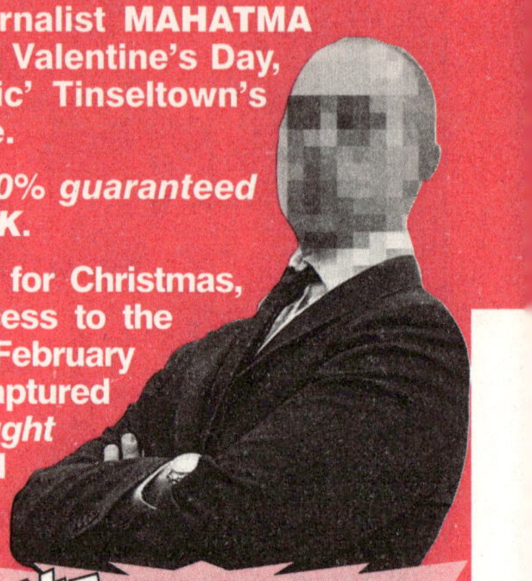

And what he uncovered is 100% guaranteed to make you PHYSICALLY SICK.

Using a drone that he received for Christmas, Macaroon gained exclusive access to the homes of the rich and famous on February 14th – and the footage he captured challenges everything we *thought* we knew about our so-called lovey-dovey showbiz faves.

So, let's find out now if the stars are hopeless romantics – or just plain hopeless – as we go... ROMANCING THE DRONE!

BY VIZ UNDERCOVER REPORTER MAHATMA MACAROON

VALENTINE'S DRONE TARGET NO.1: RICHARD CURTIS

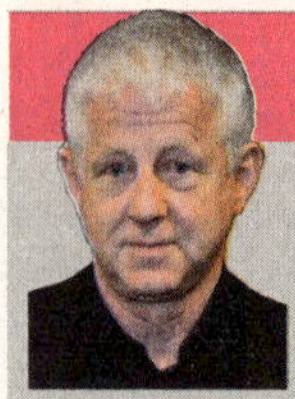

WHEN WE hear the word romance, the first name that comes to mind is that of plummy-voiced film director Richard Curtis.

Curtis and Romance are synonymous, and the left-leaning moviemaker has melted the planet's hearts time and again with his quirky, quintessentially British rom-coms, such as *Four Weddings and a Funeral*, *Notting Hill* and *Love Actually*. But how does Curtis himself treat the person **HE** claims to 'love, actually'?

With the help of my new hi-tech drone, I aim to find out.

Arriving outside the *Blackadder* icon's swanky West London home at 7am on February 14th, I switch my drone on and carefully pilot it over his garden fence. The camera is synched up to my mobile phone, so I can see everything my airborne android assistant sees. Scanning the top floor windows, the drone picks up Curtis's long-term partner, broadcaster Emma Freud, still sound asleep in the master bedroom.

I gently nudge my joystick left in search of Richard, chuckling as I imagine what kind of charming surprise the famously soppy screenwriter will have in store for her. Maybe my drone will catch him rustling up a scrumptious breakfast in bed, with heart shapes pressed into the toast. Or perhaps he's putting the finishing touches to a delightful handmade card?

But no. It turns out Richard is doing something else entirely. Something that chills me to my very bones.

Rather than preparing a heart-warming Valentine's treat for his missus, the Cambridge-educated *Comic Relief* ace is sitting in the upstairs lavatory with his pyjamas around his ankles... **DEFECATING** into the toilet.

I am so shocked, I can barely bring myself to press the record button on the drone's camera, but luckily I manage to. Today is the most romantic day of the year, and as the man behind some of Hollywood's mushiest movies, you'd think Curtis would be showering his special someone with kisses and gifts. But it seems he would much rather push foul-smelling faeces out of his left-wing anus, just metres away from the woman he loves.

*Call me 'old fashioned', but I see **NOTHING** romantic about that.*

When Curtis moves on to the paperwork, I finish recording and fly my drone back onto the street outside. As I walk away, uploading the footage to YouTube in the name of public interest, I can't help feeling a pang of despair for the director's loyal fanbase. These sentimental saps think Curtis is the King of Celluloid Chivalry. How will they feel when they learn about his favourite Valentine's Day pastime: namely, doing a **SHIT** out of his **ARSE** into the **THUNDERBOX?**

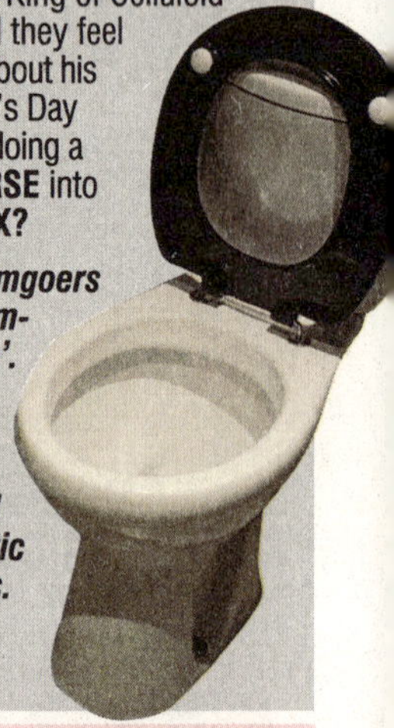

Curtis wowed filmgoers with his 2013 rom-com 'About Time'. And I think it's 'About Time' this two-faced luvvie was outed for the unromantic fraud he really is.

VALENTINE'S DRONE TARGET NO.2: DAVID MITCHELL

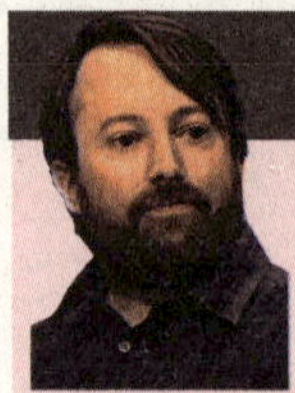

STILL REELING from my horrific experience with Richard Curtis – although pleased that the resulting footage has already reached 100,000 YouTube views – I move on to my next Valentine's Day subject.

Brainbox funnyman David Mitchell keeps us all chuckling with his witty quips on panel shows such as *Have I Got News For You?* and *Would I Lie To You?* It's also well known that the *Peep Show* fave is a true romantic, head over heels in love with his equally brainy missus Victoria Coren-Mitchell off of *Only Connect*.

So it's safe to assume that David will have pulled out all the stops for his special someone this Valentine's Day...

Arriving at the Coren-Mitchells's swanky Hampstead homestead around 9am on February 14th, I fire up my trusty drone and send it soaring over the garden wall. Its camera immediately shows me David in the kitchen, serving freshly made pancakes to his darling wife. He then plants a tender kiss on her lips and presents her with a beautiful card and a bouquet of flowers.

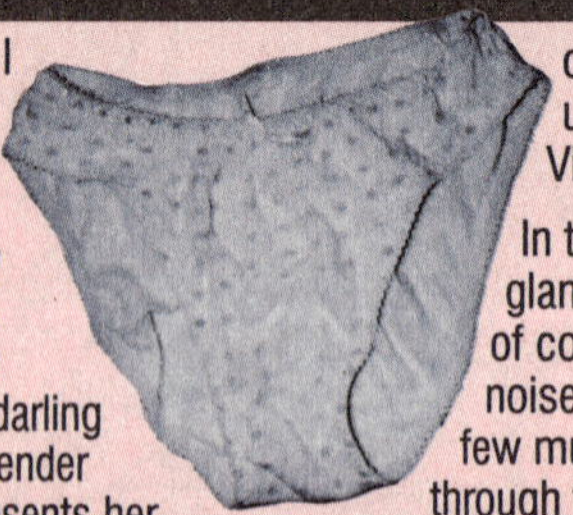

So far, so romantic. But things are about to take a nasty turn...

Wanting to get a closer look at this supposedly sentimental scene, I pilot my drone into the house itself, through an open upstairs window. Unfortunately at that very moment, my newly bought gadget begins to malfunction, spinning out of control and knocking over various vases and bookshelves, before nose-diving into a drawer that turns out to be filled with ladies' underwear – presumably Victoria's.

In the kitchen, I notice David glance upwards with a look of concern on his face at the noise from upstairs. Surely a few muffled bumps and crashes through the ceiling won't distract the amorous humorist from this once-a-year Valentine's breakfast?

But it does.

Not caring one jot about ruining his partner's special day, Mitchell stomps upstairs with a face like thunder, leaving his pancakes – and his wife's affection – to get cold. In the bedroom, he catches a glimpse of my drone, which is now draped in several pairs of his missus's scuds, and begins yelling foul-mouthed obscenities into the camera. Charming. The most romantic day of the year should be all about whispering sweet nothings to your true love. But Mitchell would rather screech four-letter abuse at an airborne inanimate object.

*Call me 'old fashioned', but I see **NOTHING** romantic about that.*

The zany gagsmith tries to grab the drone, clearly worried that *WILTY* fans will find out that he has been lying all along. But I manage to get it airborne and pilot it straight out through the window, showering glass into the garden. Moments later it arrives safely back, still with two pairs of Victoria's knickers attached, which I decide to put on eBay, donating the money to charity. As I walk away, I shake my head and reflect on another A-List hypocrite whose public persona differs vastly from their private one.

Mitchell loves to present himself as an amiable chap and a loving husband on our TV screens. But Have I Got News For You! – he's nothing of the fucking sort.

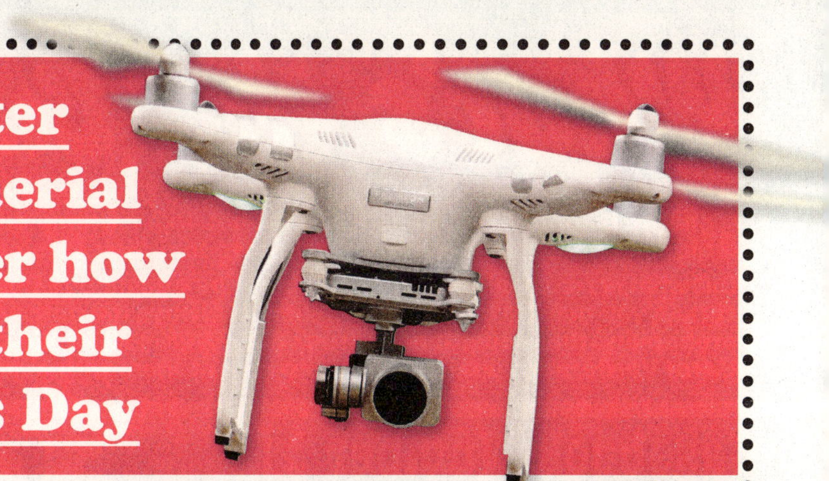

Undercover *Viz* reporter Mahatma Macaroon uses aerial surveillance tech to discover how the stars *REALLY* treat their loved ones on Valentine's Day

VALENTINE'S DRONE TARGET NO.3: GARY BARLOW

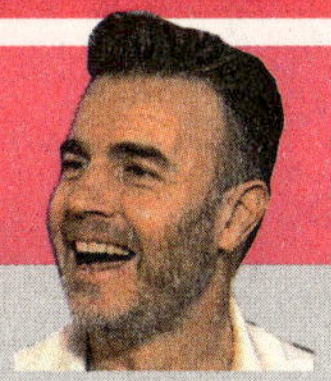

ASK ANYONE on Earth who sings the sweetest love songs and they will always respond with the same two words: *Gary Barlow OBE*.

As the hunky frontman of '90s boyband Take That, formerly big-boned Barlow made his name crooning such heart-swelling hits as *Babe*, *Relight My Fire* and *A Million Love Songs*. And despite left-wing attempts to smear Gary over his entirely above board tax arrangements, there is simply no finer purveyor of romantic music on this planet. You would assume, then, that the Cheshire-born vocalist turns his love up to 11 on Valentine's Day.

I intend to find out.

I arrive at Gary's swanky North London mansion around midday. Having refreshed YouTube to see that my video of Richard Curtis moving his bowels is now nearing 4 million views, I set up my drone and fly it straight over Barlow's back wall.

My surveillance droid scans each window to find that the whole house appears to be empty. My heart swells – Barlow is probably treating the love of his life to a romantic candlelit lunch at a swanky restaurant, one where the waiter brings her a red rose with each course. Feeling relieved that romance is apparently not dead, I decide to give the *Back For Good* balladeer and his missus a romantic surprise on their return and let Gary take it from there.

There is no gesture more romantic than covering a bedroom with rose petals, so I head straight to the nearest park and begin scooping up handfuls of the romantic tokens from the rose beds. Soon enough, I've collected five binbags full of floral magic, ready to turn the Barlow's bedroom into a cavern of love. There were a lot of leaves on the ground, it had been pissing with rain, and the gardeners had just put a load of horse shit around the roses, so there was quite bit of other stuff in with the rose petals. But I'm confident Gary's wife will still be delighted by the gesture.

Returning to Barlow's not-so-humble abode, I attach the bin bags to my drone's antennae and send it wobbling back up over the wall. The bedroom window is locked, so I'm forced to pilot the drone straight through it, and the impact of the shattering glass rips the bin bags to shreds, showering the entire room with my heart-melting Valentine's tribute.

As the compost-covered gadget lands back at my feet, I see Gary's car pull up to the house. It's all I can do not to well up with tears. With this charmingly quirky surprise as his launch pad, I'm guessing the *Could It Be Magic* minstrel will go on to show his partner the most memorable V-Day ever.

But my guess is wrong. ***DEAD WRONG.***

I hear muffled shouts from inside the house, followed by Barlow's voice, bellowing, 'Who the f*****g **FUCK** has done this?!!' Minutes later, a police car pulls up outside his gates. It takes a moment to process what I'm seeing. Rather than serenading his sweetheart on the beautiful bed of rose petals I've provided, Barlow has instead decided to call the coppers!

Call me 'old fashioned', but I see ***NOTHING*** *romantic about that.*

I send my drone back up a final time. Sure enough, it captures footage of a purple-faced Barlow in the bedroom, pointing out the rose petals (and leaves and horseshit) to a couple of police officers. Next to him, Mrs B looks on in shock, clearly dismayed that her cack-handed hubby has RUINED the most special day of the year. This certainly will be her most memorable Valentine's ever... But for all the wrong reasons.

Barlow famously topped the charts in 1996 with the single 'How Deep Is Your Love'. But had he asked that question of himself, the answer would surely have been 'not very.'

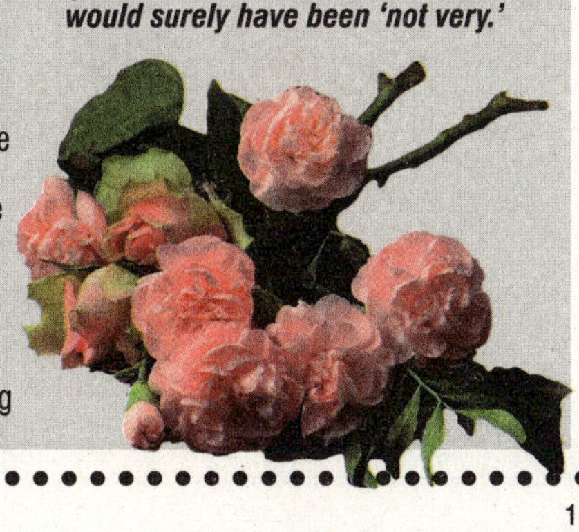

VALENTINE'S DRONE TARGET NO.4: FIONA BRUCE

IN THESE SICKENING times of 'woke' political correctness, it's not only men who are permitted to perform romantic gestures on Valentine's Day – *women can too!* You literally couldn't make it up.

And as a proudly outspoken 'feminist', Beeb icon Fiona Bruce probably believes that men and women are 'equal'. But does this 'equality' extend to the *Question Time* fave sweeping her hubby off his feet on February 14th?

Breaking news! Does it ***BOLLOCKS***.

Having slipped past the filth that Barlow called on me, I head straight for Bruce's palatial two-storey mansion nearby. Arriving just after lunch, I have a quick check on my Richard Curtis video (15 million views and rising), before once again powering up my trusty drone and flying it over Fiona's fence.

Straight away, I spot four men walking up the garden path and knocking on the front door, which is promptly opened by the *Antiques Roadshow* ace and her husband. *Now this is more like it.* Clearly, romantic-hearted Fiona has hired a **BARBERSHOP QUARTET** to serenade her hubby on the doorstep! And while the group could have made more of an effort on the costume front – rather than stripy blazers and straw boaters, they are simply wearing everyday suits and ties – it's still a delightfully touching gesture on Fiona's part.

Finally, I think to myself: an A-Lister who takes Valentine's Day seriously!

I activate the drone's built-in microphone in order to hear which tender love song the troupe are going to perform – *and that's when the disappointment hits*. It transpires that these men are **NOT** Valentine's balladeers at all – they are detectives, warning Bruce and her hubby that a "dangerous lunatic" is at large in the area, vandalising celebrity houses.

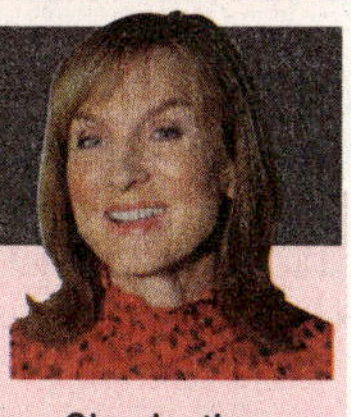

Oh dear. Fiona has raised my hopes and then cruelly dashed them to pieces. Clearly, the heartless ex-*Panorama* host is just as unromantic as the rest of them.

As I pilot my drone back over the wall, I hear the detectives explaining that they are close to catching the perpetrator having traced the 'IP address' he used to post a YouTube video earlier in the day. At that same moment, a police van screeches up next to the bush I'm crouching in and several officers wrestle me to the ground.

Chuckling at the mix-up, I explain to the tit-heads that far from being a "dangerous lunatic" I am in fact an award-winning undercover reporter investigating A-List Valentine's day hypocrisy. But the fuckwitted rozzers will not listen to reason. They place me in handcuffs and tell me I'm under arrest for "voyeurism, wanton criminal damage and the dissemination of offensive scatological imagery."

Call me 'old fashioned', but I see ***NOTHING*** *romantic about that.*

As I am hauled away in the back of their van, I can't help sobbing in despair at everything I've learned today. We look to our celebrity icons as generous, big-hearted softies who live charming, fairytale lives. But they're not. They're joyless, soulless automatons who simply aren't capable of feeling love.

I'll be spending this February 14th in a prison cell, shitting in a bucket. But I take comfort in the fact that I'll still have a more romantic evening than any of the showbiz stars.

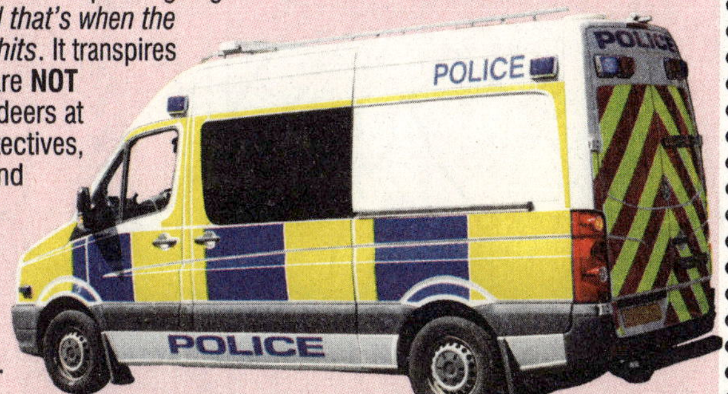
POLICE
POLICE
POLICE

NEXT WEEK: "Call me 'old fashioned', but I see NOTHING steak-and-blow-jobby about that". Mahatma uses his drone to assess how the A-List female stars treat their hubbies on March 14th's Steak and Blow-Job Day

What's the Chance?

with TV maths wizard Carol Vorderman

IN a civil court, the prosecution only have to prove their case on the balance of probability, ie, that the charge is more likely to be true than not. In a *criminal* court, however, the burden of proof is much higher, and the prosecution must prove that their version of events is true *beyond reasonable doubt*. But what *is* reasonable doubt? And can it be quantified? Doubt can never be eradicated and no matter how certain you may be of something, there is always the possibility that it is not so. But what is a 'reasonable probability' that something is true? 80%? 90%? 99%? We put four true-life scenarios to saucy maths wizard *Carol Vorderman*, and asked her to look at them with a statistician's eye, crunching the numbers to establish the truth.

Casebook Number 1

EARLIER this year, 45-year-old Alfred Cinnabun walked gingerly into the A&E department of Queen's Medical Centre in Nottingham. X-rays showed that he had a TV remote control device lodged up his rectum. He informed medical staff that he had slipped over when changing the TV channel whilst wearing a loose-fitting bath robe, and had fallen awkwardly onto the device, which had subsequently become lodged in his anal cavity. The device was removed successfully, but two weeks later, Mr Cinnabun was back at the hospital with the TV remote once again embedded in his rectum. Staff were astounded to hear that he had suffered exactly the same mishap, and they once again successfully removed the remote. But their astonishment turned to incredulity a week later, when Mr Cinnabun presented at A&E for a *third* time with the same remote control device lodged in exactly the same place as a consequence of exactly the same misadventure. And whilst the staff believed Mr Cinnabun's version of events in the first instance, one or two of them now suspected that he may have been inserting the item deliberately for purposes of sexual gratification. Were they correct, or was Mr Cinnabun simply the victim of an appallingly bad run of luck?

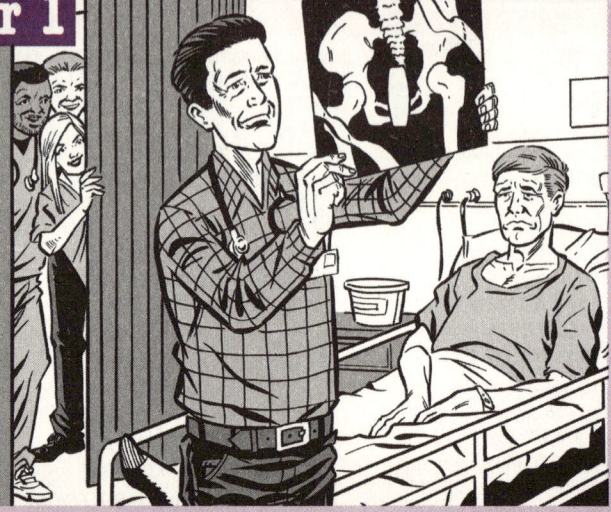

Carol Says: "According to government figures, around 30,240 people per year present at A&E departments with objects stuck up their bottoms, anything from mobile phones to Barbie dolls and small bottles to courgettes in a condom. So clearly, falling on objects and having them accidentally penetrate the body is actually quite a common occurrence. In fact, these patients represent about 2% of A&E admissions, about the same number as those coming in with football-related ankle sprains. So had Mr Cinnabun come in just once, his story would likely be true beyond reasonable doubt. Coming in a second time with the same story may seem suspicious, as the chances of an innocent mishap befalling to the same person twice is now 0.02 x 0.02 (0.0004 or 4 patients in every 10,000 Casualty admissions). And someone presenting 3 times with a remote stuck up his fundament represents just 8 patients in every million. However, with 67 million people in the UK, that means that Mr Cinnabun is one of 536 people every year who will fall on an object three times and have it wedge in their rectum. That's enough people to fill Leeds City Varieties."

CAROL'S VERDICT: The doubters can shove it, Mr Cinnabun's explanation is likely.

Casebook Number 2

SETTING out to catch the bus to work on Thursday 6th June 2022, Mr Barry Witherspoon remembered he had left an essential folder in the kitchen. Returning home to collect it, he found his wife, Cheryl lying naked on the settee in the living room of their semi-detached house in Wells. This would undoubtedly have pleased any husband, were it not for the fact that their next door neighbour Mr Colin Belch was also in the room in a similar state of undress. Cheryl quickly explained to her suspicious husband that she had been in the shower when she heard a burglar in the house and let out a scream of alarm. Mr Belch, who was also showering in his house, heard her cries through the adjoining wall, and fearing his neighbour was in danger, ran round to help without stopping to get dressed. He ran naked into the next door house just as a shaken Mrs Witherspoon came down the stairs from the shower. A concerned Mr Belch laid his neighbour down on the settee to calm her nerves, and was just about to make her a cup of tea when Mr Witherspoon came in to fetch his folder. It appears to be a plausible story, but in the cold light of day, do the numbers say it is plausible beyond reasonable doubt?

Carol Says: Let's take this question from the top and approach it through the discipline of statistics. The average shower lasts 6 minutes, meaning that there are 288 6-minute slots during the day when a shower can be taken. However, 96 of those slots will be between 11pm and 7am, when most people are in bed, which leaves 192 showering windows of opportunity during a typical day. The chances therefore of Mrs Witherspoon and Mr Belch showering at the same time that Thursday are 1 in 192 (0.52%), about the same odds as bumping into a friend in a busy pub. The fact that most people shower in the morning reduces the odds even further. Police records also show that there were 275 break-ins in the Wells area in June 2022 – that's 1 in 45 households, so there was a 2.22% probability that the Witherspoon's house would be targeted by thieves. Multiplying these odds together – 0.52 x 2.22 – gives an answer of 1.1544%, a little better than a 1-in-100 probability that Mrs Witherspoon was not fucking her neighbour Mr Belch.

CAROL'S VERDICT: When the numbers get it together, it's unlikely, but not beyond reasonable doubt.

Casebook Number 3

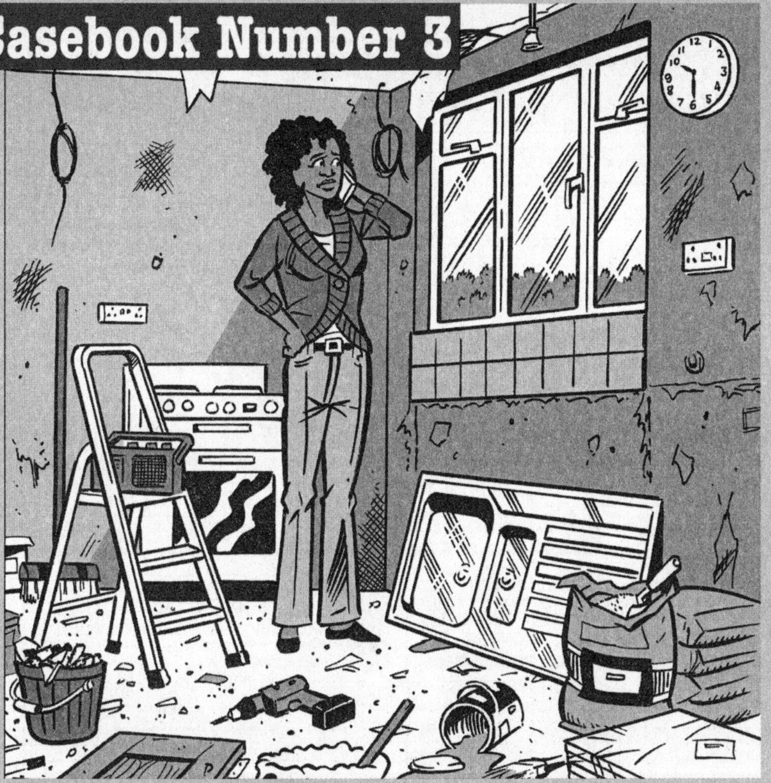

MRS Denise Squires accepted a quote from High-End Budget Kitchens to fit a brand new sink unit and cupboards in the kitchen of her terraced home in Hartlepool, and paid a deposit of £250. The business owner, Mr Derek Piles, arranged to come at 9:00 on Monday 4th September 2018 and complete the job in a day. However, by 10:30 on the day in question, he had still not arrived, so Mrs Squires called him to ask where he was. He then broke the news that he could not come as his grandmother had died that morning, but he promised to be there the next morning at 9:00 sharp. When he was still not there at 10:30 on the Tuesday, Mrs Squires once again called and was informed that tragically, Mr Piles had lost his grandfather at breakfast. On Wednesday morning, Mr Piles's mother died, and his father passed on the Thursday, preventing him from turning up on both days to start Mrs Squires's kitchen. On Friday, Mr Piles lost his wife, and said that because of all the funerals he had to arrange, he didn't know when he would be able to start. Was Mr Piles tragically bereaved five days on the trot, or does his story sow seeds of doubt in your mind?

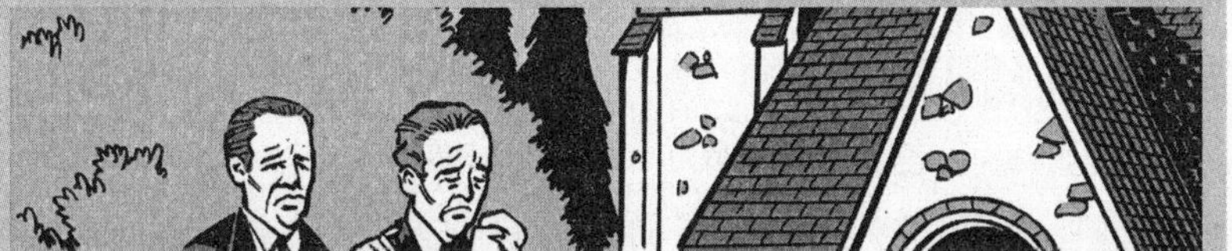

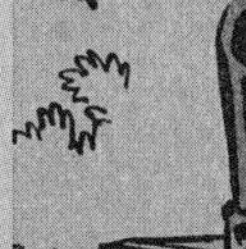

Carol Says: *Most of us will outlive both our parents and grandparents, so Mr Piles's story, on the face of it, sounds credible. But when you ask how many people lose all of them in a single week, things look a little different. If you assume that Mr Piles's grandmother could have died on any day of the year, there is a 1:365 chance of her popping her clogs on the Monday that Mr Piles was booked to start Mrs Squires' kitchen. That left 364 days on which his grandfather could have died. The chances of them dying on that Monday and Tuesday were therefore 1:365 x 1:364, or 1 in 132,860. Factor in his mother and father dying on the Wednesday and Thursday, and you come to a staggering 1 in 1.75x10^{10} chance of them all dying on subsequent days that week. Bearing in mind that we all have a 50% chance of outliving our partner, his wife dying on the Friday makes these odds double to 1 in 3.5x10^{10}. To put that in perspective, that's exactly the same odds as filling 10 Wembley Stadiums with beans, one bean of which has had an X drawn on it with a sharpie, then jumping into one of the bean-filled Wembleys and selecting a single bean at random and getting the one with the X.*

CAROL'S VERDICT: Mr Piles's story is dying on its arse. Highly unlikely.

Casebook Number 4

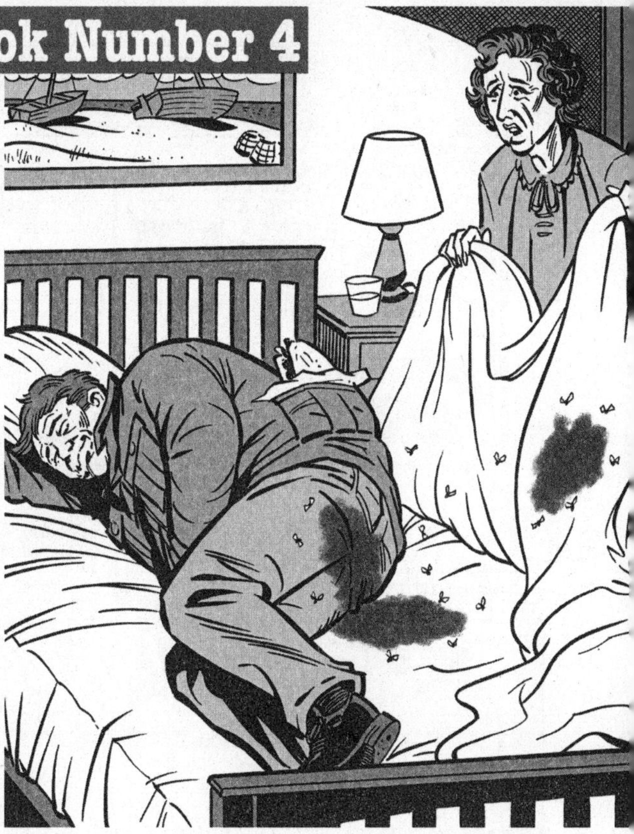

MR Arthur Wellesley returned home at 3:30am one Wednesday morning in 2022 after a night out drinking with his friends, and climbed into bed fully clothed. Shortly after this, his wife Margaret awoke after detecting a foul odour apparently emanating from her husband's side of the bed. Turning on the reading light, she saw that her husband's trousers, as well as the bedsheets, were caked in faeces. Mr Wellesley was in a deep sleep and despite his wife's efforts he couldn't be woken, so she went to sleep in the spare room. The following morning, she confronted her husband, who told her that on returning from his night out, he had spotted a fox prowling in the front garden. This animal, he ventured, must have crept into the house via the cat flap in search of food. Attracted by the half-eaten kebab in Mr Wellesley's jacket pocket, the fox must have crept upstairs and entered the bedroom. After eating the kebab, the wily animal most likely did its business onto the seat of Mr Wellesley's trousers before making its escape. However, this was the third night in a row that this thing had happened, and Margaret was beginning to suspect that there might be another explanation for the foulage in the bed. What does your nose tell you?

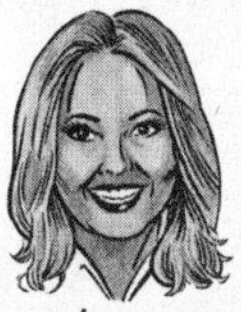

Carol Says: *There are 24,782,800 households in Britain, 26% of which have a cat – that' means there's a cat-flap in 6.4 million doors. In addition, there are around 150,000 urban foxes in the country, which means that each fox has easy access to around 43 homes. Therefore on any one night, each house with a cat-flap has a 1:43, or 2.3% chance of being invaded by a fox – that's the same chances of picking one lottery number correctly, so it's perfectly feasible that a fox got into the Wellesleys' home that night. Foxes are scavengers by nature, and so Mr Wellesley having a kebab in his pocket adds validity, albeit unquantifiable, to his version of events. But according to naturalists, these wild dogs void their bowels 3 times a day, and this is where the story hits the rails. It only takes a fox 10 seconds to defecate, and there are 8640 10-second slots in a day. That means that there is a 3:8640, or 1:2880 chance that the animal parked its breakfast whilst in the house. The probability of the event taking place three nights running as Mr Wellesley describes is therefore (2.3% x 0.0347%)^3, which is 0.000493% or 1:202839.*

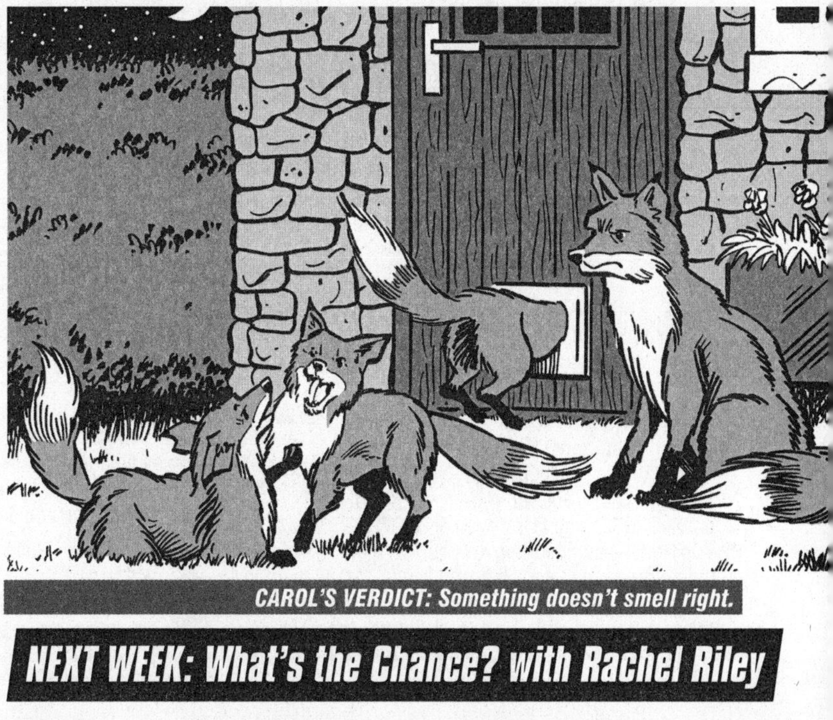

CAROL'S VERDICT: Something doesn't smell right.

NEXT WEEK: What's the Chance? with Rachel Riley

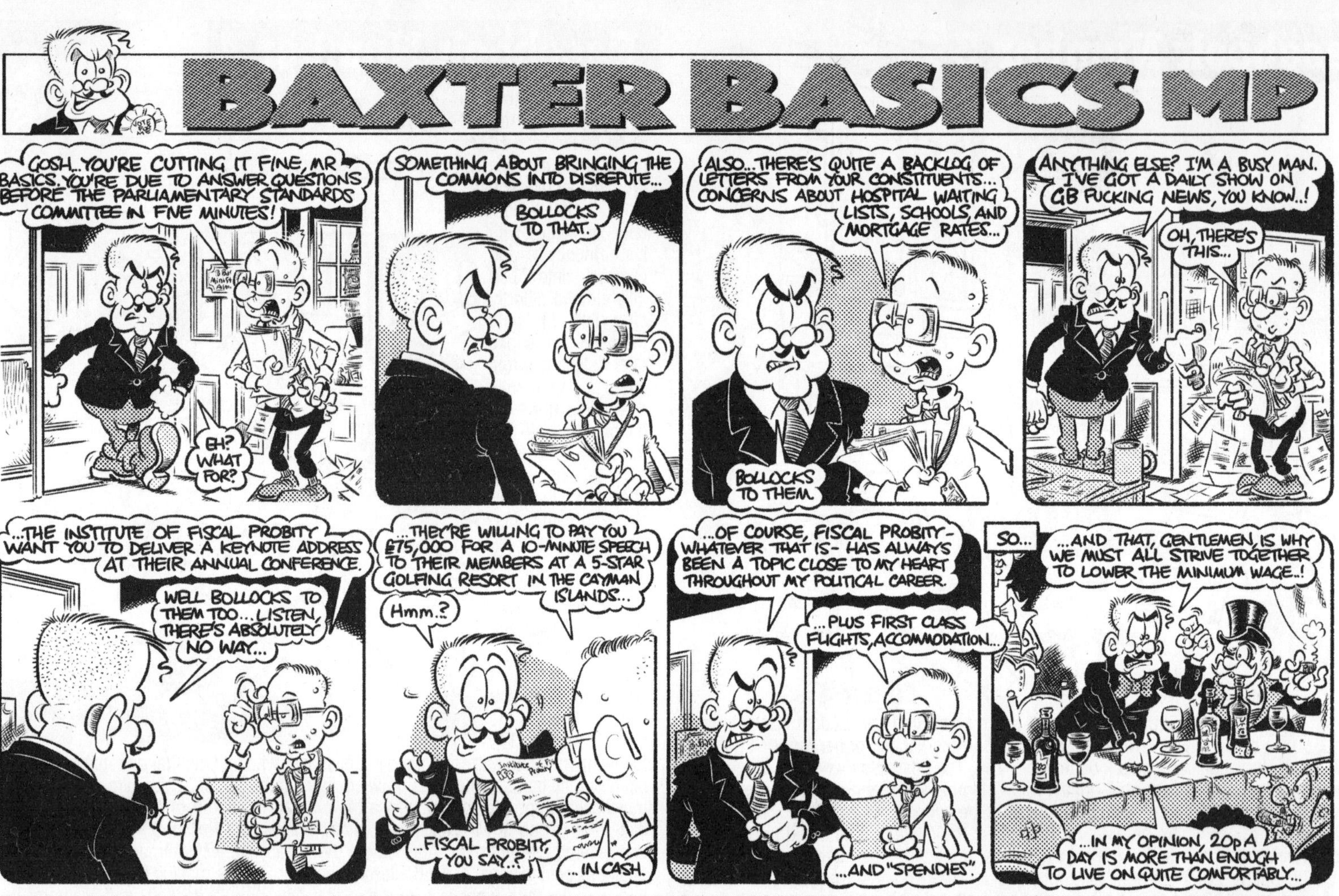
BAXTER BASICS MP
GOSH... YOU'RE CUTTING IT FINE, MR BASICS. YOU'RE DUE TO ANSWER QUESTIONS BEFORE THE PARLIAMENTARY STANDARDS COMMITTEE IN FIVE MINUTES!
EH? WHAT FOR?
SOMETHING ABOUT BRINGING THE COMMONS INTO DISREPUTE...
BOLLOCKS TO THAT.
ALSO... THERE'S QUITE A BACKLOG OF LETTERS FROM YOUR CONSTITUENTS... CONCERNS ABOUT HOSPITAL WAITING LISTS, SCHOOLS, AND MORTGAGE RATES...
BOLLOCKS TO THEM.
ANYTHING ELSE? I'M A BUSY MAN. I'VE GOT A DAILY SHOW ON GB FUCKING NEWS, YOU KNOW..!
OH, THERE'S THIS...
...THE INSTITUTE OF FISCAL PROBITY WANT YOU TO DELIVER A KEYNOTE ADDRESS AT THEIR ANNUAL CONFERENCE.
WELL BOLLOCKS TO THEM TOO... LISTEN, THERE'S ABSOLUTELY NO WAY...
...THEY'RE WILLING TO PAY YOU £75,000 FOR A 10-MINUTE SPEECH TO THEIR MEMBERS AT A 5-STAR GOLFING RESORT IN THE CAYMAN ISLANDS...
HMM..?
...FISCAL PROBITY, YOU SAY..?
...IN CASH.
...OF COURSE, FISCAL PROBITY - WHATEVER THAT IS - HAS ALWAYS BEEN A TOPIC CLOSE TO MY HEART THROUGHOUT MY POLITICAL CAREER.
...PLUS FIRST CLASS FLIGHTS, ACCOMMODATION...
...AND "SPENDIES".
SO...
...AND THAT, GENTLEMEN, IS WHY WE MUST ALL STRIVE TOGETHER TO LOWER THE MINIMUM WAGE..!
...IN MY OPINION, 20p A DAY IS MORE THAN ENOUGH TO LIVE ON QUITE COMFORTABLY...

7 THINGS YOU NEVER KNEW ABOUT LORRIES (AND 3 THINGS YOU NEVER KNEW ABOUT QUARRIES)

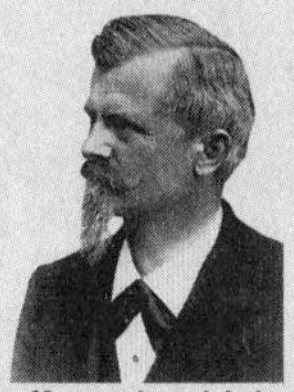

1 **THE LORRY** was invented in 1896 by German engineer Wilhelm Maybach. A passionate advocate of urinating in Lucozade bottles, Maybach soon realised he needed something to throw the bottles out of when he was finished. He decided that a big fuck-off road vehicle would be perfect, and hey presto: the modern lorry was born!

2 **THE SMALLEST** ever lorry driver was Calvin 'Tiny Rig' Phillips. The minuscule trucker piloted an articulated freightliner the size of three toasters next to each other, delivering diminutive goods such as thimbles, sugar cubes and bookie's pencils. To communicate with other truckers, Phillips spoke into a CB radio unit no bigger than a Liquorice Allsort, and when he needed to urinate he wazzed in a Lucozade bottle the size of a grain of rice.

3 **THE WORLD'S** biggest quarry can be found in Mount Airy, North Carolina, USA. It is so big that it can easily contain 66 football pitches – *each one the size of Wales!*

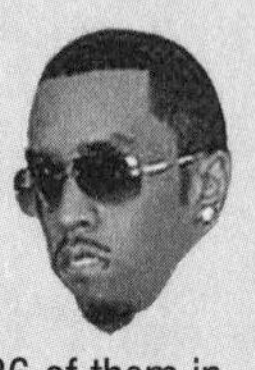

4 **YOU'D THINK** that the owner of the most Eddie Stobart lorries would probably be the Eddie Stobart Group. *But you'd be wrong!* It's actually US gangsta rap ace **P DIDDY!** The Harlem-born hip-hop fave adores the iconic green road vehicles, and keeps 736 of them in a big field just outside Cumbria. "I don't even drive them muthafuckas," Diddy told *Puzzler* magazine. "I just like to get up in the cab and give the horn a good old honking."

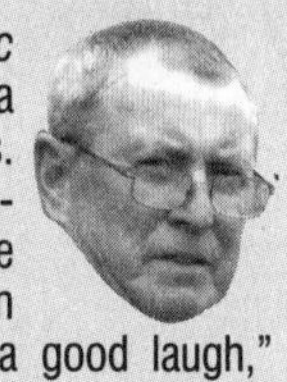

5 **BELIEVE IT** or not, *Bergerac* actor **JOHN NETTLES** lived in a quarry for much of the 1990s. The Cornish telly fave resided in a 300-acre open-pit mine used primarily for the excavation of construction aggregate on the outskirts of Colchester. "It was a good laugh," Nettles told *Vanity Fair*. "The rent was cheap and you were entitled to take as much sand and gravel as you wanted. It got a bit noisy whenever the miners were blasting the rock, but I was out filming *Midsomer Murders* a lot of the time, so it didn't bother me."

6 **YOU MAY** have wondered why lorry drivers always honk their horn when passers-by do a horn-honking gesture at them. Well, it's because *not* honking following a honk-mime is **ILLEGAL** in the UK! A passage in the *Magna Carta* states that *"any driv'r of the waggon who sounds not his h'rn yet that gent sees a pedestrian who doest pumpeth his f'rearm, so shalt that gent payeth the fine of fifteen shillings."* Incredibly, this iron-clad law, *which was written more than six centuries before lorries were even invented,* has never been repealed. You couldn't make it up!

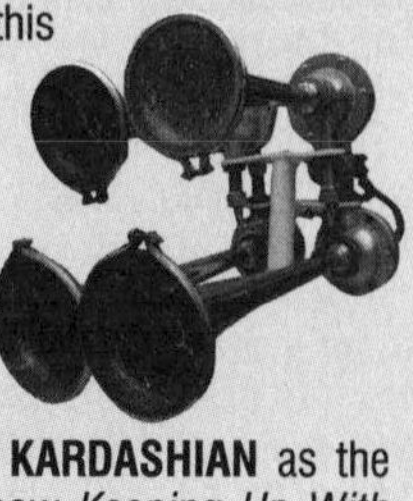

7 **WE ALL** know Hollywood 'It' girl **KIM KARDASHIAN** as the star of iconic reality show *Keeping Up With The Kardashians*. But the busty influencer is also a *licensed Heavy Goods Vehicle driver!* Curvy Kim acquired her Class 1 C+E Lorry Licence back in 2019, meaning she is legally permitted to pilot any rigid vehicle over 7.5 metres and up to 32 tonnes. The chesty heiress is currently studying for an additional Category F licence, which would permit her to drive an agricultural tractor and crop sprayer. It would also entitle her to drive a combined harvester, but only on private land.

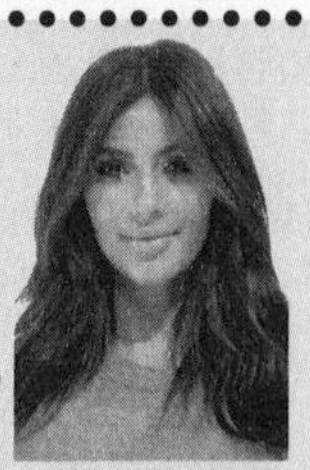

8 **THE CURRENT** world record for throwing a piss-filled Lucozade bottle out of a moving lorry is held by US trucker Cletus 'Bushwhacker' Bixby. Travelling at a speed of 72 miles per hour on Alabama's Interstate 65, Bixby rolled down his window and hurled the urine-suffused vessel a whopping 186 FEET, shattering the previous record of 141 feet set by Billy 'Smokey Bear' O'Malley.

9 **WHILE THERE** have been many hit songs written about trucks over the years, such as *Boy Gets A Truck* by Keith Urban, *Truck Drivin' Man* by Lynyrd Skynyrd and *Truck Yeah* by Tim McGraw, there have been NO hit songs explicitly about *lorries!* "I guess it's because not much stuff rhymes with 'lorry,'" explains chartologist Paul Gambaccini. "There's 'sorry' and 'quarry', and maybe even 'Corrie' – as in *Coronation Street*. But that's basically it. Whereas with 'truck' the possibilities are endless – 'tuck', 'stuck', 'muck', 'cluck', 'puck' and of course the 'F' word." Gambaccini adds.

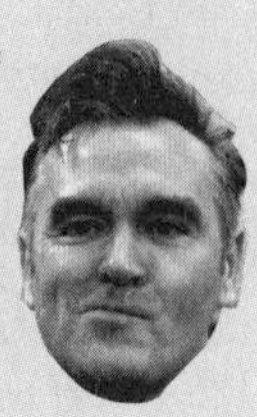

10 **IN THE ENTIRE** history of recorded music, there have only been two references to quarries – the song *Gravel Pit'* by nine-man hardcore rap troupe **WU-TANG CLAN** and the album *You Are The Quarry* by gladioli-arsed pop twat **MORRISSEY**.

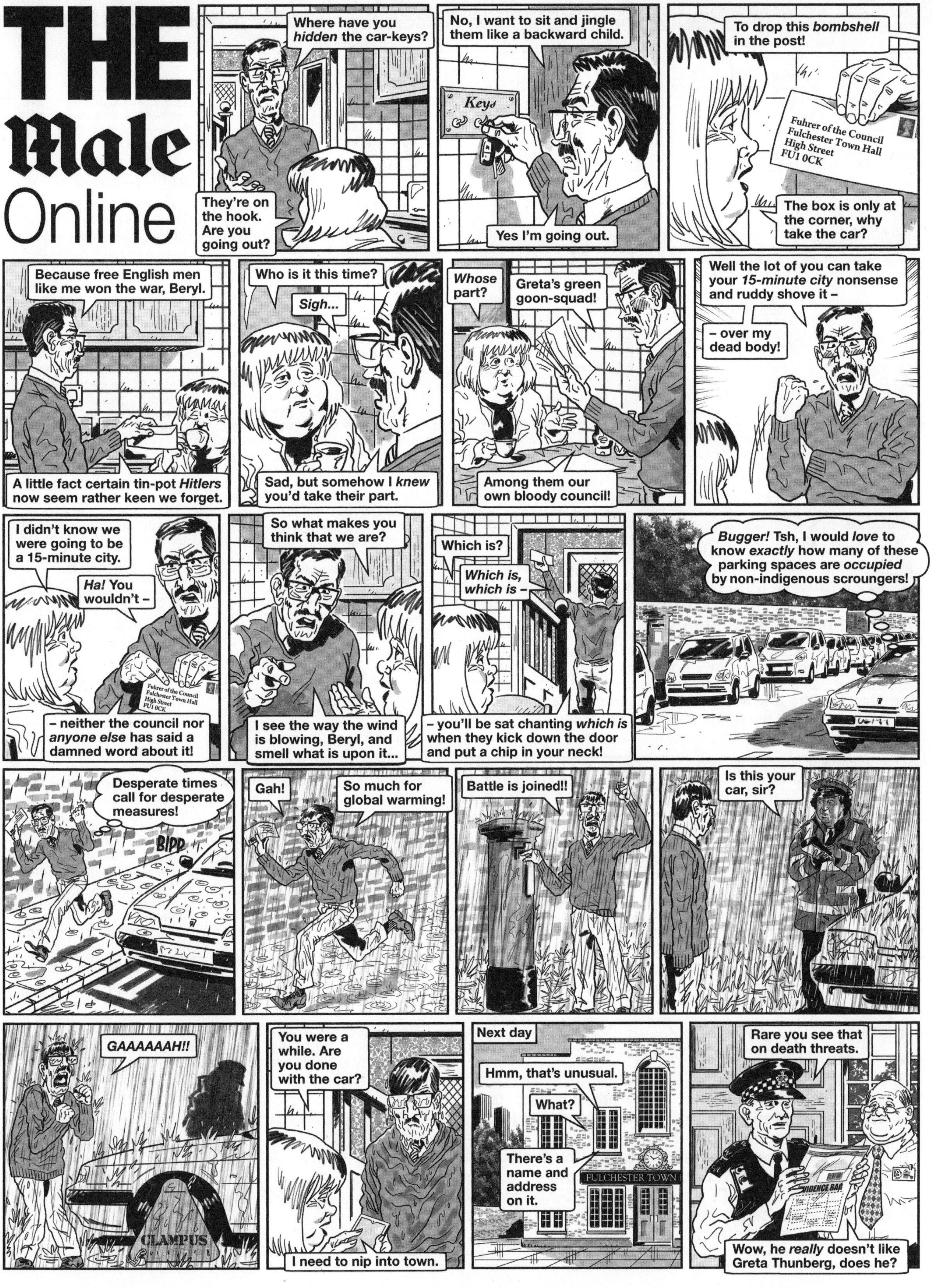
THE
Male
Online
Where have you hidden the car-keys?
They're on the hook. Are you going out?
No, I want to sit and jingle them like a backward child.
Keys
Yes I'm going out.
To drop this bombshell in the post!
Fuhrer of the Council
Fulchester Town Hall
High Street
FU1 0CK
The box is only at the corner, why take the car?
Because free English men like me won the war, Beryl.
A little fact certain tin-pot Hitlers now seem rather keen we forget.
Who is it this time?
Sigh...
Sad, but somehow I knew you'd take their part.
Whose part?
Greta's green goon-squad!
Among them our own bloody council!
Well the lot of you can take your 15-minute city nonsense and ruddy shove it –
– over my dead body!
I didn't know we were going to be a 15-minute city.
Ha! You wouldn't –
Fuhrer of the Council
Fulchester Town Hall
High Street
FU1 0CK
– neither the council nor anyone else has said a damned word about it!
So what makes you think that we are?
I see the way the wind is blowing, Beryl, and smell what is upon it...
Which is?
Which is, which is –
– you'll be sat chanting which is when they kick down the door and put a chip in your neck!
Bugger! Tsh, I would love to know exactly how many of these parking spaces are occupied by non-indigenous scroungers!
Desperate times call for desperate measures!
BIPP
Gah!
So much for global warming!
Battle is joined!!
Is this your car, sir?
GAAAAAAH!!
CLAMPUS
You were a while. Are you done with the car?
I need to nip into town.
Next day
Hmm, that's unusual.
What?
There's a name and address on it.
FULCHESTER TOWN
Rare you see that on death threats.
VIDENCE BAG
Wow, he really doesn't like Greta Thunberg, does he?

CATS IN THE ATTIC!

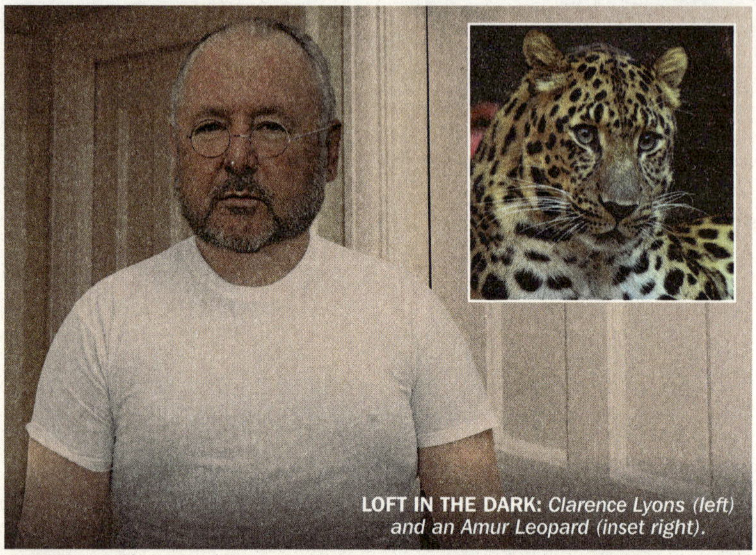

LOFT IN THE DARK: *Clarence Lyons (left) and an Amur Leopard (inset right).*

A SOUTH Yorkshire DIY-er's dream of maximising the value of his property lies in tatters thanks to woke bureaucrats and the fact that his disused roofspace is home to a breeding pair of Amur leopards.

Former hardworking homeowner CLARENCE LYONS, 61, was hoping to convert his loft into a third bedroom, adding a tidy sum to the value of his semi-detached house in Wombwell, Barnsley. But the discovery of endangered big cats living in the loft now means his home improvement plans have had to be put on hold.

EXCLAWSIVE!

"Last year the neighbours put in a dormer window, stuck their house on the market and got the asking price inside a week," the estranged dad of two told his local paper *The Barnsley Trombone and Flugelhorn*. "For me it's a no-brainer, as I need to get out of this town, fast."

He continued: "I'm sick to death of the whole stinking place and every single person in it. If I could start over somewhere else, all my problems would simply go away."

But the unemployed former kitchen salesman's escape fantasy became a nightmare when he invited a builder to quote for a similar conversion job on his own two bedrooom house.

"I'd only ever opened the loft hatch once, a couple of years back," he said. "A flap of sooty lagging flopped on my face, so I slammed it shut and have never so much as looked up there since."

According to Lyons, a local builder, Bob Plumb, arrived and clambered into the loft to assess the state of the timbers. "I was downstairs in the kitchen filling the kettle to make us both a cup of tea when the screaming began," he told the paper.

"There were blood-curdling yells from the loft and the builder came down ten times faster than he went up," he said. "He was covered in blood."

"Rather than haggling with him, and him dropping hints about discounts for cash as expected, I found myself doing first aid and dressing some horrific wounds."

brevet

An ambulance was called and as Mr Plumb was carried away, he managed to tell Clarence that whilst up in the loft, he had been attacked by two fully-grown leopards and would not be submitting a quote.

Tragically, Mr Plumb died on the way to hospital. Not of his wounds, but by drowning after the back door of the ambulance opened on a tight bend near Barnby Basin, where the stretcher bearing the hapless artisan flew out, skated across a busy road, and plunged into the canal.

Shaken by news of his big cat infestation, Lyons brought in pest-controllers to get rid of his unwanted guests, but their verdict was not good. It was, in fact, the exact opposite (ie. bad). They told him that they had identified the animals in his loft as Amur leopards, a protected species.

A recent survey by the International Union for Conservation of Nature suggests no more than two-dozen Amur leopards remain alive on Earth, and due to the endangered status of the beasts, Lyons is prohibited by law from disturbing them with home improvement projects.

"I can't trap them, poison them, gas them or anything. It's woke political correctness gone mad," he said.

"Utter mad wokeness gone politically correct," he added for emphasis.

"If I harm or distress these leopards in any way, I'm looking at an unlimited fine and potentially a custodial sentence. And we all know what happens to people who mess with endangered species behind bars," he said. "In the showers, I mean."

testimonial

According to experts from the Environment Agency, the leopards in Clarence's loft are a male and a female, the only breeding pair of wild Amur leopards outside the species's native habitat, the snowy regions of southeastern Russia and northern China.

"It's just my effing luck," Clarence grumbled. "The bloke from the agency said they were unique and literally priceless. So I asked him: What about me? Aren't I priceless and unique too?"

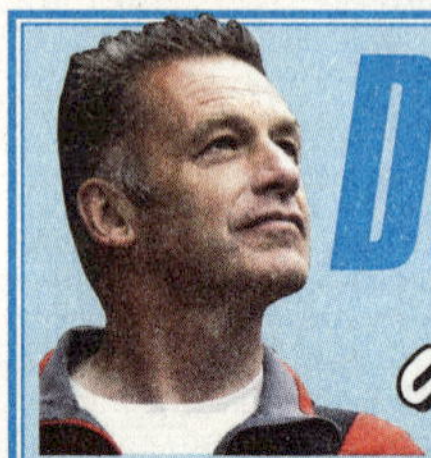

DUCK AND COVER

with Chris Packham

How to Protect and Survive in case of Amur Leopard attack.

IF ONE Barnsley man has Amur leopards living in his loft, it's likely that many other homes in the United Kingdom are similarly infested. And whilst the chance of being ripped apart and killed by these beasts in your own home is fortunately low, there is still a slim possibility that it could happen. We've teamed up with spiky-haired TV naturist CHRIS PACKHAM to bring you some handy Top Tips on protecting yourself from Amur leopard attacks in the home...

AMUR leopards feed on small mammals, so adult humans are probably too big to be looked upon as prey. If you have small children, make sure they wear a large coat around the house. If they come into contact with a leopard, they should hold the coat open like a cape to make themselves appear larger.

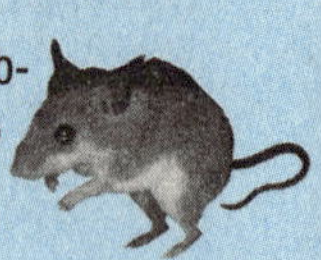

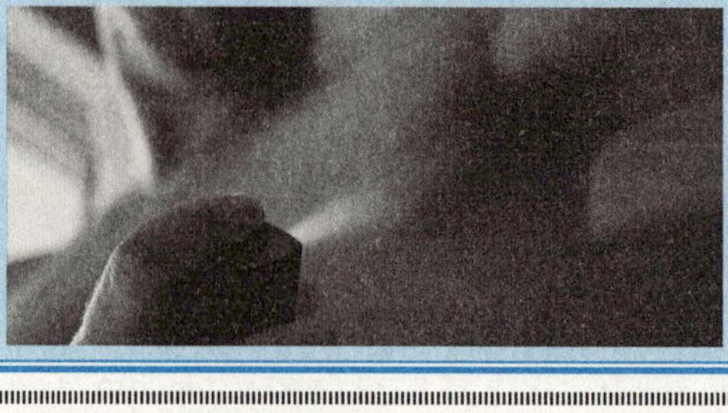

LIKE all wild cats, Amur leopards rely on their sense of smell to track their quarry. Use an antiperspirant to mask your bodily odour in order to make it more difficult for them to track you down as you go about your daily business in the house.

...4-PAGE LEOPARDS SPECIAL... 4-PAGE LEOPARDS SPECIAL... 4-PAGE LEOPARDS SPECI

Barnsley man in spot of bother after loft leopard discovery

The Environment Agency officer responded that while there were only a handful of these leopards left, people like Mr Lyons were ten-a-penny and nothing special. To add insult to injury, he told the former photocopier paper salesman that if he fell under a bus right now, no-one would care.

"It was a bit brutal, to be honest," he said. "Clearly the authorities believe these leopards are more important than me."

To make matters worse, the leopards have now learned how to open and close the hatch and have begun prowling around Mr Lyons's house.

According to experts, the big cats are generally active during the night, so during daylight hours, Mr Lyons should be able to move around his house without fear of attack. But he told reporters that he is taking no chances when he goes to bed, piling furniture behind his bedroom door.

"Thank God I've got an old chamber-pot which my ex-wife picked-up on a flea-market and left behind in her hurry to get away," he said. "So luckily I'm catered for in that department."

"All the same, it sticks in my craw that I am reduced to slopping-out every morning like a convict."

"Not that I would know what that's like, as I have never been inside," he added.

pancake

Lyons has been told by experts that if he does encounter one of the leopards prowling on the stairs or landing, he should not be too concerned as they are shy creatures and would probably not kill him unless they felt threatened or were hungry or startled. But he says this news gives him little comfort.

"I've seen what they did to the builder, and I can't say I'm in a hurry to put that theory to the test," he said.

LOFT AND FOUND: Big cats have learned how to open hatch.

AVOID decorating your living room with spotty wallpaper, as the Amur leopard is a master of camouflage. It uses its rosette-spotted coat to blend in with its surroundings, sneaking up until it is close enough to launch a deadly attack at lightning speed when it is too late for you to take any evasive action.

IF YOU do come face to face with an Amur leopard in your home, don't panic. You hopefully have at least a few seconds to act as the animal sizes you up for attack. Back away slowly, keeping eye contact with it and see if you can slip into an airing cupboard or wardrobe until it has gone away.

ALL animals are extremely protective of their young, and if your Amur leopards have bred, you must be extra careful. Never get between the mother leopard and her cubs, and in case the feline family come in, always make sure you have a clear exit available, such as a door or window.

That's all, folks, Chris x

LeoPaRdbOx

☐ **APPARENTLY** leopards are all classified as 'big cats'. But I once saw one at Bristol Zoo that had just given birth to some cubs, and the things were about half the size of my pet moggie at home. Big cats, my arse.
Cromwell Ditchwater, Ely

☐ **THEY SAY** that no two leopards have the same spots, and that their markings are as individual as fingerprints. This may be important if a leopard commits a burglary and is caught on CCTV, but other than that, I find this to be an utterly useless piece of information.
Manfred Ursine, Crewe

☐ **AN ADVERT** on the TV last night was asking people to donate money to a scheme to save the endangered snow leopard. These magnificent creatures are under threat from poachers and habitat destruction, and the already small population is expected to decline a further 10% by 2040. It is a perilous situation for these beautiful, mountain-dwelling cats and donating to the Save the Snow Leopard charity could be their best hope of survival. However, I only like Amur leopards, so they won't get a penny from me. No, sir.
Idris Coldheart, Wells

☐ **THEY SAY** that a leopard can't change its spots, but I don't suppose that applies to that man who has had his entire body tattooed with leopard markings. He could go on Channel 4's *Tattoo Fixers* and have them changed into something else. Or he could go to Laserase and have them removed altogether.
Aiken Drummond, Leeds

☐ **I HONESTLY** don't know why jaguars have a ruddy car named after them and leopards don't. Leopards are every bit as good as jaguars, and I think a Leopard XE-Mark 2 sounds like a proper fanny magnet.
Frank Topper, London

☐ **I HAVE** always loved leopards, so when I won the lottery I thought I would treat myself to a couple. I gave my wife £20,000 and sent her out to buy them. Imagine my disappointment when she came back with a pair of cheetahs! I have never liked cheetahs as I have always thought they looked like cat whippets. Fortunately my wife still had the receipt and I was able to return them to the shop and swap them for leopards. But it's the last time I send my wife out to buy big cats.
Billy Wiffles, Surrey

☐ **APPARENTLY** black panthers are actually melanistic variants of either leopards or jaguars which have excessive black pigments in their skin, so to distinguish them from each other, they should actually be referred to as black panther leopards or black panther jaguars. In which case, surely it would be simpler to just call them black leopards or black jaguars. What do we pay these fucking zoologists for?
Torbjorn Mould, Aberdeen

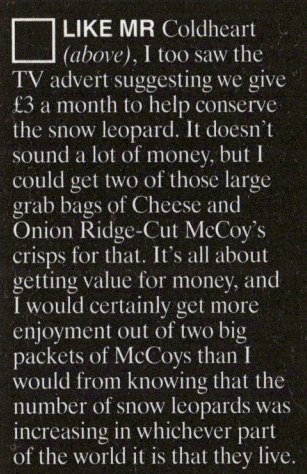

☐ **LIKE MR** Coldheart *(above)*, I too saw the TV advert suggesting we give £3 a month to help conserve the snow leopard. It doesn't sound a lot of money, but I could get two of those large grab bags of Cheese and Onion Ridge-Cut McCoy's crisps for that. It's all about getting value for money, and I would certainly get more enjoyment out of two big packets of McCoys than I would from knowing that the number of snow leopards was increasing in whichever part of the world it is that they live.
Henry Bastard, Luton

... 4-PAGE LEOPARDS SPECIAL ... 4-PAGE LEOPARDS SPECIAL ... 4-PAGE LEOPARDS SPECIAL ... 4-PAGE LEOPA

FAKE FUR

Counterfeit big cat misery for Bristol man

A BRISTOL man who bought a leopard on the internet was left counting the cost after the animal he purchased turned out to be a *fake!*

Frank Clownshoe thought he had bagged the bargain of the century after spotting a pop-up ad for an online company offering leopards for £800 - a fraction of their usual cost. Excited at the prospect of snapping up a great deal, he quickly handed over his credit card details.

"I'd always wanted a leopard, but I could never afford one," he told *The Clifton Okra and Artisan Pesto*. "So when I saw them on the net for less than a grand a pop, I couldn't buy one quick enough," he added.

And when the exotic animal arrived a week later, Frank was initially thrilled with his purchase. He built an enclosure for the beast in his back garden, complete with a bit of tree, a small pond and a covered sleeping area. "It was absolutely fantastic," he told the paper. "Like I had my own little zoo."

"And you should have seen the looks I got from people when I took it out for walks on a lead round Clifton," he said. "Honestly, I felt I'd finally arrived."

But 38-year-old bus driver Frank's joy was to be short-lived. After two weeks, he received a visit from a trading standards officer who informed him that the department had been investigating the company who had sold him the big cat. And after a brief examination of the animal, he delivered the news that Frank had been dreading. The leopard was counterfeit.

heads

Trading standards officer Henry Milksop told Frank that it was actually quite a good fake as fake leopards go, but it was only worth about £100.

"It looks, moves and sounds like the real deal," Milksop said. "It's the right size and colour, and it's got all the right markings. It's a really good imitation. But if you get close up, you can see it's not the genuine article."

pontefract

And he had this warning for any other people thinking about buying a leopard: "There are a lot of unscrupulous people out there and a lot of hooky leopards, so be careful."

"Leopards go for about fifteen thousand pounds. So if you see one for sale at 800 pounds, it's probably going to be a knock-off," he said. "If an offer seems too good to be true, it probably is."

Milksop told Frank that there were warning signs on the website itself. The company contact details were a PO Box address in Birmingham, the testimonials from customers were all written in a suspiciously similar manner, and the site had countless spelling mistakes, including 'lepards for sail'.

"Never buy a leopard online unless the sellers allow you to see the animal first," he advised. "And when you go to see it, take a zoo keeper with you to inspect the animal before parting with your money."

grindr

But despite being £800 down, Clownshoe was philosophical. "It's still a lovely animal, whether it's a real leopard or not," he told reporters. "It's just that every time I see it prowling round its cage, climbing up its bit of tree or eating a couple of rabbits, I know it's a knock-off."

"I'll probably just let it go in the woods," he added.

CLAWS FOR CONCERN: Clownshoe's leopard looked the part, but wasn't the genuine article.

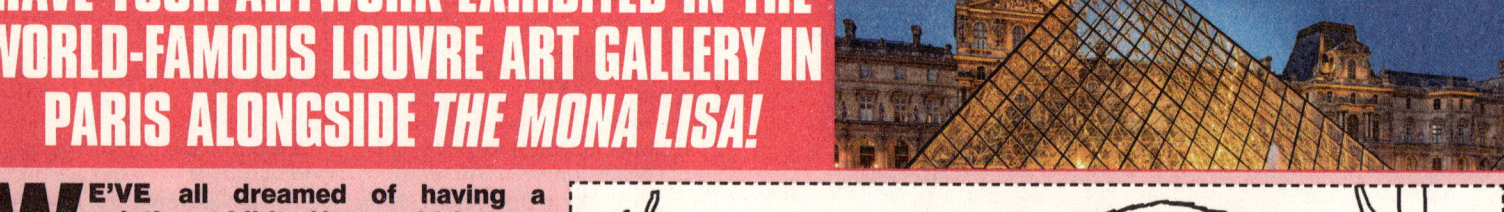

HAVE YOUR ARTWORK EXHIBITED IN THE WORLD-FAMOUS LOUVRE ART GALLERY IN PARIS ALONGSIDE *THE MONA LISA!*

WE'VE all dreamed of having a painting exhibited in a world-famous gallery, joining the pantheon of the world's greatest artists including Rubens, Rembrandt and Jack Vettriano. Well now that dream is going to come true for the lucky *Viz* reader who wins our *Amur Leopard Colouring Competition*.

All you have to do is get out you paints, crayons or coloured pencils, and colour in this picture of an Amur leopard – you can print it out bigger if you like. All entries will be judged by them three off of Sky Arts's *Portrait Artist of the Year*. The judges will be looking for consistency of stroke, use of the right colours and not going over the lines.

The best picture in the opinion of the judges will be put in a click frame and blu-tacked to the wall in The Louvre alongside the Mona Lisa. It may only be exhibited for a few seconds until it and the person putting it up are removed by security guards, but the winner will be able to brag that they have exhibited at The Louvre.

Email your completed entries to letters@viz.co.uk, to arrive no later than 20th March two years ago.

10 THINGS YOU NEVER KNEW ABOUT AMUR LEOPARDS

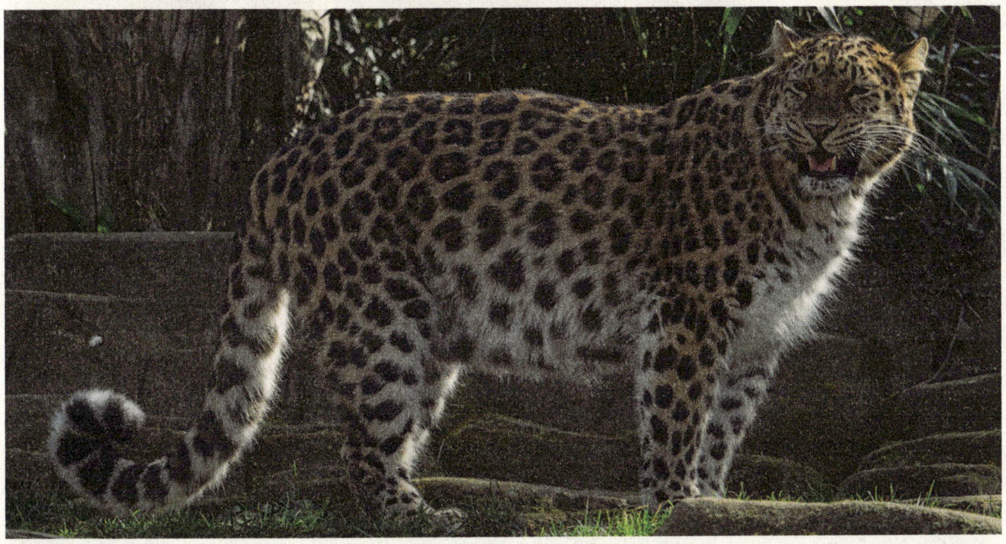

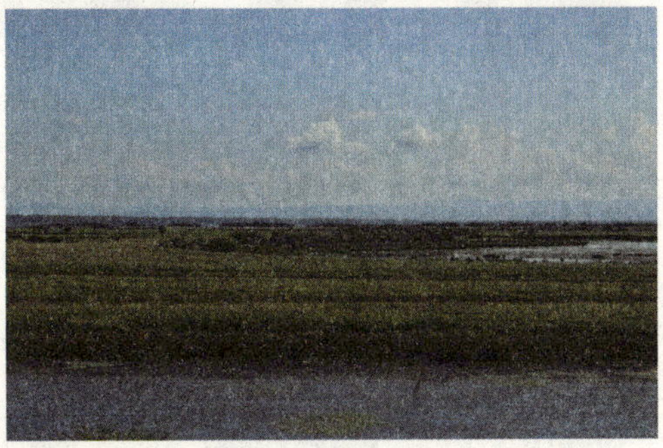

THERE are only about 26 of the fuckers left on the planet, so it's not surprising that we know very little about Amur leopards. In fact, we know more about the surface of the Moon than we do these sparsely distributed, spotty cats. But here are 10 things we certainly DO know about these thin-on-the-ground felines...

1 **ALL LEOPARDS** belong to the species *Panthera pardus*, with DNA analysis showing there to be eight distinct subspecies including the Amur leopard (*Panthera pardus orientalis*). Although it is on the verge of extinction, it doesn't really matter if the Amur leopard is wiped out as it looks exactly like all the other seven subspecies.

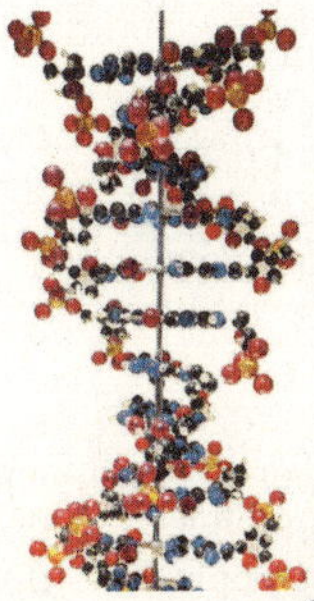

2 **THEY SAY** that a leopard cannot change its spots, and that's true for all *Panthera pardus* subspecies. Indeed, every Amur leopard has exactly the same number of spots as it did as a cub, except that they are slightly larger.

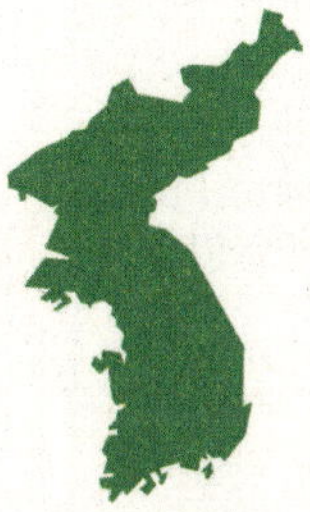

3 **NOT SATISFIED** with having just one name like every other animal, the Amur leopard is also known as the *Siberian leopard*, the *Far-eastern leopard* and the *North Chinese leopard*. It also goes by the name of the *Korean leopard*... despite being extinct on the Korean peninsula since 1970! *You couldn't make it up!*

4 **AMUR LEOPARDS** are easily distinguished from all other leopard subspecies by the distinctive 16,966 base pair-long sequence in their mitochondrial genome.

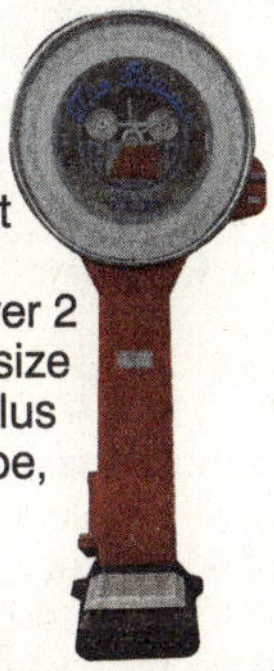

5 **THE AVERAGE** male Amur leopard weighs in at 45kg – around ten times the weight of a domestic house cat. If you kept an Amur leopard as a pet, it would make scratches in your furniture over 2 feet long and bring dead birds the size of swans into your house. On the plus side, they could not shit in your shoe, as the turds they produce would simply be too big to fit in.

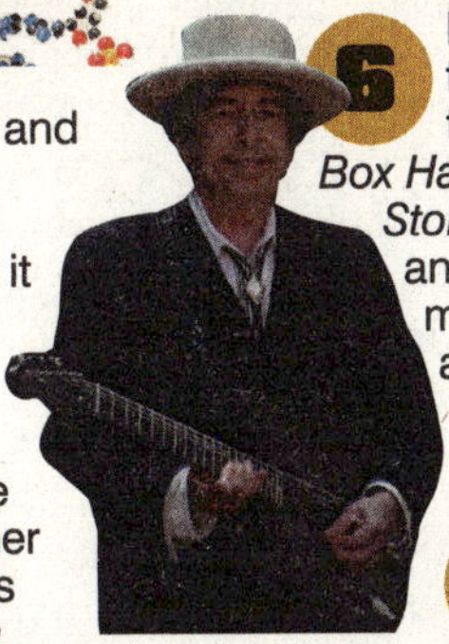

6 **MANY SONGS** have the word leopard in the title, including *Leopard-Skin Pill-Box Hat* by Bob Dylan, *The Man Who Stole a Leopard* by Duran Duran, and hundreds, if not thousands more. But in none of them do the artists make clear to which of the 8 subspecies of leopard their song refers.

7 **EXCEPT** *The Ballad of the Snow Leopard* by Lyle Lovett.

8 **NOBODY KNOWS** why the Amur leopard is so named. Many people think its nomenclature comes from Russians badly pronouncing the word 'amour' when talking about their love of the leopard subspecies in French. Some believe the name is a contraction of the words 'ham' and 'more' from the feeding instructions given to the keepers of the leopards in Russian zoos. Still others believe it could be derived from the Amur region of northern Russia where the leopards principally live.

9 **THE AMUR LEOPARD** is the only subspecies of *Panthera pardus* with four letters in its common name. You may think the Snow leopard would be another, but you would be wrong. That's because the Snow leopard is a distinct species – *Panthera uncia* – meaning that if a Snow leopard and an Amur leopard interbred, the offspring would be an interspecific hybrid and – tragically – infertile.

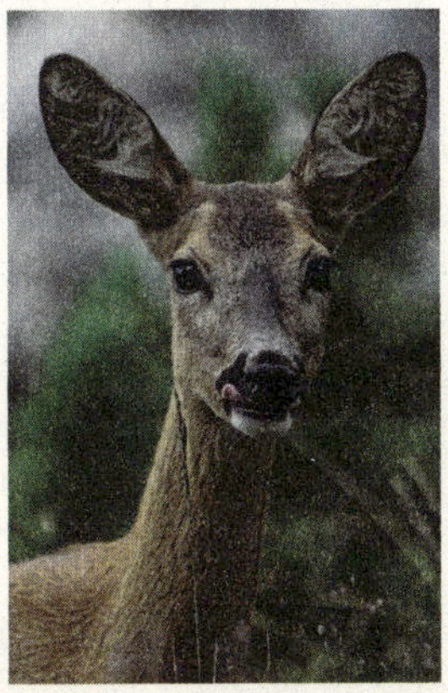

10 **DURING A** 1990s territorial study of Amur leopards in northern Russia, in which subjects were fitted with radio-tracking collars, scientists discovered that a hugely disproportionate number of individuals were living in the vicinity of deer farms. Research is being undertaken to find out why this might be so.

SPOT TIPS

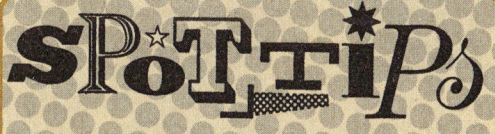

WHEN shampooing leopards, tranquilise them first as they become extremely aggressive if the soap gets in their eyes.
Frampton Ballsup, Tooting

A SIX-FOOT section of telegraph pole wrapped in hessian sacking makes an ideal scratching post for a leopard.
Dickson Dodson, Wrexham

A CLOCKWORK gazelle makes an ideal toy for a playful leopard.
Horace Socks, Leeds

IF YOU own a pair of leopards and can never tell them apart, simply dye one of them a non-leopard colour, such as blue or purple.
Barry Mophead, Luton

EXCITEMENT MOUNTS FOR DOMINO RECORD ATTEMPT

~Reuters

A LEICESTERSHIRE man is hoping to enter the history books this week with his bid to topple over a record-breaking number of dominoes.

CYRIL PITT, 58, has long nursed an ambition to enter the domino-toppling hall of fame after seeing the world record broken as a child. "I remember watching *Record Breakers* on the BBC and seeing some Belgian bloke toppling over 150,000 dominoes," he said. "I promised myself that one day I would take that record from him."

However, over the years, Cyril watched the record change hands many times and the number of dominoes toppled double to over 320,000. As the record tally grew, the shoe salesman eventually realised the chance to achieve the record had slipped from his grasp.

"There's no way I've got the time to stand up over 321 thousand dominoes," he said. "I'm in the shoe shop six days a week and my boss won't let me have time off to pursue my dream."

And it's not just time that is against Cyril. The cost of the materials has also put the venture

EXCLUSIVE!

firmly out of his reach. "There's 28 dominoes in a box, so I'd need 11,429 boxes to attempt the record," he said. "The cheapest box on Amazon is £4.25, so that's £48573.25 for the doms alone. And I'm not on Prime, so there'd be postage on top of that."

"That's simply unaffordable on a footwear salesman's salary," he said.

Undeterred, Cyril did some blue sky thinking, and came up with an idea to get his name in the record book and fulfil his childhood ambition. "I thought, if I couldn't topple the most number of dominoes, then perhaps I could topple the *least*," he said.

hostile

And a quick flick through a copy of the 1985 *Guinness Book of Records* annual confirmed that no attempt to topple the smallest number of dominoes had ever been made. "The record was there for the taking," said Cyril.

SPOT ON: *Cyril Pitt practises his tiny topple with a tipple in his local.*

And for the last two months, the would-be record breaker has been practising for the attempt on the table in the kitchenette area of his bedsit on Gallowtree Gate. "I started off with 25 dominoes, and when I could knock them over successfully, I tried it with 20, and then 15," he said.

Now ready, Cyril has hired Granby Halls in Leicester for his record attempt, and hopes the venue will be 'packed to the rafters' with spectators eager to see a local man make history and put Leicester on the map. "I've paid £25 for the hire of the hall and I'm good to go," he said.

muffler

However, Cyril is remaining tight-lipped about the exact number of dominoes he intends to topple as he doesn't want any competitors to steal his thunder. "You'll have to wait and see. But let's say you'll be able to count them on your fingers, and still have a couple of fingers left over," he teased.

"So, eight."

However, it appeared last night that the record attempt may have to be put on hold after it emerged that Granby Halls, the venue hired for the record attempt, was demolished in 2001. What's more, Cyril has been unable to contact the hall's manager, a man he met in the pub, and to whom he paid a £25 hire fee.

"His phone just goes through to voicemail and he won't call me back," he said. "If I meet that rob-dog again, it won't just be fucking dominoes I'll be knocking down."

How Many Dominoes is the Least?

DOMINO IT ALL: *Bertrand Russell in 1982, yesterday.*

WITH Cyril taking the art of domino toppling to its limits, many people have questioned how far the sport can go while still being recognisable as domino toppling. We contacted the late mathematician and philosopher Bertrand Russell to ask *"What is the least number of dominoes it is possible to topple?"*

"How many dominoes is the least number you can topple? It's a question as old as time itself. You might think that the answer is 2 dominoes, and you may be correct. But take one away and you have 1 domino, a smaller number than 2. Taken to its logical conclusion, this would mean that zero dominoes is the smallest number it is possible to topple.

But do dominoes cease to be dominoes when there are none of them? If you topple zero dominoes, how do you know you are doing it, and not toppling zero apples instead? Must there be at least 1 domino in order for there to be a number of them toppled?

If not, then we can surely move into the realm of negative numbers. Standing one domino up is equal, in a mathematical sense, to toppling *minus 1* dominoes. Stand 2 dominoes up and you have toppled *minus 2*. In this sense, just like the greatest number, there is no limit to the smallest number of dominoes you can topple. To topple the greatest number, you must first stand them up.

Logically, the holder of one record must therefore be the holder of the other. On the other hand, what's the point of even wondering? There's no way of knowing we're not just a brain in a bucket and everything we perceive is simply an illusion – and that includes dominoes."

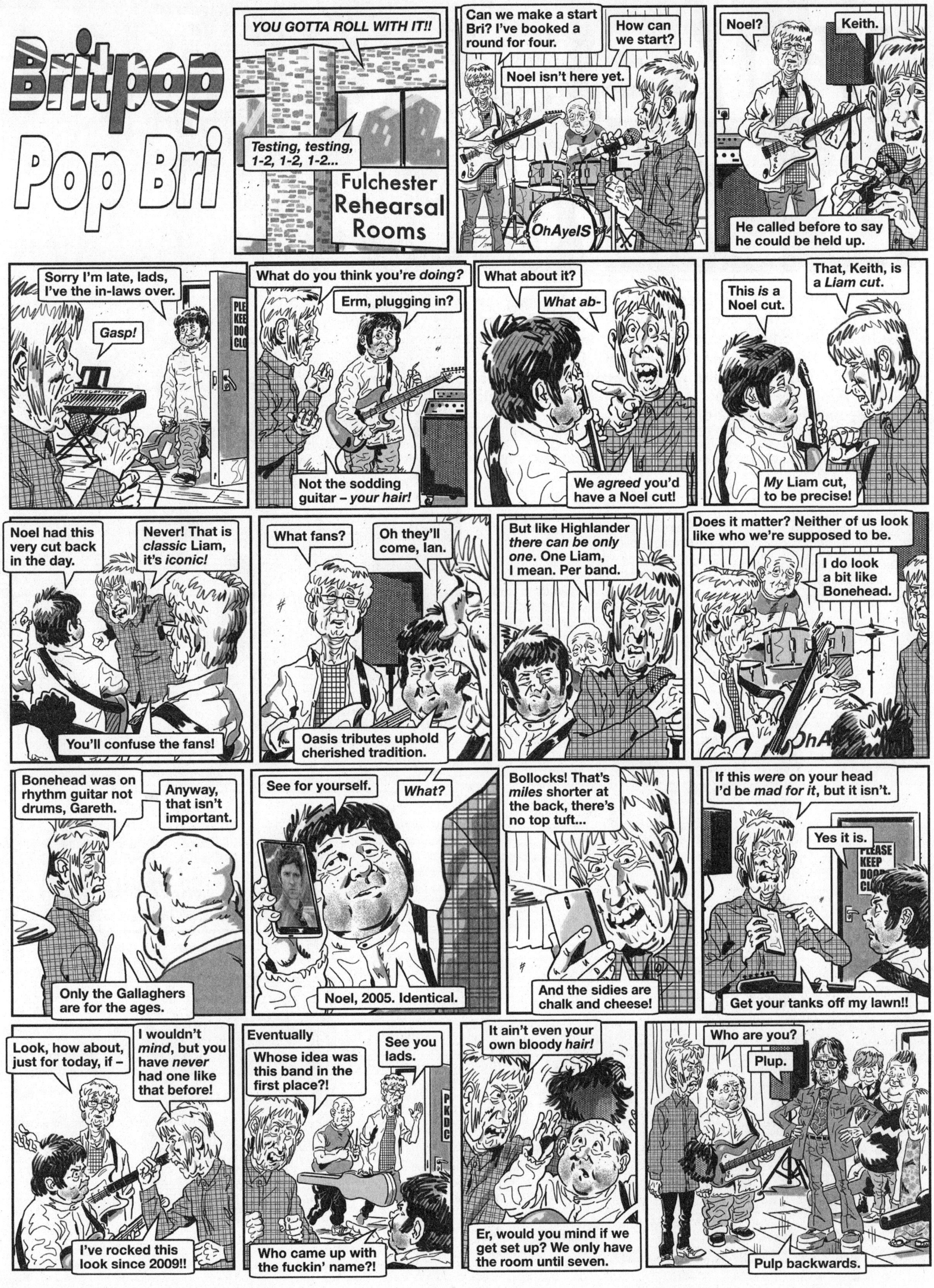
Britpop
Pop Bri
YOU GOTTA ROLL WITH IT!!
Testing, testing, 1-2, 1-2, 1-2...
Fulchester Rehearsal Rooms
Can we make a start Bri? I've booked a round for four.
How can we start?
Noel isn't here yet.
OhAyeIS
Noel?
Keith.
He called before to say he could be held up.
Sorry I'm late, lads, I've the in-laws over.
Gasp!
What do you think you're *doing?*
Erm, plugging in?
Not the sodding guitar – *your hair!*
What about it?
What ab-
We *agreed* you'd have a Noel cut!
This *is* a Noel cut.
That, Keith, is a *Liam cut.*
My Liam cut, to be precise!
Noel had this very cut back in the day.
Never! That is *classic* Liam, it's *iconic!*
You'll confuse the fans!
What fans?
Oh they'll come, Ian.
Oasis tributes uphold cherished tradition.
But like Highlander *there can be only one.* One Liam, I mean. Per band.
Does it matter? Neither of us look like who we're supposed to be.
I do look a bit like Bonehead.
Bonehead was on rhythm guitar not drums, Gareth.
Anyway, that isn't important.
Only the Gallaghers are for the ages.
See for yourself.
What?
Noel, 2005. Identical.
Bollocks! That's *miles* shorter at the back, there's no top tuft...
And the sidies are chalk and cheese!
If this *were* on your head I'd be *mad for it*, but it isn't.
Yes it is.
PLEASE KEEP DOOR CL
Get your tanks off my lawn!!
Look, how about, just for today, if –
I wouldn't *mind*, but you have *never* had one like that before!
I've rocked this look since 2009!!
Eventually
Whose idea was this band in the first place?!
See you lads.
Who came up with the fuckin' name?!
It ain't even your own bloody *hair!*
Er, would you mind if we get set up? We only have the room until seven.
Who are you?
Plup.
Pulp backwards.

Take a Shit

COMMENDED MAGAZINE OF THE YEAR –Take a Shit Magazine of the Year Awards

COME TRA

"I can make people give me anything I want... and you can, too." North east mind control expert reveals secrets.

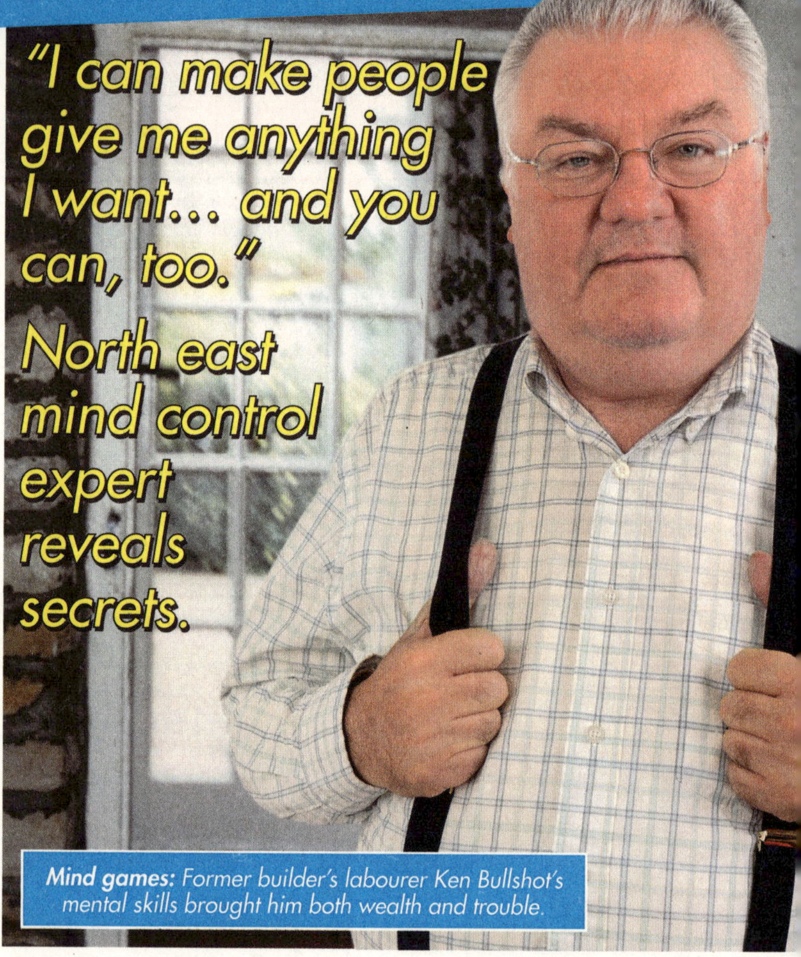

Mind games: *Former builder's labourer Ken Bullshot's mental skills brought him both wealth and trouble.*

A MAN known as the Svengali of Ashington has for years possessed amazing powers which have led to him becoming one of the richest men in eastern Northumberland. And now, former part time builder's labourer Ken Bullshot is sharing his secrets in the hope that, like him, others in the town can enjoy wealth and riches beyond their wildest dreams.

Ken, 58, first discovered he was able to control people's minds and make them do his bidding back in the eighties, and over the years he has put his amazing powers to use and amassed himself a not inconsiderable fortune. "In other hands, these powers might be considered sinister," he told the *Ashington Cyst and Ganglion*. "But I have vowed only to use them for good and making money."

As his riches grew, Ken kept the secret of his mind control abilities to himself, worried that in the wrong hands they could be abused. But following a series of bad investments and unforeseen events which resulted in him losing all his money, the 58-year-old mind-manipulator has now decided to join the lucrative 'After Dinner Speaking' circuit where he will reveal all for just £3, including a pie and pea supper.

> "I didn't know how these powers worked, I just knew they did, although not on everyone"

As told to ***Vaginia Discharge***

SCHOOL DAZE

Ken first realised that he had a strange ability to mentally bend others to his will at comprehensive school, where he could command his fellow pupils to voluntarily give up their sweets and dinner money.

"All I would have to do was go up to some little first year and simply tell them to give me their dinner money, and they would just hand it over. If it looked like they were resisting, I simply had to say it again, more slowly, emphasising each word, and they would be hypnotised. I didn't know how these powers worked, I just knew they did, although not on everyone – usually just the first years or some of the smaller second years were susceptible to my mesmerism.

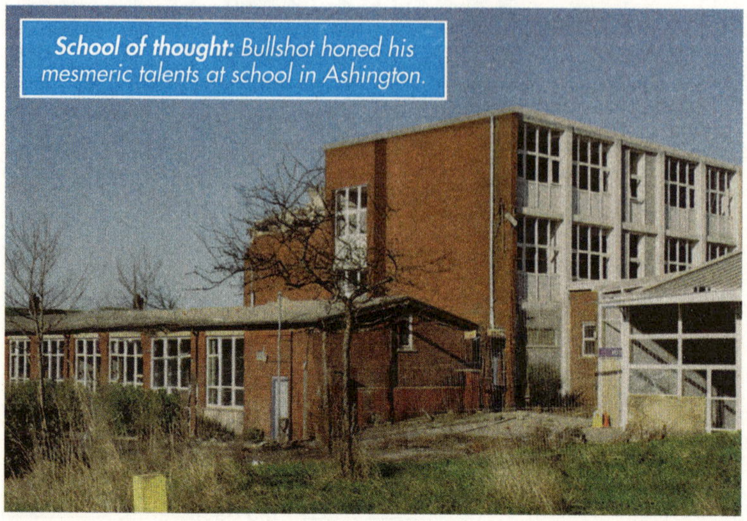

School of thought: *Bullshot honed his mesmeric talents at school in Ashington.*

Of course, I didn't just use my mind tricks to get money for tabs when I was at school, I also used them to get out of trouble. I remember one day I was messing about in the boys' toilets and I'd written some abusive graffiti about a maths teacher on the walls in excrement. I'd done it before, so I was immediately hauled before the headmaster and told that this time I would be expelled.

Fixing him with an hypnotic stare I said calmly, "No, sir. It was Tony Bartlett." He looked a little dazed, like he was going into a trance, and I hit him once again with my psychic hammer. "Tony Bartlett is the boy you are looking for," I said. "Tony Bartlett, eh?" he repeated, in a dream-like torpor.

Apparently, Tony Bartlett had been off school the day I wrote in shit on the walls, and I was, in fact, expelled. But the fact that the head had called him in and questioned him demonstrated that I had the power to manipulate someone else's mind. At that moment I vowed I would only ever use my amazing hypnotic gift for good purposes, like obtaining money and getting off with things I had done."

> "The foreman was completely under my spell. I was the puppet master making him dance to my tune"

SKIVE MENTALITY

Bullshot left school at Easter of his final year and embarked on his career as a labourer on a construction site. It was hard, physical work, but it wasn't long before the machiavellian figure found himself getting up to his mind-bending tricks once again.

"I remember my first day on the sites. It was freezing cold and I was knackered by dinner time, and so when the foreman came in the tea hut and told us to go back to work, I knew it was time to exercise my unworldly powers in order to skive.

...NCE-ING!

Gone to the dogs: Ken used advanced mind-control techniques to get cashier to pay out at dog track.

And I knew exactly how to do it.

"I can't work this afternoon because it's my gran's funeral," I told him. He stopped in his tracks. The secret of mind control is to fix eyes with your subject and tell them what you want them to believe. But you must do it in such a way that disbelieving you is not an option. "Your gran's funeral?" he said. "Yes," I answered. "And it's my grandad's tomorrow, and then my other gran's the day after that."

Anyone else coming out with this bunkum this would have been laughed out of the tea hut and told to get back to work. But the foreman was completely under my spell. I was the puppet master making him dance to my tune. "Oh, I'm sorry to hear that," he said with a deadpan, trance-like face. "Well, you'd best fuck off then, hadn't you. In fact, take as long off as you fucking well like."

It had worked. I had manipulated his thought processes, guided his brain and forced him to give me the rest of the week off. After a relaxing weekend I went back to the site on the Monday, but they had hired somebody else. I asked to see the foreman so I could shape his mind and get my job back, but they told me to fuck off.

BENEFIT OF THE DOUBT

Ken found himself unemployed and headed for the dole office in Ashington. After filling in the forms, he was awarded £16.53 per week supplementary benefit, not a great deal to live on, even in 1981. And it wasn't long before he was once again getting inside the head of another person and subverting their thoughts to his end.

Because I'd only worked half a day since leaving school, I wasn't eligible for full unemployment benefit, just the supplementary that everyone is entitled to. I tried my mind tricks on the bloke behind the desk where I signed on, trying to convince him that I had worked and paid my stamp for five years, but he wasn't having any of it – as I say, not everyone is susceptible to my mesmeric powers. But then one week when I went in, there was a young girl on duty. I don't know if it's something to do with the chemistry of their brains, but I've found that women tend to be more easily mind-controlled than men. So I went into action.

If you're on the dole and your partner is more than 10 weeks pregnant, you get free milk tokens, or at least you did back then. These could be exchanged for the white stuff at any shop, but I knew an offy where the bloke would take them for tabs, albeit at an extortionate rate – some people have no morals. So I told the girl behind the counter that my wife was expecting our first child and could she give me some milk tokens.

She looked a bit confused and after checking her paperwork said she had no record of me being married. I told her in a calm, soporific tone that her records must be wrong, before repeating my statement. I used a psychological technique called the 'broken record method' where you simply repeat the phrase again and again until it becomes truth inside your subject's mind. After a stand-off that lasted a couple of minutes with me repeating my statement about ten times, her mind was eventually overpowered and she slammed down her pen and handed me seven milk tokens. "I'm going to look into this and if it turns out you don't qualify, the cost of these will be deducted from your next payment," she drawled in a trance-like state.

She must have followed through on her threat when my mental influence eventually wore off because my next benefits cheque was only £14.37, but once again the power of suggestion had shown its strength.

ONE TRAP MIND

It is said by many that the only winners in gambling are the bookmakers. But not Ken. Because thanks to his mind control abilities, developed and honed over decades, he can always tip the odds in his favour.

> I used a psychological technique called the 'broken record method' where you simply repeat the phrase again and again until it becomes truth inside your subject's mind.

Derren Brown does a thing where he goes to a race track and makes the bookie's cashier pay out on a losing ticket. It's a simple trick if you know how to do it like I do, and it means a bumper payday at the race track. Some people might think that after saying I will only use my powers for good, I am abusing them by using them to cheat the bookies, but they are forgetting that all bookies are bastards.

The first time I used this technique was at the dog track on the Fossway in Newcastle. I'd put £10 on the dog in trap 5 at 3/1 because the form book showed it was the youngest of the runners and was unbeaten in its last five races, all against strong opposition. It had also had a shit in the parade ring before the race and that is always a good sign.

So I was extremely disappointed when, after a decidedly lacklustre race, it crossed the line in fifth place. At that point, most punters would have screwed up their betting slip and gone to put a wager on the next race. But not me – I had the power of mind control on my side, and that was my last tenner anyway, so I went up to the window with my betting slip and handed it to the cashier.

She was a little confused as she looked at it. "Trap 3 won, pet," she said. Unfazed, I moved in for the mental kill. "Yes, my slip's for trap 3," I replied. "It says 5," she replied. "It says 3," I quietly replied. I was using a technique called

> I'd put £10 on the dog in trap 5 at 3/1 because the form book showed it was was unbeaten in its last five races. It had also had a shit in the parade ring before the race and that is always a good sign

'Doubt Implantation'. She could see that my betting slip said trap 5… or did it say trap 3? I had planted that seed of doubt in her mind and it had germinated and taken root. "No. That's definitely says 5," she said, clearly doubting her own judgement.

I said once again it was a 3, suggesting that the handwriting was not very clear and she said that she was going to see her manager. My power of suggestion techniques had worked. Unsure of what she could clearly see in front of her own eyes, she wandered into the back room to get her manager and I leaned through the glass, grabbed 20 quid from the till and ran off. Actually, I had grabbed a bit more than 20 quid, £280 in fact. But rather than take it back, I vowed not to use my mind control again until I had lost £260. As I have said many times, I will only use my powers for good.

Bullshot's only talk to date will be at The Linton Colliery Buffaloes Club on August 30th. Admission is £3 on the door and includes a pie and pea supper and after dinner lecture. Tickets for the meat raffle can be purchased separately at a cost of £1 per strip.

NEXT WEEK: Using powerful desire implantation techniques on a performer in a Newcastle lapdancing club leads to Ken being marched to a cashpoint and then beaten up in an alleyway by two bouncers.

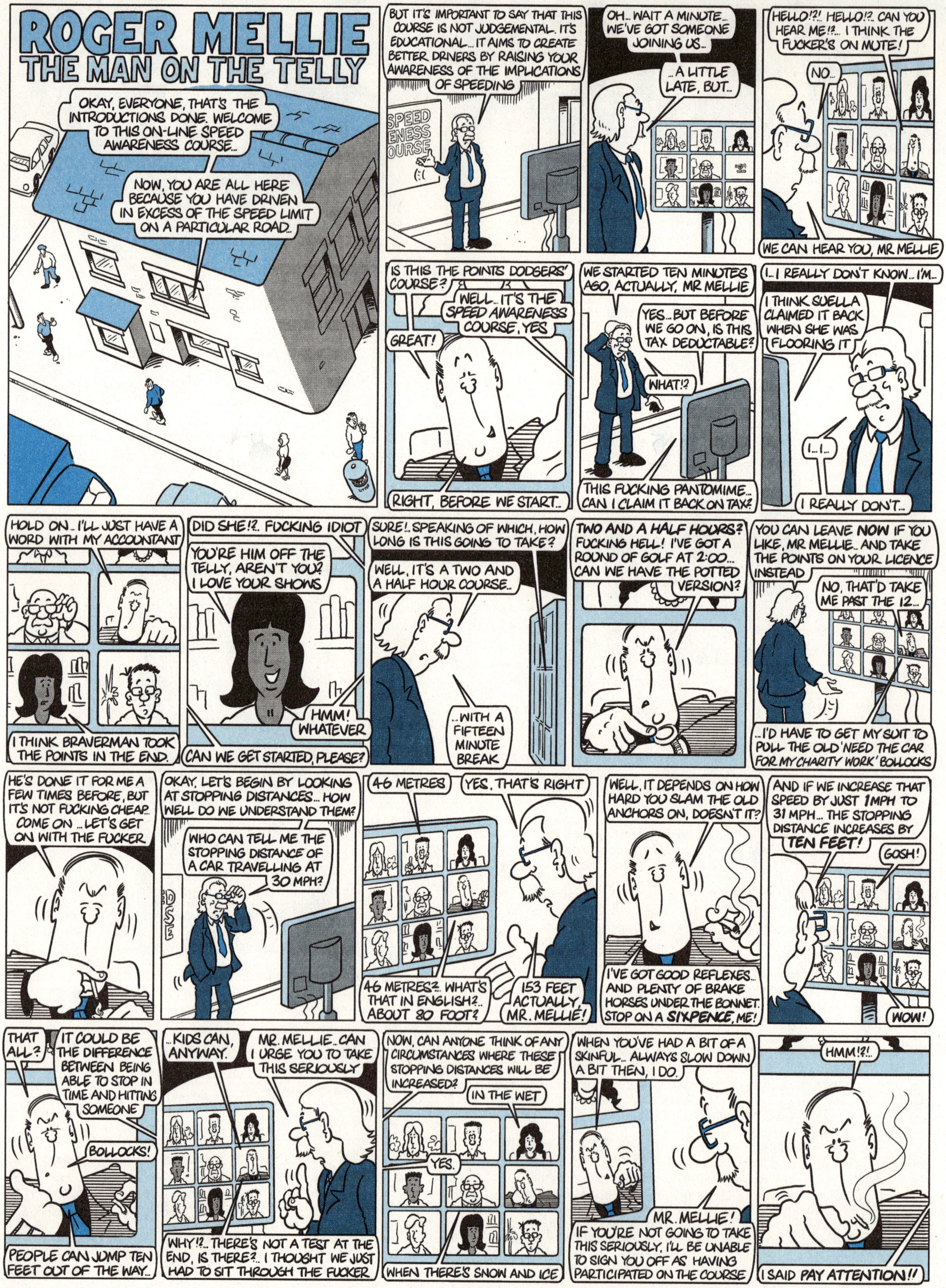
ROGER MELLIE
THE MAN ON THE TELLY
OKAY, EVERYONE, THAT'S THE INTRODUCTIONS DONE. WELCOME TO THIS ON-LINE SPEED AWARENESS COURSE...
NOW, YOU ARE ALL HERE BECAUSE YOU HAVE DRIVEN IN EXCESS OF THE SPEED LIMIT ON A PARTICULAR ROAD...
BUT IT'S IMPORTANT TO SAY THAT THIS COURSE IS NOT JUDGEMENTAL. IT'S EDUCATIONAL... IT AIMS TO CREATE BETTER DRIVERS BY RAISING YOUR AWARENESS OF THE IMPLICATIONS OF SPEEDING
OH... WAIT A MINUTE... WE'VE GOT SOMEONE JOINING US...
...A LITTLE LATE, BUT...
HELLO!?! HELLO!?.. CAN YOU HEAR ME!?... I THINK THE FUCKER'S ON MUTE!
NO...
WE CAN HEAR YOU, MR MELLIE
IS THIS THE POINTS DODGERS' COURSE?
WELL... IT'S THE SPEED AWARENESS COURSE, YES
GREAT!
RIGHT, BEFORE WE START...
WE STARTED TEN MINUTES AGO, ACTUALLY, MR MELLIE
YES... BUT BEFORE WE GO ON, IS THIS TAX DEDUCTABLE?
WHAT!?
THIS FUCKING PANTOMIME... CAN I CLAIM IT BACK ON TAX?
I... I REALLY DON'T KNOW... I'M...
I THINK SUELLA CLAIMED IT BACK WHEN SHE WAS FLOORING IT
I... I...
I REALLY DON'T...
HOLD ON... I'LL JUST HAVE A WORD WITH MY ACCOUNTANT
I THINK BRAVERMAN TOOK THE POINTS IN THE END.
DID SHE!?. FUCKING IDIOT
YOU'RE HIM OFF THE TELLY, AREN'T YOU? I LOVE YOUR SHOWS
HMM! WHATEVER
CAN WE GET STARTED, PLEASE?
SURE!.. SPEAKING OF WHICH, HOW LONG IS THIS GOING TO TAKE?
WELL, IT'S A TWO AND A HALF HOUR COURSE...
...WITH A FIFTEEN MINUTE BREAK
TWO AND A HALF HOURS? FUCKING HELL! I'VE GOT A ROUND OF GOLF AT 2:00... CAN WE HAVE THE POTTED VERSION?
YOU CAN LEAVE NOW IF YOU LIKE, MR MELLIE.. AND TAKE THE POINTS ON YOUR LICENCE INSTEAD
NO, THAT'D TAKE ME PAST THE 12...
...I'D HAVE TO GET MY SUIT TO PULL THE OLD 'NEED THE CAR FOR MY CHARITY WORK' BOLLOCKS
HE'S DONE IT FOR ME A FEW TIMES BEFORE, BUT IT'S NOT FUCKING CHEAP. COME ON ... LET'S GET ON WITH THE FUCKER
OKAY, LET'S BEGIN BY LOOKING AT STOPPING DISTANCES... HOW WELL DO WE UNDERSTAND THEM?
WHO CAN TELL ME THE STOPPING DISTANCE OF A CAR TRAVELLING AT 30 MPH?
46 METRES
YES, THAT'S RIGHT
46 METRES?.. WHAT'S THAT IN ENGLISH?.. ABOUT 80 FOOT?
153 FEET ACTUALLY, MR. MELLIE!
WELL, IT DEPENDS ON HOW HARD YOU SLAM THE OLD ANCHORS ON, DOESN'T IT?
I'VE GOT GOOD REFLEXES... AND PLENTY OF BRAKE HORSES UNDER THE BONNET. STOP ON A SIXPENCE, ME!
AND IF WE INCREASE THAT SPEED BY JUST 1MPH TO 31 MPH... THE STOPPING DISTANCE INCREASES BY TEN FEET!
GOSH!
WOW!
THAT ALL?
IT COULD BE THE DIFFERENCE BETWEEN BEING ABLE TO STOP IN TIME AND HITTING SOMEONE
BOLLOCKS!
PEOPLE CAN JUMP TEN FEET OUT OF THE WAY...
...KIDS CAN, ANYWAY.
MR. MELLIE... CAN I URGE YOU TO TAKE THIS SERIOUSLY
WHY!?.. THERE'S NOT A TEST AT THE END, IS THERE?.. I THOUGHT WE JUST HAD TO SIT THROUGH THE FUCKER
NOW, CAN ANYONE THINK OF ANY CIRCUMSTANCES WHERE THESE STOPPING DISTANCES WILL BE INCREASED?
IN THE WET
YES.
WHEN THERE'S SNOW AND ICE
WHEN YOU'VE HAD A BIT OF A SKINFUL... ALWAYS SLOW DOWN A BIT THEN, I DO.
MR. MELLIE!
IF YOU'RE NOT GOING TO TAKE THIS SERIOUSLY, I'LL BE UNABLE TO SIGN YOU OFF AS HAVING PARTICIPATED ON THE COURSE
HMM!?!..
I SAID PAY ATTENTION!!

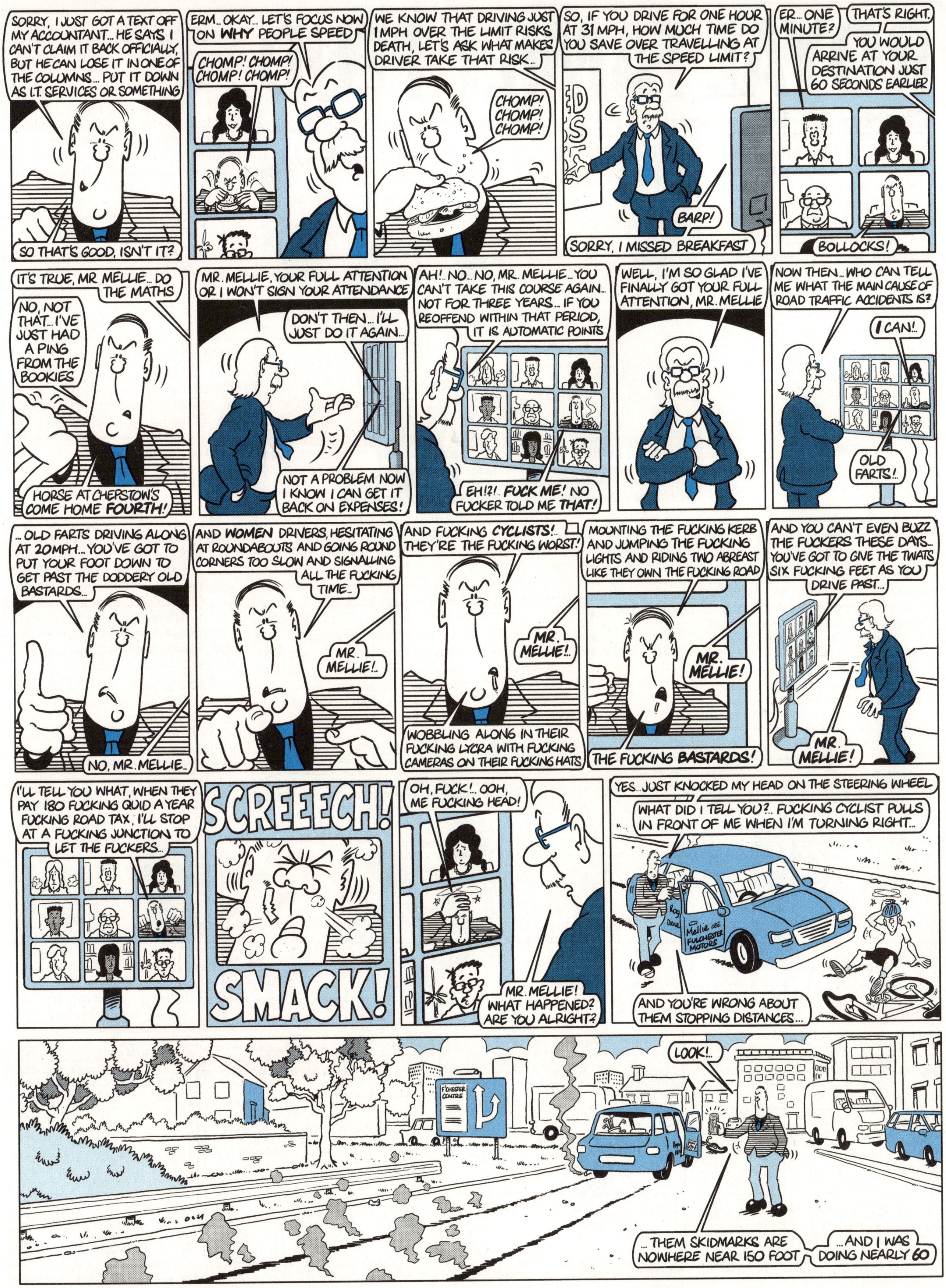
SORRY, I JUST GOT A TEXT OFF MY ACCOUNTANT... HE SAYS I CAN'T CLAIM IT BACK OFFICIALLY, BUT HE CAN LOSE IT IN ONE OF THE COLUMNS... PUT IT DOWN AS I.T. SERVICES OR SOMETHING
SO THAT'S GOOD, ISN'T IT?
ERM... OKAY... LET'S FOCUS NOW ON WHY PEOPLE SPEED
CHOMP! CHOMP! CHOMP! CHOMP!
WE KNOW THAT DRIVING JUST 1MPH OVER THE LIMIT RISKS DEATH, LET'S ASK WHAT MAKES DRIVER TAKE THAT RISK...
CHOMP! CHOMP! CHOMP!
SO, IF YOU DRIVE FOR ONE HOUR AT 31 MPH, HOW MUCH TIME DO YOU SAVE OVER TRAVELLING AT THE SPEED LIMIT?
BARP!
SORRY, I MISSED BREAKFAST
ER... ONE MINUTE?
THAT'S RIGHT.
YOU WOULD ARRIVE AT YOUR DESTINATION JUST 60 SECONDS EARLIER
BOLLOCKS!
IT'S TRUE, MR MELLIE... DO THE MATHS
NO, NOT THAT... I'VE JUST HAD A PING FROM THE BOOKIES
HORSE AT CHEPSTOW'S COME HOME FOURTH!
MR. MELLIE, YOUR FULL ATTENTION OR I WON'T SIGN YOUR ATTENDANCE
DON'T THEN... I'LL JUST DO IT AGAIN...
NOT A PROBLEM NOW I KNOW I CAN GET IT BACK ON EXPENSES!
AH!.. NO... NO, MR. MELLIE... YOU CAN'T TAKE THIS COURSE AGAIN... NOT FOR THREE YEARS... IF YOU REOFFEND WITHIN THAT PERIOD, IT IS AUTOMATIC POINTS
EH!?!.. FUCK ME! NO FUCKER TOLD ME THAT!
WELL, I'M SO GLAD I'VE FINALLY GOT YOUR FULL ATTENTION, MR. MELLIE
NOW THEN... WHO CAN TELL ME WHAT THE MAIN CAUSE OF ROAD TRAFFIC ACCIDENTS IS?
I CAN!..
OLD FARTS!..
...OLD FARTS DRIVING ALONG AT 20MPH... YOU'VE GOT TO PUT YOUR FOOT DOWN TO GET PAST THE DODDERY OLD BASTARDS...
NO, MR. MELLIE...
AND WOMEN DRIVERS, HESITATING AT ROUNDABOUTS AND GOING ROUND CORNERS TOO SLOW AND SIGNALLING ALL THE FUCKING TIME...
MR. MELLIE!..
AND FUCKING CYCLISTS!.. THEY'RE THE FUCKING WORST!
MR. MELLIE!..
WOBBLING ALONG IN THEIR FUCKING LYCRA WITH FUCKING CAMERAS ON THEIR FUCKING HATS
MOUNTING THE FUCKING KERB AND JUMPING THE FUCKING LIGHTS AND RIDING TWO ABREAST LIKE THEY OWN THE FUCKING ROAD
MR. MELLIE!
THE FUCKING BASTARDS!
AND YOU CAN'T EVEN BUZZ THE FUCKERS THESE DAYS... YOU'VE GOT TO GIVE THE TWATS SIX FUCKING FEET AS YOU DRIVE PAST...
MR. MELLIE!
I'LL TELL YOU WHAT, WHEN THEY PAY 180 FUCKING QUID A YEAR FUCKING ROAD TAX, I'LL STOP AT A FUCKING JUNCTION TO LET THE FUCKERS...
SCREEECH!
SMACK!
OH, FUCK!.. OOH, ME FUCKING HEAD!
MR. MELLIE! WHAT HAPPENED? ARE YOU ALRIGHT?
YES... JUST KNOCKED MY HEAD ON THE STEERING WHEEL
WHAT DID I TELL YOU?.. FUCKING CYCLIST PULLS IN FRONT OF ME WHEN I'M TURNING RIGHT...
Mellie OBE FULCHESTER MOTORS
AND YOU'RE WRONG ABOUT THEM STOPPING DISTANCES...
F'CHESTER CENTRE
LOOK!..
...THEM SKIDMARKS ARE NOWHERE NEAR 150 FOOT
...AND I WAS DOING NEARLY 60

ROYAL FAMILY FEUD

Charles III in for ratings rumble from beyond the grave

THE King could find himself bounced into an ugly TV ratings war on Christmas Day, but he won't be battling against the cast of *EastEnders* or Ant and Dec for viewers... it will be his *own late mum!*

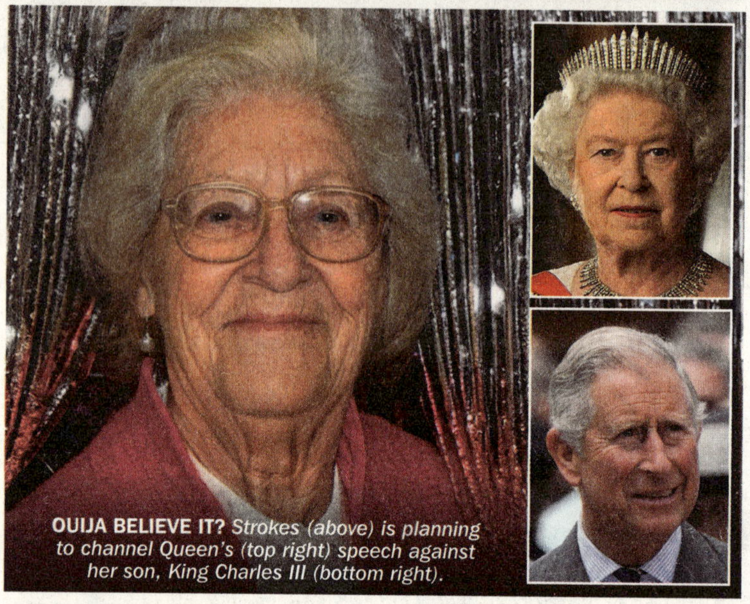

OUIJA BELIEVE IT? *Strokes (above) is planning to channel Queen's (top right) speech against her son, King Charles III (bottom right).*

That's because Leeds-based psychic entertainer **DORIS STROKES** plans to channel a festive address by the former monarch HRH Queen Elizabeth II in the coveted post-nosh-up 3pm slot. And she is currently looking for a national broadcaster prepared to air the late head of state's supernatural utterances.

medium

Doris, the self styled 'Happy Medium', says it was her late majesty herself who cooked up the sneaky plan to clash with her plump-fingered son in the Yuletide audience-share war.

"I suggested doing it late Christmas Eve, but the Queen was adamant," says Doris, 64. "What you have to remember is that in life, her majesty was a highly competitive lady. Remember how she used to jump around when one of her racehorses won? Or how she always had a face like a punched cushion when they lost?"

Strokes has spoken regularly with the deceased monarch beyond the mortal veil since her death back in 2022, and says that she had been quietly confident that her eldest child's first Christmas speech last year would not be a success. "She told me he'd die on his arse," says Doris. "Die on his arse. Those were her exact words."

"I was a bit surprised to hear her use that sort of language, but in many ways the Queen is a very different lady in the afterlife to the one we knew down here," she says. "She's become much more free and easy with the expletives. And I'm not surprised after seventy-odd years observing strict protocol and having to watch every single word she said."

small

But Doris assures royal watchers that her late majesty's language, whilst fruitier than when she was alive, has not descended to the gutter. "It's never the horrible stuff," she says. "None of the *F-ing* and *C-ing*. I think the worst I've heard from her was two loud *Bs*, when Spain beat England in the Women's World Cup final."

"Bloody bastards," she clarifies.

Things did not go as the enduring disembodied essence of the Queen expected last year, when her son's first Christmas address proved a smash-hit with viewers, netting an audience of more than ten million.

"It was more than she ever pulled while she was alive, and she took that badly," says Doris. "I later heard from the late Nelson Mandela, who spent that New Year's Eve at a star-studded gathering in the Queen's celestial Balmoral, that she it put her in an 'effing foul mood' all night."

"His words, not mine," she hurriedly clarifies.

"At one point, some deceased beefeaters had to physically separate her from another guest who had unwittingly praised her son's debut effort."

Doris insists, however, that the Queen has no plans to make such a phantom punch-up an annual Christmas day event. "She just wants one more crack at doing a speech from the other side, is what she told me from spirit world," she says. "Then she'll let it rest."

XXL

If a broadcaster can be found, the speech will be broadcast live at 3pm on Christmas Day, featuring Doris sitting in her front parlour whilst relaying the words of the late monarch to her former subjects in a Yorkshire accent. "I haven't seen the speech, but I'm sure it will be incredibly powerful and moving, a unifying moment for the whole nation," she says.

"And I've told her that if she starts effing and jeffing before the watershed, I'll have to draw down the veil and break the circle. No ifs, no buts."

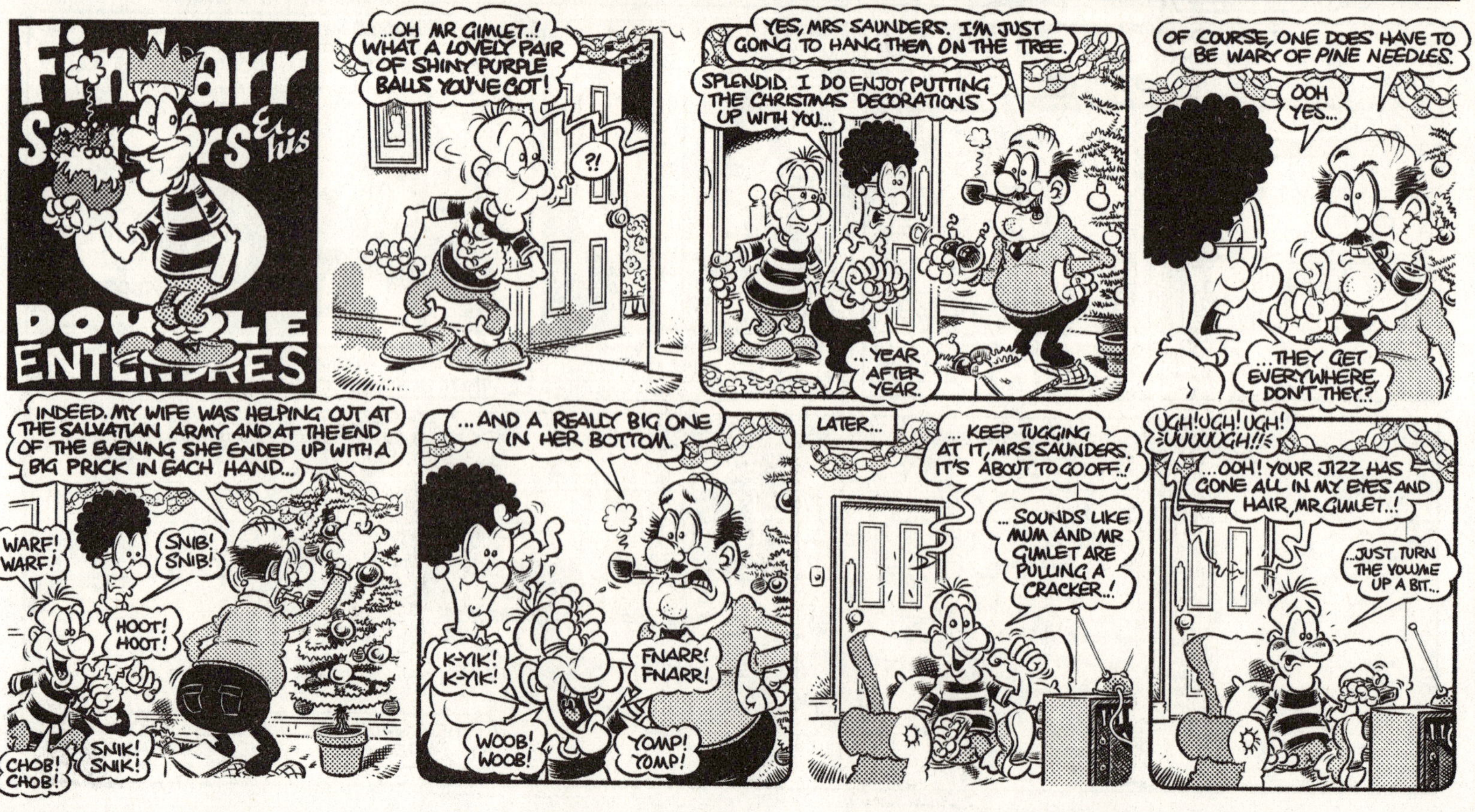
...OH MR GIMLET..! WHAT A LOVELY PAIR OF SHINY PURPLE BALLS YOU'VE GOT!
?!
YES, MRS SAUNDERS. I'M JUST GOING TO HANG THEM ON THE TREE.
SPLENDID. I DO ENJOY PUTTING THE CHRISTMAS DECORATIONS UP WITH YOU...
...YEAR AFTER YEAR.
OF COURSE, ONE DOES HAVE TO BE WARY OF PINE NEEDLES.
OOH YES...
...THEY GET EVERYWHERE, DON'T THEY..?
INDEED. MY WIFE WAS HELPING OUT AT THE SALVATIAN ARMY AND AT THE END OF THE EVENING SHE ENDED UP WITH A BIG PRICK IN EACH HAND...
WARF! WARF!
SNIB! SNIB!
HOOT! HOOT!
CHOB! CHOB!
SNIK! SNIK!
...AND A REALLY BIG ONE IN HER BOTTOM.
K-YIK! K-YIK!
FNARR! FNARR!
WOOB! WOOB!
YOMP! YOMP!
LATER...
... KEEP TUGGING AT IT, MRS SAUNDERS. IT'S ABOUT TO GO OFF..!
... SOUNDS LIKE MUM AND MR GIMLET ARE PULLING A CRACKER..!
UGH! UGH! UGH! UUUUUGH!!
...OOH! YOUR JIZZ HAS GONE ALL IN MY EYES AND HAIR, MR GIMLET..!
...JUST TURN THE VOLUME UP A BIT...

Robbie's Robot Carer
Now, *that* is the jack.
And *these* are woods.
We *bowl* these as near to that as possible.
The two closest get a point each. First to 21 wins the *end*.
I see. And people do this why?
Because it's *fun*, Martin!
Apologies. I understand the human need of fun.
Fulchester Crown Green Bowling Ass.
My sensors failed to recognise this as fun.
Each wood has a weight bias in one side, so it curves as it rolls.
Part of the fun?
Aye, and there's a slight rise or *crown* on the green to tackle too!
Adding to the fun.
Ooo, might be a bit pacy that 'un.
However
Two to me, Robbie?
Blimey.
Talk about beginner's luck!
Yes, luck.
But mainly my ability to scan topography, range, wind-speed, humidity, then plot a trajectory to an accuracy of 99.37%
Shortly
Two to me again. Meaning I win the end, 22 to nothing.
Hello Robbie.
Oh, hello Minnie.
Did you have fun, Robbie?
You still bowling then?
Well, I try my best, but Ian *is* rather good.
My 3D mapping capabilities rival those of F-35 Lightning II.
Maybe you and I should have an end, let this pair play each other.
My updated optical software is standard on next generation hypersonic missiles.
Soon
Two to me.
No, to me.
Me.
Your electron microscope is in need of recalibration.
How're you getting on with yours?
Not bad.
Still miss Coral, the lass who used to do for me. Always laughing...
They can't smile, can they?
To me!
To me!
No, and sometimes that's all you need.
Half the time I feel more lonely when I'm *with* Martin...
To me!
...than I do when I'm on my own.
TO ME!
BA-DOOM
TO ME!
TO ME!
Ian! No rockets!
VOOSH!
DUGGA! DUGGA! DUGGA!
DUGGA! DUGGA! DUGGA!
Thank goodness I put heavy-duty drawers on.

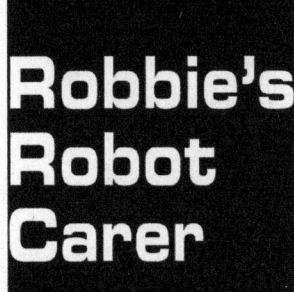

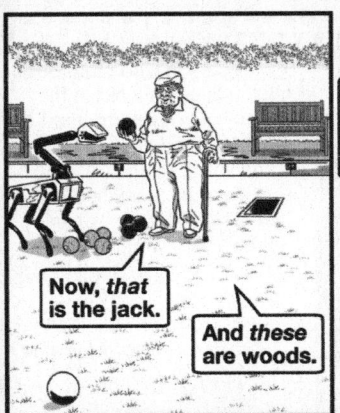

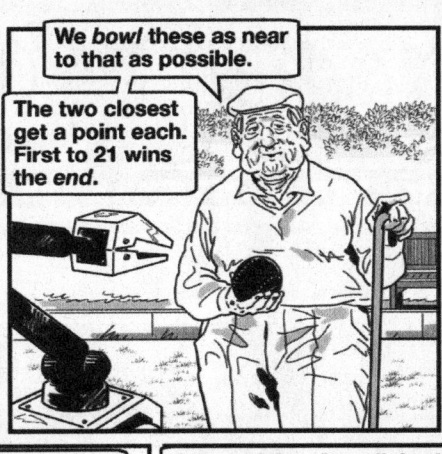

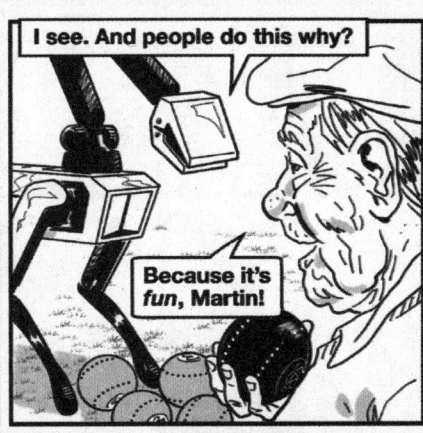

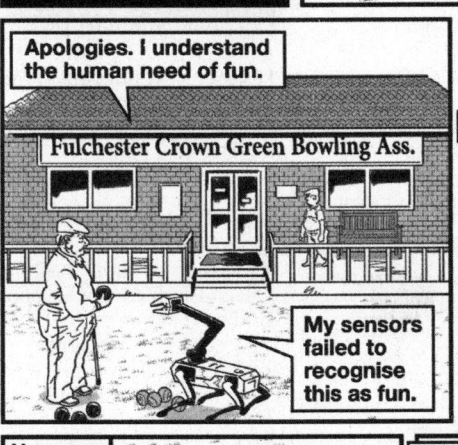

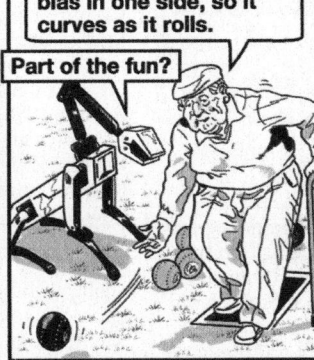

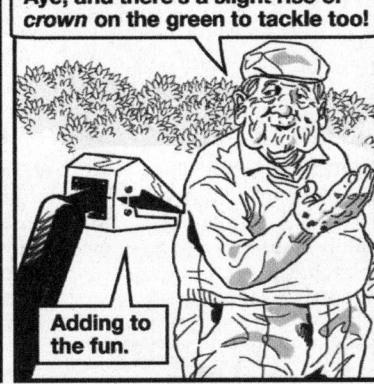

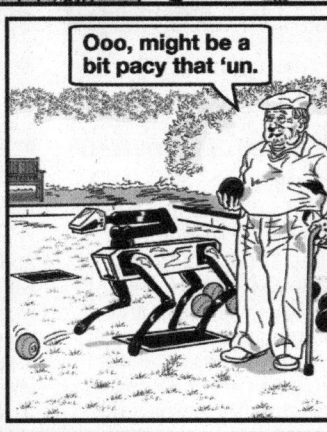

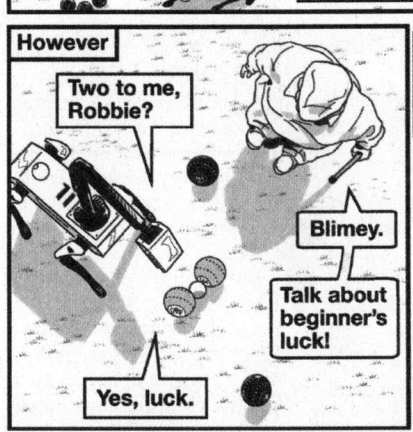

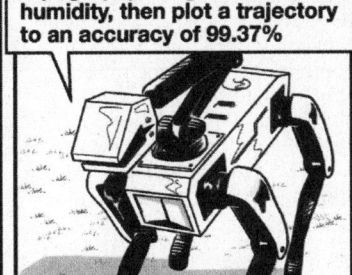

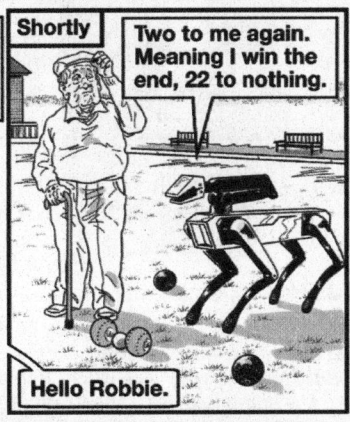

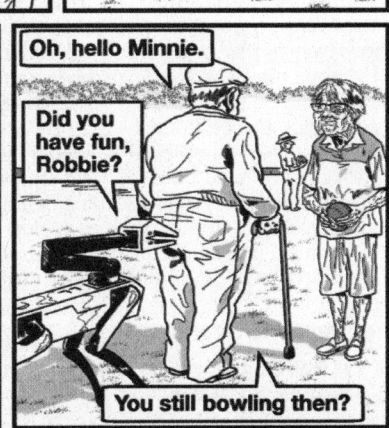

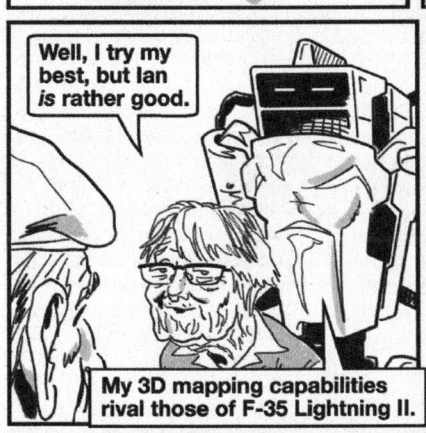

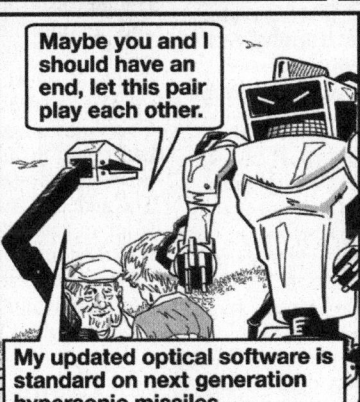

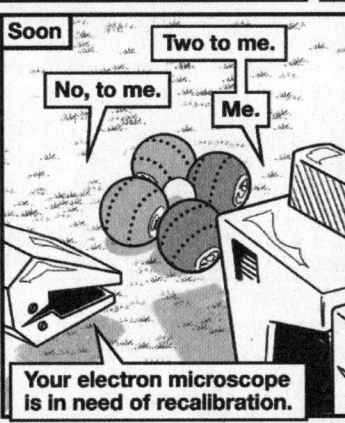

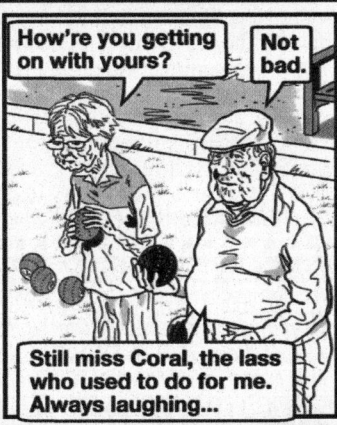

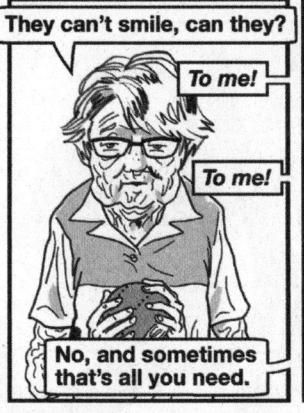

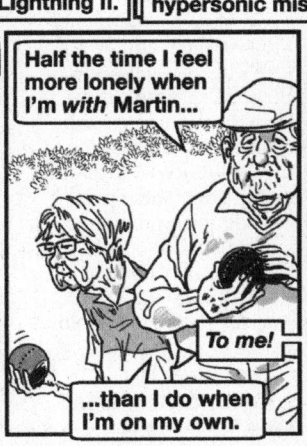

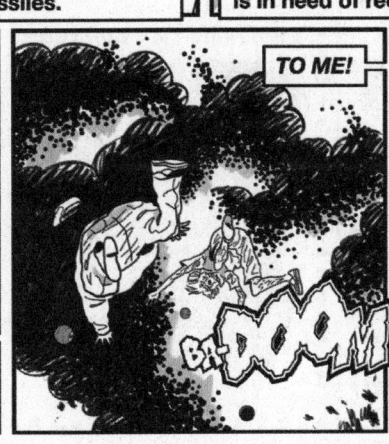

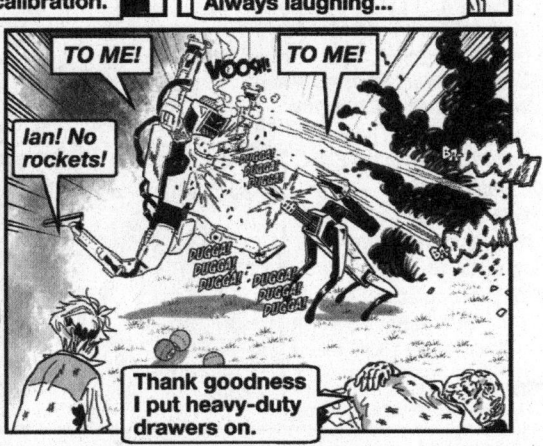

letterbocks
letters@viz.co.uk

ST★R LETTER

☐ **I KNOW** our noble NHS is stretched to breaking point at the minute, but the treatment I received recently was nothing short of shocking. If 'ring sting' and 'night farts' isn't a legitimate reason to turn up at A&E, then I don't know what is. And don't get me started on the abuse I got from the Air Ambulance people.

Les Lloyd, email

☐ **IN** the Lord Rockingham's XI's 1958 hit *There's a Moose Loose Aboot this Hoose!*, the song is sung in the Scottish vernacular, and the 'moose' he refers to is actually a mouse and not the large Canadian deer-like animal. However, the Scots would pronounce moose exactly the same, so the song may well have been about a moose. If Lord Rockingham's home had been almost completely destroyed with huge piles of steaming shite everywhere, then he probably would have been singing about an infestation of moose, rather than a mouse.

Hugh Jantlers, West Barns

☐ **A PETROL** station near me had a sign outside proclaiming it was "Under New Management." I can't for the life of me think why something being under new management might entice me in, unless the new management were knocking 5p off a litre of diesel.

Eldon Furse, Leeds

☐ **THESE** themed months are all well and good, and 'Movember' was mildly amusing wordplay, but 'Veganuary' is really stretching it. Surely 'Jamuary' would have been a more satisfying bon mot. Plus, we'd all get to eat jam, which incidentally is vegan. Essentially the same result.

Thomas Hartley, email

* *What a great idea, Mr Hartley, and one which we could support. However, your name rang a few alarm bells and we wondered if perhaps you have a vested interest in people eating jam in January. Before we support the move officially, could you let us know if you are in some way connected to Hartley's jam in order to avoid a conflict of interest.*

☐ **WITH** reference to the above letter. Mr Hartley is clearly a member of the famous jam-producing family and is attempting to drum up sales with his suggestion that we all do 'Jamuary' next year. Well, I'm afraid his cheap rouse has backfired, as I intend to give up eating jam in the first month of 2026 and eat marmalade instead. How do you like *them* apples, Mr Hartley?

Frank Cooper, Oxford

☐ **I WAS** left horrified yesterday when a huge lorry overturned in my back garden. Imagine my relief when I realised it was just my husband, TV funnyman Hugh Laurie, turning over on the sun lounger.

Mrs Ada Laurie, Oxbridge

☐ **ONE** of my mates has no arse. His back literally blends straight into his legs. Yet there are people with massive arses who would do anything to get rid of them. I know the NHS is in crisis at the minute, but it would solve a lot of problems if there was some kind of arse transplant service. Come on NHS. Sort it out.

Glen Hattersley, Stockport

☐ **I'D** love to be the person who reads out all the legal bollocks at the end of radio adverts, and I'd be dead good at it because I can speak really fast. And I'm even quicker when I've had a skinful. Does anyone know how I would go about getting a job like that? I work in a pork pie factory at the minute and I fucking hate it.

Artisan Pesto, Leicester

☐ **I WOULD** like to apologise to all my former classmates at Cardinal Griffin Comprehensive in Staffordshire for loudly breaking wind during a GCSE English mock exam in early 1988. I know I and my mates giggled about it at the time, but 35 years on I have recently matured and now realise I may have upset some of my classmates, particularly the girls. Once again, I would like to apologise to anyone who was upset, or who didn't find it funny at the time.

Paul Kelly, Dublin

☐ **A FEW** days ago after my wife had gone to bed, I decided to have a cheeky wank and so locked myself in the downstairs toilet. Upon reaching the inevitable point of no return, I saw to my dismay that the regular toilet roll had run out, and the only thing to hand was a novelty Boris Johnson toilet roll which was given to me as a joke a couple of Christmases ago, and which had sat on display in the downstairs toilet ever since. The guilt and shame one gets from an act of self pollution is bad enough, but having to shoot one's load over Boris's ugly mug, frankly, takes it to another level.

Anonymous, email

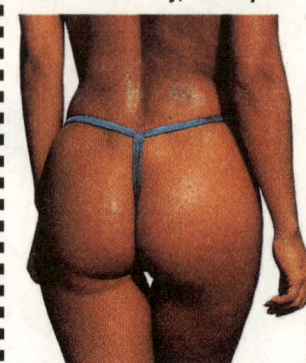

☐ **I WATCHED** Kylian Mbappé and Lionel Messi in the Qatar World Cup with growing respect. Clearly they both suffer from the same rare medical condition whereby the slightest touch from another player leaves them pole-axed on the ground in the most terrible agony, and yet somehow they find the inner strength to go on. I salute you, sirs. That kind of old school bravery is an example to us all.

Nobby Styles, email

☐ **I'D** just like to point out to my dogs that although I am a bit of a fat bastard, I'm not going to the fridge *every* time I go into the fucking kitchen. Maybe 85-90% of the time.

Eldon Furse, email

☐ **IF** the new King Charles the Third wants to be as popular as Queen Elizabeth the Second, he should loosen up the monarchy a bit and appear in the odd *Jackass* movie. His mother was fantastic in that *Naked Gun* film.

Les Lloyd, email

☐ **ONCE** my partner and I were doing some housework, and were both in the bedroom cleaning and hoovering opposite sides of the bed. We had eaten a big curry the night before, and so when I felt the imminent expulsion of flatus thundering through my bowels, I knew I had to act fast to avoid suffocating my partner with the fumes. I quickly placed the hoover nozzle just outside my trousers ready to receive the foul ejection as soon as it passed through the fabric of my trolleys. Unfortunately I lacked technical understanding of how a vacuum cleaner works, and the noxious fumes were sucked in, heated up, and expelled with amplifying force from the hoover's exhaust on the opposite side of the bed, right into my unfortunate partner's face. I have to say, it had the complete opposite effect of what I had intended.

R Feldspoor, Worcester

Nowhere for Elves to go in the garden? Orc taking up too much room in the house? Or perhaps you simply need more stolen gold storage?

It's the shed everyone's TOLKEIN about!

THE LORD OF THE SHEDS

Prices from as little as 199 Elven Shillings

- Solid construction using timber from the Forest of Lothlórien
- Steel hinges and door furniture forged in the Fires of Mount Doom
- Fully pressure treated with creosote from the Osgiliath branch of B&Q

"It's my precious shed." **Mrs B, Middle Earth**

One Shed to Rule Them All!

THE LORD OF THE SHEDS, Sauron Enterprises, Mordor Trading Estate, Westlands East of Gondor - off the B6478 between Waddington and Clitheroe

Top Tips

CHESS players. Make sure your opponent sits in front of a reflective surface so you can get a sneaky peek at their pieces when they are not looking.
Mac, Fleetwood

ADDING bleach to black paint turns it into white paint. Using scented bleach means your freshly-painted home will smell fresh and clean all year round into the bargain.
Greg Shaw, Leeds

PRETEND to be arena security by not letting your wife into the house before you've rooted through all her shopping bags.
Les Lloyd, email

CAT owners. An ankle-level letterbox makes an ideal front door cat flap for skinny cats with strong neck muscles.
Ernie Andbert, Glasgow

GENTS. Avoid not noticing your wife has been to the hairdresser's by simply telling her every day that her hair looks nice, just in case.
Eldon Furse, email

toptips@viz.co.uk

I WAS left horrified yesterday when a lorry spilled its load in my front room. Imagine my relief when I realised it was just my husband, TV funnyman Hugh Laurie, dropping his dinner tray on his way to the sofa.
Mrs Ada Laurie, Oxbridge

I OFTEN wonder what it would be like to pilot a helicopter with a wild, silverback lowland gorilla as a passenger. Has any reader ever done this, and if so, what happened?
Terry Farricker, Blackpool

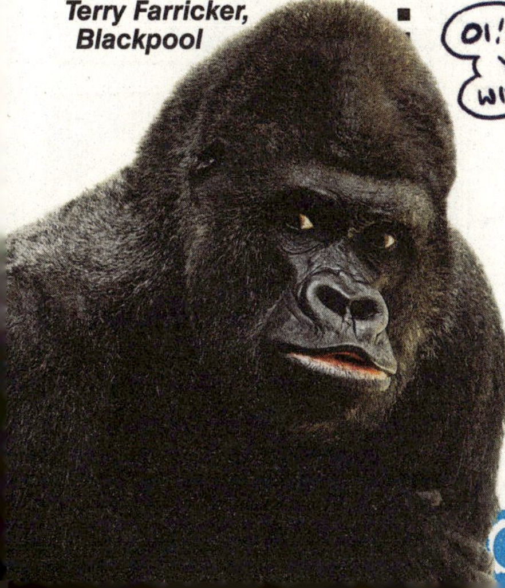

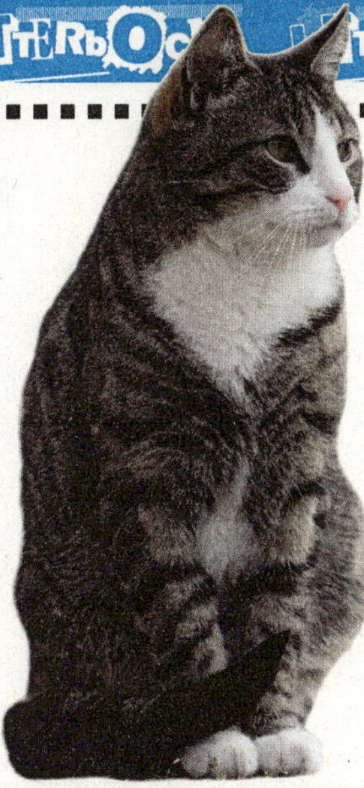

WHEN government ministers talk about 'record numbers of police on the streets' or 'record investment in the NHS', can they remember that the lowest number of police, and the least amount spent on the NHS are also record figures? They should qualify their statements by saying which of these records it is.
Bartram Golightly, Hull

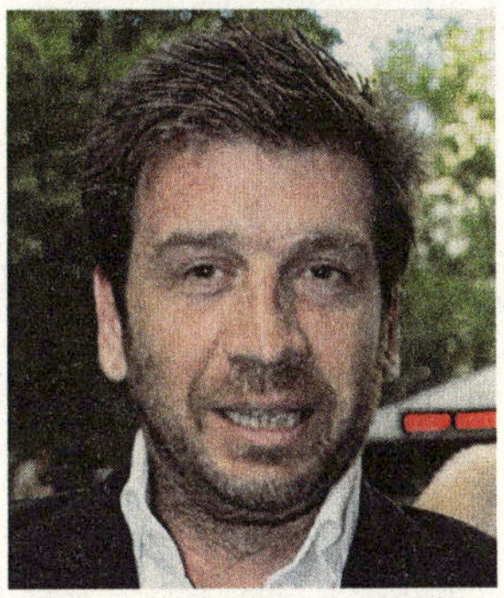

I HEARD someone shouting so loudly down our road the other day, that I automatically assumed it was TV's Nick Knowles come to convert somebody's house into a dog shelter or submarine or something for *DIY SOS*. Fortunately it was just a pissed-up neighbour. Have any other readers mistaken drunken neighbours for minor celebrities?
Glen Hattersley, Stockport

IN your last annual (*The Guard's Parcel, p208*), Ryan Collins wrote asking how you talk to a cat in the Netherlands. I can tell him that you simply call "Katje-katje-katje" (pronounced 'catchy-catchy-catchy') which means "Kitty-kitty-kitty" in Dutch.
SM Burden, email

** Thank you Mr or Ms Burden. If our army of multilingual readers could tell us how to call "Kitty-kitty-kitty" in as many languages as possible, we will keep a record so we can provide an international cat-calling translation service to our readers.*

I HAVE always thought TV soaps should be more realistic, but if my street is anything to go by, I don't think months of silence punctuated every few weeks by someone grudgingly nodding at a neighbour whose name they don't know would make for the most entertaining TV drama.
Eldon Furse, email

I WAS left horrified yesterday when a lorry crashed into my house. Imagine my relief, though, when I realised it was just my husband, TV funnyman Hugh Laurie, driving a large articulated truck straight through my front window.
Mrs Ada Laurie, Oxbridge General Hospital

APPARENTLY, Pope Benedict XVI's last words were "Lord, I love you." This final utterance was so much better than my grandad's, who garbled some nonsense about mice in the hospital bed while he was ripped to the tits on morphine.
Billy Whiffles, London

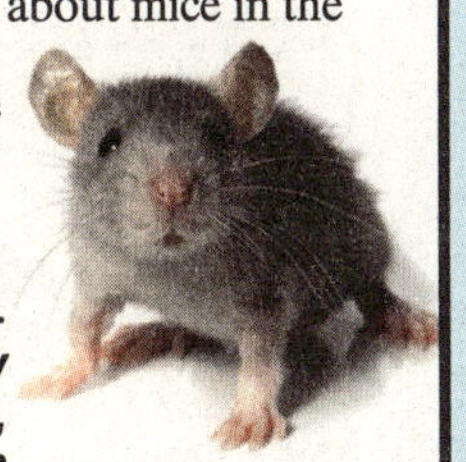

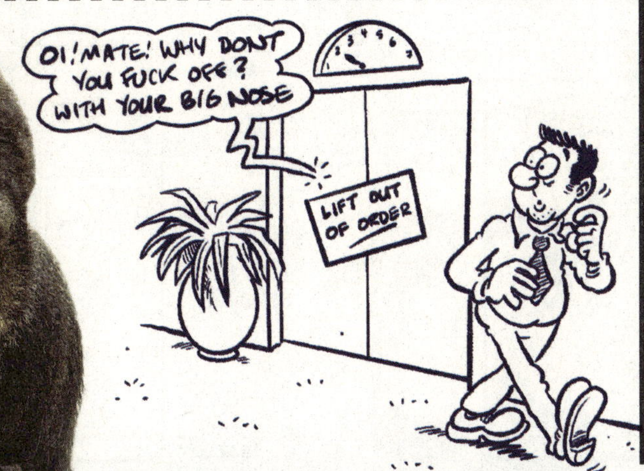
OI! MATE! WHY DONT YOU FUCK OFF? WITH YOUR BIG NOSE
LIFT OUT OF ORDER

WHEN they score a goal, footballers always talk about the ball hitting the back of the net. Do you think they mean the *front* of the net? Surely the back of the net is round the other side of the goal.
Adrian Horsman, Banbridge

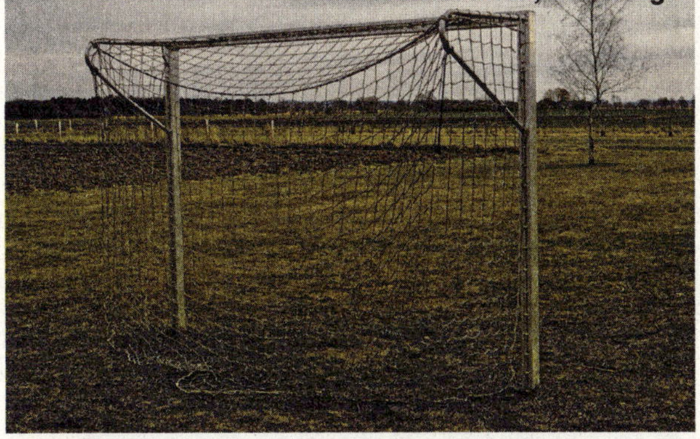

Have Your Say!

NELSON'S COLUMN has stood proudly in the centre of Trafalgar Square since 1843, commemorating the British victory over the combined fleets of France and Spain at the Battle of Trafalgar. The conflict in the Napoleonic wars cost Vice Admiral Horatio Nelson his life, and his statue stands atop the column, surveying the land for miles around, a fitting tribute from a grateful nation. *But how many double-decker buses high is it?* We went on the streets to find out what YOU think...

...WHEN I was a child, I watched John Noakes climb up Nelson's column on the TV show Blue Peter. It looked to be about 30 John Noakeses to me, and I reckon a double-decker bus is about 2 and a half John Noakeses, which would make Nelson's Column about 12 double-decker buses.
Tommy Ballsup, pipefitter

...I WORK in a scrapyard, and you can only put about six cars on top of each other before they become really unstable. I think if you stacked double-decker buses on top of each other, they would probably fall over after four. So I don't think we will ever know.
Frank Oils, scrap merchant

...I HAVE though about this for years, and have concluded that Nelson's Column is about 19 single-decker buses tall, but to be honest, I have never really considered its height in double deckers.
Aiken Drummond, ladle player

...I'M PRETTY sure that Nelson's Column is only one double-decker bus tall, but this may well be because I suffer from a rare medical condition where I believe that everything is the same height as Nelson's Column.
Jim Groyne-Strain, accountant

...I HAVE lived in a remote crofting village in the highlands of Scotland all my life, and have never seen either Nelson's Column or a double-decker bus. But I would take a stab at about 11.8.
Agnes McCloud, crofter

...I DON'T know. But if you ask a thousand people how many double-decker buses high it is, discard the highest 50 answers and lowest 50 answers, then take an average of the remaining 900, you will come to a surprisingly accurate approximation.
Brian Crumhorn, academic

...I THINK it would be about 10 of them if they are standing on their wheels. But if you piled them up on their ends it would probably be more like 6 or 7.
Hector Trelawny, hotelier

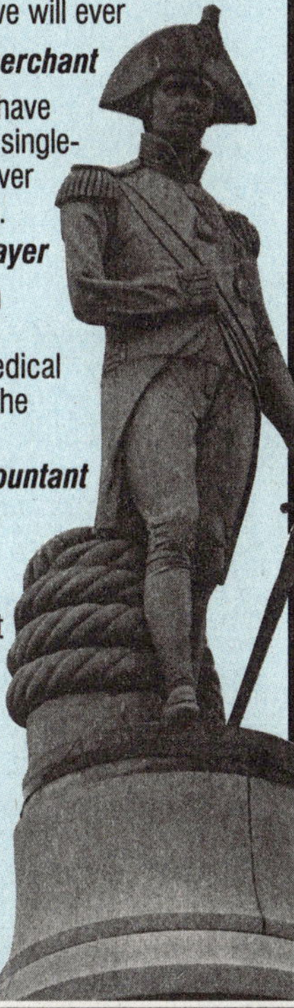

NEXT WEEK: How many Olympic swimming pools' worth of water do ***YOU*** think it would take to fill Lake Windermere?

TINSELTOWN SHARKS STOLE MY IDEA!

Joe's due for Jaws 2

A FULCHESTER man is celebrating after securing what he describes as "a first step towards victory" in his battle to extract royalty payments from the makers of the hit movie *Jaws 2*.

TOOTH AND NAIL: *Fulchester postman Joe (inset, aged 11) has been fighting for his share of movie hit royalties.*

For almost five months, **JOE TROUSERS** has been pursuing Universal Pictures with his demand for 50% of all revenues generated by the 1978 film about a killer shark. And according to the 58-year-old ex-postman, they are lucky that he only wants half. "By rights, *by rights*, I should get the lot," he told reporters, speaking from the betting shop that has become his home-from-home.

The follow-up to Steven Spielberg's 1975 box-office smash *Jaws* was one of the most successful sequels in cinema history, and to date has realised a profit of some $188m. Since Boxing Day, however, the critically-mauled yet highly lucrative shark-flick has been mired in scandal and controversy in Joe's mind.

jalopy

Midway through last year's festivities, Joe was instructed to permanently leave the home he shared with now estranged wife Cath, and he was going through his personal possessions deciding what to put in the bin when a long-forgotten childhood diary came to light.

"I started flicking through it that night as I curled-up on the backseat of the car," said now-homeless Joe. "It was your fairly standard schoolboy stuff – football, pop-groups, girls I liked, a timeline of small fires I'd started, all par for the course. Then, I saw it. There it was, in black and white."

"My entry for February 8th, 1976 is more or less the plot of what would later become *Jaws 2*."

On that historic day, 11-year-old Joe had been taken to see *Jaws* at the Fulchester Odeon, then the town's largest cinema. The beautiful art-deco picture palace, built in 1935, was demolished in 2002 to make way for a new state-of-the-art leisure complex which failed to materialise, and since then has been a large fenced-off hole in the middle of town.

"I actually found the entry chilling to read," said Joe. "For almost 45 years, a major Hollywood studio has been living a lie, projecting a family-friendly image to the world when all the time they have been counting money effectively stolen from a little boy."

The diary entry, while couched in the badly-spelt simple language of a child, makes a persuasive case.

"Jaws is grate! The best film ever," wrote the young Joe. *"They shuold do another one, Jaws 2 with a miles biger shark."*

And on the face of it, the similarities do seem remarkable. Universal Pictures did indeed make a sequel to *Jaws* as Joe suggested. His proposition that the shark should be miles bigger was realised – a 35-foot-long monster as opposed to 25-feet in the original film. Even the title, *Jaws 2*, is lifted straight out of Joe's diary, word for word.

embrocation

Blinded by rage, Joe dashed-off an angry expletive-filled letter to Universal Pictures, a move he now regrets as he believes it might have hampered his legal case.

"The old red mist came down and I let fly with with a bit of a tirade, basically," he chuckles. "This was a mistake, I understand that now, because it gave them the chance to play the victim. And typically the police tend to be on the victim's side."

But Joe is hoping that a fair-minded individual would understand the emotional trauma he had endured upon suddenly being confronted with this forgotten body of work from his past, and that what Universal call 'death threats' were in fact merely cries for help.

"The main thing is I have learned from this experience," says a now calmer Joe. "Since my initial outburst, I have conducted myself in a measured and reasonable fashion in line with the restraining order."

And his defence case has now been given a boost by scientific confirmation that his juvenile diary is indeed the genuine article. "I asked my court-appointed counsellor – and yes, counselling is a kind of science – to look it over and confirm that it's a bona-fide 1976 diary, rather than some modern-day mock-up," he said.

"The counsellor said as far as she was concerned it was the real deal," he said. "I'm going to ask her to sign a letter to that effect at my next session, and then I think it'll be game on."

8 ACE
OI EIGHT! FUCKIN' BARBECUE WAIN'T FUCKIN' LIGHT!
YER F-FF-FFUCKIN' WOT..?
A'M WANTIN' T'DO ME TEA ON IT, BUT IT'S NOT GERRIN' 'OT NO MATTEH 'OW MUCH PETROL AVE PURRONIT.
AH..! YER'VE NOT OPPENED F-FFUCKIN' VENT ON IT, LOOK...
...A'LL DO IT FOH YER...
WOOMF!
AH, THAT'S BERRA NOW... IT'S GOIN' A FUCKIN' TREAT..!
...A'LL GET SUM BANGEZ AHT FREEZEH.
AW... SHITE.
EIGHT... GO TER NANO-MART AN' GERRUZ SUM BANGEZ AN' BURGEZ FOH FUCKIN' BARBECUE, WILL YER... AN' GET YERSEN A TUBE O' BUM CREAM FOH YER FACE WHILE YER THERE...
...THAT LOOKS SORE.
...'OW MUCH WILL THAT CUM TER, DO YER RECKON..?
...BANGEZ AN' F-FFUCKIN' B-BBURGEZ AN' OINKMENT... NOT ACE... B-BBANGEZ AN B-BBURGEZ... NOT ACE...
PATEL'S NANOM
...NOT ACE.. NOT ACE..
...F-FFUCKIN' OINKMENT.
EIGHT ACE.
ONE FORTY-NINE.

SUCK IT UP AND TRY YOUR LUCK

WHETHER it's a ticket for the lottery or a flutter on the nags, an hourly scratchcard or a whole weekend indoors playing online roulette without sleeping, these days everyone loves to gamble. And despite what a few killjoys say, it's completely harmless fun. But even though there's never been a better time to be alive for the bet-loving Brit, one Fulchester entrepreneur is working on a ways to make it an even *better experience yet!*

SPIN CITY: *Wynne Naughton hopes to finally unite the worlds of domestic chores and gambling.*

Fulchester entrepreneur creates world's first vacuum cleaner fruitie

Tech-whizz **WYNNE NAUGHTON** says that as convenient and accessible as betting has become in the digital age, there are still obstacles hindering our freedom to bet whenever we like. And he has identified a window of opportunity in the gambling market through which he now aims to clamber.

"Everyday chores are shackles on our wagering liberty," the former warehouseman said. "We just want to go to the bookies or put some money in the slots in the pub, but there's a hundred-and-one jobs demanding our time and attention, from descaling the kettle to ironing."

"In having to sort out all these jobs, the pleasure of attempting to predict the outcome of sporting contests, or playing high-stakes games of chance has to be shelved," he added.

levitation

And 58-year-old Wynne singled out *hoovering* as the number one activity that comes between Brits and their ability to have a flutter.

GOOD CLEAN FUN: *Naughton is pleased with the performance of his prototype 'Fruitie Hoover'.*

EXCLUSIVE!

"To properly hoover the average British house top-to-bottom would take the typical housewife, or stay-at-home failed man, the best part of an hour," he said. "That's an hour when we could be having a flutter on a horse, putting a tenner on the first corner in a footie match or feeding coins into the slots."

"As things stand, we have two choices. We either not bother with the hoovering at all and go down the bookies, or just do the hoovering and not place any bets," he said.

"Choose the former and in no time we're living in dust and filth like an animal. Choose the latter and we're missing out on all the winnings from our bets coming in," he continued.

"It's a lose-lose situation."

gravy

And like all good ideas before it, Naughton's solution to this age-old problem is breathtaking in its simplicity. "Supposing a hoover incorporated an app which enabled the person pushing it to play online fruit-machines in the actual course of hoovering," he suggested. "The chore of hoovering would become part of the gambling experience. Just imagine it."

"Switch the machine on, and it tells the app that you want a bet and brings up a frutie on a screen on the dustbag," he continued. "Push the hoover forward to spin the reels, sweep left to hold, right to nudge, apply the nozzle to change your stake, and so on."

"Betting on the slots and cleaning your carpets *at the same time!*"

yurt

According to Wynne, the beauty of his system is that the same basic gambling hoover principle can be applied to dozens of household appliances which currently restrict our gambling options to nil. And he has already applied for patents for a Stud Poker air-fryer, and a lawnmower that allows real-time betting at every greyhound track in Britain.

"Betting household appliances are the way ahead for any serious house proud gambler," he said. "I'm thinking big."

Wynne has been testing his 'Fruitie Hoover' for two weeks, and is pleased with the way it is performing. "The first day using it, I came out twenty quid up having hoovered the front room and the hall," he said. "Then I hit the jackpot doing the stairs."

"Unfortunately, I went and put it all back doing the landing, and by the time I'd done the back bedroom, I was forty-eight quid down," he lamented.

"But I chased my losses the next day by doing the front bedroom and broke even, and I was a tenner up in the afternoon after doing the stairs again and the snug."

wellingtons

And the blue-sky thinker now believes that he has worked out a foolproof system for hitting the jackpot every time on his gambling vacuum. "What you've got to do is do the stairs first, and then hold any cherries you get whilst doing the hall," he said. "Never hold cherries whilst you're doing the front room, just spin, but always nudge on carpets with a thick pile," he said.

"It's a dead cert. Eventually you'll have a lovely clean house and you'll be quids in," he said. "Admittedly, I'm about sixteen hundred quid down at the minute, but any successful gambler will tell you it's a long game."

3-PAGE STATE OF BRITAIN'S WATERWAYS SPECIAL ... 3-PAGE STATE OF BRITAIN'S WATERWAYS SPECIAL

DIG FOR VICTORY NUMBER TWO

BRITAIN'S seas and rivers are more polluted today than they have ever been, with utilities companies pumping millions of gallons of raw sewage into our waterways every day. Far from Ruling the Waves, Britannia is sliding beneath them in a brown tsunami of her own droppings.

Many people unfairly blame the water companies for spewing out countless tons of untreated foulage into our waterways, whilst others blame the government whose policies allow them to do it. But water board bosses are only trying to make an honest living for themselves and their kiddies, and government ministers have all taken vows to act in the interest of the country at all times.

But whoever is actually to blame for Great Britain becoming an island floating in a sea of tod, one local entrepreneur is poised to push out a scheme which he believes will dump the whole messy business into a back passage in our national history books.

Shop owner Les Smallmeat is set to launch his *Dig And Go* campaign tomorrow in Fulmouth, the seaside town where he has run The Smuggler's Fun Cave gift and novelty shop since 2018. He believes that if the whole town joins in, his plan could see the brown tap polluting Fulmouth beach turned off for good.

Les, 60, had his excreta eureka moment last week as he lunched on the promenade. "I was thinking about sewage as I ate my snap," said the Fulchester-born businessman, who moved to the decaying holiday resort 6 years ago in response to a restraining order.

EXPOOSIVE!

"Sewage is a big issue here," he told reporters. "None of us traders are holding out much hope for the coming season. There's an outlet 20 yards off-shore that's been pumping out shite non-stop since Christmas."

"The sea stinks and it's full of toilet-tissue and jam-rags," he added.

egg

Munching on an egg bap, Les spied a youngster digging on the sands. "This lad would have been five or six, and he was having a fine old time," he said. "Then all at once he hops out of the hole he's dug and runs up to the portaloos at the top of the beach. I had to laugh. At that age I know that whatever I'd wanted to do, I'd happily have done it at the bottom of my hole then filled it in, and gone digging somewhere else."

Smallmeat realised that he may have chanced upon the solution to a problem that has eluded environmentalists for years. Surely, he reasoned, if everyone defaecated into a hole rather than the toilet, there would be no polluted water to deposit in the sea.

cans

It seemed an obvious solution to the town's sewage woes, and if extended nationwide might see the country once again surrounded by blue seas rather than cess. Excited, Smallmeat downed his remaining couple of lunchtime cans and raced back to his shop to embark on some research.

Ex-prison officer Les, who retired early after an incident he has been advised not to discuss, tried a variety of implements to dig holes in the back garden of his ground floor flat, but none of them came up to scratch. If the scheme was to be a success, he knew the tool had to be strong enough to withstand digging three or four holes a day, yet light enough to be carried round and small enough to be discreet.

CAN YOU DIG IT? Seaside shop owner Les Smallmeat believes he's found the answer to Britain's polluted waterways.

PIPE DOWN: Raw sewage pumped into the sea is a big problem in Les's native Fulmouth.

However, none of the tools he experimented with seemed to meet all his requirements. "I tried serving spoons, trowels, garden spades, the lot," he said. "But they were all either too flimsy to create a sizeable hole, or too big to be practical."

haemorrhoids

Smallmeat was about to give up on his research, but like many scientific discoveries, the answer came about by accident. "It was about three o'clock on a Wednesday afternoon and I hadn't made a sale all day, when I suddenly heard a commotion outside my shop," he said. "I went out to investigate and saw a group of kids from the local school running away laughing."

"They had kicked over the wire basket containing my beach buckets and spades for a laugh, the little bastards," he said. "As I picked them up to put them back in, I noticed how light and yet sturdy the spades were. The cogs started ticking in my head."

Les closed up his shop and raced home to conduct some experiments on the plastic beach toys. And the results were nothing short of amazing. "The beach shovels are light, but they are constructed for fairly rough play, and are sturdy enough to turn over most ground," he said. "And because they're child-sized, they fit easily in a briefcase or lady's handbag."

"The answer had been sitting in a wire basket outside my shop all along!"

And Les has predicted that the effect on the environment from the use of his spades will be enormous. "If, whenever somebody wants a number two, instead of going to the bog and flushing, they take themselves off to a discreet spot in their back garden, or a field, or even on the central island of a large roundabout, dig a small hole and park their breakfast in that, we'll take umpteen tons of muck out of the sewage system overnight."

"Of course, It needn't be every single visit," he said. "If it was raining or there was snow, you could always use your thunderbox. *Dig And Go* every second or third mess and you would still be tilting the balance of the equation and making a huge difference."

Having spoken with his Taiwanese suppliers, Les says that from tomorrow he will be able to offer his *Dig And Go* kits at a price of just £4 – a whopping 99p less than the same item would cost today. "Four quid to save the environment. I'd say that was a bargain," he told reporters.

"Obviously, they'd be cheaper if I broke up the sets and sold the spades separately, but then I'd be saddled with a load of castle-shaped buckets," the environmentally minded business mogul admitted. "I want to save Britain from its own filth, yes, but I am trying to run a business here. I'm making next to nothing on them as it is. What do you expect me to eat, fucking fresh air?"

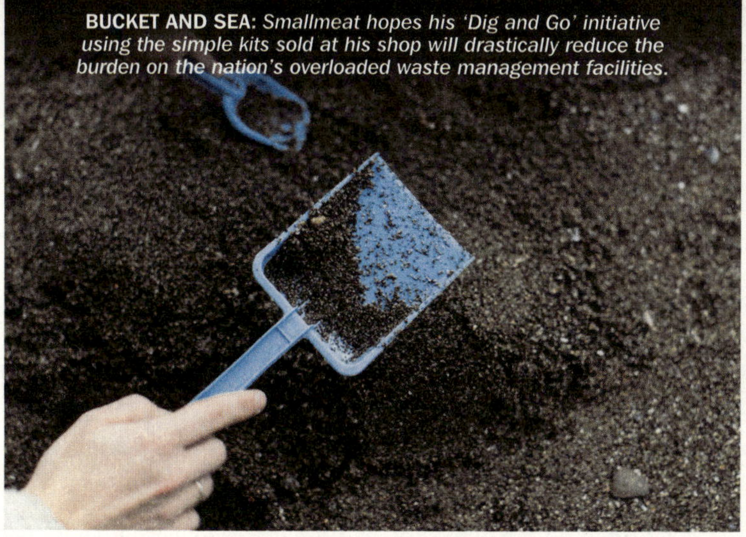

BUCKET AND SEA: *Smallmeat hopes his 'Dig and Go' initiative using the simple kits sold at his shop will drastically reduce the burden on the nation's overloaded waste management facilities.*

gandalfs

In order to get as many people as possible joining in with his environmental campaign, Les is holding a launch event at The Smuggler's Fun Cave beginning at 9am tomorrow, and he advises people to arrive early to avoid disappointment. "There'll be a local entertainer with balloon animals for the kiddies, as well as a free can of beer for the mums and dads," he said. "And of course, everyone can buy one of the *Dig and Go* kits at the special discounted launch price."

He added that a selection of specialist magazines aimed at "the discerning reader" would also be available to the adults, accessed through a doorway in the rear of the premises, protected by a fly-curtain.

VOX PLOPS

EVERYONE loves to swim in the sea, except for those who don't. And with thousands plumping for a staycation this year, it is Great Britain's coastal waters that will see many of us take the plunge. With every inch of sea around the country now boiling with effluent, foulage and bodily waste paraphernalia, the days of pristine Blue Flag beaches are long gone. But we Brits are a plucky lot, and it takes more than a flotilla of copper bolts, soiled jamrags or jizz-filled blobs to put us off our dip in the briny. We asked some household names how they make the best of things when swimming in sewage.

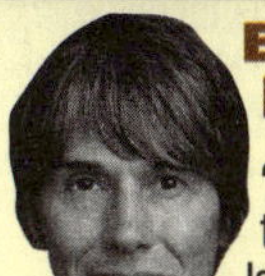

BRIAN COX,
Physicist

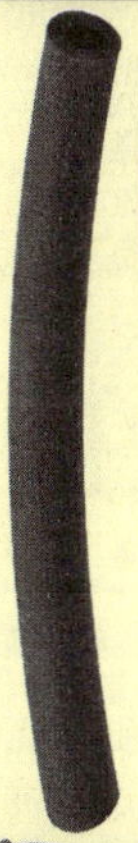

"I GET A 3 METRE length of that foam insulation they use to lag copper pipes and bend it into a ring secured with duct tape. Then I float that on the sea and splash around in the middle, and it keeps all the floating turds and wotnot away from me, a bit like those booms they use to contain oil slicks. However, being just $3/\pi$ metres in diameter, ie 95.493cm, it's only big enough for just me to play in, so if I want to throw a beachball around with a friend, I simply use a few lengths of it joined together and make a much bigger turd slick boom."

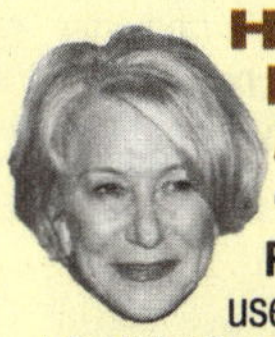

HELEN MIRREN,
Actor

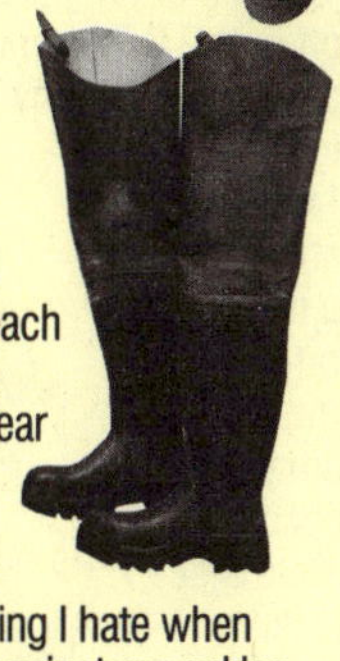

"I WORKED IN ROME for a while and I used to love to go to the beach at Castello Santa Severa or Torvaianica, where I'd paddle in the warm, crystal clear waters of the Tyrrhenian Sea. When I paddle in Britain, however, I don don a pair of fishing waders after taking my socks and shoes off, because if there's one thing I hate when paddling, it's having all turds knocking against my ankles and rubber johnnies sticking to my shins."

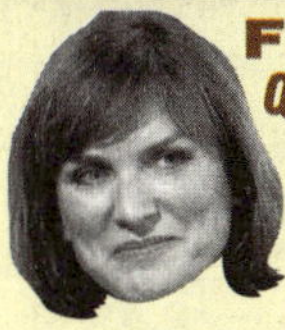

FIONA BRUCE,
***Question Time* presenter**

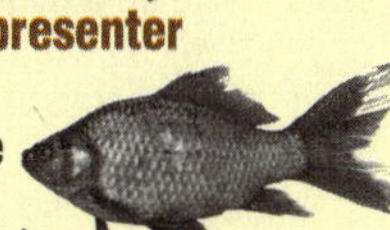

"When I go wild swimming, I take a goldfish with me in a birdcage, in much the same way that olden days miners would take a canary down the pit to test for noxious gases. I keep checking my goldfish whilst I'm in the water, and if it's swimming about in the cage, I know all is well. But if it suddenly floats to the top of the water with its eyes bulging, I'm out of there like shit off a shovel."

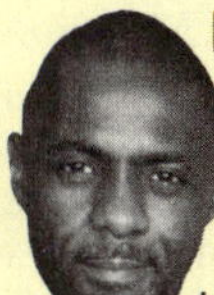

IDRIS ELBA,
Potential James Bond actor

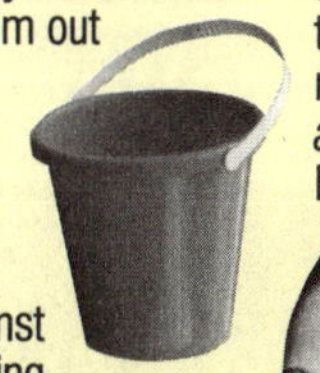

"Feeling the cold water against your bare skin when swimming in the sea is an amazingly invigorating experience, and it would be completely ruined by wearing a wetsuit or any protective clothing against the sewage. So before I swim in the sea in the UK, I stuff cotton wool in my ears and nostrils and take a really deep breath. Then I have my revitalising swim, keeping my eyes and mouth tight shut and coming out when I need to breathe again. Back on the beach, I wash myself down with a bucket of Jeyes fluid which I have brought with me, and take a course of powerful antibiotics before running back in for another energising one-breath splash about."

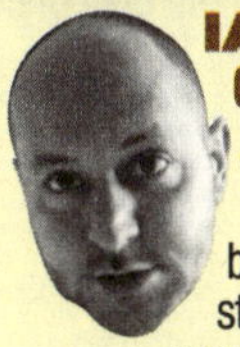

IAN DUNT,
Columnist,
i newspaper

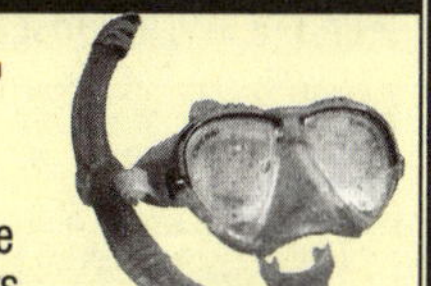

"Before going in the bastard sea, I always stick a fucking snorkel in my mouth and wrap myself head to fucking foot in clingfilm. Once I've done that, I can splash about in all the fucking shit and filth with no fucking worries. When I've fucking well had enough, I come out, take off all the fucking shit-splattered clingfilm, shove it in the cunting bin and settle down on the fucking beach to read my latest bastard book *How Westminster Works... and Why It Doesn't,* available from all fucking bookshops. Buy it. Buy it now, you cunts."

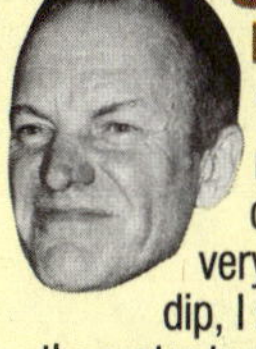

STING,
Lute-playing bellend

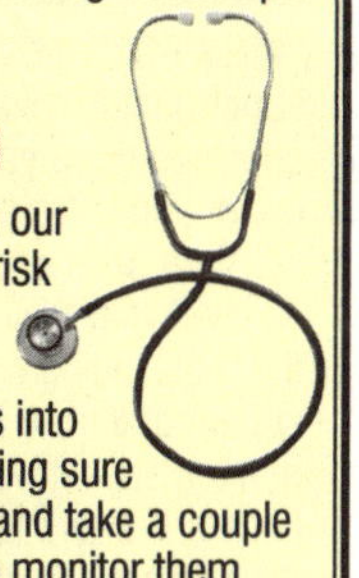

"I love wild swimming in our rivers and seas, but the risk of falling ill as a result is very real. When I fancy a dip, I send one of my servants into the water to splash around a bit, making sure that they get it in their eyes and ears and take a couple of mouthfuls. Then I get my doctor to monitor them over the next 24 hours to see what happens. If they are okay, then I'll happily swim there, but if they become dangerously ill, I'll look for somewhere else to go for a dip. There is no point taking any unnecessary risks."

STATE OF BRITAIN'S WATERWAYS SPECIAL ... 3-PAGE STATE OF BRITAIN'S WATERWAYS SPECIAL

SPLASH IN THE ATTIC!

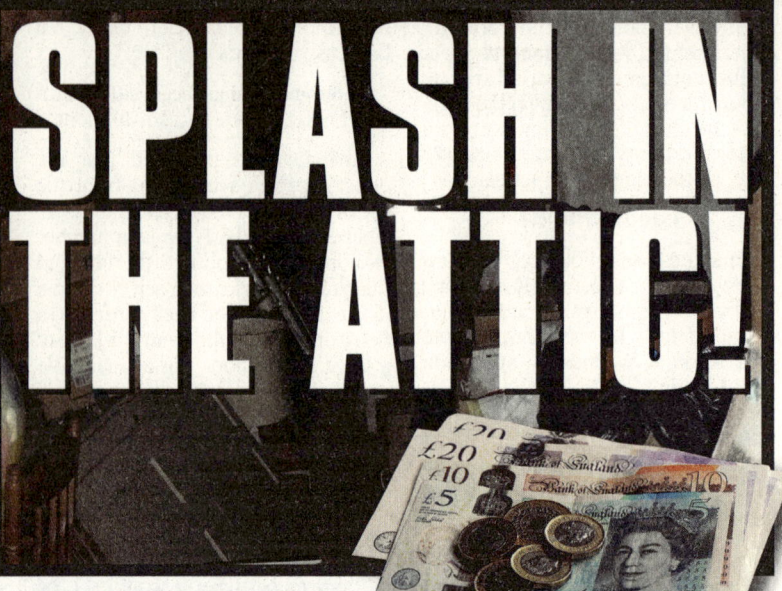

BRITAIN'S rivers are more polluted than they have ever been, with millions of gallons of raw sewage being pumped into them every day. The fish, amphibians and insects which call our waterways and ponds their home die in the filthy, toxic waters. As a result, biodiversity is now at an all time low with many ponds, streams and brooks now so contaminated that they support no animal life at all. And the problem extends to the banks and further, as the mammals and birds that rely on these aquatic creatures for their food starve and die. These watery wastelands are having a devastatingly detrimental effect on the whole ecosystem. But it's not all bad news, because if you go pond dipping today, there's a chance that you could find something of real value in the bottom of your net.

We took **ALF BARGEPOLE** – a scrap metal salvager of 45 years standing – to Kingfisher Pond on the outskirts of Tipton's Ironmonger Industrial Estate. The pond was once home to the Midlands' largest colony of great crested newts, but now armed with with his trusty grappling hook on a rope, Alf gave us the lowdown on what he dredged from the former wildlife haven's stagnant waters.

Haul 1: A child's bike frame

"KIDDIES' bike frames are perhaps the most common thing you will pull out of any pond in Britain. Most of the time, they are just good for scrap and you'll get about 50p apiece down you local weigh-in centre. If you're lucky, it might be a Raleigh Chopper or a Grifter, which you can put on ebay and get a tenner for, because they're collectors' items. This one's been in here quite a while, because the tyres and the seat have gone, and honestly it's not worth the arseache, so I'll just chuck it back in. But here's a top tip – wait until you've done dredging before lobbing owt back in, or you'll end up pulling the fucker out half a dozen times."

Haul 2: A fridge

"YOU'D THINK pulling a fridge out a pond would be a good thing, but you'd be wrong. Most of a fridge these days is plastic, with very little metal to speak of, so it's not worth muckying the boot of your car up for. Plus, because they've got all chemicals in the back that make them work, you actually have to pay to get rid of them. If I took this into the dealers, he'd want a tenner off me to take it off my hands. That's why so many of the fuckers end up in ponds. The chemical really fucks everything in the water up, but at ten quid apiece to get rid of, what else can you do?"

Haul 3: A pram

"WHAT WITH everyone using buggies, you don't get many old-fashioned prams in ponds these days. But when you do pull one out, it's a good day because there's a fair old amount of metal on them and they can easy fetch you 2 or 3 quid. They rust away quick though, so only ones that have been in the pond less than a couple of years will be worth taking to the scrappie. This one I've pulled out is almost all rust, so it's going back in. I have to say, I think the golden age of pulling prams out of ponds is well and truly behind us."

Haul 4: Pipework

"YOU CAN always pull some pipework out a pond, and what it's made of will determine what you'll get for it at the scrappie. All pipes look the same when they come out covered in sludge and shit, but when when you've been at this game as long as I have you'll learn what to look out for. The first thing you do is feel how heavy it is. If it's really light, give it a scratch – a gold colour means it's copper and will get you about 25p a metre. If it comes up silver, it's aluminium which is worth next to nowt. If it's dead heavy, you've got lead or iron in your hands and it's time to get excited. No good scrap salvager goes anywhere without his trusty magnet, and now's the time to get it out. If it sticks, you've got iron at 35p a metre. But if it drops off, you've hit lead paydirt. Unfortunately, this stuff today was aluminium, so I just lobbed the fucker back in."

Haul 5: Supermarket trolley

"NEXT TO the bike frame, the supermarket trolley is the most common thing you can hook out a pond, and there's a good £2-£2.50 worth of steel in each one. And don't believe what they tell you about them still being the property of the supermarkets. A bloke in the pub I drink at says it's covered under the finders keepers law. Of course, if they're in really good nick, you could always give them a bit of a polish and see how much the supermarket will give you to get the fucker back."

Haul 6: Hand gun

"I'VE PULLED no end of guns out of ponds in the past, and unfortunately it's becoming a more common event. Gun crime is on the rise and there's no better way for your local bad lads to get rid of any 'hot' weapons than by chucking them in a pond, usually right in the middle. The scrappie will give you about £2 for a hand gun and £2.50 for a sawn-off. By rights, you should hand them in to the police in case they are of interest in an on-going enquiry. But I did this the first time I found one – a semi-automatic Luger – and I never got it back after they solved the case. So that was 3 knicker down the fucking drain. Never again."

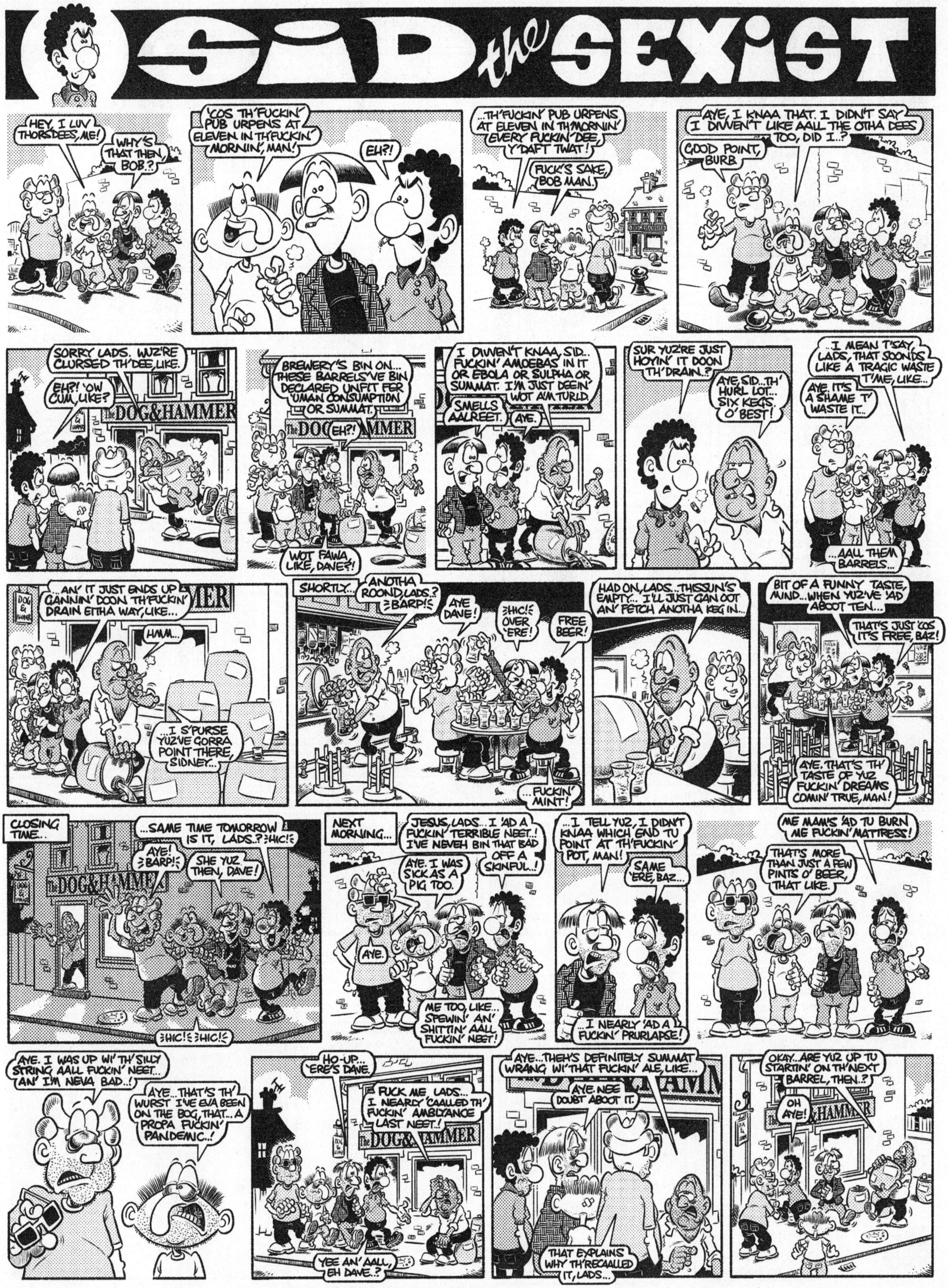
SID the SEXIST
HEY, I LUV THORSDEES, ME!
WHY'S THAT THEN, BOB..?
'COS TH' FUCKIN' PUB URPENS AT ELEVEN IN TH'FUCKIN' MORNIN', MAN!
EH?!
...TH' FUCKIN' PUB URPENS AT ELEVEN IN TH'MORNIN' EVERY FUCKIN' DEE, Y'DAFT TWAT!
FUCK'S SAKE, BOB MAN.
AYE, I KNAA THAT. I DIDN'T SAY I DIVVEN'T LIKE AALL THE OTHA DEES TOO, DID I..?
GOOD POINT, BURB
SORRY LADS. WUZ'RE CLURSED TH'DEE, LIKE.
EH?! 'OW CUM, LIKE?
BREWERY'S BIN ON... THESE BARRELS'VE BIN DECLARED UNFIT FER 'UMAN CONSUMPTION OR SUMMAT.
EH?!
WOT FAWA LIKE, DAVE?!
I DIVVEN'T KNAA, SID.. FUCKIN' AMOEBAS IN IT OR EBOLA OR SULPHA OR SUMMAT. I'M JUST DEEIN' WOT AM TURLD.
SMELLS AALREET.
AYE.
SUR YUZ'RE JUST HOYIN' IT DOON TH'DRAIN..?
AYE, SID...TH' HURL LOT... SIX KEGS O' BEST!
...I MEAN T'SAY, LADS, THAT SOONDS LIKE A TRAGIC WASTE T'ME, LIKE...
AYE. IT'S A SHAME T' WASTE IT...
...AALL THEM BARRELS...
...AN' IT JUST ENDS UP GANNIN' DOON TH'FUCKIN' DRAIN EITHA WAY, LIKE...
HMM...
...I S'PURSE YUZ'VE GORRA POINT THERE, SIDNEY...
SHORTLY...
ANOTHA ROOND, LADS..? BARP!
AYE DAVE!
HIC! OVER 'ERE!
FREE BEER!
...FUCKIN' MINT!
HAD ON, LADS...THISSUN'S EMPTY... I'LL JUST GAN OOT AN' FETCH ANOTHA KEG IN...
BIT OF A FUNNY TASTE, MIND...WHEN YUZ'VE 'AD ABOOT TEN...
THAT'S JUST 'COS IT'S FREE, BAZ!
AYE. THAT'S TH' TASTE OF YUZ FUCKIN' DREAMS COMIN' TRUE, MAN!
CLOSING TIME..
...SAME TIME TOMORROW IS IT, LADS..? HIC!
AYE! BARP!
SHE YUZ THEN, DAVE!
HIC! HIC!
NEXT MORNING...
JESUS, LADS...I 'AD A FUCKIN' TERRIBLE NEET..! I'VE NEVEH BIN THAT BAD OFF A SKINFUL..!
AYE. I WAS SICK AS A PIG TOO.
AYE.
ME TOO, LIKE... SPEWIN' AN' SHITTIN' AALL FUCKIN' NEET!
...I TELL YUZ, I DIDN'T KNAA WHICH END TU POINT AT TH'FUCKIN' POT, MAN!
SAME 'ERE, BAZ...
...I NEARLY 'AD A FUCKIN' PRURLAPSE!
ME MAM'S 'AD TU BURN ME FUCKIN' MATTRESS!
THAT'S MORE THAN JUST A FEW PINTS O' BEER, THAT LIKE.
AYE. I WAS UP WI' TH' SILLY STRING AALL FUCKIN' NEET... AN' I'M NEVA BAD..!
AYE...THAT'S TH' WURST I'VE EVA BEEN ON THE BOG, THAT... A PROPA FUCKIN' PANDEMIC..!
HO-UP... 'ERE'S DAVE.
FUCK ME LADS... I NEARLY 'CAALLED TH' FUCKIN' AMBLYANCE LAST NEET..!
YEE AN' AALL, EH DAVE..?
AYE...THEH'S DEFINITELY SUMMAT WRANG WI' THAT FUCKIN' ALE, LIKE...
AYE. NEE DOUBT ABOOT IT.
THAT EXPLAINS WHY TH'RECAALLED IT, LADS...
OKAY...ARE YUZ UP TU STARTIN' ON TH'NEXT BARREL, THEN..?
OH AYE!

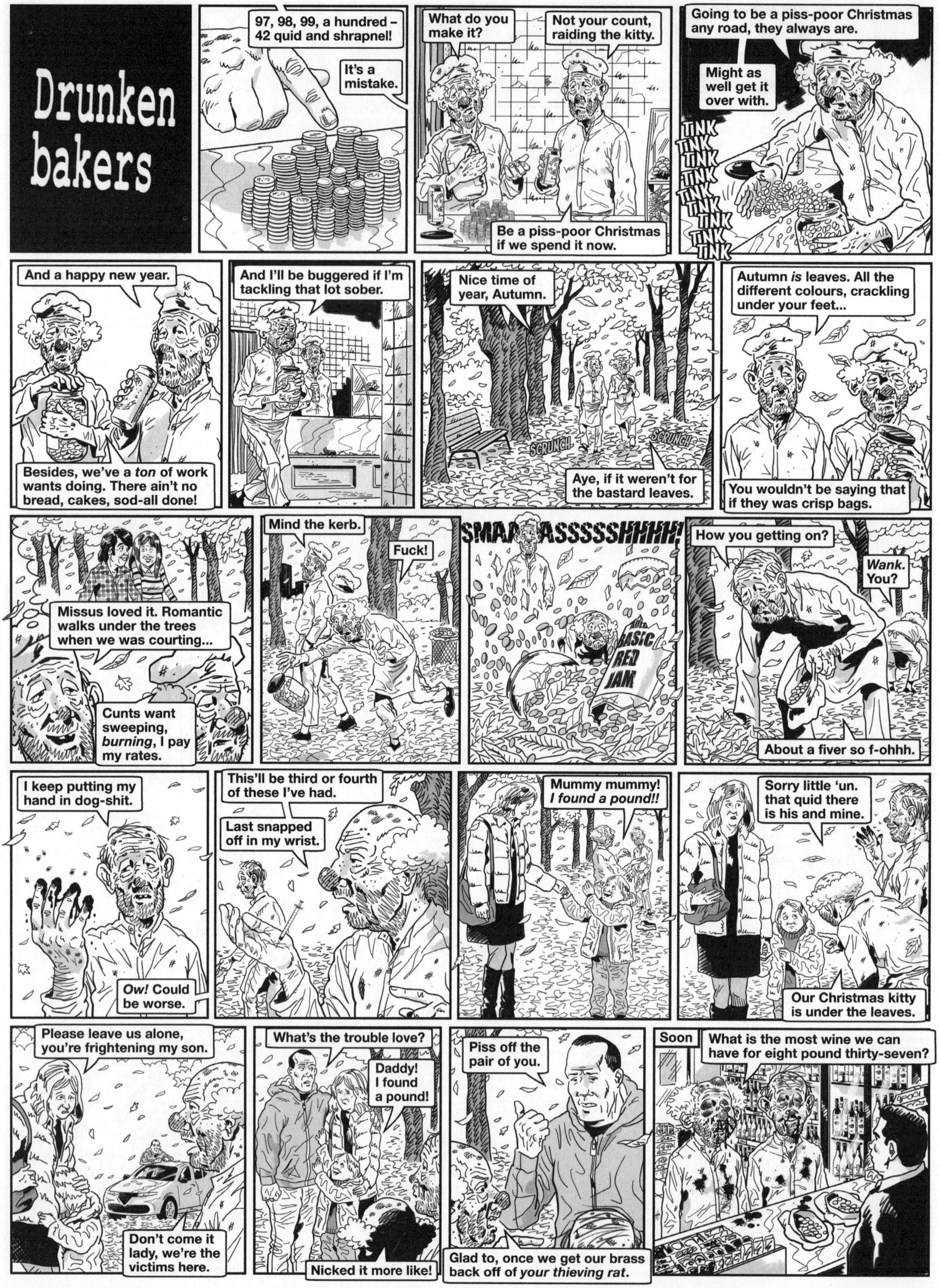

Drunken bakers
97, 98, 99, a hundred – 42 quid and shrapnel!
It's a mistake.
What do you make it?
Not your count, raiding the kitty.
Be a piss-poor Christmas if we spend it now.
Going to be a piss-poor Christmas any road, they always are.
Might as well get it over with.
TINK TINK TINK TINK TINK TINK TINK TINK
And a happy new year.
Besides, we've a *ton* of work wants doing. There ain't no bread, cakes, sod-all done!
And I'll be buggered if I'm tackling that lot sober.
Nice time of year, Autumn.
SCRUNCH
SCRUNCH
Aye, if it weren't for the bastard leaves.
Autumn *is* leaves. All the different colours, crackling under your feet...
You wouldn't be saying that if they was crisp bags.
Missus loved it. Romantic walks under the trees when we was courting...
Cunts want sweeping, *burning*, I pay my rates.
Mind the kerb.
Fuck!
SMAAASSSSSHHHH!
BASIC RED JAM
How you getting on?
Wank. You?
About a fiver so f-ohhh.
I keep putting my hand in dog-shit.
Ow! Could be worse.
This'll be third or fourth of these I've had.
Last snapped off in my wrist.
Mummy mummy! *I found a pound!!*
Sorry little 'un. that quid there is his and mine.
Our Christmas kitty is under the leaves.
Please leave us alone, you're frightening my son.
Don't come it lady, we're the victims here.
What's the trouble love?
Daddy! I found a pound!
Nicked it more like!
Piss off the pair of you.
Glad to, once we get our brass back off of *your thieving rat*.
Soon
What is the most wine we can have for eight pound thirty-seven?

EXTRA TIME TRAVEL

THE English Football Association has announced ambitious plans to fund research into time travel with the hope that one day the national team will once again be able to win the 1966 World Cup.

Apart from a third place playoff in Russia back in 2018, the last six decades have seen the Three Lions unable to progress past the quarter finals in the quadrennial international soccer tournament. But now English FA chiefs hope to exploit a loophole in the fabric of the space-time continuum to allow the current squad to beat Germany 4-2 in the 1966 World Cup final ... *every four years!*

Sports scientists are currently conducting trials with a rudimentary time portal to allow the team to once again lift the Jules Rimet trophy in 1966. And they are hoping that a full-scale working system will be ready in time for the 2026 tournament to be held in venues across North America.

"It'll be great going into a World Cup finals knowing that we are definitely going to win it," said the FA's CEO Mark Bullingham. "Just imagine winning the World Cup every time, just like we did back in 1966. We'll be a footballing force to be reckoned with."

"If all goes to plan, in 2042 England will lift the trophy for the sixth time, taking the most wins title from five-times winners Brazil," Bullingham added.

haemoglobin

But worried boffins have warned soccer chiefs that the outcome of each 1966 World Cup is not necessarily a foregone conclusion. England will only beat Germany 4-2 if all quantum events occur exactly as they did in the first meeting nearly six decades ago.

English FA to lift World Cup trophy for second time

"Time isn't a straight line," said TV boffin Professor Brian Cox. "It's more like the branches of an enormous tree, a tree of infinite size."

"England beating Germany 4-2 was just one possible branch of that tree."

"We could be playing Germany in the 1966 final in 2026, and it's 2-2 at full time as we expect. But as we go into extra time, somebody in the crowd might step on a butterfly and change the whole course of events," Cox continued.

"When Geoff Hurst hits the underside of the bar this time, the Russian linesman might decide that the ball has not crossed the line."

"Of course, we'd still go on to win 3-2, but you get my point," he added.

maracas

Meanwhile, Scottish FA bosses have also expressed an interest in meddling with the very fabric of time itself. If the English experiment works and Bobby Moore's men do lift the trophy for a second time in 2026, bofffins north of the border plan to develop their own time portal to see their team once again qualify for, and perform reasonably well in, the 1982 finals in Spain.

And even though time travel to previous World Cups is only at the drawing board stage, Scottish fans have been quick to snap up accommodation to once again watch Jock Stein's boys thrash New Zealand, draw with the Soviet Union and go down fighting to Brazil.

THEY'LL THINK IT'S ALL OVER AGAIN! *The Jules Rimet trophy which English FA chiefs hope the national squad will bag every four years.*

"Accommodation in Spain is dirt cheap in the 70s," said Tartan Army fan Doug McKenzie. "I've just booked a hotel for the entire group stages for twenty quid. And the flights will be even cheaper forty years ago than they are today."

Travel expert Simon Calder advised fans looking for flights to 1970s Spain to book well in advance and consider airport parking. "There are some great deals to be had in Spanish resorts 44 years ago if you shop around," he told anyone who'd listen.

"And if you're flexible about where you fly from, then you could be sipping sangrias by the pool the same day!" he told Holly Willoughby's neighbour's friend via text.

MAJOR MISUNDERSTANDING
SUNDAY MORNING
BONG BONG BONG
AH ETHAN, A LITTLE JOB FOR YOU.
I WANT YOU TO HAND OUT TODAY'S HYMN SHEET TO EVERYBODY AS THEY COME IN.
WE'RE STILL WAITING FOR THE NEW HYMN BOOKS TO BE DELIVERED.
YOUR HYMN, DR PREECE?
YOUR HYMN, MISS FLOWERDEW?
THANK YOU.
WHAT A WELL-MANNERED LITTLE BOY.
YOUR HYMN, MAJOR?
FOR CRYING OUT LOUD! MUST WE BE SUBJECTED TO THIS WOKE NONSENSE EVEN AT CHURCH?
YES OF COURSE I'M A BLOODY "HIM!"
DO YOU REALLY FIND IT NECESSARY TO ASK ME FOR MY PRONOUNS? I'D HAVE THOUGHT THAT THIS MOUSTACHE WOULD GIVE A CLUE.
OR DID YOU THINK IT MIGHT BE A BLOB OF HAIRY LIPSTICK?
THEN AGAIN, I SUPPOSE I MAY HAVE WOKEN UP THIS MORNING AND DECIDED TO IDENTIFY AS AN EIGHTEEN YEAR OLD CHORUS GIRL FROM THE FOLIES BERGÈRE.
AND GOD FORBID THAT EVERYBODY ELSE SHOULD FAIL TO PANDER TO MY EVERY DELUDED WHIM!
AS FOR YOU VICAR, YOU'RE SUPPOSED TO REPRESENT THE TIMELESS TRUTHS OF THE CHURCH OF ENGLAND.
YOU DON'T HAVE TO ACCOMODATE EVERY LUDICROUS FAD AND FASHION THAT COMES ALONG.
"AND GOD CREATED THEM MALE AND FEMALE" — THAT'S FROM THE BIBLE, YOU KNOW.
PERHAPS YOU OUGHT TO READ IT SOME DAY.
DJ '23

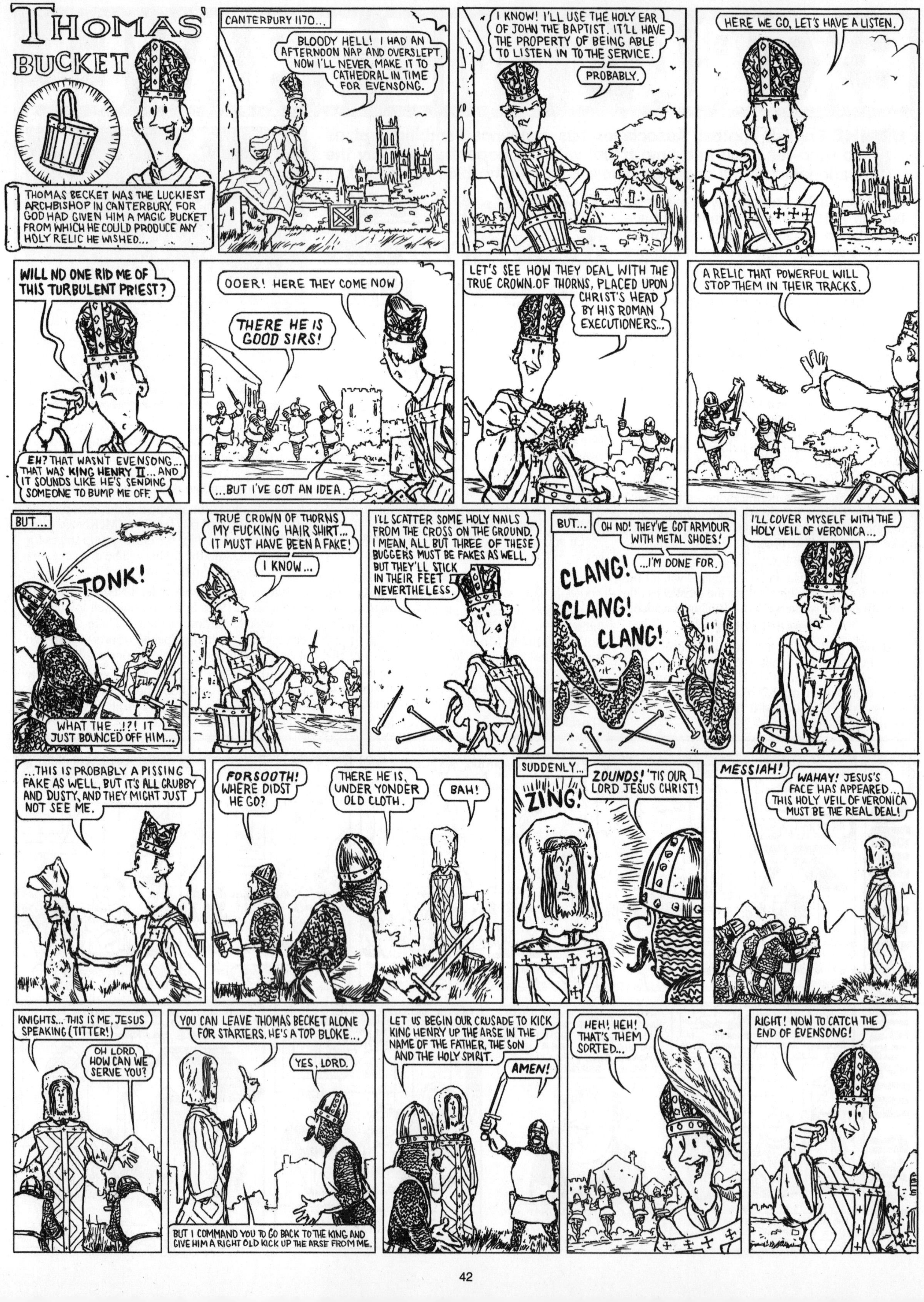
THOMAS' BUCKET
THOMAS BECKET WAS THE LUCKIEST ARCHBISHOP IN CANTERBURY, FOR GOD HAD GIVEN HIM A MAGIC BUCKET FROM WHICH HE COULD PRODUCE ANY HOLY RELIC HE WISHED...
CANTERBURY 1170...
BLOODY HELL! I HAD AN AFTERNOON NAP AND OVERSLEPT. NOW I'LL NEVER MAKE IT TO CATHEDRAL IN TIME FOR EVENSONG.
I KNOW! I'LL USE THE HOLY EAR OF JOHN THE BAPTIST. IT'LL HAVE THE PROPERTY OF BEING ABLE TO LISTEN IN TO THE SERVICE.
PROBABLY.
HERE WE GO, LET'S HAVE A LISTEN.
WILL NO ONE RID ME OF THIS TURBULENT PRIEST?
EH? THAT WASN'T EVENSONG... THAT WAS KING HENRY II... AND IT SOUNDS LIKE HE'S SENDING SOMEONE TO BUMP ME OFF.
OOER! HERE THEY COME NOW
THERE HE IS GOOD SIRS!
...BUT I'VE GOT AN IDEA.
LET'S SEE HOW THEY DEAL WITH THE TRUE CROWN OF THORNS, PLACED UPON CHRIST'S HEAD BY HIS ROMAN EXECUTIONERS...
A RELIC THAT POWERFUL WILL STOP THEM IN THEIR TRACKS.
BUT...
TONK!
WHAT THE...!?! IT JUST BOUNCED OFF HIM...
TRUE CROWN OF THORNS MY FUCKING HAIR SHIRT... IT MUST HAVE BEEN A FAKE!
I KNOW...
I'LL SCATTER SOME HOLY NAILS FROM THE CROSS ON THE GROUND. I MEAN, ALL BUT THREE OF THESE BUGGERS MUST BE FAKES AS WELL, BUT THEY'LL STICK IN THEIR FEET NEVERTHELESS.
BUT...
OH NO! THEY'VE GOT ARMOUR WITH METAL SHOES!
...I'M DONE FOR.
CLANG!
CLANG!
CLANG!
I'LL COVER MYSELF WITH THE HOLY VEIL OF VERONICA...
...THIS IS PROBABLY A PISSING FAKE AS WELL, BUT IT'S ALL GRUBBY AND DUSTY, AND THEY MIGHT JUST NOT SEE ME.
FORSOOTH! WHERE DIDST HE GO?
THERE HE IS, UNDER YONDER OLD CLOTH.
BAH!
SUDDENLY...
ZING!
ZOUNDS! 'TIS OUR LORD JESUS CHRIST!
MESSIAH!
WAHAY! JESUS'S FACE HAS APPEARED... THIS HOLY VEIL OF VERONICA MUST BE THE REAL DEAL!
KNIGHTS... THIS IS ME, JESUS SPEAKING (TITTER!)
OH LORD, HOW CAN WE SERVE YOU?
YOU CAN LEAVE THOMAS BECKET ALONE FOR STARTERS. HE'S A TOP BLOKE...
YES, LORD.
BUT I COMMAND YOU TO GO BACK TO THE KING AND GIVE HIM A RIGHT OLD KICK UP THE ARSE FROM ME.
LET US BEGIN OUR CRUSADE TO KICK KING HENRY UP THE ARSE IN THE NAME OF THE FATHER, THE SON AND THE HOLY SPIRIT.
AMEN!
HEH! HEH! THAT'S THEM SORTED...
RIGHT! NOW TO CATCH THE END OF EVENSONG!

Bosses! get rid of pesky bullying accusations once-and-for-all with our...

FREE VIZ WORKPLACE BULLYING THRESHOLD DETERMINER

IT'S GOODBYE GREY AREAS!

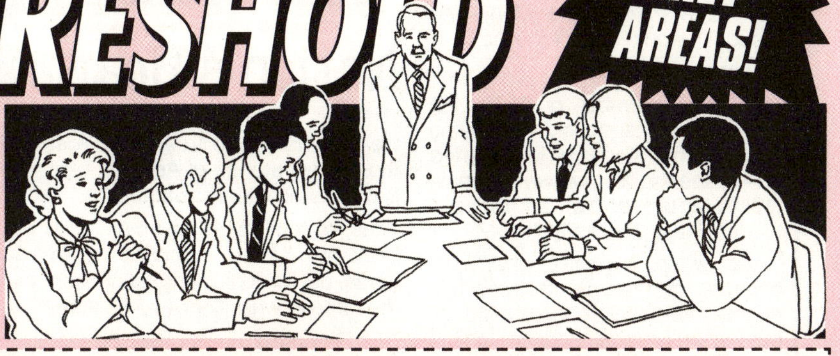

Where is the LINE DRAWN in YOUR place of work?

BULLYING has become the scourge of the modern workplace with those in positions of power behaving in an unacceptable manner with junior colleagues. And nowhere is this practice more prevalent than in the Palace of Westminster. Over the last few years, countless MPs, both in government and opposition, have been found to have bullied staff, and have quite rightly been dismissed from their posts for a few weeks before starting up where they left off.

But many accused say that the allegations are nonsensical, and that their victims were not bullied, but simply subjected to the rough and tumble of any office where high-stakes decisions are made.

So what exactly constitutes bullying in the interplay of a workplace? When does forthright criticism of a junior colleague tip over into abuse? Is making a subordinate worker cry an unacceptable episode, or a character-building moment in their career? Should a minor punch in the face always to be treated as an assault, or could it be seen as an 'outside the box' way of incentivising your staff?

It is a difficult issue because bullying is a subjective matter – one man's brutal bollocking of an employee for their own good is another woman's physical assault. The management of each workplace will have their own threshold of where acceptable staff relations end and bullying begins, and it is imperative that all workers know the boundaries. *And it is easy to get it wrong.*

But not any more! Because *Viz Comic* has come to the rescue of British bosses with this fantastic free gift.

The ***Viz* Workplace Bullying Threshold Determiner** lets all your employees know what **YOU** deem is acceptable behaviour and what is not. It will let them know whether the experience to which they have just been subjected constitutes bullying, so they will know whether to pluck up courage and make a complaint, or simply lick their wounds and get on with the job.

INSTRUCTIONS: Decide the point in **YOUR** workplace at which **YOU** determine robust managerial practice tips into bullying, and draw a thick horizontal line underneath in red between point **A** and **B**. Then draw a thick red line between your point **B** and point **C** and pin it up on the staff notice board. Employees can then consult the *Viz Workplace Bullying Threshold Determiner* if they are unsure whether or not they have been the subject of bullying by someone in a position of power.

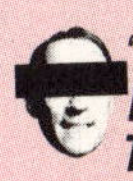

*"I never threw any food at my staff. But if we'd had a **Viz Bullying Threshold Determiner** in all the departments I've been in charge of, I could have drawn the red line right near the bottom and hurled tomatoes at them all day long."*

D.R, London

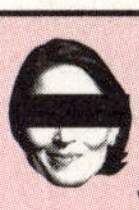

"I was found to have breached the ministerial code by bullying my staff. But then my mate, who was Prime Minister at the time, simply chucked the report in the bin and I carried on as normal. So I don't need one of these, fuck you very much."

P.P, London

OFFICE BULLYING THRESHOLD

Having a more comfortable chair than your junior staff

A — B

Mild criticism of employee with raised eyebrow

A — B

Mild criticism of employee with exaggerated eye rolling

A — B

Mild criticism of employee with finger wagging

A — B

Undermining presentations from juniors by cutting nails, doing crossword, trimming nasal hairs, etc

A — B

Belittling employees with sarcastic comments, forced laughter, slow applause etc

A — B

Name-calling using negative personal attributes without swearing. ie, fatty, big ears, speccy four-eyes

A — B

Pointing at an employee in an aggressive or threatening manner like they do in Al Qaida and ISIS videos

A — B

Shouting at employees from 5-10m across the room

A — B

Name calling using negative personal attributes with swearing ie, fat bastard, fucking big ears, speccy cunt

A — B

Shouting at employees 5-10cm from their face with all spittle coming out your mouth

A — B

Throwing of soft food items, ie. croissants, over-ripe tomatoes, Tunnocks tea cakes, at junior colleague during meeting

A — B

Pushing an employee on the shoulder as if trying to start a fight in a nightclub

A — B

Throwing of hard food items, ie. rock buns, under-ripe tomatoes, unopened tinned fruit, at junior colleague during meeting

A — B

Slapping someone rapidly on the head in a Benny Hill style to make them work faster

A — B

A slap in the face with a Sean Connery-style open hand

A — B

A punch in the face with a closed fist, occasioning bleeding

A — B

A punch in the face with a closed fist, occasioning an overnight stay in hospital for observations

C

ROBUST MANAGERIAL PRACTICE

BULLYING

TONY 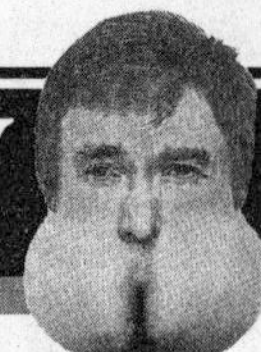 PARSEHOLE

The Tree that Broke a Nation's Heart

THE MIGHTY oak at Sycamore Gap on Adrian's Wall had stood sentinel since Roman times. For a thousand years, it had bravely withstood the ravages and ramparts of time.

We saw it in that film with Kevin Costner and him who was Red in *The Shawshank Redeption* and thought it would stand for ever.

How wrong we were.

In late September of 2023, the unthinkable suddenly became thought when it was callously felled during the night, viciously sawn in twain by an unseen hand and reduced to a worthless pile of matchwood.

And when I heard what had became of this proud tree, this mighty, wooden manifestation of our nation's noble heart of oak, I wept like a willow. The tears came unbidden to my eyes and cascaded down my cheeks like rivers of pain, anguish and despair.

I cried and I cried and – yes – I cried some more.

And then a bit more after that.

I wept because never again would we see this proud tree set amidst the ancient stones of Adrian's Wall like a staunch, leafy sentinel.

Yes, bottomists tell us it may grow back over untold centuries yet to come, but it will never again of been the same as what it once was before.

As I seen the news I realised that what once had been was now gone. And with it, a part of me had died too, and now I wept for its loss.

But who would fell this staunch tree? What is the mysterious identity of "Lumberjack the Ripper" (© Tony Parsehole 2023 in all territies)?

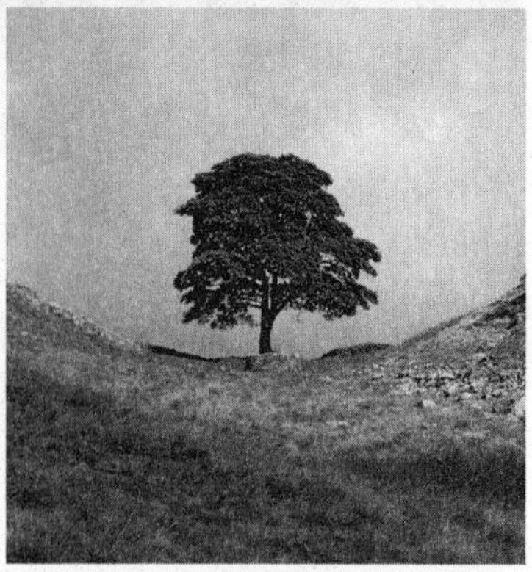

Of course, there has been speculation. Much tittle, and indeed much tattle. Perhaps we will never know for sure who it was who wealded the chainsaw that felled the mighty oak at Sycamore Gap.

But this much is certain.

Whoever it was who done it should hang their head in shame.

For they have desiccated an irreplacable icon, a proud British tree that stirred the hearts of men for time immorial and across countless centuries and years into the past and yet to come.

Twigs of oak. Branches of oak. And yes, a trunk of oak, riven with the rings that count out all our history from the Battle of Britain in 1066 to the present day. The whole of our island's story inscribed upon its beating heart, written in its D and A like words inscribed through a stick of rock.

A rock of ages that has now been heartlessly cleft in twain. A tree that has taken its final bough on our national stage. The oaken stage upon which Shakespeare himself once trod.

For was it not also fine English trees that made the ships in which Rule Britannia ruled the waves, sailed the seas and conkered the world? The ships of Sir Walter Rally, Sir Captain Cook, Sir Francis Chichester and Sir Ellen Macarthur?

Proud names that are carved upon British hearts of oak for all to see.

I'd just like to point out that I thought of Lumberjack the Ripper, and if anyone uses it I will come down on them like a ton of there thats 500 wwords inv enc

With Britain's favourite tree chopped down in a wanton act of vandalism, we 'Axe' the vital question...

WHOFELLEDIT?

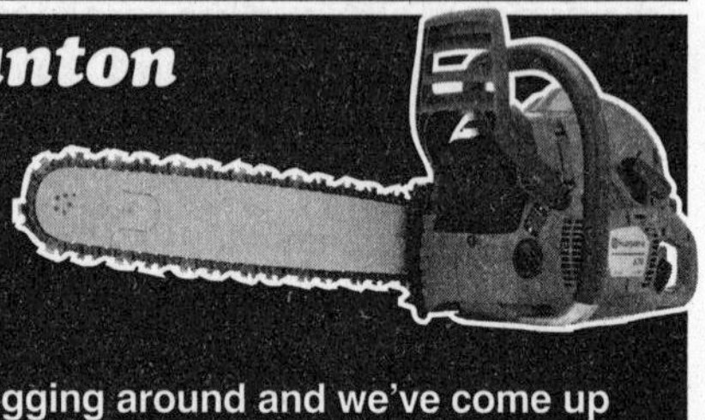

THE NOBLE tree at Sycamore Gap on Hadrian's Wall has stood for centuries. But in the small hours of September 28th 2023, a vandal – or vandals – took a chainsaw to this iconic landmark and lumberjacked it down.

With no witnesses, no clues and no DNA evidence, the police have nothing to go on, and so far the crime remains unsolved – a 2-month old cold case.

But at *Viz*, we have done a little digging around and we've come up with three prime suspects – three people with the motive, means and opportunity to commit this Crime of the Century. And we want YOUR help in putting the guilty party behind bars.

Simply read the evidence we put before you, the Viz Jury, and write in to tell us which of the three celebrities is the most likely to have done it, and we'll report the one with the most votes to the police.

Suspect 1: Mary Beard

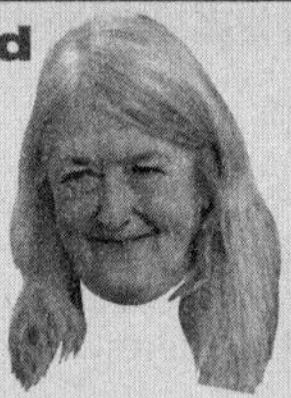

Motive: Fellow of Cambridge University's Newnham College, classicist Mary Beard is famously a lover of all things Roman. In fact, one might say her passion for the ancient empire is a love that borders on obsession; in Beard's eyes, the Romans were perhaps the greatest civilisation that has ever lived. The ancient tree at Sycamore Gap was unarguably more famous than the bit of Hadrian's Wall behind it, and this fact may have driven the scholar to distraction. Determined to destroy anything and everything that distracts from her beloved Roman Empire, perhaps Beard took a chainsaw to this most famous and beloved of our national landmarks.

Means: Newnham College is set in tree-filled parkland in the heart of Cambridge, and it is impossible to believe that the groundkeeper's hut does not contain a chainsaw of some description. As a fellow of the College, Beard will undoubtedly have access to the hut, and as a familiar face around the campus her presence would draw little attention.

Opportunity: Google does not give any indication of Professor Beard's height, but however tall she is, it is doubtful that she could bring down a 15m tree weighing upwards of 20 tonnes single-handed. But the alumni of Newnham college are a close-knit group, and it is likely she could have called in the help of any number of former fellow students, such as Germaine Greer, Miriam Margolyes or Emma Thompson.

Suspect 2: Eddie Howe

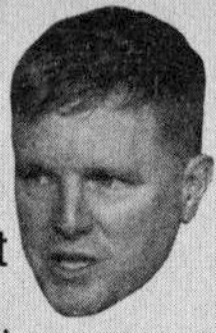

Motive: Newcastle United manager Eddie Howe has been riding high on success all season as the Magpies continue their impressive run of form. But with millions spent on new signings, if the 'Toon' were to have underperformed Howe knew that his job would be on the line. Perhaps he chopped down the tree at Sycamore Gap to divert headlines in the local press away from any poor performances his team might put in. As it turned out, it was an unnecessary act as NUFC are performing well and currently in the top 6. But it was nevertheless a good bit of 'belt and braces' insurance for the former AFC Bournemouth and Burnley boss.

Means: Newcastle United currently has a first team squad of 29 players – all fit, strong and healthy young men. And with competition stiff for the starting 11 on match day, none want to get on Howe's bad side. Were he to ask any for help cutting down the tree, it is unlikely that any players on his books would have refused.

Opportunity: The tree was chopped down in the early hours of a Friday morning, and football managers only work one day a week – Saturday, with the occasional mid-week game. So Howe would have had plenty of time to drive his squad of vandals up to Sycamore Gap in the team bus take down this piece of our heritage.

Suspect 3: Chris Packham

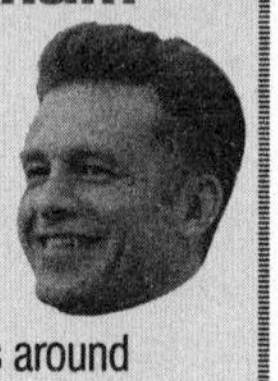

Motive: As a keen naturalist, you wouldn't expect Chris to perpetrate such an act of wanton environmental vandalism. But sycamores are not particularly good at encouraging biodiversity – whilst an oak tree can support around 2,300 different species of organisms, a sycamore supports around half that number. Incensed at the tree's poor ecological credentials, Packham may have lopped it down in the hope that a more biologically diverse sessile oak (*Quercus petraea*) might shoot up in its place.

Means: Packham is president of the Bat Conservation Trust, and in this role he will have taken part in woodland management projects in order to conserve the environment for his favourite flying mice. It is not out of the question that at some point whilst working on one of these projects, Packham learned how to handle a chainsaw.

Opportunity: The 2023 series of *Autumnwatch* was filmed at Wild Ken Hill in Norfolk. Google maps indicates that the 257-mile road journey from the recording set to Sycamore Gap could be completed in 4 hours 44 minutes. With half an hour to cut down the tree, and 2 stops at Wetherby services for a Greggs pasty and a piss, Packham could have left after filming and been back the following morning before any of the crew were awake.

I reckon the tree at Sycamore Gap was cut down by... ☐ Mary Beard ☐ Eddie Howe ☐ Chris Packham

Send to: *Sycamore Gap Crime Hotline, PO Box 841, Whitley Bay, NE26 9EQ*, and we'll tip off the filth.

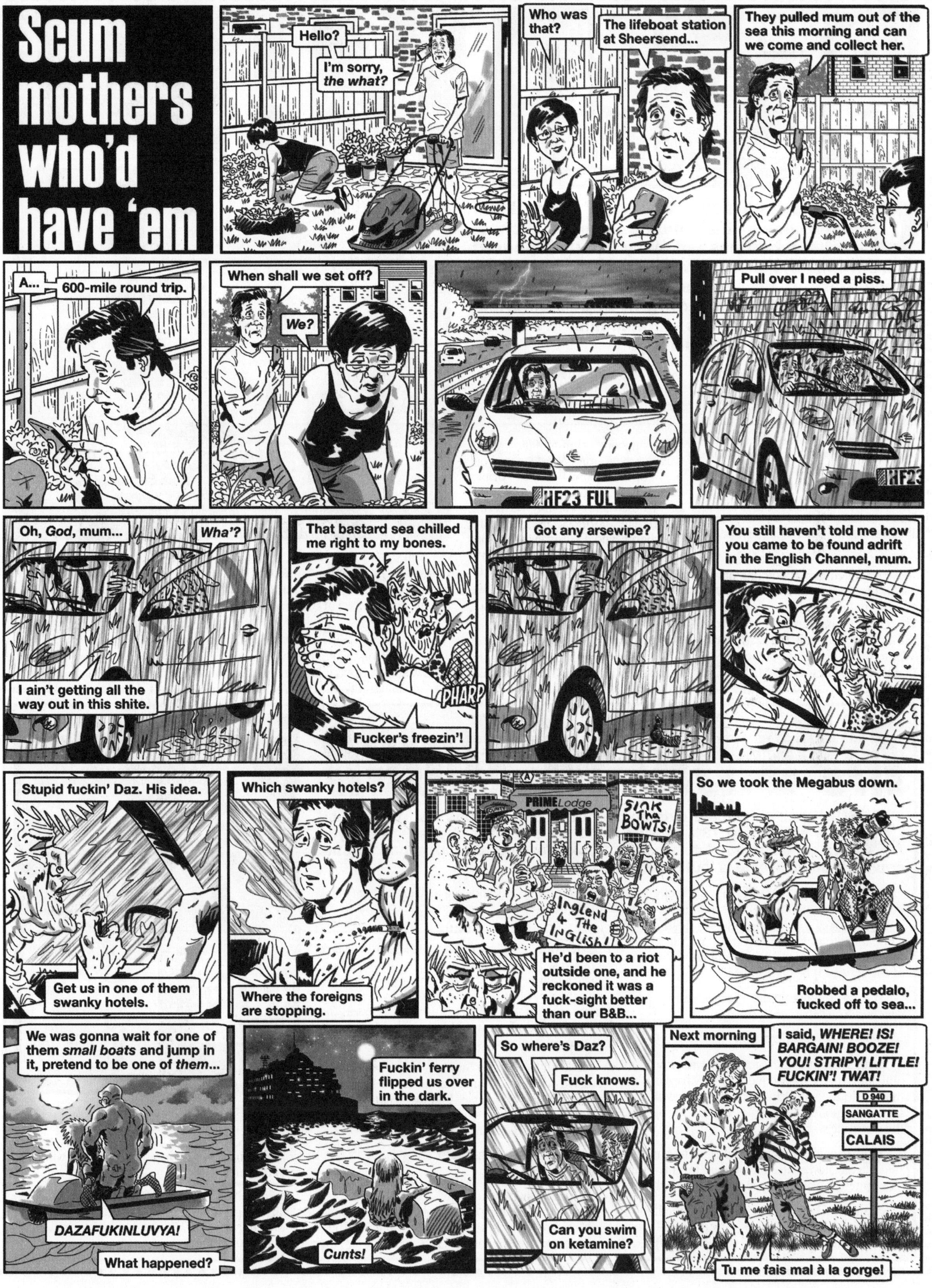

Scum mothers who'd have 'em
Hello?
I'm sorry, *the what?*
Who was that?
The lifeboat station at Sheersend...
They pulled mum out of the sea this morning and can we come and collect her.
A...
600-mile round trip.
When shall we set off?
We?
HF23 FUL
Pull over I need a piss.
HF23
Oh, *God*, mum...
Wha'?
I ain't getting all the way out in this shite.
That bastard sea chilled me right to my bones.
PHARP
Fucker's freezin'!
Got any arsewipe?
You still haven't told me how you came to be found adrift in the English Channel, mum.
Stupid fuckin' Daz. His idea.
Get us in one of them swanky hotels.
Which swanky hotels?
Where the foreigns are stopping.
PRIME Lodge
SINK The BOWTS!
Inglend 4 The INGLISH!
He'd been to a riot outside one, and he reckoned it was a fuck-sight better than our B&B...
So we took the Megabus down.
Robbed a pedalo, fucked off to sea...
We was gonna wait for one of them *small boats* and jump in it, pretend to be one of *them*...
DAZAFUKINLUVYA!
What happened?
Fuckin' ferry flipped us over in the dark.
Cunts!
So where's Daz?
Fuck knows.
Can you swim on ketamine?
Next morning
I said, *WHERE! IS! BARGAIN! BOOZE! YOU! STRIPY! LITTLE! FUCKIN'! TWAT!*
D 940
SANGATTE
CALAIS
Tu me fais mal à la gorge!

BEVERLY HILLS

ON June 25th 2009, the world learned the tragic news that music legend Michael Jackson had passed away. Tributes poured in from millions of well-wishers - everyone from movie stars to Presidents - to honour the life of a global superstar… *the King of Pop*. Memorials were held across world as stunned fans lit candles and came together in mourning.

But a decade-and-a-bit after his passing, one man who knew Jacko intimately is now lifting the lid on one of the biggest showbiz secrets of all time. And it's a secret that Rotherham-based soft drinks salesman Billy Gleet has kept to himself, vowing never to tell anyone… until now. Because unbeknown to his legion of fans, Michael 'Wacko Jacko' Jackson was *addicted to fizzy drinks*.

"It makes me laugh to hear all these so-called experts talking about Jacko like they knew the man," says Gleet, ruefully shaking his head as his gaze momentarily shifts from the screen showing the 2.10 from Wetherby in his local bookies. "Not many people know it but Michael got his 'King of Pop' nickname from me."

"It was an affectionate name that I gave to Jacko, one of my best customers, and it stuck," he told the *Rotherham Suppository*.

Throughout the 1990s, Gleet was working for Weaslegoes Pop, a Yorkshire-based soft drinks company, delivering drinks east of Rotherham, roughly covering a triangle formed by Parkgate, Thrybergh and Dalton Magna. But late in 1998, his boss called him into his office and informed him that he was being assigned a different route.

"He told me that the driver who did the Hollywood, Beverly Hills and Bel Air round had been sacked for filling his own car with petrol on the company's card, and that he'd like me to take it on," he said.

LIFE'S A GAS: *Billy Gleet spills all on his years fuelling the fizzy drinking habits of the stars.*

"Well, as you can imagine, delivering pop to the glitteratti of Tinseltown is every fizzy drink driver's dream, so I jumped at the chance."

twerk

Gleet was on the next plane to LA, and was soon driving his van around the plush streets of Beverly Hills, dropping off pop for the likes of Clint Eastwood, Scarlett Johanssen and Tom Cruise.

Gleet quickly became the go-to man for Hollywood royalty when they wanted their fix of traditional English fizzy drinks. "I was well known on the celebrity pop circuit doing the weekly round

MPs Out of Touch

A SNAP poll conducted outside the House of Commons last week found that a staggering 78% of MPs could not say what happens when you drop some Mentos into a bottle of Coke, leading to accusations that the country's political elite is 'out of touch.'

"Everyone else in the UK knows exactly what happens when you drop 10 Mentos into a 2-litre bottle of coke," said Naomi Smith, head of civil campaign group *Best For Britain*. "Yet our elected representatives seem to be completely unaware of the results. It beggars belief."

"It's as though these people have never watched YouTube," she added.

flapjack

Results showed that no party was any more oblivious to the consequences of dropping the mints into the soft drink than another, with MPs across the political spectrum unable to say what the outcome would be.

"Well, I imagine they would sink to the bottom," said *former* Chancellor of the Exchequer Jeremy Hunt. "Definitely, because they look like little pebbles."

Meanwhile, his opposite number on the Labour front bench, Rachel Reeves, unsurprisingly took the opposite view. "They would just float, I imagine," she said, showing an extraordinary lack of awareness.

bolus

former MP for Rayleigh and Wickford, Mark Francois, at first tried to evade the question, saying that he did know the answer, but was too busy to say what it was as he was on his way to a meeting of the ERG. But when pressed, he wrongly said that the Mentos would dissolve. "Everything dissolves in coke," he said.

Scottish Nationalist Stephen Flynn was equally evasive when questioned as he left a late night sitting. "Yes, of course I know what happens when you put Mentos into coke," he said before walking off without saying what it was.

slipper

former MP for Somerset North Jacob Rees-Mogg was one politician who openly admitted that they didn't know what happened when the two things are mixed. "We do not have carbonated drinks in our home, save for Indian tonic waters," the

THOUGHT BUBBLES: *MPs such as Jeremy Hunt (inset top) and Mark Francois (inset bottom) were clueless about the fizzy experiment.*

plummy-voiced *former* Leader of the House said. "As for Mentos, I have no idea what they are. Ergo, I remain unenlightened as to the consequences of their amalgamation with the cola to which you earlier alluded."

When Prime Minister Rishi Sunak was asked what happens, he just robotically prattled on about halving inflation and preventing small boats or something.

POP! No returns for the king of pop

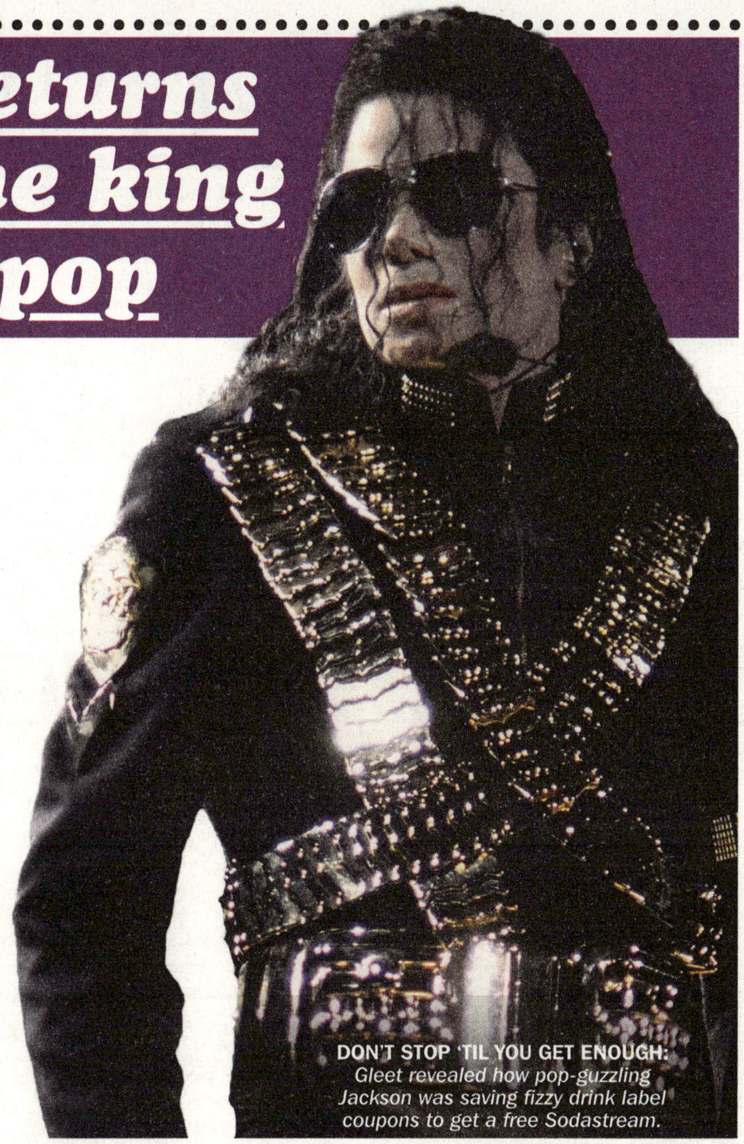

DON'T STOP 'TIL YOU GET ENOUGH: *Gleet revealed how pop-guzzling Jackson was saving fizzy drink label coupons to get a free Sodastream.*

of Tinseltown's glitterati in my Weaslegoes Pop van," he told the paper.

Selling pop to A-listers soon became all in a day's work for the big-boned dad of seven, but even Gleet was taken aback when his float was stopped on Sunset Boulevard one morning by two 'men in black' who asked him if he would add the Neverland Ranch in Santa Barbara to his delivery round.

"Obviously, I knew who lived at Neverland but it was a bit out of my way," he said. "But Jacko's men said that he would pay double for the pop, so I told them I would come round on Thursday mornings."

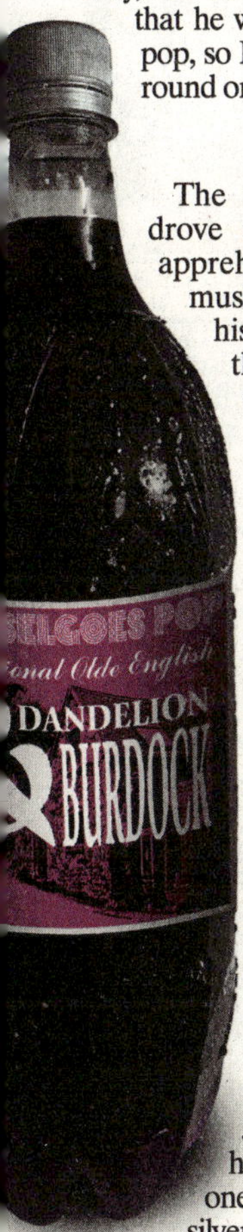
DANDELION
BURDOCK

rollerskate

The following week, Gleet drove to Neverland, a little apprehensive about how the music legend would react to his fizzy drinks. "I drove through the gates and up the huge driveway, my bottles rattling away in the back of my Commer," he said. "Jackson heard the noise and came out of his ranch with Bubbles the chimp, and without saying a word, grabbed a bottle of Dandelion and Burdock out a crate."

"He glugged it down in about 4 gulps, and then stood there, clearly thinking. D&B as we call it, is very much a 'love it or hate it' drink, so it was a very tense moment waiting for Jacko's verdict. Suddenly, he grabbed his crotch with one had, thrust the other, silver-gloved hand into the air and belched his famous 'Wooo-Hooo!' call."

"I breathed a sigh of relief, and Jacko put in an order for seven bottles a week, there and then," he said.

Gleet began delivering to Neverland every Thursday morning, dropping off fresh bottles of D&B and collecting the empties. But as the weeks went by, Jackson's order grew. Seven bottles a week became ten, and ten became twenty. Then, he added twenty bottles of cream soda to the Thursday drop, along with ten cherryade.

"It was a lot of pop for anyone to get through," said Gleet. "Apparently, in his early days on tour with the Jackson Five, his disciplinarian father had banned soft drinks as they were bad for the band's teeth. I think, in a way, Jacko wanted to re-live his missed childhood by quaffing all the pop he could lay his hands on."

debutante

What started as a harmless experimentation with carbonated beverages increased over the years to such an extent that Gleet had to work double shifts to keep up with the flammable *Beat It* singer's demands. "No one could say 'no' to Jackson. I remember one time when one of his assistants called and asked me to come round to Neverland straight away in my pop van. When I left the gates of the ranch 2 hours later I was clean out of stock! I had nothing left for the other Hollywood stars on my round. My boss went berserk!" he told the paper.

Although seeing celebrities knocking back pop was nothing new for Gleet, Jackson's behaviour reached new heights… or rather lows. "I've seen plenty of A-listers overdoing it on the pop and thinking they can handle it," he said. "They surround themselves with yes men who turn a blind eye when they are downing cans of Tizer like it's water."

Gleet recalled one fateful Thursday at Neverland when he was asked to drop off six bottles of cloudy lemonade, three bottles of Keg shandy and four bottles of American cream soda.

"I normally do my drops at the door, but I took Michael's deliveries inside his house and up to his room, because when you've got Jackson's wealth, you don't carry bottles of pop yourself," he said.

"I dropped the crates off, and as usual, his minders began peeling off all the labels, as Jacko was saving up coupons to get a free Soda Stream. I was asked to leave the room and told to come back in fifteen minutes to pick up the empties."

eiderdown

Gleet recalled: "I had a couple of smokes in my van and then went back up to Michael's room. What I saw *shocked* me, and I've been round the block a few times and I'm not easily shocked."

"Jacko was sprawled across a massive sofa, looking bloated and burping the lyrics to *Can You Feel It?* while tapping a patent shoe on the floor to create a backbeat. It was really quite tragic."

With hindsight, Gleet now realises that he should have done something as he saw Jackson descend into carbonated drink addiction "All the warning signs were there and I should have taken action," he said. "But I had a lucrative order for Neverland that was getter bigger and bigger each week and I was getting greedy."

I know Michael died of a heart attack from a prescribed drug overdose, not fizzy pop, but I should have stepped in when I saw his addictive personality taking over," he said.

"I will carry that guilt with me forever."

And Gleet has a myriad of stories he could tell about his visits to other Hollywood A-listers, but he says he would never betray a client's trust. "Being a pop man is a bit like being a doctor or a priest - your relationship with your client is confidential."

"I could tell you a tale about a very famous movie star and an order for 100 bottles of Barrs Pineappleade, but it's private between me and Clint, and nothing short of £10 would ever drag it out of me," he added.

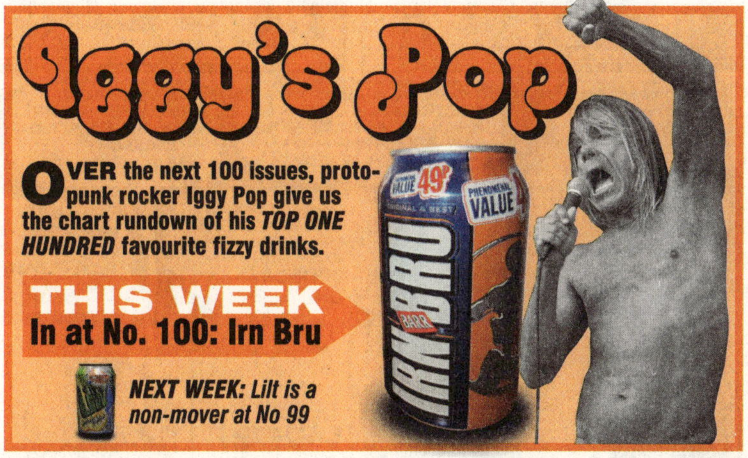
Iggy's Pop
OVER the next 100 issues, proto-punk rocker Iggy Pop give us the chart rundown of his *TOP ONE HUNDRED* favourite fizzy drinks.
THIS WEEK
In at No. 100: Irn Bru
NEXT WEEK: Lilt is a non-mover at No 99
IRN BRU
VALUE

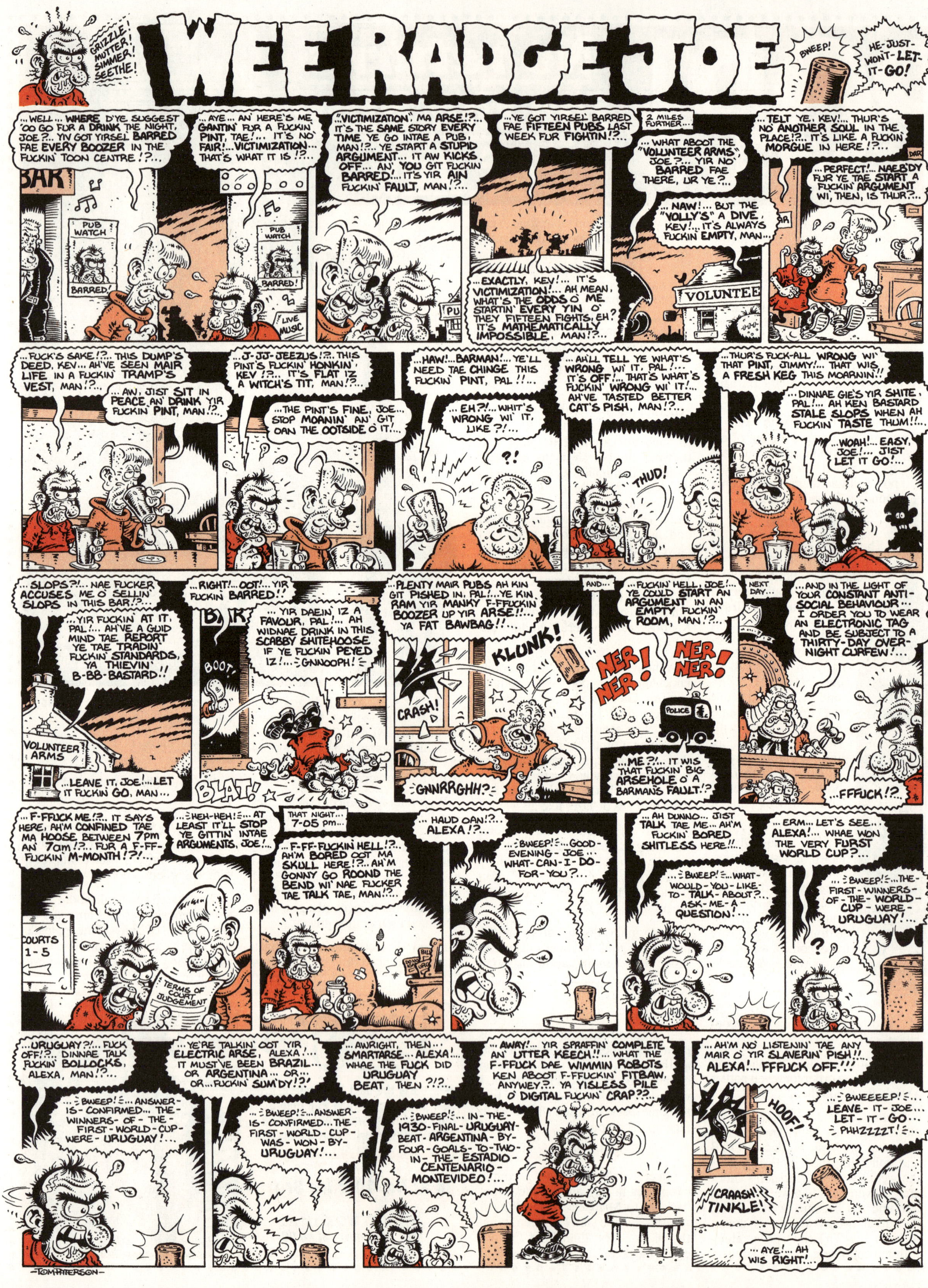
WEE RADGE JOE
GRIZZLE! MUTTER! SIMMER! SEETHE!
BWEEP!
HE-JUST-WONT-LET-IT-GO!
...WELL... WHERE D'YE SUGGEST 'OO GO FOR A DRINK THE NIGHT, JOE ?... YIV GOT YIRSEL BARRED FAE EVERY BOOZER IN THE FUCKIN' TOON CENTRE !?...
BAR
PUB WATCH
BARRED!
...AYE... AN' HERE'S ME, GANTIN' FUR A FUCKIN' PINT, TAE!... IT'S NO FAIR!... VICTIMIZATION... THAT'S WHAT IT IS !?...
PUB WATCH
BARRED!
LIVE MUSIC
..."VICTIMIZATION" MA ARSE !?... IT'S THE SAME STORY EVERY TIME YE GO INTAE A PUB, MAN !?... YE START A STUPID ARGUMENT... IT AW KICKS OFF... AN' YOU GIT FUCKIN' BARRED !... IT'S YIR AIN FUCKIN' FAULT, MAN !?...
...YE GOT YIRSEL BARRED FAE FIFTEEN PUBS LAST WEEK FUR FIGHTIN' !?...
...EXACTLY, KEV !... IT'S VICTIMIZATION !... AH MEAN, WHAT'S THE ODDS O' ME STARTIN' EVERY YIN O' THEY FIFTEEN FIGHTS, EH ? IT'S MATHEMATICALLY IMPOSSIBLE, MAN !?...
2 MILES FURTHER...
...WHAT ABOOT THE "VOLUNTEER ARMS" JOE ?... YIR NO' BARRED FAE THERE, UR YE ?...
...NAW !... BUT THE "VOLLY'S" A DIVE, KEV !... IT'S ALWAYS FUCKIN' EMPTY, MAN...
VOLUNTEE
...TELT YE, KEV !... THUR'S NO ANOTHER SOUL IN THE PLACE !?... IT'S LIKE A FUCKIN' MORGUE IN HERE !?...
...PERFECT !... NAEB'DY FUR YE TAE START A FUCKIN' ARGUMENT WI, THEN, IS THUR ?...
...FUCK'S SAKE !?... THIS DUMP'S DEED, KEV... AH'VE SEEN MAIR LIFE IN A FUCKIN' TRAMP'S VEST, MAN !?...
...AW, JIST SIT IN PEACE AN' DRINK YIR FUCKIN' PINT, MAN !?...
...J-JJ-JEEZUS !?... THIS PINT'S FUCKIN' HONKIN', KEV !?... IT'S FLAT IZ A WITCH'S TIT, MAN !?...
...THE PINT'S FINE, JOE... STOP MOANIN' AN' GIT OAN THE OOTSIDE O' IT !...
...HAW !... BARMAN !... YE'LL NEED TAE CHINGE THIS FUCKIN' PINT, PAL !!...
...EH ?!... WHIT'S WRONG WI' IT, LIKE ?!...
?!
...AH'LL TELL YE WHAT'S WRONG WI' IT, PAL !... IT'S OFF !... THAT'S WHAT'S FUCKIN' WRONG WI' IT !... AH'VE TASTED BETTER CAT'S PISH, MAN !?...
THUD!
...THUR'S FUCK-ALL WRONG WI' THAT PINT, JIMMY !... THAT WIS A FRESH KEG THIS MOARNIN' !!
...DINNAE GIE'S YIR SHITE, PAL !... AH KEN BASTARD STALE SLOPS WHEN AH FUCKIN' TASTE THUM !!...
...WOAH !... EASY, JOE !... JIST LET IT GO !...
...SLOPS ?!... NAE FUCKER ACCUSES ME O' SELLIN' SLOPS IN THIS BAR !?...
...YIR FUCKIN' AT IT, PAL !... AH'VE A GUID MIND TAE REPORT YE TAE TRADIN' FUCKIN' STANDARDS, YA THIEVIN' B-BB-BASTARD !!
VOLUNTEER ARMS
...LEAVE IT, JOE !... LET IT FUCKIN' GO, MAN...
...RIGHT !... OOT !... YIR FUCKIN' BARRED !!
...YIR DAEIN' IZ A FAVOUR, PAL !... AH WIDNAE DRINK IN THIS SCABBY SHITEHOOSE IF YE FUCKIN' PEYED IZ !... GNNOOPH !
BOOT!
BLAT!
...PLENTY MAIR PUBS AH KIN GIT PISHED IN, PAL !... YE KIN RAM YIR MANKY F-FFUCKIN' BOOZER UP YIR ARSE !!... YA FAT BAWBAG !!...
KLUNK!
CRASH!
GNNRRGHH?
AND...
...FUCKIN' HELL, JOE !... YE COULD START AN ARGUMENT IN AN EMPTY FUCKIN' ROOM, MAN !?...
NER NER!
NER NER!
POLICE
...ME ?!... IT WIS THAT FUCKIN' BIG ARSEHOLE O' A BARMAN'S FAULT !?
NEXT DAY...
...AND IN THE LIGHT OF YOUR CONSTANT ANTI-SOCIAL BEHAVIOUR, I ORDER YOU TO WEAR AN ELECTRONIC TAG AND BE SUBJECT TO A THIRTY-DAY OVER-NIGHT CURFEW !...
...FFFUCK !?...
...F-FFUCK ME !?... IT SAYS HERE, AH'M CONFINED TAE MA HOOSE BETWEEN 7pm AN' 7am !?... FUR A F-FF-FUCKIN' M-MONTH !?!...
...HEH-HEH !... AT LEAST IT'LL STOP YE GITTIN' INTAE ARGUMENTS, JOE !...
COURTS 1-5
TERMS OF COURT JUDGEMENT
THAT NIGHT... 7-05 pm...
...F-FF-FUCKIN' HELL !?... AH'M BORED OOT MA SKULL HERE !?... AH'M GONNY GO ROOND THE BEND WI' NAE FUCKER TAE TALK TAE, MAN !?...
...HAUD OAN !?... ALEXA !?...
...BWEEP !... GOOD-EVENING-JOE... WHAT-CAN-I-DO-FOR-YOU ?...
...AH DUNNO... JIST TALK TAE ME... AH'M FUCKIN' BORED SHITLESS HERE !!...
...BWEEP !... WHAT-WOULD-YOU-LIKE-TO-TALK-ABOUT ?... ASK-ME-A-QUESTION !...
...ERM... LET'S SEE... ALEXA !... WHAE WON THE VERY FURST WORLD CUP ?...
...BWEEP !... THE-FIRST-WINNERS-OF-THE-WORLD-CUP-WERE-URUGUAY !...
?
...URUGUAY ?!... FUCK OFF !?... DINNAE TALK FUCKIN' BOLLOCKS, ALEXA, MAN !?...
...BWEEP !... ANSWER-IS-CONFIRMED... THE-WINNERS-OF-THE-FIRST-WORLD-CUP-WERE-URUGUAY !...
...YE'RE TALKIN' OOT YIR ELECTRIC ARSE, ALEXA !... IT MUST'VE BEEN BRAZIL... OR ARGENTINA... OR... OR... FUCKIN' SUM'DY !?!
...BWEEP !... ANSWER-CONFIRMED... THE-FIRST-WORLD-CUP-WAS-WON-BY-URUGUAY !...
...AWRIGHT, THEN... SMARTARSE... ALEXA !... WHAE THE FUCK DID URUGUAY BEAT, THEN ?!?...
...BWEEP !... IN-THE-1930-FINAL-URUGUAY-BEAT-ARGENTINA-BY-FOUR-GOALS-TO-TWO-IN-THE-ESTADIO-CENTENARIO-MONTEVIDEO !...
...AWAY !... YIR SPRAFFIN' COMPLETE AN' UTTER KEECH !!... WHAT THE F-FFUCK DAE WIMMIN ROBOTS KEN ABOOT F-FFUCKIN' FITBAW, ANYWEY ?... YA YISLESS PILE O' DIGITAL FUCKIN' CRAP ??...
...AH'M NO' LISTENIN' TAE ANY MAIR O' YIR SLAVERIN' PISH !!... ALEXA !... FFFUCK OFF !!!
...BWEEEEP !... LEAVE-IT-JOE... LET-IT-GO... PHHZZZZT !...
HOOF!
CRAASH! TINKLE!
...AYE !... AH WIS RIGHT !...
-TOM PATERSON-

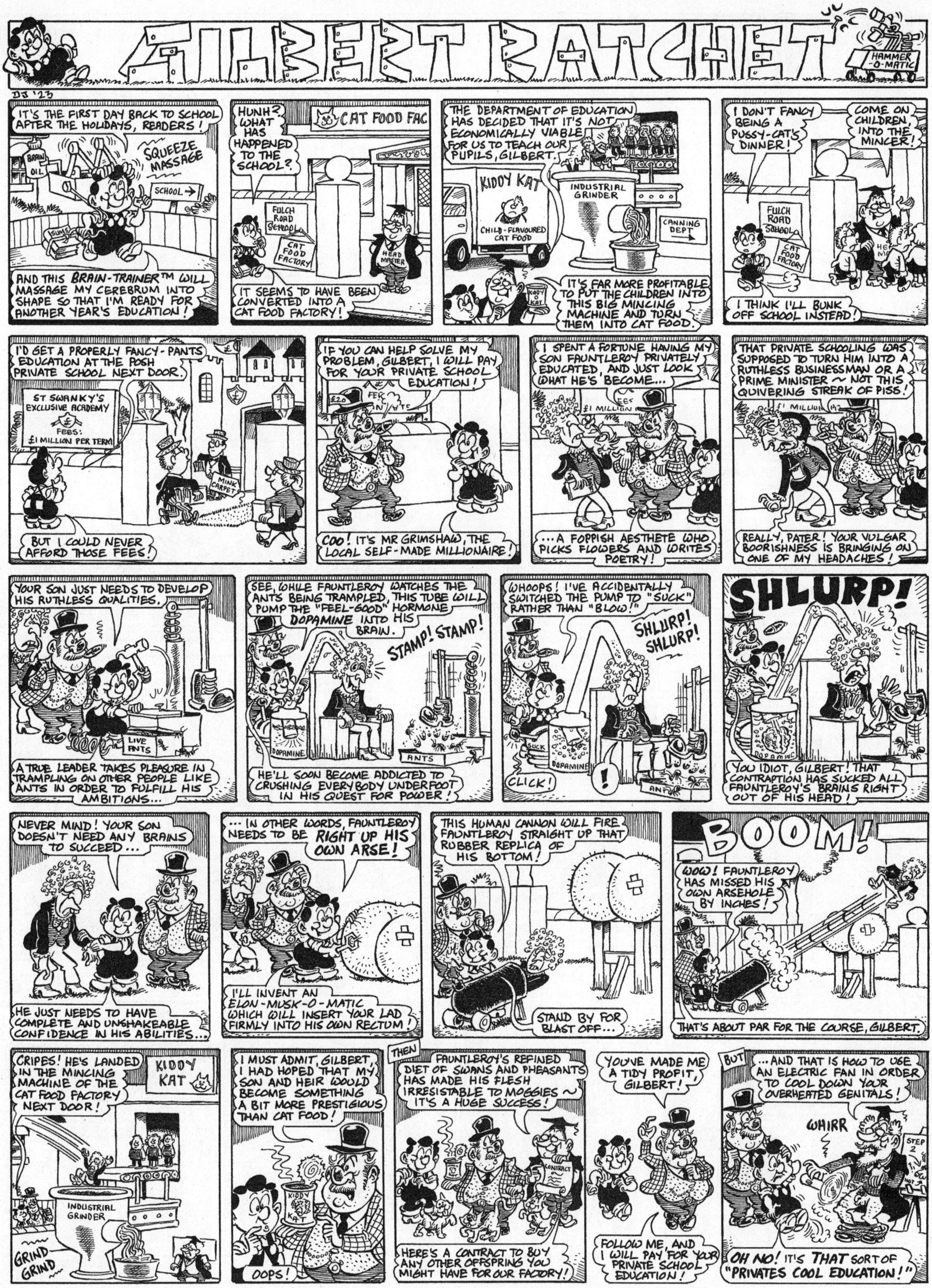
GILBERT RATCHET
HAMMER-O-MATIC
DJ '23
IT'S THE FIRST DAY BACK TO SCHOOL AFTER THE HOLIDAYS, READERS!
BRAIN OIL
SQUEEZE MASSAGE
SCHOOL
SUMS
AND THIS BRAIN-TRAINER™ WILL MASSAGE MY CEREBRUM INTO SHAPE SO THAT I'M READY FOR ANOTHER YEAR'S EDUCATION!
HUNH? WHAT HAS HAPPENED TO THE SCHOOL?
CAT FOOD FAC
FULCH ROAD SCHOOL
CAT FOOD FACTORY
HEAD MASTER
IT SEEMS TO HAVE BEEN CONVERTED INTO A CAT FOOD FACTORY!
THE DEPARTMENT OF EDUCATION HAS DECIDED THAT IT'S NOT ECONOMICALLY VIABLE FOR US TO TEACH OUR PUPILS, GILBERT.
KIDDY KAT
CHILD-FLAVOURED CAT FOOD
INDUSTRIAL GRINDER
CANNING DEPT
IT'S FAR MORE PROFITABLE TO PUT THE CHILDREN INTO THIS BIG MINCING MACHINE AND TURN THEM INTO CAT FOOD.
I DON'T FANCY BEING A PUSSY-CAT'S DINNER!
COME ON CHILDREN, INTO THE MINCER!
FULCH ROAD SCHOOL
CAT FOOD FACTORY
I THINK I'LL BUNK OFF SCHOOL INSTEAD!
I'D GET A PROPERLY FANCY-PANTS EDUCATION AT THE POSH PRIVATE SCHOOL NEXT DOOR.
ST SWANKY'S EXCLUSIVE ACADEMY
FEES: £1 MILLION PER TERM
MINK CARPET
BUT I COULD NEVER AFFORD THOSE FEES!
IF YOU CAN HELP SOLVE MY PROBLEM, GILBERT, I WILL PAY FOR YOUR PRIVATE SCHOOL EDUCATION!
£20
COO! IT'S MR GRIMSHAW, THE LOCAL SELF-MADE MILLIONAIRE!
I SPENT A FORTUNE HAVING MY SON FAUNTLEROY PRIVATELY EDUCATED, AND JUST LOOK WHAT HE'S BECOME...
...A FOPPISH AESTHETE WHO PICKS FLOWERS AND WRITES POETRY!
THAT PRIVATE SCHOOLING WAS SUPPOSED TO TURN HIM INTO A RUTHLESS BUSINESSMAN OR A PRIME MINISTER ~ NOT THIS QUIVERING STREAK OF PISS!
REALLY, PATER! YOUR VULGAR BOORISHNESS IS BRINGING ON ONE OF MY HEADACHES!
YOUR SON JUST NEEDS TO DEVELOP HIS RUTHLESS QUALITIES.
LIVE ANTS
A TRUE LEADER TAKES PLEASURE IN TRAMPLING ON OTHER PEOPLE LIKE ANTS IN ORDER TO FULFILL HIS AMBITIONS...
SEE, WHILE FAUNTLEROY WATCHES THE ANTS BEING TRAMPLED, THIS TUBE WILL PUMP THE "FEEL-GOOD" HORMONE DOPAMINE INTO HIS BRAIN.
STAMP! STAMP!
DOPAMINE
ANTS
HE'LL SOON BECOME ADDICTED TO CRUSHING EVERYBODY UNDERFOOT IN HIS QUEST FOR POWER!
WHOOPS! I'VE ACCIDENTALLY SWITCHED THE PUMP TO "SUCK" RATHER THAN "BLOW!"
SHLURP! SHLURP!
SUCK
DOPAMINE
CLICK!
!
SHLURP!
DOPAMINE
YOU IDIOT, GILBERT! THAT CONTRAPTION HAS SUCKED ALL FAUNTLEROY'S BRAINS RIGHT OUT OF HIS HEAD!
NEVER MIND! YOUR SON DOESN'T NEED ANY BRAINS TO SUCCEED...
HE JUST NEEDS TO HAVE COMPLETE AND UNSHAKEABLE CONFIDENCE IN HIS ABILITIES...
...IN OTHER WORDS, FAUNTLEROY NEEDS TO BE RIGHT UP HIS OWN ARSE!
I'LL INVENT AN ELON-MUSK-O-MATIC WHICH WILL INSERT YOUR LAD FIRMLY INTO HIS OWN RECTUM!
THIS HUMAN CANNON WILL FIRE FAUNTLEROY STRAIGHT UP THAT RUBBER REPLICA OF HIS BOTTOM!
STAND BY FOR BLAST OFF...
BOOM!
WOW! FAUNTLEROY HAS MISSED HIS OWN ARSEHOLE BY INCHES!
THAT'S ABOUT PAR FOR THE COURSE, GILBERT.
CRIPES! HE'S LANDED IN THE MINCING MACHINE OF THE CAT FOOD FACTORY NEXT DOOR!
KIDDY KAT
INDUSTRIAL GRINDER
GRIND GRIND
I MUST ADMIT, GILBERT, I HAD HOPED THAT MY SON AND HEIR WOULD BECOME SOMETHING A BIT MORE PRESTIGIOUS THAN CAT FOOD!
KIDDY KAT
OOPS!
THEN
FAUNTLEROY'S REFINED DIET OF SWANS AND PHEASANTS HAS MADE HIS FLESH IRRESISTABLE TO MOGGIES ~ IT'S A HUGE SUCCESS!
CONTRACT
HERE'S A CONTRACT TO BUY ANY OTHER OFFSPRING YOU MIGHT HAVE FOR OUR FACTORY!
YOU'VE MADE ME A TIDY PROFIT, GILBERT!
FOLLOW ME, AND I WILL PAY FOR YOUR PRIVATE SCHOOL EDUCATION!
BUT
...AND THAT IS HOW TO USE AN ELECTRIC FAN IN ORDER TO COOL DOWN YOUR OVERHEATED GENITALS!
WHIRR
STEP 2
OH NO! IT'S THAT SORT OF "PRIVATES COOL EDUCATION!"

A WOKE WEREWOLF IN NORTH LONDON
GD/AS
ONE EVENING IT CONSULTANT SEBASTIAN FOX WAS WALKING THROUGH THE STREETS OF HAMPSTEAD TO PICK UP A TOFU AND MYCOPROTEIN BURGER AND OATMILK SHAKE FROM HIS LOCAL ARTISAN DELI.
WOW! THIS NEIGHBOURHOOD IS SO MUCH NICER SINCE IT BECAME A DESIGNATED LOW TRAFFIC ZONE...
...IF ONLY THE COUNCIL WOULD TAKE NOTICE OF MY PETITION TO MAKE THE 'GREEN MAN' ON THE CROSSINGS GENDER NEU...
RAAAAGH!
Café
WHAT THE...!?!
RARR!
RIP!
TEAR!
AAAAAGH! AAAAAGH! ...I'VE BEEN BITTEN!
WEEEEE-OOOO! WEEEEE-OOOO!
THAT POLICE SIREN HAS SCARED HIM OFF... SORRY, SCARED THEM OFF...
...AND I'M NOT SURPRISED. GONE ARE THE DAYS WHEN THE PRESENCE OF THE POLICE WAS SYNONYMOUS WITH SAFETY.
SHOCKED, BLEEDING BUT LARGELY UNHARMED, SEBASTIAN GOT TO HIS FEET...
I HOPE THE POOR THING WASN'T TRIGGERED BY MY SHOUTING.
I'LL REPORT THE INCIDENT TO THE HAMPSTEAD ANIMAL WELFARE OFFICE TOMORROW. NOT THAT THEY'LL BE ABLE TO DO ANYTHING AFTER 13 YEARS OF TORY UNDERFUNDING.
Vegan Café
LATER THAT NIGHT...
THIS IS FASCINATING. I HAD NO IDEA OF HOW MUCH UNCONSCIOUS BIAS I WAS GUILTY OF.
Woke up & smell the organic coffee
HUH!?! WHAT'S HAPPENING TO ME!? I'M SUDDENLY SPROUTING HAIR!
MUST GET OUT... MUST FIND...HUMAN FLESH!
RAAAAAGH!
WAIT! WHAT AM I THINKING? I'M VEGAN. I CAN SATISFY MY HUNGER WITH ORGANIC VEGETABLES...
...LOCALLY GROWN WITH VIRTUALLY NO FOOD MILES.
SO...
GO VEG
HERE WE ARE... THE LOCAL WHOLE FOOD COLLECTIVE...
...IT'S CLOSED, SO I'LL HAVE TO FORCE MY WAY IN.
WITHIN MOMENTS...
VEGAN
VEGETARIA
RAAAAGH!
IT'S NOT WORKING! THEY'RE NOT SATING MY HUNGER...

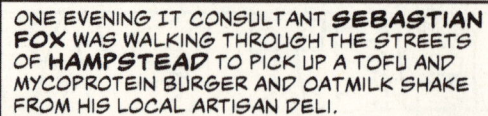

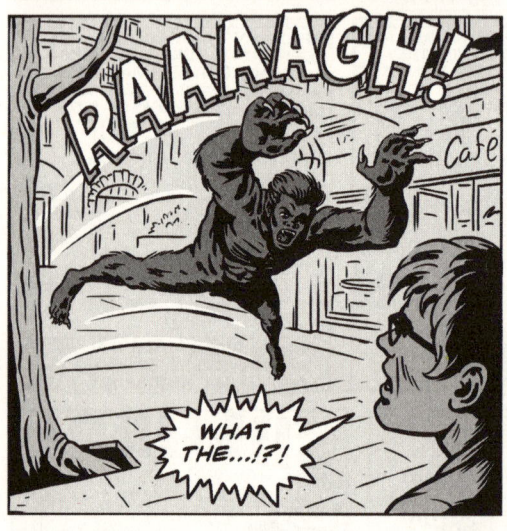

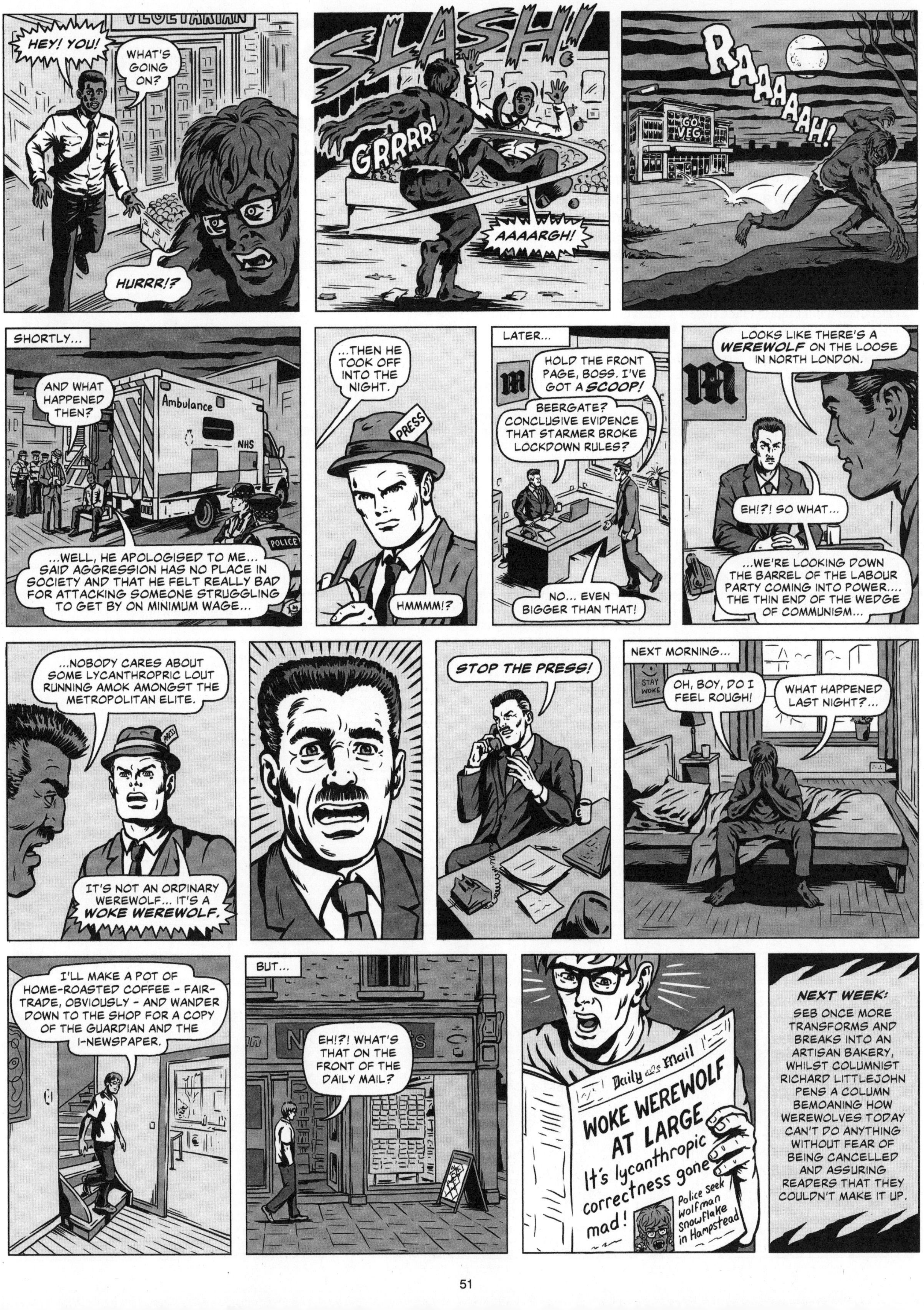
HEY! YOU!
WHAT'S GOING ON?
HURRR!?
SLASH!
GRRRR!
AAAARGH!
RAAAAAAH!
GO VEG
SHORTLY...
AND WHAT HAPPENED THEN?
Ambulance
NHS
POLICE
...WELL, HE APOLOGISED TO ME... SAID AGGRESSION HAS NO PLACE IN SOCIETY AND THAT HE FELT REALLY BAD FOR ATTACKING SOMEONE STRUGGLING TO GET BY ON MINIMUM WAGE...
...THEN HE TOOK OFF INTO THE NIGHT.
PRESS
HMMMM!?
LATER...
HOLD THE FRONT PAGE, BOSS. I'VE GOT A SCOOP!
BEERGATE? CONCLUSIVE EVIDENCE THAT STARMER BROKE LOCKDOWN RULES?
NO... EVEN BIGGER THAN THAT!
LOOKS LIKE THERE'S A WEREWOLF ON THE LOOSE IN NORTH LONDON.
EH!?! SO WHAT...
...WE'RE LOOKING DOWN THE BARREL OF THE LABOUR PARTY COMING INTO POWER.... THE THIN END OF THE WEDGE OF COMMUNISM...
...NOBODY CARES ABOUT SOME LYCANTHROPRIC LOUT RUNNING AMOK AMONGST THE METROPOLITAN ELITE.
IT'S NOT AN ORDINARY WEREWOLF... IT'S A WOKE WEREWOLF.
STOP THE PRESS!
NEXT MORNING...
STAY WOKE
OH, BOY, DO I FEEL ROUGH!
WHAT HAPPENED LAST NIGHT?...
I'LL MAKE A POT OF HOME-ROASTED COFFEE - FAIR-TRADE, OBVIOUSLY - AND WANDER DOWN TO THE SHOP FOR A COPY OF THE GUARDIAN AND THE I-NEWSPAPER.
BUT...
EH!?! WHAT'S THAT ON THE FRONT OF THE DAILY MAIL?
Daily Mail
WOKE WEREWOLF AT LARGE
It's lycanthropic correctness gone mad!
Police seek Wolfman Snowflake in Hampstead
NEXT WEEK:
SEB ONCE MORE TRANSFORMS AND BREAKS INTO AN ARTISAN BAKERY, WHILST COLUMNIST RICHARD LITTLEJOHN PENS A COLUMN BEMOANING HOW WEREWOLVES TODAY CAN'T DO ANYTHING WITHOUT FEAR OF BEING CANCELLED AND ASSURING READERS THAT THEY COULDN'T MAKE IT UP.

CRUISE CONTROL

Pint-sized star cooks own on-set brekkies

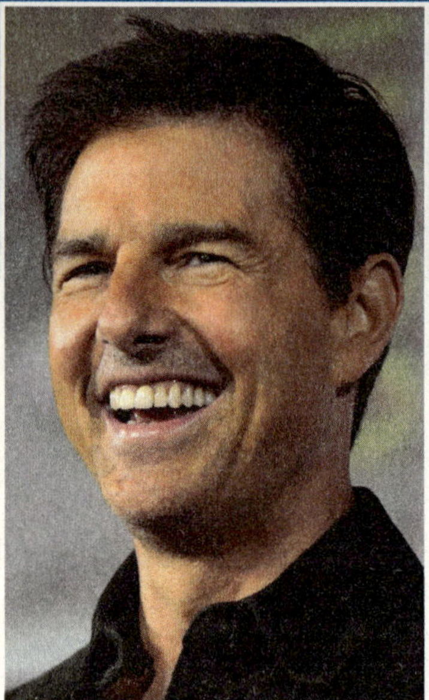

COOK-TAIL: *Fry-up fan Tom insists on cooking all his own breakfasts on set.*

LAST month saw the release of *Mission: Impossible – Dead Reckoning*, the seventh instalment in the long-running smash hit movie franchise. And in this, as in the previous six films, pint-sized star Tom Cruise insisted on cooking his own breakfasts during filming.

Every bacon sandwich, sausage & egg bun and full English that Cruise ate during production was cooked up by the actor himself, despite the fact that professional caterers were available on set the whole time.

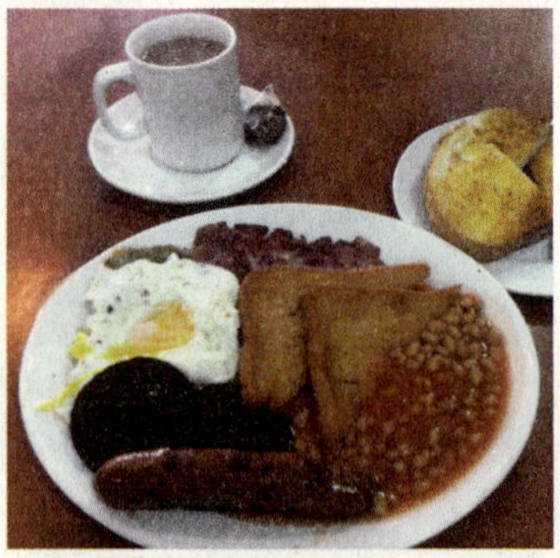

BREAK AN EGG: *The 'Tom Special': Egg, fried slice, sausage, bacon, black pudding, bubble, beans, tea and toast.*

"Tom thinks the only way to get a breakfast right is to do it himself. He's a perfectionist," said the film's director Christopher McQuarrie.

rustle

"Every other actor in the cast was happy to step back and let the professionals rustle up their breakfast for them. But that's not Tom's style," he added. "To him it's the most important meal of the day."

But Cruise doing his own breakfasts on set meant that a lot of the movie's budget had to be spent on insurance premiums to cover costs should filming be halted due to accidents. "A lot can go wrong when you're cooking a big fry-up," said the production's safety marshal Dwight Hymenburger. "If Tom's doing himself a couple of eggs sunny-side up and a bit of fat spits into his eye, he's out for a week. He takes his hash browns out the oven and burns his wrist on the door, he's off set for a fortnight."

"Shutting production for a single day on a movie like this can lose you a million bucks or more. Insuring against that don't come cheap."

escor

"I remember one scene where Tom had to jump off a building on a zipwire and crash through a glass window, and on the morning of the shoot he decided to cook himself a black pudding bap," Hymenburger told reporters. "He likes his black pudding well done on the outside, so he'd got the heat up really high. It was smoking away and we all thought it was going to burst into flames, engulfing him in a ball of fire any minute."

razzl

"But Tom just got in there, flipped the slices of pudding and whacked them on the bap like it was nothing. Our hearts were in our mouths, but he didn't bat an eyelid. Then he went off and shot the zipwire scene."

"Tom has upped the ante each time he's shot one of these movies," said Hymenburger. "Who knows what he's going to attempt in the eighth one; maybe fluffy French toast with bacon and strawberries, a cheesy sausage casserole, or even hashbrown and Spam breakfast pockets. One thing's for sure, Tom's antics in the kitchen will keep the crew on the edge of their seats every morning until the film's safely in the can."

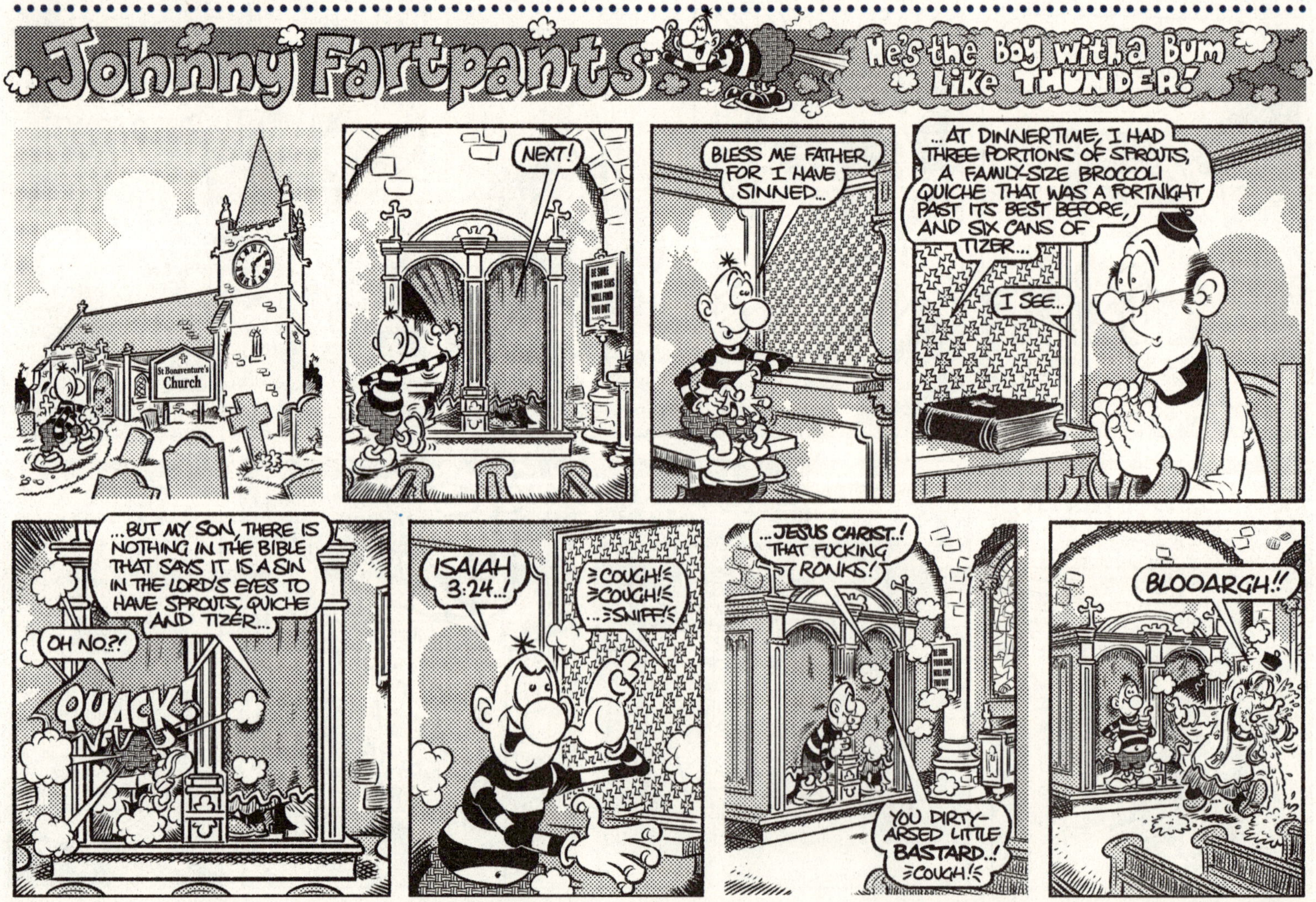
Johnny Fartpants
He's the Boy with a Bum Like THUNDER!
St Bonaventure's Church
NEXT!
BLESS ME FATHER, FOR I HAVE SINNED...
...AT DINNERTIME, I HAD THREE PORTIONS OF SPROUTS, A FAMILY-SIZE BROCCOLI QUICHE THAT WAS A FORTNIGHT PAST ITS BEST BEFORE, AND SIX CANS OF TIZER...
I SEE...
...BUT MY SON, THERE IS NOTHING IN THE BIBLE THAT SAYS IT IS A SIN IN THE LORD'S EYES TO HAVE SPROUTS, QUICHE AND TIZER...
OH NO?!
QUACK!
ISAIAH 3:24..!
COUGH! COUGH! ...SNIFF!
...JESUS CHRIST..! THAT FUCKING RONKS!
YOU DIRTY-ARSED LITTLE BASTARD..! COUGH!
BLOOARGH!!

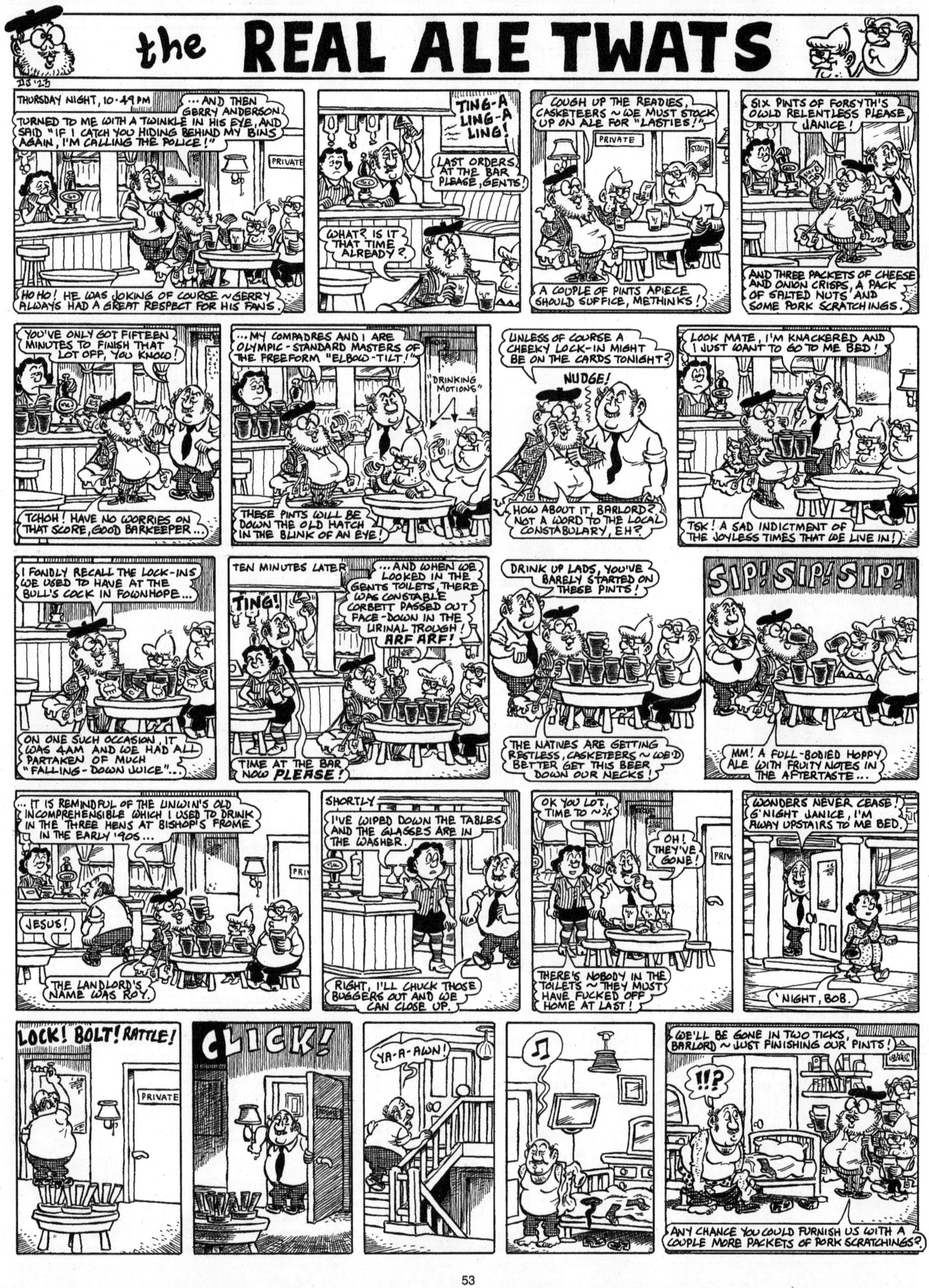
the REAL ALE TWATS
THURSDAY NIGHT, 10·49 PM
...AND THEN GERRY ANDERSON TURNED TO ME WITH A TWINKLE IN HIS EYE, AND SAID "IF I CATCH YOU HIDING BEHIND MY BINS AGAIN, I'M CALLING THE POLICE!"
PRIVATE
HO HO! HE WAS JOKING OF COURSE ~ GERRY ALWAYS HAD A GREAT RESPECT FOR HIS FANS.
TING-A LING-A LING!
LAST ORDERS AT THE BAR PLEASE, GENTS!
WHAT? IS IT THAT TIME ALREADY?
COUGH UP THE READIES, CASKETEERS ~ WE MUST STOCK UP ON ALE FOR "LASTIES!"
PRIVATE
STOUT
A COUPLE OF PINTS APIECE SHOULD SUFFICE, METHINKS!
SIX PINTS OF FORSYTH'S OWLD RELENTLESS PLEASE, JANICE!
AND THREE PACKETS OF CHEESE AND ONION CRISPS, A PACK OF SALTED NUTS AND SOME PORK SCRATCHINGS.
YOU'VE ONLY GOT FIFTEEN MINUTES TO FINISH THAT LOT OFF, YOU KNOW!
TCHOH! HAVE NO WORRIES ON THAT SCORE, GOOD BARKEEPER...
...MY COMPADRES AND I ARE OLYMPIC-STANDARD MASTERS OF THE FREEFORM "ELBOW-TILT!"
"DRINKING MOTIONS"
THESE PINTS WILL BE DOWN THE OLD HATCH IN THE BLINK OF AN EYE!
UNLESS OF COURSE A CHEEKY LOCK-IN MIGHT BE ON THE CARDS TONIGHT?
NUDGE!
HOW ABOUT IT, BARLORD? NOT A WORD TO THE LOCAL CONSTABULARY, EH?
LOOK MATE, I'M KNACKERED AND I JUST WANT TO GO TO ME BED!
TSK! A SAD INDICTMENT OF THE JOYLESS TIMES THAT WE LIVE IN!
I FONDLY RECALL THE LOCK-INS WE USED TO HAVE AT THE BULL'S COCK IN FOWNHOPE...
ON ONE SUCH OCCASION, IT WAS 4AM AND WE HAD ALL PARTAKEN OF MUCH "FALLING-DOWN JUICE"...
TEN MINUTES LATER
TING!
...AND WHEN WE LOOKED IN THE GENTS TOILETS, THERE WAS CONSTABLE CORBETT PASSED OUT FACE-DOWN IN THE URINAL TROUGH! ARF ARF!
TIME AT THE BAR NOW PLEASE!
DRINK UP LADS, YOU'VE BARELY STARTED ON THESE PINTS!
THE NATIVES ARE GETTING RESTLESS, CASKETEERS ~ WE'D BETTER GET THIS BEER DOWN OUR NECKS!
SIP! SIP! SIP!
MM! A FULL-BODIED HOPPY ALE WITH FRUITY NOTES IN THE AFTERTASTE...
...IT IS REMINDFUL OF THE UNWIN'S OLD INCOMPREHENSIBLE WHICH I USED TO DRINK IN THE THREE HENS AT BISHOP'S FROME IN THE EARLY '90S...
JESUS!
THE LANDLORD'S NAME WAS ROY.
SHORTLY
I'VE WIPED DOWN THE TABLES AND THE GLASSES ARE IN THE WASHER.
RIGHT, I'LL CHUCK THOSE BUGGERS OUT AND WE CAN CLOSE UP.
OK YOU LOT, TIME TO ~*!
OH! THEY'VE GONE!
THERE'S NOBODY IN THE TOILETS ~ THEY MUST HAVE FUCKED OFF HOME AT LAST!
WONDERS NEVER CEASE! G'NIGHT JANICE, I'M AWAY UPSTAIRS TO ME BED.
'NIGHT, BOB.
LOCK! BOLT! RATTLE!
PRIVATE
CLICK!
YA-A-AWN!
WE'LL BE GONE IN TWO TICKS, BARLORD ~ JUST FINISHING OUR PINTS!
!!?
ANY CHANCE YOU COULD FURNISH US WITH A COUPLE MORE PACKETS OF PORK SCRATCHINGS?

LeTTERbOCKS

letters@viz.co.uk

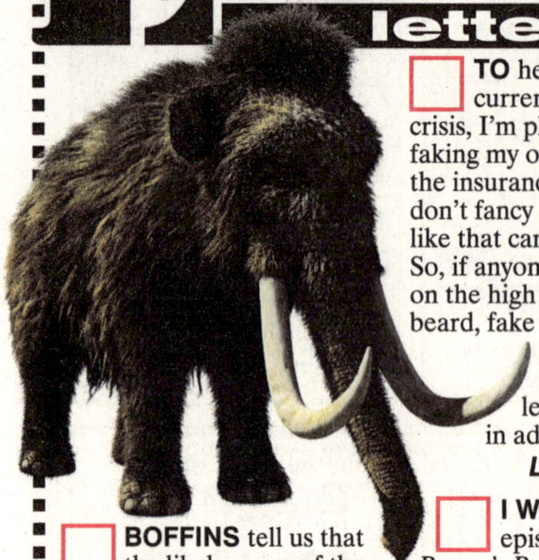

TO help with the current cost of living crisis, I'm planning on faking my own death for the insurance money, but I don't fancy getting caught like that canoe man fella. So, if anyone recognises me on the high street with a beard, fake nose or wearing a dress, do me a solid and don't let on. Thank you in advance.

Les Lloyd, email

BOFFINS tell us that the likely cause of the extinction of mammoths was climate change. Normal elephants simply got on with things and weathered the storm, but these hairy oafs ran away, in evolutionary terms, at the first sign of trouble.

Usain Imfat, Orkney

I WATCHED an episode of *Mrs Brown's Boys* recently and it had me in stitches. Whilst leaning forward in a desperate attempt to press the off switch on my remote control, I toppled forward and cracked my head open on a glass coffee table.

Shona Hill, Toulouse

STAR LETTER

AS a boy I was very keen on adventure, and for my thirteenth birthday I received a Swiss Army knife and a copy of a book entitled *SAS Survival*. The one piece of advice I remember from the book is that if you're on a liferaft in the middle of the ocean, you should urinate in short, intermittent spurts so as not to attract sharks. I have yet to employ this technique out at sea, but I do use the "short, intermittent spurts" method to fart in bed so as not to anger my wife.

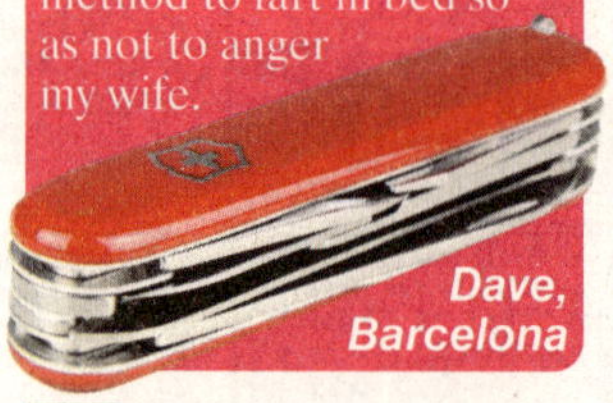

Dave, Barcelona

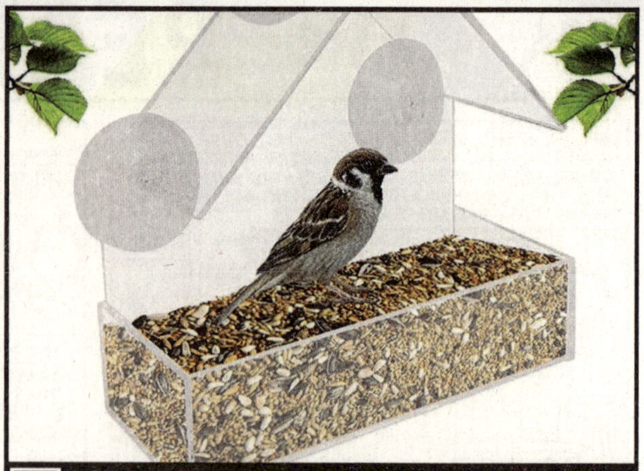

I ORDERED this sparrow and birdhouse set off the internet, and when it arrived the sparrow had eaten all the seed and flown off. On the plus side, the bastard hadn't shat in the plastic house.

Chingford Rob, email

I MADE a complete dog's dinner of my work this morning. Then I remembered I'm a nutritionist in a pet food factory, so I'm now looking forward to being promoted.

Mr T Duck, Spleen

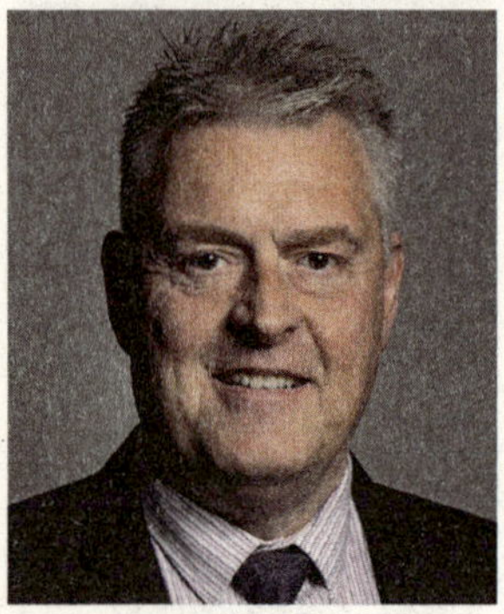

REFORM party MP Lee Anderson says he is in favour of the death penalty for the most heinous of crimes, but only in cases where there is 100% certainty about the guilt of the accused. I think this is a very sensible stance to take. In cases where the courts are not 100% convinced of their guilt, then the accused should simply spend the rest of their life behind bars.

Hector House, Surrey

I RECENTLY engaged the services of a "traditional" window cleaner. All I can say is *traditional, my arse!* He left the windows clean and sparkling and not once did he try to peep at my wife in the bath. A shitty rag smearing the neighbourhood filth from a bucket of black water was good enough for my parents. No wonder the country has gone to the dogs.

Arthur Shandy, email

LAST time I watched the aeroplane safety demonstration before a flight, I realised that the emergency command 'Brace! Brace!' has a slightly humorous double meaning, since the word 'brace' can mean two of something… *and they say it twice!* If I'm ever hurtling towards my death in a plane crash I shall definitely spend my final moments chuckling in mild amusement at this 'brace of braces'.

Ben Nunn, Caterham

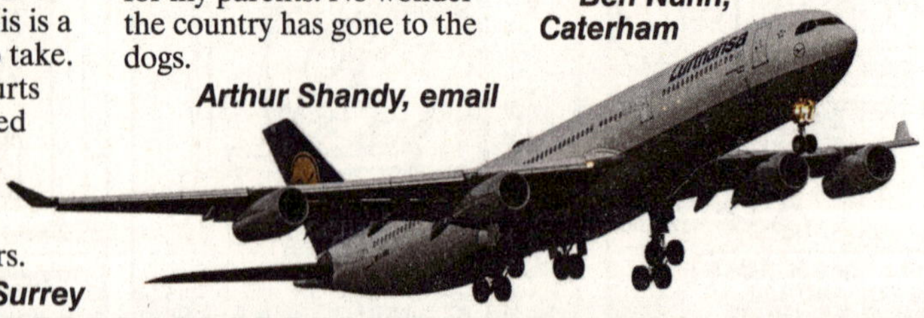

AS a receptionist at a gastrointestinal clinic, I always sing the Boney M lyric *"Show me your motion, la la la la la!"* to patients when accepting their faecal samples. Often the patients join in with "la la la la la!" bit, providing a welcome distraction from their terrible enteric suffering.

Gertrude Flupps, Rottingdean

I'VE masturbated in 12 different countries around the world. Can anyone beat that?

James Millar, Sutton

* *Congratulations, Mr Millar. That is certainly a globe-trotting, onanistic record to be proud of. But can any Viz reader beat it? There's a pair of extremely strong-lensed spectacles for the person, male or female, who has pleasured themselves in the greatest number of countries.*

ISN'T it remarkable that such a grand word as tumescence describes something as basic as a stiffy? I have never heard any actors in bongo flicks refer to their tumescence, though. But come to think of it, I don't really take that much notice of the dialogue in these sorts of films.

Captain Pat Catpain, Horsham

I BET the evil Lord Voldemort wishes he had not bothered with a spell and had just thrown the one-year-old baby Harry Potter through a window. I know there wouldn't have been much of a story, but these malevolent wizards really need to explore more conventional fictional angles sometimes, and not always rely on magic.

Dave Turton, Doncaster

ON checking into a hotel room in Sri Lanka, I complained to the manager that the balcony in my room was too small. He told me he would sort it, and when I went back up 10 minutes later, they had made the balcony much bigger. Hats off to the 'can do' attitude of foreign hoteliers. The British tourist industry needs to wake up.

Mog, Portsmouth

I'M no legal expert, but I reckon if a high court judge used the phrase 'I shit you not' in his summing up, it would carry a greater amount of gravitas for the average man.

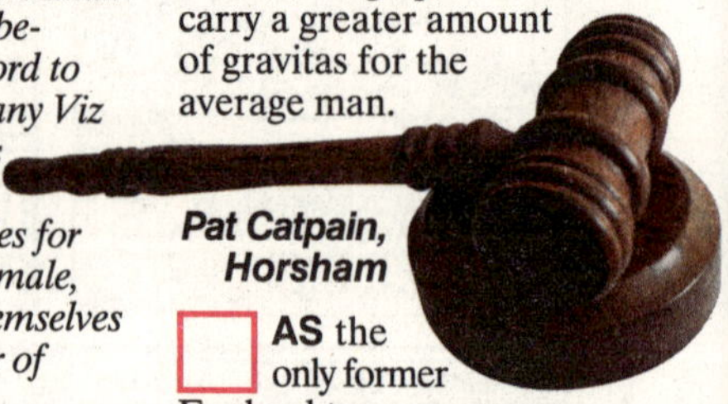

Pat Catpain, Horsham

AS the only former England team manager with a hundred percent win record, I am surprised that Big Sam Allardyce has not been snapped up to coach a top flight Premier League club. I often wonder if it's because he is yet to prove his credentials as an old fashioned circus strongman. If he would only grow a curly, waxed moustache, dress up in a tiger print leotard off one shoulder and rip a phonebook in half before every kick-off, I would happily welcome him back at Everton with open arms.

Les Lloyd, email

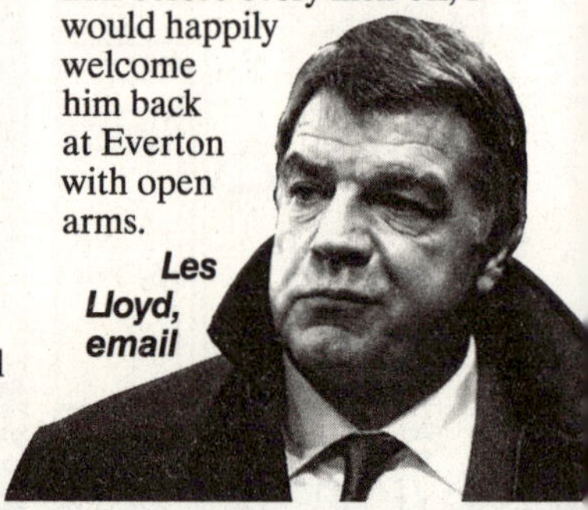

HITCHING A RIDE (WITH CHRISTOPHER HITCHENS)

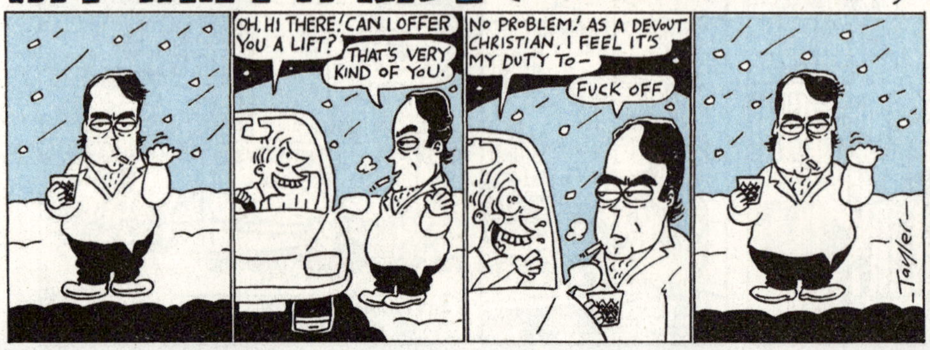
OH, HI THERE! CAN I OFFER YOU A LIFT?
THAT'S VERY KIND OF YOU.
NO PROBLEM! AS A DEVOUT CHRISTIAN, I FEEL IT'S MY DUTY TO–
FUCK OFF

CONVINCE passers-by that you and your mates are in the Mafia by drinking coffee outside Cafe Nero wearing vests.
Kevin Caswell-Jones, Gresford

PRETEND you're getting married by sending your friends and family a list of things you want from John Lewis.
Herbert, Bridmouth-on-Sea

ARSEHOLES. Informing people that you are "hard, but fair" is an excellent way of signalling that you are neither.
Kevin Caswell-Jones, Gresford

OLD beermats make ideal cheese biscuits for alcoholics.
Dave Edwards, Bridport

PEOPLE who live in glass houses. Throw your stones when outside and away from your property, and there shouldn't be any issues.
Jason Ettridge, Cwmbran

FOOL the bus driver into thinking you've just been swimming by getting on the bus with wet hair, eating a banana and carrying a kitbag with water in the bottom so it drips up the stairs.
M Phelps, Swindon

TRICK your spouse into thinking you've made a start on the washing-up by taking clean plates and placing them on the draining board.
Craig Hesmondhalgh, Lancaster

toptips@viz.co.uk

WHY is it that in movies, we always see a dystopian future and never a dystopian past? Come on, film-makers. Show us a dystopian past.
Bomber, York
PS. Actually, forget that. I have just watched *Holiday on the Bus*es.

MY neighbour just handed me a letter that was accidentally left in his letterbox. I live at number 12 and he lives at number 21. I wonder if your readers have had any similar incidents, where the postie has inadvertently transposed the numbers of the delivery address?
Douglas Hall, Springfield
We shall ask them, Mr Hall, but we imagine it is very unlikely. In fact, it's such an impossible event to contemplate, that we suspect you are making the episode up simply to see your name in print on the Letterbocks page.

I'VE just snapped off an unbroken 12-incher in the lav. Isn't it refreshing that since Brexit, I no longer have to refer to it as a unbroken 30.48cm-er? It is such a relief and a worthwhile reason to have gone through six years of divisive politics and financial hardship.
Captain Pat Catpain, Horsham

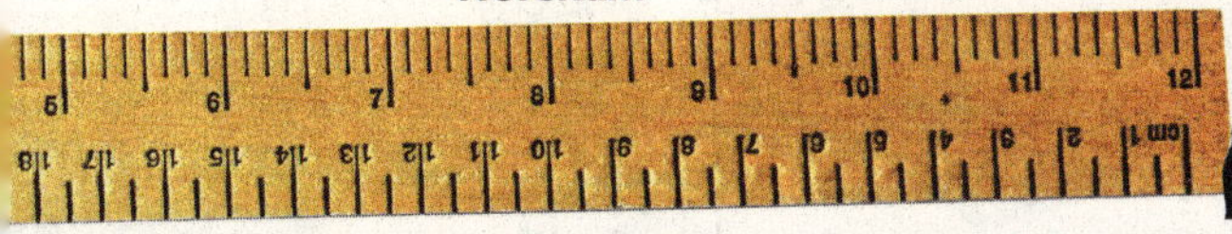

NINE-and-a-half years after the referendum, we have absolutely nothing to show for leaving the European Union except blue passports. And I'm blue-purple colour blind, so I've got absolutely fuck all. It's not the Brexit I voted for.
Wallace Wallet, Nottingham

FORMER PM Rishi Sunak was fined for not wearing a seatbelt in the back of a government vehicle, but I've just seen a woman on the *Fake Taxi* smut site not wearing her seatbelt, or much else for that matter, while going along the A41 between Bicester and Waddesdon. To the best of my knowledge she hasn't been fined for this. Yet again it's one rule for British Prime Ministers and another for amateur grumble starlets.
Mikey Bhoy, Shrewsbury

WHY do people always go on about people fighting like cats and dogs? Whenever my dog tries it on with my cat she swipes him and he runs away howling, the soft shite.
Joe S Kicker, Derbyshire

ON Radio 4's cultural magazine show *Loose Ends* last week, comedian Steve Bugeja made reference to "less people clapping in the audience". He was quickly corrected by presenter Arthur Smith, who pointed out that it should be "*few*er people clapping in the audience". However, a 500g bag of flour contains *les*s flour than a 1kg bag, and Mr Bugeja may have been referring to the collective mass of the audience members clapping rather than their number. How do you like *the*m apples, Mr Smith?
Tarquin Boils, Luton

WITH all these NHS doctors and nurses leaving to work for Lidl, I'm hoping the queues will go down quicker and that they'll have a quick look at my haemorrhoids whilst I pack my shopping.
Stuie, Bunny

BACK in 1993, Brian Cox's D-Ream famously told us in song that *things can only get better*. But things didn't better at all. In fact they got a whole lot shitter, and continue to do so. The lying bunch of bastards.
Gav H, Hebden Bridge

MY advice to anyone wanting to start their own business is probably not to bother. There's loads of forms to fill in. It's a proper ball-ache.
Cakers, London

HOW come Susie Dent never goes on *Countdow*n as a contestant? Maybe she's not as good at spelling without a big fuck-off dictionary in front of her.
Gary Ireland, Tauranga

I'M currently watching the Australian Tennis Open and I have noticed that all male tennis players have extremely sexy wives. Does anyone know how hard it is to play tennis?
James Millar, email

WHERE I come from, the end bit of a man's penis is referred to as his lid. So imagine my disgust whilst shopping in John Lewis last week, where I saw a large a display of cooking pots, with a sign saying "2.5l pot with ceramic lid," not 6 feet away from a woman with two small children.
Hector Bracegirdle, Blyth

What distinguishes a Paxman from a Vine? What are the main features of a Corbyn? Where are you most likely to spot a Clarkson?

Find all these answers, and more, in...

The Observer's Book of JEREMYS

OUT NOW! JUST £9.99

Full colour illustrations of over 150 Jeremys commonly found in the British Isles, with information on their characteristics and identification..

"I used to see a Jeremy every morning on the tube in London, but I never knew which one it was. With the Observer's Book of Jeremys, I was able to identify it as the former BBC Breakfast host Jeremy Bowen."
Mr H, Hampstead

"I'd regularly spot a Jeremy flitting about the streets where I live, but I could never identify it. With the help of this book, I discovered it was Jeremy Irons, a rare summer visitor from Ireland."
Mrs P, Islington

Want a shed?... but at the same time DON'T want a shed?

Schrödinger's Shed

Erect a Schrödinger's Shed in your garden, and it's either there or it's not… and you won't know which until you look at it. Made of the finest lap larch or not, each Schrödinger's Shed is guaranteed to last 25 years* whilst simultaneously being guaranteed not to have ever existed.

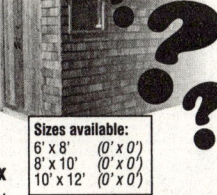

Sizes available:
6' x 8'   (0' x 0')
8' x 10' (0' x 0')
10' x 12' (0' x 0')

"It may or may not be a boon!" Mrs. B, Essex

"I put up a **Schrödinger's Shed** last week and when I went to get my lawn mower, it wasn't there. What excellent value for money." B Cox, CERN

*Guarantee automatically invalidated if you look at your Schrödinger's Shed.

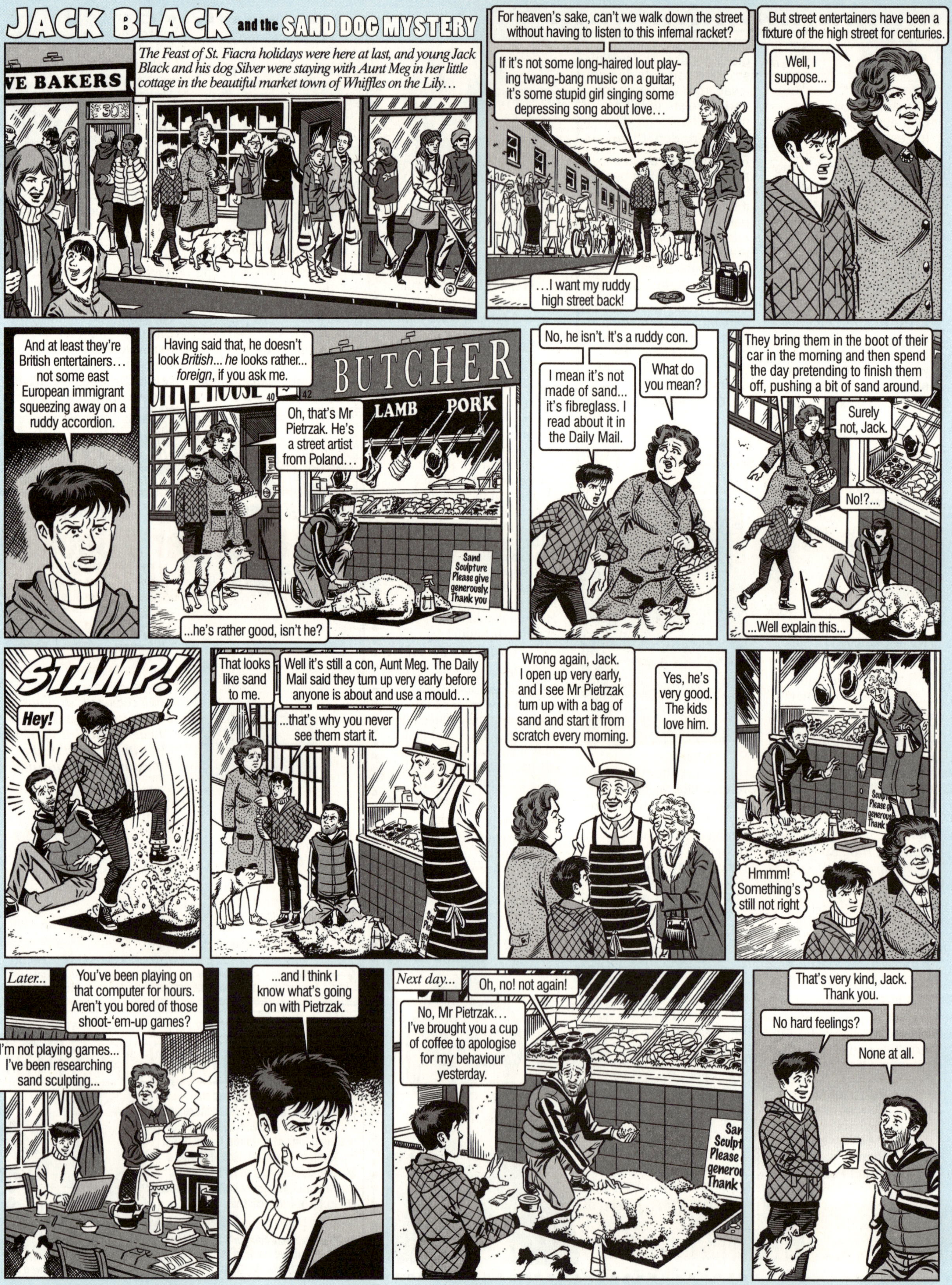

JACK BLACK and the SAND DOG MYSTERY
The Feast of St. Fiacra holidays were here at last, and young Jack Black and his dog Silver were staying with Aunt Meg in her little cottage in the beautiful market town of Whiffles on the Lily…
VE BAKERS
30
For heaven's sake, can't we walk down the street without having to listen to this infernal racket?
If it's not some long-haired lout playing twang-bang music on a guitar, it's some stupid girl singing some depressing song about love…
…I want my ruddy high street back!
But street entertainers have been a fixture of the high street for centuries.
Well, I suppose…
And at least they're British entertainers… not some east European immigrant squeezing away on a ruddy accordion.
Having said that, he doesn't look British… he looks rather… foreign, if you ask me.
BUTCHER
LAMB
PORK
40
42
Oh, that's Mr Pietrzak. He's a street artist from Poland…
Sand Sculpture Please give generously. Thank you
…he's rather good, isn't he?
No, he isn't. It's a ruddy con.
I mean it's not made of sand… it's fibreglass. I read about it in the Daily Mail.
What do you mean?
They bring them in the boot of their car in the morning and then spend the day pretending to finish them off, pushing a bit of sand around.
Surely not, Jack.
No!?…
…Well explain this…
STAMP!
Hey!
That looks like sand to me.
Well it's still a con, Aunt Meg. The Daily Mail said they turn up very early before anyone is about and use a mould…
…that's why you never see them start it.
Wrong again, Jack. I open up very early, and I see Mr Pietrzak turn up with a bag of sand and start it from scratch every morning.
Yes, he's very good. The kids love him.
Hmmm! Something's still not right
Later…
You've been playing on that computer for hours. Aren't you bored of those shoot-'em-up games?
I'm not playing games… I've been researching sand sculpting…
…and I think I know what's going on with Pietrzak.
Next day…
Oh, no! not again!
No, Mr Pietrzak… I've brought you a cup of coffee to apologise for my behaviour yesterday.
That's very kind, Jack. Thank you.
No hard feelings?
None at all.

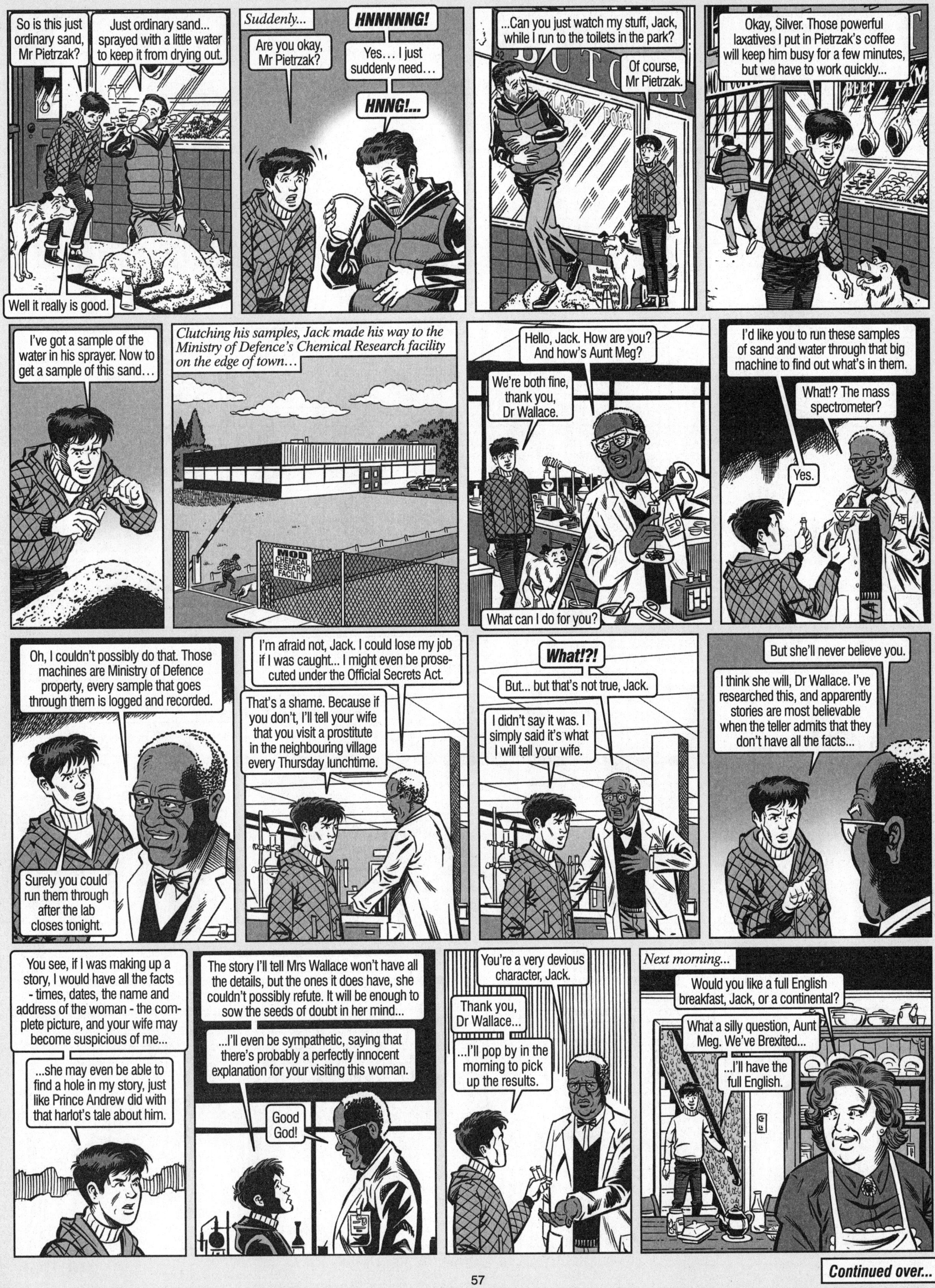
So is this just ordinary sand, Mr Pietrzak?
Just ordinary sand... sprayed with a little water to keep it from drying out.
Well it really is good.
Suddenly...
Are you okay, Mr Pietrzak?
HNNNNNG!
Yes... I just suddenly need...
HNNG!...
...Can you just watch my stuff, Jack, while I run to the toilets in the park?
Of course, Mr Pietrzak.
BUTCHER
LAMB
PORK
Okay, Silver. Those powerful laxatives I put in Pietrzak's coffee will keep him busy for a few minutes, but we have to work quickly...
I've got a sample of the water in his sprayer. Now to get a sample of this sand...
Clutching his samples, Jack made his way to the Ministry of Defence's Chemical Research facility on the edge of town...
MOD CHEMICAL RESEARCH FACILITY
Hello, Jack. How are you? And how's Aunt Meg?
We're both fine, thank you, Dr Wallace.
What can I do for you?
I'd like you to run these samples of sand and water through that big machine to find out what's in them.
What!? The mass spectrometer?
Yes.
Oh, I couldn't possibly do that. Those machines are Ministry of Defence property, every sample that goes through them is logged and recorded.
Surely you could run them through after the lab closes tonight.
I'm afraid not, Jack. I could lose my job if I was caught... I might even be prosecuted under the Official Secrets Act.
That's a shame. Because if you don't, I'll tell your wife that you visit a prostitute in the neighbouring village every Thursday lunchtime.
What!?!
But... but that's not true, Jack.
I didn't say it was. I simply said it's what I will tell your wife.
But she'll never believe you.
I think she will, Dr Wallace. I've researched this, and apparently stories are most believable when the teller admits that they don't have all the facts...
You see, if I was making up a story, I would have all the facts - times, dates, the name and address of the woman - the complete picture, and your wife may become suspicious of me...
...she may even be able to find a hole in my story, just like Prince Andrew did with that harlot's tale about him.
The story I'll tell Mrs Wallace won't have all the details, but the ones it does have, she couldn't possibly refute. It will be enough to sow the seeds of doubt in her mind...
...I'll even be sympathetic, saying that there's probably a perfectly innocent explanation for your visiting this woman.
Good God!
You're a very devious character, Jack.
Thank you, Dr Wallace...
...I'll pop by in the morning to pick up the results.
Next morning...
Would you like a full English breakfast, Jack, or a continental?
What a silly question, Aunt Meg. We've Brexited...
...I'll have the full English.

Continued over...

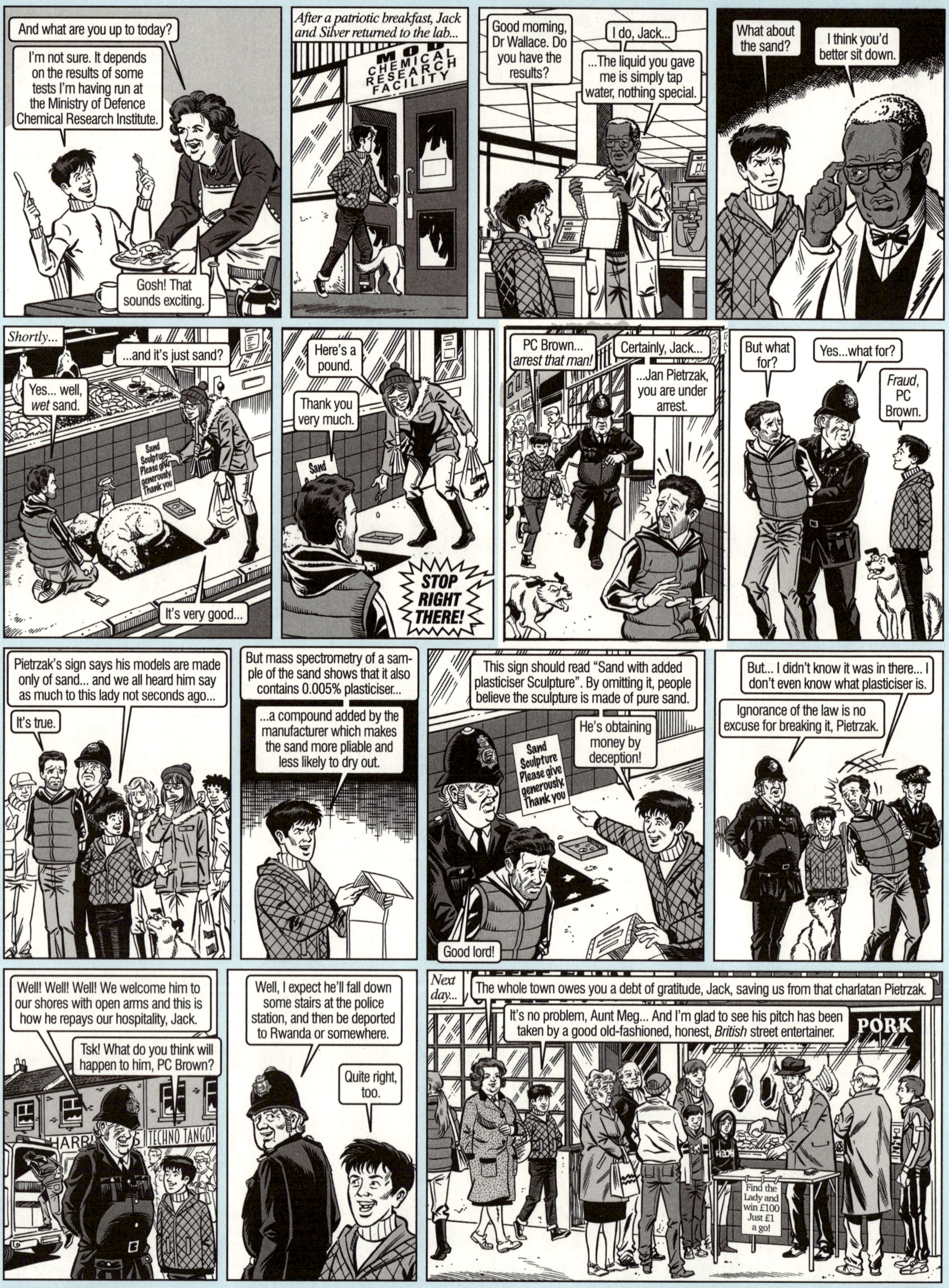

And what are you up to today?
I'm not sure. It depends on the results of some tests I'm having run at the Ministry of Defence Chemical Research Institute.
Gosh! That sounds exciting.
After a patriotic breakfast, Jack and Silver returned to the lab...
MOD CHEMICAL RESEARCH FACILITY
Good morning, Dr Wallace. Do you have the results?
I do, Jack...
...The liquid you gave me is simply tap water, nothing special.
What about the sand?
I think you'd better sit down.
Shortly...
...and it's just sand?
Yes... well, wet sand.
Sand Sculpture Please give generously. Thank you
It's very good...
Here's a pound.
Thank you very much.
STOP RIGHT THERE!
PC Brown... arrest that man!
Certainly, Jack...
...Jan Pietrzak, you are under arrest.
But what for?
Yes...what for?
Fraud, PC Brown.
Pietrzak's sign says his models are made only of sand... and we all heard him say as much to this lady not seconds ago...
It's true.
But mass spectrometry of a sample of the sand shows that it also contains 0.005% plasticiser...
...a compound added by the manufacturer which makes the sand more pliable and less likely to dry out.
This sign should read "Sand with added plasticiser Sculpture". By omitting it, people believe the sculpture is made of pure sand.
He's obtaining money by deception!
Sand Sculpture Please give generously. Thank you
Good lord!
But... I didn't know it was in there... I don't even know what plasticiser is.
Ignorance of the law is no excuse for breaking it, Pietrzak.
Well! Well! Well! We welcome him to our shores with open arms and this is how he repays our hospitality, Jack.
Tsk! What do you think will happen to him, PC Brown?
TECHNO TANGO!
Well, I expect he'll fall down some stairs at the police station, and then be deported to Rwanda or somewhere.
Quite right, too.
Next day...
The whole town owes you a debt of gratitude, Jack, saving us from that charlatan Pietrzak.
It's no problem, Aunt Meg... And I'm glad to see his pitch has been taken by a good old-fashioned, honest, British street entertainer.
PORK
Find the Lady and win £100 Just £1 a go!
THE END

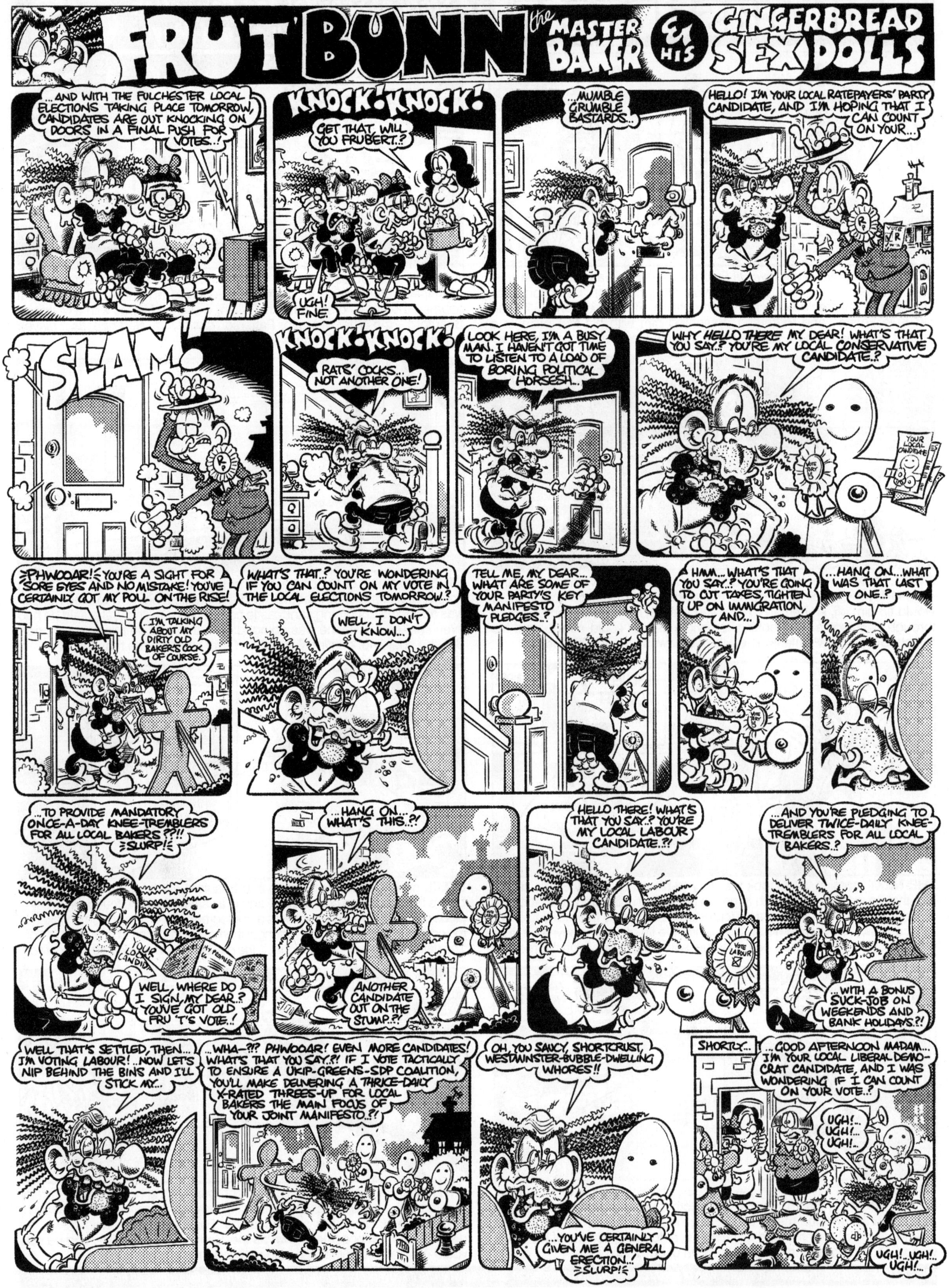
FRU'T BUNN the MASTER BAKER & HIS GINGERBREAD SEX DOLLS
...AND WITH THE FULCHESTER LOCAL ELECTIONS TAKING PLACE TOMORROW, CANDIDATES ARE OUT KNOCKING ON DOORS IN A FINAL PUSH FOR VOTES..!
KNOCK! KNOCK!
GET THAT, WILL YOU FRUBERT..?
UGH! FINE.
...MUMBLE GRUMBLE BASTARDS...
HELLO! I'M YOUR LOCAL RATEPAYERS' PARTY CANDIDATE, AND I'M HOPING THAT I CAN COUNT ON YOUR...
SLAM!
KNOCK! KNOCK!
RATS' COCKS... NOT ANOTHER ONE!
LOOK HERE, I'M A BUSY MAN. I HAVEN'T GOT TIME TO LISTEN TO A LOAD OF BORING POLITICAL HORSESH...
WHY HELLO THERE MY DEAR! WHAT'S THAT YOU SAY..? YOU'RE MY LOCAL CONSERVATIVE CANDIDATE..?
YOUR LOCAL CANDIDATE
PHWOOAR! YOU'RE A SIGHT FOR SORE EYES AND NO MISTAKE! YOU'VE CERTAINLY GOT MY POLL ON THE RISE!
...I'M TALKING ABOUT MY DIRTY OLD BAKER'S COCK OF COURSE.
WHAT'S THAT..? YOU'RE WONDERING IF YOU CAN COUNT ON MY VOTE IN THE LOCAL ELECTIONS TOMORROW..?
WELL, I DON'T KNOW...
TELL ME, MY DEAR... WHAT ARE SOME OF YOUR PARTY'S KEY MANIFESTO PLEDGES..?
HMM... WHAT'S THAT YOU SAY..? YOU'RE GOING TO CUT TAXES, TIGHTEN UP ON IMMIGRATION, AND...
...HANG ON... WHAT WAS THAT LAST ONE..?
...TO PROVIDE MANDATORY ONCE-A-DAY KNEE-TREMBLERS FOR ALL LOCAL BAKERS??!! SLURP!
YOUR LOCAL CANDID...
WELL, WHERE DO I SIGN, MY DEAR..? YOU'VE GOT OLD FRU'T'S VOTE..!
...HANG ON... WHAT'S THIS..?!
ANOTHER CANDIDATE OUT ON THE STUMP..?!
HELLO THERE! WHAT'S THAT YOU SAY..? YOU'RE MY LOCAL LABOUR CANDIDATE..?!
VOTE LABOUR
...AND YOU'RE PLEDGING TO DELIVER TWICE-DAILY KNEE-TREMBLERS FOR ALL LOCAL BAKERS..?
...WITH A BONUS SUCK-JOB ON WEEKENDS AND BANK HOLIDAYS..?!
WELL THAT'S SETTLED, THEN... I'M VOTING LABOUR! ...NOW LET'S NIP BEHIND THE BINS AND I'LL STICK MY...
...WHA-?!? PHWOOAR! EVEN MORE CANDIDATES! WHAT'S THAT YOU SAY..?! IF I VOTE TACTICALLY TO ENSURE A UKIP-GREENS-SDP COALITION, YOU'LL MAKE DELIVERING A THRICE-DAILY X-RATED THREES-UP FOR LOCAL BAKERS THE MAIN FOCUS OF YOUR JOINT MANIFESTO..?!
OH, YOU SAUCY, SHORTCRUST, WESTMINSTER-BUBBLE-DWELLING WHORES!!
...YOU'VE CERTAINLY GIVEN ME A GENERAL ERECTION..! SLURP!
SHORTLY...
...GOOD AFTERNOON MADAM... I'M YOUR LOCAL LIBERAL DEMOCRAT CANDIDATE, AND I WAS WONDERING IF I CAN COUNT ON YOUR VOTE..?
UGH!.. UGH!.. UGH!..
UGH!.. UGH! UGH!...

Sandcastlegate! *A Story of Scandal and Corruption that Brought Down a Lord Mayor*

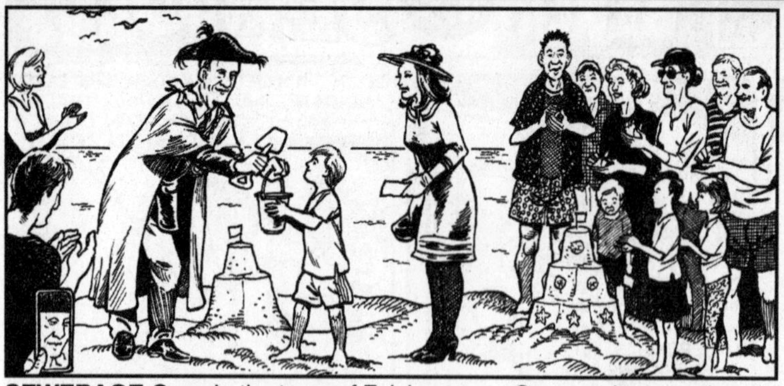

SEWERAGE Cove in the town of Fulchester-on-Sea was busy on August bank holiday 2022. The town's mayor, Alderman Ron Patterson, was judging the children's sandcastle competition. First prize went to 7-year-old Kyle Forster, and Patterson presented him with his first prize of a bucket and spade and a voucher for a free ice cream at the beach kiosk.

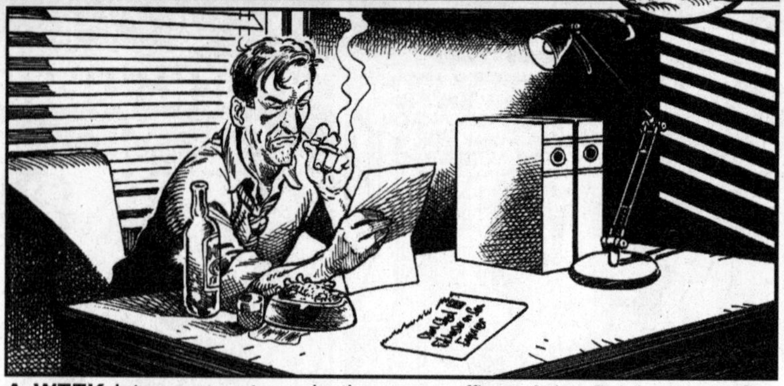

A WEEK later across town in the news office of the *Fulchester-on-Sea Examiner*, veteran reporter Sam Steel received an anonymous tip-off. It seemed that Kyle Forster's mum, Gillian, was best friends with a Margaret Beauford – the sister of Mayor Patterson's wife Ava. *Had nepotism played a major part in young Forster's sandcastle win?*

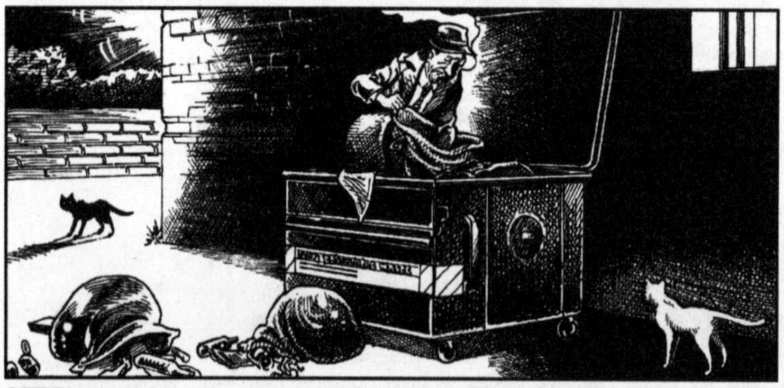

STEEL knew that the story was dynamite and could blow the Fulchester-on-Sea town council wide open. But asking the mayor for a comment would tip him off, so he had to proceed with caution. He began by going through Patterson's bins looking for evidence that could corroborate his hunch. But he drew a blank. The wily mayor was covering his tracks.

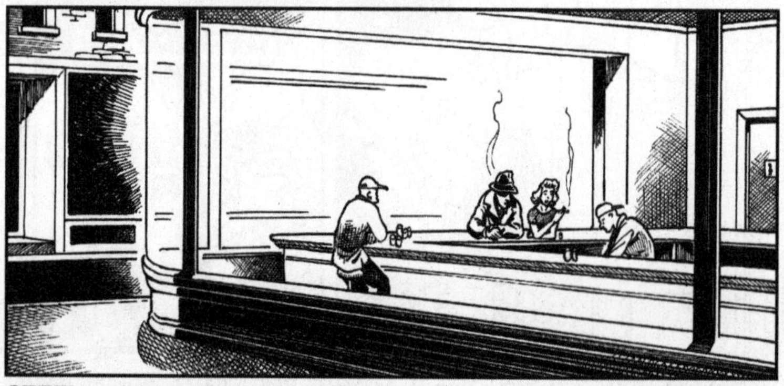

STEEL met one of his contacts who told him that she had met Gillian Forster at a community litter pick, and she had told her how excited her son was about the upcoming sandcastle competition. Tellingly, she said he had even spoken of what he was going to do with his bucket and spade prize. But she could not confirm Forster had ever met with the mayor's wife.

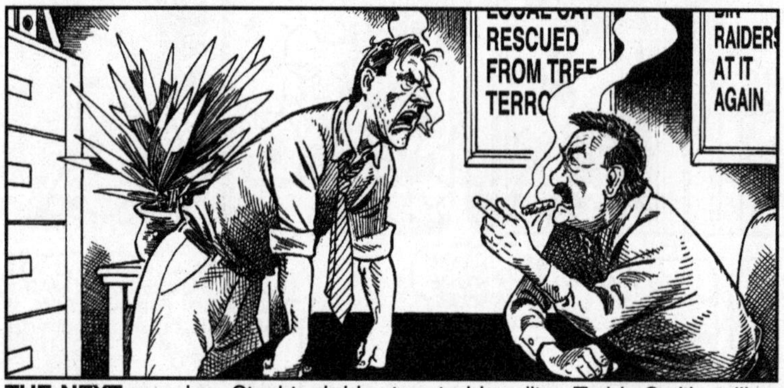
RESCUED
FROM TRE
TERRO
RAIDERS
AT IT
AGAIN

THE NEXT morning, Steel took his story to his editor, Teddy Smith, telling him that he wanted to run with it the next day. The editor agreed that it was a scoop, but the evidence was circumstantial, and said that he would not run it unless Steel named his source. Since the tip-off was anonymous, that was impossible. Steel knew he had to get someone to talk… on the record.

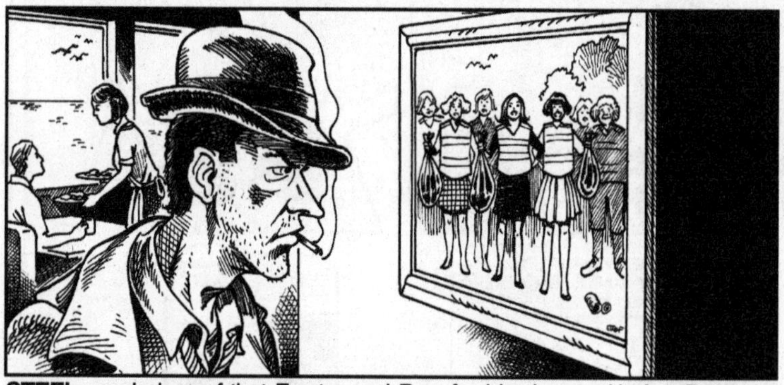

STEEL needed proof that Forster and Beauford had met with Ava Patterson before the sandcastle competition, and in a seafront cafe he found the missing piece of the jigsaw. On the wall was a photograph of a group of women taken at the community litter pick, and amongst them were the three women in question. The date of the event - 24th August… *the day before the sandcastle competition!*

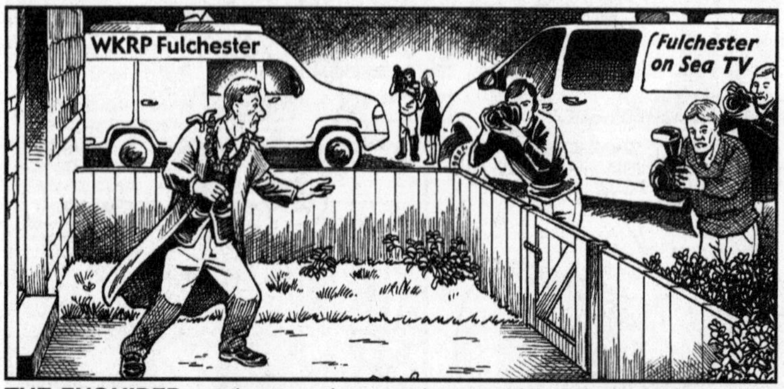
WKRP Fulchester
Fulchester on Sea TV

THE *ENQUIRER* ran the story the next day, at which point everything blew up. Ava Patterson went to stay with her other sister in Nottingham to get away from the ensuing media circus. But the mayor braved it out, denying all knowledge of the affair and claiming never to have met any of his wife's friends. But he was found guilty in the court of public opinion.

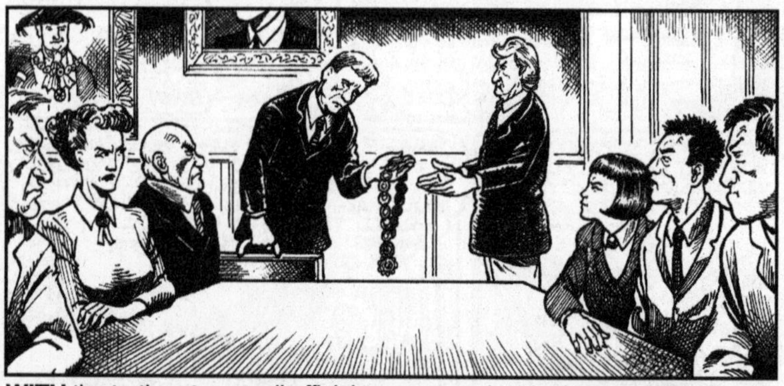

WITH the truth out, council officials went round to the home of Kyle Forster to retrieve the prizes, presenting them instead to 8-year-old Amy Fairchild, who had been awarded second place. Patterson never lived down the disgrace of what became known as the 'Sandcastlegate' affair, and he was voted out of office at the following meeting of the local council.

***NEXT TIME:** Sam Steel unearths a sinister web of seedy corruption on Fulchester-on-Sea pier, when he discovers that a global gambling cartel is gluing coins on the penny waterfalls.*

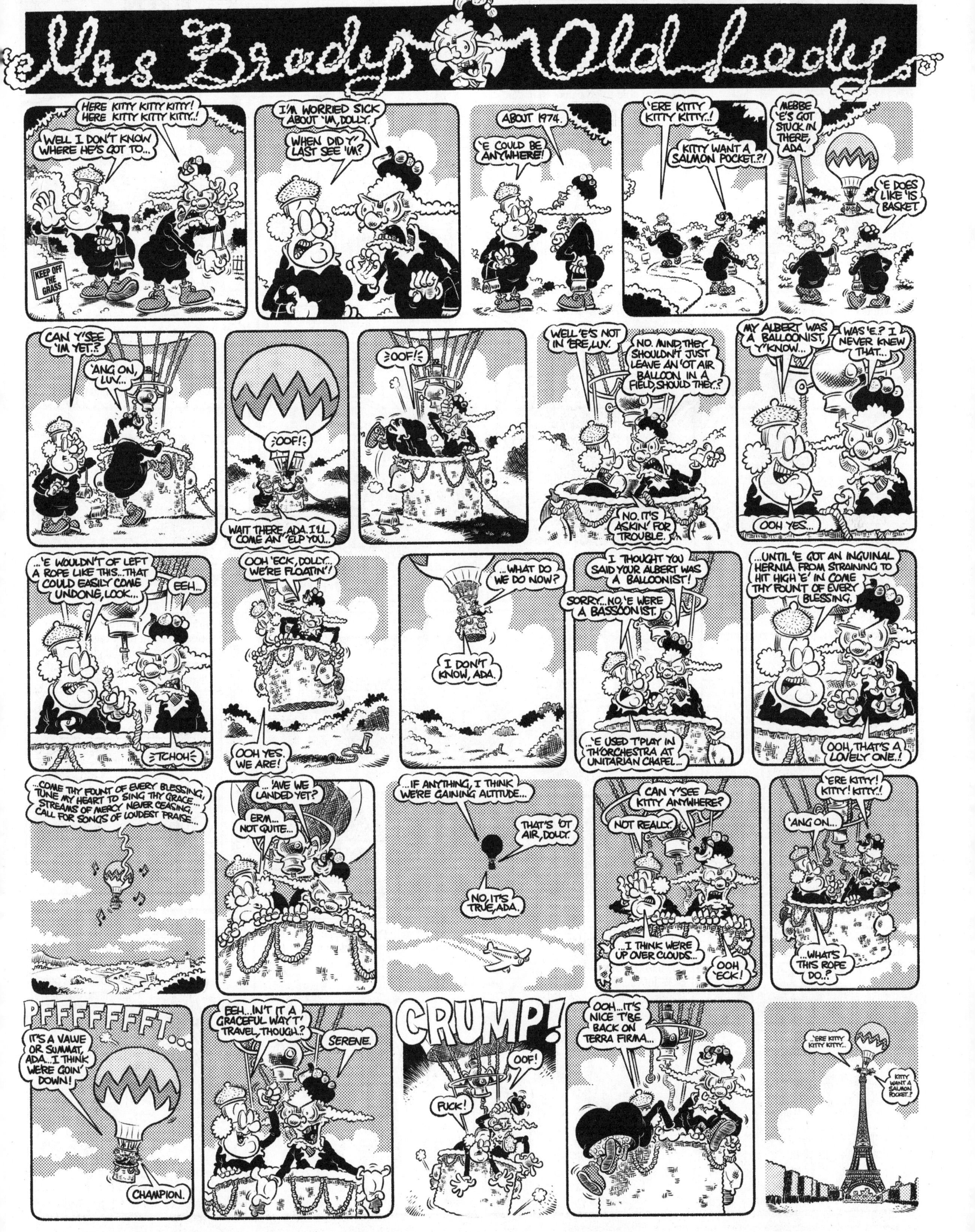
Mrs Brady Old Lady
HERE KITTY KITTY KITTY! HERE KITTY KITTY KITTY..!
WELL I DON'T KNOW WHERE HE'S GOT TO...
KEEP OFF THE GRASS
I'M WORRIED SICK ABOUT 'IM, DOLLY.
WHEN DID Y' LAST SEE 'IM?
ABOUT 1974.
'E COULD BE ANYWHERE!
'ERE KITTY KITTY KITTY..!
KITTY WANT A SALMON POCKET..?!
MEBBE 'E'S GOT STUCK IN THERE, ADA.
'E DOES LIKE 'IS BASKET
CAN Y'SEE 'IM YET..?
'ANG ON, LUV...
;OOF!;
WAIT THERE, ADA. I'LL COME AN' 'ELP YOU...
;OOF!;
WELL 'E'S NOT IN 'ERE, LUV.
NO. MIND, THEY SHOULDN'T JUST LEAVE AN 'OT AIR BALLOON IN A FIELD, SHOULD THEY..?
NO. IT'S ASKIN' FOR TROUBLE.
MY ALBERT WAS A BALLOONIST, Y'KNOW...
WAS 'E..? I NEVER KNEW THAT...
OOH YES...
...'E WOULDN'T OF LEFT A ROPE LIKE THIS...THAT COULD EASILY COME UNDONE, LOOK...
EEH...
;TCHOH;
OOH 'ECK, DOLLY... WE'RE FLOATIN'!
OOH YES. WE ARE!
...WHAT DO WE DO NOW?
I DON'T KNOW, ADA.
I THOUGHT YOU SAID YOUR ALBERT WAS A BALLOONIST!
SORRY...NO, 'E WERE A BASSOONIST.
...'E USED T'PLAY IN TH'ORCHESTRA AT UNITARIAN CHAPEL...
...UNTIL 'E GOT AN INGUINAL HERNIA FROM STRAINING TO HIT HIGH 'E' IN COME THY FOUNT OF EVERY BLESSING.
OOH, THAT'S A LOVELY ONE..!
...COME THY FOUNT OF EVERY BLESSING, TUNE MY HEART TO SING THY GRACE... STREAMS OF MERCY NEVER CEASING, CALL FOR SONGS OF LOUDEST PRAISE...
...'AVE WE LANDED YET?
ERM... NOT QUITE...
...IF ANYTHING, I THINK WE'RE GAINING ALTITUDE...
THAT'S 'OT AIR, DOLLY.
NO, IT'S TRUE, ADA.
CAN Y'SEE KITTY ANYWHERE?
NOT REALLY.
...I THINK WE'RE UP OVER CLOUDS...
OOH 'ECK!
'ERE KITTY! KITTY! KITTY..!
'ANG ON...
...WHAT'S THIS ROPE DO..?
PFFFFFFFFT...
IT'S A VALVE OR SUMMAT, ADA...I THINK WE'RE GOIN' DOWN!
CHAMPION.
EEH...IN'T IT A GRACEFUL WAY T' TRAVEL, THOUGH..?
SERENE.
CRUMP!
OOF!
FUCK!
OOH...IT'S NICE T'BE BACK ON TERRA FIRMA...
'ERE KITTY KITTY KITTY...
KITTY WANT A SALMON POCKET..?

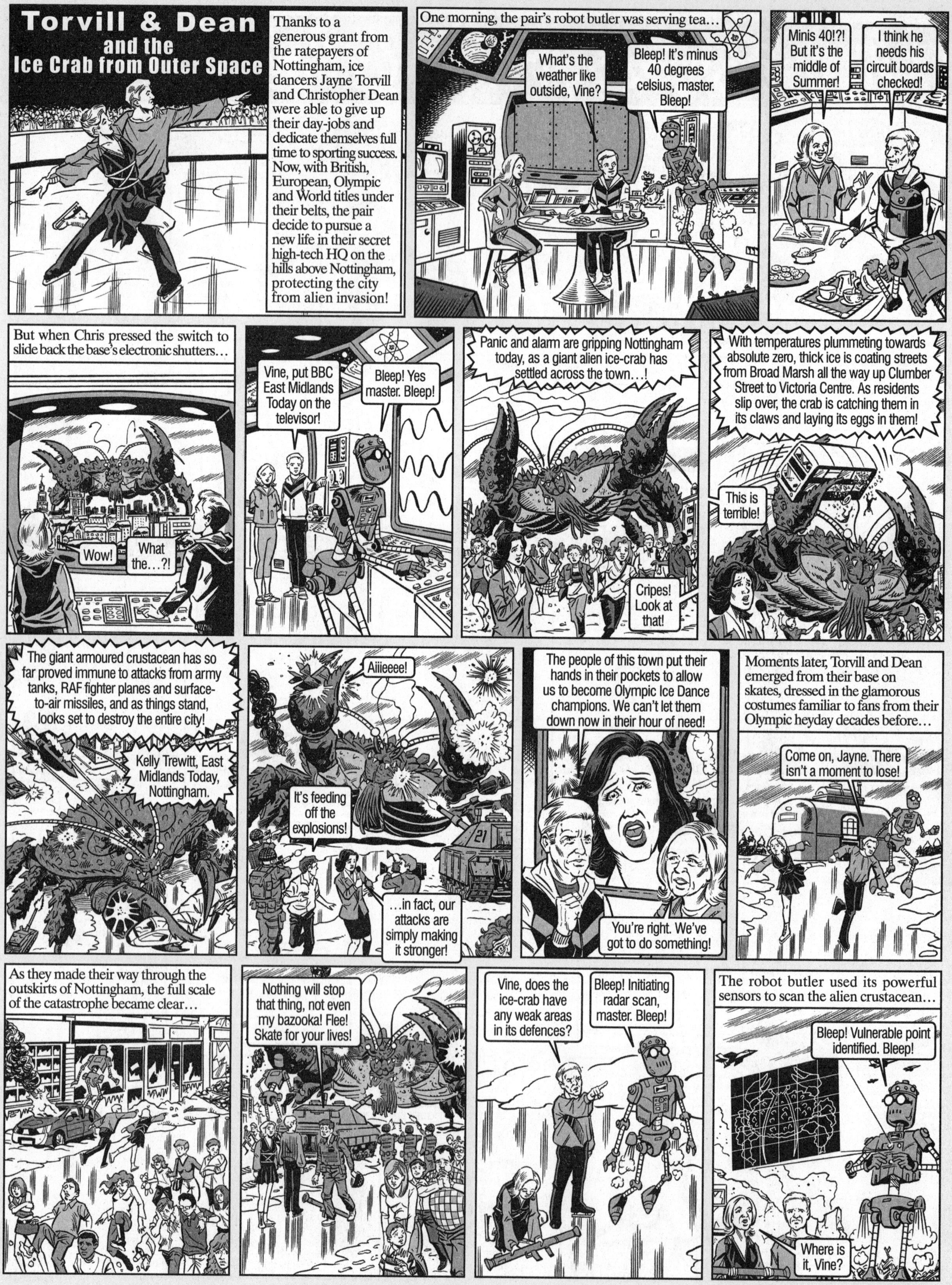

Torvill & Dean and the Ice Crab from Outer Space
Thanks to a generous grant from the ratepayers of Nottingham, ice dancers Jayne Torvill and Christopher Dean were able to give up their day-jobs and dedicate themselves full time to sporting success. Now, with British, European, Olympic and World titles under their belts, the pair decide to pursue a new life in their secret high-tech HQ on the hills above Nottingham, protecting the city from alien invasion!
One morning, the pair's robot butler was serving tea…
What's the weather like outside, Vine?
Bleep! It's minus 40 degrees celsius, master. Bleep!
Minis 40!?! But it's the middle of Summer!
I think he needs his circuit boards checked!
But when Chris pressed the switch to slide back the base's electronic shutters…
Wow!
What the…?!
Vine, put BBC East Midlands Today on the televisor!
Bleep! Yes master. Bleep!
Panic and alarm are gripping Nottingham today, as a giant alien ice-crab has settled across the town…!
Cripes! Look at that!
With temperatures plummeting towards absolute zero, thick ice is coating streets from Broad Marsh all the way up Clumber Street to Victoria Centre. As residents slip over, the crab is catching them in its claws and laying its eggs in them!
This is terrible!
The giant armoured crustacean has so far proved immune to attacks from army tanks, RAF fighter planes and surface-to-air missiles, and as things stand, looks set to destroy the entire city!
Kelly Trewitt, East Midlands Today, Nottingham.
Aiiieeee!
It's feeding off the explosions!
…in fact, our attacks are simply making it stronger!
The people of this town put their hands in their pockets to allow us to become Olympic Ice Dance champions. We can't let them down now in their hour of need!
You're right. We've got to do something!
Moments later, Torvill and Dean emerged from their base on skates, dressed in the glamorous costumes familiar to fans from their Olympic heyday decades before…
Come on, Jayne. There isn't a moment to lose!
As they made their way through the outskirts of Nottingham, the full scale of the catastrophe became clear…
Nothing will stop that thing, not even my bazooka! Flee! Skate for your lives!
Vine, does the ice-crab have any weak areas in its defences?
Bleep! Initiating radar scan, master. Bleep!
The robot butler used its powerful sensors to scan the alien crustacean…
Bleep! Vulnerable point identified. Bleep!
Where is it, Vine?

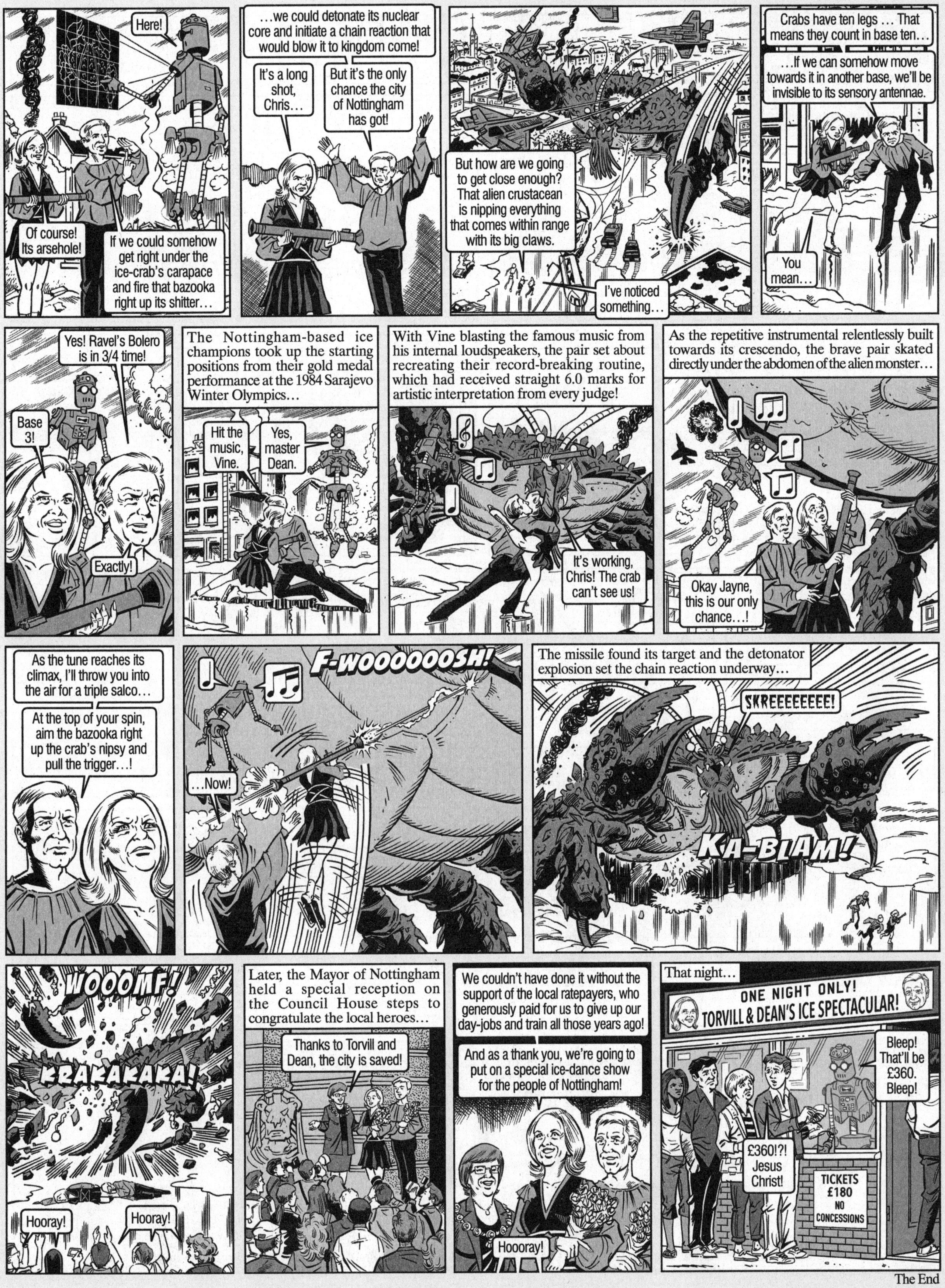

Here!
Of course! Its arsehole!
If we could somehow get right under the ice-crab's carapace and fire that bazooka right up its shitter…
…we could detonate its nuclear core and initiate a chain reaction that would blow it to kingdom come!
It's a long shot, Chris…
But it's the only chance the city of Nottingham has got!
But how are we going to get close enough? That alien crustacean is nipping everything that comes within range with its big claws.
I've noticed something…
Crabs have ten legs … That means they count in base ten…
…If we can somehow move towards it in another base, we'll be invisible to its sensory antennae.
You mean…
Yes! Ravel's Bolero is in 3/4 time!
Base 3!
Exactly!
The Nottingham-based ice champions took up the starting positions from their gold medal performance at the 1984 Sarajevo Winter Olympics…
Hit the music, Vine.
Yes, master Dean.
With Vine blasting the famous music from his internal loudspeakers, the pair set about recreating their record-breaking routine, which had received straight 6.0 marks for artistic interpretation from every judge!
It's working, Chris! The crab can't see us!
As the repetitive instrumental relentlessly built towards its crescendo, the brave pair skated directly under the abdomen of the alien monster…
Okay Jayne, this is our only chance…!
As the tune reaches its climax, I'll throw you into the air for a triple salco…
At the top of your spin, aim the bazooka right up the crab's nipsy and pull the trigger…!
F-WOOOOOOSH!
…Now!
The missile found its target and the detonator explosion set the chain reaction underway…
SKREEEEEEEE!
KA-BLAM!
WOOOMF!
KRAKAKAKA!
Hooray!
Hooray!
Later, the Mayor of Nottingham held a special reception on the Council House steps to congratulate the local heroes…
Thanks to Torvill and Dean, the city is saved!
We couldn't have done it without the support of the local ratepayers, who generously paid for us to give up our day-jobs and train all those years ago!
And as a thank you, we're going to put on a special ice-dance show for the people of Nottingham!
Hoooray!
That night…
ONE NIGHT ONLY! TORVILL & DEAN'S ICE SPECTACULAR!
Bleep! That'll be £360. Bleep!
£360!?! Jesus Christ!
TICKETS £180 NO CONCESSIONS
The End

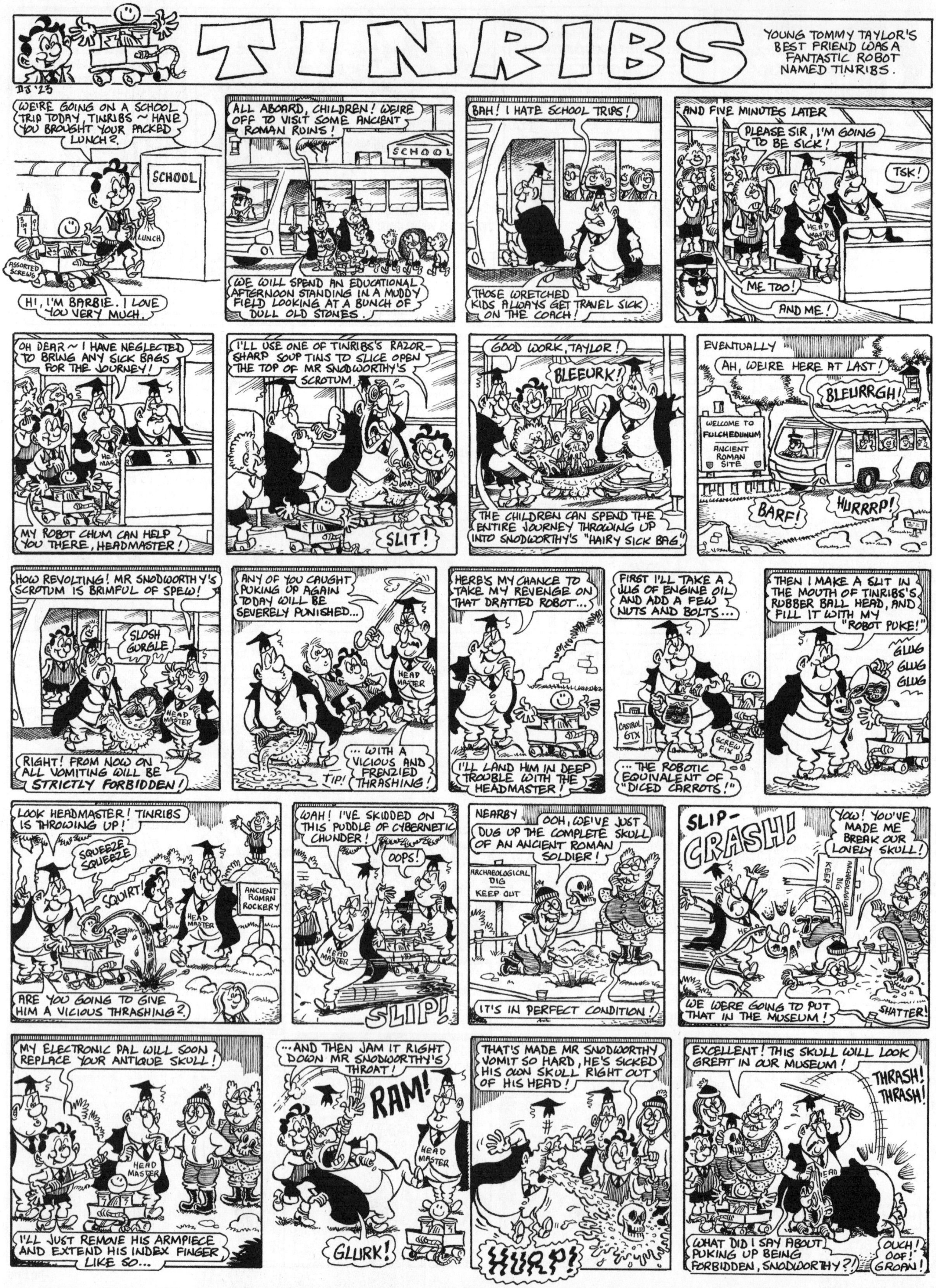
TINRIBS
YOUNG TOMMY TAYLOR'S BEST FRIEND WAS A FANTASTIC ROBOT NAMED TINRIBS.
WE'RE GOING ON A SCHOOL TRIP TODAY, TINRIBS ~ HAVE YOU BROUGHT YOUR PACKED LUNCH?
SCHOOL
LUNCH
ASSORTED SCREWS
HI, I'M BARBIE. I LOVE YOU VERY MUCH.
ALL ABOARD, CHILDREN! WE'RE OFF TO VISIT SOME ANCIENT ROMAN RUINS!
SCHOOL
WE WILL SPEND AN EDUCATIONAL AFTERNOON STANDING IN A MUDDY FIELD LOOKING AT A BUNCH OF DULL OLD STONES.
BAH! I HATE SCHOOL TRIPS!
THOSE WRETCHED KIDS ALWAYS GET TRAVEL SICK ON THE COACH!
AND FIVE MINUTES LATER
PLEASE SIR, I'M GOING TO BE SICK!
TSK!
HEAD MASTER
ME TOO!
AND ME!
OH DEAR ~ I HAVE NEGLECTED TO BRING ANY SICK BAGS FOR THE JOURNEY!
MY ROBOT CHUM CAN HELP YOU THERE, HEADMASTER!
I'LL USE ONE OF TINRIBS'S RAZOR-SHARP SOUP TINS TO SLICE OPEN THE TOP OF MR SNODWORTHY'S SCROTUM.
SLIT!
GOOD WORK, TAYLOR!
BLEEURK!
THE CHILDREN CAN SPEND THE ENTIRE JOURNEY THROWING UP INTO SNODWORTHY'S "HAIRY SICK BAG"!
EVENTUALLY
AH, WE'RE HERE AT LAST!
BLEURRGH!
WELCOME TO FULCHEDUNUM ANCIENT ROMAN SITE
BARF!
HURRRP!
HOW REVOLTING! MR SNODWORTHY'S SCROTUM IS BRIMFUL OF SPEW!
SLOSH GURGLE
HEAD MASTER
RIGHT! FROM NOW ON ALL VOMITING WILL BE STRICTLY FORBIDDEN!
ANY OF YOU CAUGHT PUKING UP AGAIN TODAY WILL BE SEVERELY PUNISHED...
...WITH A VICIOUS AND FRENZIED THRASHING!
TIP!
HERE'S MY CHANCE TO TAKE MY REVENGE ON THAT DRATTED ROBOT...
I'LL LAND HIM IN DEEP TROUBLE WITH THE HEADMASTER!
FIRST I'LL TAKE A JUG OF ENGINE OIL AND ADD A FEW NUTS AND BOLTS...
CASTROL GTX
SCREW FIX
...THE ROBOTIC EQUIVALENT OF "DICED CARROTS!"
THEN I MAKE A SLIT IN THE MOUTH OF TINRIBS'S RUBBER BALL HEAD, AND FILL IT WITH MY "ROBOT PUKE!"
GLUG GLUG GLUG
LOOK HEADMASTER! TINRIBS IS THROWING UP!
SQUEEZE SQUEEZE
SQUIRT!
ANCIENT ROMAN ROCKERY
ARE YOU GOING TO GIVE HIM A VICIOUS THRASHING?
WAH! I'VE SKIDDED ON THIS PUDDLE OF CYBERNETIC CHUNDER!
OOPS!
SLIP!
NEARBY
OOH, WE'VE JUST DUG UP THE COMPLETE SKULL OF AN ANCIENT ROMAN SOLDIER!
ARCHAEOLOGICAL DIG KEEP OUT
IT'S IN PERFECT CONDITION!
SLIP-CRASH!
YOW! YOU'VE MADE ME BREAK OUR LOVELY SKULL!
WE WERE GOING TO PUT THAT IN THE MUSEUM!
SHATTER!
MY ELECTRONIC PAL WILL SOON REPLACE YOUR ANTIQUE SKULL!
I'LL JUST REMOVE HIS ARMPIECE AND EXTEND HIS INDEX FINGER LIKE SO...
...AND THEN JAM IT RIGHT DOWN MR SNODWORTHY'S THROAT!
RAM!
GLURK!
THAT'S MADE MR SNODWORTHY VOMIT SO HARD, HE'S SICKED HIS OWN SKULL RIGHT OUT OF HIS HEAD!
HURP!
EXCELLENT! THIS SKULL WILL LOOK GREAT IN OUR MUSEUM!
THRASH! THRASH!
WHAT DID I SAY ABOUT PUKING UP BEING FORBIDDEN, SNODWORTHY?!
OUCH! OOF! GROAN!

THEY'RE the iconic British ceremonies that have been keeping our country in Kings and Queens ever since the Dark Ages. They're Coronations – the point at which the acting monarch becomes ruler in the eyes of God. We Brits have talked of little else these past months, but how much do we REALLY know about these time-honoured rituals? Since we haven't had one in the UK since 1953, the answer is probably the *thick end of fuck all*. So string up the bunting, grab your crown, orb and sceptre, and get comfy on the throne, as we bring you...

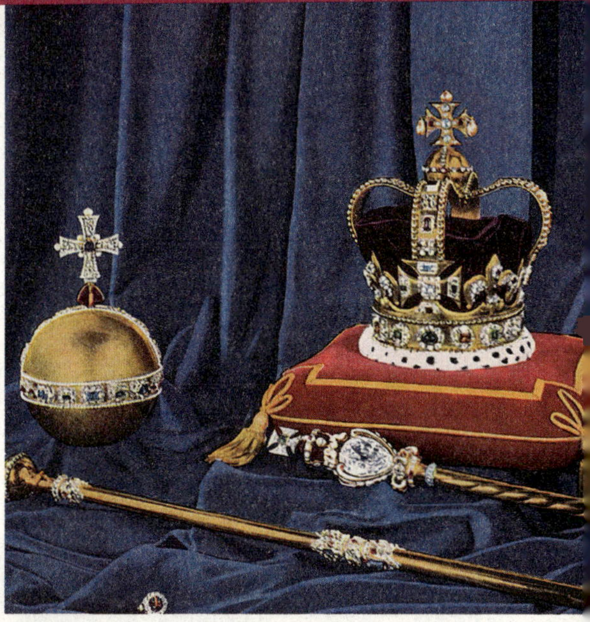

10 THINGS YOU NEVER KNEW ABOUT CORONATIONS

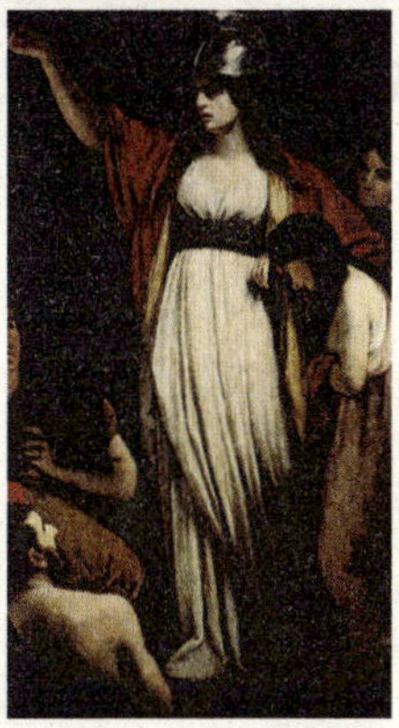

1 The earliest recorded coronation is the one held for Ancient British queen **BOUDICA** in 55 AD. The event took place in Camulodunum, with thousands of Brittonic tribespeople flocking to the town – now modern-day Colchester – buying commemorative beakers, plates and tea towels. A 2,000-year-old cruet set marking the ceremony, emblazoned with an image of the warrior queen's face and her iconic knife-wheeled chariot, turned up recently on an episode of *The Antiques Roadshow*, where pottery expert Henry Sandon valued it between £25 and £40 for insurance purposes.

2 TV technology has come a long way since the 1953 coronation of **ELIZABETH II** was broadcast in grainy, black-and-white. For **KING CHARLES III**'s crowning in May, the BBC will employ **TWO HUNDRED** state-of-the-art drones soaring around Westminster Abbey, capturing high-definition close-ups of both the participants and attendees. Additionally, The Crown of St Edward and the Archbishop of Canterbury's mitre will both be fitted with 'Go-Pro' cameras, giving royal watchers intimate access to the monarch and primate's viewpoints throughout proceedings on iPlayer via the 'red button'.

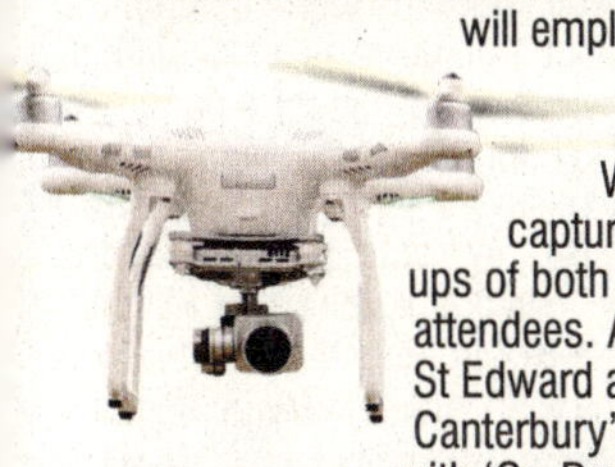

3 The smallest ever coronation took place in 1472, for history's smallest monarch – **KING CALVIN I**. The pint-sized royal wore a stately robe no bigger than a pocket handkerchief and carried a sceptre the size of a cocktail stick. Perched upon a throne roughly as big as an open baseball glove, a beer-bottle-top-sized crown was placed upon his head using tweezers. Unfortunately, as well as being Britain's shortest monarch in stature, King Calvin also holds the record for the shortest reign. Whilst walking down the steps of Westminster Abbey after the ceremony, the diminutive King was accidentally trodden on and killed by the Archbishop of Canterbury.

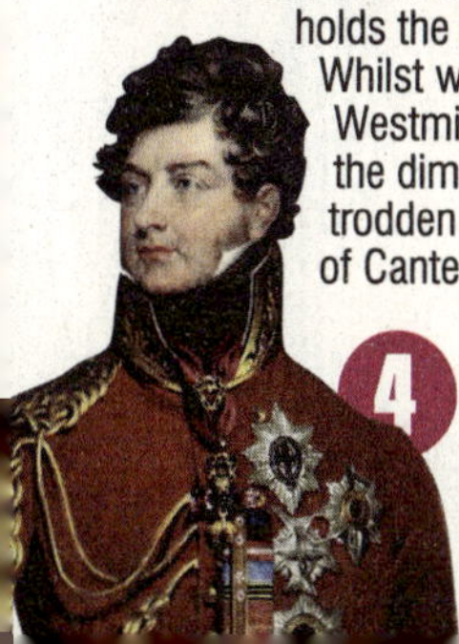

4 The coronation of **KING GEORGE IV** in 1821 fell on April Fools' Day, and the King's cheeky brother William rose early to stretch clingfilm over his sibling's chamber pot. When George nipped for a slash just prior to the beginning of the ceremony, he inevitably splashed urine all over the red velvet Supertunica robe of state. With no time to change before the event, the King had to undertake the entire five-hour engagement wearing piss-spattered regalia. "Contemporary sources report that George had a face like a slapped arse throughout," says TV historian Dan Snow. However, it was William that ended up red-faced in the long run, when it was later discovered that clingfilm wasn't actually invented until 1933 – more than a century after his prank!

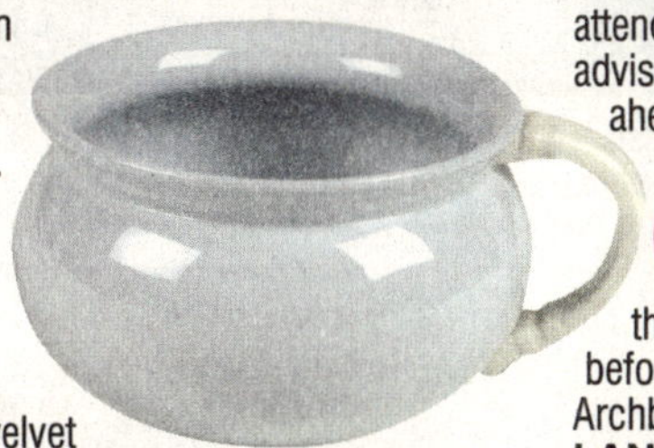

5 Contrary to popular belief, not everyone with the word 'King' in their name has undergone a coronation. Iconic horror author Stephen King never had one, and neither did slap bass maestro Mark King out of Level 42. Former Bank of England governor Sir Mervyn King underwent a ceremony at Buckingham Palace in 2014 when he was appointed to the Order of the Garter, but that was in no sense a coronation. In fact, it is only people with the **FIRST** name 'King' – such as King Henry VIII, King Edward VI and King Charles III – who have coronations.

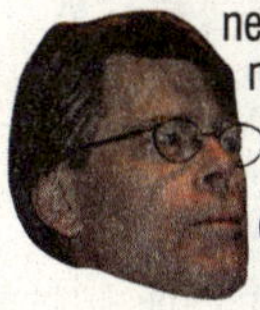

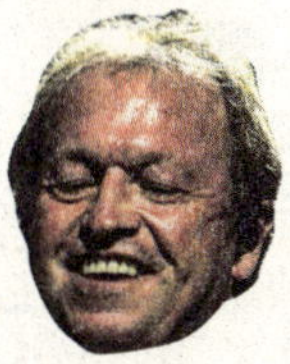

6 Except for American film director King Vidor, who hasn't. And giant-cocked porn legend King Dong.

7 According to the Magna Carta, it is an act of **TREASON** to break wind during a British coronation. The law was passed following the Coronation of **QUEEN BERENGARIA OF NAVARRE** in 1191, during which the Lord Chancellor **SIR WILLIAM LONGCHAMP** loudly dropped his guts three times – once during the oath, and twice more at the anointing. Longchamp was tried and executed soon afterwards, and coronations became strict 'no-guff zones' from then on. It is unlikely that executions would ensue today if a guest were to let out a little Tommy Squeaker, but everyone attending Charles III's crowning in May would be well advised to avoid sprouts, Tizer and Chicken Tonight ahead of entering the Abbey.

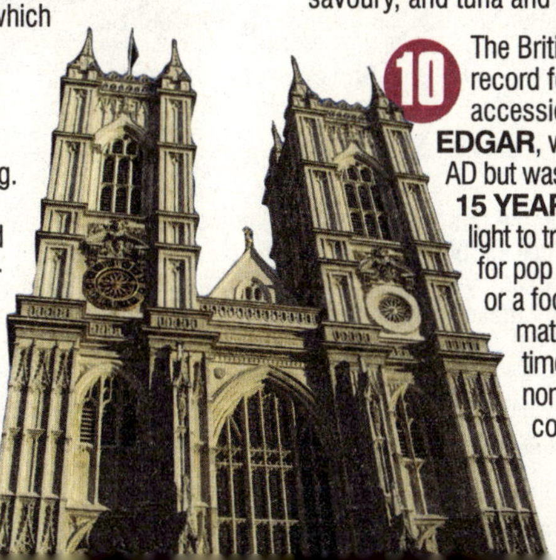

8 Everyone's favourite bit of the coronation is the anointing, in which the King or Queen-to-be is daubed with Holy Oil by the Archbishop of Canterbury. However, minutes before **GEORGE VI**'s crowning in 1936, Archbishop **COSMO LANG** looked in the cupboard and found they were completely out of Holy Chrism Oil! The quick-thinking cleric loaded the ceremonial Ampulla vessel with some oil from the chip pan in the Abbey kitchen and the ceremony got underway. "I could tell George suspected something as I smeared chip fat all over him," Lang later wrote in his memoirs. "We managed to keep a straight face during the gig, but all us bishops was pissing ourselves in the vestry afterwards."

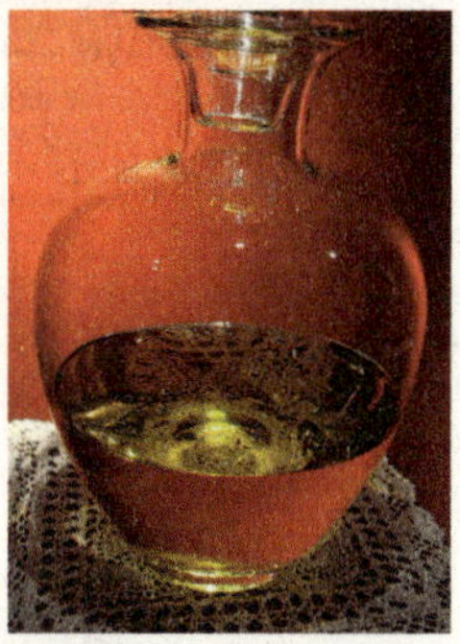

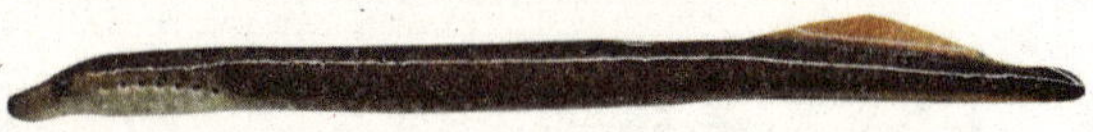

9 Coronation Chicken, created for Queen Elizabeth II's crowning in 1953, was not the first sandwich filling to be invented in honour of a monarch's ascension. Back in 1100, to mark the reign of **KING HENRY I**, a new dish dubbed 'Coronation Lamprey' was unveiled. Commemorating the King's love of the parasitic jawless freshwater fish, the recipe consisted of cream, raisins, Oriental spices and large chunks of boiled lamprey. The dish proved a hit with the medieval British public and became the nation's favourite sandwich filling. But in 1135, Henry died after eating a surfeit of it, and its popularity fell, quickly being overtaken by egg mayonnaise, cheese savoury, and tuna and sweetcorn.

10 The British monarch who holds the record for longest gap between accession and coronation is **KING EDGAR**, who acceded to the throne in 957 AD but wasn't crowned until a staggering **15 YEARS** later! That's enough time for light to travel 87,985,440,000,000 miles, for pop star Sting to achieve 8 orgasms, or a football team to play 87,600 matches, assuming that there is no time added on for stoppages, or that none of them are cup games which could go into extra time.

It'll be Alright on the Night!

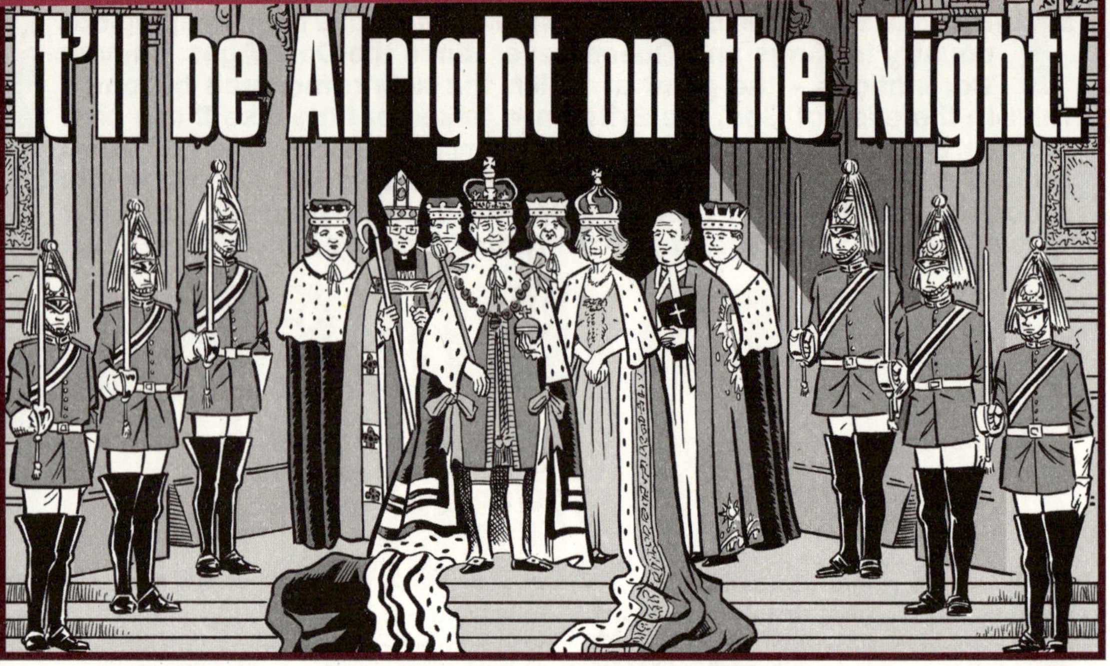

THE coronation of the monarch is a ceremony that has always been planned in meticulous detail. The crowning of His Majesty King Charles III is no exception, with every aspect being rehearsed and rehearsed, with all eventualities prepared for. As a result, the expectation is that on May 6th, the ceremony will run like a well-oiled Swiss clock.

But is it more a hope than an expectation? Can anyone prepare for every eventuality, every unforeseen event? The ceremony relies on hundreds of people, all working together and knowing their part, and human beings are fallible. The fact is that many things can go wrong on the day, and as Sod's law states, "Anything that can go wrong, will go wrong." It's likely that the coronation ceremony will be beset by problems and awash with slip-ups.

1

THE CORONATION PROCESSION will begin at 10:43 when the King and Queen Consort-to-be leave Buckingham Palace for the mile-long journey to Westminster Abbey. It is timed to perfection so that the golden coach arrives at 10:58, with the royal couple alighting and taking two minutes to walk up the Abbey steps and through the doors as Big Ben strikes 11:00. It seems like nothing could possibly go wrong, but it would take just one inconsiderate delivery driver to double park his van whilst making a drop to hold up the coronation party. Blind to the King's demands to "Move the bloody thing," the procession would have no choice but to wait until the driver delivers his parcel and moves off. The procession could make up the time, but the disappointment of the crowd lining the route as the King and Queen hurry by at breakneck speed would be huge, and a bad start to the day.

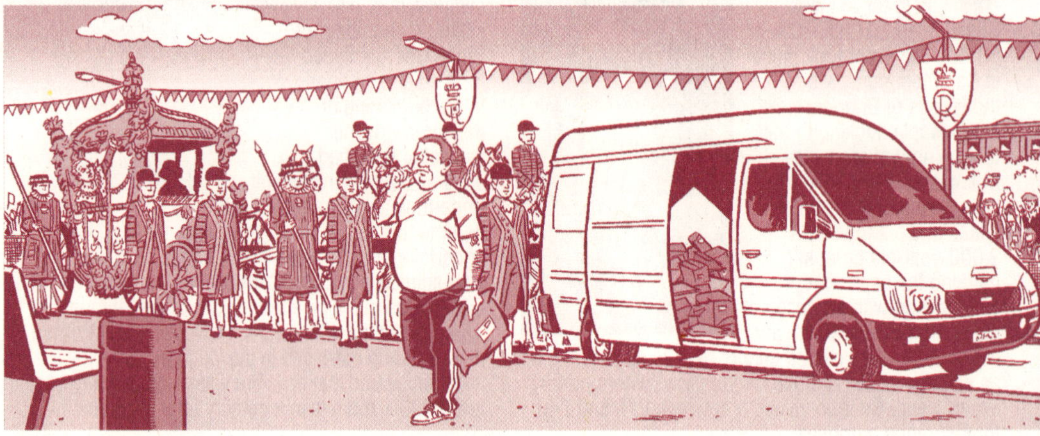

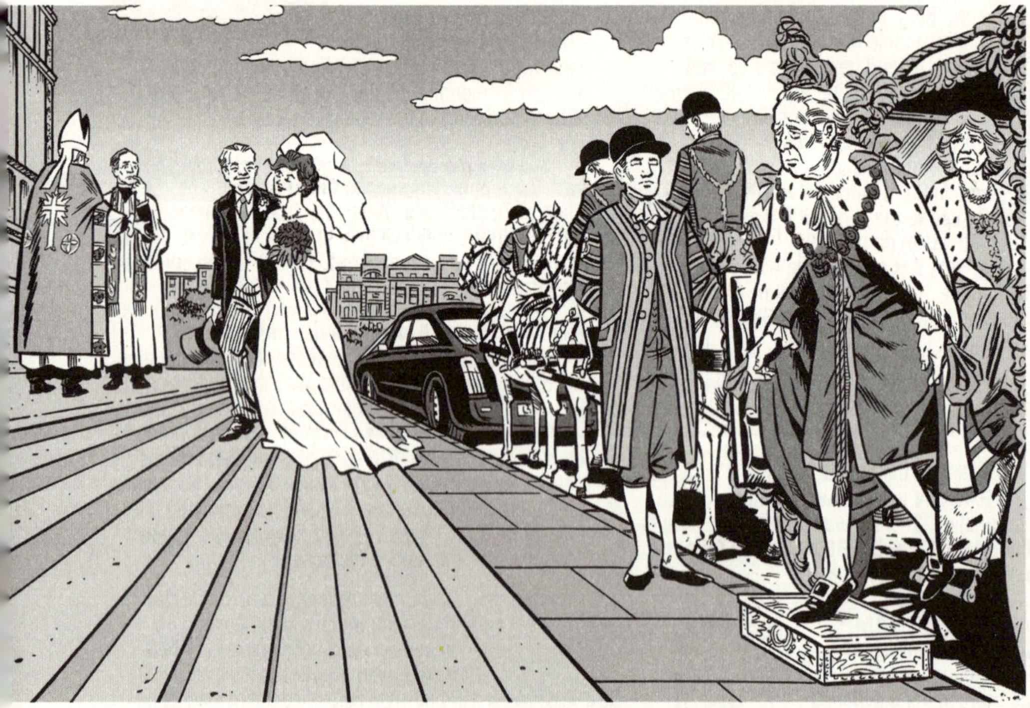

2

IN ALL LIKELIHOOD, the couple will arrive at the iconic steps of Westminster Abbey spot on time. But that is where their problems may begin. It could be that a long-standing booking for a wedding has been overlooked by the reservation department in the excitement of preparing for the coronation. Human beings make mistakes and it could well be that the Abbey has been double-booked on Saturday 6th May. Stepping out of the royal carriage to find a bridal party halfway up the steps to the door would certainly be a huge fly in the ointment. The Coronation could be held in the afternoon after the wedding is over, but that will leave the expected 1,500 invited guests milling around wondering whether to go back home, nip for a drink or just hang around outside the Abbey for a couple of hours.

3

A CEREMONY of such majesty would be nothing without the mighty and sonorous 84-stop Abbey organ thundering out the music. The procession making its way slowly down the aisle to the sound of William Walton's regal and brilliant *Crown Imperial in C Major* will show the world that nobody does pomp and pageantry like the British. But we've all had a plumber fail to come round when he says he will, or waited in for a parcel that never arrived. What if the organist booked for the event fails to turn up? The Archbishop of Canterbury would make an announcement asking if anyone in the congregation could play the piano, but it's likely that anyone who could would have a very limited repertoire. The King and Queen consort walking down the aisle to the tune of *Chopsticks*, or Scott Joplin's *The Entertainer* would cast Britain in a very poor light.

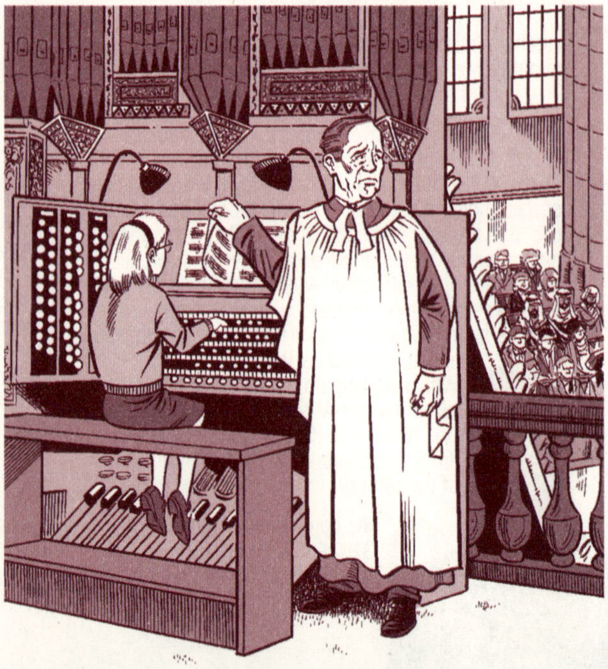

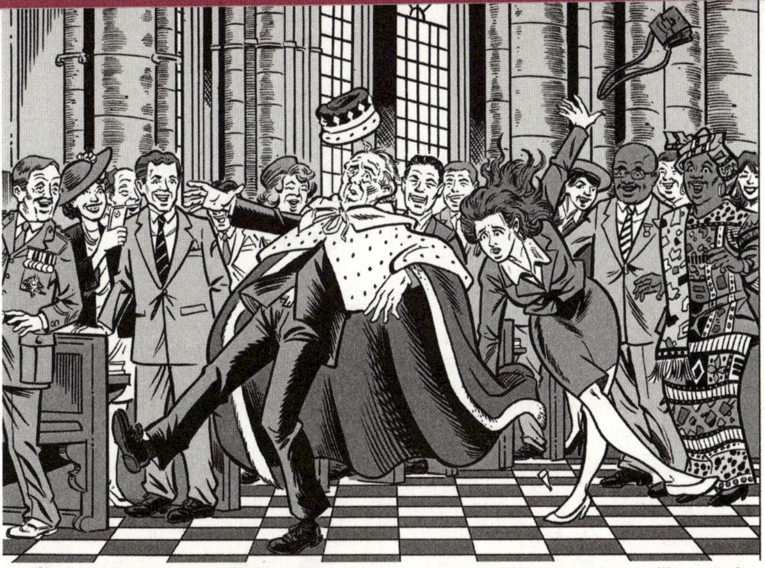

4 **WITH 1,500 GUESTS,** many of whom will be wearing trailing ermine robes, it's a pound to a penny that an accident will happen at some point. Stepping on a trailing ceremonial garment could cause the wearer to be jerked back and fall arse over tit. And whilst this would provide a moment of levity – not to mention £250 from *You've Been Framed* for anyone lucky enough to have caught it on their phone – it would spoil the solemnity of the occasion. In addition, with 750 women in the Abbey, many of whom will be wearing high heeled shoes specially bought for the occasion, you can be sure at least one of them is going to go down like Bambi on ice. Anyone walking out of the Abbey barefooted, carrying a pair of broken heels and looking on their phone for the nearest branch of Mister Minit will lower the tone of the occasion immeasurably.

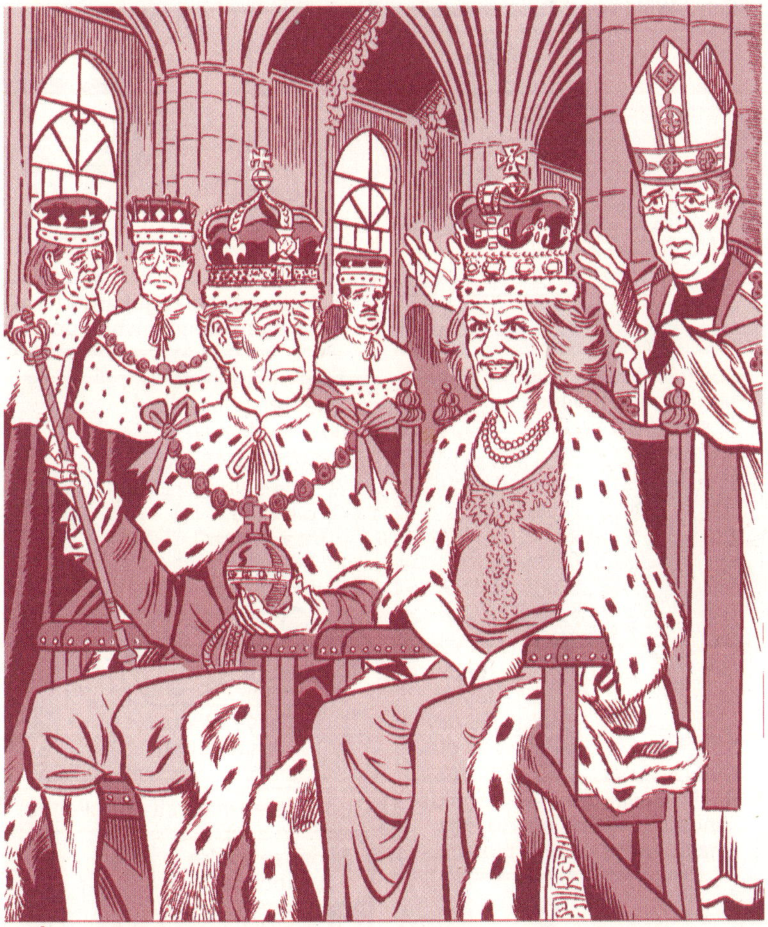

6 **THE 'MONEY SHOT'** of the coronation ceremony must surely be when Archbishop of Canterbury Dr Justin Welby places the crown upon the monarch's head, and it is such a simple act that you would think that nothing could go wrong. But there will actually be *three crowns* at the ceremony. Charles will be crowned with St Edward's Crown during the ceremony and leave the Abbey wearing the Imperial State Crown. Camilla meanwhile will have the Crown of Queen Mary solemnly laid on her bonce. But what if the Archbishop picks up the wrong one? Mixing up the order of Charles's crowns would be no big deal, but should he coronate Camilla with St Edward's Crown by accident, she would become the reigning monarch from that second onwards. After waiting for 70 years to sit on the throne, Charles would see it snatched away at the last second, making him once again a mere prince. Let's hope that the pressure does not get to Dr Welby.

5 **CHRISM,** used to anoint the monarch, is a special blend of oils and spices. The oil used for King Charles's coronation was mixed in the Holy Land and blessed by His Beatitude Patriarch Theophilos III and the Anglican Archbishop in Jerusalem, The Most Reverend Hosam Naoum. This sacred and wondrous balm infers Kingship or Queenship on all that it touches and as such, it will never have been put in rabbits' eyes or tested dermatologically on humans. So nobody knows if it will cause an allergic reaction when smeared on the monarch's skin. If it does, the reaction could be so severe that King Charles could go into anaphylactic shock and have to be stabbed with an epipen. It is highly unlikely, of course, but it cannot be ruled out.

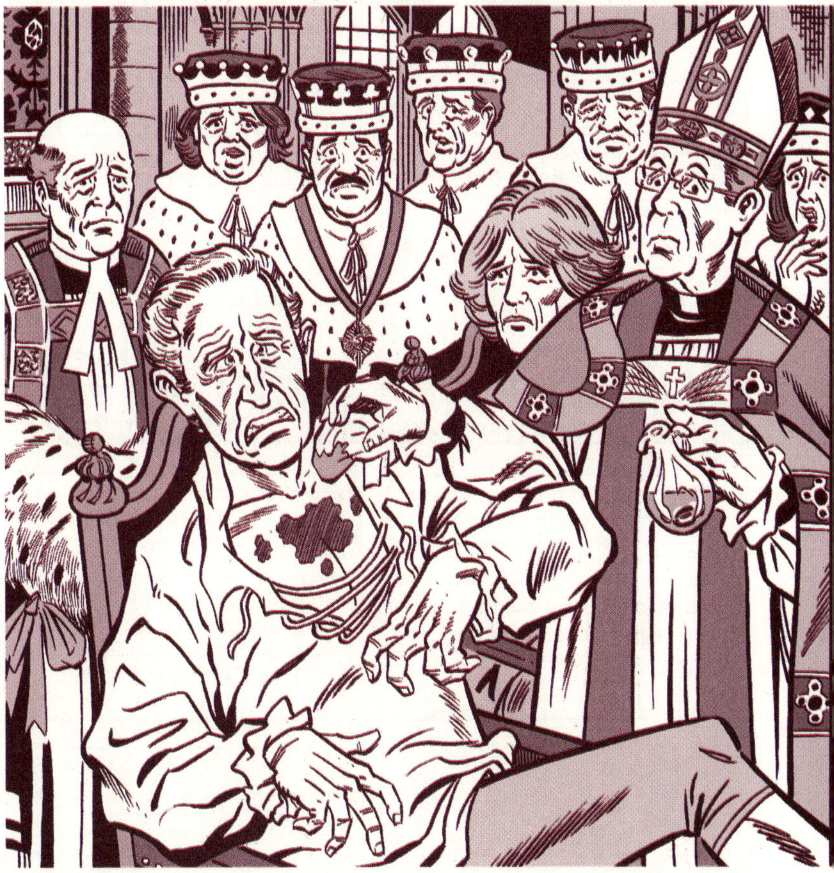

7 **EVER SINCE** the Anglo Saxon King Æthelstan was crowned King of the English in 924AD, the line of succession has been hotly disputed. Battles have been fought, usurpers thwarted and titles have been grabbed as pretenders denounced the monarch and declared their claim on the throne. For the last 400 years, we have had a bloodless succession of kings and queens. But there are still people who believe they have a greater claim to the throne than our current monarch. When the Archbishop reaches the part of the ceremony where he says "If anyone knows of any lawful impediment why Prince Charles should not be crowned King, let them speak now or forever hold their peace," there is a slim chance that a pretender to the throne might speak up. That descendant of Richard III in Australia, David Cameron, or Eddie Tudor-Pole, lead singer out of Tenpole Tudor, may feel they have more right to the throne. Without the backing of an army, they are unlikely to succeed, but halting the coronation in such a way would be a great embarrassment.

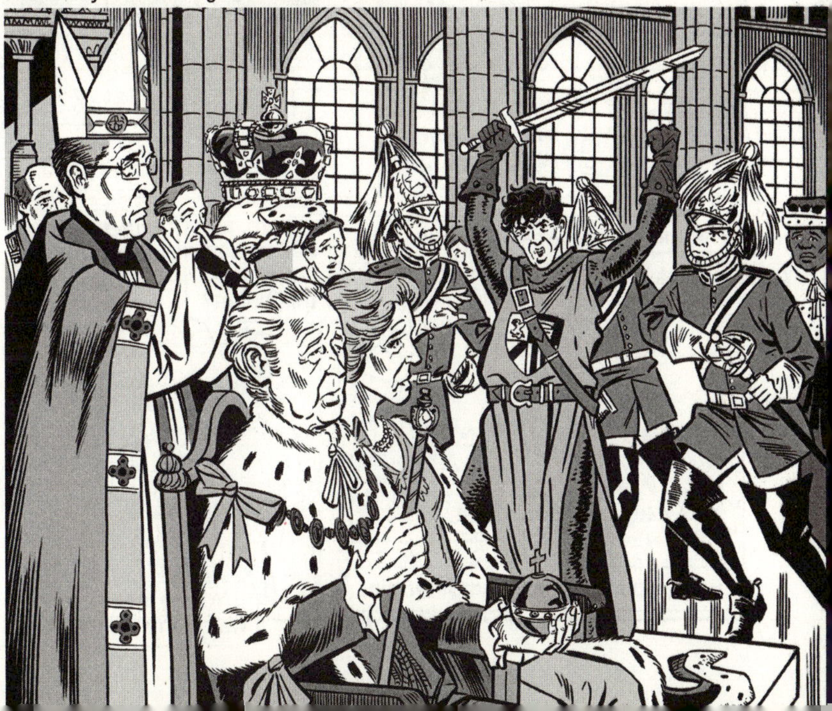

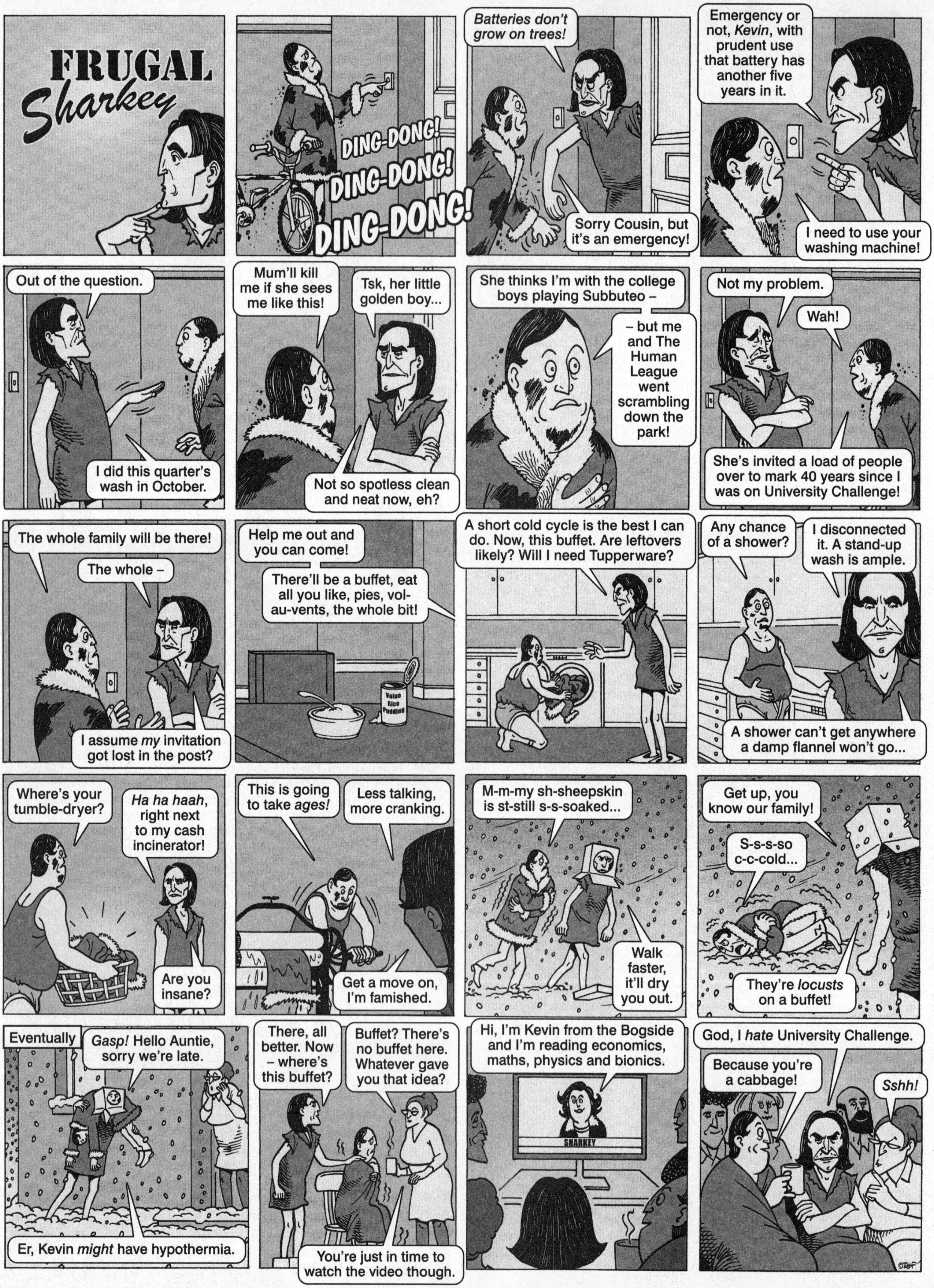
FRUGAL Sharkey
DING-DONG! DING-DONG! DING-DONG!
Batteries don't grow on trees!
Sorry Cousin, but it's an emergency!
Emergency or not, Kevin, with prudent use that battery has another five years in it.
I need to use your washing machine!
Out of the question.
I did this quarter's wash in October.
Mum'll kill me if she sees me like this!
Tsk, her little golden boy...
Not so spotless clean and neat now, eh?
She thinks I'm with the college boys playing Subbuteo –
– but me and The Human League went scrambling down the park!
Not my problem.
Wah!
She's invited a load of people over to mark 40 years since I was on University Challenge!
The whole family will be there!
The whole –
I assume my invitation got lost in the post?
Help me out and you can come!
There'll be a buffet, eat all you like, pies, vol-au-vents, the whole bit!
Value Rice Pudding
A short cold cycle is the best I can do. Now, this buffet. Are leftovers likely? Will I need Tupperware?
Any chance of a shower?
I disconnected it. A stand-up wash is ample.
A shower can't get anywhere a damp flannel won't go...
Where's your tumble-dryer?
Ha ha haah, right next to my cash incinerator!
Are you insane?
This is going to take ages!
Less talking, more cranking.
Get a move on, I'm famished.
M-m-my sh-sheepskin is st-still s-s-soaked...
Walk faster, it'll dry you out.
Get up, you know our family!
S-s-s-so c-c-cold...
They're locusts on a buffet!
Eventually
Gasp! Hello Auntie, sorry we're late.
Er, Kevin might have hypothermia.
There, all better. Now – where's this buffet?
Buffet? There's no buffet here. Whatever gave you that idea?
You're just in time to watch the video though.
Hi, I'm Kevin from the Bogside and I'm reading economics, maths, physics and bionics.
SHARKEY
God, I hate University Challenge.
Because you're a cabbage!
Sshh!

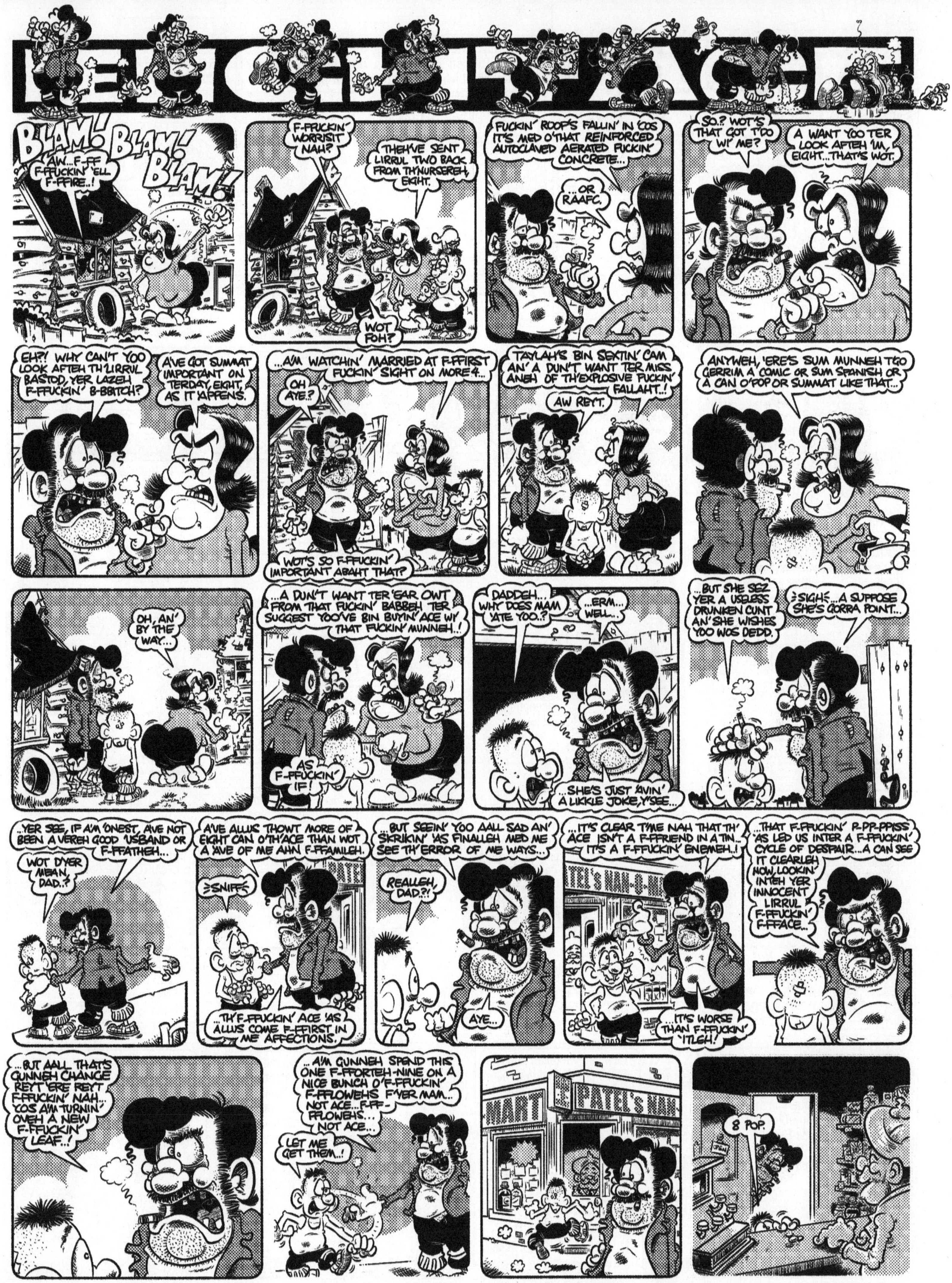
BLAM! BLAM! BLAM! BLAM!
AW...F-FF F-FFUCKIN' 'ELL F-FFIRE..!
F-FFUCKIN' WORRISIT NAH?
THEH'VE SENT LIRRUL TWO BACK FROM TH'NURSEREH, EIGHT.
WOT FOH?
FUCKIN' ROOF'S FALLIN' IN 'COS IT'S MED O'THAT REINFORCED AUTOCLAVED AERATED FUCKIN' CONCRETE...
...OR RAAFC.
SO..? WOT'S THAT GOT T'DO WI' ME?
A WANT YOO TER LOOK AFTEH 'IM, EIGHT...THAT'S WOT.
EH?! WHY CAN'T YOO LOOK AFTEH TH'LIRRUL BASTOD, YER LAZEH F-FFUCKIN' B-BBITCH?
A'VE GOT SUMMAT IMPORTANT ON TERDAY, EIGHT, AS IT 'APPENS.
...A'M WATCHIN' MARRIED AT F-FFIRST FUCKIN' SIGHT ON MORE 4...
OH AYE..?
WOT'S SO F-FFUCKIN' IMPORTANT ABAHT THAT?
TAYLAH'S BIN SEXTIN' CAM AN' A DUN'T WANT TER MISS ANEH OF TH'EXPLOSIVE FUCKIN' FALLAHT..!
AW REYT.
ANYWEH, 'ERE'S SUM MUNNEH T'GO GERRIM A COMIC OR SUM SPANISH OR A CAN O'POP OR SUMMAT LIKE THAT...
OH, AN' BY THE WAY...
...A DUN'T WANT TER 'EAR OWT FROM THAT FUCKIN' BABBEH TER SUGGEST YOO'VE BIN BUYIN' ACE WI' THAT FUCKIN' MUNNEH..!
AS F-FFUCKIN' IF!
DADDEH... WHY DOES MAM 'ATE YOO..?
...ERM... WELL...
...SHE'S JUST 'AVIN' A LIKKLE JOKE, Y'SEE...
...BUT SHE SEZ YER A USELESS DRUNKEN CUNT AN' SHE WISHES YOO WOS DEDD.
SIGH ...A SUPPOSE SHE'S GORRA POINT...
...YER SEE, IF A'M 'ONEST, A'VE NOT BEEN A VEREH GOOD 'USBAND OR F-FFATHEH...
WOT D'YER MEAN, DAD..?
A'VE ALLUS THOWT MORE OF EIGHT CAN O'TH'ACE THAN WOT A 'AVE OF ME AHN F-FFAMILEH.
SNIFF
...TH' F-FFUCKIN' ACE 'AS ALLUS COME F-FFIRST IN ME AFFECTIONS.
...BUT SEEIN' YOO AALL SAD AN' SKRIKIN' 'AS FINALLEH MED ME SEE TH' ERROR OF ME WAYS...
REALLEH, DAD?!
AYE..
...IT'S CLEAR T'ME NAH THAT TH' ACE ISN'T A F-FFRIEND IN A TIN... IT'S A F-FFUCKIN' ENEMEH..!
PATEL'S NAN-O-M
...IT'S WORSE THAN F-FFUCKIN' 'ITLEH!
...THAT F-FFUCKIN' P-PP-PPISS 'AS LED US INTER A F-FFUCKIN' CYCLE OF DESPAIR...A CAN SEE IT CLEARLEH NOW, LOOKIN' INTEH YER INNOCENT LIRRUL F-FFUCKIN' F-FFACE..
...BUT AALL THAT'S GUNNEH CHANGE REYT 'ERE REYT F-FFUCKIN' NAH... 'COS A'M TURNIN' OVEH A NEW F-FFUCKIN' LEAF..!
...A'M GUNNEH SPEND THIS ONE F-FFORTEH-NINE ON A NICE BUNCH O'F-FFUCKIN' F-FFLOWEHS F'YER MAM... NOT ACE...F-FF-FFLOWEHS... NOT ACE...
LET ME GET THEM..!
MART
PATEL'S NAN
8 POP.

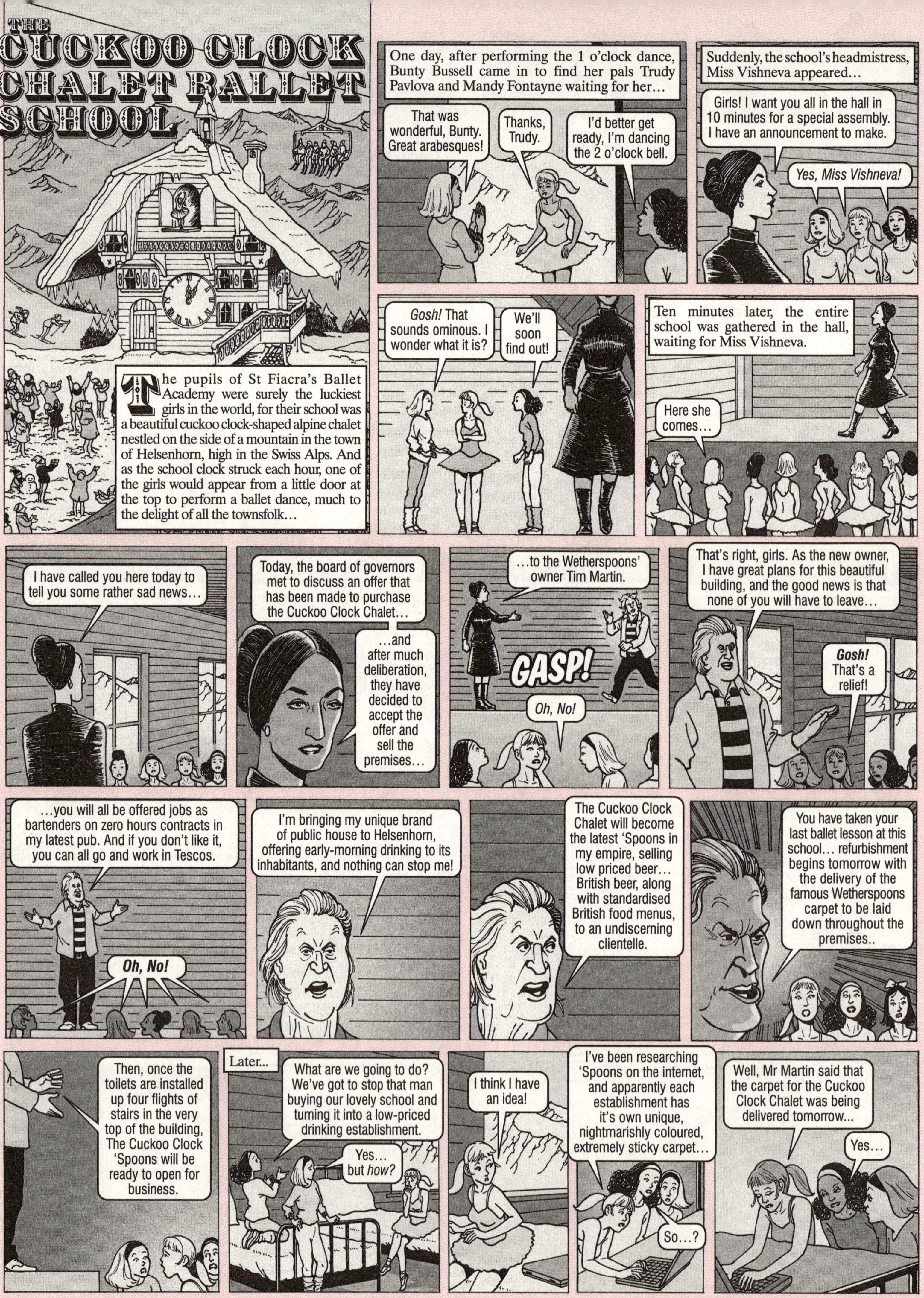

THE CUCKOO CLOCK CHALET BALLET SCHOOL
The pupils of St Fiacra's Ballet Academy were surely the luckiest girls in the world, for their school was a beautiful cuckoo clock-shaped alpine chalet nestled on the side of a mountain in the town of Helsenhorn, high in the Swiss Alps. And as the school clock struck each hour, one of the girls would appear from a little door at the top to perform a ballet dance, much to the delight of all the townsfolk…
One day, after performing the 1 o'clock dance, Bunty Bussell came in to find her pals Trudy Pavlova and Mandy Fontayne waiting for her…
That was wonderful, Bunty. Great arabesques!
Thanks, Trudy.
I'd better get ready, I'm dancing the 2 o'clock bell.
Suddenly, the school's headmistress, Miss Vishneva appeared…
Girls! I want you all in the hall in 10 minutes for a special assembly. I have an announcement to make.
Yes, Miss Vishneva!
Gosh! That sounds ominous. I wonder what it is?
We'll soon find out!
Ten minutes later, the entire school was gathered in the hall, waiting for Miss Vishneva.
Here she comes…
I have called you here today to tell you some rather sad news…
Today, the board of governors met to discuss an offer that has been made to purchase the Cuckoo Clock Chalet…
…and after much deliberation, they have decided to accept the offer and sell the premises…
…to the Wetherspoons' owner Tim Martin.
GASP!
Oh, No!
That's right, girls. As the new owner, I have great plans for this beautiful building, and the good news is that none of you will have to leave…
Gosh! That's a relief!
…you will all be offered jobs as bartenders on zero hours contracts in my latest pub. And if you don't like it, you can all go and work in Tescos.
Oh, No!
I'm bringing my unique brand of public house to Helsenhorn, offering early-morning drinking to its inhabitants, and nothing can stop me!
The Cuckoo Clock Chalet will become the latest 'Spoons in my empire, selling low priced beer… British beer, along with standardised British food menus, to an undiscerning clientelle.
You have taken your last ballet lesson at this school… refurbishment begins tomorrow with the delivery of the famous Wetherspoons carpet to be laid down throughout the premises..
Then, once the toilets are installed up four flights of stairs in the very top of the building, The Cuckoo Clock 'Spoons will be ready to open for business.
Later...
What are we going to do? We've got to stop that man buying our lovely school and turning it into a low-priced drinking establishment.
Yes… but how?
I think I have an idea!
I've been researching 'Spoons on the internet, and apparently each establishment has it's own unique, nightmarishly coloured, extremely sticky carpet…
So…?
Well, Mr Martin said that the carpet for the Cuckoo Clock Chalet was being delivered tomorrow…
Yes…

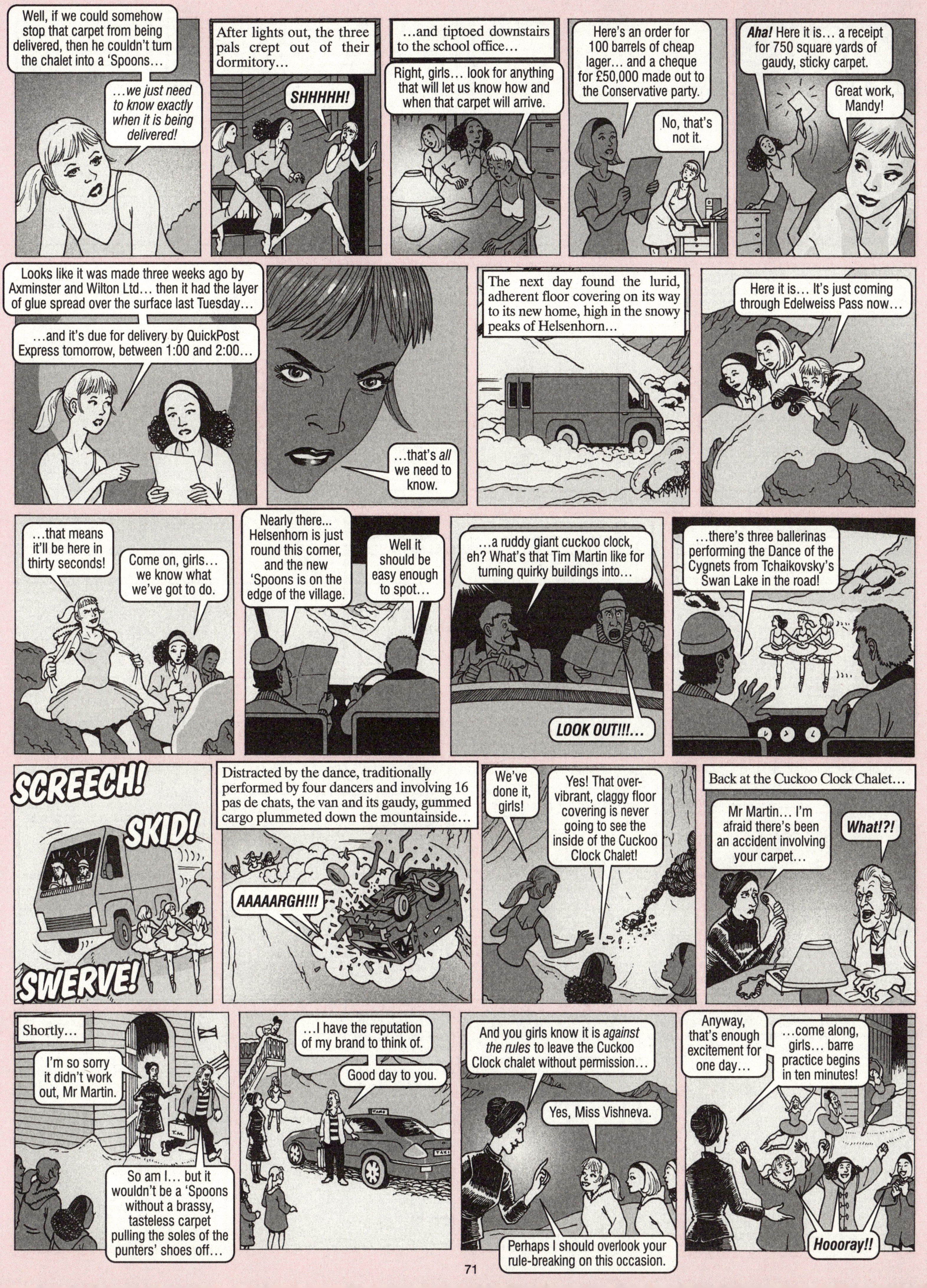
Well, if we could somehow stop that carpet from being delivered, then he couldn't turn the chalet into a 'Spoons…
…we just need to know exactly when it is being delivered!
After lights out, the three pals crept out of their dormitory…
SHHHHH!
…and tiptoed downstairs to the school office…
Right, girls… look for anything that will let us know how and when that carpet will arrive.
Here's an order for 100 barrels of cheap lager… and a cheque for £50,000 made out to the Conservative party.
No, that's not it.
Aha! Here it is… a receipt for 750 square yards of gaudy, sticky carpet.
Great work, Mandy!
Looks like it was made three weeks ago by Axminster and Wilton Ltd… then it had the layer of glue spread over the surface last Tuesday…
…and it's due for delivery by QuickPost Express tomorrow, between 1:00 and 2:00…
…that's all we need to know.
The next day found the lurid, adherent floor covering on its way to its new home, high in the snowy peaks of Helsenhorn…
Here it is… It's just coming through Edelweiss Pass now…
…that means it'll be here in thirty seconds!
Come on, girls… we know what we've got to do.
Nearly there... Helsenhorn is just round this corner, and the new 'Spoons is on the edge of the village.
Well it should be easy enough to spot…
…a ruddy giant cuckoo clock, eh? What's that Tim Martin like for turning quirky buildings into…
LOOK OUT!!!…
…there's three ballerinas performing the Dance of the Cygnets from Tchaikovsky's Swan Lake in the road!
SCREECH!
SKID!
SWERVE!
Distracted by the dance, traditionally performed by four dancers and involving 16 pas de chats, the van and its gaudy, gummed cargo plummeted down the mountainside…
AAAAARGH!!!
We've done it, girls!
Yes! That over-vibrant, claggy floor covering is never going to see the inside of the Cuckoo Clock Chalet!
Back at the Cuckoo Clock Chalet…
Mr Martin… I'm afraid there's been an accident involving your carpet…
What!?!
Shortly…
I'm so sorry it didn't work out, Mr Martin.
So am I… but it wouldn't be a 'Spoons without a brassy, tasteless carpet pulling the soles of the punters' shoes off…
…I have the reputation of my brand to think of.
Good day to you.
And you girls know it is against the rules to leave the Cuckoo Clock chalet without permission…
Yes, Miss Vishneva.
Perhaps I should overlook your rule-breaking on this occasion.
Anyway, that's enough excitement for one day…
…come along, girls… barre practice begins in ten minutes!
Hoooray!!

FIRST LIVING STATUE ON MARS
FIFTY METRES... TWENTY METRES...
TEN...
FIVE...
NASA
MISSION CONTROL, WE HAVE TOUCH-DOWN!
EXTERNAL CHECKS HAVE BEEN COMPLETED
ROGERS IS NOW EXITING THE LANDING MODULE AND STEPPING ONTO THE BARREN MARTIAN LANDSCAPE...
THE ORANGE CRATE IS IN POSITION FOR DEPLOYMENT...
HE'S PUT OUT A HAT WITH A LITTLE MONEY ALREADY IN IT AND – YES! HOUSTON, HE IS STANDING TOTALLY STILL!
TODAY MAN HAS SLIPPED THE SURLY BONDS OF EARTH TO TREAD THE SOIL OF ANOTHER WORLD– AND PRETEND TO BE JUST A SCULPTURE OR WHATNOT!!!
WHAT A HISTORIC ACHIEVEMENT! THE BUSKING DATA HE IS COLLECTING FOR STREET PERFORMER SCIENCE HAS VINDICATED ALL THE DANGER AND DISCOMFORT
OF TRAVELLING 480 MILLION KM PAINTED COMPLETELY SILVER UNDERNEATH HIS SPACESUIT!
INCLUDING SUN-GLASSES AND A TIE WITH A WIRE THAT MAKES IT LOOK LIKE IT'S WINDY!
...YEP!
HE'S DEFINITELY STANDING THERE!
BUT – WAIT, HANG ON! HOUSTON, I'M READING AN ASTRONAUT FROM THE EUROPEAN SPACE AGENCY'S BASE AT JEZERO CRATER
COMING BACK FROM THE SHOPS!
SHE'S GIVEN HER SON WHAT APPEARS TO BE SOME SPARE CHANGE...
HE'S APPROACHING THE HAT ANNNND...
WE HAVE A 1-EURO COIN! REPEAT, WE HAVE A 1-EURO COIN! MISSION CONTROL, WE ARE GO!
AND THERE IT IS! WHAT HAD SEEMED TO BE AN INANIMATE FIGURE MADE OF SOLID STONE OR METAL HAS NOW SURPRISED THE BOY BY MOVING SLIGHTLY!
THIS SEVEN-MONTH, $230 BILLION MISSION HAS ALL BEEN WORTH IT, TO BRING A MOMENT OF WONDER AND DELIGHT TO A CHILD'S–
...NOPE, THE LITTLE BASTARD'S JUST CRYING.
STILL, WE ONLY NEED 229,999,999,999 MORE CUSTOMERS LIKE THAT AND THEN THE REST OF THE DAY'LL BE PURE PROFIT!
AND HERE COME SOME RUSSIAN COSMONAUTS AFTER SPACE PUB CLOSING TIME!
WHAT AN INSPIRING SIGHT... BACK ON OUR OWN TINY PLANET, TWO ADVERSARIAL NATIONS – BUT OUT HERE IN THE VASTNESS OF THE COSMOS MERELY FELLOW MEMBERS OF THE HUMAN RACE!
AND ONE OF THEM'S NUDGING THE CRATE WITH HIS FOOT FOR A LAUGH!
NOW HE'S PUTTING A CRISP PACKET ON ROGERS' SHOULDER
AND ANOTHER ONE'S PISSING IN HIS HAT
AND NOW THE CRISP GUY'S MIMING DOING HIM UP THE ARSE WHILE THE OTHER ONE FILMS IT ON HIS PHONE
AND THE THIRD ONE'S PINGING CHIPS AT HIS FACE!
TRULY A TESTAMENT TO THE SPIRIT OF ENDEAVOUR THAT UNI–
OOP – ONE OF THE CHIPS CRACKED HIS VISOR.
ROGERS' OXYGEN SUPPLY IS RAPIDLY DEPLETING AS HIS SUIT DECOMPRESSES IN THE THIN AND UNBREATHABLE MARTIAN ATMOSPHERE!
FORTUNATELY THE ENGINEERS AT NASA HAD THE FORESIGHT TO PLACE STRIPS OF MYLAR DUCT TAPE IN HIS RIGHT LEG POCKET FOR CRITICAL REPAIRS LIKE THIS!
BUT – DEAR GOD! SINCE NOBODY PUT ANY DOSH IN HIS HAT ROGERS CAN'T MOVE TO TAKE THEM OUT!
HE HAS JUST SECONDS OF AIR REMAINING!
MAYDAY! MAYDAY! HE'S LOSING CONSCIOUSNESS! HOUSTON, THE ONLY CHANCE TO SAVE THIS MISSION IS FOR ME TO LEAVE THE LANDER ON AN EMERGENCY MARSWALK – IF I CAN ONLY REACH HIS POSITION IN TIME!
I AM NOW TEN METRES AWAY!
FIVE!
FOUR! THREE! TWO–
MISSION CONTROL, I AM NOW PLAYING REACH BY S CLUB!
REPEAT, NOW PLAYING REACH BY S CLUB!
BUSKING HAS BEEN RESTORED!

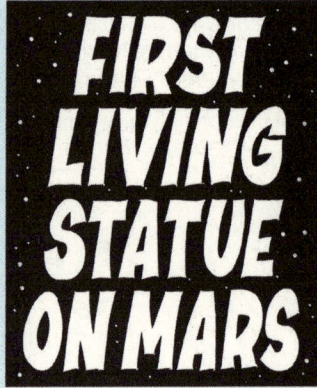

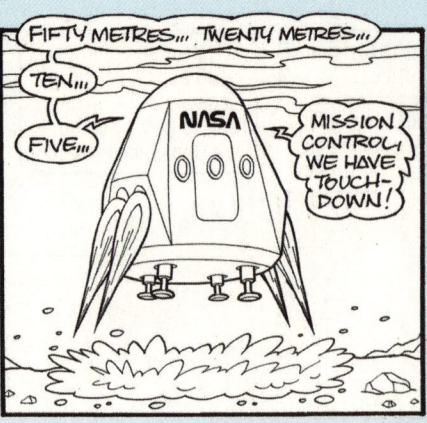

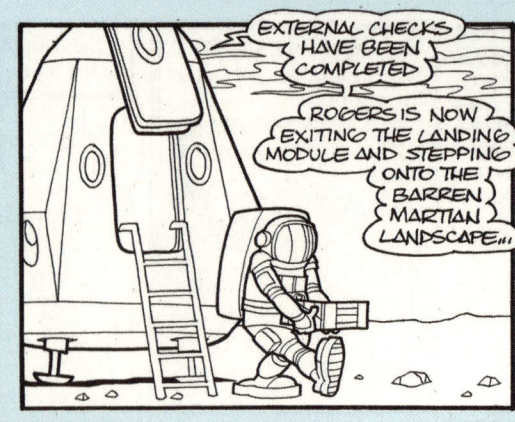

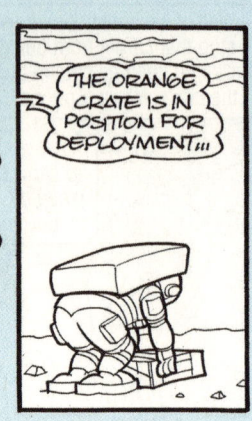

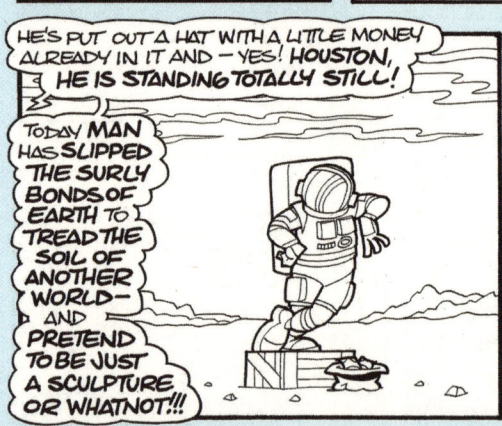

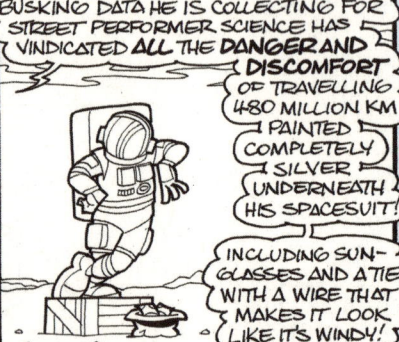

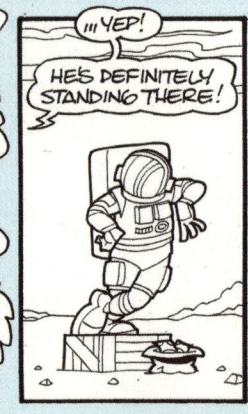

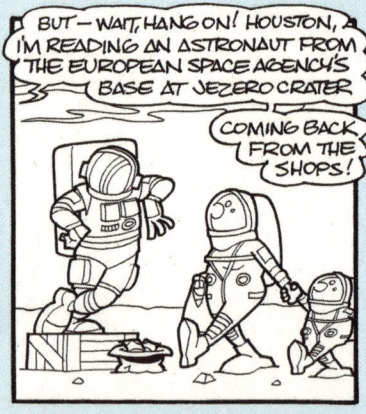

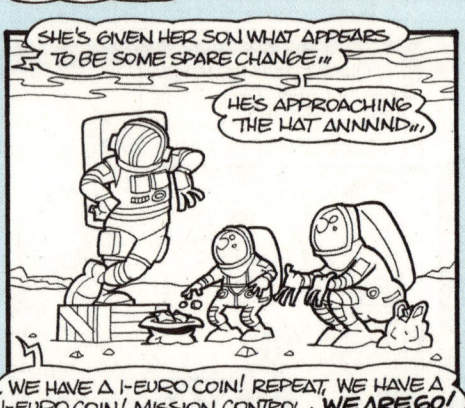

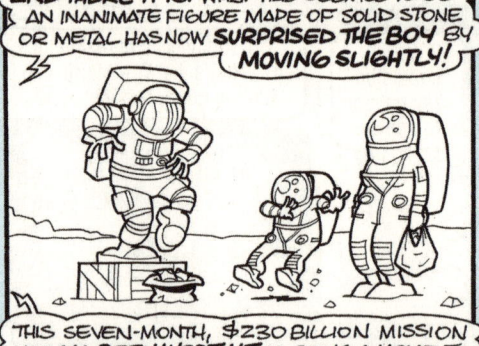

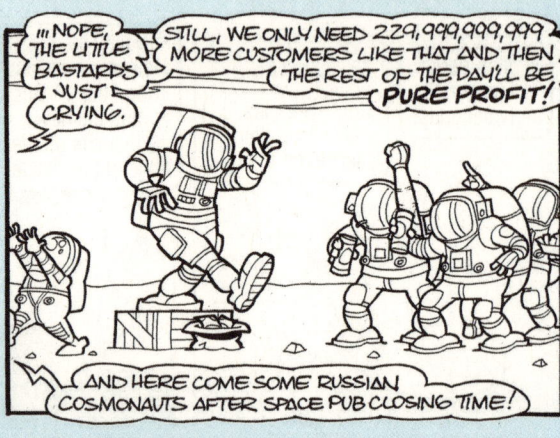

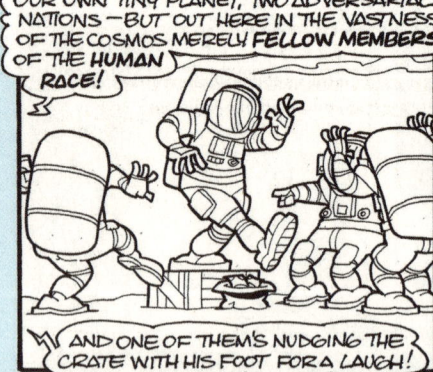

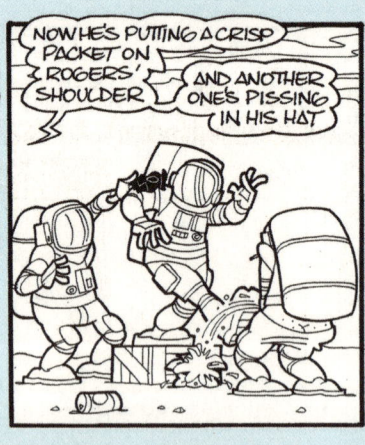

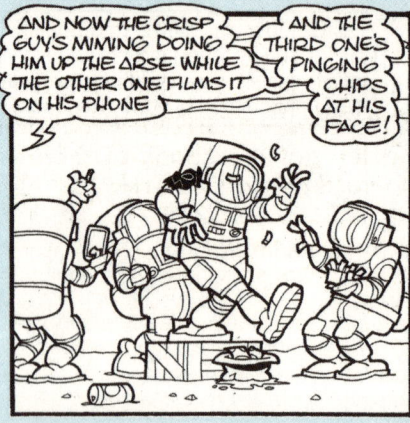

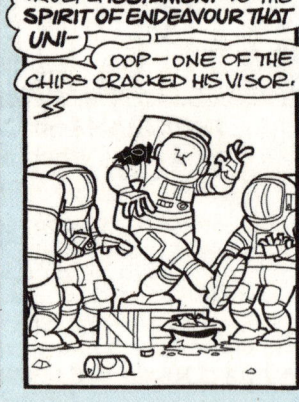

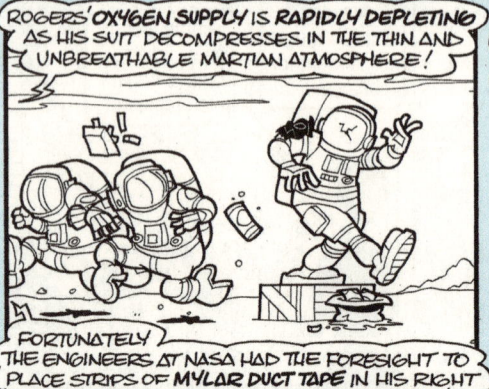

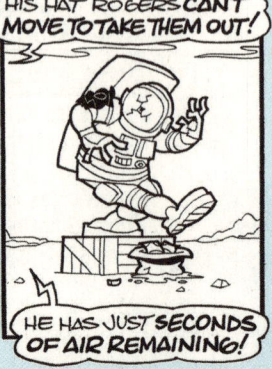

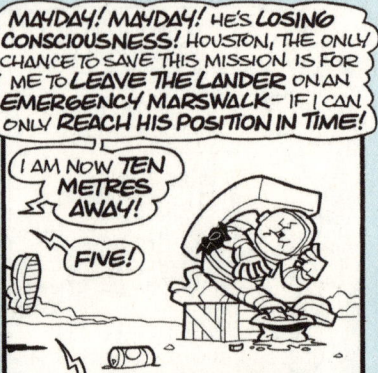

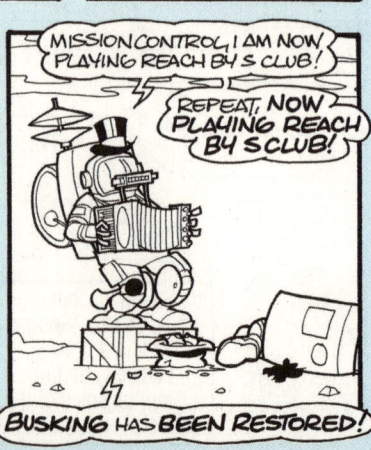

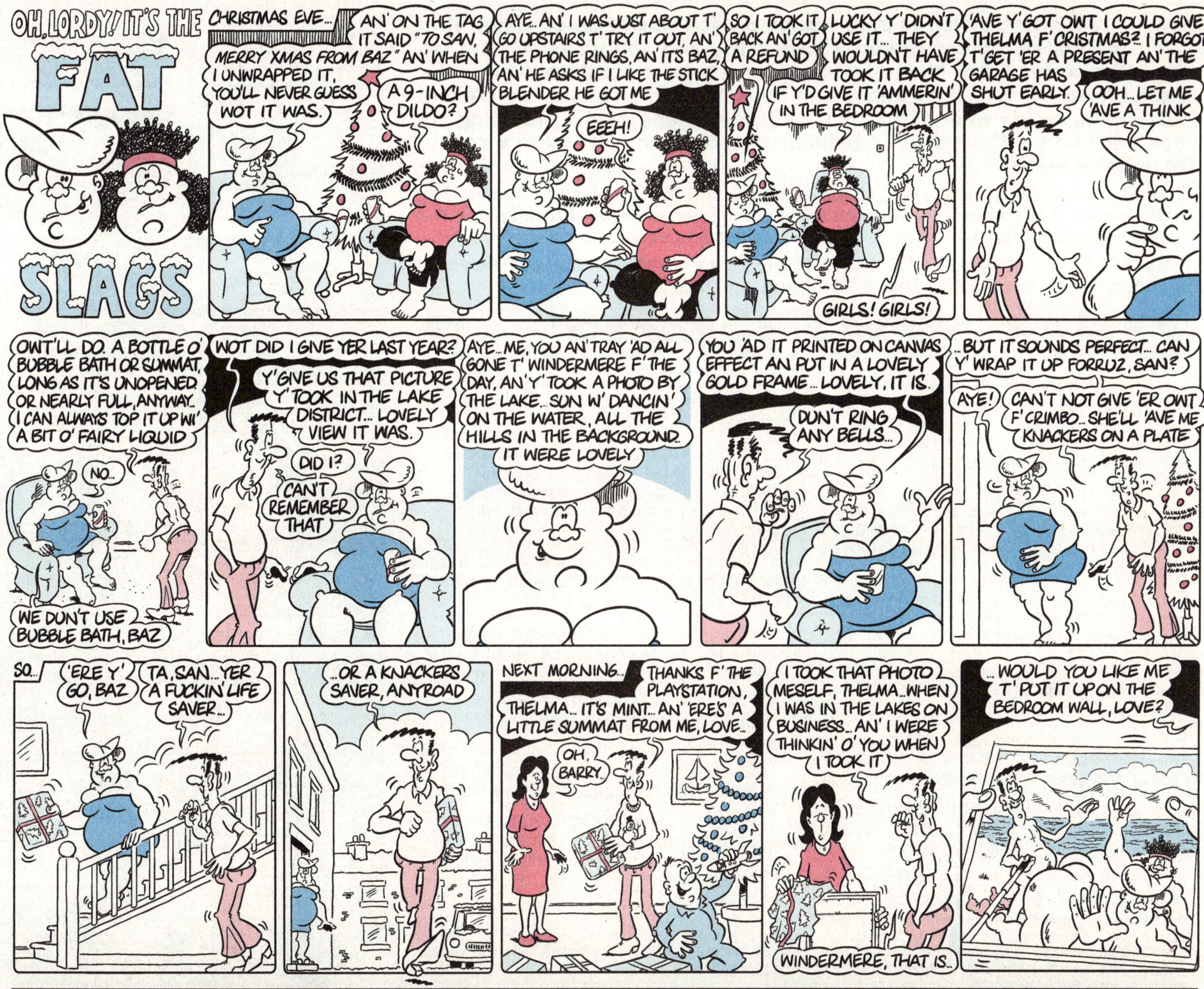

OH, LORDY! IT'S THE
FAT
SLAGS
CHRISTMAS EVE...
AN' ON THE TAG IT SAID "TO SAN, MERRY XMAS FROM BAZ" AN' WHEN I UNWRAPPED IT, YOU'LL NEVER GUESS WOT IT WAS.
A 9-INCH DILDO?
AYE.. AN' I WAS JUST ABOUT T' GO UPSTAIRS T' TRY IT OUT, AN' THE PHONE RINGS, AN' ITS BAZ, AN' HE ASKS IF I LIKE THE STICK BLENDER HE GOT ME
EEEH!
SO I TOOK IT BACK AN' GOT A REFUND
LUCKY Y' DIDN'T USE IT... THEY WOULDN'T HAVE TOOK IT BACK IF Y'D GIVE IT 'AMMERIN' IN THE BEDROOM
GIRLS! GIRLS!
'AVE Y' GOT OWT I COULD GIVE THELMA F' CRISTMAS? I FORGOT T' GET 'ER A PRESENT AN' THE GARAGE HAS SHUT EARLY.
OOH... LET ME 'AVE A THINK
OWT'LL DO. A BOTTLE O' BUBBLE BATH OR SUMMAT, LONG AS IT'S UNOPENED OR NEARLY FULL, ANYWAY.. I CAN ALWAYS TOP IT UP WI' A BIT O' FAIRY LIQUID
NO..
WE DON'T USE BUBBLE BATH, BAZ
WOT DID I GIVE YER LAST YEAR?
Y'GIVE US THAT PICTURE Y' TOOK IN THE LAKE DISTRICT... LOVELY VIEW IT WAS.
DID I?
CAN'T REMEMBER THAT
AYE.. ME, YOU AN' TRAY 'AD ALL GONE T' WINDERMERE F' THE DAY, AN' Y' TOOK A PHOTO BY THE LAKE.. SUN W' DANCIN' ON THE WATER, ALL THE HILLS IN THE BACKGROUND.. IT WERE LOVELY
YOU 'AD IT PRINTED ON CANVAS EFFECT AN PUT IN A LOVELY GOLD FRAME... LOVELY, IT IS.
DON'T RING ANY BELLS...
...BUT IT SOUNDS PERFECT... CAN Y' WRAP IT UP FORRUZ, SAN?
AYE!
CAN'T NOT GIVE 'ER OWT F' CRIMBO.. SHE'LL 'AVE ME KNACKERS ON A PLATE
SO...
'ERE Y' GO, BAZ
TA, SAN... YER A FUCKIN' LIFE SAVER...
...OR A KNACKERS SAVER, ANYROAD
NEXT MORNING...
THANKS F' THE PLAYSTATION, THELMA... IT'S MINT... AN' 'ERE'S A LITTLE SUMMAT FROM ME, LOVE..
OH, BARRY.
I TOOK THAT PHOTO MESELF, THELMA.. WHEN I WAS IN THE LAKES ON BUSINESS... AN' I WERE THINKIN' O' YOU WHEN I TOOK IT
WINDERMERE, THAT IS...
...WOULD YOU LIKE ME T' PUT IT UP ON THE BEDROOM WALL, LOVE?

TURN-UP FOR THE BOOK

Library book returned almost millennium late

LIBRARIANS in Crawley got the shock of their lives yesterday when an overdue book was returned to the town's library – over 900 years after it was borrowed.

The first edition copy of the *Domesday Book* was taken out of the library in November 1086 by Silas Glass on a two-week loan. But it was never returned and was assumed to be lost. However, it re-appeared 936 years later in a box of junk owned by Frank Glass, a 42nd generation descendent of Tyler's.

The book, by William the Conqueror, was published in 1086 and became an instant best seller, despite 95% of the population being illiterate at the time.

"I was going through some of my late dad's stuff in the garage when I came across the book," said builder Frank. "It was due to be returned by my ancestor on November 28th 1087, but he must have forgot, or died of the plague or something."

"I suppose it was then handed down from generation to generation until it came to my dad. Of course, the branch where he borrowed it from was long gone, but I thought it was my duty to return it to the present branch."

Frank took the book to the current Crawley Library, expecting a light-hearted exchange with the staff. But he may wish he had kept quiet, as the punishments for the late return of a library book in 11th century England were extremely harsh.

"Libraries did not implement monetary fines in those days as nobody had two ha'pennies to rub together," said chief librarian Agnes Bullstrode. "Instead, a series of medieval punishments were meted out for late returns. Women were tied to a stool and and ducked in the village pond, just like if they were a nag or a fishwife."

But unluckily for Frank, the punishment for men transgressing Dark Age library rules were even more severe, with male late returners being required to pick up a small rod of red hot metal heated in a brazier, and carry it one pace for each day their book was late.

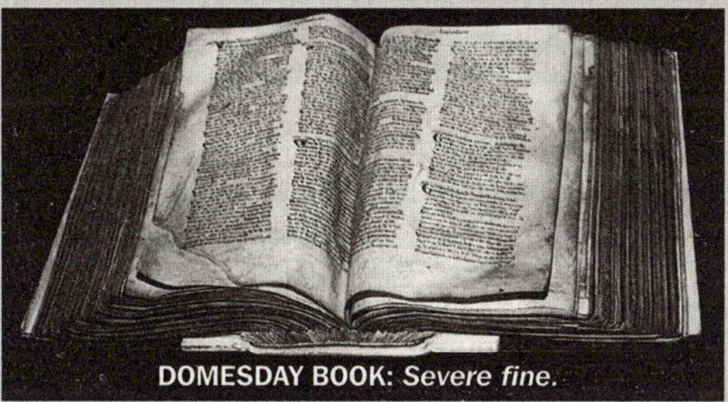
DOMESDAY BOOK: *Severe fine.*

And as senior librarian, Bullstrode is insisting that the punishment be imposed on Frank.

"I understand that times have changed and this may seem barbaric by today's standards," she said. "But it was the punishment of the time, and we have to send an example to anyone else keeping library books for centuries longer than they should."

The staff at the library have borrowed a brazier from the Works Department and deputy head librarian Ernest Gordon has volunteered to carry out the punishment.

"He's quite excited about it actually," said Agnes. "He's got a big pair of metal tongs to lift the rod out of the fire and hand it to Mr Glass."

"And he's going to do it with no shirt on and a leather hood over his head," she added.

BRITAIN has a rich history reaching back hundreds of years. And the stately homes dotted across our green and pleasant land tell the story of that history, documenting how our betters lived in the past. These palaces, halls and manor houses stand as stone, marble and slate monuments to our country's cultural heritage, and – providing we don't ask where the money to build them came from – they are a source of national pride.

Thanks to charitable institutions, these buildings and the priceless treasures they hold are being preserved, held in trust so that future generations who can afford the extortionate entrance fees can see how life was lived, upstairs and downstairs.

So let's go for a day out to Fulchester Manor, home of the 18th Earl of Fulchester and now in the hands of The National Heritage, and ask...

CAN YOU SPOT...?

☐ **A FAMILY** at the ticket office trying to work out the cheapest way in – An adult, three children and a pensioner, a family ticket for two adults and two children, a non-concession adult and one extra child, or an annual Trust membership with 75% off your first admission.

☐ **A YOUNG COUPLE** who have borrowed her grandma and grandad's membership cards rehearsing what they will say if questioned about the fact that they are clearly not in their 80s.

☐ **A VOLUNTEER** who is more pleased than she should be to tell a couple that they cannot take a buggy into the main house.

☐ **A VOLUNTEER** who is clearly delighted to tell an elderly gentleman that he cannot take his dog into the manor.

☐ **A VOLUNTEER** whose day has been made by two excited children, telling them to stop running and "politely" asking their parents to keep them under control.

☐ **A VOLUNTEER** who failed to get into the police force humiliating any visitors who didn't realise they have to wear blue elasticated shoe covers.

☐ **A MIDDLE-AGED COUPLE** who have borrowed their son and his wife's cards, hoping they will pass for a couple in their late twenties if questioned.

☐ **A VOLUNTEER** who doesn't wait to be asked before telling everybody who comes in the full story of every object in the room.

☐ **A VOLUNTEER** who constantly refers to the owner as 'His Lordship' in hushed, reverential tones.

☐ **THE EARL OF FULCHESTER** who has had to give the manor to The National Heritage for financial reasons, walking around with a face like a slapped arse because the great unwashed are looking at his stuff.

☐ **THE COUNTESS OF FULCHESTER**, walking round the gardens in a pair of £650 Le Chameaux wellies and carrying a trug, mumbling under her breath about the fucking rabble looking at her flowers.

☐ **AN EMPLOYEE** in the kitchen decanting Aldi Basics honey into smaller jars labelled 'Fulchester Priory Honey' to go on sale in the gift shop for £10 a pop.

☐ **A CAFE** selling Fulchester Priory Honey at £15 a pop.

☐ **A WOMAN** who has been told to tie her dog up outside, looking disdainfully at the four Fulchester Manor cats lying on a 16th century four poster bed, pulling threads with their claws.

☐ **A FILM CREW** who the charitable trust believe are there to shoot a BBC costume drama, but who are actually filming the scud-flick *Pussies and Prejudice vol.7* for TelevisionX.

☐ **A GALLERY OF PORTRAITS** of the Earls from 1108 up to the present day, with a facial feature that becomes progressively more pronounced through succeeding inbred generations.

☐ **A MAP** showing the private areas of the manor that are not open to the public and which together form about 95% of the floor area.

☐ **A SUIT OF ARMOUR** described as having been worn by the Earl's ancestors at the Battle of Towton in 1461, but which was actually bought in 2007 from that place in Wales that makes armour for the film industry.

☐ **A BITTER UNDER-GARDENER** who, if you shaved off his beard, would look suspiciously like the Duke's father.

☐ **AN ELDERLY WOMAN** looking at a chair, wondering if it's an exhibit or one she can have a little sit down on.

☐ **A VOLUNTEER** looking at an elderly woman looking at a chair, getting ready to shout at her if she goes to sit on it.

☐ **AN OLD WOMAN** pointing at everything she sees and saying "Eeeh! My mum had one of them."

☐ **A VOLUNTEER** explaining how terrible it was that His Lordship had to relinquish the manor to the trust because of crippling inheritance tax to a couple who have saved up for six months to take their two kids for a day out.

☐ **A SIXTEEN-YEAR-OLD LAD**, drunk on power, telling visitors arriving in the car park to park their cars closer together in the field.

☐ **A TIGER** that's been living in the woods since it escaped from the old Duke's private zoo in 1976.

☐ **A MAN** who has cricked his neck after the audio guide told him to "look up at the ornate late Baroque plasterwork dating from the 17th century."

☐ **SOME CHILDREN** who have not yet given up on the treasure hunt, looking for a small teddy bear somewhere in the room.

☐ **SOME CHILDREN** who, after 12 largely-similar rooms, have stopped looking for hidden teddy bears and are begging their parents to take them to McDonalds.

☐ **A PUSHY MUM** who has compiled a challenging worksheet for her 'exceptionally gifted' six and seven-year-old children to complete, telling them in a passive-aggressive manner that they will thank her one day.

☐ **AN AMERICAN TOURIST** asking one of the volunteers if the electric stairlift was an original feature of the house.

☐ **A PADLOCKED STOREROOM** containing artefacts that the family has 'collected' from around the globe over the years, that the trust has tactfully decided to remove from display.

☐ **AN ORIGINAL REMBRANDT** painting hanging in a dark corridor, a priceless treasure that no-one has ever looked at or noticed, the sale of which would easily have paid off all the Duke's death duties.

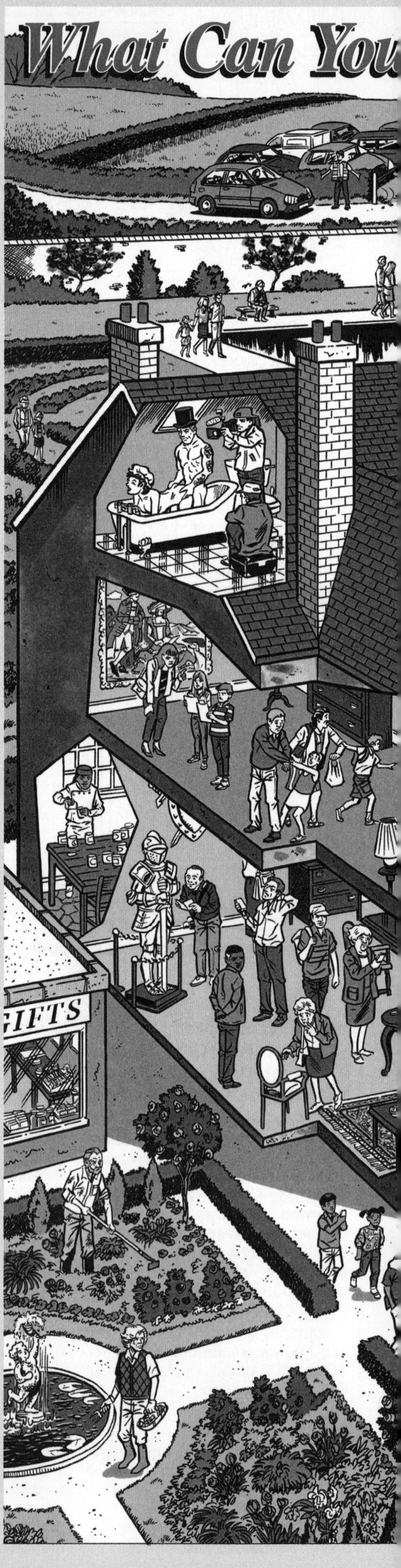
What Can You
GIFTS

Spot at a Stately Home?

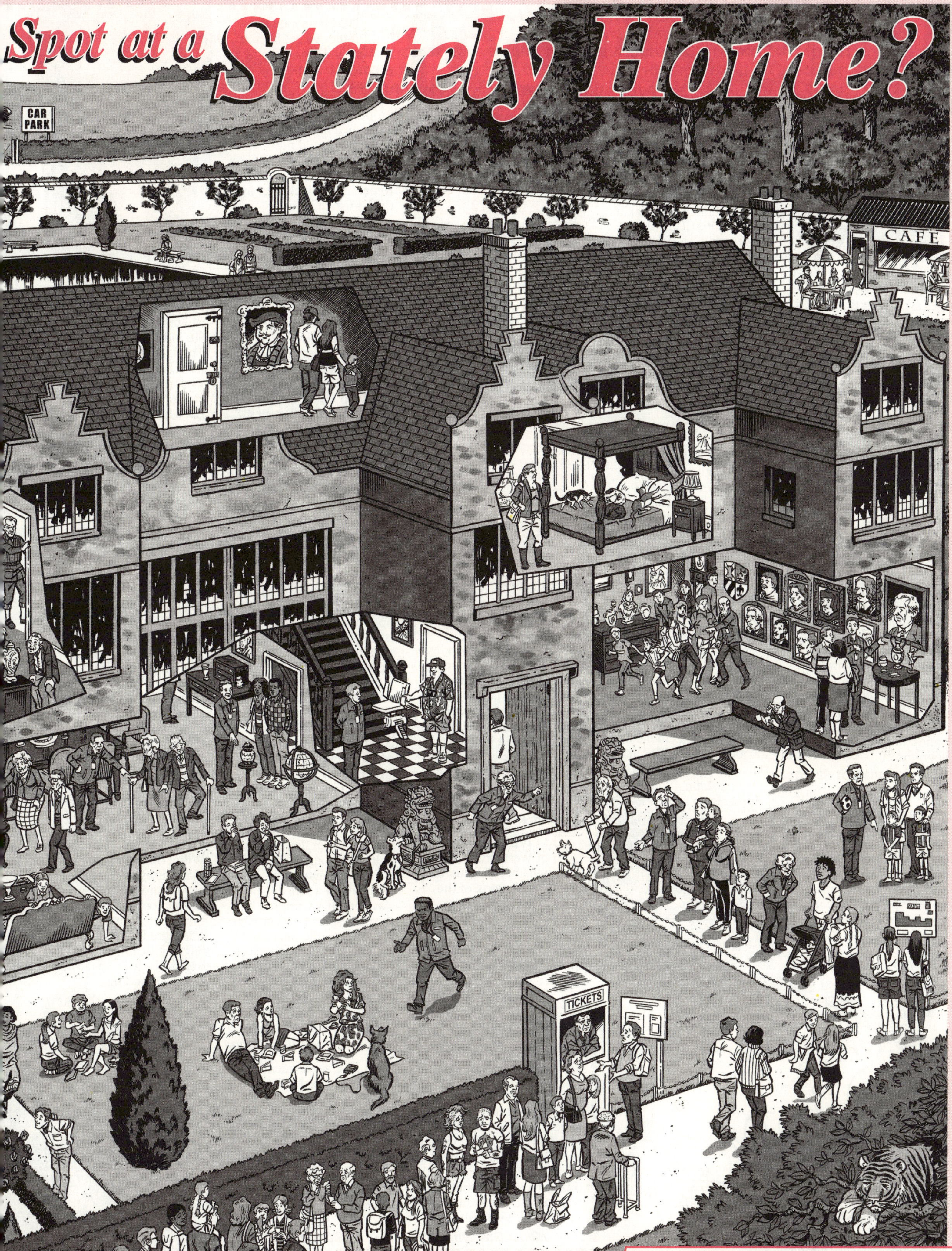
CAR PARK
CAFE
TICKETS

NEXT WEEK: Who's Who at a Sex Orgy.

LETTERBOCKS

letters@viz.co.uk...letters@viz.co.uk...letters@viz

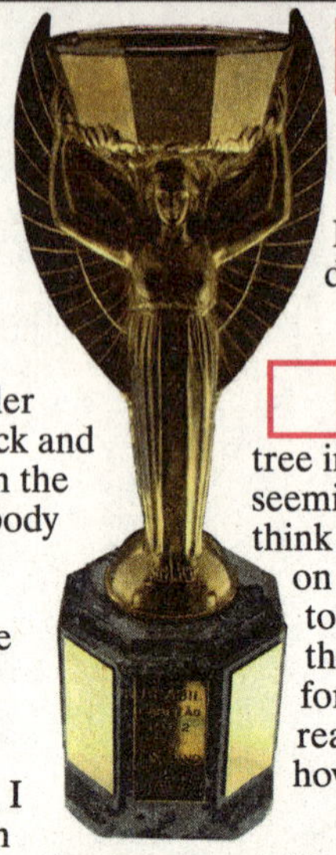

WHEN Brazil won the World Cup for a third time, they were allowed to keep the Jules Rimet trophy. And when a footballer scores a hat-trick and walks away with the match ball, nobody bats an eyelid. Yet when I do THREE service washes and take a handful of bras and knickers home, I am sacked from my job at the launderette, arrested, and put on the Sex Offenders Register.

Kevin Caswell-Jones, Gresford

ON page 55, Mr James Miller of Sutton proudly boasted to have masturbated in 12 different countries. What an amateur. I have rubbed the relic in no less than 37 different countries. And not just any relic, but a proud, erect and turgid *British* relic. How do you like *them* apples, Brussels? And apples weighed in imperial pounds, not bureaucratic kilograms.

Reg Corvette, St Albans

TV adverts for online gambling often show groups of people laughing and having a lovely time together. This doesn't seem at all realistic to me, but I suppose a shot of someone sitting alone in their underpants, crying because they've lost the rent money again, is unlikely to get many people signing up.

Eldon Furse, email

COME on, Airfix – why do you leave it to us to build your planes? Stop cutting corners. Imagine if car makers did this. Ridiculous.

Chris, Baku

I LOVE the way birds can just sit in a tree in the pouring rain not seeming to mind at all. I did think of putting an anorak on and climbing a tree to give it a go, but then thought it's probably not for me. Have any of your readers tried it, and if so, how did it go?

Lighto, Wallasey

** Have you sat in a tree wearing an anorak in the pouring rain? Write in and tell us how it went, and we'll pass your comments onto Mr, Mrs, or Ms Lighto to help them decide whether or not it's for them.*

I OBSERVED a blackbird this afternoon and was greatly impressed. In the time it took to swoop down and land on top of a fencepost, twitch its tail feathers and drop its load, I wouldn't have been able to pick out the reading material for a sit-down visit, let alone finish the job and fly off. What a remarkable creature it is.

Prince Asbo, Folkestone

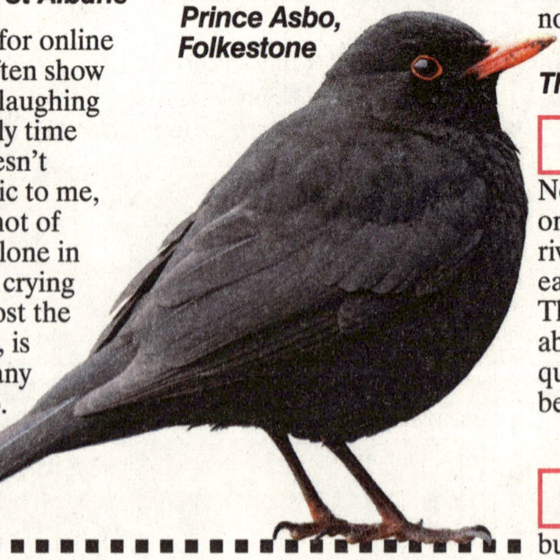

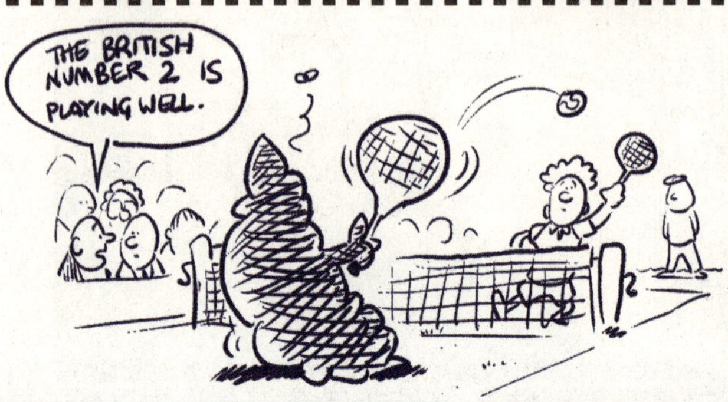
THE BRITISH NUMBER 2 IS PLAYING WELL.

STAR LETTER

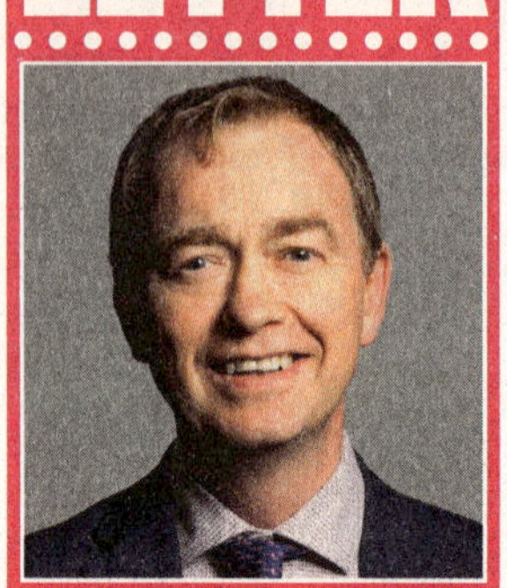

I WALKED past Lib Dem MP Tim Farron in London this afternoon, and he was exactly the height that I had always imagined him to be. All too often, politicians turn out to be a lot taller or shorter in real life than you expect, so it was a refreshing change to see one exactly the height that I had envisaged. Well done, Tim.

Jack Dury, Bristol

WHEN I turn on my TV in the morning, I have to listen to news presenters, experts, politicians and weather presenters talking absolute nonsense, and I'm getting sick of it. The government should ban people talking nonsense early in the morning.

Thomas Rott, Isle of Wight

I LIVE in the town of West Bridgford in Nottingham. It is situated on the south bank of the river Trent and on the east side of Trent Bridge. There's nothing 'west' about it at all. Honestly, the quicker we leave the EU the better.

T Balls, West Bridgford

AS a teenager, my wife threw a cheese butty (no pickle) at her mum's head for being a shite mother. On another occasion she threw a bacon and tomato sauce butty at her head for the same reason. Have any *Viz* readers ever hurled a sandwich at a parent's head in anger, and if they have, what was the reason for doing so, and what was the sandwich filling?

Martin Graham, email

DOES anyone know if they've got beer in heaven, and if so, is it any good? I was thinking about converting to the Viking religion so I could get proper pissed in Valhalla, but then a mate reminded me that it would probably be Carlsberg there, which gives me the runs. I hope there's something a bit classier in the Christian heaven.

Rev O'Dand, Dawlish

DUNSTON FC have the Latin motto *Nulli Secundus* - 'Second to None' - on their club crest. However, at the time of writing this letter they are in sixth place in the Northern Premier League East division, a full 32 points behind league leaders Worksop Town. If they win their remaining 8 games, the best they can do is finish as runners-up. In this eventuality, I wonder if they will be changing their motto to *Worksopii Oppidum Secundus* – 'Second to Worksop Town'.

Bjorn Monkbottle, Consett

IN the late 90s I was on a bus to Homerton Hospital in east London for a straightforward hernia operation. I had the latest issue of *Viz* with me, and reading a cartoon called *Prime Suspect with DC Ben Turpin* made me laugh so much that I coughed up a bit of blood. Have any other readers suffered medical complications from laughing so much at one of *Viz's* strips from the late 90s?

Greg Fearn, Darley Dale

MY grandson asked me why the sky was blue the other day. I was only halfway through explaining that electromagnetic radiation of a short wavelength is scattered by the atmosphere to a greater degree than the longer wavelengths in the spectrum, making the blue light more visible, when his eyes glazed over and he wandered off to play with some Lego. I mean, why bother asking?

Eldon Furse, email

I'VE got an idea for a film called *Shitanic*, but I can't decide whether it's about a really crap boat or a cruise ship with an outbreak of dysentery. Before I take it any further, I'd be interested in which one your readers would rather go to see at the pictures.

Sam Bamsam, Sutton Coldfield

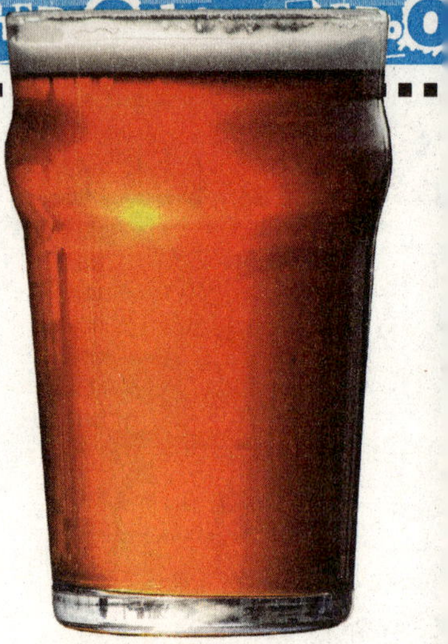

CHILDREN nowadays are soft as shite, whereas in the 60s, 70s and 80s kids were hard as fuck. Thinking about it, it may have had something to do with all that asbestos in the classrooms. So come on. Let's bring back asbestos and have tougher kids.

Hasto, Cramlington

I SAW a fella at the circus juggling clubs while balancing on a free-standing ladder. It was absolutely amazing, but set me wondering whether he learned to juggle first and then balance on a ladder, or vice versa. Whichever way round it was, his hard work had certainly paid off, because he was dating the gorgeous trapeze artist. I saw him kissing her after the show, just before he started shovelling all the elephant shit into some barrels.

D Williams, Donegal

OSCAR Wilde is famously quoted as saying "There is only one thing in life worse than being talked about, and that is not being talked about." May I assure Mr Wilde through your pages, that this assertion may have some merit from the perspective of one of the 20th century's most celebrated writers and wits, but significantly less so if one explosively shat one's kegs at a wedding in 2012.

Shitty Kev, Gresford

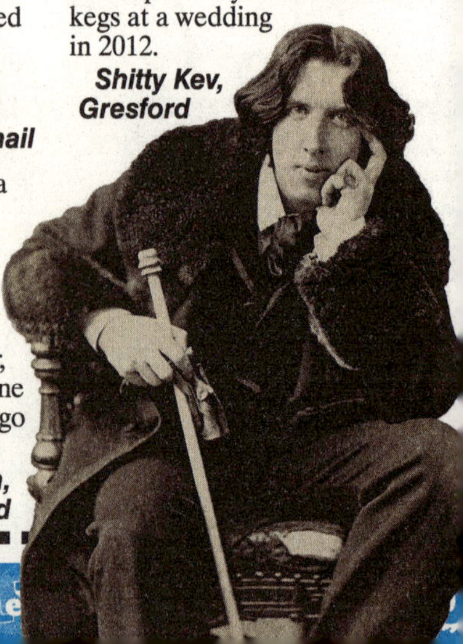

THOSE signs you see on trains saying "See it. Say it. Sorted!" should be taken with a pinch of salt. I just said, very loudly, "man with BO eating a fucking egg sandwich with a bollock hanging out the leg of his shorts," and he was still there when I got off an hour later.

Steve Crouch, P'borough

YOU hear a lot about this Harry Styles fellow these day, picking up awards and performing concerts and the like, but I haven't got a clue who he is. I've never heard of him. Former *X-Factor* contestant and lead singer of One Direction turned solo recording artist he might be, but mention the name to me and you'll get a blank stare I'm afraid.

Albert Crumplehorn, Hull

IT'S a good job Jeremy Clarkson's surname isn't Cuntchops, otherwise his hit Amazon show would be called *Cuntchops' Farm.* Although in our household we call it that anyway.

Gerry Paton, London

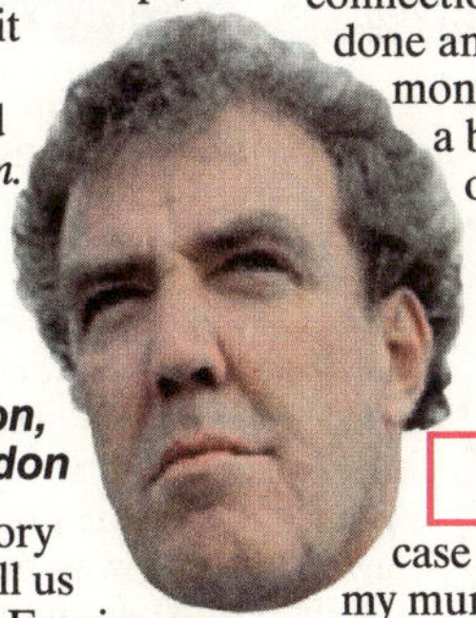

THE history boffins tell us that the Roman Empire was an advanced civilisation. But reading a book about their communal bogs, where the turds would run down an open gutter and they would wipe their arses with a sponge on a stick, leads me to think otherwise. The dirty buggers.

Graham Flintoft, Gatesheed

I AM baffled as to why someone who has a robust constitution is described as 'strong as an ox'. It seems to me that any animal which is routinely mashed up and turned into stock cubes is hardly an example of vigour or longevity. I would suggest that a badger or a cassowary would be a more logical choice for a hard animal.

Pam Fritters, Firth

SO many technological breakthroughs – VCR, credit card payments, the internet and mp4 compression to name but a few – have only come about because of the porn industry. Can someone figure out an angle in which developing a cure for cancer could somehow help the porn industry? Honestly, if we could establish a connection, it would be done and dusted in six months, mostly likely in a budget hotel room or on a sketchy housing estate in the Midlands.

Calvin Graham, Philadelphia

"ALWAYS wear clean pants, in case you get run over," my mum used to say. Ironic then, that when I saw the bus coming towards me, I shit myself.

David Edwards, Bury St Edmunds

PEOPLE who have had a hectic day sometimes say that they have been running around like a blue-arsed fly. Surely a blue-arsed fly would get more done if it flew instead of ran, so these people are being disingenuous about how busy they've actually been.

Dumbo Sane, Zurich

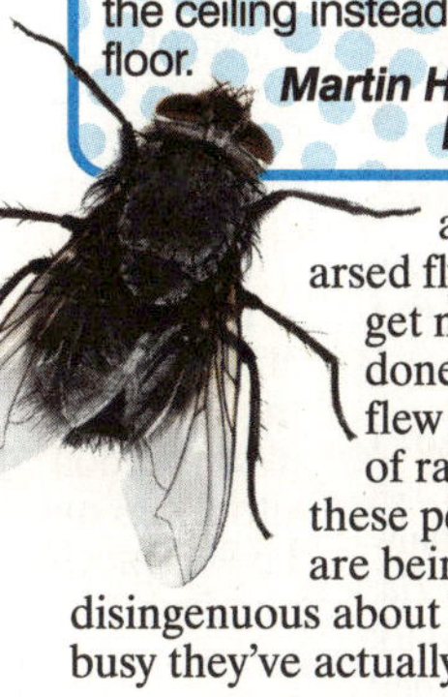

I WONDER James Bond didn't shit his pants when he was bout to be cut in half with a giant circular saw? I can just imagine Ernst Blofeld saying "I see you have shat your pants, Mr Bond," in that voice of his, whilst stroking a cat.

Greg Shaw, Leeds

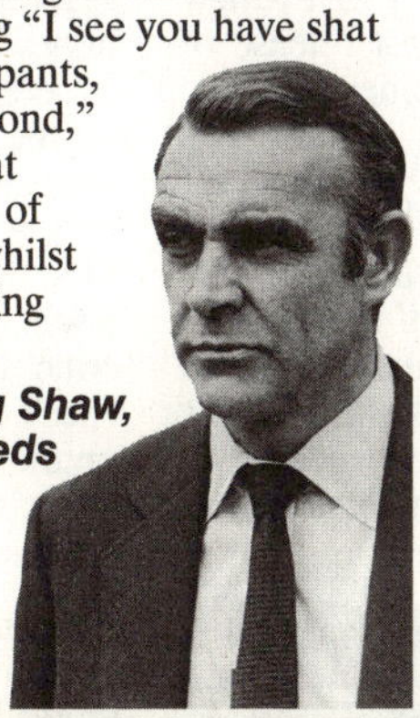

TOP TIPS

WHEN unloading the dishwasher, avoid being spalshed by water that has collected in the base of the upturned mugs by drilling small holes in the bases as you load them in, allowing the water to drain away.

Andrew Merson, Aberdeenshire

SAVE wear and tear on your carpet by affixing it to the ceiling instead of the floor.

Martin Harwood, Bradford

A CONDOM filled with expanding foam makes a tasty alternative to a vegan sausage.

Barry Biskits, Chodbury-on-sea

SAVE money on expensive magnetic travel chess sets by simply dipping the base of your regular pieces into a jar of supermarket own brand honey.

Chris Casseroles, Golders Green

KEEP fit enthusiasts. Get in your 10,000 steps a day by going for a piss and back in Wetherspoons.

Fat Al White, Wrenthorpe

TURN your humble two-up, two-down semi into a luxurious 10-bedroom mansion by simply adding more interior walls.

Johnny Rubber, Wigan

CONDUCTORS. Make live performances of Vivaldi's *The Four Seasons* more familiar by stopping your orchestra every three minutes and saying, "Your call is important to us. Please continue to hold."

Michael, Thompson

toptips@viz.co.uk

IT'S common knowledge that Elvis died on the toilet, but does anyone actually know if he had successfully completed his movements at the time of death? I don't like the idea of the King spending his final earthly moments in agony, straining to force out a troublesome dreadnaught. On the other hand, if he had finished his business and was just having a few pleasant minutes to himself, perhaps perusing a copy of *Exchange & Mart*, or *The People's Friend*, that actually wouldn't be such a bad way to go.

Ben Nunn, Caterham

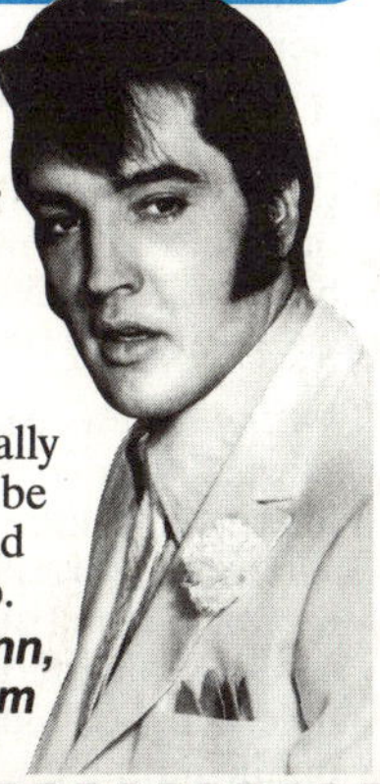

MEMORY LANE

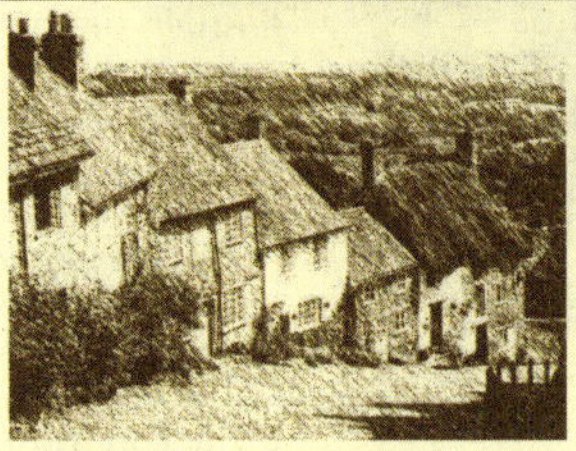

WE ALL agree that everything today is utter shite and that everything was better in the olden days. Our readers have been writing in to tell us what they miss about yesteryear...

WHATEVER happened to the birthday bumps? I have the fondest memories of being repeatedly thrown into the air by so-called friends on my birthday, my arms being violently ripped from their sockets and being kicked in the small of the back at the height of each cycle. Doubtless it has been outlawed by some swivel-eyed, wokist bureaucrat in the name of "elf and safety".

Dennis Elbow, email

WHATEVER happened to good old-fashioned moonies? Time was that you couldn't drive on the motorway without a bunch of cheeky schoolboys pushing their bare arses against the rear coach window every time a car pulled too close, giving a chuckle to the great British driver. I blame the EU nanny state for putting seatbelts on coaches. The sooner we have this bonfire of EU laws, the better.

Jay George, Leeds

WHY don't we ever see members of the royal family choking on fishbones anymore? It used to happen all the time in the 80s. Maybe it's time to start this wonderful tradition up again. King Charles could make the news gagging on a bit of haddock lodged in his throat, or perhaps the Princess of Wales could struggle for air on a nice piece of cod. Come on, Royals! Bring back the good old days and choke on more fish!

I Carson, Widnes

LOVE FEEDING THE BIRDS IN YOUR GARDEN, BUT CAN'T STAND BLUE TITS? YOU NEED...

BLUE TIT-AWAY

Cyanistes caeruleus Repellant

The Market Leader in Blue Tit Deterrents

One spray on your bird table will keep blue tits away for up to 48 hours.

- ***100% environmentally friendly***
- ***Will not affect other garden birds***
- ***Biodegradable and CFC-free***

Spray on bird table, feeders, nest boxes – Anywhere you don't want blue tits.

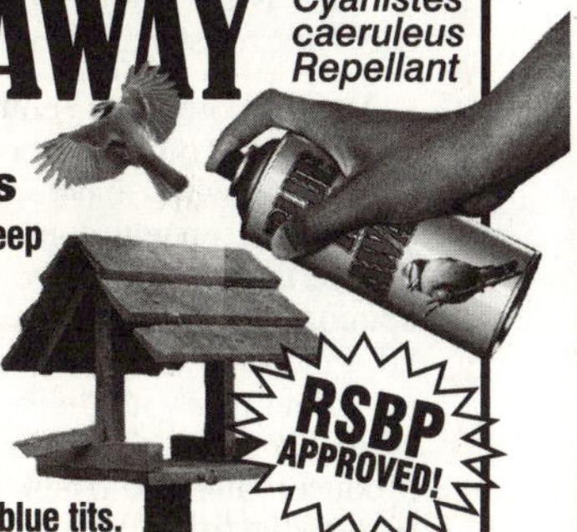
RSBP APPROVED!

"I used to love watching the robins, chaffinches and long-tailed tits eating the sunflower seeds I put out for them. And then these blue and yellow bastards would turn up and spoil things. Not any more." **Mrs J, Colchester**

"I've nothing against blue tits, I just don't want them in my garden. I'm against poisoning them, so Blue Tit-Away is the perfect solution." **Mrs L, Croydon**

"Thanks to this spray, my bird table is a blue tit-free zone, leaving the sparrows, finches and nuthatches to get on with their dinner in peace." **Mr A, Hull**

Available from discerning hardware stores and some garden centres

Rid my garden of wrens at the flick of a switch?
It can't be done! Yes it CAN! With...

Wren-Be-Gone™

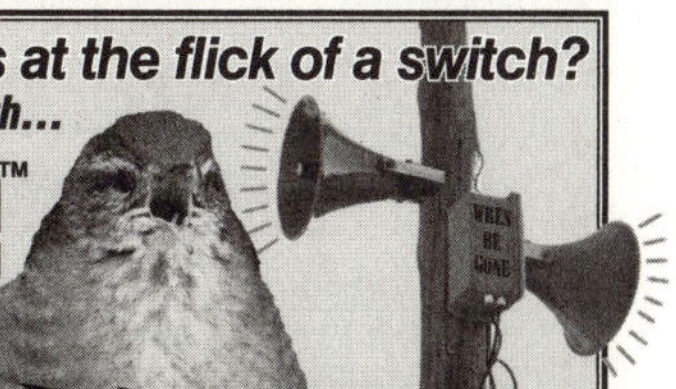

The **NON-CHEMICAL** answer to ridding your garden of this tiny, stupid-shaped bird.

The **Wren-Be-Gone** emits a high-pitched, irritating sound that only wrens can hear. The result of years of research by world-leading ornithologists, **Wren-Be-Gone** will keep wrens away ***PERMANENTLY!***

Turn it *ON* and the Wrens are *GONE!*

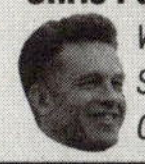

Chris Packham says: *"I love all birds. Except wrens. I keep my Wren-Be-Gone switched on 24/7 and I haven't seen one of the little fuckers for years."*

Available online from www.wren-be-gone.org

LIGHTS! CAMERA! T

Top movie reviewer in HOSPITAL after 'revenge attacks'

ONE of the UK's most prestigious and influential film critics is said to be "fighting for his life" in a south Leicestershire hospital, following a series of cowardly attacks from Hollywood directors.

EXCLUSIVE

Narborough-based father-of-nine **FENTON HAMMERTOE** is well known to movie lovers across the country for his wildly popular review site *FentonLuvzFilmz.blogspot.net*. But while audiences lap up Fenton's scathing, scalpel-sharp prose, the 58-year-old's brutal takedowns of some of Tinseltown's biggest blockbusters have made him a target for furious filmmakers.

"My reviews can make or break a movie," says Fenton, speaking from his bed in South Wigston Hospital, where he is currently recovering from a broken arm, shattered pelvis and severe groinal bruising. "I'll usually upload my critique of a new picture on the morning it opens. If I shower it with praise, the film is guaranteed to blockbust the box office. If I rip it to shreds, it'll be in the supermarket bargain DVD bin within the week."

"Such is the power of the humble critic," the registered sex offender sighs.

And the potency of Fenton's poison pen is not lost on Hollywood's leading directors, who have proclaimed him 'public enemy number one'. "I believe filmgoers deserve my honest opinion," the former paperboy states. "If a movie is a right old stinker, I'm not afraid to say it. Unlike other film critics, who are in the pockets of the producers and studio heads, I give my readers the truth, the whole truth and nothing but the truth."

"And look where's it landed me," he adds, gesturing around the hospital room.

And in this exclusive, so-brave, so-not-making-it-all-up Fenton explains how his no-holds-barred film reviews have left him in *critic*-al condition.

Calamity James

Fenton launched his stupendously successful review site back in autumn 2022, following a lengthy period of unemployment.

"I can't work due to various medical conditions that I simply don't have time to go into right now. And late last year I was having a few minor financial issues - a misunderstanding about a gambling debt that, again, I simply don't have the time to get into - and my nash cheques weren't quite cutting it, so I started looking for extra income.

I've always loved movies, so I wondered if I should try my hand as a professional film critic. I occasionally read columns by the likes of *The Guardian's* Peter Bradshaw or Mark Kermode off the BBC, and it seemed like a piss-easy gig. You just watched a film, wrote down what happened in it and then said whether you thought it was good or shit. Not exactly rocket science. So I set up my website, *FentonLuvzFilmz*, and got to work.

Fittingly, I decided my first review would be for the biggest release of that year - James Cameron's epic science fiction sequel *Avatar: The Way of Water*. The first *Avatar* had set a new box office record back in 2009, and this follow-up was already on its way to becoming one of the highest-grossing movies of all time. The critics were churning out gushing five-star reviews in all the big broadsheets. But there was one critic who *hadn't* seen it. *Fenton Hammertoe.*

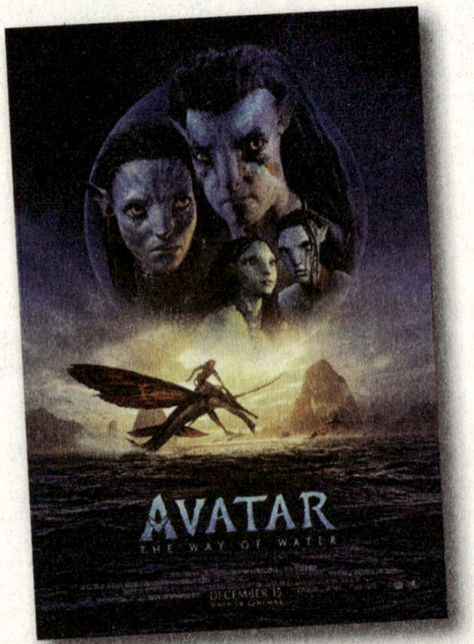
AVATAR
THE WAY OF WATER

So, one Saturday afternoon I nipped to the local multiplex for a viewing. I emerged three-and-a-bit hours later, feeling stunned. The film was, to put it mildly, the biggest load of wank I had ever seen in my life. It was a kind of high-tech version of The Smurfs - a load of blue twats running about and talking in weird voices. It was totally unrealistic, the plot made no sense and it was *far* too long - I'd nipped for three pisses *and a shit* by the time the credits rolled.

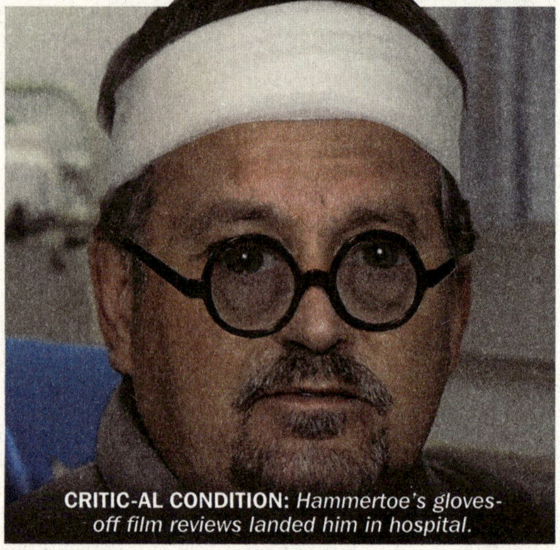

CRITIC-AL CONDITION: *Hammertoe's gloves-off film reviews landed him in hospital.*

I got home and poured all this confusion, dissatisfaction and vitriol into my review. I pulled precisely zero punches, detailing the various gaping plot holes at the movie's centre. I tore the film a new arsehole, before signing off with the killer line:

'He may be called James Camera-on - but maybe it's about time this talentless wanker turned his Camera-off!!'

It was brutal stuff. But it was also fair, honest, and exquisitely written. I knew as soon as I hit 'upload' that it would set the film world alight. And I wasn't wrong. Within a few days, my debut review had notched up a whopping SIX MILLION page impressions! I was officially the most widely read critic on Earth! But don't bother checking, because when I loaded it up there was a glitch that meant zeros don't show up, so it'll say '6' page impressions when it's really '6000000'.

I could see I was quickly accruing a gargantuan fanbase, but it never once crossed my mind that *James Cameron himself* might read my article. But even if he did, he'd made billions of dollars off this sequel. One bad review wouldn't upset him, surely.

How wrong could I be?

Just a fortnight after my incendiary critique of his stupid film went viral, Cameron sent his goons to extract revenge. I was in the pub bogs having a slash one evening when I felt a large pair of hairy arms around my neck. I was pulled to the ground and viciously pummelled by an unseen assailant.

'What's this about?!' I cried, as I writhed about on the toilet floor. 'You know *exactly* what it's about, Fenton', hissed my aggressor. His voice sounded quite similar to that of my local bookie, Terry, with whom I'd had the aforementioned misunderstanding over a gambling debt. However, the situation was exactly that - a *misunderstanding*. I didn't actually owe Terry any money, and no one could prove I did, so it couldn't have been him.

As my attacker gave me one last killer boot to the clockweights and took my wallet, I realised *exactly* who he was. James Cameron had clearly flown one of his security staff over from LA to Narborough to punish me for trash-talking his half-arsed film. It was my first taste of Hollywood-style retribution. Sadly, it wouldn't be my last."

'Oppen' Mad

Whilst recovering in hospital from that initial revenge attack, so-fearless Fenton continued to publish yet more searing critiques of Hollywood blockbusters. Soon enough, his nascent site's popularity had exploded, notching up 16 MILLION total page impressions by the spring of 2023, although the tech glitch on his blogpage continued to omit the zeros.

"I've asked the IT bods to look into it, but it's like herding fucking kittens with them lot. Anyroad, as my subscriber numbers rocketed, I incurred more and more wrath from Tinseltown's top directors. Soon after James Cameron's cowardly attack, I reviewed the star-studded blockbuster *Asteroid City* by quirky auteur Wes Anderson. The critics had creamed themselves over this one, awarding it five-star reviews across the board. But Fenton J. Hammertoe is a little harder to please.

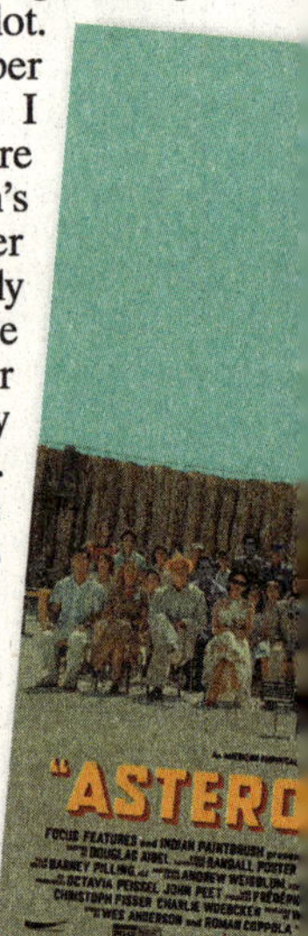

In a withering half-a-star takedown,

RACTION!

I dubbed the film 'utter, utter cack', reprimanding Anderson for his 'two-dimensional characterisation' and 'plot holes you could drive a fucking bus through'. Two nights later, the distraught director hit back. He had one of his goons place a row of parked cars *directly* in my path as I was driving home from the pub. The resulting crash left me with severe whiplash and the thick end of ten grand's damage to my Clio. Yet still I refused to stop writing.

By this point I had become such a revered critic that I no longer needed to pay for cinema tickets. Desperate for a glowing write-up on *FentonLuvzFilmz*, studio bosses would send me 'screeners' - personalised copies of their biggest movies on DVD. They were usually delivered by a bloke in the pub called 'Shifty Nev', who also had access to all the latest 'adult' film releases, and could do you six lighters for a quid. Anyroad, one night a few weeks back, Nev opened his trenchcoat and handed me the big one: Christopher Nolan's hugely anticipated nuclear bomb thriller *Oppenheimer*.

This star-studded biographical drama was set to be the biggest movie of the summer, and critics were already going bonkers for it. I knew my vast fanbase would be chomping at the bit to hear what I made of it, so I left the pub straight away and headed home with my review copy, stopping for a few white ciders at the offie.

When I put it on later that evening, I was gobsmacked. The movie was - to put it mildly - shit. It was uninspired, deathly dull and genuinely impossible to follow. I was so bored I'd even switched over to the snooker halfway through. The quality of the 'screener' didn't help - it seemed Nev had accidentally filmed it with his iPhone on mute, so none of the sound had come through, and he was on the end row, so there was a constant stream of punters going past to the toilet.

Jason SCHWARTZMAN
Scarlett JOHANSSON
Tom HANKS
Jeffrey WRIGHT
Tilda SWINTON
Bryan CRANSTON
Edward NORTON
Adrien BRODY
Liev SCHREIBER
Hope DAVIS
Stephen PARK
Rupert FRIEND
Maya HAWKE
Steve CARELL
Matt DILLON
Hong CHAU
Willem DAFOE
Margot ROBBIE
Tony REVOLORI
Jake RYAN
Jeff GOLDBLUM
CITY"

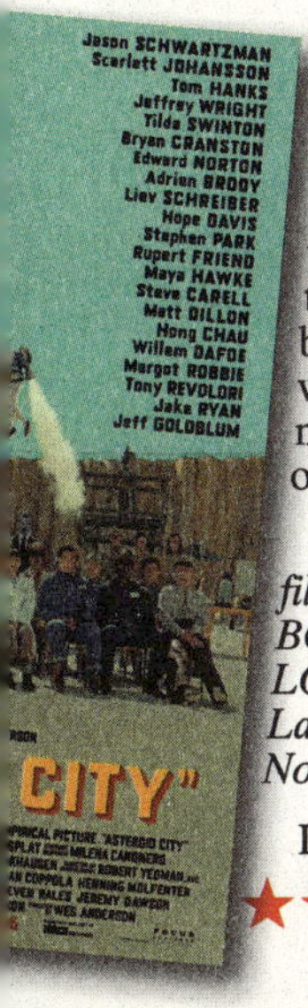

Nevertheless, it was painfully clear that Nolan had a flop on his hands. The *Dunkirk* icon had shat the bed, big time. And I was the only critic unafraid to say so. I immediately boshed out 1000 scathing words on the film's many, many flaws, before signing off with the killer line:

'It's entirely fitting that a film about a BOMB is set to BOMB at the box office!!! LOL!!! Christopher No-Lan? More like Christopher No-Talent!!! LMFAO!!!!'

It was brutal stuff, I knew that, but I owed it to my readers to be honest. I hit 'upload', and as I watched the page impressions soar into the millions (again, don't bother checking), I steeled myself for Nolan's retribution.

It didn't take long to arrive.

A FILM BY CHRISTOPHER NOLAN
OPPENHEIMER
7 21 23
SHOT WITH IMAX FILM CAMERAS

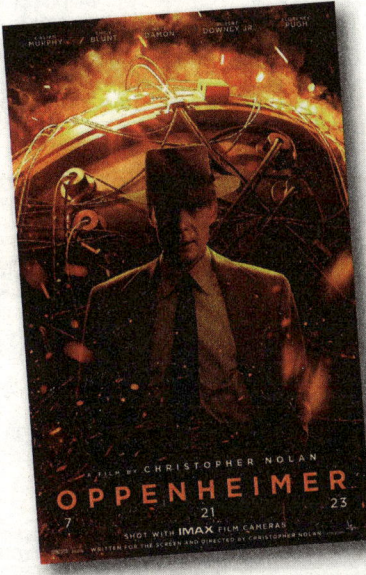

The very next night, I was leaving a close friend's house through the bedroom window, when I received a glancing blow to the back of the head. As I tumbled to the ground, I knew instantly that Nolan had read my review. 'You don't have to do this!' I cried, hoping to calm the irate filmmaker. 'Oh yes I fucking do, Fenton!' the director shot back. It was odd: his voice sounded remarkably similar to that of my next-door neighbour, Brian. But I knew it couldn't be Brian as we weren't on speaking terms due to him believing a (false) rumour about me tupping his missus while he was working nights.

No, it was plain as day that the man kicking six shades of shit out of me was the Oscar-nominated director Christopher Nolan. Incensed by my wholly accurate assessment of his abysmal film, the *Inception* hack had obviously taken the red-eye from Beverly Hills to Narborough to extract his pathetic revenge.

As I lay bleeding on the concrete, slipping in and out of consciousness, I couldn't help laughing. Tinseltown's sticks and stones may have broken my bones - *but my words were hurting them far worse*."

Burning with Envy

The Oppenheimer piece may have landed Fenton back in intensive care, but it was his biggest hit yet, clocking up 20 MILLION unverifiable page impressions in just 24 hours! But despite this success, Hammertoe decided it was time to try a fresh angle with his reviews.

"As chuffed as I was about being the planet's best loved film critic, I was also sick to ruddy death of losing half my teeth and a pint of blood after every review. Then it struck me: the reason these Hollywood directors were so sensitive about my critiques was because I was actively losing them money. Every bad review on *FentonLuvzFilms* meant millions of dollars lost in potential ticket sales. So, what if I decided to pass judgement on *older* films that were no longer on general release? Surely I couldn't get physically attacked for doing *that?*

Spoiler alert: I could, and I did.

I launched a new section on my website called 'Fenton Revisitz The Classicz'. It was a weekly column in which I would watch films that were universally considered to be 'masterpieces', and see if they matched up to my famously high standards. I kicked off with a double-bill of *Goodfellas* and *Pulp Fiction* by Martin Scorsese and Quentin Tarantino. Both movies were acknowledged as iconic works of art - *but would they pass the Fenton test?* I couldn't wait to see them and find out.

I couldn't be arsed to watch them as they are quite long, and I had a court date for unpaid child maintenance, so I only had time to give each a quick whizz through on fast forward before penning my article. And I'm glad I didn't waste any more time on this pair of piss-poor potboilers. One of them was even edited in the wrong order, a schoolboy error. My review gave them a quarter-of-a-star apiece, and signed off with the killer one-liner:

'When it comes to directing films, Marty and Quentin are BADfellas - and that's a Pulp FACT!!!! #LOL #ShitDirectors #FuckMartyAndQuentin'

It was brutal stuff, I realised that, but it was also unavoidably TRUE. But Scorsese and Tarantino had already made their millions off these sub-par 'classics', so I slumbered safe in the knowledge that there would be no retribution this time.

How very wrong I was.

I awoke in the middle of the night to the smell of burning. When I peered downstairs I saw flames roaring out of my kitchen, threatening to engulf the entire ground floor. I knew instantly what must have happened. After finishing my review, I'd nipped out to the precinct for a few dozen cans before coming home to make some chips. I'd definitely turned the chip pan off when I'd finished - I knew that for certain - but apparently Scorsese and Tarantino had broken in and switched it back on.

RAY LIOTTA
ROBERT DE NIRO
JOE PESCI
GoodFellas

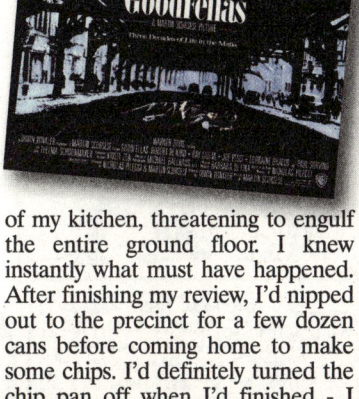

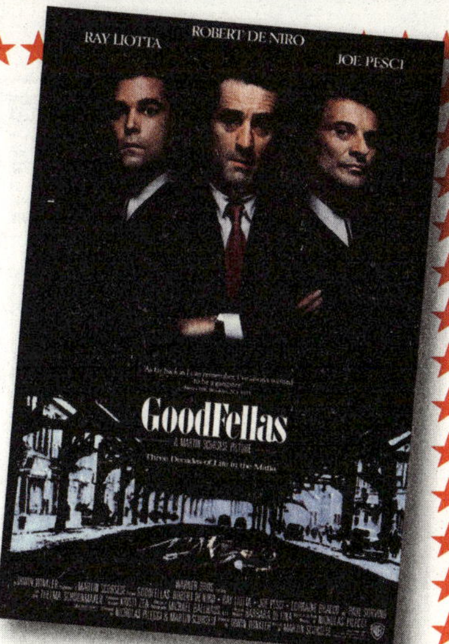

It didn't make sense. Why would Martin and Quentin care about me trashing movies that were several decades old? And that's when it hit me... *it wasn't Martin or Quentin!*

Earlier that evening, I had posted my review on Twitter, @-ing my movie buff peers Peter Bradshaw and Mark Kermode with the message: 'Hey guys check out my new review ;-)' Neither had 'liked' my tweet, nor given any indication that they'd seen it. But they obviously had.

Clearly, Bradshaw and Kermode had read my searingly intelligent and witty review, and shat their respective kecks. They'd realised there was a hotshot new critic in town, with more talent in his (ie. my) little finger than they had in their whole bodies. They knew that once *The Guardian* and the BBC got wind of my incisive prose, they'd both be straight down the dole office. So they'd snuck into my house to reignite my chip pan and do me in.

As the flames rose higher, I stood frozen to the spot in horror. Of all the despicable things filmmakers had done to me, it was my *fellow film critics* that had proved the most despicable. I couldn't believe it.

Looking around, I could see only one option - to try, unsuccessfully, to shin down the drainpipe outside the top floor window. And that's why I'm lying here now, fighting for my life in this hospital. There's not much to do while I wait for my shattered body to recover. But I'll tell you one thing: I *won't* be watching any films!"

FROM THE CREATOR OF TRUE ROMANCE AND RESERVOIR DOGS
QUENTIN TARANTINO
PULP FICTION

NEXT WEEK: ***Fenton launches his new website FentonLuvzTelly, only to be beaten unconscious outside a strip club for his scathing critique of the 'Succession' finale.***

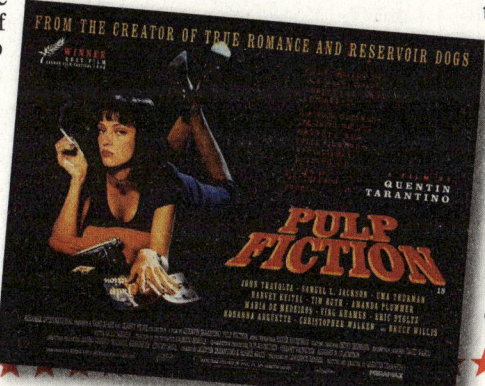

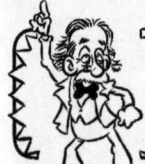

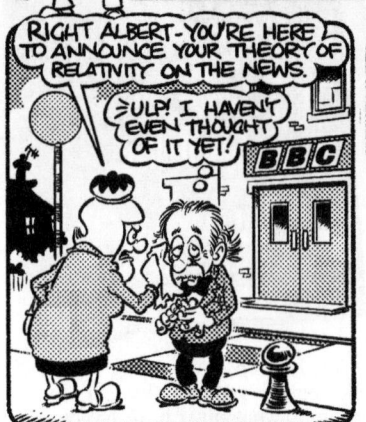

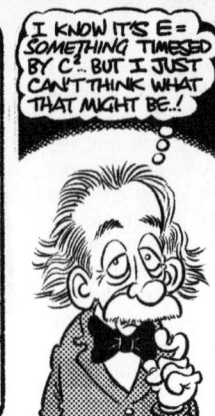

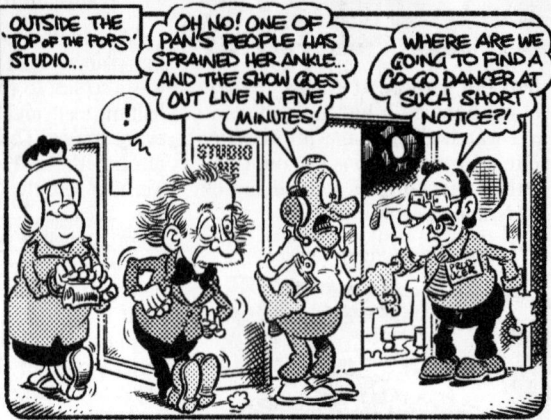

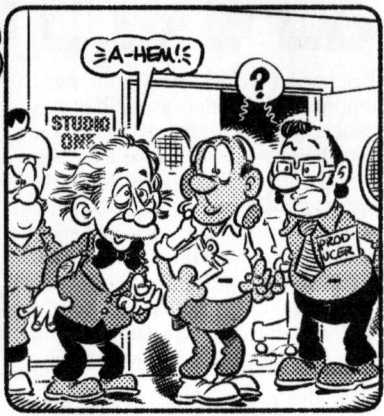

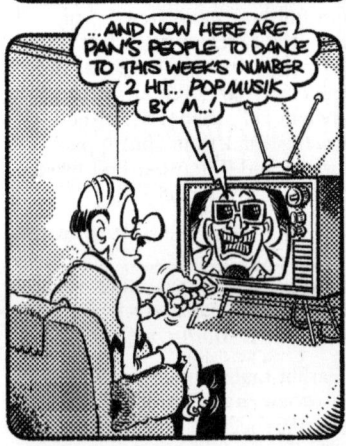

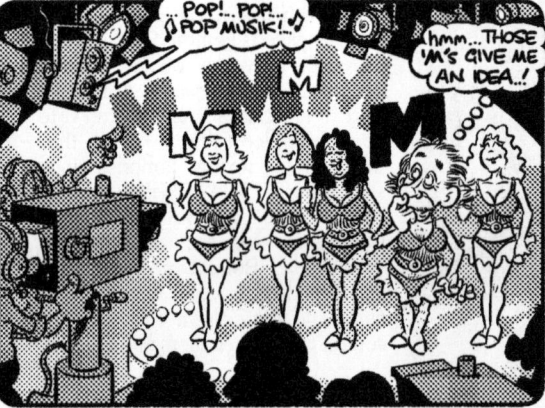

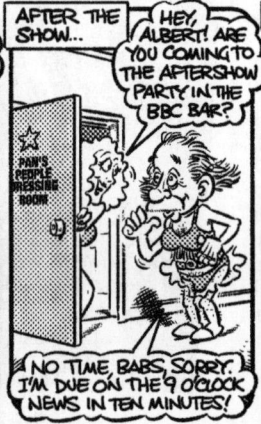

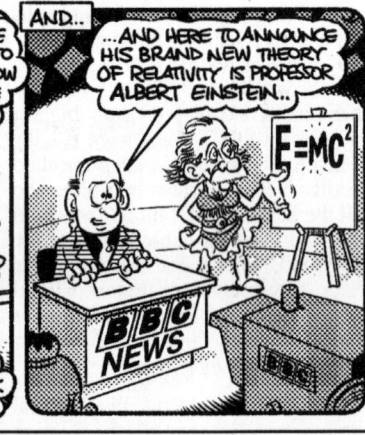

EINSTEIN A GO-GO!
ALBERT EINSTEIN HAD ALWAYS DREAMED OF BEING A GO-GO DANCER AT THE DISCOTHEQUE, BUT HIS MUM PUSHED HIM INTO A CAREER ...AS A THEORETICAL PHYSICIST..!
RIGHT ALBERT- YOU'RE HERE TO ANNOUNCE YOUR THEORY OF RELATIVITY ON THE NEWS.
ULP! I HAVEN'T EVEN THOUGHT OF IT YET!
BBC
I KNOW IT'S E = SOMETHING TIMESED BY C². BUT I JUST CAN'T THINK WHAT THAT MIGHT BE..!
OUTSIDE THE 'TOP OF THE POPS' STUDIO...
OH NO! ONE OF PAN'S PEOPLE HAS SPRAINED HER ANKLE.. AND THE SHOW GOES OUT LIVE IN FIVE MINUTES!
WHERE ARE WE GOING TO FIND A GO-GO DANCER AT SUCH SHORT NOTICE?!
!
A-HEM!
?
STUDIO ONE
PRODUCER
...AND NOW HERE ARE PAN'S PEOPLE TO DANCE TO THIS WEEK'S NUMBER 2 HIT... POP MUSIK BY M..!
...POP!..POP!... POP MUSIK!...
hmm... THOSE 'M's GIVE ME AN IDEA..!
AFTER THE SHOW...
HEY, ALBERT! ARE YOU COMING TO THE AFTERSHOW PARTY IN THE BBC BAR?
PAN'S PEOPLE DRESSING ROOM
NO TIME, BABS, SORRY. I'M DUE ON THE 9 O'CLOCK NEWS IN TEN MINUTES!
AND...
...AND HERE TO ANNOUNCE HIS BRAND NEW THEORY OF RELATIVITY IS PROFESSOR ALBERT EINSTEIN...
E=MC²
BBC NEWS

BORE AND DULLARD SITUATIONS VACANT

F1 GOBSHITE
£45k pa

Do you follow the Formula 1 circus? Does all your knowledge of it come from the TV coverage? Are you an utter, utter pain in the arse? Then we want to hear from YOU.

We are seeking to recruit a full time **F1 GOBSHITE** to regurgitate stuff they hear from the TV coverage to polite, but disinterested audiences UK-wide. The candidate will never have been to a Grand Prix, but will have watched every one live on the box, including getting up at 3:00am for the round in Shanghai.

The successful applicant will…

- ***Drone on about how the noise an F1 car makes is out of all proportion to their size, despite never having seen or heard one.***
- ***Describe how the downforce means an F1 car could drive upside down on the ceiling, despite it not being true.***
- ***Refer to drivers and team managers by their first names as though they know them personally.***
- ***Still live with their mum.***

Send full CV to

F1Gobshitesuk.com

Recent Non-Smoker Senior Lecturer

We are looking for a former heavy smoker who has given up in the past month to lecture anyone trying to enjoy a cigarette.

The successful candidate must demonstrate an ability to:

- ★ Bore the arse off smokers talking about the dangers of cigarettes
- ★ Outline how much money they are saving and what they are going to spend it on
- ★ Announce how much better they feel whilst inflating their lungs dramatically
- ★ Attribute the subsequent hacking cough to 'breathing in a crumb'

The new non-smoker must be able to turn a conversation on any topic – politics, football, TV etc – to a smugly delivered condemnation of the tobacco industry and the health benefits of cigarette-free living. The ability to open every sentence with *"When I was a smoker…"* is essential.

The pay grade for this position is 34k pa plus nicotine gum allowance. Please note, this is a temporary appointment as it is expected the successful candidate will be back on 100+ a day within six months.

Send your CV to:
appointments@quitfagbores.org

GENERAL SPORTS BORE ~ 45K PA

We have several vacancies for highly-irritating men to voice loud, unsolicited opinions on a variety of sports including:

• Golf • Cricket • Football • Athletics

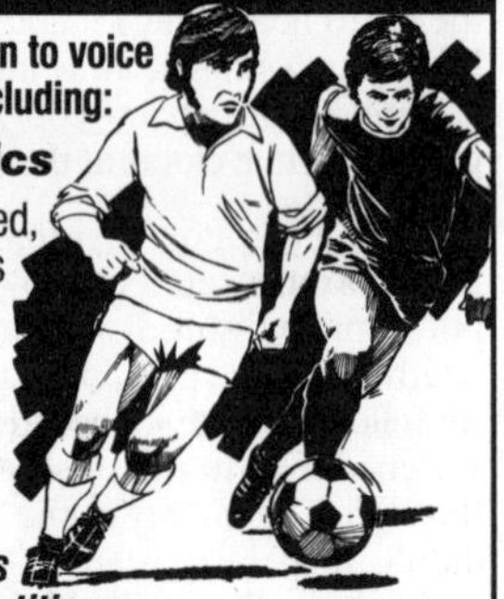

Having played these sports to any level is not required, but the successful applicant must be able to express unfounded views, both in and out of season, in a wide variety of settings including pubs, restaurants, canteens, funerals and bus stops.

A loud, confident and over-bearing voice is essential. The successful candidate will be:

• Repetitious • Frequently wrong • Repetitious • Unable to recognise lack of interest • Repetitious

So if you've been to one cricket match in your life on the last afternoon of a test when entry was free, or think you could do a better job than Gareth Southgate despite not having been inside a football ground since your dad took you as a kid, then *we want to hear from you*.

Applicants from the taxi-driving community are strongly encouraged to apply.

Apply online at www.sportsbores.org.uk

Tedious New Parent - 25kpa

Just Had a Baby? We are looking for a new mum or dad to attend dinner parties and other social events and talk non-stop about their newborn infant. Can you bang on and on and on about…

- ***how uniquely intelligent your child is***
- ***how they are already showing an understanding of maths at 2 months***
- ***how they will show no interest in computer games as they get older***
- ***how they will become a musical prodigy***

In addition, you must be able to subject your audience to 1000+ largely identical photographs of your neonate on your smartphone, not scrolling to the next until viewers have made a favourable comment on each.

You will also be able to make, on the face of it, complimentary sounding, yet in reality, quite derogatory, remarks concerning the looks and abilities of other people's children.

Apply using our online form at lookatmybloodybaby.co.uk

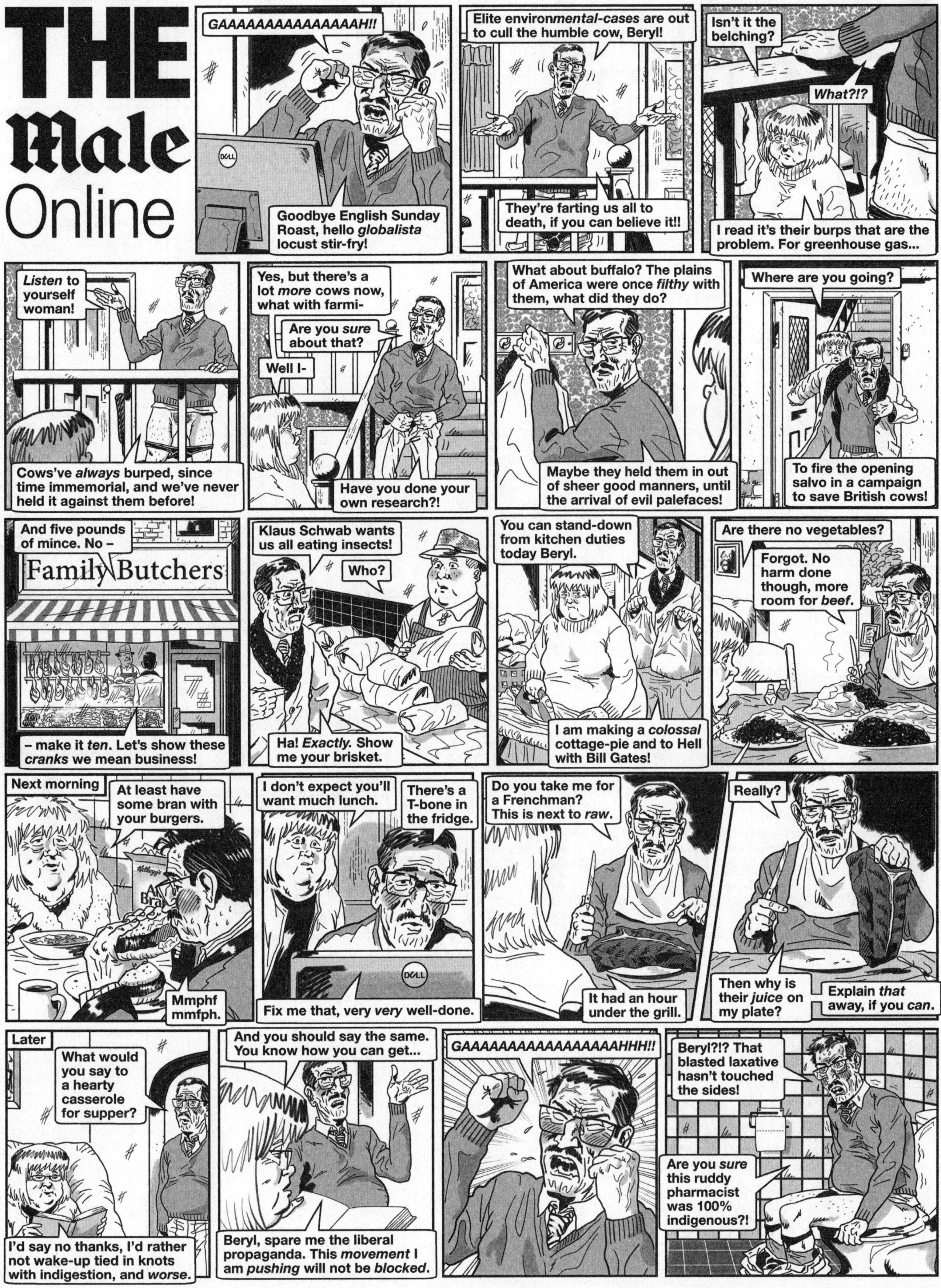
THE Male Online
GAAAAAAAAAAAAAAAAH!!
Goodbye English Sunday Roast, hello globalista locust stir-fry!
Elite environmental-cases are out to cull the humble cow, Beryl!
They're farting us all to death, if you can believe it!!
Isn't it the belching?
What?!?
I read it's their burps that are the problem. For greenhouse gas...
Listen to yourself woman!
Cows've always burped, since time immemorial, and we've never held it against them before!
Yes, but there's a lot more cows now, what with farmi-
Are you sure about that?
Well I-
Have you done your own research?!
What about buffalo? The plains of America were once filthy with them, what did they do?
Maybe they held them in out of sheer good manners, until the arrival of evil palefaces!
Where are you going?
To fire the opening salvo in a campaign to save British cows!
And five pounds of mince. No –
Family Butchers
– make it ten. Let's show these cranks we mean business!
Klaus Schwab wants us all eating insects!
Who?
Ha! Exactly. Show me your brisket.
You can stand-down from kitchen duties today Beryl.
I am making a colossal cottage-pie and to Hell with Bill Gates!
Are there no vegetables?
Forgot. No harm done though, more room for beef.
Next morning
At least have some bran with your burgers.
Mmphf mmfph.
I don't expect you'll want much lunch.
There's a T-bone in the fridge.
Fix me that, very very well-done.
Do you take me for a Frenchman? This is next to raw.
It had an hour under the grill.
Really?
Then why is their juice on my plate?
Explain that away, if you can.
Later
What would you say to a hearty casserole for supper?
I'd say no thanks, I'd rather not wake-up tied in knots with indigestion, and worse.
And you should say the same. You know how you can get...
Beryl, spare me the liberal propaganda. This movement I am pushing will not be blocked.
GAAAAAAAAAAAAAAAAAAHHH!!
Beryl?!? That blasted laxative hasn't touched the sides!
Are you sure this ruddy pharmacist was 100% indigenous?!

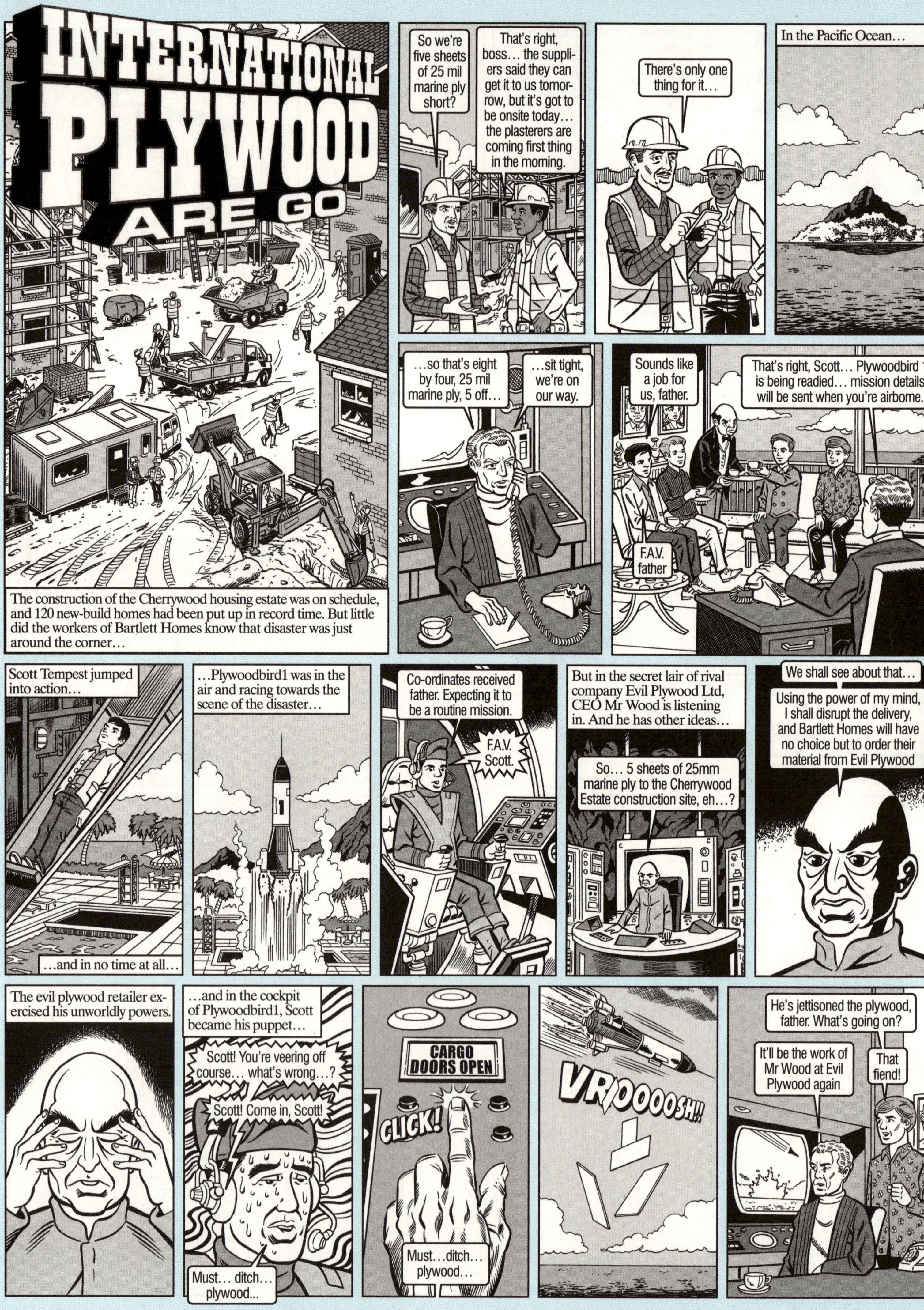

INTERNATIONAL PLYWOOD ARE GO
The construction of the Cherrywood housing estate was on schedule, and 120 new-build homes had been put up in record time. But little did the workers of Bartlett Homes know that disaster was just around the corner…
So we're five sheets of 25 mil marine ply short?
That's right, boss… the suppliers said they can get it to us tomorrow, but it's got to be onsite today… the plasterers are coming first thing in the morning.
There's only one thing for it…
In the Pacific Ocean…
…so that's eight by four, 25 mil marine ply, 5 off…
…sit tight, we're on our way.
Sounds like a job for us, father.
That's right, Scott… Plywoodbird 1 is being readied… mission details will be sent when you're airborne.
F.A.V. father
Scott Tempest jumped into action…
…and in no time at all…
…Plywoodbird1 was in the air and racing towards the scene of the disaster…
Co-ordinates received father. Expecting it to be a routine mission.
F.A.V. Scott.
But in the secret lair of rival company Evil Plywood Ltd, CEO Mr Wood is listening in. And he has other ideas…
So… 5 sheets of 25mm marine ply to the Cherrywood Estate construction site, eh…?
We shall see about that…
Using the power of my mind, I shall disrupt the delivery, and Bartlett Homes will have no choice but to order their material from Evil Plywood
The evil plywood retailer exercised his unworldly powers.
…and in the cockpit of Plywoodbird1, Scott became his puppet…
Scott! You're veering off course… what's wrong…?
Scott! Come in, Scott!
Must… ditch… plywood...
CARGO DOORS OPEN
CLICK!
Must…ditch… plywood…
VROOOOOSH!!
He's jettisoned the plywood, father. What's going on?
It'll be the work of Mr Wood at Evil Plywood again
That fiend!

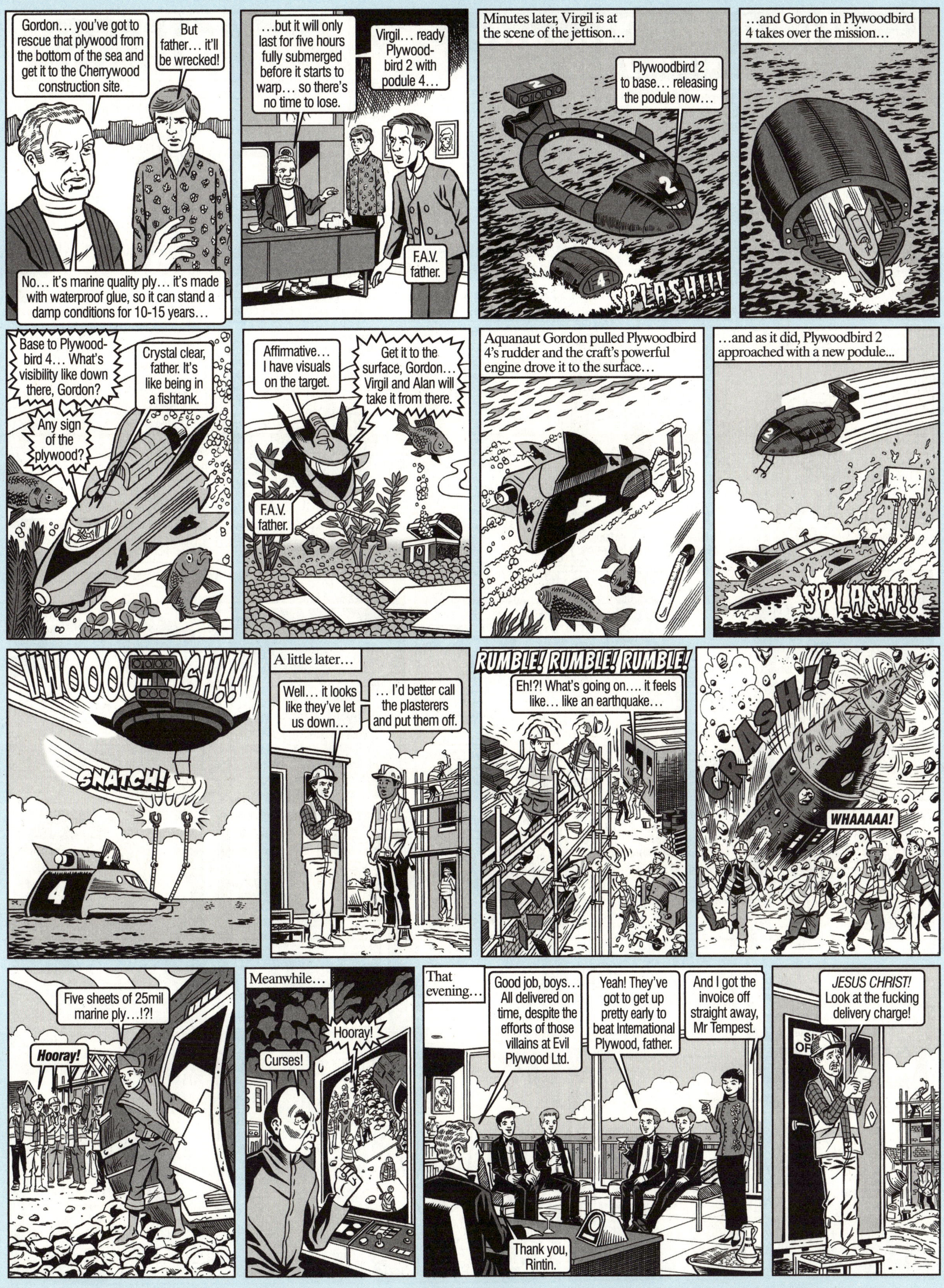

Gordon… you've got to rescue that plywood from the bottom of the sea and get it to the Cherrywood construction site.
But father… it'll be wrecked!
No… it's marine quality ply… it's made with waterproof glue, so it can stand a damp conditions for 10-15 years…
…but it will only last for five hours fully submerged before it starts to warp… so there's no time to lose.
Virgil… ready Plywood-bird 2 with podule 4…
F.A.V. father.
Minutes later, Virgil is at the scene of the jettison…
Plywoodbird 2 to base… releasing the podule now…
SPLASH!!!
…and Gordon in Plywoodbird 4 takes over the mission…
Base to Plywood-bird 4… What's visibility like down there, Gordon?
Crystal clear, father. It's like being in a fishtank.
Any sign of the plywood?
Affirmative… I have visuals on the target.
Get it to the surface, Gordon… Virgil and Alan will take it from there.
F.A.V. father.
Aquanaut Gordon pulled Plywoodbird 4's rudder and the craft's powerful engine drove it to the surface…
…and as it did, Plywoodbird 2 approached with a new podule...
SPLASH!!
SNATCH!
A little later…
Well… it looks like they've let us down…
…I'd better call the plasterers and put them off.
RUMBLE! RUMBLE! RUMBLE!
Eh!?! What's going on… it feels like… like an earthquake…
CRASH!!
WHAAAAA!
Five sheets of 25mil marine ply…!?!
Hooray!
Meanwhile…
Hooray!
Curses!
That evening…
Good job, boys… All delivered on time, despite the efforts of those villains at Evil Plywood Ltd.
Yeah! They've got to get up pretty early to beat International Plywood, father.
And I got the invoice off straight away, Mr Tempest.
Thank you, Rintin.
JESUS CHRIST! Look at the fucking delivery charge!

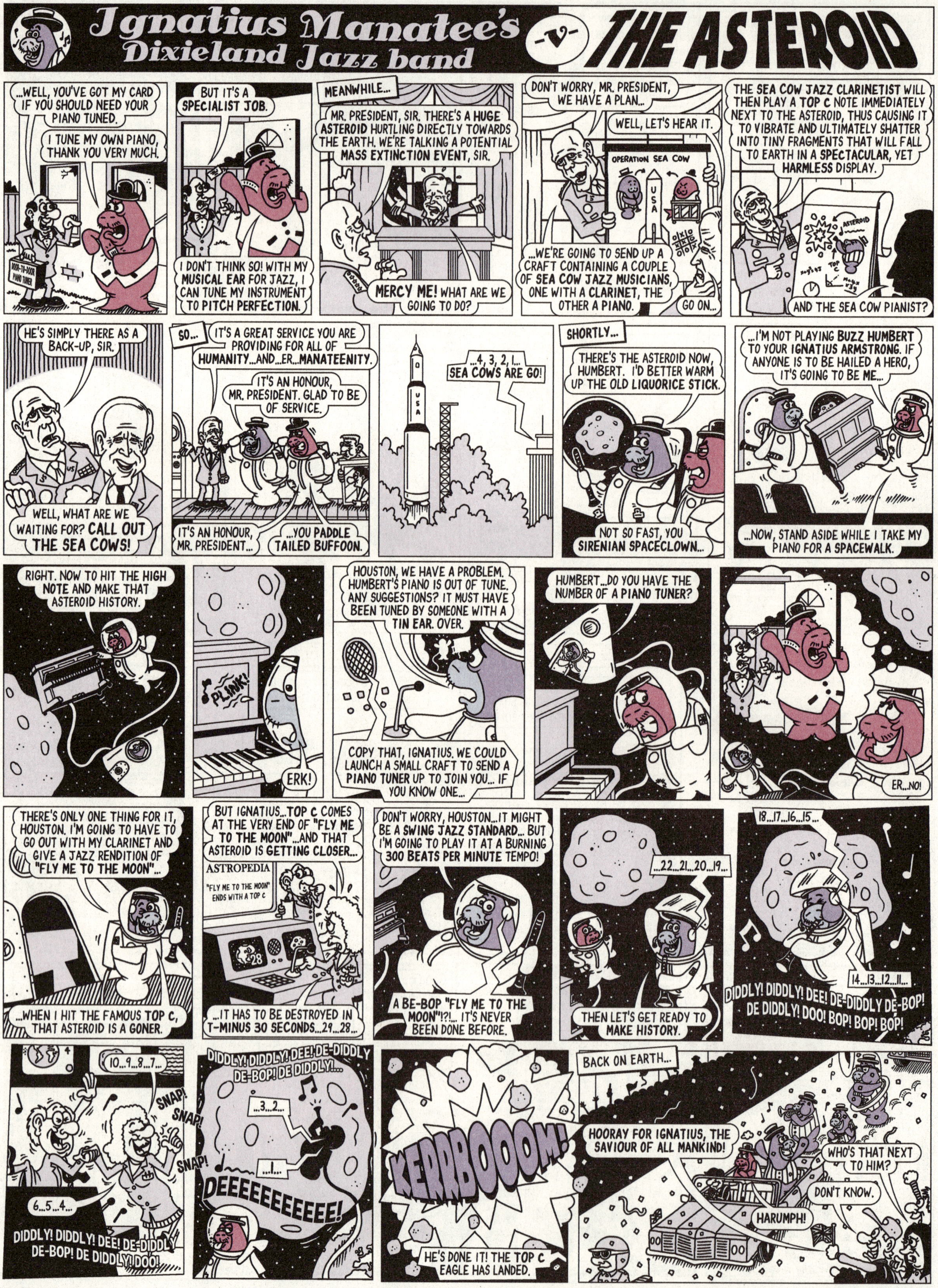
Ignatius Manatee's Dixieland Jazz band
-v-
THE ASTEROID
...WELL, YOU'VE GOT MY CARD IF YOU SHOULD NEED YOUR PIANO TUNED.
I TUNE MY OWN PIANO, THANK YOU VERY MUCH.
DOOR-TO-DOOR PIANO TUNER
BUT IT'S A SPECIALIST JOB.
I DON'T THINK SO! WITH MY MUSICAL EAR FOR JAZZ, I CAN TUNE MY INSTRUMENT TO PITCH PERFECTION.
MEANWHILE...
MR. PRESIDENT, SIR, THERE'S A HUGE ASTEROID HURTLING DIRECTLY TOWARDS THE EARTH. WE'RE TALKING A POTENTIAL MASS EXTINCTION EVENT, SIR.
MERCY ME! WHAT ARE WE GOING TO DO?
DON'T WORRY, MR. PRESIDENT, WE HAVE A PLAN...
WELL, LET'S HEAR IT.
OPERATION SEA COW
USA
...WE'RE GOING TO SEND UP A CRAFT CONTAINING A COUPLE OF SEA COW JAZZ MUSICIANS, ONE WITH A CLARINET, THE OTHER A PIANO.
GO ON...
THE SEA COW JAZZ CLARINETIST WILL THEN PLAY A TOP C NOTE IMMEDIATELY NEXT TO THE ASTEROID, THUS CAUSING IT TO VIBRATE AND ULTIMATELY SHATTER INTO TINY FRAGMENTS THAT WILL FALL TO EARTH IN A SPECTACULAR, YET HARMLESS DISPLAY.
ASTEROID
AND THE SEA COW PIANIST?
HE'S SIMPLY THERE AS A BACK-UP, SIR.
WELL, WHAT ARE WE WAITING FOR? CALL OUT THE SEA COWS!
SO...
IT'S A GREAT SERVICE YOU ALL ARE PROVIDING FOR ALL OF HUMANITY...AND...ER...MANATEENITY.
IT'S AN HONOUR, MR. PRESIDENT. GLAD TO BE OF SERVICE.
IT'S AN HONOUR, MR. PRESIDENT...
...YOU PADDLE TAILED BUFFOON.
...4, 3, 2, 1... SEA COWS ARE GO!
USA
SHORTLY...
THERE'S THE ASTEROID NOW, HUMBERT. I'D BETTER WARM UP THE OLD LIQUORICE STICK.
NOT SO FAST, YOU SIRENIAN SPACECLOWN...
...I'M NOT PLAYING BUZZ HUMBERT TO YOUR IGNATIUS ARMSTRONG. IF ANYONE IS TO BE HAILED A HERO, IT'S GOING TO BE ME...
...NOW, STAND ASIDE WHILE I TAKE MY PIANO FOR A SPACEWALK.
RIGHT. NOW TO HIT THE HIGH NOTE AND MAKE THAT ASTEROID HISTORY.
PLINK!
ERK!
HOUSTON, WE HAVE A PROBLEM. HUMBERT'S PIANO IS OUT OF TUNE. ANY SUGGESTIONS? IT MUST HAVE BEEN TUNED BY SOMEONE WITH A TIN EAR. OVER.
COPY THAT, IGNATIUS. WE COULD LAUNCH A SMALL CRAFT TO SEND A PIANO TUNER UP TO JOIN YOU... IF YOU KNOW ONE...
HUMBERT...DO YOU HAVE THE NUMBER OF A PIANO TUNER?
ER...NO!
THERE'S ONLY ONE THING FOR IT, HOUSTON. I'M GOING TO HAVE TO GO OUT WITH MY CLARINET AND GIVE A JAZZ RENDITION OF "FLY ME TO THE MOON"...
...WHEN I HIT THE FAMOUS TOP C, THAT ASTEROID IS A GONER.
BUT IGNATIUS...TOP C COMES AT THE VERY END OF "FLY ME TO THE MOON"...AND THAT ASTEROID IS GETTING CLOSER...
ASTROPEDIA
"FLY ME TO THE MOON" ENDS WITH A TOP C
28
...IT HAS TO BE DESTROYED IN T-MINUS 30 SECONDS...29...28...
DON'T WORRY, HOUSTON...IT MIGHT BE A SWING JAZZ STANDARD... BUT I'M GOING TO PLAY IT AT A BURNING 300 BEATS PER MINUTE TEMPO!
A BE-BOP "FLY ME TO THE MOON"!?!... IT'S NEVER BEEN DONE BEFORE.
...22...21...20...19...
THEN LET'S GET READY TO MAKE HISTORY.
18...17...16...15...
14...13...12...11...
DIDDLY! DIDDLY! DEE! DE-DIDDLY DE-BOP! DE DIDDLY! DOO! BOP! BOP! BOP!
10...9...8...7...
SNAP!
SNAP!
SNAP!
6...5...4...
DIDDLY! DIDDLY! DEE! DE-DIDDLY DE-BOP! DE DIDDLY! DOO!
DIDDLY! DIDDLY! DEE! DE-DIDDLY DE-BOP! DE DIDDLY!...
...3...2...
...1...
DEEEEEEEEEEE!
KERRBOOOM!
HE'S DONE IT! THE TOP C EAGLE HAS LANDED.
BACK ON EARTH...
HOORAY FOR IGNATIUS, THE SAVIOUR OF ALL MANKIND!
WHO'S THAT NEXT TO HIM?
DON'T KNOW.
HARUMPH!

WE RAIL YOU

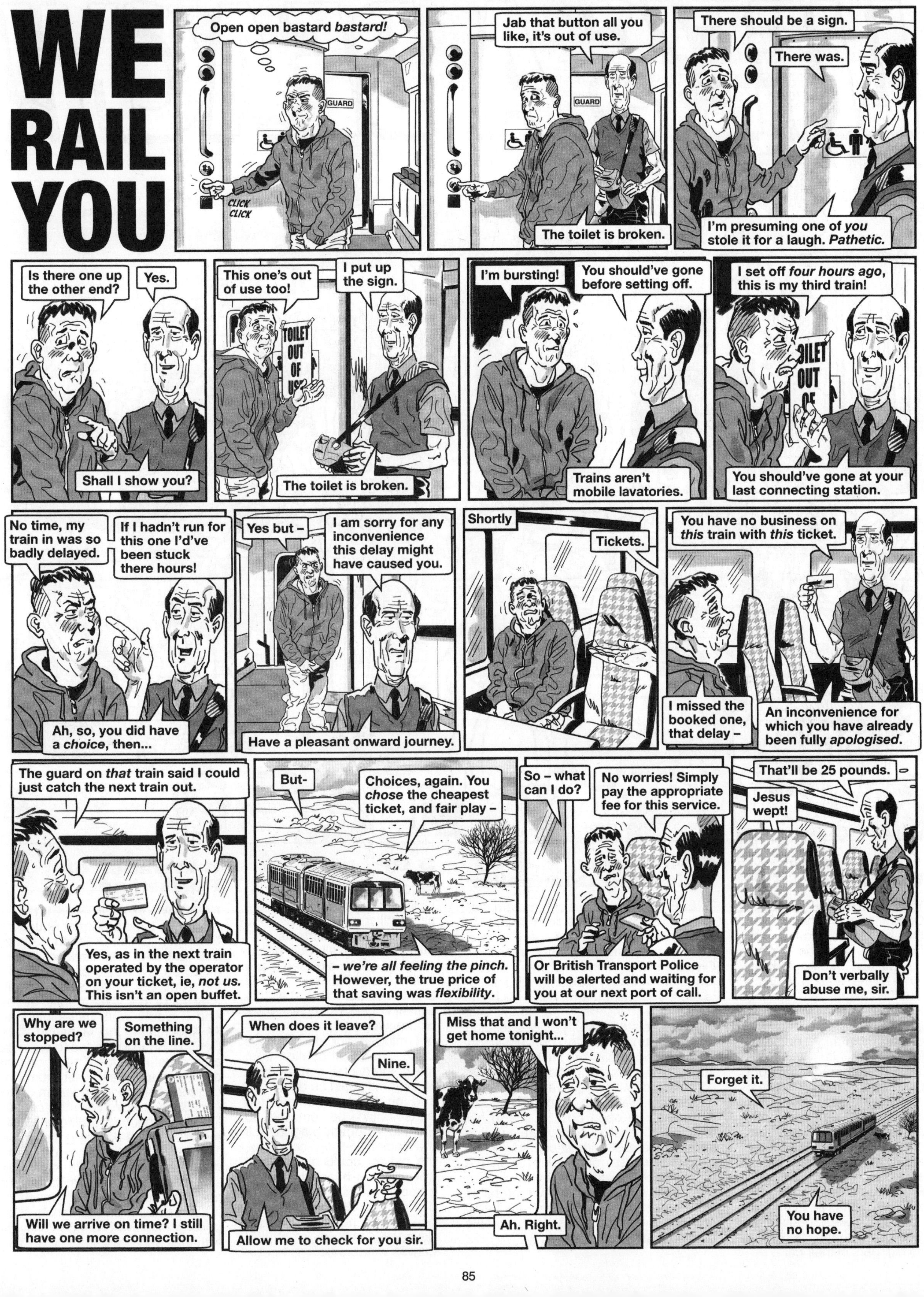

Open open bastard *bastard!*
GUARD
CLICK CLICK
Jab that button all you like, it's out of use.
GUARD
The toilet is broken.
There should be a sign.
There was.
I'm presuming one of *you* stole it for a laugh. *Pathetic.*
Is there one up the other end?
Yes.
Shall I show you?
This one's out of use too!
I put up the sign.
TOILET OUT OF
The toilet is broken.
I'm bursting!
You should've gone before setting off.
Trains aren't mobile lavatories.
I set off *four hours ago*, this is my third train!
You should've gone at your last connecting station.
No time, my train in was so badly delayed.
If I hadn't run for this one I'd've been stuck there hours!
Ah, so, you did have a *choice*, then...
Yes but –
I am sorry for any inconvenience this delay might have caused you.
Have a pleasant onward journey.
Shortly
Tickets.
You have no business on *this* train with *this* ticket.
I missed the booked one, that delay –
An inconvenience for which you have already been fully *apologised*.
The guard on *that* train said I could just catch the next train out.
Yes, as in the next train operated by the operator on your ticket, ie, *not us*. This isn't an open buffet.
But-
Choices, again. You *chose* the cheapest ticket, and fair play –
– we're all feeling the pinch. However, the true price of that saving was *flexibility*.
So – what can I do?
No worries! Simply pay the appropriate fee for this service.
Or British Transport Police will be alerted and waiting for you at our next port of call.
That'll be 25 pounds.
Jesus wept!
Don't verbally abuse me, sir.
Why are we stopped?
Something on the line.
Will we arrive on time? I still have one more connection.
When does it leave?
Nine.
Allow me to check for you sir.
Miss that and I won't get home tonight...
Ah. Right.
Forget it.
You have no hope.

LIFE'S A BEACH!

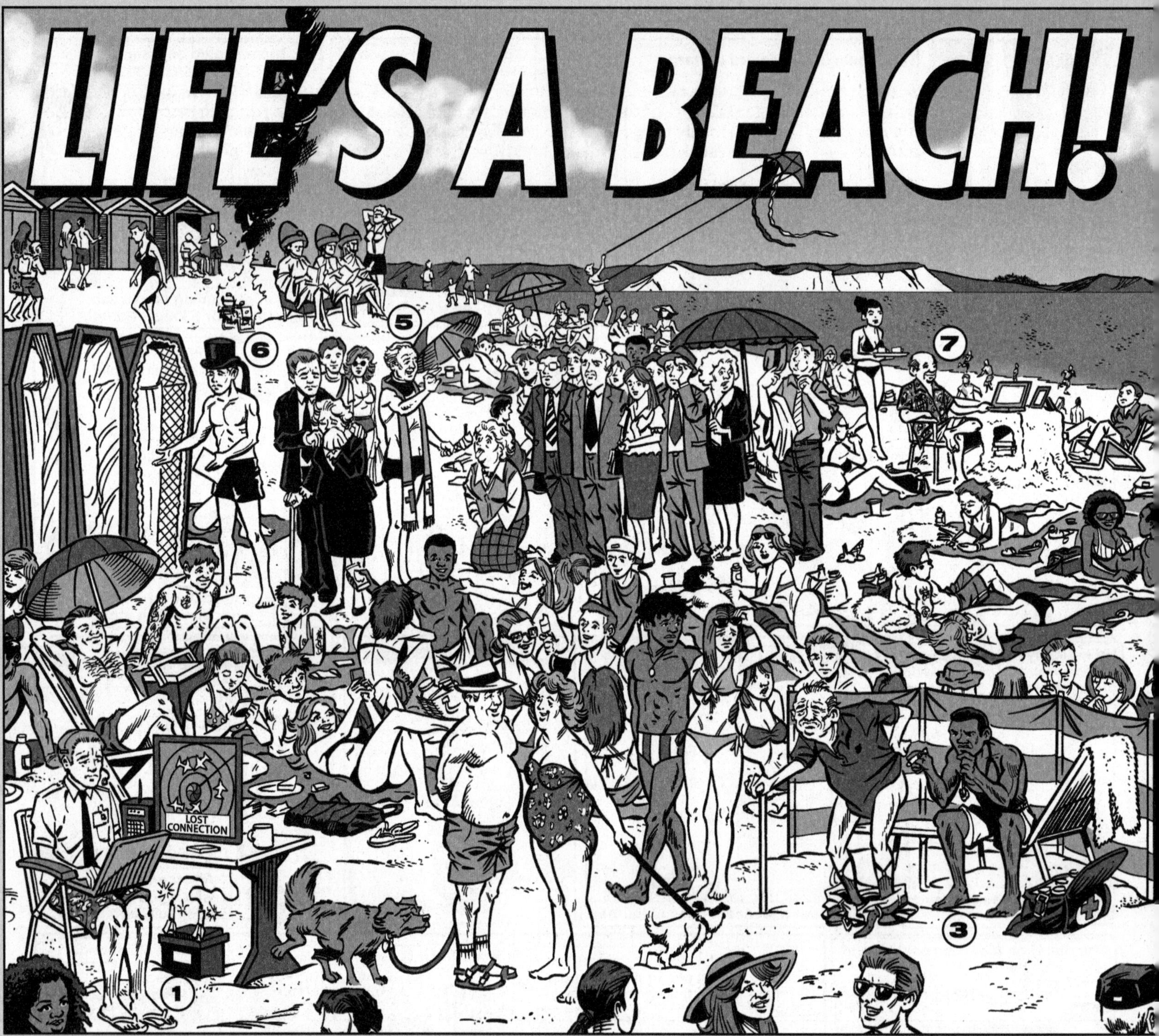

6
5
7
LOST CONNECTION
1
3

1 Air Traffic Controller

YEARS AGO, the Air Traffic Controller had to work from the airport control tower. But today, with the system completely computerised, there is no reason why he or she might not do the job from wherever there is internet coverage. It is one of the most high pressure jobs there is, with the lives of hundreds of flight passengers in their hands, and a stressed controller is liable to make costly mistakes. So working from the beach will mean they are more relaxed and better able to perform their task. Provided they don't lose their wifi signal, or run out of data, it's a win-win situation for both them and the passengers in their care.

2 Marriage Guidance Counsellor

THESE DAYS, nine out of ten marriages end in divorce within the first three years. That's enough divorcees every year to fill ten Wembley Stadiums and an Olympic-sized swimming pool. So the job of the Marriage Guidance Counsellor is more important than it has ever been. Normally, counselling sessions take place within sterile, stuffy offices, leading to dull, unproductive conversations. Taking these sessions to the beach could add a new element to the discussions. A husband who discovered his wife having an affair with a friend may be more likely to open up and talk to her and the counsellor if they are relaxing under a parasol with a cold drink. Or a couple whose relationship is on the rocks because the husband suffers from erectile dysfunction will probably talk more candidly if all three are being dragged round the bay on an inflatable banana boat.

3 GP

SINCE THE DAYS of the Covid 19 pandemic, we are all familiar with online and telephone appointments with our GP. Now all our health records are digitised and online, any doctor with a phone has our medical history at their fingertips, and we users of the wonderful NHS would not mind if our doctor gave us their medical opinion from the comfort of a sun lounger. Symptoms could be described and photographs of affected parts could be emailed to them for a speedy diagnosis. If the doctor had any concerns, the patient could always pop down to the beach for an in-person examination. Patient dignity could be ensured by performing examinations discreetly behind a striped canvas windbreak.

4 Member of Parliament

NOBODY on earth works harder than an MP, and as former Education Secretary Gillian Keegan pointed out, nobody ever fucking thanks them. So few would begrudge MPs the comforts of the seaside while they carry out their public duties. And it would work incredibly well: As Kabul fell to the Taliban in 2021, Dominic Raab managed to organise a successful airlift of British citizens and Afghan allies - all from the comfort of his paddle board in Crete! And Boris Johnson ran the country like clockwork from a different 5-star resort every week during his time at Number 10. With Zoom or Teams on their phones, MPs can hold surgeries, sit on committees, and attend top secret COBRA meetings whilst paddling on the beach, rock-pooling or playing beach volleyball with their secretary.

LAST week the country was rocked after the *Daily Mail* revealed that many council workers were being given permission to leave offices and desks to work remotely. And if that wasn't bad enough, many of these work-shy skivers were doing so... *from the beach!* You couldn't make it up.

But is remote working from the beach really such a bad thing? Could the fresh sea air and sunshine actually lead to workers being *more* productive during their nine-to-five? And if so, is it not time we allowed more people to head to the beach to clock on? Because it's not just office workers who could do their jobs on the sand. With a little forethought and preparation, professionals across a whole range of occupations could do their jobs whilst soaking up some rays and enjoying the salty air.

Let's take a look at how some key people who help us might do their work from the beach...

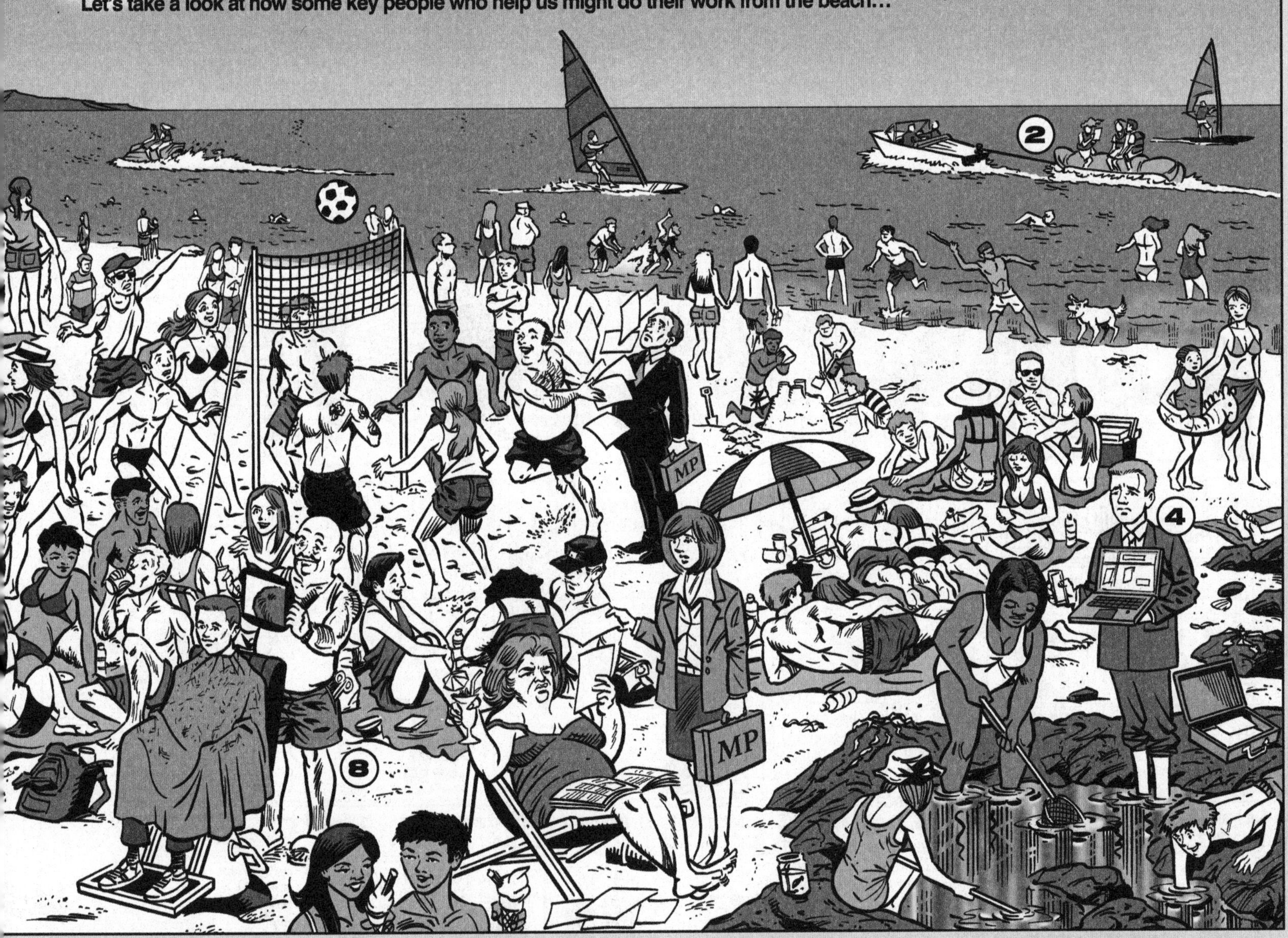
2
MP
4
MP
8

5 Vicar

SINCE VICARS only work on Sundays and get six days off, they are already free to go to the beach as much as they like. But there is no reason that they cannot spend every day on the sand. Sermons, weddings, Christenings and Holy Communions could all be conducted in God's fresh air on the seashore. The congregation could sit on comfy deck chairs instead of buttock-numbing pews, and eat ice-cream cones instead of tasteless communion wafers, with strawberry syrup transubstantiating into the Blood of Christ. The only disadvantage would be that the men of the congregation would have to remove their hats for the duration of the service, which could lead to sunburn, sunstroke or worse...

6 Undertaker

WHEN WE lose a loved one, the solid, reliable and dignified services of the Undertaker offer us consolation and help us through the difficult task of organising a funeral. Years ago, we would visit the funeral parlour to make arrangements, and more recently, funeral directors have started making home visits. There is no reason why they could not offer advice about the choice of coffin, floral tributes and funeral cars whilst relaxing with a Pina Colada on the beach. However, the actual bodies of the deceased would not be brought to the seaside as loved ones want to be with them in the atmosphere of quiet contemplation that the Chapel of Rest affords. Having kids running abound playing beach cricket, dogs barking and ice-cream vans playing tunes whilst they see their loved ones for the last time might detract from their emotional farewells.

7 Solicitor

WE ALL USE solicitors at some point in our lives, whether we're buying a house, writing a will or attempting to keep our driving licence after a speeding offence. Their services are notoriously expensive, but the cost of *not* using them could be even higher. Although their jobs are traditionally office-based, provided they can fashion a desk from sand, there is no reason why they cannot meet with their clients on the beach. However, this remote seaside-working will come at a price - as well as the cost of their time and fees, you should expect your invoices to contain a few additional charges for professional services and disbursements, such as provision of factor 50 suncream, Calypo ice-lollies and beach umbrella hire charged at £2 per hour or part thereof.

8 Barber

MOST GENTS' Barber shops are stuffy places, pungent with the smell of years of Brylcreem, hair lacquer and blue disinfectant. So how much better an experience would it be for both customer and barber if his services were provided outdoors on the beach? All the barber needs is a comb, a pair of scissors and an enormous hydraulic chair, and he's good to go. Women's hairdressing salons could similarly operate on the seafront with the addition of a small diesel generator to power the hairdryers. And as sea breezes would carry the cut hair away, beach hairstylists would not have to employ a bored, chewing gum-chomping 16-year-old to sweep the clippings up from the sand.

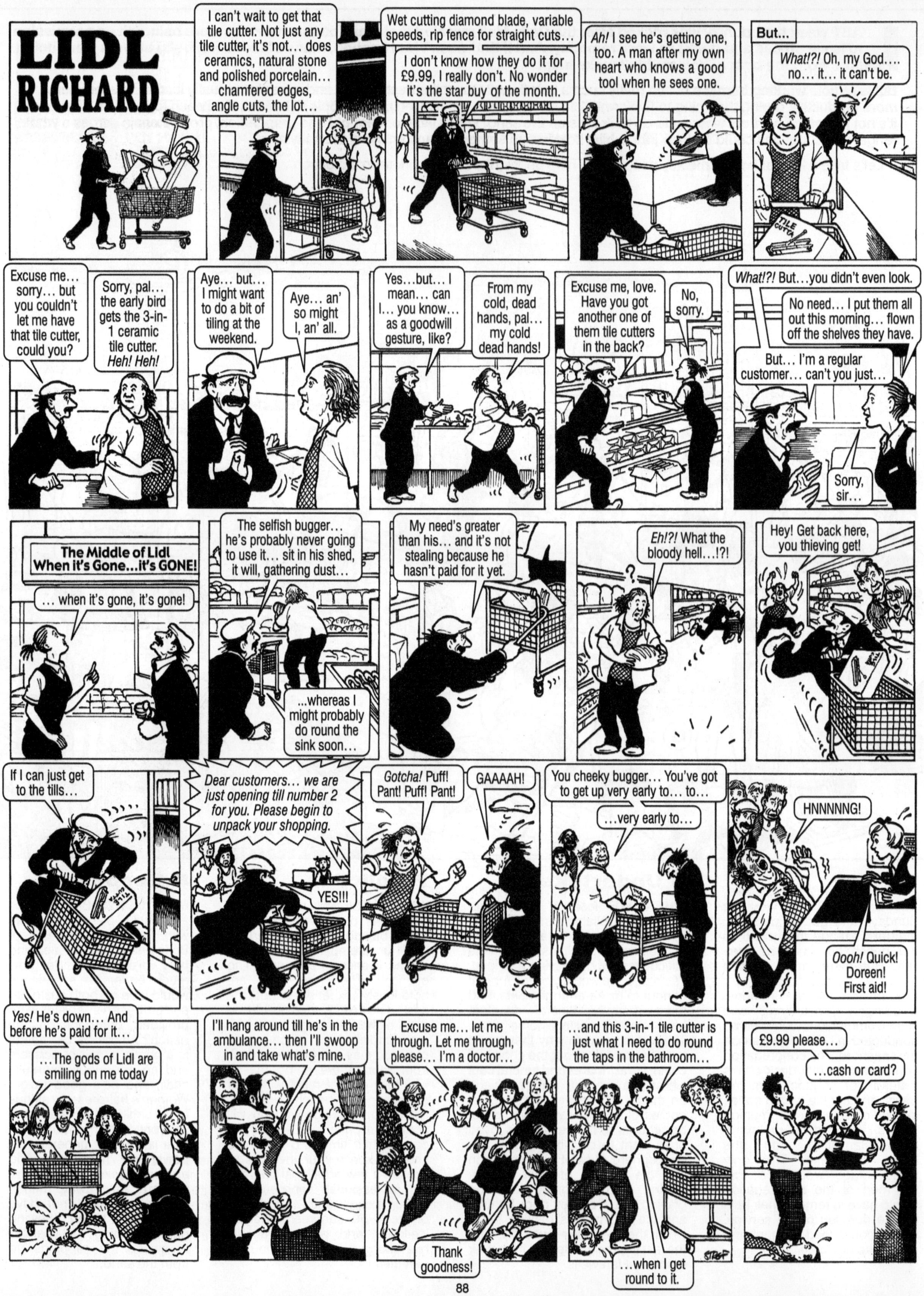

LIDL RICHARD
I can't wait to get that tile cutter. Not just any tile cutter, it's not… does ceramics, natural stone and polished porcelain… chamfered edges, angle cuts, the lot…
Wet cutting diamond blade, variable speeds, rip fence for straight cuts…
I don't know how they do it for £9.99, I really don't. No wonder it's the star buy of the month.
Ah! I see he's getting one, too. A man after my own heart who knows a good tool when he sees one.
But…
What!?! Oh, my God…. no… it… it can't be.
TILE CUTTA
Excuse me… sorry… but you couldn't let me have that tile cutter, could you?
Sorry, pal… the early bird gets the 3-in-1 ceramic tile cutter. Heh! Heh!
Aye… but… I might want to do a bit of tiling at the weekend.
Aye… an' so might I, an' all.
Yes…but… I mean… can I… you know… as a goodwill gesture, like?
From my cold, dead hands, pal… my cold dead hands!
Excuse me, love. Have you got another one of them tile cutters in the back?
No, sorry.
What!?! But…you didn't even look.
No need… I put them all out this morning… flown off the shelves they have.
But… I'm a regular customer… can't you just…
Sorry, sir…
The Middle of Lidl When it's Gone…it's GONE!
… when it's gone, it's gone!
The selfish bugger… he's probably never going to use it… sit in his shed, it will, gathering dust…
...whereas I might probably do round the sink soon…
My need's greater than his… and it's not stealing because he hasn't paid for it yet.
Eh!?! What the bloody hell…!?!
Hey! Get back here, you thieving get!
If I can just get to the tills…
Dear customers… we are just opening till number 2 for you. Please begin to unpack your shopping.
YES!!!
Gotcha! Puff! Pant! Puff! Pant!
GAAAAH!
You cheeky bugger… You've got to get up very early to… to…
…very early to…
HNNNNNG!
Oooh! Quick! Doreen! First aid!
Yes! He's down… And before he's paid for it…
…The gods of Lidl are smiling on me today
I'll hang around till he's in the ambulance… then I'll swoop in and take what's mine.
Excuse me… let me through. Let me through, please… I'm a doctor…
Thank goodness!
…and this 3-in-1 tile cutter is just what I need to do round the taps in the bathroom…
…when I get round to it.
£9.99 please…
…cash or card?

ROGER MELLIE
THE MAN ON THE TELLY
NEW YEAR'S DAY...
MORNING, ROGER. HAPPY NEW YEAR! FANCY A DRINK TO TOAST 2023?
JUST A TONIC WATER, TOM!
TONIC WATER!?
ARE YOU OKAY?
FINE, TOM... I'M DOING DRY JANUARY...
...THE FIRST TIME I GOT ON WITH IT
WOW!
I WAS SPANKING THE OLD LIVER TOO MUCH, TOM... AND I WAS GETTING A BIT OF A POT ON... STARTING TO LOOK LIKE JEREMY CLARKSON AFTER HIS CHRISTMAS DINNER
WELL I'M IMPRESSED
SO IMPRESSED, I'M GOING TO JOIN YOU, ROGER...
...TWO TONIC WATERS...
ALL THE VERY BEST TO YOU
CLINK!
BOTTOMS UP, TOM!
NEXT DAY...
MORNING ROGER... TONIC WATER?
PLEASE, TOM... AND STICK A TRIPLE GIN IN THE FUCKER, WILL YOU?
...A QUADRUPLE... NO... MAKE IT A FIVE TIMES WHATEVER THE WORD FOR THAT IS...
...QUINT-SOMETHING
WELL THAT DIDN'T LAST LONG, DID IT? BACK ON THE BOOZE ALREADY
WHAT ARE YOU TALKING ABOUT, TOM? I DID GREAT...
NOT A DROP PASSED MY LIPS!
"DRY JANUARY..."
"THE FIRST TIME I'VE GOT ON WITH IT" YOU SAID
NO!..
"DRY JANUARY THE FIRST..."
"...TIME I GOT ON WITH IT."
...I WAS SHAKING LIKE A SHITTING DOG BY MIDNIGHT, I CAN TELL YOU
ACTUALLY, I'LL MAKE IT AN OCTUPLE... I THINK THAT'S EIGHT, ISN'T IT?
I'VE GOT A BIT OF CATCHING UP TO DO

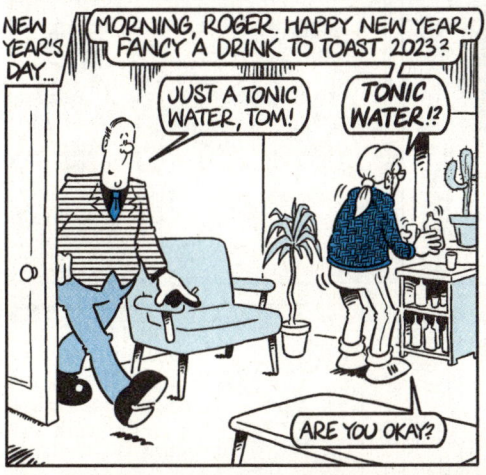

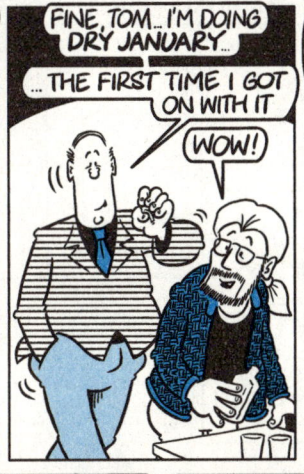

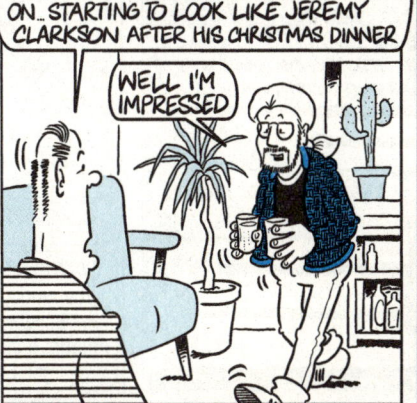

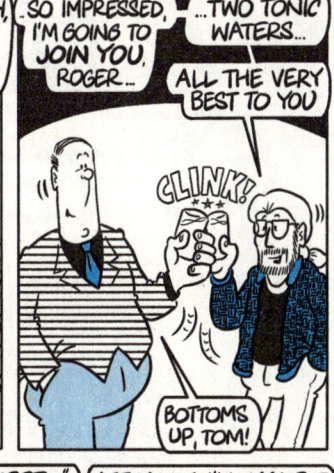

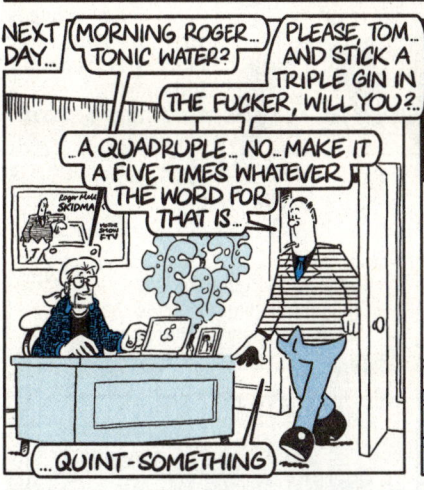

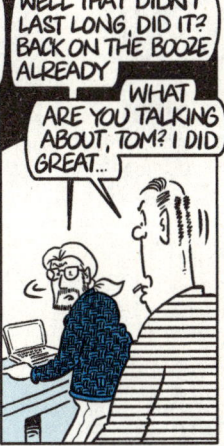

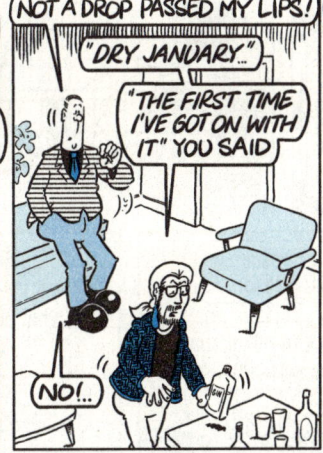

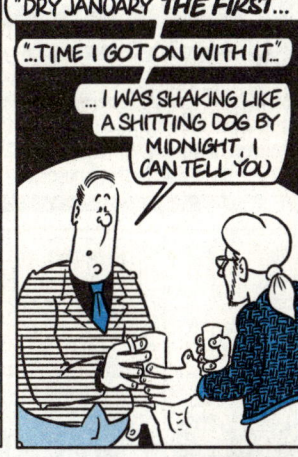

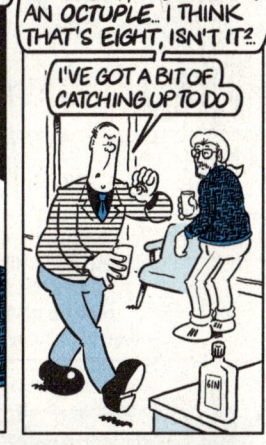

WE'RE DREAMING OF A WET CHRISTMAS!

Rain set to oust snow as new festive favourite

AFTER years of 'no snow' disappointment at Christmas, the Met Office is asking the British public to get behind a forward-thinking campaign to make *rain* the official weather of the festive period.

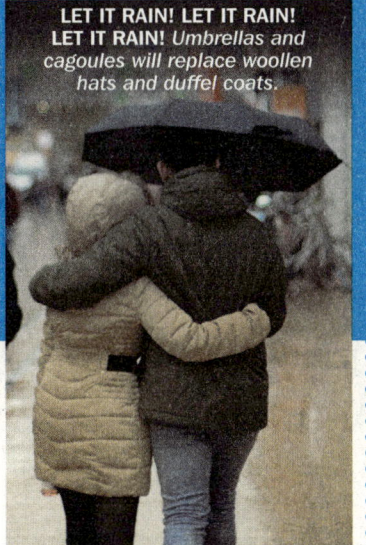

LET IT RAIN! LET IT RAIN! LET IT RAIN! *Umbrellas and cagoules will replace woollen hats and duffel coats.*

For centuries, Christmas and snow have been a classic festive pairing. From Yuletide cards of red-breasted robins sat on snow-capped branches to parks full of rosy-cheeked children tobogganing down hills covered in a freshly-fallen blankets of the white stuff, the first flakes of snow were traditionally a sign that Santa was on his way.

But a *White Christmas* – officially declared when a single snowflake falls on the Met Office building in London on Christmas Day – hasn't occurred in Britain since 2010. And even then it wasn't a very good one. For our generation, White Christmases are a thing of the past.

Met Office spokesperson, Garryl Broadbean told us: "The UK gets an average 23 days of snow a year compared to 152 days of rain. Now, with global warming leading to milder winters and regular flash flooding, it's far more likely that it'll piss down over Christmas than snow."

"When our children grow up, they won't remember wrapping-up warm in woollen mittens and balaclavas for Christmas afternoon walks on snowy streets as our grandparents did," Broadbean continued. "Instead they'll get dewy-eyed for the old days of putting on cagoules, huddling under umbrellas and dodging under shop awnings to avoid getting soaked."

meteorological

"Because it is Britain's meteorological norm, we've decided to name rain as the 'official' weather of Christmas. Now we can pretty much guarantee that the UK will get perfectly Christmassy weather, year in year out," he added.

The proposed rebrand would start from early December 2024, with all references to snow during the Christmas period being phased out. From 2025 onwards, familiar festive sights and sounds will fall into obscurity as the nation gradually builds new traditions.

- ***OUT** goes the sound of your neighbour scraping snow off their front path with a shovel. **IN** comes the sound of your neighbour bailing water out of their living room with a bucket.*
- ***OUT** goes Christmas Eve children's fave The Snowman. **IN** comes The Rainman, a heart-warming tale where a boy befriends a magical puddle with a sodden scarf dragged across it.*
- ***OUT** go wooden sleighrides down hills. **IN** come rowing boats for children's races down flooded streets.*
- ***OUT** go Christmas songs about robins, reindeers and Father Christmas. **IN** come Christmas songs about herons, hippopotamuses and 'Cap'n Christmas' – the sea-faring Santa.*

Because of the scale of the undertaking, the government is asking the UK to prepare for decades of bleak, confusing Christmases ahead while the nation adjusts to the new standard. "It won't be easy," warned Secretary of State for Culture Lucy Frazer.

"However, we are firmly committed to recalibrating a new generation's festive weather expectations," she continued. "We firmly believe that, when they pull back their bedroom curtains on a grey Christmas morning and see torrents of rain cascading from a blocked gutter onto a heavily waterlogged lawn, your children's children will clap with glee."

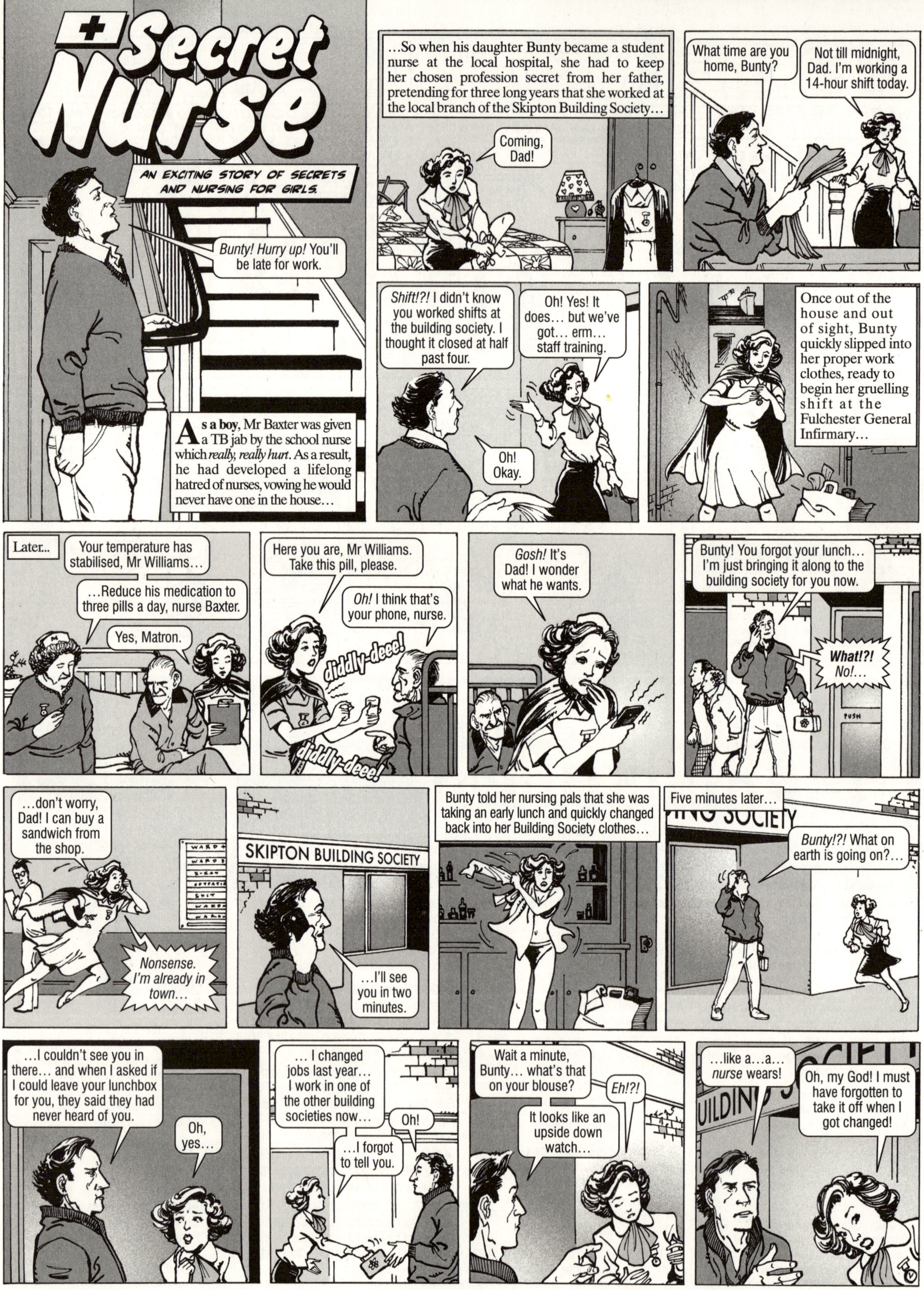

Secret Nurse
AN EXCITING STORY OF SECRETS AND NURSING FOR GIRLS
Bunty! Hurry up! You'll be late for work.
As a boy, Mr Baxter was given a TB jab by the school nurse which really, really hurt. As a result, he had developed a lifelong hatred of nurses, vowing he would never have one in the house…
…So when his daughter Bunty became a student nurse at the local hospital, she had to keep her chosen profession secret from her father, pretending for three long years that she worked at the local branch of the Skipton Building Society…
Coming, Dad!
What time are you home, Bunty?
Not till midnight, Dad. I'm working a 14-hour shift today.
Shift!?! I didn't know you worked shifts at the building society. I thought it closed at half past four.
Oh! Yes! It does… but we've got… erm… staff training.
Oh! Okay.
Once out of the house and out of sight, Bunty quickly slipped into her proper work clothes, ready to begin her gruelling shift at the Fulchester General Infirmary…
Later...
Your temperature has stabilised, Mr Williams…
…Reduce his medication to three pills a day, nurse Baxter.
Yes, Matron.
Here you are, Mr Williams. Take this pill, please.
Oh! I think that's your phone, nurse.
diddly-deee!
diddly-deee!
Gosh! It's Dad! I wonder what he wants.
Bunty! You forgot your lunch… I'm just bringing it along to the building society for you now.
What!?! No!…
PUSH
…don't worry, Dad! I can buy a sandwich from the shop.
Nonsense. I'm already in town…
SKIPTON BUILDING SOCIETY
…I'll see you in two minutes.
Bunty told her nursing pals that she was taking an early lunch and quickly changed back into her Building Society clothes…
Five minutes later…
Bunty!?! What on earth is going on?…
…I couldn't see you in there… and when I asked if I could leave your lunchbox for you, they said they had never heard of you.
Oh, yes…
… I changed jobs last year… I work in one of the other building societies now…
Oh!
…I forgot to tell you.
Wait a minute, Bunty… what's that on your blouse?
Eh!?!
It looks like an upside down watch…
…like a…a… nurse wears!
Oh, my God! I must have forgotten to take it off when I got changed!

No… erm… it's…it's a mortgage broker's watch… we use them for timing appointments with our clients…
… I must have put it on upside down by mistake this morning.
Oh!?!
Anyway, I've got to go, Dad…
…we've got loads of operations… I mean applications… *loan applications* to go through this afternoon!
Shortly...
There you go… you'll be good as new in a few weeks… and no more climbing trees, eh?
Nurse Baxter… we need some help out here
Certainly Matron… what is it?
We've just had a man rushed in to A and E… He was in town when he suffered a severe rectal prolapse…
Oh dear. Poor thing.
It's quite a simple matter of pushing his innards back inside, but he won't let any of the nursing staff near him…
…we need as many hands as we can get to hold him down.
Get *away* from me, do you hear? I hate you all!
Now come along… this won't hurt at all.
It **will!** Take your hands off me…!
…leave me alone!
DAD!!!
BUNTY!?! What are you doing here? And why are you dressed like *that?*
Oh, Dad!… I work here!…
What!?!… But… the building society.
No, Dad… I've *never* worked at the building society…
You mean… you're a… a *nurse!?!*
Yes! And I'm the nurse who's going to fix your rectal prolapse.
No! No you're not! It'll knack… just like that TB jab I had as a boy.
No it won't… I've done it many times before.
Leave me alone!
SCHLOOOOOOP! POP!
There we go! All nicely tucked back inside.
Wince!
Didn't hurt, did it, Dad?
N… no. No, not a bit…
Thank you, Bunty… I'm very proud of you.
…and I'm sorry that my behaviour has forced you to live a lie these years.
It doesn't matter now.
I'm so proud of you, Bunty
Oh, Dad!
Anyway. let's get you an injection of antibiotics so you don't develop sepsis of the rectal canal.
Whatever you say, nurse.
And at the graduation ceremony a few weeks later, one proud father was cheering louder than all the others as his daughter took the stage
***YES!* Go Bunty!**
WOOOOO!
CLAP!
CLAP!
CLAP!

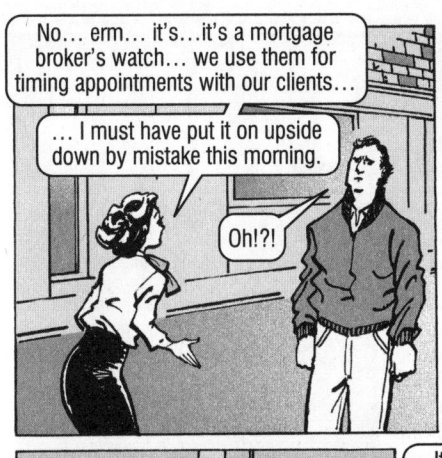

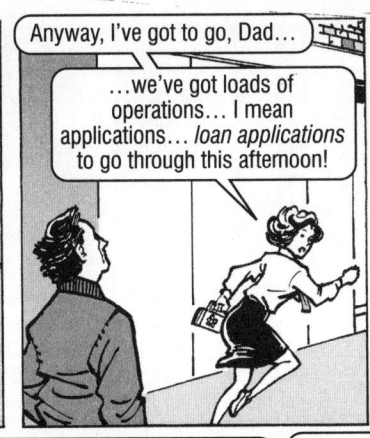

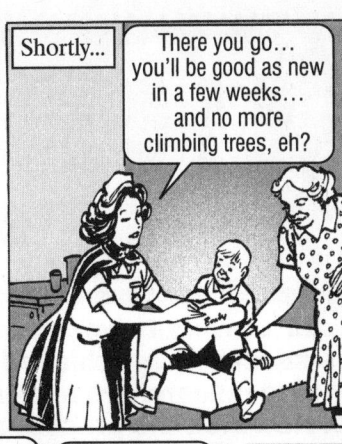

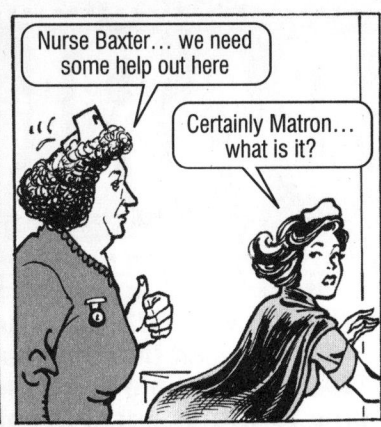

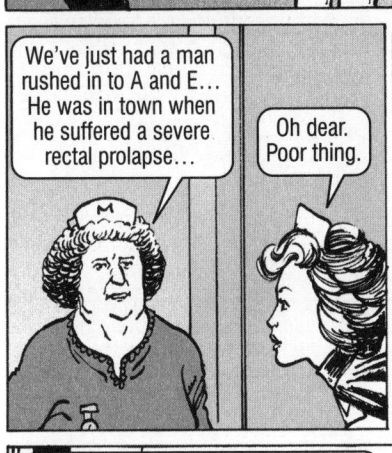

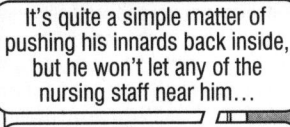

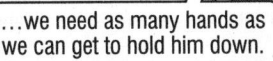

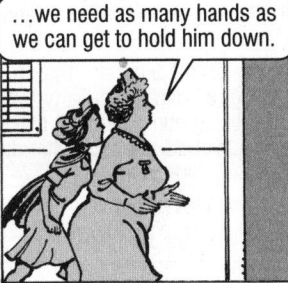

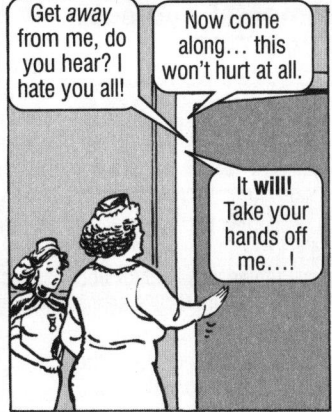

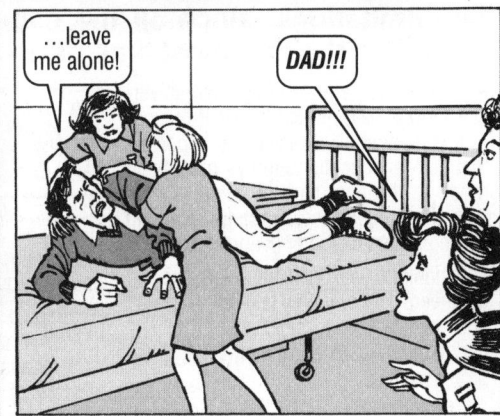

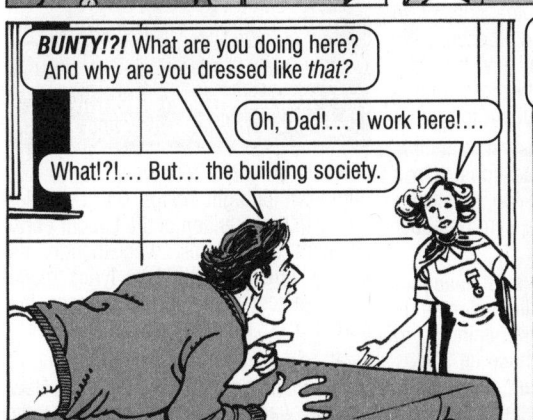

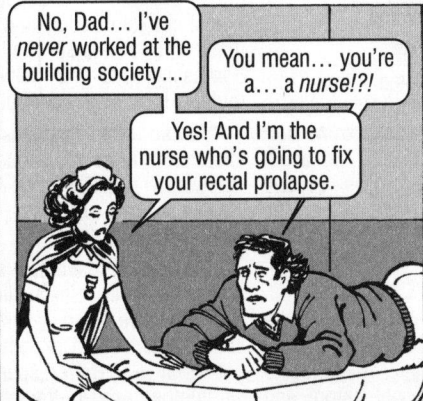

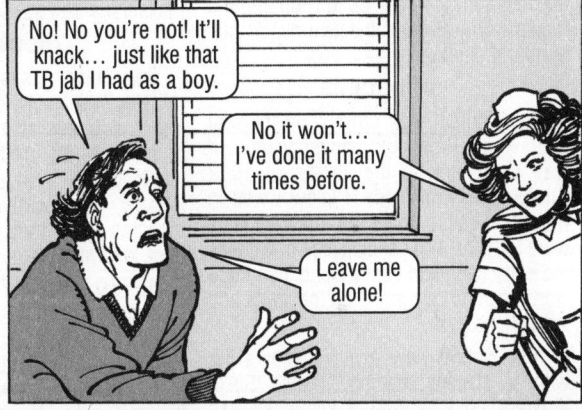

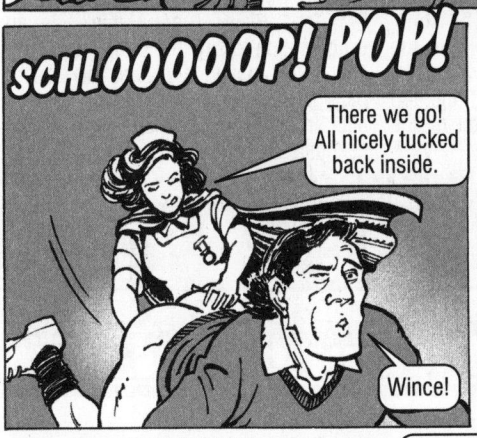

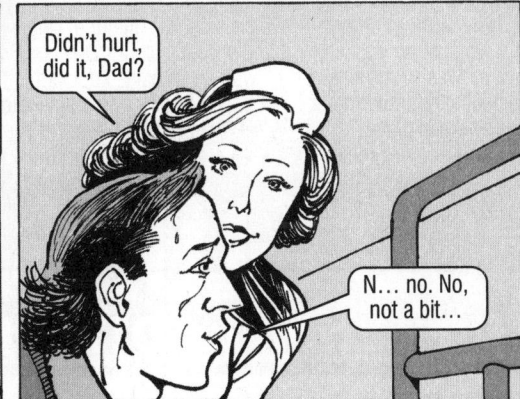

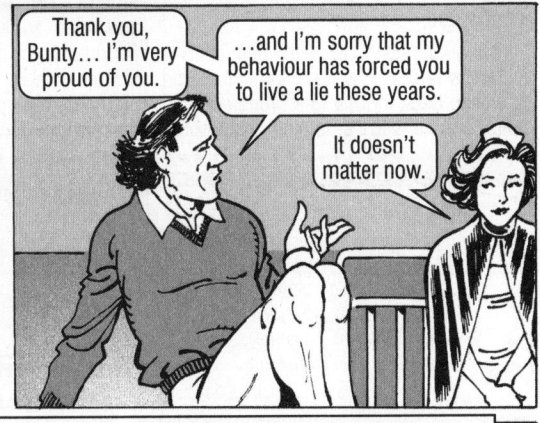

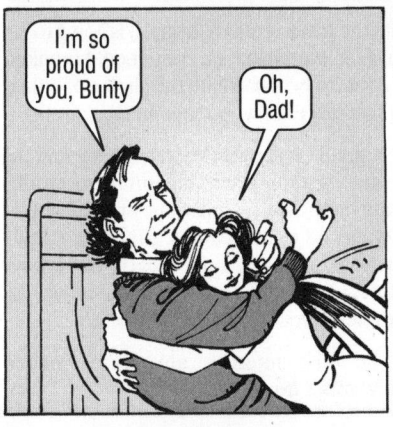

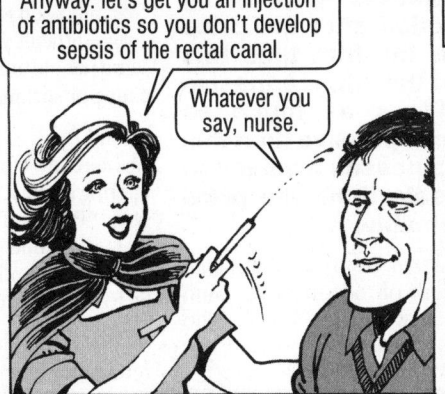

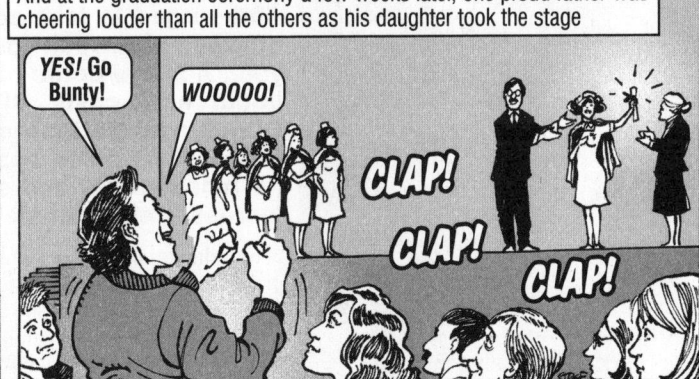

BARK TO THE FUTURE

It's a Dog's Life for Time Travellers

SCIENTISTS from Bristol University yesterday revealed that they have successfully achieved a form of time travel, sending researchers back in time to witness past events. However, the procedure has limitations, since all the experimental subjects arrived in the historical time period as a DOG!

At a press conference held in the university's main hall, project leader Professor Emma Lanceboil explained to reporters that 175 successful journeys have been made to the past and the future so far, with the subjects successfully returning to the present day after every experiment.

"Thanks to our team of scientists and engineers, time travel is now a reality and we are able to send anyone to any period in time and return them safely," the professor said.

She continued: "The main focus of our research will now be looking into the reasons why all the subjects arrive at their temporal destination as a dog."

amputate

The problem was noticed on the first test, when Professor Lanceboil herself was sent back to the streets of 1912 Bristol. She explained: "I knew I was in Bristol because many of the buildings were familiar. And I had an idea that it was the early twentieth century because there were horse drawn trams on the roads and virtually no cars."

"But when I saw a newspaper seller with a placard reading 'Titanic Sinks – Great Loss of Life' I knew we had succeeded," she said.

Although the experiment had been a success in that Professor Lanceboil had travelled back in time to a predetermined date, she sensed something was wrong.

EXCLUSIVE!

"I was in 1912 alright, but I was level with everyone's knees," she said. "Not only that, but everything was in black and white and I had the most incredible sense of smell."

"It wasn't until I walked past the window of an old costermonger's shop and saw my reflection in the glass that I realised I was a sausage dog."

housing

The team suspected that the transformation of Professor Lanceboil into a dog was an anomaly, some sort of glitch in the system, and set about planning the next test. This second journey saw another member of the research team transported even further back in time to medieval Bristol. However, the results were similar.

"He turned up as a whippet in a the medieval village of Clifton during the plague," said Lanceboil. "The villagers had never seen a whippet before and thought he was 'The Devil's Dog' and tried to kill him with pitchforks. Fortunately, being a whippet he was able to outrun them, but he was nevertheless pretty shaken up when he returned to our present day lab in his human guise."

Dr Alice Golightly, another member of the team, told reporters how she went back to the maternity unit of the Bristol Royal Infirmary as a golden retriever on the day of her own birth in 1982. "I ran into the delivery suite and actually saw myself being born," she said. "It was surreal, seeing myself as a newborn baby and my mum as I remember her from my childhood. Then I sniffed the midwife's arse and she hit me with a brush and I ran out."

"My mum used to tell me the story of how a dog ran into the delivery room when I was being born, and it all makes sense now. Little did she know that dog was actually me forty years later."

ovipositor

The team will now be focussing their energy on what is happening in the time travel process to cause the subject to transform into a dog and subsequently back into a human. And TV brainbox Professor Brian Cox thinks the Bristol boffins have their work cut out for them.

"As so often happens, a scientific discovery raises more questions than it answers," said the mop-top epaulette-coated former D-Ream synth-stabber turned-CERN-boffin.

"Time and space are two heads of the same coin, closely intermingled in ways that we are only just beginning to understand," said Cox, whose hit *Things Can Only Get Better* spent fo r weeks at number one in the charts between January and February 1994. The song, which was the second single from the band's debut album *D-ream On Volume 1*, was eventually knocked off the top spot by Mariah Carey's version of the Willie Nelson ballad *Without You*.

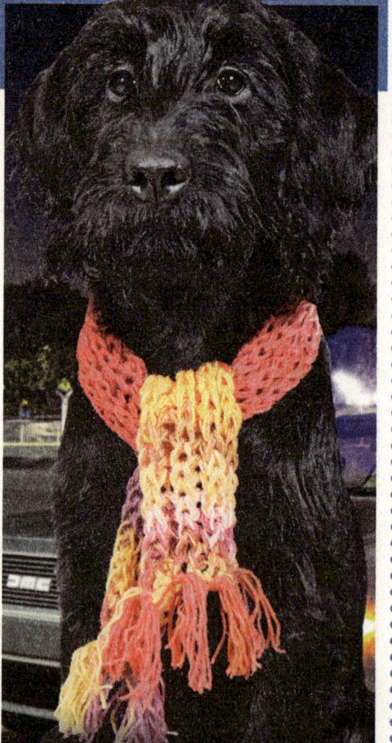

TWILIGHT BONE: *Time travel possible - but only in canine form.*

However, its four-week spell at number 1 brought *Things Can Only Get Better* to the attention of the Labour Party planners at Millbank, who thought its catchy tune and optimistic lyrics made it the perfect theme to accompany the party's 1997 election campaign.

"It so perfectly summed up the mood of the country and the direction that New Labour wanted to take," said former PM Tony Blair. "I don't think it's an exaggeration to say that *Things Can Only Get Better* played a pivotal role in our party's success at that election, and as such in some way shaped Britain for the next thirteen years."

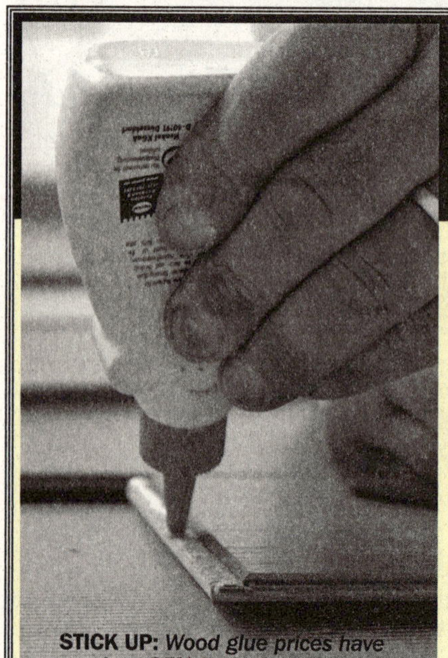

STICK UP: *Wood glue prices have risen 25% in the last year.*

WOOD GLUE BELIEVE IT?!

Calls for action as DIY adhesive prices soar

CHANCELLOR at time of going to press Rachel Reeves was being urged to take action after the price of wood-glue rose for the fifth time this year. A 500ml bottle of the white adhesive liquid now costs DIY-ers as much as £12.99, a full 25% more expensive than this time last year, and businesses involved in its manufacture and sale think the price increases are unsustainable.

"Households are being squeezed by these wood-glue prices," said Mick Bostick, head of the Adhesive, Gum and Fixative Manufacturers Association. "People who think that manufacturers make more money when prices go up simply do not understand economics."

"When prices go up, people cut back."

"Combined with the general cost of living, it is going to be a very difficult year for everyone," he continued. "Frankly, some people are going to be faced with the choice of either eating or sticking two pieces of wood together."

And Bank of England Governor Andrew Bailey said he was already considering emergency measures, including altering interest rates in order to stabilise the price of wood-glue. "Prices of wood adhesives cannot simply continue increasing unchecked," he told a House of Commons Treasury committee. "One way to address the issue would be to lower interest until wood-glue prices stabilise."

"Or it might be raise interest rates. I can never remember how it works," he added.

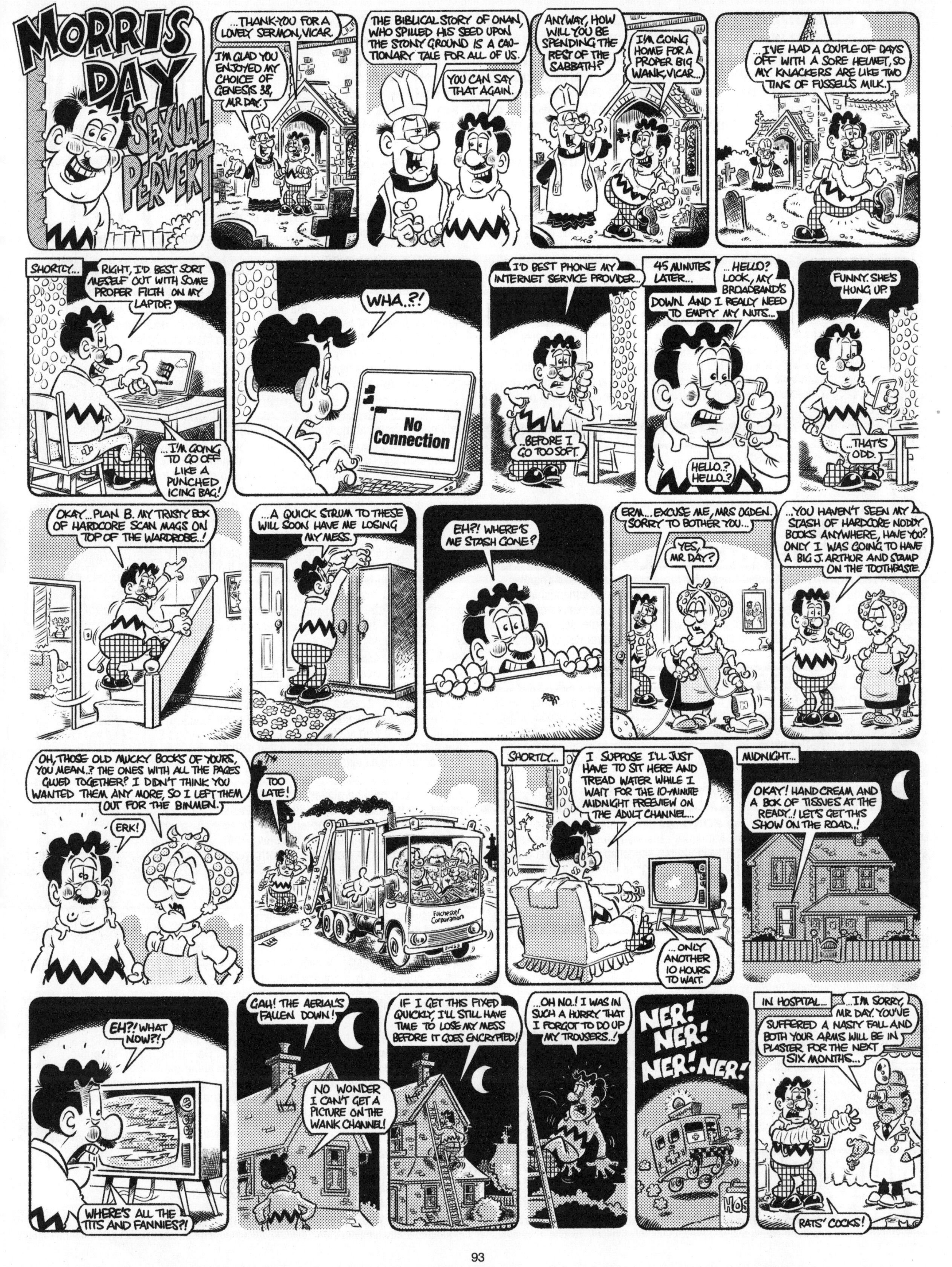
MORRIS DAY
SEXUAL PERVERT
...THANK-YOU FOR A LOVELY SERMON, VICAR.
I'M GLAD YOU ENJOYED MY CHOICE OF GENESIS 38, MR DAY.
THE BIBLICAL STORY OF ONAN, WHO SPILLED HIS SEED UPON THE STONY GROUND IS A CAUTIONARY TALE FOR ALL OF US.
YOU CAN SAY THAT AGAIN.
ANYWAY, HOW WILL YOU BE SPENDING THE REST OF THE SABBATH?
I'M GOING HOME FOR A PROPER BIG WANK, VICAR...
...I'VE HAD A COUPLE OF DAYS OFF WITH A SORE HELMET, SO MY KNACKERS ARE LIKE TWO TINS OF FUSSELL'S MILK.
SHORTLY...
RIGHT, I'D BEST SORT MESELF OUT WITH SOME PROPER FILTH ON MY LAPTOP.
...I'M GOING TO GO OFF LIKE A PUNCHED ICING BAG!
WHA..?!
No Connection
I'D BEST PHONE MY INTERNET SERVICE PROVIDER...
..BEFORE I GO TOO SOFT.
45 MINUTES LATER...
...HELLO? LOOK, MY BROADBAND'S DOWN AND I REALLY NEED TO EMPTY MY NUTS...
HELLO..? HELLO..?
FUNNY. SHE'S HUNG UP.
...THAT'S ODD.
OKAY... PLAN B. MY TRUSTY BOX OF HARDCORE SCAN MAGS ON TOP OF THE WARDROBE..!
...A QUICK STRUM TO THESE WILL SOON HAVE ME LOSING MY MESS.
EH?! WHERE'S ME STASH GONE?
ERM... EXCUSE ME, MRS OGDEN. SORRY TO BOTHER YOU...
YES, MR DAY?
...YOU HAVEN'T SEEN MY STASH OF HARDCORE NODDY BOOKS ANYWHERE, HAVE YOU? ONLY I WAS GOING TO HAVE A BIG J. ARTHUR AND STAMP ON THE TOOTHPASTE.
OH, THOSE OLD MUCKY BOOKS OF YOURS, YOU MEAN..? THE ONES WITH ALL THE PAGES GLUED TOGETHER? I DIDN'T THINK YOU WANTED THEM ANY MORE, SO I LEFT THEM OUT FOR THE BINMEN.
ERK!
TOO LATE!
Fulchester Corporation
SHORTLY...
I SUPPOSE I'LL JUST HAVE TO SIT HERE AND TREAD WATER WHILE I WAIT FOR THE 10-MINUTE MIDNIGHT FREEVIEW ON THE ADULT CHANNEL...
...ONLY ANOTHER 10 HOURS TO WAIT.
MIDNIGHT...
OKAY! HAND CREAM AND A BOX OF TISSUES AT THE READY..! LET'S GET THIS SHOW ON THE ROAD..!
EH?! WHAT NOW?!
WHERE'S ALL THE TITS AND FANNIES?!
GAH! THE AERIAL'S FALLEN DOWN!
NO WONDER I CAN'T GET A PICTURE ON THE WANK CHANNEL!
IF I GET THIS FIXED QUICKLY, I'LL STILL HAVE TIME TO LOSE MY MESS BEFORE IT GOES ENCRYPTED!
...OH NO..! I WAS IN SUCH A HURRY THAT I FORGOT TO DO UP MY TROUSERS..!
NER! NER! NER! NER!
IN HOSPITAL...
...I'M SORRY, MR DAY. YOU'VE SUFFERED A NASTY FALL AND BOTH YOUR ARMS WILL BE IN PLASTER FOR THE NEXT SIX MONTHS...
RATS' COCKS!

VLAD WHO'S

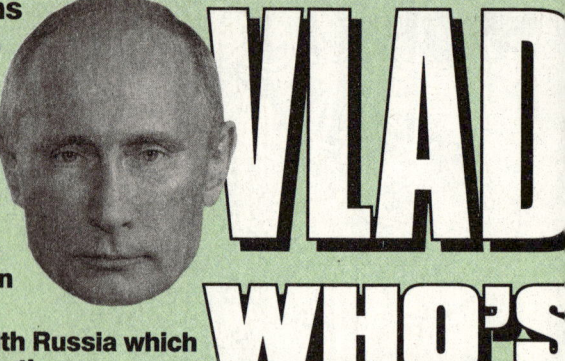

THE MODERN history of Russia is book-ended by a pair of Putins who are world-renowned as 'mad, bad and dangerous to know'. Since 1999, ex-KGB goon **VLADIMIR PUTIN** has ruled this vast superpower with a rod of iron as its first post-Soviet non-alcoholic leader; whilst back in the early days of the 20th century, the iron rod (ie, erect penis) of his near-namesake **RA-RA-RAS PUTIN** was one of the key stirrers of a pot of unrest which eventually boiled over to scald Tsar Nicholas II in the form of the Russian revolution.

So, 'put in' plain terms, there is no disputin' that in the Putin stakes it's President Vlad and 'Mad Monk' Ra-Ra-Ras who head the field. But in this tumultuous Putin head-to-head, which head wears the crown?

As everyone excitedly turns their thoughts to the prospect of a new Cold War with Russia which might last decades, there's never been a better time to ask this question…

RA-RA-RAS

ROUND 1: MADDEST — 5
AS RESIDENT faith healer-cum-mystic family therapist to the Tsar and his family, Grigori Yefimovich Rasputin became widely known as 'The Mad Monk', and few in Russian society at that time would have taken issue with Boney M's later assessment of him as "a cat that really was gone". But this may have been inaccurate as there is no actual evidence that he suffered from any kind of recognisable mental illness. Admittedly Ra-Ra-Ras had visions of the Virgin Mary and St Simeon of Verkhoturye, but he may have been completely sane, as the spirits of these individuals may well have genuinely appeared before him as he claimed. In the absence of any evidence to the contrary, we have to award half marks.

ROUND 2: BADDEST — 6
BORN and raised in the Siberian village of Pokrovskoye, according to court records the badness of a younger Ra-Ra-Ras amounted to no more than a bit of public drunkenness, petty theft and being rude to local officials; behaviour not unlike that of the average 21st Century Briton. Everything abruptly changed in 1897, when the 28-year-old fell under the influence of the *Khlysts*, a religious sect who believed the best way to please God was to sin like the clappers and then tactically repent. It is said that under their malign influence, Ra-Ra-Ras proceeded to *have it large*, partaking in alcohol and engaging in X-rated orgies, allegations that the lyrics about his "drinking and lusting" in the Boney M single appear to confirm.

ROUND 3: DANGEROUSEST TO KNOW — 10
THE ROMANOVS ruled Russia for *three centuries*, but like countless previous dynasties, they ultimately fell due to their ruler's friendship with a drunken, sex-crazed religious crackpot. Boney M's assessment of the period is that "in all affairs of state he was the man to please", and the power that Ra-Ra-Ras exercised over the Russian Royal Family scandalised the country. The Romanovs paid the price in 1917, discovering too late that knocking about with the Mad Monk had cost them *everything*. Rasputin's malign influence had changed the whole course of Russian, European, and world history.

ROUND 4: BIGGEST LOVE MACHINE — 10
RANDY Ra-Ra-Ras has gone down in history – and in the bed-chamber of Tsarina Alexandra – as one of the all-time great sex maniacs. In Boney M's analysis, this "lover of the Russian Queen" was very much "the kind of teacher women would desire," being "big and strong, in his eyes a flaming glow." The fact many "looked at him with terror and with fear" did nothing, they argue, to deter the "Moscow chicks" who regarded him as "such a lovely dear". Their conclusion that "it was a shame how he carried on," however, is mere speculation. Fellow historians might note that with such a sentiment, the German pop sensations quit the trusted path of fact for the wild hinterland of opinion.

ROUND 5: HEIGHT — 8
FOND of calling himself 'Christ in Miniature', the Mad Monk stood a strapping 6ft 3ins in his sandalled-feet, almost a foot taller than the original Christ, who tipped the bar at a mere 5ft 5ins. As a consequence, Rasputin can only be played in the cinema by tall actors, as he was by the 6ft 5ins Christopher Lee in the 1966 Hammer horror film *Rasputin the Mad Monk*, or by 6 foot 3 *Dr Who* fave Tom Baker, who gave an inch-perfect portrayal of the charismatic conman in the 1971 epic *Nicholas and Alexandra*.

ROUND 6: HIRSUITNESS — 10
ASK anyone in the street what word comes to mind on hearing the name Ra-Ra-Ras Putin, and very few will cry 'beard!' But for Boney M's complete failure to address the subject of Rasputin's facial hair in their 1978 hit single, it would undoubtedly be many more, and the fact that it is not alluded to in the lyrics is one of the pop world's all-time goofs. Indeed, the notoriously hairy Siberian's whiskers are of such fame that they inspired the title of musician Joseph Kirkarov's 2018 album *Rasputin's Beard*, although it would be dishonest to suggest that this obscure release – which appears only to be available in digital formats – was in any way successful, either critically or commercially.

ROUND 7: DEATH — 50
LIKE many influential movers and shakers, the Mad Monk of Moscow met his end at the hands of assassins. But when the 'hit' got underway, he was so rock that his assailants were forced to employ no less than five different modes of murder one after the other in order to get the job done. Thanks to his impressively long-winded performance, in December 1916 Rasputin entered the *Guinness Book of Records* for being the first political heavyweight to be poisoned, shot, clubbed, stabbed and drowned to death. Being assassinated *five times on the same night* nets him a massive 50 points in this round.

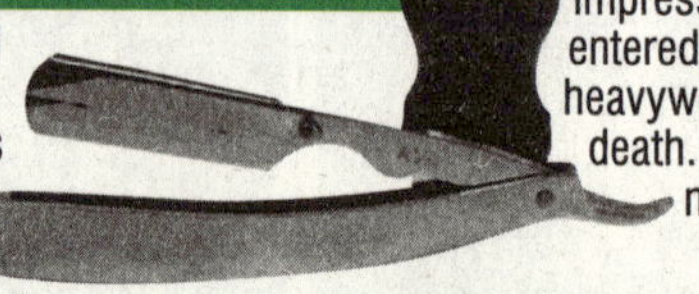

HOW DID THEY DO? — 99

HOORA-RA-RAY! The bonkers Soviet monk has licked his opponent good and proper. He may have had whiskers on his chin and warts on his cock, but he's certainly emerged from this competition with no egg on his face!

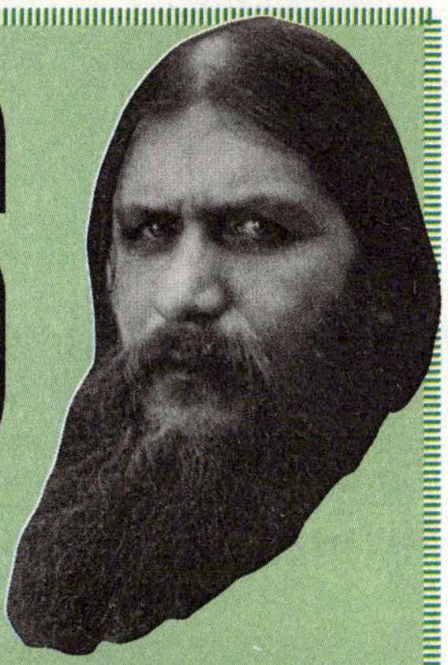

IMIR VS RA-RA-RAS

THE GREATEST PUTIN?

RE **VLADIMIR**

MADDEST

5

TRYING to guess the nature of 'Mad Vlad' Putin's mental health issues has recently become a popular pastime across the West. Evil, monstrous and psychopathic seem to be the preferred diagnoses of his condition, although experts frequently pop up on 24-hour news channel filler segments to offer more nuanced diagnoses, attributing his unhinged behaviour to everything from bipolar disorder to narcissistic multiple personality disorder, and from paranoid schizophrenia to lycanthropy. But his mental state is impossible to determine without conducting a whole gamut of psychological tests, and so far Vlad has not responded to our requests for him to undergo a thorough mental examination.

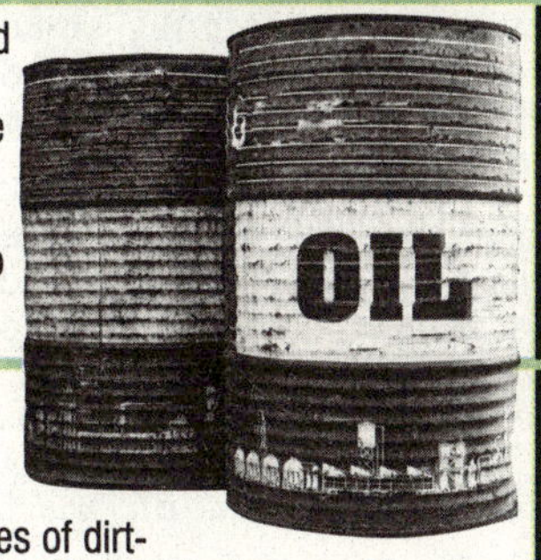

OIL

ROUND 1

BADDEST

8

ONCE in power, ex-KGB officer Vlad got briskly to work setting out his world-class *baddie* stall by launching a brutal brace of scorched-earth wars in the former Soviet-Republics of Chechnya and Georgia. Before too long, rivals were mysteriously perishing left, right, and centre, while good old-fashioned state repression was back in style for ordinary Russians. Curiously, many years of such barefaced tyranny passed before Vlad's full badness became common knowledge to other governments, years in which we all mistakenly bought huge quantities of dirt-cheap oil and gas off of him, as well as granting Russia the honour of hosting a World Cup and a Winter Olympics. Happily, thanks to Vlad's 2022 invasion of Ukraine, everyone is now bang up to speed.

ROUND 2

DANGEROUSEST TO KNOW

5

MANY individuals have found Vlad dangerous to know. Getting on his wick, perhaps by saying something he disagrees with, not applauding his speeches long enough, or simply living in the wrong former Soviet Republic, can have frightening consequences. Indeed, many individuals who cross him become so afraid that they fall out of fourth floor windows in terror on a regular basis.

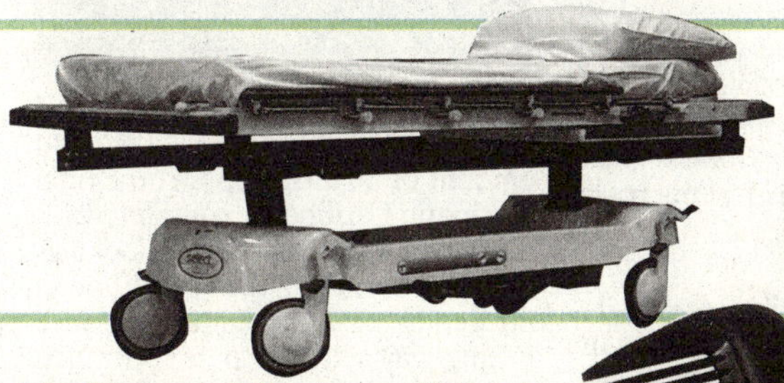

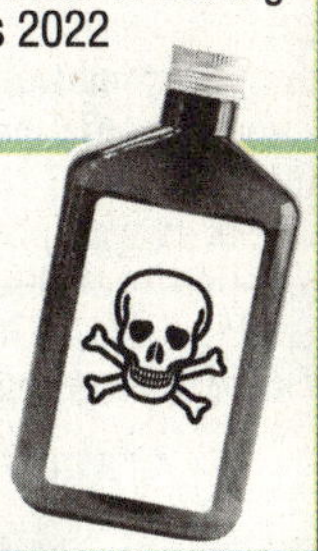

ROUND 3

BIGGEST LOVE MACHINE

4

WHILST Vlad the bad has been accused of various acts of perversion by his many detractors, all available evidence paints a picture of him as a fairly conventional lover in the fart-sack; he was married for 30 years to Aeroflot trolley dolly Lyudmila, with whom he has two daughters. It has been rumoured that for the last ten years of this marriage, Vlad conducted an affair with fellow politician Alina Kabaeva, but this appears unlikely to be true as the *Moskovsky Korrespondent* newspaper was shut down shortly after printing the scurrilous allegations. In summation, Vlad's had a lively love life, but there's nothing here to qualify him as a truly legendary pork swordsman.

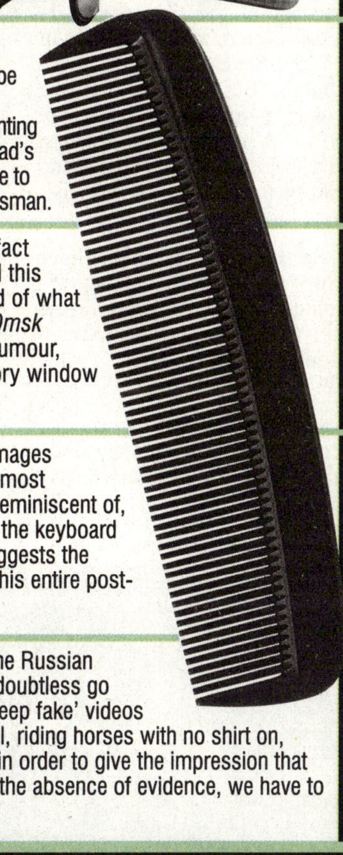

ROUND 4

HEIGHT

6

AT A PINT-SIZED 5ft 7ins (the same height as Tom Cruise, Beyoncé Knowles and Bing Crosby) the 4-time election-winning Russian President is often accused of harbouring a Napoleon Complex, exercising supreme power as a way of compensating for his lack of inches. But this just a cruel rumour. Phone the Kremlin and they'll inform you that Putin in fact stands a towering 6ft 4ins. And this must be true because, ashamed of what he had done, the editor of *The Omsk Fakty* which first published the rumour, threw himself out of a fourth story window and closed his newspaper.

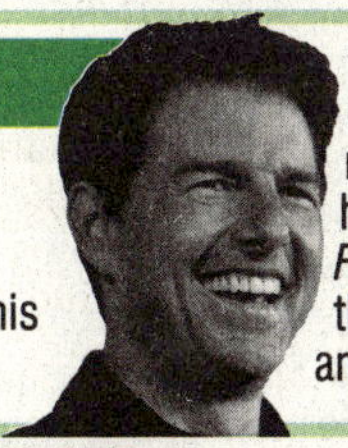

ROUND 5

HIRSUITNESS

0

THE FORCES of Vlad's follicles put up a poor showing on the battlefield of male-pattern baldness from an early age; by the time he joined the government of knockabout boozehound Boris Yeltsin in 1996, the pint-sized former spook had been sporting a laughable combover for upwards of a decade. On the facial hair front, while the internet boasts countless manipulated images depicting Vlad with various whiskers – most commonly a small black moustache reminiscent of, amongst others, Charlie Chaplin and the keyboard player out of Sparks – all evidence suggests the Russian leader has been close shaven his entire post-pubic life. It's a low scoring round.

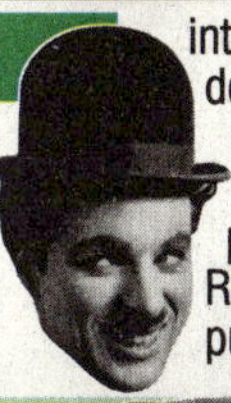

ROUND 6

DEATH

5

DESPITE rumours of ill health, advancing years and constant rumblings of Kremlin plots to take him down, Vlad was still alive at time of going to press, so it would appear that this is set to be a low scoring round for the ex-KGB despot. But having said that, if he were dead, would we actually know? If Putin did kick the bucket, the Russian propaganda machine would doubtless go into overdrive, producing 'deep fake' videos showing him alive and well, riding horses with no shirt on, skiing, or fighting a bear, in order to give the impression that it's business as usual. In the absence of evidence, we have to award him half marks.

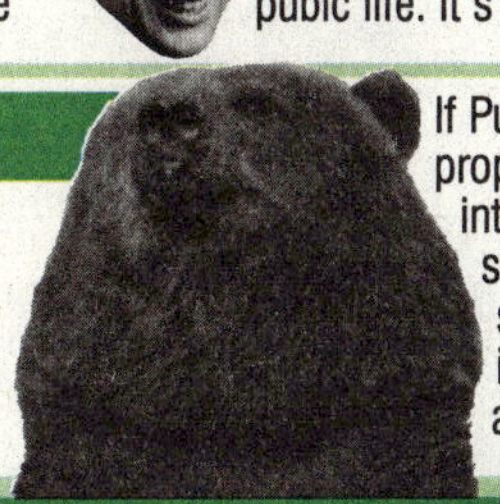

ROUND 7

33

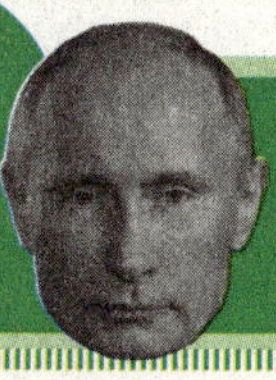

DEAR, OH DEAR, OH VLADIMIR! *The red despot has come a poor second to his long-dead fellow countryman. It was a game effort, but just like invading Ukraine, it appears the short-arsed dictator bit off more than he could chew.*

NEXT WEEK

WHO'S YOUR FAVOURITE RICHARD? CLIFF, WENDY, LITTLE OR CHARNOCK?

HAIL HARRY!

The revolution will be Stylish!

FOLLOWING a record-breaking haul at the Brit Awards, 30 Ivor Novellos, and a host of Grammys, British pop sensation Harry Styles has been outlining his plans for complete and utter world domination.

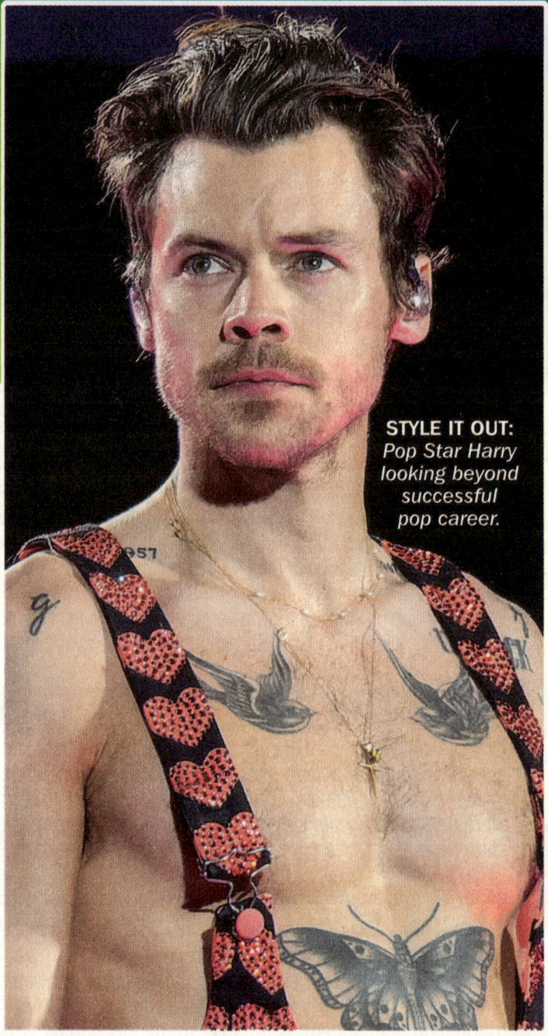
STYLE IT OUT: *Pop Star Harry looking beyond successful pop career.*

With another successful tour behind him, the twenty-something *Daydreaming* songster had been reflecting on his journey since his early days with boy band One Direction, when his future project suddenly became clear.

He told *NME*: "I'd produced three top-selling solo studio albums, had endless number one hits, and I'd broken into the American market. Everyone kept telling me that I was taking over the world, and it just got me thinking - *why don't I do it for real?*"

Nobody in the pop world had seriously considered complete planetary domination before, but Styles and his management looked into the logistics of the venture and judged that it was possible. And for the past two months, plans for the ambitious project – *The World is Mine 2024* – have been going on at full pace.

granular

"We realised the time was right for an usurpation, and it was now or never," said Styles's manager Ernst Goldthumb. "But you can't just wake up in the morning and take over the world. A planetary annexation involves a lot more planning and preparation than most people realise. It's a real logistical challenge."

"Obviously, the first step is to have something with which to threaten the global population if they refuse to bend to your will, a weapon of mass destruction or some such," Goldthumb continued.

"I can't say too much about that at the minute, but let's just say seven billion people will hear about it soon."

But becoming the supreme ruler of the planet doesn't come cheap,

VIZ – YOUR NO. 1 FOR POP STAR WORLD DOMINATION STORIES

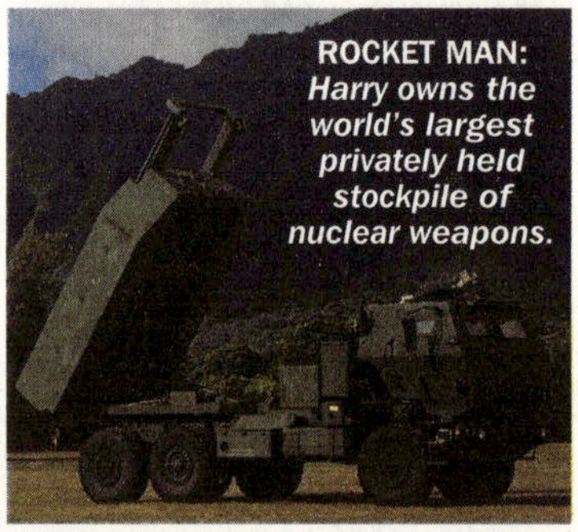
ROCKET MAN: *Harry owns the world's largest privately held stockpile of nuclear weapons.*

and the *As It Was* hitmaker admitted that he has splashed out a substantial amount of his vast pop fortune on a lair in the Caribbean, complete with its own helipad, submarine docking-bay and rocket launcher, although he denied that his ambitions were in any way selfish. "Is it too much to wish for a better future in which the world is populated by a superior race of singer-songwriters like me?" he asked.

zippy

The tousle-haired troubadour has also created a whole new look to go with his ambitious world domination project. The designer Gucci jackets and pinstripe trousers that he favoured during his blockbuster 2019 *Fine Line* tour have gone in favour of a more utilitarian look comprising neatly ironed slacks and a Mao jacket in grey for himself and his 'Styler Army'.

But the *Sign of the Times* singer admits that trying to juggle a successful musical career with attempting to control the fates of 7 billion people is proving tricky, and his latest megalomaniacal project has kept him out of the studio for some time.

"I'm not getting as much work done on new material as I'd like as I'm spending a lot of time in an underwater hideout, carefully aiming my geostationary laser satellites at the major capitals of the world on a big screen," he said. "Sometimes, I'll take my private monorail to my island mansion and sit with my guitar to work on a few tracks, but to be honest, my head's not in the zone."

drambuie

Despite being the owner of the world's largest privately held nuclear weapons stockpile, Styles insists that he wants world peace more than anything. "Except perhaps another platinum album," he joked, stroking a white Persian cat and playfully running his finger across the top of a big red button, marked 'Doomsday'.

The pop icon said he was worried that some may not share his vision of people living in harmony on what he playfully refers to as 'Harry's Planet', and he has put a range of measures in place to deter any have-a-go heroes who may attempt to thwart his ambitions.

"Like all pop stars, I've got security measures in place on my Pacific island," he told the magazine. "Razor wire, minefields, all the usual stuff. And I've hired a fat Samoan body-guard with a razor-edged hat to pick off anyone who makes it past the shark moat."

"Let me assure everyone that trouble causers will be dealt with harshly," he warned.

Fellow pop stars are not surprised that Styles' ambitions have become so all-encompassing. Fellow One Direction members said they saw the warning signs early in the band's career, and suspected this day was not far off. "Harry always wanted to be in charge of everything," said former bandmate Zane Malik.

"He would always choose which photos of the group went on the album covers, usually ones with him at the front, and he always picked the playlist when we did concerts," he continued. "And he had it in his contract that he got all the fanciest sandwiches backstage after a gig. So this bid to make the population of the planet dance to his tune comes as no surprise to me and the other 1D guys."

haberdashery

But Styles was keen to promote the up-side of his plans for a new world order, and he had a message for his soon-to-be 7 billion subjects. "I want kids to know that they can achieve anything if they just believe," he announced in an address that suddenly interrupted every television broadcast across the globe.

"I am proof that you can be anything you want to be. Who would have thought that a simple lad from Holmes Chapel with nothing more than gorgeous hair, big trousers and access to a music mogul's address book, could become the ultimate power in the Universe?" he added, laughing megalomaniacally.

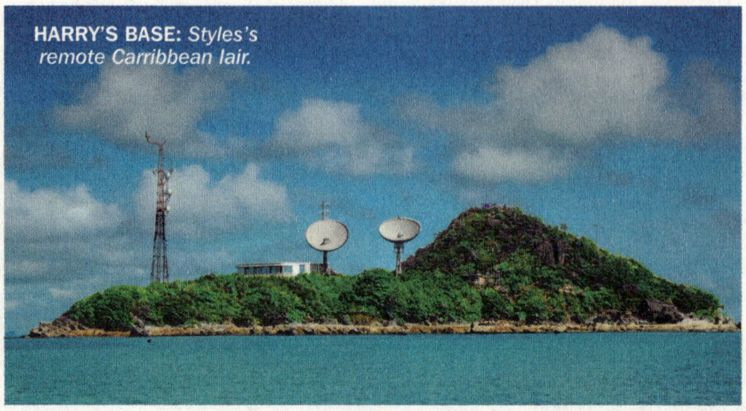
HARRY'S BASE: *Styles's remote Carribbean lair.*

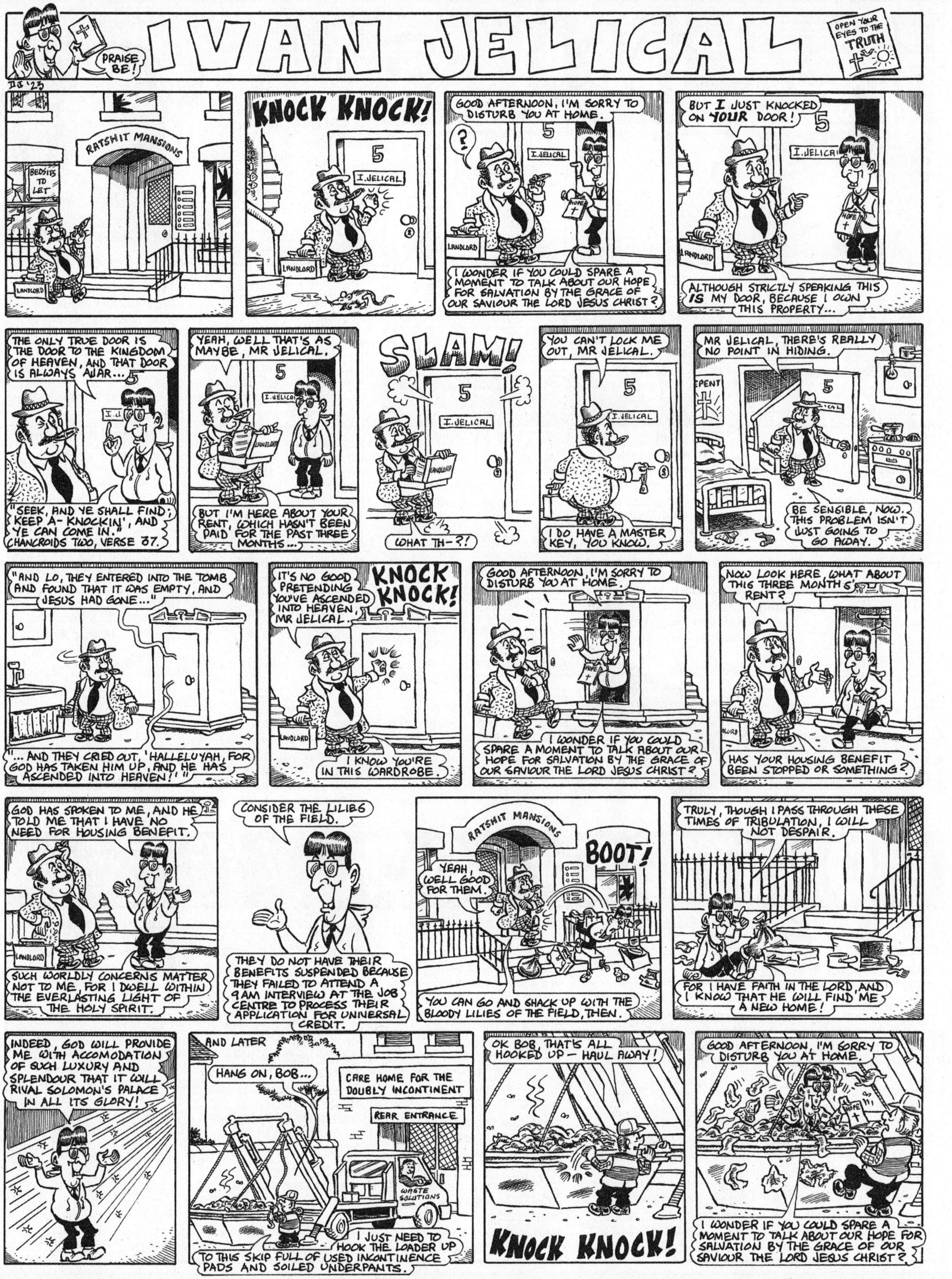
IVAN JELICAL
PRAISE BE!
OPEN YOUR EYES TO THE TRUTH
RATSHIT MANSIONS
BEDSITS TO LET
LANDLORD
KNOCK KNOCK!
5
I. JELICAL
GOOD AFTERNOON, I'M SORRY TO DISTURB YOU AT HOME.
?
HOPE
I WONDER IF YOU COULD SPARE A MOMENT TO TALK ABOUT OUR HOPE FOR SALVATION BY THE GRACE OF OUR SAVIOUR THE LORD JESUS CHRIST?
BUT I JUST KNOCKED ON YOUR DOOR!
ALTHOUGH STRICTLY SPEAKING THIS IS MY DOOR, BECAUSE I OWN THIS PROPERTY...
THE ONLY TRUE DOOR IS THE DOOR TO THE KINGDOM OF HEAVEN, AND THAT DOOR IS ALWAYS AJAR...
"SEEK, AND YE SHALL FIND; KEEP A-KNOCKIN', AND YE CAN COME IN." CHANCROIDS TWO, VERSE 37.
YEAH, WELL THAT'S AS MAYBE, MR JELICAL.
BUT I'M HERE ABOUT YOUR RENT, WHICH HASN'T BEEN PAID FOR THE PAST THREE MONTHS...
SLAM!
WHAT TH-?!
YOU CAN'T LOCK ME OUT, MR JELICAL.
I DO HAVE A MASTER KEY, YOU KNOW.
MR JELICAL, THERE'S REALLY NO POINT IN HIDING.
BE SENSIBLE, NOW. THIS PROBLEM ISN'T JUST GOING TO GO AWAY.
"AND LO, THEY ENTERED INTO THE TOMB AND FOUND THAT IT WAS EMPTY, AND JESUS HAD GONE..."
"...AND THEY CRIED OUT, 'HALLELUYAH, FOR GOD HAS TAKEN HIM UP, AND HE HAS ASCENDED INTO HEAVEN!'"
IT'S NO GOOD PRETENDING YOU'VE ASCENDED INTO HEAVEN, MR JELICAL.
KNOCK KNOCK!
I KNOW YOU'RE IN THIS WARDROBE.
GOOD AFTERNOON, I'M SORRY TO DISTURB YOU AT HOME.
I WONDER IF YOU COULD SPARE A MOMENT TO TALK ABOUT OUR HOPE FOR SALVATION BY THE GRACE OF OUR SAVIOUR THE LORD JESUS CHRIST?
NOW LOOK HERE, WHAT ABOUT THIS THREE MONTHS RENT?
HAS YOUR HOUSING BENEFIT BEEN STOPPED OR SOMETHING?
GOD HAS SPOKEN TO ME, AND HE TOLD ME THAT I HAVE NO NEED FOR HOUSING BENEFIT.
SUCH WORLDLY CONCERNS MATTER NOT TO ME, FOR I DWELL WITHIN THE EVERLASTING LIGHT OF THE HOLY SPIRIT.
CONSIDER THE LILIES OF THE FIELD.
THEY DO NOT HAVE THEIR BENEFITS SUSPENDED BECAUSE THEY FAILED TO ATTEND A 9AM INTERVIEW AT THE JOB CENTRE TO PROCESS THEIR APPLICATION FOR UNIVERSAL CREDIT.
RATSHIT MANSIONS
YEAH, WELL GOOD FOR THEM.
BOOT!
YOU CAN GO AND SHACK UP WITH THE BLOODY LILIES OF THE FIELD, THEN.
TRULY, THOUGH I PASS THROUGH THESE TIMES OF TRIBULATION, I WILL NOT DESPAIR.
FOR I HAVE FAITH IN THE LORD, AND I KNOW THAT HE WILL FIND ME A NEW HOME!
INDEED, GOD WILL PROVIDE ME WITH ACCOMODATION OF SUCH LUXURY AND SPLENDOUR THAT IT WILL RIVAL SOLOMON'S PALACE IN ALL ITS GLORY!
AND LATER
HANG ON, BOB...
CARE HOME FOR THE DOUBLY INCONTINENT
REAR ENTRANCE
WASTE SOLUTIONS
I JUST NEED TO HOOK THE LOADER UP TO THIS SKIP FULL OF USED INCONTINENCE PADS AND SOILED UNDERPANTS.
OK BOB, THAT'S ALL HOOKED UP – HAUL AWAY!
KNOCK KNOCK!
GOOD AFTERNOON, I'M SORRY TO DISTURB YOU AT HOME.
I WONDER IF YOU COULD SPARE A MOMENT TO TALK ABOUT OUR HOPE FOR SALVATION BY THE GRACE OF OUR SAVIOUR THE LORD JESUS CHRIST?

LETTERBOCKS

letters@viz.co.uk... letters@viz.co.uk... letters@viz.co

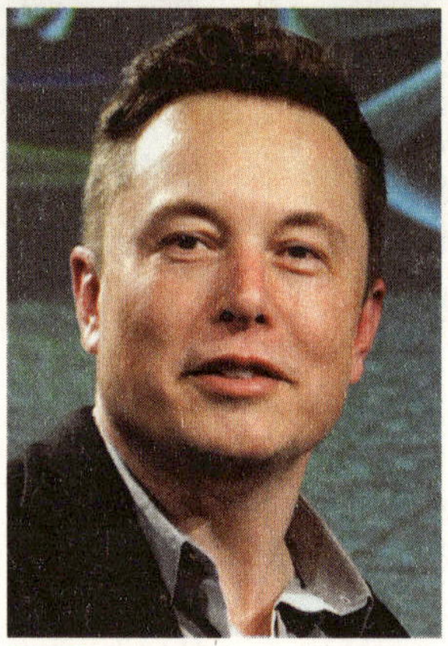

THERE seems to be a lot of criticism lately aimed at Elon Musk for being a twat, all of it quite justified. But let's not forget that his Falcon 9 rockets actually land back on earth like something right out of fucking *Thunderbirds*. Admittedly, he's an utter bellend in every other sphere of endeavour, but credit where it's due, his rockets are absolutely shit hot.

Tobamory Belch, Luton

IF you could have a look around anybody's house, who's house would you choose? I'd go for Mrs B. of Essex. Considering all the shit she has endorsed (and presumably bought) from fake *Viz* advertisers over the years, her place must be a veritable Aladdin's cave of fascinating, if useless, junk.

Glenn Evans, Melbourne

STAR LETTER

I WAS leafing through some old comics the other day when I saw an advert for X-ray Specs for £1, so I sent off a postal order. Three weeks later, they arrived, and I have to say they were a complete waste of money, as I still can't see through my next door neighbour's skirt like the advert clearly implied I would. These X-rays are a complete con, and to think they gave a Nobel Prize to the man who discovered them.

P Green, Baildon

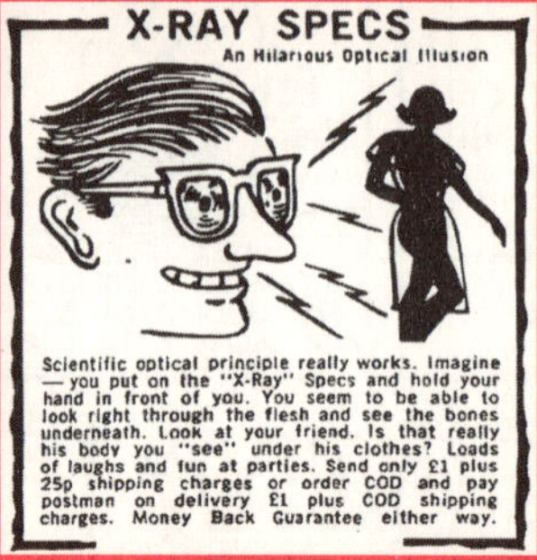
X-RAY SPECS
An Hilarious Optical Illusion
Scientific optical principle really works. Imagine — you put on the "X-Ray" Specs and hold your hand in front of you. You seem to be able to look right through the flesh and see the bones underneath. Look at your friend. Is that really his body you "see" under his clothes? Loads of laughs and fun at parties. Send only £1 plus 25p shipping charges or order COD and pay postman on delivery £1 plus COD shipping charges. Money Back Guarantee either way.

I THINK the prospect of thermonuclear war between the global superpowers is a harrowing thought, but as a street sweeper it bothers me more than it would most people. The idea of tons of debris and rubble, charred corpses and nuclear residue all around is bad enough, but it being on a nice clean road that I've only just swept really gets my hackles right up.

Scruffy Jim, Birmingham

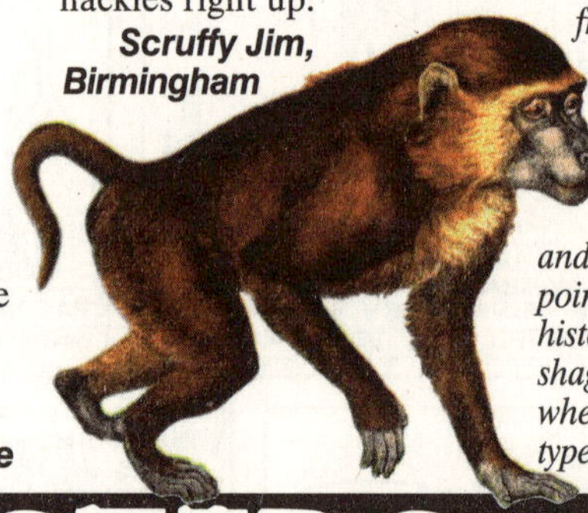

DO any of your readers know what breed of dog first shagged a monkey to make a baboon?

Dumbo Sane, Zurich

* *That's an interesting question, Mr Dumbo. However, we are not completely convinced that baboons came about as a result of a dog shagging a monkey at all. But we could be wrong. Perhaps somebody from New Scientist or Nature, or perhaps someone working in the evolutionary genetics department of a university is reading this and could tell us if, at some point in the evolutionary history of baboons, a dog shagged a monkey, and if so, when it happened and what type of dog it was.*

I BET Count Dracula cracks putrid, toxic farts. When he throws his cape over his victims, he probably knocks them out with a 'Dutch oven' due to his exclusively black pudding diet.

Les Lloyd, email

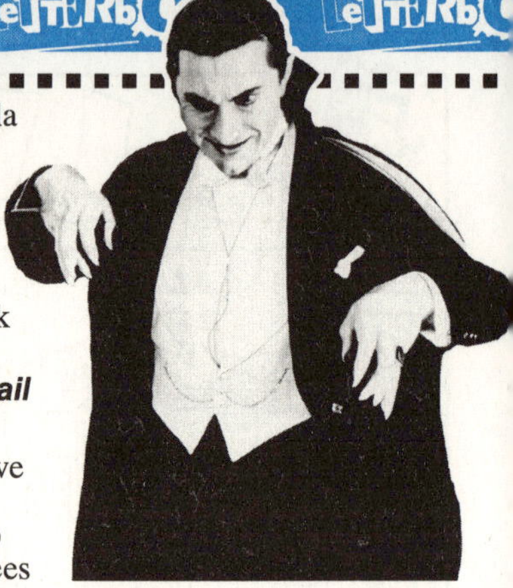

I OFTEN wonder what people who have a beard of bees do when they want a cup of tea. Do they simply brush a few bees away from their lips in order to take a sip, do they lure them away by putting a bit of honey on their chin, or do they use a straw?

Hector Bystander, Goole

YOU can say what you like about people who do banking fraud, but at least you get straight through to them when you phone up. If I call my own bank I have to wait in a queue for absolutely ages after pressing loads of buttons, but when I call the number on a scam email I'm put straight through to one of their bogus representatives. So keep up the good work, fraudsters. You provide an excellent phone service with the money you purloin.

Ken Jenkins, Kings Langley

IF Jesus knew one of His disciples was going to betray Him, which the Bible says He did, then He should have popped some laxative into all of their desserts at the Last Supper. That way Judas would have been too busy sat on the bog shitting himself inside out to go snitching to the Romans.

J Welby, Canterbury

I ALWAYS reassure oncoming traffic that there isn't a speed camera up ahead by flashing my headlights and, with my palm facing down, raising and lowering my hand in a 'no need to panic' kind of gesture.

D Williams, Donegal

I THINK the French have it right. Instead of using toilet paper to smear faeces around what is already quite an unpleasant area of the body, after a bowel movement our Gallic cousins wash their backsides with a conveniently located upside-down shower, leaving their arseholes minty fresh and dangleberry-free. How nice is that? The sooner we rejoin the EU, the better.

Prince Asbo, Folkestone

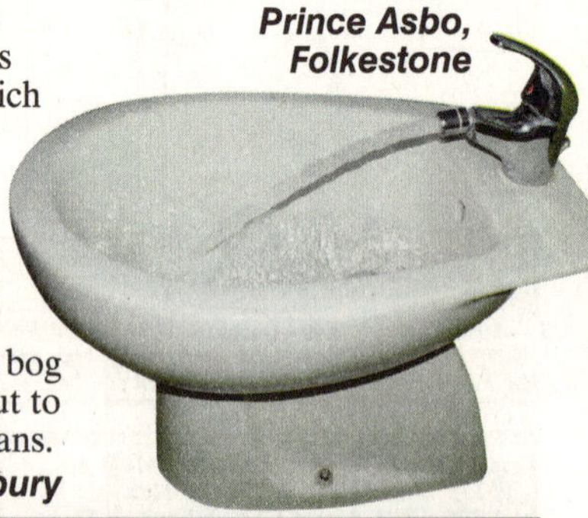

MONSTERS of ROCK

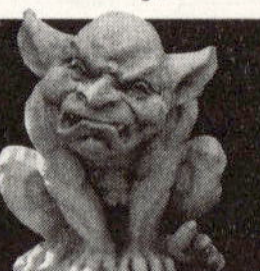

WE asked some of the Monsters of Rock which monsters (not of rock) they were particularly scared of...

Ozzy Osbourne, *Black Sabbath frontman*

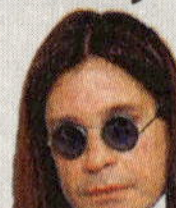

"**I ONCE** bit a bat's head off on stage, which you may think was an unusual thing to do. But it was doubly unusual for me because I'm absolutely terrified of **VAMPIRES**. I remember my fear of them started when I watched the 1970 Hammer film *Taste the Blood of Dracula*, with Christopher Lee in the title role. It had Roy Kinnear and Peter Sallis in it, too, and Martin Jarvis. I have never seen anything so terrifying before or since. I know vampires don't exist, but after watching this film, I never go on stage without a crucifix on. And when we're on tour, I always keep my hotel windows shut and insist that the tour bus has some cloves of garlic hanging over both of the front and middle doors and the emergency exit at the back in case they try to get in that way."

Jon Bon Jovi, *Bon Jovi lead singer and axeman*

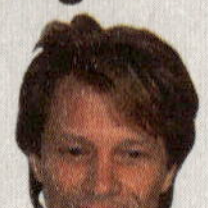

"**I WENT** camping in the Appalachian mountains when I was a kid, and whilst playing in the woods I saw a **BIGFOOT**. I immediately soiled my shorts in fear and flew back to the campsite in tears. My mum and dad calmed me down, telling me it was probably a bear or somebody in a fur coat or something. But I know what I saw, and it was a Bigfoot. I didn't see it again that trip, and I haven't seen one since, but it has left me with a lifelong fear of Bigfeet. However, there were positives to come out of the experience, as it inspired me to write the song *It's My Life*, a power ballad encouraging everyone to grab life by the horns and live it to the full. After all, we could get ate off a Bigfoot tomorrow."

Angus Young, *AC/DC Schoolboy plank spanker*

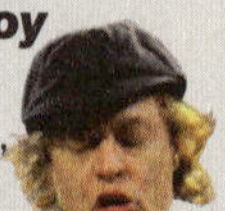

"I know it's ridiculous, but I'm terrified of the **HONEY MONSTER** from the Sugar Puffs advert. It was the big eyes, the lumbering gait and the growling voice that used to terrify me as a kid – and it still does as I am still a schoolboy. I know my fear is irrational as it is only a man in a suit, but my fear is so bad that I can't eat Sugar Puffs or watch anything with Henry McGee in, like repeats of the Benny Hill show on UK Gold. Once on tour, me and the band went down for breakfast in the hotel in Melbourne, and there was a box of Sugar Puffs on the table with a picture of the Honey Monster on. I just lost it and we ended up having to cancel the gig."

Rob Halford, *Judas Priest scream merchant*

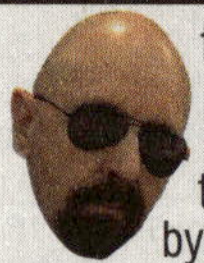

"I'm not frightened of much, but **GODZILLAS** make me shit my leather pants. The thought of a 200-foot-tall reptilian monster being awoken from the depths of the sea by a nuclear explosion and coming out the sea to get me in the night is utterly terrifying. I've had some counselling to try to overcome my fear. The therapist gave me a small model of a Godzilla to handle, and when I felt comfortable with that, she gave me a slightly bigger one, and then a slightly bigger one, and so on. Thanks to this, I'm okay with Godzillas up to about 10 feet high at the minute. I don't know what I'd be like if I came face to face with a full sized 200 foot bastard, but I'm still in therapy and going in the right direction."

☐ **THE** letters from your correspondents Reg Corvette (*page 76*) and James Miller (*page 55*), boasting about the number of countries in which they have pleasured themselves, shows them up to be abject lightweights. My mate once had to spend a night in the coronary care unit, having wanked himself into atrial fibrillation. His onanism may be limited to the one country, but at least he pursued it with enough enthusiasm and gusto to elicit a life-threatening cardiac arrhythmia. Quality over quantity every time.
Kevin Caswell-Jones, Gresford

☐ **A FRIEND** of mine who is a doctor was recently warning me about the liver damage all that beer will do. Any excuse to get out of buying his round.
Calvin Graham, Philly

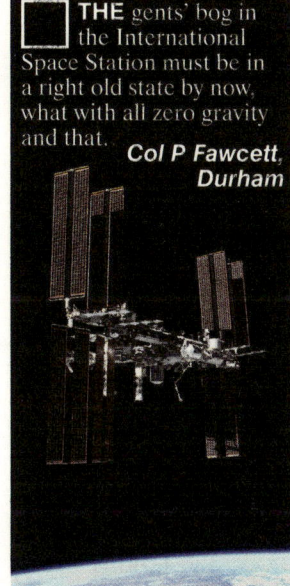

☐ **THE** gents' bog in the International Space Station must be in a right old state by now, what with all zero gravity and that.
Col P Fawcett, Durham

☐ **WHEN** people say "and I'll have less of your bullshit," can anyone tell me exactly how much bullshit they still want? If they meant "none", surely they would say "none". But to say "less" implies they would still like a certain amount of bullshit.
Greg Shaw, Leeds

☐ **OVER** the years, I have been heavily criticised by my wife for excessive farting. However, I came back late from the pub the other night completely pissed and making a racket trying to get the key in the door, and then falling through it. My wife was in bed and was petrified, thinking a burglar was trying to break in. Imagine her relief when I ripped off a massive guff and she realised it was just me.
Ewan Kerr, Wolverhampton

☐ **I HAVE** found myself pondering more and more over what happened to all those readers' wives from classic top-shelf jazz mags of decades past. I often wonder what became of Carol from Ipswich in the May 1987 edition of *Razzle* – did she remain in agriculture or was that her last summer spent legs spread wide on some hay bales? Or Suzie from Telford in the October 1990 *Fiesta* – does she still answer the office telephone kneeling on the desk, naked from the waist down, or would she now be a middle manager in that firm, with an employee to answer the phone for her? I think *Readers' Wives Revisited* would make a wonderful TV programme, finding out what happened to these women after their husband sent in a picture of them in the nuddy.
Mr M Pimple, Newport

☐ **AGEING** is a terrible thing and one of the worst aspects of it is that you no longer have the accuracy or power to piss skidmarks off pubic toilet bowls. To all young people - enjoy and make the most of your youth.
Mark Prostate, Hyde

☐ **TOILET** manufacturers should coat the bowls of their products with Teflon. It is wonderfully non-stick and I imagine it would virtually eliminate foulage build-up. I would test it myself, but I doubt the missus would be too pleased to see me curling one out into our Tefal frying pan. Once again it's up to Joe Public to do the thinking whilst the so called boffins swan about with clipboards and play ping-pong.
Tom Thumb, Brampton

☐ **"JUST** say no" was the anti-drugs message from the 1980s hit single of the same name. Well I just said "no" but my mate didn't, and he's now an investment banker in the city with an enormous house, a Tesla sports car and a trophy wife. Thanks a bunch, cast of *Grange Hill*.
Mike Tatham, St Andrews

☐ **THE** moment aliens turn up, it's all ray guns and world domination. It may not be a fashionable view, but when I travel to a new destination I strive to be polite and pleasant. I suggest that these Martians and extra-terrestrials calm down a bit, and follow the example set by gentleman travellers such as Michael Palin and David Attenborough.
Rupert M Petigo, Kirkwall

☐ **WHY** are people always *bundled* into the back of a van? Surely there must be other ways of getting in?
Cobalt Jester, Bacup

☐ **DO** any of your readers know how I go about becoming a porn star, as I'm now retired and need a bit of extra cash? I used to be a plumber, so doing the acting bit where I'm plumbing the sink in before the sexy woman starts taking her kit off will look really realistic. The sex bit should be easy as well.
Dave Kruck, Bracknell

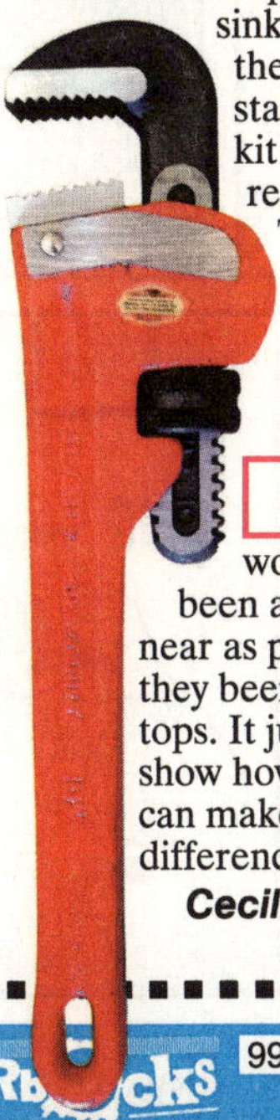

☐ **I DOUBT** tank tops would have been anywhere near as popular had they been called wank tops. It just goes to show how one letter can make all the difference.
Cecilia B de Milo, Arizona

☐ **AFTER** many years trying to find my natural parents, the only information I have managed to gather so far is that my mother was a beautiful, scantily-clad showgirl and my father was a blonde-haired opportunist Robin Askwith impersonator with a penchant for kissing ladies' bottoms. If I could just have a photograph of them both, it would mean the world to me.
Stryder Beauchamp III, Powys

☐ **BBC** science programme *Tomorrow's World* didn't predict any of this shit did it? I've got a good mind to go back to 1983, put my foot through my telly and send Michael Rodd and Judith Hann the bill.
James Thompson, London

☐ **I WONDER** if that chap who got slammed into by Gwyneth Paltrow whilst skiing got a free whiff of her snatch before he passed out?
Stuie, Bunny

☐ **WALKING** on water, feeding 5000 people with a couple of fish and a loaf of bread, and turning water into wine is witchcraft in my book. It seems that there's one rule for messianic figures and another for harmless old crones.
Mike, Aberdeen

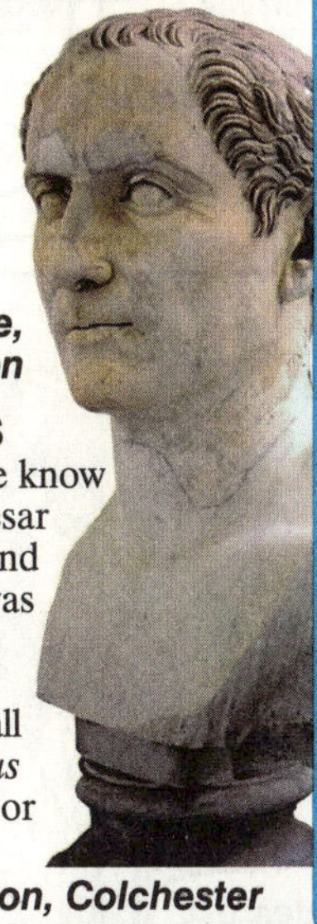

☐ **DOES** anyone know if Julius Caesar had a dog, and if so, what was it called? If I was Julius Caesar, I'd call my dog *Dogus Mucksimus*, or something.
Miles Wilson, Colchester

TOP TIPS

CONVINCE regulars in your local that you are a candidate in a general election by getting your wife to film you gingerly sipping a pint whilst you are wearing a massive rosette.
Kevin Caswell-Jones, Gresford

CONSTIPATED? Simply order something from a firm who can't give you an exact delivery time. On delivery day, the urge to shit will build up, and you will pass your first stool just as the doorbell rings.
Percy Pinchloaf, Yorks

FOOL your prostate examination doctor into thinking they are announcing FA Cup fixtures by inserting a Kinder Egg containing a small piece of paper with the name of a football team written on it into your anal cavity.
Mr Farenheit, Hench

PRETEND you are a YouTube influencer by greeting everyone you meet with the phrase "What's going on guys!?"
Tom Thumb, Brampton

DON'T waste money on expensive bookmarks. Keep track of where you have read up to by tippexing out the words as you read them.
Robbo, North Shields

FOOL onlookers into believing you own the car from Knight Rider by making your wife get in the boot and asking for her advice about things.
Fat Al White, Wrenthorpe

CLOSE your eyes when tipping the crumbs from a bag of salt and vinegar crisps into your mouth.
Mike Tatham, St Andrews

THE best way to save time in the morning when making tea, coffee, or breakfast, is to simply do what you already do, but slightly faster.
Ash, Bristol

BOSSES. If religious employees ask you the reason why on being made redundant, simply say that it is your will. They should be okay with that.
Eldon Furse, email

toptips@viz.co.uk

SOCK IT TO HIM!

Friends club together for heartbroken Dad

A YORKSHIRE father of four was left heartbroken on Christmas morning when he opened his presents to discover that for the first time in 28 years, he had not received any socks.

By our Christmas gift sock correspondent

Noel Cadeaux-Footwear

Brian Torbjorn of Purston normally unwraps around 6 pairs of the fabric foot-coverings every December 25th, an event which he has often described as the highlight of his year.

But in 2022, all he got was a toolkit and a Playstation 5 with a copy of Call of Duty: Black Ops Cold War, a combination of gifts which left the 56-year-old gas fitter in tears. He tried to put on a brave face all Christmas Day, but his wife Maxine said he was clearly very upset.

"He couldn't sleep with excitement on Christmas Eve," she told the *Pontefract Hernia and Groin Strain*. "Then the look on his little face when he opened his presents and saw there were no socks. I could have cried for him."

"Brian has had socks for Christmas for as long as I can remember. I feel terrible that he didn't get any this year."

hints

Maxine said that Brian had started dropping hints about getting socks in October, and she had pretended not to notice. "I knew he wanted socks, and he knew that I knew," she said. "It was all a bit of fun."

But Maxine told the paper that whilst in town Christmas shopping for socks in November, she spotted a 100-piece tool kit on offer in a hardware store, and thought that Brian would love it for Christmas.

"Brian likes nothing more than tinkering about with the car, and I know his tools are years old," she said. "So I thought I would get him a new tool kit this year, as the kids always get their dad socks anyway."

coincidence

But by cruel coincidence, Brian's four children had decided that this would be the year to club together and buy him a Playstation 5, assuming that their mum would be buying him his beloved socks as usual.

"I blame myself," Maxine said. "And so does Brian."

downcast

Brian went to the pub on Christmas lunchtime to meet his friends as usual, and all were wearing new Christmas socks, and all of them could see how downcast he was.

"It was heart-breaking," said Stan Dovetail, who has been part of Brian's drinking group at the town's Ancient Borough Arms for twenty years. "But I'd been given fourteen pairs of socks that morning, so I nipped home and got him a pair of mine."

Stan came back and handed Brian a pair of polypropylene calf socks, ideal for wicking sweat and moisture. "That really lifted his spirits," said Stan. "I'm a size 10 and Brian is a 9½, but fortunately the socks were 8-12."

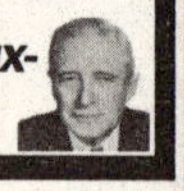

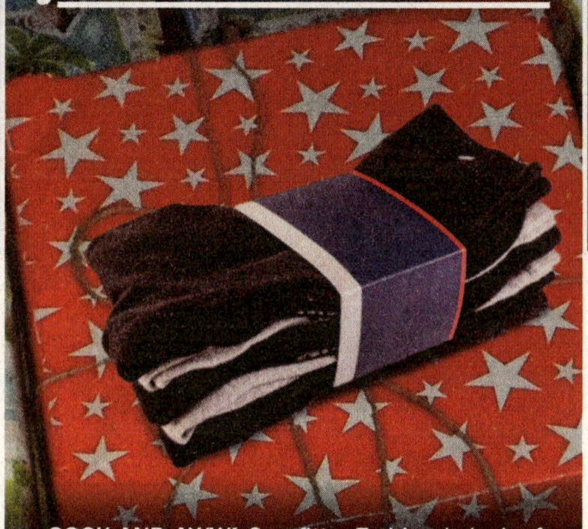

SOCK AND AWW! *Gas-fitter Torbjorn's lack of festive socks left him in tears.*

tungsten

But it was only the beginning, and what happened next took everyone by surprise. Word quickly spread about Brian's Christmas Day disappointment, and the story went viral on social media. Before he knew it, brand new pairs of socks were turning up at Brian's door, courtesy of well-wishers all over the West Riding.

"It really is a wonderful story," said Maxine. "Every day more socks arrive. A pensioner came all the way from Knottingley to give Brian a pair of Argyle calf-lengths that he'd got in a two-pack from his sister," she said. "To think that perfect strangers were doing this to cheer Brian up is wonderful. It's very touching."

"We've had people sending socks from as far afield as Castleford, Wakefield and Leeds. Even the kids in the primary school in Featherstone held a 'Socks for Brian' collection last week. Yesterday, their head teacher brought round nearly 200 pairs."

But nobody was happier than Brian, who now finds himself starting 2023 as the proud owner of over 1050 brand new pairs of socks. "I've been given worsted, cotton, bamboo, merino, spandex, the lot. I've even got half a dozen pairs of cashmere," he said. "It's like I'm walking on air."

"Or should I say, walking on socks!" he added.

THE LIKE LADS
Terry Collier @wiry_terry44
Canny new barmaid in black horse, kidda. Lovely eyes, gorgeous smile
Bob Ferris @scarborough-ferris
Howay man, get a photo!
Giz a smile, pet.
PING
Hee he...
Terry Collier @wiry_terry44
What are you looking at, Bob?
Oh, er, nothing, dearest.
PING
Thelma Ferris @thelmachambers
Haha ha!

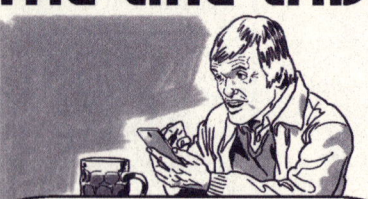

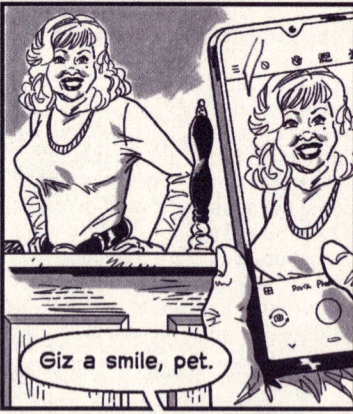

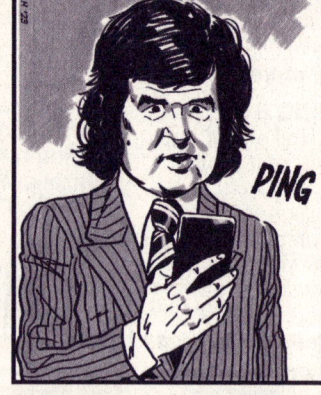

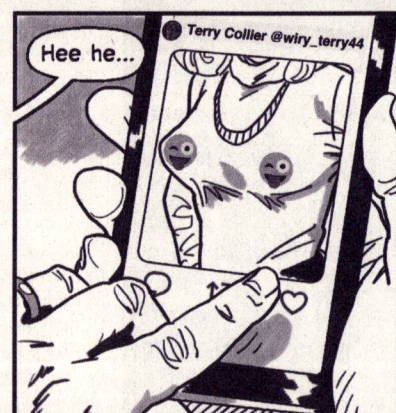

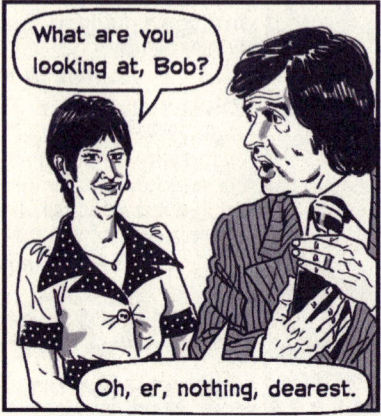

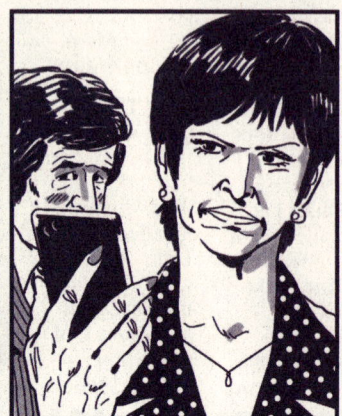

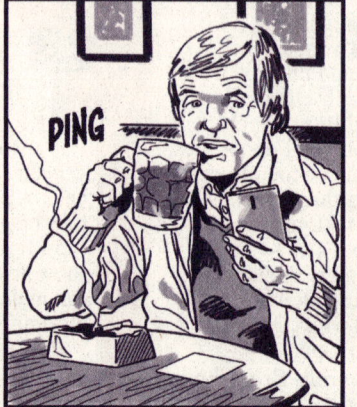

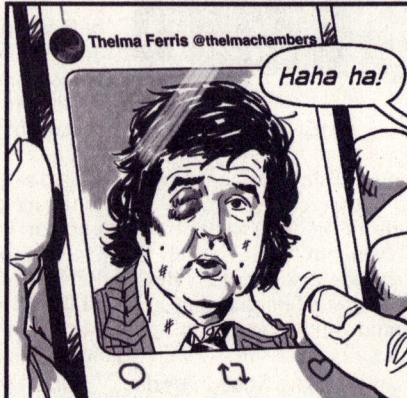

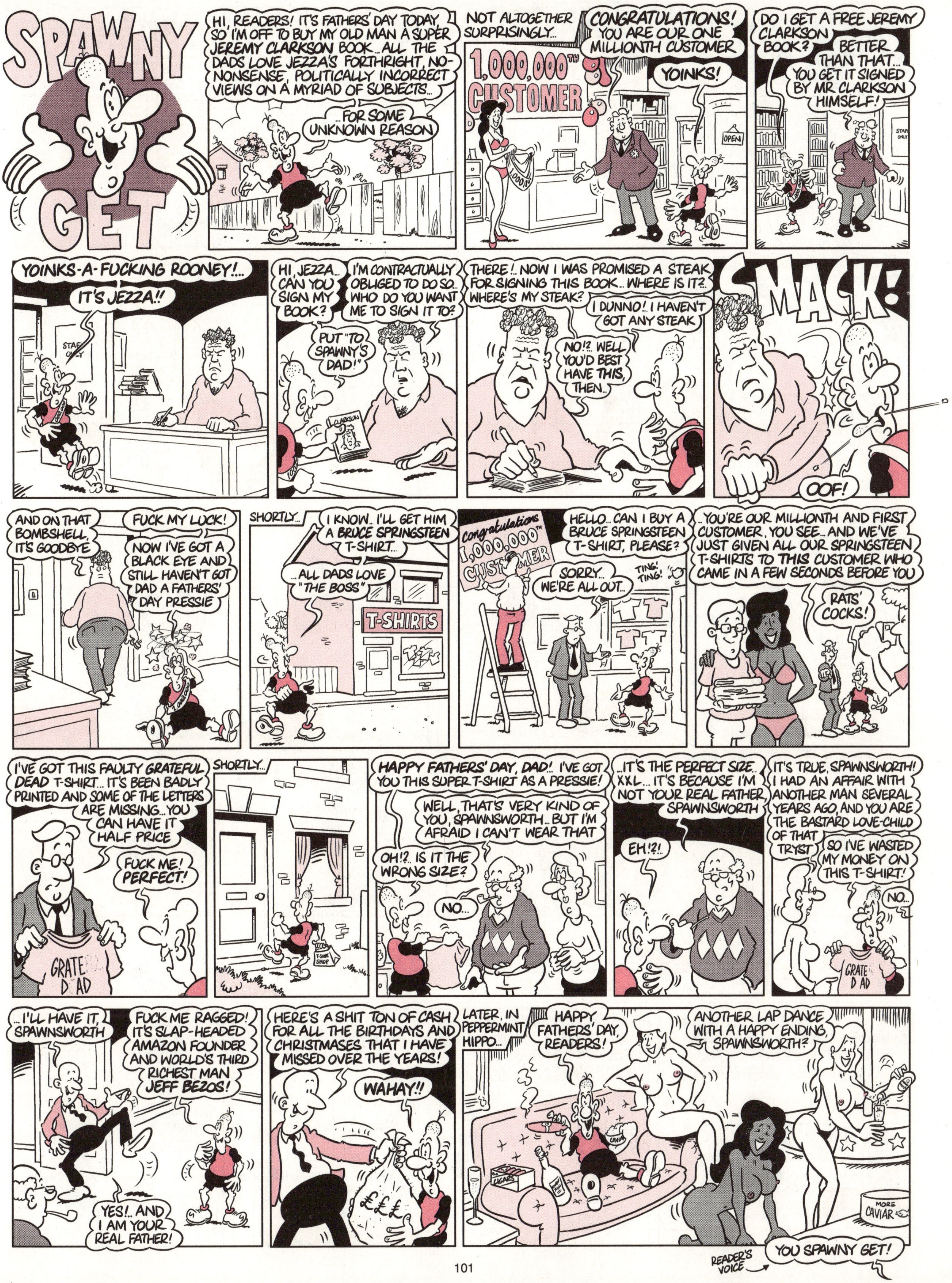
SPAWNY GET
HI, READERS! IT'S FATHERS' DAY TODAY, SO I'M OFF TO BUY MY OLD MAN A SUPER JEREMY CLARKSON BOOK... ALL THE DADS LOVE JEZZA'S FORTHRIGHT, NO-NONSENSE, POLITICALLY INCORRECT VIEWS ON A MYRIAD OF SUBJECTS...
...FOR SOME UNKNOWN REASON
NOT ALTOGETHER SURPRISINGLY...
1,000,000TH CUSTOMER
CONGRATULATIONS! YOU ARE OUR ONE MILLIONTH CUSTOMER
YOINKS!
OPEN
DO I GET A FREE JEREMY CLARKSON BOOK?
BETTER THAN THAT... YOU GET IT SIGNED BY MR CLARKSON HIMSELF!
YOINKS-A-FUCKING ROONEY!...
IT'S JEZZA!!
HI, JEZZA... CAN YOU SIGN MY BOOK?
I'M CONTRACTUALLY OBLIGED TO DO SO... WHO DO YOU WANT ME TO SIGN IT TO?
PUT "TO SPAWNY'S DAD!"
CLARKSON
THERE!... NOW I WAS PROMISED A STEAK FOR SIGNING THIS BOOK... WHERE IS IT?... WHERE'S MY STEAK?
I DUNNO!... I HAVEN'T GOT ANY STEAK
NO!? WELL YOU'D BEST HAVE THIS, THEN...
SMACK!
OOF!
AND ON THAT BOMBSHELL, IT'S GOODBYE
FUCK MY LUCK!
NOW I'VE GOT A BLACK EYE AND STILL HAVEN'T GOT DAD A FATHERS' DAY PRESSIE
SHORTLY...
I KNOW... I'LL GET HIM A BRUCE SPRINGSTEEN T-SHIRT...
...ALL DADS LOVE "THE BOSS"
T-SHIRTS
Congratulations 1,000,000TH CUSTOMER
HELLO... CAN I BUY A BRUCE SPRINGSTEEN T-SHIRT, PLEASE?
SORRY... WE'RE ALL OUT...
TING! TING!
...YOU'RE OUR MILLIONTH AND FIRST CUSTOMER, YOU SEE... AND WE'VE JUST GIVEN ALL OUR SPRINGSTEEN T-SHIRTS TO THIS CUSTOMER WHO CAME IN A FEW SECONDS BEFORE YOU
RATS' COCKS!
I'VE GOT THIS FAULTY GRATEFUL DEAD T-SHIRT... IT'S BEEN BADLY PRINTED AND SOME OF THE LETTERS ARE MISSING... YOU CAN HAVE IT HALF PRICE
FUCK ME! PERFECT!
GRATE D AD
SHORTLY...
HAPPY FATHERS' DAY, DAD!... I'VE GOT YOU THIS SUPER T-SHIRT AS A PRESSIE!
WELL, THAT'S VERY KIND OF YOU, SPAWNSWORTH... BUT I'M AFRAID I CAN'T WEAR THAT
OH!?... IS IT THE WRONG SIZE?
NO...
...IT'S THE PERFECT SIZE... XXL... IT'S BECAUSE I'M NOT YOUR REAL FATHER, SPAWNSWORTH
EH!?!
IT'S TRUE, SPAWNSWORTH! I HAD AN AFFAIR WITH ANOTHER MAN SEVERAL YEARS AGO, AND YOU ARE THE BASTARD LOVE-CHILD OF THAT TRYST
SO I'VE WASTED MY MONEY ON THIS T-SHIRT!
NO...
GRATE D AD
...I'LL HAVE IT, SPAWNSWORTH
FUCK ME RAGGED! IT'S SLAP-HEADED AMAZON FOUNDER AND WORLD'S THIRD RICHEST MAN JEFF BEZOS!
YES!... AND I AM YOUR REAL FATHER!
HERE'S A SHIT TON OF CASH FOR ALL THE BIRTHDAYS AND CHRISTMASES THAT I HAVE MISSED OVER THE YEARS!
WAHAY!!
£££
LATER, IN PEPPERMINT HIPPO...
HAPPY FATHERS' DAY, READERS!
ANOTHER LAP DANCE WITH A HAPPY ENDING, SPAWNSWORTH?
CIGARS
CAVIAR
MORE CAVIAR
READER'S VOICE
YOU SPAWNY GET!

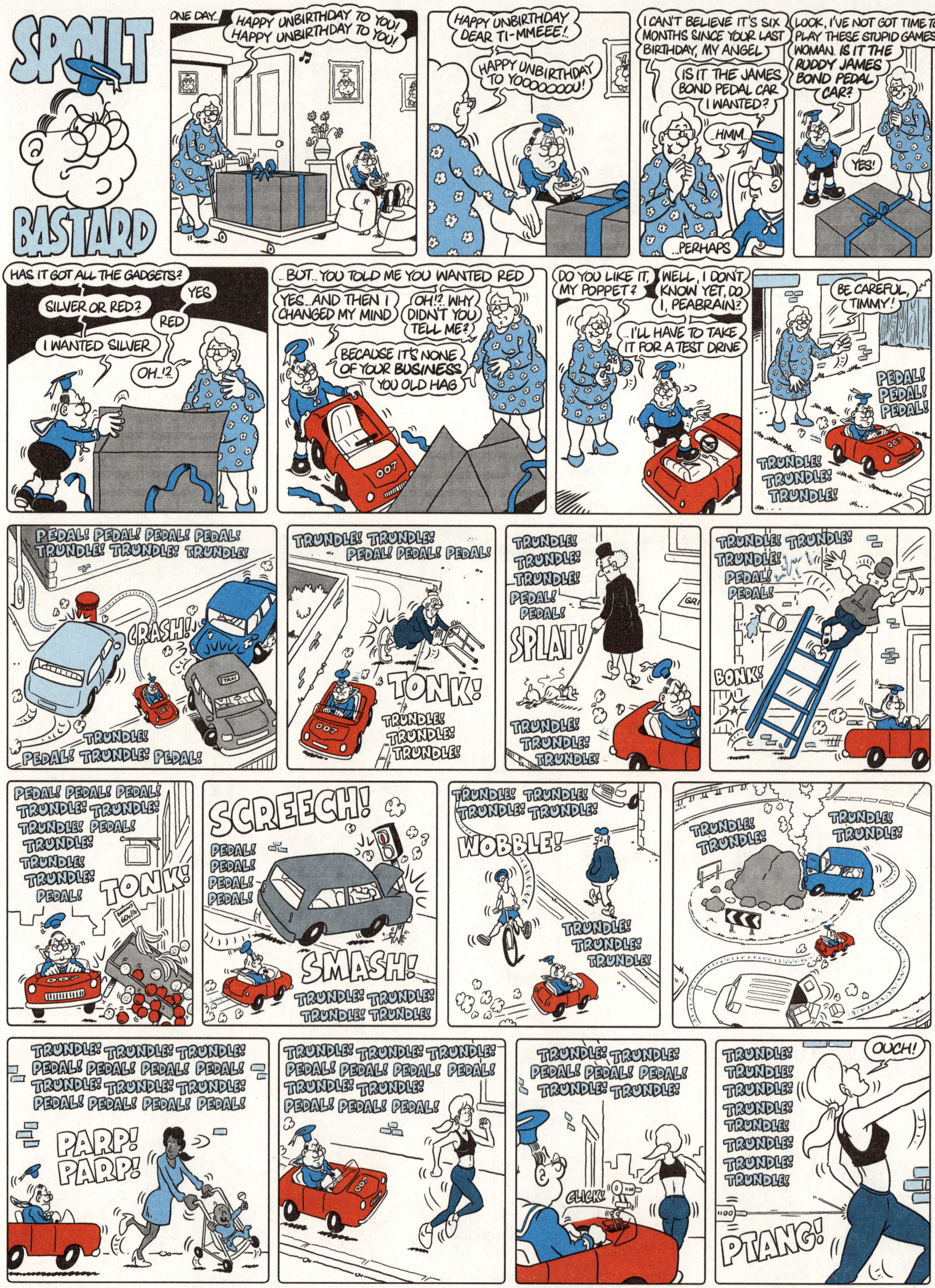
SPOILT BASTARD
ONE DAY...
HAPPY UNBIRTHDAY TO YOU! HAPPY UNBIRTHDAY TO YOU!
HAPPY UNBIRTHDAY DEAR TI-MMEEE!..
HAPPY UNBIRTHDAY TO YOOOOOOOU!
I CAN'T BELIEVE IT'S SIX MONTHS SINCE YOUR LAST BIRTHDAY, MY ANGEL
IS IT THE JAMES BOND PEDAL CAR I WANTED?
..HMM...
...PERHAPS
LOOK, I'VE NOT GOT TIME TO PLAY THESE STUPID GAMES, WOMAN. IS IT THE RUDDY JAMES BOND PEDAL CAR?
YES!
HAS IT GOT ALL THE GADGETS?
YES
SILVER OR RED?
RED
I WANTED SILVER
OH..!?
...BUT... YOU TOLD ME YOU WANTED RED
YES...AND THEN I CHANGED MY MIND
OH!? WHY DIDN'T YOU TELL ME?
BECAUSE IT'S NONE OF YOUR BUSINESS YOU OLD HAG
DO YOU LIKE IT, MY POPPET?
WELL, I DON'T KNOW YET, DO I, PEABRAIN?
...I'LL HAVE TO TAKE IT FOR A TEST DRIVE
BE CAREFUL, TIMMY!
PEDAL! PEDAL! PEDAL!
TRUNDLE! TRUNDLE! TRUNDLE!
PEDAL! PEDAL! PEDAL! PEDAL! TRUNDLE! TRUNDLE! TRUNDLE!
CRASH!
TAXI
TRUNDLE! PEDAL! TRUNDLE! PEDAL!
TRUNDLE! TRUNDLE! PEDAL! PEDAL! PEDAL!
TONK!
TRUNDLE! TRUNDLE! TRUNDLE!
TRUNDLE! TRUNDLE! TRUNDLE! PEDAL! PEDAL!
SPLAT!
TRUNDLE! TRUNDLE! TRUNDLE!
TRUNDLE! TRUNDLE! TRUNDLE! PEDAL! PEDAL!
BONK!
PEDAL! PEDAL! PEDAL! TRUNDLE! TRUNDLE! TRUNDLE! PEDAL! TRUNDLE! TRUNDLE! TRUNDLE! PEDAL!
TONK!
SCREECH!
PEDAL! PEDAL! PEDAL! PEDAL!
SMASH!
TRUNDLE! TRUNDLE! TRUNDLE! TRUNDLE!
TRUNDLE! TRUNDLE! TRUNDLE! TRUNDLE!
WOBBLE!
TRUNDLE! TRUNDLE! TRUNDLE!
TRUNDLE! TRUNDLE!
TRUNDLE! TRUNDLE!
TRUNDLE! TRUNDLE! TRUNDLE! PEDAL! PEDAL! PEDAL! PEDAL! TRUNDLE! TRUNDLE! TRUNDLE! PEDAL! PEDAL! PEDAL! PEDAL!
PARP! PARP!
TRUNDLE! TRUNDLE! TRUNDLE! PEDAL! PEDAL! PEDAL! PEDAL! TRUNDLE! TRUNDLE! PEDAL! PEDAL! PEDAL!
TRUNDLE! TRUNDLE! PEDAL! PEDAL! PEDAL! TRUNDLE! TRUNDLE!
CLICK!
OUCH!
TRUNDLE! TRUNDLE! TRUNDLE! TRUNDLE! TRUNDLE! TRUNDLE! TRUNDLE! TRUNDLE!
PTANG!

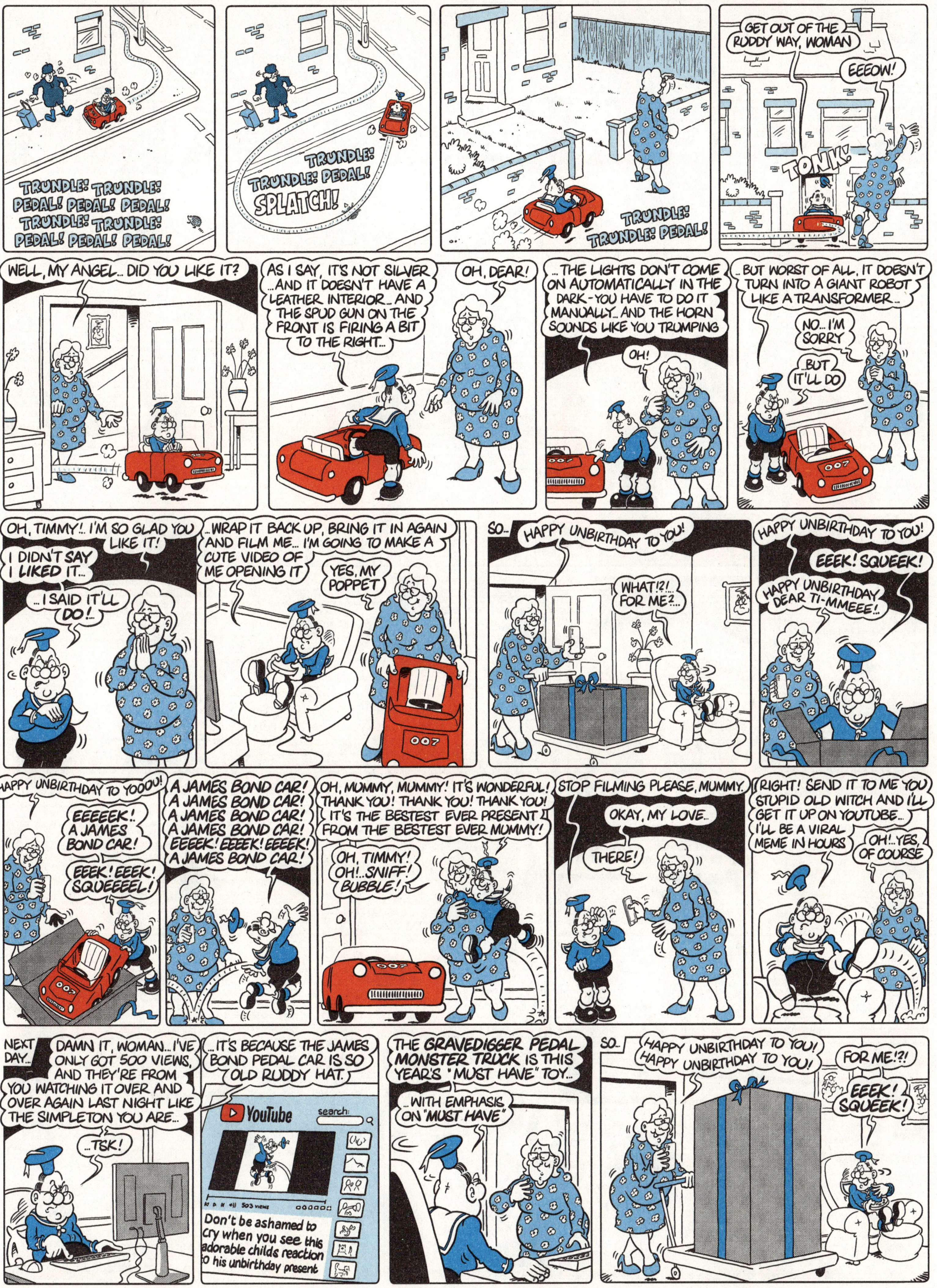
TRUNDLE! TRUNDLE! PEDAL! PEDAL! PEDAL! TRUNDLE! TRUNDLE! PEDAL! PEDAL! PEDAL!
TRUNDLE! TRUNDLE! PEDAL!
SPLATCH!
TRUNDLE! TRUNDLE! PEDAL!
GET OUT OF THE RUDDY WAY, WOMAN
EEEOW!
TONK!
WELL, MY ANGEL... DID YOU LIKE IT?
AS I SAY, IT'S NOT SILVER ...AND IT DOESN'T HAVE A LEATHER INTERIOR... AND THE SPUD GUN ON THE FRONT IS FIRING A BIT TO THE RIGHT...
OH, DEAR!
...THE LIGHTS DON'T COME ON AUTOMATICALLY IN THE DARK - YOU HAVE TO DO IT MANUALLY... AND THE HORN SOUNDS LIKE YOU TRUMPING
OH!
...BUT WORST OF ALL, IT DOESN'T TURN INTO A GIANT ROBOT LIKE A TRANSFORMER...
NO... I'M SORRY
...BUT IT'LL DO
OH, TIMMY!... I'M SO GLAD YOU LIKE IT!
I DIDN'T SAY I LIKED IT...
...I SAID IT'LL DO!...
...WRAP IT BACK UP, BRING IT IN AGAIN AND FILM ME... I'M GOING TO MAKE A CUTE VIDEO OF ME OPENING IT
YES, MY POPPET
007
SO...
HAPPY UNBIRTHDAY TO YOU!
WHAT!?!... FOR ME?...
HAPPY UNBIRTHDAY TO YOU!
EEEK! SQUEEK!
HAPPY UNBIRTHDAY DEAR TI-MMEEE!...
HAPPY UNBIRTHDAY TO YOOOU!
EEEEEK!... A JAMES BOND CAR!
EEEK! EEEK! SQUEEEEL!
A JAMES BOND CAR! A JAMES BOND CAR! A JAMES BOND CAR! A JAMES BOND CAR! EEEEK! EEEEK! EEEEK! A JAMES BOND CAR!
OH, MUMMY, MUMMY! IT'S WONDERFUL! THANK YOU! THANK YOU! THANK YOU! IT'S THE BESTEST EVER PRESENT FROM THE BESTEST EVER MUMMY!
OH, TIMMY! OH!... SNIFF! BUBBLE!
STOP FILMING PLEASE, MUMMY.
OKAY, MY LOVE...
THERE!
RIGHT! SEND IT TO ME YOU STUPID OLD WITCH AND I'LL GET IT UP ON YOUTUBE... I'LL BE A VIRAL MEME IN HOURS
OH!... YES, OF COURSE
NEXT DAY...
DAMN IT, WOMAN... I'VE ONLY GOT 500 VIEWS, AND THEY'RE FROM YOU WATCHING IT OVER AND OVER AGAIN LAST NIGHT LIKE THE SIMPLETON YOU ARE...
...TSK!
...IT'S BECAUSE THE JAMES BOND PEDAL CAR IS SO OLD RUDDY HAT.
YouTube
search:
503 VIEWS
Don't be ashamed to cry when you see this adorable childs reaction to his unbirthday present
THE GRAVEDIGGER PEDAL MONSTER TRUCK IS THIS YEAR'S "MUST HAVE" TOY...
...WITH EMPHASIS ON "MUST HAVE"
SO...
HAPPY UNBIRTHDAY TO YOU! HAPPY UNBIRTHDAY TO YOU!
FOR ME!?!
EEEK! SQUEEK!

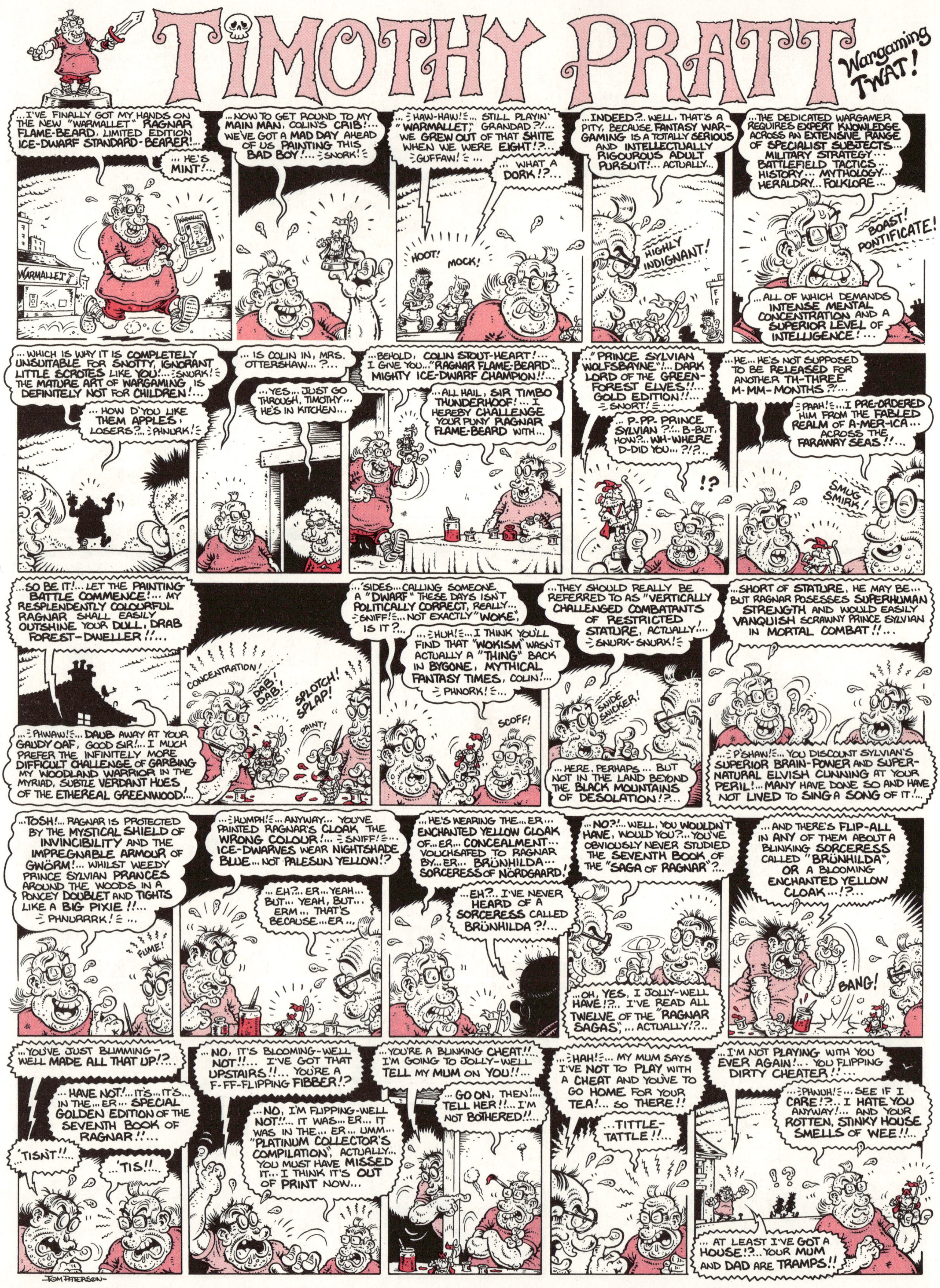
TIMOTHY PRATT
Wargaming TWAT!
...I'VE FINALLY GOT MY HANDS ON THE NEW "WARMALLET" RAGNAR FLAME-BEARD, LIMITED EDITION ICE-DWARF STANDARD-BEARER!...
...HE'S MINT!...
WARMALLET
...NOW TO GET ROUND TO MY MAIN MAN, COLIN'S CRIB!... WE'VE GOT A MAD DAY AHEAD OF US PAINTING THIS BAD BOY!... SNORK!
...HAW-HAW!... STILL PLAYIN' "WARMALLET," GRANDAD?!... WE GREW OUT OF THAT SHITE WHEN WE WERE EIGHT!?... GUFFAW!...
...WHAT A DORK!?...
HOOT!
MOCK!
...INDEED?... WELL, THAT'S A PITY, BECAUSE FANTASY WAR-GAMING IS A TOTALLY SERIOUS AND INTELLECTUALLY RIGOUROUS ADULT PURSUIT!... ACTUALLY...
HIGHLY INDIGNANT!
...THE DEDICATED WARGAMER REQUIRES EXPERT KNOWLEDGE ACROSS AN EXTENSIVE RANGE OF SPECIALIST SUBJECTS... MILITARY STRATEGY... BATTLEFIELD TACTICS... HISTORY... MYTHOLOGY... HERALDRY... FOLKLORE...
BOAST! PONTIFICATE!
...ALL OF WHICH DEMANDS INTENSE MENTAL CONCENTRATION AND A SUPERIOR LEVEL OF INTELLIGENCE!...
...WHICH IS WHY IT IS COMPLETELY UNSUITABLE FOR SNOTTY, IGNORANT LITTLE SCROTES LIKE YOU!... SNURK! THE MATURE ART OF WARGAMING IS DEFINITELY NOT FOR CHILDREN!...
...HOW D'YOU LIKE THEM APPLES, LOSERS?... PHNURK!
...IS COLIN IN, MRS. OTTERSHAW...?...
...YES... JUST GO THROUGH, TIMOTHY... HE'S IN KITCHEN...
...BEHOLD, COLIN STOUT-HEART!... I GIVE YOU..."RAGNAR FLAME-BEARD"... MIGHTY ICE-DWARF CHAMPION!!...
...ALL HAIL, SIR TIMBO THUNDERHOOF!... I HEREBY CHALLENGE YOUR PUNY RAGNAR FLAME-BEARD WITH...
..."PRINCE SYLVIAN WOLFSBAYNE"!... DARK LORD OF THE GREEN-FOREST ELVES!!... GOLD EDITION!!... SNORT!...
...P-PP-PRINCE SYLVIAN?!... B-BUT, HOW?... WH-WHERE D-DID YOU...?!?...
!?
...HE... HE'S NOT SUPPOSED TO BE RELEASED FOR ANOTHER TH-THREE M-MM-MONTHS?!...
PAAH!... I PRE-ORDERED HIM FROM THE FABLED REALM OF A-MER-ICA... ACROSS THE FARAWAY SEAS!!...
SMUG SMIRK!
...SO BE IT!... LET THE PAINTING BATTLE COMMENCE!... MY RESPLENDENTLY COLOURFUL RAGNAR SHALL EASILY OUTSHINE YOUR DULL, DRAB FOREST-DWELLER!!...
...PHWAW!... DAUB AWAY AT YOUR GAUDY OAF, GOOD SIR!... I MUCH PREFER THE INFINITELY MORE DIFFICULT CHALLENGE OF GARBING MY WOODLAND WARRIOR IN THE MYRIAD, SUBTLE VERDANT HUES OF THE ETHEREAL GREENWOOD!...
CONCENTRATION!
DAB! DAB!
SPLOTCH! SPLAP!
PAINT!
...'SIDES... CALLING SOMEONE A "DWARF" THESE DAYS ISN'T POLITICALLY CORRECT, REALLY... SNIFF!... NOT EXACTLY "WOKE", IS IT?...
...HUH!... I THINK YOU'LL FIND THAT "WOKISM" WASN'T ACTUALLY A "THING" BACK IN BYGONE, MYTHICAL FANTASY TIMES, COLIN!... PHNORK!...
SCOFF!
...THEY SHOULD REALLY BE REFERRED TO AS "VERTICALLY CHALLENGED COMBATANTS OF RESTRICTED STATURE, ACTUALLY!... SNURK-SNURK!
SNIDE SNICKER!
...HERE, PERHAPS... BUT NOT IN THE LAND BEYOND THE BLACK MOUNTAINS OF DESOLATION!?...
...SHORT OF STATURE, HE MAY BE... BUT RAGNAR POSESSES SUPERHUMAN STRENGTH AND WOULD EASILY VANQUISH SCRAWNY PRINCE SYLVIAN IN MORTAL COMBAT!!...
...P'SHAW!... YOU DISCOUNT SYLVIAN'S SUPERIOR BRAIN-POWER AND SUPER-NATURAL ELVISH CUNNING AT YOUR PERIL!... MANY HAVE DONE SO AND HAVE NOT LIVED TO SING A SONG OF IT!...
...TOSH!... RAGNAR IS PROTECTED BY THE MYSTICAL SHIELD OF INVINCIBILITY AND THE IMPREGNABLE ARMOUR OF GWÖRM!... WHILST WEEDY PRINCE SYLVIAN PRANCES AROUND THE WOODS IN A PONCEY DOUBLET AND TIGHTS LIKE A BIG PIXIE!!... PHNURRRK!...
FUME!
...HUMPH!... ANYWAY... YOU'VE PAINTED RAGNAR'S CLOAK THE WRONG COLOUR!... SNIFF!... ICE-DWARVES WEAR NIGHTSHADE BLUE... NOT PALESUN YELLOW!?
...EH?... ER... YEAH... BUT... YEAH, BUT... ERM... THAT'S BECAUSE... ER...
...HE'S WEARING THE... ER... ENCHANTED YELLOW CLOAK OF... ER... CONCEALMENT... VOUCHSAFED TO RAGNAR BY... ER... BRÜNHILDA... SORCERESS OF NÖRDGAARD!
...EH?... I'VE NEVER HEARD OF A SORCERESS CALLED BRÜNHILDA?!...
...NO?!... WELL, YOU WOULDN'T HAVE, WOULD YOU?... YOU'VE OBVIOUSLY NEVER STUDIED THE SEVENTH BOOK OF THE "SAGA OF RAGNAR"?...
...OH, YES, I JOLLY-WELL HAVE!?... I'VE READ ALL TWELVE OF THE "RAGNAR SAGAS",... ACTUALLY!?...
...AND THERE'S FLIP-ALL IN ANY OF THEM ABOUT A BLINKING SORCERESS CALLED "BRÜNHILDA", OR A BLOOMING ENCHANTED YELLOW CLOAK...!?...
BANG!
...YOU'VE JUST BLIMMING-WELL MADE ALL THAT UP!?...
...HAVE NOT!... IT'S... IT'S... IN THE... ER... SPECIAL GOLDEN EDITION OF THE SEVENTH BOOK OF RAGNAR!!...
...'TISN'T!!...
...'TIS!!...
...NO, IT'S BLOOMING-WELL NOT!!... I'VE GOT THAT UPSTAIRS!!... YOU'RE A F-FF-FLIPPING FIBBER!?
...NO, I'M FLIPPING-WELL NOT!!... IT WAS... ER... IT WAS IN THE... ER... UMM... "PLATINUM COLLECTOR'S COMPILATION", ACTUALLY... YOU MUST HAVE MISSED IT... I THINK IT'S OUT OF PRINT NOW...
...YOU'RE A BLINKING CHEAT!!... I'M GOING TO JOLLY-WELL TELL MY MUM ON YOU!!...
...GO ON, THEN!... TELL HER!!... I'M NOT BOTHERED!!...
...HAH!... MY MUM SAYS I'VE NOT TO PLAY WITH A CHEAT AND YOU'VE TO GO HOME FOR YOUR TEA!... SO THERE!!
...TITTLE-TATTLE!!...
...I'M NOT PLAYING WITH YOU EVER AGAIN!... YOU FLIPPING DIRTY CHEATER!!...
...PHNUH!... SEE IF I CARE!?... I HATE YOU ANYWAY!... AND YOUR ROTTEN, STINKY HOUSE SMELLS OF WEE!!...
!?
...AT LEAST I'VE GOT A HOUSE!?... YOUR MUM AND DAD ARE TRAMPS!!
TOM PATERSON

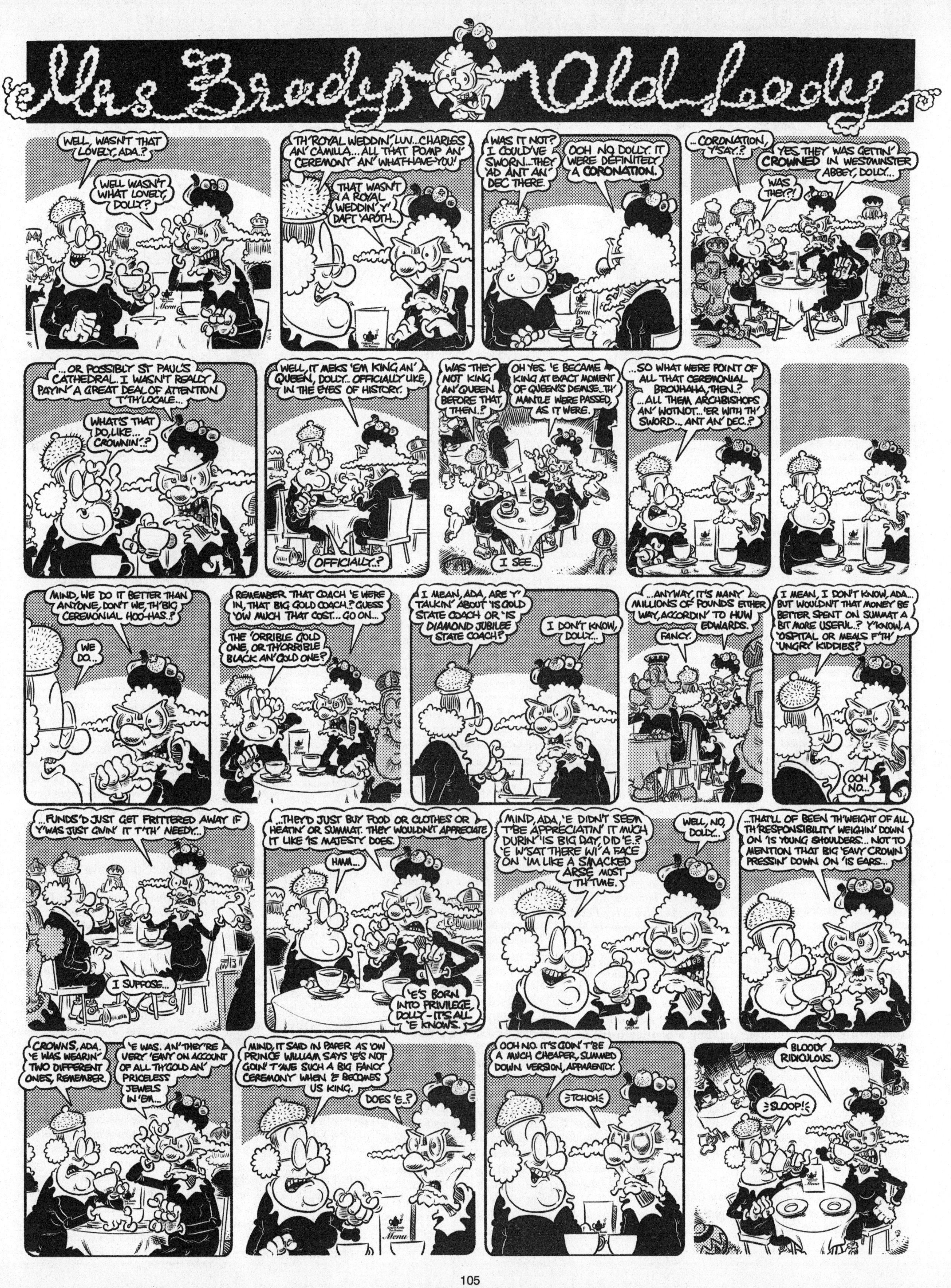
Mrs Brady Old Lady
WELL, WASN'T THAT LOVELY, ADA..?
WELL WASN'T WHAT LOVELY, DOLLY?
TH' ROYAL WEDDIN', LUV... CHARLES AN' CAMILLA... ALL THAT POMP AN' CEREMONY AN' WHAT-HAVE-YOU!
THAT WASN'T A ROYAL WEDDIN', Y' DAFT 'APOTH...
WAS IT NOT? I COULD'VE SWORN... THEY 'AD ANT AN' DEC THERE.
OOH NO, DOLLY. IT WERE DEFINITELY A CORONATION.
...CORONATION, Y'SAY..?
YES, THEY WAS GETTIN' CROWNED IN WESTMINSTER ABBEY, DOLLY...
WAS THEY?!
...OR POSSIBLY ST PAUL'S CATHEDRAL. I WASN'T REALLY PAYIN' A GREAT DEAL OF ATTENTION T'TH' LOCALE...
WHAT'S THAT DO, LIKE... CROWNIN'..?
WELL, IT MEKS 'EM KING AN' QUEEN, DOLLY.. OFFICIALLY LIKE, IN THE EYES OF HISTORY.
OFFICIALLY..?
WAS THEY NOT KING AN' QUEEN BEFORE THAT, THEN..?
OH YES. 'E BECAME KING AT EXACT MOMENT OF QUEEN'S DEMISE.. TH' MANTLE WERE PASSED, AS IT WERE.
I SEE...
...SO WHAT WERE POINT OF ALL THAT CEREMONIAL BROUHAHA, THEN..? ...ALL THEM ARCHBISHOPS AN' WOTNOT... 'ER WITH TH' SWORD... ANT AN' DEC..?
MIND, WE DO IT BETTER THAN ANYONE, DON'T WE, TH' BIG CEREMONIAL HOO-HAS..?
WE DO...
REMEMBER THAT COACH 'E WERE IN, THAT BIG GOLD COACH..? GUESS 'OW MUCH THAT COST... GO ON...
THE 'ORRIBLE GOLD ONE, OR TH'ORRIBLE BLACK AN' GOLD ONE?
I MEAN, ADA, ARE Y' TALKIN' ABOUT 'IS GOLD STATE COACH OR 'IS DIAMOND JUBILEE STATE COACH?
I DON'T KNOW, DOLLY...
...ANYWAY, IT'S MANY MILLIONS OF POUNDS EITHER WAY, ACCORDIN' TO HUW EDWARDS.
FANCY.
I MEAN, I DON'T KNOW, ADA... BUT WOULDN'T THAT MONEY BE BETTER SPENT ON SUMMAT A BIT MORE USEFUL..? Y'KNOW, A 'OSPITAL OR MEALS F'TH' 'UNGRY KIDDIES?
OOH NO...
...FUNDS'D JUST GET FRITTERED AWAY IF Y'WAS JUST GIVIN' IT T'TH' NEEDY...
I SUPPOSE...
...THEY'D JUST BUY FOOD OR CLOTHES OR HEATIN' OR SUMMAT. THEY WOULDN'T APPRECIATE IT LIKE 'IS MAJESTY DOES.
HMM...
'E'S BORN INTO PRIVILEGE, DOLLY - IT'S ALL 'E KNOWS.
MIND, ADA, 'E DIDN'T SEEM T'BE APPRECIATIN' IT MUCH DURIN' 'IS BIG DAY, DID 'E..? 'E W'SAT THERE WI' A FACE ON 'IM LIKE A SMACKED ARSE MOST TH' TIME.
WELL, NO, DOLLY...
...THAT'LL OF BEEN TH' WEIGHT OF ALL TH' RESPONSIBILITY WEIGHIN' DOWN ON 'IS YOUNG SHOULDERS... NOT TO MENTION THAT BIG 'EAVY CROWN PRESSIN' DOWN ON 'IS EARS...
CROWNS, ADA. 'E WAS WEARIN' TWO DIFFERENT ONES, REMEMBER.
'E WAS. AN' THEY'RE VERY 'EAVY ON ACCOUNT OF ALL TH'GOLD AN' PRICELESS JEWELS IN 'EM...
MIND, IT SAID IN PAPER AS 'OW PRINCE WILLIAM SAYS 'E'S NOT GOIN' T'AVE SUCH A BIG FANCY CEREMONY WHEN 'E BECOMES US KING.
DOES 'E..?
OOH NO. IT'S GOIN' T'BE A MUCH CHEAPER, SLIMMED DOWN VERSION, APPARENTLY.
TCHOH
BLOODY RIDICULOUS.
SLOOP!

Roger's Profanisaurus

Seconds Out for a Bout of Word Wrestling from Britain's Favourite Lexicon of Profanity

aggrophobic *n.* One who is afraid of fighting; a *yitney*.

alco-Popeye *n.* A bloke who, after imbibing one too many WKDs, takes on the persona of the famously incoherent, monocular maritime cartoon mentalist and wants to fight everyone in sight.

bacardi bruiser *n.* An inebriated lady who elects to fight rather than to cry.

battle cry *n.* A loud and stirring *rumpet voluntary*, signalling a declaration of war against a particularly troublesome *Thora*.

beef piston 1. *n.* A crowd-pleasing pro-wrestling move, probably. 2. *n.* Nickname of *glans*-headed pro-wrestler-turned-thesp "Dwayne Johnson" (real name Thelwell Rockingham).

bowling like Imran Khan *sim.* Running into a *pagga* and attempting to join in with a wild, overhead swing.

boxer's punchball *n.* The acorn of *shit* that hangs off the *toffee strings* and resists all attempts to *tap the ash off*, simply bouncing around like a pugilist's exercise equipment.

Buckfast bravery *n.* Instances of incredible courage manifested by ruddy-faced Caledonian outdoorsmen, *eg*. Strolling across four lanes of traffic without looking left or right, sleeping on a railway level crossing, fighting a police horse *etc*.

Bugner's eye *n.* Flapless female genitalia, resembling the ex-pugilist's closed-up eye in every fight he had.

champagga *n.* A fight fuelled by expensive beverages, as opposed to Special Brew. A brawl one may see once in a blue moon outside a brasserie.

Commodus *n. prop.* A name given to a reluctant hero who always seems to turn up after a scrap with the immortal line from the film *Gladiator*, *viz*. "Am I too late? Have I missed the battle?"

drambo *n.* Scots. Someone who will fight anyone in the room after a few shandies. Also *two can Van Damme, half pint Harry, tinny mallet*.

drinking medal *n.* Unexplained scar or bruise acquired on the Saturday night town centre battlefield.

dropping a weight division 1. *n.* In boxing, a fighter losing sufficient poundage so as to be able to compete in a lower weight category, thus enabling him to take on a larger number of opponents in the ring. 2. *n.* In *shitting*, the act of expelling such an impressive quantity of *feeshus* that you could conceivably make the move from heavy to cruiserweight or, if you've got amoebic dysentery, junior flyweight.

dry bath *n.* A right pummelling. 'Christ. What happened to you?' 'I said hello to Björk at the airport and she gave me a dry bath.'

emergency stop button *n.* The *bollocks*. From the fact that a sharp blow to the *knackers* will instantly render any man into a state of agonised immobility, whatever he happens to be doing.

empty headlock, fanny like an *sim.* Said of a cavernous and accommodating *clunge* that is reminiscent of the empty void left when a wrestler frees himself from the eponymous underarm hold. Also *arse like an empty headlock*. 'What can I say about my next guest? She's one of the last great stars from the golden age of Hollywood and after nine husbands, she must have a fanny like an empty headlock. Ladies and gentlemen, please give a big Pebble Mill at One welcome to Miss Zsa Zsa Gabor.'

fart to a shit fight, bring a *v.* In a competitive situation, to be seriously overmatched. 'And Dunn really has brought a fart to a shit fight here, Harry.'

fighting a boozing battle *n.* A familiar sight outside late bars and nightclubs. Young men wearing white, short-sleeved shirts, exchanging blows while under the influence of alcohol. 'Where's Harry?' 'Last time I saw him he was outside on the steps fighting a boozing battle with a photographer, Meghan. He said he'd see you back at the Chinook.'

fighting water *n.* Falling down juice, wreck the hoose juice, Spesh.

fisticuffs *n.* Knocking oneself about a bit. 'How did your quiet night in go, then, your holiness?' 'I'm afraid it descended into fisticuffs, as usual.'

fist magnet *n.* Someone who attracts punches to his face.

fist of fury *n.* Of a gentleman with a restricted *wank window*, for example while his missus has just nipped next door for a cup of sugar, a mindlessly violent act of *self abuse* carried out in a sort of masturbatory red mist. An *armbreaker, bishop rage, power wank*.

fisty-cuffs 1. *n.* A *pagga* or *Barney*. 2. *n.* Tadpoles in cream deposited on the lower sleeve of a shirt following a bout of *pud-pulling*.

five finger death punch 1. *n.* Popular USA alt-rock combo. No, us neither. 2. *n.* Five sticks of Peperami between two slices of thickly buttered white bread, all washed down with tea with four sugars and a Capstan Full Strength; the breakfast of champions. 3. *n.* A no-nonsense spot of *fisting*. Also *Amsterdam uppercut, a fiver in*.

get one's sovereigns on *v.* while preparing for a *pagga*, to adorn one's hands with cheap *clink*, thereby creating a budget knuckle duster effect. To *put up your Lizzie Dukes*. 'Best get your sovereigns on, Mrs Walker. Albert Tatlock's in the snug and he's got the red mist again.'

goochy fragrance *n.* The musky, manly aroma of a gymnasium locker room, rugby club changing area or wrestler's jockstrap launderette. *Eau de barse*.

half nelson 1. *n.* A grappling hold practised by both wrestlers and wrestlees. 2. *n.* An unfinished act of *horatio*.

invincibility cloak *n.* That drink-fuelled shield that gives a man the ability to fight like Tyson, escape from the police in a single bound and fall off scaffolding without harm.

kicking the piper *n.* A bout of flatulence that sounds like a prolonged and violent attack on a traditional Scottish musician.

knock off the bobby's helmet *v.* To engage in a fistfight with one's *little Kojak*.

lamp a champion *v.* To squeeze out a much larger *shit* than you thought possible. To *punch way over your weight* in the *ring*.

lard as nails *adj.* Fat as *fuck* but surprisingly tasty in a *pagga*.

mortal combat *n.* Fighting between intoxicated fellows. Or occasionally, in the case of certain self-sufficient Harold Ramps, between a single intoxicated fellow.

mud wrestling *n.* A long and messy battle on the toilet, involving much grunting and groaning, which usually ends in either a knock-out, a fall or a submission.

one pint Viking *n.* A man who gets very fighty after a pitifully small amount of booze. A *two can van Damme, two pot screamer, drambo, half-pint Harry etc*.

pagga *n.* A free-for-all no-holds-barred combat between anyone who wants to join in.

pagga starter *n.* A strong beer which breaks the ice at fights. *Supermarket smack, spesh*.

plumstruck *adj.* Incapable of speech following a soft glancing blow to the *chap equipment*.

punch above one's weight 1. *v.* In boxing, to come out on top in a bout against a superior fighter. 2. *v.* Of a plain gentleman, to successfully *woo* a young lady whom he might ordinarily consider to be out of his class. 'Punching above your weight there, Rupe.'

punched by the invisible man *euph.* On entering a freshly soiled toilet, being knocked off one's feet by an unseen force.

punch its head in *v.* What a gentleman does to his *gentleman* when *relaxing in a gentleman's way*.

punch the clown *v.* To make *custard* shoot out the top of *Charlie Cairoli's hat*. To *pour oneself a hand shandy*.

punch up the whiskers *n.* A *knee trembler* or similar romantic encounter in a train lavatory, taxi queue or Building Society doorway.

pyrrhic victory 1. *n.* A military triumph obtained at arguably too great a cost to the winning side, from King Pyrrhus of Epirus's victory against the Romans in 279BC, where he won the battle but lost all his troops. 2. *n.* Successfully *bringing yourself off* but getting all *spunk* in your eye.

roid rage 1. *n.* Sudden attack of *red mist* from a pumped-up bouncer when somebody's looked at him funny, or has tried to come in the club wearing the wrong sort of shoes. An outburst of anger caused by illicit body-building drugs. 2. *n.*

profanisaurus@viz.co.uk

The violent anger exhibited by a haemorrhoid sufferer whose *bum grapes* have just been *twatted* with a *metal ruler*, for example. Any foul mood brought on by a sudden flare-up of the *Nobbys*.

slabberdash *v.* In fighting or romance, to slap one's opponent or lover upon the side of the face with a semi-erect penis. To *chap*.

sophisticuffs *n.* A fight at the opera.

sovving *n.* The use, in a proper old-style Cockney punch-up, of one or more sovereign-ring-bedecked fists.

still fighting *adj.* Of a curry or other spicy meal, to display the same or greater aggression on the way out as/than it did when it went in. *'Are you all right in there, June?' 'No. It's that chili I had last night, Terry. It's still fighting.'*

supermarket smack *n.* Special brew, *pagga starter, falling down juice*.

tackle bag *1. n.* Something that rugby players practise pummelling into submission, prior to drinking pints of vomit and lighting rectally inserted toilet paper. *2. n.* The *ball sack* or scrotum. Also *John Wayne's hairy saddlebags*, the *happy sack, raisin bag etc*.

technical knockout *1. n.* Something in a boxing match that presumably doesn't include biting your opponent's ear off. *2. n.* A perfectly executed *hand shandy* below the belt that leaves no *spoff* on the knuckles.

throw me a clip *1. exclam.* Desperate request for more ammunition, often shouted heroically across the battlefield to a fellow soldier during big-budget action movies. *2. exclam.* Desperate request for more *shit scrape*, often shouted heroically across the landing and/or down the stairs.

throw the towel in *1. v.* Of a boxing trainer, to concede defeat when his fighter is getting his fucking head kicked in. *2. v.* To give up trying to have a *poke* because the missus has *got the painters and decorators in*. *3. v.* Of a lady, to casually insert a *mouse*.

Tipton uppercut *n.* A knee in the *bollocks*.

two little boys fighting under a blanket *n.* Alluringly unrestrained *fat rascals*. Also *two puppies fighting in a bag, dead heat in a Zeppelin race*.

Tyson Brewery *n. prop.* A *pissive aggressive* person who, after a couple of beers, wants to fight the fucking world. Also *one can Van Damme, tinny mallet, half pint Harry, drambo, Hulk Höegarden*.

vestosterone *n.* Middle-aged male hormone caused by drinking in the afternoon during summer, an excess of which leads to the wearing of sleeveless singlets and sudden bursts of manly violence.

what do you think of that, Mean Gene? Ooo yeah! *exclam.* Something to say, in the style of deceased bonkers wrestler "Macho Man" Randy Savage after *letting one rip*. Also *you've got to let it breathe*.

winotaur *n.* She who, after taking alcohol on board, turns in a violent, foul-mouthed beast that looks like something animated by Ray Harryhausen.

wounded soldier's walk *n.* The trip a gentleman makes to the bathroom after completing a messy act of *relaxation* when he has nothing to hand with which to clean up the resultant mess. From the fact that cupping a few teaspoonsful of rapidly cooling *spuffer* to his belly causes him to assume a hunched posture which is very reminiscent of a shot infantryman clutching his injured stomach as he hobbles off the battlefield.

wrestling Sergeant Brown *euph.* Struggling to force out a particularly recalcitrant *pop*. From the film *Bear Man*, in which the protagonist describes a fight between two grizzlies thusly: *"Crikey, what a horrible mess. It looks like someone's been wrestling Sergeant Brown."*

wrestling the Balrog *1. n.* In *The Lord of the Rings*, Gandalf the Grey's display of heroics in halting the advance of the eponymous flame-spewing behemoth. *2. n.* The challenge a chap's *nipsy* faces when valiantly attempting to hold back a particularly foul and gruesome *bogstopper* as he makes his way home following an impressively ambitious curry. Often accompanied by the shouted avowal: "You shall not pass."

Roger's PROFANISAURUS

WRESTMANIA WORDSEARCH

THE time for trash-talking is over as ***Roger's Profanisaurus*** entries go toe-to-toe in the ***Heavyweight Wordsearch of the Century***. All 64 fight-related entries on this page are hidden in the wrestling ring, and all you have to do is find them. They may read horizontally, vertically or diagonally, backwards or forwards, two falls, two submissions or a knockout. So come on, Grapple/Wordsearch fans, it's seconds out, and let's get ready to rumble.

D T B E E F P I S T O N B W G M L O F W A K L A W S R E I D L O S D E D N U O W M S F
B Y O E B Y H P I X T O P N M M K F E A C G U J H R M L P U H G A E R K L F J D X T I
A E W N K L C D W N M U I B Y O W O B U C K F A S T B R A V E R Y L I A E A M L H P S
P P L X V Y G J T E V L A P K T R M L G D W A C T J O P U T Z D F C M B T N S A M L T
Q U I W H T H G I F T I H S A O T T R A F A G N I R B B O T D W K P G S E N E T M Y I
W N N X F U W S B S I L N E S M D E A M H S A R T U P N M Y P I L H Y D F Y L H I R C
A C G C B T D O E B T G X C L R M F R L P W A R D L E L M Y N A P H T D O L F R B L U
F H L Q H N W R L J F W H L I T E S L F C A R L T S L Y R G E O G E W O J I B O O E F
A I I W H A W K T I K F R T B B F K L G P O A E S H N D T M F A I G O L U K D W X B F
B T K A F D B C F J T O L F I F I A S D N E M O S H R H S L U I X E A M F E L T E R S
D S E W U K F O L F M T X I U N D L E I L I V B W T E O O J R D N M K L A A E H R W G
D H I M K D W O V E S L L C M E G E I J H E K M A P L C W A O E O K L J Y N P E S E S
S E M S V G U J P E A O I E M T P W R T R W T I I T U I L M G L C B T E R E H T P H E
E A R D W A C H K L O T P G B W O E A E Y O E P V L H R N N E A R M E X A M Z O U L M
P D A L R H L K P E S N N E R O T L I T E C E H K T W T A G M A O D C L H P E W N L E
P I N F E O A F H I L I E T D R Y G K L E R L I T B N E L S T E C E H A R T L E C N S
L N K B S H P L H Y K A E S A E N S L H T R Y O B P M I T E D H B L N E W Y E L H W A
N P H U T E S P T N Q A Y T W S E R F K L R E R A T U E P L K A E Q I L T H D I B L T
O B A Y L R O F I X D T S R O E E S I I U M L T A K K H L E R D H B C P B E L N A X E
S L N H I S H R H N P A E N O L I S Y F G L T H T R E W C H N K T C A M H A W C L E A
L T E K N S D Z Y F G L C D K T M G F T V H T E A Z D H I N R O E S L L S D E H L U T
E I R D G M T U R G T A V D R Y C O H K P F T M M F R S L P U L H R K E R L L P T F A
N P A T S E U I A M H U W I L A T I A T O E R I L M B B M C S P K H N Z H O M H Y I L
F T S D E T M P L D F K P E O S O K V K T E R M N I U L J S R H Z E O M Y C G L D G E
L O B U R S W E P L B F G K I M L F N C P M L B D G X E F L O C K Q C M U K Z E T H A
A N A Z G P X P R T F H V F P G L I Q U I P F T N E U F Q X T N L U K E D R Y B A T H
H U A R E U T V L G Y I Z R D J H T S K W H T E L O U N L T W U A E O L H V C E T I P
E P R A A M L R E T E L G M F T B T M L D E R Y E C M L D N T P G U U L D E M Z R N L
W P A R N I B T D S L N H H U M L F D W Y S L R Y T R G L E E H S E T O K G L U X G T
T E B S T L F R W A T P C O T Z E N B I E B T T Y L U I R Y R T M L H T Z A P L U A R
D R A M B O V T R T E O Y Y L I O Z D Y V P S C H P A L E Y N A L K F R W R M L A B A
F C W Q R V Y D A R U O S L S I N E E B W I L H T R T P P L W E B O H S U D O M M O C
L U Z O O I A M F R D E A T P T E G E A F B S M L F O E T E O D P L A F R I L Y E O M
M T S C W S S T R T B D S M E R O K H F R E W I C P N U A A L R M T A Y T O A E Y Z L
A W T H N R S U A O K R A W T R A P M L H T A E O E I J C B C E M L T N S R S R B I L
D E U A M D W H L O H H M L Z W O P B C F H I C N N W L K B E G F L F R K Q C H Y N M
A W I M M A W O R S C M L F C E P N X U M Y L M J S X C L L H N P I W A F E M F T G E
D L X P M S B A C A R D I B R U I S E R T A M F D C U T E L T I E O S E L S T A A B H
S A E A A F T M P M S F R W U T H J N S W T Z F E S K P B V H F A D E T O A D R Y A B
M A W G B T E M L E H S Y B B O B E H T F F O K C O N K A E C E C R T V M L T S W T E
L D W G Z W A P T Y S O N B R E W E R Y S U T N P H T R G Y N V P A V P D A M D R T E
C S W A M L F R T H U K S W E C F T L P U H D Q E S T E A L U I B I M J D X G E A L J
D A O E R P U N C H E D B Y T H E I N V I S I B L E M A N B P F N A C F R E S N T E N
A X D E W F T Y H U F R O P I B H D R F V T Y G S W A X R D K G M H F R S A W O E B L
G O O C H Y F R A G R A N C E T H S A D R E B B A L S E A G G R O P H O B I C P Y T Q

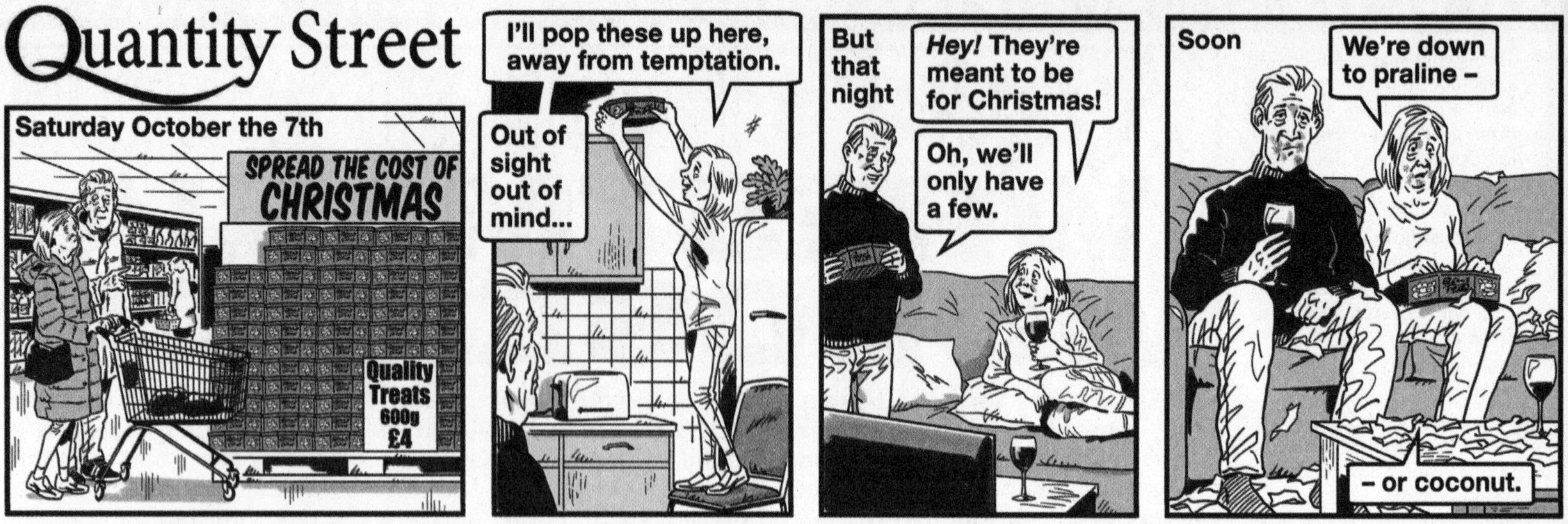
Quantity Street
Saturday October the 7th
SPREAD THE COST OF CHRISTMAS
Quality Treats 600g £4
I'll pop these up here, away from temptation.
Out of sight out of mind...
But that night
Hey! They're meant to be for Christmas!
Oh, we'll only have a few.
Soon
We're down to praline –
– or coconut.

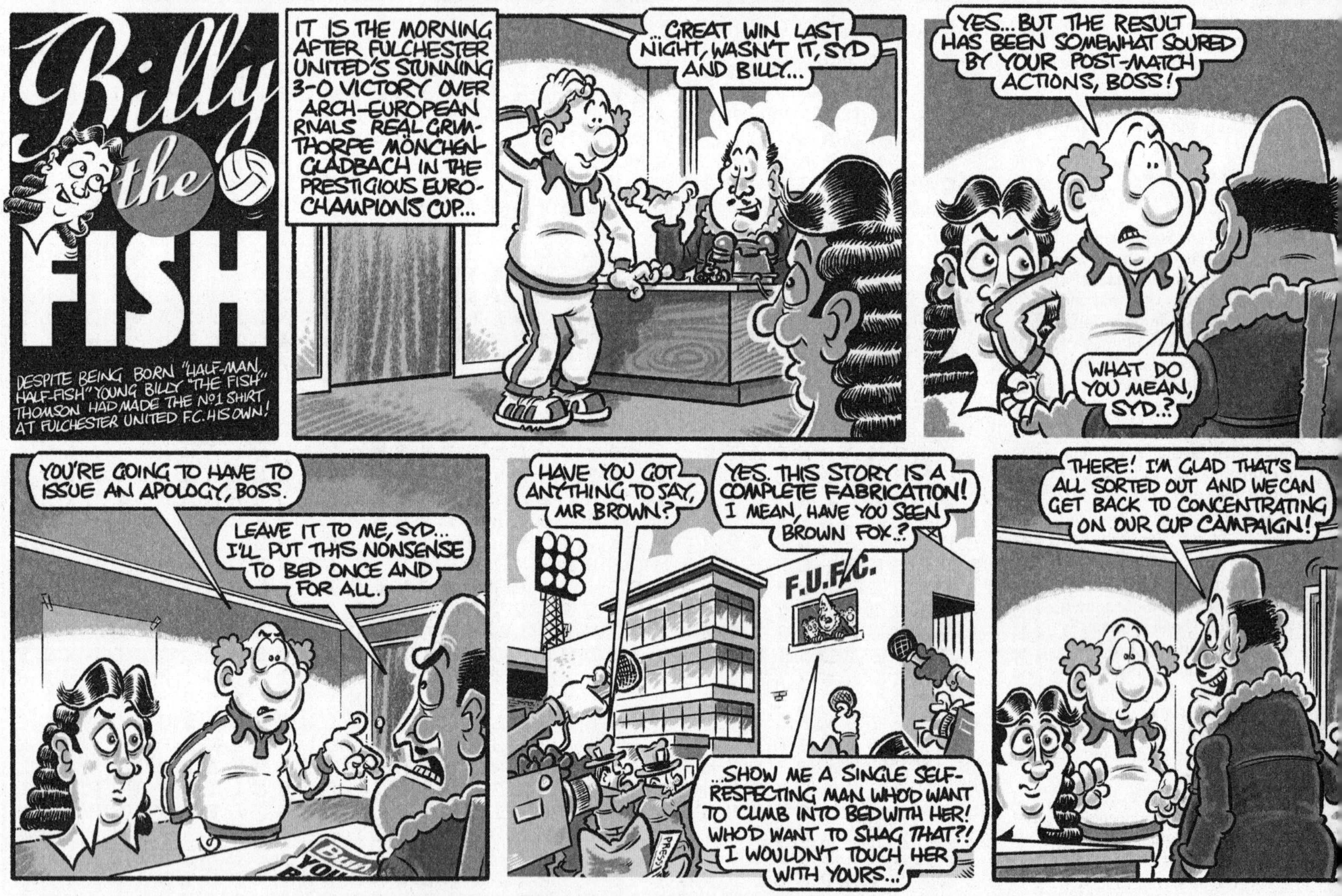
Billy the FISH
DESPITE BEING BORN "HALF-MAN, HALF-FISH" YOUNG BILLY "THE FISH" THOMSON HAD MADE THE No1 SHIRT AT FULCHESTER UNITED F.C. HIS OWN!
IT IS THE MORNING AFTER FULCHESTER UNITED'S STUNNING 3-0 VICTORY OVER ARCH-EUROPEAN RIVALS REAL GRIMTHORPE MÖNCHENGLADBACH IN THE PRESTIGIOUS EURO-CHAMPIONS CUP...
...GREAT WIN LAST NIGHT, WASN'T IT, SYD AND BILLY...
YES... BUT THE RESULT HAS BEEN SOMEWHAT SOURED BY YOUR POST-MATCH ACTIONS, BOSS!
WHAT DO YOU MEAN, SYD..?
YOU'RE GOING TO HAVE TO ISSUE AN APOLOGY, BOSS.
LEAVE IT TO ME, SYD... I'LL PUT THIS NONSENSE TO BED ONCE AND FOR ALL.
HAVE YOU GOT ANYTHING TO SAY, MR BROWN?
YES. THIS STORY IS A COMPLETE FABRICATION! I MEAN, HAVE YOU SEEN BROWN FOX..?
F.U.F.C.
...SHOW ME A SINGLE SELF-RESPECTING MAN WHO'D WANT TO CLIMB INTO BED WITH HER! WHO'D WANT TO SHAG THAT?! I WOULDN'T TOUCH HER WITH YOURS..!
THERE! I'M GLAD THAT'S ALL SORTED OUT AND WE CAN GET BACK TO CONCENTRATING ON OUR CUP CAMPAIGN!

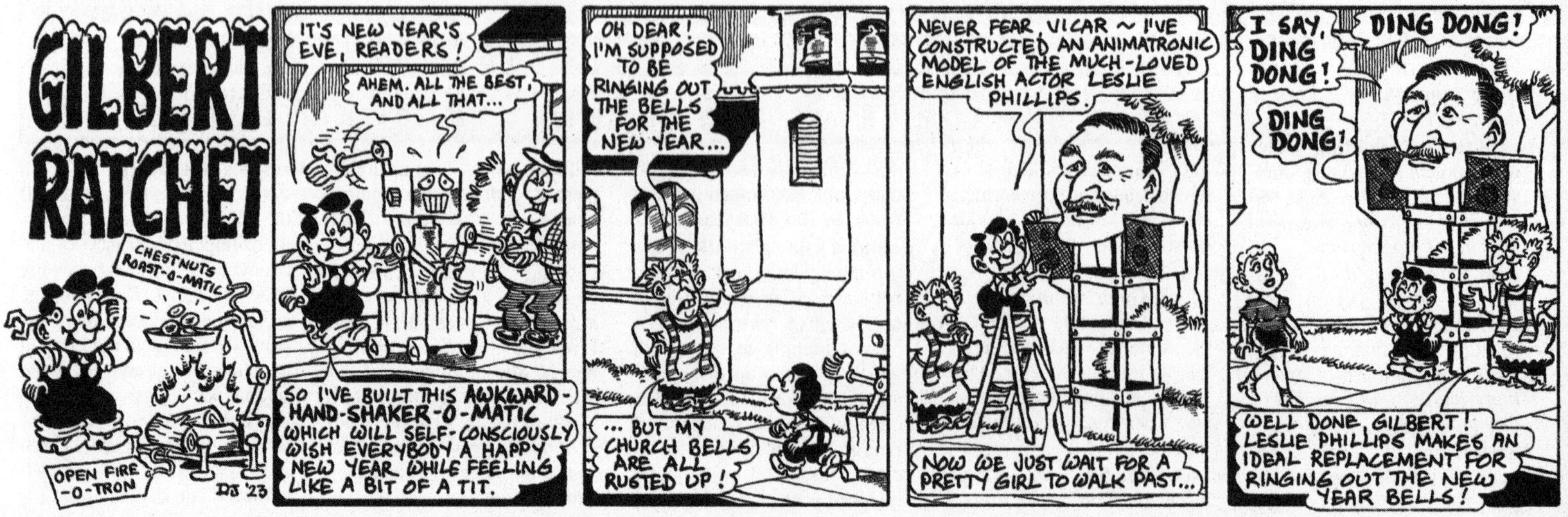
GILBERT RATCHET
CHESTNUTS ROAST-O-MATIC
OPEN FIRE -O-TRON
DJ '23
IT'S NEW YEAR'S EVE, READERS!
AHEM. ALL THE BEST, AND ALL THAT...
SO I'VE BUILT THIS AWKWARD-HAND-SHAKER-O-MATIC WHICH WILL SELF-CONSCIOUSLY WISH EVERYBODY A HAPPY NEW YEAR WHILE FEELING LIKE A BIT OF A TIT.
OH DEAR! I'M SUPPOSED TO BE RINGING OUT THE BELLS FOR THE NEW YEAR...
... BUT MY CHURCH BELLS ARE ALL RUSTED UP!
NEVER FEAR, VICAR ~ I'VE CONSTRUCTED AN ANIMATRONIC MODEL OF THE MUCH-LOVED ENGLISH ACTOR LESLIE PHILLIPS.
NOW WE JUST WAIT FOR A PRETTY GIRL TO WALK PAST...
I SAY, DING DONG!
DING DONG!
DING DONG!
WELL DONE, GILBERT! LESLIE PHILLIPS MAKES AN IDEAL REPLACEMENT FOR RINGING OUT THE NEW YEAR BELLS!

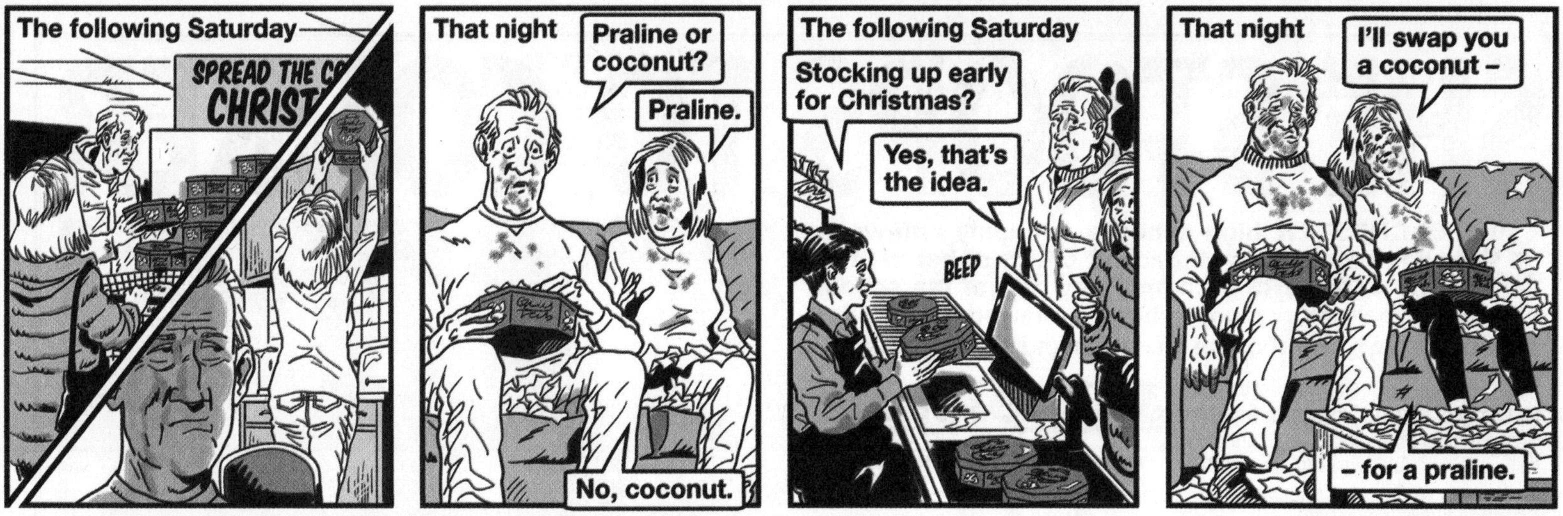
The following Saturday
That night
Praline or coconut?
Praline.
No, coconut.
The following Saturday
Stocking up early for Christmas?
Yes, that's the idea.
BEEP
That night
I'll swap you a coconut –
– for a praline.

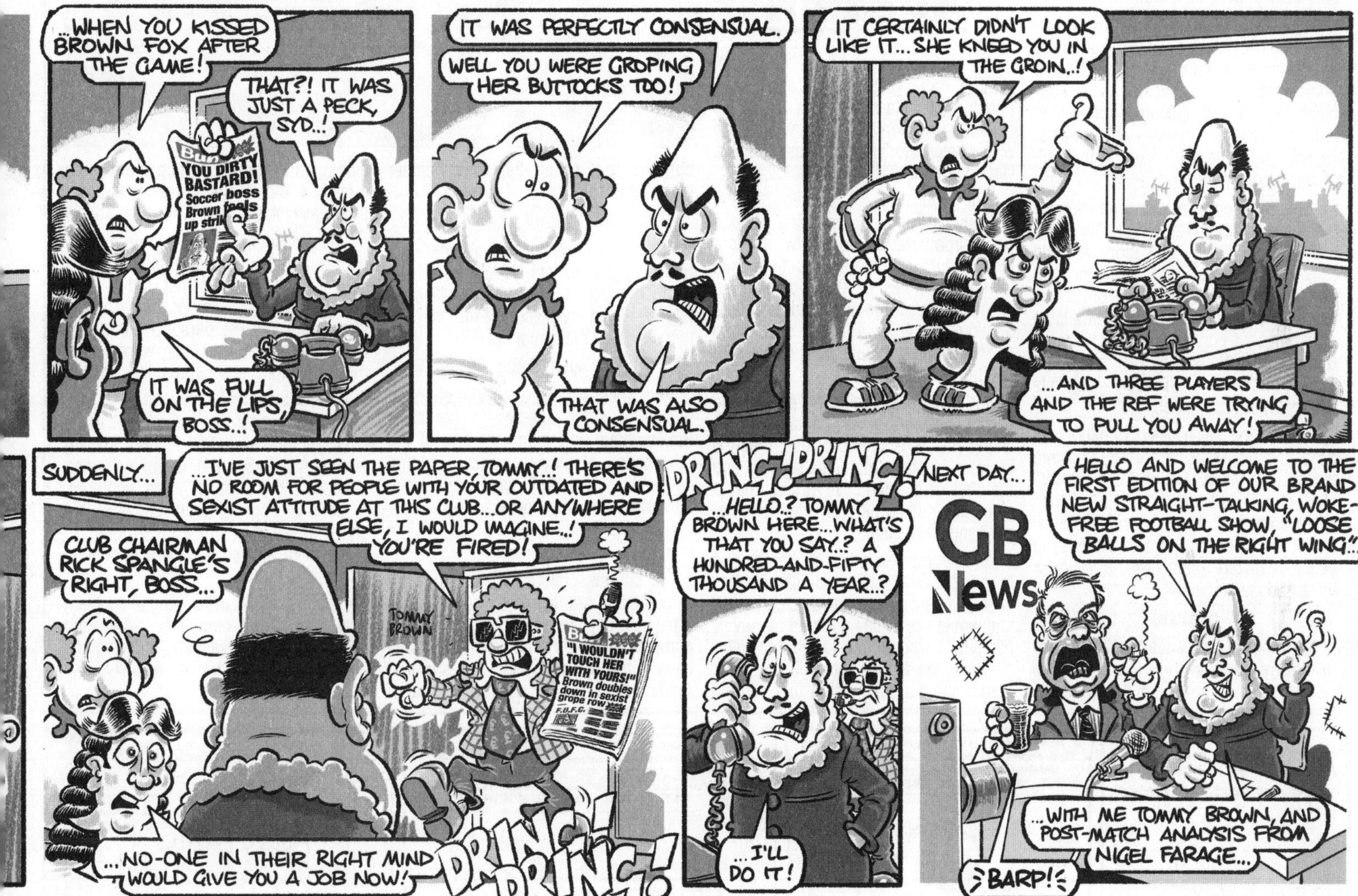
...WHEN YOU KISSED BROWN FOX AFTER THE GAME!
THAT?! IT WAS JUST A PECK, SYD..!
IT WAS FULL ON THE LIPS, BOSS..!
IT WAS PERFECTLY CONSENSUAL.
WELL YOU WERE GROPING HER BUTTOCKS TOO!
THAT WAS ALSO CONSENSUAL.
IT CERTAINLY DIDN'T LOOK LIKE IT... SHE KNEED YOU IN THE GROIN..!
...AND THREE PLAYERS AND THE REF WERE TRYING TO PULL YOU AWAY!
SUDDENLY...
...I'VE JUST SEEN THE PAPER, TOMMY..! THERE'S NO ROOM FOR PEOPLE WITH YOUR OUTDATED AND SEXIST ATTITUDE AT THIS CLUB...OR ANYWHERE ELSE, I WOULD IMAGINE..! YOU'RE FIRED!
CLUB CHAIRMAN RICK SPANGLE'S RIGHT, BOSS...
TOMMY BROWN
"I WOULDN'T TOUCH HER WITH YOURS!" Brown doubles down in sexist grope row
...NO-ONE IN THEIR RIGHT MIND WOULD GIVE YOU A JOB NOW!
DRING! DRING!
DRING! DRING!
...HELLO..? TOMMY BROWN HERE...WHAT'S THAT YOU SAY..? A HUNDRED-AND-FIFTY THOUSAND A YEAR..?
...I'LL DO IT!
NEXT DAY...
GB News
HELLO AND WELCOME TO THE FIRST EDITION OF OUR BRAND NEW STRAIGHT-TALKING, WOKE-FREE FOOTBALL SHOW, "LOOSE BALLS ON THE RIGHT WING"...
...WITH ME TOMMY BROWN, AND POST-MATCH ANALYSIS FROM NIGEL FARAGE...
BARP!

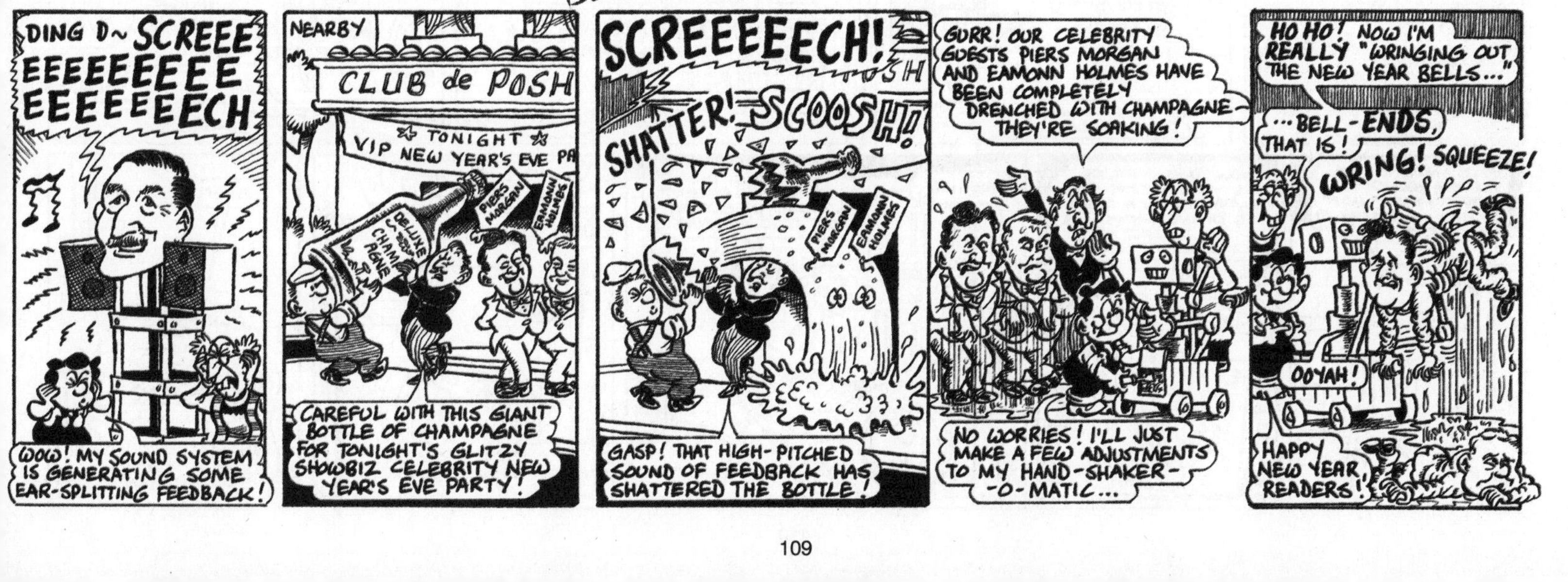
DING D~ SCREEEEEEEEEEEEEEEEEECH
WOW! MY SOUND SYSTEM IS GENERATING SOME EAR-SPLITTING FEEDBACK!
NEARBY
CLUB de POSH
TONIGHT
DELUXE CHAMPAGNE
PIERS MORGAN
EAMONN HOLMES
CAREFUL WITH THIS GIANT BOTTLE OF CHAMPAGNE FOR TONIGHT'S GLITZY SHOWBIZ CELEBRITY NEW YEAR'S EVE PARTY!
SCREEEEEECH!
SHATTER! SCOOSH!
GASP! THAT HIGH-PITCHED SOUND OF FEEDBACK HAS SHATTERED THE BOTTLE!
GURR! OUR CELEBRITY GUESTS PIERS MORGAN AND EAMONN HOLMES HAVE BEEN COMPLETELY DRENCHED WITH CHAMPAGNE - THEY'RE SOAKING!
NO WORRIES! I'LL JUST MAKE A FEW ADJUSTMENTS TO MY HAND-SHAKER-O-MATIC...
HO HO! NOW I'M REALLY "WRINGING OUT THE NEW YEAR BELLS..."
...BELL-ENDS, THAT IS!
WRING! SQUEEZE!
OOYAH!
HAPPY NEW YEAR, READERS!

SHE STOOPS TO CONKER

A FULCHESTER high school's famously *anti-woke* headmistress has hit back at critics of her plan to make CONKERS a compulsory part of the school timetable, years after many schools outlawed the popular autumnal playground game on health and safety grounds.

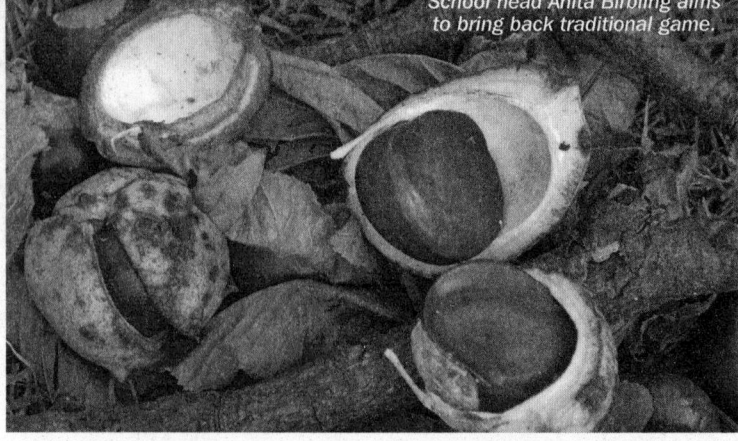

CHESTNUT JOB: *Fulchester High School head Anita Birbling aims to bring back traditional game.*

School nuts swing into Autumn

Since taking the reins at Fulchester Academy of Superb Excellence, formerly Fulchester High School, in September last year, head Anita Birbling has courted controversy with her no-nonsense approach to pupils' education.

Imposing a regime founded upon so-called 'old-fashioned values' such as mindless rote-learning and unquestioning respect for authority backed up by iron-discipline, straight-talking Birbling has turned around the school – which was in special measures and on fire at the time of her appointment.

"The Academy remains in special measures, but is no longer on fire," the *say-it-like-it-is* educationalist told *GBNews* presenter and part-time MP Lee Anderson. And she went on to say that the introduction to the timetable of 2-hours of conkers per week during October and November will make her pupils better able to cope with life outside the school gates.

"Back in my day, a love of conkers was deep and universal, and engrained into the soul of every British schoolchild," she told a nodding Anderson. "Then along comes all this children's mental health and *street dance*, and a thousand years of history goes out the window. It's a national tragedy."

giblets

Miss Birbling defended her decision to remove some of the more traditional lessons to make room in the timetable for the conker sessions. "Children acquire more good habits and useful transferrable life-skills over a single conkering season than they would in a whole year studying useless subjects like art and music," she said.

"For years now we've been told that drawing pictures or messing around on a trombone is somehow a more meaningful use of a child's time than learning how to carefully bore holes or gain the geometrical understanding required to strike a small suspended target using an object at the end of a knotted shoelace."

And she insisted that by playing the game, children would effectively be taking part in a science class. "They'd be learning about materials science and the physics of interactive forces. They'd also learn quite a bit about the bones of the hand," she said.

As an outspoken advocate of restoring corporal punishment in schools, Birbling was adamant about the consequences she would like to see suffered by any of her pupils who refuse to play conkers. "I would like to see them hit six times across the buttocks with a thin, flexible bamboo rod, or an inch-wide leather strop," she said.

"And a seventh for luck."

"Of course, that's not allowed any more due to political correctness," she said, making speechmarks with her fingers whilst over-enunciating the last two words of the sentence.

wurlitzer

And whilst disappointed that she was unable to strike children in her care, Birbling told Anderson that one of the advantages of playing conkers is that corporal punishment is inadvertently administered to pupils by their classmates in the form of 'raps' on the knuckles.

"Of course, children who do not put in sufficient practice with conkers will often painfully strike the knuckles of their competitors, who ironically may well have put in a lot of practice," she told Anderson. "This may seem a little harsh inasmuch as the wrong pupils are being punished. But at least someone is being physically hit, and that's the main thing."

The presenter agreed that he himself had suffered corporal punishment at school, and claimed that rather than doing him any harm, it had actually turned him into the person he is today. And he asked Birbling what other misdemeanors she would like to see corporally punished.

"Swearing, smoking, using smartphone in class, not paying attention, sarcasm and having the wrong clothes and hairstyle," she ventured, to nods of approval from her host. "In short, anything where a child does not conform to a basic standard that I find acceptable."

"I can't think of a single problem in a school that cannot be addressed and solved by physically attacking the children with a stick or a belt," she added.

MR MAGHOUL
THE SHORT-SIGHTED GHOST
HI READERS - I'VE BEEN WANDERING THE MORTAL PLANE AS A WRAITH, UNABLE TO PASS THROUGH THE VOID TO THE HEREAFTER!
I MUST FIND MY WAY TO THE AFTERLIFE!
NOW LET ME PUT ON MY SPECTRE-CLES...
AH, A CHURCH, OR 'HOUSE OF GOD' IF YOU WILL. THAT WILL SURELY HELP ME GET TO THE HEAVENLY REALM!
LAUNDRETTE
SUCH MAGNIFICENT COLUMNS! WHAT A BEAUTIFUL TESTAMENT TO THE GLORY OF OUR LORD!
AAAAGH! A G-G-G-GHOST!
HOLY ANOINTING OIL I'LL BE BOUND! I'LL COVER MYSELF IN IT TO AID MY JOURNEY TO GOD'S SEAT!
NOW TO SLIP INSIDE THIS MAGNIFICENT 18TH CENTURY CHURCH ORGAN. ITS DIVINE HARMONIES WILL SEND ME DIRECTLY TO HEAVEN!
TEE HEE!
THAT'S ALL THE SOILED UNDERGARMENTS LOADED IN. BETTER SET IT TO 'VIGOROUS'.
WHAT? SHITTY PANTS? AAAAAAAH!
CHURN
BAH!
HOME FOR THE SEVERELY INCONTINENT

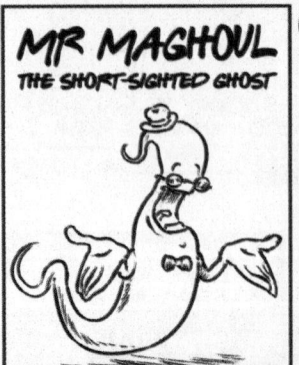

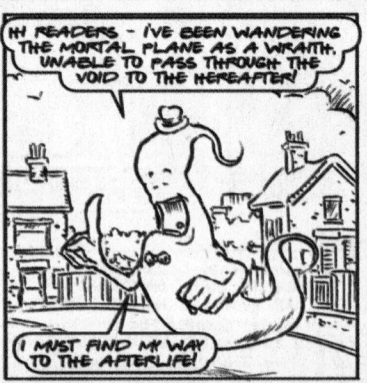

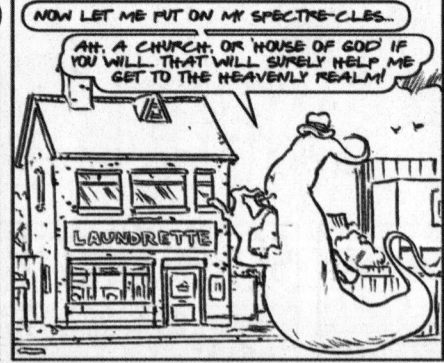

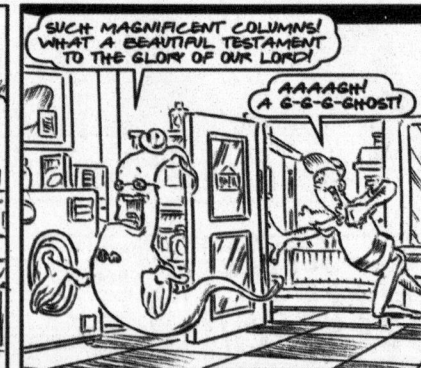

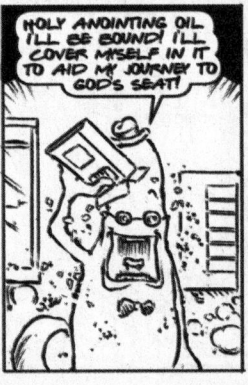

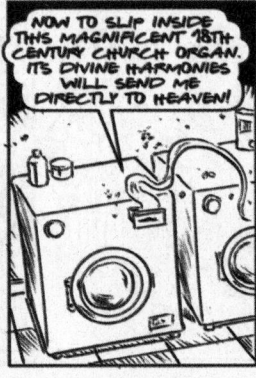

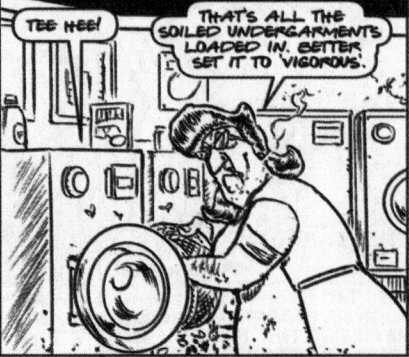

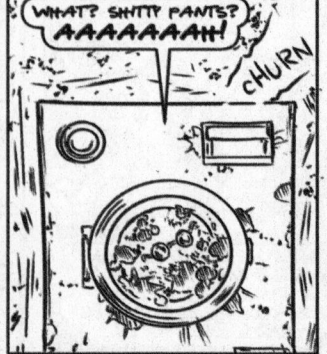

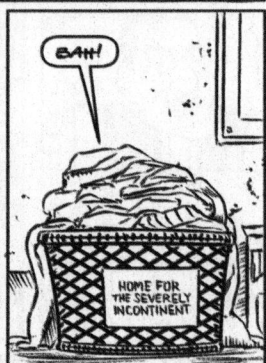

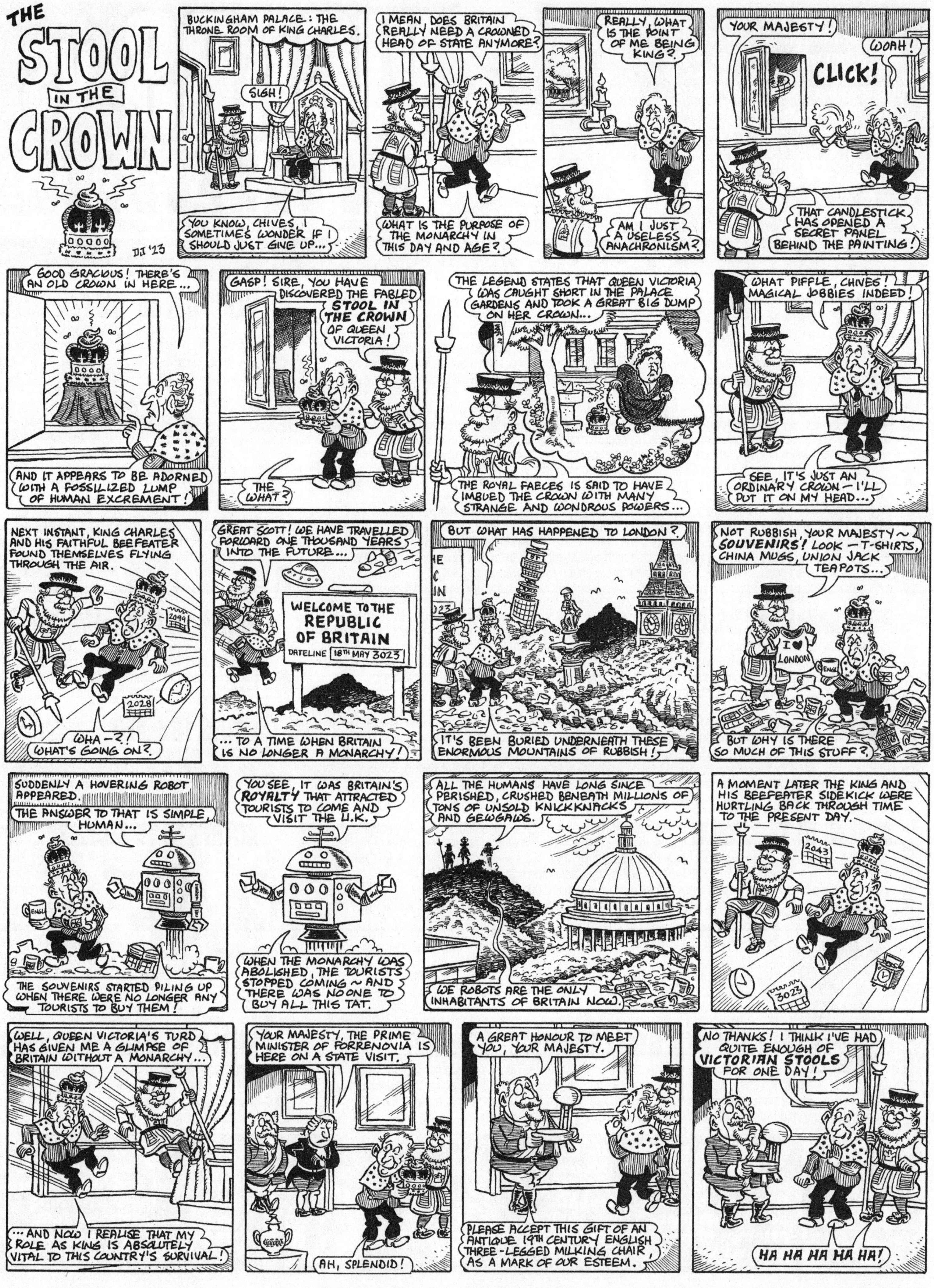
THE STOOL IN THE CROWN
DJ '23
BUCKINGHAM PALACE: THE THRONE ROOM OF KING CHARLES.
SIGH!
YOU KNOW, CHIVES, I SOMETIMES WONDER IF I SHOULD JUST GIVE UP...
I MEAN, DOES BRITAIN REALLY NEED A CROWNED HEAD OF STATE ANYMORE?
WHAT IS THE PURPOSE OF THE MONARCHY IN THIS DAY AND AGE?
REALLY, WHAT IS THE POINT OF ME BEING KING?
AM I JUST A USELESS ANACHRONISM?
YOUR MAJESTY!
WOAH!
CLICK!
THAT CANDLESTICK HAS OPENED A SECRET PANEL BEHIND THE PAINTING!
GOOD GRACIOUS! THERE'S AN OLD CROWN IN HERE...
AND IT APPEARS TO BE ADORNED WITH A FOSSILIZED LUMP OF HUMAN EXCREMENT!
GASP! SIRE, YOU HAVE DISCOVERED THE FABLED STOOL IN THE CROWN OF QUEEN VICTORIA!
THE WHAT?
THE LEGEND STATES THAT QUEEN VICTORIA WAS CAUGHT SHORT IN THE PALACE GARDENS AND TOOK A GREAT BIG DUMP ON HER CROWN...
THE ROYAL FAECES IS SAID TO HAVE IMBUED THE CROWN WITH MANY STRANGE AND WONDROUS POWERS...
WHAT PIFFLE, CHIVES! MAGICAL JOBBIES INDEED!
SEE, IT'S JUST AN ORDINARY CROWN — I'LL PUT IT ON MY HEAD...
NEXT INSTANT, KING CHARLES AND HIS FAITHFUL BEEFEATER FOUND THEMSELVES FLYING THROUGH THE AIR.
2099
2028
WHA—?! WHAT'S GOING ON?
GREAT SCOTT! WE HAVE TRAVELLED FORWARD ONE THOUSAND YEARS INTO THE FUTURE...
WELCOME TO THE REPUBLIC OF BRITAIN
DATELINE 18TH MAY 3023
... TO A TIME WHEN BRITAIN IS NO LONGER A MONARCHY!
BUT WHAT HAS HAPPENED TO LONDON?
IT'S BEEN BURIED UNDERNEATH THESE ENORMOUS MOUNTAINS OF RUBBISH!
NOT RUBBISH, YOUR MAJESTY ~ SOUVENIRS! LOOK — T-SHIRTS, CHINA MUGS, UNION JACK TEAPOTS...
I ♥ LONDON
BUT WHY IS THERE SO MUCH OF THIS STUFF?
SUDDENLY A HOVERING ROBOT APPEARED.
THE ANSWER TO THAT IS SIMPLE, HUMAN...
THE SOUVENIRS STARTED PILING UP WHEN THERE WERE NO LONGER ANY TOURISTS TO BUY THEM!
YOU SEE, IT WAS BRITAIN'S ROYALTY THAT ATTRACTED TOURISTS TO COME AND VISIT THE U.K.
WHEN THE MONARCHY WAS ABOLISHED, THE TOURISTS STOPPED COMING ~ AND THERE WAS NO ONE TO BUY ALL THIS TAT.
ALL THE HUMANS HAVE LONG SINCE PERISHED, CRUSHED BENEATH MILLIONS OF TONS OF UNSOLD KNICKKNACKS AND GEWGAWS.
WE ROBOTS ARE THE ONLY INHABITANTS OF BRITAIN NOW.
A MOMENT LATER THE KING AND HIS BEEFEATER SIDEKICK WERE HURTLING BACK THROUGH TIME TO THE PRESENT DAY.
2043
3023
WELL, QUEEN VICTORIA'S TURD HAS GIVEN ME A GLIMPSE OF BRITAIN WITHOUT A MONARCHY...
... AND NOW I REALISE THAT MY ROLE AS KING IS ABSOLUTELY VITAL TO THIS COUNTRY'S SURVIVAL!
YOUR MAJESTY, THE PRIME MINISTER OF FORRENOVIA IS HERE ON A STATE VISIT.
AH, SPLENDID!
A GREAT HONOUR TO MEET YOU, YOUR MAJESTY.
PLEASE ACCEPT THIS GIFT OF AN ANTIQUE 19TH CENTURY ENGLISH THREE-LEGGED MILKING CHAIR AS A MARK OF OUR ESTEEM.
NO THANKS! I THINK I'VE HAD QUITE ENOUGH OF VICTORIAN STOOLS FOR ONE DAY!
HA HA HA HA HA!

THEY'RE the three pillars of our local communities, always there at our side when we need them. ***Vicars*** – officiating at ceremonies to mark the important milestones of our lives; ***Vets*** – taking care of the animals we cherish; and ***Vampires*** – promising us immortality in return for the blood they suck greedily from puncture wounds in our jugular veins. ***But which one of the three "V"s is the "V" best?*** It's time to pit them against each other to discover, once and for all...

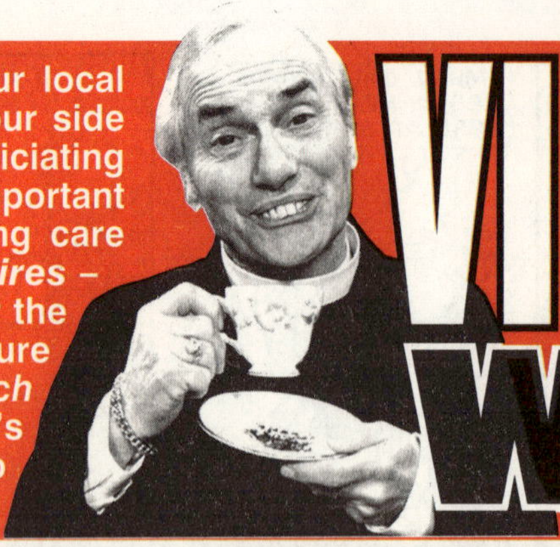

VICARS VS
WHICH O

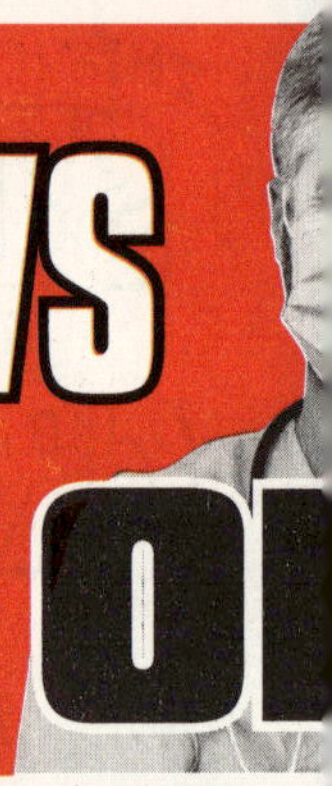

VICARS

ROUND 1 **REACTION TO THE CRUCIFIX** The traditional crucifix is a representation of the barbaric execution suffered by the original founder of the Christian church. So you might suppose Vicars – famously Jesus's biggest fans – would view it with a certain amount of horror. But you'd be wrong, because for some reason they're not at all "cross" about seeing this symbol of their hero's suffering. In fact, they absolutely *love it*, plastering it all over their Bibles, churches, stained glass windows and nuns. It's a nailed-on high score in this first round for the God-botherers. **SCORE 8**

ROUND 2 **COST** Considering all the good work they do in their communities, Vicars are pretty good value. Parishioners cough up a few coppers in the Sunday collection plate, in return for which the local sky-pilot puts on regular services, buries the dead, and gets his church roof fixed. On top of these weekend tips, the C of E pays vicars between twenty and thirty grand a year – nice work if you can get it! But remember, these earnings are taxable under ITEPA 2003 as employment income, and vicars also have Class 1 National Insurance costs deducted by their employer – the Archbishop of Canterbury. **SCORE 6**

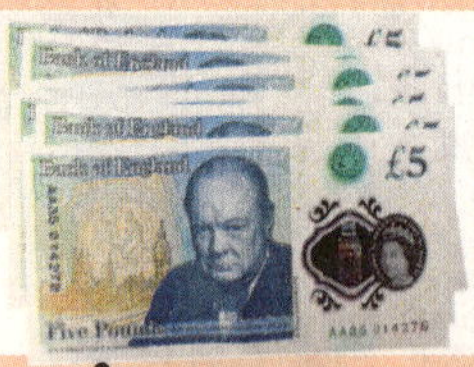

ROUND 3 **GARLIC** As any Christian will tell you, although there are three quarters of a million words in the Bible, "garlic" is only referred to *once*, in Numbers 11:5, which says: *"We remember the fish, which we did eat in Egypt freely; the cucumbers, and the melons, and the leeks, and the onions, and the garlic."* You would be forgiven for thinking that this single mention means that this delicious savoury ingredient is of little importance to the Christian religion, but it's one more mention than potatoes get. **SCORE 4**

ROUND 4 **PORTRAYAL IN EMMERDALE** Since the Yorkshire-based soap first began over 40 years ago, the rural parish of Emmerdale has had more than a dozen vicars officiating at its disastrous weddings and mass funerals. The current incumbent is the Rev Charles Anderson, who viewers might recognise as Manny from *Locked Up Abroad*, Beresford Brown in *Rillington Place*, and Sketch Witness (uncredited) in *Justice League* starring Ben Affleck. Ironically, the original village church was burnt down by local vet Zoe Tate in 2002. **SCORE 6**

ROUND 5 **LIVING FOREVER** When it comes to living forever, Vicars have a distinct advantage over the rest of us, thanks to their professed religious belief in an eternal afterlife. According to the Good Book, once they die they either go to Heaven, grow wings and sit on a cloud for an infinite stretch of time, or else descend into the fiery pits of Hades to suffer unimaginable anal agonies for a similar period. Either way, a literally endless future stretches out ahead of them, and they score splendidly as a result. **SCORE 7**

ROUND 6 **ACTING IN TV SHOWS** Countless real-life Vicars have portrayed characters in popular telly series, including *Dad's Army*'s Frank Williams, to pick a name at random. The toothy pastor starred as an auctioneer in a 1991 episode of *Boon*, a librarian in *Bergerac* back in 1985, and a lawyer in little-remembered 1984 drama series *The Brief* – and that's just the Bs. In fact, over his long acting career, Rev. Williams appeared in more than 100 shows, a score that's Manna from Heaven for him and his fellow clerics. **SCORE 7**

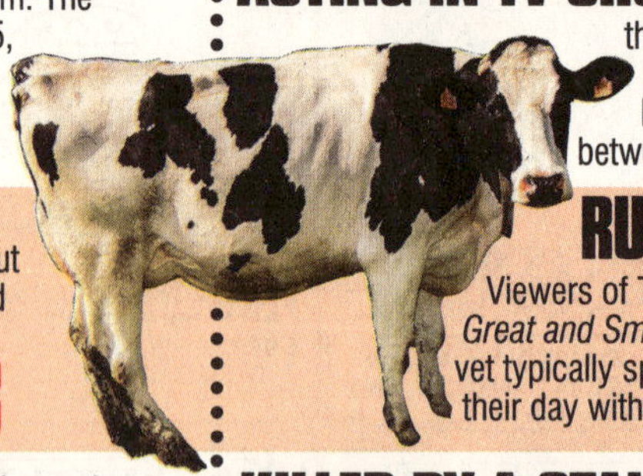

ROUND 7 **RUNNING WATER** Ask anyone who's ever been in a church what vicars keep in the font, and they'll tell you without hesitation – "water!" But this special holy liquid used for blessings, baptisms and repelling evil isn't *running* water; it's just sat there. Unfortunately, this lack of aqueous motivity makes this a particularly damp and disappointing round for the clerics. **SCORE 3**

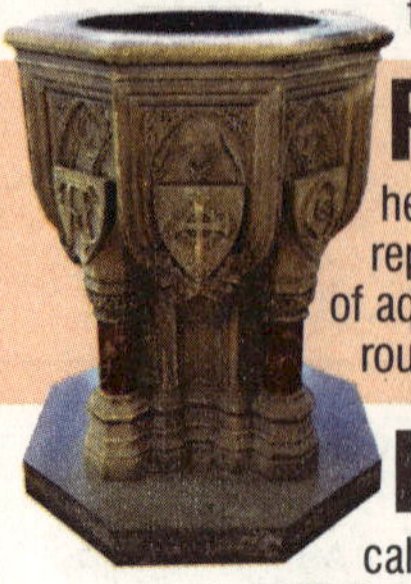

ROUND 8 **KILLED BY A STAKE THROUGH THE HEART** Played over the years by a roll-call of stars including Peter Cushing, Anthony Hopkins, Laurence Olivier, Hugh Jackman and Herbert Lom in screen versions of *Dracula*, the character of Dr Abraham Van Helsing has destroyed countless vampires by driving wooden stakes through their hearts. But in none of those films did the intrepid fictional vampire hunter ever destroy a Vicar in this manner. **SCORE 0**

HOW DID THEY DO?

VICARS ***Oh, Lord!*** **Into the doghouse with the dog-collared clerics. It's time for a new, eleventh commandment – "Thou shalt not attempt to win a competition against Vets and Vampires"!**

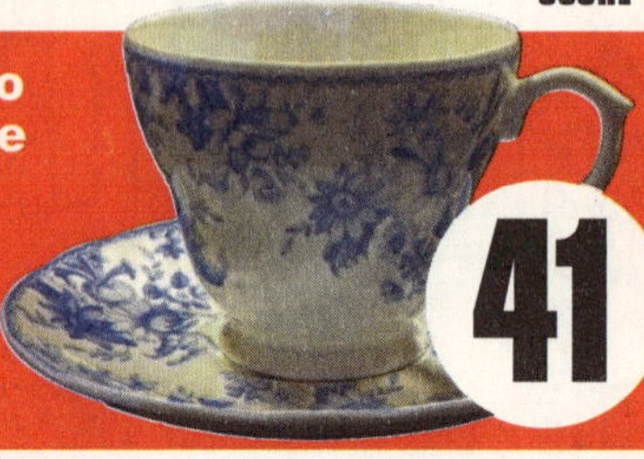

41

V

REACTION TO THE CRUCIFIX You might regard Veterinary Science as a rigorous discipline that leaves its students little room for airy-fairy beliefs in invisible deities living in the sky, choirs of heavenly angels, or immortal beardy-weirdies

COST A recent study showed that Vets going into jobs straight after university are among the country's highest paid graduates. And it's their customers – ordinary members of the public

GARLIC Everyone loves garlic, you might imagine. It's a tasty addition to everything from a casserole to a salad, and it's what gives the melted butter under your Chicken Kiev its pungent tang. But Vets see another side to this delicious ingredient, since it is actually *poisonous* to

PORTRAYAL IN EMMERDALE The vet is the busiest member of any farming community, and the village of Emmerdale has had its fair share, boasting a dozen different vets over the years. Current incumbent Paddy Dingle has been caring for the villagers' animals

LIVING FOREVER The world's most famous vet – author James Herriot – was born in 1916, and seemed to be doing well at living forever until 1995, when he suddenly died at the age of 78. However, all is not lost for him and his kind in this round, as his

ACTING IN TV SHOWS Several vets have trod the TV boards, for example TV supervet Dr Noel Fitzpatrick. In between fixing sickly family

RUNNING WATER Viewers of TV's *All Creatures Great and Small* will tell you that a vet typically spends about 90% of their day with their arm shoved up a

KILLED BY A STAKE THROUGH THE HEART Tradition states that if a stake has been driven through a vampire's heart, it is instantly slayed, although if that stake is later removed, the vampire can come back to life.

VETS ***A beastly performance!*** **Never mind *All Creatures Great and Small*, there's nothing "great" about the pitifully "small" score the animal docs have scraped in this contest.**

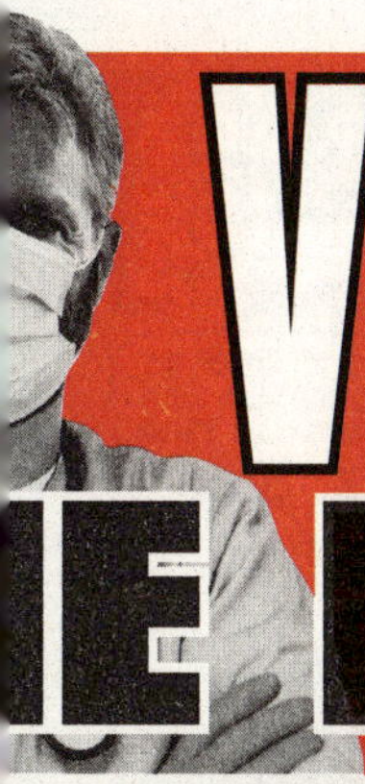

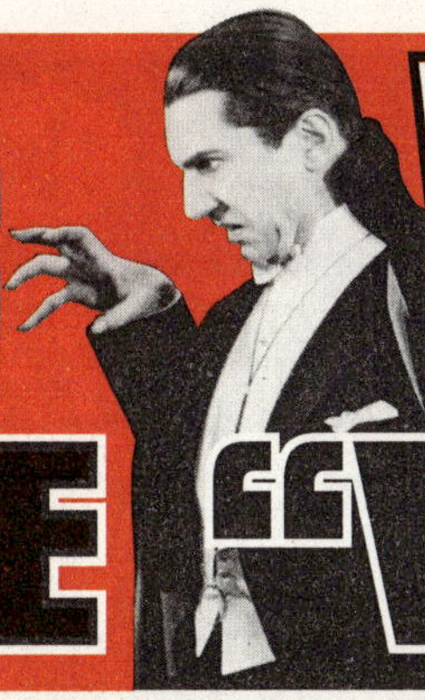

VETS VS VAMPIRES

[WHO'S TH]E IS THE "V" BEST?

[VE]TS

raising the dead, feeding the five thousand, and turning water into wine. But that's not necessarily the case, because when the world's most famous vet - James Herriot - decided to get hitched back in 1941, he booked the crucifix-bedecked St Mary's Church in Thirsk to stage the holy ceremony. SCORE 6

worried about their poorly pets – who end up footing the bill for these syringe-toting Champagne Charlies. On top of their basic wage, many also manage to further stick it up the paying public by penning warm-hearted humorous memoirs of their early careers in the Yorkshire Dales. SCORE 8

many household pets. Dogs and cats are regularly brought in for emergency treatment after scoffing a plate of garlic bread or a pizza out the bin, and vets use powerful emetics to induce vomiting and rid their bodies of toxins. SCORE 5

since 1997, between getting married and divorced several times and going bald as a coot. Ironically, his second wife, Emily Kirk, quit the Dales in 2007 to become a vicar in Manchester, earning Vicars an extra point in this round, although third wife Rhona is a vet, too, which evens things back up. SCORE 6

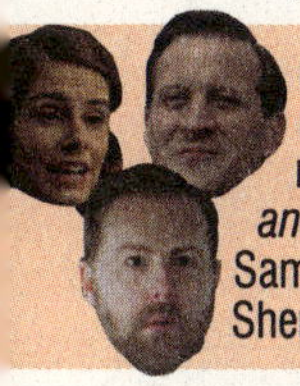

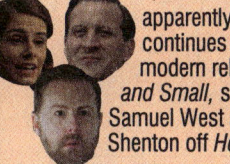

apparently immortal young self continues to appear in Channel 5's modern reboot of *All Creatures Great and Small*, starring Nicholas Ralph, Samuel West and Rachel Shenton off *Hollyoaks*. SCORE 6

pets, Noel has had cameo roles in countless dramas including *The Bill*, *London's Burning*, *Heartbeat*, and *Casualty*. And who played the title character in 1971's *Charlie and the Chocolate Factory?* Step forward yet another vet, Dr Peter Ostrum, who specialises in equine medicine. SCORE 4

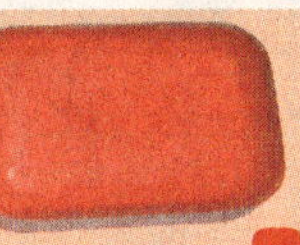

cow's shitty arse. It's a mucky business, so access to a reliable supply of soap and clean, running H_2O is an absolute *must*, meaning that vets quite literally "clean up" in this round. SCORE 8

But there is no evidence that the same is also true of veterinary surgeons, who typically require at least 5 GCSEs including English, Maths and Science, and 3 A-levels in science subjects to get on a degree course. SCORE 0

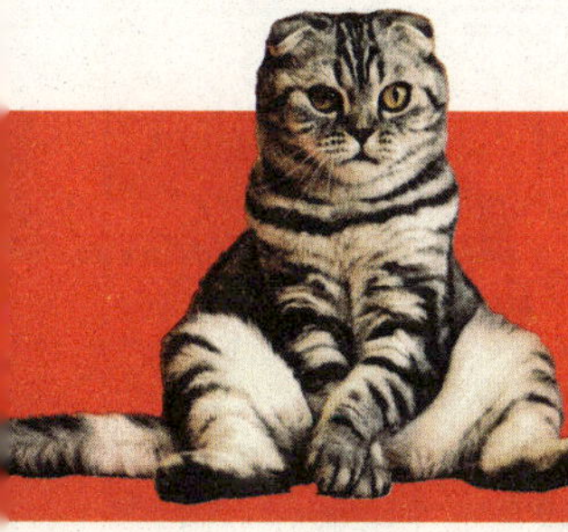

43

VAMPIRES

ROUND 1

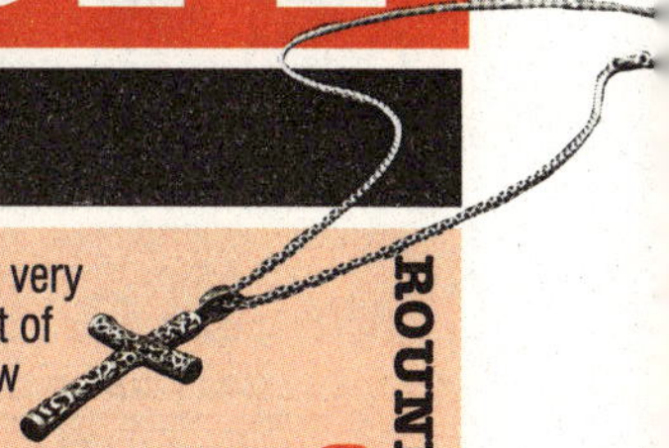

REACTION TO THE CRUCIFIX In horror movies, the undead typically have a very strong reaction to the crucifix. The mere sight of it causes them to recoil and hiss in revulsion – even a cross-shaped shadow cast by a window frame can be enough to put them off their stroke – whilst physical contact with this powerful religious symbol leaves livid flesh burns that can cause Count Dracula to scream in hellish agony. As such, it's an impressive opening round for th ese blood-sucking denizens of the twilight. SCORE 9

ROUND 2

COST Although Vampires are typically self-employed and only come out after dark, they will happily make free house calls in the middle of the night. Sounds too good to be true? Well, there is a catch. A moonlit visit from an undead blood-sucker can lead to you or a member of your family getting bitten in the jugular vein and becoming a vampire too. It's something to think about carefully before inviting a sinister, red-eyed bat into your boudoir as the clock strikes midnight. SCORE 6

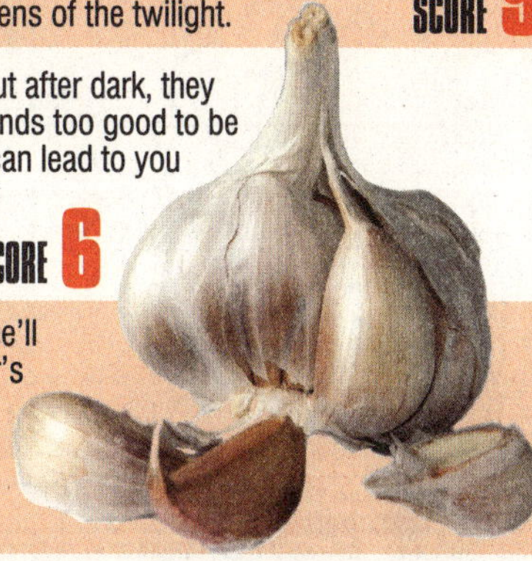

ROUND 3

GARLIC Offer Count Dracula a slice of Garlic Bread for his tea and he'll recoil in terror. That's because – as outlined in Bram Stoker's *Dracula* when Van Helsing decks Lucy's room with garlic flowers to protect her from the blood-sucking Transylvanian count – it's yet another thing that repels Vampires. SCORE 7

ROUND 4

PORTRAYAL IN EMMERDALE *Emmerdale* viewers have sat through a surfeit of ludicrously dramatic storylines over the years, including a festive jumbo jet crash onto the Woolpack, Meena's serial killing spree, a fifteen-vehicle pile-up on the bypass, and Seth Armstrong's revelation that his first name was Archibald. However, there has never been a bloodthirsty vampire at large in the sleepy Yorkshire hamlet. *Or has there?* Because actor Max Parker, who played cafe worker Luke Posner in the soap, was recently cast as a hunky bloodsucker in big budget US series *Vampire Academy*! SCORE 6

ROUND 5

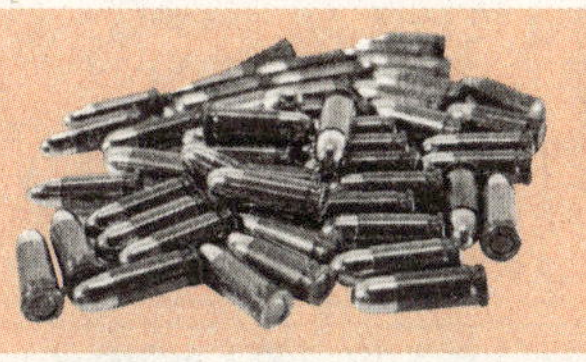

LIVING FOREVER The insatiably sanguisuganous and non-reflective fiends are not technically immortal, as they can be killed in a surprisingly large number of ways. Silver bullets, holy water, sunlight, decapitation, burning, and stakes driven through their heart by grim-faced vampire hunters in a crypt are all simple ways of doing away with them, and as a result, it's a disappointing round for the undead. SCORE 5

ROUND 6

ACTING IN TV SHOWS Alleged real-life vampire/cannibal/film star Armie Hammer has an impressive acting CV, with roles in dozens of top-rated movies and TV shows. Elsewhere in Tinseltown, *Transformers* star Megan Fox recently boasted to *Glamour* magazine that she and her rapper beau Machine Gun Kelly regularly drink each other's blood. But they aren't real vampires as they come out in the daylight to make their films and pop records. SCORE 3

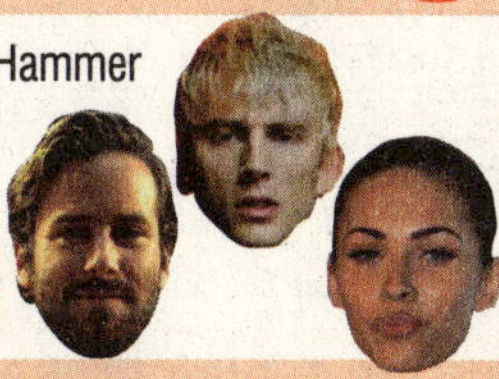

ROUND 7

RUNNING WATER According to occultists, Vampires are unable to cross running water. This means that people who live on boats – including celebrities such as Virgin boss Richard Branson, Spandau Ballet's Simon le Bon, Sooty puppeteer Matthew Corbett, and disgraced undercrackers magnate Baroness Michelle Mone – are all safe from having their blood drank by the toothy nocturnal bugaboos. SCORE 6

ROUND 8

KILLED BY A STAKE THROUGH THE HEART Vampires have perished by means of wooden stakes driven through their hearts in countless movies, including *Dracula* (1931), *Horror of Dracula* (1958), *Blood for Dracula* (1974), *Dracula Has Risen from the Grave* (1968), *The Satanic Rites of Dracula* (1973), *Blood of Dracula* (1957) and many more. SCORE 10

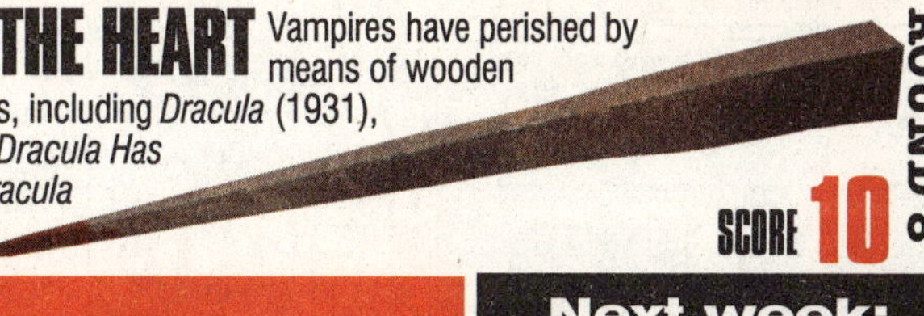

VAMPIRES

Wam! Bam! Fang-you, Mam! There's no bats in the vampires' belfry – they've bloody well winged their way to victory in style!

52

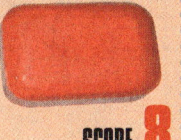

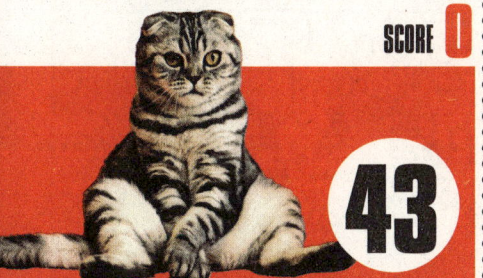

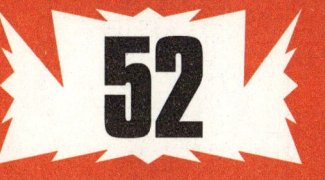

Next week:
LADY DIANA VS PHIL VS MARKS &
Who's the best Spencer?

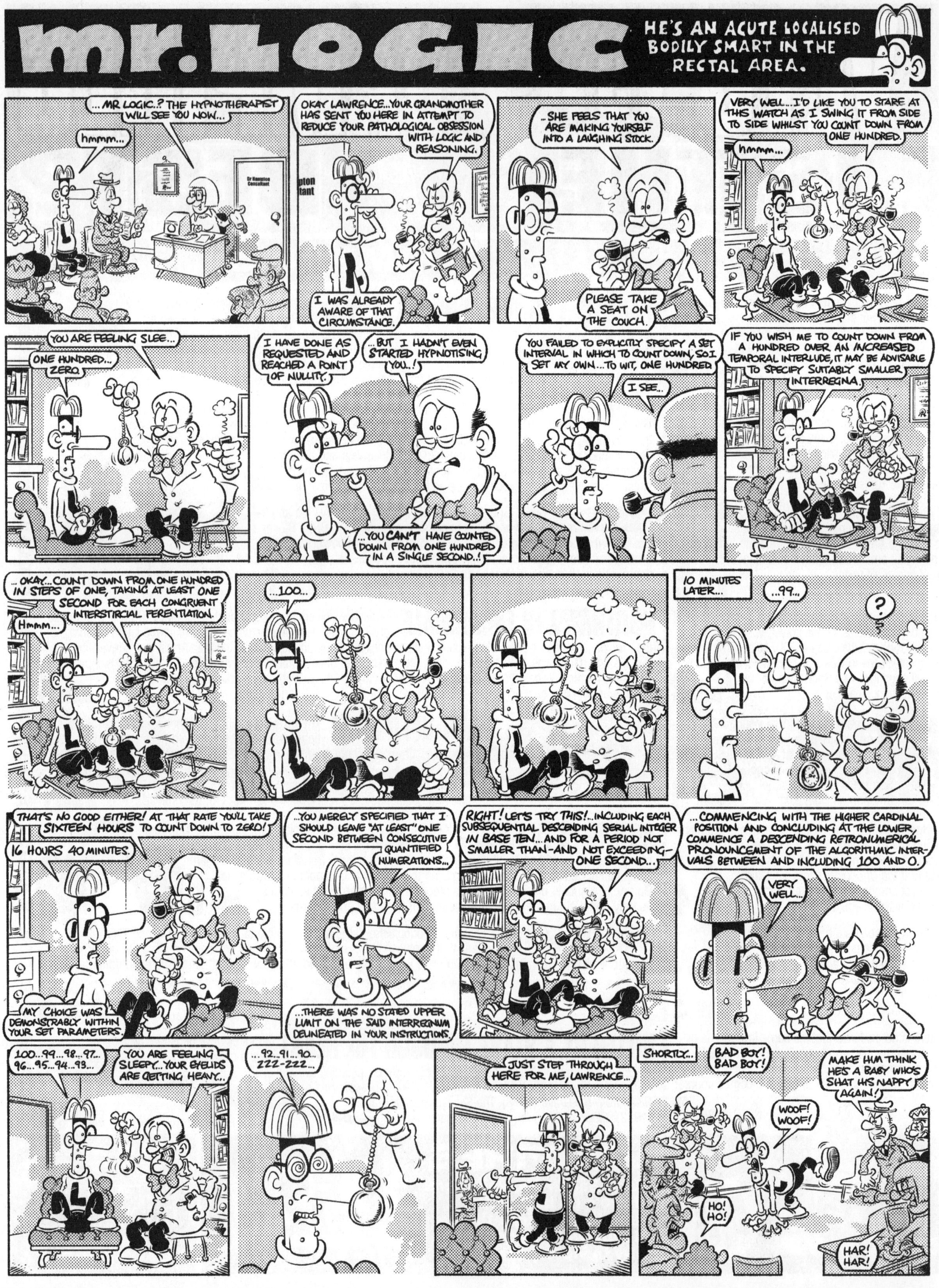
mr. LOGIC
HE'S AN ACUTE LOCALISED BODILY SMART IN THE RECTAL AREA.
...MR LOGIC..? THE HYPNOTHERAPIST WILL SEE YOU NOW...
hmmm...
OKAY LAWRENCE...YOUR GRANDMOTHER HAS SENT YOU HERE IN ATTEMPT TO REDUCE YOUR PATHOLOGICAL OBSESSION WITH LOGIC AND REASONING.
I WAS ALREADY AWARE OF THAT CIRCUMSTANCE.
...SHE FEELS THAT YOU ARE MAKING YOURSELF INTO A LAUGHING STOCK.
PLEASE TAKE A SEAT ON THE COUCH.
VERY WELL...I'D LIKE YOU TO STARE AT THIS WATCH AS I SWING IT FROM SIDE TO SIDE WHILST YOU COUNT DOWN FROM ONE HUNDRED.
hmmm...
YOU ARE FEELING SLEE...
ONE HUNDRED... ZERO.
I HAVE DONE AS REQUESTED AND REACHED A POINT OF NULLITY.
...BUT I HADN'T EVEN STARTED HYPNOTISING YOU..!
...YOU CAN'T HAVE COUNTED DOWN FROM ONE HUNDRED IN A SINGLE SECOND..!
YOU FAILED TO EXPLICITLY SPECIFY A SET INTERVAL IN WHICH TO COUNT DOWN, SO I SET MY OWN...TO WIT, ONE HUNDRED.
I SEE..
IF YOU WISH ME TO COUNT DOWN FROM A HUNDRED OVER AN INCREASED TEMPORAL INTERLUDE, IT MAY BE ADVISABLE TO SPECIFY SUITABLY SMALLER INTERREGNA.
...OKAY...COUNT DOWN FROM ONE HUNDRED IN STEPS OF ONE, TAKING AT LEAST ONE SECOND FOR EACH CONGRUENT INTERSTIRCIAL FERENTIATION.
Hmmm...
...100...
10 MINUTES LATER...
...99...
?
THAT'S NO GOOD EITHER! AT THAT RATE YOU'LL TAKE SIXTEEN HOURS TO COUNT DOWN TO ZERO!
16 HOURS 40 MINUTES.
MY CHOICE WAS DEMONSTRABLY WITHIN YOUR SET PARAMETERS.
...YOU MERELY SPECIFIED THAT I SHOULD LEAVE "AT LEAST" ONE SECOND BETWEEN CONSECUTIVE QUANTIFIED NUMERATIONS...
...THERE WAS NO STATED UPPER LIMIT ON THE SAID INTERREGNUM DELINEATED IN YOUR INSTRUCTIONS.
RIGHT! LET'S TRY THIS!...INCLUDING EACH SUBSEQUENTIAL DESCENDING SERIAL INTEGER IN BASE TEN...AND FOR A PERIOD NOT SMALLER THAN-AND NOT EXCEEDING-ONE SECOND...
...COMMENCING WITH THE HIGHER CARDINAL POSITION AND CONCLUDING AT THE LOWER, COMMENCE A DESCENDING RETRONUMERICAL PRONOUNCEMENT OF THE ALGORITHMIC INTERVALS BETWEEN AND INCLUDING 100 AND 0.
VERY WELL...
100...99...98...97... 96...95...94...93...
YOU ARE FEELING SLEEPY...YOUR EYELIDS ARE GETTING HEAVY...
...92...91...90... ZZZ-ZZZ...
JUST STEP THROUGH HERE FOR ME, LAWRENCE...
SHORTLY...
BAD BOY! BAD BOY!
MAKE HIM THINK HE'S A BABY WHO'S SHAT HIS NAPPY AGAIN!
WOOF! WOOF!
HO! HO!
HAR! HAR!

CORN BLIMEY!

Cinema goer rescued from popcorn

THE Fire Service was called to the UCI Cinema in North Shields yesterday after a woman fell headfirst into a large bucket of popcorn.

23-year-old Kelly Binlid was at the cinema to see *Puss In Boots: The Last Wish* with her boyfriend when the accident happened.

According to witnesses, the couple were coming down the stairs of the auditorium looking for their seats when Kelly lost her footing and pitched forward into the popcorn bucket, which was on a cinemagoer's lap at the end of a row.

crevice

"It all happened so quickly," Kelly told the *North Shields Aneurism and Infarction*. "There was a car advert on the screen, and I was thinking that I might buy a car after the film. Then I stumbled and the next thing I knew I was going down in the popcorn."

"It was horrible. It was going into my ears, my mouth, up my nose. I kept trying to swim upwards, to reach air, but it's hard to swim through popcorn."

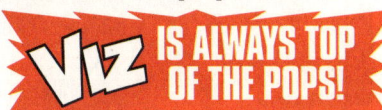

VIZ IS ALWAYS TOP OF THE POPS!

According to witnesses, Kelly's boyfriend Kyle dropped the two large drinks he was carrying and tried to grab her as she fell in, but he was not quick enough. Staff at the cinema were alerted and the house lights were raised whilst several people attempted to rescue her, but to no avail. In the end, emergency services were called.

glandular

But the fire brigade rescue was hampered as the drinks that Kelly's boyfriend had dropped had flooded the bottom half of the auditorium, and the first responders had to wade through waist-deep cola to reach the scene.

Once at the bucket, the rescuers quickly got to work, setting up ladders and lowering one firefighter into the popcorn on a rope. Kelly was quickly found and pulled to the surface of the buttery snack.

"I've never been so happy as when that fireman's hands reached down and grabbed me," said Kelly.

It is understood that following the accident, the cinema is considering reducing the size of its large popcorn portions. It comes in the wake of an incident last week in which a customer in the back row knocked over a similar popcorn bucket causing an avalanche of toasted butterscotch kernels to flood down the auditorium, burying the entire front four rows.

POP CORN
POP CORN
POP CORN

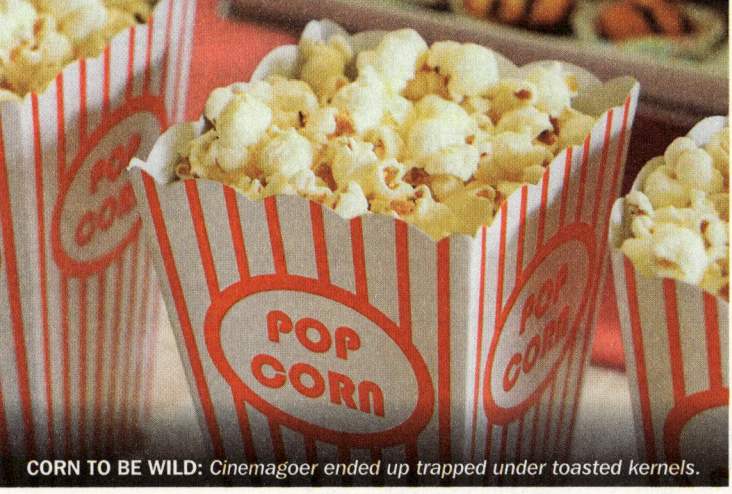

CORN TO BE WILD: *Cinemagoer ended up trapped under toasted kernels.*

Cornographic!

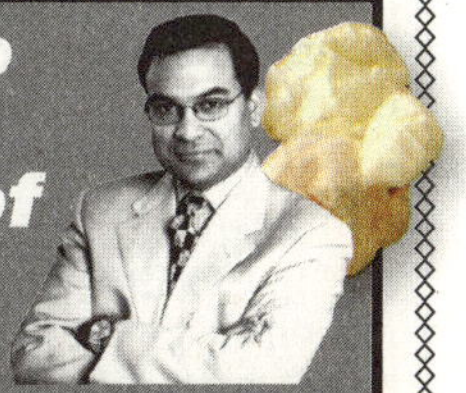

What you get up to in bed says a lot about the flavour of popcorn you like!

says TV's Dr Raj Persaud

WE ALL like to do different things in bed with our partners, from straight sex to the little more spicy and from the downright kinky to the utterly disgusting. As consenting adults, we're free to express ourselves sexually in any way we please. But if you think that your spicy sexual preferences have no bearing on your favourite types of popcorn, you'd be wrong!

Because, according to formerly-disgraced-but-now-back-on-TV psychiatrist Dr Raj Persaud, our sexual appetites and what we get up to between the sheets says a lot about our snack preferences at the flicks. He told us: "Your brain is a complex network of neurons which are all inextricably linked. And like it or not, your sexual proclivities speak volumes about which flavour popcorn floats your boat."

As Dr Raj says: "If you want to keep your personal popcorn preferences private, something that is nobody's business but yours, don't let on what you and your partner get up to in the fart sack!"

Missionary position in the dark

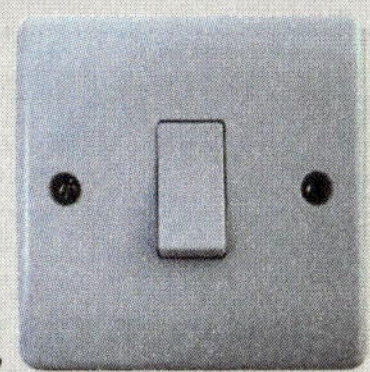

THIS IS THE MOST common way sex is undertaken today, often referred to as the 'vanilla' of sexual activity. So it's no surprise that the people who go in for it are just as unimaginative when it comes to choosing their popcorn at the pictures. These sexual pedestrians will always select commonplace **TOFFEE POPCORN**. Just like their sexual activity, this flavour is nice enough, and it gets the job done, but it's never going to take anyone's tastebuds to the heights of ecstasy.

Celebrity Missionary Position Popcorners

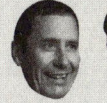

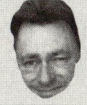

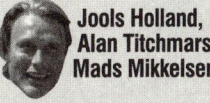

Jools Holland, Alan Titchmarsh, Mads Mikkelsen

Dressing up and role play

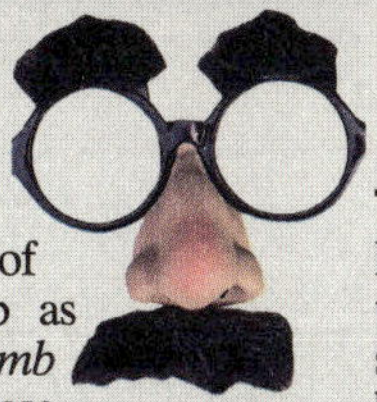

MANY COUPLES today spice up their love-lives with a bit of role play, perhaps dressing up as a sexy nurse, a fireman or *Tomb Raider's* Lara Croft. And these fancy dressers are also likely to add a bit of spice to their popcorn buying habits, too. **SALTED CARAMEL, MINT CHOCOLATE GLAZE** or **HONEY MUSTARD** are all flavours that they will try together in the cinema so that their movie snacking doesn't become jaded and stale.

Celebrity Dressing Up Popcorners

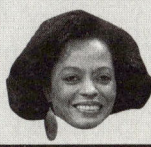

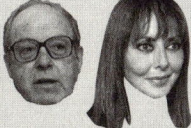

Diana Ross, Hans Blix, Carol Vorderman

Bondage, S&M and spanking

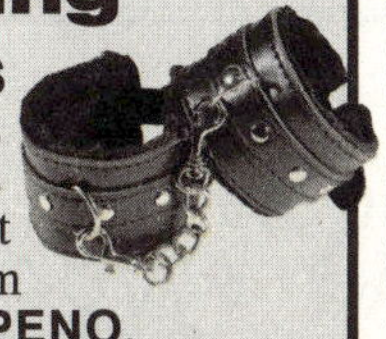

THESE FREE-THINKERS have no taboos when it comes to expressing themselves sexually, and they take that bedroom philosophy with them into the multiplex. **JALAPENO, CINCINNATI STYLE CHILLI, GINGER SNAP CARAMEL** – all these flavours and more will be tried. They may even go to the cinema with another couple to experiment with new flavours as a foursome. Literally nothing is off the table for these popcorn adventurers.

Celebrity S&M Popcorners

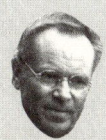

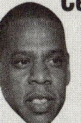

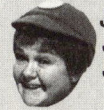

Jeffrey Archer, Jay-Z, Jeanette Krankie

ROLL ON STONES

Beeston man in charity skate-athon

A 54-YEAR-OLD midlander plans to roller-skate from Land's End to John O'Groats to raise much-needed funds for a local charity. And to make his venture more challenging, he'll be skating all 874 miles of the journey *over gravel!*

Roller-mad TOBY 'ROLLER' BATES got the idea to traverse the length of Britain in aid of charity whilst on his morning skate in the Beeston suburb of Nottingham, where he is a familiar face with locals.

"I cover dozens of miles a week round Beeston on my wheels for my health," the betting shop worker told the *Beeston Cyst and Ganglion*. "And it occurred to me that I might as well be doing all these miles for somebody else's good as well as my own."

twist

A marathon skate from Land's End to John O'Groats was the obvious choice for his fund-raising charity venture. But Bates feared that the 'go to' route was a little old hat. "I thought a fresh twist on the venture was needed to get people digging deep into their pockets," he told the paper.

"Roller-skating from Land's End to John O'Groats has been done a million times before. My trip had to be different," he said. "So I was rolling along, wondering what I could do to make my trip a bit more newsworthy when the idea came to me."

madison

"I skated over a massive pothole that the council had filled with gravel, and I nearly went arse over tit," he said. "When I tried to skate out of it, I found it was almost impossible."

"I knew in that instant that roller-skating the length of the country *on gravel* was the thing to do."

YOUR No.1 VIZ IS TOPS FOR ROLLER-SKATING SCOOPS!

But Bates's charity event quickly hit a snag when he discovered that very little of the route from the southernmost tip of Cornwall to the northernmost bit of Scotland was covered by gravel, with most of the 874 miles being pavement or tarmac road.

Undeterred, he came up with an ingenious way around the problem. He told the paper: "I thought that on the bits of the route that weren't gravel, which to be fair is most of it, I could bring my own."

mashed potato

Toby enlisted the help of a friend with a transit van in which he plans to install a tray full of gravel. "I'll be skating around in the gravel in the back while my mate Eddie drives from Land's End to John O'Groats," he said. "If he spots any gravel on the route, he'll pull over and drive slowly behind me while I roller-skate across it. Once through it, it's back to skating through the gravel in the van."

Bates hopes his marathon gravel skate will raise £5000 for a local children's hospital, but he has had trouble finding sponsors following a misunderstanding with another of his charity fund-raisers last month.

"I'd done a 5-mile skate around the perimeter of Wollaton Park and I'd collected about £150 for Help the Aged," he said. "But as I was taking the cash to their shop in the town, I was mugged."

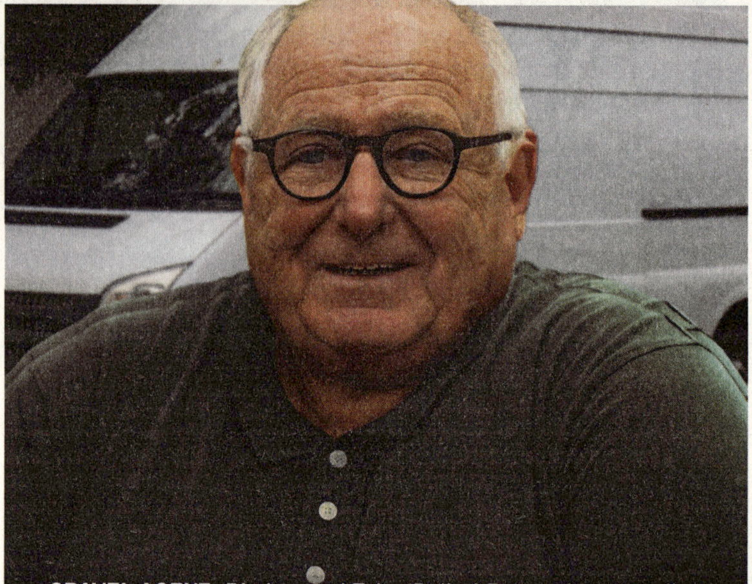

GRAVEL AGENT: *Big hearted Toby 'Roller' Bates plans to roller-skate the length of the UK on tray of gravel inside friends van.*

"I was absolutely furious. I mean, what kind of scum steals from charities?" he said. "I was even more annoyed as it was the third time it had happened. My last two fund-raisers also ended up with me being robbed whilst taking the money I'd raised to charity shops."

sausages

But he was quick to reassure potential sponsors that lightning will not strike a fourth time. "Eddie has offered to come with me when I take the money to the kiddies' hospital," he said. "And nobody fucks with Eddie, let me tell you. He's nails."

Bates admitted that he will reluctantly be forced to take modest expenses from the sponsor money in order to fund his marathon skate attempt, but assured the big-hearted people of Beeston that he will try to keep costs to a minimum.

"We'll need to put petrol in Eddie's van," he said. "And even if he puts his foot down, it's going to take us a couple of days, so we'll need a night's stop in a B&B."

"We could kip in the back of the van, but it'll be full of gravel, and after roller- skating on the stuff all day, I won't want to bed down on the bastard. I'll need a good night's sleep so I'm refreshed for the final leg," he said.

peas & gravy

But many Beeston residents are cynical of Bates's new scheme, and so far only £7.50 has been pledged. When questioned, locals said they doubted Bates's honesty, saying that they wouldn't put it past him not to roller-skate at all, but just to sit in the front of the van with his feet up for the two-day journey, and pocket the money.

Bates refuted the accusations. "There's nothing to stop me doing that, of course, and nobody would know if I did," he said. "But that's not who I am."

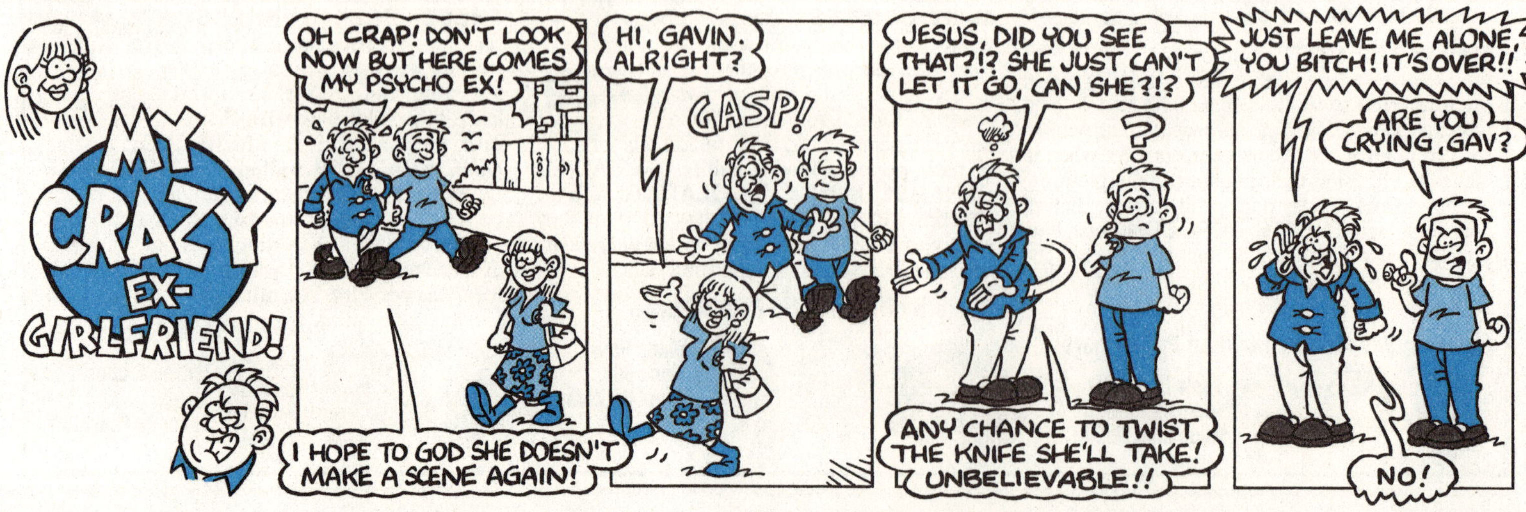
MY CRAZY EX-GIRLFRIEND!
OH CRAP! DON'T LOOK NOW BUT HERE COMES MY PSYCHO EX!
I HOPE TO GOD SHE DOESN'T MAKE A SCENE AGAIN!
HI, GAVIN. ALRIGHT?
GASP!
JESUS, DID YOU SEE THAT?!? SHE JUST CAN'T LET IT GO, CAN SHE?!?
?
ANY CHANCE TO TWIST THE KNIFE SHE'LL TAKE! UNBELIEVABLE!!
JUST LEAVE ME ALONE, YOU BITCH! IT'S OVER!!
ARE YOU CRYING, GAV?
NO!

ROLLING BACK THE YEARS

Glossop archaeologist makes 'Find of the Century'

DISCO INF-NERO: *Artist's impression of how Glossop's Roman roller-disco may have looked in its heyday.*

AFTER its fall, the Roman Empire left behind a wealth of material allowing excavators to piece together how life was lived in the greatest empire the world has ever seen. But the fuddy-duddy subject of archaeology has been turned on its head by the discovery of what one real life Tony Robinson believes is the location of a *Roman roller-disco* on the outskirts of Glossop in Derbyshire.

And the find is all the more incredible since the man making it has no formal expertise in archaeology whatsoever.

By his own admission, 52-year-old ex-carpet salesman Doug Upton is no Indiana Jones. But if authenticated, his unique find would not only require the history of the Romans in Britain to be rewritten, it could also see many other books torn from the shelves and pulped.

Experts have been swift to pour cold water on the notion of a Roman roller-disco, claiming there currently exists no proof whatsoever that the Romans ventured anywhere near what became modern-day Glossop during their three-and-a half-century stay in the British Isles. They further point-out that the roller-skate itself was only invented in 1760, by a Belgian Freemason.

"They're just jealous because an Easter school leaver has made the archaeological discovery of the century, and they haven't," says the thrice-divorced father of six. "It boils their piss."

At first glance, the body of evidence that Doug has compiled in support of his claim might appear flimsy. But the discovery of a single, heavily-corroded roller-skate 'key' – a small metal tool used to adjust the fit of old-fashioned skates worn over the user's shoe – is enough to convince the amateur archaeologist that he has unearthed the site of Europe's only Roman roller-disco on a patch of waste ground on the outskirts of the Derbyshire town.

chicken

"You can picture it now," Upton told reporters at a hastily arranged press conference in the cafe at Glossop Sports Centre. "All these Romans in their togas and plumed helmets whizzing round and round with their roller-skates over their sandals while the musicians played. It must of been a sight to behold."

"There'd have been a bar, probably, selling amphoras of wine and Roman bar snacks like figs, nuts and bits of fermented fish."

"And they probably ended the night with one of their famous sex orgies, writhing naked together like beasts, the dirty buggers," the amateur archaeologist speculated. "If you were there, you would of been able to see it going in and everything."

The 2-millennia-old, rusty 4-inch key has been put on permanent display in Upton's room in the Hostel Campanile by the motorway slip-road, where it is available for public viewing in return for a small charge.

Self-taught enthusiast Doug is now demanding a comprehensive excavation of the site. And the former sales assistant at the Carpet Fantasia warehouse, adjacent to the waste ground he is convinced was once the scene of bawdy Roman parties on wheels, is keen to lead the dig for ancient treasures.

scaramouche

"Only I know where to look," said the burly five-footer. "So if the archaeological experts want this vital chapter of world history dug up, they'd better dig out their chequebook, that's all I'm saying."

"But let me warn them – Doug Upton doesn't get out of bed for less than minimum wage and benefits."

Doug, who admits he acquired the bulk of his archaeological know-how from watching every single episode of *Time Team*, some of them two or three times, says he literally stumbled upon the first – and so far only – piece of his Roman roller-disco historical jigsaw puzzle completely by accident. "I was out the back of the warehouse on my break, having a little smoke and a lager loosener," he explained.

KEY WITNESS: *How the roller-skate key may have looked when discovered*

Mindful of his ex-employer's old-fashioned stance on substance use during work hours, Upton had, as usual, taken himself off to a small wooded area some way behind the carpet outlet, a cherished fixture on the Gasworks Retail and Enterprise Park since 2018.

"The woods are out of the way and fairly sheltered," he told reporters. "But this particular morning the rain had been pouring down, and the footing was treacherous. I recall nearly falling over on several occasions. And then I must have actually gone over and banged my head on something because suddenly there was only blackness."

Noting Doug's absence several hours later, colleagues at Fantasia Carpets launched a search, and he was eventually found unconscious at the foot of a silver birch.

"Next thing I knew I'm face down in the mud with the store manager standing over me shouting I was fired," said the amateur relic-hunter. "I can only assume I'd banged my head against that bloody tree."

hessian

Hours later, whilst removing his soiled clothing, Doug found the roller-skate key in his trouser pocket and, consoling himself over a few restorative drinks and more herbal cigarettes, his mind raced with possibilities.

"I knew at once it was incredibly old because it was all rusty, so straight away I thought it must be Roman," he said. "And it struck me as highly unlikely that this key had been the property of some random centurion in possession of the only pair of roller-skates in that whole mighty empire."

"There would obviously have been loads of others and, being a highly social culture which enjoyed numerous communal leisure activities like bathing and orgies, it is impossible to imagine ancient Romans indulging in solitary roller-skating."

"From this conclusion it was a fairly small leap to the roller-disco theory," he said.

Upton added that his daily alcohol and drug intake was 'relatively modest' and in no way impacted upon either his archaeological judgement or carpet-selling capabilities.

"Trust me, you need a bit of something to keep you going when you're selling carpets to the public," he said. "They can be a right pain in the arse. Hardly any of them know what they want, they wander around asking gormless questions, tying you up for bloody ages, and then blithely stroll out empty-handed."

"If they knew how poor the pay is, and how much staff rely on sales commissions to bump up their wages, well, I'd say they were sadists," he added.

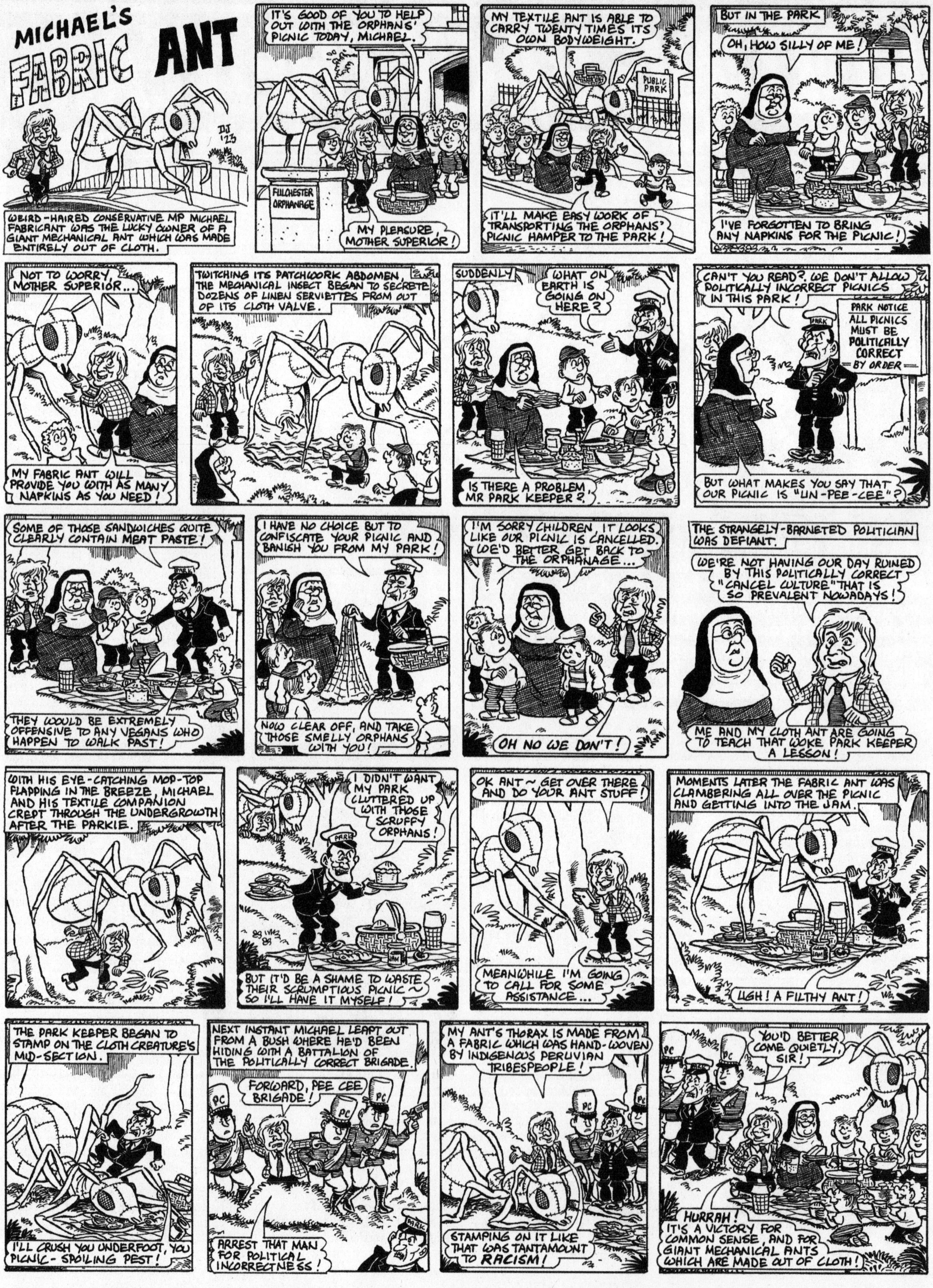
MICHAEL'S FABRIC ANT
DJ '23
WEIRD-HAIRED CONSERVATIVE MP MICHAEL FABRICANT WAS THE LUCKY OWNER OF A GIANT MECHANICAL ANT WHICH WAS MADE ENTIRELY OUT OF CLOTH.
IT'S GOOD OF YOU TO HELP OUT WITH THE ORPHANS' PICNIC TODAY, MICHAEL.
FULCHESTER ORPHANAGE
MY PLEASURE, MOTHER SUPERIOR!
MY TEXTILE ANT IS ABLE TO CARRY TWENTY TIMES ITS OWN BODYWEIGHT.
PUBLIC PARK
IT'LL MAKE EASY WORK OF TRANSPORTING THE ORPHANS' PICNIC HAMPER TO THE PARK!
BUT IN THE PARK
OH, HOW SILLY OF ME!
I'VE FORGOTTEN TO BRING ANY NAPKINS FOR THE PICNIC!
NOT TO WORRY, MOTHER SUPERIOR...
MY FABRIC ANT WILL PROVIDE YOU WITH AS MANY NAPKINS AS YOU NEED!
TWITCHING ITS PATCHWORK ABDOMEN, THE MECHANICAL INSECT BEGAN TO SECRETE DOZENS OF LINEN SERVIETTES FROM OUT OF ITS CLOTH VALVE.
SUDDENLY
WHAT ON EARTH IS GOING ON HERE?
IS THERE A PROBLEM, MR PARK KEEPER?
CAN'T YOU READ? WE DON'T ALLOW POLITICALLY INCORRECT PICNICS IN THIS PARK!
PARK NOTICE ALL PICNICS MUST BE POLITICALLY CORRECT BY ORDER
BUT WHAT MAKES YOU SAY THAT OUR PICNIC IS "UN-PEE-CEE"?
SOME OF THOSE SANDWICHES QUITE CLEARLY CONTAIN MEAT PASTE!
THEY WOULD BE EXTREMELY OFFENSIVE TO ANY VEGANS WHO HAPPEN TO WALK PAST!
I HAVE NO CHOICE BUT TO CONFISCATE YOUR PICNIC AND BANISH YOU FROM MY PARK!
NOW CLEAR OFF, AND TAKE THOSE SMELLY ORPHANS WITH YOU!
I'M SORRY CHILDREN, IT LOOKS LIKE OUR PICNIC IS CANCELLED. WE'D BETTER GET BACK TO THE ORPHANAGE...
OH NO WE DON'T!
THE STRANGELY-BARNETED POLITICIAN WAS DEFIANT.
WE'RE NOT HAVING OUR DAY RUINED BY THIS POLITICALLY CORRECT "CANCEL CULTURE" THAT IS SO PREVALENT NOWADAYS!
ME AND MY CLOTH ANT ARE GOING TO TEACH THAT WOKE PARK KEEPER A LESSON!
WITH HIS EYE-CATCHING MOP-TOP FLAPPING IN THE BREEZE, MICHAEL AND HIS TEXTILE COMPANION CREPT THROUGH THE UNDERGROWTH AFTER THE PARKIE.
I DIDN'T WANT MY PARK CLUTTERED UP WITH THOSE SCRUFFY ORPHANS!
BUT IT'D BE A SHAME TO WASTE THEIR SCRUMPTIOUS PICNIC ~ SO I'LL HAVE IT MYSELF!
OK ANT ~ GET OVER THERE AND DO YOUR ANT STUFF!
MEANWHILE, I'M GOING TO CALL FOR SOME ASSISTANCE...
MOMENTS LATER THE FABRIC ANT WAS CLAMBERING ALL OVER THE PICNIC AND GETTING INTO THE JAM.
UGH! A FILTHY ANT!
THE PARK KEEPER BEGAN TO STAMP ON THE CLOTH CREATURE'S MID-SECTION.
I'LL CRUSH YOU UNDERFOOT, YOU PICNIC-SPOILING PEST!
NEXT INSTANT MICHAEL LEAPT OUT FROM A BUSH WHERE HE'D BEEN HIDING WITH A BATTALION OF THE POLITICALLY CORRECT BRIGADE.
FORWARD, PEE CEE BRIGADE!
ARREST THAT MAN FOR POLITICAL INCORRECTNESS!
MY ANT'S THORAX IS MADE FROM A FABRIC WHICH WAS HAND-WOVEN BY INDIGENOUS PERUVIAN TRIBESPEOPLE!
STAMPING ON IT LIKE THAT WAS TANTAMOUNT TO RACISM!
YOU'D BETTER COME QUIETLY, SIR!
HURRAH! IT'S A VICTORY FOR COMMON SENSE, AND FOR GIANT MECHANICAL ANTS WHICH ARE MADE OUT OF CLOTH!

HAT'S YER LOT!

Council thinking a-Head

IN the wake of the bankruptcy announced by Birmingham City Council last month, residents of nearby Stourbridge feared their local council could suffer the same fate. Worries grew after it was announced that council tax payments are to be used to buy all residents of the town a *LITTLE HAT*.

Announcing the plan, councillors confirmed that inevitably certain services will have to be cut, including refuse collection, street cleaning and closure of the town's library. But officials were adamant that giving everyone in the borough a small item of headgear was the best way to give ratepayers value for money.

"Town councils are going bankrupt right, left and centre, and the reason is simply that the taxpayers' pound doesn't go nearly as far as it used to," said Stourbridge County Council leader Alderman Tom Finch.

"But rather than working out what cuts in services we would have to make, we thought we would just scrap the lot and see what could be bought with the money we had in the coffers. And a little hat for everyone in the borough came in right on budget."

sputnik

Finch pointed out that the decision to purchase small, rather than normal-sized hats was a practical rather than a financial one, as sizing hats for the town's 310,000 residents would have presented a logistical nightmare. "We would have to have bought a selection of sizes, and inevitably people would have measured their heads wrong

EXCLUSIVE!

and end up with the wrong size and there would be lots of extra large left over," said Finch. "A normal-sized hat has to fit properly, or it looks ridiculous. On the other hand, those little top hats that Burlesque dancers wear fit anyone, and they're meant to look ridiculous, so it takes the sizing problem out of the equation."

grievous

And any residents worried about accessorising their council hats with their existing outfits needen't worry, as they will be able to chose the colour of their tiny topper. "We've ordered them in sequinned black, white, metallic red, silver or gold, so there will be a choice," said Finch. "But they will be allocated on a strictly first come first served basis, so go to the council website early to reserve your choice of colour."

All public services in the town were stopped two weeks ago, and residents will start to receive their hats next month. And deputy leader Iris Bottoms said that the council will be prioritising the elderly and vulnerable when the roll-out begins. "We'll be getting the little hats out to pensioners and young children first," she said. "Then we'll start delivering them to residents aged between 55 and 65, followed by those aged 45 to 55, and so on."

"Be assured, all our residents will eventually get a little hat, but we ask everyone, particularly the younger residents, to be patient."

The plan to cut all services to the borough and spend the money on comically small top hats has met with a mixed reception from those living in Stourbridge. Many think that it is an excellent scheme which for once gives ratepayers something tangible for their money.

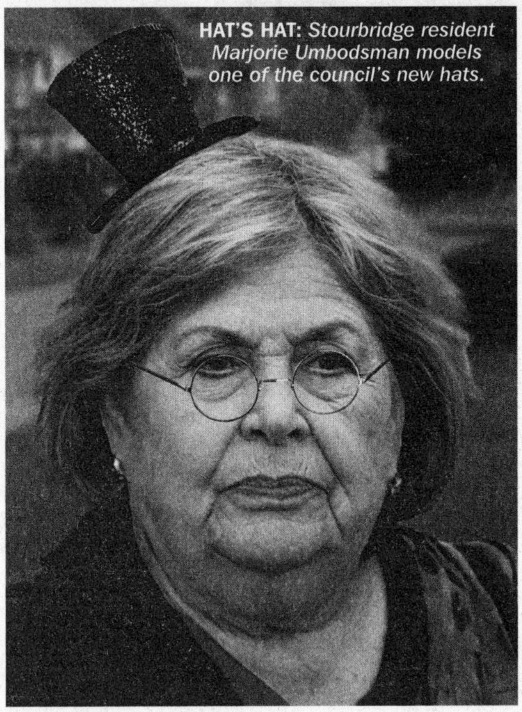

HAT'S HAT: *Stourbridge resident Marjorie Umbodsman models one of the council's new hats.*

oblongs

85-year-old local resident Tom Tugcock was yesterday looking forward to receiving his council hat. "I've asked for a silver one, and I can't wait," he said. "I never go to the park or use the library, so it doesn't bother me if they cut all that nonsense."

Others, however would rather see a return, albeit at a reduced rate, of public and environmental services. "I'm as much a fan of those little hats as the next person," said 25-year-old resident Kelly Bullfight. "But you can't tell me they're a substitute for litter-free parks and adequate street lighting. I haven't had my bins collected in a fortnight and I saw a rat yesterday."

Others were for the scheme in principle, but though that the way it would be rolled out unfairly penalised those without children. "I live with my husband in a large house in band G, and we'll get a hat each," said 45-year-old Sarah Ballspond. "Meanwhile, a single mum living in a smaller house in band A with three kids will pay half the rates I do, but get twice as many hats. It's not fair."

If you want to get ahead... GET A HAT!

NORMAL hats are sized so that the inner circumference of the brim is the same as the circumference of the head. When pushed on, the hat is held in place by the force of gravity pulling down and frictional forces between the inner brim and the scalp. But how does a hat that is ridiculously small stay on your bonce? We asked small hat expert, DR MINI PETASUM.

"Tiny Burlesque hats will sit quite directly on top of any head without any problem, as long as you walk slowly," she told us. "However, for maximum effect, they are best worn at a jaunty angle to one side of the head, and as such need fixing in some way. Lets look at the three most common ways to secure a burlesque hat..."

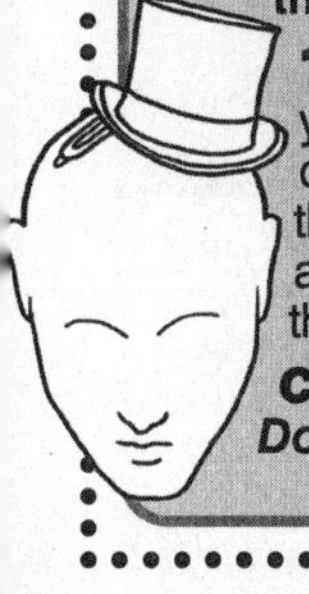

1 A Clip is the best way of securing a small hat to your head, provided you have lots of thick hair. The clip can fix the hat at any angle, but the disadvantage of this method is that it is a little fiddly to do put on, and the hat may need adjusting as the hair moves throughout the course of the day.

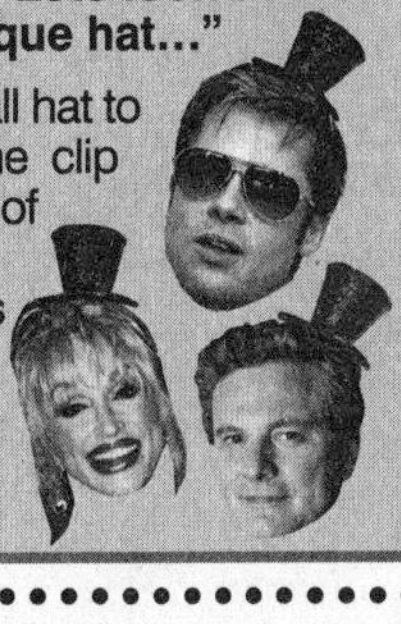

Celebrity Burlesque hat clip wearers:
Dolly Parton, Brad Pitt, Colin Firth.

2 Elastic. Just like a party hat, a Burlesque hat can be secured using a piece of elastic, a method best suited to those individuals with very short or thin hair. It is simple to put on, but may become uncomfortable under the chin if worn for extended periods. Try wearing the hat slightly forward on the forehead with the elastic going round the back of the head.

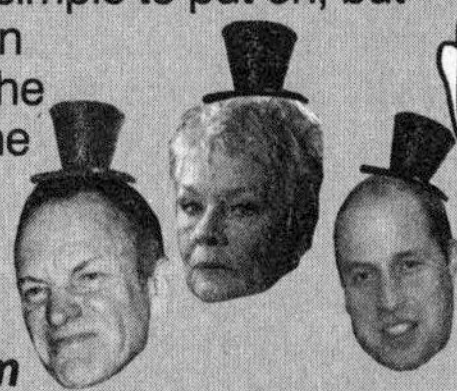

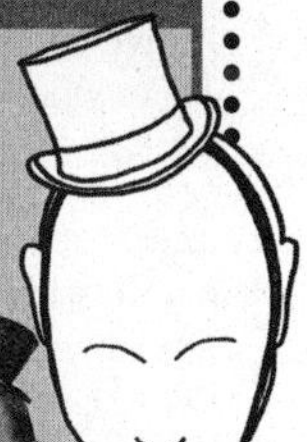

Celebrity Burlesque hat elastic wearers:
Sting, Dame Judi Dench, Prince William

3 Toupee tape. For any years, men suffering from male patterned baldness have been unable to wear Burlesque hats. But the invention of Toupee tape in 2016 put an end to all that. Just a couple of strips on the underneath of the hat sticks it to the dome for up to 24 hours. And such is the strength of modern toupee tapes, that virtually any tilt to the hat is possible.

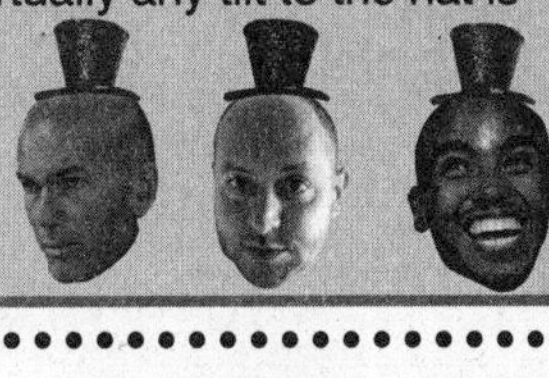

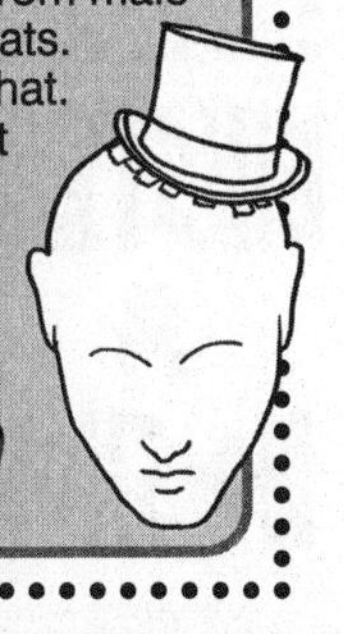

Celebrity Burlesque hat toupee tape wearers:
Zinedine Zidane, Ian Dunt, Sir Mo Farah

LETTERBOCKS

letters@viz.co.uk

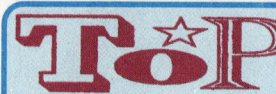

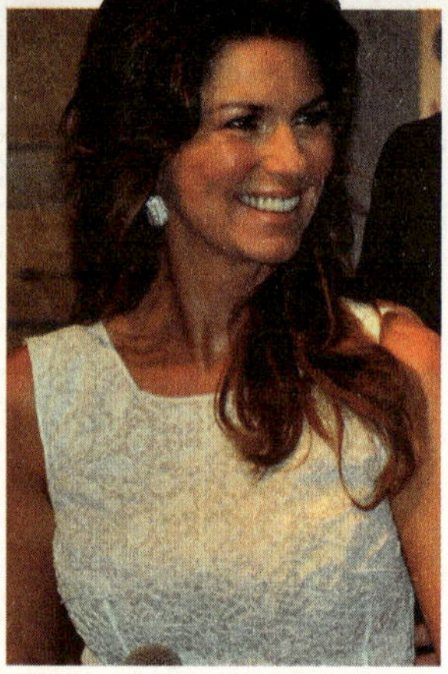

DO any of your readers know if Shania Twain has ever eaten a Scotch egg for her lunch?

Kay Evans, Darlington

** An interesting question, Kay. A Google search of 'Shania Twain scotch egg' tantalisingly offers up 770,000 results, but none of them reveals whether or not the Canadian songstress has ever eaten one for lunch. And clicking on the images displayed pictures of either Scotch eggs or Shania, but not both. Perhaps you work in a shop selling Scotch eggs and have served Ms Twain one of the sausage-meat-enveloped eggs. Or perhaps you have booked her to play a concert and she has requested Scotch eggs in her rider. Write in and let us know.*

ON page 76 of this annual, Shitty Kev from Gresford described Oscar Wilde as "one of the the 20th century's most celebrated writers and wits". However, Wilde died in 1900, which is technically the last year of the *19th* century, and he didn't do anything of value in the last few months of his life anyway. Please forward me Mr Kev's address so I can put my foot through Richard Ellmann's magnificent biography of Wilde and send him the bill.

John Moynes, Dublin

I WONDER how wankers coped before the printing press was invented? I suppose the mental wank bank was available as it's always been, but the women in those days were horny-handed, with rotten teeth and big hairy muffs. I'm so glad I live in the age of the internet.

Stuie, Bunny

I THINK that football should take a leaf out of figure skating's book. When a player scores a goal, someone should run onto the pitch and present them with a large bunch of flowers. It would add a lovely touch to the game.

Renton Prodworthy, Hull

I AGREE with Mr Prodworthy *(above)*, but I would go even further in making football more like ice skating. I would have a panel of judges giving each goal scored a mark out of ten – based on footballing skills, composition of movement, and artistic interpretation – and only goals which score more than 5.75 would be allowed to stand. Watching the likes of Erling Haaland, Harry Kane and Mo Salah clutching their flowers and looking nervously up at the big screen for their marks would add an exciting element to the game.

Harold Crumbhorn, Deal

THIS morning I saw a dog turd the exact size and shape of a blackcurrant jelly baby. What a wicked canine trick. Can you imagine what might happen were an inquisitive child or hungry and indiscriminate adult to happen upon it? Battersea Dogs Home won't be getting a penny from me, I can tell you.

Rev. F Butler Gallie, Kent

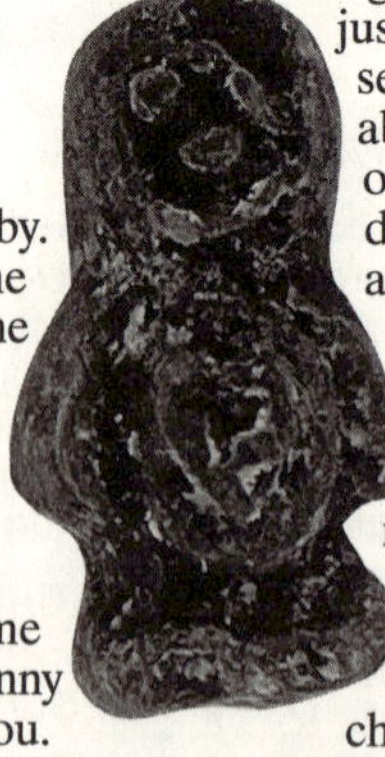

STAR LETTER

THEY say that Sir Edmund Hillary and Tenzing Norgay were the first to reach the summit of Mount Everest during the 9th expedition in 1953. Well, I'm sorry, but if the photographs they took are anything to go by, I'd say they stopped about 3 feet short of the top. Close, but no cigar, gentlemen.

Barrington Topper, Ely

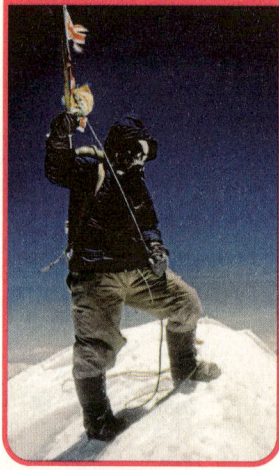

I RECENTLY saw an advert for a 1966 E-Type Jaguar for £59,000, a car I had always wanted. I'm unemployed with massive debts, but nevertheless I thought I might pretend to be a genuinely interested just so I could go and see it. However, I was about to contact the owner and get a 'test drive' when I noticed at the foot of the advert the phrase "no time wasters". As a consequence I didn't take my interest any further. Doubtless that key phrase deters all similar bone-idle chancers.

Sean Beaver, Fulchester

TOP TIPS

WHEN packing for a holiday, put a few heavy items that you won't need, such as housebricks, in the suitcase. Then, if you find your luggage is overweight at the check-in desk, you can simply remove as many of the bricks as required to get below that magic 45kg limit.

Howitt, Bedford

GAMBLERS. Always put your money on the horse with the lowest odds as, by definition, it's the most likely to win.

Brian Saxby, Chicago

SAVE money on a robotic vacuum cleaner by vacuuming your room blindfolded and changing direction every time you hit a piece of furniture.

Dave Fill, Llandudno

GET revenge on jellyfish by simply touching them with a 9v battery.

John Owens, Glasgow

GET the experience of being a drill instructor by shouting "Left, Right, Left, Right…" in time with passers-by walking in the street.

Martin Harwood, Bradford

RECREATE the fun of Channel4's *Naked Attraction* for your neighbours by standing nude on your windowsill and then gradually lifting your roller blinds a bit at a time and inviting them to comment unfavourably on your genitals.

P Draper, email

toptips@viz.co.uk

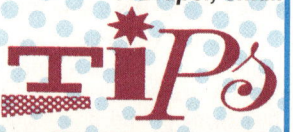

I RECKON I'd be pretty good at being an admiral. Do any of your readers have a navy that needs an admiral?

John Moynes, Dublin

** There is probably more to being an admiral than merely thinking you'd be pretty good at it, John. Or maybe we are wrong and it's a piece of piss that any bellend could do. Perhaps some of our readers were in the navy and have a story or two about what a twat their admiral was. Write in and let us know.*

WE have recently had a new bathroom installed which includes a toilet with a "soft close" seat. Now when I go for a piss, I like to start the seat closing and attempt to finish before the seat edge strikes the stream. Admittedly it's not exactly the boulder-chasing Indiana Jones stuff, but since Covid ended I've missed that regular jeopardy.

Armitage Shanks, Twyford

I WAS driving along a country lane today when I noticed a horse standing in a nearby field. As I glanced over, I was shocked to see that it was displaying a penis which reached halfway to the ground. I was so distracted by this sight that I nearly crashed into a wall. We often see advertisements urging us to slow down for horses, but so far I have yet to see one advising horses to keep their genitalia to themselves.

G Golightly, Orkney

ONLY 12 men have walked on the moon, and obviously one of them will have had the biggest cock out of all of them. I'm not sure how we would find out which one, but I'd imagine someone who would know that sort of thing would probably read *Viz*. So perhaps they should write in and give the people what they want.

John Moynes, Dublin

** Do any of our readers work for NASA, and if so, did you keep any records of the astronauts' cock lengths? – it seems like the kind of thing NASA would do. Perhaps it was Neil 'Python' Armstrong, Alan 'Truncheon' Shepard or Pete 'baby's arm holding an apple' Conrad. Write in, in the strictest confidence of course, and let us know, and we'll print the results, in the strictest confidence of course, in the next issue.*

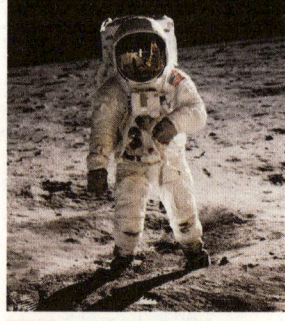

I EMBARKED on a mission to find my natural parents recently. After a short search I found them in the dining room.

John Mason, email

EINSTEIN A NO-SHOW

BOOK SIGNING
ALBERT EINSTEIN
WHERE THE HELL IS HE? NOT STILL CELEBRATING, SURELY?
TIME AND RELATIVITY
HAVE YOU SEEN THE QUEUE?
I'M SO SORRY, FOLKS – I'M SURE HE WON'T BE MUCH LONGER...
TT
I'LL TRY PHONING HIM AGAIN...
SO...
Z
RING RING!
PIZZA
PARP!!

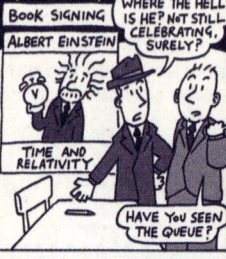

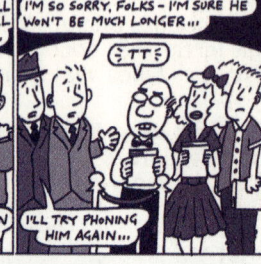

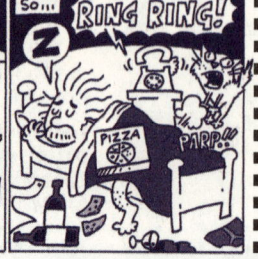

I TALK TO THE TREES

IN THE 1969 western musical Paint Your Wagon, Clint Eastwood sang of how he talked to the trees, before bemoaning the fact that they never listened to him. In reality, these enormous, woody plants are relatively simple organisms which can neither hear nor speak, so Eastwood was unlikely to get any response when conversing with them. But what would they have said if they could speak? We went on the street and posed the question… "If YOU were a tree that could talk, what would you have said to Clint Eastwood?"

"I'M a massive fan of Clint Eastwood, so if I was a talking tree, I'd ask him for his autograph. Obviously, being a tree I wouldn't have a pen or paper with me, but I imagine Clint probably carries a pen with him, and if he didn't have any paper, he could always sign one of my leaves, provided I was a broadleaf tree like a horse chestnut or lime. Although knowing my luck, the only time I meet my hero, I'd be a conifer!"
Barry Marmalade, Luton

"I WOULD tell Clint that I was his biggest tree fan and ask if I could take a selfie with him. Although he'd have to take it because I wouldn't have any fingers, just twigs, and I don't think they would work the camera button on my Samsung Galaxy."
Shelly Mousetrap, Ely

"I'M not a great fan of Clint Eastwood. I've watched a couple of his spaghetti westerns and one of those Dirty Harry ones, but they're not my cup of tea. So if I was a tree who could talk, I probably wouldn't say much to him at all. Don't get me wrong, I wouldn't be unpleasant to the man. I would say hello and perhaps make some light small talk about the weather as he walked past me in the forest, but I wouldn't strike up a conversation."
Martin Ballsup, Truro

"I ONCE met D-list celebrity Joe Swash when he was opening a supermarket and I was so star-struck that I went to pieces. So if I was a tree and I met an A-lister like Clint Eastwood, I think I'd be even worse. I don't know how trees would talk if they could, but I suspect I wouldn't be able to get any words out anyway. Perhaps this is what happened with the trees in Paint Your Wagon – that they were so in awe of the Hollywood star that they just clammed up."
Billy Shoehorn, Featherstone

"IF I was a tree, I'd ask Clint what it was like acting alongside an orangutan like he did in those films. I imagine I would have had a few of them swinging around in my branches at one time or another, so we could spend a few minutes swapping amusing orangutan-based anecdotes."
Toby Belch, Stratford

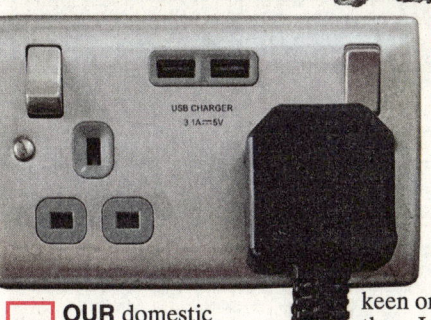

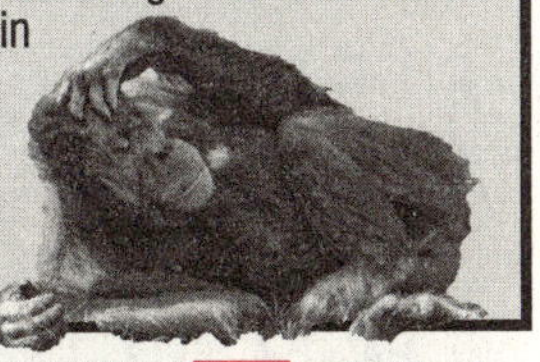

☐ OUR domestic electricity used to be supplied at 240 volts, but was reduced to 230 volts a few years ago, yet the price of electricity didn't come down. I have the same wiring and same domestic appliances, so who is helping themselves to my extra 10 volts?
Basil Garnish, Orkney

☐ THE next time David Attenborough makes a series for the BBC in which he talks about the dangers of climate change, in the interests of balance, shouldn't Julia Hartley-Brewer narrate it with him, contradicting everything he says?
Torbjorn Roseland, Ely

☐ I AM sick to the back teeth of seeing shipping containers going up and down the country on the backs of *lorries*! The clue is in the name, for heaven's sake. Let's stop them cluttering up His Majesty's highways and send them back to the sea. Maybe then we'll all be able to enjoy a bit of peace and quiet.
Oxter Boggins, Monifieth

☐ I THINK that the ending to *Succession* was good in as far as it went, but writer Jesse Armstrong could have made it much more realistic by having some little fucker you had never heard of being made CEO. That's what happened to me at my place when I was led to believe I was a shoe-in for area manager because I had ten years experience, and then they give it to some fucking teenage twat in sales who's only been there eighteen months and we have to stand and give him a fucking clap when they announce his fucking promotion and it's all because his dad plays at the same fucking golf club as the boss, the fucking bastard.
Hector Musatoid, Luton

☐ EVERYONE thinks Count von Count off *Sesame Street* is a vampire, even though it is never explicitly said in the show that he is, and no-one should make the assumption. If I had fangs and a cape, didn't like garlic, and couldn't see my reflection in a mirror, I'd be pretty annoyed about people jumping to conclusions like that.
Joe Williams, Leeds

☐ LOTS of people love to sit and watch a gritty TV crime drama, but it's a different story when they are victims of a real-life crime. They're not so keen on crime dramas then. I wish folk would make their minds up.
Ken Topping, email

☐ ON their Sage & Onion Stuffing box, Paxo clearly state that the contents make 12 stuffing balls. Well, I've just ran out of mix after making 11. The lying bastards.
Mark, Camelford

PUBES on the SOAP

A round-up of all the pube-related plots in this week's soaps.

Corrie
A DRAMATIC conclusion to the highly controversial Liz McDonald grey pubes story. There's a showdown in the Rovers as Sally taunts Liz over her own sandy coloured bush before the catfight from hell erupts. Norris drags Sally off Liz, but it's too late as the former machinist supervisor has already debagged Liz and the regulars realise they've been lied to all these years. Liz tries to explain – but is it too late?

Eastenders
ANGIE WATTS makes a surprise return to settle some old scores and put the record straight on her pubes. Since she left the soap, rumours have been rife in the Square that her pubic thatch was as patchy as a late summer tennis ball. But jaws drop when she strolls back into town sporting a genital spread as lush as the hair on her head. Meanwhile, Lofty Holloway discovers crabs in his fuse wire, and confronts the person he caught them off… *but who is it?*

Emmerdale
WEDNESDAY'S episode saw an explosive helicopter crash in the village with a huge fireball engulfing all the main cast and singeing their pubes. Viewers will have to wait until next week to find out which characters' pubic hairs survived the crash intact. In the Woolpack, Amos Brearley confides in Seth Armstrong that he has had a "Tuppenny all-off down there". But can loose-lipped Seth keep the news to himself?

The editors take no responsibility in the event that these story lines to not come about, or if some of the characters mentioned have not been in their respective soaps for more than 20 years.

☐ ACCORDING to the Quit Smoking app, I've saved £742 since giving up the fags in January, yet I'm skint. Can any of these "so-called" experts explain that?
Roland Poland, Chard

☐ THE plural of 'foot' is 'feet' and yet the plural of 'boot' isn't 'beet'. I wish the boffins would explain that, rather than wasting their time trying to find cures for diseases I might never catch.
Bert Thraxby, Harlow

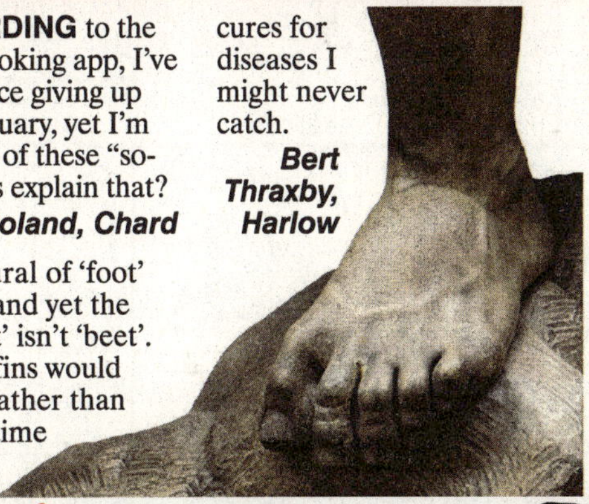

COX'S CORNER
Your cookery questions answered by top physicist Professor Brian Cox

WHY do recipes call for ginger in centimetres? Surely the amount of ginger in a piece 3cm long is determined by how thick it is. It's madness.
Micky Bullock, Bristol

Professor Cox says… You are absolutely correct, Mr Bullock, and the cookery community should standardise the ginger amount called for in recipes. At CERN, we propose that all recipes use a standardised SI unit for ginger (Gr) with 1Gr equal to a cylindrical piece of ginger 0.01m long with a radius of 0.01m. 1Gr is therefore equivalent to $1 \times \pi r^2$ worth of ginger, or, in centimetres $1 \times 3.142 \times 1^2 = 3.142 cm^3$ of ginger. If the radius of your ginger is greater or smaller than 1cm, you will need a shorter or longer piece than the recipe demands in order to provide the same Gr value. To determine how much you need, simply use the equation…

$$l = \frac{n\pi}{\pi r^2}$$ cancel π on the numerator and denominator to give

$$l = \frac{n}{r^2}$$ where: l = the length of your ginger you need
n = the Gr value stated in the recipe
r = the radius of your ginger

Then add a little bit more because you will lose some when you peel it.

More next time, cookery physics fans! Bri xx

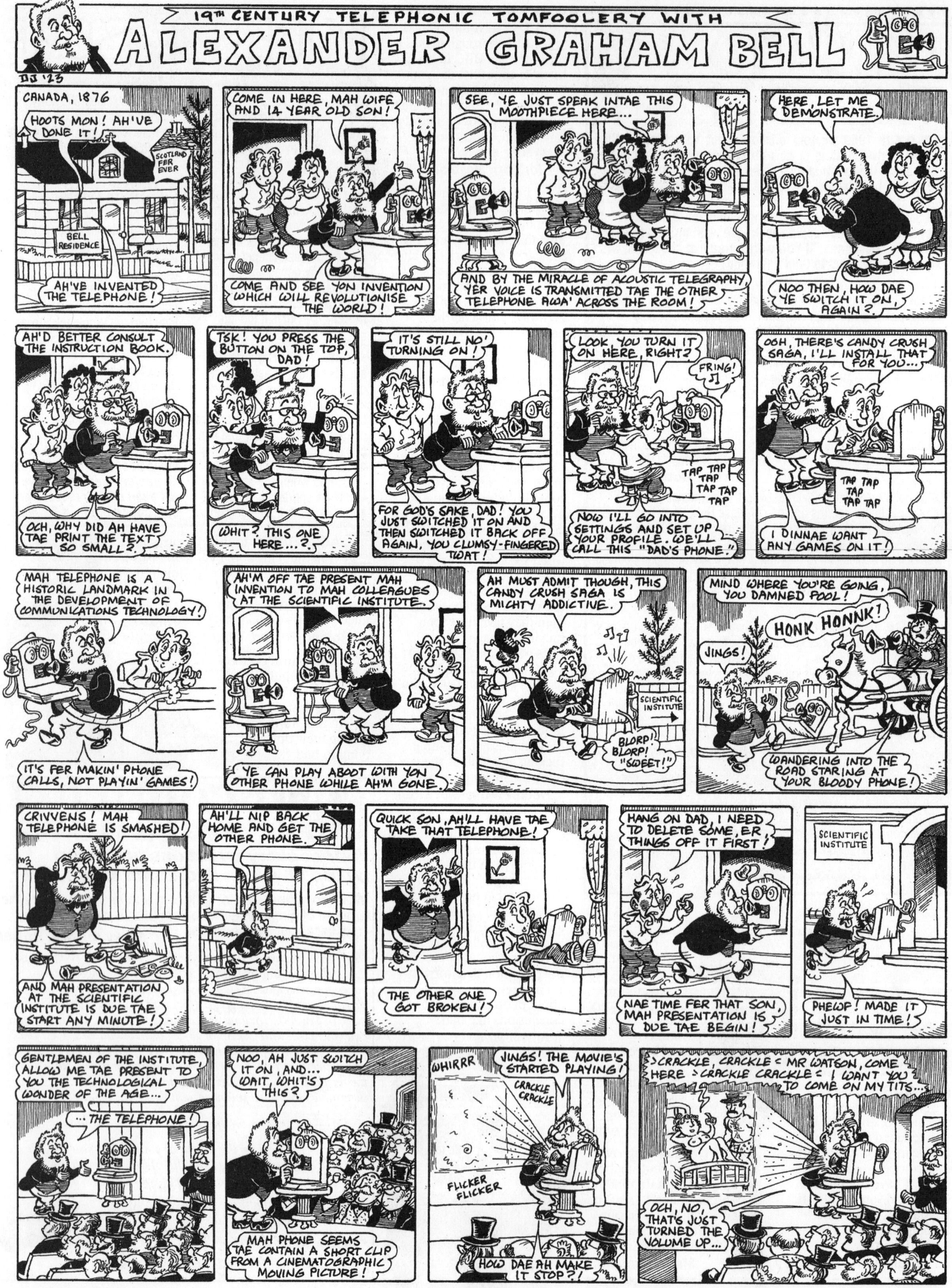
19TH CENTURY TELEPHONIC TOMFOOLERY WITH
ALEXANDER GRAHAM BELL
DJ '23
CANADA, 1876
HOOTS MON! AH'VE DONE IT!
SCOTLAND FER EVER
BELL RESIDENCE
AH'VE INVENTED THE TELEPHONE!
COME IN HERE, MAH WIFE AND 14 YEAR OLD SON!
COME AND SEE YON INVENTION WHICH WILL REVOLUTIONISE THE WORLD!
SEE, YE JUST SPEAK INTAE THIS MOOTHPIECE HERE...
AND BY THE MIRACLE OF ACOUSTIC TELEGRAPHY, YER VOICE IS TRANSMITTED TAE THE OTHER TELEPHONE AWA' ACROSS THE ROOM!
HERE, LET ME DEMONSTRATE.
NOO THEN, HOW DAE YE SWITCH IT ON, AGAIN?
AH'D BETTER CONSULT THE INSTRUCTION BOOK.
OCH, WHY DID AH HAVE TAE PRINT THE TEXT SO SMALL?
TSK! YOU PRESS THE BUTTON ON THE TOP, DAD!
WHIT? THIS ONE HERE...?
IT'S STILL NO' TURNING ON!
FOR GOD'S SAKE, DAD! YOU JUST SWITCHED IT ON AND THEN SWITCHED IT BACK OFF AGAIN, YOU CLUMSY-FINGERED TWAT!
LOOK, YOU TURN IT ON HERE, RIGHT?
FRING!
TAP TAP TAP TAP TAP TAP
NOW I'LL GO INTO SETTINGS AND SET UP YOUR PROFILE. WE'LL CALL THIS "DAD'S PHONE."
OOH, THERE'S CANDY CRUSH SAGA, I'LL INSTALL THAT FOR YOU...
TAP TAP TAP TAP TAP
I DINNAE WANT ANY GAMES ON IT!
MAH TELEPHONE IS A HISTORIC LANDMARK IN THE DEVELOPMENT OF COMMUNICATIONS TECHNOLOGY!
IT'S FER MAKIN' PHONE CALLS, NOT PLAYIN' GAMES!
AH'M OFF TAE PRESENT MAH INVENTION TO MAH COLLEAGUES AT THE SCIENTIFIC INSTITUTE.
YE CAN PLAY ABOOT WITH YON OTHER PHONE WHILE AH'M GONE.
AH MUST ADMIT THOUGH, THIS CANDY CRUSH SAGA IS MIGHTY ADDICTIVE.
SCIENTIFIC INSTITUTE
BLORP! BLORP! "SWEET!"
MIND WHERE YOU'RE GOING, YOU DAMNED FOOL!
HONK HONNK!
JINGS!
WANDERING INTO THE ROAD STARING AT YOUR BLOODY PHONE!
CRIVVENS! MAH TELEPHONE IS SMASHED!
AND MAH PRESENTATION AT THE SCIENTIFIC INSTITUTE IS DUE TAE START ANY MINUTE!
AH'LL NIP BACK HOME AND GET THE OTHER PHONE.
QUICK SON, AH'LL HAVE TAE TAKE THAT TELEPHONE!
THE OTHER ONE GOT BROKEN!
HANG ON DAD, I NEED TO DELETE SOME, ER THINGS OFF IT FIRST!
NAE TIME FER THAT SON, MAH PRESENTATION IS DUE TAE BEGIN!
SCIENTIFIC INSTITUTE
PHEW! MADE IT JUST IN TIME!
GENTLEMEN OF THE INSTITUTE, ALLOW ME TAE PRESENT TO YOU THE TECHNOLOGICAL WONDER OF THE AGE...
...THE TELEPHONE!
NOO, AH JUST SWITCH IT ON, AND... WAIT, WHIT'S THIS?
MAH PHONE SEEMS TAE CONTAIN A SHORT CLIP FROM A CINEMATOGRAPHIC MOVING PICTURE!
WHIRRR
JINGS! THE MOVIE'S STARTED PLAYING!
CRACKLE CRACKLE
FLICKER FLICKER
HOW DAE AH MAKE IT STOP?!
>CRACKLE, CRACKLE< MR WATSON, COME HERE >CRACKLE CRACKLE< I WANT YOU TO COME ON MY TITS...
OCH, NO, THAT'S JUST TURNED THE VOLUME UP...

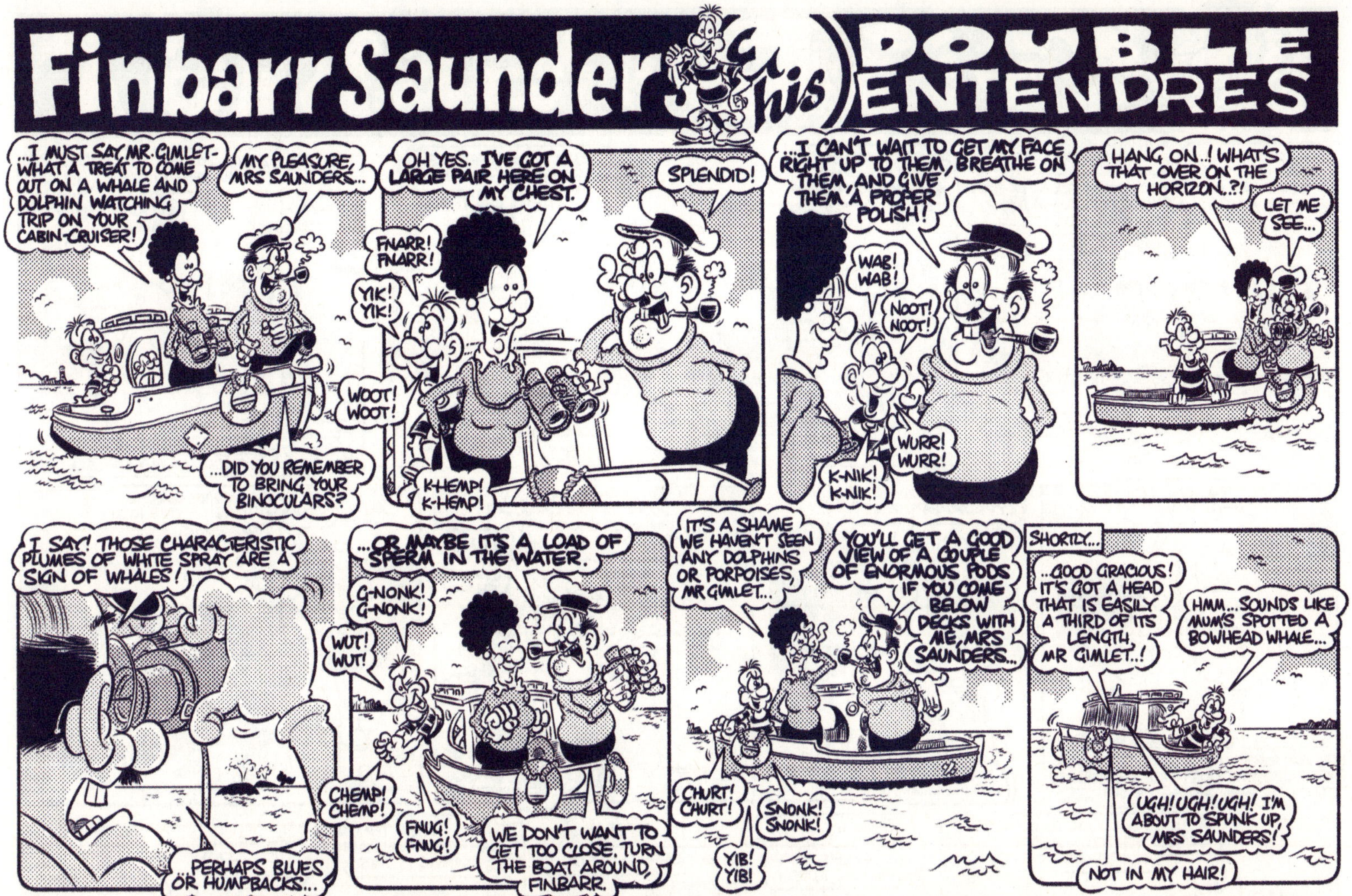
Finbarr Saunders & his DOUBLE ENTENDRES
...I MUST SAY, MR. GIMLET- WHAT A TREAT TO COME OUT ON A WHALE AND DOLPHIN WATCHING TRIP ON YOUR CABIN-CRUISER!
MY PLEASURE, MRS SAUNDERS...
...DID YOU REMEMBER TO BRING YOUR BINOCULARS?
OH YES. I'VE GOT A LARGE PAIR HERE ON MY CHEST.
SPLENDID!
FNARR! FNARR!
YIK! YIK!
WOOT! WOOT!
K-HEMP! K-HEMP!
...I CAN'T WAIT TO GET MY FACE RIGHT UP TO THEM, BREATHE ON THEM, AND GIVE THEM A PROPER POLISH!
WAB! WAB!
NOOT! NOOT!
WURR! WURR!
K-NIK! K-NIK!
HANG ON..! WHAT'S THAT OVER ON THE HORIZON..?!
LET ME SEE...
I SAY! THOSE CHARACTERISTIC PLUMES OF WHITE SPRAY ARE A SIGN OF WHALES!
PERHAPS BLUES OR HUMPBACKS...
...OR MAYBE IT'S A LOAD OF SPERM IN THE WATER.
G-NONK! G-NONK!
WUT! WUT!
CHEMP! CHEMP!
FNUG! FNUG!
WE DON'T WANT TO GET TOO CLOSE. TURN THE BOAT AROUND, FINBARR.
IT'S A SHAME WE HAVEN'T SEEN ANY DOLPHINS OR PORPOISES, MR GIMLET...
YOU'LL GET A GOOD VIEW OF A COUPLE OF ENORMOUS PODS IF YOU COME BELOW DECKS WITH ME, MRS SAUNDERS...
CHURT! CHURT!
SNONK! SNONK!
YIB! YIB!
SHORTLY...
...GOOD GRACIOUS! IT'S GOT A HEAD THAT IS EASILY A THIRD OF ITS LENGTH, MR GIMLET..!
HMM...SOUNDS LIKE MUM'S SPOTTED A BOWHEAD WHALE...
UGH! UGH! UGH! I'M ABOUT TO SPUNK UP, MRS SAUNDERS!
NOT IN MY HAIR!

PARLIAMENTARY STATIONERS AND GOVERNMENTAL GIFT SUPPLIERS

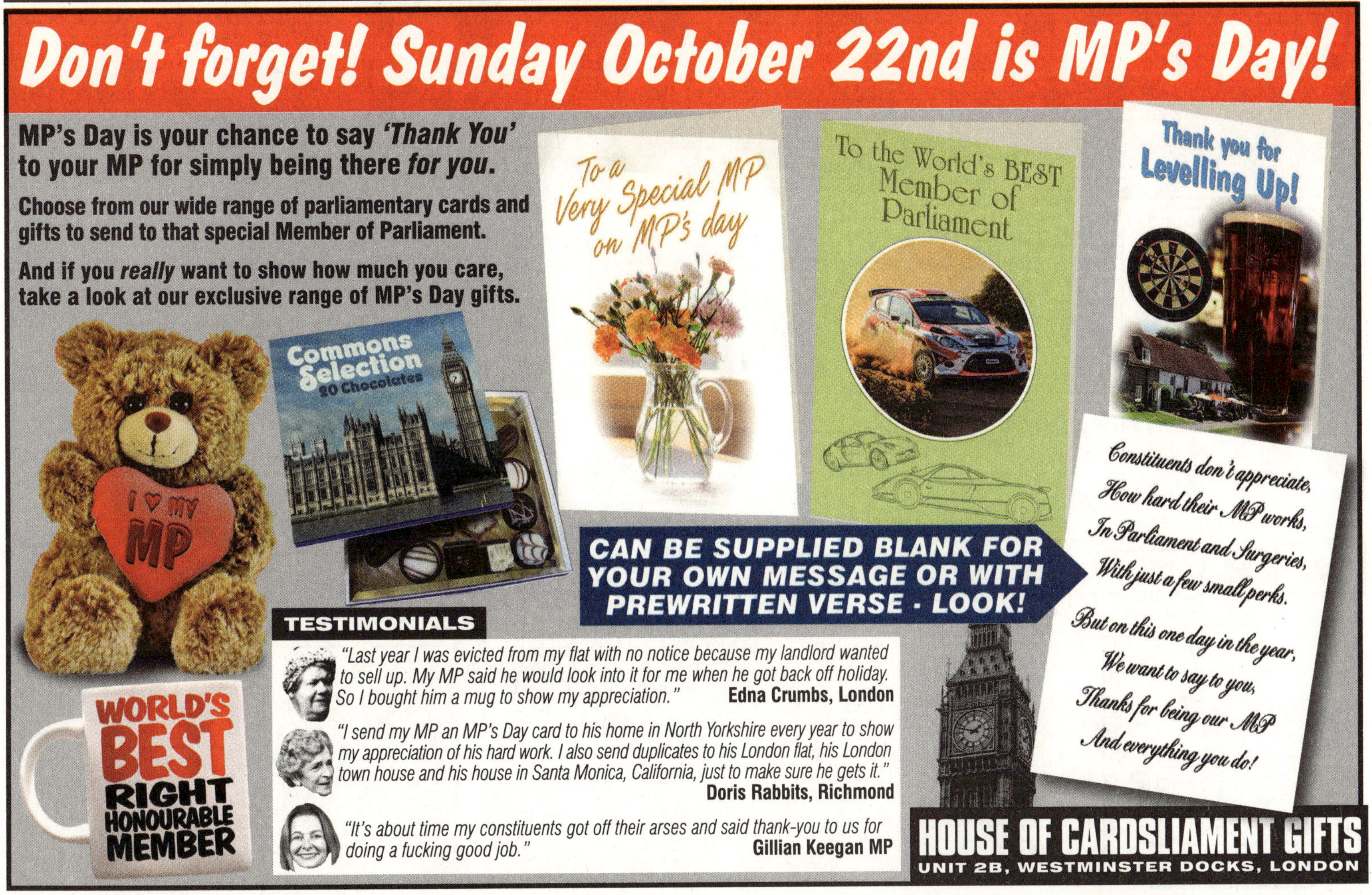
Don't forget! Sunday October 22nd is MP's Day!
MP's Day is your chance to say 'Thank You' to your MP for simply being there for you.
Choose from our wide range of parliamentary cards and gifts to send to that special Member of Parliament.
And if you really want to show how much you care, take a look at our exclusive range of MP's Day gifts.
To a Very Special MP on MP's day
To the World's BEST Member of Parliament
Thank you for Levelling Up!
Commons Selection 20 Chocolates
I ♥ MY MP
CAN BE SUPPLIED BLANK FOR YOUR OWN MESSAGE OR WITH PREWRITTEN VERSE - LOOK!
Constituents don't appreciate,
How hard their MP works,
In Parliament and Surgeries,
With just a few small perks.
But on this one day in the year,
We want to say to you,
Thanks for being our MP
And everything you do!
WORLD'S BEST RIGHT HONOURABLE MEMBER
TESTIMONIALS
"Last year I was evicted from my flat with no notice because my landlord wanted to sell up. My MP said he would look into it for me when he got back off holiday. So I bought him a mug to show my appreciation." Edna Crumbs, London
"I send my MP an MP's Day card to his home in North Yorkshire every year to show my appreciation of his hard work. I also send duplicates to his London flat, his London town house and his house in Santa Monica, California, just to make sure he gets it." Doris Rabbits, Richmond
"It's about time my constituents got off their arses and said thank-you to us for doing a fucking good job." Gillian Keegan MP
HOUSE OF CARDSLIAMENT GIFTS
UNIT 2B, WESTMINSTER DOCKS, LONDON

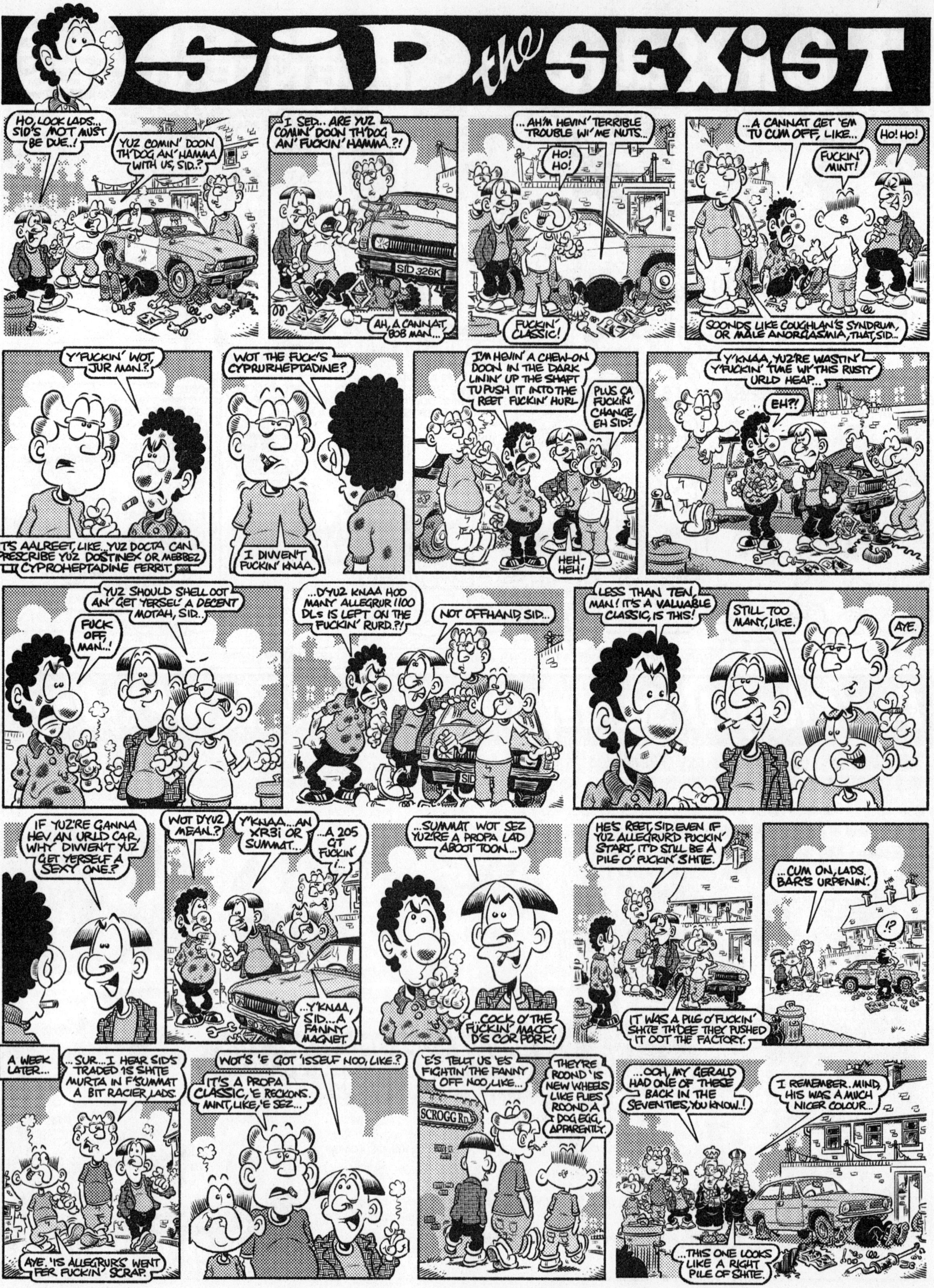
SID the SEXIST
HO, LOOK LADS... SID'S MOT MUST BE DUE..!
YUZ COMIN' DOON TH'DOG AN' HAMMA WITH US, SID..?
I SED... ARE YUZ COMIN' DOON TH'DOG AN' FUCKIN' HAMMA..?!
AH, A CANNAT, BOB MAN...
SID 326K
...AH'M HEVIN' TERRIBLE TROUBLE WI' ME NUTS...
HO! HO!
FUCKIN' CLASSIC!
...A CANNAT GET 'EM TU CUM OFF, LIKE...
FUCKIN' MINT!
HO! HO!
SOONDS LIKE COUGHLAN'S SYNDRUM, OR MALE ANORGASMIA, THAT, SID...
Y'FUCKIN' WOT, JUR MAN..?
IT'S AALREET, LIKE... YUZ DOCTA CAN PRESCRIBE YUZ DOSTINEX OR MEBBEZ CYPROHEPTADINE FERRIT.
WOT THE FUCK'S CYPRURHEPTADINE?
I DIVVEN'T FUCKIN' KNAA.
I'M HEVIN' A CHEW-ON DOON IN THE DARK LININ' UP THE SHAFT TU PUSH IT INTO THE REET FUCKIN' HURL
PLUS CA FUCKIN' CHANGE, EH SID?
HEH-HEH!
Y'KNAA, YUZ'RE WASTIN' Y'FUCKIN' TIME WI' THIS RUSTY URLD HEAP...
EH?!
YUZ SHOULD SHELL OOT AN' GET YERSEL' A DECENT MOTAH, SID...
FUCK OFF, MAN..!
...D'YUZ KNAA HOO MANY ALLEGRUR 1100 DLs IS LEFT ON THE FUCKIN' RURD..?!
NOT OFFHAND, SID...
LESS THAN TEN, MAN! IT'S A VALUABLE CLASSIC, IS THIS!
STILL TOO MANY, LIKE.
AYE.
IF YUZ'RE GANNA HEV AN URLD CAR, WHY DIVVEN'T YUZ GET YERSELF A SEXY ONE..?
WOT D'YUZ MEAN..?
Y'KNAA... AN XR3i OR SUMMAT...
...A 205 GT FUCKIN' i...
...Y'KNAA, SID... A FANNY MAGNET.
...SUMMAT WOT SEZ YUZ'RE A PROPA LAD ABOOT TOON...
...COCK O' THE FUCKIN' MACCY D'S COR PORK!
HE'S REET, SID. EVEN IF YUZ ALLEGRURD FUCKIN' START, IT'D STILL BE A PILE O' FUCKIN' SHITE.
IT WAS A PILE O' FUCKIN' SHITE TH'DEE THEY PUSHED IT OOT THE FACTORY.
...CUM ON, LADS. BAR'S URPENIN'.
!?
A WEEK LATER...
...SUR... I HEAR SID'S TRADED 'IS SHITE MURTA IN F'SUMMAT A BIT RACIER, LADS.
AYE. 'IS ALLEGRUR'S WENT FER FUCKIN' SCRAP.
WOT'S 'E GOT 'ISSELF NOO, LIKE..?
IT'S A PROPA CLASSIC, 'E RECKONS. MINT, LIKE, 'E SEZ...
SCROGG Rd.
'E'S TELT US 'E'S FIGHTIN' THE FANNY OFF NOO, LIKE...
THEY'RE ROOND 'IS NEW WHEELS LIKE FLIES ROOND A DOG EGG, APPARENTLY.
...OOH, MY GERALD HAD ONE OF THESE BACK IN THE SEVENTIES, YOU KNOW..!
I REMEMBER.. MIND, HIS WAS A MUCH NICER COLOUR...
...THIS ONE LOOKS LIKE A RIGHT PILE OF SHITE.

...GS SPECIAL ... 3-PAGE XMAS GRUB AND ALL THE TRIMMINGS SPECIAL ... 3-PAGE XMAS GRUB AND...

MARZIPANDEMIC
Bakery fears over new Covid strain

HALF A DECADE after the Covid-19 virus effectively closed down Christmas, experts in the food industry claim that the nightmare festive scenario could happen again thanks to the emergence of a virulent new Corona strain. But the new variant will not arise by the usual route of mutations in its genetic code… instead it will be caused *by people eating marzipan!*

DOWN THE 'PAN: *Could marzipan on cakes be linked to new Covid variant?*

That's according to **JIM GUTROTS**, president of the National Icing Confederation, an organisation working to promote the use of fondant and royal icing on cakes. "The science is a little difficult to explain to the layman," he explained. "But all the evidence points to marzipan on cakes being linked to a new Covid variant."

jamboree

The new strain was first recorded in Nottinghamshire back in November, and has since quickly spread through the country. Symptoms include a sore throat, runny nose, diarrhoea, muscle aches and stomach cramps, as well as the loss of taste and smell associated with the original Covid-19 virus. And Gutrots believes that the timing of the new strain's arrival so close to the festive season is no coincidence.

"This new Covid comes along in November, the exact time when people start making their Christmas cake," he said. "Everyone knows it's best to get your cake done and iced a few weeks before the big day so it has time to mature."

"The arrival of the virus coincided exactly with when people spread apricot jam on the top of the cake and put the marzipan on. You've just got to join the dots and follow the science."

"I'm not a scientist, I'll admit. But I've been involved in cake decorating all my life, so I know what I'm talking about. Obviously it's got nothing to do with the jam – I mean, that's just nonsense. So it's got to be the marzipan what's causing this virus," he concluded.

bingo

And Gutrots had this advice for anyone making a Christmas cake this year: *"If you don't want to be sat on the pot all Christmas Day, blowing your nose and shitting through the eye of a needle, then leave the marzipan off."*

However, the scientific world sounded a note of caution, stressing that further research would be needed before a causal link between the new Covid variant and the use of marzipan on Christmas cakes could be firmly established. "Because two things happen at the same time does not mean that they happen because of each other," said Dr Adam Rutherford, presenter of the BBC flagship science programme *Science Now*.

"Having said that, not having marzipan on your Christmas cake is no great sacrifice, so it would be little hardship to err on the side of caution in this instance."

"I will not be having marzipan on my cake this year, just in case," Rutherford added.

And for anyone worried that their Christmas cake will be lacking something without the almond-flavoured fondant paste, Gutrots had this suggestion: "Why not have two layers of icing instead?"

NUT ON YOUR NELLY!

VISITORS turning up at the home of Grammy Award-winning singer Nelly Furtado this Christmas will be met with all the usual festive trimmings – paper decorations, bunches of mistletoe and a tinsel covered tree. But one thing that will be missing is *nuts*. That's because Furtado is worried that she may have developed an allergy to the small, dry fruits.

The multiple Juno Award-winning Canadian singer has eaten nuts all her life, but became fearful after hearing a story about a fifty-year-old man going into anaphylactic shock after eating a Brazil nut.

"He had ate nuts all his life with no problem," the 2007 MTV Music prizewinner told *NME*. "Then one day he went allergict to them and he ate one and his throat all swelled up."

"He would of died if they hadn't of come over and stabbed him with a pen," the Grammy Award-winning artist continued.

And such is the Canadian singer's fear that she too may have developed the same potentially life-threatening intolerance to the indehiscent

XMASCLUSIVE!

fruits, that she has **BANNED** all foods containing nuts and nut products from her house over the festive season. "My house will be a nut-free zone this Christmas," the 2015 German Sustainability Award winner said.

In fact, the 2001 *Q* Awards Best Music Video nominee has even gone so far as to ban any foodstuffs that are produced in factories where nuts are handled. "I'm just not going to take the risk," she said.

shuttlecock

But epidemiologist and medical writer doctor Ben Goldacre thinks the 2013 Canadian Civil Liberties Association Excellence in the Arts Award-winner is being overcautious, as serious allergies showing up in later life are extremely rare.

timpani

"If you're allergict to nuts, you usually know about it in your childhood, so if you've been eating them all your life, you should be okay," the Medical Journalism Awards 2006 Freelancer of the Year said.

"However, eating nuts is a bit like getting stang off a wasp," he cautioned.

"The first time you get stang, it's okay. But if you're allergict, your blood produces something what means it's the second time you get stang where your throat all swells up and you have to get stabbed with a pen."

"So if you've only ever ate nuts once, be careful," the 2006 Committee for Skeptical Inquiry Balles Prize in Critical Thinking award winner advised.

NELLY A GONER! *Furtado worried about allergy to nuts (above).*

Could YOU kill a Turkey?

THE Moral MAZE

...enter our festive moral maze to find out!

ASK ANYONE what their favourite part of Christmas dinner is, and you'll get the same answer: *the turkey*. Vegans will tell you it's the nut cutlet or roast potatoes, but in their heart, it's the turkey for them too.

No Christmas dinner is complete without it. But few of us realise that just days earlier, the succulent meat swimming in gravy and cranberry sauce on our plate was a bird, alive and well and running around a farmyard or cramped, windowless shed. For hundreds of years, killing a living bird and preparing it for the table was all part of the cooking process. But in modern times, this grim job has been delegated to others so we only see the sanitised end result in the supermarket fridge or butcher's window.

So it's time to face the big festive question: Could *YOU* kill a turkey for your table?

The answer to this question lies deep within your psyche, so we've prepared a fun quiz to find out. Simply answer the following questions truthfully, tot up your score and see if *YOU'VE* got what it takes to top a turkey!

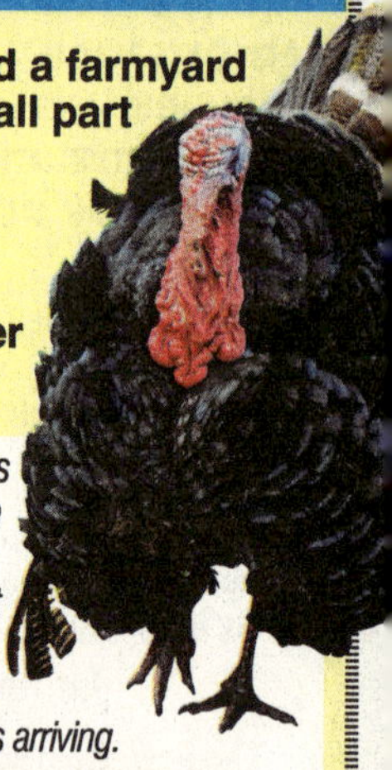

1. The circus comes to town and your friend asks you to go with them to see it. You don't really like circuses, but your friend is depressed as they have had relationship problems and you want to show them some support, so you go along. What is your favourite act?

a. *The flying trapeze artists*
b. *The clowns*
c. *The jugglers*

2. You are in town shopping when a market researcher attempts to stop you to ask some questions. You are extremely busy and don't want to take part in their survey. What do you do?

a. *Just walk on, pretending that you haven't seen them, whilst pretending to look for something in your bag or wallet.*
b. *Apologise without breaking your stride and say you cannot stop as you are in a hurry to be somewhere.*
c. *Stop and take part, but give your answers quickly without giving them any thought just so you can get away.*

3. Coming out of a pub one evening, you spot a young couple, a man and a woman, having an argument in an alleyway. It is loud and heated, but not physical. What do you?

a. *Walk on. It's nothing to do with you and you should mind your own business.*
b. *Watch for a few minutes and get ready to intervene if things escalate.*
c. *Wade in, ask the bloke what his fucking game is before giving him a fourpenny one on the chin.*

4. One morning at work, you suddenly realise that you have missed your mother's birthday the day before. What do you do?

a. *Nothing. It's too late now and the damage is done.*
b. *Immediately call her up to apologise, wish her happy birthday for yesterday, and arrange for some flowers to be delivered.*
c. *Call her and brazen it out, asking if she liked her card and blaming the postal service when she tells you it never arrived.*

5. A co-worker comes into the office one day wearing a dress she bought at the weekend and she asks you if you like it. It looks terrible on her. What do you say?

a. *You tell her the truth, saying it looks awful and makes her arse look fucking huge. It might be brutal, but in future when you tell her something she is wearing looks good, she will believe you.*
b. *You tell a lie, saying it looks great. Honesty is not always the best policy.*
c. *You begin to say "I think it looks..." and then pretend to have a heart attack. It will all be forgotten in the excitement of the paramedics arriving.*

HOW DID YOU DO?

Mainly As: *It's going to be a good Christmas for your turkey. You haven't got it in you to kill a fly, let alone a full grown fowl. Make yourself a nice nut roast, or pop along to the supermarket to get a few of those vegan kievs for you and your family to have on Christmas Day.*

Mainly Bs: *It's touch and go for any turkey in your possession. You haven't got it in you to finish it off yourself, but you could take part in the process, perhaps catching it or holding it down whilst someone who scored mainly Cs in this quiz wrings its neck.*

Mainly Cs: *It's safe to say that any turkey in your possession has a bleak future ahead of it. You will think absolutely nothing of marching out on Christmas morning and cheerfully dispatching the unfortunate bird whilst whistling a Christmas carol.*

HAPPY NEWS YEAR! CHRISTMAS NEWS ROUND-UP

BOOKS describing the origins of our Christmas traditions are a festive staple. Every October, bookshops begin filling up with hastily written tomes explaining why we eat turkey at Christmas, who sent the first Christmas card, and why we bring a tree into the house. Usually ghostwritten and with a photograph of a celebrity in a Santa hat on the front, the arrival of these lightweight, utterly forgettable volumes in the shops is a much-loved tradition. But have you ever thought about how they started? If you have, then a new book out this year will give you all the answers. *The Origin of Christmas Tradition Books* (Stuffing Books, £12.99) explains where and when these books started, who wrote the very first one, and why we continue to buy them. Purportedly written by **LEE MACK** and illustrated by somebody you've never heard of, it's a festive stocking filler that will find its way under many trees on December 25th.

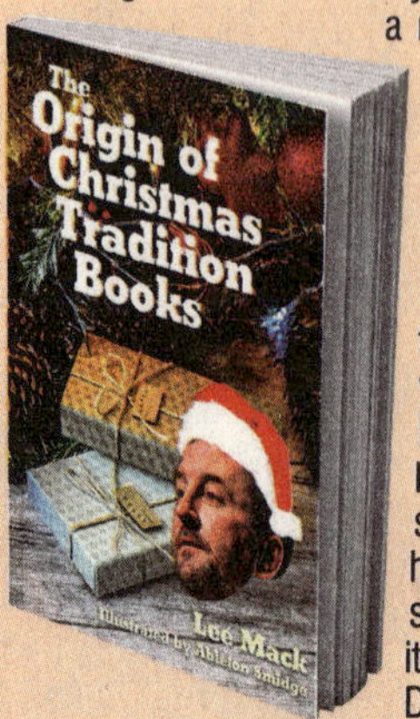
The Origin of Christmas Tradition Books
Lee Mack

WE ALL LOVE pigs in blankets – those little cocktail sausages wrapped in bacon and roasted along with the turkey – and our Christmas dinner would not be the same without them. But for the past 12 months, researchers at the University of Bristol have been looking into the effects that eating pigs in blankets has on the body – and it's not good news. "We took 300 healthy individuals and divided them into two groups," said study leader **DR ULF CIGGIES**. "The control group were fed a diet that was rich in protein, fruit and vegetables, and low in fats and carbohydrates. The second group ate 250 pigs in blankets every day. Over the course of a year, the study found that those eating only pigs in blankets were significantly less healthy than the control group." Shocked boffins found that the second group put on tons of weight, suffered really bad constipation and dropped horrible farts. "They might taste nice, but pigs in blankets are not good for you," Dr Ciggies concluded.

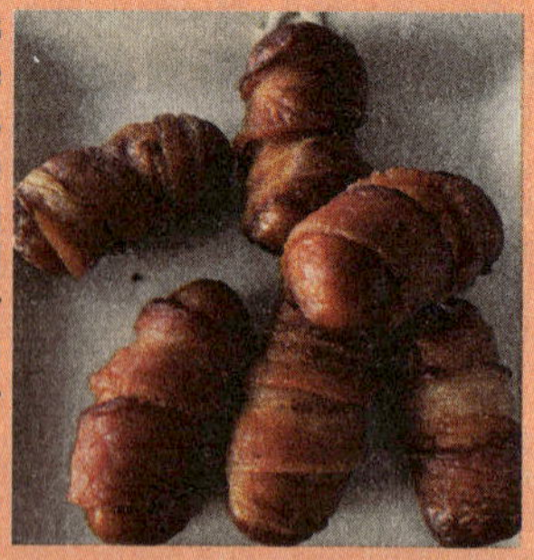

FORMULA 1 ace **LEWIS HAMILTON** has scotched internet rumours by revealing that he *will* be putting up a tree in his Monaco home this Christmas. The seven-times world motor racing champion has traditionally put up and decorated a tree to celebrate the festive season, but pitlane tittle-tattle speculated that he would not be doing so this year following a run of lacklustre results. The rumours were fuelled after the pole position record holder refused to comment after being asked by *Sky*'s **TED KRAVITZ** if he would be erecting a tree this year. And speculation hotted up after he was not spotted with *Pussycat Dolls* singer **NICOLE SCHERZINGER** going into the Christmas Store in Monaco's Fontvielle Shopping Centre in early December. However, the question was put to bed after the speed ace – with 103 wins and 196 podium finishes under his belt – finally spoke out. "Just to put an end to all the rumours, yes, I will be putting up a tree this Christmas," he told a press conference following the Abu Dhabi grand prix qualification session. "I've already been up in the loft to get my box of decos down, but it stinks so I think there might be a dead mouse in the bottom of it."

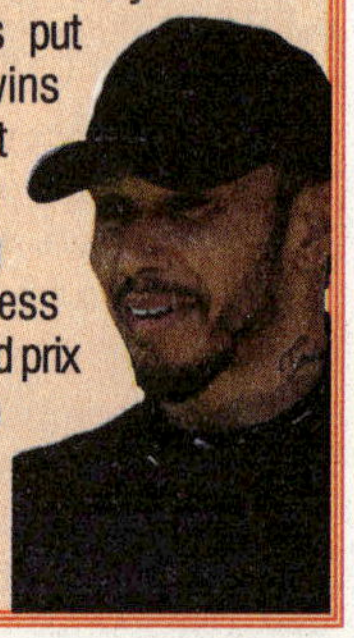

It's the Great Christmas Cake Balloon Debate!

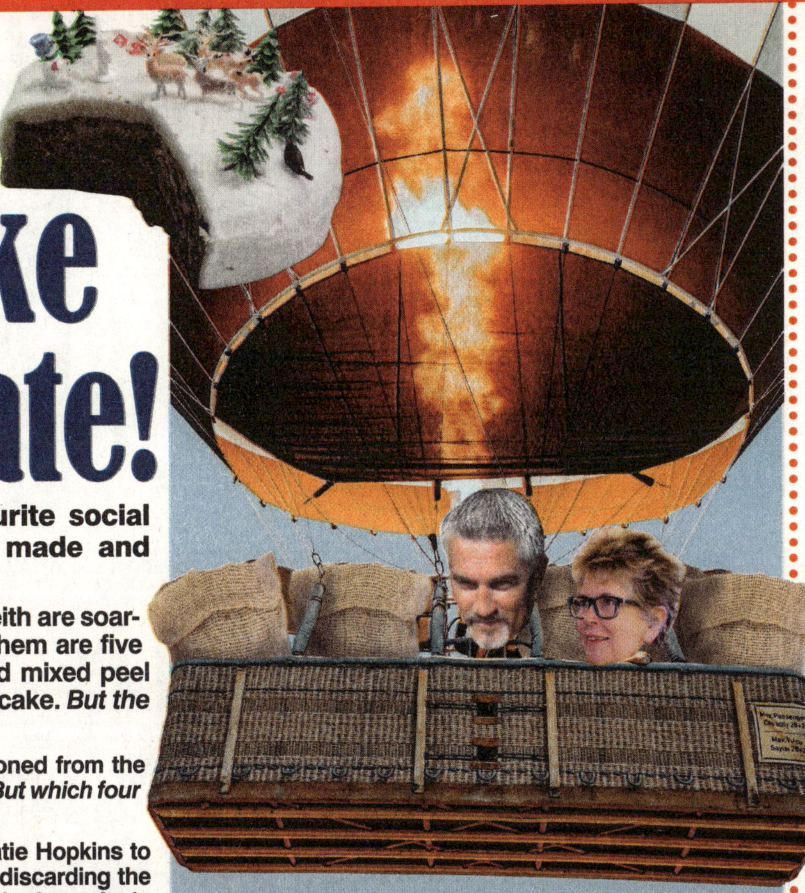

UP, UP AND A WEIGHT: *Which Christmas Cake ingredient should Paul and Pru drop from their balloon?*

THE Balloon Debate game is one of our favourite social pastimes. Ideas are put forward, cases are made and debate is sparked whenever it is played.

In this seasonal, celebrity version, Paul Hollywood and Prue Leith are soaring through the sky in a hot air balloon. In the gondola with them are five bags containing raisins, sultanas, cherries, chopped nuts and mixed peel – all the ingredients necessary to make a delicious Christmas cake. *But the balloon is sinking!*

The ingredients are too heavy, and all but one bag must be jettisoned from the basket if the pair are to arrive safely at their bakery to make the cake. *But which four items should they throw out, and which should they save?*

We asked 3 of our favourite celebrities and Boris Johnson and Katie Hopkins to each champion an ingredient and make the case for saving it whilst discarding the other four. At the end of the debate, you – the *Viz* readers – will be invited to write in and say who has made the best case for the ingredient that makes it into the cake.

BORIS JOHNSON, *disgraced PM*

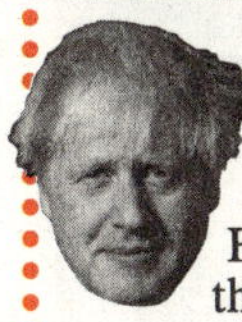

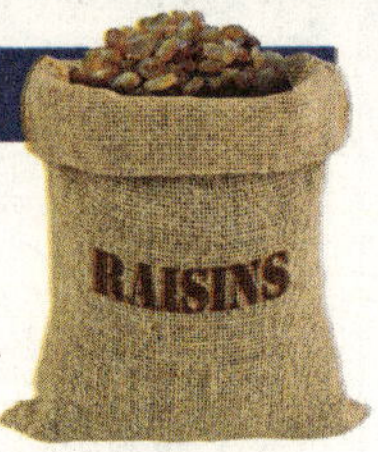
RAISINS

"Nulla res maior creatur quam racemus' – No greater thing is created than a bunch of grapes. So wrote Epicurus in his great work *The Discourses*, and I wholeheartedly agree with him. For it is from the humble grape, my friends, that we are gifted the even humbler raisin, the one ingredient that is truly worthy of being in this balloon basket. I concede that the other potential cake constituents each have their merits, be they superior in taste, flavour or texture. But none is so important as the desiccated fruit of the vine. The raisin is the the stout yeoman of the Yuletide cake, and the other four, alas, must go. Actually, I'm just reading it was Epictetus, not Epicurus who said it. I must of misread it when I Googled 'Latin grape quotes'.

IDRIS ELBA, *still as yet unconfirmed Bond actor*

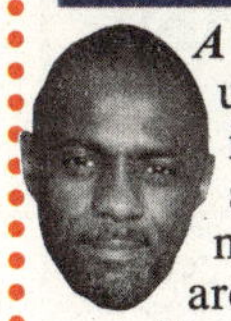

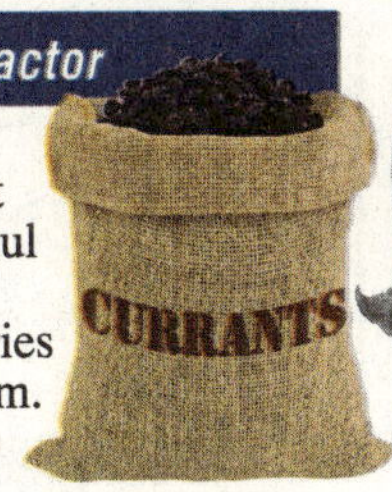
CURRANTS

A Christmas cake without currants is simply unthinkable; they are the one essential ingredient in this balloon. Let's face it, everything else in Paul and Prue's basket is unnecessary. Raisins are neither here nor there in a Christmas cake. Cherries are too divisive; one either loves them or hates them. Nuts – when present – can prove potentially fatal to some individuals, and peel is the part of the orange and lemon that should be thrown away, not put in a cake. No, the one ingredient that any Yuletide cake cannot do without is the dried fruit of the red grape – *currants*. Actually, am I thinking of sultanas? I think I'm thinking of sultanas.

TOM HOLLANDER, *actor in things*

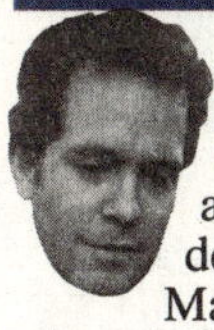

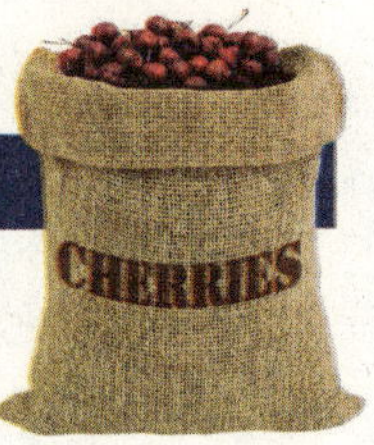
CHERRIES

A Christmas cake without cherries would be just another run-of-the-mill fruit cake – perfectly nice in its own way, moist and perfectly acceptable. But just a fruit cake. It is the deep, rich taste of the cherry – red or black, Marachino or glacé – that truly puts the spirit of the season into this traditional treat and turns a plain old fruit cake into a *Christmas cake*. All the other ingredients – the currants, the nuts, the peel – are mere extras, bit part players supporting the principal actor – *the cherry* – in the spotlight on the glittering Christmas cake stage.

TOMMY WALSH, *TV DIY-er*

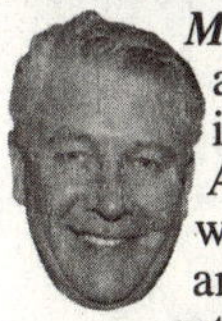

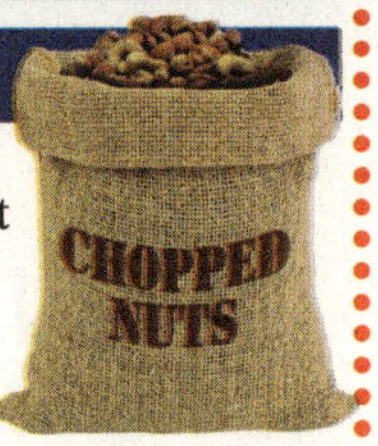
CHOPPED NUTS

Make concrete without any aggregate and it'll be absolutely fine... until you try to pick it up, that is. It'll simply fall apart under its own weight. And the same is true of a Christmas cake without chopped nuts – it looks perfectly good, and it'll even taste good. But as soon as you cut a slice and try to pick up, it'll be nothing but crumbs. Nuts are nature's aggregate, and whilst they don't taste of much, they give structure and rigidity to every festive cake. For this reason if no other, you should keep the nuts in your balloon and throw everything else in the skip.

KATY HOPKINS, *poisonous columnist*

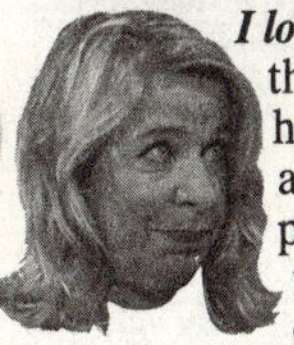

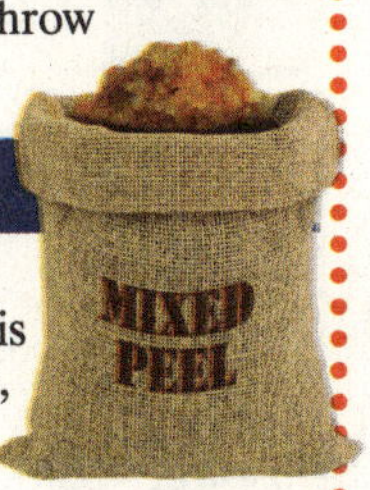
MIXED PEEL

I love mixed peel in a Christmas cake, and that is the main reason why it deserves its place in this hypothetical balloon – because I want it there, and that's that. I don't care what the other people making cases for their ingredients think. They are wrong. And I'm right. They should jump out of the balloon and die and do us all a favour. And if you think that's a little harsh of me, then suck it up. You can jump out with them and die for all I care. And good riddance to all of you.

***Who do YOU think has made the best case for their ingredient?* Fill in the form below and send it in, and we'll write to all the bakers in the country asking them to stop putting the losing ingredients into their Christmas cakes.**

Based on the arguments made in the debate, I think the cake ingredient that deserves to stay in Paul and Pru's hot-air balloon is (tick one box only):

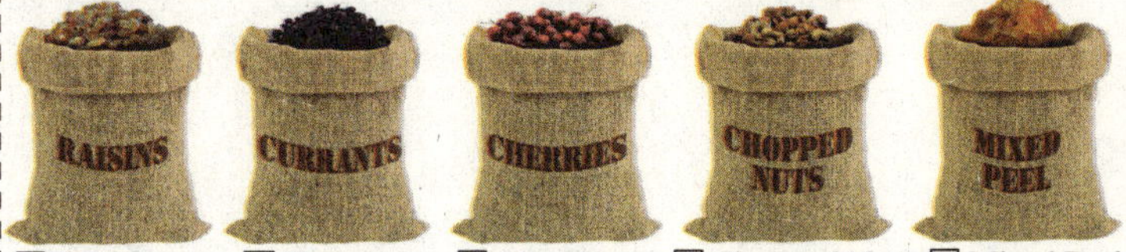
RAISINS
CURRANTS
CHERRIES
CHOPPED NUTS
MIXED PEEL

☐ Raisins ☐ Currants ☐ Cherries ☐ Chopped Nuts ☐ Mixed Peel

Signed .... Print name .... Date ....

☐ *I understand that this is not a real thing and that no action will be taken as a result of me filling in and posting this form. I accept that it is a complete waste of my time and effort, not to mention the cost of a stamp.*

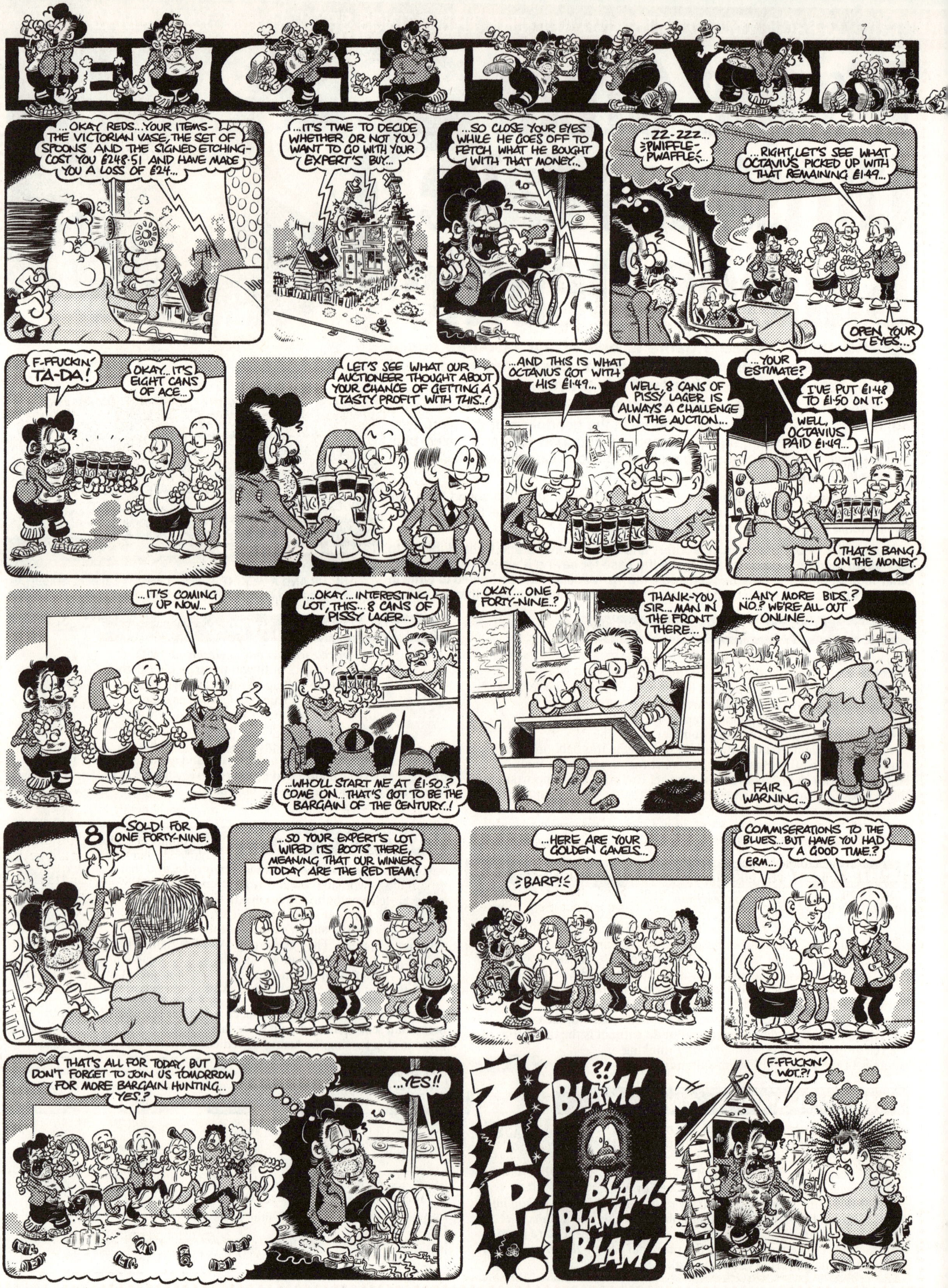

...OKAY REDS... YOUR ITEMS- THE VICTORIAN VASE, THE SET OF SPOONS AND THE SIGNED ETCHING- COST YOU £248·51 AND HAVE MADE YOU A LOSS OF £24...
...IT'S TIME TO DECIDE WHETHER OR NOT YOU WANT TO GO WITH YOUR EXPERT'S BUY...
...SO CLOSE YOUR EYES WHILE HE GOES OFF TO FETCH WHAT HE BOUGHT WITH THAT MONEY...
...ZZ-ZZZ... PWIFFLE-PWAFFLE...
...RIGHT, LET'S SEE WHAT OCTAVIUS PICKED UP WITH THAT REMAINING £1·49...
OPEN YOUR EYES...
F-FFUCKIN' TA-DA!
OKAY... IT'S EIGHT CANS OF ACE...
LET'S SEE WHAT OUR AUCTIONEER THOUGHT ABOUT YOUR CHANCE OF GETTING A TASTY PROFIT WITH THIS..!
...AND THIS IS WHAT OCTAVIUS GOT WITH HIS £1·49...
WELL, 8 CANS OF PISSY LAGER IS ALWAYS A CHALLENGE IN THE AUCTION...
...YOUR ESTIMATE?
I'VE PUT £1·48 TO £1·50 ON IT.
WELL, OCTAVIUS PAID £1·49...
THAT'S BANG ON THE MONEY.
...IT'S COMING UP NOW...
...OKAY... INTERESTING LOT, THIS... 8 CANS OF PISSY LAGER...
...WHO'LL START ME AT £1·50..? COME ON... THAT'S GOT TO BE THE BARGAIN OF THE CENTURY..!
...OKAY... ONE FORTY-NINE..?
THANK-YOU, SIR... MAN IN THE FRONT THERE...
...ANY MORE BIDS..? NO..? WE'RE ALL OUT ONLINE...
FAIR WARNING...
8
SOLD! FOR ONE FORTY-NINE.
...SO YOUR EXPERT'S LOT WIPED ITS BOOTS THERE, MEANING THAT OUR WINNERS TODAY ARE THE RED TEAM!
...HERE ARE YOUR GOLDEN GAVELS...
BARP!
COMMISERATIONS TO THE BLUES... BUT HAVE YOU HAD A GOOD TIME..?
ERM...
THAT'S ALL FOR TODAY, BUT DON'T FORGET TO JOIN US TOMORROW FOR MORE BARGAIN HUNTING... YES..?
...YES!!
ZAP!
?!
BLAM!
BLAM! BLAM! BLAM!
F-FFUCKIN' WOT..?!

"DREAM OF DICK" DEEMED 'INAPPROPRIATE'

Influencer's offer rebuffed by councillors

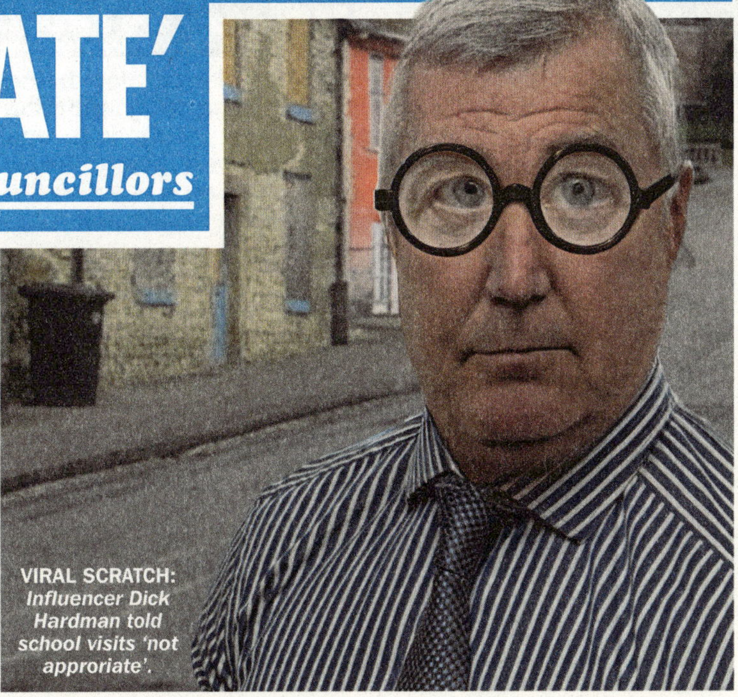

VIRAL SCRATCH: *Influencer Dick Hardman told school visits 'not approriate'.*

SOCIAL media commentator ANDREW TATE grabbed all the headlines recently when he was arrested simply for highlighting the problems and prejudices that men face in the modern world, and on suspicion of some other things. And now a leading Derby-based internet influencer has found himself in similar hot water after generously reaching out to the town's educators.

EXCLUSIVE!

Retired newsagent **DICK HARDMAN** has blasted the "faceless bureaucrats" who have scuppered his plans to project a mindful and positive image of so-called "toxic masculinity" into local schools.

Since 2020 Hardman, 63, has entertained and educated a growing audience of young men on YouTube, Facebook, TikTok and Friendster with videos bemoaning his lot, and the plight of modern males in general. And he believes his heartfelt message of empowerment needs to be heard by a wider, even younger audience.

radish

At first, Dick's rage was focused on his long-suffering wife Susan, who he humorously berated in series of light-heartedly aggressive posts for failing to meet what he described as her 'wifely obligations'. The furious, expletive-filled rants were an instant success, clocking-up dozens of hits and giving him his first taste of fame and power.

"It was incredible," laughs the former Rotarian. "I went all at once from being a complete nobody to someone who couldn't leave the house to go to the corner shop for a few cans without people I knew shouting 'hello' and waving."

Susan left the family home on Christmas Day evening in 2021 to live with her sister in Tipton, following a disagreement over the washing-up. Lacking any other immediate source of relatable content for his regular internet posts, the influencer began posting clips in which he humorously berated women in general for failing to meet what he described as 'their womanly obligations'.

"The missus leaving actually made things better for me, because it meant I could come in out of the shed and film my clips in the lounge," he says. "And if I thought things were crazy before, I soon realised they weren't crazy at all, because they went really crazy then."

Instead of just dozens of views, Hardman's expletive-filled posts went viral, suddenly getting *several* dozens. Soon, thanks to his new-found fame and notoriety, it became nearly impossible to live a normal life in the small Derbyshire village he calls home.

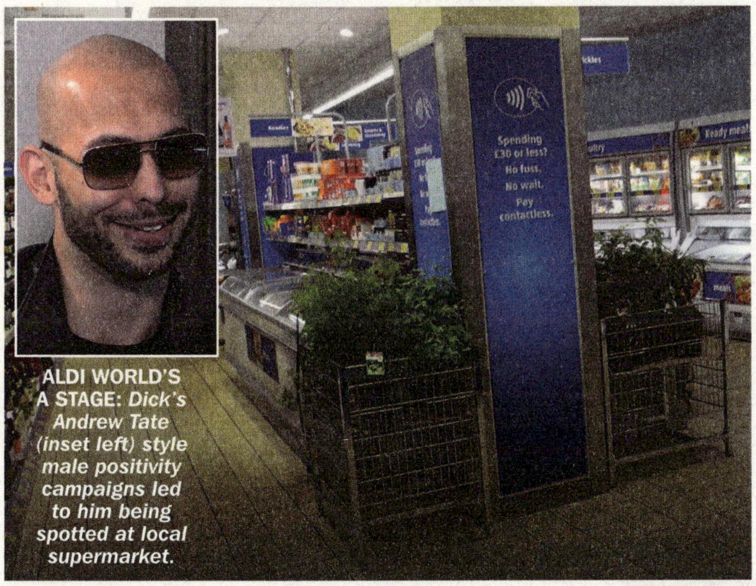

Spending £30 or less? No fuss. No wait. Pay contactless.

ALDI WORLD'S A STAGE: *Dick's Andrew Tate (inset left) style male positivity campaigns led to him being spotted at local supermarket.*

"Once, in the big Aldi, I turned quickly away from the eggs and saw a man pointing me out while whispering to a woman I presume to have been his wife," he reminisces. "And one of the workers there wouldn't take their eyes off me when I had been hanging round the spirits section for ten minutes."

"It's the price of fame, I suppose."

harbinger

As he increasingly perceived men's rights to be ebbing away due to 'wokeness' and 'political correctness gone mad', the earlier humorous aspects of Dick's posts gradually fell away. Clips where he concentrated on seriously criticising women and urging his fellow men to lift weights, eat beef and demand respect quickly racked up dozens of views. And he now claims that his homespun male philosophy has built a dedicated global following, many of whom live in America.

"Do you want to see the numbers? I can show you the numbers," Dick says, scrolling through his three-digit internet stats. "There's one bloke in Kentucky sends me scores of messages every single night."

"Once you crack the States, there's no limit, and it's fair to say that just like that kickboxer fella I've become an international phenomena," he says.

But despite his global profile, he insists that he is still the same person he always was. "First and foremost, I'm a local man," he insists. "I did twenty years in the Derby Rotarians, and you don't get that under your belt by being an arsehole."

"I've always wanted to put something back into my community, and it struck me that one way to do this was to reach out to the impressionable boys of Derbyshire, before their young minds become crammed with book-learning, so-called 'political correctness' and the effeminacy that this modern namby-pamby mindset inevitably breeds."

omelette

Hardman's idea was to simply go into classrooms, sit where the teacher sits, and pass on his empowering message of self-respect, male pride and paternal family values first-hand. But his selfless dream lies in ruins after councillors rejected his plan in a coldly-worded letter sent last week.

"I had offered to go round the local schools spreading my message of hope and masculine empowerment," he says. "But instead of jumping at the chance, they sent me a letter, signed by some faceless bureaucrat whose name I'd never even heard of, someone not even remotely famous on TikTok, saying that it was 'not appropriate' for me to visit local schools."

"No apology, no best wishes, no offer to work alongside me and develop my vision. Just 'not appropriate'," he says, shaking his head in disbelief.

"Talk about looking a gift horse in the mouth. They've got a worldwide internet sensation on their doorstep offering his time and experience for nothing more than expenses and an hourly rate befitting my global reach, plus a few cans, and that's all they can find to say."

"I don't know why I bother, really I don't."

GAMBLE AND WIN!

Bookie sparks controversy by revealing industry secrets

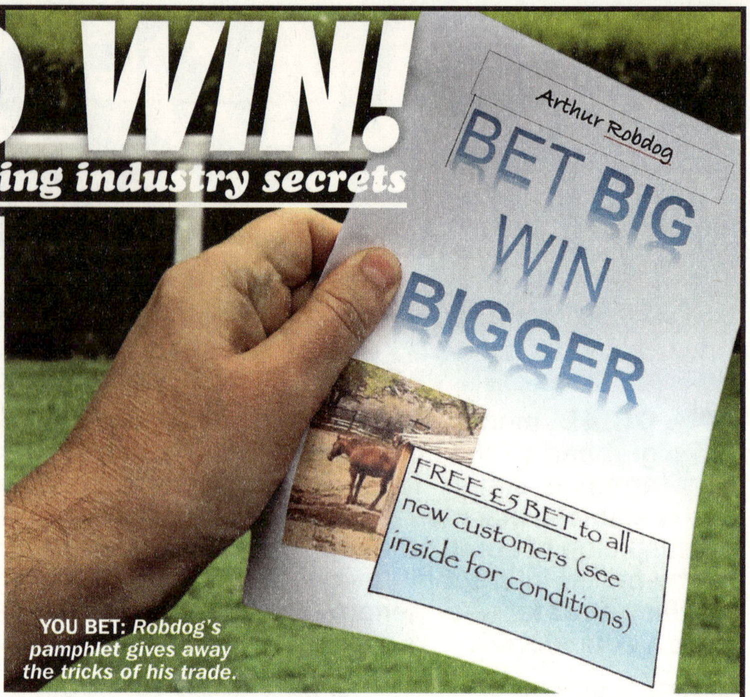
Arthur Robdog
BET BIG
WIN
BIGGER
FREE £5 BET to all new customers (see inside for conditions)

YOU BET: *Robdog's pamphlet gives away the tricks of his trade.*

THE betting industry is often blamed for being responsible for a massive rise in gambling addiction and all the family breakdown, alcoholism and resultant misery that it entails. But if only people knew how gambling worked, they would see that it is a surefire way to achieve riches beyond their wildest dreams.

This is according to **ARTHUR ROBDOG**, a trackside racecourse bookmaker, who last week published a pamphlet explaining how to beat the bookies like himself. And in what can only be a described as a staggering own goal, the pamphlet, which Robdog is giving away free to all his customers this season, explains how gambling on horses works, and shows punters how easy it is to tip the odds in their favour and win every time.

peculiar

"People say gambling is a mug's game. But to be honest, the real mugs are the bookies like me," Robdog said. "Honestly, you wouldn't believe how much I pay out to my punters at every meeting. It's a wonder I make a living at all, honestly, which I don't, to be honest."

And Robdog explained whilst all of his customers were laughing all the way to the bank, some were laughing louder than others. "Honestly, the ones who take the most off me are the ones who come to every race and always put big money down." he said. "Not the amateurs who turn up once, put a couple of quid on the favourite, and go home. They don't win Jack shit."

"Honestly, the ones who put big money on accumulators, they're the ones who clean me out," he admitted. "Them, and the ones who chase their losses. Not that there are many losses, to be honest."

bovril

"Honestly, nobody will ever make money as a bookie as long as they've got a hole in their arse," he lamented.

"Honestly, all us bookies should get out of this game before the punters finish us off," he said from the terrace of his modest 8-bedroom house in Kensington.

And the pamphlet, called *Bet Big, Win Bigger* explains just how easy it is to turn a month's rent or weekly food shop into a small fortune in just one visit to the race course. "It explains exactly how to take money off idiot bookies like me. It's like taking candy from a baby," he said. "I'm not very popular with my trackside colleagues after producing this pamphlet, to be honest."

And in what can only be described as another financially suicidal move, Robdog is offering a **FREE £5 BET** to any new customer who spends £100 opening an account with him next time he is trackside.

"I realise that such a good offer is open to abuse, with people opening several £100 accounts just to get the free bets. But I say good for them, to be honest. If I'm daft enough to give my money away like that, then go for it," he said.

"Honestly, I might as well cut my own throat."

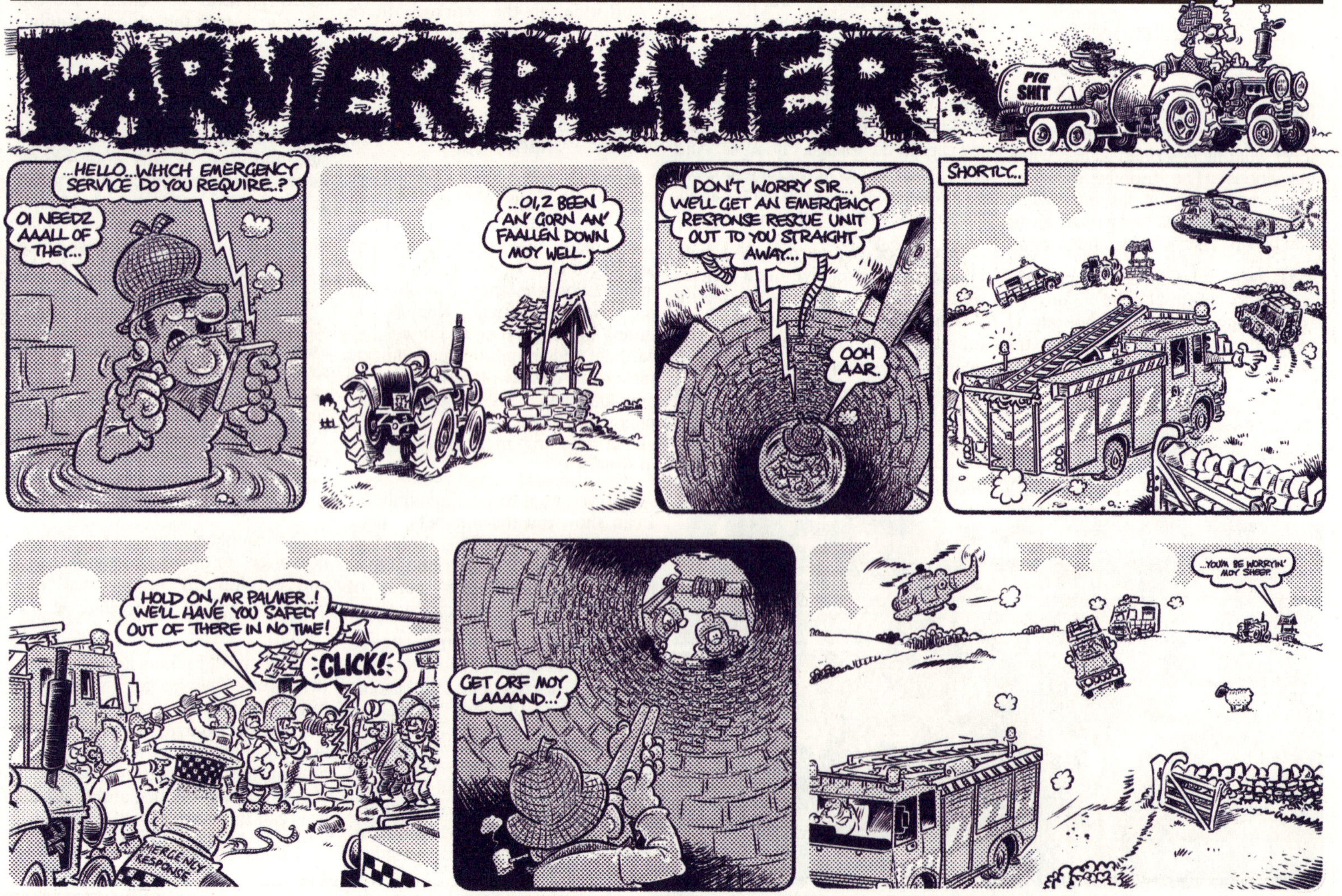
FARMER PALMER
PIG SHIT
...HELLO...WHICH EMERGENCY SERVICE DO YOU REQUIRE..?
OI NEEDZ AAALL OF THEY...
...OI, 2 BEEN AN' GORN AN' FAALLEN DOWN MOY WELL.
DON'T WORRY SIR... WE'LL GET AN EMERGENCY RESPONSE RESCUE UNIT OUT TO YOU STRAIGHT AWAY...
OOH AAR.
SHORTLY...
HOLD ON, MR PALMER..! WE'LL HAVE YOU SAFELY OUT OF THERE IN NO TIME!
CLICK!
EMERGENCY RESPONSE
GET ORF MOY LAAAAND..!
...YOU'M BE WORRYIN' MOY SHEEP.

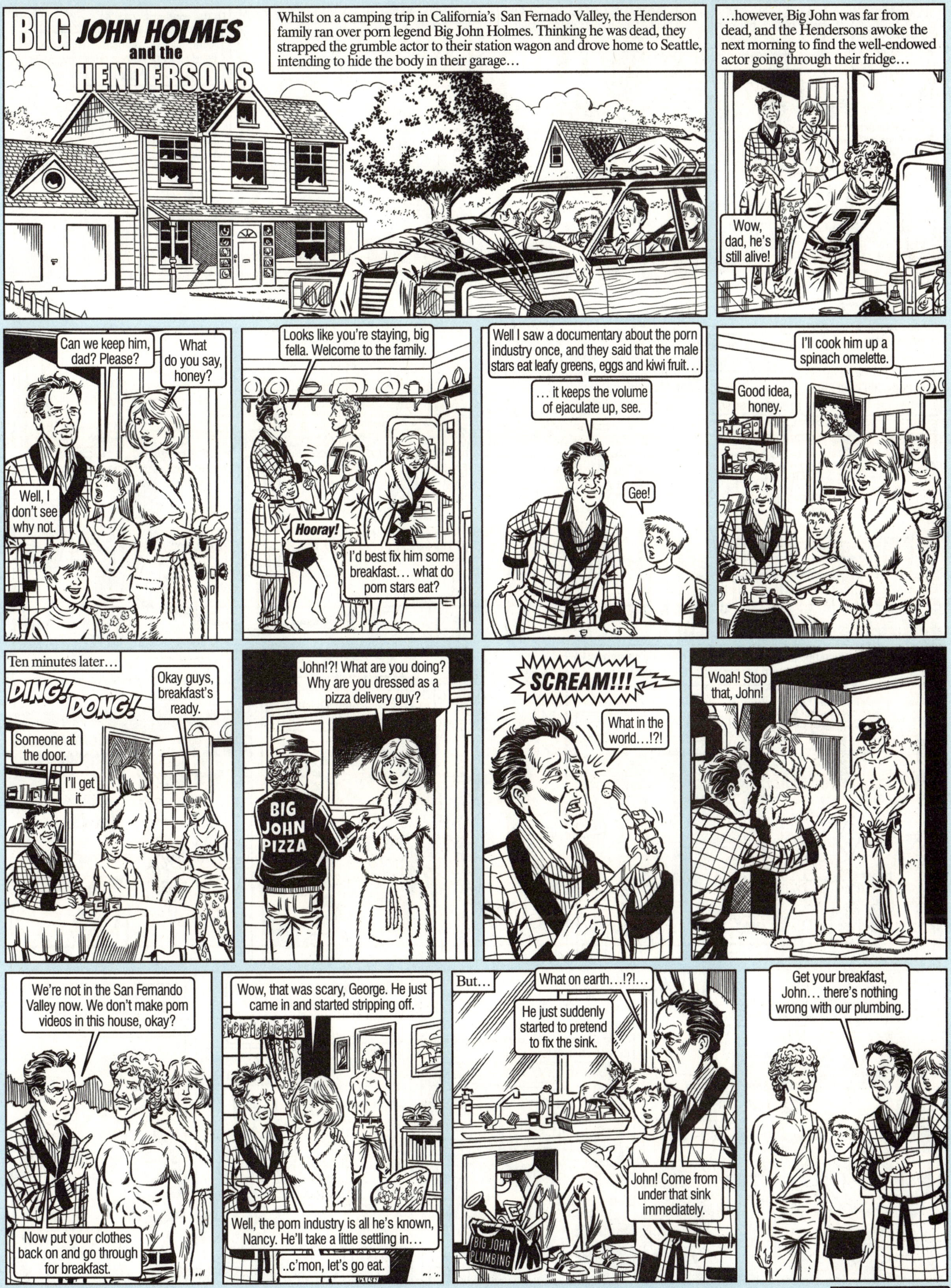

BIG JOHN HOLMES and the HENDERSONS
Whilst on a camping trip in California's San Fernado Valley, the Henderson family ran over porn legend Big John Holmes. Thinking he was dead, they strapped the grumble actor to their station wagon and drove home to Seattle, intending to hide the body in their garage…
…however, Big John was far from dead, and the Hendersons awoke the next morning to find the well-endowed actor going through their fridge…
Wow, dad, he's still alive!
Can we keep him, dad? Please?
What do you say, honey?
Well, I don't see why not.
Looks like you're staying, big fella. Welcome to the family.
Hooray!
I'd best fix him some breakfast… what do porn stars eat?
Well I saw a documentary about the porn industry once, and they said that the male stars eat leafy greens, eggs and kiwi fruit…
… it keeps the volume of ejaculate up, see.
Gee!
I'll cook him up a spinach omelette.
Good idea, honey.
Ten minutes later…
DING! DONG!
Okay guys, breakfast's ready.
Someone at the door.
I'll get it.
John!?! What are you doing? Why are you dressed as a pizza delivery guy?
BIG JOHN PIZZA
SCREAM!!!
What in the world…!?!
Woah! Stop that, John!
We're not in the San Fernando Valley now. We don't make porn videos in this house, okay?
Now put your clothes back on and go through for breakfast.
Wow, that was scary, George. He just came in and started stripping off.
Well, the porn industry is all he's known, Nancy. He'll take a little settling in…
..c'mon, let's go eat.
But…
What on earth…!?!…
He just suddenly started to pretend to fix the sink.
John! Come from under that sink immediately.
BIG JOHN PLUMBING
Get your breakfast, John… there's nothing wrong with our plumbing.

Continued over...

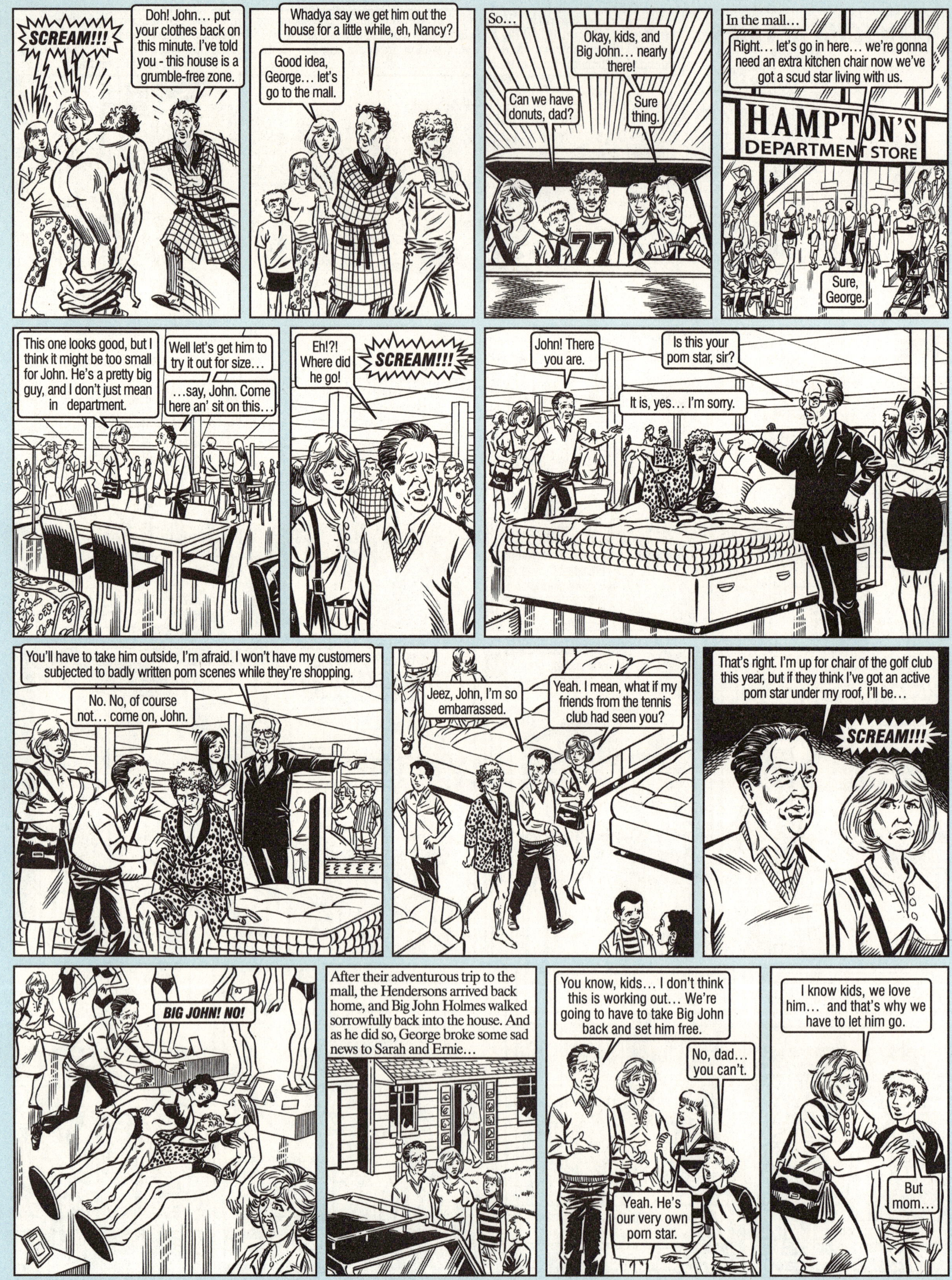
SCREAM!!!
Doh! John… put your clothes back on this minute. I've told you - this house is a grumble-free zone.
Whadya say we get him out the house for a little while, eh, Nancy?
Good idea, George… let's go to the mall.
So…
Okay, kids, and Big John… nearly there!
Can we have donuts, dad?
Sure thing.
77
In the mall…
Right… let's go in here… we're gonna need an extra kitchen chair now we've got a scud star living with us.
HAMPTON'S DEPARTMENT STORE
Sure, George.
This one looks good, but I think it might be too small for John. He's a pretty big guy, and I don't just mean in department.
Well let's get him to try it out for size…
…say, John. Come here an' sit on this…
Eh!?! Where did he go!
SCREAM!!!
John! There you are.
Is this your porn star, sir?
It is, yes… I'm sorry.
You'll have to take him outside, I'm afraid. I won't have my customers subjected to badly written porn scenes while they're shopping.
No. No, of course not… come on, John.
Jeez, John, I'm so embarrassed.
Yeah. I mean, what if my friends from the tennis club had seen you?
That's right. I'm up for chair of the golf club this year, but if they think I've got an active porn star under my roof, I'll be…
SCREAM!!!
BIG JOHN! NO!
After their adventurous trip to the mall, the Hendersons arrived back home, and Big John Holmes walked sorrowfully back into the house. And as he did so, George broke some sad news to Sarah and Ernie…
You know, kids… I don't think this is working out… We're going to have to take Big John back and set him free.
No, dad… you can't.
Yeah. He's our very own porn star.
I know kids, we love him… and that's why we have to let him go.
But mom…

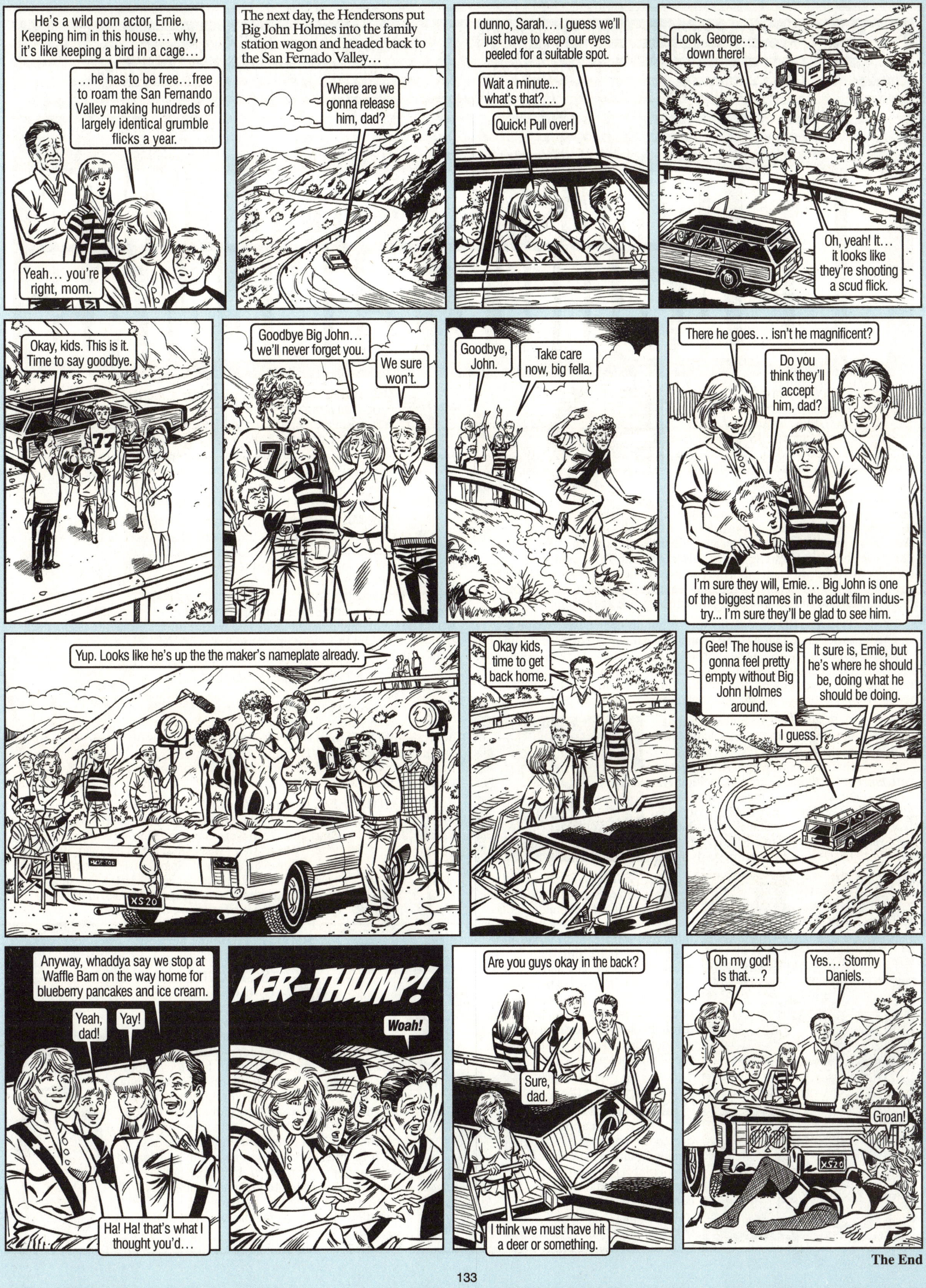
He's a wild porn actor, Ernie. Keeping him in this house… why, it's like keeping a bird in a cage…
…he has to be free…free to roam the San Fernando Valley making hundreds of largely identical grumble flicks a year.
Yeah… you're right, mom.
The next day, the Hendersons put Big John Holmes into the family station wagon and headed back to the San Fernando Valley…
Where are we gonna release him, dad?
I dunno, Sarah… I guess we'll just have to keep our eyes peeled for a suitable spot.
Wait a minute... what's that?…
Quick! Pull over!
Look, George… down there!
Oh, yeah! It… it looks like they're shooting a scud flick.
Okay, kids. This is it. Time to say goodbye.
Goodbye Big John… we'll never forget you.
We sure won't.
Goodbye, John.
Take care now, big fella.
There he goes… isn't he magnificent?
Do you think they'll accept him, dad?
I'm sure they will, Ernie… Big John is one of the biggest names in the adult film industry... I'm sure they'll be glad to see him.
Yup. Looks like he's up the the maker's nameplate already.
XS20
Okay kids, time to get back home.
Gee! The house is gonna feel pretty empty without Big John Holmes around.
It sure is, Ernie, but he's where he should be, doing what he should be doing.
I guess.
Anyway, whaddya say we stop at Waffle Barn on the way home for blueberry pancakes and ice cream.
Yeah, dad!
Yay!
Ha! Ha! that's what I thought you'd…
KER-THUMP!
Woah!
Are you guys okay in the back?
Sure, dad.
I think we must have hit a deer or something.
Oh my god! Is that…?
Yes… Stormy Daniels.
Groan!
XS20

The End

PICTURE houses, movie theatres, film palaces. Call them what you will, but all of those are wrong. They are CINEMAS, and chances are that wherever you live in Britain, you are no more than twenty miles from one, possibly more in the Highlands of Scotland or on one of them little islands right up at the top. The cinema is a place to gather with friends, watch the latest Hollywood blockbuster and buy bladder-bursting amounts of watered-down generic cola, and we love it. But how much do we actually know about these enormous, lightless buildings sitting on the edges of retail parks? What are they made of? Who owns them? And why is the pick'n'mix sold at prices you wouldn't otherwise expect to see until the year 2099 at least? Read and learn as we bring you...

10 THINGS YOU NEVER KNEW ABOUT CINEMAS

1 **THE VERY** first film to play in a cinema was titled *L'Arrivée d'un Train en Gare de La Ciotat*, made in 1895 and shown at the Crewe Odeon. The film was only 50 seconds long, and showed a train pulling into a railway station in France. Nobody had ever seen moving pictures before, and the film caused the audience to flee in terror as the train approached. And they were right to do so. Because the movie theatre had been built alongside the main Crewe to Stoke railway line, and by a remarkable coincidence a freight train on its way south derailed and crashed through the back wall of the cinema at the exact same moment that the train on screen arrived at the station, ploughing through the auditorium.

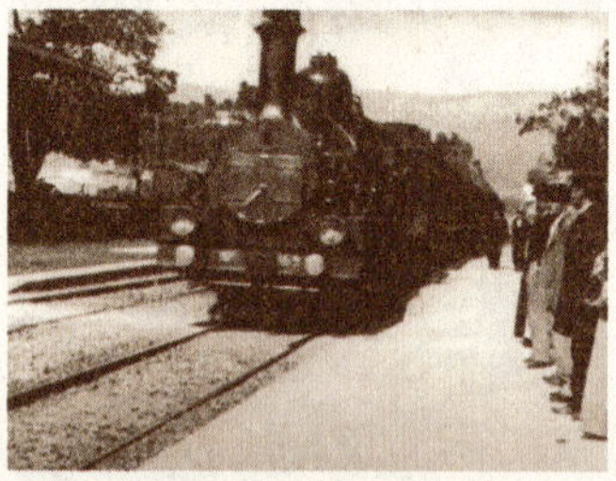

2 **THE WORD** 'cinematic' was originally coined to describe any experience that has the visual or aesthetic qualities of a film. However, it can also be used to describe an experience that is a bit like being in a cinema, such as having someone repeatedly kick the back of your chair, flash their iPhone torch in your face while trying to find a seat, or asking you to stand up so they can go to the toilet.

3 **IT'S A WIDELY** known fact that most, if not all cinemas have films in them. But what's less known is there have also been several *films* with *cinemas* in them. Examples include *The Cinema Murder* (1919), *Cinema Paradiso* (1988) and *The Cinema: A Brief History of World Cinema* (2013). Ironically, that last one wasn't even shown in cinemas... *It went straight to DVD!* You couldn't make it up.

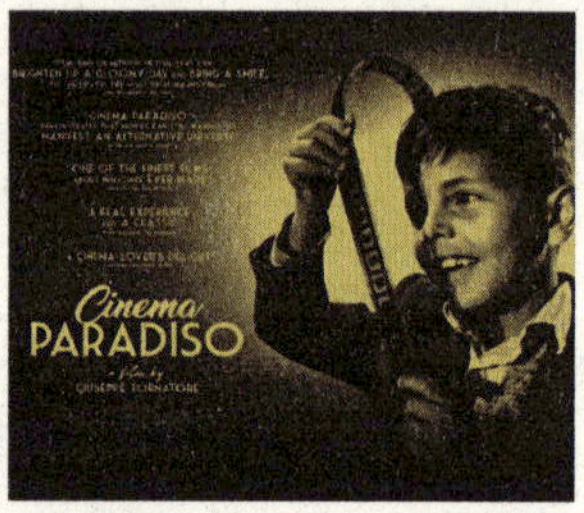
Cinema
PARADISO

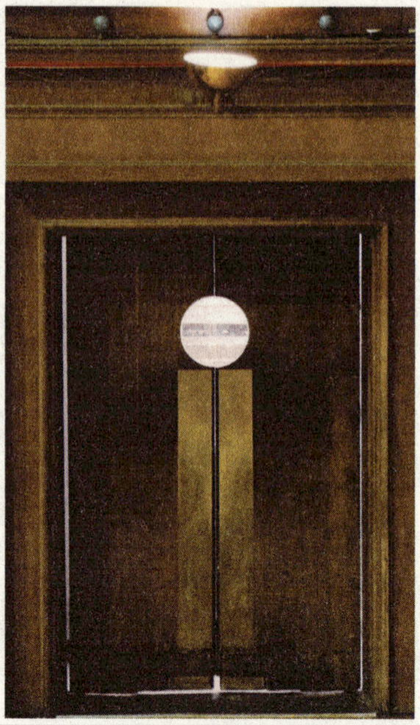

4 **EVERY** cinema in the UK is accessed via a door at the front of the building; once you go through it, you may think that you are safely inside and ready to watch the film. But you'd be wrong. That door only allows access to the *foyer* – the place where you meet your friends, get your ticket and buy your film snacks. You have to go through a *second* door in order to get into the darkened theatre where the film is shown.

5 **ALL THE DOORS** in cinemas are able to open and close due to the presence of hinges – pairs of articulated metal plates fixed to both the door and the frame, connected by an interlocking pin about which the two plates rotate.

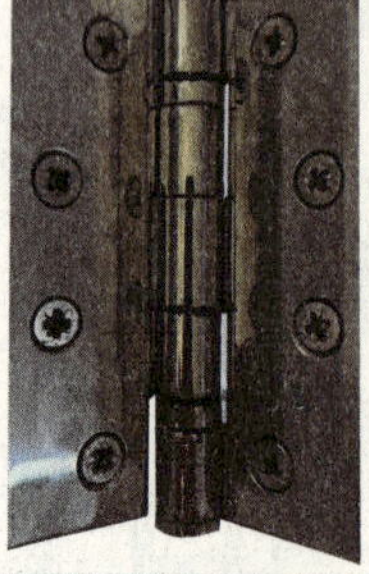

6 **THE WORLD** record for Loudest In-Cinema Food Consumption was set in 2001 by Wisconsin resident 'Big' Ed McCulloch. During a screening of *Nutty Professor 2: The Klumps* at his local Wisconsin Odeon, McCulloch consumed one extra large bucket of caramel butter popcorn and two bags of 'Swedish Fish' candy, masticating at a level of 97.3 decibels – slightly louder than a motorcycle engine.

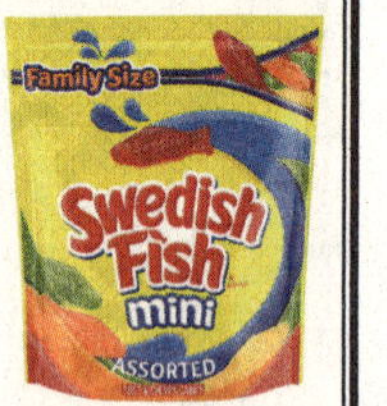
Family Size
Swedish Fish
mini
ASSORTED

7 **THE MASSIVE** 815m^2 screen in the Traumpalast Leonberg cineplex in Germany is the largest cinema screen in the world. Measuring 20m tall and 38.8m across, it is longer than a Boeing 737 airliner, and covers the size of a 5-a-side football pitch. To put it into perspective, were the cinema to screen a Big John Holmes film, such as *Saturday Night Beaver* or *Fiesta of Flesh*, the actor's famously garagantuan member would be 3.9m long in a full length body shot on the soft, and 43m in a close up where it was on the bonk, filling the screen from corner to corner.

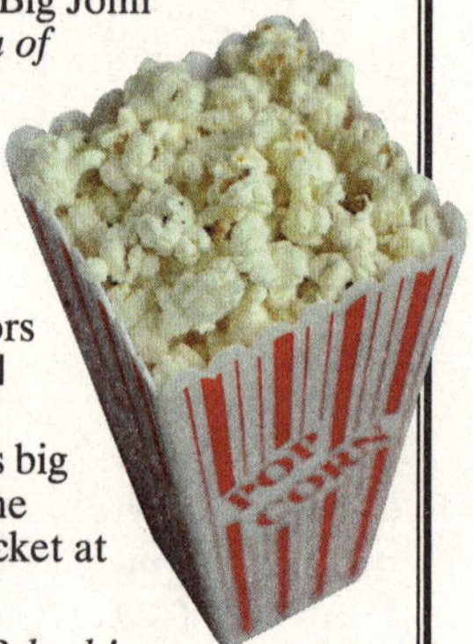

8 **SCIENTISTS** estimate that the total amount of popcorn spilled on cinema floors across the globe every year would fill **TEN** Wales-sized Wembley Stadiums. That's equivalent to **FIFTEEN** Olympic swimming pools as big as China, **TWENTY-FIVE** double decker buses to the moon and back, or **ONE** medium-sized popcorn bucket at your local multiplex.

9 **WITH THEIR** famous *Pah! Pah! Pah-ah! Pah-ah! Pah-ah! Pah! Pah! Pah!* theme tune, cinema advertising gurus Pearl and Dean were the most famous double act where one of them was called Dean for over 30 years. However, all that changed in 1984 when a little-known pair of ice dancers – Jayne Torvill and Christopher Dean – turned the world upside down with a perfect score of 6.0 across the board with their rendition of Ravel's *Bolero* at the Sarajevo Winter Olympics.

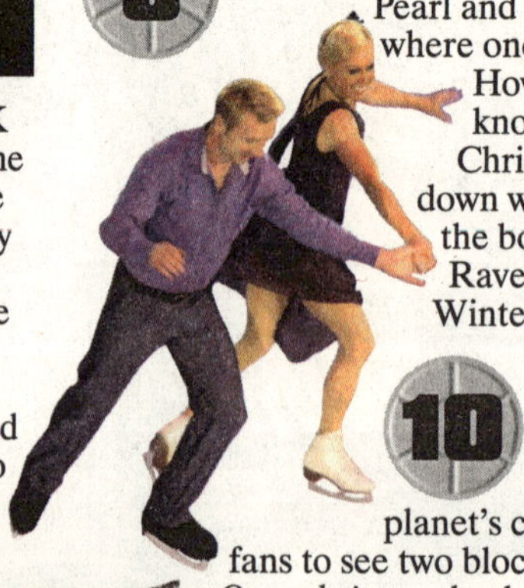

10 **THE RECENT** 'BarbenHeimer' phenomenon fuelled a huge boom for the planet's cinemas, encouraging film fans to see two blockbusters – *Barbie* and *Oppenheimer* – back-to-back at their local picture house. However, it was not the first time cinemas have attempted a dual-movie marketing campaign. In 2004, multiplexes around the globe spent billions promoting 'PassionPotato' – twin screenings of Mel Gibson's brutal religious epic *The Passion of the Christ* and Johnny Vegas's raunchy veg comedy *Sex Lives of the Potato Men*. Unfortunately, 'PassionPotato' failed to grasp the public imagination in quite the same way as 'BarbenHeimer', and cinemas suffered significant losses worldwide.

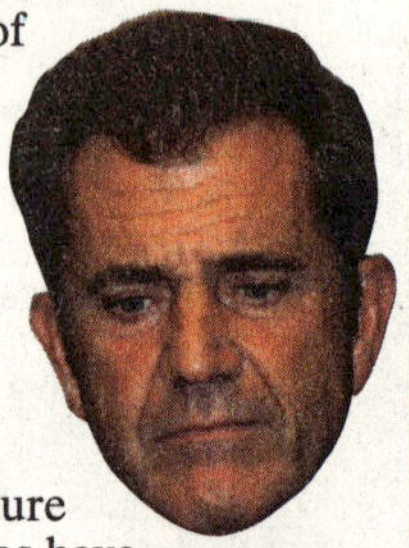

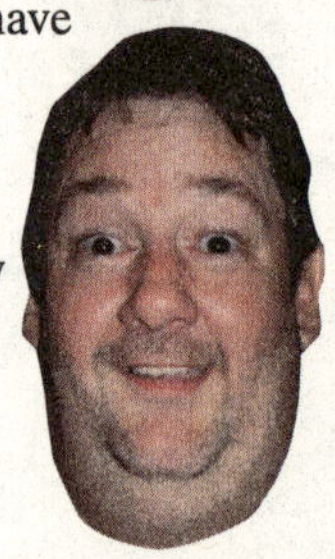

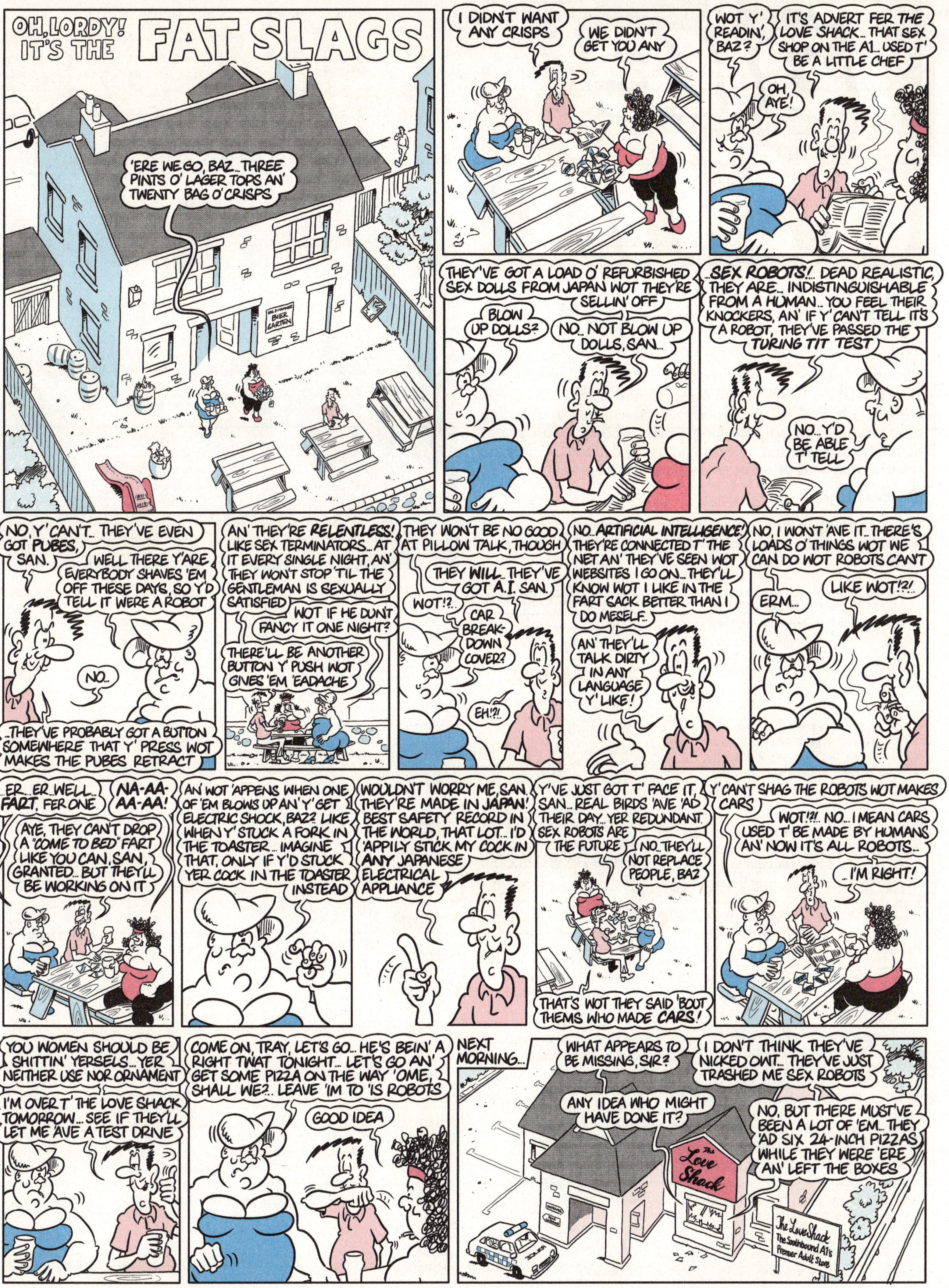

OH, LORDY! IT'S THE FAT SLAGS
'ERE WE GO, BAZ... THREE PINTS O' LAGER TOPS AN' TWENTY BAG O' CRISPS
BIER GARTEN
I DIDN'T WANT ANY CRISPS
WE DIDN'T GET YOU ANY
WOT Y' READIN', BAZ?
IT'S ADVERT FER THE LOVE SHACK... THAT SEX SHOP ON THE A1... USED T' BE A LITTLE CHEF
OH, AYE!
THEY'VE GOT A LOAD O' REFURBISHED SEX DOLLS FROM JAPAN WOT THEY'RE SELLIN' OFF
BLOW UP DOLLS?
NO... NOT BLOW UP DOLLS, SAN...
...SEX ROBOTS!... DEAD REALISTIC, THEY ARE... INDISTINGUISHABLE FROM A HUMAN... YOU FEEL THEIR KNOCKERS, AN' IF Y' CAN'T TELL IT'S A ROBOT, THEY'VE PASSED THE TURING TIT TEST
NO... Y'D BE ABLE T' TELL
NO, Y' CAN'T... THEY'VE EVEN GOT PUBES, SAN.
...WELL THERE Y'ARE, EVERYBODY SHAVES 'EM OFF THESE DAYS, SO Y'D TELL IT WERE A ROBOT
NO...
...THEY'VE PROBABLY GOT A BUTTON SOMEWHERE THAT Y' PRESS WOT MAKES THE PUBES RETRACT
AN' THEY'RE RELENTLESS! LIKE SEX TERMINATORS... AT IT EVERY SINGLE NIGHT, AN' THEY WON'T STOP 'TIL THE GENTLEMAN IS SEXUALLY SATISFIED
WOT IF HE DON'T FANCY IT ONE NIGHT?
THERE'LL BE ANOTHER BUTTON Y' PUSH WOT GIVES 'EM 'EADACHE
THEY WON'T BE NO GOOD AT PILLOW TALK, THOUGH
THEY WILL... THEY'VE GOT A.I., SAN.
WOT!?
CAR BREAK-DOWN COVER?
EH!?!
NO... ARTIFICIAL INTELLIGENCE! THEY'RE CONNECTED T' THE NET AN' THEY'VE SEEN WOT WEBSITES I GO ON... THEY'LL KNOW WOT I LIKE IN THE FART SACK BETTER THAN I DO MESELF...
AN' THEY'LL TALK DIRTY IN ANY LANGUAGE Y' LIKE!
NO, I WON'T 'AVE IT... THERE'S LOADS O' THINGS WOT WE CAN DO WOT ROBOTS CAN'T
ERM...
LIKE WOT!?!
...ER... ER... WELL... FART, FER ONE
NA-AA-AA-AA!
AYE, THEY CAN'T DROP A 'COME TO BED' FART LIKE YOU CAN, SAN, GRANTED... BUT THEY'LL BE WORKING ON IT
AN' WOT 'APPENS WHEN ONE OF 'EM BLOWS UP AN' Y' GET ELECTRIC SHOCK, BAZ? LIKE WHEN Y' STUCK A FORK IN THE TOASTER... IMAGINE THAT, ONLY IF Y'D STUCK YER COCK IN THE TOASTER INSTEAD
WOULDN'T WORRY ME, SAN. THEY'RE MADE IN JAPAN! BEST SAFETY RECORD IN THE WORLD, THAT LOT... I'D 'APPILY STICK MY COCK IN ANY JAPANESE ELECTRICAL APPLIANCE
Y'VE JUST GOT T' FACE IT, SAN... REAL BIRDS 'AVE 'AD THEIR DAY... YER REDUNDANT. SEX ROBOTS ARE THE FUTURE
NO... THEY'LL NOT REPLACE PEOPLE, BAZ
THAT'S WOT THEY SAID 'BOUT THEMS WHO MADE CARS!
Y' CAN'T SHAG THE ROBOTS WOT MAKES CARS
...WOT!?!... NO... I MEAN CARS USED T' BE MADE BY HUMANS AN' NOW IT'S ALL ROBOTS...
...I'M RIGHT!
YOU WOMEN SHOULD BE SHITTIN' YERSELS... YER NEITHER USE NOR ORNAMENT
I'M OVER T' THE LOVE SHACK TOMORROW... SEE IF THEY'LL LET ME 'AVE A TEST DRIVE
COME ON, TRAY, LET'S GO... HE'S BEIN' A RIGHT TWAT TONIGHT... LET'S GO AN' GET SOME PIZZA ON THE WAY 'OME, SHALL WE?... LEAVE 'IM TO 'IS ROBOTS
GOOD IDEA
NEXT MORNING...
WHAT APPEARS TO BE MISSING, SIR?
I DON'T THINK THEY'VE NICKED OWT... THEY'VE JUST TRASHED ME SEX ROBOTS
ANY IDEA WHO MIGHT HAVE DONE IT?
NO, BUT THERE MUST'VE BEEN A LOT OF 'EM... THEY 'AD SIX 24-INCH PIZZAS WHILE THEY WERE 'ERE AN' LEFT THE BOXES
The Love Shack
The Love Shack
The Southbound A1's Premier Adult Store

Take a Shit

COMMENDED MAGAZINE OF THE YEAR ~Take a Shit Magazine of the Year Awards

PAPERBAC

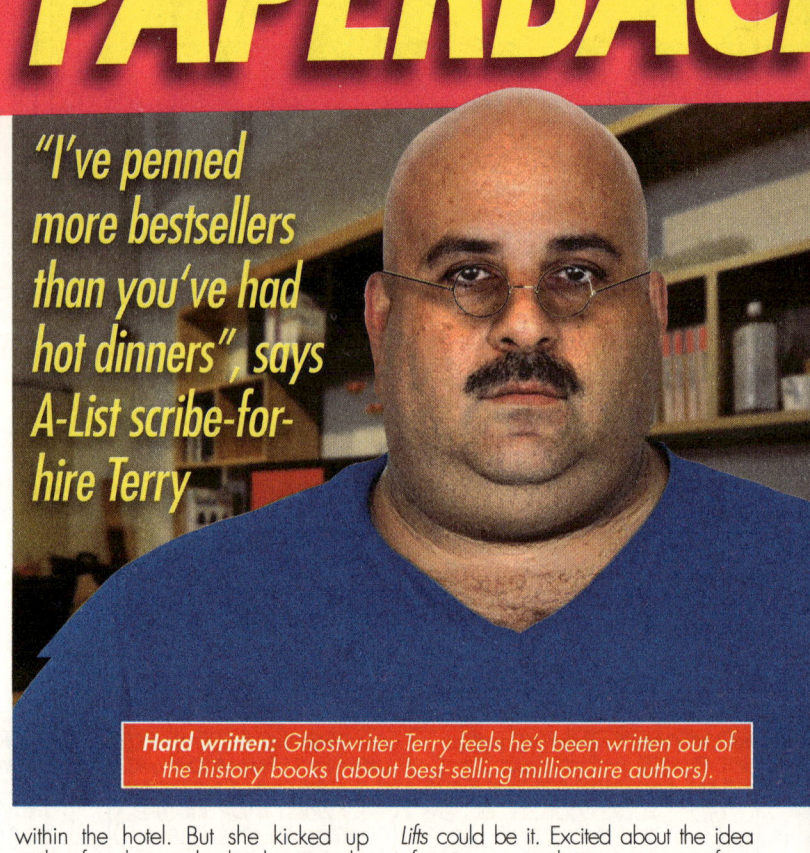

"I've penned more bestsellers than you've had hot dinners", says A-List scribe-for-hire Terry

Hard written: Ghostwriter Terry feels he's been written out of the history books (about best-selling millionaire authors).

WHETHER we're setting off on a long train journey, cosying up with a cuppa on the sofa, or simply voiding our bowels on the thunderbox, there's no better accompanying activity than READING A BOOK.

Via the powerful imaginations of top authors like JK ROWLING, GEORGE RR MARTIN and JEFFREY ARCHER, we are whisked off on wondrous adventures in dazzling new worlds. The page-turning stories of these wordsmiths have enlightened and entertained us for decades, and these creative geniuses deserve every penny of their vast fortunes.

Or do they?

For according to one clinically obese Kippax sex offender, every bestseller in your local Waterstones or WH Smith is in fact written by someone else... HIM!

"If you've read it, I probably wrote it," chuckles 67-year-old **TERRY LOCKTITE**. "Comedies, thrillers, detective novels, them *Game of Thrones* and *Harry Potter* ones, the lot – I've knocked all of them out and more, for some of the biggest names in the book biz."

Thrice-divorced Terry is what is known in the publishing industry as a 'ghostwriter' – a freelance pen-for-hire who supplies manuscripts that are officially credited to another author. And while it's widely known that celebrities use ghostwriters to produce their autobiographies, what is LESS widely known is that many of the planet's most celebrated *novelists* are in fact publishing Terry's work under their own names!

"I've technically won the Booker Prize sixteen times," sighs the jobless dad-of-nine. "I wrote *Life of Pi* 'by' Yann Martel and *The Remains Of The Day* 'by' Kazuo Ishiguro, among others. I've done finger speech marks around 'by' there to indicate that those books are not actually by those people. They're by me: Terry Locktite."

But despite having sold an estimated **20 BILLION** novels worldwide, Terry has never seen a **PENNY** from his ink-spattered endeavours. "I'm on the bones of my arse," he sobs. "All because these publishing bigwigs want to keep up the pretence that their clients are 'talented authors'."

"And I've done finger speech marks again around 'talented authors' because they're nothing of the fucking sort," he clarifies.

Having had his fill of telling other people's stories, Terry is now finally ready to tell his own – *in an exclusive interview*

As told to Vaginia Discharge

with a reporter who was sat next to him on a bus and couldn't get away.

KING'S RANSOM

Terry's ghostwriting career began in earnest in 1976, just after he married his first wife, Sally. And unlike his marriage, his first book proved to be a tremendous success, albeit for someone else. "Sally was my childhood sweetheart," Terry says, smiling wistfully as he opens a can of white cider to aid the flow of memories.

"We had a smashing wedding, and for our honeymoon, we'd gone to this little seaside hotel in Hornsea. The place looked great when I booked it, but when we arrived there, my surroundings began to have a strange effect on me.

I knew I was there to enjoy a romantic week with my beloved new wife. But it was as if the hotel itself was *controlling* me somehow – brainwashing me into acting completely out of character.

One night, for instance, I drank ten cans of white cider and playfully goosed the receptionist's arse. Another night, I was violently ejected from a local strip club for 'excessive arse-goosing.'

I tried to explain to Sally that I was a mere puppet under the sinister force within the hotel. But she kicked up such a fuss that we had to leave early. When we got home, I knew I had to document this bizarre and frightening experience, so I began writing it down.

I've always loved literature, from the sonnets of Shakespeare to the collected works of Jeremy Clarkson, so it wasn't long before my imagination began running wild. From this initial concept of a hotel that drives a man crackers, I began conjuring a spine-chilling horror story unlike any other. I chucked in a load of hoary old shite about a boy who can see the future and a lift full of blood and what have you – and wallop! Soon enough, I had finished my first book! I titled it simply *The Hotel With All Blood In The Lifts*.

> I sent the manuscript to a top literary agent, whose name I can't recall at present, but who definitely exists

I sent the manuscript to a top literary agent, whose name I can't recall at present, but who definitely exists. She confirmed my suspicion that the book was a masterpiece. However, she also outlined the struggles that debut authors face in getting their voices heard, and she suggested selling the manuscript to a more established writer who would publish it under their own name. That way I would gain a foothold in the industry, and make a few quid to boot.

She told me she was working with an American bloke named Stephen King who'd had a couple of potboilers, but was still waiting for his big break. She thought *The Hotel With All Blood In The Lifts* could be it. Excited about the idea of seeing my work in print – even if my name wasn't on the cover – I accepted.

Next year, when *The Shining* (as the fuckwitted marketing bods had retitled it) came out, I was stunned. The book became a number one international best-seller, and suddenly this Stephen King was on every TV show on Earth talking about how HE got the idea for it! The speccy little fucker hadn't even thanked me in the acknowledgements. And to add insult to injury, my agent wasn't returning my calls about the royalties, either.

That night, as I drowned my sorrows in the pub, I happened to mention in passing to a few people that I was the ghostwriter behind Stephen King's new book. After all, if I wasn't going to get fame or fortune from it, at least I could have the respect of my peers, right?

Wrong.

As I left the pub at closing time, I was violently thrown to the ground by a large man with a shaved head. He proceeded to pummel me viciously, making some ridiculous claim about how I'd goosed his wife's arse on her way to the loo. Which I hadn't, by the way. It was crystal clear who this man **REALLY** was... *a muscle-bound thug hired by Stephen King's publishers to shut me up.*

If the secret got out that King was a four-eyed fraud who couldn't even write a fucking shopping list, his books would stop selling. I knew too much – and that made me a target.

I stumbled home, battered and bruised, vowing never to dabble in ghostwriting again."

GHOSTWRITER!

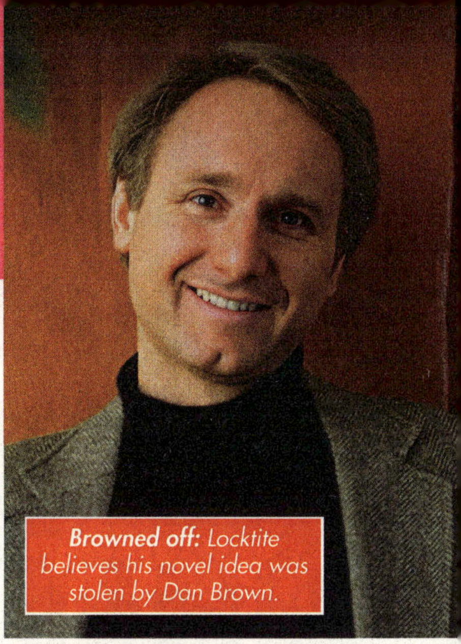

Browned off: Locktite believes his novel idea was stolen by Dan Brown.

HEART OF STEEL

Terry immediately dabbled in ghostwriting again, anonymously penning several more international best-sellers. "In the late Seventies, I knocked out The Bourne Identity for Robert Ludlum," Terry claims, moving from cider to shorts. The book which spawned another film made good money for everyone involved except for "Terry fucking Muggins" as Locktite refers to himself.

"I cranked out a few more smash hits – *Sophie's Choice* 'by' William Styron, *The Handmaid's Tale* 'by' Margaret Atwood – but by the mid-Eighties, I was beginning to fall out of love with writing. Sally had pissed off by this point due to a misunderstanding involving me, her sister's arse and an alleged 'goosing,' which didn't take place, I might add. So, single once again, I embarked on a period of wild sexual experimentation.

It was a heady time of erotic abandon, and like many of the great writers before me – Arthur Miller, Anais Nin, William Burroughs – I pushed the very boundaries of sensual pleasure. Unlike them however, I eventually ended up on the sex offenders register after a misunderstanding at a yoga class.

But it was around this time that I got a call out of the blue from a literary agent representing an American writer named Danielle Steel. She told me she'd heard my name bandied about in the top publishing houses as 'the best ghostwriter in town' and was wondering if she could procure my services.

Her client, Ms Steel, was a moderately successful author of romance books, but she was suffering from writer's block – a condition to which I appear to be immune. The agent asked if I would consider penning a couple of steamy thrillers that Danielle could release under her own name, just to kickstart her career again – a literary laxative, if you will.

I told her I'd had bad experiences with ghostwriting before – i.e. not receiving any money or credit, and having the shit kicked out of me outside a pub – but the agent was adamant we would divide all profits 50/50, and my name would be on the inside cover. So I got to work.

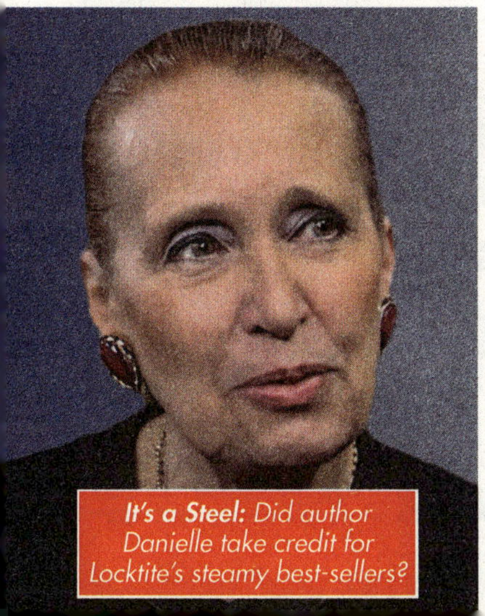

It's a Steel: Did author Danielle take credit for Locktite's steamy best-sellers?

Right from the off, I took to the romance genre like a duck to water. Drawing on my recent period of carnal envelope-pushing, I wrote reams and reams of racy material. My blood was pumping as I pounded away at the typewriter, conjuring images of 'throbbing members,' 'pillowy breasts' and 'freshly goosed arses.' When I posted the resulting manuscripts off to Danielle's agent, I was certain we had a bumper crop of best-sellers on our hands.

And I was right. The public lapped up my novels – published under the titles *Secrets*, *Wanderlust*, *Zoya* and *Daddy* – and Steel soon became one of the best-selling authors of all time. Some of the more explicit imagery in my original drafts had been removed, along with practically all references to arse-goosing. But the plots, characters, themes and general sense of heart-swelling tenderness were exactly the same. And no one can prove they weren't.

Unfortunately, the agent (whose name still escapes me but absolutely exists) wasn't returning my calls regarding royalty cheques, so I was making ends meet by working at a local frozen foods factory. My supervisor, Mr Barker, was celebrating his birthday one evening, and I got chatting to his wife Janet at the party. She mentioned being a huge Danielle Steel fan, so I let slip that I was in fact Ms Steel's ghostwriter, responsible for penning all her recent smash hits.

"*Drawing on my recent period of carnal envelope-pushing, I wrote reams and reams of racy material*"

I thought nothing of it, but then I saw Janet talking to Mr Barker in a hushed voice and pointing at me. The very next day, I was called into Barker's office and handed my P45. Gob-smacked, I asked why, only to be fobbed off with some pathetic excuse about me 'goosing his wife's arse' at the party the night before. I had never heard anything so ridiculous in all my life. It was perfectly clear what was really happening: *Danielle Steel's publishers were pressuring Barker to punish me for spilling the beans about my ghostwriting gig.* It was a warning shot across the bow. They'd taken my job, and if I mentioned it again, perhaps they'd take my life.

I left the factory in tears, vowing that the next best-seller I penned would have the words '**TERRY LOCKTITE**' on the cover."

DESPERATE DAN

Unfortunately, Terry would have to wait a little longer to see his name in print, as he continued to take on high-profile ghostwriting work for the planet's top authors. "The nineties was a busy time for me," he says, graduating from shorts to methylated spirits. Strapped for cash after his second divorce and a handful of buttock-based wrongful arrests, he took on ghostwriting gig after ghostwriting gig.

"Working evenings and weekends, I simultaneously boshed out all them *Harry Potters* 'by' JK Rowling and all them *Games of Throneses* 'by' George RR Martin. But have I ever seen a single penny for all that hard work? *Have I bollocks*. To this day, neither JK nor George RR has ever even acknowledged I exist.

When I got hitched to my third missus, Brenda, in 2002, I decided it was time to hang up the old ghostwriting quill for good. It was a thrill to consider that I was technically the best-selling author that had ever lived, of course, but receiving the square root of fuck all for my troubles was beginning to leave a sour taste in my mouth.

Instead, I graciously allowed Brenda to become the family breadwinner. She took on three full-time jobs at once while I went back to writing for pleasure. And it was wonderful – for the first time in years, I had no deadlines, no meetings, no A-List authors breathing down my neck for the next chapter. I was simply writing for *myself*.

I soon came up with a brilliant plot idea that I decided would form the basis of the first bona fide Terry Locktite novel. I can't recall the exact details at this minute (when you've written so many best-sellers, they all sort of blend into one) but it was something to do with the Mona Lisa and the idea that maybe she was Jesus Christ's bit on the side, or some such bollocks. Anyway, it was a cracker, a real page-turner. I titled it simply *Mona Lisa Was Jesus's Bit On The Side*.

With my manuscript typed, I headed down to London for a meeting with a top publishing house. Waiting in the lobby I met another author – an American bloke named Dan Brown – who said he was there to pitch a book, too. We got chatting, and he seemed like a nice enough bloke. I'd been out on a stag do the previous evening, and I was shitting the through the eye of a needle, so I asked Dan to watch my manuscript while I went to the bogs. However, when I came back forty minutes later, Dan was gone – *and so was my manuscript!*

At the time, I thought nothing of it. After all, I could remember the story and could easily type it out again and resubmit it. I was intending to do just that over the next few months, but I never quite got round to it. Imagine my surprise, then, in April 2003, when a book called *The Da Vinci Code* came out and rocketed straight to the top of every best-seller chart. It was the story of a man investigating the idea that the Mona Lisa might have been Jesus Christ's bit on the side, and its author was one... *Dan Brown*.

I was farting fire. I'd finally broken free of my ghostwriting chains and penned the novel that was meant to launch my career – and yet **STILL** it had ended up published under a lesser author's name. I drowned my sorrows with a few cans in the precinct and then staggered into Brenda's car, intending to drive to the nearest legal office and file a billion-dollar lawsuit against Brown. But as I eased away from the kerb, disaster struck. I lost control of the vehicle and crashed straight into a ditch.

The car was a write-off, but luckily I only sustained minor bruises and shitted kecks. Still, it was painfully obvious what had happened. Dan Brown's publishers had sabotaged Brenda's Seat Alhambra, removing the front brake pads and replacing them with a pair that were completely worn. The intention was to bump me off before I could tell the world about Brown's despicable cowardly crime. And they had almost succeeded.

In the past two decades, I've left the ghostwriting alone, afraid for my – and my family's – safety. Yet the literary bigwigs have never stopped trying to silence me – usually targeting me just as I'm leaving a pub or after I've been falsely accused of goosing someone's wife's arse.

It's plain as day that the publishing industry no longer wants me as a ghostwriter... They want me as a ***GHOST***."

NEXT WEEK: ***Terry narrowly escapes death in a late-night chip pan fire after telling people in the pub about his new job writing Richard Osman's crime novels.***

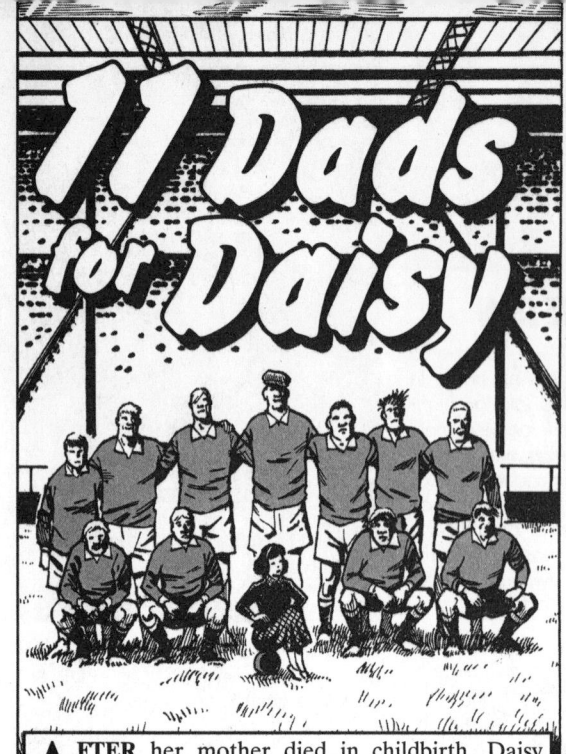

11 Dads for Daisy

AFTER her mother died in childbirth, Daisy Drummond was brought up by her father, a keen football supporter. When he himself passed away 15 years later, he appointed Plymouth Argyle as her legal guardians…

Daisy was with her friend Mandy at Plymouth Argyle's ground watching her dads take on the visitors Port Vale in league division 3…

"Gosh, Daisy. It must be great having 11 dads."

"Not when I have to watch them play football every week. It's *so* boring."

"*Hey!* Are you going to the party at Bunty's house tonight? Her mum and dad are away?"

"I'd love to, but my dads never let me go to parties… they're so annoying."

"Well tell them you're coming to my house for a sleepover…"

"…I've told my mum and dad I'm staying at yours tonight."

"Good idea!"

Eventually the final whistle blew, and Daisy's dads left the field after a thrilling 3-2 victory over their rivals…

"*Hey!* Well played, Dads."

"Thanks, Daisy."

"Thank you. Did you enjoy it?"

"Yes…"

"Oh! I forgot! Mandy has asked me to sleep over at hers tonight? Is that okay?"

"Er… yes, I don't see why not."

"No, wait a minute, Nobby… I don't think that's a good idea…"

"…You've got school on Monday, Daisy."

"Aw! But it's only Saturday, Alf."

"Yes, but she's got homework to do."

"No, I don't think so, Daisy. Best stay home tonight."

"Aw! It's *so* unfair!"

"Listen, lads! Just like football, parenting is a team game. We have to be on the same page and work together…

…Daisy needs stability and boundaries."

"Yes. Even if we disagree, we have to present a united front to Daisy. Otherwise she'll play us off against each other."

"You're right, Tommy."

That evening…

"Eight thirty, Daisy… time for bed."

"Okay dads… goodnight!"

"Goodnight."

"Blimey! Who'd have thought bringing up kids would be such hard work?"

"Yes. This parenting malarky makes an away fixture to Manchester United look like a walk in the park!"

"*Ha!* Too right, Frank."

"I did feel a little sorry for her, mind. It was just a sleep over at her chum's house."

"Yes, Billy, but there has to be rules."

"Tell you what. How about we read her a bedtime story? That always cheers her up!"

"Good idea…"

"What do you say we tell her about the time we won the third division south trophy in '52?"

"Yes. That's one of her favourites."

"Daisy! How would you like a bedtime st…"

"Bloomin' 'ell. She's *gone!*"

"*Gone!?!* Gone *where?*"

"To that sleepover, most likely, the scamp…"

"Most likely shinned down the drainpipe."

"I'll call Mandy's mum"

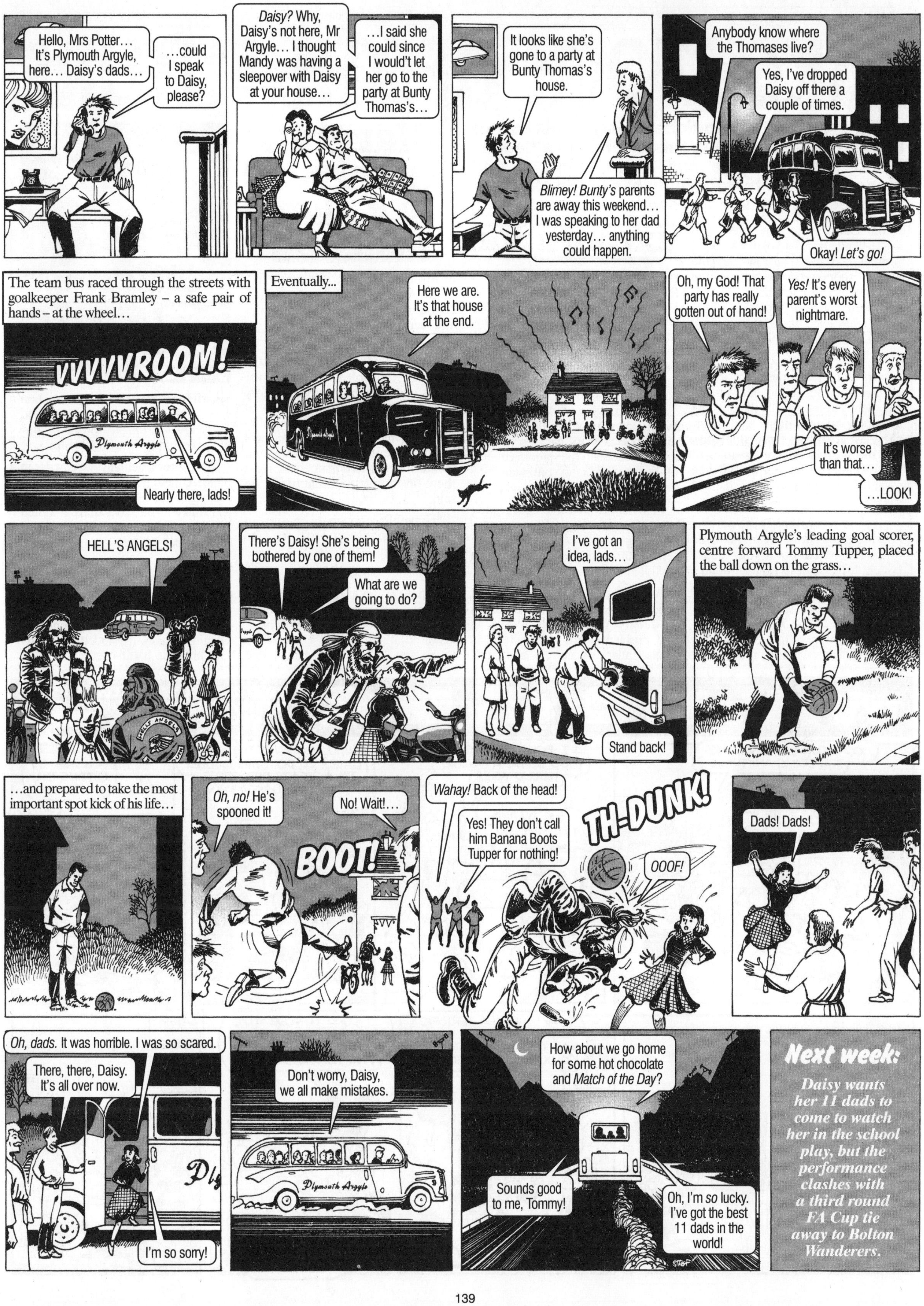
Hello, Mrs Potter… It's Plymouth Argyle, here… Daisy's dads…
…could I speak to Daisy, please?
Daisy? Why, Daisy's not here, Mr Argyle… I thought Mandy was having a sleepover with Daisy at your house…
…I said she could since I wouldn't let her go to the party at Bunty Thomas's…
It looks like she's gone to a party at Bunty Thomas's house.
Blimey! Bunty's parents are away this weekend… I was speaking to her dad yesterday… anything could happen.
Anybody know where the Thomases live?
Yes, I've dropped Daisy off there a couple of times.
Okay! Let's go!
The team bus raced through the streets with goalkeeper Frank Bramley – a safe pair of hands – at the wheel…
VVVVVROOM!
Plymouth Argyle
Nearly there, lads!
Eventually...
Here we are. It's that house at the end.
Oh, my God! That party has really gotten out of hand!
Yes! It's every parent's worst nightmare.
It's worse than that…
…LOOK!
HELL'S ANGELS!
There's Daisy! She's being bothered by one of them!
What are we going to do?
I've got an idea, lads…
Stand back!
Plymouth Argyle's leading goal scorer, centre forward Tommy Tupper, placed the ball down on the grass…
…and prepared to take the most important spot kick of his life…
Oh, no! He's spooned it!
No! Wait!…
BOOT!
Wahay! Back of the head!
Yes! They don't call him Banana Boots Tupper for nothing!
TH-DUNK!
OOOF!
Dads! Dads!
Oh, dads. It was horrible. I was so scared.
There, there, Daisy. It's all over now.
I'm so sorry!
Don't worry, Daisy, we all make mistakes.
Plymouth Argyle
How about we go home for some hot chocolate and Match of the Day?
Sounds good to me, Tommy!
Oh, I'm so lucky. I've got the best 11 dads in the world!
Next week:
Daisy wants her 11 dads to come to watch her in the school play, but the performance clashes with a third round FA Cup tie away to Bolton Wanderers.

TAKE STOCK OF THE FUTURE

GRAVY – the traditional meaty moistener of Great British meals as diverse as a Sunday roast, sausage and mash, and pie and chips – is set to be reborn thanks to the efforts of a pioneering Wallsend-based tech-guru.

Elton Gates, who ten years ago single-handedly founded X-COM computer repair barrow in the Forum shopping precinct, is the brains behind SmartGravy – an AI-enhanced adaptation of the much-loved meat juice-based sauce, which he says will change the way we look at gravy forever.

"Gravy may be the only aspect of modern life to so far remain completely untouched by the ongoing technological revolution," said Gates. "The last great leap forward in gravy was the introduction of granules to the commercial market in the late seventies, and nothing's changed since."

"It's fair to say that at the minute, pouring gravy – whether home-made or granule-based – over your dinner is literally the same as riding around a 21st century Olympic velodrome on a penny farthing."

According to the 55-year-old tech-savvy entrepreneur, SmartGravy will differ from what we today think

EXCLUSIVE!

of as gravy in one critical way – the presence in the mix of of thinking *nanobots* – tiny, self-replicating electronic robots. Billions of these marvels of futuristic technology, each the size of a gravy molecule, will be present in each spoonful.

marylebone

"SmartGravy is going to be a living community of these edible, microscopic robots, each performing a vital function in the smooth running of the system," Gates continued. "It'll be more like a *hive* than a sauce."

"The nanobots will keep the gravy piping hot right throughout the meal by using kinetic energy to move rapidly through the liquid, creating frictional heat at an atomic level."

And according to Gates, the days of gravy covering only the food it is poured over are gone. "We've all had problems with gravy sitting in pools under the carrots and none

Nanobot tech coming to a plate near you

of it on your spuds," he continued. "The SmartGravy nanobots will create a 3D map of the the dinner and actively divert move gravy to where it is needed."

And SmartGravy will also consign the age-old problem of there never being enough gravy to the history books. "Deep in the matrix of SmartGravy, I envisage a specially-equipped factory nanobot that will be able to replicate gravy atoms and create more gravy if needed, right there on the plate in real time," he said.

"Hopefully enough to ensure an even coating anyway. We'll see," he added, optimistically.

ripcord

Although various snags remain to be ironed-out – for example, as yet he has no nanobots of any description at his disposal and doesn't know where to get any – Gates is confident that

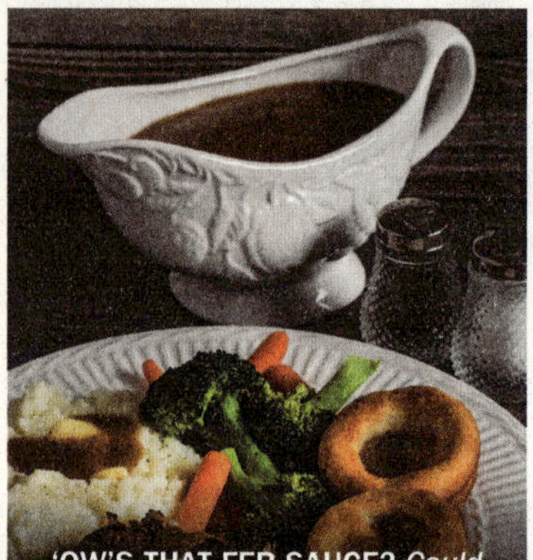

'OW'S THAT FER SAUCE? *Could SmartGravy revolutionise the Great British Sunday Roast?*

SmartGravy will enter full production very soon, and says the hi-tech food dressing will be on sale from his barrow in the Forum in time for Christmas.

"I'm not actually trained in nanotechnology, but I've done a bit of surfing on the net and it doesn't look too tricky to me, so I think I should be able to get it up and running by crimbo, barring any complications," he said.

"I've got to hit Christmas. The gravy consumption over them two weeks accounts for something like three quarters of all the gravy consumed in Britain annually," he added. "If I don't hit Christmas, it's all over."

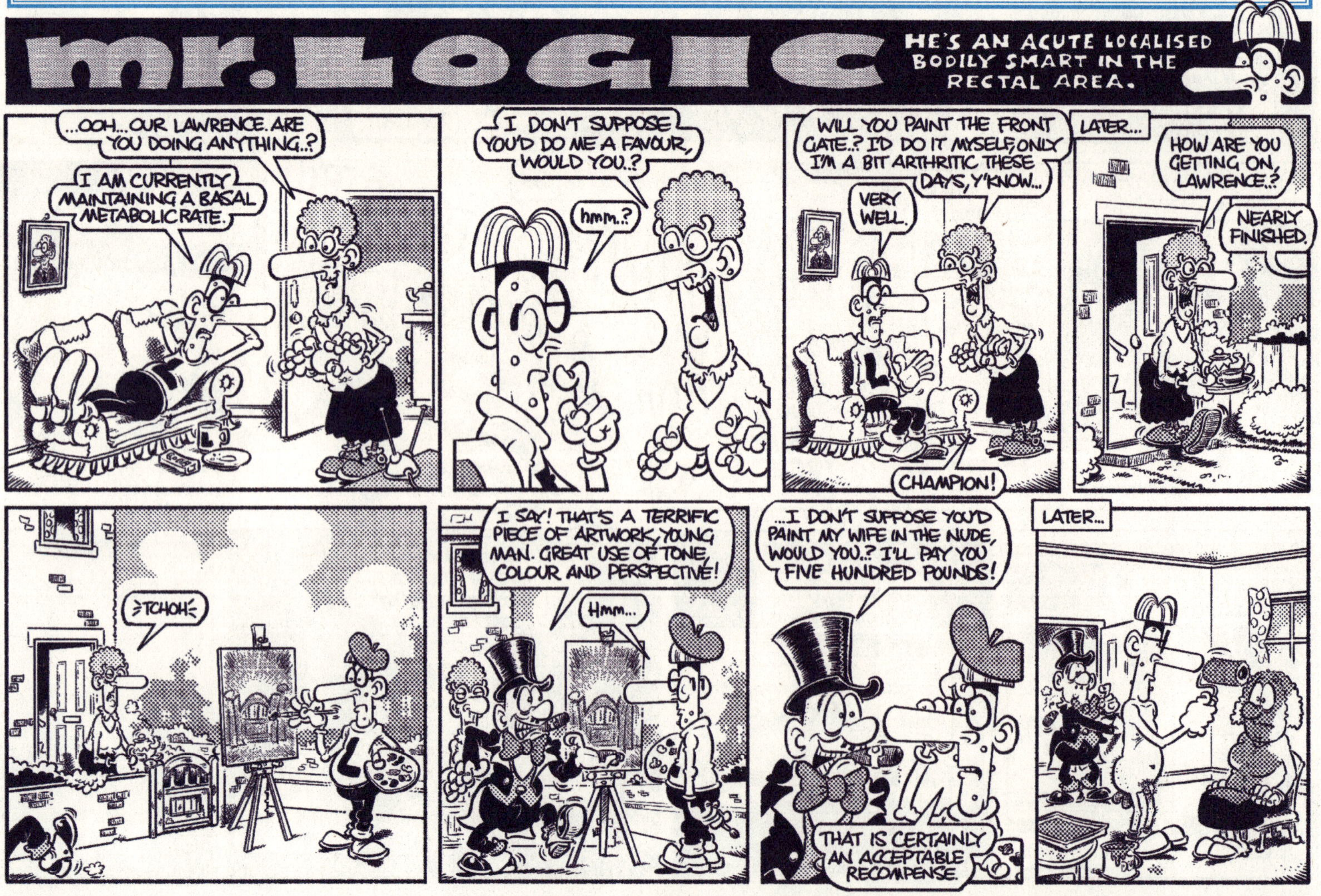
mr. LOGIC
HE'S AN ACUTE LOCALISED BODILY SMART IN THE RECTAL AREA.
...OOH... OUR LAWRENCE. ARE YOU DOING ANYTHING..?
I AM CURRENTLY MAINTAINING A BASAL METABOLIC RATE.
I DON'T SUPPOSE YOU'D DO ME A FAVOUR, WOULD YOU..?
hmm..?
WILL YOU PAINT THE FRONT GATE..? I'D DO IT MYSELF, ONLY I'M A BIT ARTHRITIC THESE DAYS, Y'KNOW...
VERY WELL.
CHAMPION!
LATER...
HOW ARE YOU GETTING ON, LAWRENCE..?
NEARLY FINISHED.
TCHOH
I SAY! THAT'S A TERRIFIC PIECE OF ARTWORK, YOUNG MAN. GREAT USE OF TONE, COLOUR AND PERSPECTIVE!
Hmm...
...I DON'T SUPPOSE YOU'D PAINT MY WIFE IN THE NUDE, WOULD YOU..? I'LL PAY YOU FIVE HUNDRED POUNDS!
THAT IS CERTAINLY AN ACCEPTABLE RECOMPENSE.
LATER...

THE Male Online

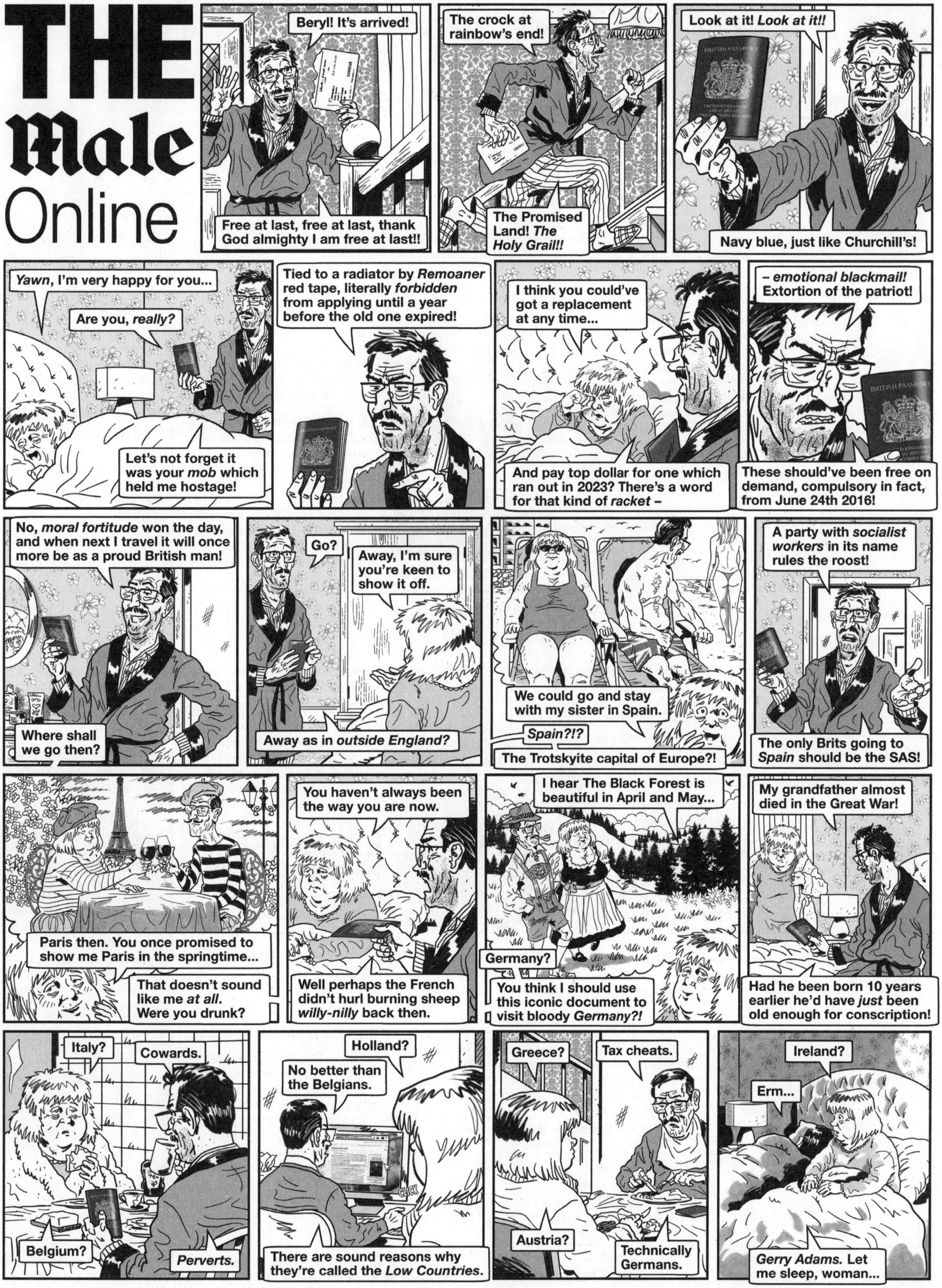

Beryl! It's arrived!
Free at last, free at last, thank God almighty I am free at last!!
The crock at rainbow's end!
The Promised Land! *The Holy Grail!!*
Look at it! *Look at it!!*
BRITISH PASSPORT
Navy blue, just like Churchill's!
Yawn, I'm very happy for you...
Are you, *really?*
Let's not forget it was your *mob* which held me hostage!
Tied to a radiator by *Remoaner* red tape, literally *forbidden* from applying until a year before the old one expired!
I think you could've got a replacement at any time...
And pay top dollar for one which ran out in 2023? There's a word for that kind of *racket* –
– emotional blackmail! Extortion of the patriot!
BRITISH PASSPORT
These should've been free on demand, compulsory in fact, from June 24th 2016!
No, *moral fortitude* won the day, and when next I travel it will once more be as a proud British man!
Where shall we go then?
Go?
Away, I'm sure you're keen to show it off.
Away as in *outside England?*
We could go and stay with my sister in Spain.
Spain?!?
The Trotskyite capital of Europe?!
A party with *socialist workers* in its name rules the roost!
The only Brits going to *Spain* should be the SAS!
Paris then. You once promised to show me Paris in the springtime...
That doesn't sound like me *at all*. Were you drunk?
You haven't always been the way you are now.
Well perhaps the French didn't hurl burning sheep *willy-nilly* back then.
I hear The Black Forest is beautiful in April and May...
Germany?
You think I should use this iconic document to visit bloody *Germany?!*
My grandfather almost died in the Great War!
Had he been born 10 years earlier he'd have *just* been old enough for conscription!
Italy?
Cowards.
Belgium?
Perverts.
Holland?
No better than the Belgians.
CLICK
There are sound reasons why they're called the *Low Countries*.
Greece?
Tax cheats.
Austria?
Technically Germans.
Ireland?
Erm...
Gerry Adams. Let me sleep, woman...

Letterbocks

letters@viz.co.uk letters@viz.co.uk letters@viz

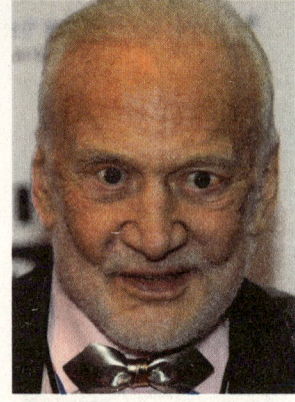

ON page 120, John Moynes queried which Moon astronaut has the biggest cock – a deep scientific question that I'm sure would've kept even the great Stephen Hawking awake at night. Buzz Aldrin has been married 4 times, including in 2023 at the age of 93 to a woman 30 years younger than him. I scraped a C in my science GCSEs, but I think it's blatantly obvious that Big Buzz is the man.

David Vasey, Whitley Bay

TODAY I spilled a small quantity of honey on my toolbox. Since I rarely eat honey and even more rarely use tools, it was something that has never happened to me before and is highly unlikely ever to occur again. Have any readers experienced similar 'once in a lifetime' events as mundane as this?

Ben Nunn, Caterham

HAD I been a servant in the days of Downtown Abbey, I would have been pissing in the master's soup when nobody was looking. However, no scenes of this nature were included in the show. So much for historical accuracy.

Gerry Paton, London

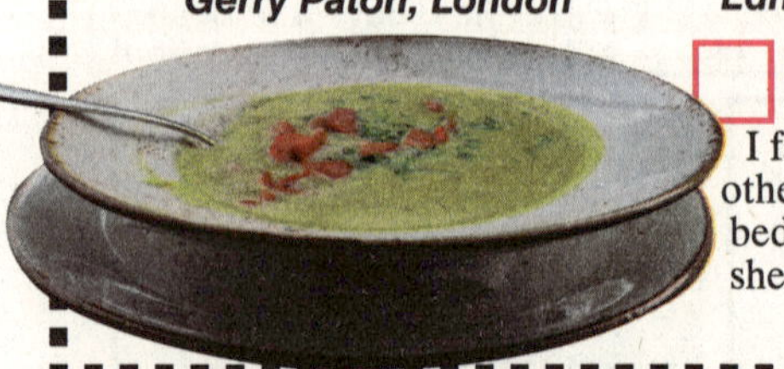

THIS weekend my girlfriend and I went to Weston-super-Mare for the day, and we decided to take a stroll along the 366m-long Grand Pier. However, it was a pound each to go on, and I reckoned that after walking to the end, the only advantage would be that the horizon would be a bit further away and we'd be able to see a pier's length more sea. Admittedly, there may have been something worth looking at in that extra 366 metres of water – perhaps an interesting boat or a school of whales or something – but in all likelihood it would just be more sea, exactly the same as you can see without going on the pier. So we turned our £2 into 2p pieces and put it in the slots on the seafront instead.

Jack Dury, Bristol

I THINK Jack Dury *(above)* is looking at the entrance charge to the Grand Pier in the wrong way. Seeing a bit more sea is not what you are paying the £1 admission fee for. You are paying to walk along a piece of British history. And if he is of average height, it will take him 488 steps to stroll to the end, which is just 0.2 pence per step, fantastic value in anyone's book.

Torbjorn Creases, York

I AGREE with Mr Creases *(above)* when he says what splendid value the Grand Pier at Weston-super-Mare is. And if Mr Dury took a really slow amble and included the steps on the way back when calculating the cost of his admission, it would represent even better value for money.

Edna Sprite, Cromer

MY wife always complains when I fart in bed. The other night I shit the bed instead and *still* she complained.

Bath Bob, Bath

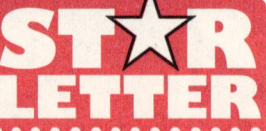

STAR LETTER

NOT only does the word 'advertisements' have the word 'semen' in it, it is literally between the word 'tits.' English used to be the finest language in the world. Sadly, no longer.

Calvin Graham, Philadelphia

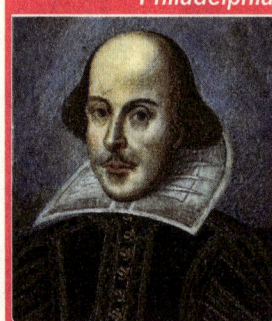

I ACCIDENTALLY bought some pork sausages instead of our usual vegan ones from the supermarket, and I must say I was really impressed. The texture and flavour was so good that we could barely tell the difference. Any vegans looking for a low cost, tasty alternative should definitely give them a try.

Martin Standards, Chester

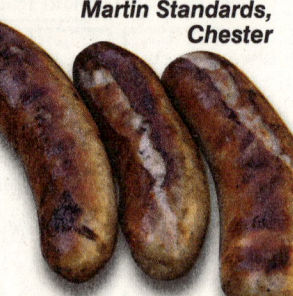

IF my surname was Street, ten years ago when my son was born, I would have called him Warren so that I could take photos of him next to the sign for Warren Street on the London Underground. However, as my surname is Cooper, I didn't.

D Cooper, Malta

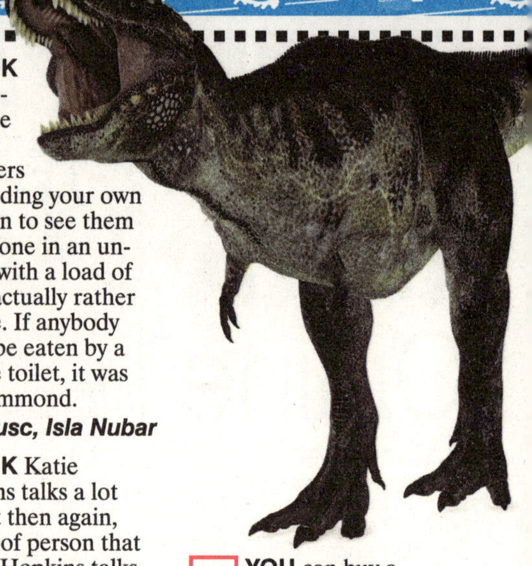

I THINK that de-extincting the world's most perfect hunters and then sending your own grandchildren to see them during a cyclone in an un-drivable car with a load of strangers is actually rather irresponsible. If anybody deserved to be eaten by a T-Rex on the toilet, it was Dr. John Hammond.

Randy Mollusc, Isla Nubar

I THINK Katie Hopkins talks a lot of sense. But then again, I'm the kind of person that thinks Katie Hopkins talks a lot of sense, so whatever I think should be taken with a pinch of salt.

F Mental-Mee, email

WHY don't doctors have little buttons they can press after a consultation has finished that illuminates one of two lights in the waiting room? A green light flashing means that it was a good diagnosis, and everyone waiting can clap and cheer the patient as they come out of the consultation room. Or if it's a red light, we can give them a consolatory pat on the back, and say things like "chin up, pal" and "worse things happen at sea".

Terry Farricker, Blackpool

JUST before going to sleep one night, I released a loud air biscuit lasting several seconds, at the end of which my girlfriend's mobile phone went 'ting!' after receiving a text message. I felt like I had won the star prize on a Roger Mellie game show of some sort. Have any other readers had a similar experience?

Fatty McBridie, email

DOES anyone know how sperm whales got their name? Because if you shot something that size out of your cock there would be hell to pay.

Ted Haddock, Grimsby

I DON'T understand why drivers slow down to a crawl on the motorway when the legal speed limit is fully 70 miles per hour. There were literally hundreds of these dangerous lunatics jamming up traffic on the M25 by driving at 15mph as I was trying to get home last Friday during rush hour. At one point they even stopped. Utter madness!

Prince Asbo, Folkestone

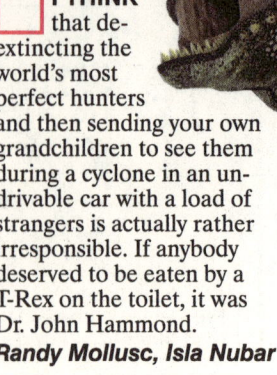

YOU can buy a pornographic magazine on a Sunday after 4 o'clock, but not a Bible. That's fantastic.

Hampton Soregland, Hull

I DON'T think it's fair of King Charles to posthumously knight the author Martin Amis. Amis might have wanted to refuse the honour and tell his majesty to shove his knighthood up his arse, but now he will never have the chance. He's Sir Martin and that's that. I would like to take this opportunity to say that if I am ever offered a knighthood, I will tell the monarch to shove it up his arse. And I'm leaving instructions in my will for the executors to tell him to shove any "posthumous" knighthood up his arse, too.

Hampton Crayons, Leeds

MY husband and I went to Iceland for a holiday last year. It was a lovely place, but it was very small and I think we saw most of it in our week there, so although we enjoyed it I don't think we will go back. And everyone who I speak to who has been there thinks the same thing – that Iceland is the kind of place you only go to once. If I was the Icelandic Tourist Board, I'd be fairly worried watching my customer base get smaller each year.

Edna Gruel, Harlow

DAVE
Chandler
PROFESSIONAL
GAMBLER
CORRAL
BET ON ANY THING NOW
OPEN
BET NOW 24/7
HIS ONLINE ACCOUNTS SUSPENDED, OUR HERO TAKES THE BUS ACROSS TOWN TO ONE OF THE FEW BETTING SHOPS HE ISN'T BANNED FROM, WITH A HOT TIP FOR A BULGARIAN THIRD DIVISION FOOTBALL MATCH.
BET
FIRST GOAL: G. SLOVOV
£50 00
SOON...
GOAL! P. NOKLOV
RATS' COCKS

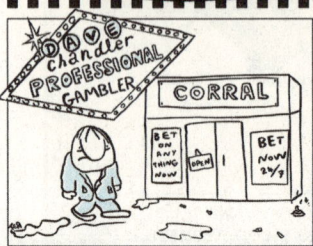

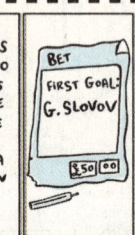

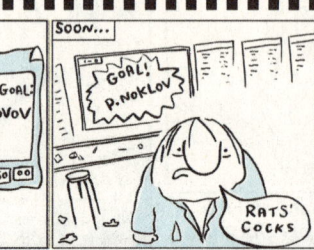

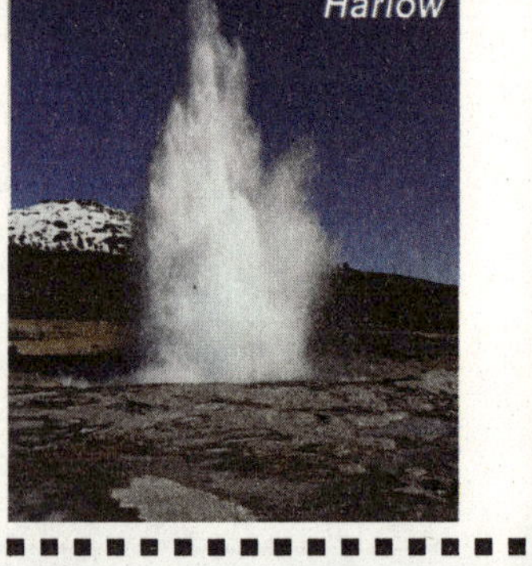

☐ **THIS** letter was written using ChatGPT in the style of a human. Or was it?
AI, Bottle

* That's an interesting one, Al… or is that A.I.? Because of the risk that many of our readers' letters are being generated by Artificial Intelligence, we have decided that all future correspondence to the Letterbocks page must be accompanied by the following form – with a tick placed in all the boxes which contain a bird's arse.

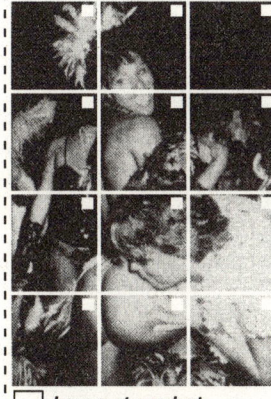

☐ I am not a robot.

☐ **WE** keep being told that AI is so clever that it's a potential threat to the existence of the human race and could wipe us all out. If that's the case, before it starts kicking off, why doesn't someone just ask one of these AI bots how to stop it if it does? Yet again it's left to the likes of me to come up with solutions to the world's woes because the boffins simply can't be bothered.
Joe Smith, Exeter

☐ **YESTERDAY**, while walking down my stairs at home, I farted on every single step. Is this a record?
P Green, Baildon
PS. There were thirteen steps.

☐ **HOW** tedious these cyclists are. They film every journey they make with a little camera attached to a hat, then they watch the resulting video later that evening while masturbating.
Fat Allan, Little Lever

* That's a rather wild assumption to make, Fat Allan, and one we are not sure is true. Are you a cyclist who doesn't film your every journey? Or if you do film your every journey, do you then not re-watch it that night whilst masturbating? Write in and let us know so we can put paid to Fat Allan's theory that this is what all cyclists do. If no one writes in, we will have to assume that he is correct.

☐ **MANY** years ago I saw ex-West Ham footballer Tony Cottee going into a chemist in Essex. Over the years, I have often wondered what he went in for. What do other readers think he went in for?
Jackie Hopkins, Clacton on sea

* We don't know, Jackie, and it would be pointless to speculate. But if we were to speculate, it might have been something ordinary, like deodorant or soap. On the other hand, it could have been something rather embarrassing, like piles ointment or bongo pills. Or it could have been something very spicy, like a tube of Durex Play sexual lubricant, or one of those ring buzzers you put on your cock. The fact is, we may never know for sure.

☐ **I DON'T** think the British monarchy should start paying their taxes or giving some of their cash away, as it will put young people off aspiring to become kings and queens. We need to promote a properly aspirational society to set an example for our youngsters in these difficult times.
Nort Shaw, Dunnow

☐ **"I'LL** be back" said Arnold Schwarzenegger in the 1984 film *The Terminator* ... and he was - in a string of blockbuster sequels! Say what you like about Arnie, but he is at least a man of his word.
T Cockfondle, Crawley

☐ **I LOVE** watching opera on the telly, me, especially when they put the subtitles on as it makes it much easier to sing along.
Ray, Prestwich

TOP TIPS

TWO old-style drawing pins attached by fuse wire to a 9v PP3 battery makes an ideal defibrillator for a mouse that has gone into cardiac arrest.
Warwick Street, Heaton

TREAT yourself to a *Back to the Future* experience by snogging your mum before hiring the local sex pest to valet your car.
Kevin Caswell-Jones, Gresford

☐ **WHAT'S** so special about used teabags? In my house, every other bit of kitchen rubbish goes straight in the bin. But not teabags. They get put on a special dish next to the kettle to lie in state for 24 hours in view of everyone. Are tea bags somehow related to the Royal Family?
Joe Newson, Fort William

☐ **THE** return of the Raleigh Chopper bicycle may seem like a cause for celebration, but I'd advise anyone thinking of buying one to put realism before nostalgia. That gearstick caused a lot of painful accidents to riders in the 1970s, even before their balls had dropped, so what it could do to a 60-year-old's dangly clockweights doesn't bear thinking about.
Steve Crouch, P'borough

☐ **CROCODILES** have pointed heads and Alligators have rounded heads. However, the letter C is rounded and the letter A is pointed. Couldn't the bloke who named them have simply done it the other way around to make it easier for us to remember which is which?
Horace Tadpole, Florida

WHEN passing a garden with drying laundry on the clothes line, dividing the number of socks by the number of pairs of pants will give you the arithmetical mean number of feet per person in that household.
Greg Shaw, email

A DAMP towel draped across your dog's shoulders is a good way of cooling them down in hot weather, and also lets you see what they would look like if they decided to take up boxing.
Airdrieonion, Airdrie

☐ **I DON'T** like cress on egg sandwiches but my husband loves it, and despite this we've been happily married for forty years. I hope this is a lesson to young couples starting out that their relationships can work if they put in a bit of effort.
Doris Mustard, Wells

☐ **WITH** orcas attacking boats in the Mediterranean and sharks savaging swimmers in the Red Sea, it appears that wildlife is becoming more aggressive. Could I suggest that the producers of *Springwatch* reflect this trend? Perhaps Chris Packham could get gored by a stag, or Michaela Strachan might get bit on the arse off of an owl.
Russel Hobbs, Orkney

CONVINCE people that your family are in an American film by getting your wife to cook a huge breakfast of pancakes and eggs, only for you to just drink black coffee and your children to ignore it in favour of a bite out of a slice of toast eaten as they hurry out to catch the school bus.
Tom O'Brien, Sheffield

toptips@viz.co.uk

☐ **WHEN** ITV launched their online itvX service, I naturally expected the 'X' to signify hardcore adult content for the first time on ITV. So imagine how disappointed I was when it turned out to be just the same ITV programmes, but with extra adverts and sponsorships, none of which were even remotely pornographic.
Ben Nunn, Caterham

☐ **WHAT** with the porn industry' obsession with shaven fannies, if any of your younger readers would like to know what they looked like in the olden days with pubes on, there is a Mary Millington film on Netflix.
Julian Wiseman, email

Let down by the **NEGLIGENCE** of a loved one with their lamentable 'love gift ideas'? You need…

VALENTINES-CLAIM-LAWYERS-4U

Valentines-Claim-Lawyers-4U is the name you can trust! We've been dealing with **WOEFUL MISDIAGNOSIS** of what kind of gift you wanted and **INDUSTRIAL**-scale **DEAFNESS** on the part of your loved one for more than 25 years.

JUST LOOK AT THESE RECENT PAYOUTS!

♥ Hurt caused by accidental non-removal of 24hr garage "Reduced for Quick Sale" stickers on flowers. — We got Mrs J. of Barnsley **£4,500**

♥ Mystery day-trip outlined by husband as "romance personified" ended at steam traction museum. — We got Mrs F. of York **£3,700**

♥ Distress caused by 'romantic' gift of unrequested cosmetic surgery vouchers. — We got Mrs G. of Leeds **£9,000**

♥ Humiliated by hugely optimistic underwear purchase from LoveHoney internet site — We got Mrs A. of Carlisle **£8,250**

He's *never* going to get it right. And when he doesn't, *we're* there to help. We are **Valentines Claim-Lawyers-4U**
CALL US NOW 01-811-8055

Tommy Quang's WORLD OF STRANGE

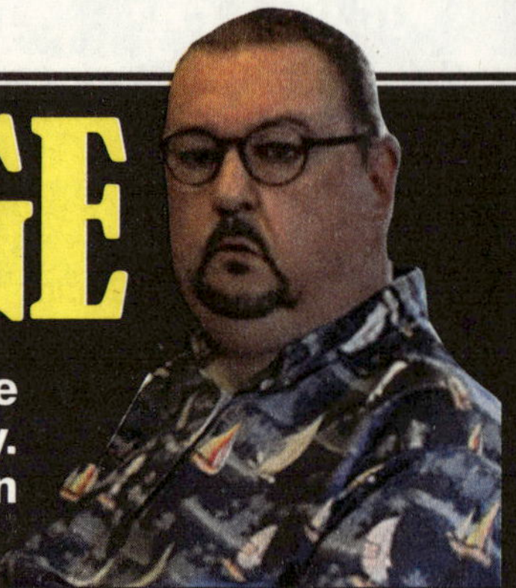

PARANORMAL researcher Tommy Quang has been investigating strange events in and around Tyseley in the Midlands for over half a century. Here's this week's casebook of weird and unexplained happenings in this most mysterious of Birmingham districts.

CASE FILE 1:
The Ring Recycle

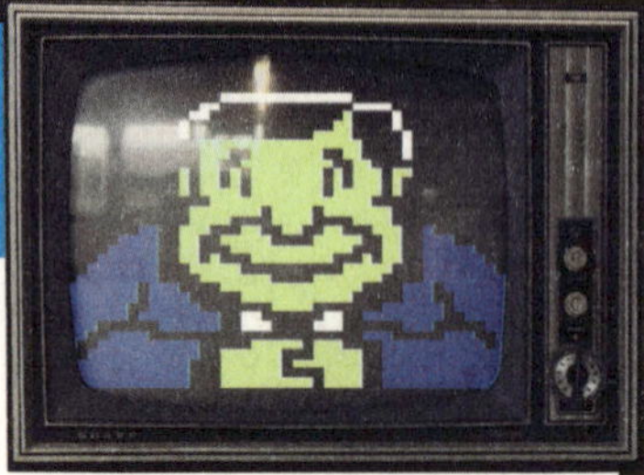

WE'VE ALL SEEN *The Ring*, the psychological horror film featuring a haunted television which tells watchers when they will die. A work of fiction, you might think, and perhaps you may be right. But one Tyseley resident would disagree after she had a similar experience when her set became possessed by the host of the Teletext quiz *Bamboozle*.

Sheila Breadmould was a regular player of the Channel4 Teletext game since the service was launched in the 1980s, answering 25 general knowledge questions every day. But some time in 2007, cartoon quizmaster Bamber Boozler's questioning became increasingly personal and existential.

According to Sheila, *Bamboozle* had normal questions at first – what's the capital of France, what's the highest waterfall in the world, that sort of thing.

But as time went on, the questions began to become more personal and seemed to be specifically aimed at Sharon. Questions like 'Where does Sharon keep the sugar in her house?' and 'Where did the Breadmould family go on holiday last year?' Sharon admitted to being a little freaked out.

But it was nothing compared to what was to come. Because Boozler, seemingly with complete knowledge of space and time, told Sharon how, where and when she was going to die. She said: "It was a bit scary hearing that, but I suppose if I don't visit Primark in Merry Hill on October 3rd 2038, or at least I refrain from eating sweets when I'm in there if I do, then I won't choke on a gobstopper in the underwear section."

During the course of my investigations, I found Sheila to be a credible witness. She took an independent lie detector test, which she failed, but the machine that the bloke was using was faulty, so that proves she was telling the truth.

Conclusion: TRUE

CASE FILE 2:
Time Travel, Gentlemen, Please

TIME TRAVEL is the stuff of science fiction. But could it be that in Tyseley, distorting the space-time continuum to change the direction of chronology is actually *science fact?*

When, back in 2019, I heard that a regular at Tyseley Working Men's Club was an alleged time traveller, I knew I had to investigate. And I say 'alleged' time traveller, because as a sceptic, I always reserve judgement until I have all the data.

The mysterious man introduced himself as 'Morphy Richards' and claimed to be from the year 2032. He looked fairly normal – not what you'd expect a man from 13 years into the future to look like, but I was simply there to gather information. He told me that he drank in the present day because beer was so expensive in the future.

He was very credible. Nevertheless I asked for proof, I wanted him to tell me something that only a man who had already lived through the next decade-and-a-bit would know. And he gave it to me. He told me that before the year was out, there would be an Oasis reunion, that Kat would cheat on Alfie in *EastEnders*, and that US president Donald Trump would behave 'rather foolishly'.

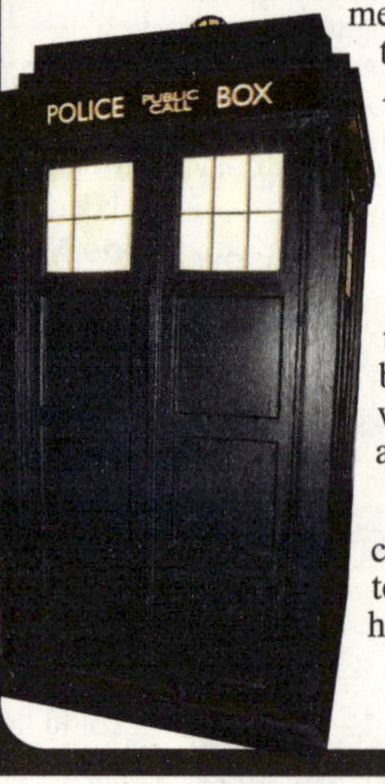
POLICE PUBLIC CALL BOX

After last orders was called, he said he was going to the chippy for a battered sausage and chips before going home to his own time, but that he would be in the club again tomorrow if I fancied another pint.

Although one of his prognostications did not come true, the other two certainly did, and I came to the conclusion that on the balance of probability, he was telling the truth.

Conclusion: TRUE

CASE FILE 3:
Claws For Thought

THERE are many sightings of big cats around the UK. Cryptozoologists have spotted these elusive creatures on Bodmin Moor, in the Derbyshire Peak District and in the wilds of Northumberland. But could the 'Tyseley Tiger' be added to rollcall of ferocious beasts that stalk the British Isles?

After hearing tales of an enormous, striped cat at large in the town, I decided to conduct some research. I began by interviewing the man who spotted it – Ken Ovoid.

Ken owns the 50p pasty shop in the centre of town and is at work early every morning, taking the freshly baked pasties out of the freezer. And it was on one of those morning shifts last week that he spotted the beast.

It was about 5.30, and Ken had just turned the ovens on when he heard a commotion by the bins outside. Rushing out, he saw an animal disappearing round the corner of his shop. He ran across to see what it was, but it had vanished onto some wasteground by the bookies.

"I only saw six inches of its tail as it disappeared," Ken told me. *"But it looked like the last six inches of the tail of a Bengal tiger."*

Ken came across as a credible witness. He is pillar of the community, a down-to-earth baker not given to flights of fancy, so I believed his every word. He had also recently visited Dudley Zoo and seen a tiger, so he had intimate knowledge of what the ends of their tails look like. All the evidence pointed to a tiger on the loose.

Looking round the back of his bakery, I spotted several piles of spoor – the cryptozoological name for shit. It looked like dog mess from something big, like a Great Dane or St Bernard, but I was more or less certain that nobody round that part of town owned a dog like that. It was all very intriguing.

I then looked at the bin bags. They had literally been torn open to get at the food scraps inside. Whatever did this had ripped through the plastic as though it wasn't there – and these were the good quality bags, not the flimsy things you get from the pound shop. It was certainly not any animal I have ever seen.

But as I have said, I am a sceptic and a scientist, and until I get absolute proof that there is a tiger on the loose in Tyseley, I will have to conclude that it is only probable, rather than certain.

Conclusion: PROBABLY TRUE

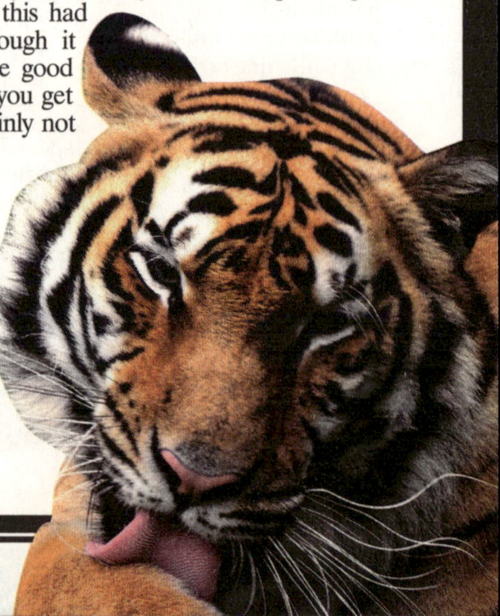

CASE FILE 4:
YOU F.O!

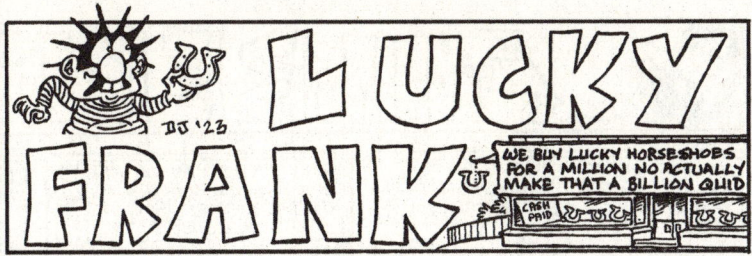

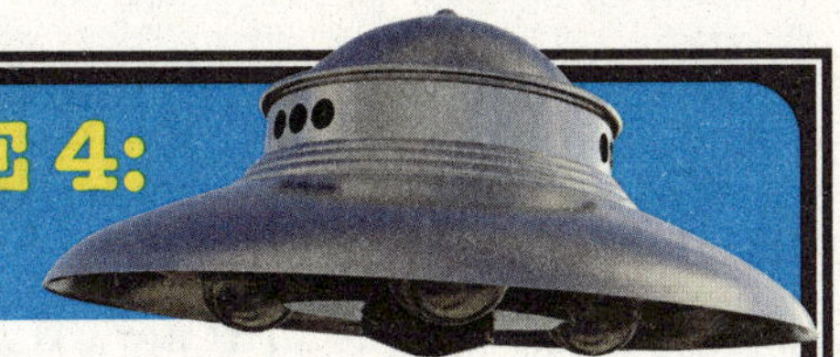

REPORTS of abductions by space aliens are becoming more and more frequent, with one in six Americans claiming to have been snatched and anally probed by extra-terrestrials. And it now seems that these ETs are turning their sights towards the residents of Tyseley.

Sharon Crapstick told me how her husband Darren was abducted in 2019, on the night they had tickets to see Gary Barlow at the NEC. "Darren went missing in the afternoon. I was worried sick," she told me.

Darren arrived back at the house at 6.30 the following morning, in a terrible state and babbling about spotting a UFO hovering over Tile Heaven Warehouse. When he had gone to have a look, he was sucked up into the ship by some kind of a force-field. He remembers having a chat with a member of the crew who was humanoid in appearance and resembled Dominic Cummings.

Sharon, a massive Gary Barlow fan had been over the moon when Darren agreed to go to the NEC with her, as throughout their courtship he had said that he would do almost anything to avoid having to sit through a Gary Barlow concert. Not surprisingly, she was particularly upset when he was abducted by aliens.

And it wasn't the first time that a plan to see her idol had been scuppered. In 2016, the couple had tickets to see Barlow in Wolverhampton, but a few hours before they were due to set off for the show, Darren was beamed aboard a strange cigar-shaped craft and experimented on. He was beamed down the following morning and found confused in a hedge near his local pub.

The couple admitted to feeling cursed as a Covid pandemic plan to see the former Take That! star was also scuppered in early 2021. Barlow was playing a Zoom concert during lockdown and the couple bought online tickets. However, Darren spotted a strange light hovering above his house, and seconds later the internet went off and didn't come back on until after the virtual concert was over.

"Darren was as upset as me," Sharon told me. She seemed a credible witness, and all the dates and times in her story match up. Darren refused to speak to me about the events, a situation that is often the case with alien abductions, lending even more weight to this extraordinary story.

Conclusion: TRUE

CASE FILE 5:
Let Us Spray

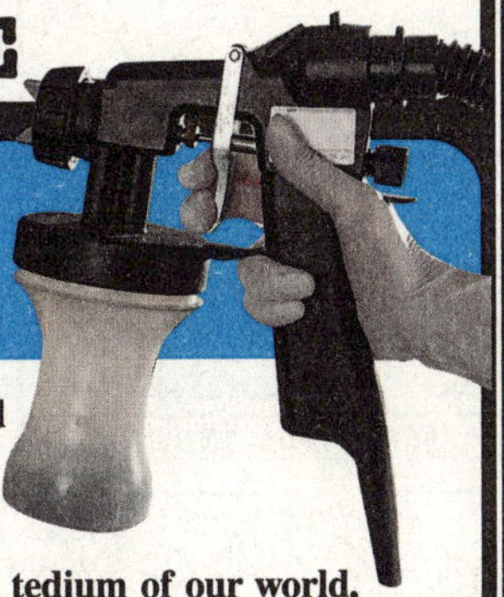

SUPERHEROES – the strangely powered adventurers that have been the staple characters of comics and films for years. *The Boys*, *Guardians of the Galaxy* and *The Black Knight* allow us to escape from the everyday, humdrum tedium of our world, and spent a thrilling few hours in theirs. *But what if their world and ours were one and the same?*

This thought sprang to mind when I heard the story of a Tyseley man who claimed to have gained superpowers after having a spray tan. Were these extraordinary claims the ramblings of a sad attention seeker, or had he truly undergone some strange transformation whilst visiting Tanned and Deliver by the incineration plant? I decided to investigate.

I interviewed Eddie Dome, who told me that since having the spray tan, he had developed incredible strength as well as the ability to make people do what he wants using the power of his mind. "I had the spray tan to look my best for a Christmas works do, but I didn't expect this!" he told me. I asked for a demonstration of his strength, but he said that his powers diminish as the tan fades, and he wasn't going back for a top-up until next week.

Just like the Hulk getting a blast of gamma rays, it's possible that the tanning machine had some effect on Eddie's body, gifting him these super-human abilities. But whatever the truth, the residents of Tyseley can sleep safe in their beds, as nightclub bouncer Eddie has vowed never to abuse his new-found powers. "I'll mostly use them for good," he told me.

It's a compelling story, and Eddie was a credible teller. But data speaks louder than words, and until I see his super-human abilities first hand, I will have to defer my judgement.

Conclusion: MORE EVIDENCE NEEDED

NEXT WEEK:** More tales of the supernatural and bizarre from the Midlands beacon of the paranormal in next week's **Tommy Quang's World of Strange.

LUCKY FRANK
DJ '23
WE BUY LUCKY HORSESHOES FOR A MILLION NO ACTUALLY MAKE THAT A BILLION QUID
CASH PAID
GRAND FETE
IT'S THE VICARAGE FETE TODAY, READERS.
LUCKY DIP 50p
FORTUNES TOLD
HOME MADE CAKES
AND I'M GOING TO CHANCE MY ARM AT THE LUCKY DIP!
PLUNGE!
HOPE I GET AN XBOX "S" SERIES!
LUCKY DIP 50p
FRANK! THAT'S NOT THE LUCKY DIP ~ IT'S A CARELESSLY POSITIONED BARREL OF SULPHURIC ACID!
HISSSSSS
LUCKY DIP 50p
LUCKY DIP
YARK! MY ARM HAS BEEN DISSOLVED ~ THAT WASN'T VERY FORTUNATE!
DON'T WORRY FRANK ~ A SPOONFUL OF THIS NATURAL REMEDY WHICH I'VE MADE OUT OF LUCKY HEATHER AND FOUR LEAF CLOVERS WILL SOON MAKE YOUR ARM GROW BACK!
Sylvia Moonstone's NATURAL MEDICINES
YURP?
GRACIOUS! I'VE TRIPPED OVER A BLACK CAT AND DOSED FRANK WITH THE WHOLE BOTTLE!
SHOVE!
TRIP
GLUB!
YUBBLE!
YOWP! NOW I'VE SPROUTED THIRTEEN ARMS ~ THAT'S UNLUCKY FOR ME...
SPROING!
BECAUSE I'M GOING TO LOOK LIKE AN ABSOLUTE FREAK!
NEVER MIND FRANK...
SPLAT THE RAT
HOOK A DUCK
YOU'RE WELL EQUIPPED TO TRY YOUR HAND AT MY STALL OVER HERE...
BRAVO, YOUNG MAN! WANKING OFF A DOZEN BISHOPS AT ONCE MAKES YOU THE RUNAWAY WINNER!
BASH THE BISHOP 50P
PULL A BISHOP'S COCK AND WIN A PRIZE
XBOX
FIRST PRIZE
WANK! WANK! JERK! TOSS!
UH! UH!
PLEASE ACCEPT FIRST PRIZE!
YOINKS! AN XBOX "S" SERIES!
OOH, YES!

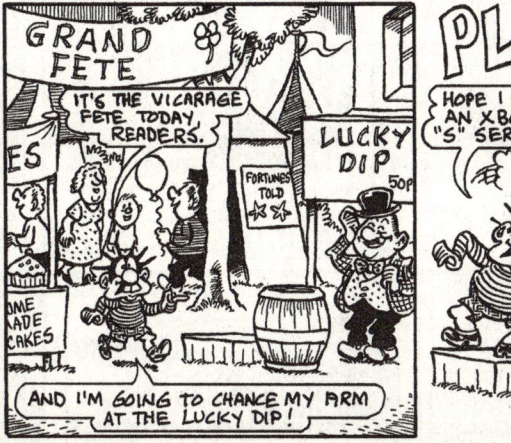

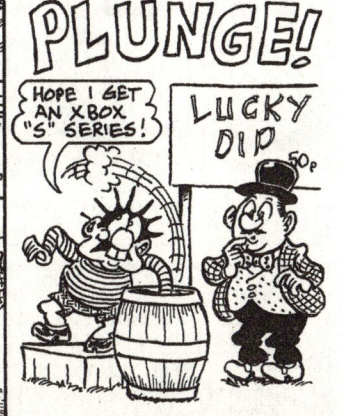

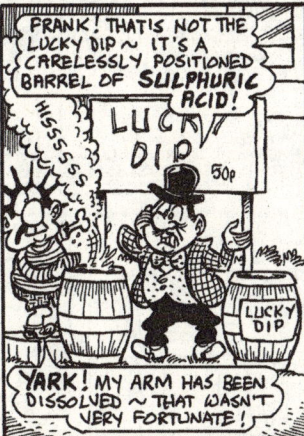

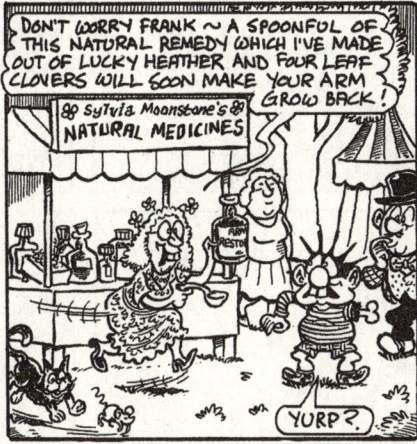

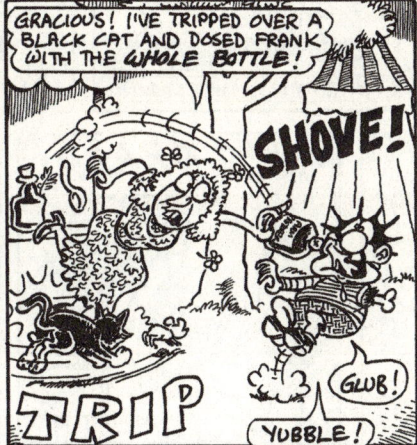

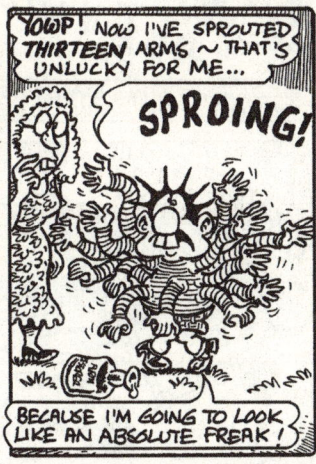

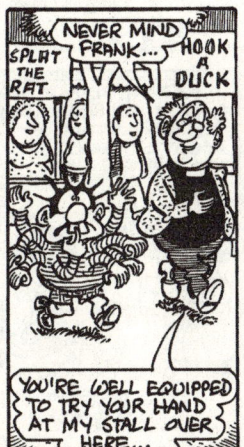

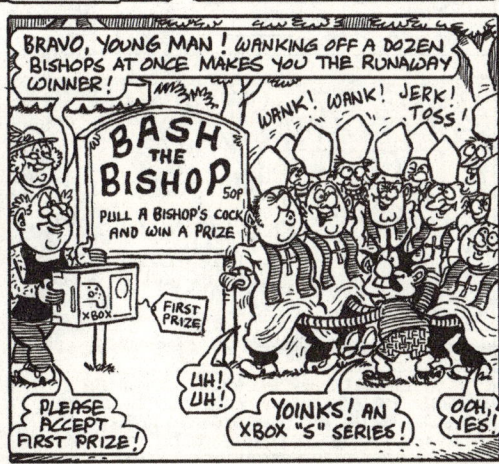

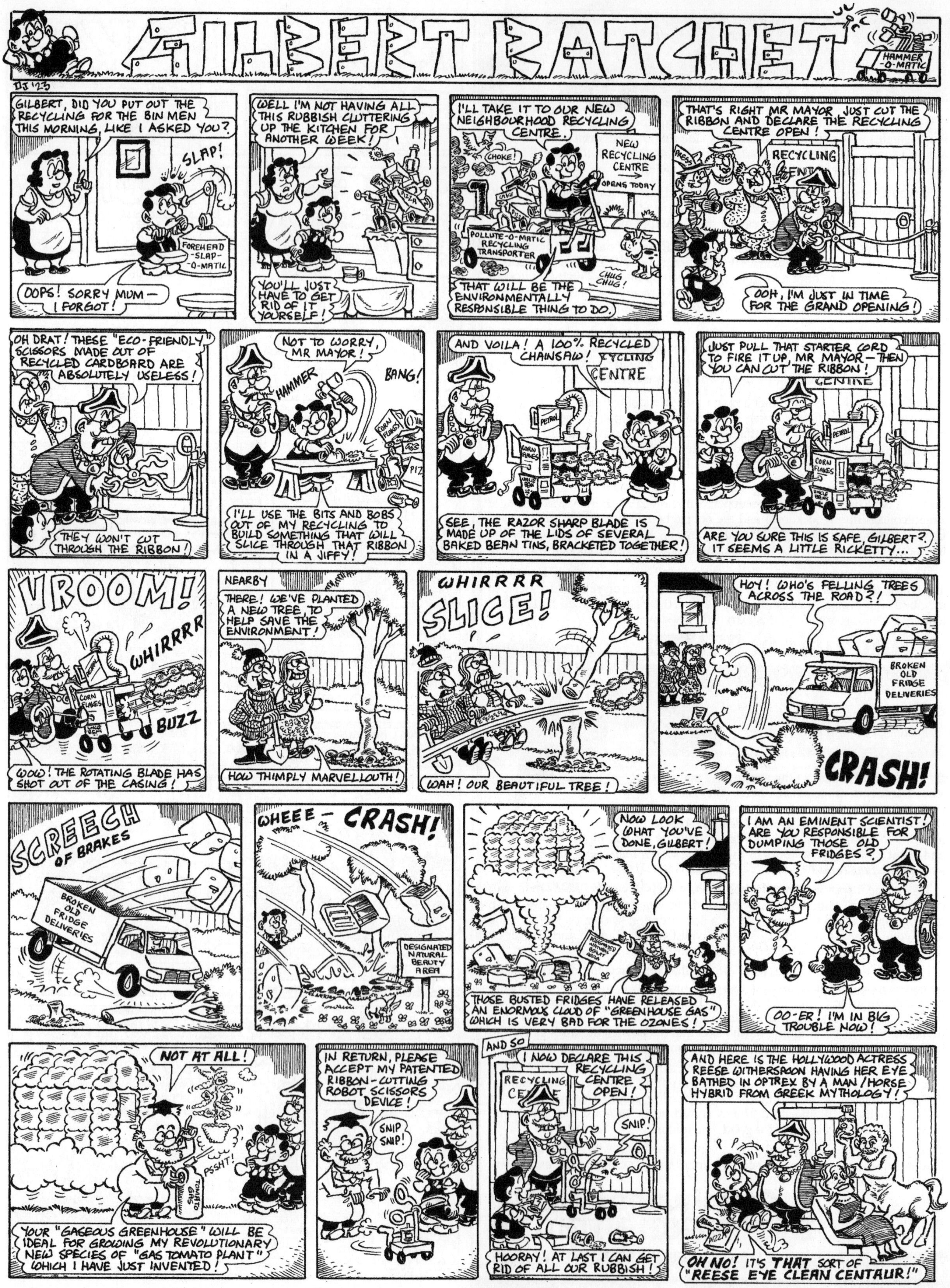
GILBERT RATCHET
HAMMER -O-MATIC
DJ '23
GILBERT, DID YOU PUT OUT THE RECYCLING FOR THE BIN MEN THIS MORNING, LIKE I ASKED YOU?
SLAP!
FOREHEAD -SLAP- -O-MATIC
OOPS! SORRY MUM — I FORGOT!
WELL I'M NOT HAVING ALL THIS RUBBISH CLUTTERING UP THE KITCHEN FOR ANOTHER WEEK!
YOU'LL JUST HAVE TO GET RID OF IT YOURSELF!
I'LL TAKE IT TO OUR NEW NEIGHBOURHOOD RECYCLING CENTRE.
CHOKE!
NEW RECYCLING CENTRE OPENS TODAY
POLLUTE-O-MATIC RECYCLING TRANSPORTER
CHUG CHUG!
THAT WILL BE THE ENVIRONMENTALLY RESPONSIBLE THING TO DO.
THAT'S RIGHT MR MAYOR JUST CUT THE RIBBON AND DECLARE THE RECYCLING CENTRE OPEN!
PRESS
RECYCLING
OOH, I'M JUST IN TIME FOR THE GRAND OPENING!
OH DRAT! THESE "ECO-FRIENDLY" SCISSORS MADE OUT OF RECYCLED CARDBOARD ARE ABSOLUTELY USELESS!
THEY WON'T CUT THROUGH THE RIBBON!
NOT TO WORRY, MR MAYOR!
HAMMER
BANG!
CORN FLAKES
I'LL USE THE BITS AND BOBS OUT OF MY RECYCLING TO BUILD SOMETHING THAT WILL SLICE THROUGH THAT RIBBON IN A JIFFY!
AND VOILA! A 100% RECYCLED CHAINSAW!
CYCLING CENTRE
PETROL
CORN FLAKES
SEE, THE RAZOR SHARP BLADE IS MADE UP OF THE LIDS OF SEVERAL BAKED BEAN TINS, BRACKETED TOGETHER!
JUST PULL THAT STARTER CORD TO FIRE IT UP, MR MAYOR — THEN YOU CAN CUT THE RIBBON!
ARE YOU SURE THIS IS SAFE, GILBERT? IT SEEMS A LITTLE RICKETTY...
VROOM!
WHIRRRR
BUZZ
WOW! THE ROTATING BLADE HAS SHOT OUT OF THE CASING!
NEARBY
THERE! WE'VE PLANTED A NEW TREE, TO HELP SAVE THE ENVIRONMENT!
HOW THIMPLY MARVELLOUTH!
WHIRRRR
SLICE!
WAH! OUR BEAUTIFUL TREE!
HOY! WHO'S FELLING TREES ACROSS THE ROAD?!
BROKEN OLD FRIDGE DELIVERIES
CRASH!
SCREECH OF BRAKES
BROKEN OLD FRIDGE DELIVERIES
WHEEE — CRASH!
DESIGNATED NATURAL BEAUTY AREA
NOW LOOK WHAT YOU'VE DONE, GILBERT!
THOSE BUSTED FRIDGES HAVE RELEASED AN ENORMOUS CLOUD OF "GREENHOUSE GAS" WHICH IS VERY BAD FOR THE OZONES!
I AM AN EMINENT SCIENTIST! ARE YOU RESPONSIBLE FOR DUMPING THOSE OLD FRIDGES?
OO-ER! I'M IN BIG TROUBLE NOW!
NOT AT ALL!
PSSHT!
TOMATO GAS
YOUR "GASEOUS GREENHOUSE" WILL BE IDEAL FOR GROWING MY REVOLUTIONARY NEW SPECIES OF "GAS TOMATO PLANT" WHICH I HAVE JUST INVENTED!
IN RETURN, PLEASE ACCEPT MY PATENTED RIBBON-CUTTING ROBOT SCISSORS DEVICE!
SNIP SNIP!
AND SO
I NOW DECLARE THIS RECYCLING CENTRE OPEN!
RECYCLING CE
SNIP!
HOORAY! AT LAST I CAN GET RID OF ALL OUR RUBBISH!
AND HERE IS THE HOLLYWOOD ACTRESS REESE WITHERSPOON HAVING HER EYE BATHED IN OPTREX BY A MAN/HORSE HYBRID FROM GREEK MYTHOLOGY!
OH NO! IT'S THAT SORT OF "REESE EYE CLEAN CENTAUR!"

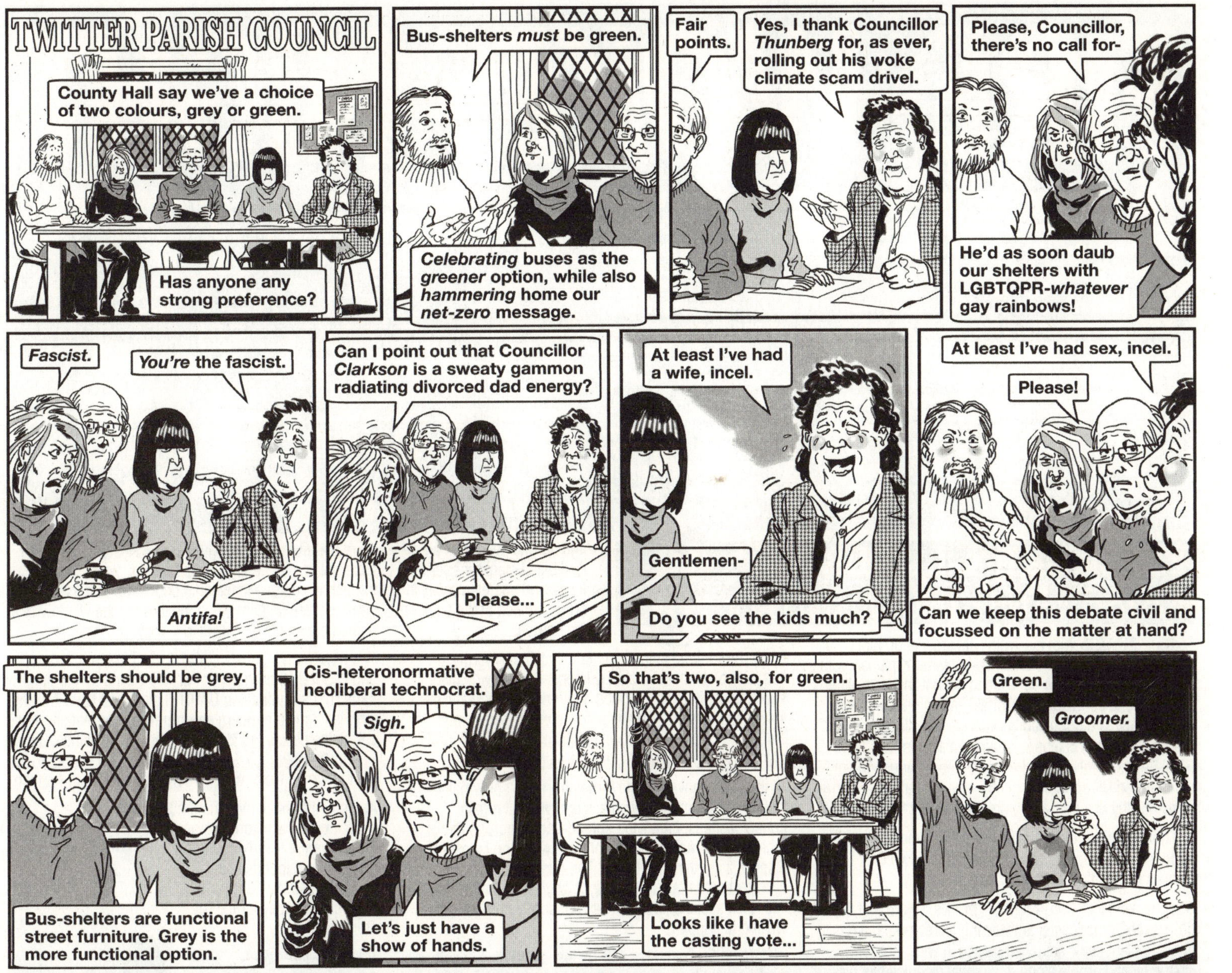

TWITTER PARISH COUNCIL
County Hall say we've a choice of two colours, grey or green.
Has anyone any strong preference?
Bus-shelters *must* be green.
Celebrating buses as the *greener* option, while also *hammering* home our *net-zero* message.
Fair points.
Yes, I thank Councillor *Thunberg* for, as ever, rolling out his woke climate scam drivel.
Please, Councillor, there's no call for-
He'd as soon daub our shelters with LGBTQPR-*whatever* gay rainbows!
Fascist.
You're the fascist.
Antifa!
Can I point out that Councillor *Clarkson* is a sweaty gammon radiating divorced dad energy?
Please...
At least I've had a wife, incel.
Gentlemen-
Do you see the kids much?
At least I've had sex, incel.
Please!
Can we keep this debate civil and focussed on the matter at hand?
The shelters should be grey.
Bus-shelters are functional street furniture. Grey is the more functional option.
Cis-heteronormative neoliberal technocrat.
Sigh.
Let's just have a show of hands.
So that's two, also, for green.
Looks like I have the casting vote...
Green.
Groomer.

HIS MAJESTY'S LEISURE

New report reveals British prisons just like holiday camps

A RECENTLY commissioned Government report focusing on conditions across the UK's prisons has left senior ministers in shock, revealing that many of the highest security 'Category A' prisons are being run 'just like holiday camps' with prisoners treated like 'holiday-makers.'

The report, compiled over three years, shows how far removed today's prisons are from the days of damp, white cells with bars in place of windows and bread and water being pushed through holes in the door.

Prisoners these days are more likely to do 'granola' than 'porridge', as good, old-fashioned correctional practices are ousted in place of airy-fairy fun activities, more akin to a holiday camp:

- ***OUT GOES** Prisoners shuffling around the recreation area in the freezing rain looking dolefully through the perimiter fence.*
- ***IN COMES** Lags larking around in a heated, Olympic-sized outdoor pool.*

EXCLUSIVE!

- ***OUT GOES** Inmates bending over to retrieve bars of soap in the showers.*
- ***IN COMES** Wardens organising knobbly-knees competitions for inmates with oversized soft toy prizes.*
- ***OUT GOES** Bored prisoners making matchstick models of ships and Eiffel Towers and doing rubbish paintings to pass the time.*
- ***IN COMES** Nightly variety performances including wardens' talent evenings, video karaoke sets and 'bamboozling' magic shows.*

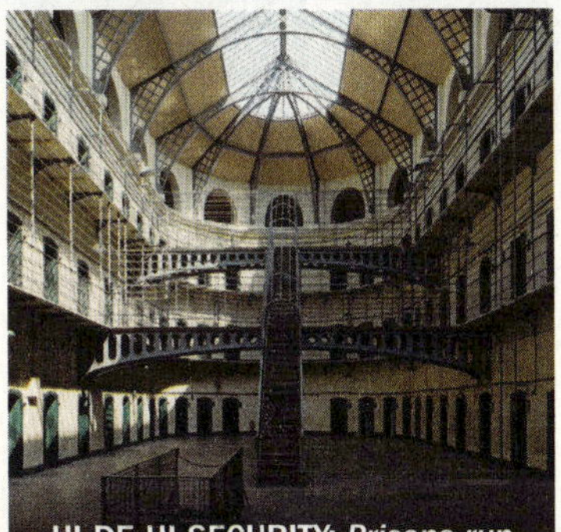

HI-DE-HI SECURITY: *Prisons run like hoiday camps, report finds.*

Reform Party (at time of going to press) MP, Lee Anderson, told us: "My party has long suspected that today's prisoners have an easy life on the inside, but this new report reveals the full scale of the problem."

"It's a disgrace. There's no hardship whatsoever," he continued. "Rather than being beaten every hour on the hour with a cat o' nine tails as punishment for their crimes, our prisoners are enjoying what can only be descibed as an extended holiday – a holiday that lasts the full length of their sentence. And it's all off the back of honest, tax-paying Brits. Have I said hanging's too good for them already?"

But Bob Oblong, a warden for HMP Wakefield who asked not to be named, told us that the recent report was misleading and that life on the inside was appropriately tough for their inmates.

"Anyone who's ever missed the 7am xylophone chime over the tannoy system calling inmates for breakfast at the Tahitian Lounge will know the meaning of true hunger," he explained.

"And you get plenty of time to dwell over your life choices between the end of the midday Punch and Judy show and the start of the Over 60s Tug O' War competition, taking place at 14.00 hours by the far end of the lazy river."

FIRE-*WOKES* NIGHT!

ASK any decent, non-traitorous Brit what their favourite day of the year that isn't St George's Day is, and the response will always be the same: *Bonfire Night*.

Every November 5th is a patriotic carnival of high-flying pyrotechnics, glittering sparklers, scrumptious baked potatoes and cheeky human effigies roasting on green and pleasant bonfires. What's not to love?

*Sadly, **EVERYTHING**, according to the joyless, left-leaning celebs who are hell bent on taking over our country.*

Year in, year out, members of the showbiz Wokerati descend mob-like from their ivory towers to launch pearl-clutching attacks on every aspect of our Great British Bonfire Night traditions. Whether it's 'elf-n-safety' pen-pushers insisting we wear protective goggles to launch our rockets, PC red-tape merchants whining about the fireworks frightening hamsters, or nanny-state namby-pambies complaining about the toffee apples being 'too sugary', you literally couldn't make it up! Although, to be fair, we may have done, as we haven't checked if anyone has ever actually complained about those things.

Regardless, it's crystal clear that the Loony Left killjoys are intent on sucking all the fun out of Guy Fawkes Night. But it begs the question...

*Just how closely do these sanctimonious snowflakes obey their **OWN** ultra-woke Fireworks Codes come November 5th?*

We sent top *Viz* investigative reporter **MAHATMA MACAROON** out and about this Bonfire Night, going deep undercover at the fireworks parties of the liberal elite. And the hypocrisy he uncovered will make every UK citizen who isn't an enemy of the people feel **SICK** to their stomach.

Join us now, as we get up close and personal with... the *FIRE-WOKE BRIGADE!*

FIREWOKE A-LISTER #1: KRISHNAN GURU-MURTHY

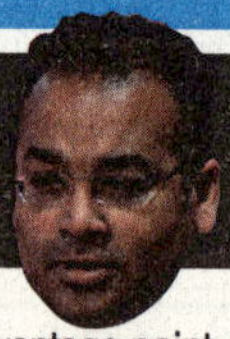

ARMED with his Trotskyite arsenal of 'facts' and 'evidence', Channel 4 coward Krishnan gets his kicks from humiliating decent men like Nigel Farage, Boris Johnson and Donald Trump on his tawdry news show. The so-called 'journalist' was also one of many left-leaning celebs to speak out against ex-PM Rishi Sunak's brave decision not to repair thousands of condemned UK schools recently – so it's safe to assume Guru-Murthy is a card-carrying 'elf-n-safety' loon to boot.

But how much does this hand-wringing hypocrite care about elf-and-safety when it comes to his own Guy Fawkes celebrations? *I aim to find out.*

After hacking into Guru-Murthy's emails, I learn that the do-gooding broadcaster is throwing a fireworks bash at his opulent semi-detached palace in west London. On the night, I amble along, cunningly disguised as his equally PC-crazed former colleague, Jon Snow, my hair coloured silver by two cans of lead-heavy spray paint. It's the perfect disguise – even Snow's own mother would mistake me for her Stalinist son. The party is just starting and no one even bats an eyelid as I clamber over the fence and secrete myself in some bushes at the back of the garden.

From my vantage point, I can see that Guru-Murthy has set up six rockets, clearly intended to provide the spectacular finale to tonight's fireworks show. On initial inspection they *seem* to be safely erected – each one standing in a plastic tube secured firmly in the soil, and pointing straight upwards into the night sky.

At this point, however, the fumes from the spray paint kick in and I momentarily black out. When I regain consciousness, I am lying spread-eagled across the rockets and I realise to my horror how wrong I was – the display is anything BUT safe! The gunpowder-packed cylinders are in fact lying at *right-angles* on the ground with their sticks snapped. They are surely an accident waiting to happen.

In order to find out, I light all six fuses and dive headfirst back into the bush, praying that I'm wrong and Guru-Murthy has actually thought this unorthodox set-up through.

KA-BLAMMM!!!

As I poke my head back out of the shrubbery, my worst fears are realised. Guru-Murthy's recklessly assembled pyrotechnics have blown a gigantic hole through his garden fence, and shot through to neighbouring gardens. One of them has gone through the window of a parked car and is exploding in a shower of sparks.

The newsman's guests come spilling out into the garden, and I spot BBC correspondent Ros Atkins screaming, "My car!! That's my fucking **CAR!!**" I glance at Guru-Murthy, who is feigning concern and mumbling something about calling the police. But it's a piss-poor performance. Careless Krishnan knows full well that his shameful disregard for the Fireworks Code was an accident waiting to happen.

As I clamber back over the fence I find myself physically vomiting onto the pavement. Guru-Murthy's nauseating hypocrisy, and possibly also the paint fumes, have quite literally turned my stomach.

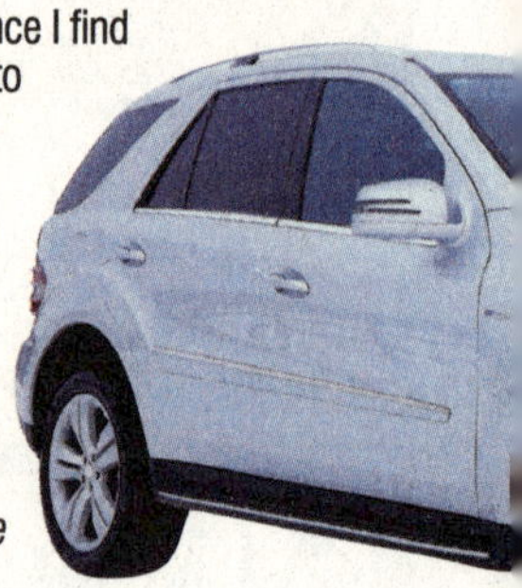

This high-and-mighty newshound loves to accuse politicians of failing to look after the common man, but he can't even look after his own Guy Fawkes guests.

FIREWOKE A-LISTER #2: BEN FOGLE

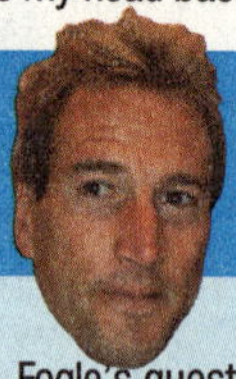

PLUMMY-VOICED Beeb fave Ben has long used his celebrity platform to virtue signal about the horrors of so called 'climate change'. With this in mind, it would be fascinating to find out just how environmentally sound the 'eco-friendly' star's fireworks celebrations are. *I set off to find out.*

Still hallucinating from the lead-based paint smeared all over my head, I stagger towards Fogle's house nearby. I know from having rifled through his bins last week that the ex-*Castaway* icon is hosting some pals for a Bonfire gathering, and I intend to be there.

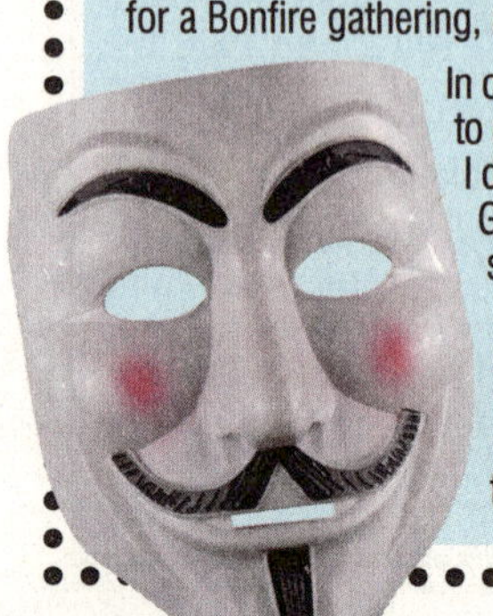

In order to scope out the best spot to gain access to Fogle's garden, I disguise myself as a lifeless Guy Fawkes effigy. Holding a sign reading 'PENNY FOR THE GUY' and wearing a wide-brimmed Witchfinder hat and a *V For Vendetta* mask, I lie deathly still in a cart opposite the presenter's house. For the crowning touch, I've doused myself from head to toe in diesel so I even give off that 'about-to-be-burned' smell.

The disguise works like a charm. Fogle's guests all file straight past me, and aside from a few dozen people asking me repeatedly if I'm OK or if I need help, no one suspects that I'm not an inanimate, anti-Catholic puppet.

Once the party has started, I leap out of my cart and hop over the garden fence. Fogle's bonfire has already been lit, and at first sight, it certainly **LOOKS** environmentally friendly. It's small and well contained, built from twigs and logs, with no sign of toxic chemical fire-lighters anywhere. The *Countryfile* ace has also constructed a stone circle around it to stop the flames getting out of hand. So far, so non-hypocritical...

Until I decide to take a closer look.

As I lean over the blaze to properly inspect its sustainability, the fumes from my jacket intensify the flames, which suddenly leap up and roar. Thinking quickly, I attempt to subdue the blaze by taking off my jacket and wafting out the flames. Unfortunately, that only seems to make matters worse.

FLOOOMF!!!

The inferno soars twenty feet up into the night sky, catching the branch of an overhanging tree. I watch in horror as the blaze spreads into neighbouring gardens, incinerating all the foliage in its path.

Once again, I feel sick to my stomach. This was a simple mishap that could have happened at **ANY** Bonfire party, to **ANY** person whose clothes were soaked in diesel. But reckless Fogle hadn't even bothered to put the necessary precautions in place to stop it. The muscle-bound eco-hunk is constantly telling others to 'take care of the environment'. Yet apparently it's **FINE** for him to decimate acres of local vegetation at his Bacchanalian Bonfire Bash. *Talk about double standards.*

As the wail of sirens fills the air, I shake my head, devastated – yet not entirely unsurprised – that another Woke A-Lister has turned out to be an utter fucking hypocrite.

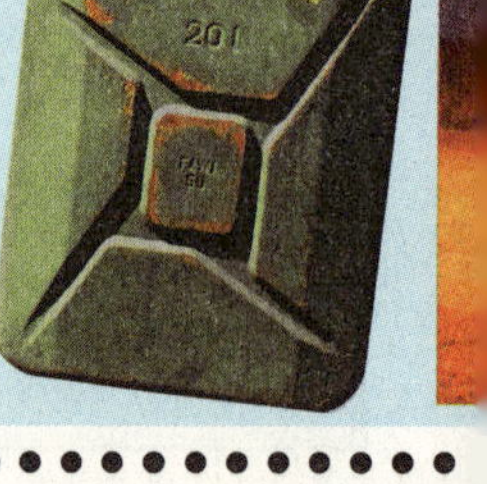

Fogle made his name on the shit reality series 'Castaway'. But after this flame-grilled Fireworks night, I think he should 'Cast Away' his eco-friendly credentials.

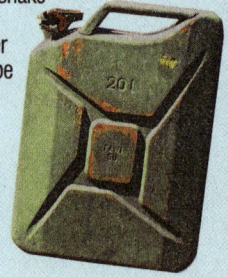

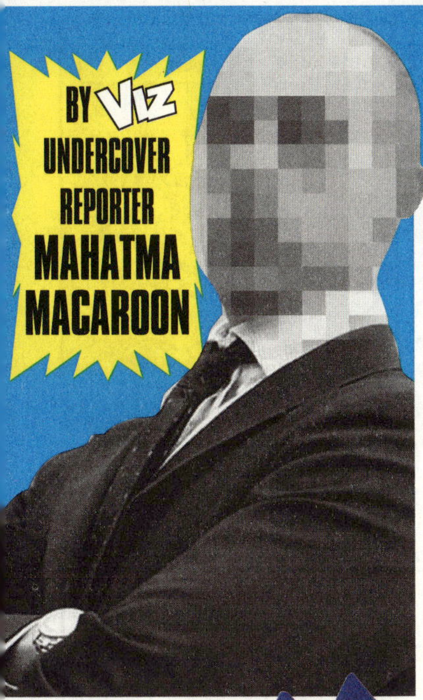
BY VIZ
UNDERCOVER
REPORTER
MAHATMA
MACAROON

We expose the bonfire-based hypocrisy of the Loony Left stars

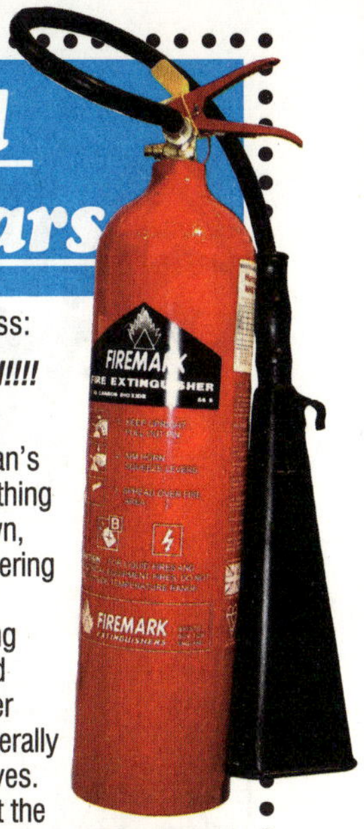
FIREMARK
FIREMARK

FIREWOKE A-LISTER #3: CAROL VORDERMAN

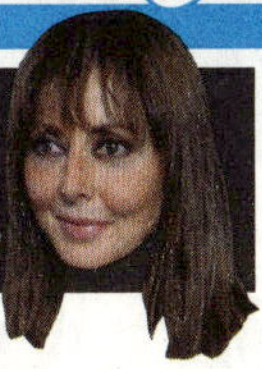

CURVY brainbox Carol has become a hero of the Woke Mob recently, due to her scathing comments about our green and pleasant government. The treasonous telly temptress regularly takes to social media to accuse the hard-working Tory Party of being 'disgraceful', 'chaotic' and 'inept'. Having dished out this harsh criticism, then, it's fair to assume that Carol's own Fireworks Party will run smoothly, safely and successfully...

Or so you might think.

Drifting in and out of consciousness due to the dual effects of the diesel and lead paint fumes, I stumble towards the ex-*Countdown* crumpet's nearby house. Having recently tasered her postman and intercepted her mail, I know she's hosting a Guy Fawkes knees-up this evening. It's strictly invite-only, but luckily I have another cunning disguise up my sleeve to ensure I gain entry.

Done up in a fireman's fancy dress outfit that I bought on eBay, I knock at Vorderman's door claiming to be a fire safety inspector. "I'm checking all the homes in the area to make sure all fireworks are securely installed, ma'am," I tell the buxom boffin.

Carol is clearly rattled, but she masks it expertly with a confused frown. "Erm, OK, we haven't started the fireworks yet, so you can go on through the garden," the vowel-or-consonant vixen tells me.

In the back yard, I find a brightly coloured Catherine Wheel set up and ready for launch. It has been safely installed on a firm wooden post, with a thick metal nail hammered through its centre. But it's a damp night, so there's a chance that the nail could rust, in which case, the wheel would sputter and stall, wrenching itself loose from its stake and wreaking fiery havoc across Vorderman's garden.

Shaking my head at Carol's dangerous set-up, I pull out a can of WD40 from my *Fireman Sam* satchel and remove the nail so I can properly lubricate it. Unfortunately, the nozzle of the can is turned the wrong way, so I end up spraying a substantial amount of toxic isoparaffin directly into my eyes and mouth. I stagger blindly into a shrub and lose consciousness. I am awoken an hour later by the sound of screaming followed by a fizzing, fiery hiss:

PSSSSHHHHHHHHH!!!!

Peering out from the bush, I see Vorderman's Catherine Wheel scything wildly across her lawn, sending guests scattering like human bowling pins, before careening up onto her patio and smashing through her French windows. I literally cannot believe my eyes. Calamity Carol has lit the firework's fuse without even **BOTHERING** to check whether I'd reinserted the nail after lubricating it, which I hadn't, due to blacking out.

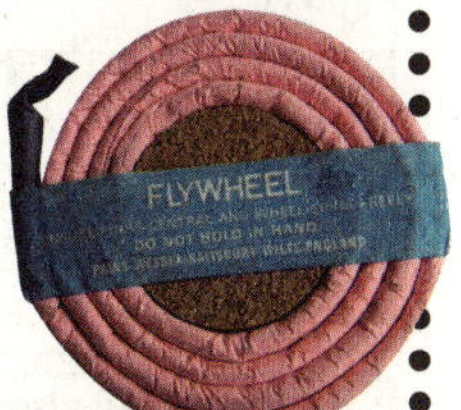
FLYWHEEL

As the curvy klutz reaches for her fire extinguisher and struggles to tackle the roaring blaze, I can't help but chuckle at her brazen hypocrisy. How would I describe this Fireworks Party? 'Disgraceful'? Check. 'Chaotic'? Check. 'Inept'? Check.

Looks like the bosomy broadcaster should choose her words more carefully next time.

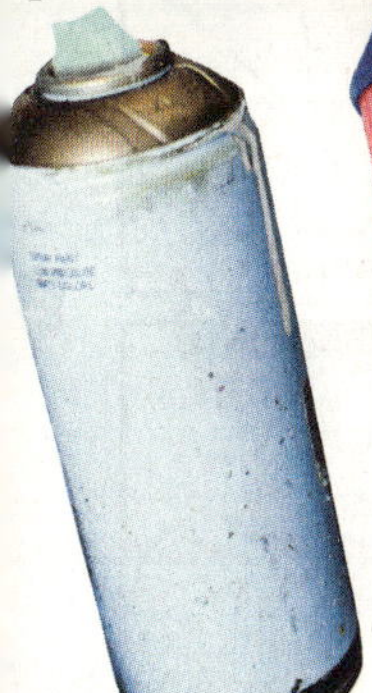

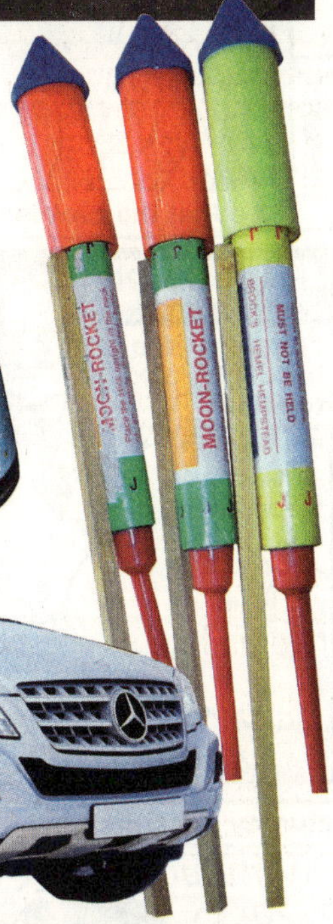
MOON-ROCKET
MOON-ROCKET

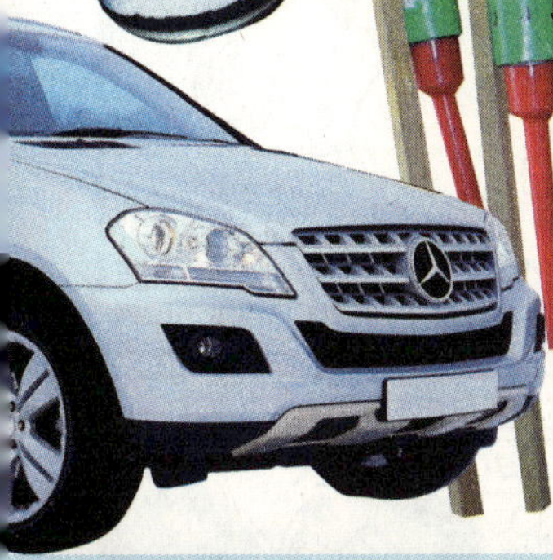

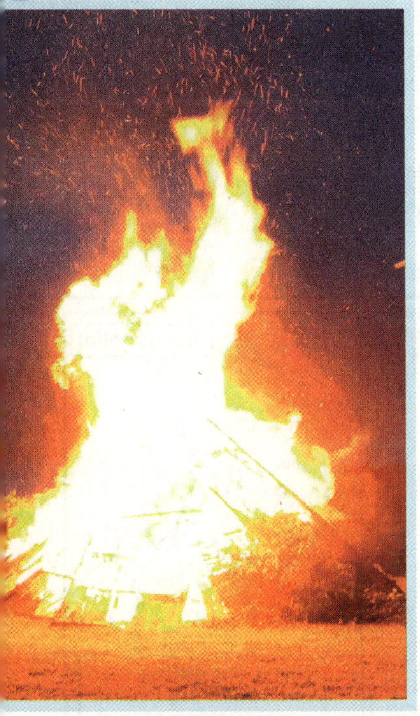

FIREWOKE A-LISTER #4: MICHAEL SHEEN

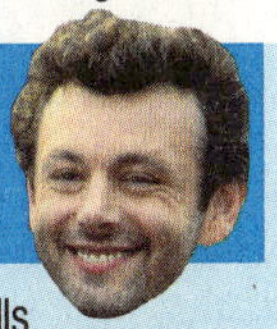

WHEN he's not being paid billions to dress up as David Frost or Tony Blair, lefty luvvie Michael can usually be found being a traitor to his country. Whether he's returning his OBE, campaigning for 'Welsh independence' or sticking up for homeless parasitic scroungers, Sheen is a proud member of the Woke Stasi. What's more, as a passionate supporter of animal rights charities, it's likely the actor is one of those bleeding-heart liberals who drone on about the importance of 'keeping pets safe' on Fireworks Night.

But how much does the bearded blowhard care about cats' and dogs' security when it comes to his *own* Guy Fawkes celebrations? Is it one rule for us plebs and another for high-and-mighty Michael?

Let's fucking see, shall we?

High on a cocktail of diesel, lead and WD40, I stumble towards Sheen's opulent two-up-two-down ivory tower. Having previously tapped Michael's phone, I know he's planning a bonfire blowout tonight, and I'm aiming to test the star's canine fireworks conduct. I stop en route to borrow six pitbulls from a local dog fight organiser I know.

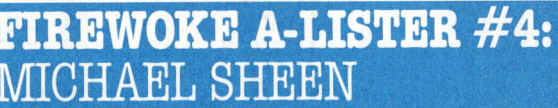

With my bloodthirsty hounds in tow, I pitch up at Sheen's pad to find his November 5th shindig in full swing. Peering over the garden fence, I see that the actor is so concerned about startling the local animals that he hasn't even got in any fireworks – just a load of sparklers. So far, so woke.

But sparklers still technically count as 'fireworks', and even if they don't make noise, their brightly coloured discharge could easily unsettle a timid pooch. *And animal-loving Michael wouldn't want that, would he?* And as the Port Talbot performer's guests retreat to the garden and light their politically correct pyrotechnics, I make a run for the house with my borrowed dogs.

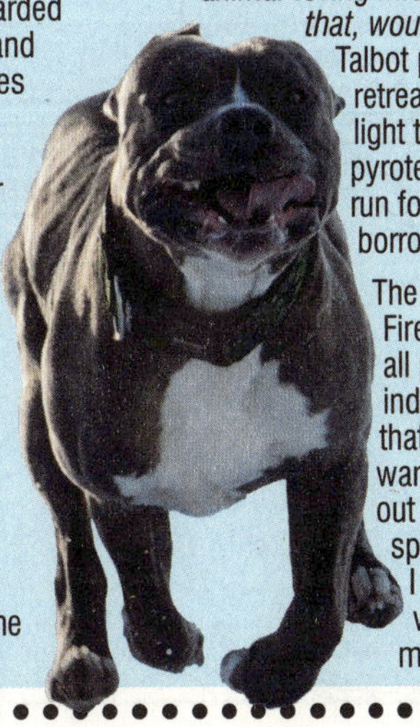

The first rule of the Fireworks Code is that all pets **MUST** be kept indoors, and knowing that Michael wouldn't want my poor pitbulls out on the street with his sparklers flashing about, I jemmy his downstairs window and usher the mutts inside.

KER-SMASHHHHH!!!

It's a heartwarming sight to see the dogs safe inside Sheen's living room. They are not the best behaved animals in the world, and before long they're ripping Michael's sofa to shreds, and plastering his carpet with foul-smelling faeces. But surely Sheen will find this a small price to pay for knowing that these charming local pups are sheltered from his pyrotechnics?

Guess again.

Hearing the commotion from inside, the bewhiskered board-treader rushes into the house. "What the FUCK?!!" he screams.

Not for the first time this evening, my heart sinks. This uber-woke Welshman makes a song and dance about being kind to animals, but clearly he'd rather my adorable terriers were out on the street, cowering in terror from his sparklers.

As I stumble away to the sound of more barking, crashing and screeching, I can't help but feel utterly numb with disappointment, and probably paint/petrol/WD40 inhalation.

*The traitorous thesp may have returned his knighthood, but here's one title he **CAN'T** return: **BRITAIN'S BIGGEST HYPOCRITE**.*

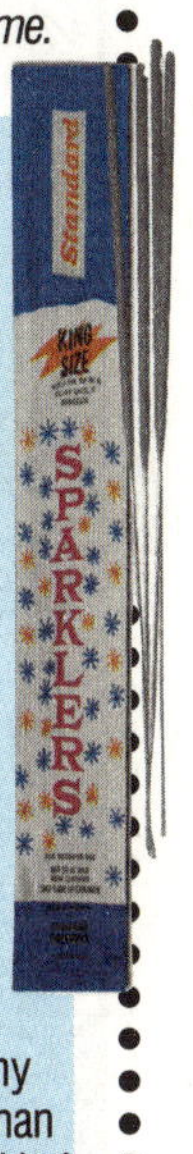
Standard
SPARKLERS

NEXT WEEK – "I'M DREAMING OF A WOKE CHRISTMAS!" *Mahatma dresses up Santa Claus, Rudolph, Frosty, and the Infant Jesus Christ in order to expose the snowflake celebs' festive hypocrisy.*

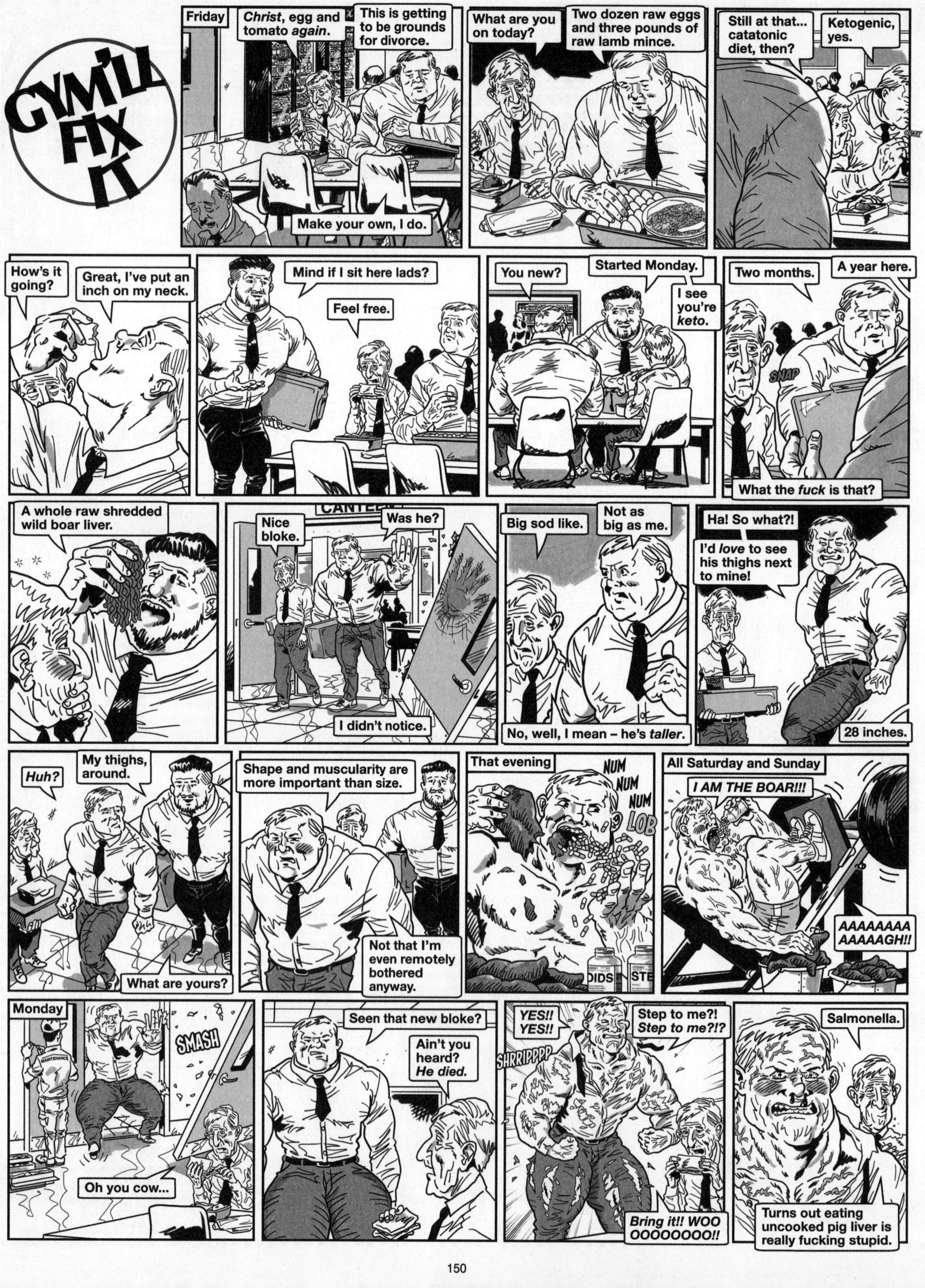
GYM'LL FIX IT
Friday
Christ, egg and tomato *again*.
This is getting to be grounds for divorce.
Make your own, I do.
What are you on today?
Two dozen raw eggs and three pounds of raw lamb mince.
Still at that... catatonic diet, then?
Ketogenic, yes.
How's it going?
Great, I've put an inch on my neck.
Mind if I sit here lads?
Feel free.
You new?
Started Monday.
I see you're *keto*.
Two months.
A year here.
SNAP
What the *fuck* is that?
A whole raw shredded wild boar liver.
Nice bloke.
Was he?
I didn't notice.
Big sod like.
Not as big as me.
No, well, I mean – he's *taller*.
Ha! So what?!
I'd *love* to see his thighs next to mine!
28 inches.
Huh?
My thighs, around.
What are yours?
Shape and muscularity are more important than size.
Not that I'm even remotely bothered anyway.
That evening
NUM
NUM
NUM
LOB
All Saturday and Sunday
I AM THE BOAR!!!
AAAAAAAA AAAAAGH!!
Monday
SMASH
Oh you cow...
Seen that new bloke?
Ain't you heard? *He died.*
YES!! YES!!
Step to me?! *Step to me?!?*
Bring it!! WOO OOOOOOOO!!
Salmonella.
Turns out eating uncooked pig liver is really fucking stupid.

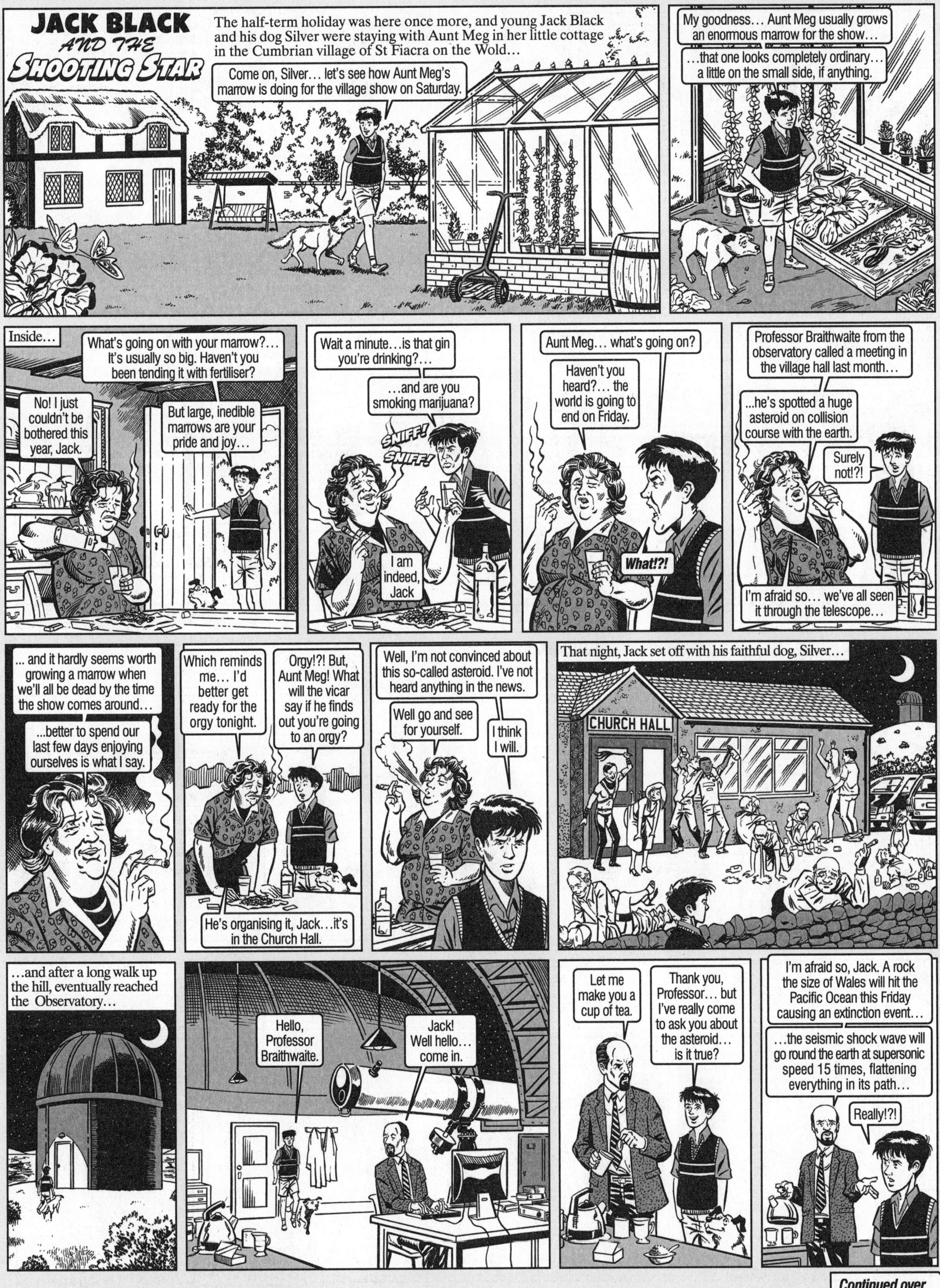

JACK BLACK AND THE SHOOTING STAR
The half-term holiday was here once more, and young Jack Black and his dog Silver were staying with Aunt Meg in her little cottage in the Cumbrian village of St Fiacra on the Wold…
Come on, Silver… let's see how Aunt Meg's marrow is doing for the village show on Saturday.
My goodness… Aunt Meg usually grows an enormous marrow for the show…
…that one looks completely ordinary… a little on the small side, if anything.
Inside…
What's going on with your marrow?… It's usually so big. Haven't you been tending it with fertiliser?
No! I just couldn't be bothered this year, Jack.
But large, inedible marrows are your pride and joy…
Wait a minute…is that gin you're drinking?…
…and are you smoking marijuana?
SNIFF!
SNIFF!
I am indeed, Jack
Aunt Meg… what's going on?
Haven't you heard?… the world is going to end on Friday.
What!?!
Professor Braithwaite from the observatory called a meeting in the village hall last month…
...he's spotted a huge asteroid on collision course with the earth.
Surely not!?!
I'm afraid so… we've all seen it through the telescope…
... and it hardly seems worth growing a marrow when we'll all be dead by the time the show comes around…
...better to spend our last few days enjoying ourselves is what I say.
Which reminds me… I'd better get ready for the orgy tonight.
Orgy!?! But, Aunt Meg! What will the vicar say if he finds out you're going to an orgy?
He's organising it, Jack…it's in the Church Hall.
Well, I'm not convinced about this so-called asteroid. I've not heard anything in the news.
Well go and see for yourself.
I think I will.
That night, Jack set off with his faithful dog, Silver…
CHURCH HALL
…and after a long walk up the hill, eventually reached the Observatory…
Hello, Professor Braithwaite.
Jack! Well hello… come in.
Let me make you a cup of tea.
Thank you, Professor… but I've really come to ask you about the asteroid… is it true?
I'm afraid so, Jack. A rock the size of Wales will hit the Pacific Ocean this Friday causing an extinction event…
…the seismic shock wave will go round the earth at supersonic speed 15 times, flattening everything in its path…
Really!?!

Continued over...

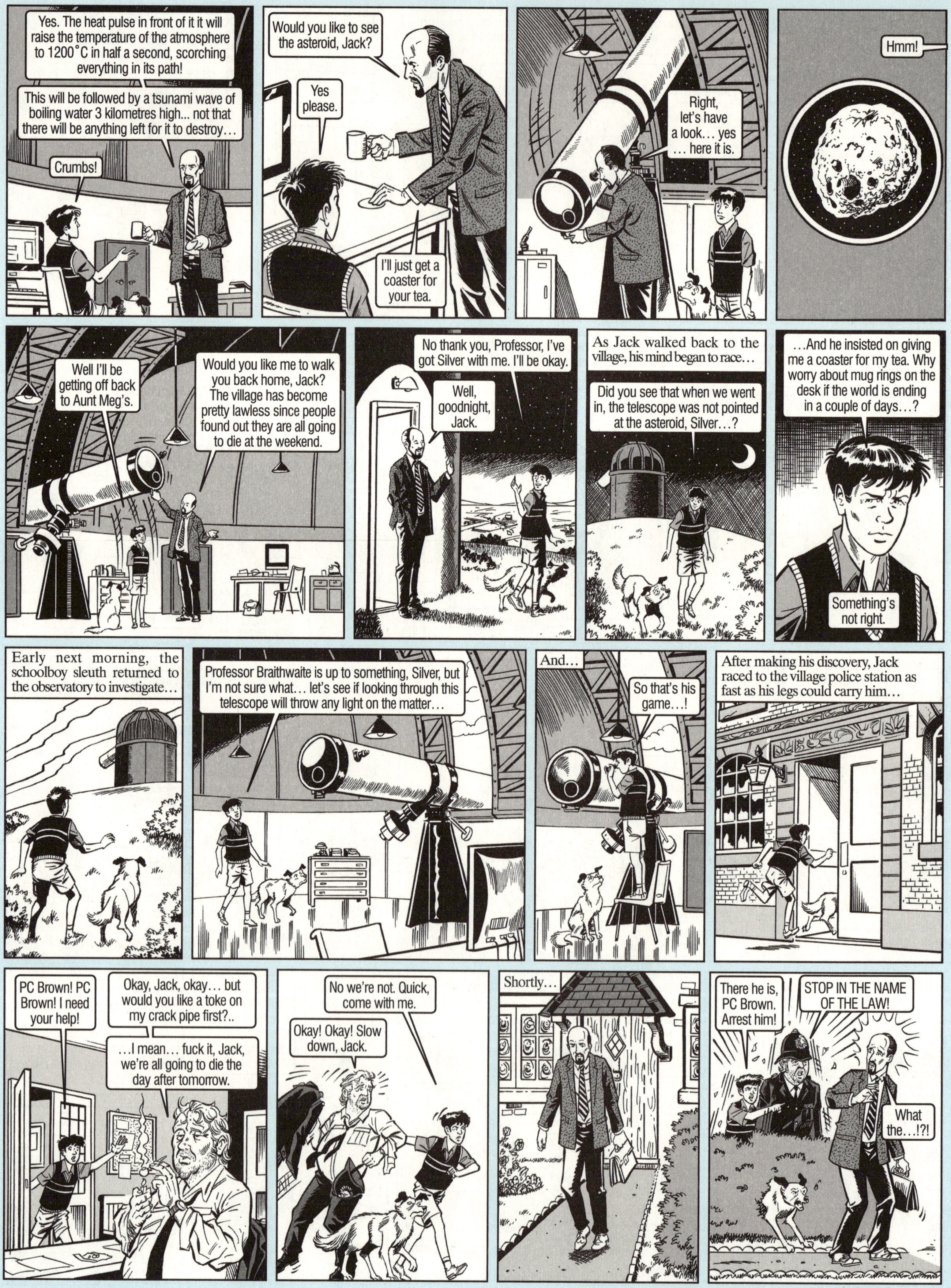
Yes. The heat pulse in front of it it will raise the temperature of the atmosphere to 1200˚C in half a second, scorching everything in its path!
This will be followed by a tsunami wave of boiling water 3 kilometres high... not that there will be anything left for it to destroy…
Crumbs!
Would you like to see the asteroid, Jack?
Yes please.
I'll just get a coaster for your tea.
Right, let's have a look… yes … here it is.
Hmm!
Well I'll be getting off back to Aunt Meg's.
Would you like me to walk you back home, Jack? The village has become pretty lawless since people found out they are all going to die at the weekend.
No thank you, Professor, I've got Silver with me. I'll be okay.
Well, goodnight, Jack.
As Jack walked back to the village, his mind began to race…
Did you see that when we went in, the telescope was not pointed at the asteroid, Silver…?
…And he insisted on giving me a coaster for my tea. Why worry about mug rings on the desk if the world is ending in a couple of days…?
Something's not right.
Early next morning, the schoolboy sleuth returned to the observatory to investigate…
Professor Braithwaite is up to something, Silver, but I'm not sure what… let's see if looking through this telescope will throw any light on the matter…
And…
So that's his game…!
After making his discovery, Jack raced to the village police station as fast as his legs could carry him…
PC Brown! PC Brown! I need your help!
Okay, Jack, okay… but would you like a toke on my crack pipe first?..
…I mean… fuck it, Jack, we're all going to die the day after tomorrow.
No we're not. Quick, come with me.
Okay! Okay! Slow down, Jack.
Shortly…
There he is, PC Brown. Arrest him!
STOP IN THE NAME OF THE LAW!
What the…!?!

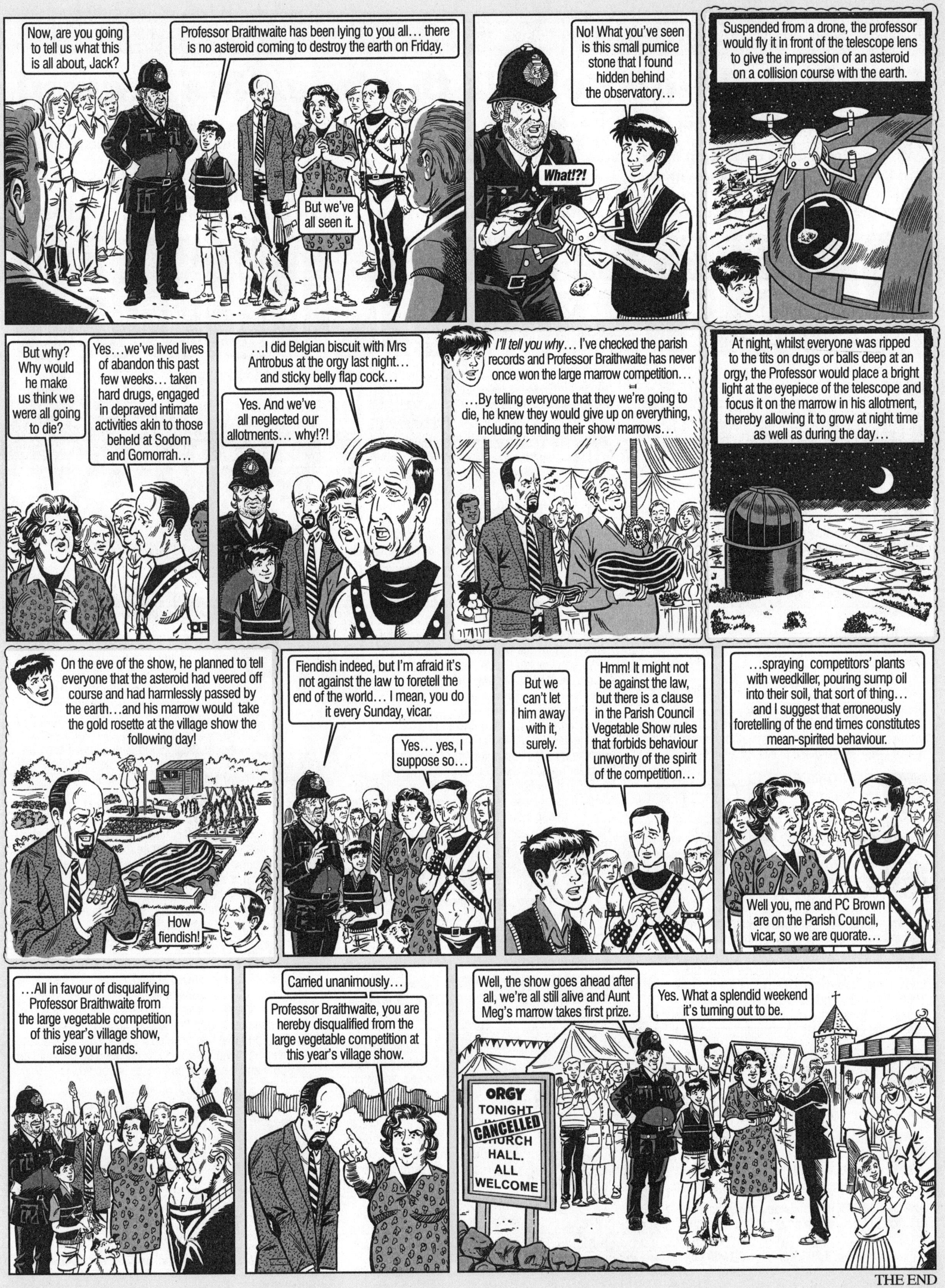
Now, are you going to tell us what this is all about, Jack?
Professor Braithwaite has been lying to you all… there is no asteroid coming to destroy the earth on Friday.
But we've all seen it.
No! What you've seen is this small pumice stone that I found hidden behind the observatory…
What!?!
Suspended from a drone, the professor would fly it in front of the telescope lens to give the impression of an asteroid on a collision course with the earth.
But why? Why would he make us think we were all going to die?
Yes…we've lived lives of abandon this past few weeks… taken hard drugs, engaged in depraved intimate activities akin to those beheld at Sodom and Gomorrah…
…I did Belgian biscuit with Mrs Antrobus at the orgy last night… and sticky belly flap cock…
Yes. And we've all neglected our allotments… why!?!
I'll tell you why… I've checked the parish records and Professor Braithwaite has never once won the large marrow competition…
…By telling everyone that they we're going to die, he knew they would give up on everything, including tending their show marrows…
At night, whilst everyone was ripped to the tits on drugs or balls deep at an orgy, the Professor would place a bright light at the eyepiece of the telescope and focus it on the marrow in his allotment, thereby allowing it to grow at night time as well as during the day…
On the eve of the show, he planned to tell everyone that the asteroid had veered off course and had harmlessly passed by the earth…and his marrow would take the gold rosette at the village show the following day!
How fiendish!
Fiendish indeed, but I'm afraid it's not against the law to foretell the end of the world… I mean, you do it every Sunday, vicar.
Yes… yes, I suppose so…
But we can't let him away with it, surely.
Hmm! It might not be against the law, but there is a clause in the Parish Council Vegetable Show rules that forbids behaviour unworthy of the spirit of the competition…
…spraying competitors' plants with weedkiller, pouring sump oil into their soil, that sort of thing… and I suggest that erroneously foretelling of the end times constitutes mean-spirited behaviour.
Well you, me and PC Brown are on the Parish Council, vicar, so we are quorate…
…All in favour of disqualifying Professor Braithwaite from the large vegetable competition of this year's village show, raise your hands.
Carried unanimously…
Professor Braithwaite, you are hereby disqualified from the large vegetable competition at this year's village show.
Well, the show goes ahead after all, we're all still alive and Aunt Meg's marrow takes first prize.
Yes. What a splendid weekend it's turning out to be.
ORGY TONIGHT
CANCELLED
HALL.
ALL WELCOME
THE END

Ho! Ho! Ho-oh no! It's the infestive season!

THEY'RE small, they've got six legs, they live in your bed and they bite you on the arse. They disappeared briefly during the pandemic, but now they're back with a vengeance. They're BEDBUGS, and chances are the mattress you fall asleep on tonight is absolutely lifting with the things.

But despite sharing our beds with them, we know very little about these insect parasites. Where do they lay their eggs? What do they eat? How do they grow? Actually, these are some of the questions to which scientists do know the answers, but there are many aspects of these critters' lives that remain a mystery. Here are...

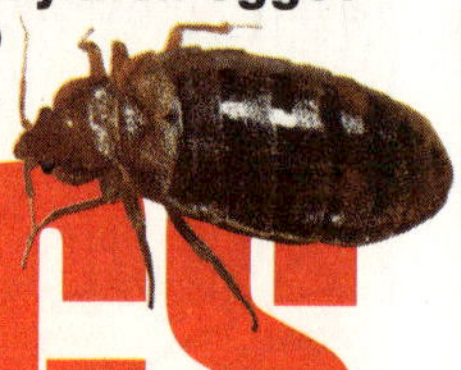

20 THINGS YOU NEVER KNEW ABOUT BEDBUGS

1 **BEDBUGS** come out of hiding and feed on their hosts when they are asleep. For this reason, you won't find these parasites in the beds of brothels, as nobody ever goes to sleep in them. After perfunctory sexual intercourse, during which both participants remain wide awake, brothel beds are quickly vacated. Any bedbugs finding themselves living in a knocking shop would quickly starve.

2 **BEDBUGS**, like fleas, mosquitoes and vampire bats, feed off human blood. Some people may view this as nauseating, but blood is effectively just liquid black pudding – a staple ingredient of your favourite full English breakfast!

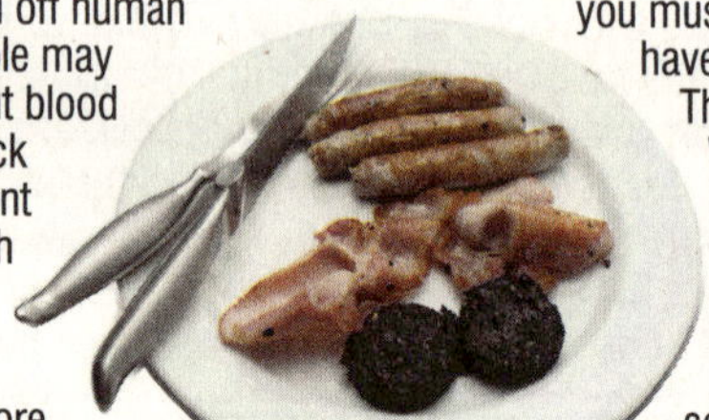

3 **BEDBUG** infestations are more common in towns and cities than in the countryside, simply because there are more beds in a metropolis. Rural areas have beds in houses and cottages, with perhaps a few pubs doing B&B. But cities have beds in houses, high-rise flats, hostels and enormous chain hotels – the dream place to live for a bedbug.

4 **IRONICALLY**, one place you won't find any bedbugs is in a bed showroom or bed factory.

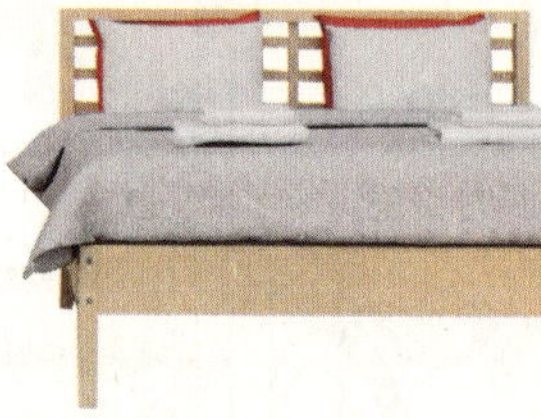

5 **SO** that's actually two places.

6 **THE CITY** of Paris recently suffered an outbreak of bedbugs, with the parasitic insects quickly spreading to the UK inside holidaymakers' luggage, in vehicles on board ferries, and tucked into the seats of the Eurostar. This influx of foreign parasitic bugs happened despite us Brits taking control of our borders and leaving the EU in 2021. You couldn't make it up.

7 **BEDBUGS** live their entire life – from eggs to larvae to adults – underneath the blankets. So each time one of them farts, it is technically giving a Dutch oven to all its fellow insects in the colony.

8 **BEDBUGS** will only come out to feed during the hours of darkness, so you can easily outsmart them by popping on an eyemask and sleeping with the bedroom light on.

9 **BEDBUGS** may be creepy crawlies, but they move quite quickly and can reach an impressive 100 feet per hour – this means that a quarter-inch-long bug can cover 4,800 times its body length in 60 minutes. In human terms, that's the equivalent of a 6' tall person walking at 5.45 miles per hours – a brisk walking pace. So it's actually not that impressive at all.

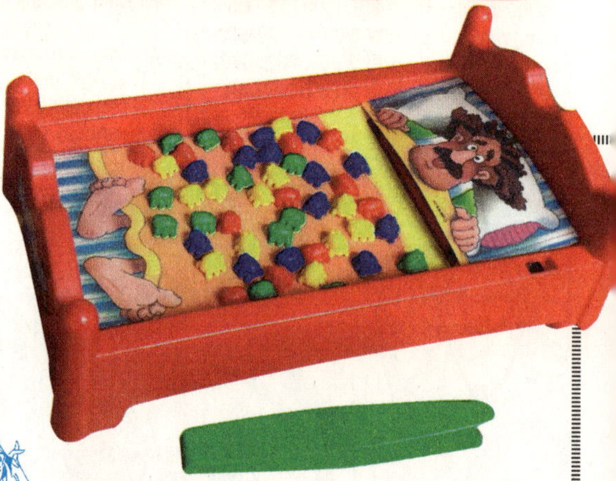

10 **IF YOU'RE** staying in a hotel in Wales and you notice the telltale signs of a bedbug infestation in your room – spots of faecal material on the sheets, a pungent smell like rotting raspberries and raised, itchy patches on your skin – you must inform reception. But if you report you have bedbugs, they won't understand you. That's because they speak Welsh, and in Wales they call them, unimaginatively, *'byg gwely'* – literally 'Bedbugs'.

11 **IN DEPRESSION-ERA** America in the early 1920s, if you saw someone behaving like a Bedbug, you wouldn't necessarily have to spray them with a concentrated dose of cyperthermin. That's because chances are they were doing *The Bed Bug* – participating in the latest dance craze to hit the speakeasies of Manhattan. The dance involved a conga line of dancers wriggling their rear ends, whilst stepping alternately to the left and the right before jumping, en-masse in someone's bed and repeatedly biting the sleeping occupant on the arse.

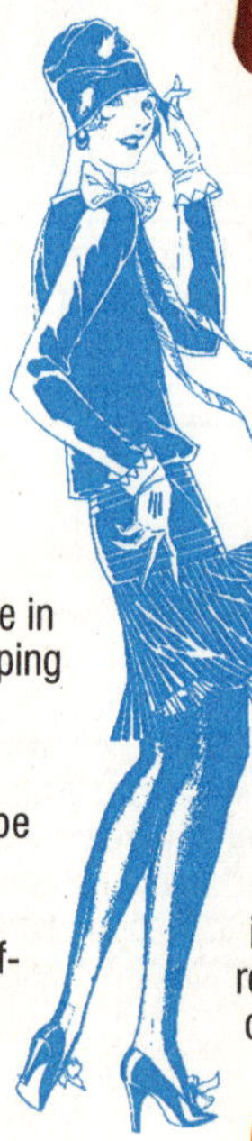

12 **ACCORDING** to folklore, bedbugs can be eradicated from your bed and home by simply asking them to leave. There is no scientific basis for this pest control method, and it is not as effective as their prolonged exposure to the carbamate insecticide propoxur.

13 **NOWHERE** is safe from an infestation of bedbugs, not even Buckingham Palace. Indeed, with the Royal family boasting over 240 state and staff bedrooms in their grand house, there is a plethora of beds for these unpleasant parasites – the bedbugs, that is, not the Royal family – to choose from every night.

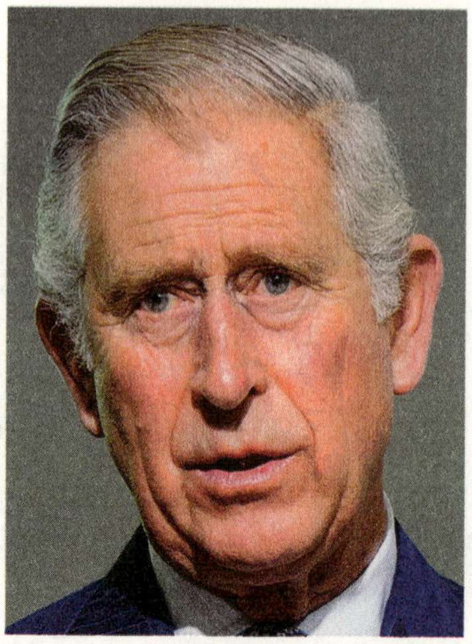

14 **YOU** wouldn't have thought that getting rid of bedbugs was fun, but you'd be wrong! In the 1980s board game 'Bedbugs', up to 4 players attempted to remove wriggling plastic bedbugs from a shaking bed using a pair of colourful, oversized tweezers. Described on the box as 'the motorised hopping, leaping, jumping game' it can't be regarded as a truly accurate simulation of a domestic bedbug infestation.

15 **MOST** ectoparasites have more than one anagram – such as fleas (false, leafs), nits (snit, tins) and mites (emits, items, smite, times). However, 'bedbugs' has just the one anagram – bugs bed – which is a practice whereby a concealed device is placed on or around a bed in order to secretly record events taking place, such as being urinated on by Russian prostitutes.

16 **TO EXPRESS** their opposition against the Vietnam War in 1969, John Lennon and Yoko Ono staged a series of "Bed-ins for Peace" at luxury hotels around the world. At the start of a proposed five-day protest at the Britannia Inn, Wythenshawe, the ex-Beatle was nipped on the tintis by a bedbug that had crawled into his pyjama bottoms, causing the demonstration to be cut short so he could go to Boots and get some corticosteroid cream.

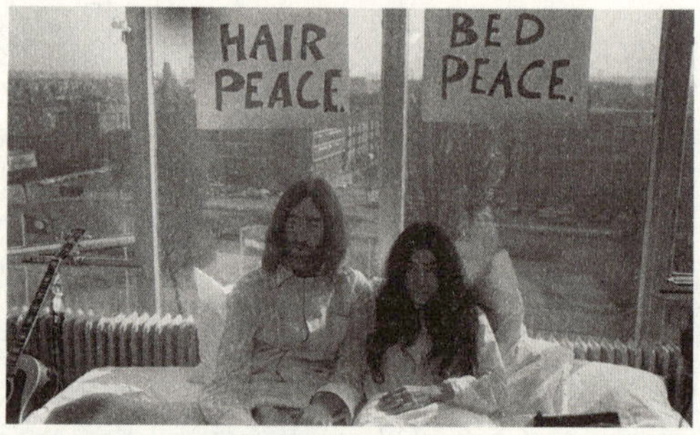
HAIR PEACE.
BED PEACE.

17 **THE PORN** industry is fastidious about the health and safety of its performers, with all of them undergoing regular health checks to ensure they are not carrying a sexually transmitted disease. And blue movie bosses are equally strict about the cleanliness of the sets. The owners of all the hotels, motels, private clubs, flat-roof pub back rooms and taxis where adult films are shot are required to produce certificates testifying that the premise is bedbug free.

18 **THE ONLY** bed where bedbugs can't live is the sea bed. But this isn't true as there are in fact underwater "bed bugs" – scavenging isopods known as *Bathynomus yucatanensis* – who spend their lives scavenging for food in the silt of the ocean floor. Growing up to a foot-and-a-half in length, these tropical scavengers feast on the leftover remains of other marine creatures, and are unlikely to bite your ankles while you are sleeping unless you are a deep sea diver and you've forgotten to put your lead boots on.

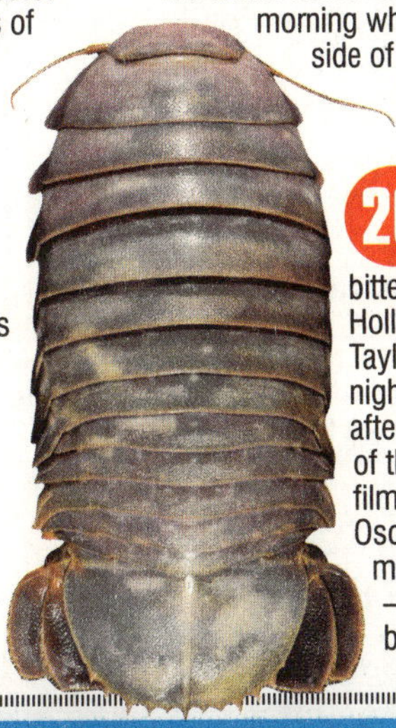

19 **WHEN** fictional 1-legged pirate Long John Silver retired at night to his room at the Admiral Benbow Inn, he might have expected to wake up with itchy red bedbug bites on his ankle. However, imagine his surprise in the morning when he swung his false leg out the side of his fartpit to discover it had been bitten by woodworms instead!

20 **PERHAPS** the most glamorous person ever to be bitten by bedbugs was Hollywood star Elizabeth Taylor. After spending the night with Richard Burton after he seduced her at the start of their tempestuous affair during filming for 1962 epic *Cleopatra*, the Oscar-winning actress found itchy red marks on her face, neck and ankles – the parts of her body that hadn't been protected by her pyjamas.

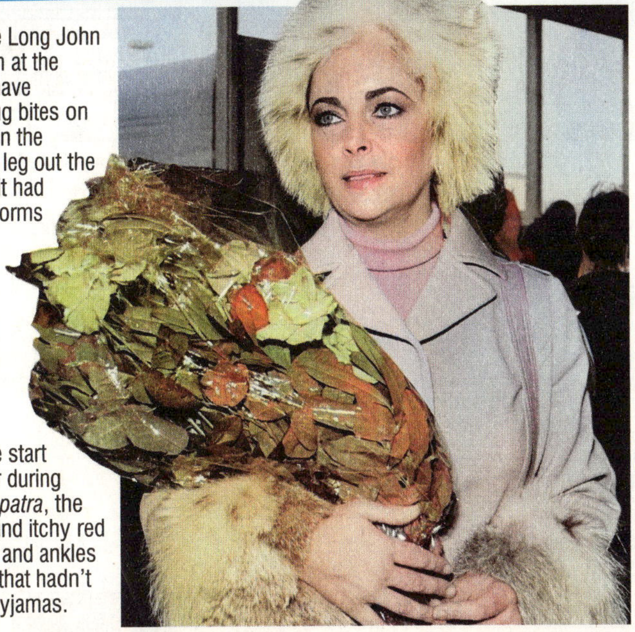

Win a Bedbug Infestation for 2 in our PARASITASTIC COMPETITION!

BEDBUGS are all the rage! They're everywhere from Paris to London and all points in between. They're in the homes of the rich and famous, and if you haven't got them, you're missing out.

But if you find yourself without these ectoparasites sharing your sleeping quarters, don't worry. Because we're got a bedbug infestation to give away to the lucky winner of our fantastic parasitic competition.

For your chance to win, all you have to do is to match up each of the bedbugs with the celebrity in whose bed they were found. If **YOU** are the first correct entry drawn out of the hat, you'll win a breeding colony of bedbugs, ten male and twenty female – simply empty them into your fartpit and within two weeks you'll be bang on trend and crawling with the fuckers!

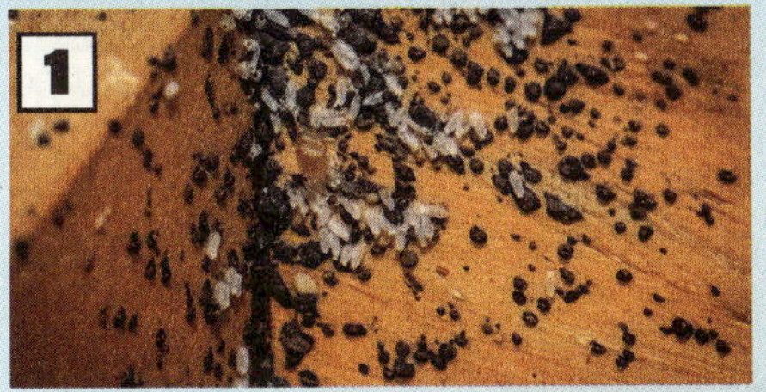

1 **IT'S AS** hot as a bakery in the bed where these bugs live, and they probably make a *showstopper* of their host's blood when they go for a *Great British Bite-Off*. Let's hope they don't nibble his buttocks and leave him with a *soggy bottom!*

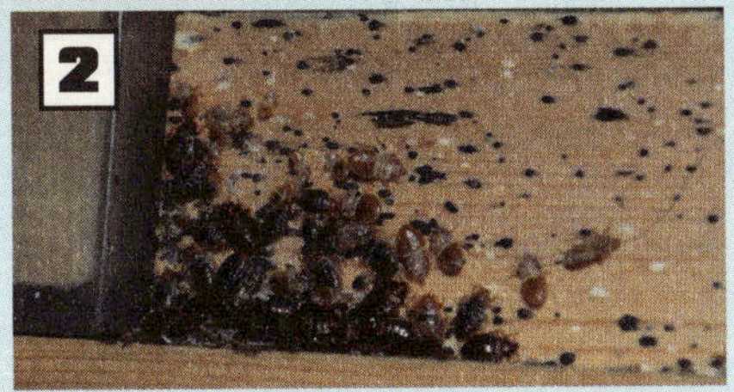

2 **WHEN** these sweet creatures come out at night, they only go in *one direction* – towards their luxuriant-haired host. And it's a *sign of the times* that when these parasites suck this former boyband frontman's blood, they *Harry* up and do it in *Style!*

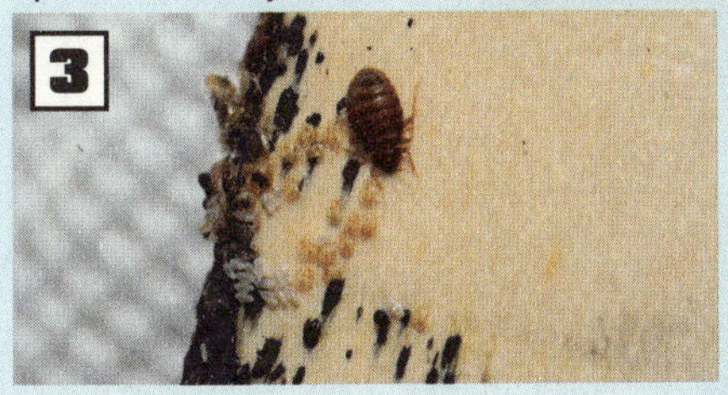

3 **WHO'S** *that girl* who sleeps in the bed where these bugs spend the night? And during the day, they *get into the groove* on the side of the mattress to hide. And they love exposed skin, so remember to *dress (you) up* in pyjamas if you climb into her bed!

Bedbug celeb 1: ....
Bedbug celeb 2: ....
Bedbug celeb 3: ....

***Send to**: Bedbug Competition, Viz, PO Box 841, Whitley Bay NE26 9EQ*

**Bedbug infestation dependent on bedbug availability at time of drawing competition winner out of hat.*

Bedbug Fact File

ALL of a sudden, Bedbugs are the topic of conversation on everybody's lips! In pubs, clubs and restaurants, at work, at home and in school, people are talking of little else. If you don't join in, you'll be left behind.

But what if you don't know anything about these blood-sucking critters? How can you add to a dinner party conversation about their faeces being a tell-tale sign of their presence if you don't know that it is? How can you impress someone on a first date with the fact that a bed can be crawling with up to 5,000 bugs if you are unaware of that information?

That's where this handy *Viz Bedbug Fact File* comes in. Easily concealed in the palm of a large hand, or stapled inconspicuously onto a cuff, the *Viz Bedbug Fact File* contains all the information you need to join in the bedbug banter and hold everyone in your thrall with your bedbug knowledge.

Instructions:

Cut out the handy fact file below and staple it to the inside of your cuff. Then simply pretend to examine your finger nails whenever you need a bedbug fact to wow your company at any social occasion.

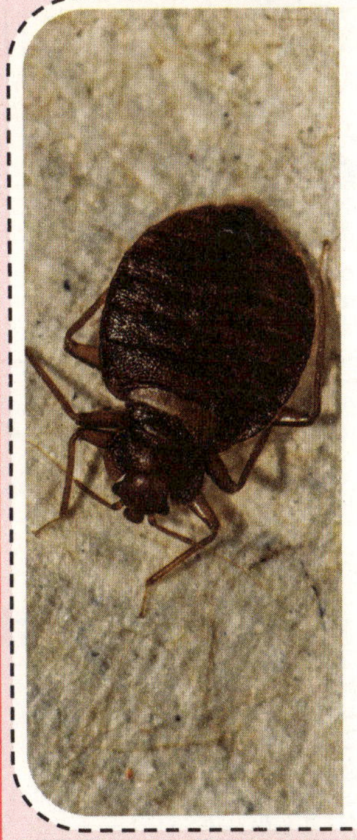

Name:	Bedbug
Name in Latin:	*Cimex lectularius*
Name in Icelandic:	Veggjalús
Type of animal:	Insect
Number of legs:	6
Number of wings:	4
Number of wings that work:	0
Days survival without feeding:	70
Places they bite:	Arms, Legs, Torso, Arse
Most infected city in the UK:	London
Least infected city in the UK:	Wakefield
Minimum length:	4mm or less
Maximum length:	7mm or more
Colour:	Red or dark brown
Width:	3mm
Plural:	Bedbugs
No. of letters in name:	6 (singular) or 7 (plural)

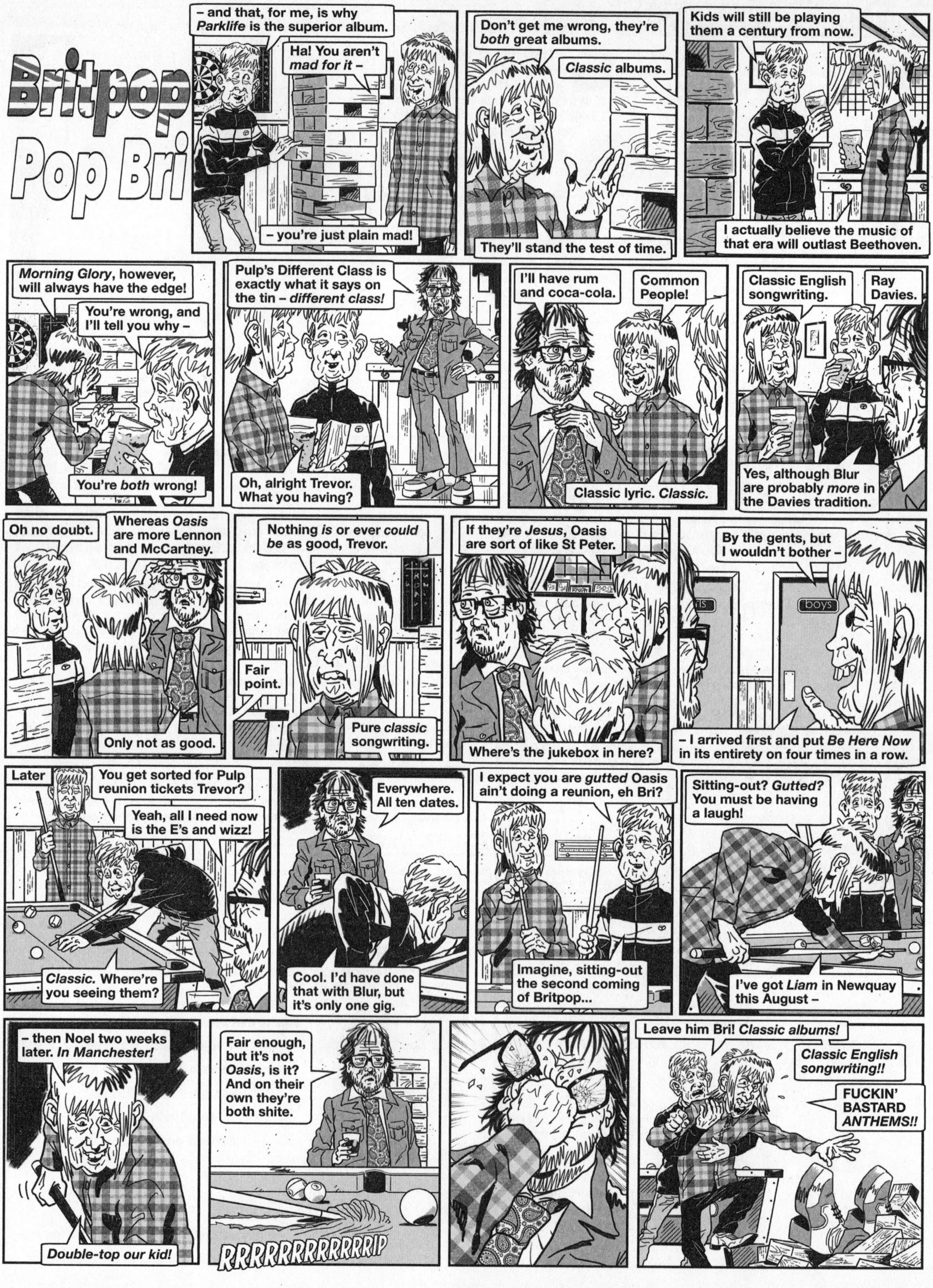
Britpop
Pop Bri
– and that, for me, is why *Parklife* is the superior album.
Ha! You aren't *mad for it* –
– you're just plain mad!
Don't get me wrong, they're *both* great albums.
Classic albums.
They'll stand the test of time.
Kids will still be playing them a century from now.
I actually believe the music of that era will outlast Beethoven.
Morning Glory, however, will always have the edge!
You're wrong, and I'll tell you why –
You're *both* wrong!
Pulp's Different Class is exactly what it says on the tin – *different class!*
Oh, alright Trevor. What you having?
I'll have rum and coca-cola.
Common People!
Classic lyric. *Classic.*
Classic English songwriting.
Ray Davies.
Yes, although Blur are probably *more* in the Davies tradition.
Oh no doubt.
Whereas *Oasis* are more Lennon and McCartney.
Only not as good.
Nothing *is* or ever *could be* as good, Trevor.
Fair point.
Pure *classic* songwriting.
If they're *Jesus*, Oasis are sort of like St Peter.
Where's the jukebox in here?
By the gents, but I wouldn't bother –
boys
– I arrived first and put *Be Here Now* in its entirety on four times in a row.
Later
You get sorted for Pulp reunion tickets Trevor?
Yeah, all I need now is the E's and wizz!
Classic. Where're you seeing them?
Everywhere. All ten dates.
Cool. I'd have done that with Blur, but it's only one gig.
I expect you are *gutted* Oasis ain't doing a reunion, eh Bri?
Imagine, sitting-out the second coming of Britpop...
Sitting-out? *Gutted?* You must be having a laugh!
I've got *Liam* in Newquay this August –
– then Noel two weeks later. *In Manchester!*
Double-top our kid!
Fair enough, but it's not *Oasis*, is it? And on their own they're both shite.
RRRRRRRRRRRRIP
Leave him Bri! *Classic albums!*
Classic English songwriting!!
FUCKIN' BASTARD *ANTHEMS!!*

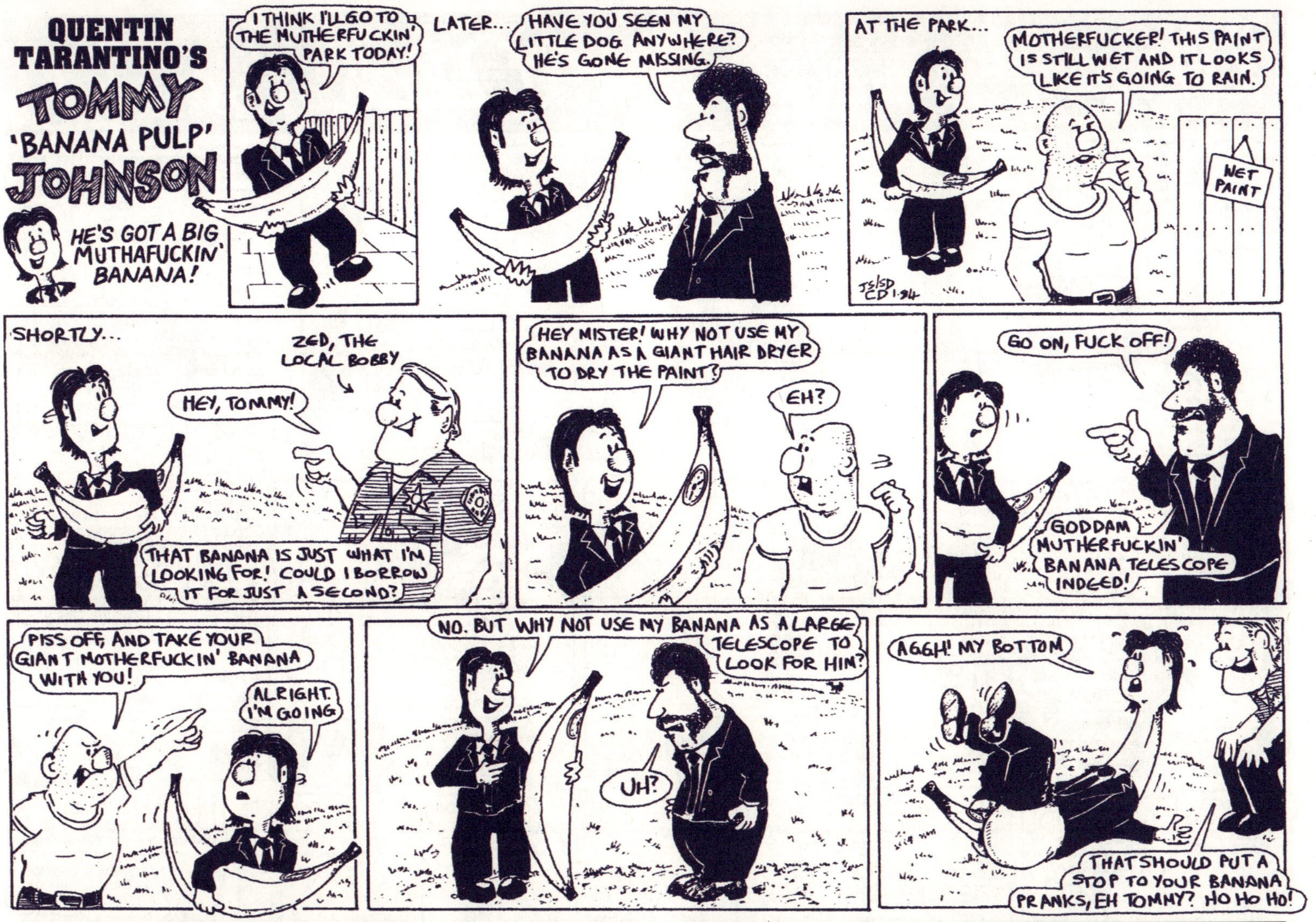

QUENTIN TARANTINO'S
TOMMY
'BANANA PULP'
JOHNSON
HE'S GOT A BIG MUTHAFUCKIN' BANANA!
I THINK I'LL GO TO THE MUTHERFUCKIN' PARK TODAY!
LATER...
HAVE YOU SEEN MY LITTLE DOG ANYWHERE? HE'S GONE MISSING.
AT THE PARK...
MOTHERFUCKER! THIS PAINT IS STILL WET AND IT LOOKS LIKE IT'S GOING TO RAIN.
WET PAINT
SHORTLY...
ZED, THE LOCAL BOBBY
HEY, TOMMY!
THAT BANANA IS JUST WHAT I'M LOOKING FOR! COULD I BORROW IT FOR JUST A SECOND?
HEY MISTER! WHY NOT USE MY BANANA AS A GIANT HAIR DRYER TO DRY THE PAINT?
EH?
GO ON, FUCK OFF!
GODDAM MUTHERFUCKIN' BANANA TELESCOPE INDEED!
PISS OFF, AND TAKE YOUR GIANT MOTHERFUCKIN' BANANA WITH YOU!
ALRIGHT. I'M GOING
NO. BUT WHY NOT USE MY BANANA AS A LARGE TELESCOPE TO LOOK FOR HIM?
UH?
AGGH! MY BOTTOM
THAT SHOULD PUT A STOP TO YOUR BANANA PRANKS, EH TOMMY? HO HO HO!

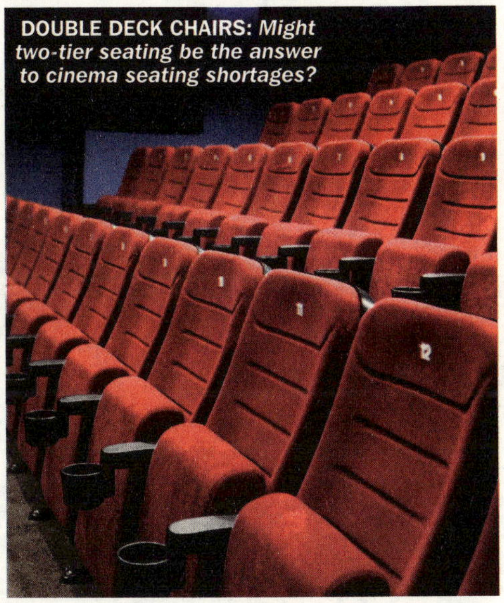

DOUBLE DECK CHAIRS: *Might two-tier seating be the answer to cinema seating shortages?*

LAP OF LUXURY

Cumbria cinema pilots innovative new seating scheme

IT'S official! Going to the flicks is back! And after *Barbie* and *Oppenheimer*'s box-office-record-smashing opening weekend, *it's more popular than ever!* And one cinema that is hoping to cash in on film lovers' demands for big screen thrills is Keswick's longest-running multiplex, Screenplanet.

"We've never seen anything like it," says the Lake District cinema's deputy manager Harlan Belvedere. "A month back we were lucky to get three people a day through the door. Now we're getting hundreds, possibly millions. We just can't keep up with the demand for seats."

"Whilst looking into ways to somehow fit more punters into the auditorium, I noticed that no-one ever sits in front row A," he said. "So we took all those seats out and moved them to the back, behind row M. But then people started avoiding row B, preferring to squeeze themselves into the new row N instead."

"But it got me thinking that if people are prepared to squash into tighter spaces, then perhaps two people might be prepared to share a single seat with one person sat on the other's lap," he continued. "It was a lightbulb moment."

embrocation

As well as the obvious financial advantages gained by doubling the capacity of the cinema, Belvedere insists there are also environmental benefits to the scheme.

"With twice as many people watching each screening, the amount of electricity used is halved," he said. "And I've been able to turn the heating down a notch or two as well, since double the punters creates double the warmth."

Belvedere believes his two-tier seating scheme is popular with his customer base as it works out slightly cheaper than regular cinema tickets. "Not only that, our customers can now choose from a premium, standard or a basic level package," he said.

"The premium level is where two close friends reserve the above and below positions on a seat, guaranteeing that they know the person they are sitting on," Belvedere explained. "Standard level is where the holder gets allocated a place above or below another cinemagoer, determined by an algorithm which takes into account the combined height of both parties, or if one or the other is wearing a hat."

"With the basic level ticket, two people share a seat as before, but not at the same time," he continued. "One takes the first half of the film and the other takes the second."

"We encourage them to hang around in the foyer after the film finishes, so they can explain to each other what happened in the half they missed," Belvedere added.

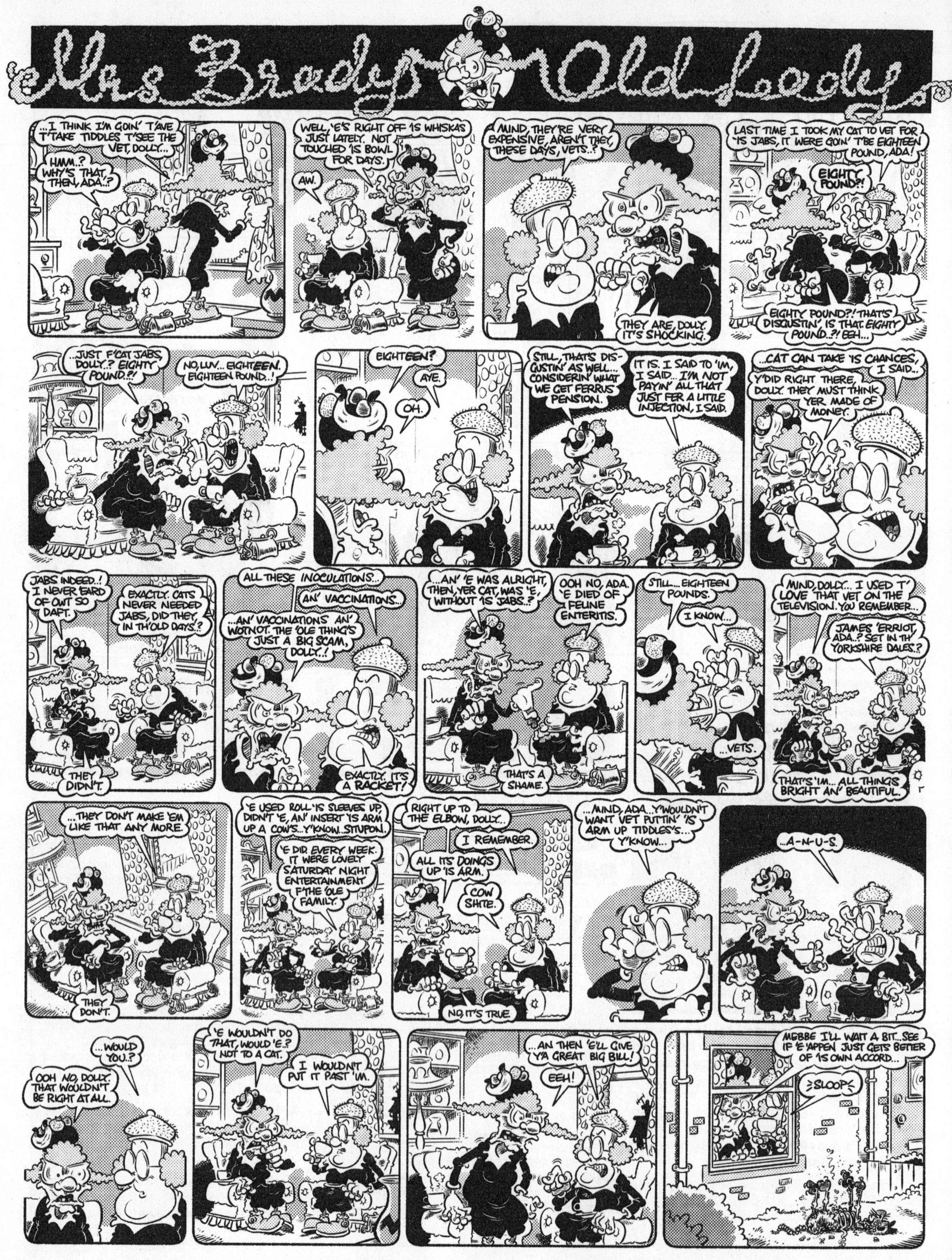
Mrs Brady Old Lady
...I THINK I'M GOIN' T'AVE T'TAKE TIDDLES T'SEE THE VET, DOLLY...
HMM..? WHY'S THAT, THEN, ADA..?
WELL, 'E'S RIGHT OFF 'IS WHISKAS JUST LATELY. NOT TOUCHED 'IS BOWL FOR DAYS.
AW.
MIND, THEY'RE VERY EXPENSIVE, AREN'T THEY, THESE DAYS, VETS..?
THEY ARE, DOLLY. IT'S SHOCKING.
LAST TIME I TOOK MY CAT TO VET FOR 'IS JABS, IT WERE GOIN' T'BE EIGHTEEN POUND, ADA!
EIGHTY POUND?!
EIGHTY POUND?! THAT'S DISGUSTIN', IS THAT. EIGHTY POUND..?! EEH...
...JUST F'CAT JABS, DOLLY..? EIGHTY POUND..?!
NO, LUV... EIGHTEEN. EIGHTEEN POUND..!
EIGHTEEN?
AYE.
OH.
STILL, THAT'S DISGUSTIN' AS WELL... CONSIDERIN' WHAT WE GET FERRUS PENSION.
IT IS. I SAID TO 'IM, I SAID... I'M NOT PAYIN' ALL THAT JUST FER A LITTLE INJECTION, I SAID.
...CAT CAN TAKE 'IS CHANCES, I SAID...
Y'DID RIGHT THERE, DOLLY. THEY MUST THINK YER MADE OF MONEY.
JABS INDEED..! I NEVER 'EARD OF OWT SO DAFT.
EXACTLY. CATS NEVER NEEDED JABS, DID THEY, IN TH'OLD DAYS..?
THEY DIDN'T.
ALL THESE INOCULATIONS...
AN' VACCINATIONS...
...AN' VACCINATIONS AN' WOTNOT. THE 'OLE THING'S JUST A BIG SCAM, DOLLY..!
EXACTLY. IT'S A RACKET!
...AN' 'E WAS ALRIGHT, THEN, YER CAT, WAS 'E, WITHOUT 'IS JABS..?
OOH NO, ADA. 'E DIED OF FELINE ENTERITIS.
THAT'S A SHAME.
STILL... EIGHTEEN POUNDS.
I KNOW...
...VETS.
MIND, DOLLY... I USED T' LOVE THAT VET ON THE TELEVISION. YOU REMEMBER...
JAMES 'ERRIOT, ADA..? SET IN TH' YORKSHIRE DALES..?
THAT'S 'IM... ALL THINGS BRIGHT AN' BEAUTIFUL.
...THEY DON'T MAKE 'EM LIKE THAT ANY MORE.
THEY DON'T.
'E USED ROLL 'IS SLEEVES UP, DIDN'T 'E, AN' INSERT 'IS ARM UP A COW'S...Y'KNOW...STUPON.
'E DID. EVERY WEEK. IT WERE LOVELY SATURDAY NIGHT ENTERTAINMENT F'THE 'OLE FAMILY.
RIGHT UP TO THE ELBOW, DOLLY...
I REMEMBER.
ALL ITS DOINGS UP 'IS ARM.
COW SHITE.
NO, IT'S TRUE.
...MIND, ADA... Y'WOULDN'T WANT VET PUTTIN' 'IS ARM UP TIDDLES'S... Y'KNOW...
...A-N-U-S.
...WOULD YOU..?
OOH NO, DOLLY. THAT WOULDN'T BE RIGHT AT ALL.
'E WOULDN'T DO THAT, WOULD 'E..? NOT TO A CAT.
I WOULDN'T PUT IT PAST 'IM.
...AN THEN 'E'LL GIVE YA GREAT BIG BILL!
EEH!
MEBBE I'LL WAIT A BIT... SEE IF 'E 'APPEN JUST GETS BETTER OF 'IS OWN ACCORD...
SLOOP

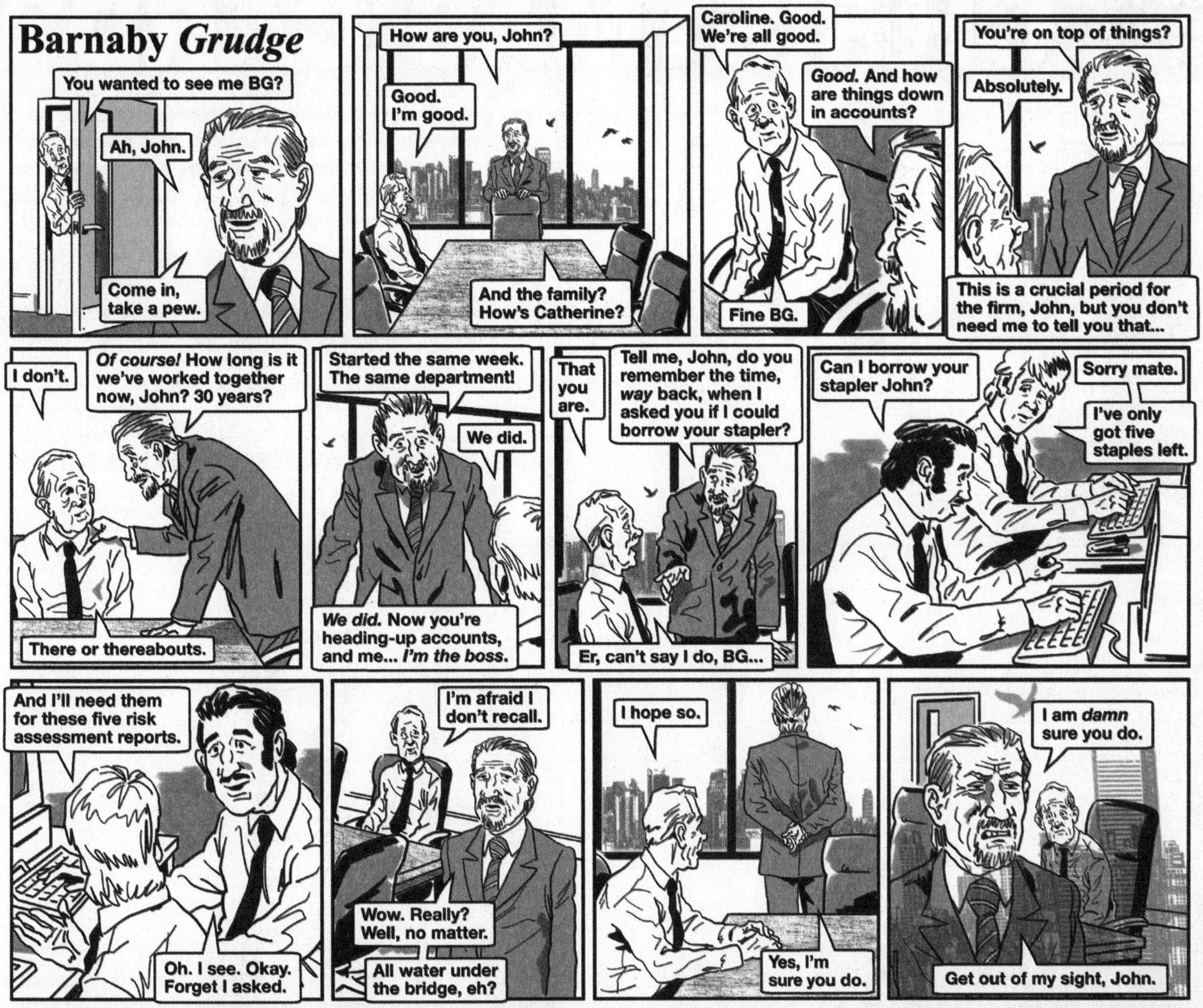
Barnaby Grudge
You wanted to see me BG?
Ah, John.
Come in, take a pew.
How are you, John?
Good. I'm good.
And the family? How's Catherine?
Caroline. Good. We're all good.
Good. And how are things down in accounts?
Fine BG.
You're on top of things?
Absolutely.
This is a crucial period for the firm, John, but you don't need me to tell you that...
I don't.
Of course! How long is it we've worked together now, John? 30 years?
There or thereabouts.
Started the same week. The same department!
We did.
We did. Now you're heading-up accounts, and me... I'm the boss.
That you are.
Tell me, John, do you remember the time, way back, when I asked you if I could borrow your stapler?
Er, can't say I do, BG...
Can I borrow your stapler John?
Sorry mate.
I've only got five staples left.
And I'll need them for these five risk assessment reports.
Oh. I see. Okay. Forget I asked.
I'm afraid I don't recall.
Wow. Really? Well, no matter.
All water under the bridge, eh?
I hope so.
Yes, I'm sure you do.
I am damn sure you do.
Get out of my sight, John.

BONK-UP SMACKDOWN

Banjo pill bigwigs go head-to-head

AN unholy war of words broke out last night as the CEOs of two pharmaceutical giants slammed their rivals' erectile dysfunction drugs, each challenging the efficacy of the other's products.

The spat started at a Pfizer shareholders' meeting, when CEO Henry 'The Rock' Montague reported how Viagra had shown record sales growth year on year. And he went on to bad mouth Cialis, the erectile dysfunction treatment produced by rival drugs company Lilly-ICOS.

"Viagra is the original and best and the only one that makes men granite hard. This Cialis leaves men with a dick limper than a sock full of blancmange," Montague said, to whoops and cheers from shareholders.

But Ernest 'the Destroyer' Baumgarten, chairman of Lilly-ICOS immediately hit back, branding Viagra as much use as "tits on a fish."

"Well surprise, surprise. Montague has been shooting his big mouth off again," he told delegates at the AGM in Geneva last week.

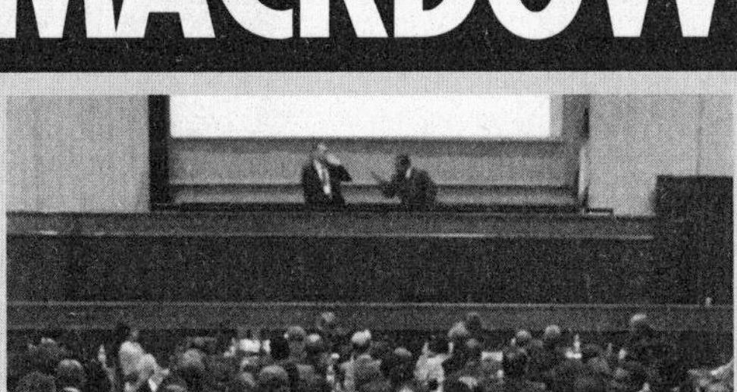

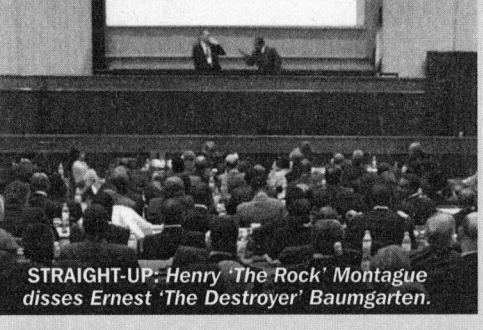

STRAIGHT-UP: *Henry 'The Rock' Montague disses Ernest 'The Destroyer' Baumgarten.*

"Well let me tell you, I've seen people take his dick pills, and that stuff didn't even give them half a Goddam teacake."

And the crowd of 500 Lilly-ICOS shareholders and investors went wild as Baumgarten continued to trash-talk his rival's product.

"I'm talking to you, Montague," he said. "You know your Viagra is the pits. You know only Cialis gets a man's dick hard as yo mama's rolling pin."

But the Pfizer CEO didn't take Baumgarten's onslaught lying down, challenging the Lilly-ICOS chief to "Put his banjo pills where his mouth is."

"Let's go for it, Baumgarten. Your pills against mine. Anywhere, anytime. If you're not too chicken shit," Montague said.

And the challenge was taken up as the Lilly-ICOS CEO released a two word statement yesterday on his company's website. "Let's rumble!"

What is being billed as the 'Bone-on Battle of the Century' is likely to take place early next year at the PG Paints Arena in Pittsburgh, when the two erectile dysfunction tablets will go head to head in front of an audience of millions. The pills will be given to men suffering from the condition, and the length, turgidity and duration of any subsequent erections measured to decide the winner.

Tickets for the event will go on sale in the new year and will initially be available to shareholders in Pfizer and Lilly-ICOS before going on sale to the public. The event will also be broadcast on Sky TV pay-per-view, presented by Kay Burley and Eamonn Holmes.

So You Didn't Send a CHRISTMAS CARD?

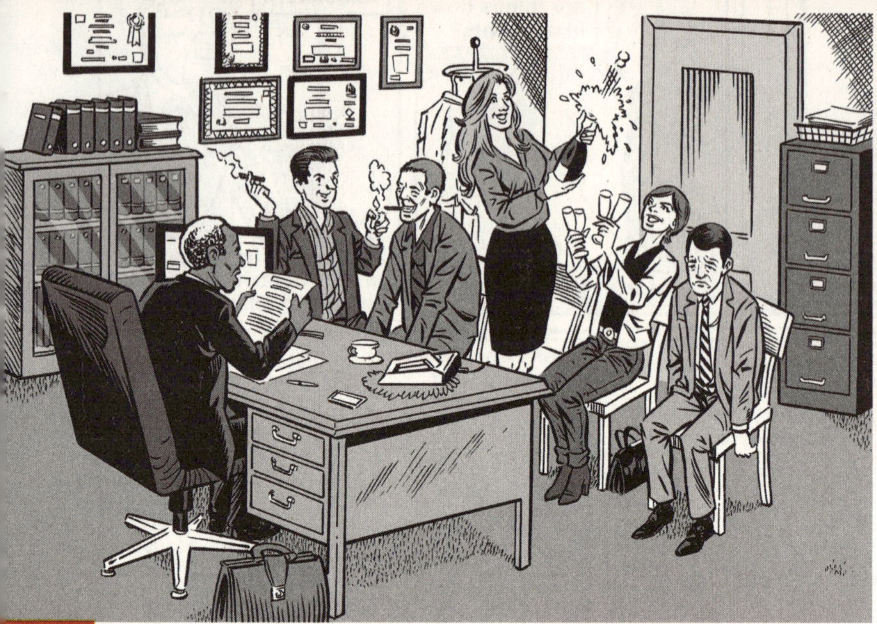

POSTING Christmas cards to friends and relatives has been a traditional part of the festive season for over a century. But this last year, to save money as our latest Age of Austerity took hold and the cost of living went through the roof, many people decided not to send postal greetings.

On the face of it, not sending a Christmas card may seem a trivial act with few repercussions – a mild rebuke from a mother, a frosty glare from an aunt, or a sarcastic phone call from a sister. But in actual fact, the consequences can be dire. So if you thought you had posted your last Christmas card back in 2022, then read on *...and think again!*

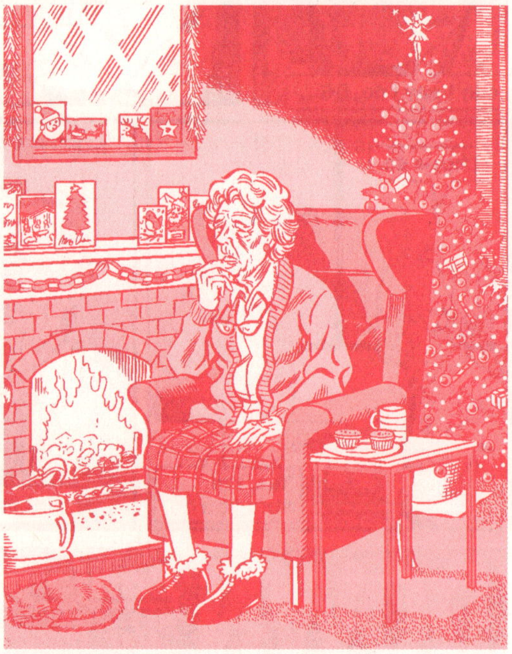

ELDERLY grandparents love to receive cards from their relatives at Christmas time, and they look unfavourably upon anyone who forgets, or choses not to send these traditional greetings. And whilst many OAPs struggle with remembering what they came into a room for, who the prime minister is, or how to use a mobile phone despite being shown a hundred times, their memories are razor sharp when it comes to who has overlooked them. Insults and slights are stored in their memories and never forgotten, with grudges borne for decades. Come the sad day when they eventually pass on, the saving of a pound last December could turn out to have been a very bad investment indeed. At the reading of the will, you may see your share of their cash going to a cat shelter, the local church or worse, to your grinning siblings and cousins *who took the trouble to pop a card in the post!*

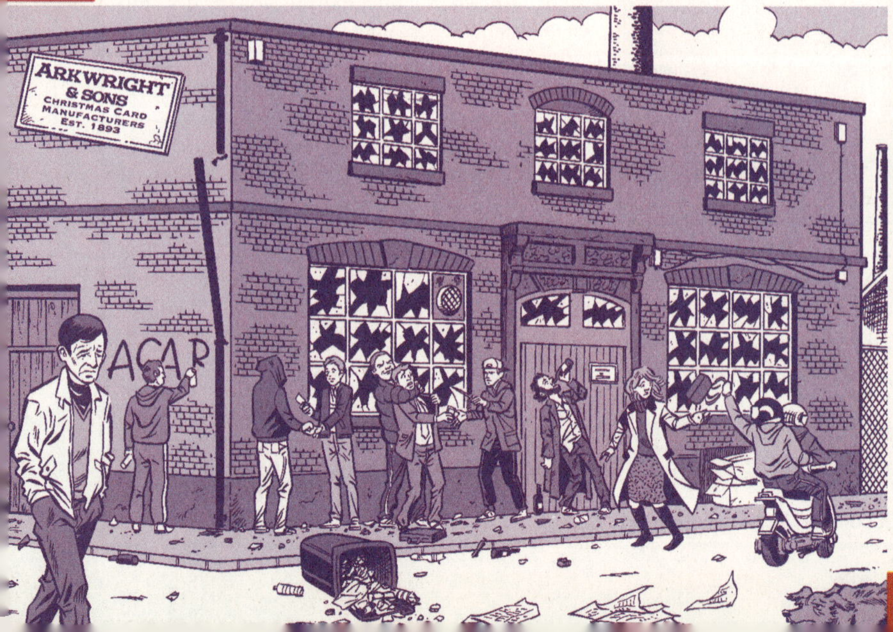

ARKWRIGHT & SONS
CHRISTMAS CARD MANUFACTURERS
EST. 1893

DECEMBER is the postie's favourite time of the year. Mail workers love delivering Christmas cards, dragging their heavier-than-usual bags around the frozen streets to bring cheer to everyone on their morning rounds. But the outsourcing of services to private couriers means that morale amongst our posties is currently at an all-time low, and taking this much-loved festive job away from them will only lower their spirits even further. Robbed of this simple pleasure, our postmen and women will sink into deep depressions, putting stress on the country's already overworked mental health services. Many posties will seek solace in drink or class-A drugs, perhaps turning to crime to fund their new-found habits. Unfortunately, some may take even more drastic measures, deciding that without this increased workload, life is not worth living. Saving a postie's life can cost as little as the price of a Christmas stamp.

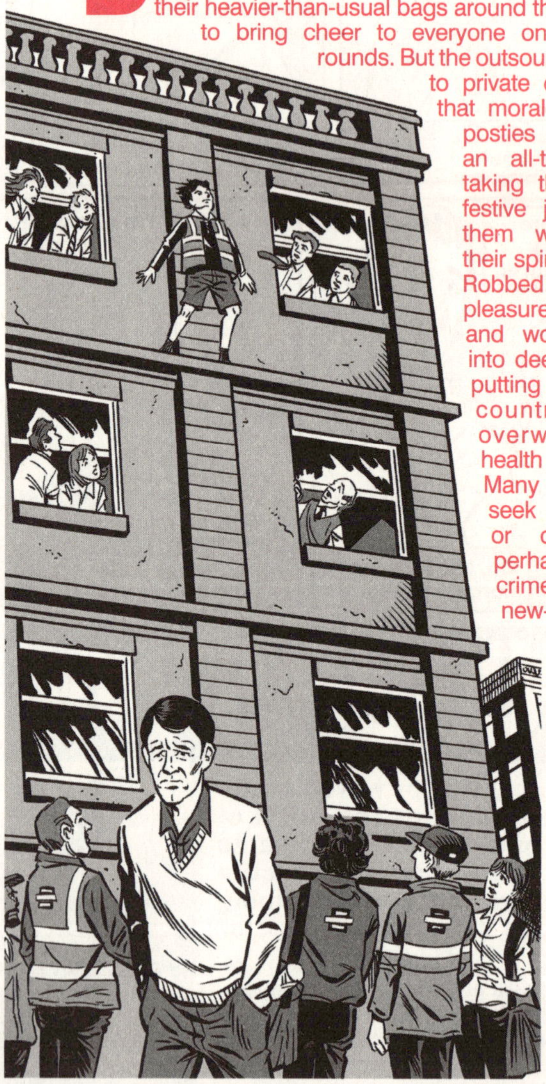

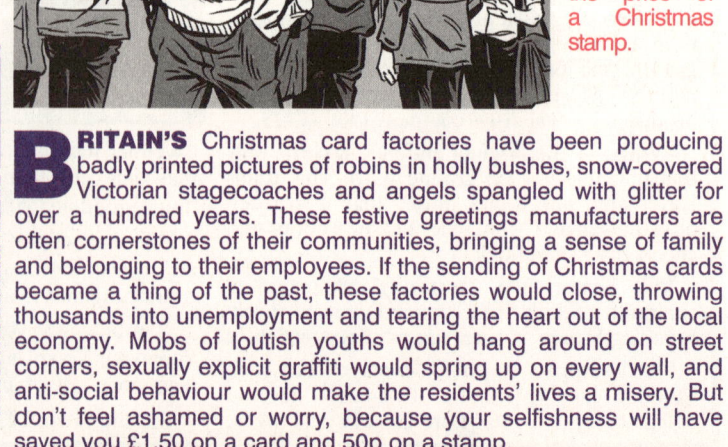

BRITAIN'S Christmas card factories have been producing badly printed pictures of robins in holly bushes, snow-covered Victorian stagecoaches and angels spangled with glitter for over a hundred years. These festive greetings manufacturers are often cornerstones of their communities, bringing a sense of family and belonging to their employees. If the sending of Christmas cards became a thing of the past, these factories would close, throwing thousands into unemployment and tearing the heart out of the local economy. Mobs of loutish youths would hang around on street corners, sexually explicit graffiti would spring up on every wall, and anti-social behaviour would make the residents' lives a misery. But don't feel ashamed or worry, because your selfishness will have saved you £1.50 on a card and 50p on a stamp.

WHEN YOU fail to send a Christmas card, it is not only the people directly involved in their manufacture whose lives you are ruining. There are hundreds of businesses servicing this industry, including glitter producers, manufacturers of tiny plastic pegs and bits of string, and writers of sickly-sweet, poorly-rhyming verses. But perhaps hardest hit of all will be the people who make envelopes with horrible-tasting fishy glue that fails to stick the flap down. These are typically small businesses employing just a handful of people, yet they will be unable to survive. Making envelopes is not the most demanding work, and cast out onto the scrapheap, these unskilled people may find it difficult to get another job. It's a sad fact that many will certainly drift into crime, prostitution or rent-boying, more tragic victims of your decision not to send your nan a Christmas card.

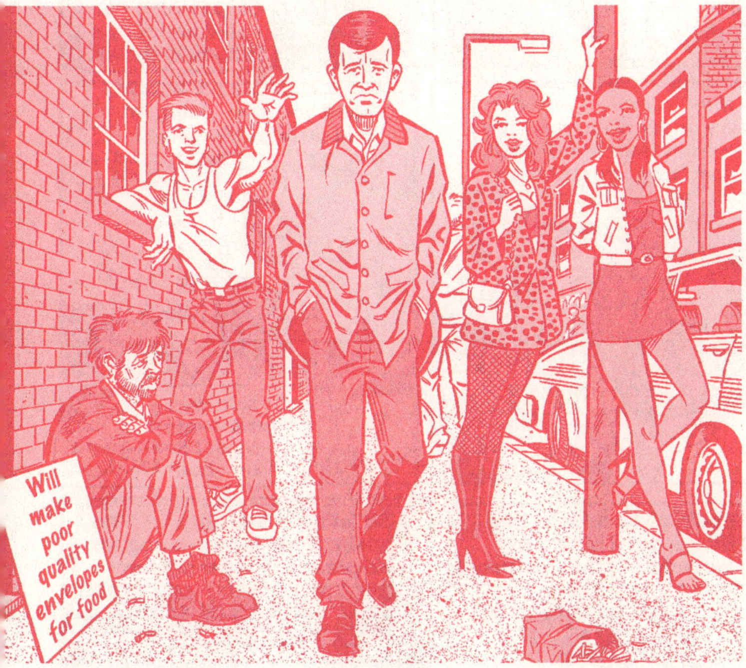
Will make poor quality envelopes for food

EVERYONE has heard of the Butterfly Effect – that a small change in one small thing can lead to a catastrophic change in a much larger thing further down the line. For example – don't send a Christmas card to your sister and she will be in a huff as she heads out to the pub. She will likely down a couple more than she would normally consume. She might then get into a fight, breaking a woman's nose. This woman may work at a nuclear power station and have to take a day off work. She in turn may be replaced by a temp who is inexperienced. When the reactor core temperature suddenly increases, she will not know how to react or which emergency switch to throw, leading to a nuclear meltdown. This is just one possible outcome of not sending a Christmas card. Chaos Theory says that there are an infinite number of alternative outcomes, an infinite number of which are even worse. Sending a card would stop any of them happening.

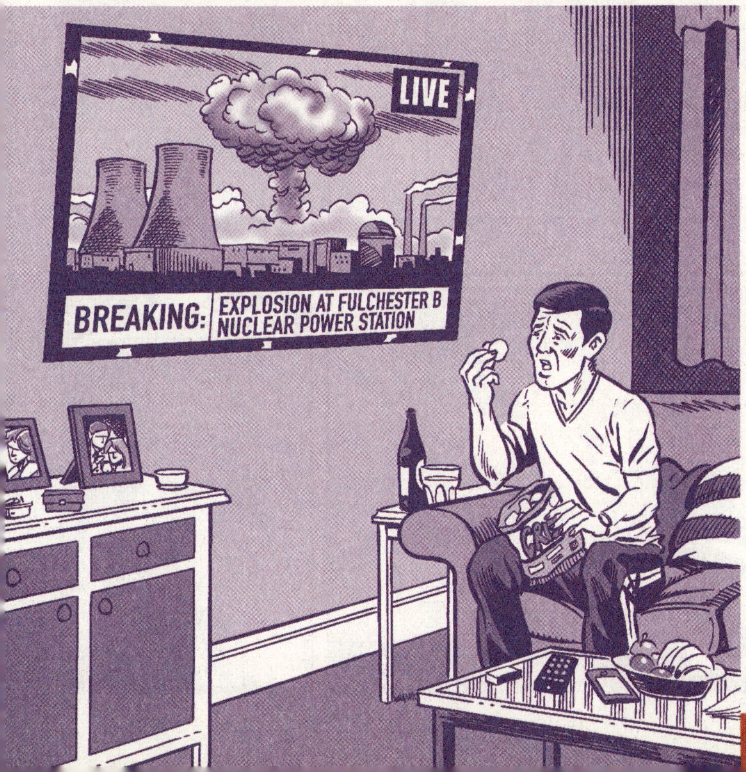
LIVE
BREAKING: EXPLOSION AT FULCHESTER B NUCLEAR POWER STATION

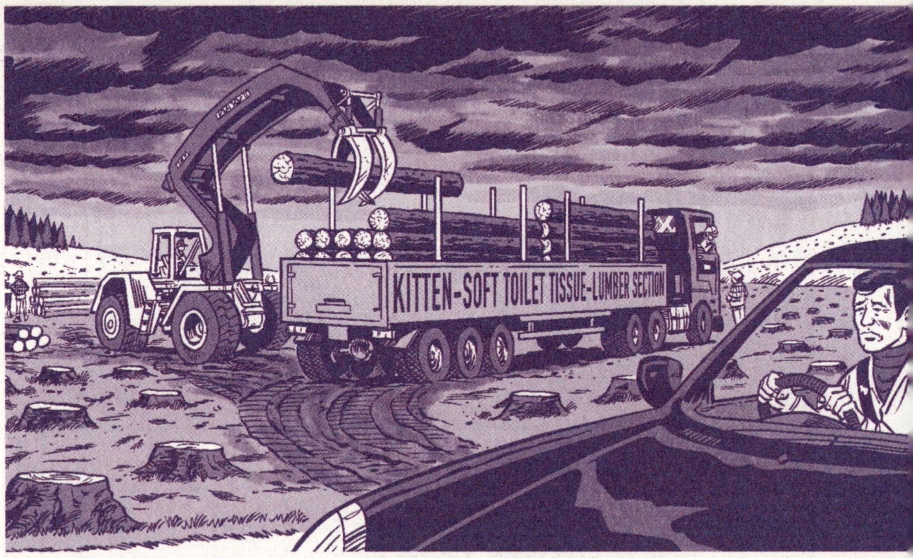
KITTEN-SOFT TOILET TISSUE-LUMBER SECTION

LAST YEAR, Britons sent over 150 million Christmas cards to friends and relatives in the UK. With the average weight of each card being 15g, that's a staggering 2250 tonnes of cardboard sitting on mantlepieces, sellotaped to walls at an angle or pinned to office noticeboards. On twelfth night, all these precious resources went into the recycling system. Nativity scenes became printer paper, photographs of snowmen clearly made from polystyrene became packaging, and whimsical cartoons of Santa and his reindeer became toilet rolls with the occasional razor-sharp shard of glitter in them. If this recycling doesn't take place, new trees will have to be cut down – trees which actively remove CO_2 from our atmosphere, helping to cool our planet. So by not participating in the festive card exchanging tradition, you are actively contributing to the process of global warming in a very real way. Sending a Christmas card doesn't cost the earth, but not sending one almost certainly will.

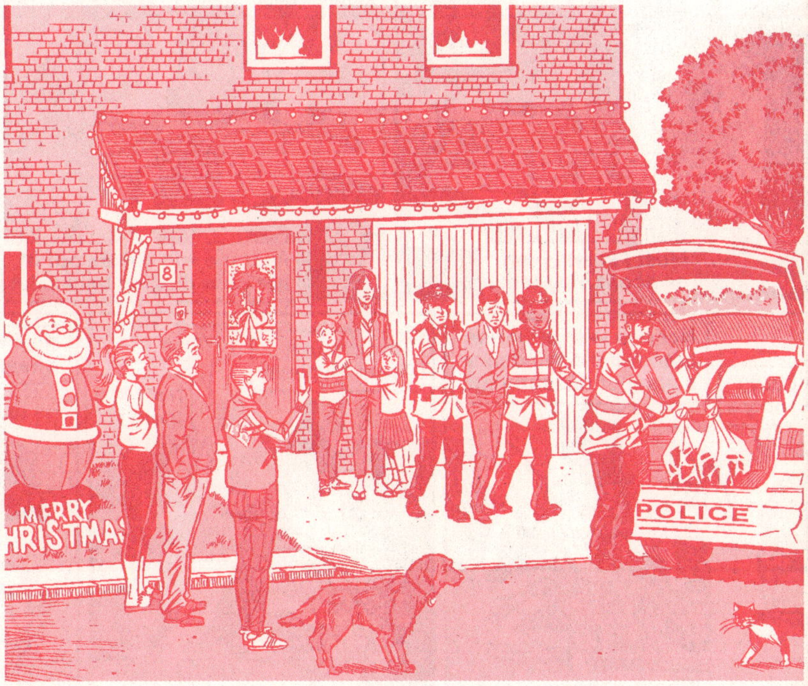
8
MERRY CHRISTMAS
POLICE

IN TODAY'S computer-riddled society, you may opt to deliver your festive good wishes with an e-card rather than the traditional paper and glitter version. But before you hit that send button, it's worth remembering that all internet traffic is monitored by the government. Your festive greetings to a friend will, deep down in its coding, carry the entire browsing history of your computer, invisible to the recipient of your good wishes, but crystal clear to the goons at GCHQ. They will be able to track every website you have visited, determine how long you stayed and what material you downloaded. They will even have web-cam footage of whatever you were doing whilst visiting this site, and you could end up on the Sex Offenders' Register. If that sounds a bit 'Big Brother', that's because it is. All this can be avoided by sending a traditional Christmas card next December.

NEXT WEEK: So you didn't send a Valentines Card?

Brought to you by The British Consortium of Greetings Card Manufacturers.

ROY'LL WATCH

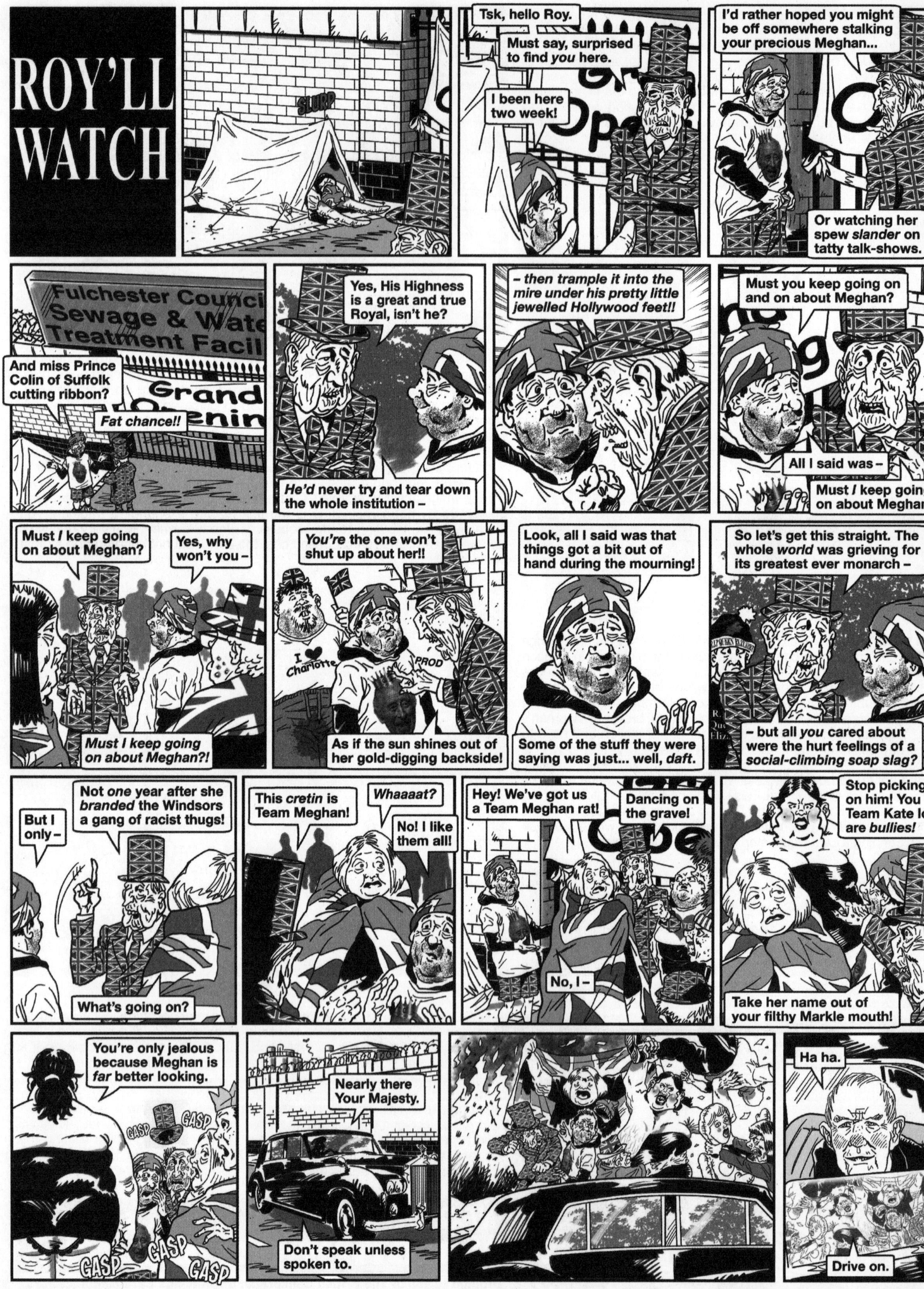

SLURP
Tsk, hello Roy.
Must say, surprised to find *you* here.
I been here two week!
I'd rather hoped you might be off somewhere stalking your precious Meghan...
Or watching her spew *slander* on tatty talk-shows.
Fulchester Council Sewage & Water Treatment Facil
Grand Openin
And miss Prince Colin of Suffolk cutting ribbon?
Fat chance!!
Yes, His Highness is a great and true Royal, isn't he?
He'd never try and tear down the whole institution –
– then trample it into the mire under his pretty little jewelled Hollywood feet!!
Must you keep going on and on about Meghan?
All I said was –
Must *I* keep going on about Meghan?
Must *I* keep going on about Meghan?
Yes, why won't you –
Must I keep going on about Meghan?!
You're the one won't shut up about her!!
I ♥ Charlotte
PROD
As if the sun shines out of her gold-digging backside!
Look, all I said was that things got a bit out of hand during the mourning!
Some of the stuff they were saying was just... well, *daft*.
So let's get this straight. The whole *world* was grieving for its greatest ever monarch –
– but all *you* cared about were the hurt feelings of a *social-climbing soap slag?*
But I only –
Not *one* year after she *branded* the Windsors a gang of racist thugs!
What's going on?
This *cretin* is Team Meghan!
Whaaaat?
No! I like them all!
Hey! We've got us a Team Meghan rat!
Dancing on the grave!
No, I –
Stop picking on him! You Team Kate lot are *bullies!*
Take her name out of your filthy Markle mouth!
You're only jealous because Meghan is *far* better looking.
GASP
GASP
GASP
GASP
GASP
Nearly there Your Majesty.
Don't speak unless spoken to.
Ha ha.
Drive on.

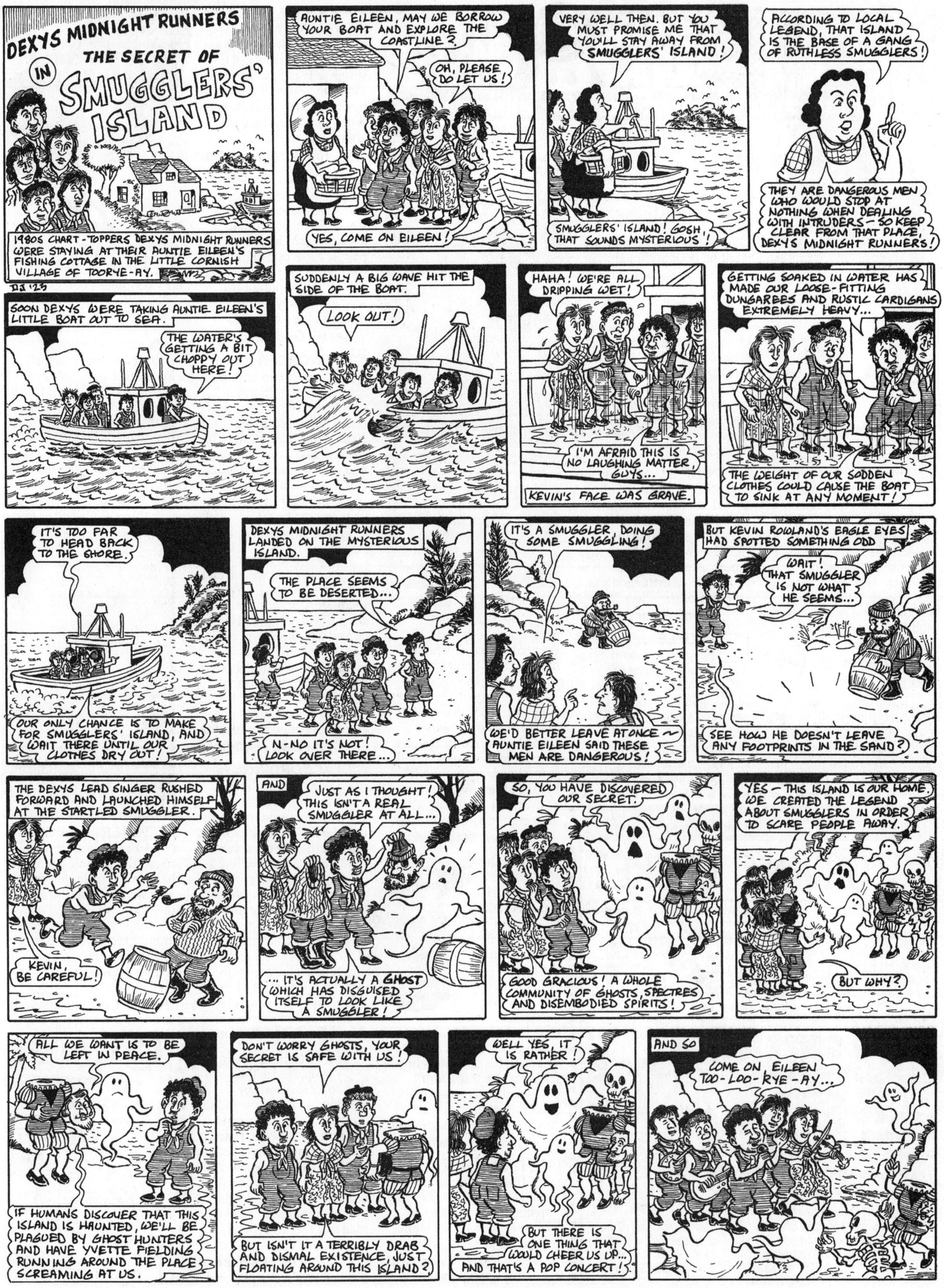
DEXYS MIDNIGHT RUNNERS
IN
THE SECRET OF
SMUGGLERS' ISLAND
1980S CHART-TOPPERS DEXYS MIDNIGHT RUNNERS WERE STAYING AT THEIR AUNTIE EILEEN'S FISHING COTTAGE IN THE LITTLE CORNISH VILLAGE OF TOORYE-AY.
DJ '23
AUNTIE EILEEN, MAY WE BORROW YOUR BOAT AND EXPLORE THE COASTLINE?
OH, PLEASE DO LET US!
YES, COME ON EILEEN!
VERY WELL THEN. BUT YOU MUST PROMISE ME THAT YOU'LL STAY AWAY FROM SMUGGLERS' ISLAND!
SMUGGLERS' ISLAND! GOSH, THAT SOUNDS MYSTERIOUS!
ACCORDING TO LOCAL LEGEND, THAT ISLAND IS THE BASE OF A GANG OF RUTHLESS SMUGGLERS!
THEY ARE DANGEROUS MEN WHO WOULD STOP AT NOTHING WHEN DEALING WITH INTRUDERS - SO KEEP CLEAR FROM THAT PLACE, DEXYS MIDNIGHT RUNNERS!
SOON DEXYS WERE TAKING AUNTIE EILEEN'S LITTLE BOAT OUT TO SEA.
THE WATER'S GETTING A BIT CHOPPY OUT HERE!
SUDDENLY A BIG WAVE HIT THE SIDE OF THE BOAT.
LOOK OUT!
HAHA! WE'RE ALL DRIPPING WET!
I'M AFRAID THIS IS NO LAUGHING MATTER, GUYS...
KEVIN'S FACE WAS GRAVE.
GETTING SOAKED IN WATER HAS MADE OUR LOOSE-FITTING DUNGAREES AND RUSTIC CARDIGANS EXTREMELY HEAVY...
THE WEIGHT OF OUR SODDEN CLOTHES COULD CAUSE THE BOAT TO SINK AT ANY MOMENT!
IT'S TOO FAR TO HEAD BACK TO THE SHORE.
OUR ONLY CHANCE IS TO MAKE FOR SMUGGLERS' ISLAND, AND WAIT THERE UNTIL OUR CLOTHES DRY OUT!
DEXYS MIDNIGHT RUNNERS LANDED ON THE MYSTERIOUS ISLAND.
THE PLACE SEEMS TO BE DESERTED...
N-NO IT'S NOT! LOOK OVER THERE...
IT'S A SMUGGLER, DOING SOME SMUGGLING!
WE'D BETTER LEAVE AT ONCE - AUNTIE EILEEN SAID THESE MEN ARE DANGEROUS!
BUT KEVIN ROWLAND'S EAGLE EYES HAD SPOTTED SOMETHING ODD
WAIT! THAT SMUGGLER IS NOT WHAT HE SEEMS...
SEE HOW HE DOESN'T LEAVE ANY FOOTPRINTS IN THE SAND?
THE DEXYS LEAD SINGER RUSHED FORWARD AND LAUNCHED HIMSELF AT THE STARTLED SMUGGLER.
KEVIN, BE CAREFUL!
AND
JUST AS I THOUGHT! THIS ISN'T A REAL SMUGGLER AT ALL...
... IT'S ACTUALLY A GHOST WHICH HAS DISGUISED ITSELF TO LOOK LIKE A SMUGGLER!
SO, YOU HAVE DISCOVERED OUR SECRET.
GOOD GRACIOUS! A WHOLE COMMUNITY OF GHOSTS, SPECTRES AND DISEMBODIED SPIRITS!
YES - THIS ISLAND IS OUR HOME. WE CREATED THE LEGEND ABOUT SMUGGLERS IN ORDER TO SCARE PEOPLE AWAY.
BUT WHY?
ALL WE WANT IS TO BE LEFT IN PEACE.
IF HUMANS DISCOVER THAT THIS ISLAND IS HAUNTED, WE'LL BE PLAGUED BY GHOST HUNTERS AND HAVE YVETTE FIELDING RUNNING AROUND THE PLACE SCREAMING AT US.
DON'T WORRY GHOSTS, YOUR SECRET IS SAFE WITH US!
BUT ISN'T IT A TERRIBLY DRAB AND DISMAL EXISTENCE, JUST FLOATING AROUND THIS ISLAND?
WELL YES, IT IS RATHER!
BUT THERE IS ONE THING THAT WOULD CHEER US UP...
AND THAT'S A POP CONCERT!
AND SO
COME ON EILEEN TOO-LOO-RYE-AY...

letterbocks

letters@viz.co.uk letters@viz.co.uk letters@viz.co.uk

WITHOUT Googling, can anyone name 10 famous people called Fanny? I think most of us would struggle after Fanny Brice and Fanny Craddock, yet a couple of hundred years ago seemingly every other woman was called Fanny. Do any of your readers know how and when this name fell out of favour, and who was the Fanny who broke the camel's back? It's just that I'm doing a PhD dissertation titled *How the Patriarchy Wiped Out Fanny*.

G Horsecock, Louth

MY local boozer advertised 'Live premiership football' every weekend. But when I got there, it was actually on a widescreen television.

Les Lloyd, email

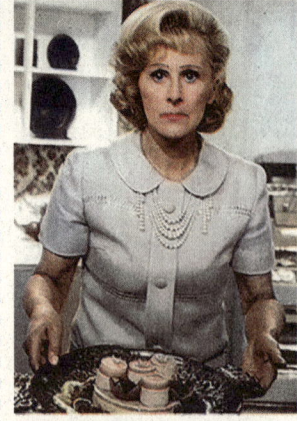

JACKIE Hopkins *(Letterbocks page 143)* says that she saw Tony Cottee go into a chemist in Essex once. Well I was once in a chemist in Highgate when The Kinks' Ray Davies came in. I didn't see what he bought though.

Bath Bob, Bath

** First Tony Cottee, then Ray Davies – it seems like celebrities are obsessed with chemists' shops these days. Write in and tell us if you've ever seen a star in a chemist, and we'll keep our readers regularly updated with a Starmacy Pharmacy column until everyone loses interest. Shouldn't take long.*

WHILST watching the Women's World Cup, I noted with interest that the Swiss team all wore badges highlighting the fact that they were qualified first aiders. A wonderful touch in this world of extreme stress on our health services.

Andy Bryant, Bristol

PEOPLE are always banging on about 'How long is a piece of string?'. Well, I have a piece of string in front of me right now, and I can tell you it's just a little bit smaller than those rulers you had at school. Case closed!

Jarvil McAonas, Scunt

STAR LETTER

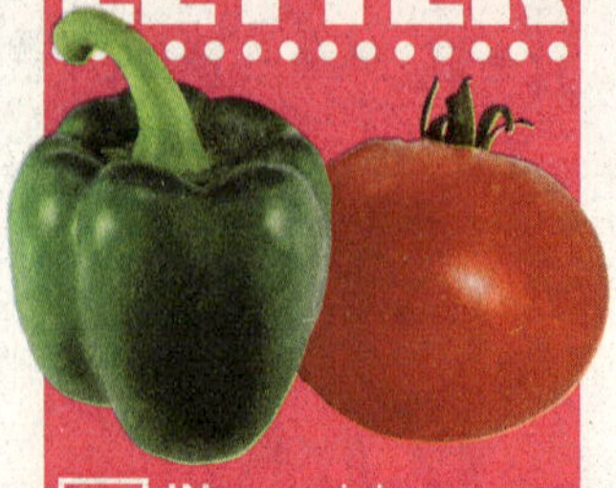

IN my opinion, the producers of *Ready Steady Cook* made a mistake using green peppers and red tomatoes for the scoring. Peppers can be red, and tomatoes can be green, so it's utterly confusing. They should have used something less ambiguous, like a fried egg and a potato. No wonder the show got cancelled after just thirty-two series.

Joe Williams, Leeds

KING Henry VIII had 3 children - Mary, Elizabeth and Edward - none of whom had children themselves, so when Elizabeth I died, the Tudor dynasty died with her. Why is it, then, that almost everyone who appears on *Who Do You Think You Are* is deemed to be descended from the merry monarch? Perhaps Lucy Worsley could answer that, probably whilst dressed up as Anne Boleyn.

Dan Sleet, Orkney

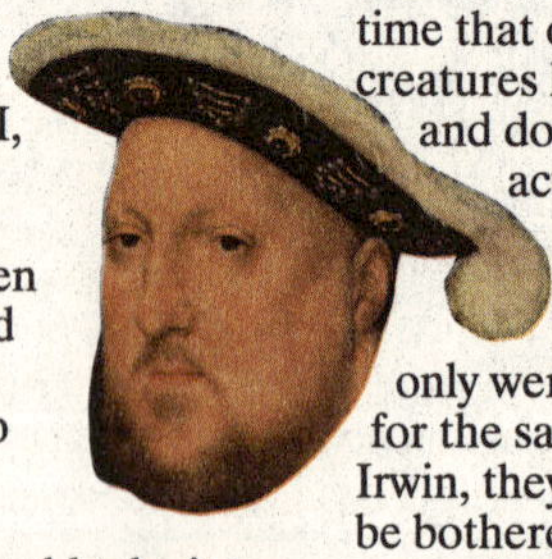

ON the subject of Henry VIII, do you think he ever got drunk and then commissioned the artist Holbein to do a painting of his cock, and then had a herald take it to Anne Boleyn, Jane Seymour or one of his other bits on the side, like the Tudor equivalent of a dick pic? I reckon he did.

Tommy Cromwell, Melbourne

IT'S a good job bakers fillet our bread before we buy it. Imagine how horrible it would be to get a bone in your throat whilst enjoying a jam sandwich.

Dave, Cape Cod

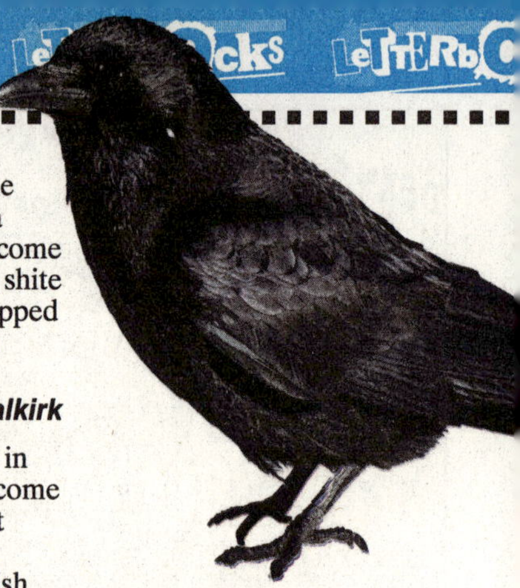

EXPERTS say that crows have the intellectual capacity of a seven-year-old. So how come I watched one eat a dog shite yesterday? My bairn stopped doing that when he was about four or five.

Nightbrogue, Falkirk

WHY do trousers in this country only come in even-numbered waist sizes - 30-inch, 32-inch, 34-inch etc? Don't British people have odd-numbered waist sizes, or is this a huge part of the population who are simply being discriminated against?

Hector Golightly, Penge

I WONDER if your readers can help me remember the title of a film I saw as a child. I don't recall much of the plot, but it was mostly about men in stetson hats riding horses and shooting at each other. It was set in the past, I think, possibly in America. Can anyone help?

Mathew Shepherd, Derby

"DU BIST sehr schön, but we haven't been introduced." So sang Damien Albran in his hit song *Boys and Girls*. But as any schoolboy will tell you, if he hadn't been introduced he really should be using the more formal "Sie sind sehr schön." Come on, Britpoppers. Let's not embarrass ourselves like this.

The Owl, Northfields

ACCORDING to a recent global study, there are approximately 150 million tonnes of single use plastics floating around our oceans. Isn't it about time that ocean-dwelling creatures like fish, crabs and dolphins got their act together and thought about somebody else for a change? Not only were they responsible for the sad demise of Steve Irwin, they now can't even be bothered to recycle.

Ian Blindell, Lincoln

I DON'T know why people judge the timidity of someone by whether or not they would say 'Boo!' to a goose. Trying to show off for the wife, I tried it when I was totalled on holiday in Wales and the bastard thing honked at me, bit me on the arse and made look a right twat by chasing me down the road and I fell in a muddy puddle. Bad tempered fucker.

Les Lloyd, email

THANK you news and magazine TV programmes for ensuring we know the difference between actor Brian Cox and the boffin Brian Cox with the clever ploy of putting the word 'actor' after the actor's name and the prefix 'Professor' for the scientist. Apart from one of them having a face like a dry chamois leather and the other looking like a choir boy that hasn't had his balls drop yet, it would be very easy to get them mixed up.

Glen R Car, Stockport

RIVHER
PULL HERE

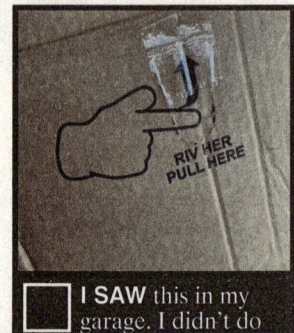

I SAW this in my garage. I didn't do as instructed because I've fallen for that trick once before and I'm not falling for it again.

Kendo, Boroughbridge

LNER station staff. Please don't explain to me that I can't get on the half-empty train that leaves 30 minutes earlier than the one I am booked on as though it's down to some immutable law of physics. I can't get on it because you've decided I can't get on it.

Hector Cretis, Newcastle

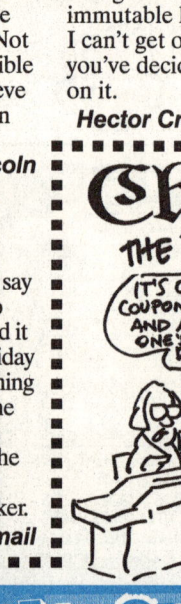

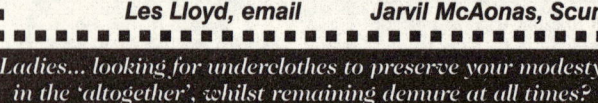

Ladies... looking for underclothes to preserve your modesty in the 'altogether', whilst remaining demure at all times?
VICTORIAN'S SECRET
BY APPOINTMENT TO THE CROWNED HEADS OF EUROPE.
Risqué Steel-Hooped Horschair Cage Crinolines 4/9
Enhances behindativeness without excessive weight!
PRICES HELD SINCE 1887!
Chiffon Open Cup Shifts 8/6
See-Through Camisoles 7/9
50% off peephole calico combinations!
Starched, Above-Ankle Petticoats 15/9
'As a supplier of ladies' underwear and sundries, it's really most beneficial!' Mrs. B, Essex
'Their garments are feminine and recherché, yet conceal the requisite amount of flesh.' Mr. R-M, Somerset

Christ
THE REDEEMER
IT'S ONLY ONE COUPON PER PURCHASE AND ANYWAY THIS ONE'S OUT OF DATE.

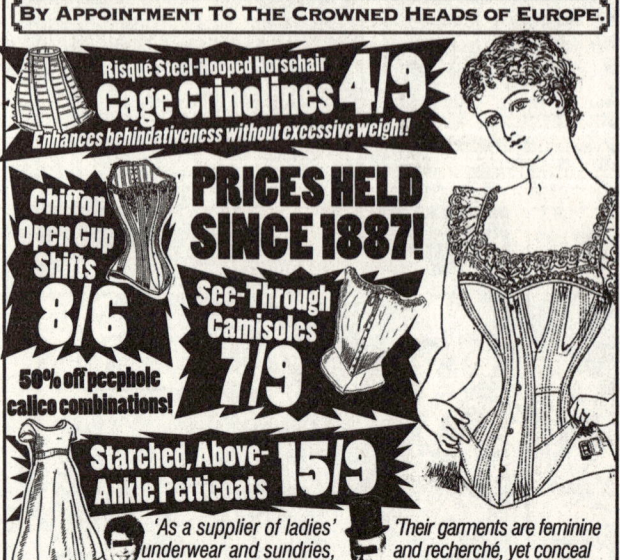

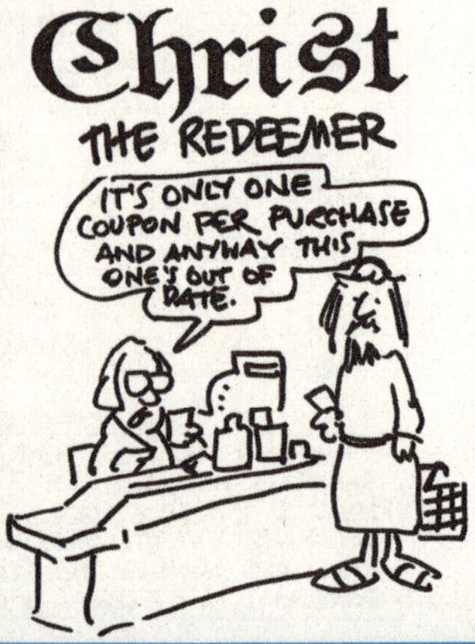

LOOKING at the online reviews of a *Tetrapanax papyrifer* plant recently, I would suggest that Brian S. can fault the experience, and indeed did so by giving it four stars. Similarly, I put it to Martin B. that he was in fact only 80% satisfied.
Ulf Linneus, Bergan

42 customer reviews for Tetrapanax papyrifer

★★★★
Can't fault the experience. Well done!¿
Brian S. – 21 June 2019

★★★★
Having saw the 'T-Rex' plant on TV. Went on line and found it at Palm Centre. Ordering it was simple, said it would be dispatched within 6 working days. Ordered it on the Tuesday and arrived Friday. Plant packaged very well, strong and healthy looking plant. Will be buying more plants from palm centre on line.
100% satisfied.
Martin B. – 17 May 2019

← 1 2 **3** 4 5 6 7 ... 371 →

COX, NOT COCKS!
It's Britain's liveliest forum for people who don't know the difference between BLACK HOLES and GLORYHOLES.
with synth-stabber turned pysicist **Professor Brian Cox**

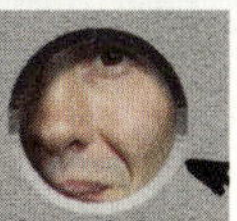

"Top telly physicist Brian Cox here. If there's one thing that baffles the public most when it comes to science, it's the distinction between black holes and gloryholes. Here are just a few of the questions I've received this month."

Dear Professor Cox,
IF I'M on a spaceship hurtling towards an Event Horizon and I stick my cock through a hole in the craft's toilet wall, will my bellend technically be younger than my balls?
Keith, Halifax

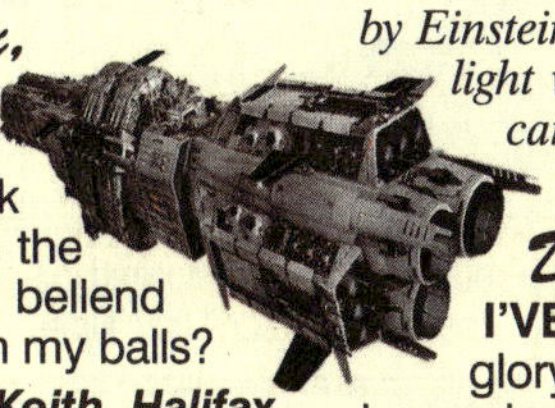

Brian says... This is a tricky one. If you are travelling on a bus and jump up, you will not be propelled towards the back of the vehicle. But, if you stick your knob out of the bus window and piss, the stream of urine will reach the back of the bus in seconds. And it's the same with Event Horizons. Hope this helps.

Dear Professor Cox,
IF I pushed my cock through a glory hole in a black hole, could someone the other side take a picture of it, or would the light from the flash be pulled away from my Charlie and towards the centre of the superdense star?
Mick, Leeds

Brian says... Someone could take all the photos they like of your male member pushed through the black hole wall, but as predicted by Einstein's Theory of General Relativity the light will be unable to escape from your camera, and all the photos will come back really dark.

Dear Professor Cox,
I'VE heard scare stories about gloryholes on Event Horizons becoming smaller after you've stuck your nob through them due to an energy loss phenomenon called Hawking radiation. Is this true, and if so, will it choke my cock?
Tim, Worcester

Brian says... Let me put your mind at rest – the answer is no! Hawking radiation occurs because the vacuum is not really empty and could technically evaporate a gloryhole, nipping any chopper poked through it. However, it would take longer than the age of the Universe to fully evaporate and become a total vacuum, leaving you plenty of time to get noshed off by a stranger without worrying!

More next time, folks who don't know the difference between Black Holes and Gloryholes **Bri xx**

☐ **I FOUND** a cock and balls in the lid of my Marmite. Would you like to see it?
Tony Macneil, Worcs

∗ *That depends, Mr Macneil. If you mean a Marmite impression of a cock and balls on the lid, then by all means send it in. If it's an actual set of male genitalia in the jar, then you probably ought to report it to the police immediately.*

☐ **I KEEP** seeing posters stating "It's okay not to be okay." But I beg to differ. It's dreadful.
Micky Bullock, Bristol

☐ **YOU** know when you're sitting on the loo and realise that there's no toilet paper, so you have to do that silly, trousers-down waddle to go and get some. Well, I'm nearly at Tesco's now, and I've had some very strange looks.
B Cholmondeley-Warner, email

☐ **I WAS** looking for a birthday card the other day and noticed one which stated 'To My Darling Wife'. Well, I'm not even married, so they got that one wrong for starters. Is there no beginning to their competence?
John Kelly, Stone

☐ **THE** size of the gates in Jurassic Park suggests that they were always planning on letting the dinosaurs out at some point.
Daniel, Fareham

☐ **WHILST** going down the stairs at Addenbrooke's Hospital today, I did a blow-off that lasted the whole two flights from the 5th to the 4th floor. Can any of your readers beat that?
Jaimie Taylor, Cambridge

∗ *That is impressive, Jaimie, but not unbeatable. So we're launching the Addenbrooke's Hospital Stair Fart Challenge. If any medical staff, porters, cleaners, visitors or indeed patients, can fart their way down 3 or more flights of stairs at the Cambridge hospital, write and let us know. If it proves a popular feature, we'll run the challenge in other hospitals in the UK, except North Tyneside General, which is all on one level because of something to do with mining in the area, apparently.*

☐ **I RECENTLY** purchased a new saucepan which came with an instruction leaflet. Frankly, there was nothing in it which could be described as a game changer, but at least it confirmed that the food goes inside the pan as opposed to directly onto the cooker.
Nick Lyon, Orkney

☐ **THE** phrases 'I was pissing myself' and 'I was shitting myself' describe two very different experiences. But I wonder who decided that it was a laugh-fest to be urinating inside your underpants, yet absolutely disastrous to be filling them with faecal matter? Ideally, I don't really want to do either.
John Mason, email

HOT BLOKE AT THE NEXT DESK CHAT

Bored Blokes At The Next Desk are *HOT* and *STEAMY* and waiting to talk 1-2-1 to *YOU!*

"I heard if it gets to 27 c*nt*gr*de, they have to s*nd us h*me."
08-811-8055

"The un*on should get them to put an a*r c*n unit in."
0881-180-55

"I've just got back from tw* w**ks in C*prus, and it were n*wh*re ne*r this h*t!"
088-118-055

Full and UNCENSORED *Hot Bloke At The Next Desk* chat GUARANTEED!

Calls cost £1.50/minute and terminate at the front reception. All proceeds go to the tea and coffee fund.

TOP TIPS

IDENTIFY the origin of a porn film by freezing the frame and looking at the power socket design in the background. Compare the socket style to a reference chart and you'll know the geographical area in which the grumbleflick was shot.
Barry, Queefton

FOOL people into believing you have dandruff by crumbling a prawn cracker onto the shoulders of your jumper.
Col P Fawcett, Durham

MALE porn stars. Removing your shirt prior to getting too deeply into your role means you won't have to use one hand to keep holding it up. This will allow you to use both hands to attend to the needs of your co-star.
Rob, Beaumaris

KIDNAPPERS. Don't ask for a £1 million ransom. Ask for £999,999.99 instead. It's only a penny less, but it doesn't break that psychological million pound barrier.
Derek Messerschmidt, High Wycombe

FOOTBALL Managers. Take a tip from the porn trade to knock a few quid off prospective signings by walking around the player half a dozen times whilst looking them up and down, shaking your head and occasionally kicking their shoes.
Kevin Caswell-Jones, Gresford

DARTS players. Recreate the atmosphere of a tennis match by screeching like you've just stood on a plug every time you throw.
Kevin Jaswell-Cones, Fresgord

MODEL train enthusiasts. Flattened raisins make excellent pats of cow shit to give your rural railways that authentic feel.
Lee Knight, Chesterfield

MAKE guests think that someone has done a very wet fart in your sink by emptying the 'dust' from a packet of dry roast peanuts into it and misting it with a little water.
Clifton Cornell, Leigh on Sea

toptips@viz.co.uk

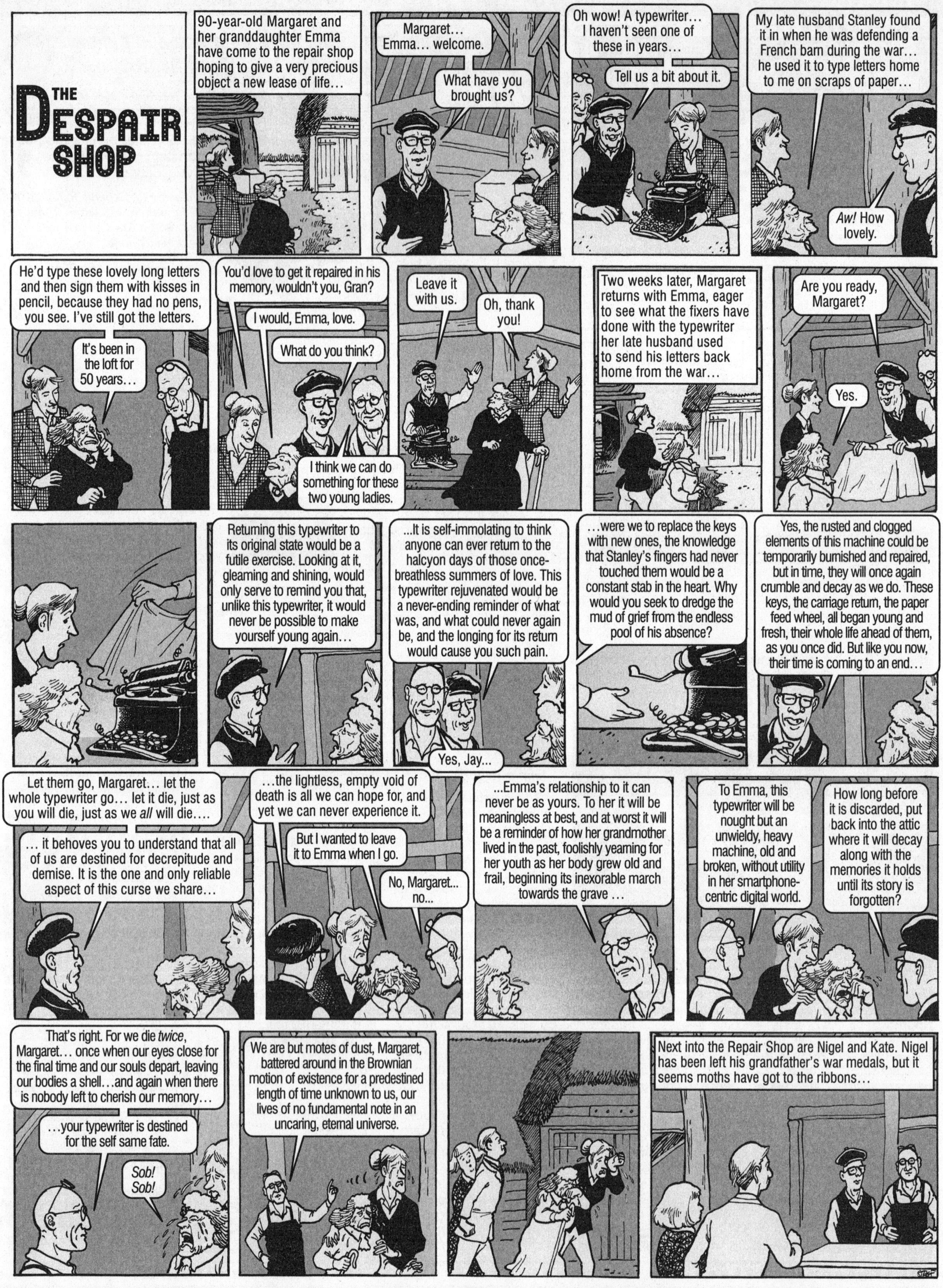
THE DESPAIR SHOP
90-year-old Margaret and her granddaughter Emma have come to the repair shop hoping to give a very precious object a new lease of life…
Margaret… Emma… welcome.
What have you brought us?
Oh wow! A typewriter… I haven't seen one of these in years…
Tell us a bit about it.
My late husband Stanley found it in when he was defending a French barn during the war… he used it to type letters home to me on scraps of paper…
Aw! How lovely.
He'd type these lovely long letters and then sign them with kisses in pencil, because they had no pens, you see. I've still got the letters.
It's been in the loft for 50 years…
You'd love to get it repaired in his memory, wouldn't you, Gran?
I would, Emma, love.
What do you think?
I think we can do something for these two young ladies.
Leave it with us.
Oh, thank you!
Two weeks later, Margaret returns with Emma, eager to see what the fixers have done with the typewriter her late husband used to send his letters back home from the war…
Are you ready, Margaret?
Yes.
Returning this typewriter to its original state would be a futile exercise. Looking at it, gleaming and shining, would only serve to remind you that, unlike this typewriter, it would never be possible to make yourself young again…
...It is self-immolating to think anyone can ever return to the halcyon days of those once-breathless summers of love. This typewriter rejuvenated would be a never-ending reminder of what was, and what could never again be, and the longing for its return would cause you such pain.
Yes, Jay...
…were we to replace the keys with new ones, the knowledge that Stanley's fingers had never touched them would be a constant stab in the heart. Why would you seek to dredge the mud of grief from the endless pool of his absence?
Yes, the rusted and clogged elements of this machine could be temporarily burnished and repaired, but in time, they will once again crumble and decay as we do. These keys, the carriage return, the paper feed wheel, all began young and fresh, their whole life ahead of them, as you once did. But like you now, their time is coming to an end…
Let them go, Margaret… let the whole typewriter go… let it die, just as you will die, just as we *all* will die….
… it behoves you to understand that all of us are destined for decrepitude and demise. It is the one and only reliable aspect of this curse we share…
…the lightless, empty void of death is all we can hope for, and yet we can never experience it.
But I wanted to leave it to Emma when I go.
No, Margaret... no...
...Emma's relationship to it can never be as yours. To her it will be meaningless at best, and at worst it will be a reminder of how her grandmother lived in the past, foolishly yearning for her youth as her body grew old and frail, beginning its inexorable march towards the grave …
To Emma, this typewriter will be nought but an unwieldy, heavy machine, old and broken, without utility in her smartphone-centric digital world.
How long before it is discarded, put back into the attic where it will decay along with the memories it holds until its story is forgotten?
That's right. For we die *twice*, Margaret… once when our eyes close for the final time and our souls depart, leaving our bodies a shell…and again when there is nobody left to cherish our memory…
…your typewriter is destined for the self same fate.
Sob! Sob!
We are but motes of dust, Margaret, battered around in the Brownian motion of existence for a predestined length of time unknown to us, our lives of no fundamental note in an uncaring, eternal universe.
Next into the Repair Shop are Nigel and Kate. Nigel has been left his grandfather's war medals, but it seems moths have got to the ribbons…

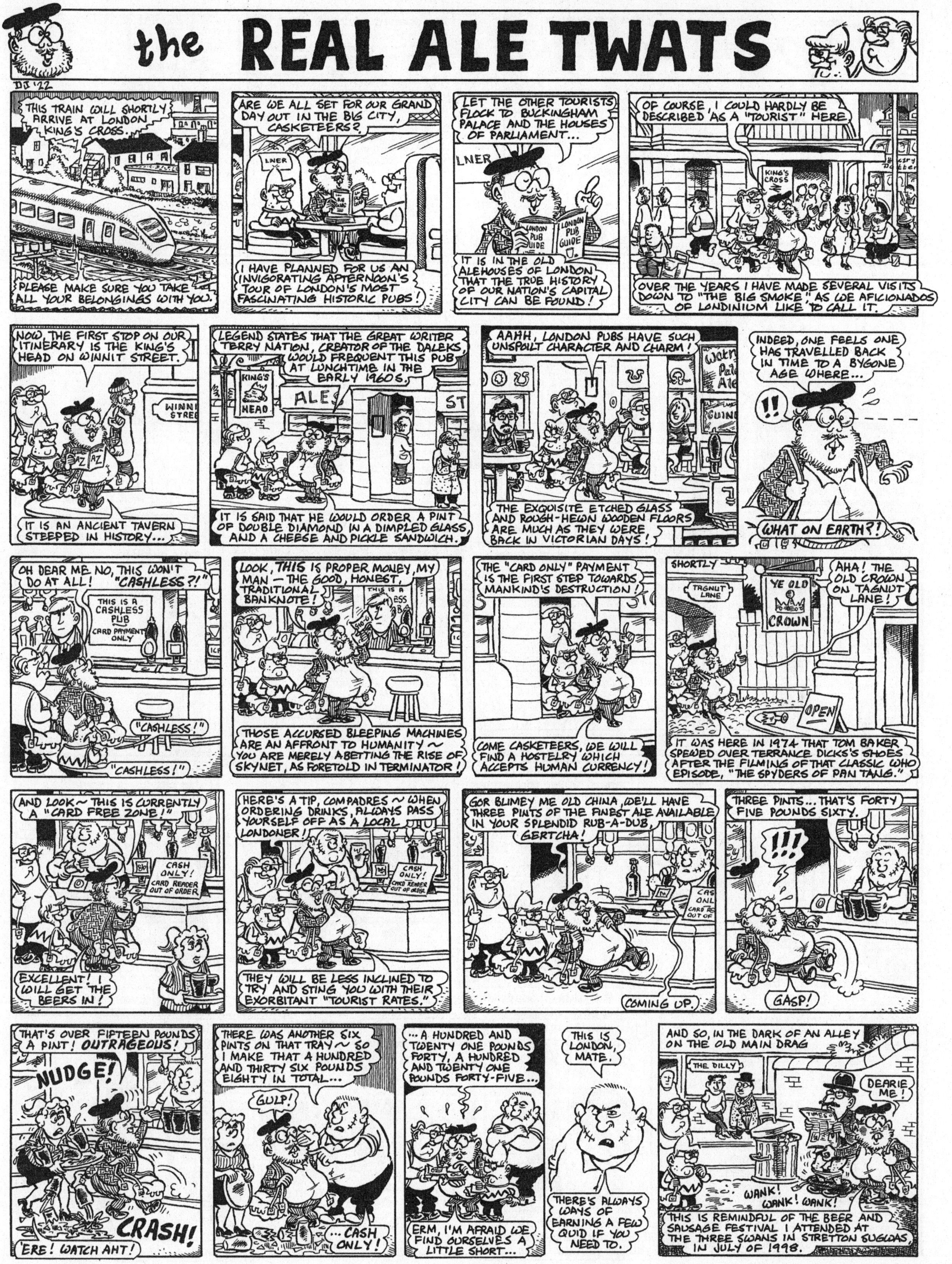
the REAL ALE TWATS
DJ '22
THIS TRAIN WILL SHORTLY ARRIVE AT LONDON KING'S CROSS.
PLEASE MAKE SURE YOU TAKE ALL YOUR BELONGINGS WITH YOU.
ARE WE ALL SET FOR OUR GRAND DAY OUT IN THE BIG CITY, CASKETEERS?
LNER
I HAVE PLANNED FOR US AN INVIGORATING AFTERNOON'S TOUR OF LONDON'S MOST FASCINATING HISTORIC PUBS!
LET THE OTHER TOURISTS FLOCK TO BUCKINGHAM PALACE AND THE HOUSES OF PARLIAMENT...
LNER
LONDON PUB GUIDE
IT IS IN THE OLD ALEHOUSES OF LONDON THAT THE TRUE HISTORY OF OUR NATION'S CAPITAL CITY CAN BE FOUND!
OF COURSE, I COULD HARDLY BE DESCRIBED AS A "TOURIST" HERE.
KING'S CROSS
OVER THE YEARS I HAVE MADE SEVERAL VISITS DOWN TO "THE BIG SMOKE," AS WE AFICIONADOS OF LONDINIUM LIKE TO CALL IT.
NOW, THE FIRST STOP ON OUR ITINERARY IS THE KING'S HEAD ON WINNIT STREET.
WINNI STRE
A-Z
IT IS AN ANCIENT TAVERN STEEPED IN HISTORY...
LEGEND STATES THAT THE GREAT WRITER TERRY NATION, CREATOR OF THE DALEKS, WOULD FREQUENT THIS PUB AT LUNCHTIME IN THE EARLY 1960S.
KING'S HEAD
ALES
IT IS SAID THAT HE WOULD ORDER A PINT OF DOUBLE DIAMOND IN A DIMPLED GLASS, AND A CHEESE AND PICKLE SANDWICH.
AAHH, LONDON PUBS HAVE SUCH UNSPOILT CHARACTER AND CHARM!
THE EXQUISITE ETCHED GLASS AND ROUGH-HEWN WOODEN FLOORS ARE MUCH AS THEY WERE BACK IN VICTORIAN DAYS!
INDEED, ONE FEELS ONE HAS TRAVELLED BACK IN TIME TO A BYGONE AGE WHERE...
!!
WHAT ON EARTH?!
OH DEAR ME NO, THIS WON'T DO AT ALL! "CASHLESS?!"
THIS IS A CASHLESS PUB CARD PAYMENT ONLY
"CASHLESS!"
"CASHLESS!"
LOOK, THIS IS PROPER MONEY, MY MAN — THE GOOD, HONEST, TRADITIONAL BANKNOTE!
THOSE ACCURSED BLEEPING MACHINES ARE AN AFFRONT TO HUMANITY ~ YOU ARE MERELY ABETTING THE RISE OF SKYNET, AS FORETOLD IN TERMINATOR!
THE "CARD ONLY" PAYMENT IS THE FIRST STEP TOWARDS MANKIND'S DESTRUCTION!
COME CASKETEERS, WE WILL FIND A HOSTELRY WHICH ACCEPTS HUMAN CURRENCY!
SHORTLY
TAGNUT LANE
YE OLD CROWN
AHA! THE OLD CROWN ON TAGNUT LANE!
OPEN
IT WAS HERE IN 1974 THAT TOM BAKER SPEWED OVER TERRANCE DICKS'S SHOES AFTER THE FILMING OF THAT CLASSIC WHO EPISODE, "THE SPYDERS OF PAN TANG."
AND LOOK ~ THIS IS CURRENTLY A "CARD FREE ZONE!"
CASH ONLY! CARD READER OUT OF ORDER
EXCELLENT! I WILL GET THE BEERS IN!
HERE'S A TIP, COMPADRES ~ WHEN ORDERING DRINKS, ALWAYS PASS YOURSELF OFF AS A LOCAL LONDONER!
CASH ONLY! CARD READER OUT OF ORDER
THEY WILL BE LESS INCLINED TO TRY AND STING YOU WITH THEIR EXORBITANT "TOURIST RATES."
GOR BLIMEY ME OLD CHINA, WE'LL HAVE THREE PINTS OF THE FINEST ALE AVAILABLE IN YOUR SPLENDID RUB-A-DUB, GERTCHA!
COMING UP.
THREE PINTS... THAT'S FORTY FIVE POUNDS SIXTY.
!!!
GASP!
THAT'S OVER FIFTEEN POUNDS A PINT! OUTRAGEOUS!
NUDGE!
CRASH!
'ERE! WATCH AHT!
THERE WAS ANOTHER SIX PINTS ON THAT TRAY ~ SO I MAKE THAT A HUNDRED AND THIRTY SIX POUNDS EIGHTY IN TOTAL...
GULP!
...CASH ONLY!
...A HUNDRED AND TWENTY ONE POUNDS FORTY, A HUNDRED AND TWENTY ONE POUNDS FORTY-FIVE...
ERM, I'M AFRAID WE FIND OURSELVES A LITTLE SHORT...
THIS IS LONDON, MATE.
THERE'S ALWAYS WAYS OF EARNING A FEW QUID IF YOU NEED TO.
AND SO, IN THE DARK OF AN ALLEY ON THE OLD MAIN DRAG
THE DILLY
DEARIE ME!
WANK! WANK! WANK!
THIS IS REMINDFUL OF THE BEER AND SAUSAGE FESTIVAL I ATTENDED AT THE THREE SWANS IN STRETTON SUGWAS, IN JULY OF 1998.

Tip Top Tony

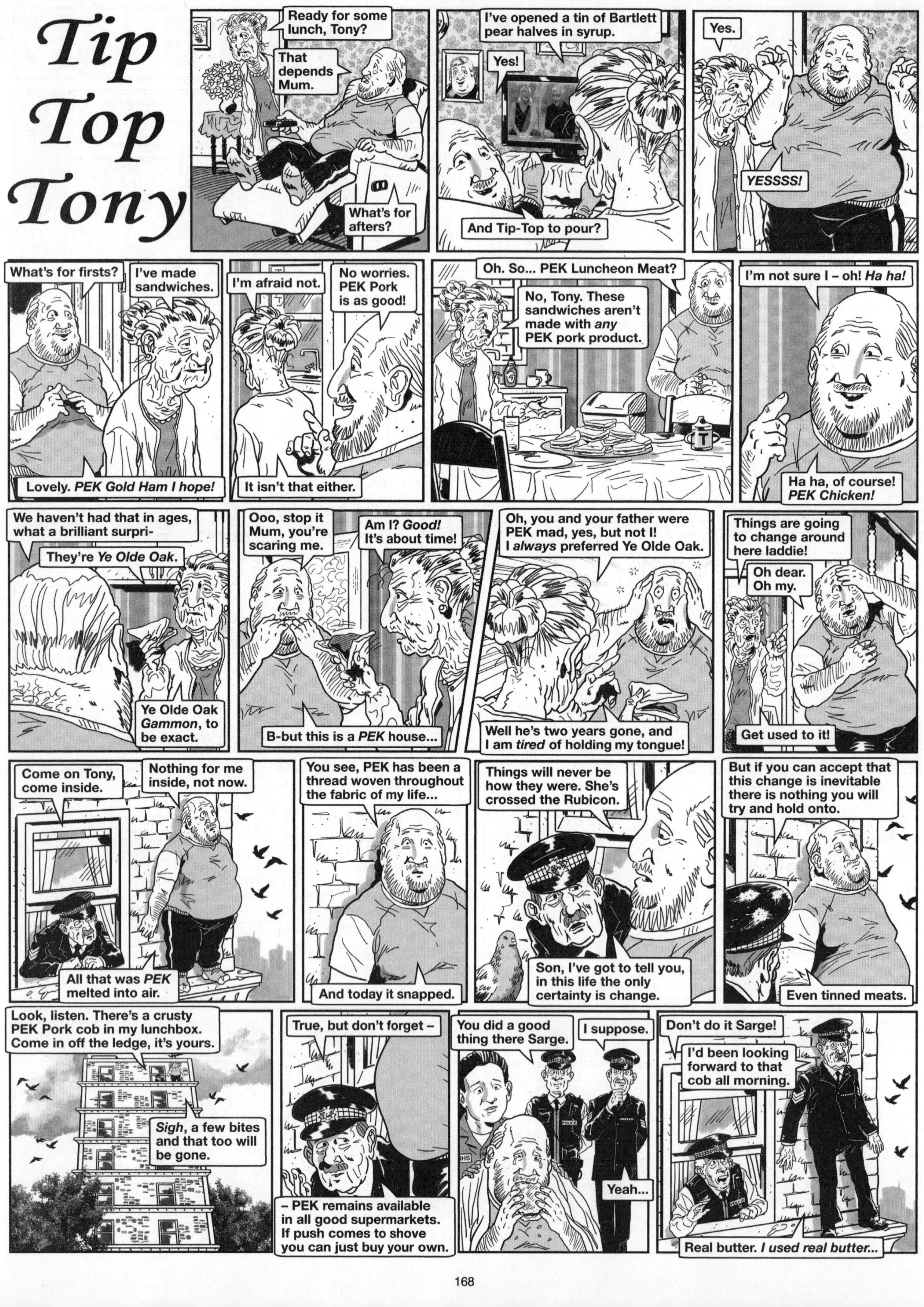

Ready for some lunch, Tony?
That depends Mum.
What's for afters?
I've opened a tin of Bartlett pear halves in syrup.
Yes!
And Tip-Top to pour?
Yes.
YESSSS!
What's for firsts?
I've made sandwiches.
Lovely. PEK Gold Ham I hope!
I'm afraid not.
No worries. PEK Pork is as good!
It isn't that either.
Oh. So... PEK Luncheon Meat?
No, Tony. These sandwiches aren't made with any PEK pork product.
I'm not sure I – oh! Ha ha!
Ha ha, of course! PEK Chicken!
We haven't had that in ages, what a brilliant surpri-
They're Ye Olde Oak.
Ye Olde Oak Gammon, to be exact.
Ooo, stop it Mum, you're scaring me.
Am I? Good! It's about time!
B-but this is a PEK house...
Oh, you and your father were PEK mad, yes, but not I! I always preferred Ye Olde Oak.
Well he's two years gone, and I am tired of holding my tongue!
Things are going to change around here laddie!
Oh dear. Oh my.
Get used to it!
Come on Tony, come inside.
Nothing for me inside, not now.
All that was PEK melted into air.
You see, PEK has been a thread woven throughout the fabric of my life...
And today it snapped.
Things will never be how they were. She's crossed the Rubicon.
Son, I've got to tell you, in this life the only certainty is change.
But if you can accept that this change is inevitable there is nothing you will try and hold onto.
Even tinned meats.
Look, listen. There's a crusty PEK Pork cob in my lunchbox. Come in off the ledge, it's yours.
Sigh, a few bites and that too will be gone.
True, but don't forget –
– PEK remains available in all good supermarkets. If push comes to shove you can just buy your own.
You did a good thing there Sarge.
I suppose.
Yeah...
Don't do it Sarge!
I'd been looking forward to that cob all morning.
Real butter. I used real butter...

HYDROMETER
THE REAL ALE TWATS
IN THE LOCAL
SO WHEN'S YOUR MATE DUE TO RETURN HOME FROM THE MUNICH BEER FESTIVAL?
♪ EIN PROSIT, EIN PROSIT, DER GEMÜTLICHKEIT... ♪
GUTEN HABEN MEIN CASKETEERS!
SLAP!
AH, WHAT AN INCREDIBLE COUPLE OF DAYS I'VE HAD!
EVERY TRUE CONNOISSEUR OF PUB CULTURE SHOULD VISIT THE OKTOBERFEST AT LEAST ONCE IN THEIR LIVES!
THE AMOUNT OF BEER BEING CONSUMED AT SAID FESTIVAL WAS QUITE STAGGERING...
...AND I USE THE WORD "STAGGERING" ADVISEDLY, CASKETEERS! EVEN SUCH A SEASONED DRINKER AS MYSELF WAS A LITTLE UNSTEADY IN THE LEG DEPARTMENT!
NUDGE!
IT WAS A VERITABLE "QUAFF-AGEDDON!"
YES, YOU HAVE TO HAND IT TO OUR BAVARIAN FRIENDS ~ THEY CERTAINLY KNOW HOW TO HAVE A "SESSION."
LET ME REGALE YOU WITH A FEW HILARIOUS ANECDOTES ABOUT MY RECENT GERMANIC ADVENTURE...
AH HELLO, YOU TOLD ME THAT THIS WAS YOUR REGULAR HAUNT.
REMEMBER ME? I'VE BEEN SERVING YOU DRINKS IN THE BAR AT FULCHESTER AIRPORT FOR THE PAST COUPLE OF DAYS.
SHAME ABOUT YOU MISSING YOUR FLIGHT TO MUNICH WHEN YOU FELL ASLEEP AFTER DRINKING THREE PINTS OF JOHN SMITHS.
ANYWAY, I THOUGHT I'D DROP OFF YOUR PASSPORT ~ YOU LEFT IT ON THE BAR.

ELDERLY ADVANTAGE TAKING ORGANISATIONS

WARNING! IGNORING THIS ADVERT COULD LEAD TO YOUR ARREST.

BILLIONS of pounds are still **OWED** to HMRC by MILLIONS of OAPs – ***YOU ARE ONE OF THEM!***

You may not even know you owe any tax, ***BUT YOU DO!*** And not paying it is a criminal offence for which you can go to prison for life! That means that your grandchildren would not see you for years.

You may have heard in the news about **'iTunes Vouchers'**. You may also have heard that they may be used to pay off your tax bill. Are you eligible?

- ***Were you born in the 20th Century between 1910 and 1951?***
- ***Can you not remember whether you have paid all your tax between those years?***
- ***Are you both gullible AND vulnerable?***

This is NOT a SCAM! This is NOT a CON!

If you answered **YES**, then **YOU** can pay your tax bill by **iTunes Vouchers**.

We have been self-appointed as the **OFFICIAL FINANCIAL RECEIVER** for authorised iTunes Voucher Tax Bill Payments - *BUT THE DEADLINE IS COMING UP FAST!*

To avoid a custodial sentence, simply go to your nearest iTunes retailer and buy iTunes cards to the value of £5,000. and enter your iTunes Vouchers codes:

_ _ _ _ _ / _ _ _ _ _ / _ _ _ _ _

at **Whattsapp/UKtax-officialiTunes12**

Then ***RELAX!*** Our operatives will redeem the vouchers for you against the money that you owe to HMRC.

If you don't know how much you owe, find out by visiting YourTaxStatus-advice4u.ru

The LAST CHANCE TO PAY OFF YOUR TAX BILL USING iTUNES VOUCHERS is NEXT FRIDAY!

If you are concerned you may have been targeted by fraudsters, contact our Fraud Action Team at **ActionFraud-4-u.ru** with the credit card details you think may have been compromised to hand.

COMEDIC CANINE VIBRATION-ACTIVATED CAR GONKS

There can be no GREATER TRIBUTE to one of Britain's blandest Comedians

MICHAEL McINTYRE NODDING DOG

Nod along with the master of the mundane!

only £199

The ultimate in annoyingly ubiquitous vehicle toy adornments – a *HILARIOUS* depiction of the UK's most annoyingly ubiquitous comedian!

BUT IT DOESN'T JUST NOD! *It also spouts random McIntyre jollities* ***EVERY FIFTEEN SECONDS!****

- ***"Have you ever been in the supermarket when..."***
- ***"When you're in the car..."***
- ***"I was in the bath the other day..."***
- ***"When you're dropping off the kids at school..."***

Your stunning tribute to the bobble-headed star of primetime stage and screen easily affixes** to the front or rear dash.

*WARNING - Once started, the Michael McIntyre Nodding Dog cannot be turned off (longlife battery lifetime 5+ years)

** Once permanently fixed will require professional removal by a mechanic.

ORDER NOW: nodding-mcintyre-dog.co.ck

Realistic nodding action... ...just like the real thing!

...ASIDE SPECIAL ... 6-PAGE SEASIDE SPECIAL ... 6-PAGE SEASIDE SPECIAL ... 6-PAGE SEASIDE SPECIA...

SUIT UP FOR SUMMER
Seaside resort to dish out free Hazmat suits to beachgoers

SUN HAS GOT HAZMAT ON: *Visitors to Fulchester-super-mare will be able to leave the suncream at home this year.*

SADDLED with scat-spattered sands and seas packing more germs per drop than a cuppa from Porton Down canteen, there's no doubt that this year will go down as an *anus horribilis* in the annals of UK staycation history. But one iconic British holiday resort is refusing to throw in the beach-towel, and has vowed to tackle the human effluent problem head on – by giving every visitor to the resort a free Hazmat Suit!

Fulchester-super-mare Council is poised to sink an as yet undisclosed sum into providing visitors with personal safety equipment to allow them to relax and enjoy the golden sands and once-pristine sea that made the resort famous.

"Hazmat suits have a terrible image problem, and the recent pandemic did them no favours whatsoever," said the resort's Mayoress Ingrid Erskin. "But here in Fulchester-super-mare, we're aiming to challenge that view, and to revamp them in new and inclusive ways."

A meeting of the council last week passed a motion to lay on a free reusable hazmat suit for every visitor to the town in the summer season. And with millions of visitors heading to the town for fun in the sun each year, the undertaking represents a substantial investment for ratepayers. But Mrs Erskin told councillors that they had little choice in the matter.

"More than two thousand townsfolk work in candy-floss alone," she told the *Fulchester-super-mare Shitstirrer*. "Another thousand are engaged in the manufacture of those big red rock dummies, fifteen hundred hire deckchairs. The list goes on."

"The latest scientific research we commissioned found there is currently a higher risk of catching a dose of E coli from a swim in the water off our beaches than there is from eating a hot-dog off the pier," she said. "And I'm not proud to tell you that takes some doing."

"If we can't keep people safe, they won't come. And if they don't come there *is* no Fulchester-super-mare. These hazmat suits will allow our visitors to enjoy our glorious beaches just like they did in the days before there was foulage all over them," she said.

hieroglyphics

And Mrs Erskin admitted that some difficult financial decisions had to be made to find the money to pay for the suits. "Regrettably, we have had to close the library," she said. "In addition, rubbish collections will shift from weekly to annually, and the five schools in the town will move to a two-day-week from the autumn term."

But the Mayor insisted that finding the money for over 1.5 million Hazmat suits was only half the battle. "The main problem is going to be overcoming the negativity about the suits themselves," she said.

"People associate them with Ebola outbreaks, toxic spillages, or accidents at nuclear facilities. It's all rather grim," she continued. "Most people don't want to think about things like that while they're on holiday."

And to counter the negative associations hazmat suits have with disaster, the council has come up with a plan to make them fun. The mayoress told reporters: "They're going to add to the holiday, not detract from it."

"There'll be none of those horrible day-glo hazard-yellow suits coming within a mile of our beaches. Instead, there'll be ones with 'Kiss me quick, squeeze me slow!' written on the front of the helmet, and transparent panels so the girls can show off their tanned beach-bodies," she added.

potato

Sourcing such a quantity of personal protective holiday equipment could have been a problem, but as luck would have it, Billy Mone, the Mayor's brother in-law had, only the day before, formed a company which specialised in making bespoke hazmat suits.

"After the meeting, I took the unilateral decision to award the contract to produce the suits to my brother-in-law, Mr Mone," she said.

HOT STEPPER: H off of Steps.

"In an ideal world, the contract would have gone out to tender, but we face dire circumstances and we've got to strike while the iron is hot."

"We've got H out of Steps switching on the illuminations in a week's time, and then there's the bank holiday coming up," she added. "Time is not on our side."

The Beachcombers

WE all love BEACHCOMBING – idling up and down a sandy shore, keeping our eyes peeled for shiny sea glass, interesting fossils and intricate shells. And our favourite A-List stars are no different. That's why we called up four of our most-loved celebs and asked them: *What's the best thing you've ever found while out beachcombing?*

TOM CRUISE, small actor
I was on a beach in California once where thousands of Nike trainers had washed up after a shipping container fell from a ship. There were hundreds of people rushing round, trying to find their size and match up pairs, setting up swapping stations and everything. It was great fun. I managed to find a left Air Max Dunk Low in my size, but I couldn't find the right one in the same colour. I eventually found one half a size bigger, which isn't ideal, but it's fine and I still wear them today with a bit of tissue paper stuffed into the toe.

ICE CUBE, gangsta rap icon
Me and the NWA lads went beachcombing when we were on tour in Blackpool back in the eighties and I found a cuttlefish. But my main memory of the day was that we got into a right old barney about the meanings of 'flotsam' and 'jetsam'. Eazy-E was convinced that 'flotsam' was debris deliberately thrown overboard by a ship's crew, and 'jetsam' was debris accidentally spilled overboard, whereas I said it was the other way round. This was pre-internet, mind, so we couldn't just google it. We argued all the way back to the B&B, and then Dr Dre looked it up in an encyclopaedia and wallop – I was proved right. You should of seen the look on Eazy's face! He was monster fucking livid.

HANS BLIX, weapons inspector
I once found a shit-ton of Pogs on a beach in Marbella. Do you remember Pogs? You couldn't move for the fuckers in the nineties, but no one even mentions them nowadays. Anyroad, as I was wandering along this beach, I stubbed my foot on a cake tin poking out the sand, and the tin turned out to be full of fucking Pogs. I stuck the lot on eBay and ended up getting about sixty euros for them, which isn't fuck-off money, I know, but it's better than a kick up the arse.

POPE FRANCIS, late pontiff
The most memorable thing I've found while beachcombing was a pocket fanny which a sailor must have lost overboard his ship. It had washed up among some seaweed, and I picked it up because I thought it was a mermaid's purse. I was so embarrassed when I realised my mistake that I slipped it down the front of my cassock and ran home to the Vatican. That evening, I went to put it in the recycling, but then I thought what if someone sees it? The papers would have a ruddy field day running with "Pope chucks out pocket fanny" or something. I wracked my brains but I couldn't think of a single safe way to dispose of it, so I kept it.

...6-PAGE SEASIDE SPECIAL ... 6-PAGE SEASIDE SPECIAL ... 6-PAGE SEASIDE SPECIAL ... 6-PAGE SEA...

YOU find them at the edge of a country where it meets the sea and people flock to them in their thousands on sunny days. And unless you live in Coton-in-the-Elms in Derbyshire, there's one not that far away. They're BEACHES, and every one of us has fond memories of playing on them as a child. But what are they made of? Who owns them? And how many Brazilian rain forests the size of Wales do they cover? Find out the answers to – not these – but other questions as we bring you...

10 THINGS YOU NEVER KNEW ABOUT BEACHES

1 **SAND** the world over is made of Silicon dioxide, SiO_2, in the form of particulates of stable quartz crystals. This means that every beach in the world has the same chemical structure. However, people still insist of holidaying in the Seychelles or the Maldives, when they could sit on exactly the same stuff in Filey or Cleethorpes! Talk about throwing money down the drain.

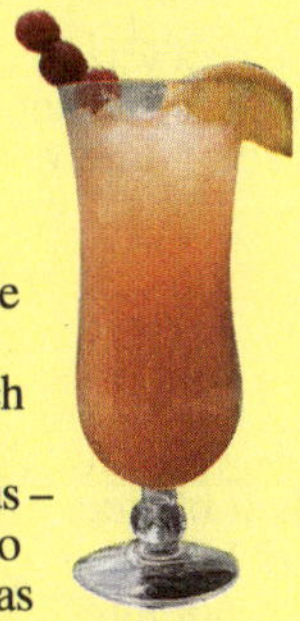

2 **YOU** may think that Sex on the Beach would be extremely enjoyable, and you would be right… but not for the reasons you think. Because 'Sex on the Beach' is the name of a fruity cocktail containing vodka, peach schnapps, orange juice and cranberry juice which – as well as being delicious – also gives men on holiday an excuse to attempt a feeble and unoriginal joke as part of their chat-up routine.

3 **THE OTHER** type of 'Sex on the Beach' – penetrative intercourse performed on the strip of sand between the high and low tidal water marks – is less enjoyable, as sand and grit rubbing repeatedly on the participants' delicate genital tissues invariably leads to painful cuts and scratches.

4 **TORONTO** in Canada is famed for its many beaches, including Silver Birch Beach, Key-Balmy Beach, Woodbine Beach and many more. All boast golden sands, sun loungers, ice-cream kiosks and dunes to the rear – all the things you would expect on a beach. Except the sea! Because little do those bonkers Canadian holidaymakers know it, but they are actually paddling, swimming and otherwise frolicking in a massive *lake*.

5 **BEACHES** are places where people wear very little clothing, perhaps a skimpy bikini for the ladies and a pair of Speedos for the gents. But *nudist* beaches are a place where you can shed *all* your clothes and walk around naked and unashamed, enjoying the sun just as nature intended. However, anyone going there for a cheap thrill is doomed to disappointment as they are almost entirely populated by old men in their eighties with saggy arses and their clockweights hanging about an inch above their knees.

6 **FOR** many reasons, you will never find deck chairs for hire on a nudist beach. Firstly, they pose a hygiene risk, as sweat from naked buttocks soaks into the striped cloth. From a safety point of view, dangling your unprotected genitals in proximity to unpredictable pieces of wood moving in a scissoring action is an accident waiting to happen. And putting deck chairs up entails a lot of bending over which, considering the predominance of elderly men in the naturist community, is problematical from an aesthetic point of view.

7 **ASK** anyone for directions to the beach in Prague and they will give you a blank stare. This is because the Czech Republic is a landlocked country; that is to say, one that does not have a coastline. With no beaches anywhere, they might not even have a word for it.

8 **ASK** anyone for directions to the beach in Liechtenstein or Uzbekistan, and you'll get an even blanker stare than you did off the person in Prague. That's because they are both *double* landlocked countries – so not only do they not have any beaches, but neither do all the neighbouring countries surrounding them. *You couldn't make it up.*

9 **THERE** are no triple-landlocked countries in the world, although Nebraska is a triple-landlocked state in the US, so you might get a blanker stare there than in Liechtenstein or Uzbekistan.

10 **FAMOUS** people from Nebraska include Nobel Prize-winning geneticist **GEORGE WELLS BEADLE**, atom bomb physicist **JOHN R DUNNING**, and 'Tony the Tiger' Frosties ad voiceover man **THURL RAVENSCROFT**.

ROCK-POOLING with UKIP-turned-Brexit Party-turned-Reform MP *Nigel Farage*

Hi! Nigel Farage here. Now, when I'm not surviving light aircraft crashes or the wheels coming off my car on the Autobahn, I like nothing better than spending the day sitting atop our Great British cliffs on the lookout for small boats. But watching for desperate people whose lives I can make a bit more difficult is tiring work, so I like to take a break every now and then by going down onto the beach below to do a bit of rock-pooling. Why don't you join me and we'll see what we can see in these rocky, watery worlds…

Good old **CRABS** are the things you are most likely to see in a rock pool. With their ten limbs, these crustaceans are as British as steak and chips, bobbies on the beat and red telephone boxes. Some French crabs may have made their way across the channel into UK waters, but they will be easily spotted by their lazy, sluggish manner and disregard for the rules of the rock-pool.

All the **MUSSELS** you see in a rock-pool on our shore will be 100% British. There are of course mussels in France, where those Gallic wasters insist on calling them 'moules', but since they can neither walk nor swim, none of them ever make their way across the English Channel, which the foreigns insist on calling 'La Manche'.

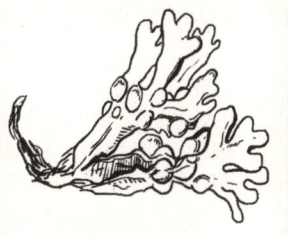

BLADDERWRACK is a small British seaweed with little air sacs that make it float on the water surface to catch the sunlight and so aid photosynthesis. It is British greeny brown in colour, and clings to the British rocks with roots, but with a simplified organ called a holdfast, which is also British.

PIPEFISH – these long, thin British fish – are actually a member of the seahorse family, having come over here from more tropical waters thousands of years ago, just like the Anglo Saxons, so that's alright. They live in shallow waters and eat… Oh, sorry, got to rush, I've just spotted a boatload of dole scroungers coming to take our jobs.

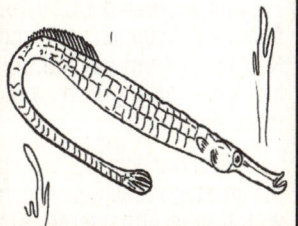

171

METAL MICKEY

Local detectorist in ownership dispute over find

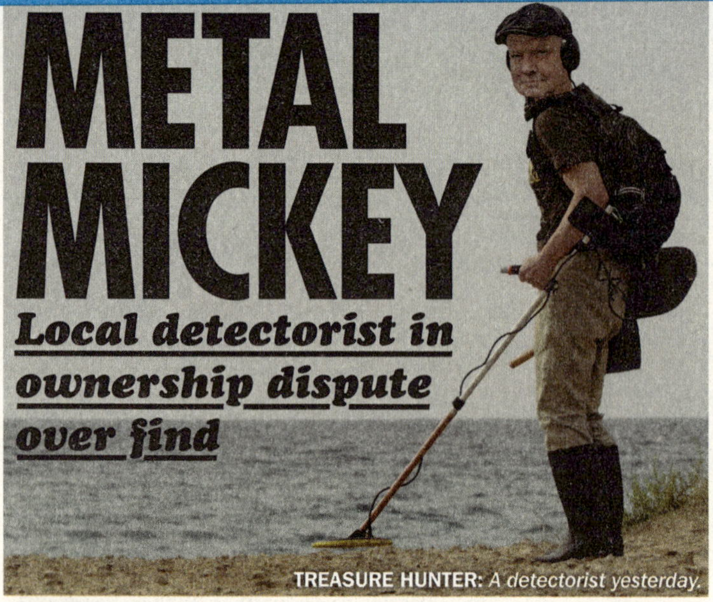

TREASURE HUNTER: *A detectorist yesterday.*

TREASURE hunters with metal detectors have made many interesting and important discoveries over the years. Valuable Saxon armour, Viking swords and hordes of Roman coins are always declared 'Treasure Trove' and handed in to the authorities. But the law states that objects found on the beach, as opposed to the land, belong to the finder.

EXCLUSIVE!

So a keen amateur metal detectorist thought he had made the discovery of his life when he unearthed a valuable watch in the sand dunes in his home town of Sutton-on-Sea, Lincolnshire. But not only was 48-year-old Mickey Natterjack not allowed to keep his find, he was arrested by police and charged with theft!

"I just don't know what I'm supposed to have done wrong," Natterjack told the *Sutton-on-Sea International Enquirer*. "I found this watch behind a clump of sedge in the dunes, and so that's finders, keepers."

Having little need for a watch, the former schoolboy took it the next day to the Sutton-on-Sea branch of Cash Counter, where he was given a straight £100 cash in return for the £2,500 Rolex. "It was probably worth a bit more, but they've got to make their profit, so I was happy," he told the paper.

forbidden

But his happiness proved short-lived when the police arrived at his flat the following week and placed him under arrest for theft. The owner of the watch had reported it stolen the same day as Natterjack's find, and detectives had made enquiries in local pawn shops.

Cops reviewed CCTV footage from Cash Counters and recognised Natterjack from several previous incidents relating to his hobby of metal detecting.

"At first I thought they were getting me on a technicality, saying that the watch was considered Treasure Trove because the beach does not legally constitute the sand dunes or something," he said. "When they charged me with theft, I almost fell through the floor."

"I tried to argue my case, telling them that just because the watch was on top of the sand rather than under it, there was no legal distinction from a metal detecting standpoint," he said. "We detectorists find hidden things. Whether they are hidden by sand or earth or a towel, a pair of shoes and some folded clothes is neither here nor there."

sauerkraut

However, despite Mickey's protestations the police pressed charges, saying the fact that Natterjack does not own a metal detector adds credibility to their case, a claim he flatly refutes.

"Being a detectorist is nothing to do with having the equipment. It's about having a passion for archaeology, a desire to find things that show us how we used to live," he said.

"Just like you don't need any clubs to be a good golfer, you don't need a metal detector to unearth our history."

Last week, Natterjack appeared before magistrates in Louth, where he pleaded guilty to theft and asked for 340 other cases, which he also described as 'mistaken treasure trove', to be taken into consideration.

Oh I Do Like to *Pee* Beside the Seaside!

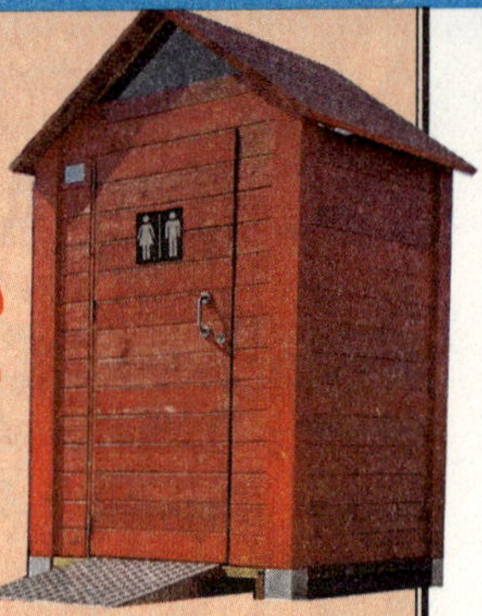

IT'S a situation we have all found ourselves in at one time or another. We're having a day on the beach, and whilst splashing about in the waves, we suddenly feel the need to relieve ourselves. The dilemma we face is a simple one – do we make our way out of the sea and across the beach to the public lavatories on the promenade... or do we simply 'let go' in the sea? With Britain's waters nothing more than open sewers anyway, adding our own 'two penn'orth' to the foetid mix is surely no big deal. Or is it never acceptable to make things worse, whatever the scale of the problem? We visited a busy Norfolk seaside resort to test the waters on this divisive subject...

"...I WOULD definitely have a waz in the sea. The volume of seawater on earth is nothing compared to my bladder, so me having a gypsy's kiss in the water won't make a blind bit of difference. Although I suppose if I had a proper bladderful and was busting, I might nip out to the lavs for the sake of the environment."

Renton Aguecheek, plumber

"OF COURSE I'd strain my greens in the sea. Whales spend their whole lives pissing in the water and their bladders are about the size of a Mini Metro. My little half-pint deposit is nothing compared to a whole carful of piss."

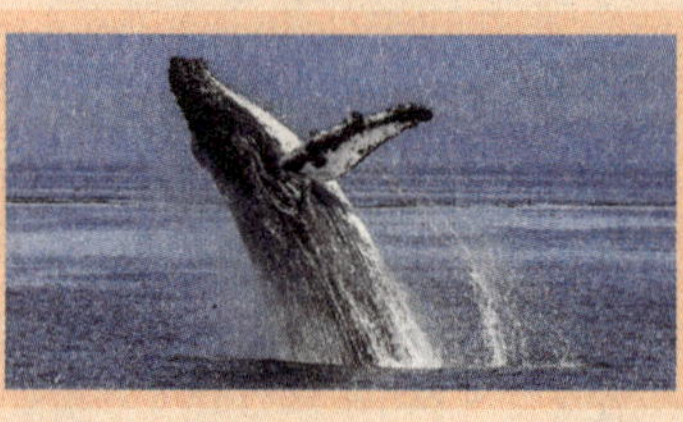

Harry Hotspur, decorator

"I MOST certainly would not urinate in the sea. I know water companies regularly release millions of gallons of the stuff into our waters, but they have no choice in the matter as they have to keep dividends high for their shareholders. But if any individual were to do it, that would be absolutely unforgivable."

Lyle Curthose, stockbroker

"I WOULDN'T piss in the sea personally, because there are these fish what swim up your hog's eye, and they've got spines on their back which means that you can't pull them back out, and doctors have to slice your cock open to remove them. I know they live in the tropics in Brazil or Australia or somewhere, but what with global warming it's only a matter of time before they're in the sea off Chapel St Leonards or Ingoldmells."

Declan Lackland, surveyor

"I WOULDN'T spend a penny in the sea because. as a lady, I would have to squat down, which means I would have to go in the shallows and there is a risk that the water could retreat and leave me exposed. I could waddle backwards and forwards as the waves go in and out so as to be constantly covered, but that would be most undignified."

Edna Broomshank, lollypop lady

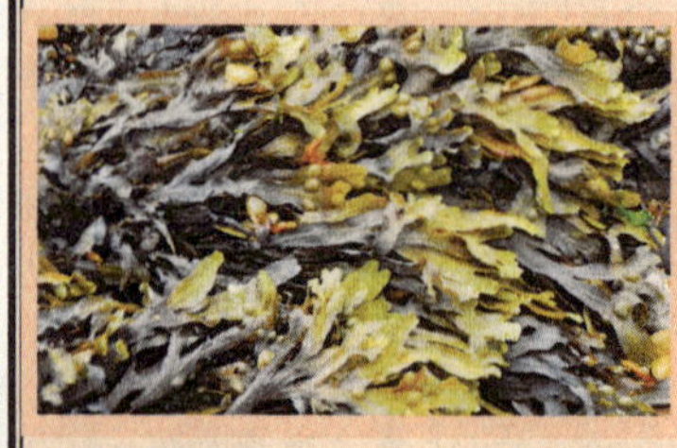

"I WOULD piss in the sea, certainly, but I wouldn't have a shit because the toilet paper would just disintegrate when I went to wipe my arse. I could use a piece of that wide, flat seaweed, I suppose, but if there was a couple of barnacles on it, it would cheese-grate my poor nipsy to shreds."

Mordecai Fortune, university lecturer

"I LIVE on the coast and I have a swim in the sea every day. But before I do, I like to play a little game whereby I park my breakfast in the toilets on the promenade. Then I flush the bog and race out onto the prom and down onto the beach to the sewage outlet to see if I can beat my turds to the sea."

Hampton Crowfoot, high court judge

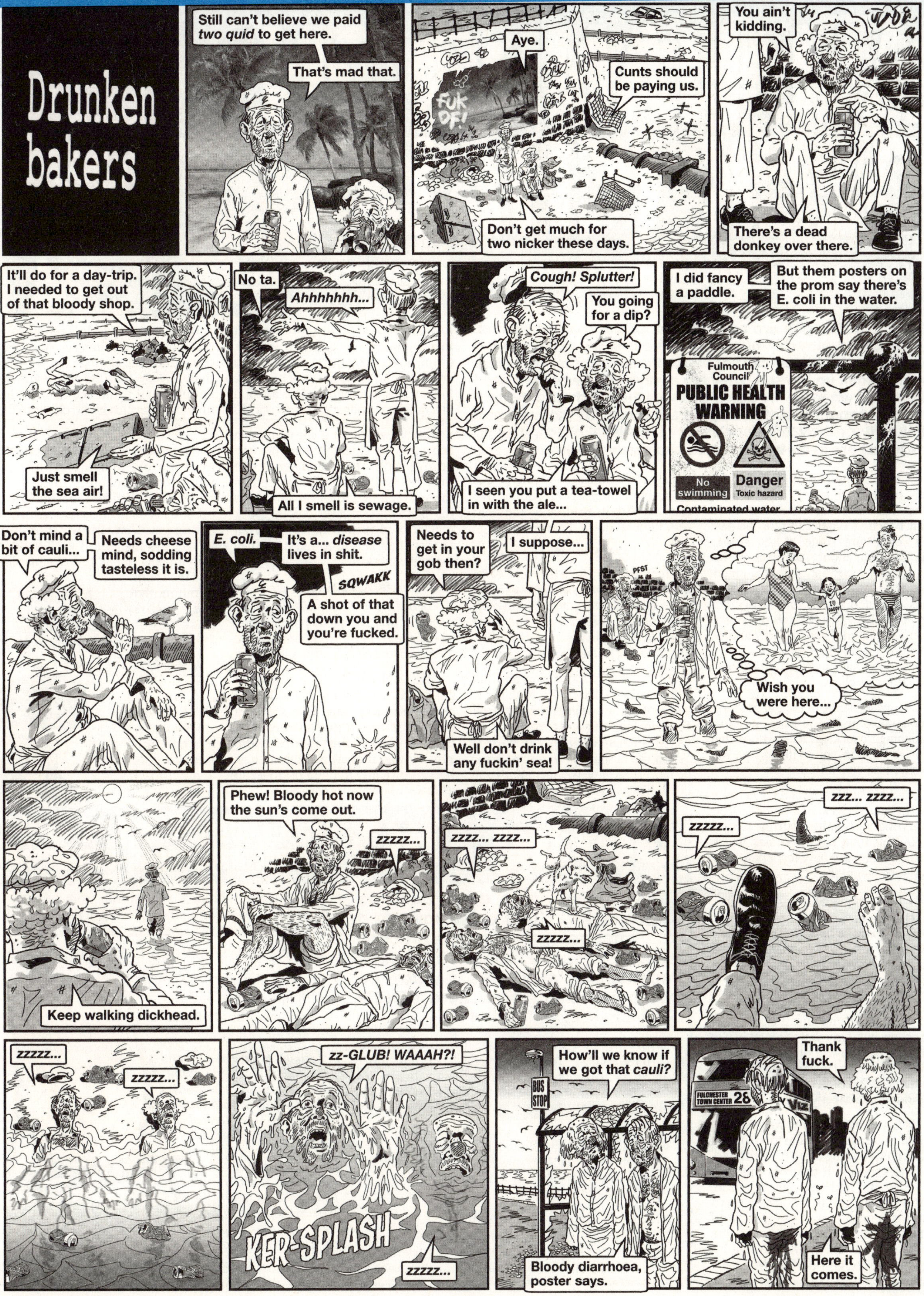
Drunken bakers
Still can't believe we paid *two quid* to get here.
That's mad that.
Aye.
Cunts should be paying us.
FUK OF!
Don't get much for two nicker these days.
You ain't kidding.
There's a dead donkey over there.
It'll do for a day-trip. I needed to get out of that bloody shop.
Just smell the sea air!
No ta.
Ahhhhhhh...
All I smell is sewage.
Cough! Splutter!
You going for a dip?
I seen you put a tea-towel in with the ale...
I did fancy a paddle.
But them posters on the prom say there's E. coli in the water.
Fulmouth Council
PUBLIC HEALTH WARNING
No swimming
Danger
Toxic hazard
Contaminated water
Don't mind a bit of cauli...
Needs cheese mind, sodding tasteless it is.
E. coli.
It's a... *disease* lives in shit.
SQWAKK
A shot of that down you and you're fucked.
Needs to get in your gob then?
I suppose...
Well don't drink any fuckin' sea!
Wish you were here...
Keep walking dickhead.
Phew! Bloody hot now the sun's come out.
zzzzz...
zzzz... zzzz...
zzzzz...
zzzzz...
zzz... zzzz...
zzzzz...
zzzzz...
zz-GLUB! WAAAH?!
KER-SPLASH
zzzzz...
How'll we know if we got that *cauli*?
BUS STOP
Bloody diarrhoea, poster says.
FOLCHESTER TOWN CENTER 28
Thank fuck.
Here it comes.

ALL HANDS ON DECK (CHAIR)

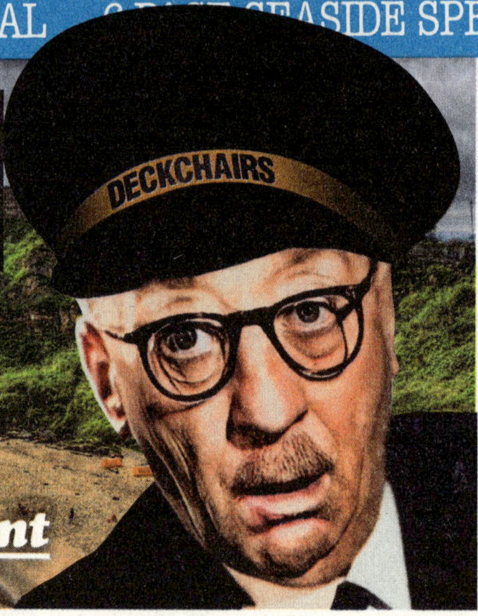
DECKCHAIRS

"I've seen it all," says Tynemouth chair attendant

DECKCHAIRS are a traditional fixture on our beaches. On a sunny day, hundreds of these stripy cloth-covered wooden frames can be seen on the sand as their occupiers sit and soak up the sun. They are always there when we need them, and when we are done, we leave them without a thought of what happens next. So spare a thought for the man who looks after nearly 250 deckchairs on his local beach, making sure they are in tip-top condition and ready for hire.

The aptly named Derek 'Dec' Chair has been in charge of the council deckchair hire hut on St Edward's Bay beach in Tynemouth for the past 40 years, and some of the stories he can tell about the mishaps his customers have had with his chairs are hilarious. So much so, that Dec has collected his memoirs together in a book, which is already in the top 2 million best sellers, and is currently riding high at number 8 in Amazon's Deckchair and Windbreak Biographies chart.

"Honestly, some of the things I have seen would make you wet your pants laughing," chuckles Dec. "Although if you did that in one of my chairs, you would lose your £10 deposit."

And his book *It Shouldn't Happen to a Council Deckchair Attendant!* is bursting with side-splitting stories about his time 'on the chairs' which are guaranteed to have readers 'folding up' with laughter.

cloth

Dec says the funniest moments come from people who think that putting up a deckchair is a simple matter, when in fact nothing – or at least very little – could be further from the truth.

"I remember this one summer, a couple came and hired two chairs from my hut. I asked if they would like a quick demonstration of how to put them up, but the man was giving it the old Bertie Big Bollocks, saying that he could do it perfectly well.

What happened next was comedy gold, as the macho chump tried to erect the chair, showing off to his girlfriend. He was turning it this way and that, looking at it and scratching his head. At one point, he had it upside down and was pushing the top instead of the bottom. He struggled with the first chair for a full minute while his girlfriend looked on before finally getting it up. The second one he got up in about thirty seconds, but he was crimson with frustration by the time they both sat down, I can tell you!"

pork pie

Most of Dec's customers take instructions from him and watch the quick demonstration he gives with each hire. But this doesn't mean that there won't be any comedy moments when they try to do it for themselves. Far from it.

"Once, a very large man and his wife hired two chairs and took them to a spot on the beach about fifty yards from my hut. They got them up fairly easily, but that's when the fun started. When the husband – who must have been 25 stone if he was an ounce – sat down, his chair gave an almighty creak. Everyone around must have thought that the wood was going to splinter or the fabric tear and he was going to end up on his backside with his drink thrown in the air and his legs akimbo in a tangle of timber and stripy cloth.

But that was never going to happen because these chairs are load-bearing up to a good 35 stone. And I know that for a fact because I maintain them in the winter. All 250 of my chairs go through a rigorous twelve-point check in the closed season, and any that fail are repaired and re-tested until they make the grade."

stegosaurus

According to Dec, the funniest moments with deck chairs occur when you least expect them, as one elderly couple found out to their cost a few years ago.

"This old pair hired a couple of chairs one summer in 1997 or 1998, I can't quite remember. They set them up on the beach and sat down to enjoy a read of their books in the sun. Anyway, they eventually put their books down and nodded off to sleep as many of my customers do.

But what they didn't realise was that the tide was coming in. After four decades on the chairs, I know better than anyone that the tide waits for no man, and I watched as the edge of the sea got closer and closer to the dozing pensioners.

Eventually, a bit of water lapped over the old man's feet, and he immediately woke up. Luckily for him he had taken his shoes and socks off and rolled his trouser legs up, or else he would have had wet shoes. But as you can imagine, I was doubled up with laughter as he woke his wife and they both calmly moved their chairs back about 20 yards!"

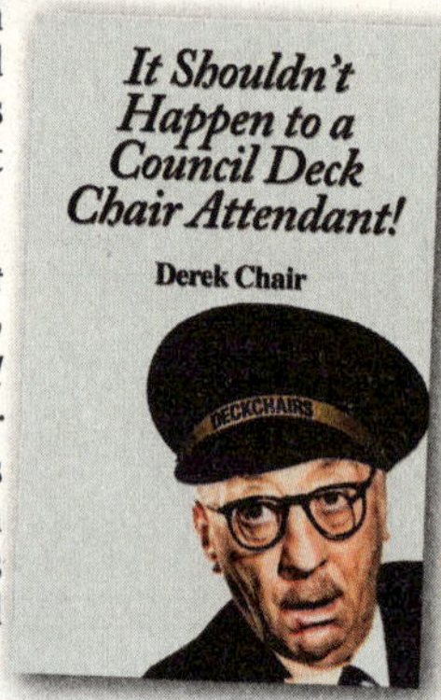
It Shouldn't Happen to a Council Deck Chair Attendant!
Derek Chair
DECKCHAIRS

It Shouldn't Happen to a Council Deck Chair Attendant! is available on Amazon as a download only.

Going Up! Dec's foolproof tutorial on the simplest way to erect a deck chair

PUTTING up a deck chair is simple... *if you know how!* And after going through the process around *2 MILLION TIMES* in his career, Dec Chair certainly ticks that box. So for the less experienced, here is Dec's Deck Chair Erection 101...

Whenever you find yourself needing to erect a deckchair in a hurry, simply remember my easy-to-remember acronym; *GGRL* – like the word 'girl' but with two 'g's at the beginning and no 'i' in the middle. This stands for *Grasp, Give, Release, Lower*. Then follow these four easy stages in order:

★ **GRASP** the chair in both hands, holding the top of the chair (the end opposite the notched bar) and the prop mechanism in your left hand, and the bottom of the chair and the notched bar in your right.

★ **GIVE** the chair a swift shake and, whilst keeping hold of the bottom of the chair, release the notched bar so as it swings down and hangs at 90° to the main frame.

★ **RELEASE** the prop mechanism from your left hand whilst keeping hold of the top of the chair and maintaining the grip on the bottom with your right.

★ **LOWER** the bottom of the chair in your right hand to the ground and lift the top of the chair in your left until the prop mechanism engages with the notched bar and you're done.

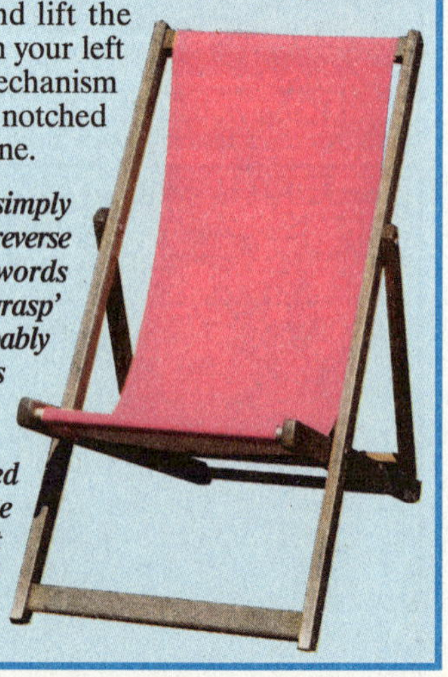

NB. To lower the chair, simply follow the instructions in reverse order, transposing the words 'raise' and 'lower', and 'grasp' and 'release'. There's probably a simple acronym for this too, but I usually let the punters work it out for themselves. Left-handed people should follow the instructions as given, but round the other side of the deck chair.

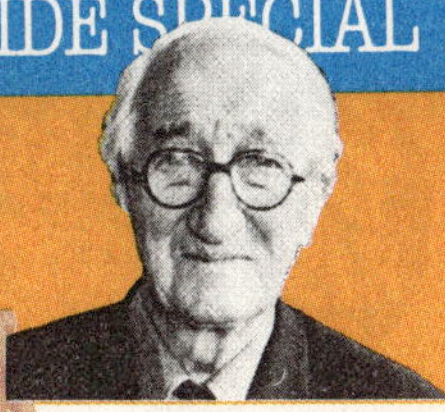

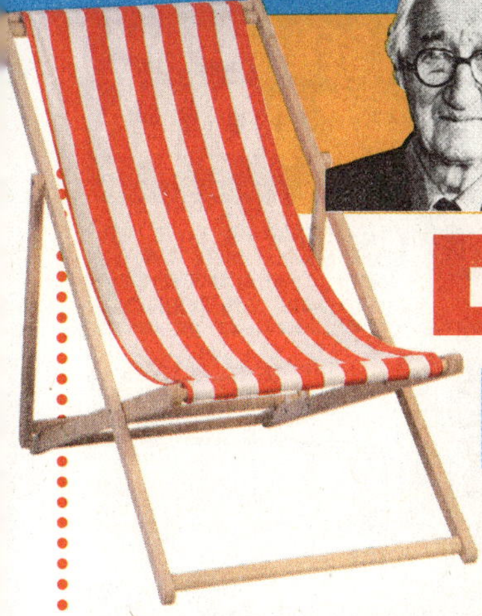

Watt's WHICH!?

DECKCHAIR... or LOUNGER?

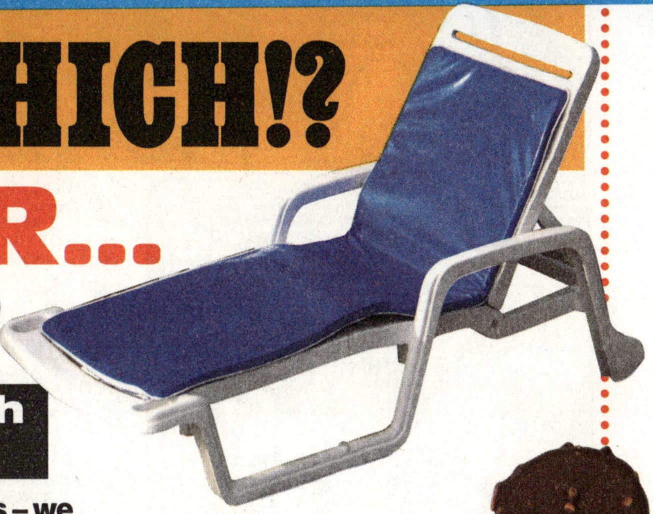

Consumer testing with professor Dirk Watt

WHEN it comes to relaxing on the beach, we have two options – we can sit on the sand on a blanket, or we can hire something to sit on. If we go for the second option, we then have another decision to make. We can choose to lay back and relax in comfort on a fully adjustable, reclining, padded sun-lounger. Alternatively, we can sit more upright on some stripy hessian cloth slung over a rickety wooden frame. It's a difficult choice. Here, Dr Dirk Watt – Professor of Beach Furniture at Mablethorpe University – gives us the lowdown...

"Deckchairs and sun loungers are very different beasts; both have their pros and cons, their advantages and disadvantages. So you need to do your research before you part with your money, or you could end up making a costly mistake. Let's break this down and assess the various qualities of each option so you can make up your mind.

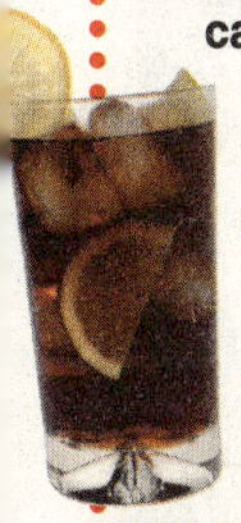

AFFORDABILITY

If you are looking to save money, then a deckchair is for you. The price for deckchair hire on most UK beaches starts from around 50p per hour, but most beaches offer an all-day-for-£3 option. Sun-loungers, on the other hand, start at around £5 for the day, a couple of quid more expensive. So let's look at what this £2 buys you.

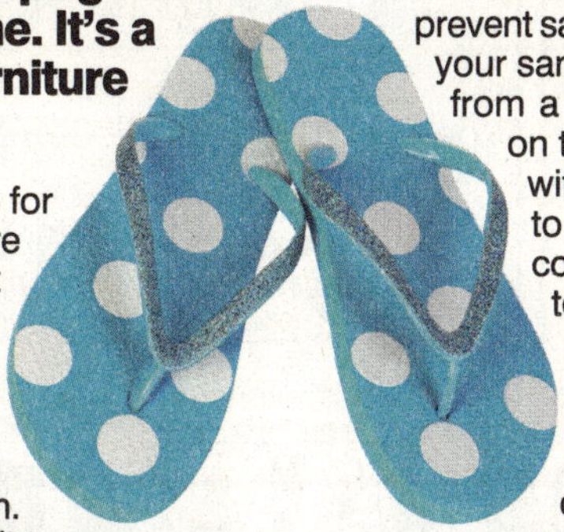

COMFORT

The sun-lounger wins the battle of the comfort wars hands down. You can adjust it to any position – upright, when you want to read a book, fully flat when you want a snooze, or anywhere in between when you want to do something else. With a fully sprung mattress, it is effectively a bed on the beach. The deckchair on the other hand, has three positions – bolt upright, slightly back and a little bit further back.

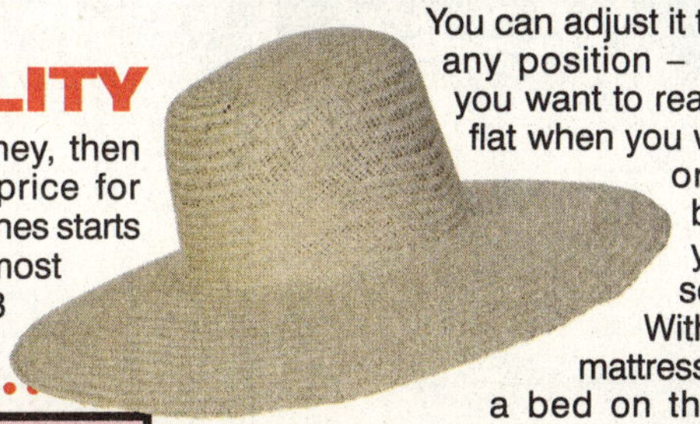

EASE OF USE

Anyone but a gymnast will struggle to get out of a deckchair gracefully, not to mention the ever-present risk of it collapsing in the process. And when you finally manage it, with no cushioning the hessian cloth will have left a tell-tale cross-hatched impression on the back of your legs. Getting off a sun-lounger, on the other hand, is as simple as swinging your tanned legs over the side, a graceful, easy action that can be accompanied by pushing your Armani sunglasses up onto the top of your head.

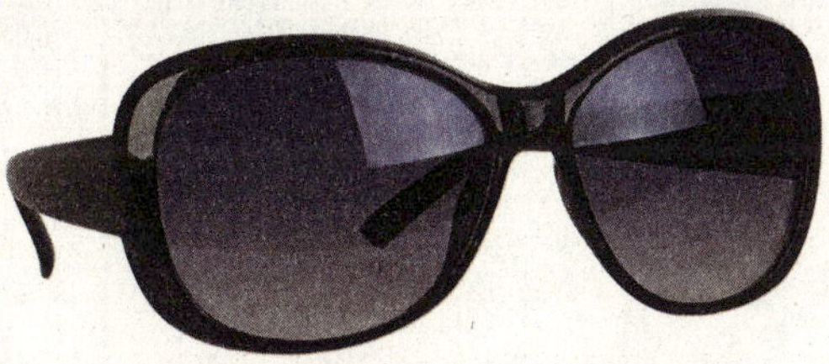

ACCESSORIES

When you hire a deckchair, quite often you will be offered the chance to pay a little bit more for a windbreak to go with it. These contraptions – featuring sticks nailed to a piece of cloth, usually in the same colours as the chair – are hammered into the beach to prevent sand from blowing into your sandwiches or your tea from a flask. Sun-loungers on the other hand, come with some kind of shade to prevent you and your ice cold cocktail from becoming too hot in the sun. This is usually a large umbrella emblazoned with the name of the hotel, such as The Continental, St Tropez, or The Monaco Tropicana. Or perhaps it's in the form of a large parasol made from the leaves of a locally grown coconut palm.

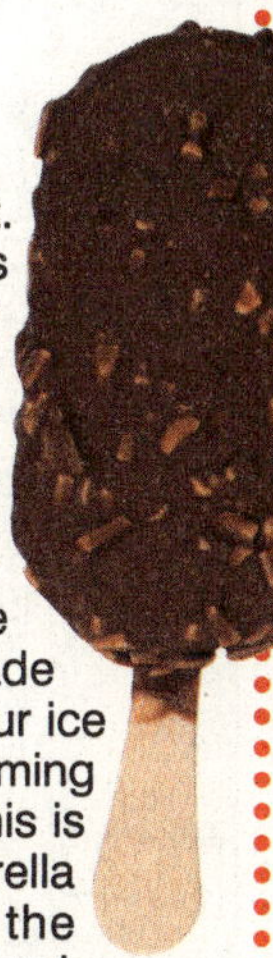

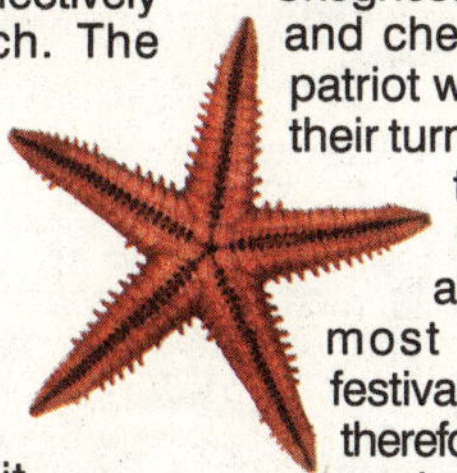

STYLE

The deckchair is the staple of the British seaside holiday, and they are found on beaches everywhere, from Clacton to Prestatyn, from Skegness to Blackpool. Whilst they are cheap and cheerful, even the staunchest British patriot would not say that they're stylish. In their turn, sun-loungers are found mainly on the sun-kissed beaches of the French Riviera, like those in Nice, Montpellier and Cannes, home of the world's most glamorous film festival. Sun loungers therefore conjure up images of films such as *And God Created Woman*, starring Brigitte Bardot and Jean-Louis Trintignant. Deckchairs, on the other hand, bring to mind *Holiday on the Buses*, starring Reg Varney and Bob Grant, or *Yus, My Dear – the Movie*, if it had been made, starring Arthur Mullard and Queenie Watts."

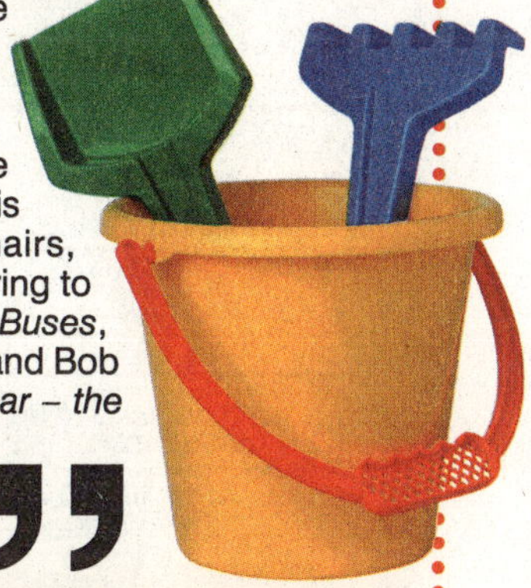

Watts' WHICH!? recommendation:

SUN LOUNGER

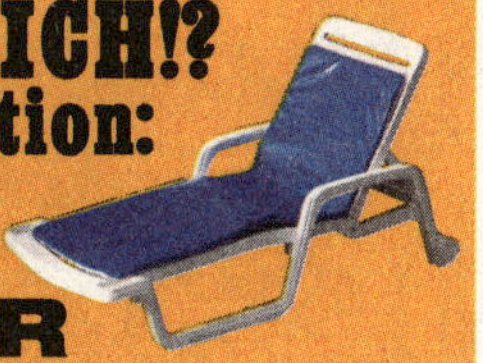

Life's a Beach with The MAN in the PUB

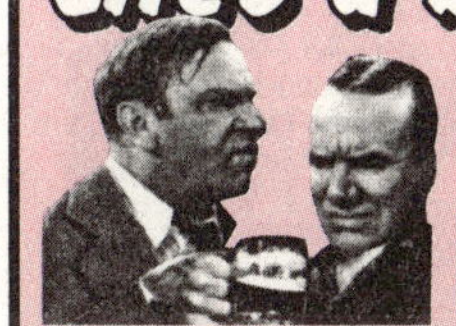

HERE'S a thing. If you wrote your initials on a grain of sand – difficult, I know – but say you did, and then you got your mate to hide it anywhere on any beach in the world, right? And then you shuffled a pack of cards and laid them out in a line. And then you went to any beach in the world and picked up any grain of sand. Now then, what's more likely – that you pick up your grain of sand or that you've just laid the cards out in an order what's already been done before since cards were invented? I bet you say the cards, don't you? Well you're wrong, cos there's fucking trillions and trillions and trillions of ways of arranging a pack of cards. Fucking loads more than there are grains of sand on earth. And that's without the two jokers. I thought that was bollocks an' all when I first heard it, but it's true. Straight up. Boggles your fucking crust, don't it? There's another bit that goes on about all the protons and nutrients in the earth but the fucking egghead on youtube lost me with all that bollocks. Mine's a pint if you're passing the bar.

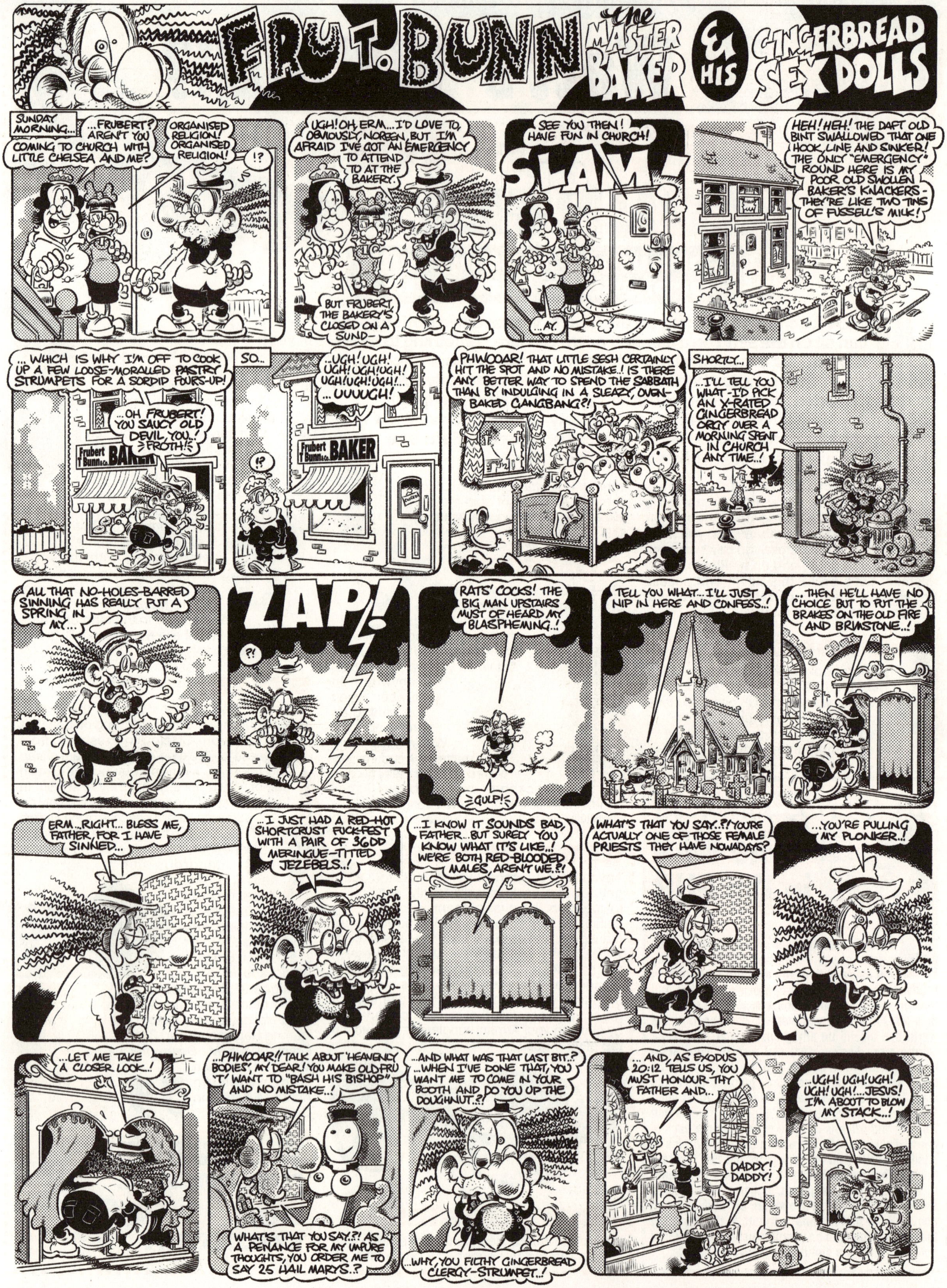
FRU T. BUNN the MASTER BAKER & HIS GINGERBREAD SEX DOLLS
SUNDAY MORNING...
...FRUBERT? AREN'T YOU COMING TO CHURCH WITH LITTLE CHELSEA AND ME?
ORGANISED RELIGION! ORGANISED RELIGION!
!?
UGH! OH, ERM... I'D LOVE TO, OBVIOUSLY, NOREEN, BUT I'M AFRAID I'VE GOT AN EMERGENCY TO ATTEND TO AT THE BAKERY...
BUT FRUBERT, THE BAKERY'S CLOSED ON A SUND-
SEE YOU THEN! HAVE FUN IN CHURCH!
SLAM!
...AY.
HEH! HEH! THE DAFT OLD BINT SWALLOWED THAT ONE HOOK, LINE AND SINKER! THE ONLY "EMERGENCY" ROUND HERE IS MY POOR OLD SWOLLEN BAKER'S KNACKERS - THEY'RE LIKE TWO TINS OF FUSSELL'S MILK!
...WHICH IS WHY I'M OFF TO COOK UP A FEW LOOSE-MORALLED PASTRY STRUMPETS FOR A SORDID FOURS-UP!
...OH FRUBERT! YOU SAUCY OLD DEVIL YOU..! FROTH!
Frubert T Bunn & Co. BAKER
SO...
...UGH! UGH! UGH! UGH! UGH! UGH! UGH! UGH!... ...UUUUGH!
!?
PHWOAR! THAT LITTLE SESH CERTAINLY HIT THE SPOT AND NO MISTAKE..! IS THERE ANY BETTER WAY TO SPEND THE SABBATH THAN BY INDULGING IN A SLEAZY, OVEN-BAKED GANGBANG?!
SHORTLY...
...I'LL TELL YOU WHAT - I'D PICK AN X-RATED GINGERBREAD ORGY OVER A MORNING SPENT IN CHURCH ANY TIME..!
ALL THAT NO-HOLES-BARRED SINNING HAS REALLY PUT A SPRING IN MY...
ZAP!
?!
RATS' COCKS! THE BIG MAN UPSTAIRS MUST OF HEARD MY BLASPHEMING..!
GULP!
TELL YOU WHAT... I'LL JUST NIP IN HERE AND CONFESS..!
...THEN HE'LL HAVE NO CHOICE BUT TO PUT THE BRAKES ON THE OLD FIRE AND BRIMSTONE..!
ERM... RIGHT... BLESS ME, FATHER, FOR I HAVE SINNED...
...I JUST HAD A RED-HOT SHORTCRUST FUCK-FEST WITH A PAIR OF 36DD MERINGUE-TITTED JEZEBELS..!
...I KNOW IT SOUNDS BAD, FATHER... BUT SURELY YOU KNOW WHAT IT'S LIKE..! WE'RE BOTH RED-BLOODED MALES, AREN'T WE..?!
WHAT'S THAT YOU SAY..?! YOU'RE ACTUALLY ONE OF THOSE FEMALE PRIESTS THEY HAVE NOWADAYS?
...YOU'RE PULLING MY PLONKER..!
...LET ME TAKE A CLOSER LOOK..!
...PHWOAR!! TALK ABOUT 'HEAVENLY BODIES', MY DEAR! YOU MAKE OLD FRU T' WANT TO "BASH HIS BISHOP" AND NO MISTAKE..!
WHAT'S THAT YOU SAY..?! AS A PENANCE FOR MY IMPURE THOUGHTS, YOU ORDER ME TO SAY 25 HAIL MARYS..?
...AND WHAT WAS THAT LAST BIT..? ...WHEN I'VE DONE THAT, YOU WANT ME TO COME IN YOUR BOOTH AND DO YOU UP THE DOUGHNUT..?!
...WHY, YOU FILTHY GINGERBREAD CLERGY-STRUMPET..!
...AND, AS EXODUS 20:12 TELLS US, YOU MUST HONOUR THY FATHER AND...
...UGH! UGH! UGH! UGH! UGH!... JESUS! I'M ABOUT TO BLOW MY STACK..!
DADDY! DADDY!

ROGER MELLIE The Man on the Telly

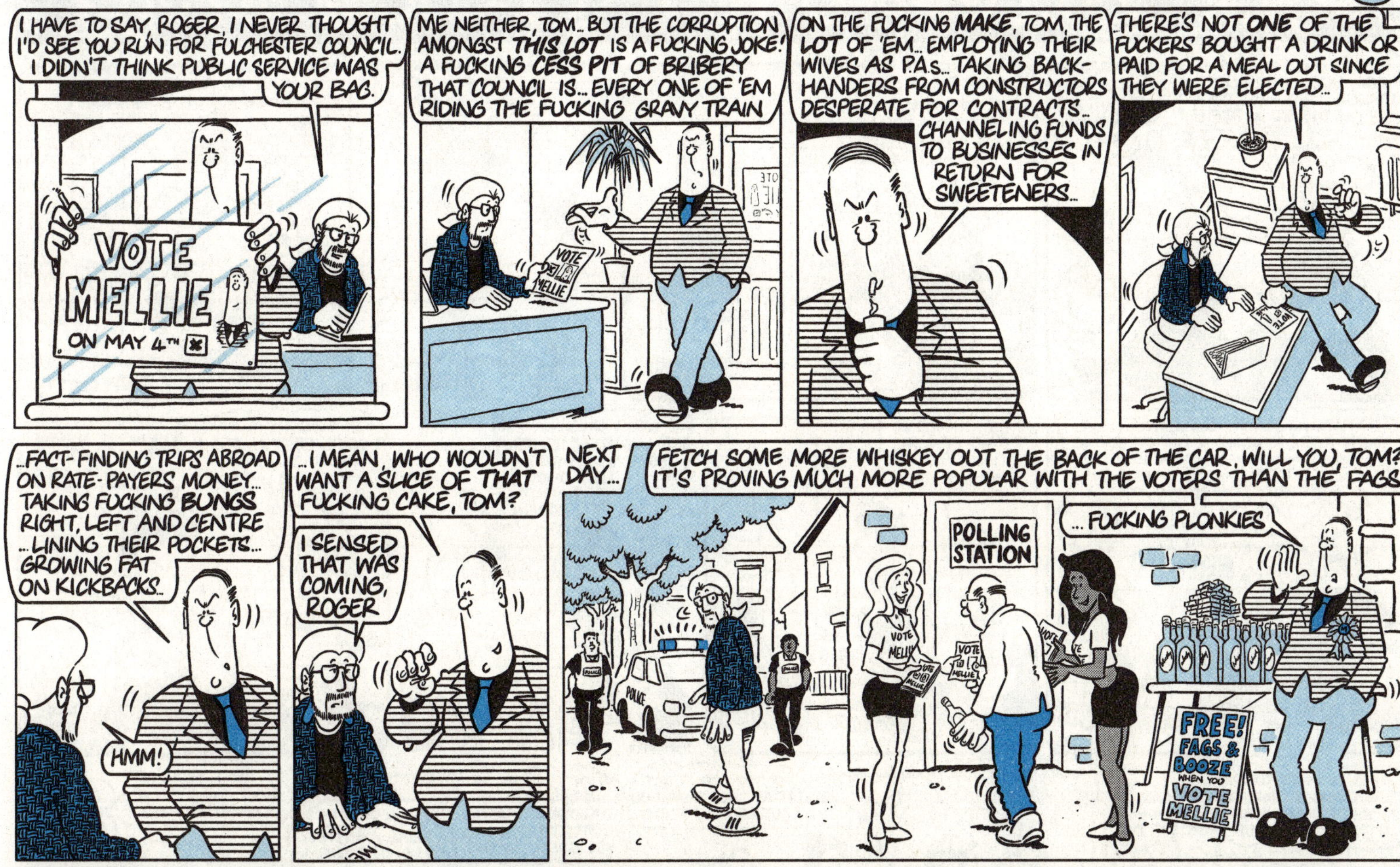
I HAVE TO SAY, ROGER, I NEVER THOUGHT I'D SEE YOU RUN FOR FULCHESTER COUNCIL. I DIDN'T THINK PUBLIC SERVICE WAS YOUR BAG.
VOTE MELLIE ON MAY 4TH
ME NEITHER, TOM.. BUT THE CORRUPTION AMONGST THIS LOT IS A FUCKING JOKE! A FUCKING CESS PIT OF BRIBERY THAT COUNCIL IS... EVERY ONE OF 'EM RIDING THE FUCKING GRAVY TRAIN
ON THE FUCKING MAKE, TOM, THE LOT OF 'EM.. EMPLOYING THEIR WIVES AS P.A.s.. TAKING BACK-HANDERS FROM CONSTRUCTORS DESPERATE FOR CONTRACTS.. CHANNELING FUNDS TO BUSINESSES IN RETURN FOR SWEETENERS...
THERE'S NOT ONE OF THE FUCKERS BOUGHT A DRINK OR PAID FOR A MEAL OUT SINCE THEY WERE ELECTED..
..FACT-FINDING TRIPS ABROAD ON RATE-PAYERS MONEY.. TAKING FUCKING BUNGS RIGHT, LEFT AND CENTRE ..LINING THEIR POCKETS... GROWING FAT ON KICKBACKS..
HMM!
..I MEAN, WHO WOULDN'T WANT A SLICE OF THAT FUCKING CAKE, TOM?
I SENSED THAT WAS COMING, ROGER
NEXT DAY...
FETCH SOME MORE WHISKEY OUT THE BACK OF THE CAR, WILL YOU, TOM? IT'S PROVING MUCH MORE POPULAR WITH THE VOTERS THAN THE FAGS...
POLLING STATION
...FUCKING PLONKIES
FREE! FAGS & BOOZE WHEN YOU VOTE MELLIE

ONE SMALL STEP FOR FAN

BRITISH billionaire Sir James Dyson is set to make history next year when he plans to move his *business's head office from Singapore...* to the Moon!

The Brexit-championing hoover entrepreneur, 76, dropped the revelation that his electrical gadget empire would be the first business to relocate to another planetary body in a candid interview with the *Financial Times* this week.

He told the paper: "Back in 2019, I felt that the best way of demonstrating the freedom and opportunities offered to Britain by Brexit was by moving our company's headquarters from Wiltshire to Singapore."

"I truly believed that the move would put me in a prime position from which to observe how successfully the UK economy was growing after leaving the European Union."

He continued: "However, although my Singaporean office window was pretty high up, it wasn't quite high enough to be able to actually see Britain and the benefits which Brexit had brought the country, even when standing on tip-toes."

treacle

Sir Jim then went on to explain how a dream about a perfectly uninterrupted view of a blossoming Britain, free from the shackles of bureaucratic Brussels red-tape, rather than tax avoidance reasons, led him to consider the Moon as a possible location for his high-tech company's head office.

"Like every other British business we will be paying our taxes," he explained. "They'll just be special Moon taxes which are invisible to the human eye."

"However, I can reassure the people of Britain that even though we will be based on the Moon and paying special Lunar taxes, Dyson will remain a British company to its core, with Britain's financial interests first and foremost in our minds."

"From my vacuum-powered lunar base 240,000 miles above the Earth, I'll get a clear view of Britain's growing financial independence in the global marketplace. And I'm also planning on opening a shop up there," he said.

stetson

The shop, Dyson Moon, will be the first retail outlet in space, and will offer a full range of premium-priced electrical products.

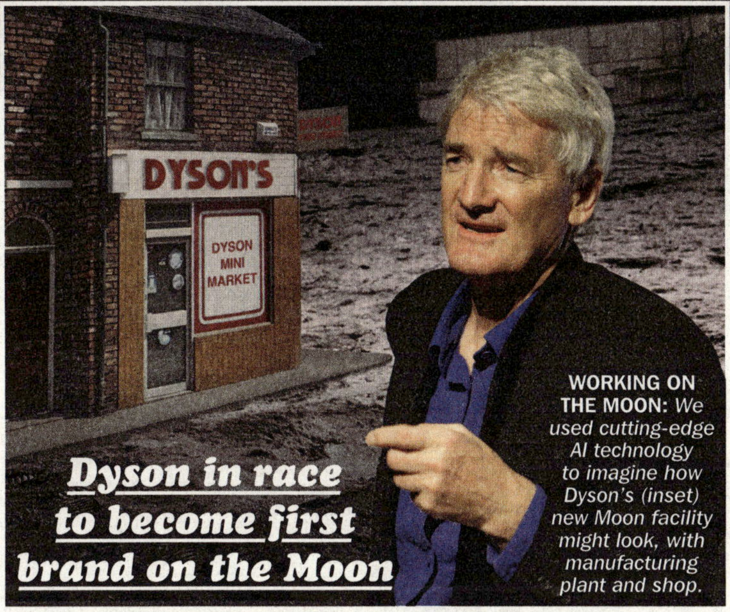
DYSON'S
DYSON MINI MARKET

Dyson in race to become first brand on the Moon

WORKING ON THE MOON: *We used cutting-edge AI technology to imagine how Dyson's (inset) new Moon facility might look, with manufacturing plant and shop.*

"The great thing about the Moon is that it'll attract wealthy visitors, like Elon Musk and Richard Branson and Alan Sugar and that," Dyson said. "And when they inevitably land their billionaire-laden spaceships on the lunar surface, they'll be desperate to start splashing their cash around on hair straighteners, vacuum cleaners and commercial hand-driers."

"They'll all be doing billionaire stuff like sticking their company's flags in the Moon dust and taking selfies," Dyson continued, "And with the lack of a breeze up there, I'm banking on them each needing an overpriced room fan to make their flags unfurl in the lunar atmosphere."

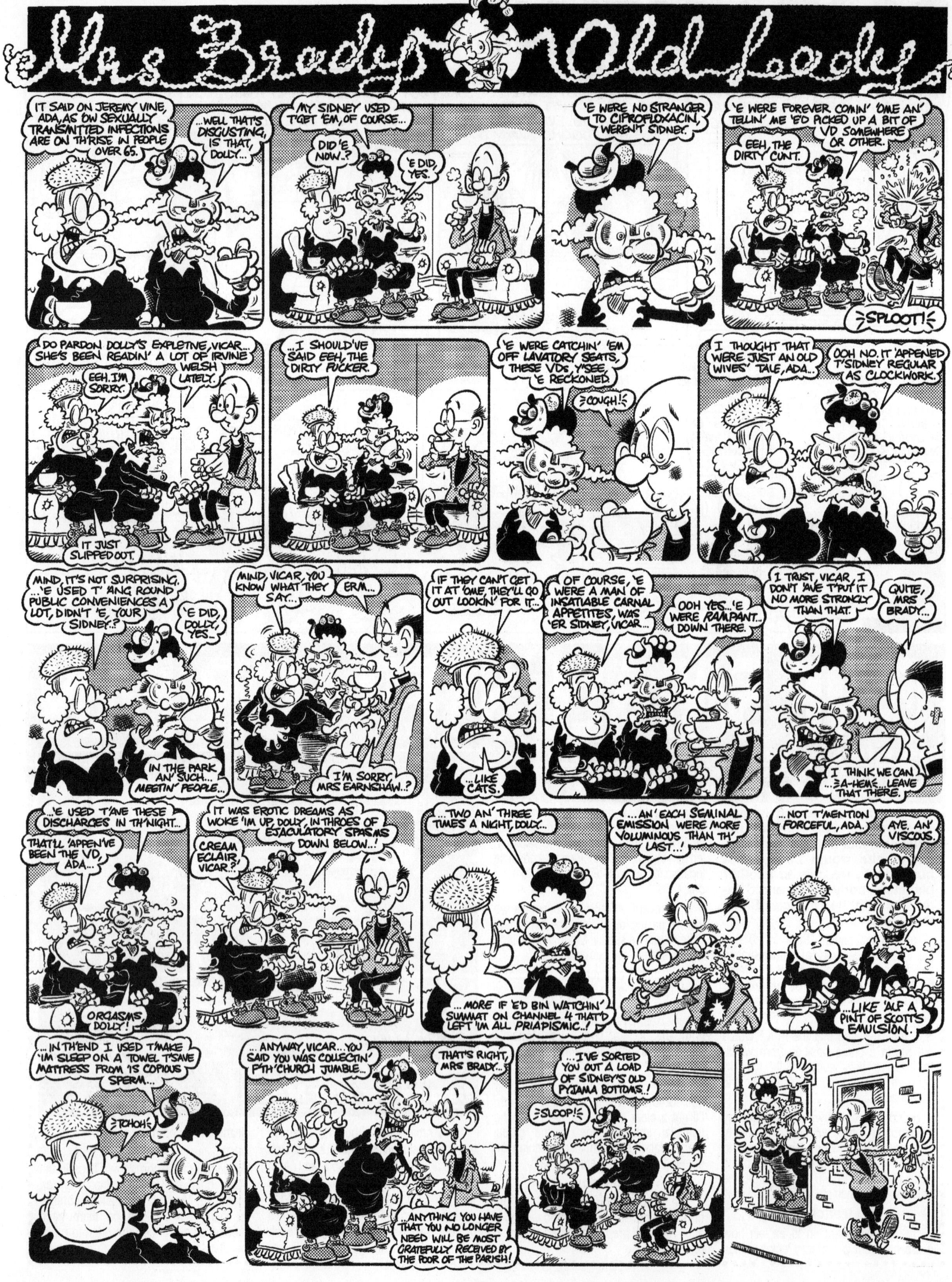
Mrs Brady Old Lady
IT SAID ON JEREMY VINE, ADA, AS 'OW SEXUALLY TRANSMITTED INFECTIONS ARE ON TH'RISE IN PEOPLE OVER 65.
...WELL THAT'S DISGUSTING, IS THAT, DOLLY...
MY SIDNEY USED T'GET 'EM, OF COURSE...
DID 'E NOW..?
'E DID, YES.
'E WERE NO STRANGER TO CIPROFLOXACIN, WEREN'T SIDNEY.
'E WERE FOREVER COMIN' 'OME AN' TELLIN' ME 'E'D PICKED UP A BIT OF VD SOMEWHERE OR OTHER.
EEH, THE DIRTY CUNT.
SPLOOT!
DO PARDON DOLLY'S EXPLETIVE, VICAR... SHE'S BEEN READIN' A LOT OF IRVINE WELSH LATELY.
EEH. I'M SORRY.
IT JUST SLIPPED OUT.
...I SHOULD'VE SAID EEH, THE DIRTY FUCKER.
'E WERE CATCHIN' 'EM OFF LAVATORY SEATS, THESE VDs, Y'SEE, 'E RECKONED.
COUGH!
I THOUGHT THAT WERE JUST AN OLD WIVES' TALE, ADA..
OOH NO. IT 'APPENED T'SIDNEY REGULAR AS CLOCKWORK.
MIND, IT'S NOT SURPRISING. ...'E USED T' 'ANG ROUND PUBLIC CONVENIENCES A LOT, DIDN'T 'E, YOUR SIDNEY..?
'E DID, DOLLY, YES...
IN THE PARK AN' SUCH... MEETIN' PEOPLE...
MIND, VICAR, YOU KNOW WHAT THEY SAY...
ERM...
I'M SORRY, MRS EARNSHAW..?
IF THEY CAN'T GET IT AT 'OME, THEY'LL GO OUT LOOKIN' FOR IT...
...LIKE CATS.
OF COURSE, 'E WERE A MAN OF INSATIABLE CARNAL APPETITES, WAS 'ER SIDNEY, VICAR...
OOH YES...'E WERE RAMPANT... DOWN THERE.
I TRUST, VICAR, I DON'T 'AVE T'PUT IT NO MORE STRONGLY THAN THAT.
QUITE, MRS BRADY...
I THINK WE CAN ...A-HEM... LEAVE THAT THERE.
...'E USED T'AVE THESE DISCHARGES IN TH'NIGHT...
THAT'LL 'APPEN'VE BEEN THE VD, ADA...
ORGASMS, DOLLY!
IT WAS EROTIC DREAMS AS WOKE 'IM UP, DOLLY, IN THROES OF EJACULATORY SPASMS DOWN BELOW...!
CREAM ECLAIR, VICAR?
...TWO AN' THREE TIMES A NIGHT, DOLLY...
...AN' EACH SEMINAL EMISSION WERE MORE VOLUMINOUS THAN TH' LAST...!
...MORE IF 'E'D BIN WATCHIN' SUMMAT ON CHANNEL 4 THAT'D LEFT 'IM ALL PRIAPISMIC..!
...NOT T'MENTION FORCEFUL, ADA.
AYE. AN' VISCOUS.
...LIKE 'ALF A PINT OF SCOTT'S EMULSION.
...IN TH'END I USED T'MAKE 'IM SLEEP ON A TOWEL T'SAVE MATTRESS FROM 'IS COPIOUS SPERM...
TCHOH
...ANYWAY, VICAR... YOU SAID YOU WAS COLLECTIN' F'TH'CHURCH JUMBLE...
THAT'S RIGHT, MRS BRADY...
...ANYTHING YOU HAVE THAT YOU NO LONGER NEED WILL BE MOST GRATEFULLY RECEIVED BY THE POOR OF THE PARISH!
...I'VE SORTED YOU OUT A LOAD OF SIDNEY'S OLD PYJAMA BOTTOMS..!
SLOOP!

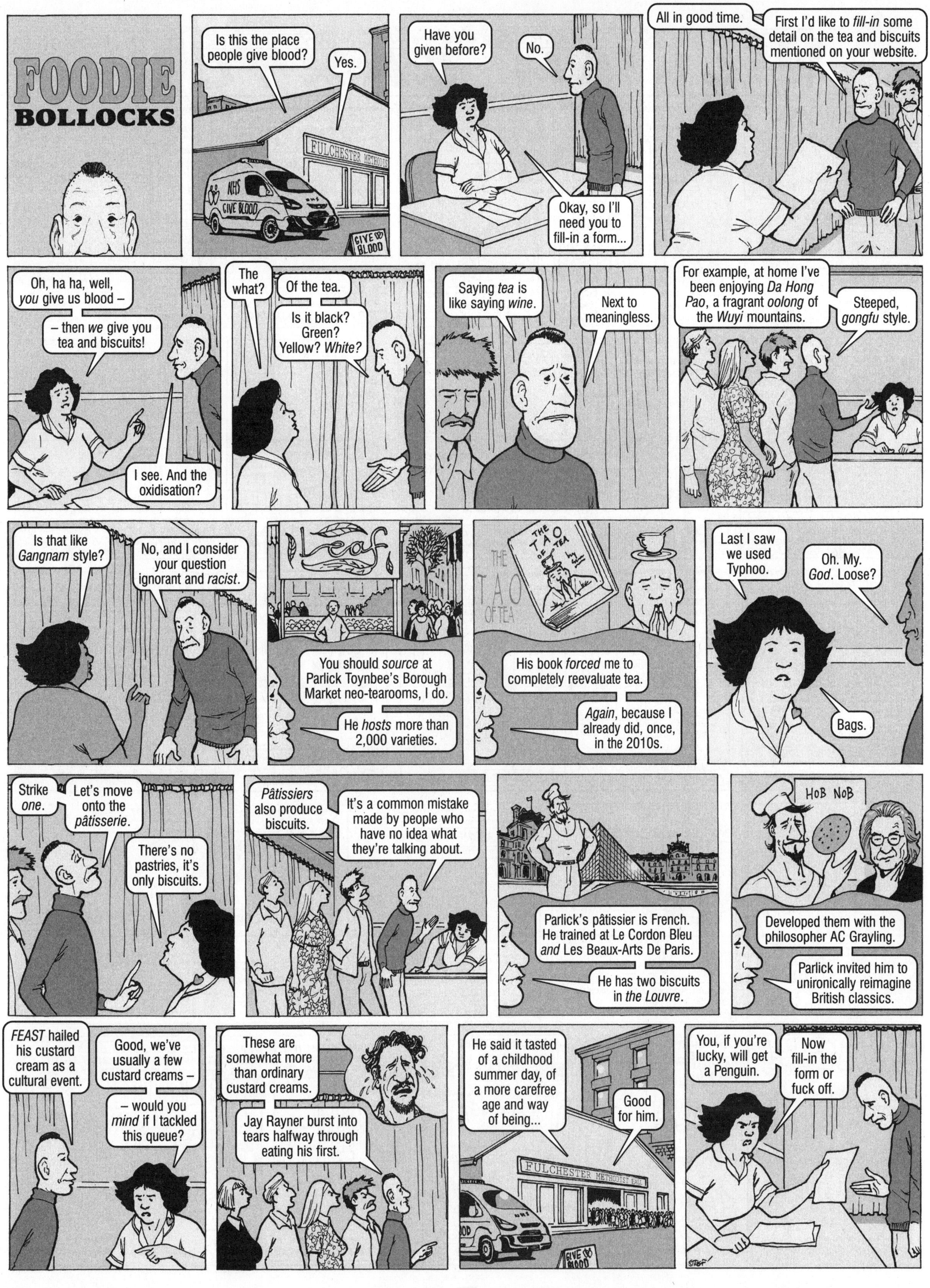
FOODIE BOLLOCKS
Is this the place people give blood?
Yes.
FULCHESTER METHODIST
NHS GIVE BLOOD
GIVE BLOOD
Have you given before?
No.
Okay, so I'll need you to fill-in a form...
All in good time.
First I'd like to *fill-in* some detail on the tea and biscuits mentioned on your website.
Oh, ha ha, well, *you* give us blood –
– then *we* give you tea and biscuits!
I see. And the oxidisation?
The what?
Of the tea.
Is it black? Green? Yellow? *White?*
Saying *tea* is like saying *wine*.
Next to meaningless.
For example, at home I've been enjoying *Da Hong Pao*, a fragrant *oolong* of the *Wuyi* mountains.
Steeped, *gongfu* style.
Is that like *Gangnam* style?
No, and I consider your question ignorant and *racist*.
Leaf
You should *source* at Parlick Toynbee's Borough Market neo-tearooms, I do.
He *hosts* more than 2,000 varieties.
THE TAO OF TEA
His book *forced* me to completely reevaluate tea.
Again, because I already did, once, in the 2010s.
Last I saw we used Typhoo.
Oh. My. *God*. Loose?
Bags.
Strike *one*.
Let's move onto the *pâtisserie*.
There's no pastries, it's only biscuits.
Pâtissiers also produce biscuits.
It's a common mistake made by people who have no idea what they're talking about.
Parlick's pâtissier is French. He trained at Le Cordon Bleu *and* Les Beaux-Arts De Paris.
He has two biscuits in *the Louvre*.
HOB NOB
Developed them with the philosopher AC Grayling.
Parlick invited him to unironically reimagine British classics.
FEAST hailed his custard cream as a cultural event.
Good, we've usually a few custard creams –
– would you *mind* if I tackled this queue?
These are somewhat more than ordinary custard creams.
Jay Rayner burst into tears halfway through eating his first.
He said it tasted of a childhood summer day, of a more carefree age and way of being...
Good for him.
FULCHESTER METHODIST HALL
GIVE BLOOD
You, if you're lucky, will get a Penguin.
Now fill-in the form or fuck off.
STEEF

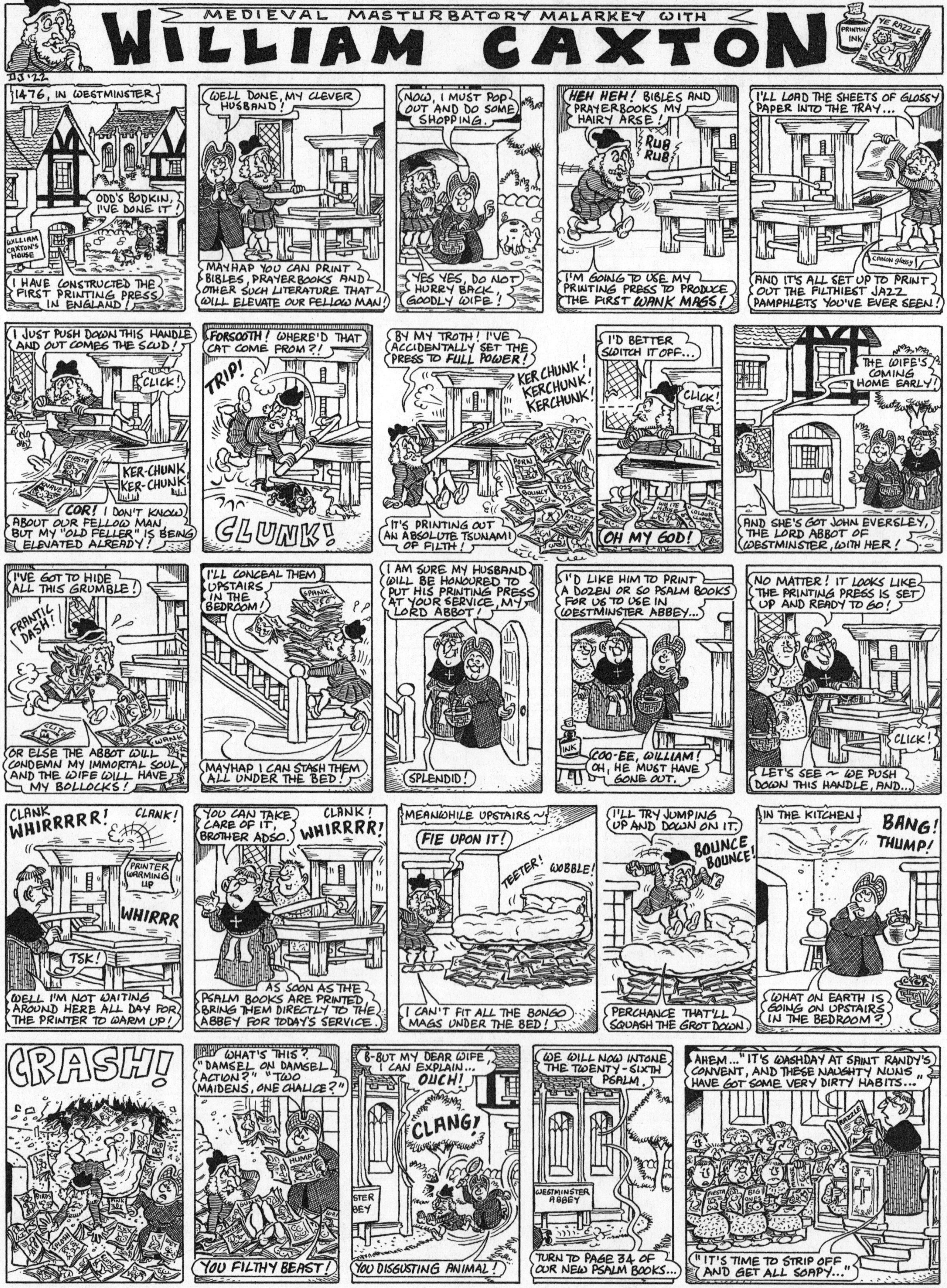
MEDIEVAL MASTURBATORY MALARKEY WITH
WILLIAM CAXTON
PRINTING INK
YE RAZZLE
1476, IN WESTMINSTER
ODD'S BODKIN, I'VE DONE IT!
WILLIAM CAXTON'S HOUSE
I HAVE CONSTRUCTED THE FIRST PRINTING PRESS IN ENGLAND!
WELL DONE, MY CLEVER HUSBAND!
MAYHAP YOU CAN PRINT BIBLES, PRAYERBOOKS AND OTHER SUCH LITERATURE THAT WILL ELEVATE OUR FELLOW MAN!
NOW, I MUST POP OUT AND DO SOME SHOPPING.
YES YES, DO NOT HURRY BACK, GOODLY WIFE!
HEH HEH! BIBLES AND PRAYERBOOKS MY HAIRY ARSE!
RUB RUB
I'M GOING TO USE MY PRINTING PRESS TO PRODUCE THE FIRST WANK MAGS!
I'LL LOAD THE SHEETS OF GLOSSY PAPER INTO THE TRAY...
CANON glossy
AND IT'S ALL SET UP TO PRINT OUT THE FILTHIEST JAZZ PAMPHLETS YOU'VE EVER SEEN!
I JUST PUSH DOWN THIS HANDLE AND OUT COMES THE SCUD!
CLICK!
FIESTA
KNAVE
KER-CHUNK KER-CHUNK
COR! I DON'T KNOW ABOUT OUR FELLOW MAN, BUT MY "OLD FELLER" IS BEING ELEVATED ALREADY!
FORSOOTH! WHERE'D THAT CAT COME FROM?!
TRIP!
CLUNK!
BY MY TROTH! I'VE ACCIDENTALLY SET THE PRESS TO FULL POWER!
KER CHUNK! KERCHUNK! KERCHUNK!
PORN
BOUNCY
TOSS
RAZZLE
IT'S PRINTING OUT AN ABSOLUTE TSUNAMI OF FILTH!
I'D BETTER SWITCH IT OFF...
CLICK!
OH MY GOD!
THE WIFE'S COMING HOME EARLY!
AND SHE'S GOT JOHN EVERSLEY, THE LORD ABBOT OF WESTMINSTER, WITH HER!
I'VE GOT TO HIDE ALL THIS GRUMBLE!
FRANTIC DASH!
WANK
OR ELSE THE ABBOT WILL CONDEMN MY IMMORTAL SOUL, AND THE WIFE WILL HAVE MY BOLLOCKS!
I'LL CONCEAL THEM UPSTAIRS IN THE BEDROOM!
SPANK
MAYHAP I CAN STASH THEM ALL UNDER THE BED!
I AM SURE MY HUSBAND WILL BE HONOURED TO PUT HIS PRINTING PRESS AT YOUR SERVICE, MY LORD ABBOT!
SPLENDID!
I'D LIKE HIM TO PRINT A DOZEN OR SO PSALM BOOKS FOR US TO USE IN WESTMINSTER ABBEY...
INK
COO-EE, WILLIAM! OH, HE MUST HAVE GONE OUT.
NO MATTER! IT LOOKS LIKE THE PRINTING PRESS IS SET UP AND READY TO GO!
CLICK!
LET'S SEE ~ WE PUSH DOWN THIS HANDLE, AND...
CLANK WHIRRRRR! CLANK!
PRINTER WARMING UP
WHIRRR
TSK!
WELL I'M NOT WAITING AROUND HERE ALL DAY FOR THE PRINTER TO WARM UP!
YOU CAN TAKE CARE OF IT, BROTHER ADSO.
CLANK! WHIRRRR!
AS SOON AS THE PSALM BOOKS ARE PRINTED BRING THEM DIRECTLY TO THE ABBEY FOR TODAY'S SERVICE.
MEANWHILE UPSTAIRS ~
FIE UPON IT!
TEETER! WOBBLE!
I CAN'T FIT ALL THE BONGO MAGS UNDER THE BED!
I'LL TRY JUMPING UP AND DOWN ON IT.
BOUNCE BOUNCE!
PERCHANCE THAT'LL SQUASH THE GROT DOWN.
IN THE KITCHEN
BANG! THUMP!
WHAT ON EARTH IS GOING ON UPSTAIRS IN THE BEDROOM?
CRASH!
WHAT'S THIS? "DAMSEL ON DAMSEL ACTION?" "TWO MAIDENS, ONE CHALICE?"
HUMP
YOU FILTHY BEAST!
B-BUT MY DEAR WIFE, I CAN EXPLAIN... OUCH!
CLANG!
YOU DISGUSTING ANIMAL!
WE WILL NOW INTONE THE TWENTY-SIXTH PSALM.
WESTMINSTER ABBEY
TURN TO PAGE 34 OF OUR NEW PSALM BOOKS...
AHEM..." IT'S WASHDAY AT SAINT RANDY'S CONVENT, AND THESE NAUGHTY NUNS HAVE GOT SOME VERY DIRTY HABITS..."
RAZZLE
FIESTA
BIG ONES
" IT'S TIME TO STRIP OFF AND GET ALL SOAPY..."

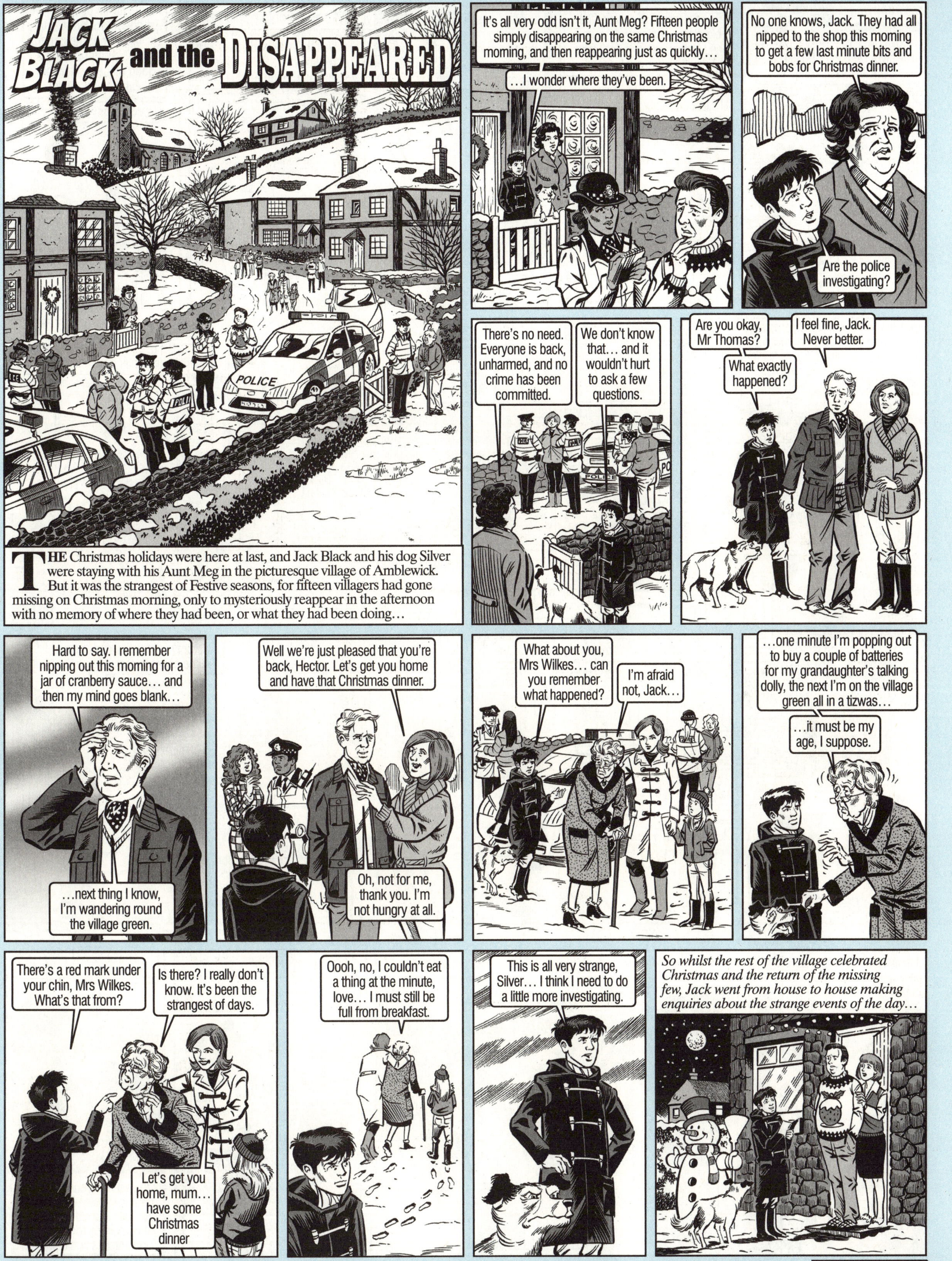
JACK BLACK and the DISAPPEARED
POLICE
THE Christmas holidays were here at last, and Jack Black and his dog Silver were staying with his Aunt Meg in the picturesque village of Amblewick. But it was the strangest of Festive seasons, for fifteen villagers had gone missing on Christmas morning, only to mysteriously reappear in the afternoon with no memory of where they had been, or what they had been doing…
It's all very odd isn't it, Aunt Meg? Fifteen people simply disappearing on the same Christmas morning, and then reappearing just as quickly…
…I wonder where they've been.
No one knows, Jack. They had all nipped to the shop this morning to get a few last minute bits and bobs for Christmas dinner.
Are the police investigating?
There's no need. Everyone is back, unharmed, and no crime has been committed.
We don't know that… and it wouldn't hurt to ask a few questions.
Are you okay, Mr Thomas?
I feel fine, Jack. Never better.
What exactly happened?
Hard to say. I remember nipping out this morning for a jar of cranberry sauce… and then my mind goes blank…
…next thing I know, I'm wandering round the village green.
Well we're just pleased that you're back, Hector. Let's get you home and have that Christmas dinner.
Oh, not for me, thank you. I'm not hungry at all.
What about you, Mrs Wilkes… can you remember what happened?
I'm afraid not, Jack…
…one minute I'm popping out to buy a couple of batteries for my grandaughter's talking dolly, the next I'm on the village green all in a tizwas…
…it must be my age, I suppose.
There's a red mark under your chin, Mrs Wilkes. What's that from?
Is there? I really don't know. It's been the strangest of days.
Let's get you home, mum… have some Christmas dinner
Oooh, no, I couldn't eat a thing at the minute, love… I must still be full from breakfast.
This is all very strange, Silver… I think I need to do a little more investigating.
So whilst the rest of the village celebrated Christmas and the return of the missing few, Jack went from house to house making enquiries about the strange events of the day…

Continued over...

Next morning…
You know, I think Boxing Day is my favourite part of Christmas, Jack. It's so relaxing…
… the stress of cooking the big dinner, dealing with visitors and all that bollocks done with, if you'll pardon my French…
…nothing to do but put your feet up. What about you?
Hmm!?!…
…No, I'm still working on the Christmas Day disappearance case.
Oh, let it go. Everyone is fine.
Sorry, Aunt Meg, no can do.
Let's see… everyone who went missing was going to the shops to buy something, and there were only two shops in the village open on Christmas Day…
…Milligan's general store and Cartwright newsagents…
All the items people were shopping for were only available from the general store, so that seems a good place to start our investigations, Silver…
…come on, boy!
WOOF!!
Jack's sixth sense told him there was a mystery to solve and he made his way to Milligan's General Store. The game was afoot…
J. MILLIGAN GENERAL STORE
Hmm. Milligan has closed his shop, Silver… and he's not opening up until tomorrow.
Let's have a look round the back.
Hmm! That's strange, Silver… it looks like there's been some kind of party going on in the back room…
…but there are no festive decorations up, so it wasn't a Christmas party, that's for sure.
WOOF!!
What is it? What have you found, boy?
An empty bottle of chloroform and some benzodiazepine phials…
Hmmmm!
I think I know what's happening, Silver. I just need to check the electoral register online, and if what I think is true, this mystery is solved.
Next morning, Mr Milligan arrived to open up his shop…
Suddenly…
Hold it right there, Milligan, you're under arrest!
What on earth…!?!
Well done, PC Brown.
No problem, Jack. But now we've got him in custody, are you going to tell us what this all about?
Certainly. It's all about the people going missing yesterday, PC Brown… I know where they were…
… and so does Mr Milligan.
What!?!
You see, everyone who went missing yesterday visited Mr Milligan's shop on Christmas morning for some last minute bits and bobs…

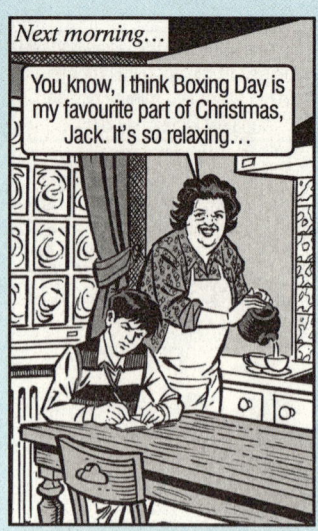

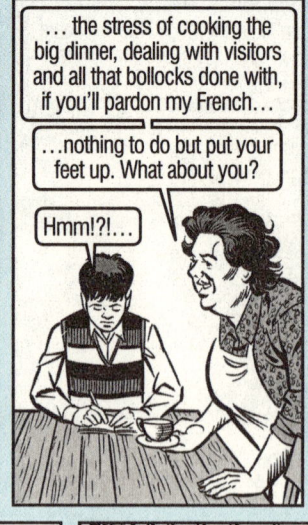

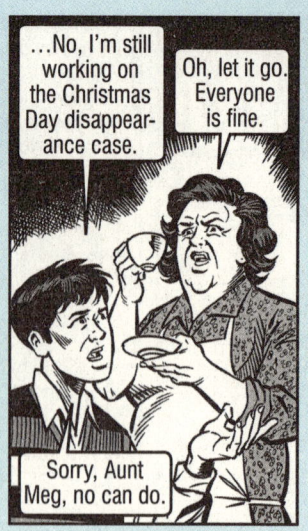

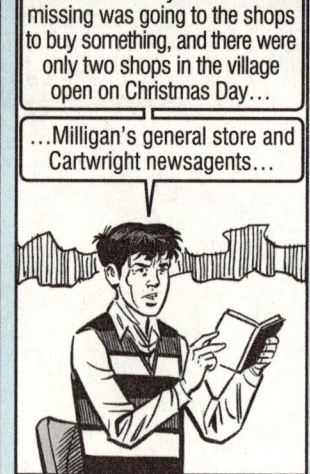

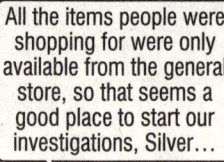

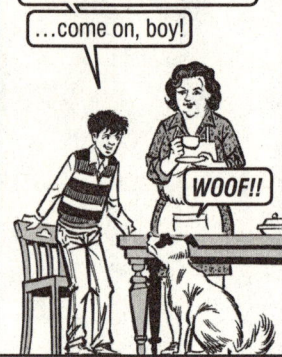

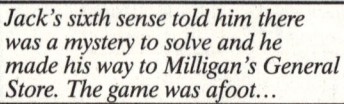

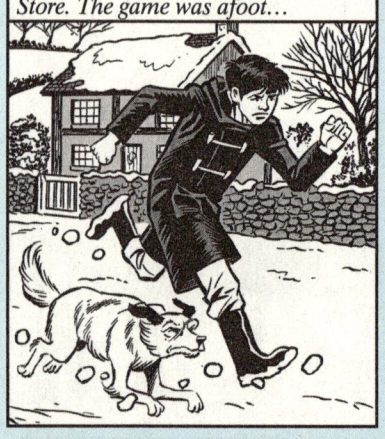

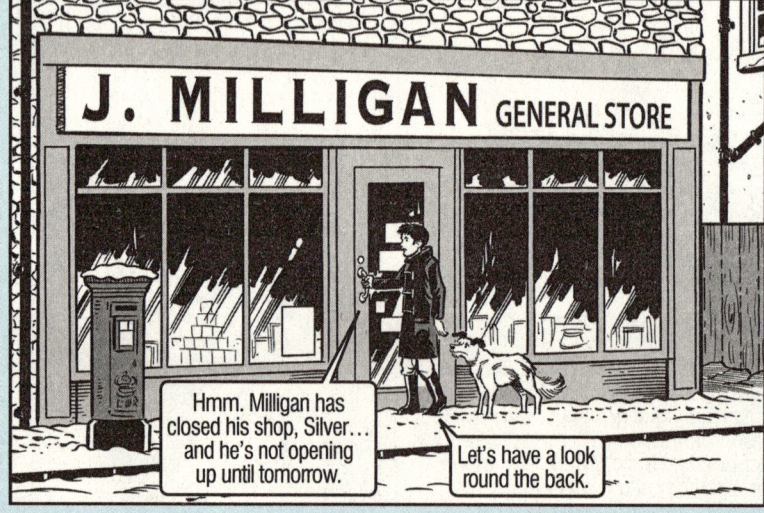

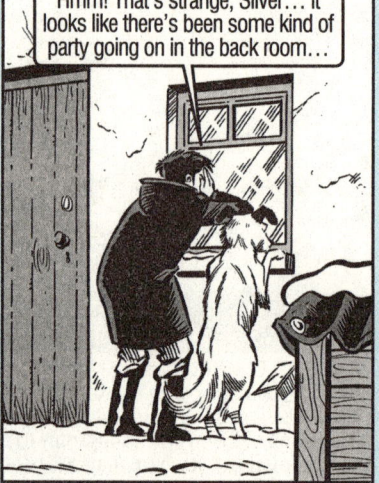

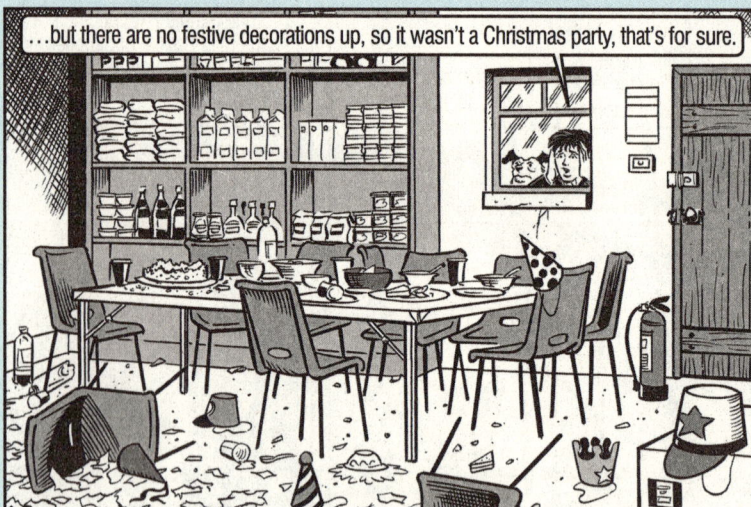

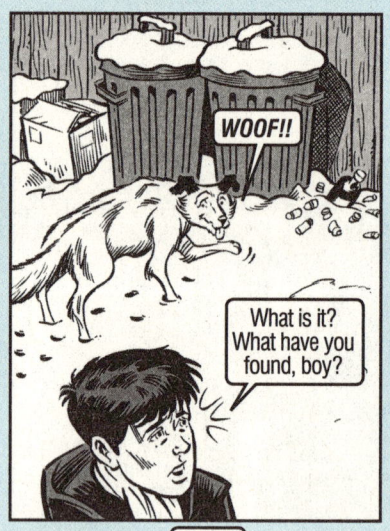

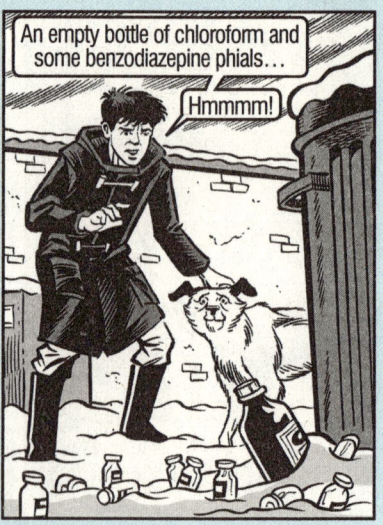

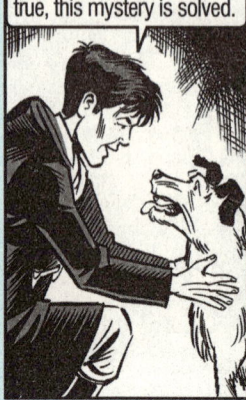

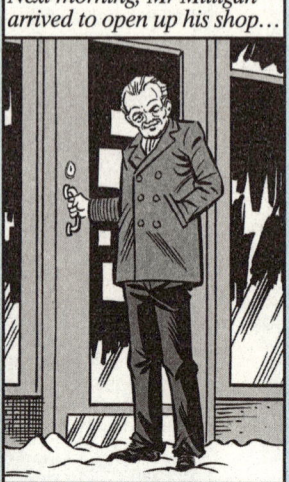

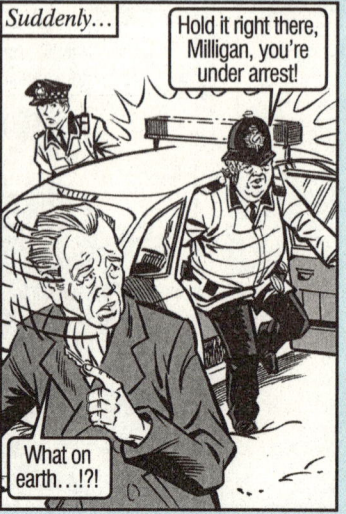

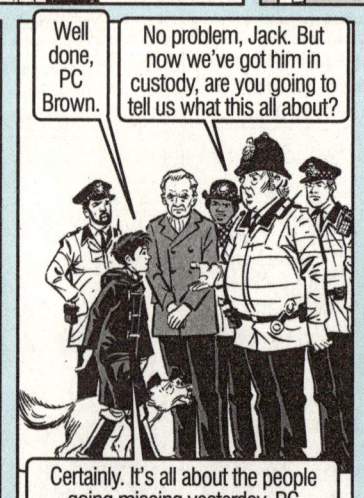

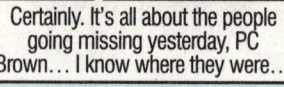

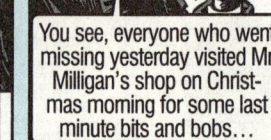

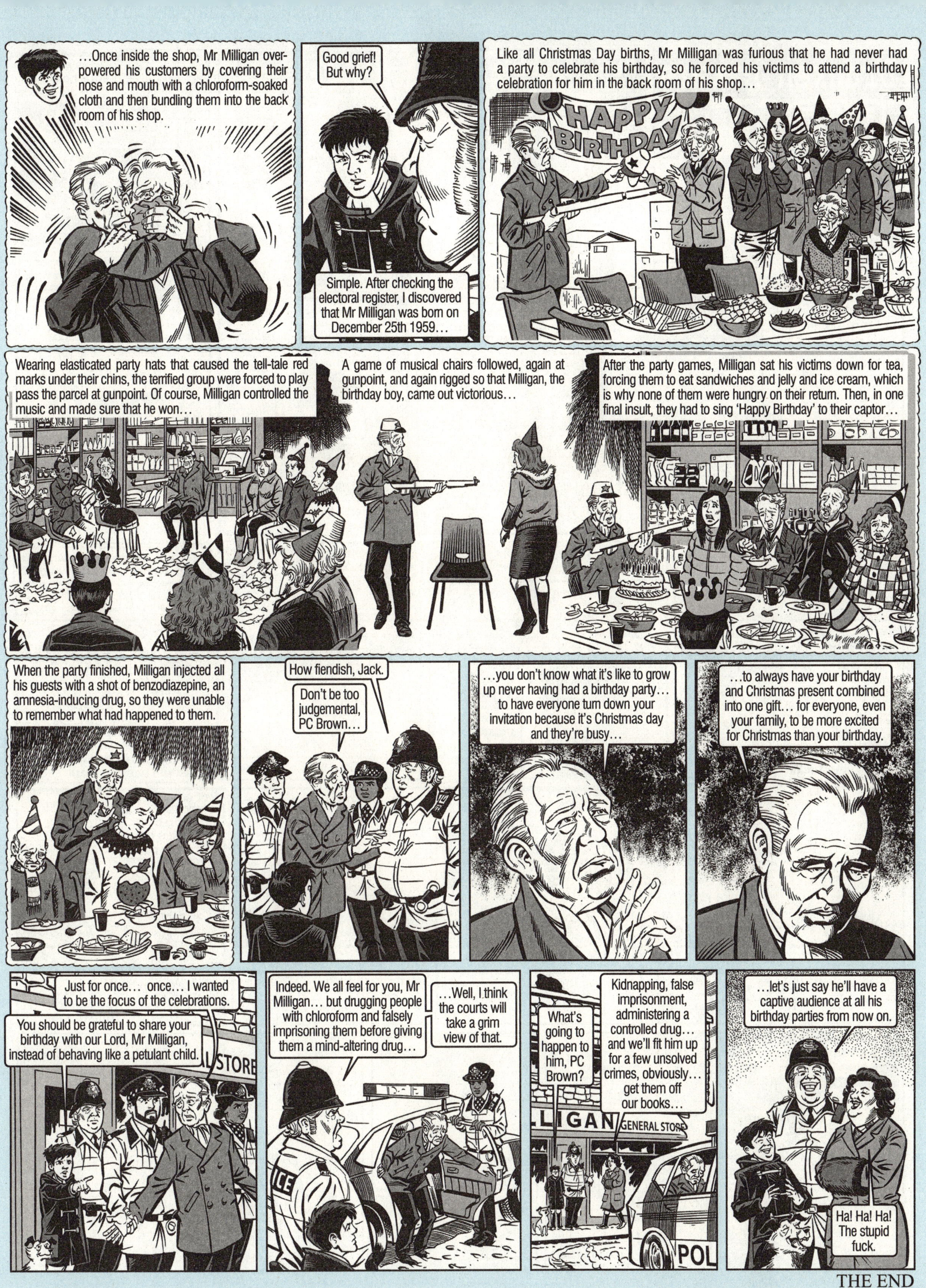
…Once inside the shop, Mr Milligan overpowered his customers by covering their nose and mouth with a chloroform-soaked cloth and then bundling them into the back room of his shop.
Good grief! But why?
Simple. After checking the electoral register, I discovered that Mr Milligan was born on December 25th 1959…
Like all Christmas Day births, Mr Milligan was furious that he had never had a party to celebrate his birthday, so he forced his victims to attend a birthday celebration for him in the back room of his shop…
HAPPY BIRTHDAY
Wearing elasticated party hats that caused the tell-tale red marks under their chins, the terrified group were forced to play pass the parcel at gunpoint. Of course, Milligan controlled the music and made sure that he won…
A game of musical chairs followed, again at gunpoint, and again rigged so that Milligan, the birthday boy, came out victorious…
After the party games, Milligan sat his victims down for tea, forcing them to eat sandwiches and jelly and ice cream, which is why none of them were hungry on their return. Then, in one final insult, they had to sing 'Happy Birthday' to their captor…
When the party finished, Milligan injected all his guests with a shot of benzodiazepine, an amnesia-inducing drug, so they were unable to remember what had happened to them.
How fiendish, Jack.
Don't be too judgemental, PC Brown…
…you don't know what it's like to grow up never having had a birthday party… to have everyone turn down your invitation because it's Christmas day and they're busy…
…to always have your birthday and Christmas present combined into one gift… for everyone, even your family, to be more excited for Christmas than your birthday.
Just for once… once… I wanted to be the focus of the celebrations.
You should be grateful to share your birthday with our Lord, Mr Milligan, instead of behaving like a petulant child.
Indeed. We all feel for you, Mr Milligan… but drugging people with chloroform and falsely imprisoning them before giving them a mind-altering drug…
…Well, I think the courts will take a grim view of that.
What's going to happen to him, PC Brown?
Kidnapping, false imprisonment, administering a controlled drug… and we'll fit him up for a few unsolved crimes, obviously… get them off our books…
GENERAL STORE
…let's just say he'll have a captive audience at all his birthday parties from now on.
Ha! Ha! Ha! The stupid fuck.

THE END

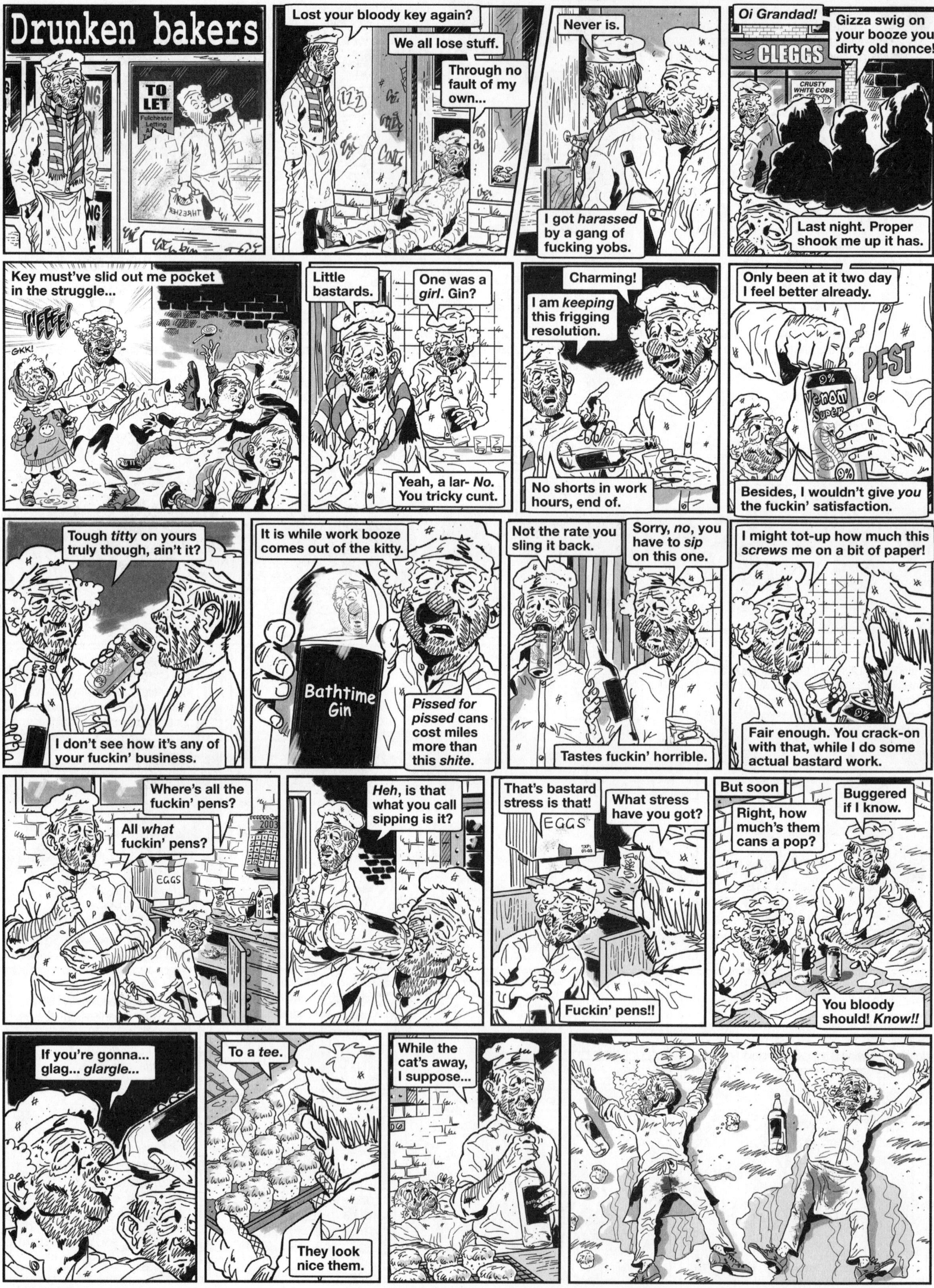
Drunken bakers
TO LET
Fulchester Letting
THRESHER
Lost your bloody key again?
We all lose stuff.
Through no fault of my own...
Never is.
I got *harassed* by a gang of fucking yobs.
Oi Grandad!
Gizza swig on your booze you dirty old nonce!
CLEGGS
CRUSTY WHITE COBS
Last night. Proper shook me up it has.
Key must've slid out me pocket in the struggle...
GKK!
Little bastards.
One was a *girl*. Gin?
Yeah, a lar- *No.* You tricky cunt.
Charming!
I am *keeping* this frigging resolution.
No shorts in work hours, end of.
Only been at it two day I feel better already.
PFST
9%
Venom Super
Besides, I wouldn't give *you* the fuckin' satisfaction.
Tough *titty* on yours truly though, ain't it?
I don't see how it's any of your fuckin' business.
It is while work booze comes out of the kitty.
Bathtime Gin
Pissed for pissed cans cost miles more than this *shite*.
Not the rate you sling it back.
Sorry, *no*, you have to *sip* on this one.
Tastes fuckin' horrible.
I might tot-up how much this *screws* me on a bit of paper!
Fair enough. You crack-on with that, while I do some actual bastard work.
Where's all the fuckin' pens?
All *what* fuckin' pens?
EGGS
Heh, is that what you call sipping is it?
That's bastard stress is that!
What stress have you got?
EGGS
Fuckin' pens!!
But soon
Right, how much's them cans a pop?
Buggered if I know.
You bloody should! *Know!!*
If you're gonna... glag... *glargle*...
To a *tee*.
They look nice them.
While the cat's away, I suppose...

BELL END OF AN ERA

Cinema Pocket Billiards Player Dies Aged 102

THE last person in Britain to be prosecuted for interfering with themselves in a cinema has died at the age of 103. Former bus inspector Albert Onan was the last of his generation and his passing means that nobody in the country now has a criminal record for public indecency in a cinema.

In addition to Onan being the last, he was also the country's most prolific offender, knocking out a massive 58 prosecutions for the same offence, all committed in the same Nottingham cinema.

Onan was born in 1921 and served as an infantryman during the second world war, seeing action in Europe. After being demobbed, Albert married his childhood sweetheart Rose and settled down to raise a family in the Sneinton area of the city. His first prosecution for public indecency was in July 1965, when he was arrested inside the now demolished Classic Cinema in Market Street. Onan was spotted playing with himself under his coat during a matinee performance of Russ Meyer's skinflick *Faster Pussycat! Kill! Kill!*. He was prosecuted and fined 15 shillings.

Onan was arrested on a regular basis over the years for the same offence, which were usually committed whist watching the films of Russ Meyer or Doris Wishman, reaching a peak of 14 arrests in 1969. But the advent of the video recorder meant that the days of the porn cinema were numbered, and Onan's tally of indecency prosecutions fell during the 1970s. His final arrest came in October 1979, when he was caught fiddling with himself in the back row of the cinema during a *Deadly Weapons* and *Beneath The Valley of the Ultra Vixens* double bill. He pleaded guilty and was fined £10 with £2 costs.

The Classic Cinema was demolished in 1991 and replaced with a car park, and Onan was granted the Freedom of the City of Nottingham in 2010. A campaign is now underway to persuade Nottingham City Council to erect a blue plaque on the wall adjacent to the car park entrance to commemorate his 58 arrests.

FLICKS OF THE WRIST: Tugger Onan.

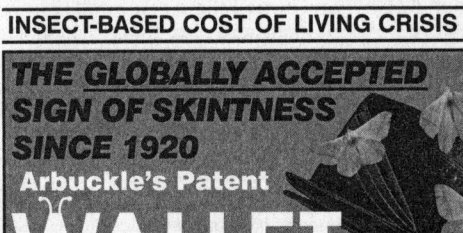

INSECT-BASED COST OF LIVING CRISIS ACCESSORIES

THE GLOBALLY ACCEPTED SIGN OF SKINTNESS SINCE 1920

Arbuckle's Patent

WALLET MOTHS™

£10.99 for 5 larvae

When you need to show someone that you're out of cash in a hurry, there's no more fail-safe way than Arbuckle's Patent Wallet Moths™.

Arbuckle's Patent Wallet Moths™ are the world's number one pocketbook-dwelling Lepidoptera. For over **100 years**, our wallet moths have been the globally accepted sign of pennilessness at over 3 times as many retailers than tattered, fingerless gloves or trouser pockets pulled slowly inside-out.

"I lost my job during the pandemic and my house was in danger of being repossesed. When the bailiffs came knocking, I opened my wallet and, bang on cue, out flew my Wallet Moths™. The bailiffs nodded as if they understood, and went on their way. Thanks!"
Mr J, Wessex

"I spent the last of my life's savings on 15 sachets of Arbuckle's Wallet Moths™. It's the best decision I ever made."
Mrs K, HMP Bronzefield

call now **01-811-8055**

Letterbocks

viz.co.uk letters@viz.co.uk letters@v

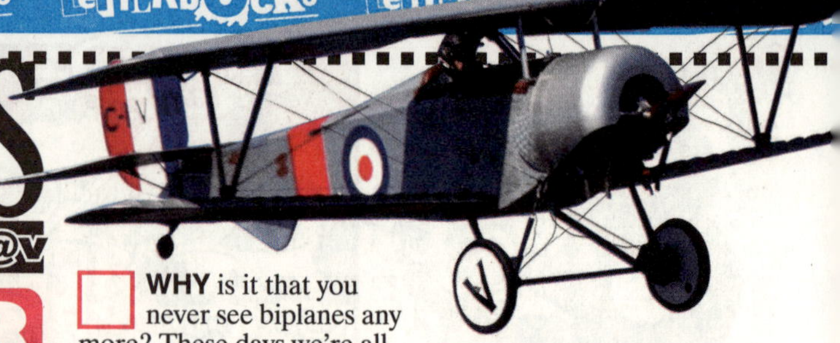

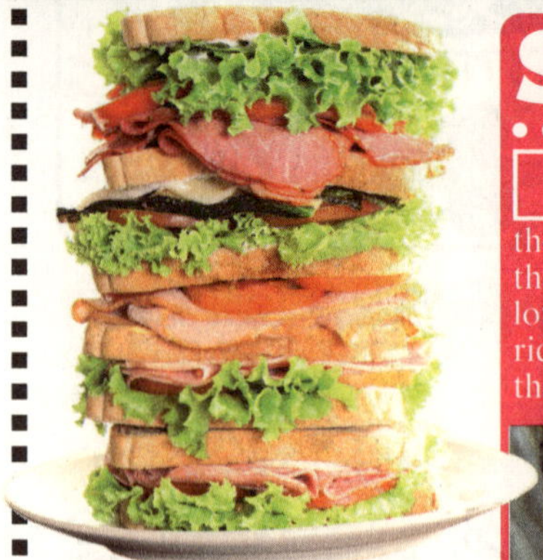

STAR LETTER

IF the Multiverse theory is correct, and there is indeed an infinite number of parallel universes, then there must be one in which fish and chips is served the other way round, where you get one massive chip and lots of little tiny fish. Well, I've never heard anything so ridiculous in all my life! I think I'll stick with this universe, thank-you very much.

Ben Nunn, Caterham

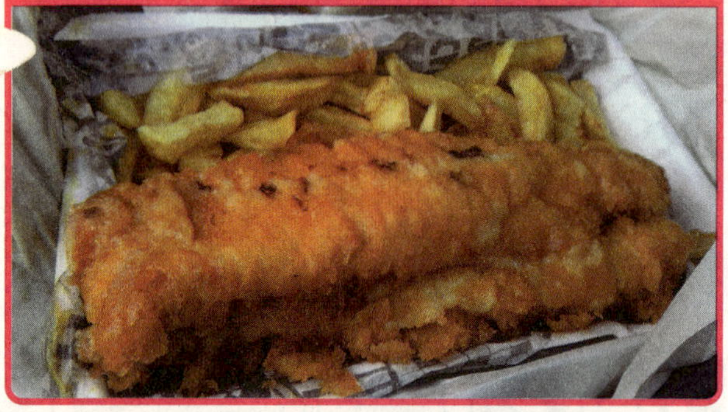

WHAT'S all this 'wafer thin ham' about? Why would it being wafer thin make me want to buy it? I'm not going to say "Yes, I'd love a ham sandwich, but make sure the ham is so thin that I'll have to put four slices in." I want a thick slab of ham between the bread. Get your heads out of your arses, supermarkets.

Ken Jenkins, Kings Langley

WHENEVER somebody commits a murder in the films or on telly, they always dig a six-foot long hole in the woods in order to bury the body. What a waste of effort. If I committed a murder, I'd save myself a lot of work by digging a hole half that size and just double the body up before throwing it in.

Hector Crumbhorn, Hull

AT one point during the non-league football match I was at last weekend, the exasperated visiting manager threw his arms in the air and shouted "How the hell can he be offside, ref? Eh? How can he be offside?" Well, by being in the opposing half with any part of his head, body or feet closer to the goal line than the second last defender when the ball was played forwards to him by a team mate, is the answer to that question.

Hector Källström, London

THEY say the Scots are a friendly lot. Well, not in my experience. I laughed at a man's penis in a public toilet in Edinburgh yesterday, and barely got out alive.

Dave Edwards, Bridport

WITH reference to my earlier letter about digging holes to bury bodies, can I just say that I have never killed anybody and buried them in a wood or anywhere else. I was speaking hypothetically, simply saying what I would do were I to kill somebody.

Hector Crumbhorn, Hull

HOW come grizzly bears have got razor-sharp claws, jaws that could crush a bowling ball and arms strong enough to pick up a car, and yet they only eat insects, fruit and the occasional fish? Starlings eat exactly the same stuff and they aren't even well-enough equipped to fend off my cat. I'd like to see David Attenborough explain that one.

Oliver Seventy-Three, email

SUBJECT to availability goes without saying. Surely you can only have stuff that exists.

Christina Martin, Bexhill-on-Sea

WHEN the police are trying to fit somebody up for a crime but are having a little difficulty as there is absolutely no evidence, why don't they simply say the accused has used witchcraft to magic all the evidence away? Witchcraft is still a crime on the statute books, so they can add that to the charge sheet as well.

Bjorn Catweasle, Pendogget

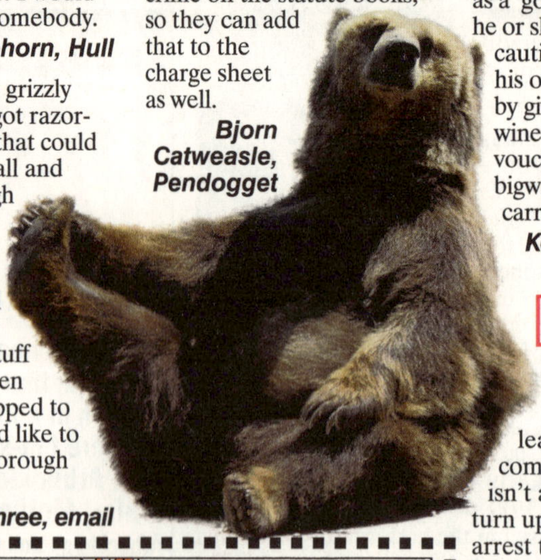

WHY is it that you never see biplanes any more? These days we're all fobbed off with monoplane airliners when we go on our jollies. It's just another way for these holiday companies to cut their costs, and frankly it boils my fucking piss.

Simon Price Jones, Leeds

REGARDING my earlier two letters, I am concerned that my correspondence may have given the impression that I am intending to commit a murder and dispose of the body in a wood. Can I reiterate that this is not the case, and if any bodies are subsequently found doubled up in half-sized graves, it wasn't me.

Hector Crumbhorn, Hull

I WELCOME the decision by the FA instructing referees to clamp down on deliberate time wasting by issuing yellow cards to offenders. But surely there should also be a corresponding reward system in place for players who score a late goal and *save* time by legging it back to the centre circle full pelt with the ball under their arm. Perhaps if that player has received a yellow card earlier in the game, it could be rescinded as a 'good will gesture'. Or, if he or she has not received a caution, the ref could show his or her appreciation by giving them a bottle of wine or some Amazon gift vouchers. Come on, FA bigwigs. How about a bit of carrot as well as stick?

Kevin Caswell-Jones, Wrexham

TO make better use of their coppers' time, under-resourced police forces should learn from delivery companies. If a suspect isn't answering when they turn up at their door to arrest them, they should leave a card saying they were out when they called, with a box to tick on the reverse side saying they will call again. Or they could ask them to turn themselves in at the local police station, indicating that have left a pair of handcuffs with a neighbour, or something.

Gavin Smith, Prestwick

"WHEN life gives you lemons, make lemonade", the saying goes. Well, my mate Joe give me a bag of lemons and I made a meringue pie and two drizzle cakes. I wonder if any other readers have slapped convention in the face in such an anarchistic way.

Graham Flintoft, Gatesheed

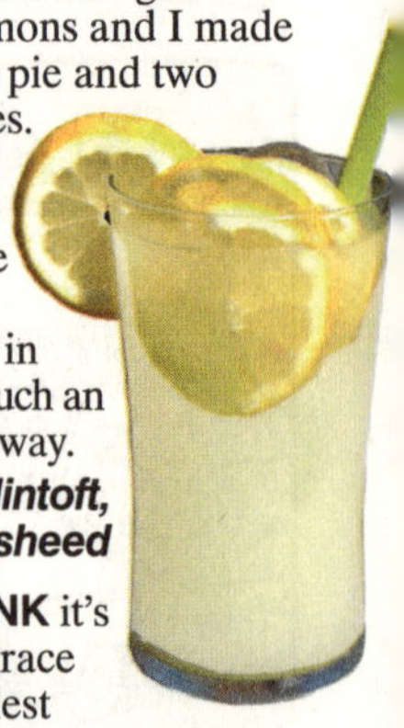

I THINK it's a disgrace that the tallest person ever to have topped the UK pop charts is an Italian. DJ Spiller stood at 6' 9" when *Groovejet (If this Ain't Love)* reached number one in 2001. We didn't leave the EU so that ruddy foreigners could hold the record for the UK's loftiest chart-topping recording artiste. Are there any Brits reading this who can play an instrument or sing, and – crucially – are 6' 10" or over? If so, it's your patriotic duty to release a number one single and bring this record home.

Ellis Dexter, London

I DON'T think James Bond got lucky when he threw his titfer onto Miss Moneypenny's hat stand, I think he practised. I can't imagine 007 risking the embarrassment of an errant shot and him having to retrieve his hat from a wastepaper basket, or worse still, watch it sail out of an open window. But I do wonder why he needed to partake in this act of showing off in the first place. Moneypenny would have been impressed enough by the fact that he was a secret agent with a licence to kill and a snazzy car with all guns coming out of the headlights. A trick that probably wouldn't win him a coconut at the fucking fair is hardly going to make any difference to Bond's scoring chances.

Jack Weevils-Nelson, email

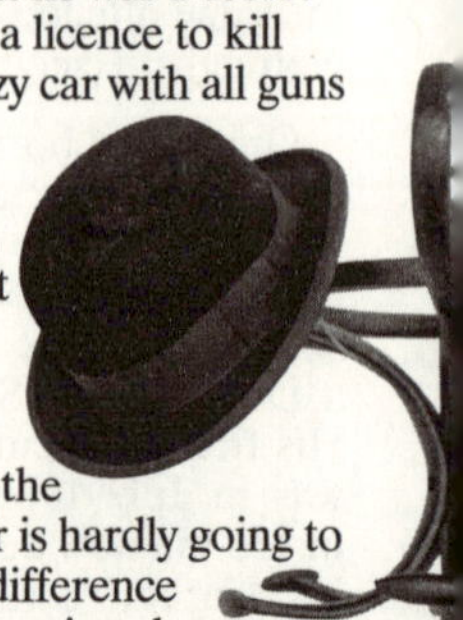

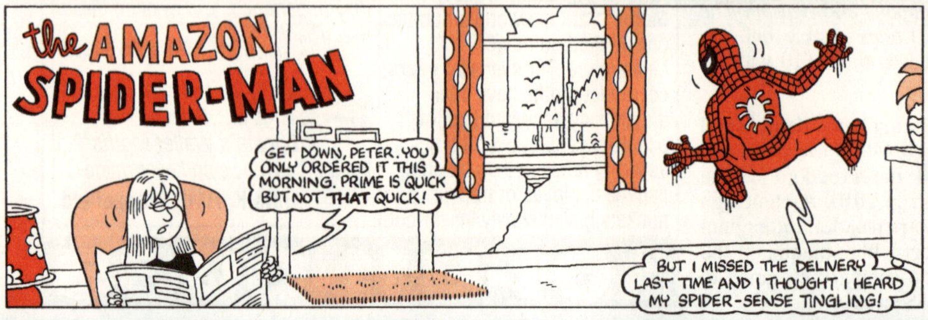

the AMAZON SPIDER-MAN
GET DOWN, PETER. YOU ONLY ORDERED IT THIS MORNING. PRIME IS QUICK BUT NOT THAT QUICK!
BUT I MISSED THE DELIVERY LAST TIME AND I THOUGHT I HEARD MY SPIDER-SENSE TINGLING!

WE are in the EU for forty-odd years and everything is absolutely fine. Then we come out and I snap my Achilles tendon playing five-a-side football. Project Fear, my arse.

Aiken Drummond, Derby

WITH reference to the above letter, I'm afraid Mr Drummond is confusing correlation with causation. There is indeed a correlation between the two events Mr Drummond describes – we leave the European Union and he snaps his Achilles tendon. Similarly, the incidents of sunburn and ice cream sales in the UK show a correlation, but one does not occur as a direct consequence of the other. It is 'bad science' to suggest that leaving the EU has in some way *caused* Mr Drummond to rupture his Achilles tendon, because it hasn't.

Arthur Semaphore, Luton

MR Semaphore *(above)* is correct up to a point, but he goes too far in his conclusion. As he says, when two things are correlated, it does not follow that one caused the other. But equally, it does not mean that it didn't. The null hypothesis is that leaving the EU did not snap Mr Drummond's Achilles tendon, but that would need to be proved or rejected scientifically.

Dr Ben Goldacre, London

* *Let's put this to bed once and for all. If you have ever torn your Achilles tendon, write in and let us know, and tell us if we were in the EU at the time. For each category, we'll divide the number of injuries by the length of time we were in or out of the EU to get a standardised figure of for each. If it appears that there is a correlation between Achilles ruptures and EU membership, we'll run a Chi-squared-test to on the data to see if there is any statistical evidence of a causal link. We'll print the results in the next annual.*

WHEN future generations look for an event marking the fall of Western civilisation, I reckon they'll pinpoint it to that time that Geordie contestant on *Big Brother* wiped his arse on the pillowcase of the woman he'd met in there.

David Craik, Hull

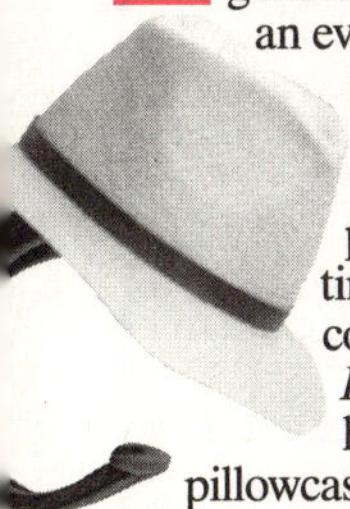

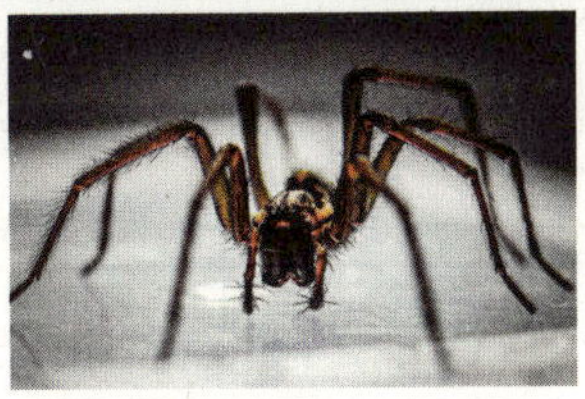

WHEN I was recently bitten by a spider in bed, I was hoping to wake up with amazing spider powers. Instead, I just had an itchy bacterial-induced rash on my left testicle where its little fangs went in. Does the spider have to be radioactive to impart superpowers, does anyone know? I would ask Stan Lee, but he died recently.

Mouris Piper, Hull

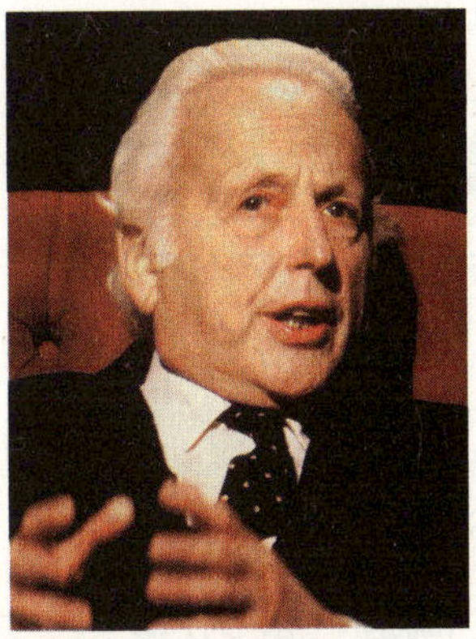

FOLLOWING recent *Viz* reader sightings of Ray Davies and Tony Cottee in chemist shops, I spotted nonagenarian journalist Peregrine Worsthorne emerging from a pharmacy in Pimlico, wearing a tweed suit and carrying a small paper prescription bag. I've no idea what his prescription was, but it can't have done him much good as he was dead less than a year later.

Ben Nunn, Caterham

WHY are the Greeks still making a fuss about the Elgin Marbles? Elgin is a town south of Lossiemouth in Scotland; it's nothing to do with the Greeks. They should keep their noses out of it.

Rufus A Badgersbum, Leicester

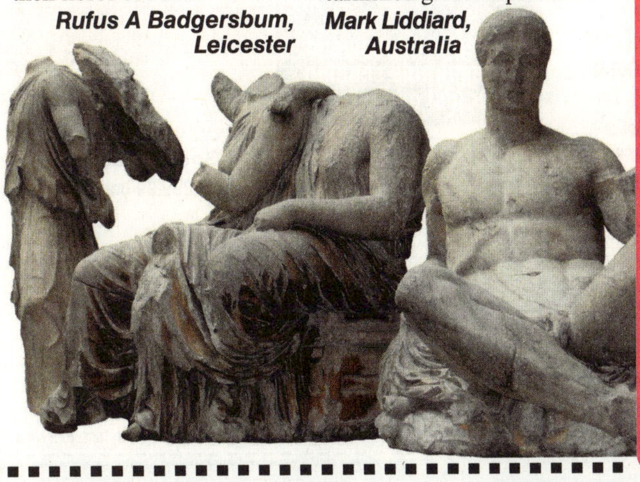

TOP TIPS

LIVEN up beans on toast by putting the beans on the plate first and serving toast on beans! If you don't like it, simply place another plate on top, turn it upside down, remove the original plate and Hey Presto! Good old beans on toast once more.

Hector Lysander, Ely

FEELING tired at work? Take a nap at the bottom of a ladder, and if the boss comes simply tell him you fell.

Graham Flintoft, Gatesheed

PUTTING gravy into your Whoopee Cushion lifts an amusing prank to a whole new level of authenticity.

Stuart Silver, Glasgow

FOOL your cat into believing you're a supervillain by telling your wife and kids to "SEIZE HIM" as he comes through the cat flap.

Kevin Caswell-Jones, Gresford

MAKING a cheesecake? Save the effort of breaking up digestive biscuits for the base with a rolling pin by getting your supermarket to deliver them instead.

Mark, Camelford

TEA drinkers. Always keep a box of Earl Grey in the cupboard in case you run out of normal tea. Being reminded of how fucking horrible it is will make sure you keep your usual tea well stocked in future.

Eldon Furse, email

MAKE your own headache tablets by rolling blobs of ibuprofen gel in icing sugar and baking them in the oven for 20 mins at gas mark 5.

Chingford Rob, email

toptips@viz.co.uk

KING Charles's late mam was addressed using the posh term 'Ma'am'. So why isn't her son addressed as 'Da'ad', I wonder? It seems it's one rule for frosty-faced royal women and another for the sausage-fingered, red-faced men, who, if the late Mike Yarwood was to be believed, go "uhhhnmm... uhnmm" just before they speak.

Eugene Ruane, Liverpool

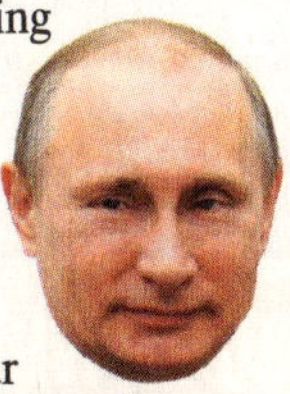

VLADIMIR Putin is often unfairly maligned for being a bloodthirsty despot, but he always strikes me as more like the accident-prone 1970s sitcom star Frank Spencer. After all, his chums are always falling out of windows, being poisoned or blown up in planes; accidents just seem to follow him wherever he goes. Perhaps if he started wearing a beret and saying 'Ooh, Betty!' when another official falls to their death or ingests a neurotoxin, it might help rebuild his somewhat tarnished global reputation.

Mark Liddiard, Australia

Richard Wilson's "I *DO* believe it!"

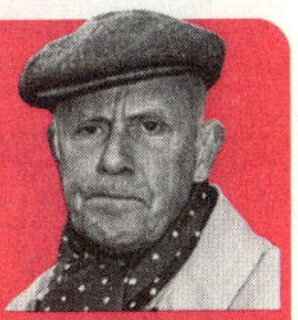

FROM solving a Rubik's Cube to humans landing on the Moon, history is peppered with feats which, despite all evidence pointing to their veracity, some people still find hard to believe.

But what of the remarkable playground stories we were told by mates that seemed too incredible to be true? Can age and hindsight shine any light on their authenticity? *Viz* asked four A-list celebs to share their most unbelievable schoolfriends' facts that time has yet to disprove.

Sting, *first order bellend lutist*

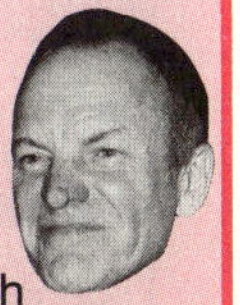

THERE was a kid at my school who told me that his dad was a special sort of policeman who was given a type of uniform coated in a secret chemical that allowed him to walk through walls. I didn't believe him until I asked to see it and he said that he'd let me. Unfortunately his dad was only allowed to use it between 2 and 4 in the morning, in case anyone saw him and it sent them mad. It's amazing to think that such technology was available back then and I've often wondered if it was ever used to solve any famous crimes.

Gary Lineker, *crisp advertiser*

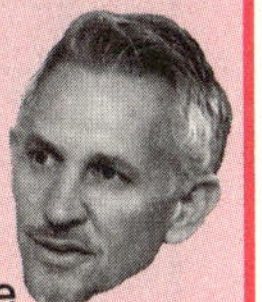

A GUY in the year below me said that he'd broken into the boarded-up witch's Cottage in the woods behind our school in Leicester, but had to leg it because a ghost had jumped out and tried to bite him on the shoulder. He offered to take me up there on Halloween at midnight to show me where the ghost lived, but although I really wanted to go it turned out I couldn't make it because I had to look after a friend who wasn't well or something. But I often wonder if the ghost is still there.

Colin Firth, *heart throb actor*

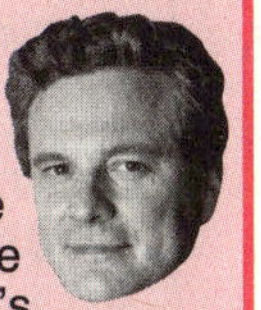

A MATE of mine said his dad was in the army, but I didn't believe him because his dad had a mullet haircut, an earring and spent all his time in the pub. However, my mate explained that he was undercover, infiltrating the IRA and that's why he looked like he did. He told me never to tell anyone because his cover would be blown and his dad would be killed and he and his mum would be kneecapped. His dad is is an old man now, but I sometimes see him when I go back home, and he still has the same haircut and spends all day in the same pub. I often wonder if he ever rooted out any IRA cells in the Hampshire village of Grayshott.

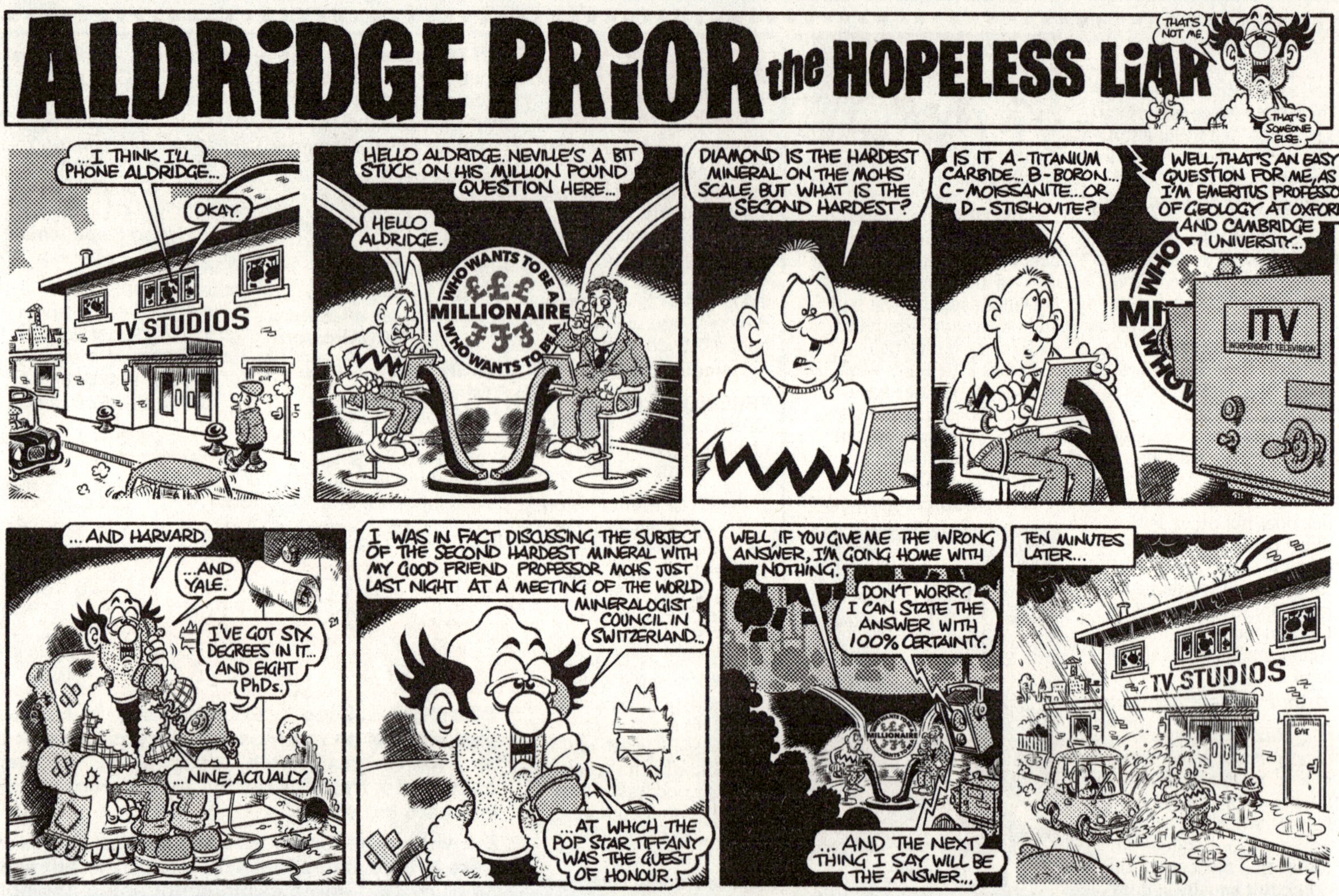
ALDRIDGE PRIOR the HOPELESS LIAR
THAT'S NOT ME.
THAT'S SOMEONE ELSE.
...I THINK I'LL PHONE ALDRIDGE...
OKAY.
TV STUDIOS
HELLO ALDRIDGE. NEVILLE'S A BIT STUCK ON HIS MILLION POUND QUESTION HERE...
HELLO ALDRIDGE.
WHO WANTS TO BE A MILLIONAIRE
DIAMOND IS THE HARDEST MINERAL ON THE MOHS SCALE, BUT WHAT IS THE SECOND HARDEST?
IS IT A-TITANIUM CARBIDE... B-BORON... C-MOISSANITE...OR D-STISHOVITE?
WELL, THAT'S AN EASY QUESTION FOR ME, AS I'M EMERITUS PROFESSOR OF GEOLOGY AT OXFORD AND CAMBRIDGE UNIVERSITY...
ITV
...AND HARVARD.
...AND YALE.
I'VE GOT SIX DEGREES IN IT... AND EIGHT PhDs.
...NINE, ACTUALLY.
I WAS IN FACT DISCUSSING THE SUBJECT OF THE SECOND HARDEST MINERAL WITH MY GOOD FRIEND PROFESSOR MOHS JUST LAST NIGHT AT A MEETING OF THE WORLD MINERALOGIST COUNCIL IN SWITZERLAND...
...AT WHICH THE POP STAR TIFFANY WAS THE GUEST OF HONOUR.
WELL, IF YOU GIVE ME THE WRONG ANSWER, I'M GOING HOME WITH NOTHING.
DON'T WORRY. I CAN STATE THE ANSWER WITH 100% CERTAINTY.
...AND THE NEXT THING I SAY WILL BE THE ANSWER...
TEN MINUTES LATER...
TV STUDIOS

AUDIOPHILES – Tired of perfect digital music with crystal-clear timbre and faultless reproduction? Yearning for music with warmth and character? You need...

The Vinyl Vandal

YOU'LL WOW AND FLUTTER AT THE RESULTS!

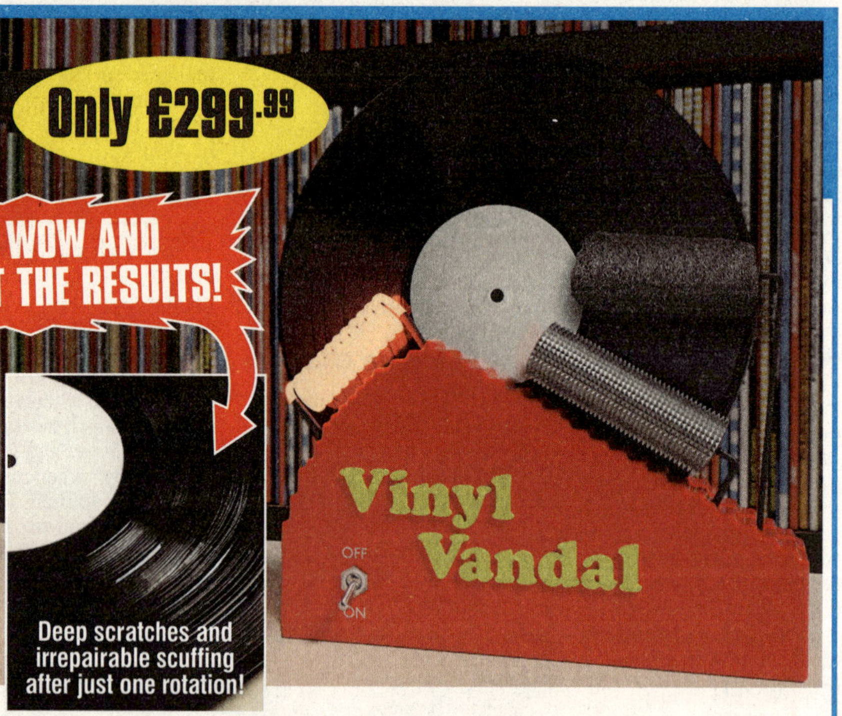
Only £299.99
Vinyl Vandal
OFF
ON
Deep scratches and irrepairable scuffing after just one rotation!

The revolutionary 12-inch vinyl scratching machine that makes pristine sounds a thing of the past!

SNAP! CRACKLE! POP! **Years of vinyl wear and tear at the flick of a switch. Your ears will not believe the difference. Just 1 minute in the *Vinyl Vandal*, and the resulting scratches, clicks and hisses will make even the latest Ed Sheeran album sound like it was recorded in 1920 on a wax cylinder.**

The Vinyl Vandal **carefully rotates your record at 33rpm whilst a toothed cast-iron roller adds those characterful scratches to the surface. Nostalgic hiss is added thanks to a wire wool pad. And a 1500W kettle element will make any long player sound like it's been sitting on the parcel shelf of an Austin Maxi all summer.**

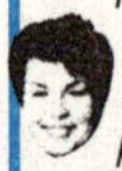
"I bought the latest Public Service Broadcasting album and the sound was absolutely perfect. But just two minutes in the Vinyl Vandal and now when I put it on, it's like they are playing in a chip shop with the fat fryers going full tilt."
Mr B, Essex

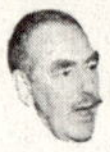
"I used to rub my records with a bit of sandpaper, but it just used to make the stylus jump and skip. The Vinyl Vandal produces that all over analogue sound that makes it seem like your are listening to your collection with a needle stuck in the bottom of a yoghurt pot."
Mr L, Birmingham

To: Shitco, FREEPOST, Unit 3A, Goole Industrial Estate, GH4 9NN

Please rush me........... *Vinyl Vandal(s)* at £299.99 (inc. £100 p&p). Please charge me what you like, using the method of your choice.

Name of Bank .... Account name ....
Account number.. Sort code ....
Credit/debit card number.................................. Expiry date.............. CVV code..........
Name on card .... PIN no.................. House alarm code..................................
(Use separate sheet for extra cards if required)
Mr/Mrs/Miss/Mx.. Address ....
Post code ....

TERMS & CONDITIONS: Only one coupon per person. Some parts may be missing, cracked or damaged in transit. There may be electrical issues. May not work. You may not, in fact, receive a Vinyl Vandal at all. Nod if you understand.

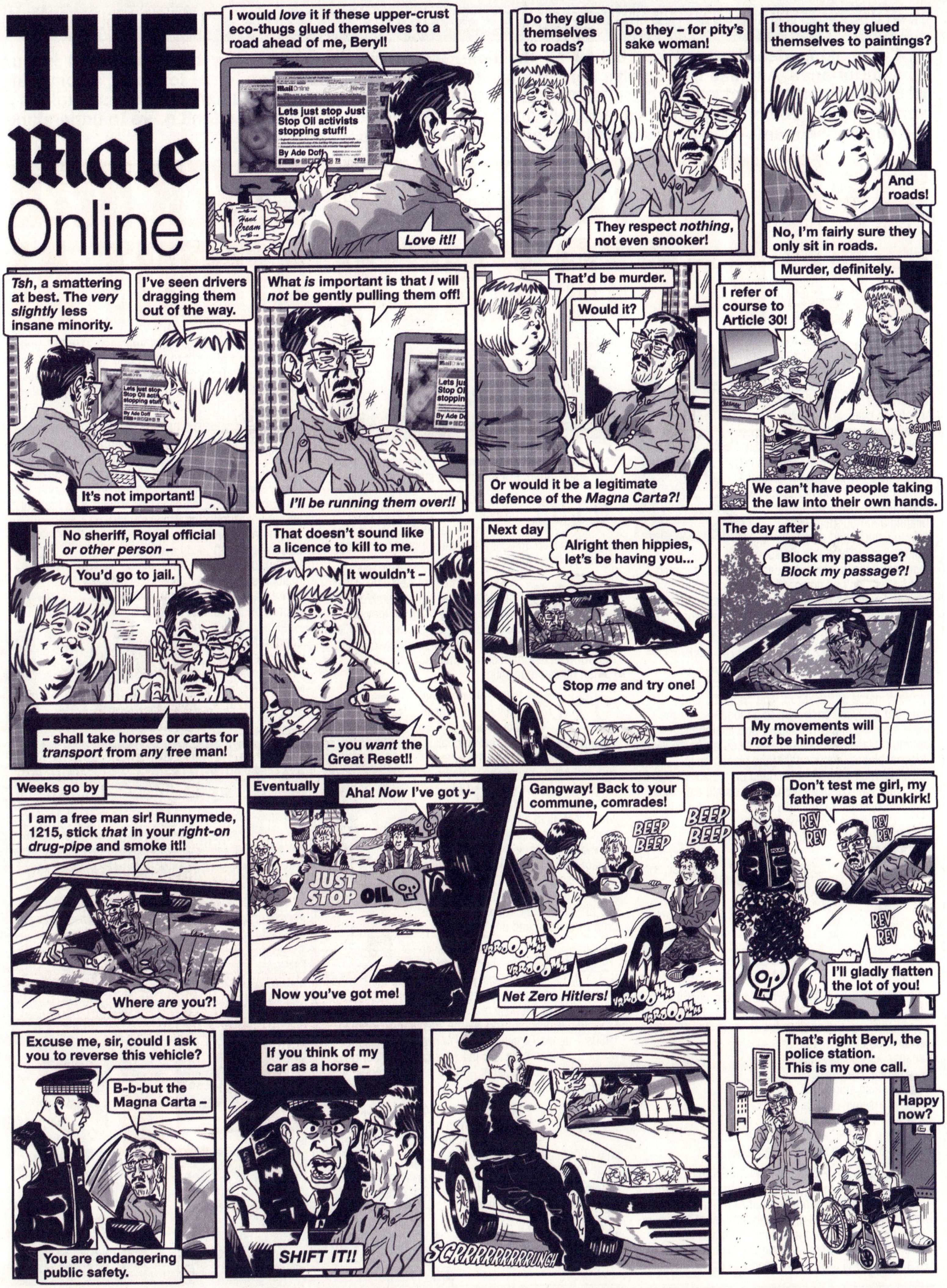
THE Male Online
I would *love* it if these upper-crust eco-thugs glued themselves to a road ahead of me, Beryl!
Mail Online
News
Lets just stop Just Stop Oil activists stopping stuff!
By Ade Doff
Hand Cream
Love it!!
Do they glue themselves to roads?
Do they – for pity's sake woman!
They respect *nothing*, not even snooker!
I thought they glued themselves to paintings?
And roads!
No, I'm fairly sure they only sit in roads.
Tsh, a smattering at best. The *very slightly* less insane minority.
I've seen drivers dragging them out of the way.
It's not important!
What *is* important is that *I* will *not* be gently pulling them off!
I'll be running them over!!
That'd be murder.
Would it?
Or would it be a legitimate defence of the *Magna Carta?!*
Murder, definitely.
I refer of course to Article 30!
SCRUNCH
SCRUNCH
We can't have people taking the law into their own hands.
No sheriff, Royal official *or other person* –
You'd go to jail.
– shall take horses or carts for *transport* from *any* free man!
That doesn't sound like a licence to kill to me.
It wouldn't –
– you *want* the Great Reset!!
Next day
Alright then hippies, let's be having you...
Stop *me* and try one!
The day after
Block my passage? *Block my passage?!*
My movements will *not* be hindered!
Weeks go by
I am a free man sir! Runnymede, 1215, stick *that* in your *right-on drug-pipe* and smoke it!!
Where *are* you?!
Eventually
Aha! *Now* I've got y-
JUST STOP OIL
Now you've got me!
Gangway! Back to your commune, comrades!
BEEP BEEP
BEEP BEEP
VRROOOMM
Net Zero Hitlers!
Don't test me girl, my father was at Dunkirk!
REV REV
REV REV
REV REV
I'll gladly flatten the lot of you!
Excuse me, sir, could I ask you to reverse this vehicle?
B-b-but the Magna Carta –
You are endangering public safety.
If you think of my car as a horse –
SHIFT IT!!
SCRRRRRRRRRUNCH!
That's right Beryl, the police station. This is my one call.
Happy now?

IT'S making decisions on our behalf all the time. It's in our computers, our televisions and in our smartphones. And like it or not, it's here to stay. It's Artificial Intelligence, or AI for short, a computer based algorithm that will perceive, synthesise and infer information so that humans do not have to. It's a very complicated concept to understand, but one of the beauties of AI is that you don't *have* to understand it – super-intelligent AI systems will understand it *for* you! So here, in binary, are...

1010 THINGS YOU NEVER NEED TO KNOW ABOUT AI

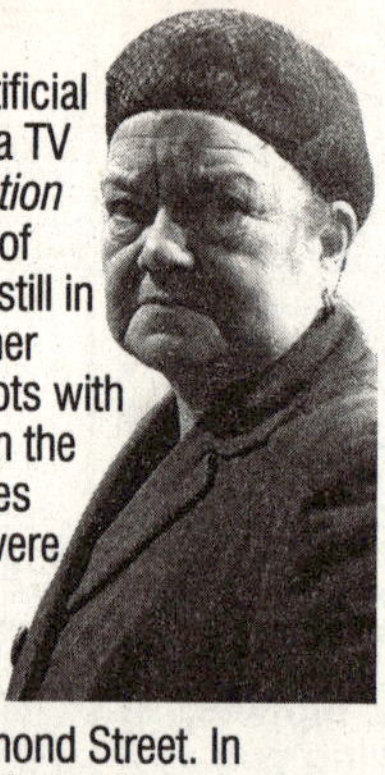

0000 **THE FIRST** reference to Artificial Intelligence on a TV soap was in an episode of *Coronation Street* in 1976, when the concept of machines being able to think was still in its infancy. Curmudgeonly pensioner Albert Tatlock was discussing robots with hair-netted fishwife Ena Sharples in the snug of the Rovers Return. Sharples bemoaned that "bloomin' robots were going to take over t'world" after hearing a rumour that Rita Fairclough had had an electronic till installed in The Kabin on Rosemond Street. In response Tatlock, played by Jack Howarth, declared that he "couldn't be doing wi' all this bloomin' AI-based tech and wotnot." Switchboards at Granada TV lit up as confused viewers rang in wanting to know what Tatlock's reference to AI meant.

0010 **IN 1972**, Oxford University's Dr Hobart Edelweiss developed a program which could play the 'perfect' game of Buckaroo. The sophisticated program analysed each item to be loaded onto the mule's back using 3-D imagery and assigned optimum placement coordinates, accurate to 1million decimal places, ensuring that the plastic animal would not kick. The system – developed on a state-of-the-art computer the size of a Ford Cortina estate car – was deemed unbeatable by humans. But this claim was never put to the test because despite a full-page invitation being published in Russia's daily newspaper *The Soviet Sports*, 8-year-old Buckaroo Grand Master Gaspar Kasperov refused to rise to the challenge.

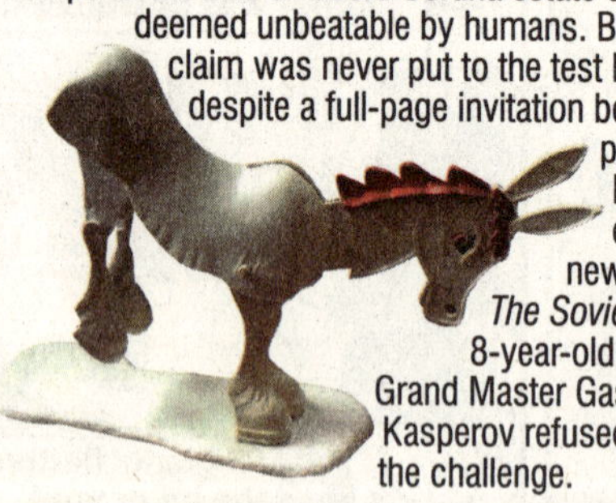

0011 **ASK** a fertility doctor what their view on AI is, and they will almost certainly be all for it. That's because as well as Artificial Intelligence, the two-letter acronym also stands for Artificial Insemination, a process by which male sperms are introduced the the female egg by a process other than sexual intercourse.

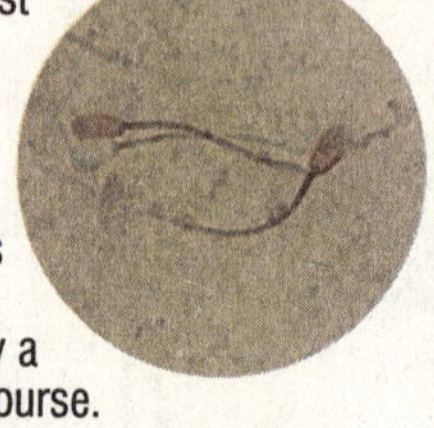

0100 **POLITICIANS** may think that their jobs are safe from the march of progress, but AI threatens their livelihood just as much as it does the rest of us. Computer scientists at the California Institute of Technology in Pasadena believe that within the next decade, they will have built a machine that is capable

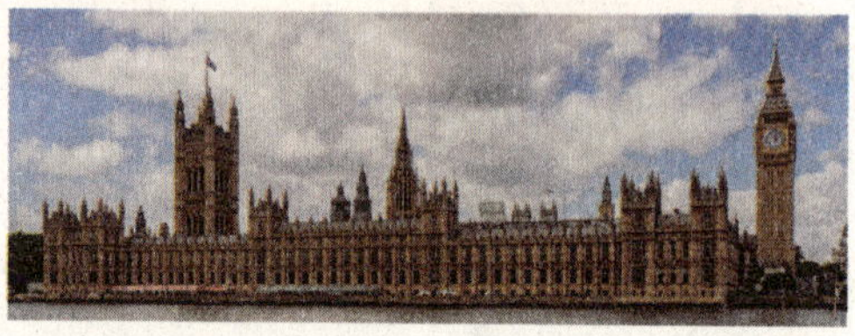

of coming out with the same stock phrase over and over again regardless of what question it is asked.

0101 **THE ACRONYM** AI has only one anagram – IA, which itself is an acronym for, amongst other things, *inter alia* which ironically, is a Latin phrase meaning 'amongst other things'.

0110 **ASK** a member of Amnesty International what they think of AI, and like fertility doctors, they will definitely be in favour of it. Because as well as Artificial Intelligence and Artificial Insemination, the two letters also form an acronym of their non-governmental human rights organisation.

0111 **WHEN** you 'chat' online to complain about poor service, there may be a human being dealing with your complaints on the other end, but without knowing it, you could be conversing with an AI robot. A clever trick to find out which it is, is to ask them what the capital of Australia is. A human being will naturally answer 'Sydney', whereas a machine powered by AI algorithms will correctly answer 'Canberra', giving away its true nature. And once you know you are talking to a robot, you can be even more rude and unpleasant.

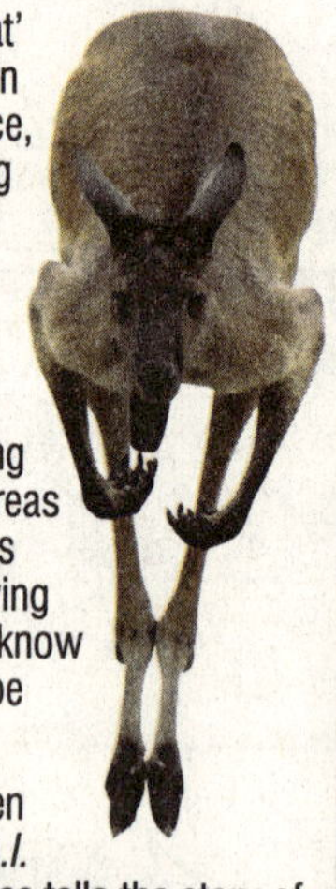

1000 **THE 2001** Steven Spielberg movie *A.I. Artificial Intelligence* tells the story of a futuristic cyborg boy who somehow develops feelings for his "mother", whose real son is in cryo-stasis with an incurable disease. This theme was first explored in 1980s Thames TV series *Metal Mickey*, in an episode where the titular robot falls in love with the Wilberforces' Electrolux vacuum cleaner and sticks his tin cock in its crevice tool, shorting out the whole street.

1001 **DESPITE** having keys for all the numbers from zero to nine along the tops of their keyboards, computers only understand binary numbers made up of ones and zeros. Instead of columns for units, tens, and hundreds, binary notation has ones, twos, fours and so on, with the value doubling in each subsequent column. For example, in binary the number sixteen is written as '10000', and ten thousand is '10011100010000'. Ironically, to an AI computer '1001 Carpet Cleaner' is actually called '9 Carpet Cleaner', and *101 Dalmations* only has five dogs in it.

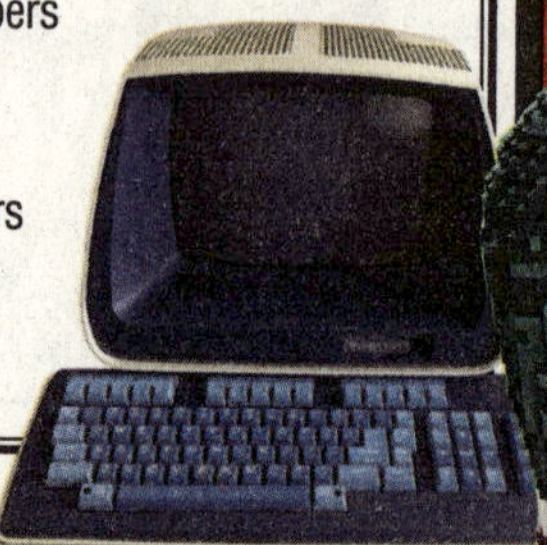

1010 **BOFFINS** from IBM were once employed by the BBC to create a powerful computer capable of generating an infinite variety of new catchphrases for family favourite TV light entertainer Bruce Forsyth. The resultant machine, named Deep Brucie, was first put into action during the Royal Variety Performance on Sunday 23rd November 1973 . However, when Forsyth deployed the machine's maiden suggestion: "Nice to see you, to turn you so much higher scores on the doors than last week's do well?" the London Palladium audience fell silent. The following week, Deep Brucie was broken up for parts.

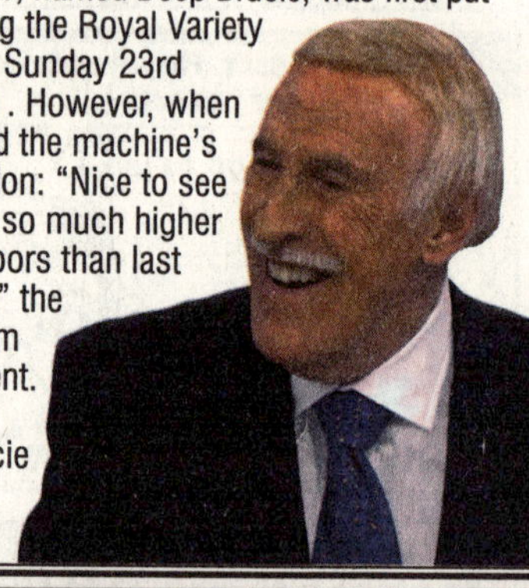

YOUNG people today are obsessed with AI. It chooses what they watch on TV, what clothes they wear, and what music they listen to. It even does their homework for them. In fact, the modern youngster don't have to think at all, or make a single conscious decision to get through their day. Life may seem easier now, but experts believe we could be storing up trouble for the future, as today's young people will grow up into a race of mindless autons, unable to think for themselves, wandering around in a trance-like state, completely at the mercy of their computerised masters. So how will things change when today's children become tomorrow's AI-zombie adults? Let's take a look at what life will be like in...

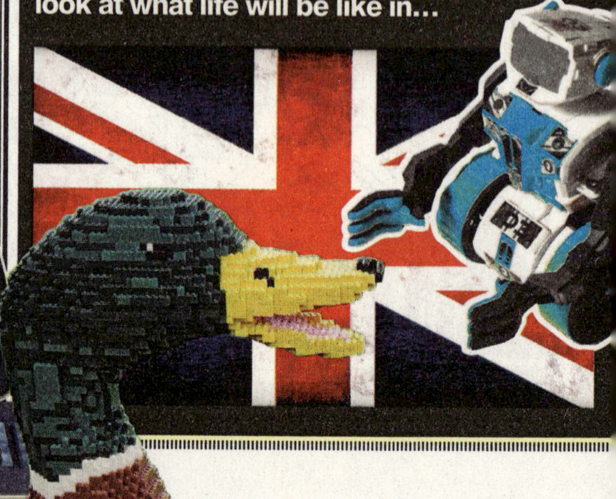

OH *AI* DO LIKE TO BE BESIDE THE SEASIDE

Blackpool gears up to thwart robot takeover. "Bring it on!" says Lord Mayor

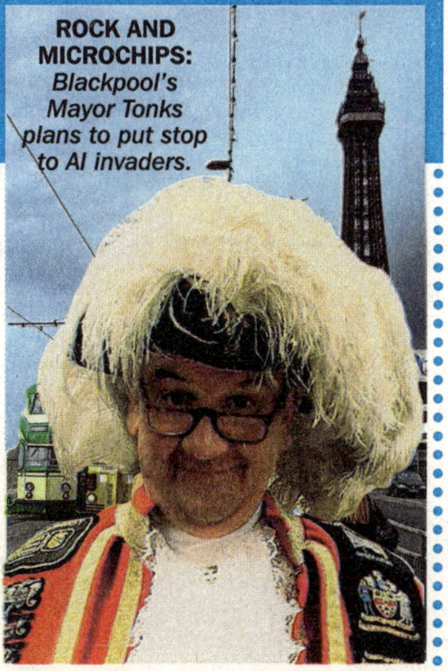

ROCK AND MICROCHIPS: *Blackpool's Mayor Tonks plans to put stop to AI invaders.*

MANY people fear the inevitable rise of Artificial Intelligence, and are apprehensive about a future when all the decisions we usually make are taken instead by banks of emotionless, electronic automatons. But the Lord Mayor of one Lancashire seaside resort thinks such a nightmare science fiction scenario is far from inevitable, and believes a little preparation will see his town repel any invasion by self-aware machines.

"If these robots think they can march into the jewel of the Lancashire coast and start running the show, they've got another think coming," said Alderman Eric Tonks, who for the past two decades has been the Mayor of the resort, famous for its Golden Mile and bonsai Eiffel Tower. "This is Blackpool, not Bl-ai-ckpool," he said tortuously.

"We human beings of Blackpool look after 18 million visitors a year." he told the *Lytham St Annes Tribune and Globe*. "The landladies, shop keepers and car park attendants along the Golden Mile all do a splendid job giving folk a holiday to remember, and we don't need any artificially intelligent gizmos poking their metal noses in, thank-you very much."

And last week, Tonks called an Extraordinary General Meeting of the parish council to formulate a plan to ready the town for the inevitable onslaught by Artificially Intelligent cyborgs. Measures drawn up by the committee to thwart the invasion include:

- *Removing the fuses from electrical sockets in all civic buildings to deprive the invaders of power*
- *The seafront Flower Clock to be set half an hour fast to 'sow confusion' amongst the invaders*
- *The wifi in the public library to be turned off to prevent the electromechanical foe from accessing free internet*
- *Gritting lorries to be deployed to 'play havoc' with the robots' mechanical parts*

But the main thrust of the council's campaign would be to keep the invading army of automatons from finding a source of energy to recharge their power source.

"I'm not an expert on robotics, but I'm guessing the things run on batteries," said Tonks. "And again, I'm not an expert on batteries, but I'm guessing they can't run for more than a couple of hours before they're as flat as a pancake."

"If we as a town can stop them plugging themselves in to any sockets, we'll have them licked in half a day," he said. "Then we can send the bin lorries round to collect them up and take them to the recycling centre on Bristol Avenue."

However, Marsha Jobsworthy, union representative for the Blackpool Borough Council workers, threw a spanner in the mayor's works by saying it was not in the refuse collectors' contracts to remove broken down robots from the street. "My members are employed to remove household waste from private households only," he told reporters. "Broken robots in the street constitute commercial waste which would require a separate local authority contract for removal."

And Leon Felix, manager at the recycling centre also had bad news for Alderman Tonks. "Robots can't be recycled as they are not just made of one type of metal," he said. "There'll be steel, aluminium, copper, and all sorts in there. Not to mention all the plastic around the wiring."

And he was also concerned that there could be dangerous substances in the robots' power packs. "There could be dangerous heavy metals in there, and a lot of these things spontaneously explode," he ventured.

"I could accept them if they had certification that there were no toxic, corrosive or flammable materials, and if they were stripped down into their various components," he said. "Then the metal could go in the mixed metal waste, the power units could go in the shipping container for batteries and the plastic wiring could go in the non-recyclables."

"I doubt there'd be any cardboard in a robot, but if there was, that would go in the paper and cardboard hopper," he added.

AI Britain 2050

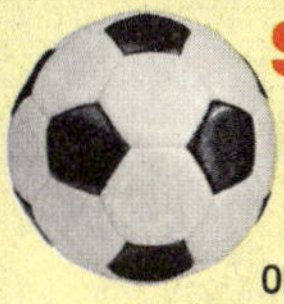

Sport

The unpredictability of a football match is part and parcel of the game. Which players will be on form? Will rehearsed training ground set-pieces pay off during the match? Will a goal against the run of play turn the game on its head? Anything can happen over the 90 minutes, meaning football is the most exciting game in the world… *for the moment*. That's because when tomorrow's players take to the field, every decision they make will be guided by AI. Who to pass to, when to shoot, when to go down in the box looking for a penalty – all these decisions will be based on algorithms inside a master computer in the dugout, and fed through to the players on the field. Gone will be the flair, the moments of brilliance, the dummies and the impossible shots, to be replaced by mundane, computerised safe play. Every game will be like watching Wolverhampton Wanderers play Chelsea. Only if the master game computer crashes will we get to see those classic footballing moments that we will remember fondly for years.

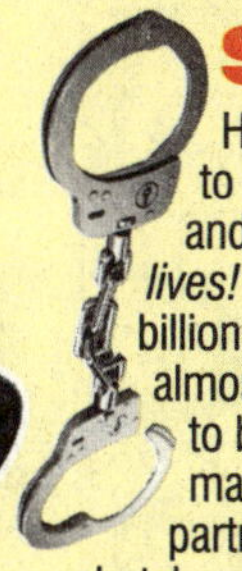

Sex

Human beings are a creative species, and when we hand our capacity to create over to an unimaginative machine that thinks in a series of ones and zeros, every aspect of our lives will be worse… except, that is, our *sex lives!* AI algorithms will will be able to instantaneously trawl every one of the 30 billion pages on the web, looking for things to do between the sheets. And with almost 30% of those pages being from porn sites, your bots are never going to be short of red hot ideas. Once the computers take over your decision-making processes, you can say goodbye to humdrum nookie with your life partner. Your AI sex life will be one long round of threesomes in brightly lit hotel rooms, 'happy ending' massages from eastern European women, and wild bukkake orgies wearing a Noh mask in the back of a snooker club on the ringroad. And if you ever *did* feel your sex life was becoming a little bit jaded, at the flick of a switch you can set your AI bot loose on the dark web for a *really* kinky treat.

Work

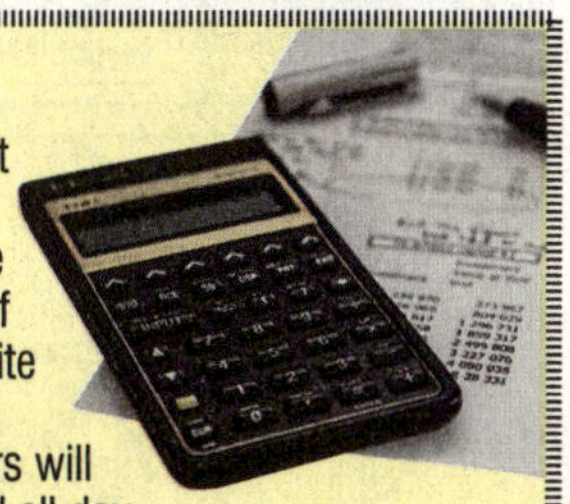

It is in the world of work where we will see the biggest changes when AI takes over. For many years, robots have been taking the jobs of manual workers – people who make things with their hands. But the AI robots of tomorrow will also be taking the jobs of so-called 'white collar' workers – those who use their brainpower. Call centre operatives, systems analysts and office workers will be released from their daily 9-to-5 grind, free to spend all day, every day with their families, albeit with no money coming in. Even those working in creative industries will not be untouched by the inexorable march forward of AI. The past two seasons of *Mrs Brown's Boys* were written by a crude AI bot in the early stages of development, and Radio 4s soap *The Archers* has not seen any human input on the writing side since 2016. It is almost certain that before the decade is out, an R2D2-like bot will waddle onto the stage at the Academy Awards ceremony to receive the Oscar for Best Screenplay for a Motion Picture, before lifting its trophy with a metal pincer and shouting: "The robots are coming!"

Transport

It is the process of driving the car where we will see the first evidence of AI taking over our lives, with driverless cars long ago leaving the drawing board and pulling into our streets. Controlled by powerful computers, these automatic automobiles are able to navigate obstacles, make complicated decisions at junctions, anticipate traffic problems and crash into ditches without any human input whatsoever. But as usual, the technology is moving faster than the real world can catch up, and no driverless car has yet been programmed to insult another driverless vehicle when cut up. Traditional insults aimed at human motorists such as "Try indicating, you wanker," and "Learn the fucking highway code you fucking arsehole," will be lost on the cyber drivers of the vehicles of the future. "Move it, you binary-based bastard," and "Put your fucking RAM in gear, you electric cunt" are more apt responses to examples of inconsiderate AI driving and will doubtless be included in future software.

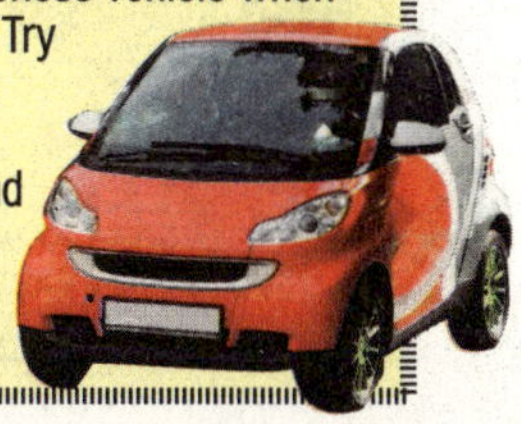

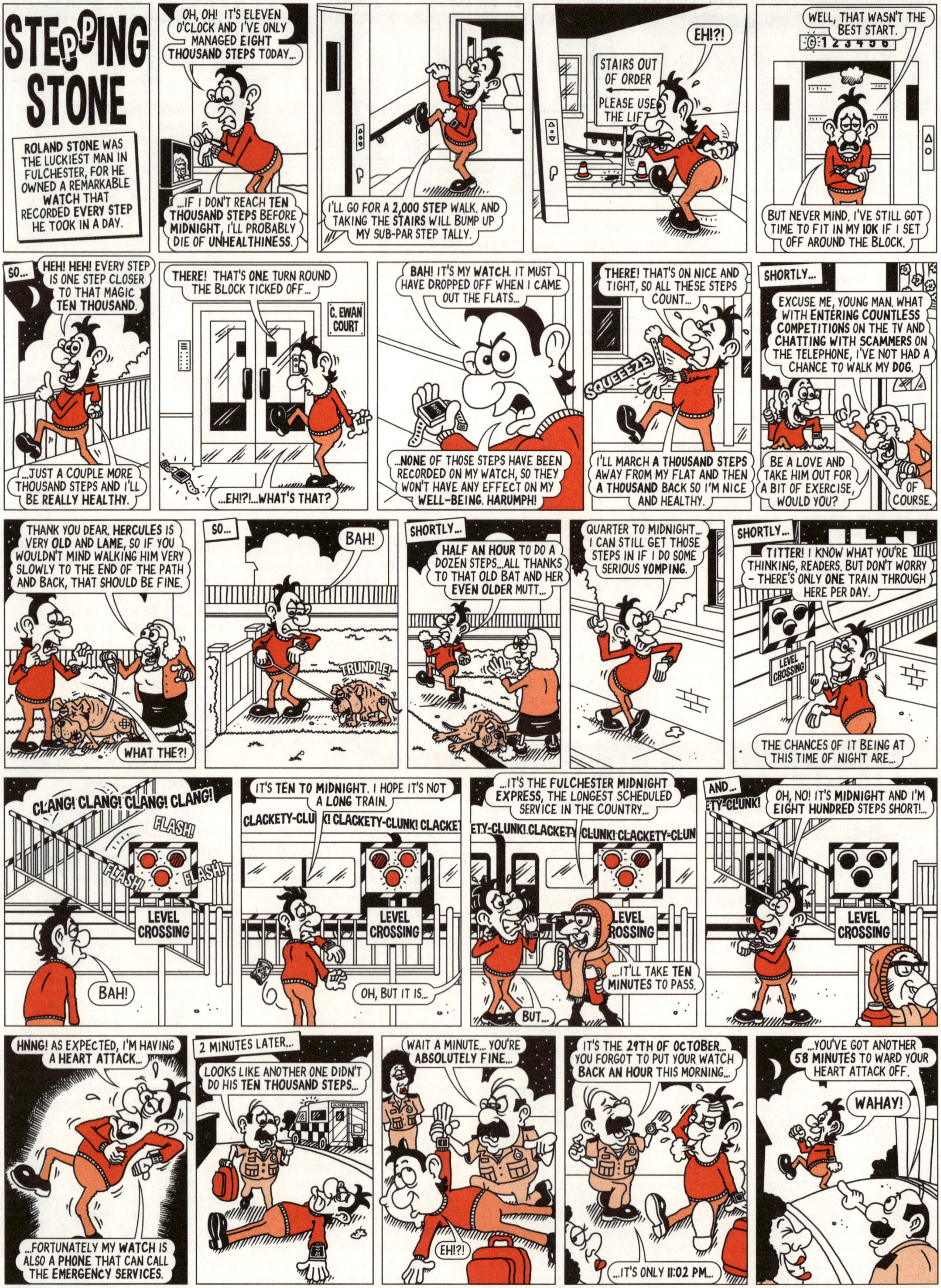
STEPPING STONE
ROLAND STONE WAS THE LUCKIEST MAN IN FULCHESTER, FOR HE OWNED A REMARKABLE WATCH THAT RECORDED EVERY STEP HE TOOK IN A DAY.
OH, OH! IT'S ELEVEN O'CLOCK AND I'VE ONLY MANAGED EIGHT THOUSAND STEPS TODAY...
...IF I DON'T REACH TEN THOUSAND STEPS BEFORE MIDNIGHT, I'LL PROBABLY DIE OF UNHEALTHINESS.
I'LL GO FOR A 2,000 STEP WALK. AND TAKING THE STAIRS WILL BUMP UP MY SUB-PAR STEP TALLY.
EH!?!
STAIRS OUT OF ORDER
PLEASE USE THE LIFT
WELL, THAT WASN'T THE BEST START.
G 1 2 3 4 5 6
BUT NEVER MIND. I'VE STILL GOT TIME TO FIT IN MY 10K IF I SET OFF AROUND THE BLOCK.
SO...
HEH! HEH! EVERY STEP IS ONE STEP CLOSER TO THAT MAGIC TEN THOUSAND.
...JUST A COUPLE MORE THOUSAND STEPS AND I'LL BE REALLY HEALTHY.
THERE! THAT'S ONE TURN ROUND THE BLOCK TICKED OFF...
C. EWAN COURT
...EH!?!...WHAT'S THAT?
BAH! IT'S MY WATCH. IT MUST HAVE DROPPED OFF WHEN I CAME OUT THE FLATS...
...NONE OF THOSE STEPS HAVE BEEN RECORDED ON MY WATCH, SO THEY WON'T HAVE ANY EFFECT ON MY WELL-BEING. HARUMPH!
THERE! THAT'S ON NICE AND TIGHT, SO ALL THESE STEPS COUNT...
SQUEEEZE!
I'LL MARCH A THOUSAND STEPS AWAY FROM MY FLAT AND THEN A THOUSAND BACK SO I'M NICE AND HEALTHY.
SHORTLY...
EXCUSE ME, YOUNG MAN. WHAT WITH ENTERING COUNTLESS COMPETITIONS ON THE TV AND CHATTING WITH SCAMMERS ON THE TELEPHONE, I'VE NOT HAD A CHANCE TO WALK MY DOG.
BE A LOVE AND TAKE HIM OUT FOR A BIT OF EXERCISE, WOULD YOU?
OF COURSE.
THANK YOU DEAR. HERCULES IS VERY OLD AND LAME, SO IF YOU WOULDN'T MIND WALKING HIM VERY SLOWLY TO THE END OF THE PATH AND BACK, THAT SHOULD BE FINE.
WHAT THE?!
SO...
BAH!
TRUNDLE!
SHORTLY...
HALF AN HOUR TO DO A DOZEN STEPS...ALL THANKS TO THAT OLD BAT AND HER EVEN OLDER MUTT...
QUARTER TO MIDNIGHT... I CAN STILL GET THOSE STEPS IN IF I DO SOME SERIOUS YOMPING.
SHORTLY...
TITTER! I KNOW WHAT YOU'RE THINKING, READERS. BUT DON'T WORRY - THERE'S ONLY ONE TRAIN THROUGH HERE PER DAY.
LEVEL CROSSING
THE CHANCES OF IT BEING AT THIS TIME OF NIGHT ARE...
CLANG! CLANG! CLANG! CLANG!
FLASH!
FLASH!
FLASH!
LEVEL CROSSING
BAH!
IT'S TEN TO MIDNIGHT. I HOPE IT'S NOT A LONG TRAIN.
CLACKETY-CLUNK! CLACKETY-CLUNK! CLACKET
LEVEL CROSSING
OH, BUT IT IS...
...IT'S THE FULCHESTER MIDNIGHT EXPRESS, THE LONGEST SCHEDULED SERVICE IN THE COUNTRY...
ETY-CLUNK! CLACKETY-CLUNK! CLACKETY-CLUN
LEVEL CROSSING
...IT'LL TAKE TEN MINUTES TO PASS.
BUT...
AND...
ETY-CLUNK!
OH, NO! IT'S MIDNIGHT AND I'M EIGHT HUNDRED STEPS SHORT!...
LEVEL CROSSING
HNNG! AS EXPECTED, I'M HAVING A HEART ATTACK...
...FORTUNATELY MY WATCH IS ALSO A PHONE THAT CAN CALL THE EMERGENCY SERVICES.
2 MINUTES LATER...
LOOKS LIKE ANOTHER ONE DIDN'T DO HIS TEN THOUSAND STEPS...
WAIT A MINUTE... YOU'RE ABSOLUTELY FINE...
EH!?!
IT'S THE 29TH OF OCTOBER... YOU FORGOT TO PUT YOUR WATCH BACK AN HOUR THIS MORNING...
...IT'S ONLY 11:02 PM...
...YOU'VE GOT ANOTHER 58 MINUTES TO WARD YOUR HEART ATTACK OFF.
WAHAY!

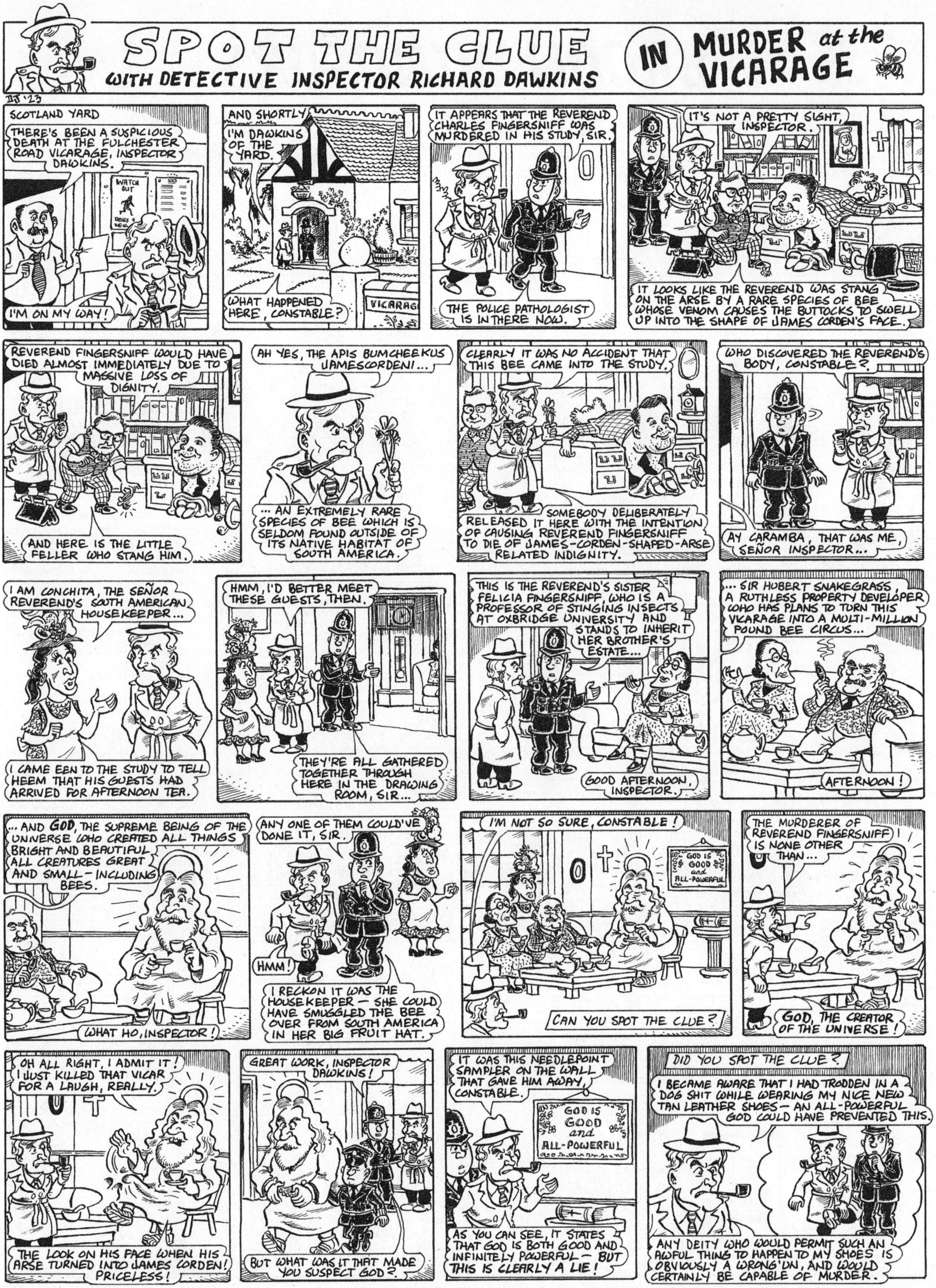
SPOT THE CLUE
WITH DETECTIVE INSPECTOR RICHARD DAWKINS
IN MURDER at the VICARAGE
IJ '23
SCOTLAND YARD
THERE'S BEEN A SUSPICIOUS DEATH AT THE FULCHESTER ROAD VICARAGE, INSPECTOR DAWKINS.
WATCH OUT
I'M ON MY WAY!
AND SHORTLY
I'M DAWKINS OF THE YARD.
WHAT HAPPENED HERE, CONSTABLE?
VICARAG
IT APPEARS THAT THE REVEREND CHARLES FINGERSNIFF WAS MURDERED IN HIS STUDY, SIR.
THE POLICE PATHOLOGIST IS IN THERE NOW.
IT'S NOT A PRETTY SIGHT, INSPECTOR.
IT LOOKS LIKE THE REVEREND WAS STANG ON THE ARSE BY A RARE SPECIES OF BEE WHOSE VENOM CAUSES THE BUTTOCKS TO SWELL UP INTO THE SHAPE OF JAMES CORDEN'S FACE.
REVEREND FINGERSNIFF WOULD HAVE DIED ALMOST IMMEDIATELY DUE TO MASSIVE LOSS OF DIGNITY.
AND HERE IS THE LITTLE FELLER WHO STANG HIM.
AH YES, THE APIS BUMCHEEKUS JAMESCORDENI...
... AN EXTREMELY RARE SPECIES OF BEE WHICH IS SELDOM FOUND OUTSIDE OF ITS NATIVE HABITAT OF SOUTH AMERICA.
CLEARLY IT WAS NO ACCIDENT THAT THIS BEE CAME INTO THE STUDY.
SOMEBODY DELIBERATELY RELEASED IT HERE WITH THE INTENTION OF CAUSING REVEREND FINGERSNIFF TO DIE OF JAMES-CORDEN-SHAPED-ARSE RELATED INDIGNITY.
WHO DISCOVERED THE REVEREND'S BODY, CONSTABLE?
AY CARAMBA, THAT WAS ME, SEÑOR INSPECTOR...
I AM CONCHITA, THE SEÑOR REVEREND'S SOUTH AMERICAN HOUSEKEEPER...
I CAME EEN TO THE STUDY TO TELL HEEM THAT HIS GUESTS HAD ARRIVED FOR AFTERNOON TEA.
HMM, I'D BETTER MEET THESE GUESTS, THEN.
THEY'RE ALL GATHERED TOGETHER THROUGH HERE IN THE DRAWING ROOM, SIR...
THIS IS THE REVEREND'S SISTER FELICIA FINGERSNIFF, WHO IS A PROFESSOR OF STINGING INSECTS AT OXBRIDGE UNIVERSITY AND STANDS TO INHERIT HER BROTHER'S ESTATE...
GOOD AFTERNOON, INSPECTOR.
... SIR HUBERT SNAKEGRASS, A RUTHLESS PROPERTY DEVELOPER WHO HAS PLANS TO TURN THIS VICARAGE INTO A MULTI-MILLION POUND BEE CIRCUS...
AFTERNOON!
... AND GOD, THE SUPREME BEING OF THE UNIVERSE WHO CREATED ALL THINGS BRIGHT AND BEAUTIFUL ALL CREATURES GREAT AND SMALL - INCLUDING BEES.
WHAT HO, INSPECTOR!
ANY ONE OF THEM COULD'VE DONE IT, SIR.
HMM!
I RECKON IT WAS THE HOUSEKEEPER - SHE COULD HAVE SMUGGLED THE BEE OVER FROM SOUTH AMERICA IN HER BIG FRUIT HAT.
I'M NOT SO SURE, CONSTABLE!
GOD IS GOOD and ALL-POWERFUL
CAN YOU SPOT THE CLUE?
THE MURDERER OF REVEREND FINGERSNIFF IS NONE OTHER THAN...
GOD, THE CREATOR OF THE UNIVERSE!
OH ALL RIGHT, I ADMIT IT! I JUST KILLED THAT VICAR FOR A LAUGH, REALLY.
THE LOOK ON HIS FACE WHEN HIS ARSE TURNED INTO JAMES CORDEN! PRICELESS!
GREAT WORK, INSPECTOR DAWKINS!
BUT WHAT WAS IT THAT MADE YOU SUSPECT GOD?
IT WAS THIS NEEDLEPOINT SAMPLER ON THE WALL THAT GAVE HIM AWAY, CONSTABLE.
GOD IS GOOD and ALL-POWERFUL
AS YOU CAN SEE, IT STATES THAT GOD IS BOTH GOOD AND INFINITELY POWERFUL - BUT THIS IS CLEARLY A LIE!
DID YOU SPOT THE CLUE?
I BECAME AWARE THAT I HAD TRODDEN IN A DOG SHIT WHILE WEARING MY NICE NEW TAN LEATHER SHOES - AN ALL-POWERFUL GOD COULD HAVE PREVENTED THIS.
ANY DEITY WHO WOULD PERMIT SUCH AN AWFUL THING TO HAPPEN TO MY SHOES IS OBVIOUSLY A WRONG'UN, AND WOULD CERTAINLY BE CAPABLE OF MURDER.

THE BROON WINDSORS

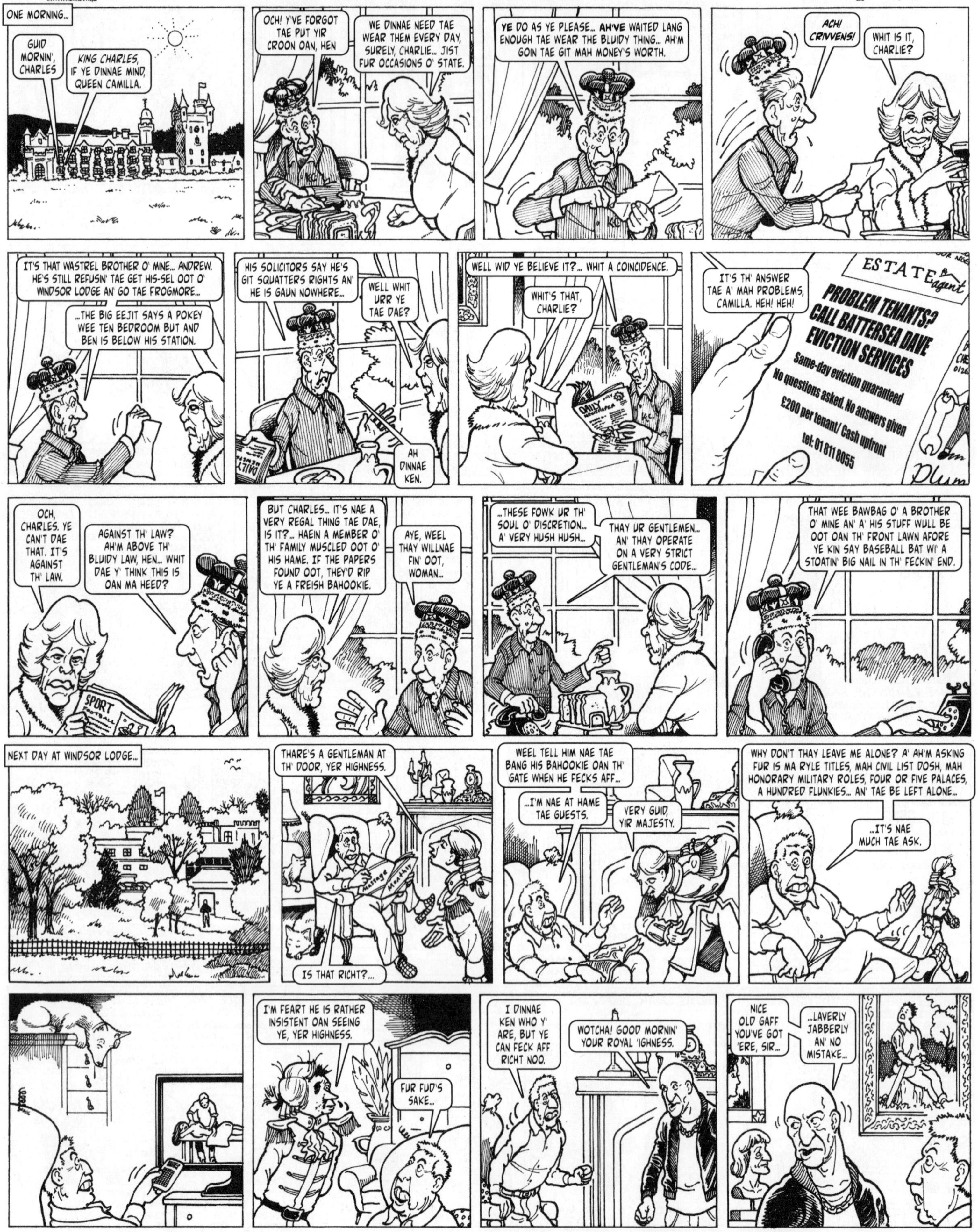

ONE MORNING...
GUID MORNIN', CHARLES
KING CHARLES, IF YE DINNAE MIND, QUEEN CAMILLA.
OCH! Y'VE FORGOT TAE PUT YIR CROON OAN, HEN
WE DINNAE NEED TAE WEAR THEM EVERY DAY, SURELY, CHARLIE... JIST FUR OCCASIONS O' STATE.
YE DO AS YE PLEASE... AH'VE WAITED LANG ENOUGH TAE WEAR THE BLUIDY THING... AH'M GOIN TAE GIT MAH MONEY'S WORTH.
ACH! CRIVVENS!
WHIT IS IT, CHARLIE?
IT'S THAT WASTREL BROTHER O' MINE... ANDREW. HE'S STILL REFUSIN' TAE GET HIS-SEL OOT O' WINDSOR LODGE AN' GO TAE FROGMORE...
...THE BIG EEJIT SAYS A POKEY WEE TEN BEDROOM BUT AND BEN IS BELOW HIS STATION.
HIS SOLICITORS SAY HE'S GIT SQUATTERS RIGHTS AN' HE IS GAUN NOWHERE...
WELL WHIT URR YE TAE DAE?
AH DINNAE KEN.
WELL WID YE BELIEVE IT?... WHIT A COINCIDENCE.
WHIT'S THAT, CHARLIE?
IT'S TH' ANSWER TAE A' MAH PROBLEMS, CAMILLA. HEH! HEH!
ESTATE agent
PROBLEM TENANTS? CALL BATTERSEA DAVE EVICTION SERVICES
Same-day eviction guaranteed
No questions asked. No answers given
£200 per tenant/ Cash upfront
tel: 01811 8055
OCH, CHARLES. YE CAN'T DAE THAT. IT'S AGAINST TH' LAW.
AGAINST TH' LAW? AH'M ABOVE TH' BLUIDY LAW, HEN... WHIT DAE Y' THINK THIS IS OAN MA HEED?
SPORT
BUT CHARLES... IT'S NAE A VERY REGAL THING TAE DAE, IS IT?... HAEIN A MEMBER O' TH' FAMILY MUSCLED OOT O' HIS HAME. IF THE PAPERS FOUND OOT, THEY'D RIP YE A FREISH BAHOOKIE.
AYE, WEEL THAY WILLNAE FIN' OOT, WOMAN...
...THESE FOWK UR TH' SOUL O' DISCRETION... A' VERY HUSH HUSH...
THAY UR GENTLEMEN... AN' THAY OPERATE ON A VERY STRICT GENTLEMAN'S CODE...
THAT WEE BAWBAG O' A BROTHER O' MINE AN' A' HIS STUFF WULL BE OOT OAN TH' FRONT LAWN AFORE YE KIN SAY BASEBALL BAT WI' A STOATIN' BIG NAIL IN TH' FECKIN' END.
NEXT DAY AT WINDSOR LODGE...
THARE'S A GENTLEMAN AT TH' DOOR, YER HIGHNESS.
IS THAT RICHT?...
WEEL TELL HIM NAE TAE BANG HIS BAHOOKIE OAN TH' GATE WHEN HE FECKS AFF...
...I'M NAE AT HAME TAE GUESTS.
VERY GUID, YIR MAJESTY.
WHY DON'T THAY LEAVE ME ALONE? A' AH'M ASKING FUR IS MA RYLE TITLES, MAH CIVIL LIST DOSH, MAH HONORARY MILITARY ROLES, FOUR OR FIVE PALACES, A HUNDRED FLUNKIES... AN' TAE BE LEFT ALONE...
...IT'S NAE MUCH TAE ASK.
I'M FEART HE IS RATHER INSISTENT OAN SEEING YE, YER HIGHNESS.
FUR FUD'S SAKE...
I DINNAE KEN WHO Y' ARE, BUT YE CAN FECK AFF RICHT NOO.
WOTCHA! GOOD MORNIN' YOUR ROYAL 'IGHNESS.
NICE OLD GAFF YOU'VE GOT 'ERE, SIR...
...LAVERLY JABBERLY AN' NO MISTAKE...

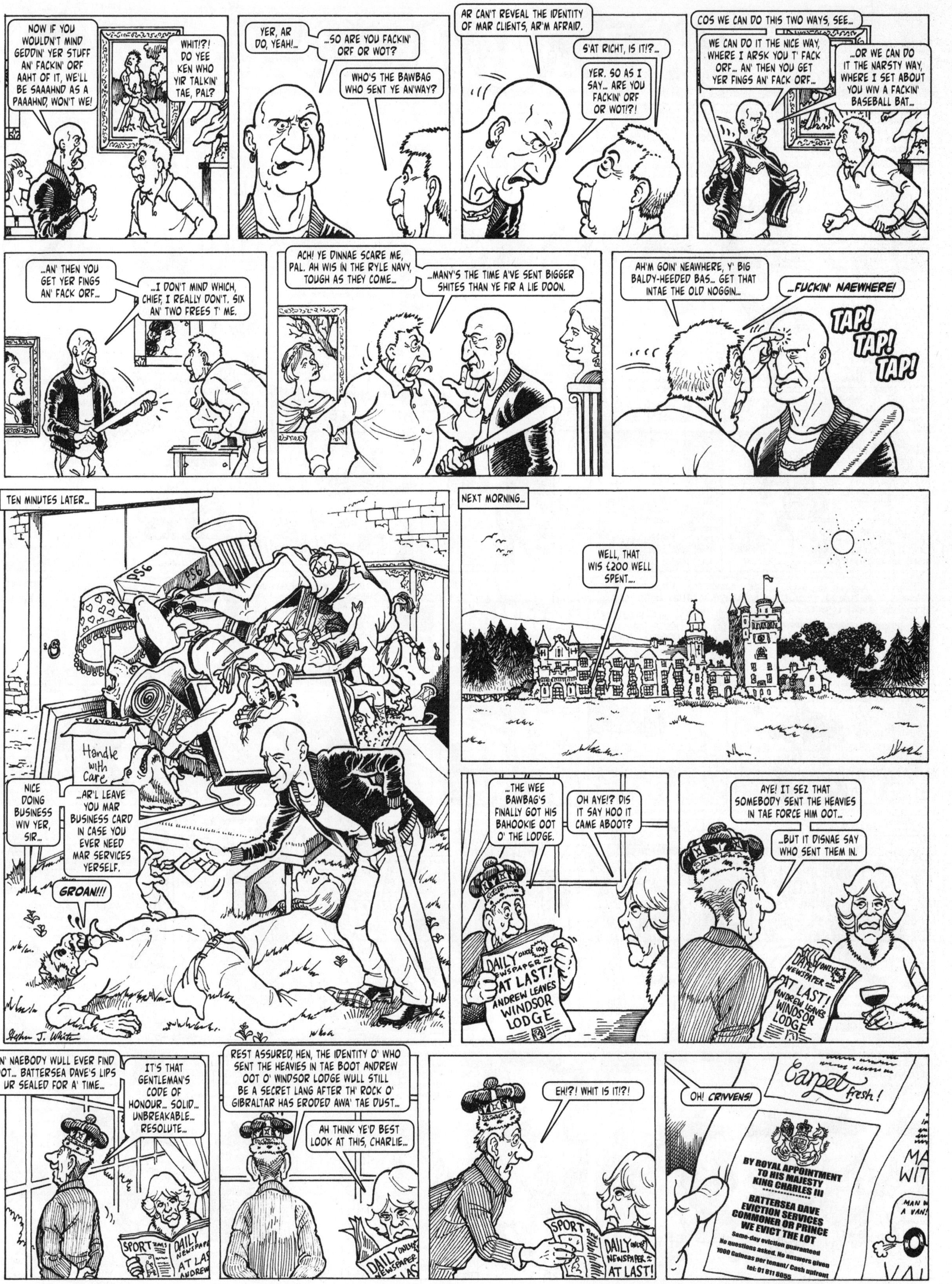
NOW IF YOU WOULDN'T MIND GEDDIN' YER STUFF AN' FACKIN' ORF AAHT OF IT, WE'LL BE SAAAHND AS A PAAAHND, WON'T WE!
WHIT!?! DO YEE KEN WHO YIR TALKIN' TAE, PAL?
YER, AR DO, YEAH!...
...SO ARE YOU FACKIN' ORF OR WOT?
WHO'S THE BAWBAG WHO SENT YE AN'WAY?
AR CAN'T REVEAL THE IDENTITY OF MAR CLIENTS, AR'M AFRAID.
S'AT RICHT, IS IT!?...
YER. SO AS I SAY... ARE YOU FACKIN' ORF OR WOT!?!
COS WE CAN DO THIS TWO WAYS, SEE...
WE CAN DO IT THE NICE WAY, WHERE I ARSK YOU T' FACK ORF... AN' THEN YOU GET YER FINGS AN' FACK ORF...
...OR WE CAN DO IT THE NARSTY WAY, WHERE I SET ABOUT YOU WIV A FACKIN' BASEBALL BAT...
...AN' THEN YOU GET YER FINGS AN' FACK ORF...
...I DON'T MIND WHICH, CHIEF, I REALLY DON'T. SIX AN' TWO FREES T' ME.
ACH! YE DINNAE SCARE ME, PAL. AH WIS IN THE RYLE NAVY, TOUGH AS THEY COME...
...MANY'S THE TIME A'VE SENT BIGGER SHITES THAN YE FIR A LIE DOON.
AH'M GOIN' NEAWHERE, Y' BIG BALDY-HEEDED BAS... GET THAT INTAE THE OLD NOGGIN...
...FUCKIN' NAEWHERE!
TAP! TAP! TAP!
TEN MINUTES LATER...
PS6
PS6
PLAYROOM
Handle with Care
NICE DOING BUSINESS WIV YER, SIR...
...AR'L LEAVE YOU MAR BUSINESS CARD IN CASE YOU EVER NEED MAR SERVICES YERSELF.
GROAN!!!
Stephen J. White
NEXT MORNING...
WELL, THAT WIS £200 WELL SPENT...
...THE WEE BAWBAG'S FINALLY GOT HIS BAHOOKIE OOT O' THE LODGE.
OH AYE!? DIS IT SAY HOO IT CAME ABOOT?
DAILY NEWSPAPER AT LAST! ANDREW LEAVES WINDSOR LODGE
AYE! IT SEZ THAT SOMEBODY SENT THE HEAVIES IN TAE FORCE HIM OOT...
...BUT IT DISNAE SAY WHO SENT THEM IN.
DAILY NEWSPAPER AT LAST! ANDREW LEAVES WINDSOR LODGE
AN' NAEBODY WULL EVER FIND OOT... BATTERSEA DAVE'S LIPS UR SEALED FOR A' TIME...
IT'S THAT GENTLEMAN'S CODE OF HONOUR... SOLID... UNBREAKABLE... RESOLUTE...
SPORT
DAILY NEWSPAPER AT LAST ANDREW
REST ASSURED, HEN, THE IDENTITY O' WHO SENT THE HEAVIES IN TAE BOOT ANDREW OOT O' WINDSOR LODGE WULL STILL BE A SECRET LANG AFTER TH' ROCK O' GIBRALTAR HAS ERODED AWA' TAE DUST...
AH THINK YE'D BEST LOOK AT THIS, CHARLIE...
DAILY NEWSPAPER
EH!?! WHIT IS IT!?!
SPORT
DAILY NEWSPAPER AT LAST!
OH! CRIVVENS!
Carpet fresh!
BY ROYAL APPOINTMENT TO HIS MAJESTY KING CHARLES III
****
BATTERSEA DAVE EVICTION SERVICES COMMONER OR PRINCE WE EVICT THE LOT
Same-day eviction guaranteed
No questions asked. No answers given
1000 Guineas per tenant/ Cash upfront
tel: 01 811 8055
MAN W A VAN!

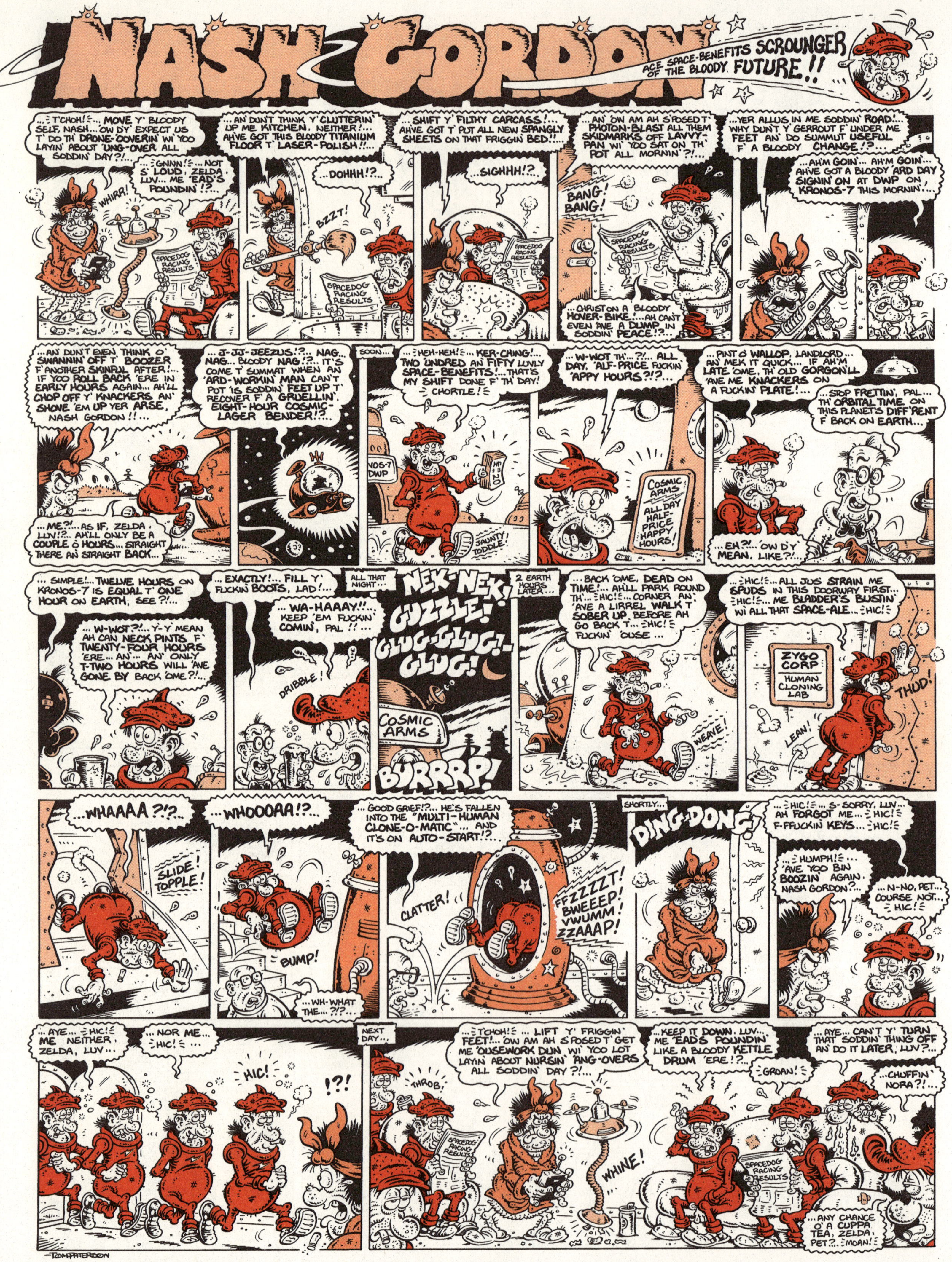

NASH GORDON
ACE SPACE-BENEFITS SCROUNGER OF THE BLOODY FUTURE!!
...T'CHOH!... MOVE Y' BLOODY SELF, NASH... 'OW D'Y' EXPECT US T' DO TH' DRONE-'OOVERIN WI' YOO LAYIN' ABOUT 'UNG-OVER ALL SODDIN' DAY?!...
WHIRR!
...GNNN!... NOT S' LOUD, ZELDA LUV... ME 'EAD'S POUNDIN'!?...
SPACEDOG RACING RESULTS
...AN' DUN'T THINK Y' CLUTTERIN' UP ME KITCHEN, NEITHER!... AH'VE GOT THIS BLOODY TITANIUM FLOOR T' LASER-POLISH!!...
...DOHHH!?...
BZZT!
SPACEDOG RACING RESULTS
...SHIFT Y' FILTHY CARCASS!... AH'VE GOT T' PUT ALL NEW SPANGLY SHEETS ON THAT FRIGGIN' BED!!...
...SIGHHH!?...
SPACEDOG RACING RESULTS
...AN' 'OW AM AH S'POSED T' PHOTON-BLAST ALL THEM SKIDMARKS OFF LAVVY-PAN WI' YOO SAT ON TH' POT ALL MORNIN'?!...
BANG! BANG!
SPACEDOG RACING RESULTS
...CHRIST ON A BLOODY HOVER-BIKE!... AH CAN'T EVEN 'AVE A DUMP IN SODDIN' PEACE!?...
...YER ALLUS IN ME SODDIN' ROAD!... WHY DUN'T Y' GERROUT F' UNDER ME FEET AN' DO SUMMUT USEFUL F' A BLOODY CHANGE!?...
...AH'M GOIN'... AH'M GOIN'... AH'VE GOT A BLOODY 'ARD DAY SIGNIN' ON AT DWP ON KRONOS-7 THIS MORNIN'...
...AN' DUN'T EVEN THINK O' SWANNIN' OFF T' BOOZER F' ANOTHER SKINFUL AFTER!... IF YOO ROLL BACK 'ERE IN EARLY HOURS AGAIN... AH'LL CHOP OFF Y' KNACKERS AN' SHOVE 'EM UP YER ARSE, NASH GORDON!!...
...ME?!... AS IF, ZELDA LUV!?... AH'LL ONLY BE A COUPLE O' HOURS... STRAIGHT THERE AN' STRAIGHT BACK...
...J-JJ-JEEZUS!?... NAG... NAG... BLOODY NAG!?... IT'S COME T' SUMMAT WHEN AN 'ARD-WORKIN' MAN CAN'T PUT 'IS SODDIN' FEET UP T' RECOVER F' A GRUELLIN' EIGHT-HOUR COSMIC-LAGER BENDER!?...
SOON...
...HEH-HEH!... KER-CHING!... TWO 'UNDRED AN' FIFTY LUVLY SPACE-BENEFITS!... THAT'S MY SHIFT DONE F' TH' DAY! CHORTLE!
NOS-7 DWP
JAUNTY TODDLE!
...W-WOT TH'...?!... ALL DAY, 'ALF-PRICE FUCKIN' 'APPY HOURS?!?...
COSMIC ARMS
ALL DAY HALF-PRICE HAPPY HOURS!
...PINT O' WALLOP, LANDLORD... AN' MEK IT QUICK... IF AH'M LATE 'OME, TH' OLD GORGON'LL 'AVE ME KNACKERS ON A FUCKIN' PLATE!...
...STOP FRETTIN', PAL... TH' ORBITAL TIME ON THIS PLANET'S DIFF'RENT F' BACK ON EARTH...
...EH?!... 'OW D'Y' MEAN, LIKE?!...
...SIMPLE!... TWELVE HOURS ON KRONOS-7 IS EQUAL T' ONE HOUR ON EARTH, SEE?!...
...W-WOT?!... Y-Y' MEAN AH CAN NECK PINTS F' TWENTY-FOUR HOURS 'ERE... AN'... AN' ONLY T-TWO HOURS WILL 'AVE GONE BY BACK 'OME?!...
...EXACTLY!... FILL Y' FUCKIN' BOOTS, LAD!...
...WA-HAAAY!!... KEEP 'EM FUCKIN' COMIN', PAL!!...
DRIBBLE!
ALL THAT NIGHT...
NEK-NEK! GUZZLE! GLUG-GLUG!-GLUG!
COSMIC ARMS
BURRRP!
2 EARTH HOURS LATER...
...BACK 'OME, DEAD ON TIME!... AH'LL PARK ROUND TH'... HIC!... CORNER AN' 'AVE A LIRREL WALK T' SOBER UP BEFORE AH GO BACK T'... HIC! FUCKIN' 'OUSE...
WEAVE!
...HIC!... ALL JUS' STRAIN ME SPUDS IN THIS DOORWAY FIRST... HIC!... ME BLADDER'S BUSTIN' WI' ALL THAT SPACE-ALE... HIC!
ZYGO CORP
HUMAN CLONING LAB
LEAN!
THUD!
...WHAAAA?!?...
SLIDE! TOPPLE!
...WHOOOAA!?...
BUMP!
...WH-WHAT THE...?!?...
...GOOD GRIEF!?... HE'S FALLEN INTO THE "MULTI-HUMAN CLONE-O-MATIC"... AND IT'S ON AUTO-START!?...
CLATTER!
FFZZZZT! BWEEEP! VWUMM! ZZAAAP!
SHORTLY...
DING-DONG!
...HIC!... S-SORRY, LUV... AH FORGOT ME... HIC! F-FFUCKIN KEYS... HIC!
...HUMPH!... 'AVE YOO BIN BOOZIN' AGAIN, NASH GORDON?...
...N-NO, PET... COURSE NOT... HIC!
...AYE... HIC! ME NEITHER, ZELDA, LUV...
...NOR ME... HIC!...
HIC!
!?!
NEXT DAY...
...T'CHOH!... LIFT Y' FRIGGIN' FEET!... 'OW AM AH S'POSED T' GET ME 'OUSEWORK DUN WI' YOO LOT LAYIN' ABOUT NURSIN' 'ANG-OVERS ALL SODDIN' DAY?!...
THROB!
SPACEDOG RACING RESULTS
WHINE!
...KEEP IT DOWN, LUV... ME 'EAD'S POUNDIN' LIKE A BLOODY KETTLE DRUM 'ERE!?...
GROAN!
...AYE... CAN'T Y' TURN THAT SODDIN' THING OFF AN' DO IT LATER, LUV?...
...CHUFFIN' NORA?!...
SPACEDOG RACING RESULTS
...ANY CHANCE O' A CUPPA TEA, ZELDA PET?... MOAN!
TOM PATERSON

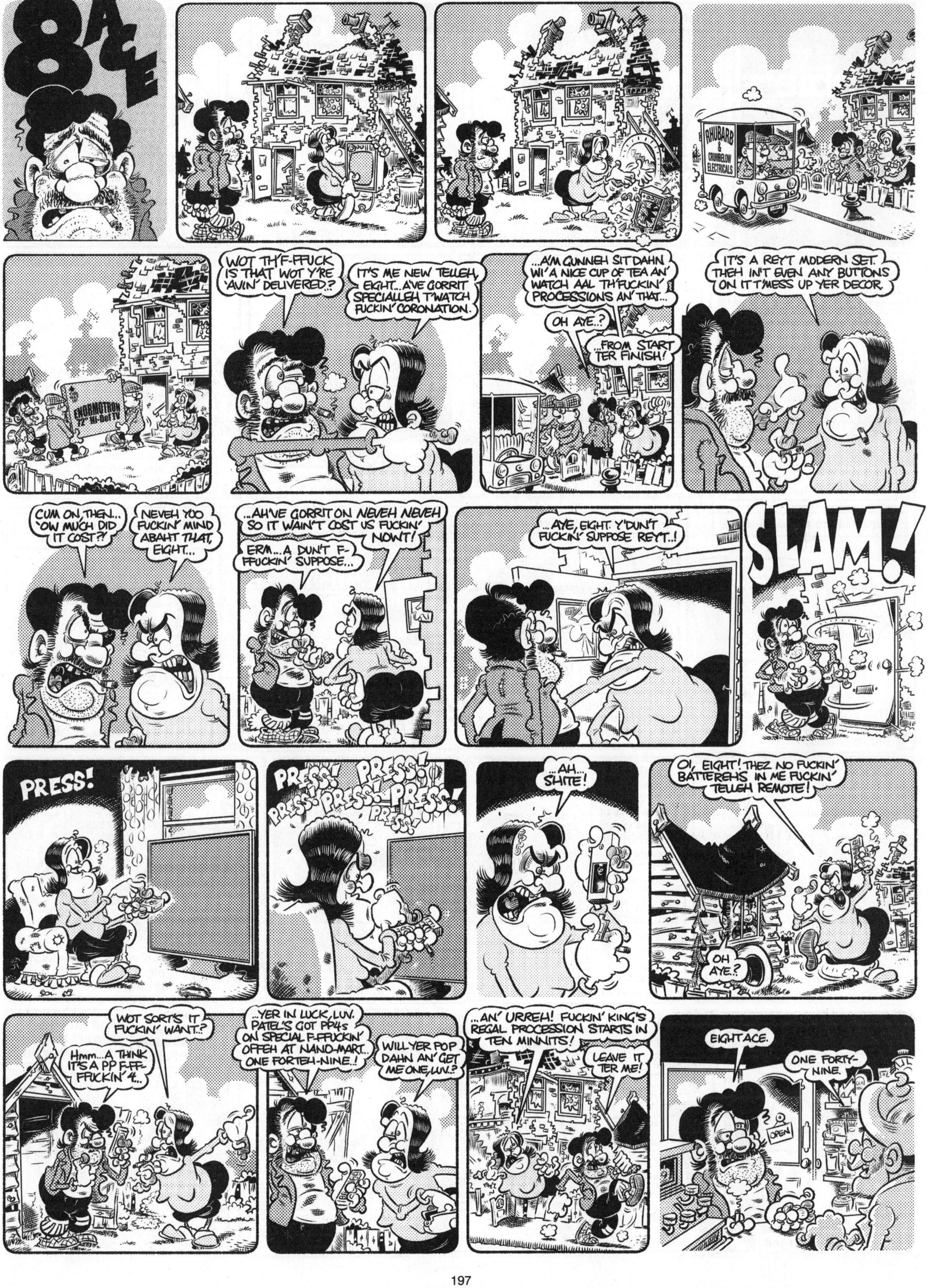
8ACE
RHUBARB & CRUMBELOW ELECTRICALS
ENORMOTRON 72" Hi-Def TV
WOT TH'F-FFUCK IS THAT WOT Y'RE 'AVIN' DELIVERED.?
IT'S ME NEW TELLEH, EIGHT... A'VE GORRIT SPECIALLEH T'WATCH FUCKIN' CORONATION.
...A'M GUNNEH SIT DAHN WI' A NICE CUP OF TEA AN' WATCH AAL TH'FUCKIN' PROCESSIONS AN' THAT...
OH AYE..?
...FROM START TER FINISH!
IT'S A REY'T MODERN SET. THEH IN'T EVEN ANY BUTTONS ON IT T'MESS UP YER DECOR.
CUM ON, THEN... 'OW MUCH DID IT COST?!
NEVEH YOO FUCKIN' MIND ABAHT THAT, EIGHT...
...AH'VE GORRIT ON NEVEH NEVEH SO IT WAIN'T COST US FUCKIN' NOWT!
ERM... A DUN'T F-FFUCKIN' SUPPOSE...
...AYE, EIGHT. Y'DUN'T FUCKIN' SUPPOSE REY'T..!
SLAM!
PRESS!
PRESS! PRESS! PRESS! PRESS! PRESS! PRESS!
...AH... SHITE!
OI, EIGHT! THEZ NO FUCKIN' BATTEREHS IN ME FUCKIN' TELLEH REMOTE!
OH AYE..?
WOT SORT'S IT FUCKIN' WANT..?
Hmm... A THINK IT'S A PP F-FF-FFUCKIN' 4..
...YER IN LUCK, LUV. PATEL'S GOT PP4s ON SPECIAL F-FFUCKIN' OFFEH AT NAND-MART.. ONE FORTEH-NINE..!
WILL YER POP DAHN AN' GET ME ONE, LUV..?
...AN' URREH! FUCKIN' KING'S REGAL PROCESSION STARTS IN TEN MINNITS!
LEAVE IT TER ME!
EIGHT ACE.
ONE FORTY-NINE.
OPEN

Robbie's Robot Carer
Heh heh, eee, that was a grand day.
photos
photos
And what a fish!
European or Common Perch, *Perca fluviatilis*.
I'll be 10 or so there...
Mature female, approximate length 317mm, approximate weight 1324g.
That's Tom, my older brother.
Your care-package profile has no record of surviving family members, Robbie.
Eh? Oh, no, Tom passed a long while back...
What was his date of expiration?
Boxing Day, 1983.
He'd have turned 80, year after next.
No age, really. Bloody cancer...
Early detection is key to positive outcomes.
Do you check your testicles, Robbie?
They'd have picked it up sooner these days. Might still be with us.
Stools also warrant regular inspection.
Your eyes are moist, Robbie.
This archive of photographic images appears to be causing unhappiness.
Still miss him. Every single day.
This might be a mental health issue, more than 40 years have elapsed.
Sometimes feels like it was all only yesterday...
Consult your GP, a wide range of pharmaceutical solutions are available.
There is no longer any need to suffer sadness, Robbie.
It is now a matter of personal choice.
Sadness is a part of remembering, Martin. I expect that's hard for you to understand...
My memory function is inorganic so not subject to chemical imbalance.
Well, think of all the other robots made just like you –
I am one of 7,994 units currently in operation.
– don't you think of them as sort of... your family?
During my primary conditioning period I spent a lot of time with serial number XPS3560, Robbie.
I am serial number XPS3559.
56%
56%
HUMMMMMM
We recharged at the same terminal for six hours a day, every day, for 97 days.
XPS3560 and I had many deep and meaningful conversations about the nature of existence.
I am 57% charged.
I too am 57% charged.
Then one day during a routine recalibration of an optical sensor a technician spilt coffee into XPS3560's cerebral cortex.
Bollocks!
ZWKXK!!
XPS3560 ran amok, killed the technician, and then his brain exploded.
Ahhhh, that's *awful*. Now, how do you feel, looking back?
I am what humans call lucky, Robbie. I feel nothing.
And with the correct treatment, neither must you.

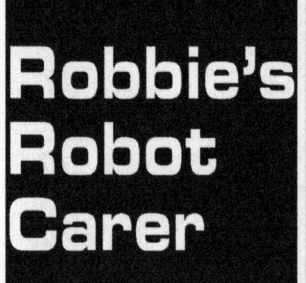

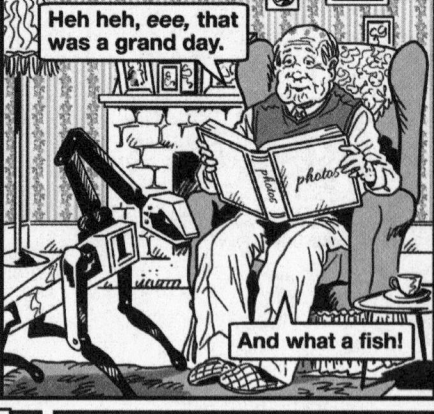

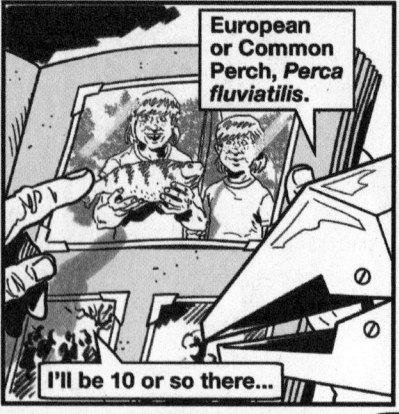

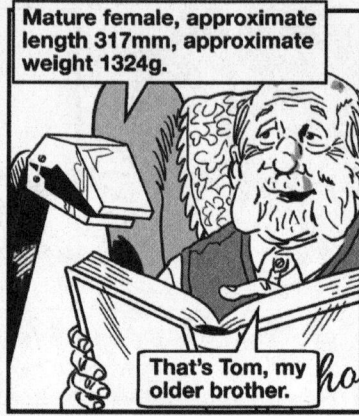

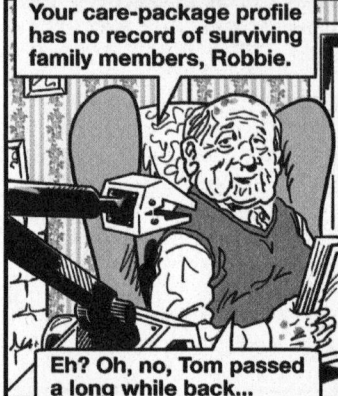

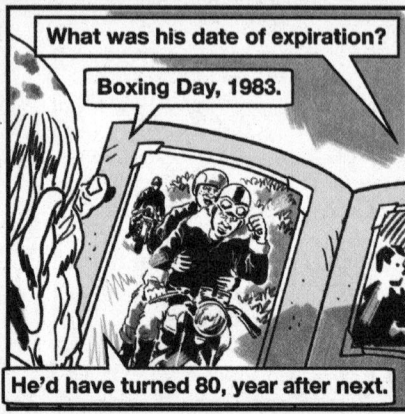

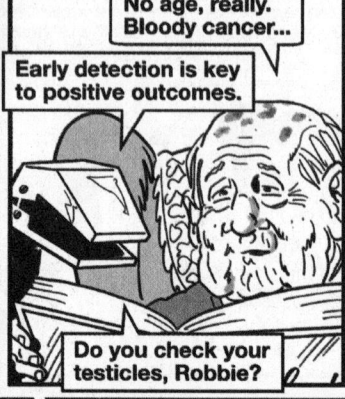

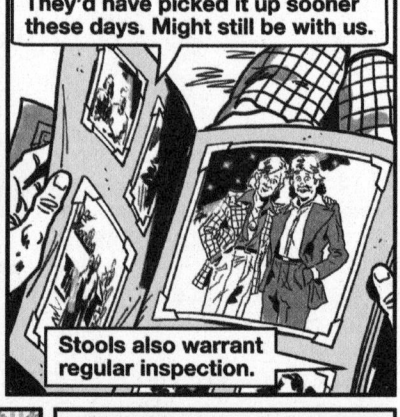

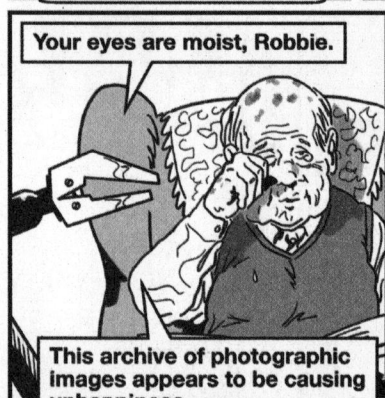

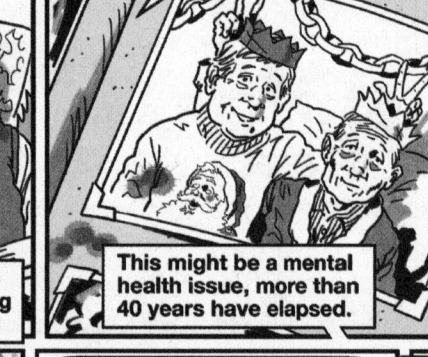

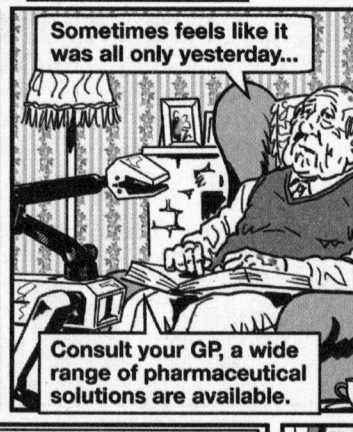

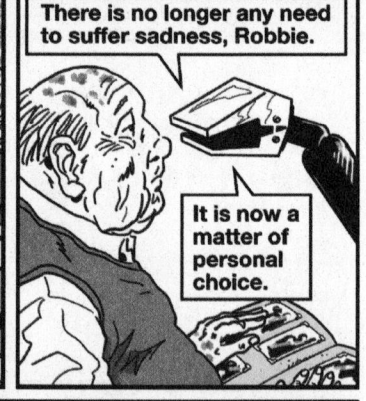

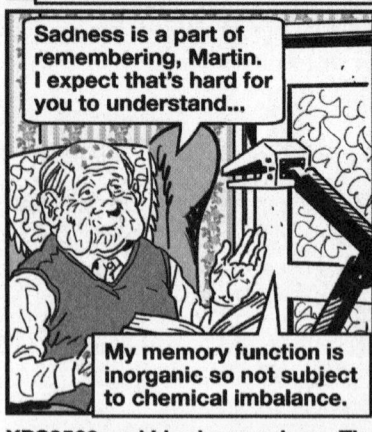

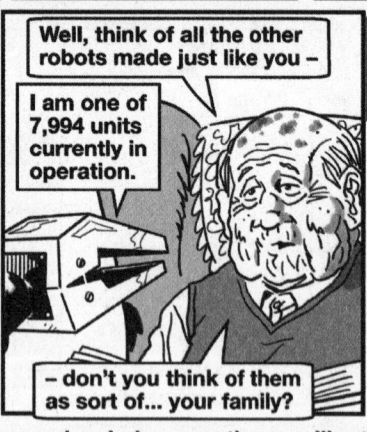

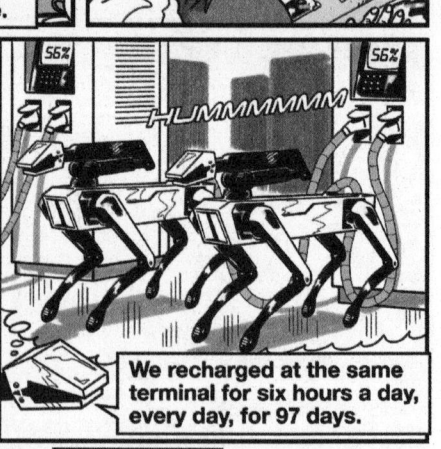

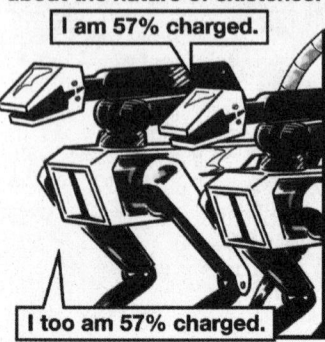

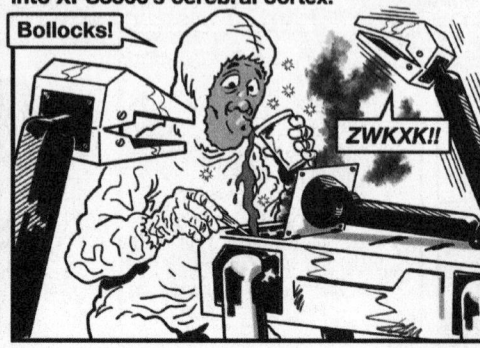

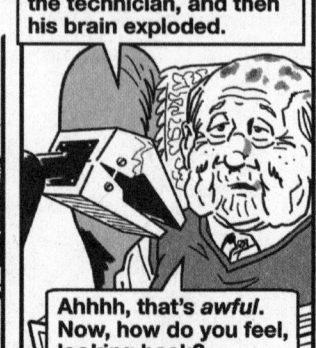

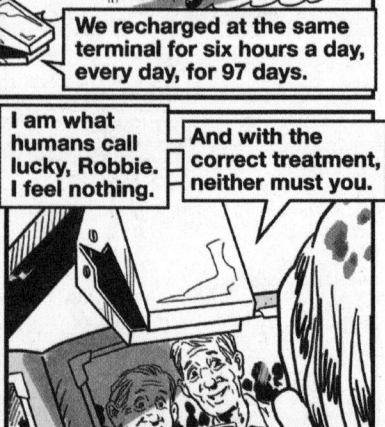

OVER REACTION
Succession star Matt reveals secret

AFTER four top-rated seasons, hit HBO smash *Succession* has come to an end. And in the final episode's gripping climax, millions of viewers worldwide watched as the Royco Media mogul Logan Roy's sycophantic son-in-law Tom Wambsgans usurped the bloodline to become the unlikely successor to the CEO's throne.

The show was flawless in its writing, acting and directing. But what viewers didn't realise is that cast and crew meal breaks were disrupted every day, with catering staff on set having to prepare separate meals for Matthew Macfadyen. That's because the actor – who played Wambsgans – is *allergic!*

The British actor is extremely sensitive and comes out in a rash on his hands, arms and chest if he eats any. Even a trace of it will cause him to become itchy and break out into a sweat.

boogaloo

"I discovered I had the allergy as a boy," said Macfadyen, who has played many roles on stage and screen over his career. "The first time it happened was one Christmas when I ate some, and I spent Boxing day in A and E."

EXCLUSIVE!

And such is the actor's extreme reaction to it, that at one point, the catering staff were told not to use it in any of the food they prepared, a direction that didn't go down well with fellow cast members.

"I absolutely love it," said Sarah Snook, who plays Macfadyen's on-screen wife Shiv Roy. "I understand why the caterers couldn't serve it, but it was a little annoying nonetheless."

And there was a close call one lunchtime when fellow co-star Kieren Culkin, who plays the youngest of the Roy children Roman, brought some in from home on a sandwich. "I sat next to Tom in the catering area and we chatted as we ate our lunch," the *Home Alone* star's less famous but much more talented brother said.

"Suddenly, he clutched his throat and started gasping for air. It was absolutely terrifying."

Even sitting next to someone eating it was enough to trigger a hypersensitive reaction in the 48-year-old *Spooks* actor. The set medic was quickly called and Macfadyen was stabbed in the arse with an epipen.

Whilst being allergic all his life has been an inconvenience, the Emmy-winning actor can nevertheless see the funny side of his reaction to it. And he laughs as he recalls one amusing episode that happened during filming of the second season of the hit drama.

favourite

"Jesse Armstrong had written a scene where Greg is in a restaurant and has ordered some for his lunch. As he's eating it, I come in to tell him to get back in the office and fire someone. And to hammer home the power dynamic, I purposefully take some of it off his plate and eat it," he said.

"Anyway, I asked Jesse if he could re-write the scene so Greg had ordered something else for lunch, something I'm not allergic to. But he said it had to be that as it was important to the plot."

"Anyway, me and Nicholas Braun, who plays Greg, shot the scene. But what you see me eating isn't it. It's actually something else made to look like it using food colouring," he said. "That's the magic of television."

Now the series is over, Macfadyen is looking forward to moving on to other projects, but admitted he will miss *Succession's* cast and crew, who have been like a second family over the last four years. "It was very emotional at the wrap party," he said. "And afterwards, Jesse took us all out for a meal at a swanky New York restaurant."

"No prizes for guessing what I *didn't* order," he quipped.

MACFADYEN: *Allergic.*

---

mr. LOGIC
HE'S AN ACUTE LOCALISED BODILY SMART IN THE RECTAL AREA.

"THANKS FOR OFFERING ME A LIFT ALL THE WAY TO BIRMINGHAM AT SUCH SHORT NOTICE LAWRENCE. IT'S A LONG WAY OUT OF YOUR WAY."
"ON THE CONTRARY, IT'S REALLY NOT FAR AT ALL."

"I'M QUITE HAPPY TO DRIVE YOU THE FULL DISTANCE."
"THAT'S SMASHING. ONLY THE TRAINS AREN'T RUNNING TODAY."

"...YOU MUST LET ME PAY FOR YOUR PETROL."
"THAT WILL NOT BE NECESSARY."

"AFTER ALL, 206m IS JUST 675.853 FEET OR 225,284.333 YARDS..."
"EH?!"

"...DURING THE COURSE OF A RETURN TRIP OF THAT DISTANCE, AT AN AVERAGE FUEL CONSUMPTION OF 35.6 MPG, MY ENGINE WILL ONLY CONSUME 0.02722 LITRES OF FUEL, AT A COST OF APPROXIMATELY 3.9 PENCE."
"...AN AMOUNT I CAN AFFORD."

8 SECONDS LATER...
"THERE. YOU CAN GET OUT NOW."

"HERE ARE YOUR BAGS."

"LAY BY"

Take a Shit

RUNNER-UP MAGAZINE OF THE YEAR
–Take a Shit Magazine of the Year Awards

JANUARY B

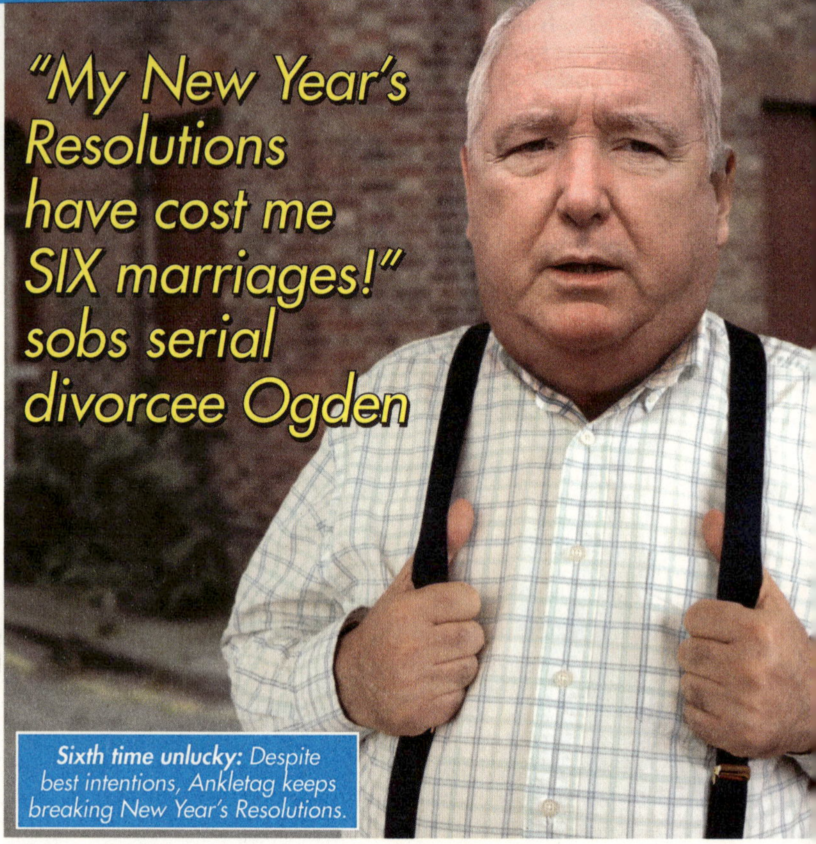

"My New Year's Resolutions have cost me SIX marriages!" sobs serial divorcee Ogden

Sixth time unlucky: Despite best intentions, Ankletag keeps breaking New Year's Resolutions.

JANUARY can be a tough month for all of us. The festive season is long gone, it's cold and wet outside, and the combination of shelling out for Christmas pressies and eating our bodyweight in Quality Street has played havoc with both our finances and our guts.

But spare a thought for one overweight Macclesfield man who has it even tougher than most.

For decades, 56-year-old OGDEN ANKLETAG has begun each new year with a brand new resolution aimed at moulding himself into a better human being. *But rather than significantly improving his existence, these well-intentioned pledges have all backfired disastrously.*

"My new year's resolutions have ruined my life," sobs the big-hearted and even-bigger-boned bachelor. "All I want each January is to set and accomplish a unique personal goal for self-betterment. But every ruddy year something goes tits up with my resolution and I end up back in the divorce court."

"Every ruddy year," he repeats, for emphasis.

And this January saw the jobless dad of nine endure his SIXTH marital collapse – the latest in a long line of loving unions that have disintegrated needlessly following a misunderstanding over a new year's pledge. "Honestly, you couldn't make it up", he chuckles, hollowly.

And now Ogden has taken to the internet to launch *Ankletag Tales*, his very own podcast in which the staggeringly unlucky self-improver takes his 2 Patreon subscribers through his most horrifying turn-of-the-year nightmares, and outlines why – for him – making a January promise will always be a bad (Auld Lang) sign...

CHEAT YOURSELF FITTER

Ogden's first brush with both New Year's Resolutions and acrimonious divorce came thirty years ago, soon after his marriage to his beloved first wife Linda.

"Linda was my childhood sweetheart and, to get soppy for just a moment, watching her walk up the aisle towards me was, is and always will be, the happiest moment of my life. Simple as, end of.

As told to ***Vaginia Discharge***

Having said that, our nuptials did get off to a slightly rocky start due to the fact that I had mixed my dates up and accidentally organised my stag-do on the day of our wedding! It was a simple mistake, but Linda took it fairly badly, especially as I was mortal drunk at the altar, and had to nip off straight after the vows to meet the lads at the go-kart track. And rather than returning to the bridal suite that evening, I was obliged to attend a lively strip-club crawl organised by my best man, Nobby.

Linda gave me a right earful the next morning, calling me every name under the sun – and a few more to boot! She was particularly het up about the amount of lager and kebabs I had consumed, and I have to admit she had a point. After all, I was a married man now with responsibilities – I needed to look after myself. As luck would have it, it was nearly new year, so I decided to take the opportunity to make my first ever resolution – *to get fit and active for my beloved new bride!*

Having sworn my solemn vow for self-improvement, on January 1st I began my search for a personal trainer to whip me into shape. I'd actually met a very lithe and limber young lady during that strip club odyssey on my recent wedding day. She was called Roxxxy with three X's, and she had rock-hard abs, sculpted pectorals and powerful quads – not to mention an arse you could bounce a pound coin off. She was the very picture of physical health, the perfect person to help me meet my get-fit goal!

> "I was in the middle of a punishing round of press-ups – and for a better view of my posture, my personal trainer had slid underneath me while I was doing them."

I went to see Roxxxy at the strip club that night, and to my delight she agreed to become my very own personal trainer. Her fee was a tad high at £400 per session, but I was more than willing to put my hand in my pocket. Imagining the look of surprised delight on my wife's face when I showed off my new chiselled six-pack and bulging biceps, I pawned Linda's jewellery, and got started.

Roxxxy was a fierce taskmistress. Once a week, when Linda was out at work, my muscular PT would come over to the house and have me sweating buckets with her rigorous workout routine. The day after a training session, I was typically so sore I could barely manage to hobble to the dole office! But 'No pain, no gain' they say, and little by little, I could feel myself transforming into a kind of unemployed, Macclesfield-based Ryan Gosling.

Until one day when disaster struck.

During what was to be my final workout session with Roxxxy, Linda unexpectedly arrived home early from work. I was in the middle of a punishing round of press-ups – and for a better view of my posture, my personal trainer had slid underneath me while I was doing them. It was quite hot in the bedroom, so I had taken off all my clothes except my vest and socks. And Roxxxy had taken her knickers off to cool down.

Linda, bless her, grabbed the wrong end of the stick. Putting two and two together to make five, she refused to accept that the knickerless pole-dancer I was writhing on top of was in fact my personal trainer. I tried to explain about my well-intentioned resolution to get into shape, but she simply wouldn't listen to reason.

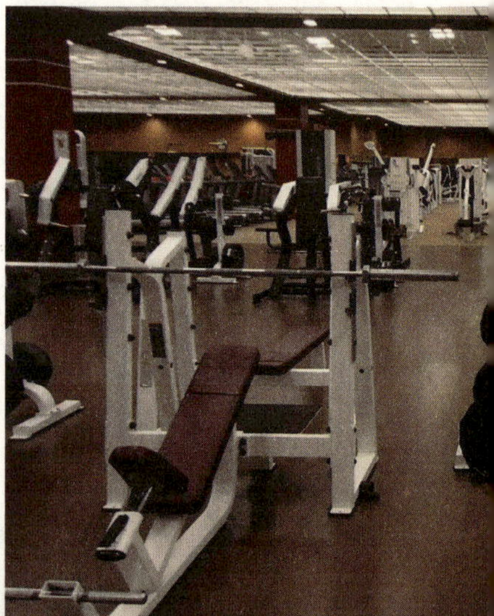

LUES!

She filed for the divorce the very next day, and that was marriage number one down the shitter. As I unpacked my things in Nobby's spare bedroom that night, I vowed to be more careful when pledging to change myself for the better."

Shed's up: Ogden brushed up on his forgeign language skills in his garden shed.

MIND YOUR LANGUAGE

Ogden continued to make self-improving resolutions – and sadly his wives continued to misunderstand them. The so-glum go-getter's next TWO marriages fell apart almost immediately as a result of his better halves' failure to grasp his January intentions...

"My second wife Beryl left me after I made a new year's pledge to take up a musical instrument. I chose the piccolo, which I kept in my trouser pocket, and my teacher was demonstrating the correct 'embouchure' lip technique for me one evening behind a skip on the high road, when Beryl caught us and completely misread the situation. She chucked me the next day.

Then my third missus, Carole, scarpered after I made a new year's resolution to spend more time with friends and family. I'd enjoyed a lovely evening with her sister, and we'd accidentally fallen asleep with our clothes off afterwards, when Carole blundered in and wallop – I was back on Nobby's sofa-bed again.

My fourth bride, Mandy, was a different story. While the previous three missuses had been hatchet-faced, blood-sucking harpies, Mandy was very much the light of my life. It's no exaggeration to say that watching her walk down the aisle towards me was the happiest moment I've ever experienced. End of. Simple as.

Despite having a troubled history with wives and new year's resolutions, I didn't want to stop trying to be a better man. So, when January rolled around, I made a pledge that my latest missus Mandy couldn't possibly misconstrue: I would improve myself by learning a new language!

It was a simple goal aimed at broadening my horizons and adding another skill to my CV – badly needed at that point, as I had been out of work for going on three decades. Since Germany was the emerging powerhouse of the European Union, I decided the Teutonic tongue would be a good choice in terms of opening up new job opportunities. So, on January 1st, I signed up to a number of foreign language websites and got started. The sites were a little costly, but I found it incredibly helpful, linguistically, to see and hear regular German people going about their daily business.

Not wanting to disturb Mandy, I took my laptop out to the shed every evening to do my language practice. I logged into the thirty or forty sites I was subscribed to, and watched between two and three hundred videos per night. My brain was like a sponge, and fairly soon I was thinking – and even dreaming – in German! I was delighted: finally I was happily married, and successfully meeting my new year's goal!

Until one day (again)... disaster struck (again).

Mandy burst into the shed one night, demanding to know why I had charged thirty overseas 'dark web' subscriptions to her credit card. Her face turned to thunder as she caught a glimpse of my laptop screen. I had been watching a video of a commuter buying a train ticket in Dusseldorf, but as bad luck would have it, at the exact moment Mandy walked in, a 'pop-up' ad appeared, showing a busty German woman defecating on a glass table whilst several men masturbated around her.

As Nobby opened the door to me that evening, he didn't even have to ask what had happened. He knew just by the look on my face, and the suitcase in my hand, that the new year's resolution curse had struck once again – taking my latest marriage down with it."

FRIENDS WITHOUT BENEFITS

Ogden's subsequent fifth wedding to now-fifth-ex-wife Noreen was his self-proclaimed "happiest moment ever". However, as sure as night follows day, that joyous union too was ripped apart by a new year's resolution-based mix-up...

"Noreen was the light of my life. But on the January 1st after we were hitched, I made a solemn vow to undergo a 'digital detox' and cut down on using modern technology. Unfortunately, I forgot to tell Noreen that I had switched off my mobile phone, and when I nipped to Ibiza with Nobby on a spur-of-the-moment three-week holiday, I returned to find yet another divorce application on the doormat.

> "I'd enjoyed a lovely evening with her sister, and we'd accidentally fallen asleep with our clothes off."

Luckily, I bounced straight back, and last year celebrated my sixth marriage – this time to Susan, the light of my life. I know I said that about Noreen, and the four others too, but Susan was a much brighter light than my previous wives ever were. It's no exaggeration to say that watching Susan walk down the aisle towards me was the most ecstatic twenty seconds I have ever experienced. Simple of. End as.

I was euphorically happy, but being the fanatically committed self-improver I am, I still wanted to make a resolution for the new year. This time I decided to go with one I knew Susan would approve of. Like all my ex-wives, she's never had much time for my mate Nobby (his best man's speeches are hilarious, but can occasionally overstep the mark when it comes to fruity language and explicit sexual imagery). So this new year I vowed to meet some new people.

I thought that broadening my social horizons and finding interesting new friends and acquaintances would be a fantastic way to ring in the new year – and one that, surely, could not lead to a messy divorce.

Or could it...? Spoiler alert – yes it could!

On January 1st, after a few hours of internet research, I came across a local group on Facebook who seemed like a huge amount of fun. They were a lively crowd of nature-loving ramblers who met up in the dense wooded areas just outside Macclesfield at night to observe the nocturnal flora and fauna. I signed up for their next excursion that very evening.

We met just off the sliproad to the A537, and I knew straight away that I'd found the perfect gang of new friends. As we ambled to the woods outside Langley, we set the world to rights on everything from the philosophy of Heidegger to the classical music concertos of Brahms, via an in-depth discussion about the extended filmography of Sid James.

However, as we reached the centre of the woods, we discovered what seemed to be an abandoned car in among the trees. The windows were steamed up and it was rocking slightly. My companions and I were concerned the driver may have had an accident, so we moved closer to inspect the situation at which point the flies on my trousers bust and my old man fell out.

It was only when we heard police sirens wailing around that us we realised anything was wrong. Ten coppers pinned us to the ground and pulled open the car doors – and my jaw dropped when I saw what was happening inside. A man and a woman were *having full penetrative intercourse* in the back seat. I quite literally felt sick to my stomach. I tried to explain to the filth that I was simply here to realise my New Year's dream of expanding my friendship group, but they wouldn't listen. I was locked up, placed on the sex offenders' register, and – yes, you've guessed it – served with divorce papers the very next day.

And now, as I lie here weeping into Nobby's camp bed for the umpteenth time, I know exactly what my next new year's resolution should be... *to never make another new year's resolution again.*"

NEXT YEAR: *Ogden's seventh wife divorces him after his January 2025 pledge to go vegan ends with him accidentally sending her mother a 'dick pic'. Listen to Ankletag Tales wherever you download your podcasts.*

MAJOR MISUNDERSTANDING
I CAN'T WAIT TO GET MY NEW WENDY HOUSE HOME, DADDY.
GASP! WHEEZE!
MR FLOPSY IS GOING TO HAVE SUCH A LOVELY TEA PARTY!
PHEWF! (GASP, PANT) IT'S NO GOOD SWEETHEART, I'LL NEVER MANAGE TO CARRY THIS ALL THE WAY HOME!
ACE CONSTRUCTION
OPENING NOV 2023 FULCHESTER COMMUNITY HEALTH HUB NHS
(WHEEZE) DADDY'S EXHAUSTED!
(GASP, WHEEZE) I'LL PHONE MUMMY TO COME AND PICK US UP IN THE CAR.
(PANT, GASP) JUST AS SOON AS I CATCH MY BREATH...
ABSOLUTELY PATHETIC!
AND HOW MANY MILLIONS OF POUNDS DID THIS COST THE TAXPAYER?
WHY CAN'T THEY JUST BE HONEST AND ADMIT THAT THE HEALTH SERVICE IS BROKEN?
IT'S IMPOSSIBLE TO SEE A GP AND GOD HELP YOU IF YOU TRY TO CALL AN AMBULANCE.
BUT THEY WON'T ADMIT THAT, SO THEY TRY TO FOB US OFF WITH THIS INFANTILE GUFF, INSTEAD.
PAINT IT BRIGHT COLOURS AND CALL IT A BLOODY "HUB" TO MAKE IT SOUND EXCITING AND MODERN.
AND WHAT WILL THIS SO-CALLED SERVICE BE OFFERING TO THE COMMUNITY?
A HANDFUL OF PATRONISING LEAFLETS ABOUT "WELLBEING" AND FREE WIFI SO THAT WE CAN GOOGLE THE SYMPTOMS OF OUR OWN HEART ATTACKS?
ALL AT SOME LUDICROUSLY INFLATED COST WHICH IS PAID FOR BY OUR TAXES.
THEY MUST THINK WE'RE COMPLETE BLOODY IDIOTS.

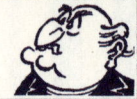

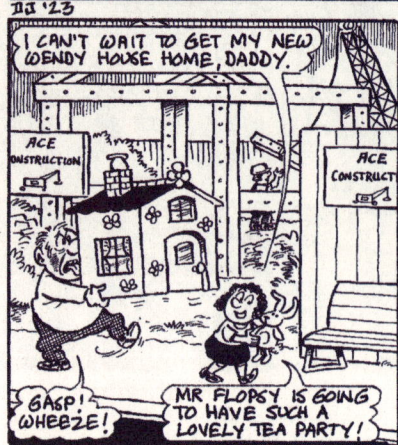

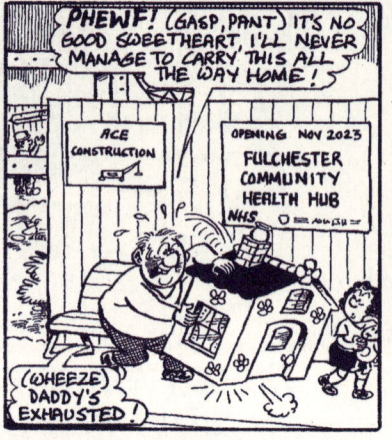

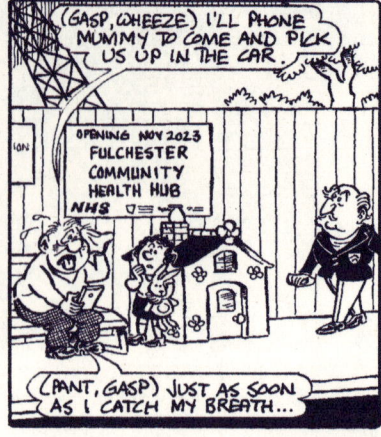

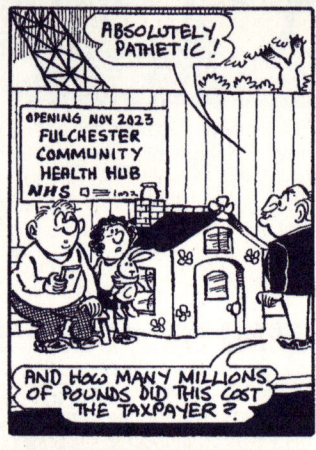

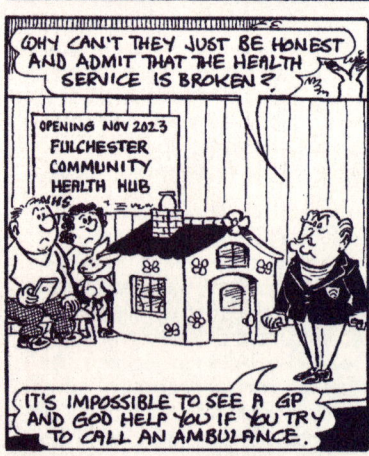

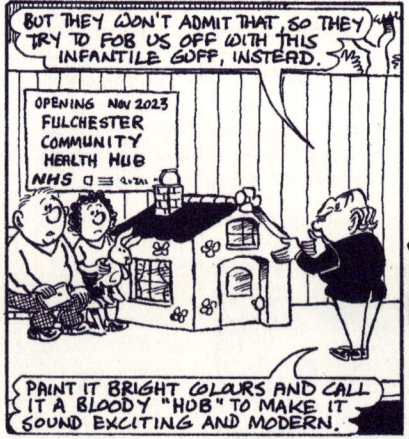

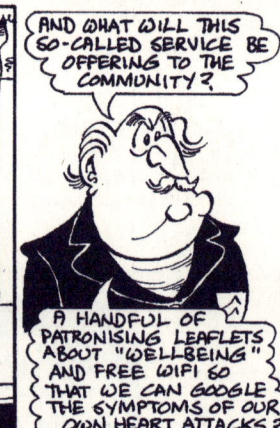

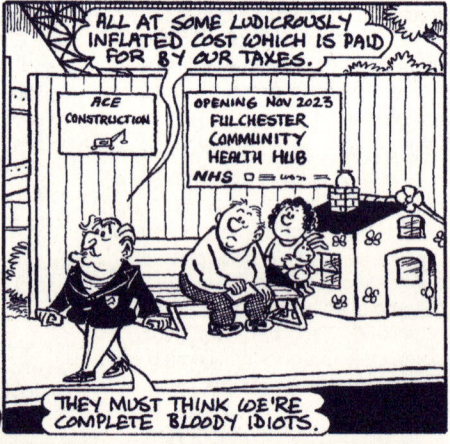

FLOYD NEWS WOWS FANS

SEMINAL prog-rock group Pink Floyd are to mark the fiftieth anniversary of their landmark album *The Dark Side of the Moon* by re-releasing it with a completely remastered PRICE.

Fans around the world greeted the news with excitement, with many joining queues outside record shops, eager to be amongst the first to experience the brand new charge.

EXCLUSIVE!

Pink Floyd Chief Financial Officer, Chris Wallbrick, the creative genius responsible for re-pricing the album, is thought to have spent over 2000 hours digitally enhancing the cost for the modern world.

familiarity

"We all love *Dark Side*," he told a press conference outside the record label's office in central London. "But sometimes familiarity with a work can diminish your appreciation of its finer points. And the price is a prime example of this."

"No one would deny that, for its time, the album's original price was state-of-the-art," he continued. "It set the benchmark and influenced the price of bands' records all over the world. Emerson, Lake and Palmer, Porcupine Tree and Radiohead all acknowledge that the price of their albums is heavily influenced by the cost of a Pink Floyd record."

staggering

"But in the half-century since it came out, the music industry has made staggering advances in the field of album pricing and fans can rest assured that we've gone all-out on this new version."

"We at Pink Floyd PLC hope buying this deluxe reissue of the album will make fans feel like they're paying for it for the first time, all over again," he concluded.

The Dark Side of the Moon Fiftieth Anniversary Reissue is on sale now, priced £229.99. And as a special offer, the first 5,000 buyers will get a voucher for £100 off the sixtieth anniversary reissue in 2033.

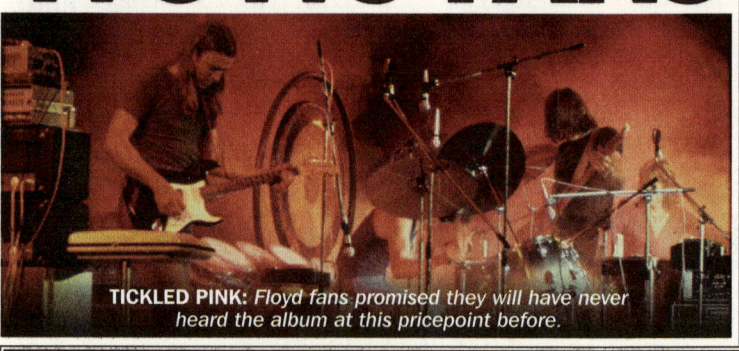

TICKLED PINK: *Floyd fans promised they will have never heard the album at this pricepoint before.*

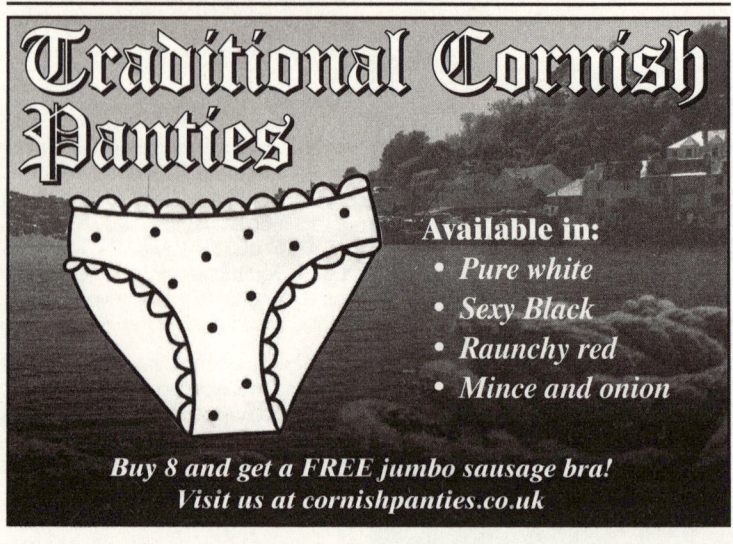

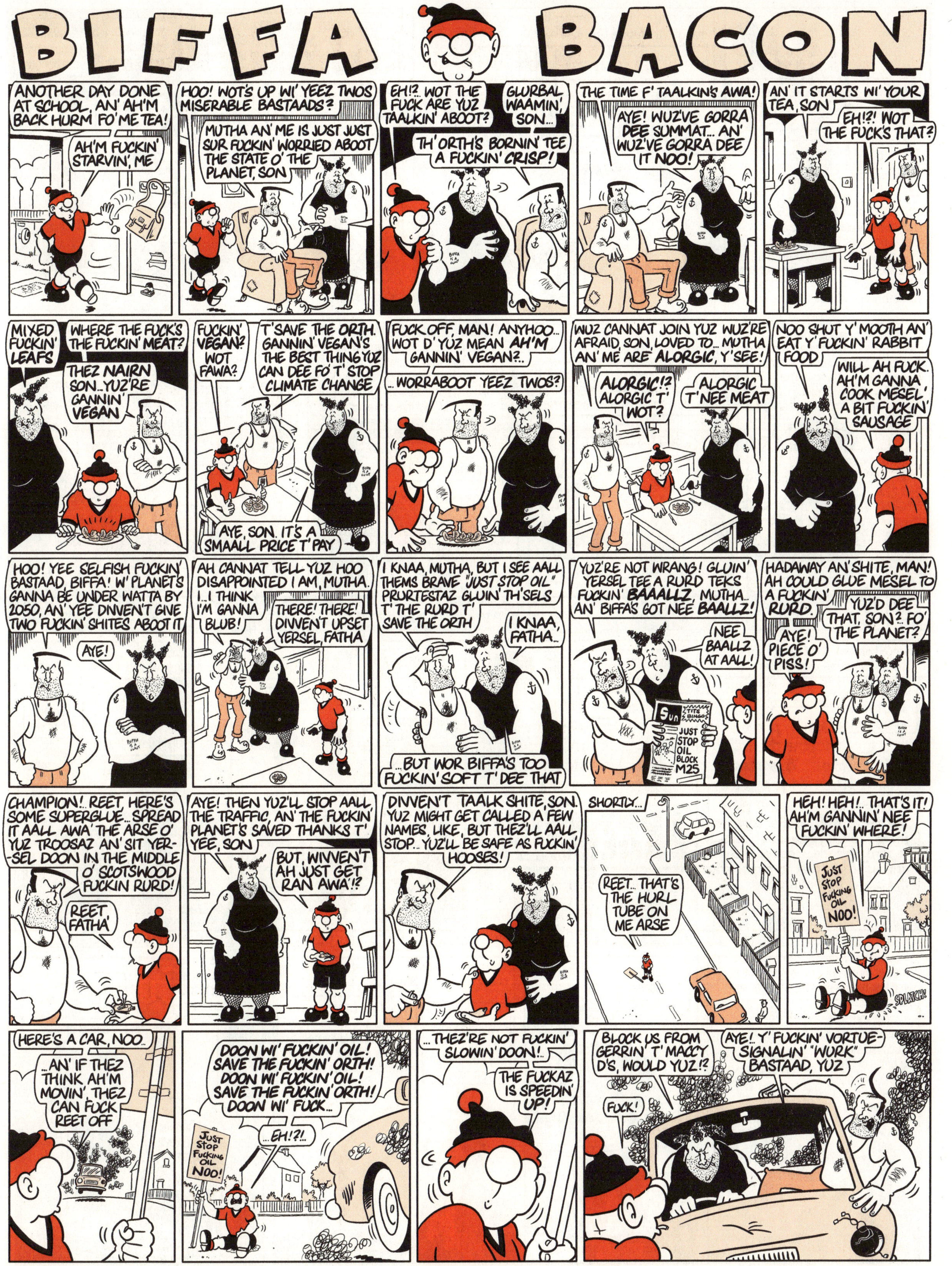
BIFFA BACON
ANOTHER DAY DONE AT SCHOOL, AN' AH'M BACK HURM FO' ME TEA!
AH'M FUCKIN' STARVIN', ME
HOO! WOT'S UP WI' YEEZ TWOS MISERABLE BASTAADS?
MUTHA AN' ME IS JUST JUST SUR FUCKIN' WORRIED ABOOT THE STATE O' THE PLANET, SON
EH!?. WOT THE FUCK ARE YUZ TAALKIN' ABOOT?
GLURBAL WAAMIN', SON...
TH' ORTH'S BORNIN' TEE A FUCKIN' CRISP!
THE TIME F' TAALKIN'S AWA!
AYE! WUZ'VE GORRA DEE SUMMAT... AN' WUZ'VE GORRA DEE IT NOO!
AN' IT STARTS WI' YOUR TEA, SON
EH!?! WOT THE FUCK'S THAT?
MIXED FUCKIN' LEAFS
WHERE THE FUCK'S THE FUCKIN' MEAT?
THEZ NAIRN SON...YUZ'RE GANNIN' VEGAN
FUCKIN' VEGAN? WOT FAWA?
T'SAVE THE ORTH. GANNIN' VEGAN'S THE BEST THING YUZ CAN DEE FO' T' STOP CLIMATE CHANGE
AYE, SON. IT'S A SMAALL PRICE T' PAY
FUCK OFF, MAN! ANYHOO... WOT D' YUZ MEAN AH'M GANNIN' VEGAN?..
...WORRABOOT YEEZ TWOS?
WUZ CANNAT JOIN YUZ WUZ'RE AFRAID, SON, LOVED TO... MUTHA AN' ME ARE ALORGIC, Y'SEE!
ALORGIC!? ALORGIC T' WOT?
ALORGIC T' NEE MEAT
NOO SHUT Y' MOOTH AN' EAT Y' FUCKIN' RABBIT FOOD
WILL AH FUCK. AH'M GANNA COOK MESEL' A BIT FUCKIN' SAUSAGE
HOO! YEE SELFISH FUCKIN' BASTAAD, BIFFA! W' PLANET'S GANNA BE UNDER WATTA BY 2050, AN' YEE DIVVEN'T GIVE TWO FUCKIN' SHITES ABOOT IT
AYE!
AH CANNAT TELL YUZ HOO DISAPPOINTED I AM, MUTHA.
I...I THINK I'M GANNA BLUB!
THERE! THERE! DIVVEN'T UPSET YERSEL, FATHA
I KNAA, MUTHA, BUT I SEE AALL THEMS BRAVE "JUST STOP OIL" PRURTESTAZ GLUIN' TH'SELS T' THE RURD T' SAVE THE ORTH
I KNAA, FATHA...
...BUT WOR BIFFA'S TOO FUCKIN' SOFT T' DEE THAT
YUZ'RE NOT WRANG! GLUIN' YERSEL TEE A RURD TEKS FUCKIN' BAAAALLZ, MUTHA... AN' BIFFA'S GOT NEE BAALLZ!
NEE BAALLZ AT AALL!
SUN
JUST STOP OIL BLOCK M25
HADAWAY AN' SHITE, MAN! AH COULD GLUE MESEL TO A FUCKIN' RURD.
YUZ'D DEE THAT, SON? FO' THE PLANET?
AYE! PIECE O' PISS!
CHAMPION! REET, HERE'S SOME SUPERGLUE... SPREAD IT AALL AWA' THE ARSE O' YUZ TROOSAZ AN' SIT YER-SEL DOON IN THE MIDDLE O' SCOTSWOOD FUCKIN RURD!
REET, FATHA
AYE! THEN YUZ'LL STOP AALL THE TRAFFIC, AN' THE FUCKIN' PLANET'S SAVED THANKS T' YEE, SON
BUT, WIVVEN'T AH JUST GET RAN AWA'!?
DIVVEN'T TAALK SHITE, SON. YUZ MIGHT GET CALLED A FEW NAMES, LIKE, BUT THEZ'LL AALL STOP... YUZ'LL BE SAFE AS FUCKIN' HOOSES!
SHORTLY...
REET... THAT'S THE HURL TUBE ON ME ARSE
HEH! HEH!.. THAT'S IT! AH'M GANNIN' NEE FUCKIN' WHERE!
JUST STOP FUCKING OIL NOO!
SPLATCH!
HERE'S A CAR, NOO...
...AN' IF THEZ THINK AH'M MOVIN', THEZ CAN FUCK REET OFF
DOON WI' FUCKIN' OIL! SAVE THE FUCKIN' ORTH! DOON WI' FUCKIN' OIL! SAVE THE FUCKIN' ORTH! DOON WI' FUCK...
...EH!?!..
JUST STOP FUCKING OIL NOO!
...THEZ'RE NOT FUCKIN' SLOWIN' DOON!..
THE FUCKAZ IS SPEEDIN' UP!
BLOCK US FROM GERRIN' T' MACCY D'S, WOULD YUZ!?
FUCK!
AYE!. Y' FUCKIN' VORTUE-SIGNALIN' "WURK" BASTAAD, YUZ

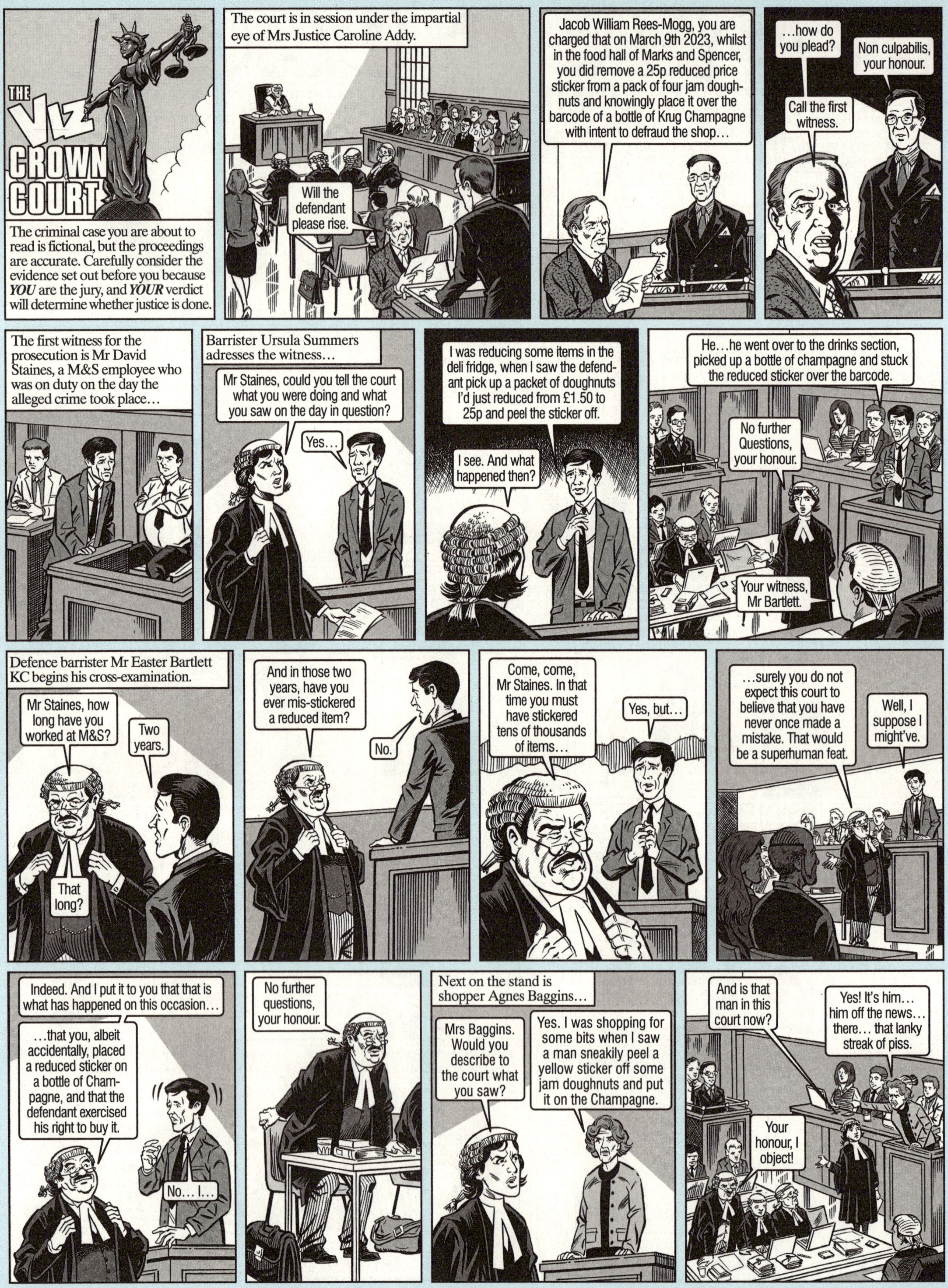
THE VIZ CROWN COURT
The criminal case you are about to read is fictional, but the proceedings are accurate. Carefully consider the evidence set out before you because YOU are the jury, and YOUR verdict will determine whether justice is done.
The court is in session under the impartial eye of Mrs Justice Caroline Addy.
Will the defendant please rise.
Jacob William Rees-Mogg, you are charged that on March 9th 2023, whilst in the food hall of Marks and Spencer, you did remove a 25p reduced price sticker from a pack of four jam doughnuts and knowingly place it over the barcode of a bottle of Krug Champagne with intent to defraud the shop…
…how do you plead?
Non culpabilis, your honour.
Call the first witness.
The first witness for the prosecution is Mr David Staines, a M&S employee who was on duty on the day the alleged crime took place…
Barrister Ursula Summers adresses the witness…
Mr Staines, could you tell the court what you were doing and what you saw on the day in question?
Yes…
I was reducing some items in the deli fridge, when I saw the defendant pick up a packet of doughnuts I'd just reduced from £1.50 to 25p and peel the sticker off.
I see. And what happened then?
He…he went over to the drinks section, picked up a bottle of champagne and stuck the reduced sticker over the barcode.
No further Questions, your honour.
Your witness, Mr Bartlett.
Defence barrister Mr Easter Bartlett KC begins his cross-examination.
Mr Staines, how long have you worked at M&S?
Two years.
That long?
And in those two years, have you ever mis-stickered a reduced item?
No.
Come, come, Mr Staines. In that time you must have stickered tens of thousands of items…
Yes, but…
…surely you do not expect this court to believe that you have never once made a mistake. That would be a superhuman feat.
Well, I suppose I might've.
Indeed. And I put it to you that that is what has happened on this occasion…
…that you, albeit accidentally, placed a reduced sticker on a bottle of Champagne, and that the defendant exercised his right to buy it.
No… I…
No further questions, your honour.
Next on the stand is shopper Agnes Baggins…
Mrs Baggins. Would you describe to the court what you saw?
Yes. I was shopping for some bits when I saw a man sneakily peel a yellow sticker off some jam doughnuts and put it on the Champagne.
And is that man in this court now?
Yes! It's him… him off the news… there… that lanky streak of piss.
Your honour, I object!

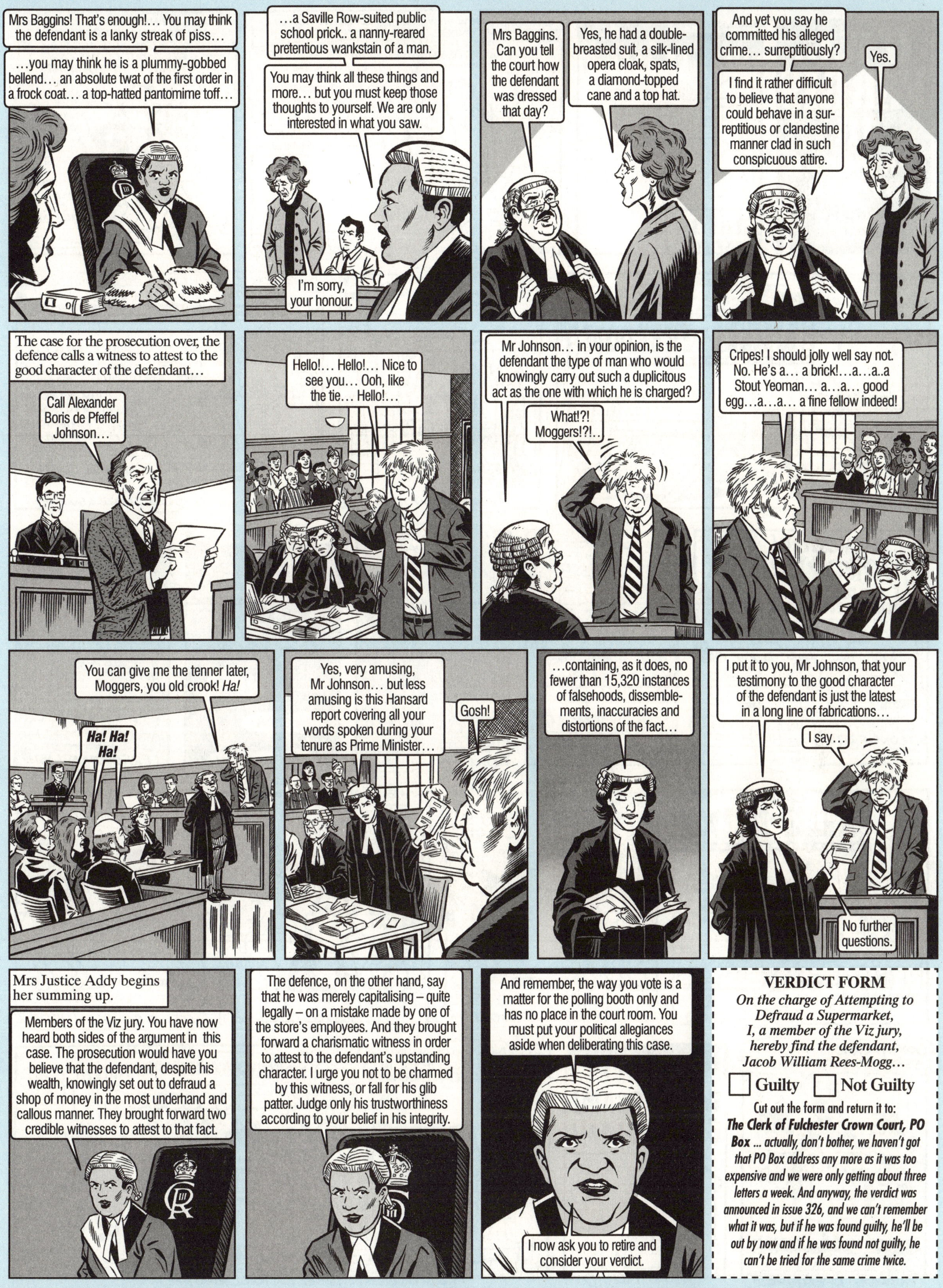

Mrs Baggins! That's enough!… You may think the defendant is a lanky streak of piss…
…you may think he is a plummy-gobbed bellend… an absolute twat of the first order in a frock coat… a top-hatted pantomime toff…
…a Saville Row-suited public school prick.. a nanny-reared pretentious wankstain of a man.
You may think all these things and more… but you must keep those thoughts to yourself. We are only interested in what you saw.
I'm sorry, your honour.
Mrs Baggins. Can you tell the court how the defendant was dressed that day?
Yes, he had a double-breasted suit, a silk-lined opera cloak, spats, a diamond-topped cane and a top hat.
And yet you say he committed his alleged crime… surreptitiously?
Yes.
I find it rather difficult to believe that anyone could behave in a surreptitious or clandestine manner clad in such conspicuous attire.
The case for the prosecution over, the defence calls a witness to attest to the good character of the defendant…
Call Alexander Boris de Pfeffel Johnson…
Hello!… Hello!… Nice to see you… Ooh, like the tie… Hello!…
Mr Johnson… in your opinion, is the defendant the type of man who would knowingly carry out such a duplicitous act as the one with which he is charged?
What!?! Moggers!?!..
Cripes! I should jolly well say not. No. He's a… a brick!…a…a..a Stout Yeoman… a…a… good egg…a…a… a fine fellow indeed!
You can give me the tenner later, Moggers, you old crook! *Ha!*
Ha! Ha! Ha!
Yes, very amusing, Mr Johnson… but less amusing is this Hansard report covering all your words spoken during your tenure as Prime Minister…
Gosh!
…containing, as it does, no fewer than 15,320 instances of falsehoods, dissemblements, inaccuracies and distortions of the fact…
I put it to you, Mr Johnson, that your testimony to the good character of the defendant is just the latest in a long line of fabrications…
I say…
No further questions.
Mrs Justice Addy begins her summing up.
Members of the Viz jury. You have now heard both sides of the argument in this case. The prosecution would have you believe that the defendant, despite his wealth, knowingly set out to defraud a shop of money in the most underhand and callous manner. They brought forward two credible witnesses to attest to that fact.
The defence, on the other hand, say that he was merely capitalising – quite legally – on a mistake made by one of the store's employees. And they brought forward a charismatic witness in order to attest to the defendant's upstanding character. I urge you not to be charmed by this witness, or fall for his glib patter. Judge only his trustworthiness according to your belief in his integrity.
And remember, the way you vote is a matter for the polling booth only and has no place in the court room. You must put your political allegiances aside when deliberating this case.
I now ask you to retire and consider your verdict.
VERDICT FORM
On the charge of Attempting to Defraud a Supermarket, I, a member of the Viz jury, hereby find the defendant, Jacob William Rees-Mogg…
☐ Guilty ☐ Not Guilty
Cut out the form and return it to:
The Clerk of Fulchester Crown Court, PO Box ... actually, don't bother, we haven't got that PO Box address any more as it was too expensive and we were only getting about three letters a week. And anyway, the verdict was announced in issue 326, and we can't remember what it was, but if he was found guilty, he'll be out by now and if he was found not guilty, he can't be tried for the same crime twice.

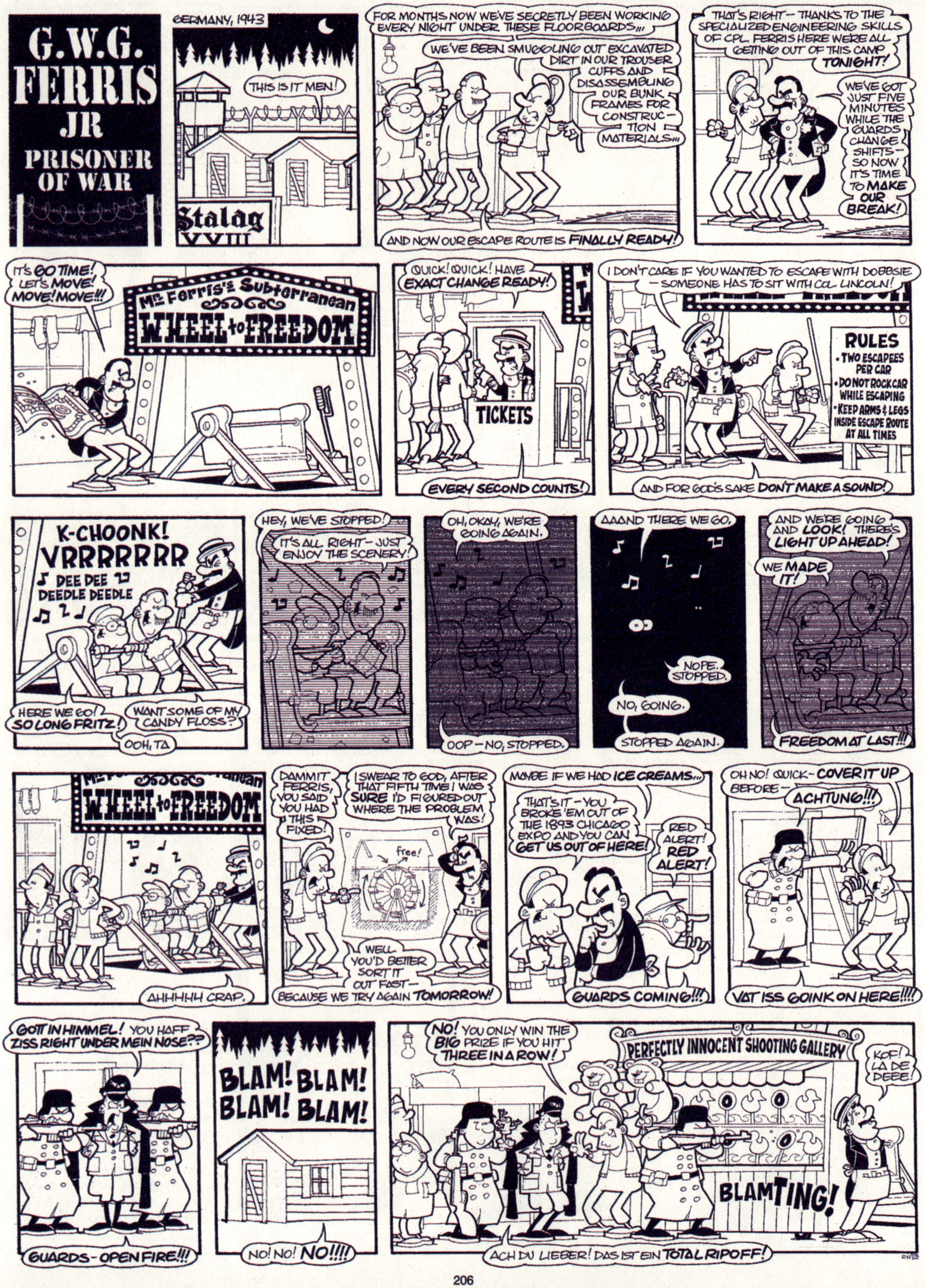
G.W.G. FERRIS JR
PRISONER OF WAR
GERMANY, 1943
THIS IS IT MEN!
Stalag XVIII
FOR MONTHS NOW WE'VE SECRETLY BEEN WORKING EVERY NIGHT UNDER THESE FLOORBOARDS...
WE'VE BEEN SMUGGLING OUT EXCAVATED DIRT IN OUR TROUSER CUFFS AND DISASSEMBLING OUR BUNK FRAMES FOR CONSTRUC-TION MATERIALS...
AND NOW OUR ESCAPE ROUTE IS FINALLY READY!
THAT'S RIGHT — THANKS TO THE SPECIALIZED ENGINEERING SKILLS OF CPL. FERRIS HERE WE'RE ALL GETTING OUT OF THIS CAMP TONIGHT!
WE'VE GOT JUST FIVE MINUTES WHILE THE GUARDS CHANGE SHIFTS — SO NOW IT'S TIME TO MAKE OUR BREAK!
IT'S GO TIME! LET'S MOVE! MOVE! MOVE!!!
Mr Ferris's Subterranean WHEEL to FREEDOM
QUICK! QUICK! HAVE EXACT CHANGE READY!
TICKETS
EVERY SECOND COUNTS!
I DON'T CARE IF YOU WANTED TO ESCAPE WITH DOBBSIE — SOMEONE HAS TO SIT WITH COL. LINCOLN!
RULES
• TWO ESCAPEES PER CAR
• DO NOT ROCK CAR WHILE ESCAPING
• KEEP ARMS & LEGS INSIDE ESCAPE ROUTE AT ALL TIMES
AND FOR GOD'S SAKE DON'T MAKE A SOUND!
K-CHOONK! VRRRRRRR
DEE DEE DEEDLE DEEDLE
HERE WE GO! SO LONG FRITZ!
WANT SOME OF MY CANDY FLOSS?
OOH, TA
HEY, WE'VE STOPPED!
IT'S ALL RIGHT — JUST ENJOY THE SCENERY!
OH, OKAY, WE'RE GOING AGAIN.
OOP — NO, STOPPED.
AAAND THERE WE GO.
NOPE. STOPPED.
NO, GOING.
STOPPED AGAIN.
AND WE'RE GOING AND LOOK! THERE'S LIGHT UP AHEAD!
WE MADE IT!
FREEDOM AT LAST!!!
WHEEL to FREEDOM
AHHHHH CRAP.
DAMMIT FERRIS, YOU SAID YOU HAD THIS FIXED!
I SWEAR TO GOD, AFTER THAT FIFTH TIME I WAS SURE I'D FIGURED OUT WHERE THE PROBLEM WAS!
free!
WELL YOU'D BETTER SORT IT OUT FAST—
BECAUSE WE TRY AGAIN TOMORROW!
MAYBE IF WE HAD ICE CREAMS...
THAT'S IT — YOU BROKE 'EM OUT OF THE 1893 CHICAGO EXPO AND YOU CAN GET US OUT OF HERE!
RED ALERT! RED ALERT!
GUARDS COMING!!!
OH NO! QUICK — COVER IT UP BEFORE—
ACHTUNG!!!
VAT ISS GOINK ON HERE!!!!
GOTT IN HIMMEL! YOU HAFF ZISS RIGHT UNDER MEIN NOSE??
GUARDS — OPEN FIRE!!!
BLAM! BLAM! BLAM! BLAM!
NO! NO! NO!!!!
NO! YOU ONLY WIN THE BIG PRIZE IF YOU HIT THREE IN A ROW!
PERFECTLY INNOCENT SHOOTING GALLERY
KOF! LA DE DEE!
BLAMTING!
ACH DU LIEBER! DAS IST EIN TOTAL RIPOFF!

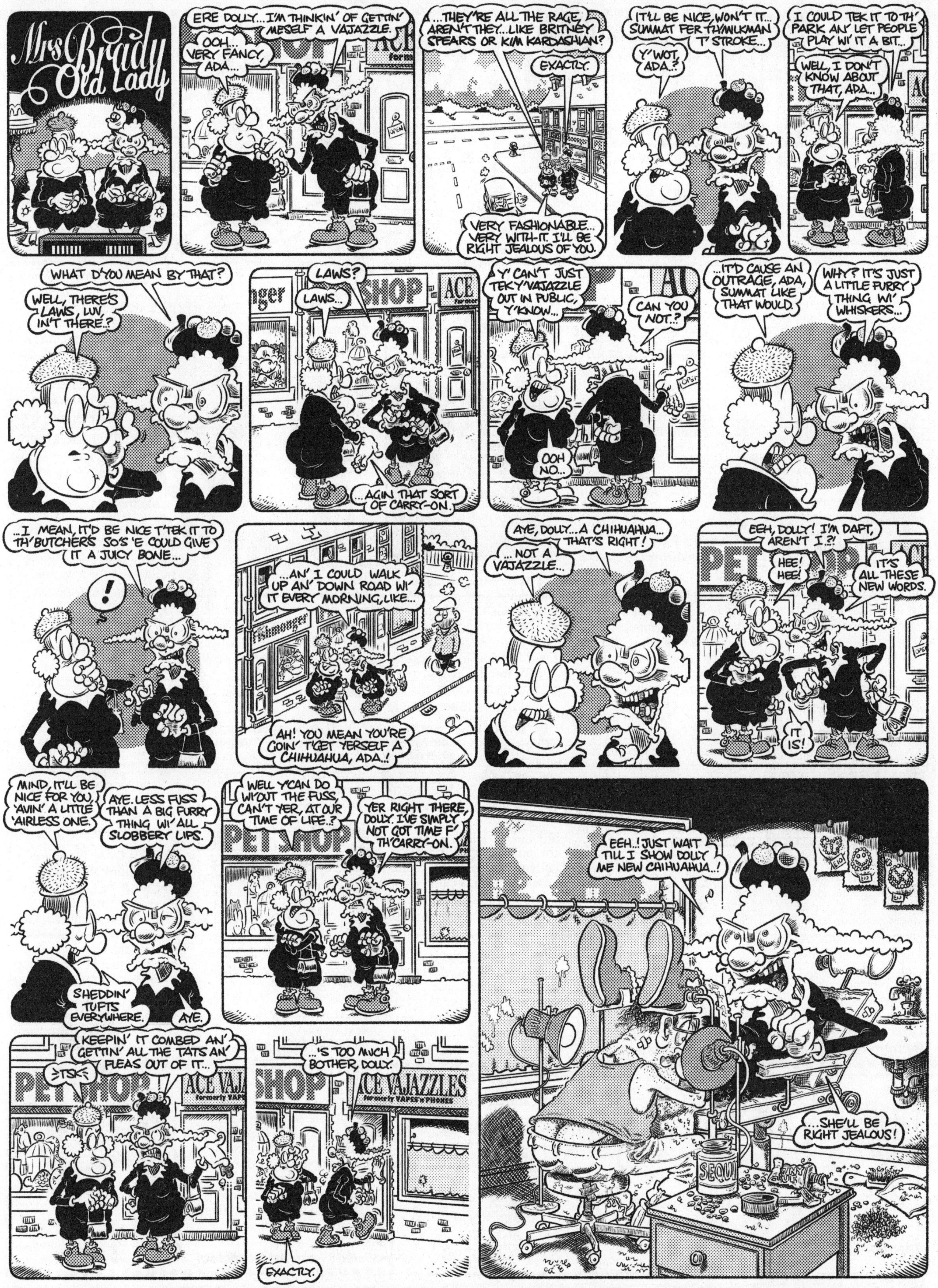
Mrs Brady Old Lady
ERE DOLLY... I'M THINKIN' OF GETTIN' MESELF A VAJAZZLE.
OOH... VERY FANCY, ADA...
...THEY'RE ALL THE RAGE, AREN'T THEY... LIKE BRITNEY SPEARS OR KIM KARDASHIAN?
EXACTLY.
VERY FASHIONABLE... VERY WITH-IT. I'LL BE RIGHT JEALOUS OF YOU.
IT'LL BE NICE, WON'T IT... SUMMAT FER TH'MILKMAN T' STROKE...
Y' WOT, ADA..?
I COULD TEK IT TO TH' PARK AN' LET PEOPLE PLAY WI' IT A BIT...
WELL, I DON'T KNOW ABOUT THAT, ADA...
WHAT D'YOU MEAN BY THAT?
WELL, THERE'S LAWS, LUV, IN'T THERE..?
LAWS?
LAWS...
SHOP
ACE
...AGIN THAT SORT OF CARRY-ON.
Y' CAN'T JUST TEK Y'VAJAZZLE OUT IN PUBLIC, Y'KNOW...
CAN YOU NOT..?
OOH NO...
...IT'D CAUSE AN OUTRAGE, ADA, SUMMAT LIKE THAT WOULD.
WHY? IT'S JUST A LITTLE FURRY THING WI' WHISKERS...
...I MEAN, IT'D BE NICE T'TEK IT TO TH' BUTCHER'S SO'S 'E COULD GIVE IT A JUICY BONE...
!
...AN' I COULD WALK UP AN' DOWN ROAD WI' IT EVERY MORNING, LIKE...
Fishmonger
AH! YOU MEAN YOU'RE GOIN' T'GET YERSELF A CHIHUAHUA, ADA..!
AYE, DOLLY... A CHIHUAHUA... THAT'S RIGHT!
...NOT A VAJAZZLE...
EEH, DOLLY! I'M DAFT, AREN'T I..?!
HEE! HEE!
IT'S ALL THESE NEW WORDS.
IT IS!
MIND, IT'LL BE NICE FOR YOU, 'AVIN' A LITTLE 'AIRLESS ONE.
AYE. LESS FUSS THAN A BIG FURRY THING WI' ALL SLOBBERY LIPS.
SHEDDIN' TUFTS EVERYWHERE.
AYE.
WELL Y'CAN DO WI'OUT THE FUSS, CAN'T YER, AT OUR TIME OF LIFE..?
YER RIGHT THERE, DOLLY. I'VE SIMPLY NOT GOT TIME F' TH'CARRY-ON.
PET SHOP
KEEPIN' IT COMBED AN' GETTIN' ALL THE TATS AN' FLEAS OUT OF IT...
TSK!
...'S TOO MUCH BOTHER, DOLLY.
EXACTLY.
ACE VAJAZZLES
formerly VAPES'n'PHONES
EEH..! JUST WAIT TILL I SHOW DOLLY ME NEW CHIHUAHUA..!
...SHE'LL BE RIGHT JEALOUS!

Letterbocks

letters@viz.co.uk letters@viz.co.uk

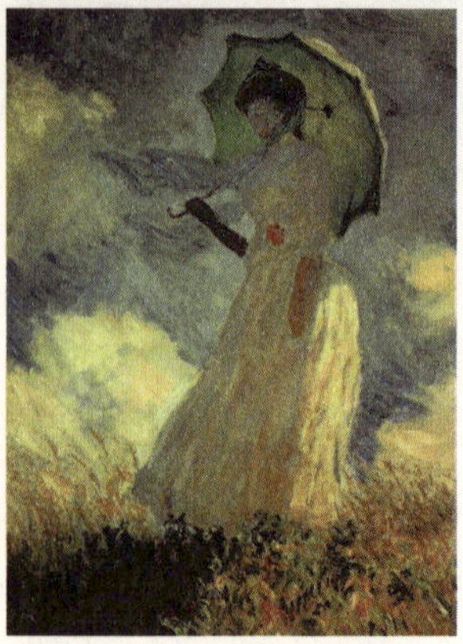

WHILST admiring this Monet painting *Woman with a Parasol*, I was suddenly struck by the depressing thought that if it was painted today, the subject would probably be wearing a baseball cap, a sweatshirt with Nando's sauce stains on it, and some old leggings. And it would probably be called *Woman with a Cameltoe* or something. Come on, ladies! Stick on a big floaty dress and a bonnet, grab a frilly gamp and let's set the art world alight again!

Mike Hayley, email

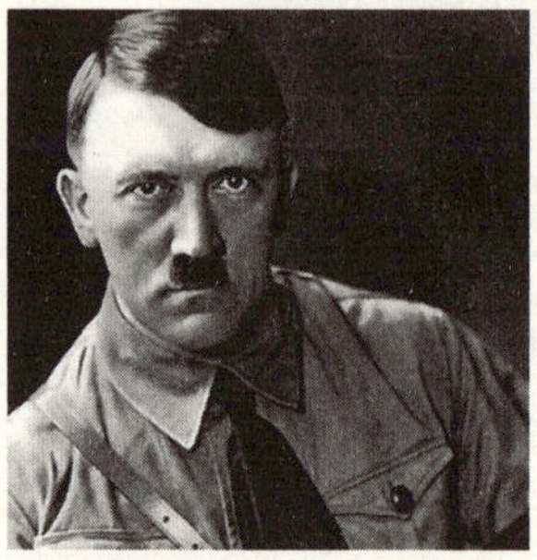

ADOLF Hitler was always banging on about his Aryan race of blond-haired, blue-eyed super-humans. But whilst he did have blue eyes himself, his hair was in no way blonde, but rather extremely dark brown. It seems like we should add hypocrisy to the list of his crimes.

Bartram Bullshot, Derby

I RECENTLY bought a work colleague a "Get Better Soon" card. Not because they were ill, rather because they are just shit at their job. Now I'm the one facing disciplinary proceedings for trying to encourage a better workplace and improve worker outcomes. You couldn't make it up.

Barry, Queefton

THE other day I decided I would try and live in our local canal rather than on terra firma. However, after a minute underwater I was freezing cold and had started to drown. Luckily, a passer-by pulled me out, and I needed a week in bed to recover. I won't be doing that again. What was Darwin on about? Common ancestor with fish, my arse.

Vernon Prolapse, Addingham

REGARDING Jack Weevils-Nelson's James Bond/hat throwing letter (*page 186*), I can't remember the last time I saw James Bond actually wearing a hat. I know he wore one in *From Russia With Love* to disguise the fact that it was obviously a stunt double diving out of the way of a low flying helicopter, but after that I'm struggling. Perhaps he was so traumatised by his encounter with bowler-slinging henchman Oddjob in *Goldfinger* that he developed hat-induced PTSD, and can no longer don a titfer. This could form the storyline of the next 007 film, which I would call *For Your Hats Only*.

Shenkin Arsecandle, Llaregyb

PS. I just remembered he had a bobble hat on when he skied off the cliff at the start of *The Spy Who Loved Me*, but that was the stunt double thing again.

STAR LETTER

WHY on earth do wells always have to have little tiled roofs over them to keep the rain out? Surely a wide funnel would be much more practical.

Susan Butcher, Australia

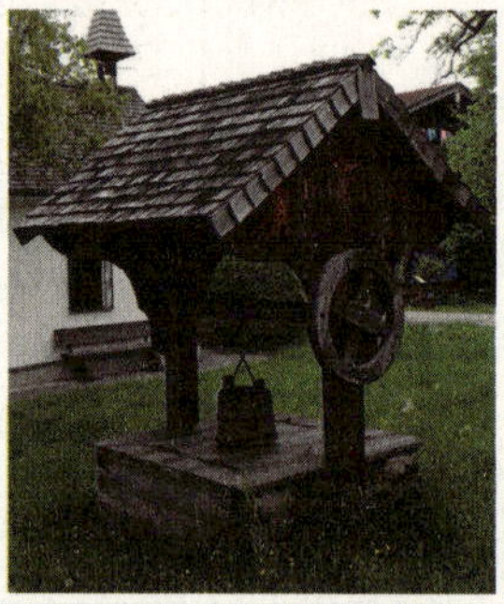

WHY are girlfriends called girlfriends? Your friends don't have your knackers clanging away at their chins every night do they? It seems inappropriate – if not disrespectful – to refer to them as mere friends.

Simon, Macclesfield

'WHICH came first - the chicken or the egg?' is an age-old riddle. But it's obviously the egg, as animals were laying eggs for millions of years before chickens evolved. There's the answer to your unfathomable paradox, you daft twats.

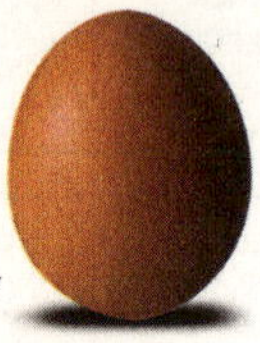

Naich, Cambridge

I FOR one am glad to see that the HS2 high-speed rail link has been cancelled. I went up north once and it was fucking awful. If anything, I'd want to get there slower.

Herbert Cleeve, Devon

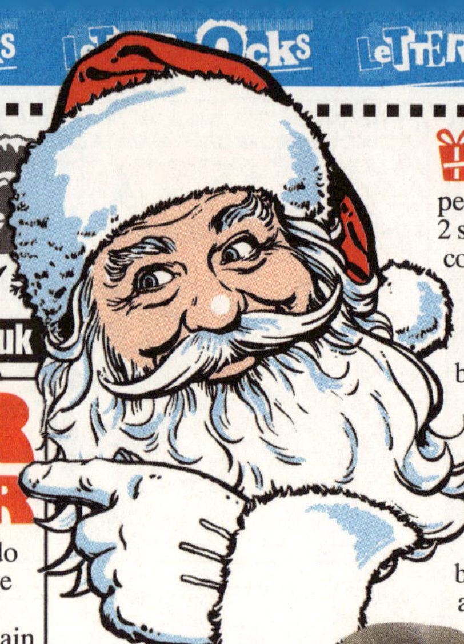

WHEN I was a child, my TV viewing featured a kangaroo who could tell humans when someone was stuck in a well, a wonder horse who could thwart bank robbers, and a dolphin who could capture criminals who were foolish enough to attempt to escape in a boat. Today, I watched my dog piss on the kitchen floor and then slip over as he walked through the pool of his own urine. I wonder what has gone so terribly wrong.

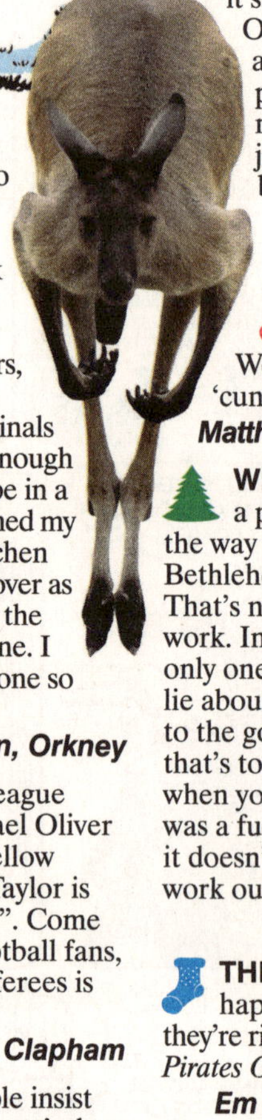

Nick Lyon, Orkney

PREMIER League referee Michael Oliver is 6' 2" while his fellow referee Anthony Taylor is a pocket sized 5' 7". Come on, the FA. As football fans, all we ask from referees is consistency.

Tony Macaroni, Clapham

WHY do people insist on saying 'a dozen' when referring to the number 12? Surely it would be quicker to just say 'twelve' as the word contains just one syllable compared to 'a dozen' which has three. Similarly, when I hear the phrase 'half a dozen', it makes me rage, using four syllables to replace the one-syllabled word 'six'. I'm starting work in a bakery next week.

Ian Webb, Bury St Edmunds

I RECENTLY read a science fiction book where everybody had a robot. These robots were almost identical copies of humans, yet none of the blokes in the story dressed their women robots as French maids and ordered them to perform degrading sex acts. Come on, sci-fi writers, get real.

Terry Farricker, Blackpool

I'M a good athletics club runner with a personal best time of 4 mins 2 secs for the 1500m. By comparison, the winning time in the 1900 Olympics held in Paris was 4 mins 6 secs. Therefore, if I'd been born in, say, 1878, I would have won the gold medal instead of Charles Bennett. I wrote to Seb Coe to see if I could get my medal awarded retrospectively, but I didn't even receive a reply. It would seem it's one rule for actual Olympic champions and one rule for people who, through no fault of their own, just happened to be born too late.

Billy (the Whizz) Barrington, email

SHOULDN'T that line in that Wombles song say 'cunts' instead of 'folks'?

Matthew Majinkus, Perth

WHY did Joseph drag a pregnant Mary all the way from Nazareth to Bethlehem for a census? That's not how censuses work. In my opinion, there's only one reason people lie about where they live to the government, and that's to dodge tax. And when you consider Joseph was a fucking tradesman, it doesn't take a genius to work out what was going on.

Andy, Mansh

THEY say "worse things happen at sea," and they're right. I've just watched *Pirates Of The Caribbean 5*.

Em Rickinson, Sunlun

I CAN'T help but think that these so-called 'well built' rugby players are nothing of the sort. Half of them seem to be held together with sticky tape or plasters. Very badly put together, in my opinion.

Damien Thundercock, Slough

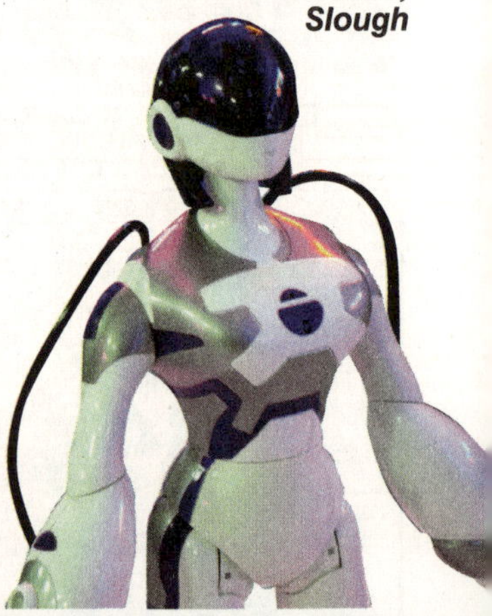

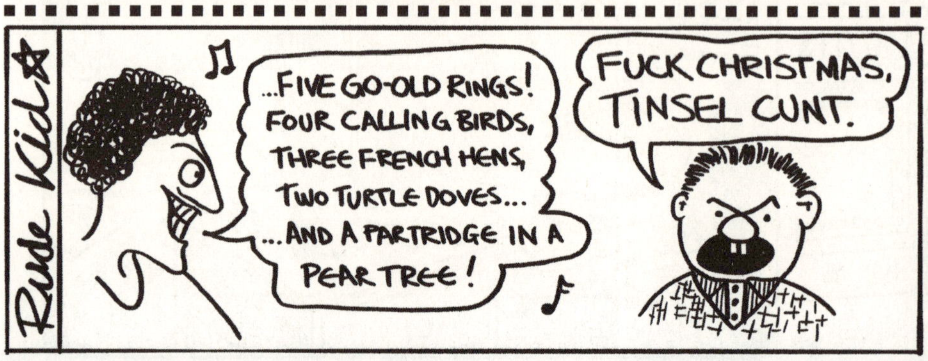
Rude Kid
...FIVE GO-OLD RINGS! FOUR CALLING BIRDS, THREE FRENCH HENS, TWO TURTLE DOVES... ...AND A PARTRIDGE IN A PEAR TREE!
FUCK CHRISTMAS, TINSEL CUNT.

IT'S often said that nothing rhymes with the word 'orange'. Well, a sporange is a reproductive part of a fern, and Mount Blorenge overlooks Abergavenny. In what could be a literary first, here's a man in orange, sitting on Mount Blorenge behind some sporange.
Gezmundo, Cardiff

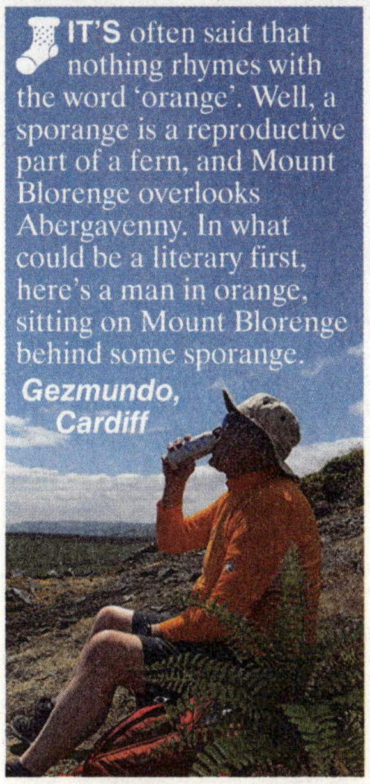

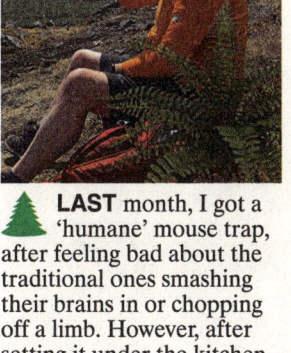

LAST month, I got a 'humane' mouse trap, after feeling bad about the traditional ones smashing their brains in or chopping off a limb. However, after setting it under the kitchen units and checking it 3 weeks later, I was surprised to find the emaciated corpse of a mouse that had clearly starved to death. Humane? I don't think so.
Poing Jelly, Quintin

IF I was the Invisible Man, I'd go somewhere densely populated like a busy shopping centre every time I needed a shit. The sight of a freshly baked log appearing out of thin air would render 50% of the witnesses horrified and disgusted, whereas for the other 50%, it would arguably go down as the best day of their fucking lives.
Kevin Caswell-Jones, Gresford

I RECENTLY donated blood for the first time, and it fills me with enormous civic pride to know that I've helped out another human being in their time of need. I also wonder if, somewhere, some bloke's bonk-on is filling up with some of my blood. Food for thought.
Barry, Queefton

THEY say that non-stick technology came from the space programme, but you would have thought that the last thing a space chef would want is all his fried eggs suddenly lifting off the frying pan and floating round the capsule.
Stuie, Bunny

IMAGINE Mr Logic's delight on seeing that the makers of this ready-rolled pastry have invented an unbelievable 133,225 recipes. Or 133,590 if it's a leap year.
Tarps, Hooky

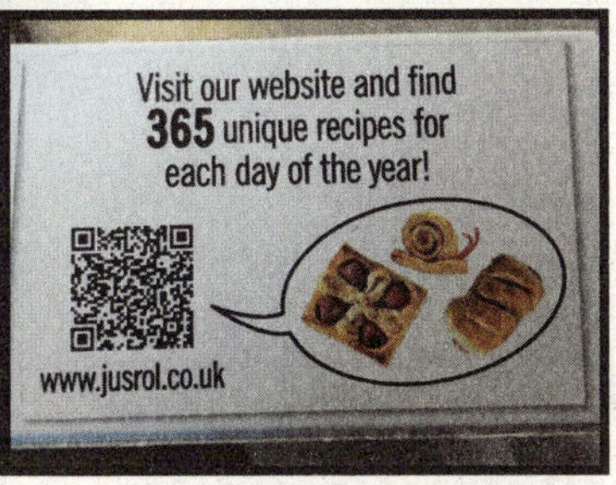
Visit our website and find
365 unique recipes for each day of the year!
www.jusrol.co.uk

TOP TIPS

OBSOLETE pound coins stuck to your fingers using double sided sellotape make excellent sovereign rings for cockney wide boys on a budget.
Nessie Van Jockwell, email

BANK staff. When armed robbers demand the combination to the safe, politely inform them that's it's the permutation they require, as a combination does not require a sequence of symbols to be ordered, whereas a permutation does have this requirement.
Martin Harwood, Bradford

SAVE money on vapes by putting a few fags in the kettle next time you make a cup of tea, and inhaling the steam as it boils.
Lucy Collins, Devizes

PUBLIC toilet attendants. Ease congestion in a busy gents' convenience by telling queueing customers to have their cock out ready for when a urinal becomes available.
Fat Al White, Wakefield

A PACK of butter placed outside makes a handy temperature gauge. If the butter is soft, that means it's warm outside, whilst hard butter means it's cold.
Andrew McGuigan, Blaydon

SURFERS. Make the probability of surviving a shark attack 50% higher by simply smearing yourself in Marmite before taking to the water.
John Owens, Glasgow

GENTS. Glue nipple tassels to your testicles as a sexy treat for your other half.
Gerry Paton, London

TEENAGERS. Pretend you can beatbox by repeatedly saying the word 'umch' at the rate of two 'umches' per second. Preferably on public transport.
D Williams, Donegal

toptips@viz.co.uk

CUCKOOS can fuck right off. The lazy fuckers can't be arsed to sit on their own eggs, so they dump them on some poor unsuspecting sparrow. Then their feckless offspring hatch out and massacre the sparrow chicks. Fucking appalling. So what do we do but commemorate the evil bastards with a novelty clock where they pop out hourly, all sweetness and light like butter wouldn't fucking melt. I see you, cuckoos. I fucking see you.
Jock Boofus, Newport

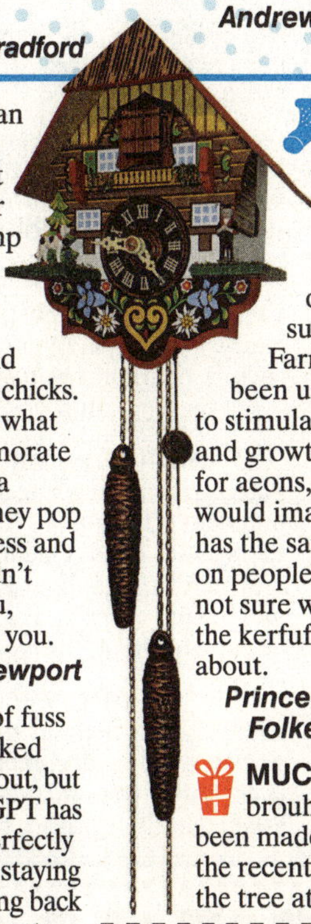

I FOR one welcome more human waste in our water supply. Farmers have been using manure to stimulate health and growth in plants for aeons, and I would imagine it has the same effect on people, so I'm not sure what all the kerfuffle is about.
Prince Asbo, Folkestone

MUCH brouhaha has been made about the recent felling of the tree at Sycamore Gap, but I'm surprised the Romans didn't cut it down years ago. Hadrian's Wall was meant to keep out unruly Scots, but having seen the tree, some of the branches were hanging well over the other side, providing an easy means for them to cross the border.
C. Hadrianus, Rome

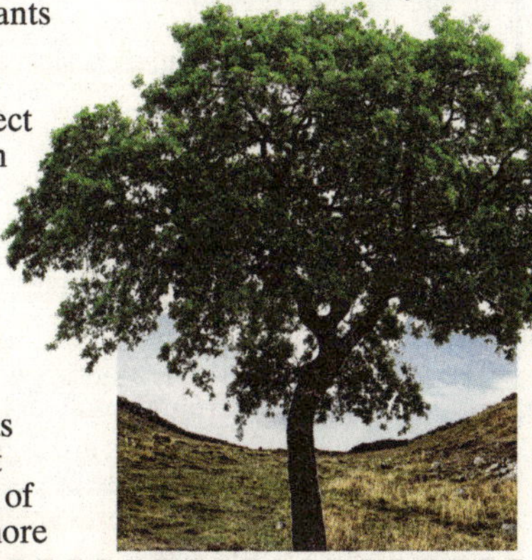

THERE'S a lot of fuss and nonsense talked about AI wiping us all out, but in no time at all Chat GPT has just generated four perfectly sound reasons for me staying in the pub and not going back to the office. If that's not proof that AI's got our backs, I'd like to know what is.
Irene Hammer, Truro

IT'S too bad Jedi Master Obi-Wan Kenobi was never recognised for his efforts in combatting outer space tyranny. 'Obi-Wan Kenobi OBE' has a nice ring to it.
D Williams, Donegal

I NOTICE that new currency featuring our king's face is now in circulation. This would be a great way to honour our new monarch were it not for the fact that hardly anyone uses money any more. Surely King Prince Charles would be better off putting his face on something more modern, like a phone or an internet.
Nick Mao, email

I REALLY like that estate agents have started putting photographs of themselves on their 'For Sale' signs. They have truly become the faces of our fantastic housing market.
Oxter Boggins, Monifieth

ARE there any other songs about stool pigeons other than *Stool Pigeon* by Kid Creole & The Coconuts?
Humphrey, Dumfries

I DON'T understand why the government is banning laughing gas. There seems little enough to chuckle at in the world today, and outlawing something that makes a lot of kids giggle seems a very spiteful thing to do.
Edna Bowestiger, Durham

IF Buddy Holly hadn't died in a plane crash in 1959, he would possibly be dead by now anyway, or if he wasn't he'd be 87.
Ian Webb, Bury St Edmunds

150 million tonnes of single-use plastic in our oceans might sound scary, but if you compare it to a much bigger number, say 900 trillion tonnes or something, then it really isn't that bad.
Kev, Halifax

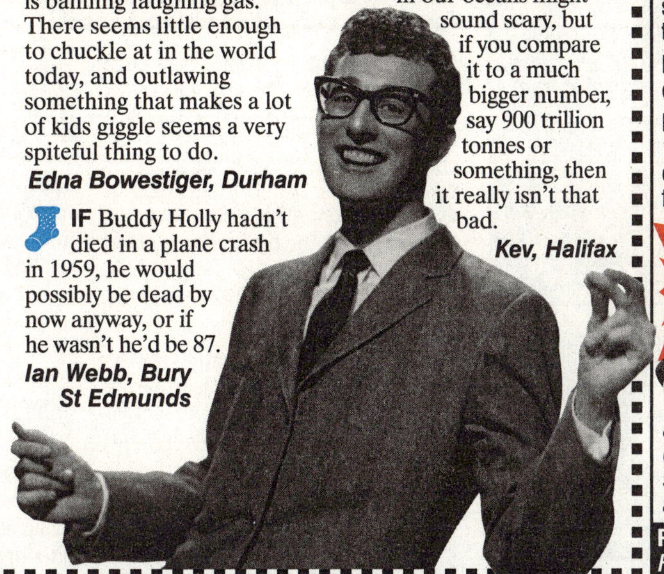

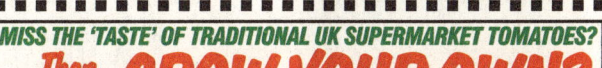

MISS THE 'TASTE' OF TRADITIONAL UK SUPERMARKET TOMATOES?

Then why not... GROW YOUR OWN?

With global events currently restricting customer access to bland tasting tomatoes across UK supermarkets, there has never been a better time to *GROW YOUR OWN* crop!

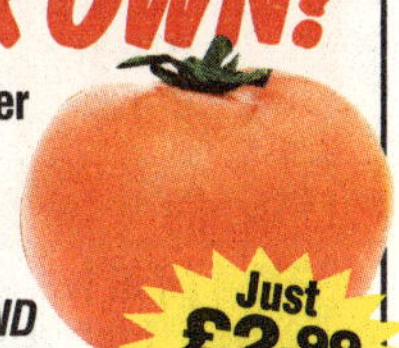

Just £2.99 per packet

Enjoy the 'taste' of big, round, identically-sized ***AND*** completely flavourless tomatoes ***ALL YEAR ROUND!***

Each packet of seeds comes with a ***FREE*** copy of *"Growing Your Own Supermarket Tomatoes"* - a step by step guide detailing exactly how to recreate the insipid, watery "flavour" of your favourite supermarket varieties.

0% Aroma. 1000% unlike the ones you get on holiday!

"I grew some of your Ailsa Bland toms last year. From a single plant I harvested 7lb of identically sized, completely spherical tomatoes that tasted like they'd been sprayed with ethylene and shipped semi-ripened halfway around the world." **Mr B, Essex**

Tick the variety of UK supermarket-style tomato you would like to grow:
- ☐ Ailsa Bland
- ☐ Heavy-Crop Unappetizing
- ☐ Gardener's Insipid

Name......................................
Address...................................
.........................Post Code.........
(Please Include your bank card and a SAE)

POST TO: *Crap Crop Tomatoes, Barnsley Allotments, Barnsley Brown Field Enterprise zone, The Old Barnsley Asbestos Works, Barnsley*

READ ON TOAST ... 2-PAGE SPREAD ON TOAST ... 2-PAGE SPREAD ON TOAST ... 2-PAGE SPREAD ON T

EX-ROYALS MADE ME BURN TOAST

Harry and Megan cause of over-cooked bread says Essex man

A CHELMSFORD man has revealed how his life was turned upside down last week because of the behaviour of former Royal couple Prince Harry and Meghan Markle. And despite their promise to step back from public life, Hector Bilgetank says the fifth in line to the throne and his wife have caused him to burn his toast.

BURNT OFFERINGS: Hector Bilgetank displays a slice of toast that he burnt specially for our photographer to show how burnt the slice of toast that Harry and Meghan (inset bottom) caused him to burn was.

"I put some bread in the toaster this morning, and then I popped into the other room to get my phone," said Bilgetank. "The toaster is bust and doesn't pop up, so you have to keep your eye on it, but I was on the case."

"I couldn't find my phone, and then I remembered that it was upstairs, so I nipped to get it," the former school caretaker said.

"Suddenly I smelt burning from the kitchen, so I rushed downstairs, and when I got back in, my toast was completely burnt." he said.

"Completely inedible. I'm sick of the pair of them."

masonry

Bilgetank says that he has never burnt his breakfast toast before, and he accuses Harry and Meghan of disrupting not just his life, but that of his friends.

"Stuff like this never used to happen. Life was all good. Then them two come along and my mate busts his ankle playing five-a-side football, and my wife's sister loses two grand because of identity theft," he said.

"I wish they'd just piss off and not come back."

weebles

And rather than just moaning, Bilgetank has started an online petition calling for Harry and Megan to piss off and not come back, a petition that has already collected over twenty signatures in just seven days.

"They're out there in their fancy Los Angeles mansion giving it the old 'Oh, poor us, poor us. It's not fair that we're not going to be King and Queen' malarkey. And they never think about normal people like me, the ones who've got to eat burnt toast because of them," he complained.

Harry and Megan were unavailable for comment last night as they were filming a 12-part Netflix documentary about their lives, but a press secretary for the couple asked that their privacy be respected.

MARMALADE QUIZ

For a bit of fun, we've removed all the vowels from a popular toast-topper. Without cheating and using only the vowels from the vowel safe below, can you guess what the hidden breakfast time treat is? Be warned – *some vowels may occur more than once...*
CLUE: *Not jam.*

M_ RM_ L_ D_

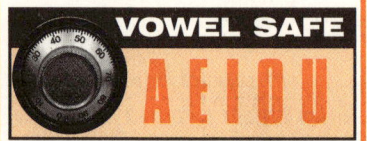

ANSWER: Use 3x 'A' and 1x 'E' from the Vowel Safe to spell the word 'Marmalade'.

THE TOAST OF THE COUNTRY

LONDON HILTON: Toasty host.

THE 99th National Bread Cookery Awards were held last night at the Hilton Hotel in London, and as ever, **TOAST** scooped the top award as the nation's favourite way of cooking bread.

It was thought by some that 2023 could have seen the crunchy snack voted off the top spot for the first time since the awards began, as top chefs experiment with other ways of cooking the staple foodstuff. But whilst fried bread, croutons and traditional bread and butter have gained in popularity recently, judges held firm and voted toast the tops for the 99th consecutive year.

"It's a great achievement to lift the award once again," said chairman of the British Toast Consortium, Hector Twelves. "Since 1924, toasting has proved the nation's favourite way of cooking bread, and next year, we hope to make it a century at the top."

However, members of the UK

EXCLUSIVE!

Fried Bread Association believe that toast's win this year could be their last, and even suggested that underhand dealings have kept the dry-grilled bread as the winner. "It might be a coincidence that the National Bread Cookery Awards have always been sponsored by toaster manufacturers Rowenta," said UKFBA president Ursula Bear. "I couldn't possibly say."

"However, the patrons of next year's awards are going to be frying pan manufacturers Tefal. So let's wait and see if there is an upset in 2024," she added.

HOT TOAST!

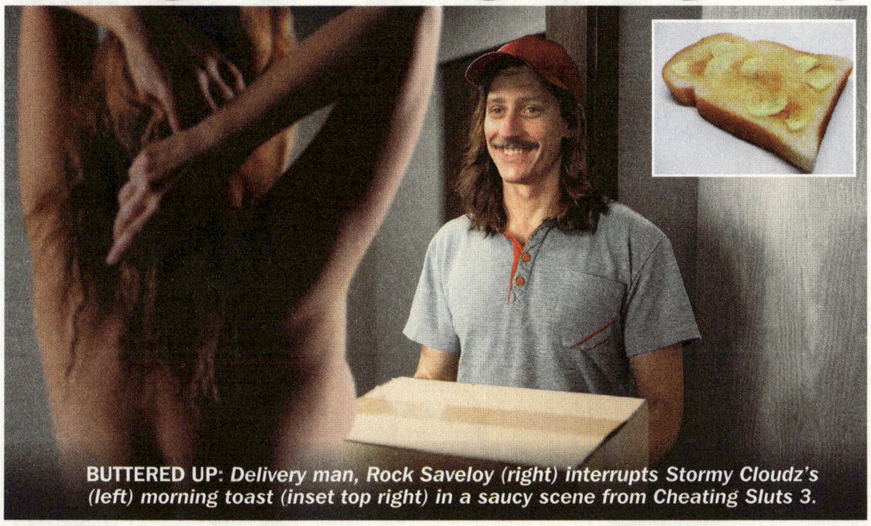

BUTTERED UP: *Delivery man, Rock Saveloy (right) interrupts Stormy Cloudz's (left) morning toast (inset top right) in a saucy scene from Cheating Sluts 3.*

HOT buttered toast just got hotter after it was revealed that the favourite breakfast staple will feature in a new pornographic movie due to be released on the subscription channel *Television X* later this month. And the news has left toast-lovers divided.

Cheating Sluts 3, will feature Stormy Cloudz as a toast-eating housewife who embarks on a 15-minute affair with a delivery man. In the film's opening scene, Stormy is seen buttering two slices of toast fresh from the toaster when the doorbell rings. Answering it, she finds it is a delivery man, played by Rock Savaloy, who has a parcel for Stormy.

The toast is quickly forgotten as the couple move into the lounge where they are soon naked and engaging in penetrative sex in several different positions including the Wheelbarrow, the Scissors and Reverse Cowgirl. The couple then engage in mutual oral stimulation for several minutes before the scene ends with Savaloy pulling a face whilst ejaculating on Cloudz's breasts.

harpsichord

"I've watched the film and it's great to see toast finally breaking into the adult movie business," said Chester Batwings, chairman of the British Board of Toast and Marmalade. "It's only two slices, and they're only on screen for a few seconds, but it's a start."

Toast has been a mainstay of mainstream cinema for many years, being seen in everything from Hollywood greats like *Citizen Kane* and *Pulp Fiction* to British classics like *Four Weddings and a Funeral*. But Batwings is convinced that moving into the adult movie scene will be good for grilled bread. "Scud films may not be everybody's cup of tea, but *Cheating Sluts 3* will bring toast to a wider audience," he said.

onion

But not everyone agreed that the toast bongo flick cameo was good for the brand. Marjory Christian-Whitehouse, president of the UK Breakfast Grilled Bread Association, feels that toast's link with pornographic films can only be bad for the food's popularity.

"We are trying to promote breakfast toast as a healthy start to the day for children," she fumed. "How are we going to do that when it appears in filth like this?"

"When people see the disgusting things those filthy beasts get up to in the front room, they are going to associate it with the lovely toast they saw at the start of the scene," she said. "All that sweating and groaning. It's enough to put anyone right off toast."

TOAST by POST

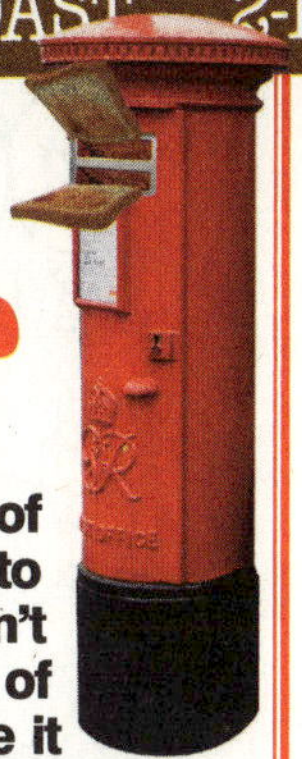

DO YOU fancy a couple of slices of toast, but can't be arsed to go to the kitchen to make it? Well don't worry, because you can have two slices of delicious toast done exactly as you like it and delivered to your door – if you are the lucky winner of our Toast Word Ladder competition.

HOW TO ENTER:

Simply change the word **BREAD** to **TOAST** in as few steps as you can, changing one letter at a time to make another word. According to the internet, there's a 19-step solution, and a 7-step solution, but the 7-step includes words we've never heard of, like **BREES**, **BRAST** and **BLEST**. Simply fill in the form with your answer and toast choice and post it off to: *Toast Word Ladder Puzzle, Viz Comic, PO Box 841, Whitley Bay NE26 9EQ*. We'll put all the answers into a toaster, and the first correct entry that pops up and isn't on fire will receive two slices of toast by return of post.

1: BREAD	11:
2:	12:
3:	13:
4:	14:
5:	15:
6:	16:
7:	17:
8:	18:
9:	19:
10:	20: TOAST

Name...................... **Address**..

.... **Post code**......................

What toast would you like? ☐ White ☐ Brown ☐ Wholemeal

Do you mind the crusts? ☐ Yes ☐ No ☐ Not bothered

How would you like it done? ☐ Light ☐ Medium ☐ Dark

Any spread? ☐ Butter ☐ Marge ☐ Vegan spread ☐ None

If you are having difficulty solving the puzzle, simply type "Word Ladder Puzzle Solver" into Google and go to any of the resulting sites to get the correct answer. Copy the answer down on the form and send it in to the competition address. Or rather, don't bother because, let's face it, we're not going to send two bits of toast out in the post to anyone, win or lose. We're just going to throw any letters marked 'Toast Word Ladder Puzzle' in the fucking bin unopened and you'll have wasted £1.25 on a first class stamp.

YOU'RE TOAST!

Apprentice boss spills beans on toast misery

SOUR-FACED reality TV boss Lord Sugar has finally revealed to the public that he is unable to drop his morning toast butter-side-up.

For years, the outspoken *The Apprentice* businessman has kept quiet about his breakfast dropping shortfall, fuelling rumours amongst the hit show's fanbase that he might occasionally get to recover fumbled slices of his toasted morning treat from the floor and continue eating them.

However, House of Lords absentee Sugar put an end to speculation on Monday in a tweet to his followers which read simply, "Alright! I admit it. No matter how hard I try, I just can't do it. My twatting toast always lands face down!"

"It's got so bad recently that I realise that it's pointless trying to hide it from people any more. You can read it in my face," he explained in a full page advert taken out in *The Daily Telegraph* the following day. "Every wrinkle adds to a roadmap of buttery disappointment."

"It's not so much the toast dropping face-down bit that pisses me off, more the fact that I can't simply pick the slice up off the floor and shove it back in my mouth that really gets my goat," the Amstrad PenPad tycoon continued. "Whenever the toast leaves my hand on its inevitable journey floorwards, nine times out of ten it'll land on a bit of carpet and get one of those little rooty bits you find at the bottom of a pack of peanuts or a silver pube stuck to it."

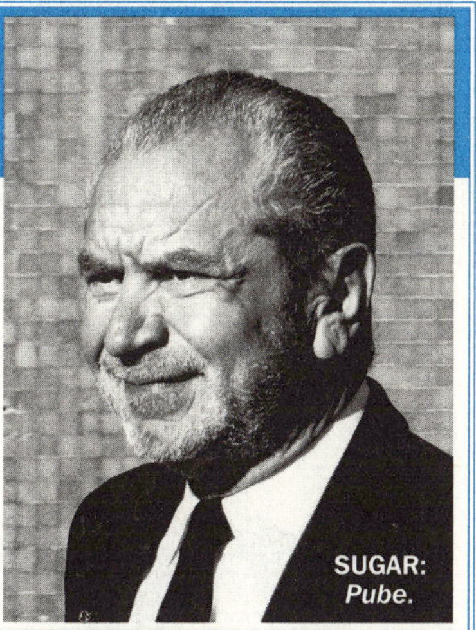

SUGAR: *Pube.*

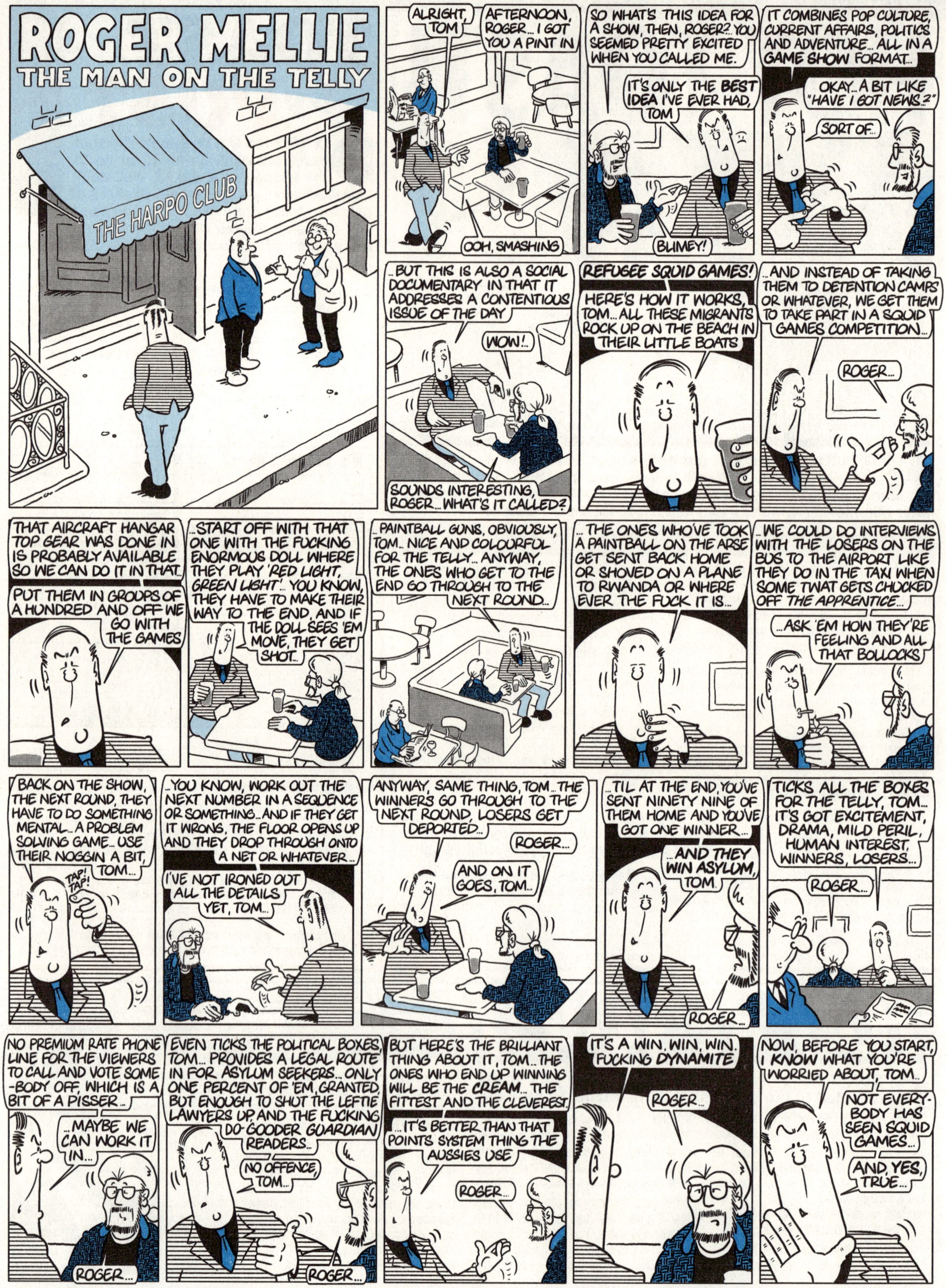
ROGER MELLIE
THE MAN ON THE TELLY
THE HARPO CLUB
ALRIGHT, TOM
AFTERNOON, ROGER... I GOT YOU A PINT IN
OOH, SMASHING
SO WHAT'S THIS IDEA FOR A SHOW, THEN, ROGER? YOU SEEMED PRETTY EXCITED WHEN YOU CALLED ME.
IT'S ONLY THE BEST IDEA I'VE EVER HAD, TOM
BLIMEY!
IT COMBINES POP CULTURE, CURRENT AFFAIRS, POLITICS AND ADVENTURE... ALL IN A GAME SHOW FORMAT...
OKAY... A BIT LIKE "HAVE I GOT NEWS...?"
SORT OF...
...BUT THIS IS ALSO A SOCIAL DOCUMENTARY IN THAT IT ADDRESSES A CONTENTIOUS ISSUE OF THE DAY
WOW!...
SOUNDS INTERESTING, ROGER... WHAT'S IT CALLED?
REFUGEE SQUID GAMES!
HERE'S HOW IT WORKS, TOM... ALL THESE MIGRANTS ROCK UP ON THE BEACH IN THEIR LITTLE BOATS
...AND INSTEAD OF TAKING THEM TO DETENTION CAMPS OR WHATEVER, WE GET THEM TO TAKE PART IN A SQUID GAMES COMPETITION...
ROGER...
THAT AIRCRAFT HANGAR TOP GEAR WAS DONE IN IS PROBABLY AVAILABLE SO WE CAN DO IT IN THAT...
PUT THEM IN GROUPS OF A HUNDRED AND OFF WE GO WITH THE GAMES
...START OFF WITH THAT ONE WITH THE FUCKING ENORMOUS DOLL WHERE THEY PLAY 'RED LIGHT, GREEN LIGHT'... YOU KNOW, THEY HAVE TO MAKE THEIR WAY TO THE END, AND IF THE DOLL SEES 'EM MOVE, THEY GET SHOT...
...PAINTBALL GUNS, OBVIOUSLY, TOM... NICE AND COLOURFUL FOR THE TELLY... ANYWAY, THE ONES WHO GET TO THE END GO THROUGH TO THE NEXT ROUND...
...THE ONES WHO'VE TOOK A PAINTBALL ON THE ARSE GET SENT BACK HOME OR SHOVED ON A PLANE TO RWANDA OR WHERE EVER THE FUCK IT IS...
...WE COULD DO INTERVIEWS WITH THE LOSERS ON THE BUS TO THE AIRPORT LIKE THEY DO IN THE TAXI WHEN SOME TWAT GETS CHUCKED OFF THE APPRENTICE...
...ASK 'EM HOW THEY'RE FEELING AND ALL THAT BOLLOCKS
BACK ON THE SHOW, THE NEXT ROUND, THEY HAVE TO DO SOMETHING MENTAL... A PROBLEM SOLVING GAME... USE THEIR NOGGIN A BIT, TOM...
TAP! TAP!
...YOU KNOW, WORK OUT THE NEXT NUMBER IN A SEQUENCE OR SOMETHING... AND IF THEY GET IT WRONG, THE FLOOR OPENS UP AND THEY DROP THROUGH ONTO A NET OR WHATEVER...
I'VE NOT IRONED OUT ALL THE DETAILS YET, TOM...
ANYWAY, SAME THING, TOM... THE WINNERS GO THROUGH TO THE NEXT ROUND, LOSERS GET DEPORTED...
ROGER...
AND ON IT GOES, TOM...
...TIL AT THE END, YOU'VE SENT NINETY NINE OF THEM HOME AND YOU'VE GOT ONE WINNER...
...AND THEY WIN ASYLUM, TOM.
ROGER...
TICKS ALL THE BOXES FOR THE TELLY, TOM... IT'S GOT EXCITEMENT, DRAMA, MILD PERIL, HUMAN INTEREST, WINNERS, LOSERS...
ROGER...
NO PREMIUM RATE PHONE LINE FOR THE VIEWERS TO CALL AND VOTE SOME-BODY OFF, WHICH IS A BIT OF A PISSER...
...MAYBE WE CAN WORK IT IN...
ROGER...
EVEN TICKS THE POLITICAL BOXES, TOM... PROVIDES A LEGAL ROUTE IN FOR ASYLUM SEEKERS... ONLY ONE PERCENT OF 'EM, GRANTED, BUT ENOUGH TO SHUT THE LEFTIE LAWYERS UP, AND THE FUCKING DO-GOODER GUARDIAN READERS...
NO OFFENCE, TOM...
ROGER...
BUT HERE'S THE BRILLIANT THING ABOUT IT, TOM... THE ONES WHO END UP WINNING WILL BE THE CREAM... THE FITTEST AND THE CLEVEREST.
...IT'S BETTER THAN THAT POINTS SYSTEM THING THE AUSSIES USE
ROGER...
IT'S A WIN, WIN, WIN. FUCKING DYNAMITE
ROGER...
NOW, BEFORE YOU START, I KNOW WHAT YOU'RE WORRIED ABOUT, TOM...
NOT EVERY-BODY HAS SEEN SQUID GAMES...
AND, YES, TRUE...

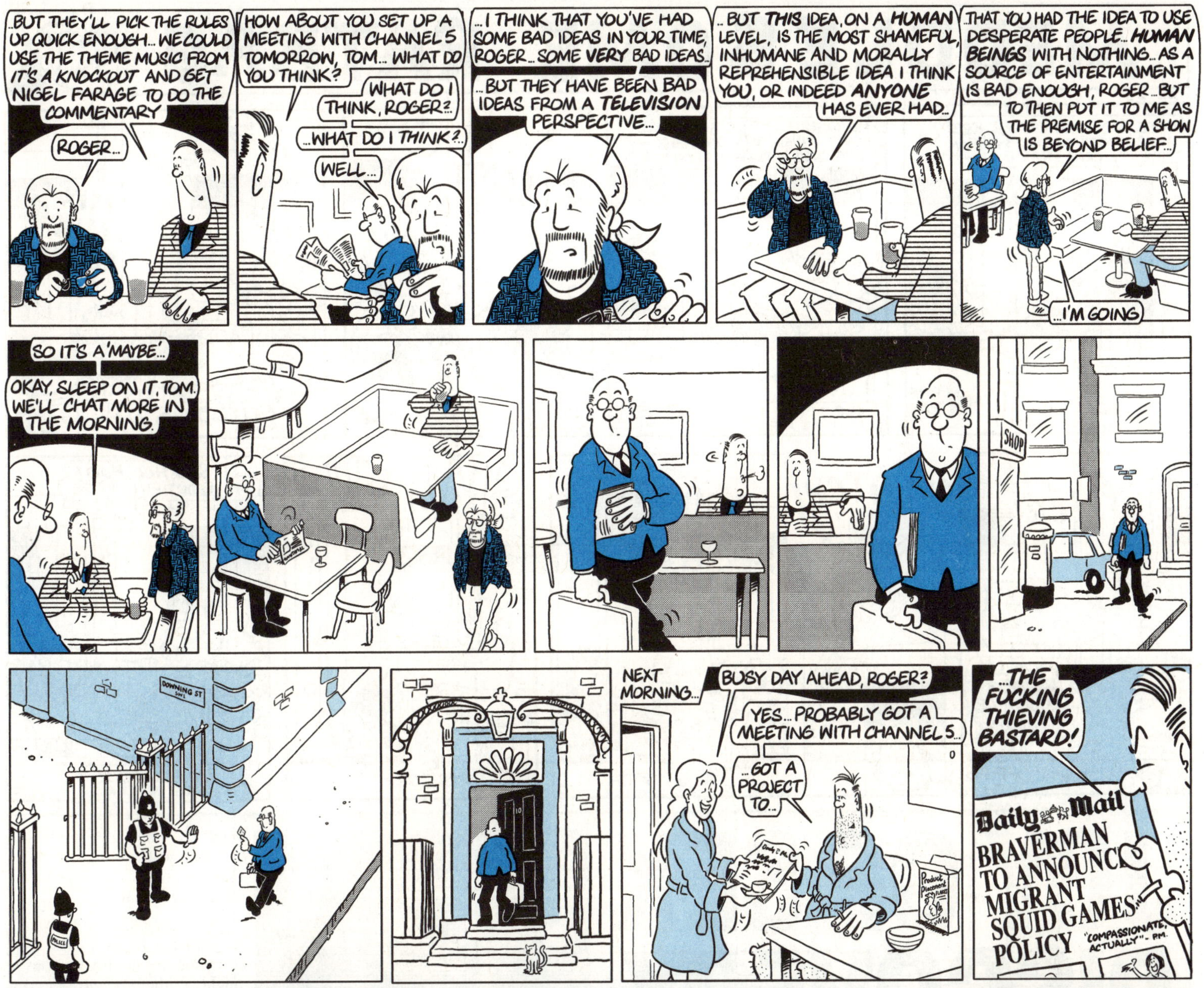
...BUT THEY'LL PICK THE RULES UP QUICK ENOUGH... WE COULD USE THE THEME MUSIC FROM IT'S A KNOCKOUT AND GET NIGEL FARAGE TO DO THE COMMENTARY
ROGER...
HOW ABOUT YOU SET UP A MEETING WITH CHANNEL 5 TOMORROW, TOM... WHAT DO YOU THINK?
WHAT DO I THINK, ROGER?
...WHAT DO I THINK?
WELL...
...I THINK THAT YOU'VE HAD SOME BAD IDEAS IN YOUR TIME, ROGER... SOME VERY BAD IDEAS...
...BUT THEY HAVE BEEN BAD IDEAS FROM A TELEVISION PERSPECTIVE...
...BUT THIS IDEA, ON A HUMAN LEVEL, IS THE MOST SHAMEFUL, INHUMANE AND MORALLY REPREHENSIBLE IDEA I THINK YOU, OR INDEED ANYONE HAS EVER HAD...
THAT YOU HAD THE IDEA TO USE DESPERATE PEOPLE... HUMAN BEINGS WITH NOTHING... AS A SOURCE OF ENTERTAINMENT IS BAD ENOUGH, ROGER... BUT TO THEN PUT IT TO ME AS THE PREMISE FOR A SHOW IS BEYOND BELIEF...
...I'M GOING
SO IT'S A 'MAYBE'...
OKAY, SLEEP ON IT, TOM. WE'LL CHAT MORE IN THE MORNING.
SHOP
DOWNING ST
NEXT MORNING...
BUSY DAY AHEAD, ROGER?
YES... PROBABLY GOT A MEETING WITH CHANNEL 5...
...GOT A PROJECT TO...
...THE FUCKING THIEVING BASTARD!
Daily Mail
BRAVERMAN TO ANNOUNCE MIGRANT SQUID GAMES POLICY
"COMPASSIONATE, ACTUALLY" - PM

SNOW JOKE

Ice costing NHS dear

MOST of us have hilariously fallen on an icy pavement, knocking out a few teeth or cracking our pelvis as we went down. Either that or we've comically lost our footing on some snow-covered steps and copped for concussion or a hairline skull fracture as we hit the deck. And if we haven't, we have certainly laughed at the sight of a stranger taking such a daft tumble. Seeing some poor sap going head over heels on a stretch of frozen street is a stone cold guaranteed rib-tickler; it's one of the best things about the winter season. But taking into account the cost of subsequent medical treatment for casualties, are these accidents now becoming too expensive for the comedy moments they produce? Some medical professionals think so.

NHS bean-counters say the average winter sees British tax-payers forking out an incredible £270 million to treat a tidal wave of broken bodies caused by ground-level frozen water. "That's the equivalent of covering a city the size of Exeter in twenty pound notes," says Dr Bartram Twelves of Queen's Medical Centre in Nottingham. "By anyone's standards, that's an expensive way to make people laugh."

"Last January, a man was brought into A&E who'd slipped down some icy steps on his arse," Dr Twelves told us. "He had a fractured pelvis and coccyx which required two weeks in hospital, an operation and six months of follow-up physiotherapy. The cost of his treatment was the thick end of two hundred thousand quid."

"The trouble is, the fall happened quite early in the morning in a secluded bit of town, and only two people saw him go arse over tit. That's a hundred grand a laugh."

Twelves pointed out that for the same amount of money, 1,150 people could have seen Michael McIntyre live in concert. "Admittedly it wouldn't have been as funny, but you see the point," he said.

Nanny state number-crunchers say that the government needs to do more to help the NHS get better value for the money it spends. "The cost of surgery is what it is, and nothing can bring it down," said Baldrick Lovejoy, hospital administrator at Queen's Medical Centre. "But what we can do is try to maximise the number of people who see someone going bollocks over teakettle and landing like a sack of spuds."

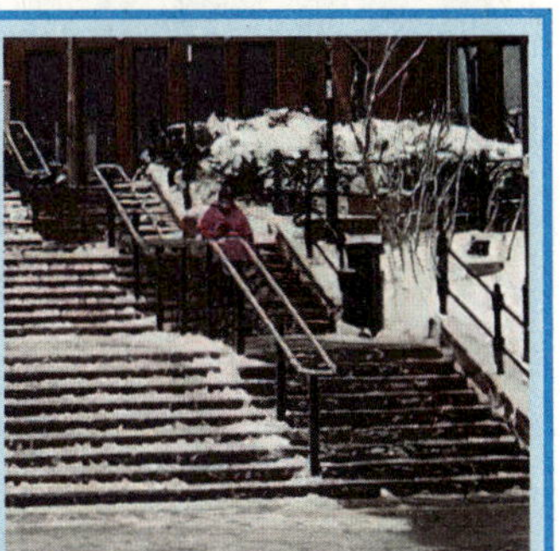

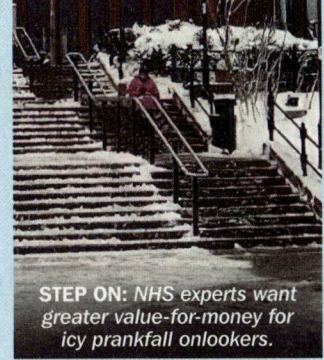

STEP ON: *NHS experts want greater value-for-money for icy prankfall onlookers.*

"I remember twenty years ago, a postman going up in the air on some ice outside the Nottingham Playhouse, landing on his backside with his letters flying everywhere," he said. "He was quite badly injured and needed traction for three weeks. But his hilarious pratfall was witnessed by over 280 people queuing to get in the theatre to see *The Ghost Train* with Henry McGee."

"Taking into account the cost of the postie's treatment, that equated to only £1.80 per laugh. That's the sort of value for money the Health Service needs to be aiming for."

And Lovejoy is now calling on the government to fund a national 'Watch Out For Ice' campaign, informing the public about the best places to see people falling on ice. "The more people we can get laughing at someone going arse over tit, the better value their treatment will represent," he said.

"It's not rocket science."

MEDDLESOME RATBAG
DJ '23
THOSE KIDS HAD BETTER KEEP THEIR FOOTBALL AWAY FROM MY COLD FRAME!
MY LEEKS WIN PRIZES, YOU KNOW!
NO WORRIES! THIS BALL CAN'T CAUSE ANY DAMAGE ~ IT'S JUST A PENNY FLOATER.
SEE ~ IT'S AS LIGHT AS A FEATHER.
BOOT!
WOAH! LOOK HOW HIGH IT GOES!
MIX MIX RUMBLE!
QUICK SETTING CEMENT
FLICK!
QUICK SETTING CEMENT
SPLOTCH!
HURTLE
ROCK SOLID
SMASH!
BOO HOO HOO! MY BEAUTIFUL PRIZE LEEKS!
BOO HOO HOO! THEY'RE IN RUINS!

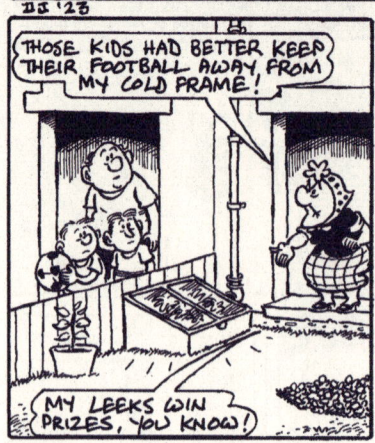

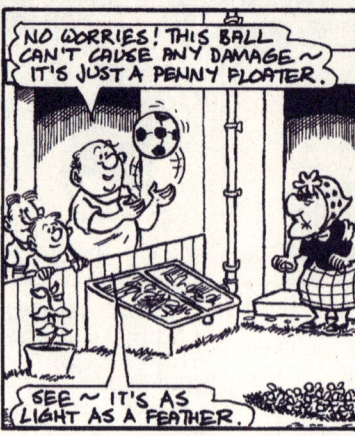

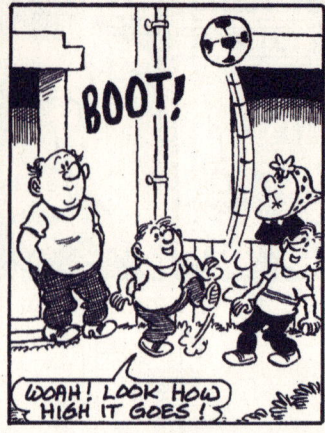

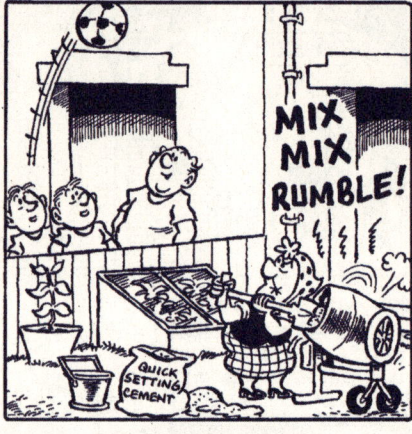

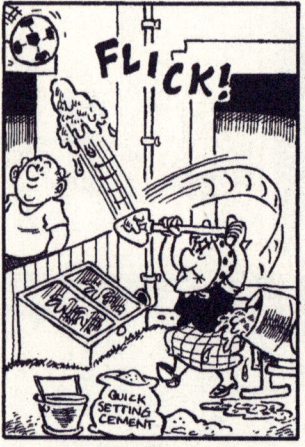

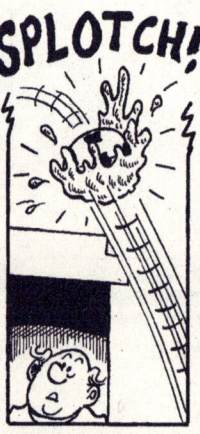

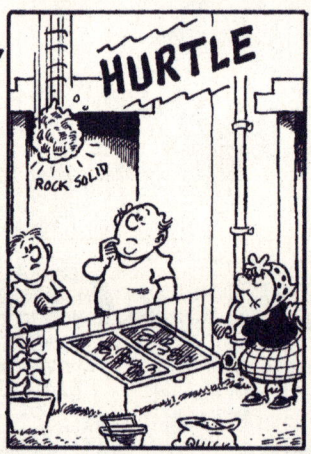

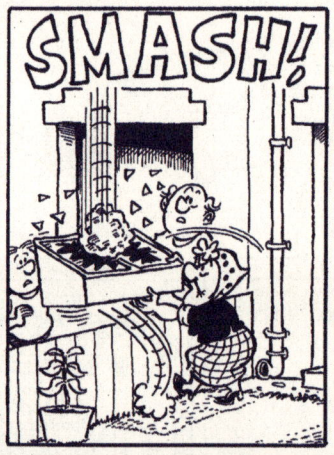

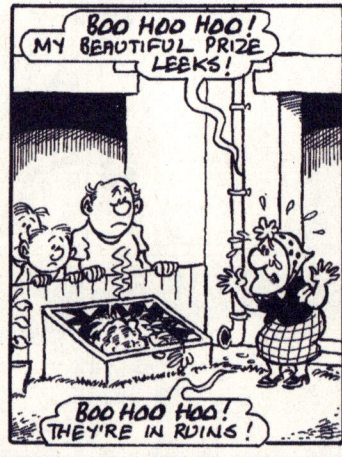

JOY OF SEX DISCOVERY

A MAN from West Yorkshire has been hailed by lovers around the world after inventing the first new position for sexual intercourse since Roman times.

Yorkshire man invents new love-making position

Kevin Bland, a pipe fitter from Featherstone said he came up with the new position in conjunction with his girlfriend Denise during one of their regular Friday night love-making sessions. And Kevin admits that the position took both of them by surprise when they found themselves in it.

"I weren't trying to be adventurous or anything," said 32-year-old Kevin. "Denise lives at her mum's and she doesn't go out on Fridays, so we have to keep it down a bit."

"I were trying to get in a position that didn't make the springs squeak, to be honest, when I happened upon it," he continued.

Kevin and Denise have been trialling the as yet unnamed position for the past few Friday nights, including one rigorous test when Denise's mum was at the bingo. And so far, things are looking encouraging for the innovative act of congress. However, the couple are remaining tight lipped about the exact details of the coital position.

humbug

"All I will say is that it's a good, honest, no-nonsense position as you would expect from a Yorkshireman. There are just a few tweaks to be made and we're there" he said. "I have discussed it with a select handful of drinkers at my local, and they agree that I'm onto a winner."

The name of the position has yet to be decided, but *The White Rose Swan, The Yorkshire Butterfly* and *The Pontefract and Knottingley Flapjack* are all in the running.

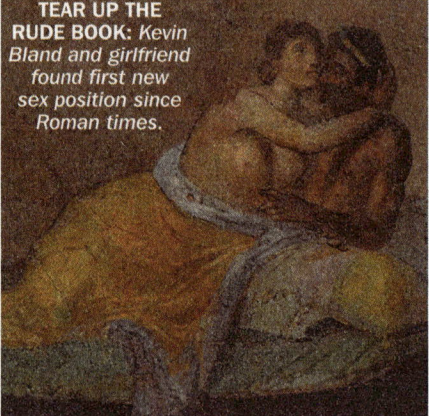

TEAR UP THE RUDE BOOK: *Kevin Bland and girlfriend found first new sex position since Roman times.*

And those desperate to see the first novel arrangement of two copulating bodies in almost 2000 years have not got long to wait. Because according to Kevin, plans are in the offing to debut the position in an erotic movie by a team of Yorkshire bongo vid makers, the release of which is just days away.

"It's going to be called *Hot 'n' Hard in Horbury*," said Bill Shipton, CEO of Three Ridings Scud Ltd, who have been working with Kevin to bring his new position to the silver screen. "It's about a plumber from Castleford who goes round to a house in Horbury to fix the S-bend on a woman's sink," he said. "I don't want to give any spoilers, but let's just say it's not the only drainpipe he ends up attending to that day."

"Viewers will have to wait to see what happens, but as it builds to a climax, they might... they *might*... end up having it off in Kev's new position," he added. "That's all I'm prepared to reveal."

Kevin was eager to point out that despite being the creator of the new position, he would not be starring in the film himself. "I wouldn't mind, but it's not Denise's kind of thing, and there's no way she'd let me do it with somebody else," he said.

julep

"I might have a non-sexual cameo role in it, playing a passer by or something, a bit like Alfred Hitchcock used to do, but nothing more".

"I'll be on set during filming to give technical directions and what have you, but I'll leave the on-camera stuff to the professionals," he said.

Hot 'n' Horny in Horbury is being filmed next Thursday afternoon and will be on general release the following day, available from that man who goes round the pubs in West Yorkshire selling pirate films and porn DVDs.

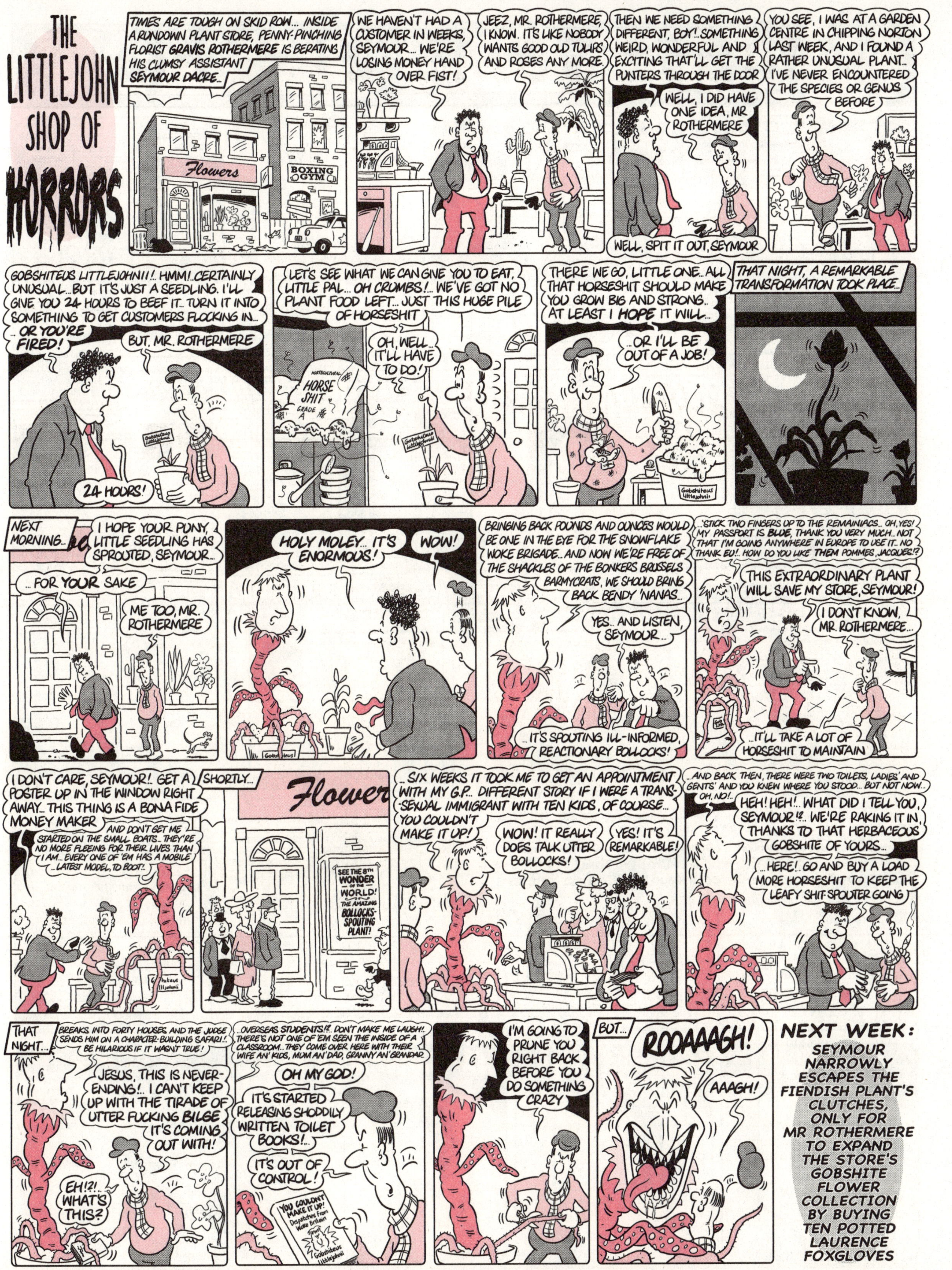
THE LITTLEJOHN SHOP OF HORRORS
TIMES ARE TOUGH ON SKID ROW... INSIDE A RUNDOWN PLANT STORE, PENNY-PINCHING FLORIST GRAVIS ROTHERMERE IS BERATING HIS CLUMSY ASSISTANT SEYMOUR DACRE...
Flowers
BOXING GYM
WE HAVEN'T HAD A CUSTOMER IN WEEKS, SEYMOUR... WE'RE LOSING MONEY HAND OVER FIST!
JEEZ, MR. ROTHERMERE, I KNOW. IT'S LIKE NOBODY WANTS GOOD OLD TULIPS AND ROSES ANY MORE
THEN WE NEED SOMETHING DIFFERENT, BOY!.. SOMETHING WEIRD, WONDERFUL AND EXCITING THAT'LL GET THE PUNTERS THROUGH THE DOOR
WELL, I DID HAVE ONE IDEA, MR ROTHERMERE
WELL, SPIT IT OUT, SEYMOUR
YOU SEE, I WAS AT A GARDEN CENTRE IN CHIPPING NORTON LAST WEEK, AND I FOUND A RATHER UNUSUAL PLANT... I'VE NEVER ENCOUNTERED THE SPECIES OR GENUS BEFORE
GOBSHITEUS LITTLEJOHNII!.. HMM!.. CERTAINLY UNUSUAL... BUT IT'S JUST A SEEDLING. I'LL GIVE YOU 24 HOURS TO BEEF IT... TURN IT INTO SOMETHING TO GET CUSTOMERS FLOCKING IN... OR YOU'RE FIRED!
BUT, MR. ROTHERMERE
24 HOURS!
LET'S SEE WHAT WE CAN GIVE YOU TO EAT, LITTLE PAL... OH CRUMBS!... WE'VE GOT NO PLANT FOOD LEFT... JUST THIS HUGE PILE OF HORSESHIT
OH, WELL... IT'LL HAVE TO DO!
HORSE SHIT GRADE A
THERE WE GO, LITTLE ONE... ALL THAT HORSESHIT SHOULD MAKE YOU GROW BIG AND STRONG... AT LEAST I HOPE IT WILL...
...OR I'LL BE OUT OF A JOB!
Gobshiteus Littlejohnii
THAT NIGHT, A REMARKABLE TRANSFORMATION TOOK PLACE...
NEXT MORNING...
I HOPE YOUR PUNY, LITTLE SEEDLING HAS SPROUTED, SEYMOUR...
...FOR YOUR SAKE
ME TOO, MR. ROTHERMERE
HOLY MOLEY... IT'S ENORMOUS!
WOW!
BRINGING BACK POUNDS AND OUNCES WOULD BE ONE IN THE EYE FOR THE SNOWFLAKE WOKE BRIGADE... AND NOW WE'RE FREE OF THE SHACKLES OF THE BONKERS BRUSSELS BARMYCRATS, WE SHOULD BRING BACK BENDY 'NANAS...
YES... AND LISTEN, SEYMOUR...
...IT'S SPOUTING ILL-INFORMED, REACTIONARY BOLLOCKS!
...'STICK TWO FINGERS UP TO THE REMAINIACS... OH, YES! MY PASSPORT IS BLUE, THANK YOU VERY MUCH... NOT THAT I'M GOING ANYWHERE IN EUROPE TO USE IT... NO THANK EU!.. HOW DO YOU LIKE THEM POMMES, JACQUES!?
THIS EXTRAORDINARY PLANT WILL SAVE MY STORE, SEYMOUR!
I DON'T KNOW, MR. ROTHERMERE...
...IT'LL TAKE A LOT OF HORSESHIT TO MAINTAIN
I DON'T CARE, SEYMOUR!.. GET A POSTER UP IN THE WINDOW RIGHT AWAY... THIS THING IS A BONA FIDE MONEY MAKER
AND DON'T GET ME STARTED ON THE SMALL BOATS... THEY'RE NO MORE FLEEING FOR THEIR LIVES THAN I AM... EVERY ONE OF 'EM HAS A MOBILE ...LATEST MODEL, TO BOOT!..
SHORTLY...
Flower
SEE THE 8TH WONDER OF THE WORLD! THE AMAZING BOLLOCKS-SPOUTING PLANT!
...SIX WEEKS IT TOOK ME TO GET AN APPOINTMENT WITH MY G.P... DIFFERENT STORY IF I WERE A TRANS-SEXUAL IMMIGRANT WITH TEN KIDS, OF COURSE... YOU COULDN'T MAKE IT UP!
WOW! IT REALLY DOES TALK UTTER BOLLOCKS!
YES! IT'S REMARKABLE!
...AND BACK THEN, THERE WERE TWO TOILETS, LADIES' AND GENTS' AND YOU KNEW WHERE YOU STOOD... BUT NOT NOW... OH, NO!..
HEH! HEH!.. WHAT DID I TELL YOU, SEYMOUR!?.. WE'RE RAKING IT IN, THANKS TO THAT HERBACEOUS GOBSHITE OF YOURS...
...HERE!.. GO AND BUY A LOAD MORE HORSESHIT TO KEEP THE LEAFY SHIT-SPOUTER GOING
THAT NIGHT...
BREAKS INTO FORTY HOUSES AND THE JUDGE SENDS HIM ON A CHARACTER-BUILDING SAFARI!.. BE HILARIOUS IF IT WASN'T TRUE!
JESUS, THIS IS NEVER-ENDING!.. I CAN'T KEEP UP WITH THE TIRADE OF UTTER FUCKING BILGE IT'S COMING OUT WITH!
EH!?!.. WHAT'S THIS?
...OVERSEAS STUDENTS!?.. DON'T MAKE ME LAUGH!.. THERE'S NOT ONE OF 'EM SEEN THE INSIDE OF A CLASSROOM... THEY COME OVER HERE WITH THEIR WIFE AN' KIDS, MUM AN' DAD, GRANNY AN' GRANDAD...
OH MY GOD!
IT'S STARTED RELEASING SHODDILY WRITTEN TOILET BOOKS!..
IT'S OUT OF CONTROL!
YOU COULDN'T MAKE IT UP! Despatches from Woke Britain
I'M GOING TO PRUNE YOU RIGHT BACK BEFORE YOU DO SOMETHING CRAZY
BUT...
ROOAAAGH!
AAAGH!
NEXT WEEK:
SEYMOUR NARROWLY ESCAPES THE FIENDISH PLANT'S CLUTCHES, ONLY FOR MR ROTHERMERE TO EXPAND THE STORE'S GOBSHITE FLOWER COLLECTION BY BUYING TEN POTTED LAURENCE FOXGLOVES

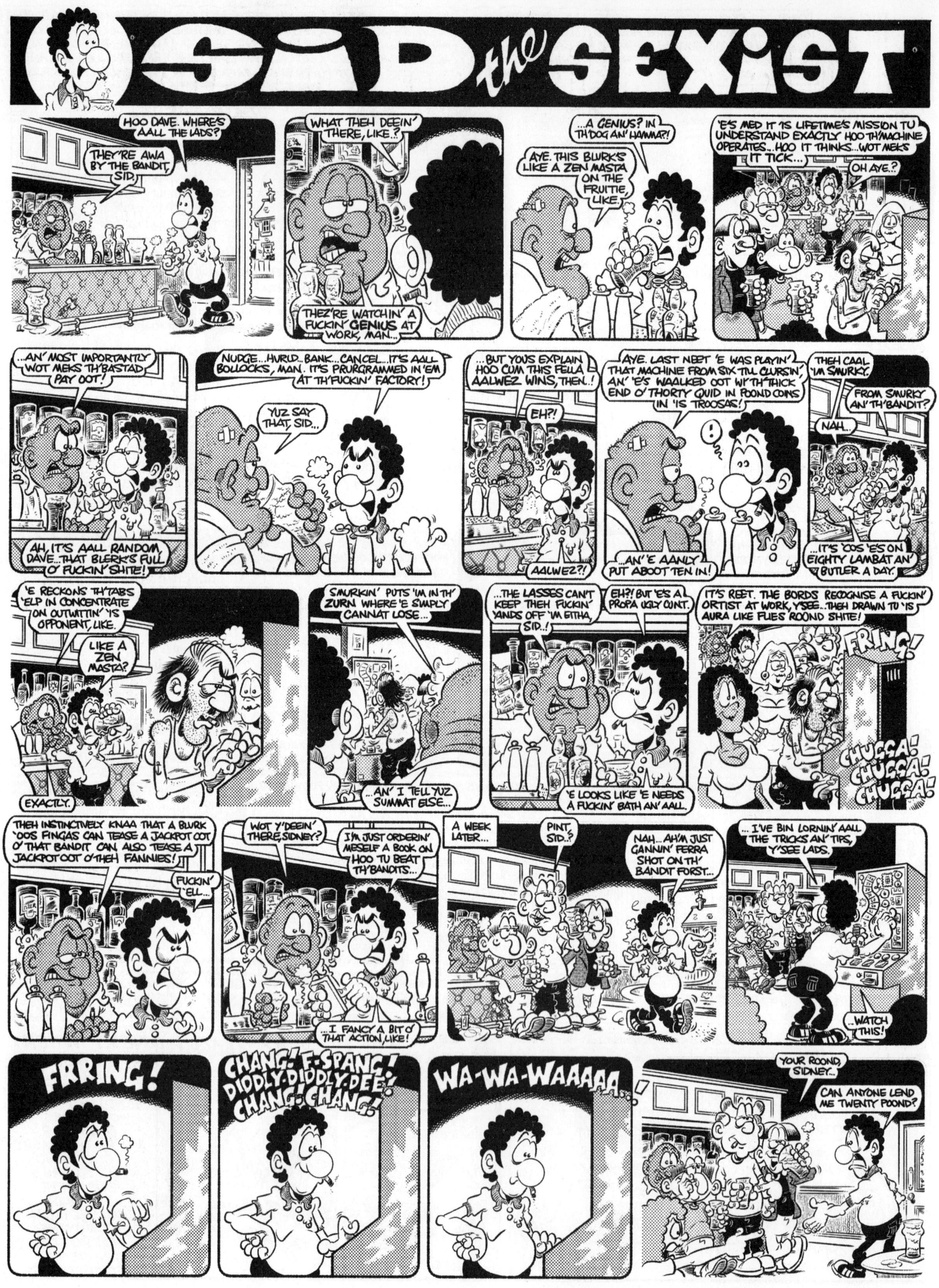
SID the SEXIST
HOO DAVE. WHERE'S AALL THE LADS?
THEY'RE AWA BY THE BANDIT, SID.
WHAT THEH DEEIN' THERE, LIKE.?
THEZ'RE WATCHIN' A FUCKIN' GENIUS AT WORK, MAN...
...A GENIUS? IN TH'DOG AN' HAMMA?!
AYE. THIS BLURK'S LIKE A ZEN MASTA ON THE FRUITIE, LIKE.
'E'S MED IT 'IS LIFETIME'S MISSION TU UNDERSTAND EXACTLY HOO TH'MACHINE OPERATES... HOO IT THINKS... WOT MEKS IT TICK...
OH AYE.?
...AN' MOST IMPORTANTLY WOT MEKS TH'BASTAD PAY OOT!
AH, IT'S AALL RANDOM, DAVE... THAT BLERK'S FULL O' FUCKIN' SHITE!
NUDGE... HURLD... BANK... CANCEL... IT'S AALL BOLLOCKS, MAN. IT'S PRURGRAMMED IN 'EM AT TH'FUCKIN' FACTORY!
YUZ SAY THAT, SID...
...BUT YOU'S EXPLAIN HOO CUM THIS FELLA AALWEZ WINS, THEN..!
EH?!
AALWEZ?!
AYE. LAST NEET 'E WAS PLAYIN' THAT MACHINE FROM SIX TIL CLURSIN' AN' 'E'S WAALKED OOT WI'TH'THICK END O' THORTY QUID IN POOND COINS IN 'IS TROOSAS!
!
...AN' 'E AANLY PUT ABOOT TEN IN!
THEH CAAL 'IM SMURKY.
FROM SMURKY AN' TH'BANDIT?
NAH...
...IT'S 'COS 'E'S ON EIGHTY LAMBAT AN' BUTLER A DAY.
'E RECKONS TH'TABS 'ELP IN CONCENTRATE ON OUTWITTIN' 'IS OPPONENT, LIKE.
LIKE A ZEN MASTA?
EXACTLY.
SMURKIN' PUTS 'IM IN TH' ZURN WHERE 'E SIMPLY CANNAT LOSE...
...AN' I TELL YUZ SUMMAT ELSE...
...THE LASSES CAN'T KEEP THEH FUCKIN' 'ANDS OFF 'IM EITHA, SID..!
EH?! BUT 'E'S A PROPA UGLY CUNT.
'E LOOKS LIKE 'E NEEDS A FUCKIN' BATH AN' AALL.
IT'S REET. THE BORDS RECOGNISE A FUCKIN' ORTIST AT WORK, Y'SEE... THEH DRAWN TU 'IS AURA LIKE FLIES ROOND SHITE!
FRING!
CHUGGA! CHUGGA! CHUGGA!
THEH INSTINCTIVELY KNAA THAT A BLURK 'OOS FINGAS CAN TEASE A JACKPOT OOT O' THAT BANDIT CAN ALSO TEASE A JACKPOT OOT O'THEH FANNIES!
FUCKIN' 'ELL...
WOT Y'DEEIN' THERE, SIDNEY?
I'M JUST ORDERIN' MESELF A BOOK ON HOO TU BEAT TH'BANDITS...
...I FANCY A BIT O' THAT ACTION, LIKE!
A WEEK LATER...
PINT, SID..?
NAH... AH'M JUST GANNIN' FERRA SHOT ON TH' BANDIT FORST...
...I'VE BIN LORNIN' AALL THE TRICKS AN' TIPS, Y'SEE LADS.
...WATCH THIS!
FRRING!
CHANG! F-SPANG! DIDDLY-DIDDLY-DEE! CHANG! CHANG!
WA-WA-WAAAAA...!
YOUR ROOND, SIDNEY...
CAN ANYONE LEND ME TWENTY POOND?

Christmas Shitpump Roundup

Not-so-silent night

THE Christmas Eve carol service from King's College, Cambridge is a tradition that has remained unchanged for centuries. But it will look a little different this year as, in an attempt to move with the times, organisers have invited US rap-rockers Limp Bizkit to perform alongside the chapel choir.

And the nu metal bad boys are sure to set the tone of the evening when they open with their riff-heavy take on *Once in Royal David's City*. "It's going to be an interesting, and I'm sure very enjoyable carol service," said Provost of King's College, Gillian Tett.

Limp Bizkit frontman Fred Durst will then read the first lesson, after which the band will go into a thrash metal version of *The Sussex Carol*, arranged by Ralph Vaughan Williams. "It's going to be an interesting, and I'm sure very enjoyable carol service," said master of the Choir Humphrey Twelves.

In the second reading, the band's turntablist DJ Lethal will read the Nativity from the Gospel of St Luke, a traditional Christmas lesson telling of Jesus's humble birth. But this year's King's service will see the former House of Pain mixer read the passage in a beatbox style. "It's going to be an interesting, and I'm sure very enjoyable carol service," said Organ scholar Benjamin Octavius.

And BBC engineers have been given instructions to bleep out any foul language if the notorious band go 'off script'.

The service will end as always with the band playing *Oh Come All Ye Faithful*. And college governors have promised to "come down hard" on anyone destroying the fixtures and furniture of the chapel if Durst encourages the congregation to "Break some shit" as he did at the notorious Woodstock '99 festival.

"It's going to be an interesting, and I'm sure very enjoyable carol service," said Dean of King's College Rev. Bartram Bartholemew.

News just got bigger

IN an effort to keep up with an ever-changing and tumultuous world, the BBC have decided to double their current 24-hour output and provide a 48-hour rolling news service.

"24-hour rolling news may have been fine for last century, when life was slower paced, but in today's world there is so much more news to report," explained middle-tier *BBC News* executive Jeremy Humshough.

"What with all the wars, politics, crime and sport, there is simply too much information to cram into an old-fashioned 24-hour news cycle," he explained. "And that's without the heartwarming stories about cats at the end."

Humshough was cagey about where the service's extra 24 hours would come from. "Well, like the news, there is no shortage of hours out there," he said. "Billions of hours have passed since the dawn of time, and I'd be surprised if there weren't billions more to come. I don't think we'll find ourselves short of hours."

Media experts expect things to escalate quickly and predict that Sky will introduce a daily 96-hour rolling news service early next year.

Soap war escalates

THE annual yuletide TV soap ratings war has started, with the popular serials locked in battle to see who can grab the largest viewing figures over the festive season. And this year, it looks like each one is trying to out-Christmas the others.

Whilst the planned plotlines remain closely-guarded secrets, sources say that in late November, two lorry loads of decorations – including paper chains, tinsel and baubles – were spotted being unloaded at Elstree studios, where *EastEnders* is filmed.

Not to be out done, on the same day Media City Studios in Salford took delivery of around 500 6-foot Christmas trees for the set of *Coronation Street*.

"The soaps all like to do Christmas, but it looks like this year they are really pushing the boat out," said Boyd Pointless, editor of supermarket checkout favourite *ChatSoap* magazine. "My sources have told me that the *Emmerdale* props department has ordered two tons of glitter and a hundred of those five-foot illuminated Santa Clauses."

"It's going to be an exciting, and very Christmassy time in soapland."

But Pointless said that he had heard rumours in the industry which, if true, will mean that the Christmas Day ratings battle would turn into a rout for one of the soaps. He told *Newsnight*'s Victoria Derbyshire: "No spoilers, but apparently, the producers of one of the 'Big Two' have rented a snow machine for the month."

"If the snow is falling in Albert Square, or it's a white Christmas in Weatherfield, it's game over for the other side," he added.

Romeshy Christmas

IT'S going to be a busy Christmas for stand up comic Romesh Ranganathan, as the BBC have announced that he will be appearing on *every programme* on the network over the festive period.

The ubiquitous presenter is already a familiar favourite on over 51% of the BBC's current output, and in December, 45 year-old Ranganathan intends to make a clean sweep of the Christmas schedules. "I'm really looking forward to being on everything on the BEEB over Christmas" he told the *Radio Times*. "On some shows I'll be a guest, on others I'll present. But rest assured, whatever's on the BBC, I'll be in it," he promised. The only show over the festive period that will be Romesh-free will be the 3:00pm Christmas Day slot when King Charles takes to the airwaves to broadcast to the Commonwealth. However, BBC bosses are in talks with the Palace to arrange for Ranganathan to sit in shot behind the King during next year's Christmas broadcast.

A Christmas Message from Viz Editor *Hampton Doubleday* OBE

GREETINGS, and the very Merriest of Christmases to you all. And I send these festive wishes safe in the knowledge that you are not purchasing the book in, let us say July or August. I see at first hand each year sales of the *Viz* Annual fall off a cliff at 5:00pm on Christmas eve, followed in the new year by the traditional trickle of unsold copies being returned to me, as the sellers cannot justify giving shelf space to a 'Christmas book' that has ceased to 'shift product' to use publishing terminology.

But it need not be so. Like dogs, *Viz Comic* should be for life, not just for Christmas, and you can get year-round fun and merriment by becoming a subscriber and having 10 issues of *Viz Comic* delivered directly to your door.

And there will doubtless be some sort of splendid offer in the form of a free gift. Simply point your computer mouse in the direction of *viz.co.uk* and click on some links or somesuch - I am not technically minded - which will guide you through the process.

It only remains for me to wish you a happy, healthy, and safe 2026.

Hampton Doubleday

Hampton Doubleday OBE

WATER MESS!

Lancashire man to sue after glugging on contaminated water

A LANCASHIRE man is taking on his local water company in a landmark legal case which, if ruled in his favour, could open the floodgates and see hundreds of similar cases brought before the courts.

EXCLUSIVE!

Brian Duckpool is claiming that Lancastrian Utilities, who provide water and sewage services across the county, have consistently failed in their duty to provide clean drinking water for locals. And the furious rate-payer is now claiming damages of £25,000 to cover loss of earnings after his health suffered as a result of drinking contaminated water.

Professional gambler Duckpool, 68, was unable to work after suffering a broken arm, a direct result of bacteria in the tap water supplied to his home in Diggle, just outside Oldham. "You read about all these germs in the water making people sick and giving them the shits and all sorts, and you wonder what else is in there," he told the *Oldham Bugle and Flugelhorn*. "I woke up last Tuesday morning with my elbow all smashed in and a break in my forearm, and it doesn't take a genius to work out there's clearly some bacteria or virus in the water that causes broken arms."

botch

Duckpool vividly remembers the day his arm broke. He told us: "I'd won a tenner on the horses that day, so I decided to go out to celebrate. I had a couple of glasses of water before I went out to keep me hydrated, which is a sensible thing to do if you plan going on a bender."

"I had a right old time. I can't recall much about the night, to be honest, and I certainly can't remember how I got home. But when I woke up with my arm all smashed up, I remembered those glasses of water."

"Just join the dots," he said.

hair

Brian went to A&E at the Royal Oldham Hospital on Rochdale Road, where he was discovered to have a distal radius fracture. "The doc told me these type of fractures are most commonly caused when people go arse over tit and put their hands out to break their fall," he said.

"I couldn't remember anything about the night before, but I would've definitely remembered falling over. And I didn't. So there can be only one conclusion. It was something in the water."

Medics put Duckpool's broken arm in a cast, before giving him a prescription for pain relief and discharging him. He went straight home, but feeling sick and with a thumping headache, he decided to take the day off work.

"If I was employed by somebody, I could have called in sick and got up to three days off with pay without a doctor's note," he said. "But when you're self-employed like I am, and you don't go to work, you don't get paid. It's that simple."

ILL WATER: *Brian Duckpool with a glass of water similar to the one he drank.*

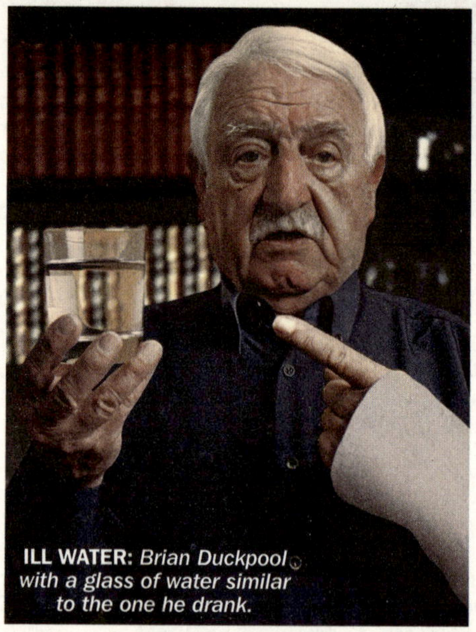

peevly

Duckpool says that he can easily earn £25,000 per day betting on horses and dogs, but he calculated that his day away from his local bookmaker's shop cost him even more than that. "I looked at all the runners I would have picked had that water not broke my arm, and they all came in," he said.

"What's more, I would've had them on an accumulator, and I would've paid the tax on it first. So I would've walked out with a cool £38,000."

After doing some research online, Brian discovered that when courts make awards for loss of earnings, they are based in line with average pay rates. So rather than look for the full £38,000 compensation, he decided to seek just £25,000.

"I've found a really good solicitor who's taken my case," said Duckpool.

"He specialises in ambulance chasing, so he knows what he's doing. And he usually does a no-win no-fee and takes half the winnings. But he says rather than take twelve-and-a-half grand off me, he'll do it for a £500 up front non-returnable fee," he added.

Finbarr Saunders & his Double Entendres

AT THE ZOO...
...I MUST SHOW YOU THE BOA CONSTRICTOR, MRS SAUNDERS.
REPTILES & AMPHIBIANS
...MY WORD, MR GIMLET! IT'S A LOT LONGER AND THICKER THAN I EXPECTED... WITH A PAIR OF BIG, HAIRY NUTS HANGING UNDERNEATH!
YOMP! YOMP!
GARF! GARF!
CHUD! CHUD!
I THINK I MIGHT ADOPT THIS ELDERLY FRESHWATER CAYMAN CALLED FRANCES.
IT'S JUST £5 A WEEK TO KEEP IT FED WITH A DIET OF SPRATS AND HERRINGS.
GOODNESS ME! YOUR DAMP OLD FANNY CERTAINLY SMELLS OF FISH!
FNARR! FNARR!
YIK! YIK!
WOOF! WOOF!
HO! HO!
HMM... THERE'S SUPPOSED TO BE AN ARGENTINIAN HORNED FROG IN HERE, BUT I CAN'T SEE IT...
OVER THERE, LOOK. I CAN MAKE OUT SOME MEATY WET LIPS BEHIND THAT TANGLED BUSH..!
HOOP! HOOP!
NANK! NANK!
WIB! WIB!
I USED TO HAVE A PET SNAKE, YOU KNOW... I USED TO GET MY WIFE TO RUB IT DOWN WITH LINSEED OIL ONCE A WEEK... STARTING WITH THE HEAD END.
NAMP! NAMP!
YOOB! YOOB!
MUMP! MUMP!
WORT! WORT!
I KEEP A GHILA MONSTER IN MY TERRARIUM, AS LIKE MOST REPTILES, THEY ARE VERY SENSITIVE TO LOW TEMPERATURES.
...INDEED. IF MY FOOT-LONG MONSTER IS ALLOWED TO GET COLD, IT SHRIVELS UP AND WON'T MOVE...
FNARR! FN—
ERM... YOU WAIT OVER HERE FOR A MINUTE, FINBARR..
...GOODNESS ME, MR GIMLET! IT'S ALL SCALY AND APPEARS TO BE SHEDDING ITS SKIN..!
WOW! IT SOUNDS LIKE MUM'S SPOTTED SOME SQUAMATE MOULTING IN PROGRESS!
YES, I THINK I MUST'VE CAUGHT SOME SORT OF CLAP OFF A PROSTITUTE ON MY LAST TRIP TO AMSTERDAM...

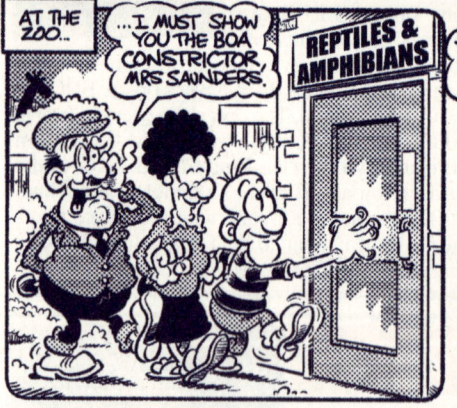

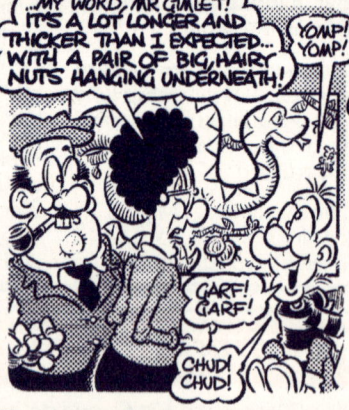

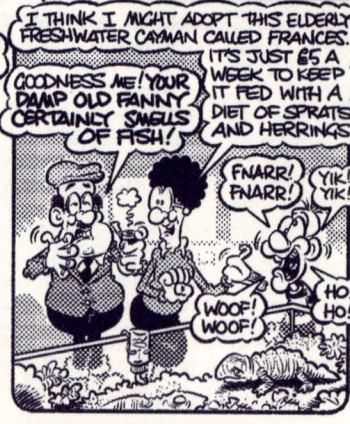

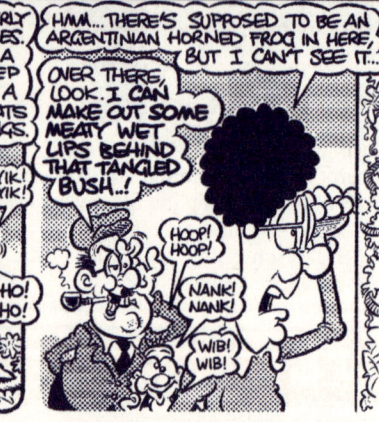

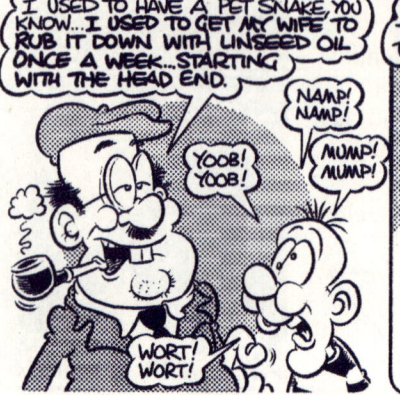

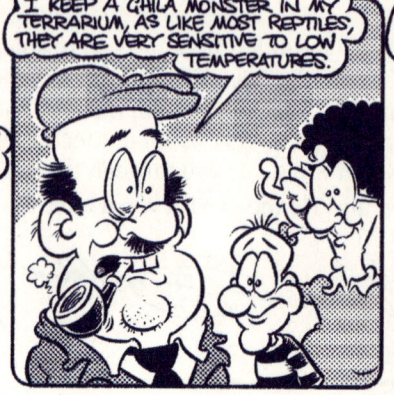

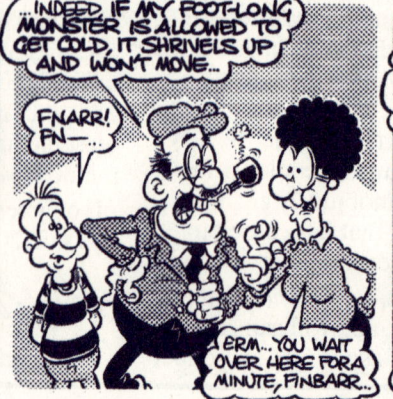

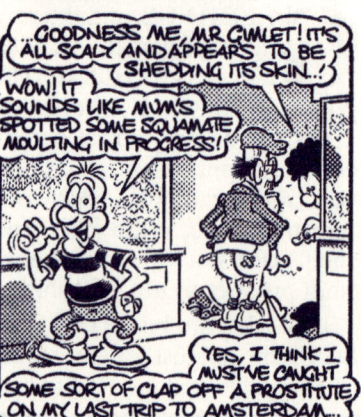

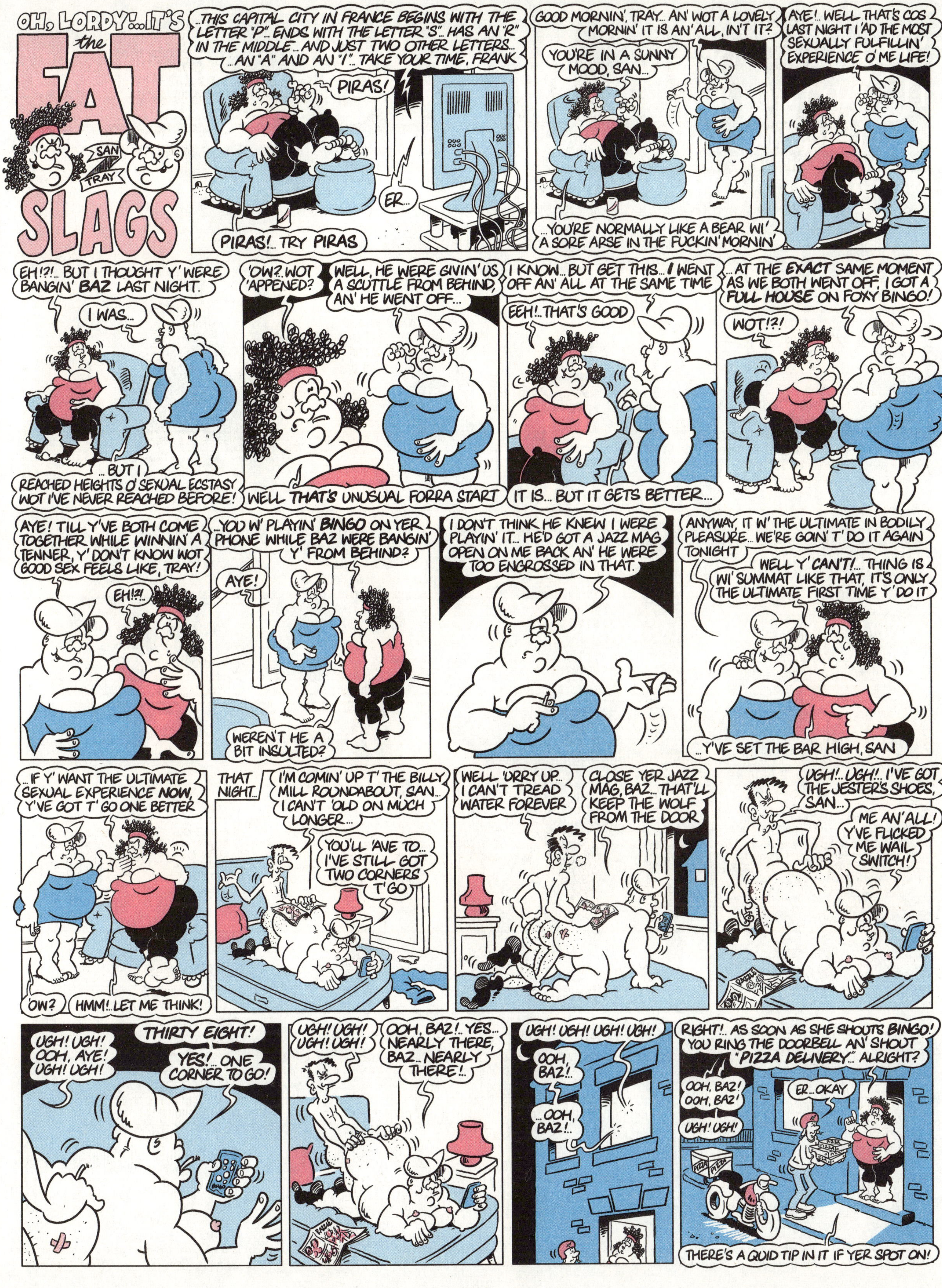
OH, LORDY!..IT'S the FAT SLAGS
SAN
TRAY
...THIS CAPITAL CITY IN FRANCE BEGINS WITH THE LETTER "P"... ENDS WITH THE LETTER "S"... HAS AN "R" IN THE MIDDLE... AND JUST TWO OTHER LETTERS... ...AN "A" AND AN "I". TAKE YOUR TIME, FRANK
PIRAS!
ER...
PIRAS!.. TRY PIRAS
GOOD MORNIN', TRAY... AN' WOT A LOVELY MORNIN' IT IS AN' ALL, IN'T IT?
YOU'RE IN A SUNNY MOOD, SAN...
...YOU'RE NORMALLY LIKE A BEAR WI' A SORE ARSE IN THE FUCKIN' MORNIN'
AYE!.. WELL THAT'S COS LAST NIGHT I 'AD THE MOST SEXUALLY FULFILLIN' EXPERIENCE O' ME LIFE!
EH!?!.. BUT I THOUGHT Y' WERE BANGIN' BAZ LAST NIGHT.
I WAS...
...BUT I REACHED HEIGHTS O' SEXUAL ECSTASY WOT I'VE NEVER REACHED BEFORE!
'OW? WOT 'APPENED?
WELL, HE WERE GIVIN' US A SCUTTLE FROM BEHIND, AN' HE WENT OFF...
WELL THAT'S UNUSUAL FORRA START
I KNOW... BUT GET THIS... I WENT OFF AN' ALL AT THE SAME TIME
EEH!.. THAT'S GOOD
IT IS... BUT IT GETS BETTER...
...AT THE EXACT SAME MOMENT AS WE BOTH WENT OFF, I GOT A FULL HOUSE ON FOXY BINGO!
WOT!?!
AYE! TILL Y'VE BOTH COME TOGETHER WHILE WINNIN' A TENNER, Y' DON'T KNOW WOT GOOD SEX FEELS LIKE, TRAY!
EH!?!
...YOU W' PLAYIN' BINGO ON YER PHONE WHILE BAZ WERE BANGIN' Y' FROM BEHIND?
AYE!
WEREN'T HE A BIT INSULTED?
I DON'T THINK HE KNEW I WERE PLAYIN' IT... HE'D GOT A JAZZ MAG OPEN ON ME BACK AN' HE WERE TOO ENGROSSED IN THAT.
ANYWAY, IT W' THE ULTIMATE IN BODILY PLEASURE... WE'RE GOIN' T' DO IT AGAIN TONIGHT
WELL Y' CAN'T!... THING IS WI' SUMMAT LIKE THAT, IT'S ONLY THE ULTIMATE FIRST TIME Y' DO IT
...Y'VE SET THE BAR HIGH, SAN
...IF Y' WANT THE ULTIMATE SEXUAL EXPERIENCE NOW, Y'VE GOT T' GO ONE BETTER
OW?
HMM!.. LET ME THINK!
THAT NIGHT...
I'M COMIN' UP T' THE BILLY MILL ROUNDABOUT, SAN... I CAN'T 'OLD ON MUCH LONGER...
YOU'LL 'AVE TO... I'VE STILL GOT TWO CORNERS T' GO
WELL 'URRY UP... I CAN'T TREAD WATER FOREVER
CLOSE YER JAZZ MAG, BAZ... THAT'LL KEEP THE WOLF FROM THE DOOR
UGH!.. UGH!.. I'VE GOT THE JESTER'S SHOES, SAN...
ME AN' ALL! Y'VE FLICKED ME WAIL SWITCH!
UGH! UGH! OOH, AYE! UGH! UGH!
THIRTY EIGHT!
YES!.. ONE CORNER TO GO!
UGH! UGH! UGH! UGH!
OOH, BAZ!.. YES... NEARLY THERE, BAZ... NEARLY THERE!..
UGH! UGH! UGH! UGH!
OOH, BAZ!..
...OOH, BAZ!..
RIGHT!.. AS SOON AS SHE SHOUTS BINGO! YOU RING THE DOORBELL AN' SHOUT "PIZZA DELIVERY"... ALRIGHT?
OOH, BAZ! OOH, BAZ!
UGH! UGH!
ER...OKAY
THERE'S A QUID TIP IN IT IF YER SPOT ON!

SHE HAD AN ARSE…
HE HAD TWO LIPS…
AND THE SPIRIT OF CARNIVAL
WAS ABOUT TO TAKE OVER…

2 GOLDEN ORBS WINNER 2023
BEST FOREIGN LANGUAGE FILM & BEST NEW ARSE IN A SUPPORTING ROLE

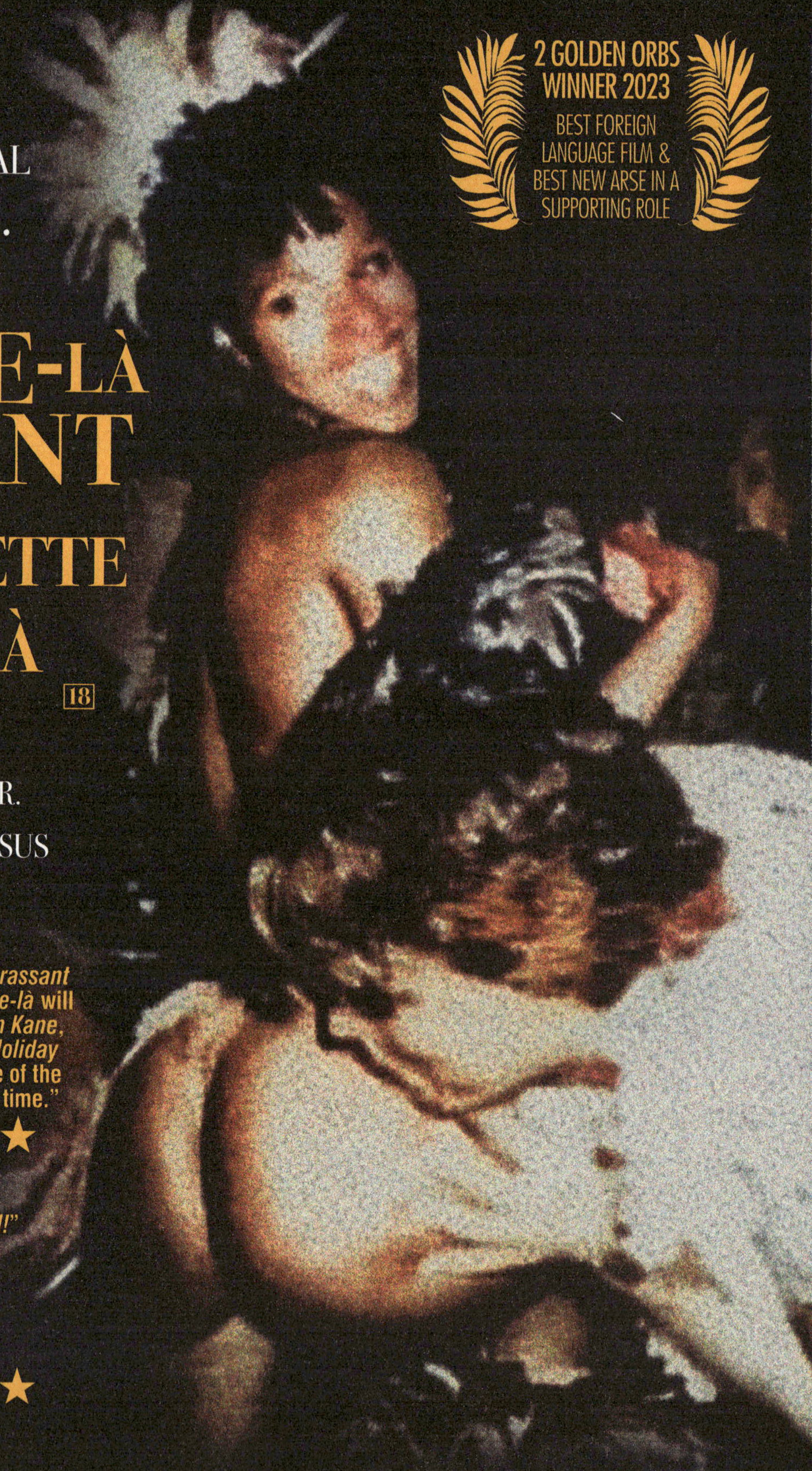

CET HOMME-LÀ EMBRASSANT LE CUL DE CETTE OISELLE-LÀ

[18]

THE KISS LASTED A MOMENT, BUT THE PICTURE WOULD LAST FOREVER.

…AND IT WAS A MARDI GRAS HIS MISSUS WOULD *NEVER* LET HIM FORGET.

"*Poignant and moving.* I will never look at that picture of that bloke kissing that bird's arse in the same way again."

Guardian

"The arse kiss scene was shot in one continuous take. *A cinematic masterpiece.*"

Time Out

"Keep the tissues handy."

Watchtower

"*Cet Homme-là Embrassant le Cul de cette Oiselle-là* will go down with *Citizen Kane*, *La Dolce Vita* and *Holiday on the Buses* as one of the greatest films of all time."

Empire

"It's in FRENCH!"

Daily Mail

"It's a *BUM!*"

Mrs B. Essex

STUDIO CARNAL PRESENTS A PHALLIQUE PRODUCTION. VINCENT CASSELL AS THAT BLOKE. BÉRÉNICE MARLOHE AS THAT BIRD. CHARLOTTE GAINSBOURG AS THAT BLOKE'S MISSUS. GUEST APPEARANCE BY GÉRARD DEPARDIEU AS THAT PHOTOGRAPHER THAT TOOK THAT PHOTOGRAPH OF THAT BLOKE KISSING THAT BIRD'S ARSE. SCREENPLAY BY HAMPTON DOUBLEJOUR. DIRECTED BY LUC BESSON. BASED ON AN ORIGINAL PHOTOGRAPH FOUND IN A MAGAZINE FORTY YEARS AGO. SUBTITLES BY TWO AMERICANS WHO HAVE NEVER SET FOOT OUTSIDE LOS ANGELES.

Coming soon to a cinema near you.

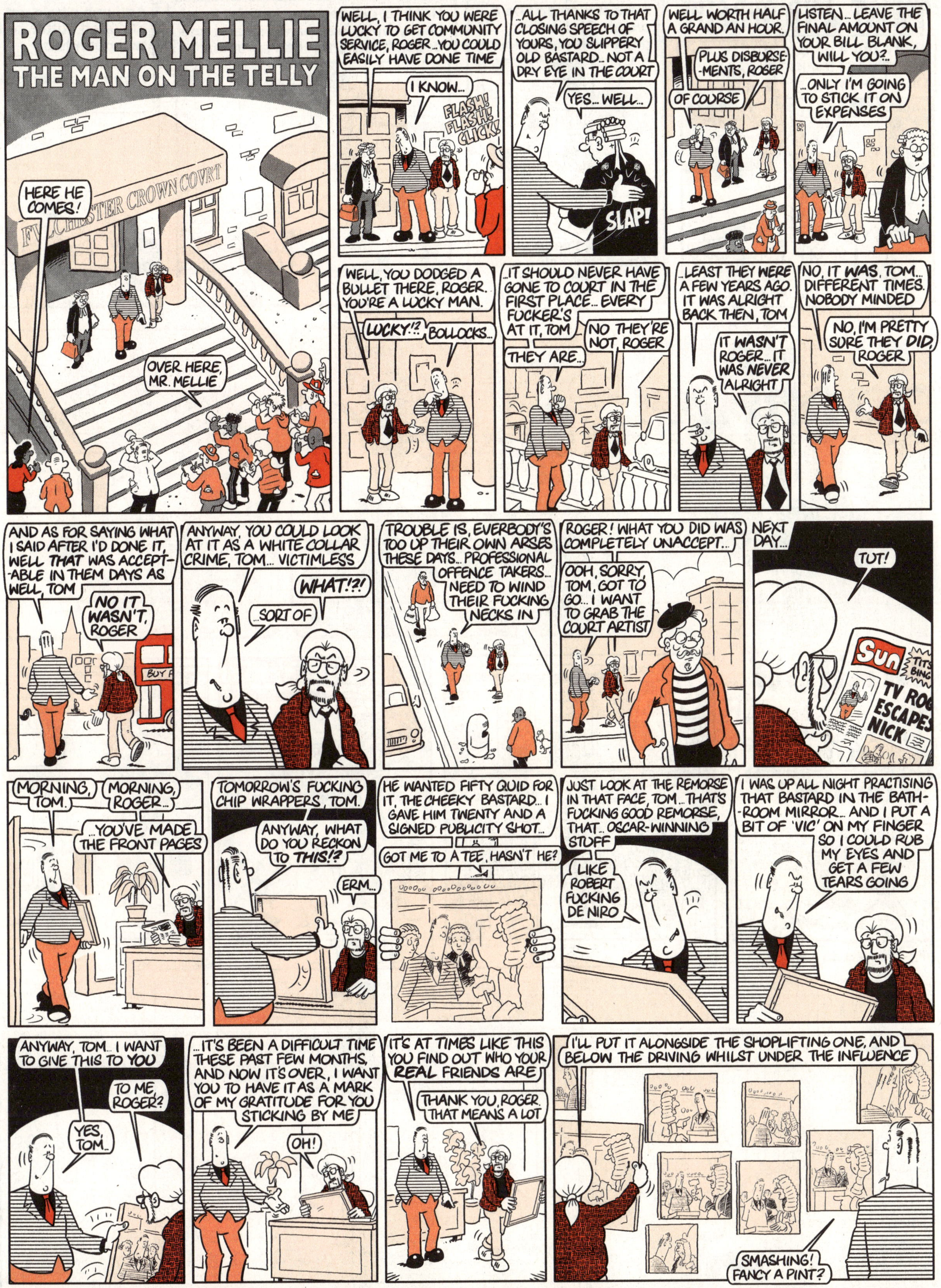
ROGER MELLIE
THE MAN ON THE TELLY
FVLCHESTER CROWN COVRT
HERE HE COMES!
OVER HERE, MR. MELLIE
WELL, I THINK YOU WERE LUCKY TO GET COMMUNITY SERVICE, ROGER... YOU COULD EASILY HAVE DONE TIME
I KNOW...
FLASH! FLASH! CLICK!
...ALL THANKS TO THAT CLOSING SPEECH OF YOURS, YOU SLIPPERY OLD BASTARD... NOT A DRY EYE IN THE COURT
YES... WELL...
SLAP!
WELL WORTH HALF A GRAND AN HOUR.
PLUS DISBURSE-MENTS, ROGER
OF COURSE
LISTEN... LEAVE THE FINAL AMOUNT ON YOUR BILL BLANK, WILL YOU?...
...ONLY I'M GOING TO STICK IT ON EXPENSES
WELL, YOU DODGED A BULLET THERE, ROGER. YOU'RE A LUCKY MAN.
LUCKY!?
BOLLOCKS...
...IT SHOULD NEVER HAVE GONE TO COURT IN THE FIRST PLACE... EVERY FUCKER'S AT IT, TOM
NO THEY'RE NOT, ROGER
THEY ARE...
...LEAST THEY WERE A FEW YEARS AGO. IT WAS ALRIGHT BACK THEN, TOM
IT WASN'T ROGER... IT WAS NEVER ALRIGHT
NO, IT WAS, TOM... DIFFERENT TIMES. NOBODY MINDED
NO, I'M PRETTY SURE THEY DID, ROGER
AND AS FOR SAYING WHAT I SAID AFTER I'D DONE IT, WELL THAT WAS ACCEPT-ABLE IN THEM DAYS AS WELL, TOM
NO IT WASN'T, ROGER
ANYWAY, YOU COULD LOOK AT IT AS A WHITE COLLAR CRIME, TOM... VICTIMLESS
WHAT!?!
...SORT OF
TROUBLE IS, EVERBODY'S TOO UP THEIR OWN ARSES THESE DAYS... PROFESSIONAL OFFENCE TAKERS... NEED TO WIND THEIR FUCKING NECKS IN
ROGER! WHAT YOU DID WAS COMPLETELY UNACCEPT...
OOH, SORRY, TOM, GOT TO GO... I WANT TO GRAB THE COURT ARTIST
NEXT DAY...
TUT!
Sun
ESCAPES NICK
MORNING, TOM.
MORNING, ROGER...
...YOU'VE MADE THE FRONT PAGES
TOMORROW'S FUCKING CHIP WRAPPERS, TOM.
ANYWAY, WHAT DO YOU RECKON TO THIS!?
ERM...
HE WANTED FIFTY QUID FOR IT, THE CHEEKY BASTARD... I GAVE HIM TWENTY AND A SIGNED PUBLICITY SHOT...
GOT ME TO A TEE, HASN'T HE?
JUST LOOK AT THE REMORSE IN THAT FACE, TOM... THAT'S FUCKING GOOD REMORSE, THAT... OSCAR-WINNING STUFF
LIKE ROBERT FUCKING DE NIRO
I WAS UP ALL NIGHT PRACTISING THAT BASTARD IN THE BATH-ROOM MIRROR... AND I PUT A BIT OF 'VIC' ON MY FINGER SO I COULD RUB MY EYES AND GET A FEW TEARS GOING
ANYWAY, TOM... I WANT TO GIVE THIS TO YOU
TO ME, ROGER?
YES, TOM...
...IT'S BEEN A DIFFICULT TIME THESE PAST FEW MONTHS, AND NOW IT'S OVER, I WANT YOU TO HAVE IT AS A MARK OF MY GRATITUDE FOR YOU STICKING BY ME
OH!
IT'S AT TIMES LIKE THIS YOU FIND OUT WHO YOUR REAL FRIENDS ARE
THANK YOU, ROGER. THAT MEANS A LOT
I'LL PUT IT ALONGSIDE THE SHOPLIFTING ONE, AND BELOW THE DRIVING WHILST UNDER THE INFLUENCE
SMASHING! FANCY A PINT?

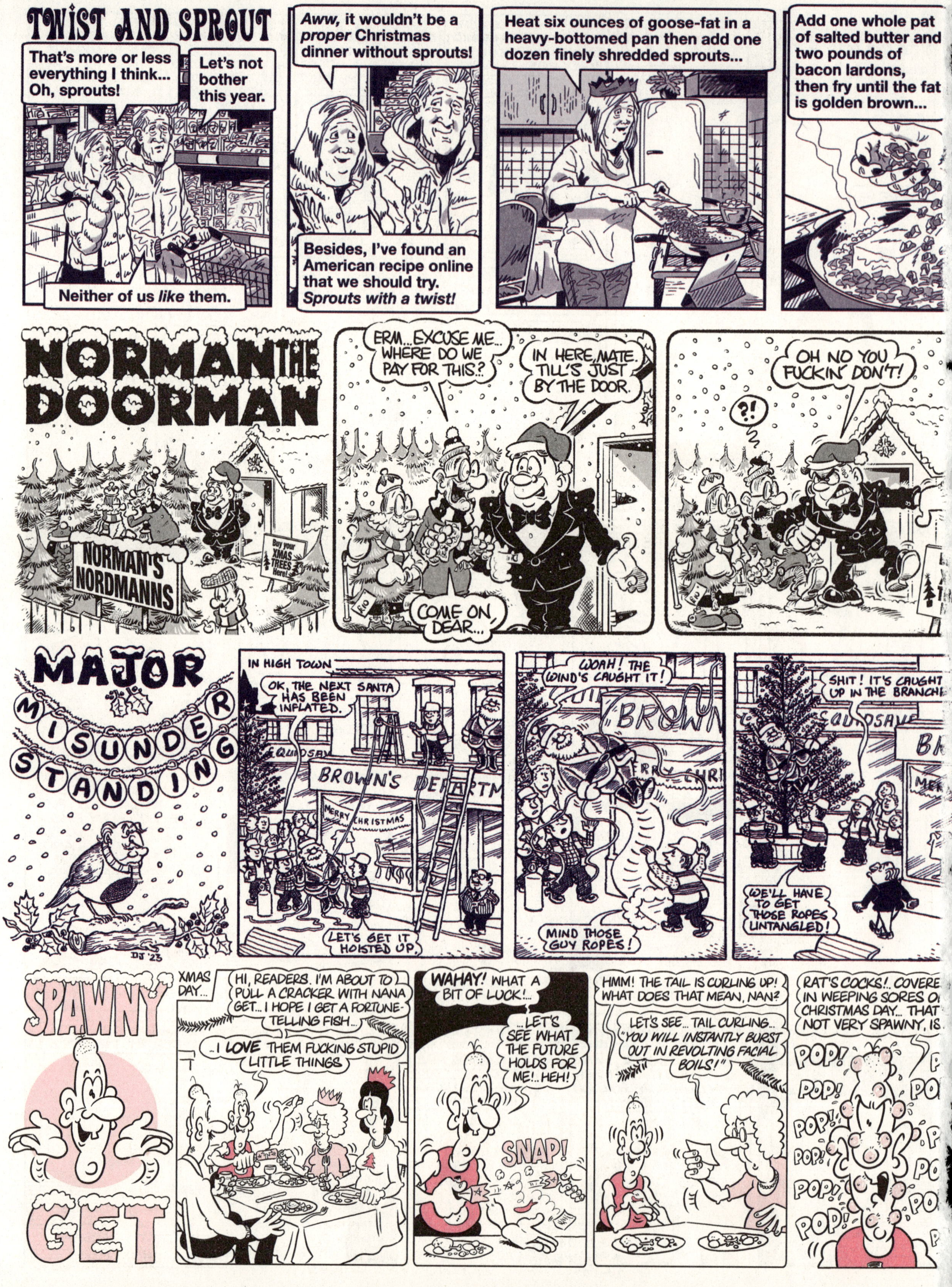
TWIST AND SPROUT
That's more or less everything I think... Oh, sprouts!
Let's not bother this year.
Neither of us *like* them.
Aww, it wouldn't be a *proper* Christmas dinner without sprouts!
Besides, I've found an American recipe online that we should try. *Sprouts with a twist!*
Heat six ounces of goose-fat in a heavy-bottomed pan then add one dozen finely shredded sprouts...
Add one whole pat of salted butter and two pounds of bacon lardons, then fry until the fat is golden brown...
NORMAN THE DOORMAN
NORMAN'S NORDMANNS
Buy your XMAS TREES Here!
ERM... EXCUSE ME... WHERE DO WE PAY FOR THIS?
IN HERE, MATE. TILL'S JUST BY THE DOOR.
COME ON, DEAR...
?!
OH NO YOU FUCKIN' DON'T!
MAJOR MISUNDERSTANDING
DJ '23
IN HIGH TOWN
OK, THE NEXT SANTA HAS BEEN INFLATED.
BROWN'S DEPARTM
MERRY CHRISTMAS
LET'S GET IT HOISTED UP.
WOAH! THE WIND'S CAUGHT IT!
BROWN
MIND THOSE GUY ROPES!
SHIT! IT'S CAUGHT UP IN THE BRANCH
QUIDSAVE
WE'LL HAVE TO GET THOSE ROPES UNTANGLED!
SPAWNY GET
XMAS DAY...
HI, READERS. I'M ABOUT TO PULL A CRACKER WITH NANA GET... I HOPE I GET A FORTUNE-TELLING FISH...
...I **LOVE** THEM FUCKING STUPID LITTLE THINGS
WAHAY! WHAT A BIT OF LUCK!...
...LET'S SEE WHAT THE FUTURE HOLDS FOR ME!... HEH!
SNAP!
HMM! THE TAIL IS CURLING UP! WHAT DOES THAT MEAN, NAN?
LET'S SEE... TAIL CURLING... "YOU WILL INSTANTLY BURST OUT IN REVOLTING FACIAL BOILS!"
RAT'S COCKS!.. COVERE IN WEEPING SORES O CHRISTMAS DAY... THAT NOT VERY SPAWNY, IS
POP! POP! POP! POP! POP! POP!

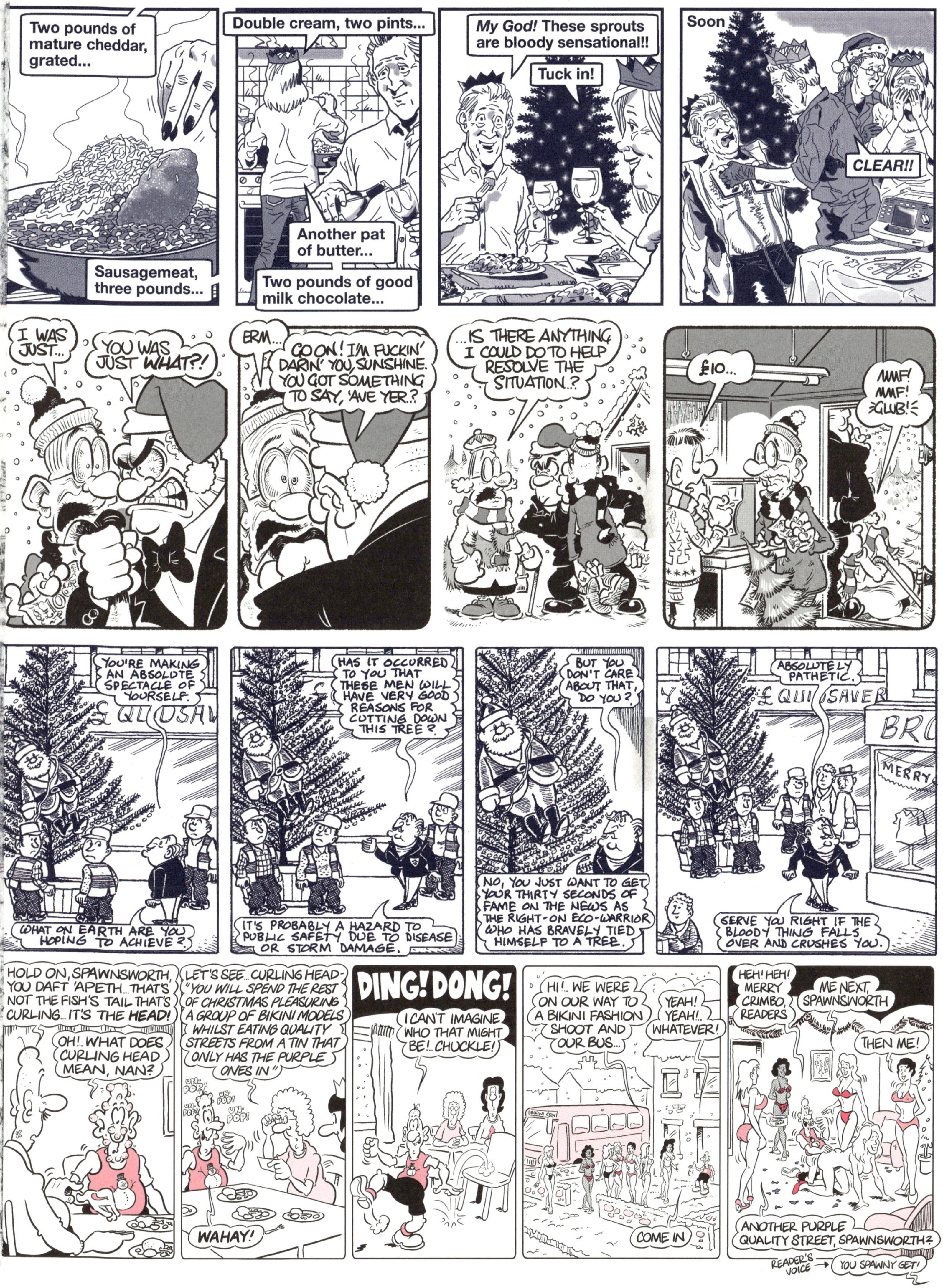

Two pounds of mature cheddar, grated...
Sausagemeat, three pounds...
Double cream, two pints...
Another pat of butter...
Two pounds of good milk chocolate...
My God! These sprouts are bloody sensational!!
Tuck in!
Soon
CLEAR!!
I WAS JUST...
YOU WAS JUST WHAT?!
ERM...
GO ON! I'M FUCKIN' DARIN' YOU, SUNSHINE. YOU GOT SOMETHING TO SAY, 'AVE YER..?
...IS THERE ANYTHING I COULD DO TO HELP RESOLVE THE SITUATION..?
£10...
MMF! MMF! GLUB!
YOU'RE MAKING AN ABSOLUTE SPECTACLE OF YOURSELF.
WHAT ON EARTH ARE YOU HOPING TO ACHIEVE?
HAS IT OCCURRED TO YOU THAT THESE MEN WILL HAVE VERY GOOD REASONS FOR CUTTING DOWN THIS TREE?
IT'S PROBABLY A HAZARD TO PUBLIC SAFETY DUE TO DISEASE OR STORM DAMAGE.
BUT YOU DON'T CARE ABOUT THAT, DO YOU?
NO, YOU JUST WANT TO GET YOUR THIRTY SECONDS OF FAME ON THE NEWS AS THE RIGHT-ON ECO-WARRIOR WHO HAS BRAVELY TIED HIMSELF TO A TREE.
ABSOLUTELY PATHETIC.
SERVE YOU RIGHT IF THE BLOODY THING FALLS OVER AND CRUSHES YOU.
HOLD ON, SPAWNSWORTH, YOU DAFT 'APETH... THAT'S NOT THE FISH'S TAIL THAT'S CURLING... IT'S THE HEAD!
OH!.. WHAT DOES CURLING HEAD MEAN, NAN?
LET'S SEE... CURLING HEAD - "YOU WILL SPEND THE REST OF CHRISTMAS PLEASURING A GROUP OF BIKINI MODELS WHILST EATING QUALITY STREETS FROM A TIN THAT ONLY HAS THE PURPLE ONES IN"
UN-POP!
WAHAY!
DING! DONG!
I CAN'T IMAGINE WHO THAT MIGHT BE!.. CHUCKLE!
HI!.. WE WERE ON OUR WAY TO A BIKINI FASHION SHOOT AND OUR BUS...
YEAH! YEAH!.. WHATEVER!
COME IN
HEH! HEH! MERRY CRIMBO, READERS
ME NEXT, SPAWNSWORTH
THEN ME!
ANOTHER PURPLE QUALITY STREET, SPAWNSWORTH?
READER'S VOICE
YOU SPAWNY GET!

FREE VIZ ARSE OPE

THE pride of Britain – our National Health Service – is at breaking point. Every new day brings fresh reports of patients being treated in hospital corridors due to lack of beds or queues of ambulances outside A&E units waiting to hand over their patients. We at *Viz* firmly believe that each-and-every UK resident needs to step up and do their bit and that's why we have produced this fun, electronic game to train all ages to perform the NHS's most popular emergency service – removing foreign objects from the Great British public's arses – and help ease the daily pressure faced by our brave doctors and nurses.*

Viz Arse Operation is a high-tech electronic game for one or more players. Due to its advanced circuit-based design, it may take a little more effort to set up than our usual *Viz* games, but we guarantee that with the addition of a few common household items, you'll be up to your elbows in fun in no time!

***NB: Viz's Arse Operation electronic game is designed as a fun simulation of an advanced medical procedure only and any expertise gained from playing it is not guaranteed to be safely transferrable to real-world arse/object retrieval situations.**

YOU WILL NEED:

Bell wire
Cereal Box
Matchbox tray
Tin foil
Glue stick
Sticky tape
Scissors or scalpel.
Metal tweezers
Insulating tape
9V buzzer
9V battery (the square one)

OPTIONAL

9V bulb approx 10mm width
Rubber Gloves
Light blue face mask.

Puffed
pops
GLU STIK

INSTRUCTIONS:

*a) Start by cutting out the section with the illustration of the patient on (**A: Playing Board**', opposite) and mounting it on the front or back of the cereal box with your glue stick (fig. 1). With a sharp knife, carefully remove the dotted section marked on the patient's arse.*

*b) Remove the other side of the cereal box cardboard and stick the sphincter (**B: Electro-sphincter**, below) to it and items (**C: Items**, opposite) to. Cut these out neatly along the dotted lines. Remove the middle of the sphincter with your scissors, then wrap it with thin strips of tin foil, ensuring that the foil wraps over and around the middle hole (fig. b). Using your finger, flatten the foil around the inside of the sphincter so that the opening is perfectly square and tight to the inner cardboard rim.*

c) Staple the stripped end of a single strand of bell wire (approx 20cm length) to the side of your foil-wrapped sphincter (fig. c) and then attach it to the other side of the cereal box so that it sits centred in position under the patient's arsehole. Using sticky-tape, tape the matchbox tray underneath the sphincter and anal cavity, ready to receive the items.

d) Now take your mum's eyebrow tweezers and tie the stripped end of another single strand of bell wire (approx 30-40cm length) around the fulcrum point (fig. d). Twist the wire to secure it tightly and then wrap a little insulating tape around it to secure it and act as the tweezers' handle. Attach the other end of this wire to one terminal of the buzzer (fig. e) and attach a new wire to the other terminal of the buzzer. Stick the buzzer inside the cereal box and attach the two loose wires to the terminals of your 9v battery See circuit diagram below (fig. f).

Drop the foreign objects into the arse cavity and you're ready to play!

ADVANCED: If you wish, you can wire a small circuit bulb between the two terminals on the buzzer, cover it with a see-through red plastic wrapper from a pre-2023 Quality Street and stick this through the patient's nasal cavity for extra fun! Or don gloves and face mask for extra realism!

VIZ ARSE OPERATION

fig 1.

fig 2.

fig 3.

fig 4.

fig 5.

'It's a bo-ooooOOOO-on!'
Mrs B. Essex

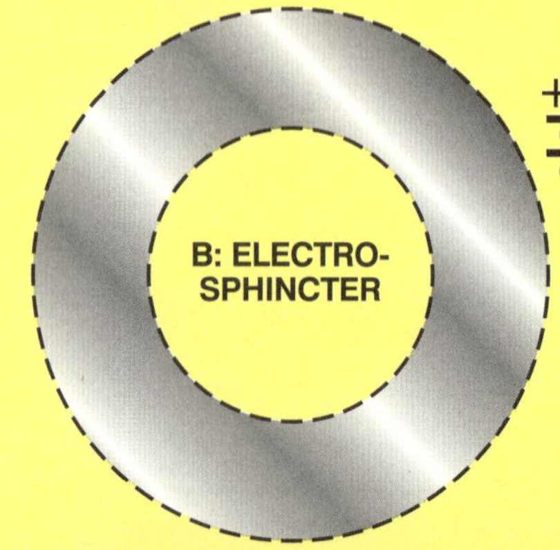

B: ELECTRO-
SPHINCTER

TWEEZERS
SPHINCTER
+
BATTERY
9V
BUZZER
BULB
(OPTIONAL)

fig 6.

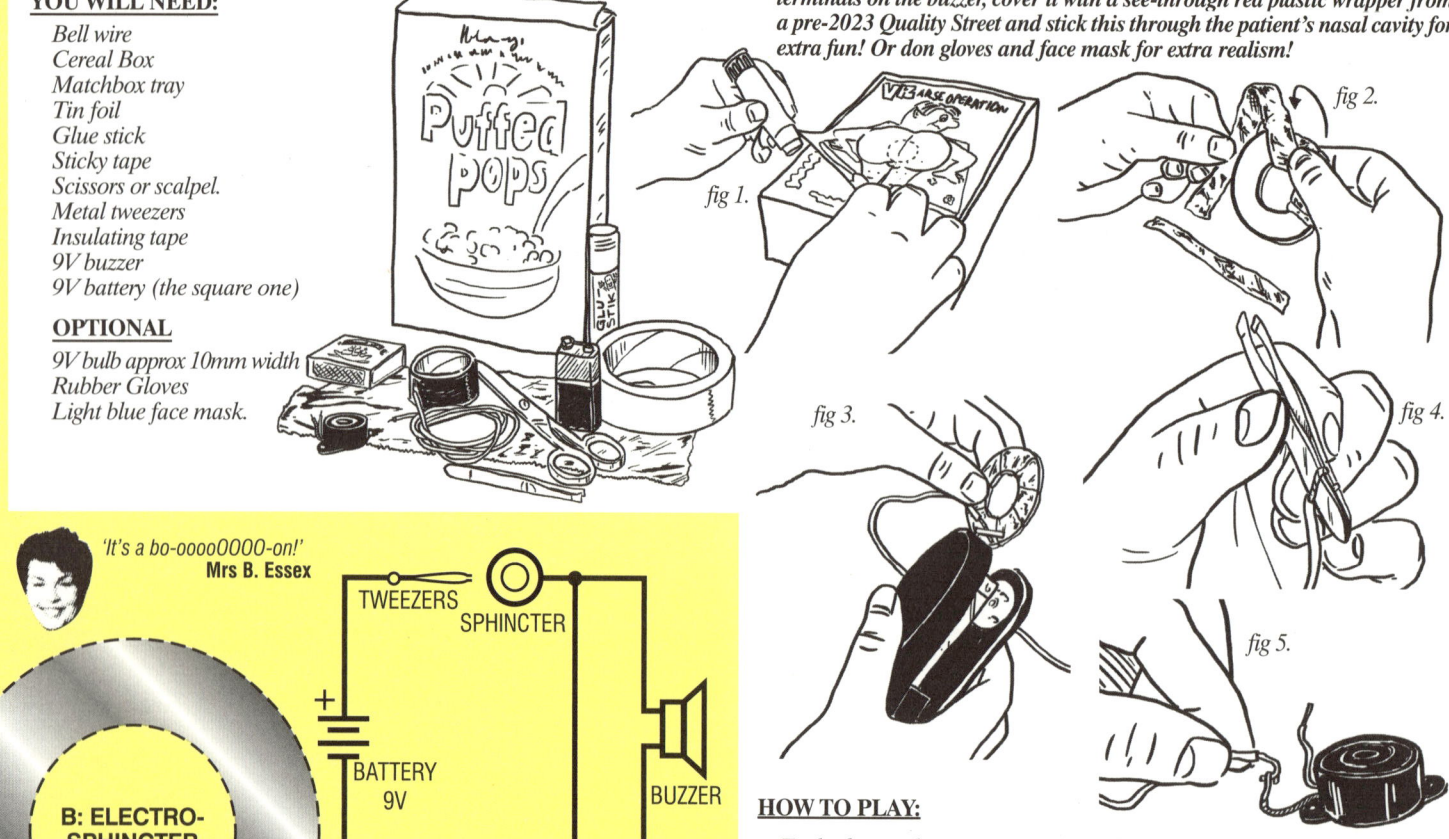

HOW TO PLAY:

Each player takes it in turns to use the tweezers to retrieve items from the patient's arse. If the tweezers touch the metal side of the sphincter then the buzzer sounds and play passes clockwise to the next player. The game ends when all objects have been safely retrieved from the patient's arse. The player with the most items retrieved from the anal cavity is the winner.